Charlie Calvert's Learn JBuilder™

Charlie Calvert
and Margie Calvert

Wordware Publishing, Inc.

Library of Congress Cataloging-in-Publication Data

Calvert, Charles.
Charlie Calvert's Learn JBuilder / by Charlie Calvert and Margie Calvert.
p. cm.
ISBN 1-55622-330-7
1. Java (Computer program language). 2. JBuilder. I. Title: Learn JBuilder.
II. Calvert, Margie. III. Title.
QA76.73.J38 C355 2002
005.13'3--dc2 2002009969
CIP

2320 Los Rios Boulevard
Plano, Texas 75074

Printed in the United States of America

ISBN 1-55622-330-7
10 9 8 7 6 5 4 3 2 1
0209

All inquiries for volume purchases of this book should be addressed to Wordware Publishing, Inc., at the above address. Telephone inquiries may be made by calling:

(972) 423-0090

Contents

Part III: JBuilder Fundamentals

Dedications

To my brother Jim: good friend, sage advisor.
Charlie Calvert

To my loving and wonderful mother, Clazine Masselink.
Margie Calvert

Acknowledgments

I would like to thank Wes Beckwith at Wordware, who put up with me when I was not at my best. Beth Kohler did a wonderful job editing the book and always acted with inspiring professional skill and poise. And a special thanks to Jim Hill for putting this title together and for all the wonderful books he has helped create.

Thanks to Lonnie Heinke for helping Margie to learn the Java language. Thanks to Dan Horn for some timely tech support and for teaching Charlie how to be a better programmer. Thanks to everyone in the Java and Linux communities for their inspiration and support. Thanks to Dean Williams for his patience and good humor. Thanks to everyone at Borland who helped create JBuilder. It is a great tool and easily the world's best Java development environment. Both John Kaster and Anders Ohlsson provided support above and beyond the call of duty while this book was under development.

Charlie and Margie would like to thank each other for simply surviving this mammoth undertaking without entirely losing their sense of perspective or sense of humor.

Part I

Getting Started

Chapter 1

Introduction

Charlie Calvert

This book is designed to be a companion for JBuilder developers. Keep it by your desk, use it for a quick reference, browse the code samples, and use it whenever you need to see how a particular feature of JBuilder works. Or, if you wish, you can read it through from beginning to end and get a complete overview of a very powerful Java programming tool.

Style and Intended Audience

This book contains a general introduction and overview of JBuilder for beginning, intermediate, and advanced programmers. I assume that readers of this book know how to program but know nothing about JBuilder.

Professional programmers and serious students of the language will feel at home with this text; it is designed to focus on the issues you need to know in order to do your work.

If you are taking a beginning-level Java course and want to learn how to use JBuilder, there is also plenty of material in here that you will find useful. I know a good deal about the kinds of things you will want to do with JBuilder, and every effort has been made to include that information.

The book should be divided about equally between discursive sections and sections that are intended to be interactive. I've also tried to keep most of the chapters fairly short and include one or more example programs for most of the non-introductory chapters. As a result, I would recommend taking the 10 or 15 minutes required to read a chapter through from beginning to end. Then fire up the computer, and see if you can duplicate the programs or exercises described in that chapter.

In most cases, I include brief tutorials or example programs within the chapters. I think it is an excellent idea to try to recreate the sample programs on your own. In the early chapters, which are dedicated to describing the product, I recommend seeing if you can locate the features described and use them yourself.

In short, I think this book will be most useful to you if you combine periods of reading the text with periods of hands-on computer use. Reading is a very valuable exercise, but nothing is more important than actually getting your hands dirty with JBuilder itself and some code.

Having said all this, I want to add that I really do try to create readable chapters. I want you to have a sense that this is not just a tutorial or a reference, but a book that you can actually read with at least some small degree of pleasure.

Content

The book is divided into the following sections:

Part I: Getting Started Learn about the JBuilder IDE and how to perform basic functions inside it.

Part II: Java Language A primer on the basic syntax of the Java language.

Part III: JBuilder Fundamentals Learn how to create simple applications and applets using JBuilder. Read about using the UI Designer to create the interface for your application. If you are interested in Swing basics, this is a good section of the book to explore.

Part IV: Project Architecture Contains an overview of the techniques, conventions, and syntax used by the programs found in this book. It is also a primer on the basic facts regarding correct programming in Java.

Part V: Project Management How to manage simple and complex applications in JBuilder. Many developers are used to creating Java programs from the command line; this section explains how to create applications of all shapes and sizes inside of JBuilder. If you are in a Java 101 course, Chapter 23, "Building Simple Applications," may be very helpful for you. If you feel you don't fully understand packages, this is the place to turn if you want to get all that business straight once and for all. In this section, I also discuss deploying applications.

Part VI: Testing, Debugging, and Maintenance Learn how to use the powerful tools in JBuilder to keep your program bug free.

Part VII: JavaBeans How to create reusable components. Event handling is covered in this section.

Part VIII: Databases How to create applications that access SQL databases. The JBuilder database tools are part of JBuilder SE and Enterprise editions. As a result, this is the one section of the book that will not be much help to users of JBuilder Personal. You can write great database code in JBuilder Personal, but you have to do the work by hand. JBuilder won't get in your way, but neither will it offer you much help.

The appendix lists technical resources.

The Purpose of the Book

As you can see from the previous section, the vast majority of this book is simply about using JBuilder. The Java language itself is discussed only in Part III: JBuilder Fundamentals. Part VII: JavaBeans has many language-specific sections, but it also has long passages on using the JBuilder JavaBeans Express. Part V: Project Management includes long passages on working with packages and import statements, so it is also relatively language specific.

The primary purpose of the book, however, is to describe JBuilder. JBuilder is a very large product with many powerful capabilities. Even getting a general feeling for what it can do for you is a major undertaking.

Since JBuilder is the center of focus in this book, I now want to move on to a new section of the chapter that describes JBuilder itself. After reading that section, you should have some sense of what this book contains.

JBuilder Overview

JBuilder is a tool that can help you build robust, easy-to-maintain applications. It does this through three primary means:

- It provides a powerful editor and debugger. The editor and related tools, such as CodeInsight, can help you explore your code and discover the available objects and methods found in your program. You can also automatically explore methods or objects in the JDK or in any third-party tool you might be using. If you use JBuilder, you never have to wonder how or where a class is defined or how or where a variable is defined. JBuilder always knows about all the valid identifiers in your program. It can take you to their declaration instantly. The debugger allows you to step through your code, explore the threads in your program, view variables in depth, view a stack trace of your program, and perform many other useful tasks.

- JBuilder can help you generate the interface to your program via a series of visual design tools. These tools can relieve you of the need to memorize or look up many of the details of how the AWT and Swing libraries are constructed. The tools generate standard Java code and do not lock you into a proprietary format.
- JBuilder also contains a series of wizards that can help you automate certain repetitive tasks. For instance, JBuilder makes it easy for you to generate Javadoc, which is a way of commenting your code. It can also help create JAR files and help you deploy your application. Other tools in the advanced versions of JBuilder can help you create database applications or distributed applications.

All but the last of these subjects will be covered in depth in this book.

JBuilder is not a magic bullet that can turn a bad programmer into a good programmer. I believe that it can help students learn about Java and it can help speed the production of applications. It cannot, however, make a lazy programmer into a good programmer any more than a word processor can make a bad writer into a good writer. A good editor can make a good writer into a better writer, and a good programming tool can make a good programmer into a better programmer. There is no substitute for learning good programming techniques and the rules that govern the Java language.

JBuilder cannot magically replace the need for a programmer to know the details of the Java language. Rather, JBuilder can help you create programs more quickly and with less struggle. Again, the analogy is to a good word processor. Ernest Hemingway was going to be a great writer whether he used a quill, a typewriter, or a word processor. However, a good writer can produce clean text more quickly with a word processor than with a pen and paper.

There is plenty of complexity in any serious programming task. If JBuilder can lighten the burden for a programmer in certain areas of development, then that is a good thing.

Most of the advanced features in JBuilder can be used or abandoned, depending on your tastes. But even if you rejected 75 percent of the features in JBuilder, you would still be better off using JBuilder than you would using Notepad, or even a powerful editor like emacs or Visual Slick Edit. My point is that the base features found in the editor and the debugger alone are enough to convert any sensible person from text editor and command-line application production to JBuilder application production.

The Myth of the Proprietary Format

Some people have the idea that JBuilder is trapping them inside some sort of proprietary format. This is simply not true. Most JBuilder applications that I have built compile absolutely fine from the command line with nothing more than the standard Sun JDK.

It is possible to add specialized Borland classes to your projects if you so desire, but you don't have to use them if you don't want to. And of course those specialized Borland classes compile fine with the Sun JDK, so long as you include the proper JAR files in your project. If you don't want to use the Borland classes, you don't have to. You are not giving up any features of JBuilder if you don't use them. They are simply available to use if you want, just as other third-party tools such as Xerces, JUnit, or Ant are there to use. In most of the book, I make almost no use of specialized code from Borland. The only major exception is the database section, which relies heavily on very useful libraries from Borland. You do not, however, have to pay royalties for using the database tools that I discuss.

NOTE: There is one Borland Java database tool called JDataStore that does cost money to use. JDataStore is not, however, a subject I cover in this book. I like the JDataStore technology, but I want to focus this book on using JBuilder to create typical Java applications. I didn't want to complicate matters by including proprietary code.

I also discuss both JUnit and Ant, which are open source products. Like the Borland database tools, they are not part of the JDK. However, using them is common practice in the Java programming world.

The JBuilder visual tools, and some of the wizards, will generate code for you automatically. In nearly all cases, the code being generated is absolutely standard Java. If you don't like the code that JBuilder generated, you can always edit it or replace it with your own code. JBuilder won't hinder you from making such changes.

Valid Java code will compile fine inside of JBuilder, regardless of how you structure your program. However, there are a few very simple rules you can follow to help you produce code that is fully compatible with JBuilder's tools. Most of these rules involve simply ensuring that you follow basic Java programming conventions, such as not placing more than one class intended to be displayed visually in a single source file. This is something you should do whether you use JBuilder or not.

There is, however, one method, called jbInit, in which you place much of the initialization code for your visual components. The use of this method is not complicated, and it should not disturb the architecture of most programs. If you don't want to use the method, your code will still compile fine inside JBuilder. However, you won't be able to take advantage of all of JBuilder's visual tools unless you include it and use it properly.

Overall, however, JBuilder is simply a tool for helping you write standard Java code exactly as it is taught by Sun in their documentation, books, and tutorials. There is nothing proprietary about any of the code you produce with JBuilder. Outside of the database section, almost all of the code in this book will compile as is, with nothing more than the Sun JDK. The few cases where you do need Borland classes to help you compile your programs are inserted explicitly for one of two reasons:

1. To show you how to use a Borland class that I think is very helpful
2. To show you how to use Borland classes if you want to include them

In most cases, however, there is no real downside to using the Borland code on the rare occasions when it is added to your programs by the JBuilder wizards. And if you don't like it, just delete it.

NOTE: To find out if you are using Borland code, look at the important statements at the top of your files and see if any of them include the words "com.borland." Most of the time you won't find any Borland import statements. But if you do find them, and you don't like them, just delete them and any associated code. In the text of this book, I will explain in depth the rare occasions when these are likely to appear.

Project Management

A major subject in this text is the techniques that JBuilder uses for handling project maintenance. These sections of the text will cover proper Java programming techniques, program architecture and design, unit testing, and the technologies JBuilder uses for managing projects.

If you have had any experience at all with Java programming, then you know at least something about packages and the classpaths. In some ways, these subjects are to Java much as pointers are to C or C++. Packages and classpaths are a stumbling block for beginners, but once you understand them, they are also one of the most useful and powerful features of the language.

JBuilder would not be an effective Java development environment if it did not help you work with both packages and classpaths. In fact, once you properly understand how to use JBuilder, this whole complicated facet of Java development can be automated by the IDE. This is particularly true if you can afford to buy the Enterprise or SE editions of JBuilder 7. These products contain wonderful refactoring tools that can instantly help you rename or move packages and classes. In the process, the refactoring tools will help you resolve all of the references to these packages or classes that exist in your program.

Whether you have the refactoring tools or not, packages and classpaths still play a major part in Java programming in general and JBuilder programming in particular. As a result, these subjects will be explored in depth in Part V: Project Management.

A Word about the Editions of JBuilder

I worked at Borland for over eight years, and hence I know a lot about the way the company works. One of the subjects of constant irritation to Borland users is the decisions the marketing department makes about which features go into which products. In particular, JBuilder has Personal, SE (what used to be called Professional), and Enterprise editions of JBuilder. The pricing for these various products varies greatly.

As a rule, I know the Borland developers and marketing team try to place appropriate level tools with appropriate level products. For instance, the Enterprise product is made up primarily of features of interest to enterprise level developers, the SE edition contains features for professional developers who don't need multi-tier support, and the Personal version is a bare-bones product with just enough features to make the product useful without stealing the market from the high-end versions. The Personal version would be appropriate for a student or developer who was building applications that did not rely on databases or multi-tier features.

NOTE: You can build very big, very powerful applications with the JBuilder Personal edition. There is no limit on the size or complexity of the projects you can develop with the Personal version. And since Java is a free language, there are no significant limitations on the APIs that are available in the Personal version. But if you want to move into web development or multi-tier development, you will find the features in the SE or Enterprise editions useful. They aren't necessary, but they are useful. You could still build a database or web-based application with the Personal edition, but the process would be more complicated.

The following quote is from the Borland web site: "JBuilder Personal is a fully functional, entry-level version of JBuilder for personal, non-commercial use. The JBuilder Personal license does not expire." For an explication of what that phrase means, you should talk to a Borland employee. From my point of view, the only real catch with the Personal edition is that it makes it more difficult for you to switch JDKs. See the end of Chapter 3 for more on switching the JDK used by your applets and applications when run from inside of JBuilder. JBuilder 7 ships with Sun's JDK 1.3.1. As I will explain later in the book, you can run it on other JDKs, but you may or may not have problems with the product under those circumstances. All editions of the product run by default on top of 1.3.1, but they let you develop your applications against whatever JDK you want to use, from the very oldest to the most recent, which was 1.4.0 at the time of publication.

The decision to buy the SE edition of JBuilder hinges on your dedication to Java and application development. If you work all day long, 365 days a year, on Java development, it is worthwhile to invest in the SE edition of the product. If you just program on weekends, or if you consider Delphi, Perl, or C++ to be your primary language, then maybe the Personal edition would make more sense for you.

NOTE: A considerable amount of work in this text is dedicated to meeting the needs of the users of JBuilder Personal and to keeping the text up to date. For instance, almost all the non-database programs on the CD compile unchanged in JBuilder 7 Personal. However, JBuilder has a very short release cycle, often less than six months in length. Release of the Personal edition often lags behind the release of the other editions, so that this short cycle is compressed even further. As a result, the screen shots of the Personal edition and some very minor points about the way it works may not correspond exactly with the feature set of JBuilder Personal 7. Because JBuilder 8 will be out by the time most readers get this book, visit www.wordware.com/calvert for updates covering that product. You may also visit my web site at http://www.elvenware.com, which contains links to a site at http://sourceforge.net/projects/elvenware that has updated source code in zip format and in a CVS repository. I should also be writing regular Java articles that may address this issue on the Borland web site at http://community.borland.com/java.

By agreement with my editor, this book is primarily about the SE and Personal level editions of JBuilder. If you want to learn specifically about Enterprise level features, then you should read *JBuilder 7.0 EJB Programming* from Wordware Publishing.

About Java

My goal in writing this book is to explain not Java, but JBuilder. There is, however, no clear line demarcating where a description of the Java language leaves off and a description of the JBuilder environment begins. Quite often, the two subjects are very closely linked.

JBuilder can help students learn the syntax and structure of the Java language. If you know how to use JBuilder, it can answer many of your questions about the basic syntax of the language without forcing you to open a book or peek in a help file.

My primary goal will be to explain JBuilder itself. But I will explain basic Java syntax and some of the knottier syntactical problems that confront Java programmers.

NOTE: If you have a teacher who discourages you from using JBuilder because it is "cheating," I suppose you will have to follow his or her advice, but I am not sure I agree. JBuilder considerably simplifies the act of creating the interface for your program, and it can automate certain other tasks. However, it doesn't make programming "easy," and it will not solve all your problems. To me, the suggestion that JBuilder is "cheating" is a bit like a cook insisting that you aren't really cooking unless you cook over an open fire. This whole business about stoves, gas and electric burners, ovens — all of that — is nothing but "cheating." Real cooks cook on an open fire! Well, maybe. But though a stove can help you cook, using a stove does not mean that your cooking task will now be easy. There are still plenty of challenges involved in making a good meal, even if you do have a tool that simplifies certain parts of the process. Similarly, JBuilder is a good tool for programmers, but using it doesn't mean that there are no challenges left in the art of programming. Here is another analogy. A bicycle or a car is a good tool for people who need to travel. You can still get across town without a car, but if you are a busy person with a job to do, a car can be quite useful. The same is true of JBuilder; if you have real work to do, then you ought to use whatever tools are available. And don't worry, there will still be plenty of challenges for you to face, even if you master all the features found in JBuilder.

The Changing Java Specification

I want to say a few things regarding my approach to the Java language. You can use this information to help you understand some of the decisions I made when writing this book.

Java is an easy language to learn, but a hard language to master. The creators of Java went out of their way to make the basic syntax of the language as easy to use as possible. They did not, however, draw a line in the sand that says the language will get only so complex and then go no further. Instead, they have continually piled new APIs on top of the original Java specification. Each new layer adds new power to the language but also additional complexity. Java is not a single static specification, but a moving target that constantly evolves.

In some cases, the new features in the Java language have been clear winners. For instance, the addition of new XML or Regular Expression APIs to Java 1.4 is a ripe plum that adds power to the language.

But the evolution of the language has not always been quite so straightforward. The Java GUI itself is a case in point. Originally, Sun created something called the AWT, or the Abstract Window Toolkit. This API was used to add buttons, list boxes, and other visual components to Java applets and applications. It was remarkably easy to use. AWT helped many beginning Java programmers build powerful applets and applications.

AWT was not without flaws in both its interface and underlying implementation. As a result, this standard was in large part replaced with something called Swing. Unfortunately, the code you wrote for Swing components was not the same as the code you wrote to run AWT components. In short, you had to rewrite parts of your program if you wanted to move from AWT to Swing. Arguments with Microsoft over the distribution of the JRE meant that there was also trouble using swing in applets.

Issues like this caused trouble for Java programmers. Other troubles occurred because of the complexity of certain advanced features in the Java language.

Java Language Lawyers

A language lawyer is someone who attempts to dictate to others what they should or should not do when using a language. These people provide a valuable service by analyzing the syntax of a language. Nonetheless, it is always a bit frightening when they find fertile ground in a particular language. One wants a language to have a clearly defined syntax, and the need for close parsing of terms can be a bad sign.

Java language lawyers recommend that you write lines of code that look like this:

```
String value = "This is a string";
```

These same sanctioned soothsayers suggest that you do not write code that looks like this:

```
String value = new String("This is a string");
```

The issue here is that writing a string literal actually creates an instance of a string, so the second example creates not one, but two, instances of the string — clearly a wasteful practice, but one that a newcomer to the language would have a hard time intuiting.

Another interesting case comes up when you are working with arrays of objects. In Java, you are not supposed to need to worry about memory management. The garbage collector is supposed to handle everything for you.

The only problem is that it doesn't always handle things for you quite the way you might suppose. If you have a class that maintains an array of objects, and you give that class methods such as add and remove, you might be creating a "memory leak." In particular, you should not write code like this:

```
class myClass
{
      private Object[]  myArray;

      public Object removeLastItem()
      {
            int lastIndex = myArray.length - 1;
            Object result = myArray[lastIndex];
            return result;
      }
}
```

Instead, your code should look like this:

```
class myClass
{
      private Object[]  myArray;

      public Object removeLastItem()
      {
            int lastIndex = myArray.length - 1;
            Object result = myArray[lastIndex];
            myArray[lastIndex] = null;
            return result;
      }
}
```

In the latter case, the code explicitly frees up the memory in the array associated with the element that you are going to return by setting a value to null. If you do not free up the memory explicitly, the Java machine would likely leave it stranded.

In short, there are cases when you should free up memory in Java, and there are other cases when you can just let the garbage collector handle the matter on its own. The problem, of course, is that it is sometimes more difficult to know when to deallocate and when not to deallocate than it is to simply go ahead and deallocate all the time, as one would in other languages.

This Book and the Java Language

Most experienced Java programmers can pick their way through its complex features with amazing dexterity. Programmers new to the language, however, have to come to terms with many of these subjects, and they have not always found the process easy. There are no insurmountable hurdles here, but in the end, it turns out that Java is not quite as simple a language as it appears to be at first glance.

As an author, I have tried to pick the simplest way through these often rather complex subjects. When making judgments, I use three yardsticks:

- What is the simplest, cleanest syntax to use for solving a particular problem?
- What solution will best fit in with JBuilder's tools?
- What solutions are most likely to remain viable over time? How can I avoid using obsolete or deprecated code? How can I write code likely to fit in with Sun's future plans for the language?

Clearly, it will not be possible for me to always come up with solutions that will fit the taste of every reader of this book. I ask, however, that you try to keep an open mind and recognize that in Java, as much as in any language, there are multiple solutions to each particular problem.

Whenever I am in doubt, I always go back to rule 1, which is my guiding light as a programmer: Keep your code as simple as possible. I don't always live up to this high standard, but it is what I strive to achieve. In my mind, the ability to write clean, simple code is the greatest virtue a programmer can possibly possess.

NOTE: If you are interested in reading more about the Java language and how to use it correctly, see Chapter 20, "Composing Java."

JBuilder and Swing

While discussing the structure and intended audience of this book, I should, perhaps, say a few more words about my use of Swing. I touched on this subject in the previous section of the text, but I want to explore it in more depth.

Swing lies very much at the heart of this book. There are a number of existing books on Swing, but this book has a special take on the subject since it shows how to use the JBuilder graphical development tools to build Swing applications. In particular, one part of JBuilder is a "what you see is what you get" editor for Swing (and old-style AWT) Java applications.

Working with some features of Swing, such as layout managers, can be very frustrating if you don't have a tool like JBuilder that lets you manipulate the UI for your application with a mouse. In general, being able to "paint" your components onto a container is easier than having to write the code by hand.

Nevertheless, it is not always immediately obvious how to use some Swing features inside JBuilder. Sun built Swing first, and then Borland came along and built JBuilder. As a result, the Sun team was not always thinking how best to build components from the point of view of a GUI development tool. This made Borland's job a bit harder.

Borland's efforts to create a smooth encapsulation of Swing is a subject that I will return to in a number of places throughout this book. Overall, they have done a superb job, but I will try to point out the places where the going gets a bit sticky.

What Do I Think of Java?

I have included the above comments to give you some feeling for how I approach Java programming. This is a big, powerful, complex language, and in this day and age it would not do for me to simply become a cheerleader for Sun or Borland. Both Java and JBuilder are great products. They do, however, have their flaws. As an author, I regard it as my duty to point out these flaws when they are troublesome and help you find the best ways to work around them.

Overall, however, you are reading an author who is very enthusiastic about Java. I have been working with the language for four or five years now, and I have come to really appreciate its virtues. I am particularly appreciative of the fact that Java provides such strong cross platform support. I love Linux, and both JBuilder and Java perform well on that platform.

I should also add that I am one of a small but growing number of developers who believe in using Java not just as a back end, but as a tool for building user-friendly applications and applets. Java has matured greatly over the years, and it is amazing to see what you can do with this language if you put your mind to it.

JBuilder itself is written entirely in Java. If you have any doubts that you can build serious applications with this product, then I ask you to just spend some time with JBuilder. From its editor and its debugger to remarkable features such as CodeInsight, it is an amazing example of what you can do with the Java language.

This is the end of the technical discussion in this chapter. I just want to add a few more quick points, and then we will be ready to move on to the next chapter, which starts examining JBuilder itself.

What Do I Think of Bill and Linus?

I try to maintain a neutral attitude toward the OS wars. I don't want to take a pro Linux and anti-Microsoft stance in this book. I like both platforms, and want to see them both succeed. I believe competition between the two platforms, rather than domination by either platform, is best for us all in the long run. If you are a Java programmer, there is little reason to prefer one platform over the other. They are both great places to run Java programs.

All of the programs on the CD have been tested successfully on both platforms. They should run without a problem on Linux, Windows, and most other Java platforms.

Unfortunately I did not have access to an Apple machine, as I think I would have very much enjoyed working with OS X. The fact that it is built on top of BSD is incredibly intriguing.

Companion CD/Author Contact

All of the example programs mentioned in this text are contained on the CD that is included with this book. You can also download the source code from my web site at www.elvenware.com. A description of how to run the code is included on the CD and on my web site.

To report technical problems with the code, you can write me at ccalvert@yahoo.com. I cannot give help with specific programming problems not related to bugs in my code, nor can I help with homework assignments. Just writing to say "hi" is fine. I am also interested in comments such as "This chapter was helpful," or "I couldn't understand the chapter on *x*," or "I loved the section on such and such, please include more of this," or "This was a waste of time," or "I wish you had covered such and such," or "This was too advanced," or "This was at just the right level," or "I hate it when you do so and so," or "Here is a much better version of program *x*," or "Your book was fabulous. Because I read it, I got a cabinet-level job as head of computer planning for the US government, my hair is no longer gray but has a natural color similar to a five-year-old's, I stand an inch taller, my health problems have disappeared, and all my investments have tripled in value." I may or may not respond to these types of comments, but I am interested in receiving them.

I Am Not a Lawyer

There are various legal rapids that one must navigate when releasing source code. For instance, you might want to include code from Borland's redistributable files, from an open source project, or from some other source. I try to help you with the technical end of that process, showing you how to include code from third parties in your projects. Many third parties expect and want you to be able to do that. I, however, am not a lawyer, and nothing I say is meant to imply that I am a lawyer or that I understand anything about the legal issues involved in such matters. You are responsible for the code you distribute, and I cannot help you decide what is legal and what is not legal. Regardless of anything else I might say in this text, the bottom line is that I have no knowledge of such matters, I do not mean to imply that I have knowledge of such matters, and the entire onus of distributing other people's source lies firmly on your shoulders.

When it comes to my code, on the other hand, you are more than welcome to compile it into your programs. You don't have to give me any credit if you want to include my code in your programs. I'm a technical writer, and I expect you to use my source in your code. I ask, however, that you do not distribute my sample programs unchanged or only slightly modified and claim that they are your work. In particular, you should not base another book, tutorial, or educational tool on the work I have included with this text.

My — or is It Our? — Writing Style

This book was written by Margie and Charlie Calvert. We are a happily married couple who both love technology and books. Charlie wrote the majority of the book, but some of the chapters, particularly in Part I: Getting Started, feature major contributions from Margie. All of the chapters contain at least some work by both of us.

If the chapter is written by Margie and Charlie, then Margie did most of the work on the chapter. Her name is listed first not just because we list feminine names first, but because she is the primary author of the chapter. This usually means she wrote 75 or 80 percent of the chapter. If it is written by either Margie or Charlie, then the credited author did at least 85 percent of the work on that chapter. In these chapters, the uncredited author may still have written 10 to 15 percent of the chapter. As I said earlier, there are no chapters in this text that do not contain at least some work by both of us.

Charlie did most of the development for this book on Windows XP Pro, though he did do a significant amount of work on Linux and a very small amount of work on Windows 2000. Ninety percent of the database code was written first on Linux and only tested on Windows. Margie worked on Windows 2000 or Linux. All of the code was tested on both Linux and Windows.

NOTE: Both Margie and Charlie were running Red Hat Linux 7.2. Both versions were kept up to date either by using the Red Hat Network or by explicitly visiting various sites. For instance, Charlie manually installed KDE 3.0 and switched his GNOME desktop Ximian using their auto-installation tools.

Much of the first draft of the text was written in HTML on Linux, but as we got closer to the final date, we had to convert to Microsoft Word to meet the publisher's requirements. Word bound us tighter to Windows and made it more difficult for us to work in Linux. Toward the end of the project, the release of CrossOver Office and Open Office significantly improved our ability to work on Word files in Linux.

NOTE: JBuilder runs fine on Linux under GNOME. The release of KDE 3.0 was a major boon for those who want to use JBuilder but prefer KDE.

As a rule, we use the convention of writing as if there were only one author. For instance, the text generally uses the first-person singular pronoun (I) rather than the plural (we). The major reason for this is to avoid the appearance of using the royal "we," as if this were an 18th century tract or a novel by Thomas Pynchon.

When I do use the first-person plural, then I usually mean you and me: that is, the reader and the author. I suppose this too could be viewed as something of an affectation, but I mean no harm by it. I simply want to give you the sense that we are working on a project together, which is in fact the way I view the situation. I am trying to help you understand JBuilder, and I can never hope to succeed unless we both decide to work together. When I am engaged in the act of writing, I am quite literally addressing an imaginary individual: the typical reader of this book. As far as I'm concerned, we really have worked together on this book.

As I said at the beginning of this chapter, the real title of this book could be "The JBuilder Companion," though it may not say as much on the cover. Surprisingly enough, authors have little control over such matters in the technical writing world. But let's not get hung up on that kind of thing. We're here to write code, to explore JBuilder, and to ooh and ah over cool technologies whenever and wherever we find them.

NOTE: There is one quirk of my writing style that you might find confusing. I find simple declarative sentences much easier to read than lengthy sentences that contain many subclauses and parenthetical asides. This is particularly true when discussing a conceptually difficult topic such as programming. (Like sloppy code, long parenthetical sentences are easy to write but hard to read.) As a result, you may think important information is missing from one paragraph or sentence, only to find it plainly stated in the next.

If possible, sit down and read an entire chapter at a single sitting. I've made the chapters short specifically to help you swallow them whole in simple, easy-to-digest bites. If that is not possible, then try to read a whole section of a chapter through from beginning to end.

The point I wish to make is that you may read a sentence or paragraph and get no hint from it that additional information on the topic under discussion is available in the next sentence or paragraph. Even if you are rushed, try to push on at least a little further in the text and see if I am really done discussing a topic. I try to organize my text logically. If the next paragraph is clearly about a new topic, then that may provide a hint that I am through discussing the subject at hand.

Summary

I like computers, I like writing code, I like Java, I like JBuilder, and I like the act of composing words into sentences, sentences into paragraphs, and paragraphs into chapters. My hope is that some of my personal enjoyment for this subject and for writing will be communicated to you through these pages and that you too can find joy in working with JBuilder, Java, and computers.

If you find yourself getting bogged down in some complicated section of the text, then just move on to the next section, or better yet, put this book aside and start writing code. Recall the last part of the book that you understood, and try to write code that duplicates it. If possible, try to recreate the programs you read about without looking at the text. (Looking at the pictures is okay.) It may seem like a peculiar exercise, but I promise you that it will yield results.

If that fails, then pick up a project, any kind of project, that interests you, and make it come to life with the tools provided by the Java language. That is what this text is all about: writing code. Nothing is more important, or more fun, than getting out there and actually writing code.

Chapter 2

Setup and Configuration

Charlie Calvert

In this chapter you will learn how to set up and configure JBuilder. Most of the information I present in this chapter comes in the form of hints and suggestions, rather than a step-by-step analysis of the install procedure.

One of the most important passages in this chapter comes at the very end, when I talk about codebox.jar. CodeBox is a set of utility routines used by many of the programs that accompany this book. You simply have to get codebox.jar set up correctly or you won't be able to use many of the example programs.

Install Overview

The install process for JBuilder is simple. It is what is commonly called a forehead install, meaning that you could (at least in theory) install the product by inserting the CD into your computer and hitting the Enter key once with your forehead! Well, okay, it's not quite that simple, but if all goes well it should not be difficult.

The registration process can be a bit trickier in some cases, but there isn't much I can do to help you with it. If you have problems, the best thing you can do is go to www.borland.com and look for information. Note in particular that there is an install newsgroup at forums.borland.com, called borland.public.install.jbuilder. This newsgroup should answer most of your questions. If you are having a problem with the install, so are other people, and discussions about the topic will come up on the forum.

For more information on newsgroups, try http://www.borland.com/newsgroups/.

NOTE: JBuilder ships with a zip file on the install CD that contains the full product. The few times when I have had trouble with recent JBuilder installs, I have found that unpacking this zip file solved all my problems very quickly. A more detailed discussion of this feature is included later in this chapter in the section called "The Alternate Install from a Zip File." If you have troubles, you might also refer to the index.html file in the root of the JBuilder CD.

Hardware Requirements

On the Intel platforms, it is my opinion that JBuilder starts being useful on a 400 MHz or above machine. You will also want at least 256 MB of RAM. These aren't the minimum requirements; they are just my personal view of what you need to feel moderately comfortable with this tool.

The development for this book was done primarily on a machine that ran at 800 MHz and had 448 MB of RAM. I noticed significant improvements in the way JBuilder behaved when I moved from 192 MB of RAM to 448.

The more RAM you can put on your machine, the better. In fact, the more powerful your machine is, the better off you will be. You don't need the fastest machine on the market, but getting a powerful machine in the 2 GHz range with 512 MB of RAM would not be overkill. In fact, that sounds like a good development machine — if you can afford it.

NOTE: At the time of publication, the hottest AMD chip was the Athlon XP 2600+, and the hottest chip from Intel was 2.8 GHz. If you have picked up this book several years after its publication, then perhaps you can get a sense of the relative speeds of the machine you need compared to the speeds current at publication time.

Installing the JDK

JBuilder comes with its own version of the Sun JDK. By default the JDK will be installed in the same directory tree as JBuilder during the regular install. For instance, if you install JBuilder in the c:\jbuilder7 directory, the JDK should be found in c:\jbuilder7\jdk1.3.1\ or some similar location.

NOTE: Charlie installed his copy of JBuilder in a directory called g:\jb7. He kept his source code in the c:\users\charlie\srcjava directory. As a result, you may find references to the g:\jb7 or srcjava directories in this book, in screen shots, and in batch files on the CD. Margie put her version of JBuilder in the Utilities directory on her E drive. Many of her source files are kept in the Documents and Settings directory on her C drive. You will find various references to her setup scattered throughout this book.

JBuilder allows you to use any available modern JDK for development. By default, you will use the JDK that ships with the product. However, you can run your apps against other JDKs if you prefer. Most of the development of this book was run against beta and release candidate versions of Java 1.4.

As you probably know, JBuilder is built entirely in Java. Therefore, it needs a version of the Java JRE to run. You can configure which JRE JBuilder uses, but I would recommend sticking with the one that ships with the product. I will explain more about this kind of configuration later in this chapter in the section called "Configuring JBuilder from the Command Line." On Linux, some people prefer to run JBuilder on top of the IBM JDK.

The point here is to distinguish the JRE on which JBuilder is running and the JDK you use when compiling your applications inside of JBuilder. When writing this book, I ran JBuilder on top of the JRE 1.3.1 that JBuilder 7 ships with, but I tested my applications against the JDK 1.4 beta. JBuilder has no problems running on top of one JRE and then letting you compile and debug your applications using another version of the JDK. It is designed to allow you to do precisely that.

Like JBuilder, the install of most JDKs is very simple. Usually, it's pretty much a matter of downloading a file, clicking on it, and pressing the OK button. It's just another forehead install, so I'm not going to walk you through it. You can get Sun's latest JDK from java.sun.com, and you can search the IBM site for the phrase "Developer Kit" or "DeveloperWorks" if you want a copy of their fast JDK.

The JBuilder Install

In the next few sections I will give some hints that may prove useful when you are installing JBuilder. As I said earlier, it is unlikely that you will have trouble with this process. Nonetheless, there are a few tips to pass on, and so I will include them here. I will start with the downloading and installing of JBuilder Personal. If you already have a JBuilder CD, you can skip that section.

When reading the next few pages, please make a distinction between installing JBuilder and configuring it. Some basic configuration issues are discussed in this chapter. But when it comes to fine-tuning the IDE, those issues are discussed in other parts of this book. Many of them will be covered in the next few chapters on the IDE and the editor. Some other configuration issues, involving classpaths and directories, will be covered in Part V: Project Management.

Downloading and Installing JBuilder Personal Edition

The Personal edition of JBuilder is free. You can download it from the Borland web site, go through a brief registration process, and then install the tool on your system.

NOTE: You can also order a CD containing JBuilder Personal edition from the Borland web site. At the time of publication, the price was approximately $9.95 U.S.

To get started, go to http://www.borland.com/products/downloads/download_jbuilder.html. You will need to perform two downloads, one for the product and one for the documentation.

First, click on the link to download the most recent edition of JBuilder. You will be guided through the steps required to download the file, which include registering, answering a questionnaire, and downloading the compressed files. To use the product, you will need a license key, which will be emailed to you.

After you have downloaded and extracted the compressed files, run **per_install.exe** (or the equivalent file for your platform) to install the JBuilder Personal edition. In Windows and in most versions of Linux, you can do this by double-clicking on it from a file browser.

Before you run JBuilder Personal for the first time, open your email and find the message you received from Borland with the subject "Borland Product Registration." Save the attachment, "reg61.txt," to your home directory. If you are using MS Windows, this would probably be C:\Documents and Settings\your_login_name; in Linux, it will be home/your login name. If for some reason the email arrived without the attachment, you can save the entire email as "reg61.txt" to your home directory.

In the bin folder in the directory where you installed JBuilder, find JBuilderW.exe (Windows) or jbuilder (Linux) and run it. Again, you can accomplish this by double-clicking in the Windows Explorer or KDE Konquerer. The appropriate menu items should also have been added to your Start menu. That's all there is to it. JBuilder will open.

Notes on Installing JBuilder for Windows

This section covers some hints on installing JBuilder from a CD. In most cases, you will simply insert the CD and the install process will launch automatically, or you will click on the install_windows.exe file in the root directory of the CD.

By default, the install program will set up a directory for your projects in the c:\Documents and Settings\UserName\jbprojects directory. I don't like doing development in directories that have spaces in their path names. Yet, in this case, there is an argument for staying with the default directories. The issue here stems from the fact that Java doesn't fully understand the Windows directory system. Java only knows as much about the DOS file system as it absolutely has to know, and nothing more. In particular, it knows the parts of the file system that behave exactly the same as the file systems on other OSs. One concept that just about every OS supports is the idea of a home directory for a user. For better or worse (and it's mostly for worse), Windows has made the user's home directory the c:\Documents and

Settings\UserName directory. To put it mildly, this is not as easy to use as the default Linux /home/UserName directory scheme.

NOTE: If you are like me, you will find it impossible to tolerate Bill's choice in this matter. The little-known solution is to move your home directory to a new location. To do this, you need to edit one entry in your registry:

```
HKEY_LOCAL_MACHINE\SOFTWARE\Microsoft\Windows NT\CurrentVersion\ProfileList
```

There will be several entries under this key. Find the one that has a ProfileImagePath that points to your home directory. It probably says something like this: %SystemDrive%\Documents and Settings\Margie, where Margie is the user name. This is the entry you need to modify.

Here are the steps you should take when modifying the entry:

- Decide if you are an experienced Windows user. If you are not, then just skip this whole process for now.
- Decide how many programs or settings on your computer hard-code in references to the Documents and Settings directory. Good Windows citizens never hard code this information, but use %USERPROFILE% instead when referencing this directory. (Java programmers call System.getProfile("user.home") to retrieve the same information.) You have to face the fact that changing this entry could cause poorly designed programs to not run correctly. I had almost no problems of this type, but your system may be different than mine.
- Copy (don't move) everything from your current Documents and Settings/UserName directory to the location where you want these files to reside. After you are sure your changes are working, then you can delete your original user home directory. You probably won't be completely sure that everything is okay until two or three weeks after you make these changes.
- Now sign on as another user, such as the administrator.
- Make the changes in the registry to the ProfileList entry, as described above, and then sign back on as yourself. If everything looks normal, then you completed the process successfully.

To be doubly sure everything is okay, go to a command line, type **set**, and make sure that the environment variable USERPROFILE is set to your new home directory. Don't set it yourself; the changes you made in the registry should have made the change for you.

If things look all wrong, then sign on as the administrator again, change the ProfileList registry setting back to what it was, and resign yourself to living with Bill's deranged plans.

For Microsoft's take on this subject, try this URL: http://support.microsoft.com/default.aspx?scid=KB;EN-US;Q236621.

If the URL doesn't work for you, then search on this subject: Cannot Move or Rename the Documents and Settings Folder (Q236621). Usually just entering Q236621 should be enough to help you find the article when searching in MSDN, Google, or another search engine.

That's all I have to say about installing on Windows. If you need more help, see the section on installing from the zip file included on the CD later in this chapter.

Notes on Installing JBuilder on Linux

I did not log in as root when I installed JBuilder. Instead, I stayed logged in as charlie. I would recommend that you also do not install JBuilder when you are logged in as root.

I use JBuilder under GNOME, and for now, I would recommend that you do the same. JBuilder runs fine under other windowing schemes, but at the time of publication, the CodeInsight feature did not work correctly under KDE.

You can probably perform a forehead install of JBuilder on Linux. However, if you do have trouble with the install, then try the alternate install procedure, described in the next section.

Some people find that JBuilder runs better on some Linux distributions when it runs on top of the IBM, rather than the Sun, JRE. A description of how to configure JBuilder to use a different JRE is included in the section titled "Configuring JBuilder from the Command Line."

The Alternate Install from a Zip File

In this section I describe the simple steps to take if the regular install process does not work for you. The emphasis in this description is on Linux users, since I doubt that you will encounter problems with the install on Windows. The steps outlined here involve working with zip files.

NOTE: I'm sure you know about working with zip files. On the off chance that you don't, here are some simple tips to get started. On Windows, you can use a shareware product called WinZip, readily available on www.download.com. Most Linux distributions ship with a program called unzip. If it is not available on your system, you can pick up a free copy at http://freshmeat.net. Windows XP handles zip files automatically now too, but I'm addicted to a command-line version of the zip utility, so I am not familiar with the quality of what the Windows GUI currently has to offer.

To install from a zip file, first go to the alt_setup directory on the JBuilder CD. Locate the JBuilder7.zip file you find there. Unzip the files in this archive into your preferred home directory for JBuilder. On my Linux machine I chose a directory called /home/charlie/jb7. On Windows, I would install to the root directory of your preferred partition. For instance, you might try the d:\jb7 directory. Whatever you choose, make sure there are no spaces in the path to the directory where you install JBuilder. This is especially important on Windows.

Under your newly created JBuilder 7 directory, there are now directories with names like bin_linux, bin_solaris, and bin_windows. Delete the directories that do not apply to you. For instance, on Linux, delete the bin_solaris and bin_windows directories; rename the bin_linux directory to bin.

Edit the jdk.config file in the JBuilder 7 bin directory so that javapath points to the location where you have the JDK 1.3.1 installed. Now change the value of addpath to the location where you have JDK 1.3.1 installed. In some cases, the path might look like this: /home/charlie/jb7/jdk1.3.1.

You can read more about this zip file install process in the index.html file in the root of the JBuilder CD.

Checking to Make Sure Basic Applets and Applications Run

At this stage, you should have JBuilder set up on your system. What you need now is a test to confirm that all is working properly. The following represents a quick test of that type. If you can run it without trouble, then your basic install and configuration has been completed. All of the steps covered here will be reviewed in more detail in other chapters.

See Figures 2-1 and 2-2 for help running through these steps to test your system:

1. Choose **File | New Project**. The Project Wizard will appear. Don't step through the wizard. Instead, just click the **Finish** button.
2. Choose **File | New** to bring up the Object Gallery.
3. On the first page of the Object Gallery, choose **Application** to bring up the Application Wizard.
4. Don't step through the wizard. Instead, just choose the **Finish** button. A sample application will be generated for you automatically.

5. Choose **Run | Run** from the menu, or press the **F9** button. (You can also press the green arrow on the toolbar.)

If an empty application appears on the top of JBuilder, things are set up correctly on your system. By default, the application will have the words "Frame Title" on the caption bar.

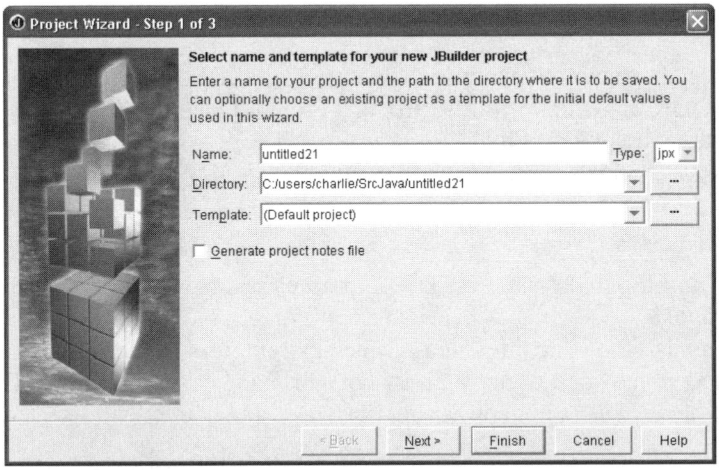

Figure 2-1: Create a new project by first choosing File | New Project and then pressing the Finish button.

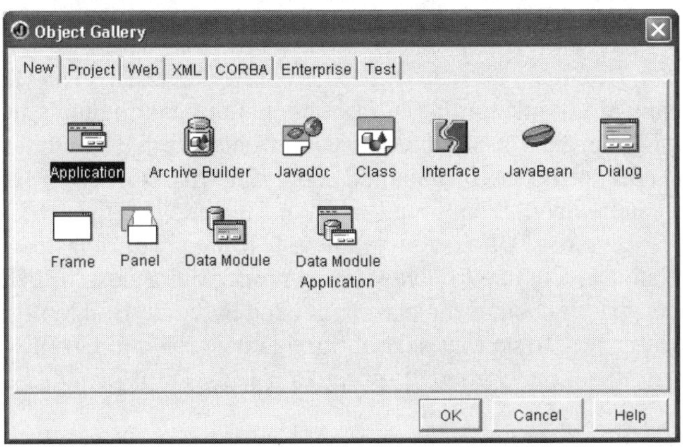

Figure 2-2: Choosing the Application Wizard from the Object Gallery

If the process described in this section took a long time to execute, then you probably do not have enough RAM on your system. As I mentioned earlier, even a 400 MHz machine is powerful enough to run JBuilder. If things are slow, make sure you have at least 256 MB of memory or more if possible.

Configuring JBuilder from the Command Line

Some portions of JBuilder are most easily configured from the command line. I will cover those options in this chapter. In the next chapter, you will learn more about configuring the IDE itself from inside of JBuilder. A discussion of configuring JBuilder to work with particular classpaths and directories is included in Part V: Project Management.

Most developers, and particularly beginning and intermediate level developers, will want to use the options discussed in the next chapter. However, you should be aware of the command-line options mentioned here, particularly if you are an advanced user.

In the JBuilder bin directory, you will find two files called jdk.config and jbuilder.config. These files allow you to make certain changes to the environment that JBuilder uses. You can read about these files, and the commands used inside them, in a file called /jbuilder/bin/config_readme.txt.

The JDK.config file allows you to configure which JDK the IDE will use. As stated earlier, I would stick with the JDK that ships with the product, though I have heard some people say that the IBM JDK can be helpful on Linux.

Here is the line you should change in the jdk.config file if you want the IDE to use a different JDK:

```
javapath ../jdk1.3.1/bin/java
```

Once again, this has nothing to do with the JDK your applications will use; this is only the JDK that the IDE will use.

Notice that you can use the jdk.config file to pass in parameters to the Java Virtual Machine. For instance, if you want to use a proxy port, or make other changes to the standard setup, you can do so here. This is not something that most developers will ever need to worry about.

The jbuilder.config file includes other options for setting up the IDE. It begins with this statement:

```
include jdk.config
```

This statement inserts a copy of the jdk.config file into the jbuilder.config file. You could, of course, insert an alternate file here if you wanted to experiment with JDK configurations without taking a chance on corrupting the original jdk.config file that ships with JBuilder.

The JBuilder config file can be used to configure the JAR files used by the IDE. Please note that this is the proper way to give the IDE access to these JAR files. There is another mechanism, called a library file, that you will use to give your own program access to JAR files or class files. In particular, don't try to change the classpath used by your JBuilder applications by editing this file. The correct way to do that sort of thing is described in Chapter 27, "Working with JAR Files," in the section titled "Setting Your ClassPath: JBuilder Library Files."

The simplest way to give JBuilder access to a set of JAR files is to use the addjars or addpath macro:

```
addjars ../patch
addpath ../lib/sqltools.jar
```

The first of these lines of code adds all the JAR files in the ../patch directory to the list of JAR files that JBuilder can access. The second line adds a single JAR file to the list of JAR files the IDE can access. If you wanted, for instance, to give JBuilder access to all the JAR files that InterClient uses, you could add them using either of these techniques.

Getting Memory Set Up Right

If you are working with a big project, and particularly if you are using the UML feature that comes in the advanced versions of JBuilder, you may find that memory inside the IDE is a bit tight. You can give the IDE a bit more headroom by changing the minimum and maximum heap size used by the Java VM. Here are the relevant lines from JBuilder config:

```
# Tune this VM to provide enough headroom to work on large

# applications

vmparam -Xms8m

vmparam -Xmx128m
```

With a big project, you might want to run with -Xmx256m, but it all depends on what your experiments reveal to be best for your system.

NOTE: If you find these parameters passed in to the JVM to be a bit esoteric, you should not feel bad. Most people don't know about them. To learn more, go to the command prompt and type java -X. This will let you see non-standard options to the Java VM. Here are the options available to you with the 1.3.1 vm on Windows:

-Xmixed — mixed mode execution (default)
-Xint — interpreted mode execution only
-Xbootclasspath:<directories and zip/jar files separated by ;> — set search path for bootstrap classes and resources
-Xbootclasspath/a:<directories and zip/jar files separated by ;> — append to end of bootstrap class path
-Xbootclasspath/p:<directories and zip/jar files separated by ;> — prepend in front of bootstrap class path
-Xnoclassgc — disable class garbage collection
-Xincgc — enable incremental garbage collection
-Xbatch — disable background compilation
-Xms<size> — set initial Java heap size
-Xmx<size> — set maximum Java heap size
-Xss<size> — set java thread stack size
-Xprof — output cpu profiling data
-Xrunhprof[:help]|[:<option>=<value>, ...] — perform JVMPI heap, cpu, or monitor profiling
-Xdebug — enable remote debugging
-Xfuture — enable strictest checks, anticipating future default
-Xrs — reduce use of OS signals by Java/VM (see documentation)

Problems with font.properties

Particularly if you are running on Linux, you may get messages when you compile that look like this:

```
Font specified in font.properties not found \
[–symbol-medium-r-normal–*-%d-*-*-p-*-adobe-fontspecific]
```

There are two ways to fix this problem:

First, go to almost any available Windows machine and find the file called symbol.ttf. This is probably located in your winnt/fonts directory or windows/fonts directory. Switch back to your Linux machine and copy the symbol.ttf font into the ../jdk1.X.X/jre/lib/fonts directory, and then add the following line to the fonts.dir file from that directory:

```
symbol.ttf -urw-symbol-medium-r-normal—0-0-0-0-p-0-adobe-fontspecific
```

When you are done, increment the number at the top of the file. Now the problem should go away.

The other alternative is to edit the font.properties file, removing all the references to the missing font. This usually involves commenting out the many lines that reference the fonts noted as missing when you try to compile.

Using Ant

When viewing the source on the CD, you may find some files called build.xml. These files are part of the configuration for a utility called Ant.

Ant is a tool from the Jakarta project that can help you with the build process. If you are familiar with the various make utilities that exist in this world, you can think of Ant as a Java implementation of make. The big difference between make and Ant is that Ant uses a very clean, XML-based syntax for controlling the build process. Make, on the other hand, uses a syntax that is only slightly less arcane than Assembler.

NOTE: Some versions of make are so evil that the very mention of the word might send shivers down the spine of some developers. If my mentioning Ant and make in the same sentence has caused your blood to chill, I want to assure you that Ant is much friendlier than make. Conversely, if you have mastered make, you may think that you don't need Ant. If you really, truly, have mastered make and can whip out makefiles with no problems, than Ant probably has nothing to offer you. But if you know make, and yet spend a lot of time tracking down silly syntactical problems in your makefiles, then you will be glad to know that Ant is much friendlier. I have never found an Ant build file to fail simply because of misplaced white space, while such problems are pretty much the norm when working with some versions of make.

You do not need Ant or make to compile any of the projects in this book. In fact, JBuilder makes compiling your applications and creating JAR files effortless from either the IDE or the command line. But there are some tasks you can do with a tool like make or Ant that you can't do from inside the JBuilder IDE, such as deleting and copying files as part of the build process or running other processes after you build.

NOTE: I've only recently come to realize that JBuilder 7 actually uses Ant as part of its standard build process. As a result, you can now do quite remarkable things from inside JBuilder, even if you do not include Ant build files. However, JBuilder 7 Enterprise has built-in tools for integrating Ant files directly into your project as first-class citizens. Simply add them to your list of files in the project pane. Note also that you can choose Project | Project Properties from the JBuilder menu, then turn to the Run page, edit a run-time configuration, and choose Clean as your build target at the bottom of your page. If you close the dialogs and choose the green run button, this new make option will completely delete your classes directory. This can be very helpful if you think JBuilder is not properly recognizing changes you have made to your files. If you want, you can set up one run-time configuration explicitly for cleaning up your build and another for normal runs.

Here is the home page for the Ant project, followed by the home page for the Apache Jakarta project:

http://jakarta.apache.org/ant/index.html
http://jakarta.apache.org/

Ant can give you very fine-tuned control over the build process. It allows you to do things like create directories, delete directories, build JAR files, and otherwise configure most of the details of the build process. Most of these things can also be done from inside of JBuilder, but

Ant gives you a bit more control and also provides a means of co-developing your project with people who don't use JBuilder.

It is possible to integrate Ant into JBuilder via a tool called AntRunner. You can download the code for AntRunner from this site: http://antrunner.sourceforge.net/. The integration process is very simple and involves little more than moving three JAR files into the JBuilder lib/ext and /doc directories and editing one line in a configuration file. When you are done, items will be added to the JBuilder menus to allow you to use Ant from inside the IDE.

NOTE: As a user of 4NT, I had a little trouble setting up Ant on Windows the first time I used it. (It ran flawlessly on Linux.) After installing Ant on Windows, a bin directory is created. This directory has a file in it called Ant.bat. This is the file you run whenever you want to use Ant. It has a line that should read like this:

```
if "%@eval[2+2]" == "4" goto setup4NT
```

In my installation of Ant, the @ symbol in the above line was missing. This caused me some trouble until I finally tracked down the problem.

This book is about JBuilder, not Ant. As a result, I won't say much more about Ant in this text. However, I would definitely consider spending the few hours it takes to install and get up to speed on this product. If your shop is using Java heavily, then it almost certainly should also be using Ant.

CodeBox

Many of the projects in this book use a utility file called codebox.jar. CodeBox contains reusable code that I have written. Here you will find simple math routines, string manipulation routines, routines for opening and closing files, simple routines for pulling down information from the web, and more.

I use CodeBox a lot in this book. If you don't have this JAR file set up properly, many of the projects in this book will not work. Setting up CodeBox properly involves making sure codebox.jar is on your class path. In JBuilder, a file is on your classpath if it is referenced in a library.

To set up CodeBox, choose **Tools | Configure Libraries** from the JBuilder menu. Click the **New** button to bring up the New Library Wizard. Give the library the name **codebox**. The best location for it is probably User Home, which is the default value in the New Library Wizard. Click the **Add** button, and search for the JAR file. It comes on the CD with this book, or you can download it from www.elvenware.com. It doesn't matter where on your hard drive you place codebox.jar, but I would recommend placing it in an easy-to-find directory that has no spaces in its path. I end up putting a number of other JAR files in the same directory with codebox.jar.

After you have browsed for and located codebox.jar, click **OK** in the Select One or More Directories dialog. Then click **OK** to close the New Library Wizard. The Configure Library Wizard should now have a new node in it called codebox. In the right-hand portion of the dialog, you should be able to see the complete JAR file name, including its path. Click **OK** to close the Configure Library dialog.

Once you have set the codebox library in your User Home directory, you can use CodeBox in any project you create. I will talk about creating projects in the next chapter. There you will learn that you can choose Project | Project Properties and then turn to the Required Libraries page on the Paths page. Click the **Add** button, and add in the new codebox library that you just created. The end effect of this procedure is to put codebox.jar on your classpath.

A more in-depth discussion of using libraries is included in Part V: Project Management. There you will learn a great deal about how to configure class paths and how to set up packages.

Summary

In this chapter you learned how to install JBuilder and learned a few basic terms that are necessary for an understanding of the remaining chapters in this text. At the end of the chapter, I also added a few notes explaining how I have customized my environment. Even if you choose other options than those I have outlined here, I would hope that you can still use these notes as a jumping-off place when figuring out how to set up the environment to suit your own purposes.

However, you can learn additional details about the install process by reading the index.html file found in the root of the JBuilder CD. You should also take at least a cursory glance at the release notes file found on the JBuilder CD. Again, the simplest way to get to the release notes is by first opening up the index.html file in the root of the JBuilder CD.

In general, it is a bad idea to start asking questions on the JBuilder newsgroups without first checking to see if your question is answered in the release notes. The release notes are perhaps the only place where the developers of JBuilder can speak directly to users. A big company like Borland erects a marketing wall around their product, but don't forget that it is developed by plain old developers just like you. Whenever you can get directly in touch with them, that is a good thing.

Chapter 3

Creating Default Applications and Applets

Charlie and Margie Calvert

In this chapter you are going to learn how to create default applications and applets in JBuilder. The term "default application or applet" refers to the simplest possible application or applet that you will create in JBuilder if you use the application or applet wizards.

If you are new to JBuilder, this chapter should help you get started using the product. Here you will find the foundations on which most of the programs in this book are built.

This chapter is going to be referred to many times throughout the book. In almost every chapter you are going to have the chance to build example programs. The descriptions of how to create many of those projects will begin by asking you to create a default application or applet. In many cases, rather than describing the same opening steps over and over again, I will ask you to refer to this chapter. Once you have the default application or applet built, you can return to the text and learn how to add new features to the foundation code described in this chapter.

Examining the other side of the coin, I want to assure you that this book examines many of the features touched on in this chapter in considerable depth. The point of this chapter is just to give you a cookbook for creating simple applications or applets. I try to describe many of the fundamental questions you might have about these programs, but I do not go into any significant depth on the underlying technologies. Text describing the IDE, project management, the structure of default JBuilder applications and applets, etc., is included in the appropriate sections of the book. Here I only want to answer the basic questions you might have about creating simple JBuilder programs.

Overview

In this section of the chapter you will get an overview of the basic steps that are part of creating both applications and applets. The process of creating an application or applet in JBuilder often starts with the creation of a new project.

Creating a new project means that you are doing two things:

- Creating a JPR/JPX file
- Creating a directory to house the file

Optionally you may also create an HTML file that you can use to describe the project. This file is called the project notes file. In the example programs for this book, this HTML file will either have the same name as the project or be called overview.html.

You don't have to do anything special to create the directory and its JPR/JPX file. If you step through the Project Wizard, JBuilder will create them both for you. In fact, the main purpose of the JBuilder Project Wizard is to create these two items in the simplest manner possible.

After creating the project, the next step is to add one or more applications or applets to the project. As a rule, you only have one application or applet in each project. However, it is not wrong, or incorrect, to put multiple applications in one project. It is simply a matter of doing what seems most reasonable.

Creating a New Project

Begin by choosing **File | New Project** from the JBuilder menu. Alternatively, you can choose **File | New** and then choose **Project** from the Project page of the Object Gallery. In either case, you will end up in the Project Wizard, the first page of which is shown in Figure 3-1.

NOTE: If you already have a project open in JBuilder, you might want to choose File | Close Projects to close any projects you already have open. If you need to have more than one project open, it is sometimes useful to choose Window | New Browser to pop up another browser. You could then place your additional project in its own space. JBuilder will let you open/create an almost unlimited number of projects, but for simplicity it is sometimes easier to just work with one at a time. If you are low on RAM, closing projects can sometimes help. But if you choose Window | New Browser, rather than opening up a new instance of JBuilder, you don't really use that much memory.

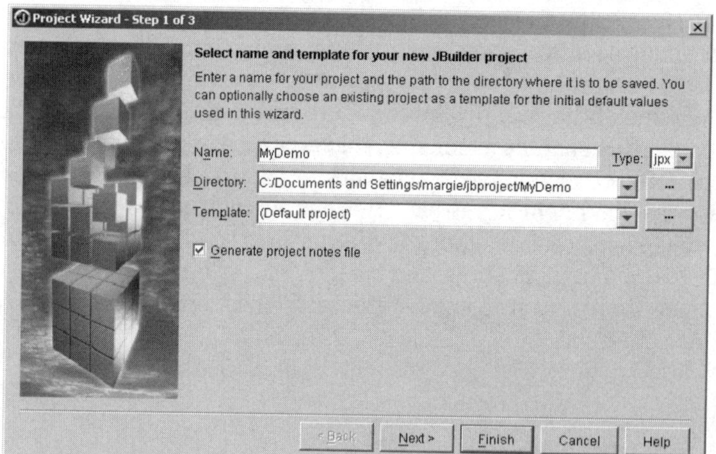

Figure 3-1: Using the first page of the Project Wizard to change the default name of a project from untitledx to MyDemo

There are only a few fields that you need to edit when creating a default project. In particular, you need to name the new directory in which your project will be located and then name the JPR or JPX file you will place inside it. You will name both the JPR or JPX file and the directory when you change the Name field in page one of the Project Wizard.

NOTE: A JPR file is an ordinary text file; a JPX file is a text file in XML format. My sense is that the team is moving toward JPX files and will eventually want to phase out JPR files.

By default, JBuilder creates projects in a directory called untitled*x*, where *x* is a scalar value larger than 0. For instance, the name field might be set to untitled1 or untitled2, etc. You will usually want to rename this value to something more meaningful. Figure 3-1 shows the Name field in the Project Wizard altered so that the project resides not in a directory called untitledx but in a directory called MyDemo.

NOTE: I tend to put all my untitled projects in one directory tree and all my named projects in another directory tree. My untitled projects are usually scrap code that I create on the fly when I want to test something. If I ever create something with an untitled name that I want to keep, I try to use the refactoring tools described later in this book, along with the techniques described in the part on project management, to move the project to the directory tree where I keep my valued projects. Then I periodically delete the projects in the untitled section. My point is that it is a good and healthy thing to create lots of temporary projects where you test out ideas. Creating temporary projects to test ideas, potential bugs, new technologies, etc., is a great virtue.

When you name your project, you will want to capitalize the first letter of the project name. The convention in this book is that a JPX or JPR file should have the same name as the main class in your project. Class names are capitalized and use camel caps: CamelCaps, MyDemo, MyProject. The project name should follow the same conventions. The fact that JBuilder uses lowercase letters to name the untitled*x* projects is confusing. However, if you look at the samples directory that comes with JBuilder, all of the projects are named using capital letters. The Welcome project that appears when you first load JBuilder is a good example of this. At any rate, it is the convention used in this book, and I believe it is a good one.

While you are in Step 1 of the Project Wizard, notice the check box that allows you to generate a project notes file. I recommend that you check this box. The project notes file is quite handy for adding any notes that you may wish to accompany the application, such as information about the purpose and architecture of the application. I try to use these files quite liberally in the projects included on the CD for this book.

Click the **Next** button to move to the next page of the Project Wizard. If you know that you are not going to make changes on pages two and three of the Project Wizard, you have the option of clicking **Finish** to exit the Project Wizard and create a project at this time.

The second page of the Project Wizard allows you to change the structure of your project itself. This page gives you the ability to set paths and required libraries. If you need to make these adjustments to the project later, you will be able to access the same dialogs on the Paths page of the Project Properties or Default Project Properties dialog. You would reach this, once you have created a project, by choosing **Project | Project Properties** or **Project | Default Project Properties**.

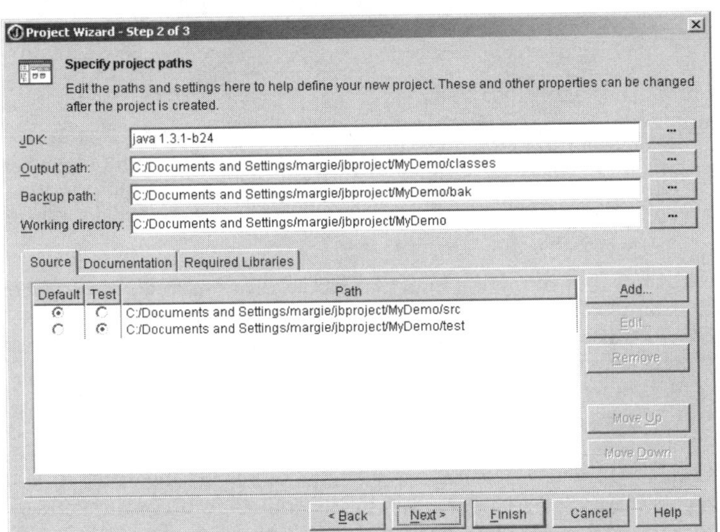

Figure 3-2: Accept the default settings in the second page of the Project Wizard.

In this case, we want to stick with the default values for your project's structure. As a result, no changes should be made to the second page in the Project Wizard, and you can just click through to the next page by clicking **Next.**

NOTE: Many of the projects in this book use codebox.jar, which contains a set of utility routines that ship with this book. A description of how to use codebox.jar is included at the end of Chapter 2, "Setup and Configuration." More is said about CodeBox in various other parts of the book, particularly in the part on project management.

The third page in the Project Wizard allows you to edit the text that will appear in the comments that JBuilder puts by default at the top of your source files. This is an entirely intuitive process and needs no explanation from me. Once you have filled in the appropriate information, click **Finish** to create the project and exit the Project Wizard.

If you do not fill out the comment section at this point, you have the option to add it later, once you have created the project. To do this, choose **Project | Project Properties** and turn to the General page, which will present the same dialog. You may find it useful to have JBuilder place some of this information in your projects by default. If you would like to choose that option, turn to **Project | Default Project Properties** and enter, for instance, your name and company on the General page. Once you have done this, JBuilder will insert that information into the header comments of each project you create from that point on.

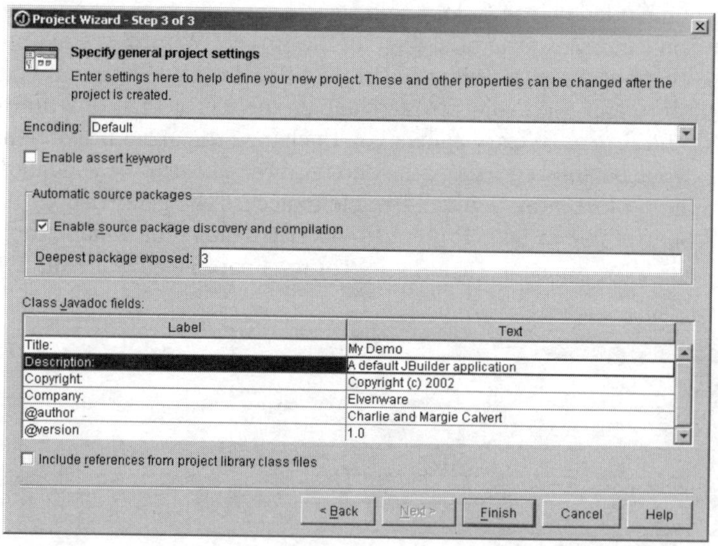

Figure 3-3: You will most likely want to fill in your own information on the third page of the Project Wizard.

NOTE: None of the decisions that you make in the Project Wizard are final. Part V: Project Management will explain, for example, how you can change the root directory in which your projects are stored (in Chapter 24, "The Structure of a Default JBuilder Project") and how to rename your project (in Chapter 31, "Refactoring and UML").

Optional Step to Facilitate Javadoc Documentation

Once you exit the Project Wizard, your newly created directory, jpx/jpr file, and optional html file will be ready to use. You will see MyDemo.jpx in the top-left side of the screen in the project pane; beneath it is a file called MyDemo.html. Figure 3-4 shows the new project as it will appear after you have double-clicked on the MyDemo.html file. The MyDemo.html file is the file you created when you chose the Generate project notes file option in Step 1 of the Project Wizard. If you entered information into the third page of the Project Wizard, that information will be part of this file and displayed on the screen, as shown in Figure 3-4.

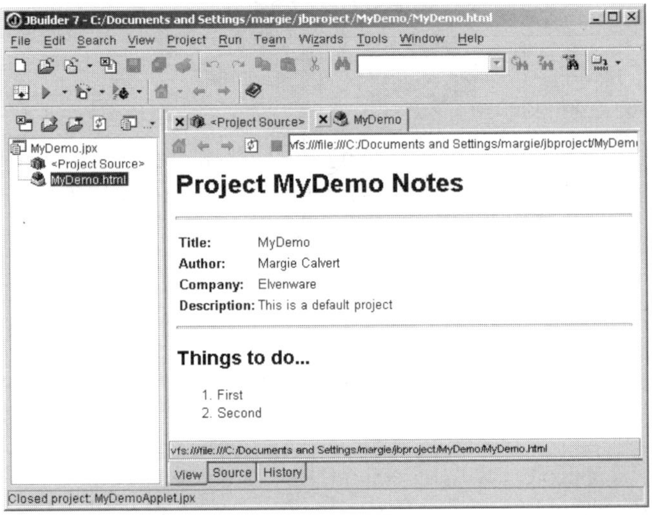

Figure 3-4: The IDE as it appears after you have created a new project

The optional step that we will take here is to rename the MyDemo.html file to overview.html. To do this, make sure that MyDemo.html is highlighted, and then choose **File | Save As.** In the Name field of the dialog that pops up, type **overview.html.** Choose **Delete source file and remove from project** and **Add saved file to project.** The dialog should look like Figure 3-5. Click **OK** to save your changes.

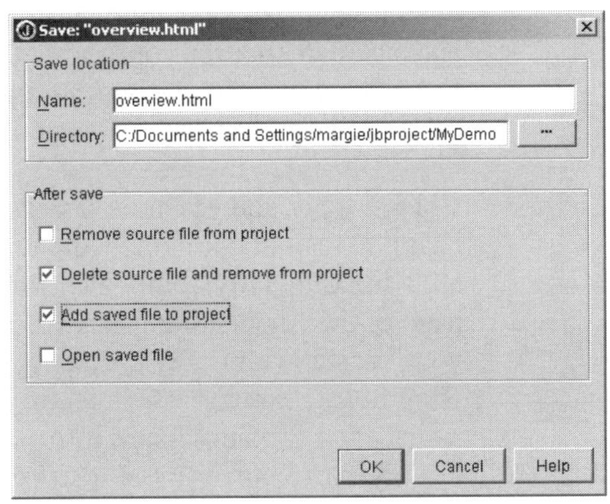

Figure 3-5: The Save dialog has some very nice features that allow you to delete the original file and add the new file to the project.

NOTE: There is actually a reason why you might want to rename your project notes file to overview.html. In particular, this will help it fit in with the Javadoc standards. For more information about the overview.html file, see Chapter 21, "Comments and Javadoc."

Creating a New Application

After you have created a project, you will almost always want to insert an application or applet into it. To insert an application, begin by selecting **File | New.** On the first page of the Object Gallery, shown in Figure 3-6, select **Application** by double-clicking it. The dialog shown in Figure 3-7 will appear.

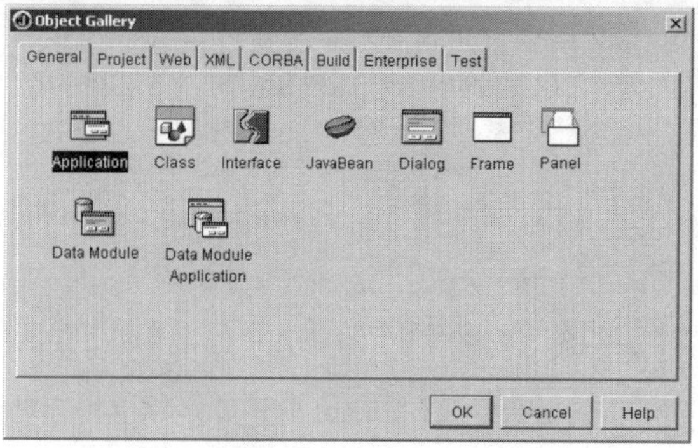

Figure 3-6: The Object Gallery of JBuilder 7. Here you will find wizards for creating a new application, a new class, a new JavaBean, and several other options.

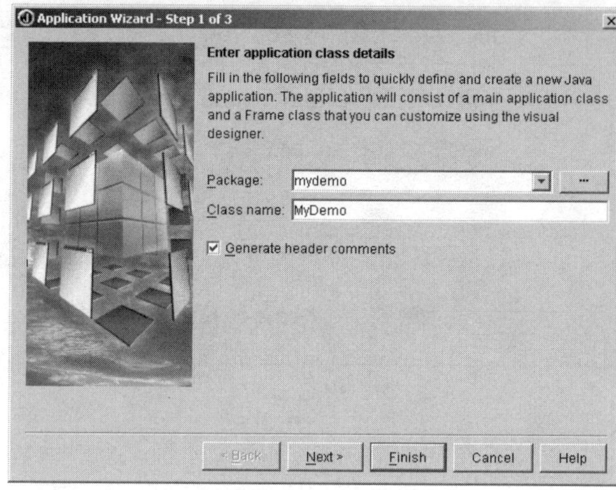

Figure 3-7: Changing the name of an application from Application1 to MyDemo on the first page of the Application Wizard

The application you add to your project will, by default, have a name like Application*x*. Again, the value *x* will be an integer value larger than 0. (In this book, we will tend not to use this default name, as explained in the next paragraph.) The files created will reside by default in a package named after your project. For instance, they might be in a directory called untitled*x*. In our case, we are placing them in a directory called MyDemo, since that was the name we gave the project in the previous section. More particularly, your Java source code will reside in MyDemo/src/mydemo/.

Figure 3-7 shows the first page of the Application Wizard. In the Class Name field, we have changed the default name, Application1, to MyDemo. JBuilder will use this information to create a file called MyDemo.java, which will contain the main class for your application. This page of the Application Wizard also allows you to change the name of the main package for your project. Generally speaking, you will not want to do this. Notice the check box for generating header comments. Selecting this check box will insert the information from the third page of the Project Wizard into your application. Make sure that the check box is selected and click **Next** to move to the next page of the wizard.

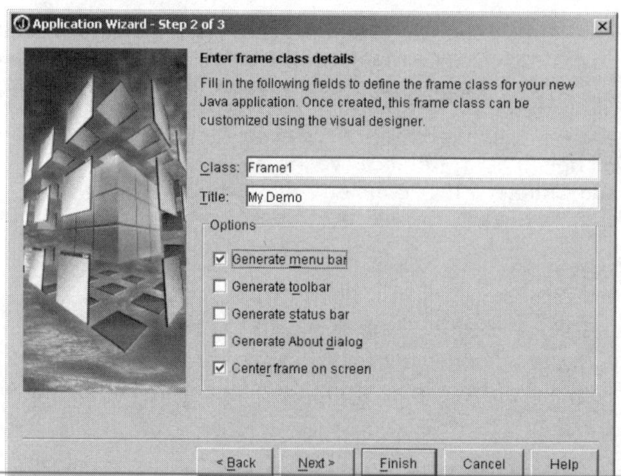

Figure 3-8: The second page of the Application Wizard

On the second page of the Application Wizard, shown in Figure 3-8, you can change the name for the main frame of your project. Generally speaking, Frame1 works just as well as any other name. Furthermore, it is useful to always give the main frame of your project the same name, as it will help you and others easily locate it. JBuilder will create a file named Frame1.java if you leave the default name.

The words that you enter into the Title field of this page will appear at the top of your application when it is running. The frame holds the graphical user interface for your application. When you run your application, the frame will pop up, displaying your interface with the title you select as the caption. You do not need to use camel caps in the Title field and should enter the title just as you wish it to display. In this case, type **My Demo** in the Title field.

Before you move on, notice that with a simple check, you can generate a menu bar for your application. You can also choose other options to customize the appearance and function of your frame. For instance, you can decide whether or not to automatically generate a toolbar, a status bar, or an "About" dialog, as well as whether or not you want to center your frame in the middle of the screen when it appears.

At this point, you have finished creating a default application. Click **Finish** to exit the wizard. You can now click the green run button on the toolbar to run your application. Or, if you prefer, choose **Run | Run Project** from the menu. The hot key for this option is F9.

NOTE: If you are interested in creating even simpler projects, such as a basic Hello World application, you should turn to Chapter 23, "Building Simple Applications." There you will also find more information on the meaning and function of all the files generated by the Project and Application wizards.

Remember that JBuilder does not contain any black boxes. If you set the name of a directory in JBuilder or if you set the name of a class, you are not writing your changes in stone. Even if you exit JBuilder, you can still change the name of that directory or the name of that class exactly as you would when working with any other directory on your system or any other piece of Java source code. The JBuilder wizards are Borland's way of helping you fill in the parts of your code that you would have to type out or create for yourself anyway. The developers of JBuilder are religious about ensuring that development in the environment involves no black boxes or deep secrets. After all, they are developers themselves, and they want exactly the same kinds of flexibility in project development that you would want.

In Chapter 31, you will learn how to automatically change package or class names in your project. Refactoring changes not only the name of a single directory or a single class but also all references to that class or package throughout your project.

Creating a New Applet

Now you know how to create an application in JBuilder. The next step is to learn how to build an applet. This section of the chapter is fairly short, as creating an applet is very much like creating an application. I recommend, however, that you read through the previous section first, as it contains tips that are skipped in this section or only mentioned in passing.

Before you create the applet, create a new project using the instructions outlined earlier in this chapter. Name the project **MyDemoApplet**.

Select **File | New** from the JBuilder menu to open the Object Gallery, shown in Figure 3-9. Turn to the third page of the Object Gallery, which is labeled Web, and choose **Applet** by double-clicking on it. (In the Personal edition of JBuilder 6, the Applet icon is not on the Web page. Instead it is on the first page of the Object Gallery, which in that version of the project was called the New page.)

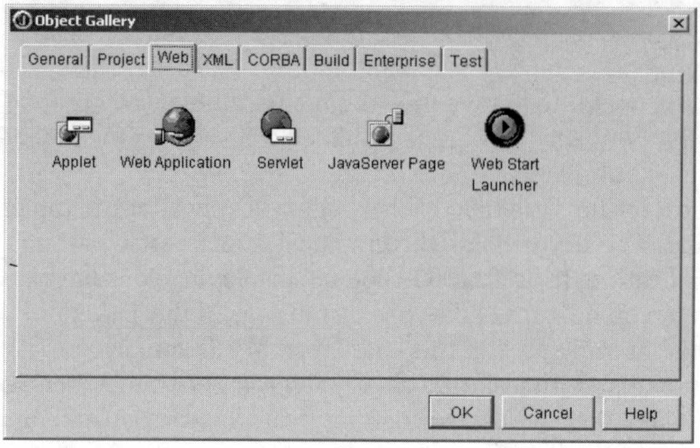

Figure 3-9: The Applet Wizard is found on the Web page of the Object Gallery.

A wizard will appear with several pages of options. There is little need to step through the other pages. Instead, check **Generate Header Comments** and uncheck the other options. In the Class Name field, rename the applet to **MyDemoApplet**. Leave the default values for the other fields. Click the **Finish** button. When you are done, your project should look like Figure 3-10.

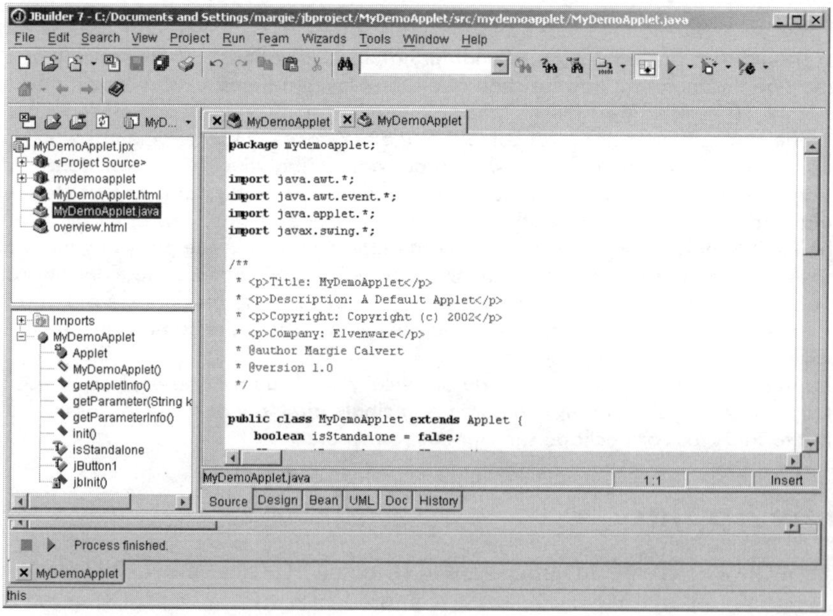

Figure 3-10: A default applet has been added to the project.

The code for the applet is shown in Listing 3-1. There is no need to do more than just glance at the code.

Listing 3-1: The default applet code generated by JBuilder

```
package mydemoapplet;

import java.awt.*;
import java.awt.event.*;
import java.applet.*;
```

```
import javax.swing.*;

/**
 * <p>Title: MyDemoApplet</p>
 * <p>Description: A default applet</p>
 * <p>Copyright: Copyright (c) 2002</p>
 * <p>Company: Elvenware</p>
 * @author Margie Calvert
 * @version 1.0
 */

public class MyDemoApplet extends Applet {
    boolean isStandalone = false;
    //Get a parameter value
    public String getParameter(String key, String def) {
        return isStandalone ? System.getProperty(key, def) :
            (getParameter(key) != null ? getParameter(key) : def);
    }

    //Construct the applet
    public MyDemoApplet() {
    }
    //Initialize the applet
    public void init() {
        try {
            jbInit();
        }
        catch(Exception e) {
            e.printStackTrace();
        }
    }
    //Component initialization
    private void jbInit() throws Exception {
    }
    //Get Applet information
    public String getAppletInfo() {
        return "Applet Information";
    }
    //Get parameter info
    public String[][] getParameterInfo() {
        return null;
    }
}
```

Viewing Your Applet

JBuilder has a built-in mechanism for viewing your applet. Before you can try this out, you will need to put something in your applet. If you find the instructions here confusing, don't worry, as the chapters after this will give you the vocabulary and knowledge to navigate JBuilder's visual tools. However, chances are that you will be able to follow these directions.

To try this out, focus MyDemoApplet.java by double-clicking on it. Click on the **Design** tab, which is located somewhere near the bottom of the middle of your screen. This will move you to a different display called design view, shown in Figure 3-11.

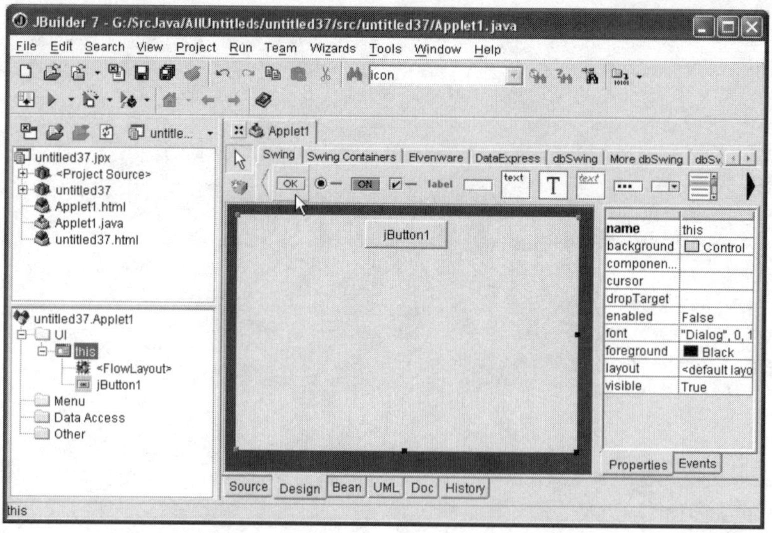

Figure 3-11: Design view in the JBuilder IDE. Here you can use the visual tools to "paint" the interface for your application.

You will see many tabs stretching across the top-right area of the screen below the toolbars. On the tabs are names like Swing, Swing Containers, and Data Express. Just under the word Swing is a little rectangle that contains the text OK. This is an icon. If you run your cursor over the icon, a little box will appear containing the words "javax.swing.JButton." Click once on the icon and then once in the square, light-colored area beneath it. You should see a button appear. Figure 3-11 shows the moment after a button has been dropped down. The cursor was moved back over the icon so that you can easily find it.

If you were able to successfully drop down a button, click the **Source** tab, which is right next to the Design tab near the bottom of the middle area of your screen. Once you click on this tab, you should be back to the view you had in Figure 3-10.

If you double-click on MyDemoApplet.html, you should see something similar to what you just created in design view, as shown in Figure 3-12. In this view, you are seeing a live version of your applet displayed in a web page.

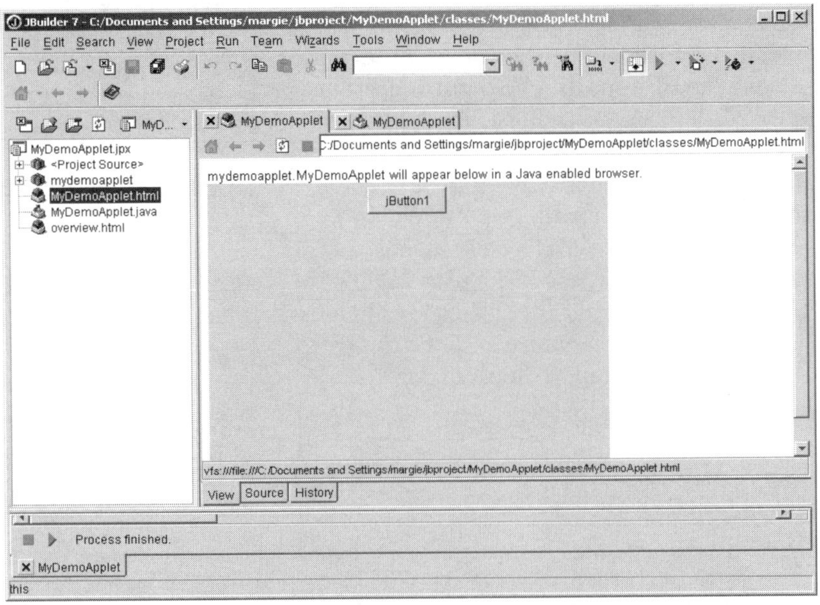

Figure 3-12: MyDemoApplet.html

NOTE: If you did not rename your project notes file to overview.html, as recommended in the section of this chapter titled "The Steps for Creating a New Project," you probably have two MyDemoApplet.html files. You can fix this by following the instructions in that section. Just make sure you rename the correct file to overview.html!

There are several ways to run the applet. You can right-click on **MyDemoApplet.html** and choose **Run using "MyDemoApplet"** from the context menu. You can also press the green run button, select **F9**, or select **Run | Run Project** from the menu.

NOTE: You can learn about deploying an applet in a JAR file in Chapter 28.

Viewing the Applet Through a Browser

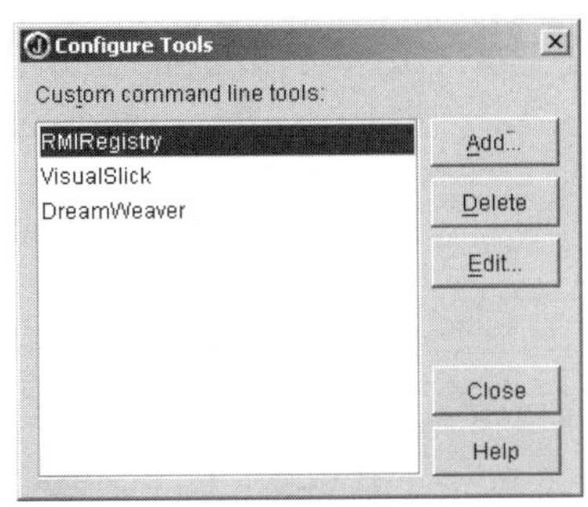

Figure 3-13: The Configure Tools dialog

If you click the Run button in JBuilder, then by default, your applet will appear in either Borland's AppletTestbed or a JDK tool called an appletviewer. The one flaw in using either of these tools is that the applet may not display exactly as it will in a browser. If you wish to view your applet in a browser, you can reconfigure JBuilder so that this option is easily accessible to you.

Choose **Tools | Configure Tools** from the JBuilder menu. A dialog will pop up that looks something like Figure 3-13.

Click the **Add** button to move to the Add Tool dialog, shown in Figure 3-15. In the Title field, write a short name for the tool you are adding. In this case, we are adding Internet Explorer, which we are abbreviating as IE. Whatever you put in the Title field will appear on the Tools menu, so be fairly brief. Use the ellipsis button for the Program field to browse to the place in your hard drive where your browser's .exe file is stored. Click the **Insert Macro** button and choose the **$Filepath – File path** macro in the Select Macro dialog, as shown in Figure 3-14. Click **OK** to confirm your selection.

In the Parameters field, you may need to put quotes around the macro name: "$Filepath." On the Windows platform, these quotes can help Bill's code-meisters deal with any spaces that might be part of the path leading to your project. The completed Add Tool dialog should look something like what you see in Figure 3-15. Click **OK** to exit the dialog. Close the Configure Tools dialog.

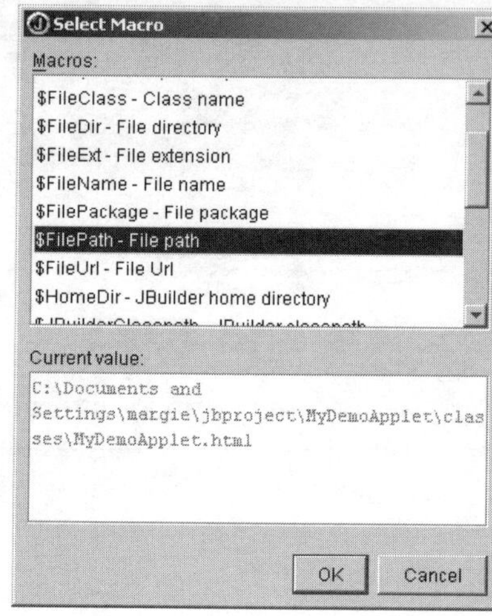

Figure 3-14: The Select Macro dialog

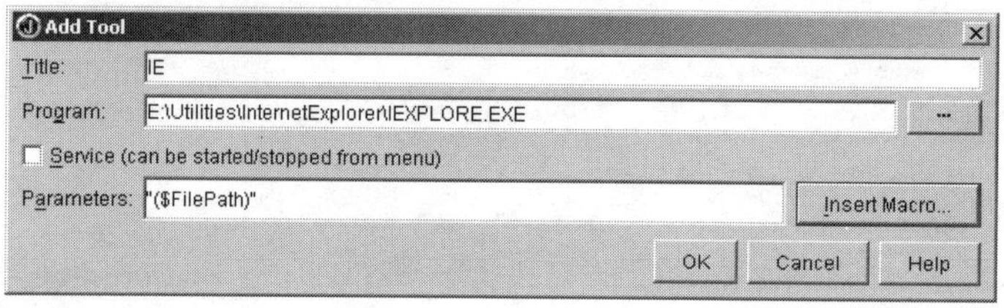

Figure 3-15: The Add Tool dialog

Double-click on **MyDemoApplet.html** to focus it in the content pane. Then choose **Tools | IE**. The applet should display in Internet Explorer.

NOTE: You can use the steps we have just gone through to link many different kinds of tools to JBuilder. Going through this fairly simple process can really save you time. For instance, on Windows, I always hook in Dreamweaver and Visual Slick Edit. I use Dreamweaver to update the project notes file. On Linux, I hook in Visual Slick Edit, and use the Composer section of Netscape 6 as my HTML editor. If you pass in -edit $FilePath, you can get Netscape to open up with your HTML file ready to edit in Composer. JBuilder is very smart in Windows about noting that you have changed your files in a second editor. On Linux, JBuilder is quite smart about this, but you might want to keep your eye on it to make sure it stays in line.

JDK Switching for Applications and Applets

Intermediate and advanced developers will be pleased to know that JBuilder allows you to run your programs from the IDE either on top of the default JDK that ships with JBuilder or on top of the JDK of your choosing. By default, JBuilder 7 uses JDK 1.3.1. To run your program on top of another JDK, first download and install the JDK you want to use from java.sun.com or from some other site of your choosing, such as the IBM site or blackdown sites (www.blackdown.org). Most JDKs have simple forehead installs.

It is now time to select the JDK you want to use when you run your program from inside of JBuilder. I'll discuss JBuilder SE and Enterprise first and then a second technique you can use in the Personal edition and the more expensive editions.

In JBuilder SE and Enterprise, choose **Project | Project Properties** and click the ellipsis button next to the JDK label on the Paths page. Here you can select any existing JDKs you have already registered with JBuilder. To register a new JDK, click the **New** button and browse to the place on your hard drive where you have installed the JDK you want to use.

Select the root drive for the installation and click **OK**. Your new JDK should now be registered, and you can select it.

For more information on switching JDKs, including how to switch JDKs if you are using the Personal edition of the project, see Chapter 5, "JBuilder Product Overview," and read the section near the end of the chapter called "The Tools Menu." In particular, see Figures 5-14 and 5-15.

Applets and JDKS

Here is a tip for intermediate and advanced programmers who are creating applets. The old 1.1x versions of the Sun JDK did not include Swing. As a result, you may want to test your applet not under the default JBuilder 7 JDK 1.3.1, but under an older version of the JDK.

Switch to the JDK you want to use, as described in the previous section. Create a new applet, but in the first page of the Applet Wizard, set the base class to **java.applet.Applet**, not javax.swing.JApplet. By choosing applet rather than JApplet, you are aiming for compatibility with the old JDKs, such as 1.1.x. Swing was not introduced until JDK 1.2.

When creating your applet, always choose controls from the AWT page of the component palette and not from the Swing page. If you have chosen an earlier JDK, such as 1.1.x, your applet will not compile if you chose items from the Swing page. This is the behavior you want, since it proves that your applet will run under older JDKs.

People choose older JDKs because Microsoft used to ship a JVM with Windows that is compatible with JREs 1.1.x but not with newer JREs. Since Microsoft creates our most popular OSs, these older JREs got very wide distribution. Please note that Windows XP does not ship by default with any JDK, though it will keep an installed JDK if you upgrade from older versions of Windows rather than doing a clean install.

If you are testing a JDK 1.1.x applet using JDK switching, you should download a JDK 1.1.x version of Swing found in a file called swingall.jar. You can find the file on the http://java.sun.com site. Create a library that references your new JAR file, and add it to your project using the Project | Project Properties | Required Libraries command found in the JBuilder menus. JBuilder library files are described in Chapter 27.

Applets and Automatically Installing JREs at Run Time

Finally, advanced programmers should note that you can create an HTML page for an applet that will, if necessary, download an updated JRE automatically. Given that Microsoft no longer ships JRE 1.1.x support with Windows, you might want to use this technique to automatically download a new JRE that supports Swing. In particular, see the htmlconverter.jar file that ships in the lib directory of most modern JDKs and also the convert.jar file you can download from the Sun web site: http://java.sun.com/products/plugin/converter.html.

You can also read about this subject on the Sun web site at the following URLs:

http://java.sun.com/products/jfc/tsc/articles/converter/converter.html
http://java.sun.com/products/plugin/index.html
http://java.sun.com/products/plugin/versions.html

This technique seems to work quite well, particularly for Windows developers, even if they are using Netscape or Mozilla. However, you should be aware that the JRE install is rather large. As a result, users with slow modems may have trouble with the long download. If you have a fast DSL or T1 connection, this technology works beautifully.

NOTE: The Java JDK includes the Java run time and source, while the JRE includes only the Java run time.

Summary

In this chapter you learned how to create a default project, an application, and an applet. You learned to rename the project notes file in the project. You also learned at least two different ways to view your applets.

Chapter 4

Using the IDE

Margie Calvert

This chapter presents an overview of the core of the JBuilder IDE, a set of interconnected tools called the AppBrowser. It also describes certain generally useful features of the product, such as how to automate the process of creating a class.

The next chapter will give a general overview of all the features of the product that are not part of the AppBrowser. Chapters scattered throughout the rest of the book will focus on other major features of JBuilder, such as the editor, the UI designer, BeansExpress, the debugger, and so on. Some of these latter features are actually part of the AppBrowser. My plan is to give you an overview of these features in this chapter, while an in-depth look is reserved for later portions of the book.

If you are new to JBuilder, this will be one of this book's most important chapters. It will familiarize you with the basic layout of this powerful programming tool.

There are a number of features in this chapter that I did not know much about before sitting down to write this book. JBuilder is a huge product, and it is easy to overlook even some of its most important tools. As a result, I would suggest taking the time to peruse this chapter, even if you think you know the basic facts about the product.

Defining Our Terms: The IDE and AppBrowser

It is now time to begin developing a vocabulary for describing the JBuilder environment. This section of the text is dedicated to giving you that terminology. When done, we can use our shared knowledge to describe the various tools found in the JBuilder IDE.

Naturally enough, the first term on the list is IDE. An *IDE* is an integrated development environment. The "development environment" part of the term means that the IDE is a program that can be used to develop applications, applets, web services, or similar tools. The "integrated" part of the acronym means that JBuilder has an integrated set of development tools. Most importantly, it combines an editor and a debugger.

There are, however, a number of other important tools that are part of the IDE, including a code browser, numerous wizards, and a context-sensitive help system. The help system even has an extension called CodeInsight that will allow you to automatically discover the methods and classes in the JDK or custom objects at design time without having to look in the help.

NOTE: I will explain CodeInsight in depth in Chapter 7, "Using the Editor." A brief introduction to this feature appears in this chapter, near the end of the section called "Automation: Creating a Class."

Borland is famous for creating good IDEs. In the past, however, Borland developed IDEs primarily for the Windows platform. JBuilder is built entirely in Java. As a result, it was relatively easy to port to other platforms. In fact, the chief architect for JBuilder has pointed out that it was really an extremely easy port. Once it was up and running on one platform, it ran nearly unchanged on other platforms. JBuilder is a stunning example of what you can do with Java if you have the needed skill and vision.

The AppBrowser

Now that you understand the term IDE, the next step is to become familiar with the AppBrowser. The official Borland documentation uses both the terms IDE and AppBrowser. At times, the distinction between these two elements in the documentation becomes blurred, and it is possible that the marketing team means to use the terms interchangeably.

For the purposes of this book, I will define the IDE as the entirety of JBuilder exclusive of the compiler, while I will call the AppBrowser the set of four interlocking windows called the *project pane*, *structure pane*, *content pane*, and *message pane*. The content pane is controlled by the file view tabs.

The top of the IDE contains the menus. Directly beneath the menus is a set of small icons collectively called the toolbar. The main items on the toolbar allow you to open and close projects, save files and projects, and compile and run your project.

Beneath the toolbar is the AppBrowser. The AppBrowser is divided into five sections, as shown in Figure 4-1. It is important that you learn the name of each of these sections, as I will refer to them constantly throughout this book.

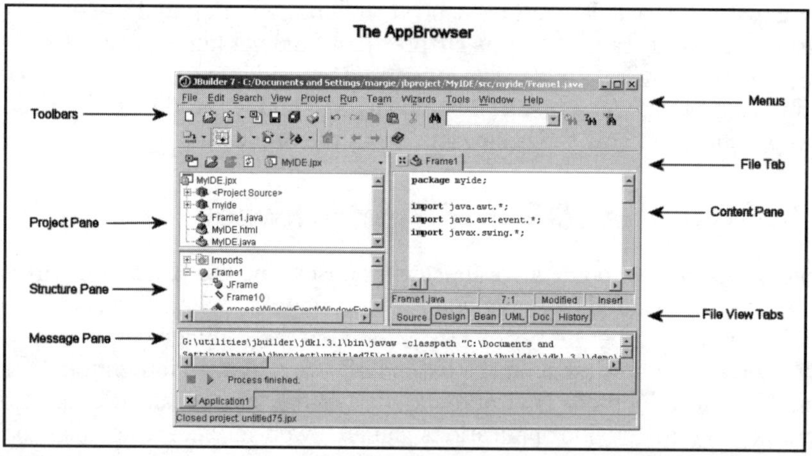

Figure 4-1: The AppBrowser consists of several components whose names play a major role in this book.

The area on the right, where you see your source code, HTML files, and visual design tools, is called the *content pane*, or sometimes the *editor*. When you are in design mode, this is where the *UI designer* appears.

NOTE: Throughout the book I will frequently refer to the area to the right of the project pane and structure pane as the content pane. At various times it may hold the editor, the UI designer, the columns editor, BeansExpress, or various other tools. But I will often call it simply the content pane.

To the left of the editor are two windows called the *project pane* and the *structure pane*. Note that the project pane is above the structure pane.

The project pane, at the top left of the editor, contains a list of the files in your project. Just below the project pane is the structure pane. The centrally important structure pane contains an analysis of the source code, objects, or components found in the file you have selected.

The *message pane* is down along the bottom of the IDE, and the *file view tabs* are between the message pane and the content pane.

You can make the project pane appear or disappear by pressing Ctrl+Alt+P. You can make the structure pane appear or disappear by pressing Ctrl+Alt+S. (Sometimes this latter feature gets a bit sticky when you want the structure pane to reappear. If you have trouble with it, try executing the key combination and then selecting another class in the project pane.) You can make the message pane appear or disappear by pressing Ctrl+Alt+M. The Ctrl+Alt+Z key combination toggles them all simultaneously. This last hot key is particularly useful when you want the editor to take up as much screen real estate as possible. Wise developers will find it worth their while to memorize all these keystrokes.

NOTE: You can restructure the appearance of the AppBrowser manually by moving the boundaries of the windows with a mouse. The content pane, project pane, structure pane, and message pane can completely disappear if you do this. If you are having trouble finding part of the IDE, it may have been removed from the screen in this way. In that case, you will need to use your mouse to once more make it visible. Go to a boundary, left-click, and drag. To free the screen from clutter, many of the illustrations in this book collapse the IDE in this way, or they use the hot keys mentioned above.

Exploring a Simple Project

At this stage, you might consider opening JBuilder itself and creating a default applet so that you can begin navigating through the IDE. If you need help creating the applet, turn to Chapter 3. After you are done, the IDE should look as it does in Figure 4-2.

If you are viewing a Java source file, the structure pane shows a list of todo statements, classes, import statements, methods, and data. Icons designating the type of data being displayed are shown in the structure and content panes.

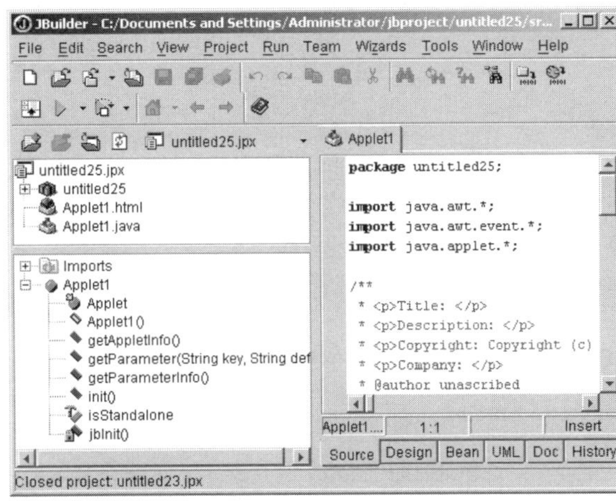

Figure 4-2: The JBuilder environment with a simple applet project loaded in it. Note that the message pane is hidden.

NOTE: The JBuilder help does a good job of defining what each of the icons in the structure and content panes mean. To find these sections of the help, you can choose Help | JBuilder Environment from the menu. Turn to the index page in the help, and type in the words "structure pane." Press Enter. You will be taken to a graphical listing and description of the icons.

In Figure 4-2, a filename, such as Applet1.java, shows up in the project pane. In the structure pane, you can see that Applet1 is the name of one of the classes in the currently selected file. The Applet1 class has methods called getAppletInfo(), getParameter(), etc. For now, it is not important that you understand what all these words mean. Just note that you can see the files in your project, and you can browse the classes declared in your files.

If you select an HTML file in the project pane, the structure pane will disappear, and you will be able to view the contents of the HTML file, including any applets it may contain, in the content pane. To try this out, double-click on **Applet1.html**. When you do this, the structure pane disappears and the file view tabs change. For instance, the tabs that say Source, Design,

Bean, and so on in Figure 4-2 are now changed to View, Source, and History, as shown in Figure 4-3. This change occurs because JBuilder is adapting to the type of data displayed in the content pane.

JBuilder has a built-in HTML code browser, shown in Figure 4-4. If you press the Source tab beneath the content pane when an HTML file is selected, you can see the source for the HTML file, and the structure pane reappears and shows the HTML tags.

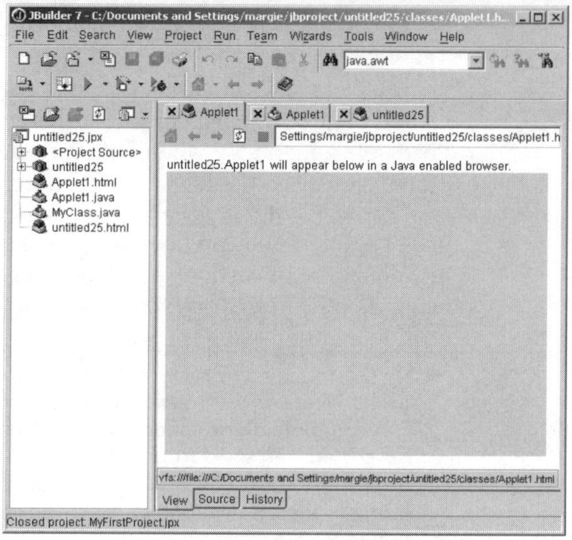

Figure 4-3: The structure pane disappears when you view the output of the HTML file.

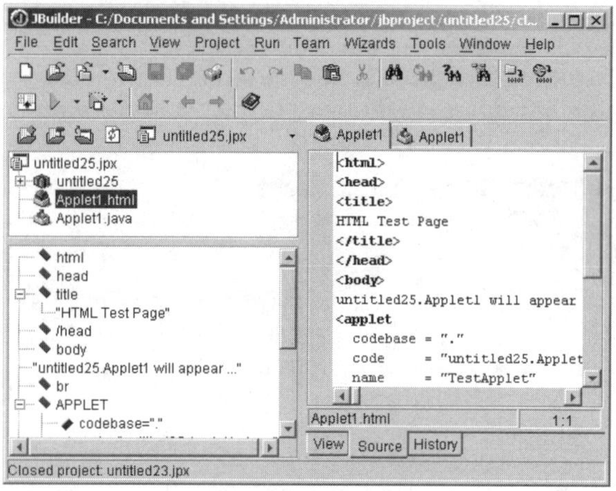

Figure 4-4: The HTML browser. Notice that the structure pane is visible, and the HTML in your file has been parsed.

When JBuilder appears as it does in Figure 4-4, you can use the structure pane to navigate through the HTML code in the content pane. For instance, if you click on the br tag in the structure pane, you will be taken to the place in the editor (content pane) where that tag is listed.

A similar capability is available when you are viewing a java source file. To see this trait in action, open Applet1.java.

Once you have focused a java source file in the content pane, try clicking on the elements in the structure pane. For instance, click on getParameterInfo() in Applet1.java. The view in the content pane will shift, if necessary, to display the declaration for this method, which will be highlighted in the content pane, as shown in Figure 4-5.

If you want to search the structure pane for a code element, move your cursor to the structure pane and start typing a name. A tool tip box will appear and JBuilder will use an incremental search to move the focus to various elements in the structure pane.

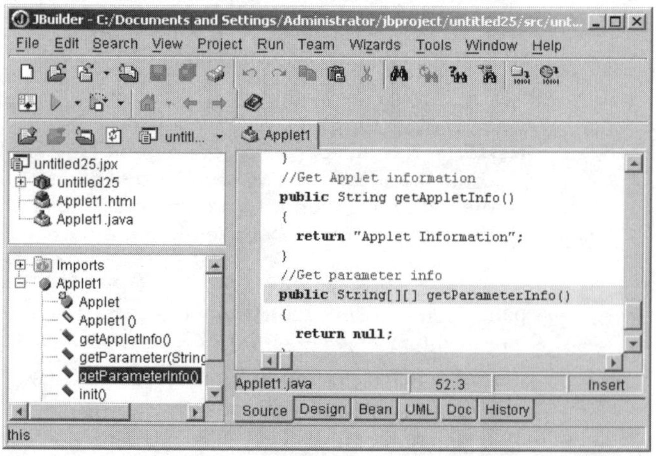

Figure 4-5: The structure pane acts as a navigation tool. Clicking on getParameterInfo() in the structure pane takes you to the implementation of that method.

NOTE: You can alter the appearance and sort order of the items in the structure pane by right-clicking on the structure pane and choosing Properties. You can decide to group items alphabetically or by the order of their appearance in your source file. You can also choose to sort their values by their access type, such as private, public, or protected. Other useful refinements of this type are available on the Properties page for the structure pane.

It turns out that there are other things you will do inside the structure pane besides navigate through a source file. For instance, you can view todo items in the structure pane, as covered in Chapter 7. You can use the structure pane when you are designing a user interface with the UI designer. In particular, if you press the Design tab, go into design mode, and drop controls such as a JButton or a JTextField onto your applet, you will be able to navigate from one control to another using the structure pane.

NOTE: Because the structure pane is so powerful, and it is used by so many different features of the product, you will find that a complete discussion of its use is spread throughout many sections of this book. You will read about the structure pane in this chapter and Chapters 6 and 7.

The Message Pane

Beneath the project pane, the structure pane, and the content pane is an area called the message pane. This is where error messages and messages from JBuilder to the developer appear.

The message pane is also where information about your class path appears when you launch an application from the IDE. If you print things to standard out in your application, they will appear here. When you compile your project, any error messages or warnings caused by your code will be shown in the message pane. If you choose to debug your project, the debugger interface will pop up in the message pane. These possibilities do not completely exhaust the functions of the message pane, which is also involved in version control, unit testing, refactoring code, and other miscellaneous tasks.

NOTE: As mentioned earlier, you can toggle the visibility of the message pane by pressing Ctrl+Alt+M. Once again, I suggest you memorize this keystroke. An icon on the JBuilder 7 toolbar can be used to toggle the visibility of the message pane. Users of older versions of JBuilder can go to http://homepages.borland.com/bstone/index.html and download a tool that will add a similar icon to your toolbar. The URL in question references the home page of Blake Stone, who is the chief architect of JBuilder. Since he developed this tool, you can feel comfortable about adding it to your development environment. The tool in question was developed with the JBuilder OpenTools API, which is discussed in Chapter 32. The OpenTools API allows you to build extensions to JBuilder.

On the toolbar, which is located under the menu, there is an icon in the shape of a green triangle. (In Figure 4-6, you can see this icon slightly offset to the left beneath the word Edit.) If you click this triangle, JBuilder will compile and run your project. Do this now with the applet you have created. Figure 4-6 should approximate the result of the compile as shown in the IDE. Notice that the message pane has appeared beneath the editor, and it contains information about how JBuilder launched your application. It shows the parameters passed to javaw, including the classpath, a Borland version of the appletviewer command, and the main class of your project.

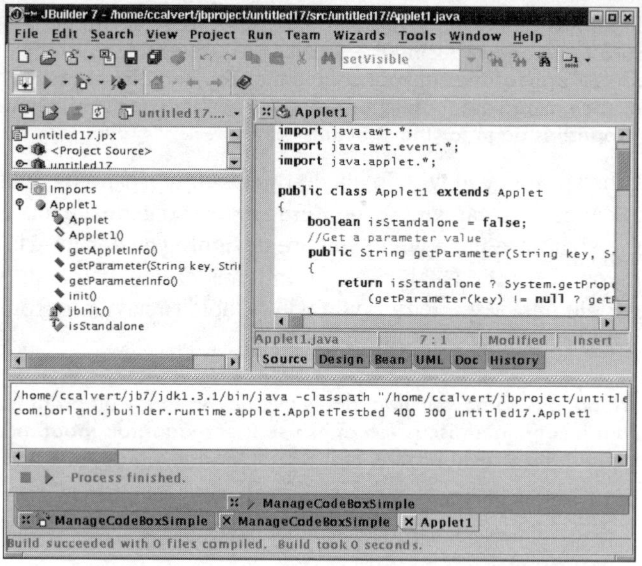

Figure 4-6: In the message pane, you can see that JBuilder is installed in the \home\ccalvert\jb7 directory, and that the current JDK is version 1.3.1.

NOTE: You may need to add a library to your project to expand your class path. This is discussed in Chapter 27 in the section called "Setting Your ClassPath: JBuilder Library Files."

When looking at Figure 4-6, note that you can see the statement used to launch javaw. Clearly, this is just a standard command for launching an applet with the Sun JDK. My point is that JBuilder is keeping you close to the JDK by using the same tools you would use if you were launching the application from the command prompt.

NOTE: In Figure 4-6, there is a reference to a Borland class called AppletTestbed. If you went to the command line and retyped this line using Sun's appletviewer instead of AppletTestbed, the command would work equally well, as long as you were in the right directory.

The File View Tabs

The file view tabs appear at the bottom of the content pane. If the message pane is visible, the content tabs will be above it, as shown in Figure 4-6.

By default, the content pane will be open to source view. If you click on the Design tab, the UI designer will become visible, as shown in Figure 4-7. This view allows you to take advantage of JBuilder's visual design tools. Notice that in Figure 4-7, a JButton, a JTextPane, and a JSlider have been dropped on the UI designer. You can see references to these objects in the structure pane. The UI

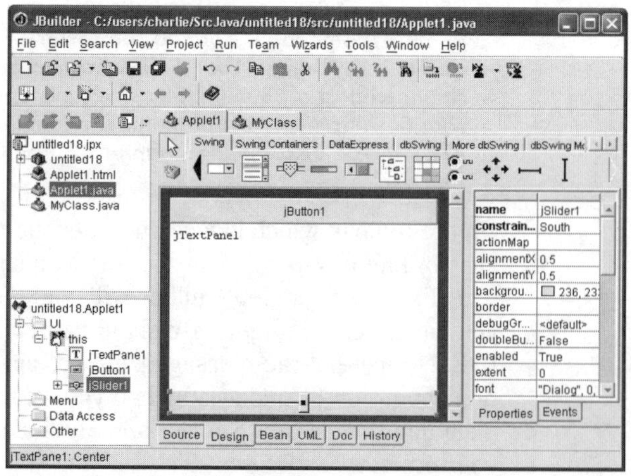

Figure 4-7: The UI designer appears in the content pane, above the file view tabs and to the right of the structure and project panes. The Inspector is to the right of the UI designer.

designer is covered in detail in Chapter 6. For now, just be aware that it exists and try to develop some sense of what it does for you.

The file view tab to the right of the Design tab is labeled Bean. This tab allows you to see the attributes of a JavaBean file and access a part of JBuilder called BeansExpress. BeansExpress is discussed in detail in Part VII: JavaBeans. In Figure 4-8, you can see a portion of BeansExpress.

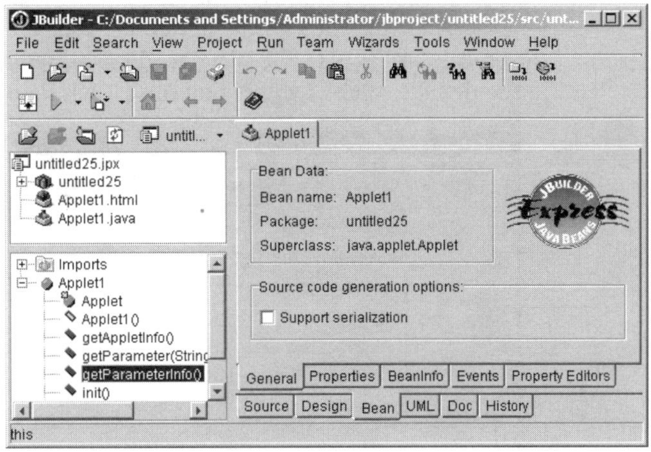

Figure 4-8: The opening page of BeansExpress. The core functionality of BeansExpress is on the Properties, BeanInfo, Events, and Property Editors pages.

In JBuilder SE and Enterprise versions only, you can modify a bean with the tools in this view. In these versions of the product, you can use the JavaBean Wizard (available through File | New | JavaBean) to create a bean. You can then tweak its visual appearance in the UI designer and change its properties in the Bean page of the content pane.

The tab after the Bean tab shows you a UML diagram of your currently selected objects. The UML (short for Unified Modeling Language) tab displays package and class diagrams and helps you visualize the structure of your code. This is an Enterprise-level tool and is not available in the other versions of the product. It is discussed in Chapter 31, "Refactoring and UML."

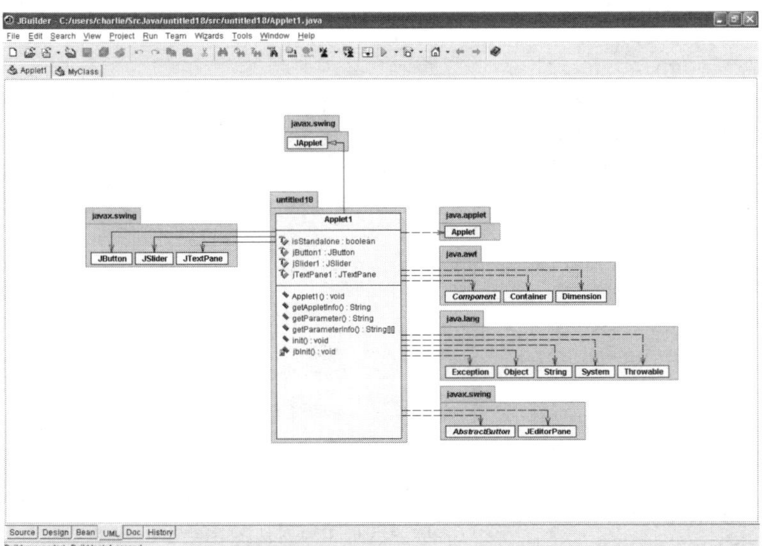

Figure 4-9: The UML Browser is available only in the Enterprise version of JBuilder.

Next to the UML pane, you will find the Doc tab. Here is where the documentation you generate using Javadoc will appear. If you are not clear on what that means, don't worry. Chapter 21 covers this subject in detail. Just be aware that you can achieve very complete documentation of your code by using the Javadoc utility that ships with the Sun JDK, and JBuilder automates this process for you. The Doc pane will show the documentation for the file you have open in the editor.

In Figure 4-10, I have run the Javadoc Wizard using all the default values to produce Javadoc for the files in this project. If you have the Javadoc Wizard in your version of JBuilder, you can probably run it successfully by opening it from the Wizards menu and accepting all the default values by pressing the Finish button on its first page.

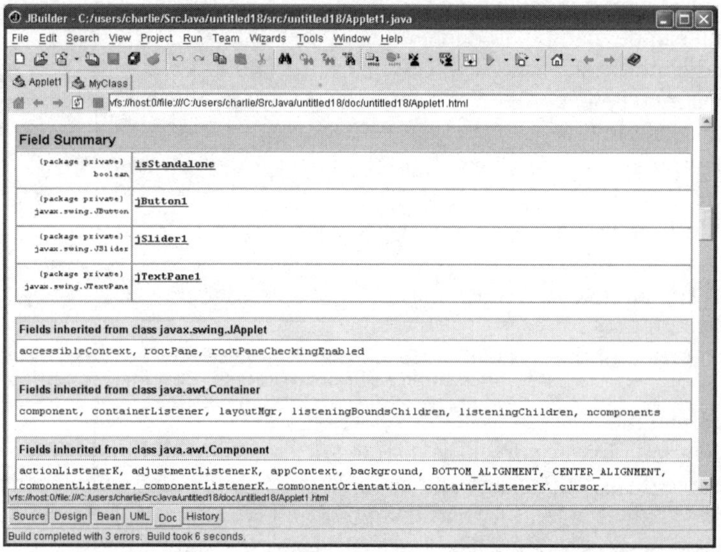

Figure 4-10: The Doc pane displaying a portion of the Javadoc file for the Applet1.java

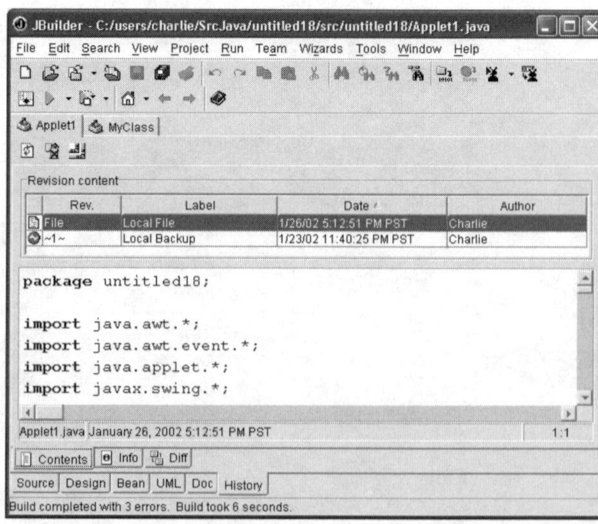

Figure 4-11: The top of the History view shows that there is one up-to-date copy of Applet1.java and one backup copy stored in the bak directory.

To the right of the Doc pane is the History tab, which is very useful for version control. Although some of the features available through this tab are SE and Enterprise level only, the page is available in all versions of JBuilder. The contents page displays the versions of the active file that are currently in play and allows you to sort through them in various ways.

The files stored in your History window exist on disk in your bak directory, which is created by default with every JBuilder project you create. In the part of this book on project management, you will learn how to move this directory if you so desire. For now, you can just use this tab to move through the versions of a file that you have created.

Figure 4-11 is a bit misleading, in that normally the History window will show many backup copies of your source file rather than just one. These backup copies are made automatically by JBuilder when you save your project.

Related to this subject is the Compare Files tool, found by selecting Compare Files from the File menu in the Enterprise version of JBuilder. This tool will either let you compare two files side by side or give you a merged view with the differences highlighted. To get a feel for this, you can use the application you just created.

Choose **File | Compare Files**. A dialog will pop up, prompting you to select the old file. Choose one of the files from the bak directory, such as Applet1.java~1~. Now you will be prompted to pick a new file. Choose **Applet1.java**.

You will be presented with a view of both files that you have chosen, side by side. Each has its own scroll bar and can be manipulated individually. You can select whether they will be tiled vertically or horizontally and whether to synchronize their movement. Now click on the Diff View tab at the top of the pane. You will see one color-coded file that illustrates the differences between the two files. This tool can be very helpful when you are comparing different versions of the same file, as shown in Figure 4-12.

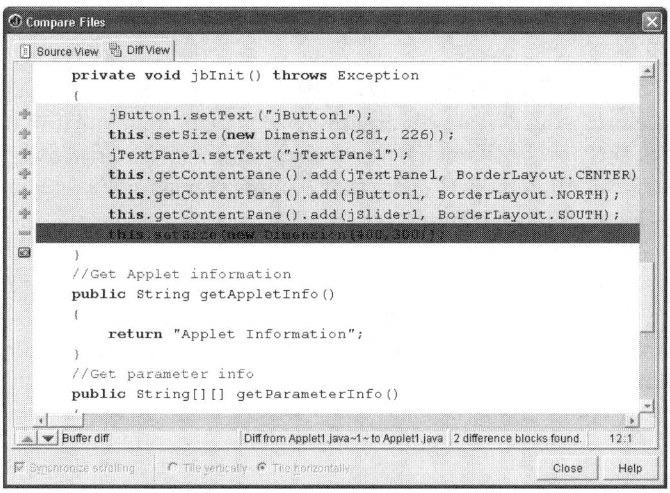

Figure 4-12: The Diff View screen shows the differences between two files.

Figure 4-12 shows the difference between Applet1.java before and after I dropped down the controls that you can see in Figure 4-7, which illustrated the UI designer. I dropped down a JTextPane, a JButton, and a JSlider. Part of the code for instantiating these objects can be seen in Figure 4-12. The point here is that we are comparing the version of Applet1.java that did not contain these controls with the version that did contain these controls.

Automation: Creating a Class

At this stage, you know some of the basic facts about using the JBuilder AppBrowser and IDE. I want to end the chapter by showing you how to use the built-in tools to create a class in JBuilder. This task will give you a sense of how Borland envisions the development process inside their IDE.

Creating a class is just one of the many tasks that JBuilder can automate for us. By singling out this one feature, I want to not only show you how one particular JBuilder tool works but also present an example of the style of programming common in JBuilder.

One of the big goals of this book is to make sure you learn how to use the tools in JBuilder, rather than just treating it as a glorified editor. Clearly, you could simply create a class by hand, typing in each word at the keyboard. However, JBuilder can help automate this task. You are not really using JBuilder to its full extent unless you understand how to use its tools to automate processes that you used to do by hand.

The following tasks are among the many that can be automated in one or more versions of JBuilder:

- Creating a class
- Creating variable or data names
- Creating getter and setter methods for your data
- Moving classes from one package to another
- Globally renaming a package, data member, or class
- Inserting and formatting the import statements at the top of your file
- Stubbing out the methods in an interface that you need to implement
- Generating Javadoc
- Deploying your application
- Creating event handlers
- Creating BeanInfo and other features of the JavaBeans specification

My point here is that automating the process of creating a class is not an isolated example, but rather an illustration of the flow of the work process in JBuilder. Nevertheless, creating classes in JBuilder is one of the fundamental tasks that you must master if you want to follow the text in the rest of this book. So the example not only illustrates a general principle, but also a specific and very useful task.

To create a class, choose **File | New** to bring up the Object Gallery. On the General page, choose the **Class** icon and click **OK**. These actions will start the Class Wizard.

In the Class Wizard, you can perform a number of tasks, such as naming your class, choosing the ancestor of your class, and choosing to change the name of the package where your class will reside. Since you are adding the class to your current package, leave the default setting for the package field. Do, however, change the name of the class. In this case, call it **MyClass**.

To choose a base class for your class, click on the ellipsis button and select **javax.swing.table.AbstractTableModel** from the base class dialog, as shown in Figure 4-13. Leave the default settings for the options at the bottom of the dialog, as shown in Figure 4-14. In particular, make sure the **Override Abstract Methods** box is checked. Now click **OK**.

NOTE: I will use the term "ellipsis button" quite frequently in this book. All users of this book will be familiar with what an ellipsis button looks like, but you may not be used to hearing it called an ellipsis button. An ellipsis is a series of three periods: .... An ellipsis button is a button that has no text on it other than an ellipsis symbol. As you know, this kind of button is used as a symbol to indicate that selecting it will bring up some kind of dialog. Usually this dialog will allow you to browse through a series of options, such as filenames, colors, text strings, and so on.

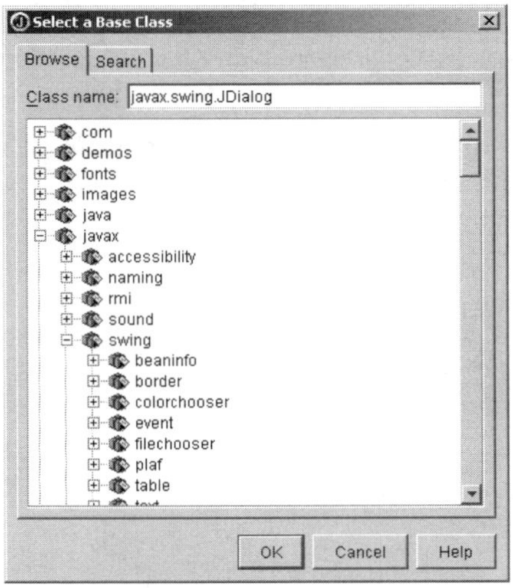

Figure 4-13: Browsing through the base class dialog to find the ancestor for your new class. Working with dialogs of this type is a common JBuilder task.

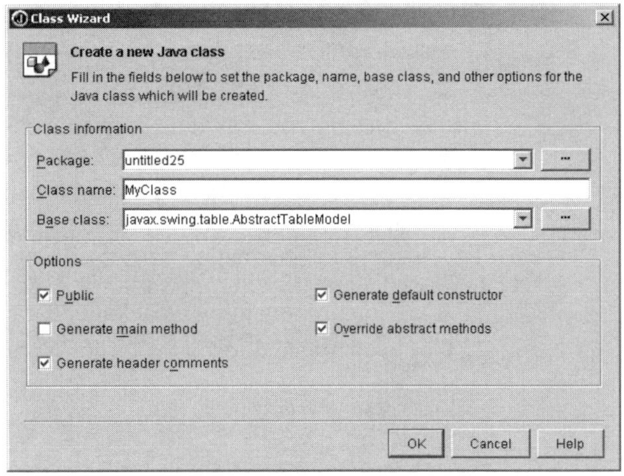

Figure 4-14: The Class Wizard will help you define the features of the class you want to create.

After you finish with the Class Wizard, notice that there is a new tab on the content pane labeled MyClass, as shown in Figure 4-15. The new class is visible in source view, ready for you to begin working on it. It appears in the project pane on the upper-left side of the content pane and also in the structure pane on the lower left of the content pane. The structure pane may contain error messages. You will learn how to deal with these later in this discussion. In short, most of the features of the AppBrowser have changed to help you explore, understand, and work with the source for your new class.

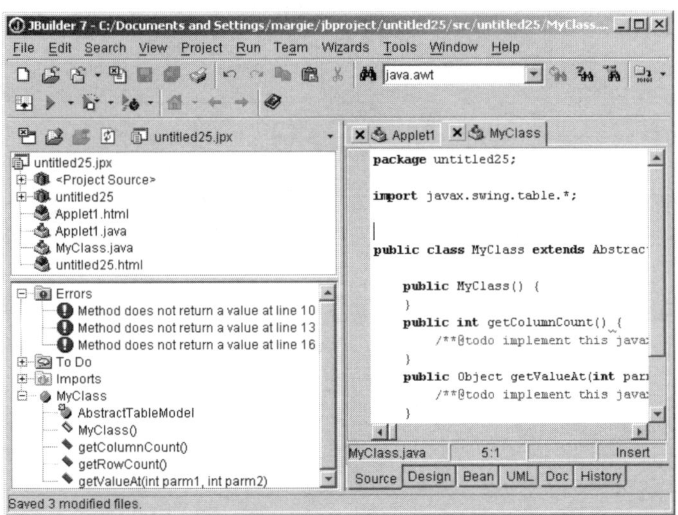

Figure 4-15: A new class called MyClass has been added to the project, and the windows of the AppBrowser now contain information about this new class.

NOTE: When you see the wide changes in the JBuilder environment that occur when you create a class, I want to remind you that this tool is developed entirely in Java. All of the parsing of files, editing of text, changing of tabs, morphing of UI features — everything — is done in Java.

The next thing you would do with this class is to begin editing it and integrating it with your program. A discussion of that process does not belong in this chapter. However, you might want to take a look at the full listing for the generated source, as shown in Listing 4-1. The methods of this class that you need to implement were automatically stubbed out for you. This is done in accordance with the rules of inheritance when you work with interfaces. Inheritance will be covered in more depth later in the book.

Listing 4-1: The stubbed-out methods in MyClass were declared in the standard interface called TableModel.

```
package untitled25;

import javax.swing.table.*;


/**
 * <p>Title: </p>
 * <p>Description: </p>
 * <p>Copyright: Copyright (c) 2002 Charlie Calvert</p>
 * <p>Company: Elvenware (www.elvenware.com)</p>
 * @author Charlie Calvert
 * @version 1.0
 */

public class MyClass extends AbstractTableModel
{

    public MyClass()
    {
    }

    public int getColumnCount()
    {
        /**@todo: implement this javax.swing.table.AbstractTableModel
      abstract method*/
    }

    public Object getValueAt(int parm1, int parm2)
    {
        /**@todo: implement this javax.swing.table.AbstractTableModel
      abstract method*/
    }

    public int getRowCount()
    {
        /**@todo: implement this javax.swing.table.AbstractTableModel
      abstract method*/
    }
}
```

The code generated in Listing 4-1 will not compile automatically. The problem is that all three methods in the class return a value, but JBuilder did not generate the return statements for you. Java considers it an error not to return a value from a method that is declared to return a value. To correct the problem, change each method to return a value:

```
public int getColumnCount()
{
    /**@todo: implement this javax.swing.table.AbstractTableModel
    abstract method*/
    return 0;
}

public Object getValueAt(int parm1, int parm2)
{
    /**@todo: implement this javax.swing.table.AbstractTableModel
    abstract method*/
    return null;
}

public int getRowCount()
{
    /**@todo: implement this javax.swing.table.AbstractTableModel
    abstract method*/
    return 0;
}
```

If you know something about Java, you will realize that methods such as getColumnCount(), getValueAt(), and getRowCount() must have been declared as abstract methods or as part of an interface from which MyClass descends. As it turns out, these are all methods of an interface. Exploring this interface will be explained in the next section.

I deliberately asked you to descend from the relatively complex class called AbstractTableModel. My reasons for this were twofold:

- It demonstrates that JBuilder is doing more than just creating a simple descendant of a class; it also analyzes the class and discovers the abstract methods that need to be overridden.
- It demonstrates that JBuilder's tools are not really meant to help you "cheat," to help people who don't know Java to somehow produce applications. In particular, it takes a certain amount of knowledge to know what to do with a class such as this AbstractTableModel descendant. JBuilder does help you write code, but its tools can only be used properly by someone who has a fairly deep understanding of Java. (For those of you who don't know much about the language, I include a few chapters on Java syntax in Part II: Java Language. I will also explain many complex parts of the language when I use them.)

After reading this section of the chapter, I hope that all readers understand how to use JBuilder tools to create a new class. Those who have a deeper understanding of Java should also begin to see how to use the JBuilder tools to smooth the way when working with some of the intermediate and advanced features of the Java language.

A Brief Introduction to CodeInsight

In the previous section you learned how to generate a class declaration in JBuilder. The class that was generated turned out to be quite complex, in part because it implements an interface it inherited from an ancestor class. JBuilder can help you unravel this complexity. In particular, you can use one of the many features of a JBuilder tool called CodeInsight to find the name of this interface and see its declaration.

NOTE: Newcomers to Java, and some intermediate-level Java programmers, may not fully understand all this talk about abstract methods, interfaces, and implementations. If that is the case, I would not worry too much. A more complete explanation of these subjects will appear in Chapter 8. For now, step through the process being discussed and try to get a general sense of what is going on. The main point here is to show you some of the tools that JBuilder provides for you. A deep understanding of the subject matter is not yet necessary.

Here is how to find out about the interface your new class has inherited. These principles illustrate how to explore the declaration for any class or data declared in your program.

Place your mouse over **AbstractTableModel** in this line of text from Listing 4-1:

```
public class MyClass extends AbstractTableModel
```

Right-click and choose **FindDefinition** from the pop-up menu that appears. You should be taken automatically to the declaration in the JDK for AbstractTableModel. The first line of that class looks like this:

```
public abstract class AbstractTableModel implements TableModel, Serializable
```

This line states that AbstractTableModel implements an interface called TableModel. Place your mouse over the word **TableModel** and right-click to bring up a menu. Again choose **FindDefinition** from the available options in the pop-up menu. You will be taken to the declaration for TableModel. Now you can view the declaration for the interface that dictates portions of the structure of the class you created.

You can use this technique with any variable found in your programs. For instance, if you have found a variable called myString in your program, you can right-click on it and be taken to the declaration for that particular identifier. It does not matter if the item was declared in the current method, as a field of the current class, as a type declared in another source file, or as a field declared in another source file — in all cases JBuilder will take you to the appropriate declaration. Even if the source for the file in question is not available, JBuilder will still try to recreate the public declarations from that file and show them to you. This is a very powerful tool, one that I use every day.

Summary

In this chapter you have been given an overview of the heart of the JBuilder environment, which is called the AppBrowser. In some cases, a particular feature was explored in some depth, while in other cases the text did little more than point out its presence. Most of these features will be explored in more depth later in this book.

The chapter ended with a look at the process for automating the creation of a class in JBuilder. This subject was intended to illustrate a general principle of JBuilder development. JBuilder is designed to help you automate many tasks that you might otherwise have to do by hand. The art of using JBuilder properly is in large part the art of learning about these automation tools and getting into the habit of taking advantage of their power.

Chapter 5

JBuilder Product Overview

Margie Calvert

This chapter covers the features in JBuilder that are not part of the AppBrowser. It also contains some basic facts about configuring your system.

Almost all the commands available in JBuilder can be accessed through the menu system. As a result, a review of the menu system provides a broad overview of all the features in the product that are not part of the AppBrowser, as that term was defined near the beginning of the previous chapter. In other words, here are all the features of the product other than those that are part of the project pane, structure pane, content pane, message pane, or file view tabs.

I have made an attempt to divide the text into clearly demarcated sections, each with its own subtitle. You should be able to browse these pages quickly, stopping to read the sections that interest you carefully.

The balancing act in writing this chapter was to avoid belaboring the obvious without skipping over important facts. I'm assuming the readers of this book are fairly sophisticated computer users, so I'm not going to spend time discussing how to use a relatively intuitive feature. On the other hand, I don't want to overlook something that can be of great help to many readers of this book.

I am ashamed to say that I learned some important things about JBuilder while researching this chapter. Don't make the same mistake that I did and assume that you can simply discover all the important tools in the IDE for yourself. You can probably read the whole chapter in 15 or 20 minutes. Unless you are already an expert on JBuilder, there are bound to be a few sections that point you to some tools that can save you a good deal of time. You don't want to waste time implementing something by hand when it can be automated by JBuilder.

The sections of the text near the end of the chapter on customizing the JBuilder environment should be of general interest to most readers. Here you will find out how to define the syntax used by JBuilder when it generates code for you and information about setting tabs and carriage returns, as well as tweaking many other features of the editor and the content pane.

All readers of the book should make sure they are familiar with the features discussed in the following sections of the text:

- "The Test Page," where testing your program with an extreme programming tool called JUnit is discussed. This same subject is covered in more depth in its own chapter.
- "The Search Menu," where a powerful incremental search feature is discussed.
- "Customizing the JBuilder Environment," where code formatting options are discussed, including the options I used when creating the code for this book.
- "The Tools Menu," where you will learn how to call your favorite editor, such as emacs, from inside JBuilder. When the editor appears, your current source file will be ready to edit inside it. Changes you make to the file should be automatically reflected inside of JBuilder. You can call any third-party tool from this menu; I just mention

editors as an example of what you can do with this extension to the JBuilder IDE. For instance, I often call Dreamweaver from JBuilder.

- You should also glance at the brief section at the end of the chapter titled "The OpenTools API." This is an introduction to a subject covered in more depth in its own chapter.

The File Menu

Let's start with a few tips about using the File menu, which is shown in Figure 5-1.

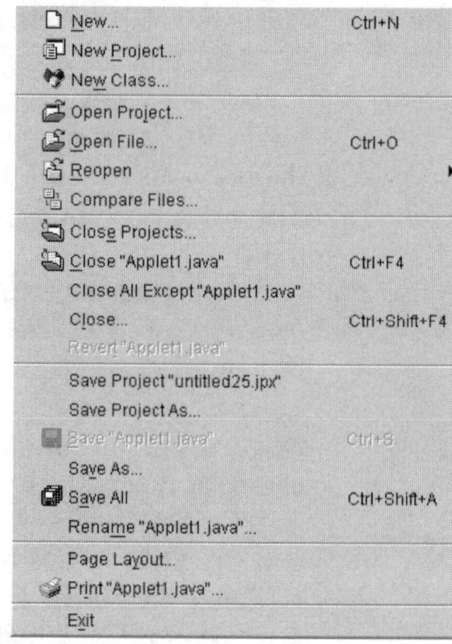

Figure 5-1: The File menu contains many powerful tools, including the frequently used Reopen option.

- It is sometimes a good idea to close any project you are in before opening a new project, unless you have some good reason for keeping them both open at the same time. The more memory you have on your machine, the less concern you need to have about this issue. To close projects, choose **File | Close Projects**. Choose **All** in the dialog box to close all the projects. See also the Window | New Browser option, discussed in the Window menu section near the end of this chapter.
- You can print directly from JBuilder (use File | Print), and you can set the layout before printing as well (use File | Page Layout). If you have the Enterprise version of JBuilder, you should be able to print out the UML drawings and then tape them or tack them up above your desk.
- Another good habit is to use the File | Save All command frequently. Choosing this option minimizes your risk of losing data. The toolbar has icons that become disabled when your files are saved. Use the icons as a reference when you want to be sure you have saved all your files.
- When working with the File menu, be aware of whether you are creating, opening, saving, or closing a file, project, class, or other object. File | Save As will save the file that is active in the content pane. It will not save your project.
- Beware of trying to change the name of your project through File | Save Project As. Instead, I suggest using the Windows Explorer, the KDE Konqueror, or a similar tool to move the base directory in your project and all the directories beneath it from one location to another on your hard drive. If you do this, JBuilder should handle everything else for you automatically. As mentioned earlier, these subjects will be explored in depth in Part V: Project Management.

The Object Gallery — Personal, SE, and Enterprise Versions

To reach the Object Gallery, choose **File | New**. The Object Gallery contains many wizards that are very helpful to you. In general, if you are going to be adding an object to your project that has some repetitive, boilerplate code as part of its structure, you should check the Object

Gallery to see if you can access a wizard for creating it. The following is a brief overview of the pages of the Object Gallery. As you are viewing the figures, be aware that they are from the Enterprise version of JBuilder.

NOTE: JBuilder Help has a useful guide to all of the features of JBuilder that are accessible through the Object Gallery. Choose Help | Help Topics and turn to the index page. At the top of the index page is a field allowing you to search for your topic. Type the words "Object Gallery," and JBuilder will bring you to a listing of all the pages of the Object Gallery that will identify the editions in which the various features are available.

The General Page

On this page you will find wizards that can create many of the objects you use most frequently. In the Personal version of the product, you will find wizards for applications and classes here. SE and Enterprise versions of the product will have wizards for creating many other objects as well. Because you will use this page whenever you start a new application, bean, or class, you may visit it frequently.

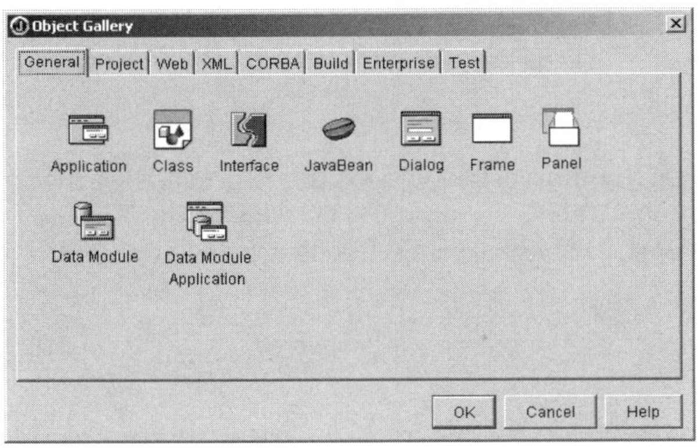

Figure 5-2: The General page

The Project Page

This page contains various options for creating or importing a project. Again, you may visit this page frequently, as you will create a project for nearly all the code you write. The wizard for importing a project, called Project for Existing Code, is available in SE and Enterprise editions. The wizards for connecting to and importing from CVS, VSS, or ClearCase are all Enterprise version options.

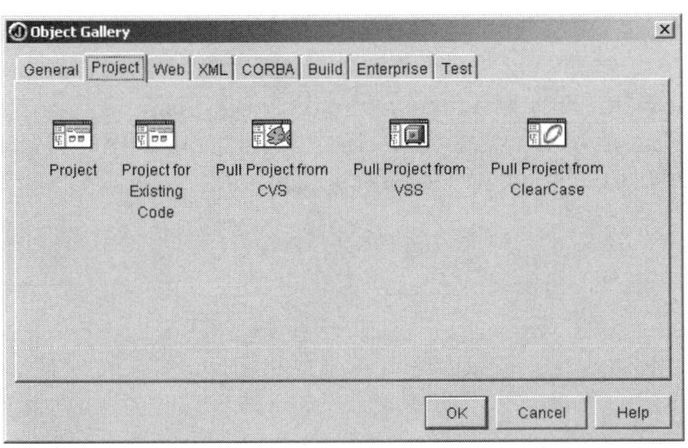

Figure 5-3: The Project page

The Web Page

The Web page contains objects that are focused on the Internet. You may have already accessed this page to use the Applet Wizard. In the Enterprise edition of JBuilder, shortcuts to other object wizards on this page will help you access the Web Start Launcher Wizard and create web applications, servlets, and JavaServer pages.

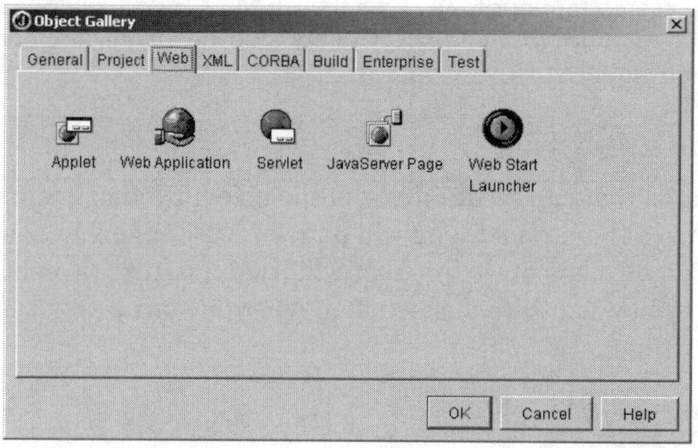

Figure 5-4: The Web page

The XML Page

The XML page is available only in the Enterprise version of the product. This page gives you shortcuts to wizards for the Cocoon Web Application, DTD to XML, and XML to DTD. Here you will also find Databinding, XML-DBMS, and SAX Handler.

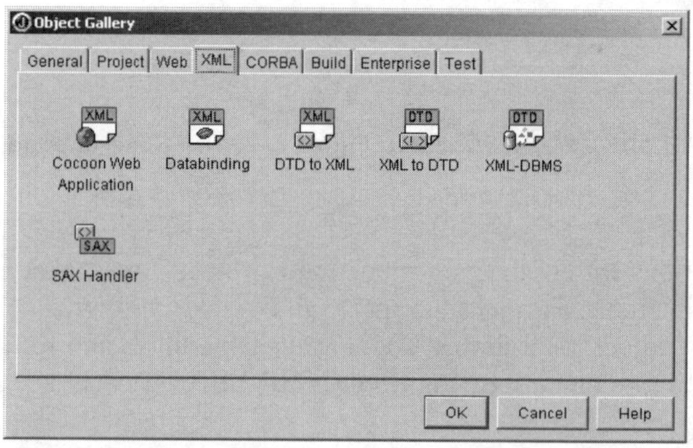

Figure 5-5: The XML page

The CORBA Page

The CORBA page is Enterprise level only and focuses on distributed application development. Among the offerings are Sample IDL, CORBA Client Interface, CORBA Server Interface, HTML CORBA Client, and CORBA Server Application.

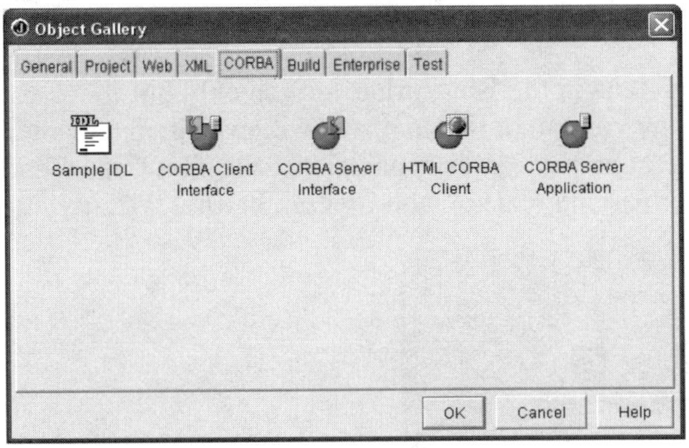

Figure 5-6: The CORBA page

The Build Page

On this page, you will find the Archive Builder, the Javadoc Wizard, and the Native Executable Wizard in both the SE and Enterprise versions of the product. Chapter 21, "Comments and Javadoc," instructs you in using the Javadoc Wizard to create documentation for your projects. You will find out how to use the Archive Builder in Chapter 28, "Deploying Applets, Applications, and Java Executables." The Native Executable Wizard is actually the same as the Native Executable archive type in the Archive Builder. The External Build Task Wizard is available only in the Enterprise edition of the product.

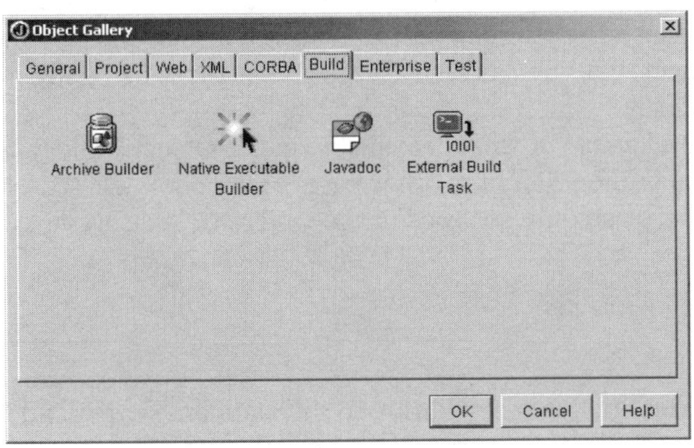

Figure 5-7: The Build page

The Enterprise Page

The Enterprise page, shown in Figure 5-8, focuses on Enterprise JavaBeans, and includes EJB Module, EJB Module from Descriptors, Enterprise JavaBean1.x, EJB 1.x Entity Bean Modeler, EJB 2.0 Bean Designer, EJB Test Client, EAR, and JMS. The options on this page are available only in the Enterprise level version of JBuilder.

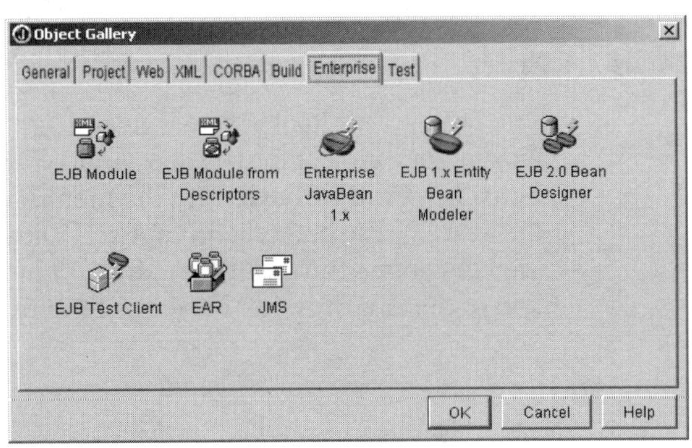

Figure 5-8: The Enterprise page

The Test Page

The Test page, shown in Figure 5-9, is in the Enterprise version only, but there are features here that can be accessed from any version of JBuilder, as I will explain in a moment. This page contains tools for creating test beds for your applications: the Test Case, Test Suite, JDBC Fixture, JNDI Fixture, Comparison Fixture, and Custom Fixture wizards.

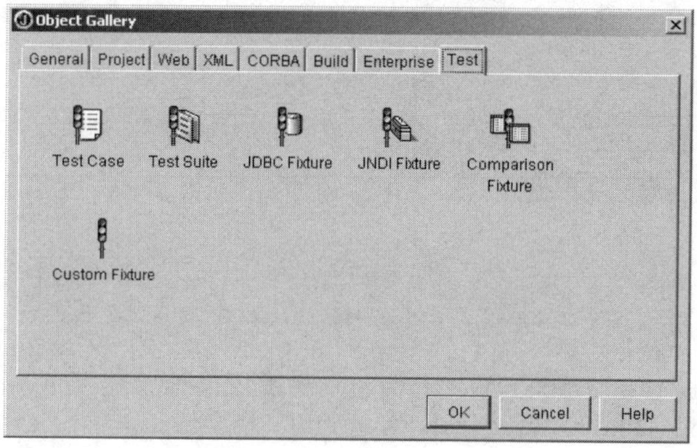

Figure 5-9: The Test page from the Object Gallery

The Test page includes wrappers around an open source tool called JUnit, which is very popular in the extreme programming community. I will discuss it in detail in Part VI: Testing, Debugging, and Maintenance. Because JUnit is an open source tool, you do not need any particular version of JBuilder to use it. The JBuilder features shown in the Object Gallery make it easier to use JUnit in your project, but you can also access the features manually. That process will be described in Chapter 30.

You should now have a general sense of what is available in the Object Gallery. Many of these features will be discussed in more detail in other parts of the book. On the other hand, some of the features in the Enterprise only sections of the Object Gallery are not covered in this book.

The Search Menu

The Search menu contains interesting tools in addition to the standard search and replace utilities. Here you will find advanced tools for searching through multiple documents, as well as tools that allow you to browse the classes available to your application.

Find in Path

The Find in Path tool is a very useful "grep-like" utility that allows you to search multiple files in your project for the occurrence of a string. To get a feeling for how it works, choose **Search | Find in Path** from the menu. A dialog will pop up. Leave the default settings for the search path, and type **java.awt.** A search on this topic will show you which files in your project contain the string "java.awt." The results can be seen in the message pane at the bottom of the AppBrowser. I use this feature nearly every day, often multiple times a day.

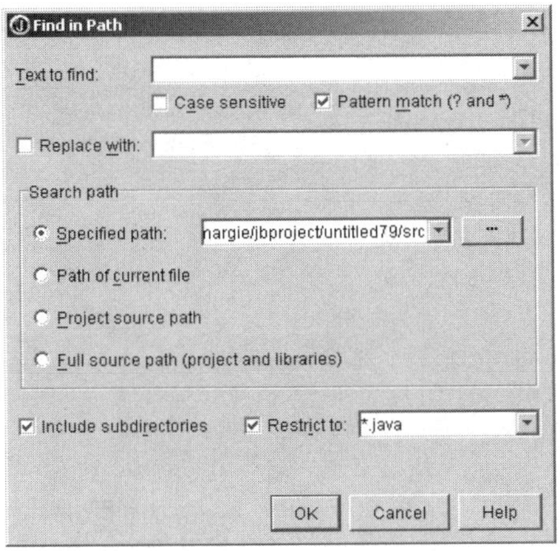

Figure 5-10: The Find in Path dialog

Incremental Search

Choosing this tool allows you to type a few letters of a word and find the next instance of the word in your code. For instance, if you type **is**, it finds the first instance of a word in your code that contains the letters "is." If you then type the letter **t**, JBuilder will find the first instance of your code that begins with the letters "ist." This kind of tool should be very familiar to users of emacs. In JBuilder, by default, the hot key for accessing this tool is Ctrl+E. To cycle through the items in your document that match the text you have typed in, press Ctrl+E multiple times.

Go to Line

The Go to Line option from the Search menu lets you find a line in the editor. By default, the hot key for this tool is Ctrl+G.

You should not, however, have to use this tool to find errors in your code. When JBuilder finds a syntax error in your code, it reports it in the message pane. Simply click on the relevant line in the message pane, and you will be taken to the place in your code where that error occurred.

Find Classes

Find Classes allows you to see, at a glance, the classes that are in the JDK or your project or in any JAR files or class files that your project is using. If you select a file in the Find Classes dialog, and the source for that file is available, then it will be brought up automatically in the content pane. If the source is not available, JBuilder will usually give you an outline of the class, showing everything but the implementation of the methods and the declaration of the private data found in the class. The hot key for Find Classes is Ctrl+– (minus).

The Project Menu

The Project menu, shown in Figure 5-11, allows you to manage your project and add or delete files. It also contains the make and rebuild commands. While the rebuild command compiles all files in the project, the make command only compiles the files that had changes made to them (that is, the source modules whose .class files have become out of date). For most purposes, the make command is quicker and is therefore used more. However, at times when you are struggling with a project and nothing seems to work right, a rebuild command can sometimes make a difference.

Choose **Project | Project Properties** to bring up the very important Project Properties dialog. This dialog is key to managing your project. Here you can set paths, choose run, debug and build options, set the code style, and make other critical decisions about your project. While the Project Properties dialog defines the settings for the current project, the Default Project Properties dialog lets you make decisions that will affect each new project that you create.

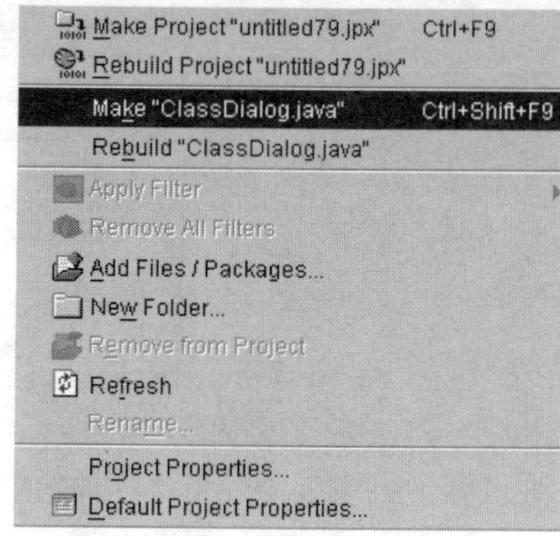

Figure 5-11: The Project menu has features that most developers use on a daily basis.

The next section, on customizing the JBuilder environment, covers many portions of this dialog. Other major sections of the Project Properties dialog are discussed in Part V: Project Management.

Customizing the JBuilder Environment

As a rule, I try to follow the most commonly used Java programming conventions. However, there are a few things I do that differ slightly from the norm. Fortunately, you can configure how JBuilder handles these features in the Project Properties dialog.

NOTE: I'm not suggesting that my way of doing things is best. I'm just letting you know what I've done to customize my environment. If you choose to make the same changes I made, you can more easily follow my examples. If you have other preferences, hopefully you won't find my personal tastes in these matters too distracting. In all cases, my decisions are based on my conception of how to write code that is as clean and easy to read as possible.

On the Project menu, choose **Default Project Properties** and turn to the Code Style page, as shown in Figure 5-12.

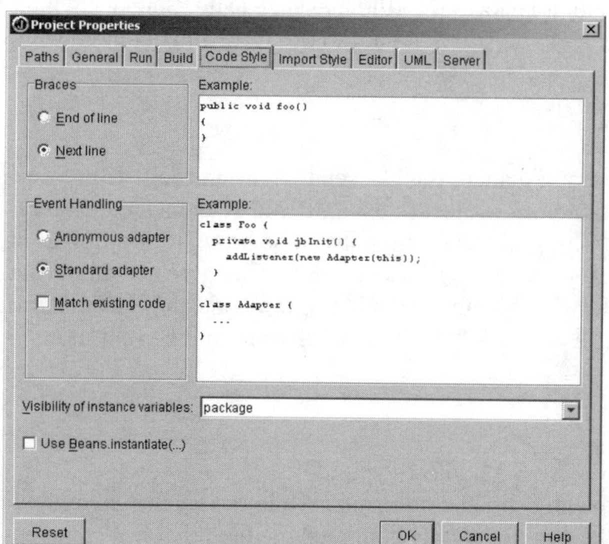

Figure 5-12: Configuring JBuilder with the Code Style page

The Code Style page is divided into two main sections called Braces and Event Handling. In the Braces section, I prefer to choose Next Line, though the End of Line selection is probably the preferred technique for the majority of Java programmers. More specifically, this option tells JBuilder to produce code that looks like this:

```
void Foo()
{
}
```

If you select the default option, your code will look like this:

```
void Foo() {
}
```

Neither technique is wrong. You can choose the one that you prefer. I personally find the first style easier to read, but perhaps this is nothing more than a matter of habit.

NOTE: There are tools called source code beautifiers that can automatically format your code in either of the above styles. I use a beautifier that is built into a product called Visual Slick Edit, but I am sure you can find free beautifiers on the web. Some of them are included in open source JBuilder OpenTools, which can be added into the IDE. The open source tools mentioned in Chapter 31, "Refactoring and UML," may be helpful in this regard.

On the Code Style page, I also prefer to use the Standard adapter rather than Anonymous adapter when handling events. I like this option because it is easy for me to read, and I also believe it will be easier for you to understand.

This is not the proper point in the text to begin discussing standard and anonymous adaptors. This subject is discussed in depth in Chapter 14, "Event Handling."

NOTE: Many readers will be interested in knowing how to set up tab settings in the editor and how to define whether JBuilder uses Windows style, Unix style, or Mac style carriage returns and linefeeds. Both of these subjects are covered near the beginning of Chapter 7, "Using the Editor."

The Run Menu

The Run command tells JBuilder to compile and run the project. The Run menu contains many debugging tools. Debugging a project is covered in Part VI: Testing, Debugging, and Maintenance.

The Team Menu

This menu allows you to access version control systems such as CVS directly from JBuilder. You can coordinate the efforts of team members who are working on the same project using the commands on this menu. This subject is covered in more detail in Chapter 26, "Team Development." The Team menu is a JBuilder Enterprise feature. But once again, CVS is an open source project, and you can use CVS whether or not you have the Enterprise version. The Enterprise version of JBuilder simply makes it easier for you to use CVS. In fact, it might contain the best available interface to CVS.

The Wizards Menu

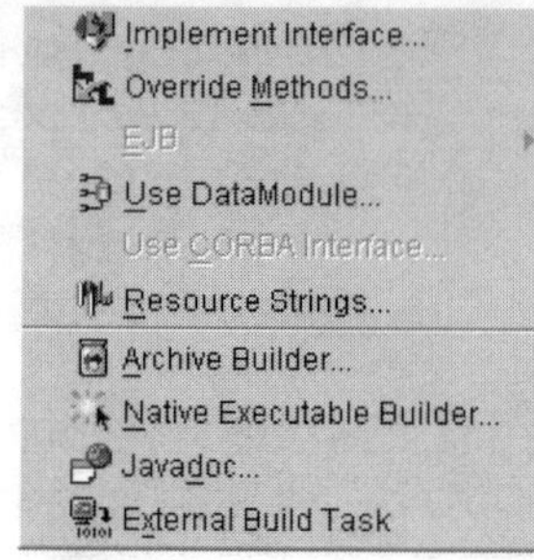

Figure 5-13: The Wizards menu

Some of the items on the Wizards menu also appear in the Object Gallery. All of the wizards on this menu are features of JBuilder SE and/or Enterprise. The extremely useful Archive Builder is discussed in Parts V and VIII. Javadoc is discussed in Chapter 21, "Comments and Javadoc." Override methods, implement interfaces, and resource strings are discussed in Chapter 7, "Using the Editor." The Use DataModule Wizard is discussed in Part VIII: Databases.

The Tools Menu

The Tools menu allows you to configure the IDE, the editor, libraries, JDKs, your toolbox, and the component palette. All of these tools are included in the Personal version of JBuilder.

In the IDE options, you can:

- Set the look and feel of the IDE to Windows, Metal, or Motif
- Change the look and feel of the tabs on the content pane
- Change the color of error messages
- Turn sound effects on or off
- Configure Web, XML, and UML output and behavior
- Configure the EJB designer
- View and, to some degree, customize the types of files that the editor understands

NOTE: The JBuilder editor recognizes a wide variety of file types, from Java source files and XML and HTML files to graphic files of type JPG, GIF, and PNG. It provides appropriate syntax highlighting when possible and shows the images for recognized graphics formats. Some of the types it recognizes might surprise you, such as C and C++ files.

The Editor options give you many possible choices:

- You can set the color scheme for the editor.
- You can select the font and font size for the text in the editor.
- This is also a place where you can configure tabs. (Carriage returns and linefeeds are configured in the Project Properties menu.)
- Here you can also choose the type of key mapping that you prefer: CUA, emacs, Visual Studio, Brief, or two key mappings for Mac programmers.
- Other options, such as search, save, and smart key preferences, can be configured here. The smart key options affect the way the editor works when you hit the Tab, Home, and End keys. For instance, it defines whether hitting the Home key takes you to the beginning of a line or to the first non-white space character in a line. The End key performs the same task for the end of a line. Smart Tab defines whether or not to line up tabs on the defined tab stops or on the indent of the previous non-blank line.
- The editor has a feature called Code Templates that can allow you to quickly and easily insert snippets of code into your editor. This is discussed in Chapter 7.

NOTE: If some of the options in the editor seem too fussy for you, stick with the defaults. If the behavior of the editor is driving you buggy, look at the Editor Options on the first page of the Tools | Editor Options dialog. Also, see the following section on adding third-party tools to the Tools menu.

The Tools | Configure JDK option is very important to all users of JBuilder Personal edition. Here you can change the JDK that your product uses. The JBuilder Personal edition can only target one JDK, so if you want to use JDK 1.4.0 instead of 1.3.1, you need to switch using the Configure JDKs dialog box, shown in Figure 5-14. The Configure JDKs dialog box will display when you choose Tools | Configure JDK.

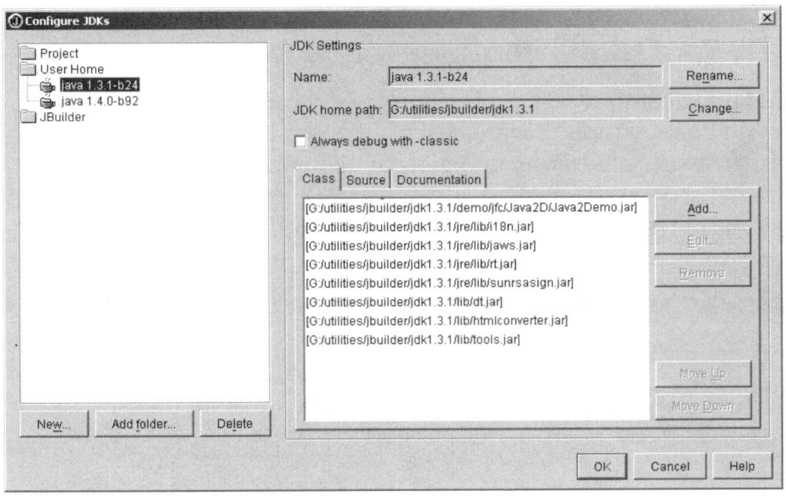

Figure 5-14: The Configure JDKs dialog box

Browse to the directory where you have stored your JDK by clicking on the **Change** button to the right of the JDK Home Path field. This will open the Select Directory dialog box, shown in Figure 5-15.

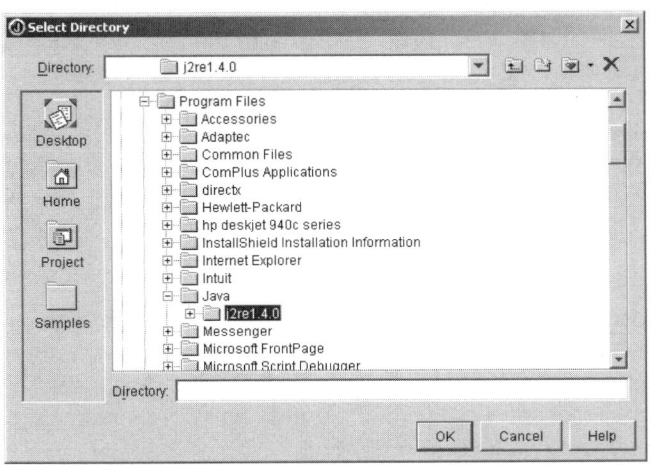

Figure 5-15: The Select Directory dialog box

Click **OK** to confirm your selection. Click **OK** again to complete the process. If you wish to double-check to be sure that this process worked, choose **Project | Project Properties**. The JDK you just selected should appear in the JDK field.

NOTE: You won't be able to switch JDKs unless you have first installed the JDK you wish to use. You can download new or old JDKs from http://java.sun.com. As a rule, the installation for a JDK is a simple forehead install. In other words, the install is so simple that you could probably run it with your forehead. See the index.html file on the JBuilder CD for a note on JDKs and the Windows registry.

In addition to the basic features in the Editor and IDE Options menu, the Tools menu also provides Enterprise and SE version tools to help you examine JavaBeans and work with databases. Several of the tools, including Enterprise Deployment and Create EJB Client JAR, are only found in the Enterprise version of the product. The database tools will be covered in Part VIII: Databases.

Adding a Third-Party Tool to the JBuilder Menu System

Many developers will want to access a favorite text editor for performing certain tasks. For instance, you might be very familiar with emacs, Kate, Visual Slick Edit, or some other editor, and simply prefer to do certain editing tasks inside that tool.

To access a third-party editor or some other tool, such as Dreamweaver from JBuilder, first choose **Tools | Configure Tools** from the menu. Click the **Add** button to bring up the dialog shown in Figure 5-16.

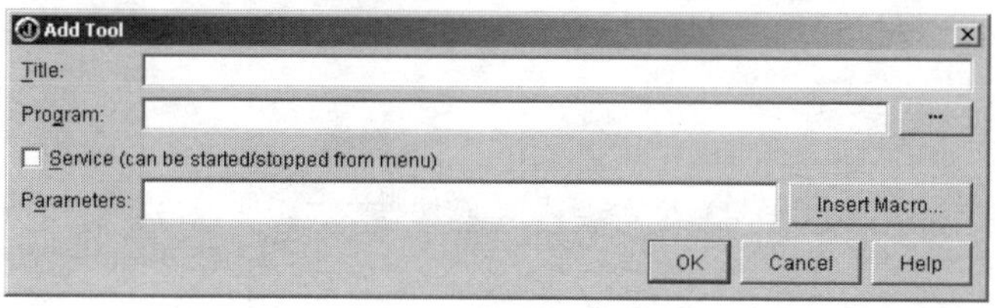

Figure 5-16: Adding a third-party tool to the JBuilder menu system

Type in the name of your tool in the Title field. Browse for the tool itself using the ellipsis button next to the Program field.

At this stage, you have set things up so that JBuilder will launch your third-party tool. However, in this case, you want to do more. You want to have your third-party editor open up the file that is currently focused in JBuilder. To do this, choose the FilePath macro from the list of available macros.

NOTE: If you start experimenting with the various built-in macros that you can choose, you will see that JBuilder shows the command each macro generates inside this dialog. Using this viewer, you can quickly become familiar with the many powerful macros available to you when you launch a third-party tool. In this case, however, you want to use the FilePath macro. If necessary, put quotes around the macro so that Windows will know how to handle paths that contain spaces: "($FilePath)."

Click the **OK** button to close the current dialog, and then click the **Close** button to close the Configure Tools dialog. Now when you open the JBuilder Tools menu, a new item will be available. If you select this item, your editor of choice will be opened. Assuming you can pass in a filename as a parameter to this editor, the editor should currently be ready to edit the same file that you were viewing in JBuilder.

When you are through using your editor, JBuilder should automatically reflect the changes you made while in your third-party editor. In practice, this latter feature can be a bit shaky on some platforms. In Windows, it should work perfectly, but on some Linux distributions, with certain JDKs, I have had a little trouble. In such worst-case scenarios, the simplest thing to do is close the file you're working on in JBuilder and reopen it from the File | Reopen menu. The changes you made should now be visible.

NOTE: There have been several places in the text where I have mentioned that a particular feature might not work perfectly on some platforms. In Linux, the situation can get very complicated quite quickly. For instance, a particular JDK might not work perfectly if running on top of a particular version of Libc, GNOME, or KDE. If JBuilder is running on top of an unstable JDK, anything might happen. Who is at fault? Is it the JDK? Is it Libc? Is it GNOME or KDE? Is it JBuilder? Well, it can be very difficult to decide exactly where the blame should fall or if it is even fair to assign blame in such situations. In my opinion, JBuilder running on Windows is a remarkably clean product, particularly in its core features found in the Personal and SE versions. On Linux, I have had trouble using CodeInsight on KDE 2.0. However, KDE 3.0 handled CodeInsight without mishap. If you have problems, I suggest that you sign on to the JBuilder forums at http://www.borland.com/ forums, and ask questions and share your experience. Quite often someone else will have encountered your problem and will be able to give you a solution or workaround. For what it's worth, I find that JBuilder on Linux runs better with each release of JBuilder, Libc, the Linux kernel, GNOME, and KDE. As I said earlier, I find that I can now comfortably do serious work inside JBuilder on Linux.

The Window Menu

I use the Window menu mostly for switching between multiple projects — if I have more than one project open at a time. This is also a quick and easy way to switch between the files in your project without having to use the mouse.

The New Browser command gives the appearance of creating a new instance of JBuilder. As far as I can tell, opening up a new browser does not require the same kind of memory hit on your system as opening up a second instance of JBuilder. Certainly it opens up a second AppBrowser very quickly, while starting a second instance of JBuilder itself can take a significant period of time. If you have opened a browser through the New Browser command, choosing Exit from the File menu closes all associated instances of JBuilder. Choosing this menu item is a good solution for those who wish to keep more than one project open at a time or wish to have two views of the same project.

Notice that you are able to cascade, tile, minimize, or restore your browsers through the commands on the Window menu.

The Help Menu

JBuilder has an excellent help system that provides detailed information on any part of the JBuilder IDE and many parts of the JDK. On the menu are useful topics such as the JBuilder environment, tutorials, and references on the Java language, Swing, and DataExpress, among others. If you have a question about JBuilder that relates to any of the topics on the menu, you will find relevant information by clicking on the topic.

For more narrow-gauge questions, choose **Help | Help Topics.** Then, in the JBuilder Help dialog, click on the **Index** tab. Now type the name of your topic, such as **editor.** You will be provided with a list of index entries that include the word "editor." Choose the one you want by left-clicking on the entry.

The OpenTools API

Now that you know what you can do with the JBuilder IDE, you may still have a list of additional features that you wish were included. As it happens, the OpenTools API allows you to build extensions to JBuilder. This is a very powerful feature but too complicated to be explained in this chapter. It is covered in Chapter 32, "Introduction to the OpenTools API."

You should definitely explore the world of free, shareware, and commercial add-ons to JBuilder that are implemented through the OpenTools API. Some of these add-ons, such as AntRunner, have long been part of my day-to-day programming experience. (As of JBuilder 7, Ant is integrated into JBuilder Enterprise. AntRunner is still helpful for owners of the SE and Personal editions.)

As you will find out later on, adding an OpenTool to JBuilder usually involves little more than copying a JAR file into the appropriate directory and then restarting JBuilder. To begin finding these add-ons, read the appropriate sections of the book, browse the CD that accompanies this book, go to Google and perform a search on JBuilder OpenTools, view the repository of such tools found on http://codecentral.borland.com, and browse the Companion CD that comes with some versions of JBuilder.

NOTE: The Companion CD is a second CD that comes inside the JBuilder product box. It contains materials from third parties.

Summary

This chapter featured an overview of the major features found in the JBuilder IDE. In some cases, a particular feature was explored in depth, while in other cases the text did little more than point out the presence of a particular feature. Many sections of the chapter simply referred you to other chapters of this book where a feature is discussed in more detail.

The main point of the chapter was simply to make you aware of what was available to you as a developer. JBuilder is a very large tool, and it is quite possible to work with it for years without knowing that it has a particular capability that can save you hours of time. In this chapter you got an overview that hopefully focused on at least the most important of those features.

Chapter 6

The UI Designer

Margie and Charlie Calvert

In this chapter you will learn the basic facts that you need to know to design the interface for your application. JBuilder eases this task by providing you with a "WYSIWYG" toolset for creating your program's interface. You may find, however, that not everything about the UI designer (user interface designer) is quite as simple and obvious as it might appear after a cursory appraisal.

Interface composition in JBuilder takes place inside a tool called the *UI designer.* Developers use this tool when they want to drop buttons, list boxes, check boxes, and other UI elements onto a JFrame, JPanel, or other visual container. In JBuilder you can actually "draw" these elements with the mouse, rather than being forced to create them with lines of code. Alternatively, you can visually place the tools inside the structure pane. Of course, you can also use the editor to write UI code by hand if you so wish, but usually the visual tools present a much simpler way of performing the same task. In either case, you end up with the same type of code; it is just a question of how you want to create it.

NOTE: When I say you end up with the same type of code, my point is not that the visual designer will perform every task the same way you would were you writing the code by hand. In a language as complex as Java, there are sometimes many ways to reach a single destination. The developers of JBuilder were therefore forced to make some decisions. At times, JBuilder may produce code that is identical to what you would have created by hand, and other times it may produce code that is quite different. If you don't like the code JBuilder produces automatically, you can always edit it by hand to suit your tastes. As long as your edits produce valid Java code, JBuilder will still compile and run your program.

Overall, the UI designer is easy to use. However, there are a few tricks you need to master before you can fully utilize its capabilities. This holds true even for experienced users of other visual programming tools, such as Delphi, VB, or C++Builder. These seasoned developers might come to JBuilder with certain expectations, many of which might be frustrated if they don't know a few important facts about how to use the JBuilder visual designers.

As I mention elsewhere in the text, the Java visual components were not tailor-made to be used in a visual tool such as JBuilder. As a result, you won't find a seamless fit between the visual design environment and the Java Swing components.

One of the main purposes of this text is to show how to overcome any difficulties you may encounter when using the visual tools. The text aims to help you become comfortable with the JBuilder UI designer and its ability to manipulate Swing objects. If you learn a few simple tricks and some problem areas to avoid, you will soon find that you can create powerful visual interfaces quickly and easily.

More specifically, this chapter will cover the following topics:

- How to drop and arrange components on the UI designer
- How to use the Inspector to examine the components you drop on the UI designer

- How to use Java layouts to configure the arrangement of your components
- How to use the designer to create standard and pop-up menus

A discussion of the best way to work with particular components will be reserved primarily for Part III: JBuilder Fundamentals. There you will learn about list boxes, check boxes, panels, and other controls in some detail. Near the end of this chapter, you will find out how to use a JTabbedPane.

NOTE: Many of these controls are very easy to use. For instance, you can drop a JTabbedPane on a frame. To add pages to the JTabbedPane, drop JPanels on top of the JTabbedPane.

Believe it or not, there are large numbers of JBuilder users who don't really understand the UI designer. This is one of the most powerful tools in the product, and if you can fully grasp what it can do for you, it will be very much to your advantage.

A Theory of Interface Design

Before getting started, I want to cover an important point of theory. Most Java developers are probably familiar with the concept of a model-view-controller (MVC) architecture. This theory states that one should keep the visual part of a component separate from the data stored in the component. For instance, Java makes a clear distinction between the container used to hold the list of strings in a list box and the visual drawing tools that paint the list box on the screen. The first part, the data, is the *model* part of the model-view architecture. The second part, the painted components visible on the screen, is the *view* part of the model-view architecture. The *controller* part of the model-view-controller architecture is the event code that ties the model and view parts of a component together.

NOTE: In various parts of this text, including this chapter and Parts III and VII, you will encounter more information about the Swing model-view-controller architecture.

I want to draw an analogy between correct application development and correct component development. I believe you should separate the UI code for your program from the core logic of your program. A list box's UI is separated from the list that it maintains. It is my opinion that in most applications you should not mix up your UI code with the code that actually drives your application.

You should get input from the user in one class and process that input in a separate class. Respond to button clicks and other user input in one file and process that information in a separate class. The response to a button click should often be a single line of code that calls a method of another object to actually handle the click.

Suppose you want to create a grep-like application designed to allow the user to scan the files in multiple directories looking for a piece of text. This application might be used to search through all the source files in your project looking for references to the word "applet."

When constructing this imaginary application, I believe that you should have one class, which is usually either a JFrame or a JPanel descendant, that will handle the input from the user. Then, once you have gathered all the user's input, you should create a separate class whose sole purpose is to iterate over a series of files. Perhaps you would even want a third class for processing each of the files that you find.

Every class you create should have one purpose. If you create a class that does two, three, four, five, or more separate tasks, then your design is getting sloppy. (Sometimes you are under so much time pressure that this can't be helped, but you should try to do the right thing! If you design your application correctly, it will end up saving you time in the long run. Typically, efforts in this regard are rewarded many times over.)

You should get input from the user in one class and then process that input in a separate class. Program logic should not be part of any class that is designed to get input from the user. That class already has a purpose: to get input. Don't also try to process the data in the same class.

Just as a Swing component should have a model part and a view part, an application should have an input part that gives the user an interface and a separate class or classes that handle the data the user passes to you.

Classes that get input from a user usually get input regarding very disparate functions. For instance, one part of your interface might allow the user to open a file, another to edit the file, and a third to search across your hard drive. If you put code for doing those things into the same class that got input from the user, that single class would be doing three or four different tasks. If you create objects that do five different things, you might as well not use OOP at all.

Hopefully this little bit of theory that I have interjected into the text will make sense to you right away. If not, you will find that I discuss this whole subject in more depth in Chapter 20, "Composing Java."

I don't want to belabor this point too much, but let me restate it in a different way in the hopes that my point will become absolutely clear. JBuilder is a useful tool. However, you should not let it dictate the architecture of your application. You will find that JBuilder tempts you to center your entire application around a single JFrame descendant on which you place a series of JButtons and JTextFields. Unless your program is very simple, don't give in to this temptation. Instead, use the JFrame descendant as a place to get input from the user, and then move the various pieces of functionality in your program off to their own classes. The watchwords are *partition* and *divide and conquer. Refactoring* is also an important term in this context.

UI Designer Basics

The preliminaries are now out of the way, and we can begin exploring the UI designer itself. Create a standard Java application, as explained in Chapter 3, "Creating Default Applications and Applets." To access the designer, first use the project pane to focus Frame1 or some other Java source file that has a visual interface. For instance, you might want to focus a JApplet, JFrame, or a JPanel descendant. Any standard JBuilder application or applet will contain at least one of these objects. For the purposes of this discussion, just focus Frame1 from your project.

NOTE: If you try to focus a class such as an Object descendant that has no visual element, then you won't see anything very interesting in the UI designer. It is not really a mistake to bring up such a file in the UI designer, and sometimes there can even be a purpose to it. For instance, the data modules discussed in Part VIII are non-visual components that can be edited extensively in design mode. Most of the time, however, it only makes sense to click the Design tab when you are working with a class that descends from JApplet, JFrame, JPanel, or one of the other visual component classes.

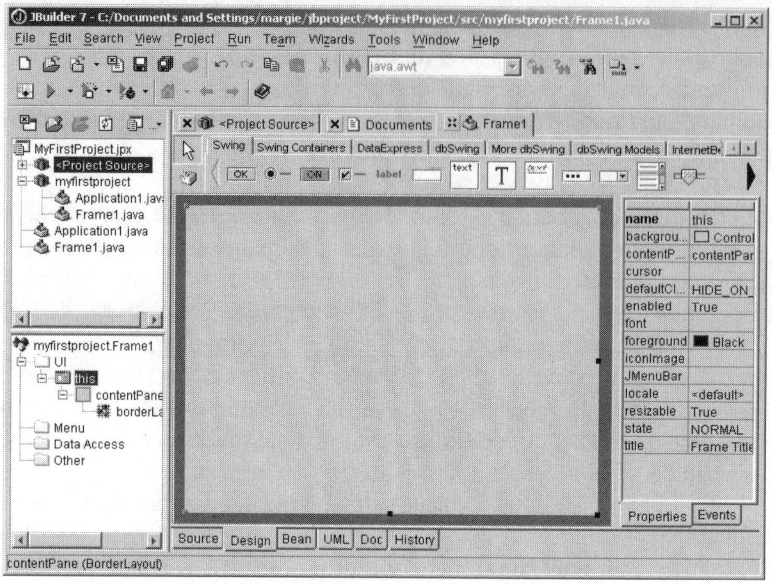

Figure 6-1: The UI designer focused on a simple descendant of a JFrame. Nothing has been dropped on the JFrame, so its surface is blank.

In Figure 6-1, notice that the project pane, the structure pane, the menu bar, and the toolbar remain visible. The project pane is unchanged from what you would see in a default JBuilder application. The structure pane, however, has changed from what you see when looking at a source file to showing the subcomponents of the JFrame descendant currently open in the content pane.

The component tree in the structure pane now shows four named folders, which will be empty or contain information relating to a particular part of the focused class. The UI folder will contain any UI components that are part of this JFrame descendant.

In this case, the UI folder lists an object created by Sun called the contentPane. It turns out that every JFrame descendant, by default, contains a JPanel instance that JBuilder will call the contentPane. This JPanel control is the container that actually holds the controls you drop onto Frame1. One of JBuilder's tasks is to give you a handle to this container.

NOTE: Please note that the JPanel contentPane is not the same as the JBuilder content pane. The JBuilder project pane, structure pane, and content pane exist in one world that was created by Borland. The JPanel and its contentPane exist in an entirely different world that was created by Sun. The similarity of the two names is purely coincidental or perhaps a bit unfortunate. As I mentioned earlier, JBuilder was created by Borland, and Swing was created by Sun. As a result, there are times when the two worlds don't mesh perfectly. This is perhaps a rather minor instance of one of those occasions.

A JPanel object always has a layout associated with it. Later in this chapter, you will learn about layouts in general and BorderLayouts in particular. If you are new to layouts, you may find the subject less than entirely intuitive. The basic idea behind them, however, is that a Java application may need to be displayed on many different platforms. As a result, you want to place components in flexible and resizeable relationships to one another, rather than at specific x and y locations. Layouts, discussed in depth in Part III: JBuilder Fundamentals, make it possible for you to do this.

Dropping Components on the UI Designer

It is now time to actually begin using the UI designer for its intended purpose. In the next few paragraphs, you will learn how to drop a component onto the designer.

Stretching across the top of the UI designer is the component palette, which contains pages of icons associated with various components. All of the components on the first page of the component palette are part of Swing.

Figure 6-2: The component palette open to the Swing page with icons for a JButton, JRadioButton, JToggleButton, JTextArea, and other Swing components

At the far-right side of the component palette, you may see two small arrows set off on buttons and pointing in opposite directions. Clicking on these arrows will reveal additional pages. (If the resolution of your screen is high enough, the buttons may not be needed and will therefore not be visible.) Beneath them, you will notice a large black triangular arrow pointing to the right. (If your resolution is high enough or the number of components on the page small enough, this arrow may be grayed out.) Clicking on this arrow will show additional component icons on the current page — in this case, the Swing page. A similar arrow on the left side of the component palette lets you browse back to the left across the page you are on.

By default, the component palette will be open to the Swing page, identified by a tab that is visible next to the selection tool (white arrow in Figure 6-3). The first component on the left side of the swing page is a JButton. If you move your cursor over it, a tool tip help item will appear identifying it as javax.swing.JButton. Click on the JButton icon and move your cursor to the UI designer, which is located beneath the component palette, and click again. Your button will appear in the UI designer, as shown in Figure 6-3.

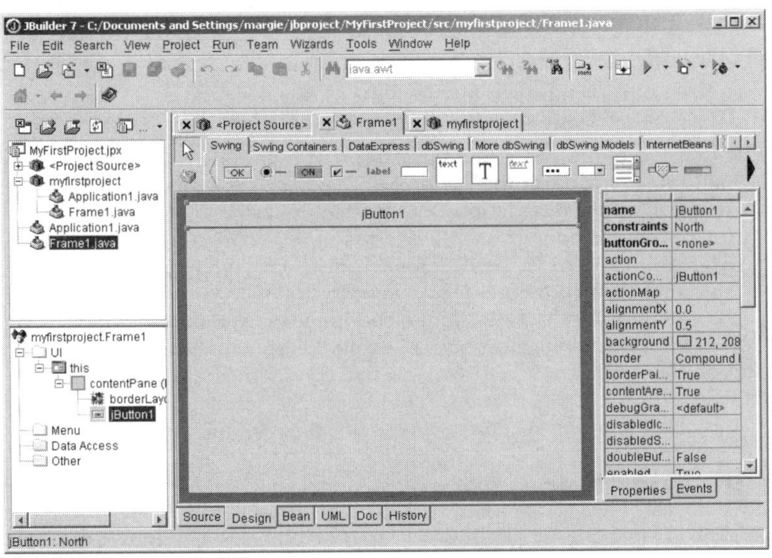

Figure 6-3: A JButton in the UI designer

Take a moment to notice what has happened. Look, for instance, at the structure pane. The UI folder now contains a new item called jButton1. This is the name that JBuilder automatically assigned to the component you dropped onto the contentPane. It created this name by taking the name of the component you dropped and adding a 1 to it. You dropped a JButton, and so the name of the component is jButton1. If you dropped a second JButton, it would be named jButton2 (not jButtonToo, a name I would have been delighted to see!).

NOTE: Needless to say, the developers of JBuilder did not think that jButton1 was a good name for a component. They simply had to ensure that if you dropped multiple components on a form, each one would have a unique name. Once again, don't let JBuilder dictate the structure or names in your application. You should take control of the naming conventions in your program. All JBuilder has done is come up with an algorithm that ensures that each component will have a unique name so that your code will compile. Having a unique name, however, is not enough. Your components should have meaningful names.

jButton1 is a child of the contentPane. It sits on top of the contentPane. It is therefore depicted that way in the structure pane, as seen in Figure 6-3. As you begin developing more complex applications, the order in which components appear in the structure pane will become crucially important.

Let's spend some more time studying Figure 6-3. Look now at the tabs above the component palette. The file that is currently focused is Frame1.java. You need to always be aware of which file is currently focused in the editor. You can use either the project pane or the tabs above the component palette to change that focus.

Now look to the right of the UI designer, and you will see the Inspector. This tool is explained in more depth later in this chapter and also in Part III: JBuilder Fundamentals. But for now, you can see that it displays information about the button that you have dropped onto Frame1. It will always display information about the currently selected component. In this case, you can see the name of the component, which is jButton1. You can also see its orientation to the north part of the BorderLayout. Other information is also in evidence.

You can use the Inspector to change the properties of your components. As mentioned earlier, in a real application, you will want to change the name of jButton1 to a name that is more meaningful to you, such as fileOpenButton, sortButton, or what have you. Later in this chapter, you will see how the Inspector can help you make this change. Or, if you prefer, you can make the change in the source code.

NOTE: On the far-left side of the component palette, next to the word "Swing," is a white arrow called the selection tool. You can use this to "unload" your cursor so that it can be used to select items on the UI designer, rather than to insert items into the UI designer. In particular, if you click on the JButton icon on the component palette and then click on the UI designer, an instance of the JButton control will usually appear in the designer. Sometimes you may click on JButton by mistake or change your mind after you click on it. If you want to "unload" your cursor so that it will not start dropping components onto the UI designer, click once on the selection tool.

After you click on the selection tool, you will be able to use your cursor to "select" components on the visual part of the UI designer. For instance, you can then click once on jButton1 to select it. You can tell it is selected because its properties appear in the Inspector. More on the selection tool is found later in this chapter in the section on multi-selecting components.

Viewing the Source JBuilder Generates

While you worked in the UI designer, JBuilder generated the Java code necessary to create the component you dropped onto Frame1. It is important to understand that JBuilder is not painting its version of what these components should look like onto the screen. Instead, it is generating code and instantiating instances of these components based on that code. These are real, live components that you see on the UI designer.

Return to source view and take a look at the editor. Here you will find the contentPane and jButton1 declarations, as shown in Figure 6-4.

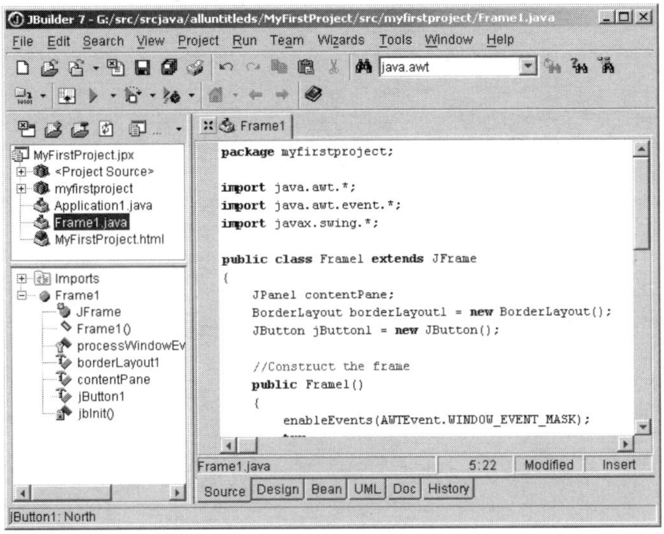

Figure 6-4: The source view shows the code behind the visual components.

Listing 6-1 shows the complete source code of Frame1 after you have dropped a JButton on it. I want to spend several paragraphs studying this code, as it is essential that you understand how it is structured. When studying Listing 6-1, you might note that I removed the comments that JBuilder normally inserts into such code by default. I also removed a commented-out line that JBuilder normally inserts into the beginning of the jbInit method for working with icons. These deletions were made in order to give you an uncluttered view of this important bit of source code.

Listing 6-1: A simple JFrame descendant containing a single button created in the UI designer

```
package untitled19;

import java.awt.*;
import java.awt.event.*;
import javax.swing.*;

public class Frame1 extends JFrame
{
    JPanel contentPane;
    BorderLayout borderLayout1 = new BorderLayout();
    JButton JButton1 = new JButton();

    //Construct the frame
    public Frame1()
    {
        enableEvents(AWTEvent.WINDOW_EVENT_MASK);
        try
        {
            jbInit();
        }
        catch(Exception e)
        {
            e.printStackTrace();
        }
    }

    //Component initialization
    private void jbInit() throws Exception
```

```
    {
        contentPane = (JPanel) this.getContentPane();
        JButton1.setText("JButton1");
        contentPane.setLayout(borderLayout1);
        this.setSize(new Dimension(281, 251));
        this.setTitle("Frame Title");
        contentPane.add(JButton1, BorderLayout.NORTH);
    }

    //Overridden so we can exit when window is closed
    protected void processWindowEvent(WindowEvent e)
    {
        super.processWindowEvent(e);
        if (e.getID() == WindowEvent.WINDOW_CLOSING)
        {
            System.exit(0);
        }
    }
}
```

As I said earlier, there are many different ways to solve certain problems in a language as complex as Java. Since JBuilder is generating code for you, it was necessary for the developers of the product to pick some particular style and stick with it. It is time to analyze certain specific elements of that style.

NOTE: It is easy to disagree with the decisions the JBuilder developers made when it came time to generate code. I personally, however, don't think it is wise to begin regarding these decisions with contempt. Most of the people in key positions on the JBuilder team were and are very bright people with many years of programming experience behind them. Don't get the idea that some mid-level bureaucrat in JBuilder marketing created this product. The members of the JBuilder team do not always make the best possible decisions, but they rarely make decisions that make absolutely no sense at all. On the whole, this is an excellent product, and the IDE you see represents the culmination of a series of good decisions on many complicated individual issues.

The Constructor for Frame1

It is now time to begin analyzing code. You might think that there is little reason to discuss code in a chapter on the UI designer. It turns out that this is not the case. You need to understand quite a bit of Java code before you can fully appreciate what is happening in the UI designer. After all, the purpose of the UI designer is to generate code.

Let's begin by looking at the constructor for Frame1:

```
public Frame1()
{
    enableEvents(AWTEvent.WINDOW_EVENT_MASK);
    try
    {
        jbInit();
    }
    catch(Exception e)
    {
        e.printStackTrace();
```

```
        }
    }
```

This code is boilerplate JBuilder code, and you need to make sure you are comfortable with it. The first line in the method is a call to enableEvents. This call helps ensure that your application closes properly. I will discuss this call last after covering the other code in this file.

After the call to enableEvents there is a try..catch block. This code does nothing more than call a method named jbInit and then catch any exceptions that might occur inside of jbInit. More specifically, if any errors occur in jbInit, the call to printStackTrace will display the location of the problem to the developer.

Understanding jbInit

jbInit is one of the cornerstones of JBuilder development. It is where component initialization occurs.

jbInit is not a documented part of the Java language, but it is a coding convention that plays an important role in JBuilder. jbInit is the method JBuilder expects you to use whenever you are writing code that defines the visual appearance of your app. Define your visual code elsewhere, and you probably won't be able to edit that code in the UI designer. Instead, you will have to edit the code by hand.

On the other side of the coin, we can define jbInit as the method in which JBuilder will insert the code it generates when you are working in the UI designer. For instance, if you drop a JButton on the UI designer, JBuilder will insert the code for configuring this button into jbInit. (The code for instantiating the button does not go in jbInit.)

NOTE: Don't let what I have said in this paragraph confuse you. jbInit is perfectly valid Java code. It is, however, a product of Borland R&D, not Sun R&D.

Here is what jbInit looks like in our simple program:

```
// Data fields of the Frame1 object
JPanel contentPane;
BorderLayout borderLayout1 = new BorderLayout();
JButton jButton1 = new JButton();

// ... Code omitted here for brevity

private void jbInit() throws Exception
{
    contentPane = (JPanel) this.getContentPane();
    JButton1.setText("jButton1");
    contentPane.setLayout(borderLayout1);
    this.setSize(new Dimension(281, 251));
    this.setTitle("Frame Title");
    contentPane.add(jButton1, BorderLayout.NORTH);
}
```

The first line of code in the body of the jbInit method retrieves the JPanel component that is built into all JFrames. JBuilder needs a handle to this component because, by default, it will add all the buttons, list boxes, and other controls that you drop on the UI designer to the contentPane.

The second line of code sets the text, or label, for jButton1:

```
JButton1.setText("jButton1");
```

Note that this is exactly the same code you would use were you coding by hand.

This is a simple line of code, but there is actually quite a bit that needs to be said about it. First, notice that the button itself was created above when it was declared as a member of your class:

```
JButton jButton1 = new JButton();
```

Now look back up at the call to jButton1.setText("jButton1"). You can change this value in one of two ways:

1. You can use the Inspector, as described later in this chapter. If you use the Inspector, then you are using the visual tools to change the values in your code.
2. Alternatively, you can edit the text of your source file itself:

```
JButton1.setText("fileOpenButton");
```

If you then press the Design tab, you will see that the visual appearance of your button has changed to reflect the changes you made in code. You don't have to press the Compile button in order to have this happen. JBuilder parses the code you have typed and makes changes in the designer to reflect the current status of the buffer where your source code is stored.

NOTE: If you can't quite visualize what I just described, please perform the following steps in JBuilder:

1. Drop a button on a JFrame descendant.
2. Press the Source tab. Edit the call to jButton1.setText so that the string that is being set in the text field does not read "jButton1."
3. Now go back to design mode and look at your button. The text should have changed to reflect the edits you made while in source mode.

NOTE: I have, on occasion, and particularly in older versions of the product, seen JBuilder fail to automatically update the designer to reflect changes I made while in the editor. If this happens to you, save your work and hit the Compile button. If that fails to help, then run your application and see if JBuilder sets things up correctly at run time.

If all else fails, try closing and reopening JBuilder. If memory is tight on your system, sometimes JBuilder will not perform perfectly if it stays open for too long. (Uh-oh!) Remember my discussion of memory requirements for JBuilder. Anything less that 256 MB of memory would strain JBuilder and potentially cause problems of the kind discussed here. On my machine, which has 448 MB of RAM on it, this problem rarely occurs.

The rest of the code in our sample jbInit method is standard Java fare. As a result, I'm not going to discuss it any further at this stage.

The key point to grasp is that the code associated with the UI designer is placed here. Similar code placed in other parts of your program won't necessarily be reflected in the UI designer. As a result, if you want to convert a non-JBuilder program to JBuilder, often one of your first tasks is to move all this UI-type code into a method called jbInit, which is called from the constructor of your JFrame or JPanel descendant. Code that you call from jbInit will also appear in the UI designer. As a result, you could "convert" an application to JBuilder by simply calling the method where you initialize UI components from a method called jbInit.

More on Editing UI Code by Hand

I am going to add some to the text you read earlier and emphasize certain points by repeating them. My goal is to make sure you understand some very important points about the UI designer.

The UI designer and the editor interact with each other. If you type in the code to instantiate a visual component in the editor, the component will become visible when you switch to design mode.

To try this, turn to source view and write code to create an instance of a JButton. At the top of the code for Frame1, right under the declaration for jButton1, type:

```
JButton myButton = new JButton();
```

In the jbInit() method, under the similar lines of code referring to jButton1, type in the following lines:

```
myButton.setText("My Button");
contentPane.add(myButton, BorderLayout.SOUTH);
```

Now switch to design view. myButton will appear at the bottom of the UI designer.

The following code listing will help you see where to insert the code for myButton.

Listing 6-2: Frame1 source code after adding myButton

```
package myfirstproject;

import java.awt.*;
import java.awt.event.*;
import javax.swing.*;

public class Frame1 extends JFrame
{
  JPanel contentPane;
  BorderLayout borderLayout1 = new BorderLayout();
  JButton JButton1 = new JButton();
  JButton myButton = new JButton();

  //Construct the frame
  public Frame1()
  {
    enableEvents(AWTEvent.WINDOW_EVENT_MASK);
    try
    {
      jbInit();
    }
    catch(Exception e)
    {
      e.printStackTrace();
    }
  }

  //Component initialization
  private void jbInit() throws Exception
  {
```

```
    contentPane = (JPanel) this.getContentPane();
    JButton1.setText("JButton1");
    myButton.setText("My Button");
    contentPane.setLayout(borderLayout1);
    this.setSize(new Dimension(400, 300));
    this.setTitle("Frame Title");
    contentPane.add(JButton1, BorderLayout.NORTH);
    contentPane.add(myButton, BorderLayout.SOUTH);
  }

  //Overridden so we can exit when window is closed
  protected void processWindowEvent(WindowEvent e)
  {
    super.processWindowEvent(e);
    if (e.getID() == WindowEvent.WINDOW_CLOSING)
    {
      System.exit(0);
    }
  }
}
```

This code would not work properly if you did not include the last two lines in jbInit. For instance, the following code works fine at run time, but it does not work as expected in the UI designer:

```
  public Frame1()
  {
    enableEvents(AWTEvent.WINDOW_EVENT_MASK);
    try
    {
      myButton.setText("My Button");
      jbInit();
    }
    catch(Exception e)
    {
      e.printStackTrace();
    }
  }

  //Component initialization
  private void jbInit() throws Exception
  {
    contentPane = (JPanel) this.getContentPane();
    JButton1.setText("JButton1");
    contentPane.setLayout(borderLayout1);
    this.setSize(new Dimension(400, 300));
    this.setTitle("Frame Title");
    contentPane.add(JButton1, BorderLayout.NORTH);
    contentPane.add(myButton, BorderLayout.SOUTH);
  }
```

In this code block, I have moved myButton.setText from jbInit to the constructor. As far as Java is concerned, the move I made is totally legal. It is still valid Java code. JBuilder will compile the code fine, and if you select the JBuilder Run option, the program will appear correctly at run time. But it will not show up correctly at design time. No errors will occur, but you simply do not see the text on the button you have created. The following code, however, will work as expected at design time:

```
//Component initialization
private void jbInit() throws Exception
{
      contentPane = (JPanel) this.getContentPane();
      contentPane.setLayout(borderLayout1);
      setButtonText();
      contentPane.add(myButton);
      this.setSize(new Dimension(400, 300));
      this.setTitle("Frame Title");
}

private void setButtonText()
{
      myButton.setText("Sam");
}
```

Here the call to myButton.setText is not inside of jbInit, but it is called from jbInit. JBuilder understands your intention.

I think this last example, of calling a method from jbInit, can be fairly significant. The issue here is that jbInit can become very long and complicated in programs that have a complicated interface. If you want, you can break those long jbInit methods up into several blocks, using the technique shown here.

The following takes a block of code from jbInit having to do with tabbed panes and moves it into its own method:

```
private void jbInit() throws Exception
{
      contentPane = (JPanel) this.getContentPane();
      contentPane.setLayout(borderLayout1);
      // … code omitted here for brevity
      doTabbedPane();
      this.setSize(new Dimension(400, 300));
      this.setTitle("Frame Title");
}

private void doTabbedPane()
{
      contentPane.add(jTabbedPane1, BorderLayout.CENTER);
      jTabbedPane1.add(JPanel1,  "JPanel1");
      jTabbedPane1.add(JPanel2,  "JPanel2");
      jTabbedPane1.add(JPanel3,  "JPanel3");
}
```

One of the important points about the technique shown here is that it combines a certain amount of visual programming with a certain amount of standard editing. You would normally design the tabs in the UI designer, but to create the doTabbedPane method in code, use the

JBuilder text editor. This is the way things are supposed to work in JBuilder. You should be able to move freely between code and the visual tools.

Finally, I want to reemphasize the theoretical design issues discussed earlier in the chapter. Because jbInit can become so huge, it tends to clutter up the class in which it belongs. Even if you clean up the code using the methods shown in this section, it will still tend to overwhelm any other code found in this class. As a result, I think you should only put UI code in Frame1 descendants. Program logic belongs elsewhere.

Coming to Terms with processWindowEvent

As you recall, the first line in the constructor for Frame1 calls a method of java.awt.Component called enableEvents. Most objects will not get a particular kind of event unless they explicitly register a listener for it. This method says that Frame1 should get WINDOW_EVENT_MASK messages even though the component has not registered a listener of this type. (The subject of listeners and events will be discussed in Chapters 14 and 15.)

Look down at the bottom of Listing 6-1. You will see a method called processWindowEvent.

Here is the JBuilder-generated version of the call to processWindowEvent as it appears in Frame1.java:

```
//Overridden so we can exit when window is closed
protected void processWindowEvent(WindowEvent e)
{
    super.processWindowEvent(e);
    if (e.getID() == WindowEvent.WINDOW_CLOSING)
    {
        System.exit(0);
    }
}
```

I will explain what this method does in just a few moments. But for now, you only need to know that the processWindowEvent method will never be called if the class does not first call enableEvents and pass in a parameter of AWTEvent.WINDOW_EVENT_MASK.

Here is a grossly oversimplified version of enableEvents as it appears in the Java JDK file called Component.java:

```
protected final void enableEvents(long eventsToEnable)
{
    eventMask |= eventsToEnable;
}
```

After this method is called, JBuilder tracks what events it needs to send to your program in a variable called eventMask. It sends these events to your program via a virtual method called processWindowEvent.

One of the first things you might notice about the processWindowEvent method in Frame1 is that it calls super.processWindowEvent. This means that there is an ancestor object in the hierarchy tree for Frame1 that also contains a method called processWindowEvent.

Here are the objects from which Frame1 descends:

```
java.lang.Object
  |
  +-java.awt.Component
      |
```

```
+-java.awt.Container
      |
      +-java.awt.Window
            |
            +-java.awt.Frame
                  |
                  +-javax.swing.JFrame
                        |
                        +-Frame1
```

As you can see, Frame1 has a fairly rich ancestry. All of the objects in Frame1's ancestry are part of the Java JDK. They were all written by Sun, and they are all part of every standard Java VM. It is not important at this time that you understand all of the objects in this hierarchy, only that you know that the hierarchy exists.

NOTE: In Chapter 7, you will find out how to use JBuilder to discover a hierarchy of the type shown here.

If you study the objects in Frame1's ancestry, you will find out that JFrame itself contains an instance of the processWindowEvent method. In JFrame's version of processWindowEvent, a certain key behavior for this type of window is defined:

```
protected void processWindowEvent(WindowEvent e)
{
    super.processWindowEvent(e);

    if (e.getID() == WindowEvent.WINDOW_CLOSING)
    {
        switch(defaultCloseOperation)
        {
          case HIDE_ON_CLOSE:
             setVisible(false);
             break;
          case DISPOSE_ON_CLOSE:
             setVisible(false);
             dispose();
             break;
          case DO_NOTHING_ON_CLOSE:
             default:
             break;
          case EXIT_ON_CLOSE:
            System.exit(0);
            break;
        }
    }
}
```

You can see that this method responds to certain events by doing things such as making the window invisible and, in one case, disposing the window.

It turns out that processWindowEvent is called by a method called processEvent, which is declared in another ancestor of Frame1 called Window.java:

```
protected void processEvent(AWTEvent e)
{
      if (e instanceof WindowEvent)
      {
            processWindowEvent((WindowEvent)e);
            return;
      }
      super.processEvent(e);
}
```

processEvent itself is called in class Component, which is the base class of any class that can appear on the screen. processEvent will not be called unless the method eventEnabled returns true:

```
    boolean eventEnabled(AWTEvent e) {
        switch(e.id) {
          case WindowEvent.WINDOW_OPENED:
          case WindowEvent.WINDOW_CLOSING:
          case WindowEvent.WINDOW_CLOSED:
          case WindowEvent.WINDOW_ICONIFIED:
          case WindowEvent.WINDOW_DEICONIFIED:
          case WindowEvent.WINDOW_ACTIVATED:
          case WindowEvent.WINDOW_DEACTIVATED:
            if ((eventMask & AWTEvent.WINDOW_EVENT_MASK) != 0 ||
                windowListener != null) {
                return true;
            }
            return false;
          default:
            break;
        }
        return super.eventEnabled(e);
    }
```

Study this method carefully, and you will see that it returns true if WINDOW_EVENT_MASK is present. This is the event we initially asked the system to look for.

To sum up: Component.java will not call processEvent unless enableEvents has been called and has specifically made it clear that a particular kind of event should be processed. That is why the call in our constructor to enableEvent is so important:

```
enableEvents(AWTEvent.WINDOW_EVENT_MASK);
```

Without the call to enableEvents, processEvent and processWindowEvent would never be called. The purpose of the call to processWindowEvent is very obvious if you study the method itself. The key line is shown here:

```
System.exit(0);
```

This code ensures that your program will exit when this window closes. If you did not include this line of code, the window would close, but the program would still stay in memory.

I know that it takes a bit of mental exercise to follow all this, but if you have done so, then you should now have a clear sense of the relationship between the call to enableEvents and the method in Frame1 called processWindowEvent.

NOTE: Beginning level programmers are probably a bit angry at me for getting them involved in an examination of such a complex object hierarchy. However, more experienced programmers who are new to Java might find this analysis rather comforting. In particular, it reveals that Java has an object hierarchy very similar to the kind of code found in Borland's class hierarchies for Owl or the VCL. Many of these big class hierarchies for complex window-based objects tend to look and feel the same. Whether they are written in Pascal, C++, or Java, they all tend to act more or less the same way. So here comes another one!

Visual Programming Tricks and Techniques

I promise there will be no more sections in this chapter quite as trying as the one you just read. As a peace offering, I'll present you with two simple descriptions of how to multi-select components in the UI designer and how to delete components.

Multi-Selecting Components

Suppose that you wanted to drop several buttons on the UI designer in quick succession. Go to design view, press **Shift**, and click on the **JButton** icon in the component palette. Now click twice on the UI designer. A JButton will appear for each click. To deselect the **JButton**, click on the selection tool, which is the white arrow on the top left of the component palette.

Deleting Components

If you want to delete a component, you can delete it in source view. Move to source view and delete this line of code:

```
JButton myButton = new JButton();
```

Now return to design view. myButton will no longer be on the panel. Of course, if you were deleting myButton from your code, you would want to clean up the rest of the references to myButton in your source code. The visual tools trump the manual programming tools in this case, since they will perform this cleanup for you.

In design view, there are multiple ways to delete a component. You can select it in the structure pane and then use Ctrl+X, or you can right-click on its name in the structure pane and choose Cut from the pop-up menu or right-click on the component in the UI designer and choose Cut. Selecting the component in either the UI designer or the structure pane and pressing the Delete key on your keyboard will also work. Note that you can use the Ctrl key to select multiple components for a deletion if you are using the structure pane.

NOTE: You can undo the deletion by selecting Ctrl+Z. JBuilder's visual design tools are extremely powerful when it comes to undoing changes in the visual designer. Often you can undo a half hour's work just by hitting Ctrl+Z multiple times. What I have said about the visual designer is also true about the editor, but the effect is not quite so dramatic.

The Structure Pane Rules!

The last normal paragraph in the previous section is really very important because it emphasizes the importance of using the structure pane. I generally find that the structure pane is the simplest way to manipulate a graphical component in JBuilder. In a tool like Delphi, the designer itself is easiest to use. But in JBuilder, as you will see again and again in this book, the structure pane is what is most important.

In a sense, the UI designer is really just a visual confirmation of what you do in the structure pane. In tools such as Delphi, you design your component on the form in which it will appear. To some degree, the same is true of JBuilder. But as you get more experienced at working with components in visual design mode, you will come to see that it is the structure pane that is most useful, and the UI designer itself is really only there to help you see that your design is working out as you planned.

When I drop a button on a JFrame descendant, it is often simplest for me to drop it not on the JFrame itself, but on the listing for the JFrame in the structure pane. In relatively simple designs, it is perhaps six of one, half a dozen of the other, as far as the choice you make. But in complex visual interfaces, it becomes harder and harder to simply paint your components onto the UI designer with the mouse. Instead, I find I have more control using the structure pane.

Why is this? The answer to that question really lies in the chapters on layout managers in Part III. The short explanation is simply that components in JBuilder are not placed at particular x and y coordinates but rather in relationship to one another. The structure pane gives you a better conceptual understanding of that relationship than the content pane does.

It would seem that painting things with the mouse would be easier than working in the non-graphical structure pane. But in many cases, the more obvious, more intuitive technique is not the best technique when creating your user interface. The counter-intuitive aspect of this issue is especially strong for Delphi or VB developers, who are really used to painting their interfaces directly on a form.

The rest of this chapter briefly covers the Inspector and the event mechanisms that are part of the UI designer. These sections of text are really just introductions to subjects that will be covered in more depth in Part III: JBuilder Fundamentals.

The Inspector

On the right side of the screen is the Inspector. Using the Inspector, you will be able to set properties for components and also generate event stubs for them. Drop a component onto the panel, and look to the right at the Inspector. The Inspector will display the most recently generated or selected component by default. Select another component by clicking on it either in the UI designer or the structure pane. The Inspector will shift its focus to the selected component.

By default, the Inspector will be open to the Properties page. Check for this by looking at the bottom of the Inspector where the Properties tab should be selected. The properties are listed in alphabetical order, except for name, constraints, and buttonGroup.

Let's alter some of jButton1's characteristics in the Inspector. Select **jButton1** by clicking on it in the structure pane. Now click on the word **name** at the top of the Inspector. This will select the text field adjacent to it. Press **Delete** to get rid of the name jButton1, and then type in **myButton** and press **Enter**. You have just renamed the button. Switch to source view, and you will see the following code:

```
JButton myButton = new JButton();
```

Go back to design view. To change the text on the button, scroll to the text property and repeat the process, typing **My Button** in the setText method of the text field.

NOTE: My Button (two words) is legal as a caption for a component. The name of the component, however, must contain no spaces.

Now go back to the Inspector. Tweak the look of the button by changing the background property. Move to the background property in the Inspector and choose **blue** from the drop-down list. Find the foreground property and change the foreground to **cyan**. Then change the font by moving to the font property and clicking in the field to its right. An ellipsis will appear. Click on it to move to the Font dialog box. Choose the type and size of font that you want, and click **OK**.

The Properties page in the Inspector is a complicated and powerful tool. Hopefully, I have said enough to get you acquainted with it. In later chapters, you will read more about this tool. The next section discusses the Events page of the Inspector.

Creating a Simple Event Handler

Events are a complicated subject, one that will be dealt with in its own chapters, "Event Handling" and "Firing Events." For now, I'm going to only show you a simple example of what you can do in the Events page.

When you associate an event with a button, you are defining the behavior the button will have when someone clicks on it. It is called an *event handler* because it handles the event that occurs when a user clicks on a button.

To add an event to myButton, move your cursor to the bottom of the Inspector and select the Events page. Click in the field to the right of the event you want to use and press enter. JBuilder will create a code stub for the event with all of the boilerplate event code written for you and move you to the editor. If you want the actionPerformed event for a component, you can double-click on the component in the UI designer, and JBuilder will create the event stub. Here is what the code looks like:

```
void jButton1_actionPerformed(ActionEvent e)
{

}
```

You would write code between the curly braces to define what the button does. For instance, you might write code that looks like this:

```
void jButton1_actionPerformed(ActionEvent e)
{
    JOptionPane.showMessageDialog(this, "Little pretty infant wiles");
}
```

You can now run the program, click on the button, and see the text from William Blake appear in its own window.

It turns out that there is more code generated when you create an event than what I have shown you here. However, for now, it will do to simply give you this simple bit of functionality to use in your own programs.

Using JTabbedPane

To end the chapter, let's take a moment to see how to use JTabbedPane. Create a new default application, as shown in Chapter 3.

Focus **Frame1** in the project pane and switch to design mode. Turn to the Swing Containers page of the component palette and drop down a **JTabbedPane**. From the same page of the component palette, drop down a **JPanel** onto the JTabbedPane. Now click again on the

JPanel component in the component palette. This time, drop the panel on the word jTabbedPane1 in the structure pane.

Each JPanel that you dropped down on the JTabbedPane created a new page. At this stage, you should have a JTabbedPane with two pages on it, as shown in Figure 6-5.

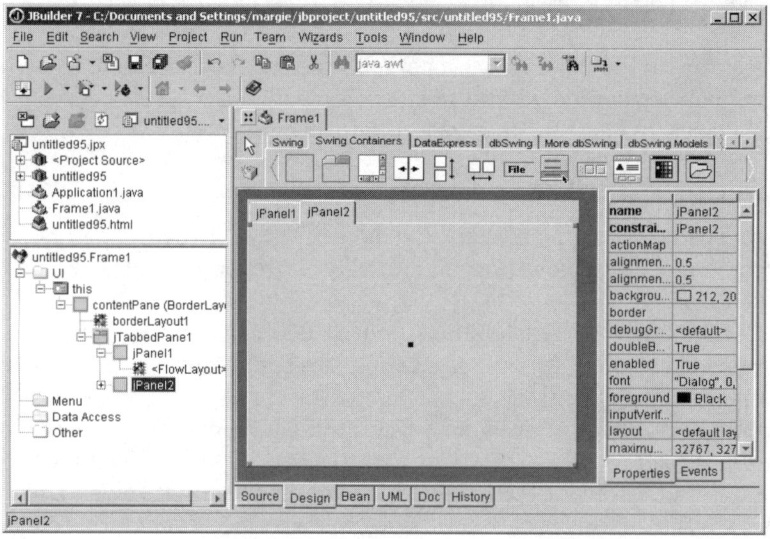

Figure 6-5: A JTabbedPane with two JPanels dropped on top of it to create pages

You can switch back and forth between the two pages of the JTabbedPane by selecting the JPanel objects in the structure pane.

Select the first page. Set the layout for jPanel1 to **BorderLayout**. Drop down a **JTextArea**. Set its constraints property to **Center**. Find a block of text that you want to display in the JTextArea. Copy it to the clipboard. Select the text property of the JTextArea and paste the selection you made into the property editor. (Use the appropriate hot key, such as Ctrl+V, to paste the text.) Press **Enter** once, and the text you selected should appear in the control, similar to Figure 6-6.

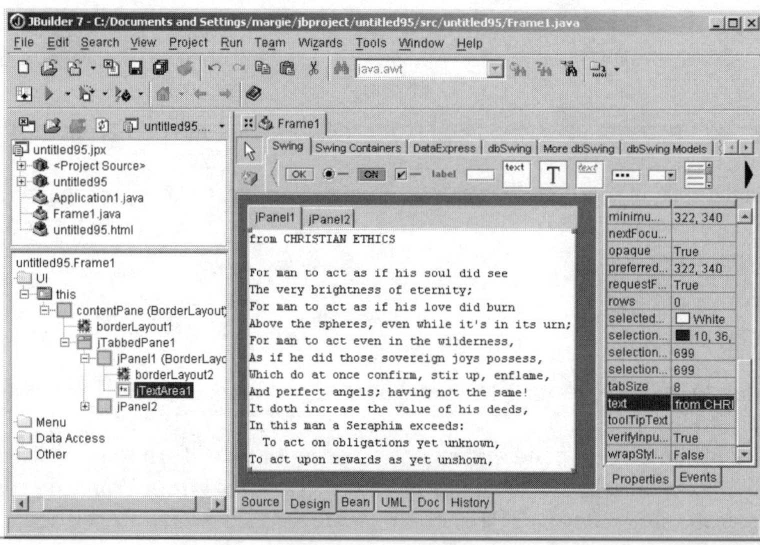

Figure 6-6: The text of a poem by Thomas Traherne shown in one page of a JTabbedPane

Turn to the second page of the JTabbedPane, and repeat the actions that you performed on the first page, only this time enter in some other block of text. Run the program. You should be able to move back and forth between the two tabbed pages.

You can rename the captions found on the tabs of the pages by editing the constraints property for jPanel1 and jPanel2. The final program at run time is shown in Figure 6-7. The source for the program is found on the CD under the name TabbedPaneExample.

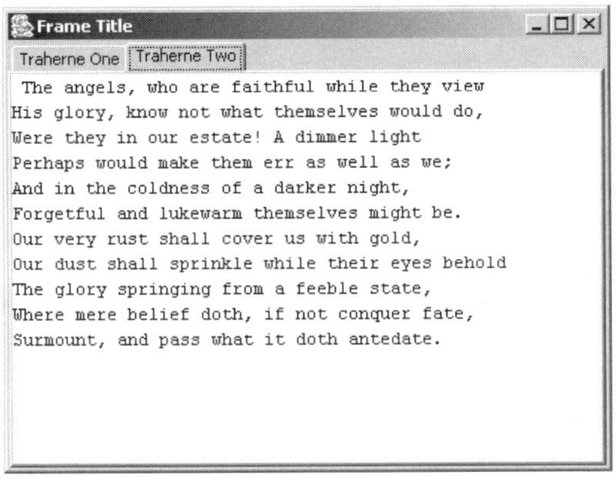

Figure 6-7: The TabbedPaneExample at run time

Setting Your ClassPath inside the IDE

You may need to add a library to your project to expand your classpath. This is discussed in Chapter 27 in the "Setting Your ClassPath: JBuilder Library Files" section.

Summary

You now know the basics about creating a user interface in JBuilder. As easy as the first steps may be, you will find that it can soon become considerably more complex than it appears at first. We have already touched on a few issues that can confuse developers, such as the primacy of jbInit and the potential for that method to become very large and complex.

The next step for students of the UI designer will occur in Chapter 12, "Layout Managers." Layout managers are one of the most important subjects encountered in this book, one that can prove to be a stumbling block to newcomers if they don't have the inclination to treat the matter with considerable respect.

This whole discussion of the complex nature of interface design in JBuilder will continue throughout Part III: JBuilder Fundamentals. There you will come face to face with the complexities generated by the powerful model-view-controller architecture that lies behind Swing.

For now, however, you can rest easy with the knowledge you have about the basic mechanisms at work in the UI designer. This is one of the most powerful parts of JBuilder, one that can save you a huge amount of time. As you come to understand it better throughout the course of this book, you will find that it is really a very flexible tool, as long as you use it wisely.

Chapter 7

Using the Editor

Charlie Calvert

In this chapter you will learn how to use the editor. Here you will find the tools for writing and editing code. Some of these tools provide context-sensitive support for helping you find the classes, methods, and parameters that you need. Effective and knowledgeable use of the many tools in the editor is essential if you want to use JBuilder properly.

When I worked at Borland, I was once sent to a conference to cover JBuilder in a booth. The product was new at the time, and I frankly didn't know much about it. In a desperate attempt to stick with something that I actually understood, I ended up covering the editor (and debugger) in great detail. To my amazement, this was a big hit with a number of people who had been used to doing everything with a text editor and the command line. They just couldn't believe what the JBuilder editor had to offer.

Most of the tools described in this chapter are available in all versions of JBuilder. The fact that they are present in the low-end versions of JBuilder does not make them any less useful. In fact, many of the technologies described in this chapter form the core capabilities on which your day-to-day use of the product must stand.

Subjects covered in this chapter include:

- Code templates
- Automatically inserting and optimizing imports
- CodeInsight, MemberInsight, and related technologies
- Automatically inserting the proper try..catch blocks in your program
- An introduction to Javadoc, a subject covered in depth in Chapter 21
- Viewing class libraries
- Customizing hot keys

I'm going to start by discussing some of the simpler tools, such as code templates and customizing keystrokes. With these basics out of the way, I will move on to the heart of the chapter, which is a study of CodeInsight and various methods for automatically and intelligently inserting code into your source files. The end of the chapter covers some wizards that automate tasks commonly performed inside a text editor.

Key Mapping

When working with a new editor, one of the first questions many developers ask is, "Does it support the keystrokes in my favorite tool?" The second question they ask is if JBuilder key mappings are customizable. Fortunately, JBuilder supports a range of editor key mappings, and you can add new key mappings of your own and customize existing key mappings.

NOTE: A key mapping defines the special keystrokes used in an editor. For instance, Ctrl+V is mapped to the Paste command in many editors. But there are differences from editor to editor in the hot keys used for deleting characters, cutting and pasting, saving documents, etc. It's getting control over these differences that concerns us now.

The first task you need to learn is how to select the key mapping that you prefer. From the JBuilder menu, choose **Tools | Editor Options**, and turn to the Editor page. Drop down the **Keymap** list, as shown in Figure 7-1. You can see that you are able to choose from CUA, Brief, Emacs, Macintosh, Macintosh CodeWarrior, and Visual Studio key mappings.

There is a Customize button to the right of the keymap field. Click that button to customize the keystrokes for your editor. This is also one of the best ways to learn what keystrokes are available for your editor. The other method is to choose Help | Keyboard mappings from the JBuilder menu.

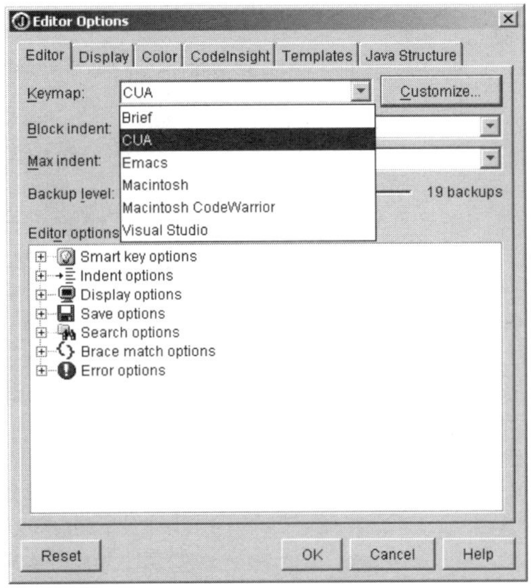

Figure 7-1: Selecting your favorite key mapping

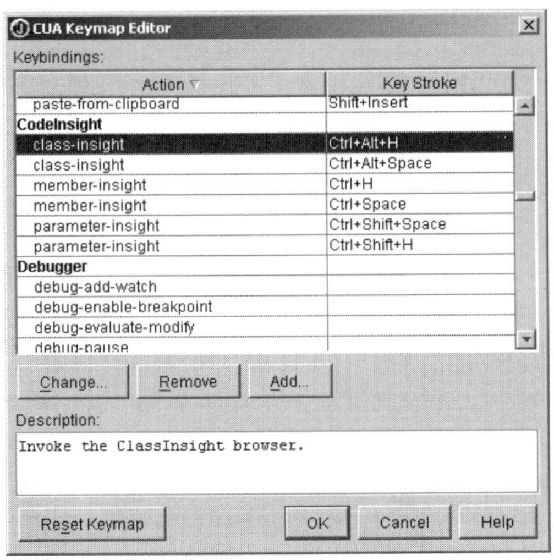

Figure 7-2: Viewing the Keymap editor. Here you can view the settings for your hot keys and edit them.

To edit a particular value, simply select it in the Keymap Editor dialog, and press the **Add** button. A new dialog will appear, as shown in Figure 7-3. When using this editor, it is simplest to select the event type of Key Pressed. Then you can simply press the keystrokes you want to use, and JBuilder will record them automatically.

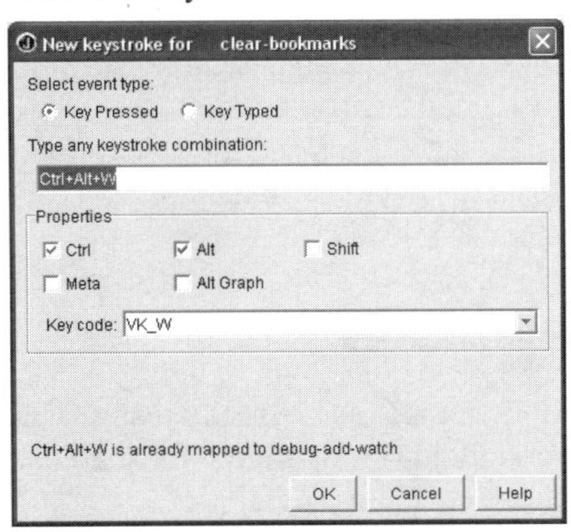

Figure 7-3: Adding a new keystroke to the editor

Notice that the keystroke chosen in Figure 7-3 causes a conflict with another custom keystroke I created for adding watches. In cases like this, JBuilder will allow you to either select a new keystroke or override the existing keystroke. If you select a keystroke that is unique, a message will appear at the bottom of the dialog stating "No conflicts."

You can completely customize your keystrokes in JBuilder by creating your own OpenTool. Two sample OpenTool implementations of keymap bindings ship with JBuilder in the Samples/OpenTools directory.

Creating your own key bindings is fairly simple but tedious. Here is example code for creating a single binding:

```
new KeymapManager.KeyActionBinding(KeyStroke.getKeyStroke(
    KeyEvent.VK_O,
    Event.CTRL_MASK),
    BrowserFile.ACTION_FileOpen),
```

You can create your own custom actions. Creating custom actions could be considered a technique for scripting macros. See the UserEmacsActions.java sample for a regrettably complex example of how to proceed. The other example that ships with the product, UserCUA, provides little help with custom actions but does provide a much simpler template for creating your own key mappings.

JBuilder and Macros

There are, of course, a number of powerful editors available for programmers. Some, such as emacs and Visual Slick Edit, provide relatively easy-to-use macro languages that give you a capability that can only be achieved in JBuilder by using the JBuilder OpenTools libraries, as described in the previous section. The OpenTools APIs are wonderful, but many developers will consider them too complex for macro development.

NOTE: A JBuilder team member said that features are added to JBuilder based on two requirements: user demand and ease of implementation. If a certain valuable but not essential feature such as macros takes X months to develop, while five other features of relatively equal value can also be produced in the same period of time, the team will go for the latter option on the grounds that it gives them the most bang for the buck. Still, I wish there were macros in JBuilder.

If you really need a macro language, just call emacs, Visual Slick Edit, or some other tool from JBuilder, as described in the section called "Adding a Third-Party Tool to the JBuilder Menu System" from Chapter 5. This subject is alluded to again later in this chapter in the section called "Integration with emacs and Other Editors."

There is at least one OpenTools implementation of macros available for free download. The tool was developed by Luke Hutteman. You should be able to download it from here: http://codecentral.borland.com/codecentral/ccweb.exe/listing?id=15582.

As far as I can see, the tool provides no scripting capabilities and will not save your macros. However, it will let you play back a series of keystrokes. This feature used to be built into older versions of JBuilder.

Code Templates

Code templates are really just a simple, yet useful, mechanism for inserting snippets of code directly into your source files. To use JBuilder effectively, you need to know at least a few of these code templates.

NOTE: Code templates are a relatively simple-minded technology compared to the CodeInsight technologies. Yet, sometimes a simple solution is all you need.

The technology behind code templates is both extensible and easy to understand. Code templates allow you to type in an abbreviation for a command and expand the abbreviation when you press Ctrl+J. (The hot key may differ if you are using something other than the default key mappings, but most of them seem to be mapped to Ctrl+J.)

If you type in the letters **ifb** and then press **Ctrl+J**, the following code will be inserted into your program:

```
if ()
{

}
```

Furthermore, your cursor position will be moved into the open parenthesis after the word "if." This is usually where you want to begin typing.

If you type in the word **if** and then press **Ctrl+J**, a CodeInsight window will pop open, as shown in Figure 7-4.

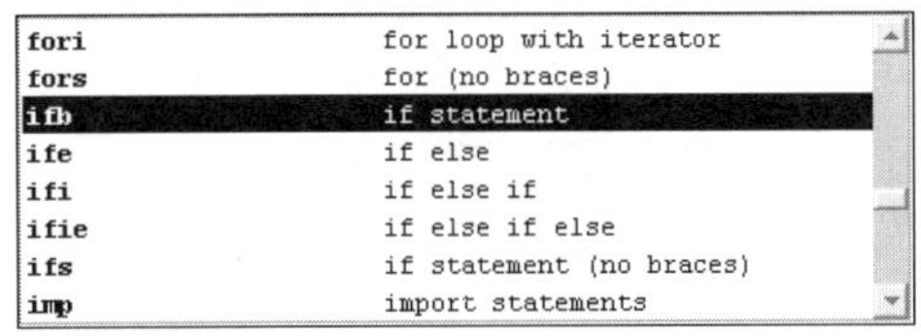

Figure 7-4: Using CodeInsight to help you choose between a series of code templates

If you look at the options in the CodeInsight window, you will see that there are several different if statements that you can use. For instance, the one that reads "ifie" looks like this:

```
if ()
{

}
else if ()
{

}
else
{

}
```

The forb code template expands to code that looks like this:

```
for (; ; )
{

}
```

Many of the commands have a b version and an s version. For instance, there is a forb and fors and an ifb and ifs. The "b" versions include the curly braces after them, as in the previous example. The "s" versions, on the other hand, omit the curly braces:

```
for (; ; )
```

NOTE: I assume that "b" stands for braces and "s" for short, but I don't think this is documented anywhere.

Some other useful options include the abbreviation sys, which inserts the following code:

```
System.err.println("");
```

...and tryc, which inserts this code:

```
try
{

}
catch (Exception ex)
{

}
```

There are many other useful templates. However, it is difficult to learn them all at once. To ease your task, I would suggest that you focus on the following list of Charlie's 15 favorite templates:

classp	Insert a public class
err	system.err.println
forb	for statement with curly braces
ifb	if statement with curly braces
ife	if else statement with curly braces
imp	The most common import statements
iter	Use an iterator for working with containers
main	main statement
switchs	Switch statement without default option
switchd	Switch statement with default option
addXXX	addaction adds an ActionListener, addawt adds an AWTEventListener, etc.
todo	/** @todo */
tryc	try catch block
tryf	try catch finally block
whileb	while block with curly braces

NOTE: Learning to use a tool well is often a bit of work. It's an annoying task at first, but you should try to catch yourself if you ever start typing in an if, for, or while statement from scratch. With code templates around, it's a waste of time to type out System.err.println in full. Instead, you should type sys and then press Ctrl+J. In the long run, developing these kinds of habits will save you time.

If you choose Tools | Editor Options | Templates from the menu, you can view all the available code templates and their abbreviations.

You can also add new templates here, if you wish. For instance, you might want to add one called sysout, which will type in System.out.println(). I will not talk you through the process of adding code templates, as it is very intuitive. It is very important, but nonetheless intuitive.

Setting Up Tabs

If you work in a shared programming environment, your team undoubtedly has some conventions about whether or not to use tabs and about how many spaces there should be when you indent. I discussed this subject briefly in an earlier chapter, but here I will cover it in more depth.

JBuilder can be quite intelligent about these matters. Choose **Tools | Editor Options**, and turn to the Editor page. If you want to use tabs and have each indent by four spaces, set the **Block Indent** and **Tab** size to **4**. Open up **Indent Options** and check **Smart indent** and **Use tab character**.

Go down to the save options, and choose **Strip trailing white space** and **Change leading spaces to tabs.** This latter option is a particularly powerful means of ensuring that you do not accidentally place space characters where you mean to place tabs.

I won't bore you by explaining in detail how you can achieve the opposite effects choosing the opposite options. Note, however, that there is a Change leading tabs to spaces option.

Under the Brace match Options, choose **Generate closing curly brace** and **Enable brace match highlighting**.

In general, you will find that many of the options found in the Editor page of this dialog are quite useful. The smart key options might prove to be particularly useful to a certain kind of developer. If you turn on Smart home key, for instance, hitting the Home key will take you to the first non-blank character on a line rather than back to the beginning of the line itself.

Setting Up Carriage Returns and Linefeeds

As mentioned in an earlier chapter, you can have JBuilder use UNIX style, Windows style, or Mac style carriage returns and linefeeds. Or, if you prefer, it can automatically adopt itself to the style in your current file. Choose **Project | Project Properties**, and turn to the Editor page to adjust these settings.

Error Insight

If JBuilder 7 and above finds an error in your code, it underlines it in red, much as Microsoft Word underlines misspellings in red. If you put your cursor over the error, you can often get a tip explaining what is wrong. The errors should also appear at the top of the structure pane.

The red underlines are mostly useful simply because they remind you that something about your code is not quite right. If you are an experienced developer, just the sight of the red underline should be all you need to help you understand what is wrong.

Letting JBuilder Write Your try..catch Blocks

In JBuilder 7 and above, if you right-click on code that needs to be surrounded by a try..catch block, JBuilder will insert the necessary code for you automatically. Usually it will automatically detect the kind of statements that you want to catch and insert the appropriate type into your code. Thus, it will not write a catch (Exception ex) statement when what you want is a catch (IOException ex) statement.

An example might help you understand how this works. Suppose you enter the following code:

```
File f = new File("c:\\sam.txt");
if (f.createNewFile());
```

If you right-click on createNewFile and choose the appropriate menu item, JBuilder will automatically insert the following code:

```
File f = new File("c:\\sam.txt");

try
{
  if (f.createNewFile());
}
catch (IOException ex)
{
}
```

Letting JBuilder Write Your Import Statements

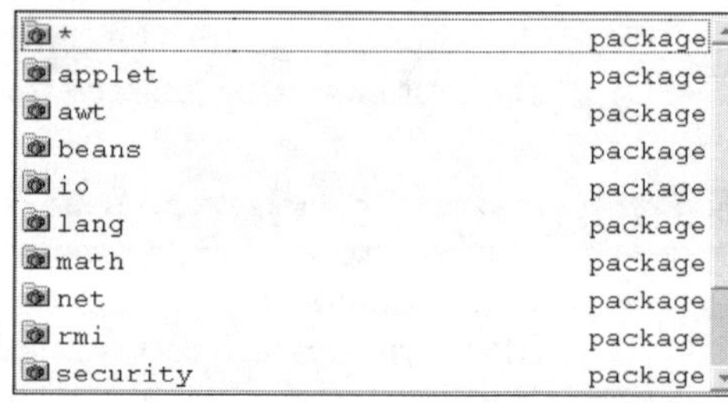

Figure 7-5: The list that pops up when you are typing in an import statement

Part of CodeInsight will help you enter import statements. For instance, if you type import java., then JBuilder will automatically pop up a list of classes that can help you complete your statement, as shown in Figure 7-5.

The list shown in Figure 7-5 is not a list of all classes available on your classpath. Rather, it is an intelligently filtered list showing only the classes on your classpath that can be used in this particular context. For instance, if you type **import java.**, you will see all the classes or packages in the java package (directory) and not any of those from the com package, the javax package, or any other packages.

There is a kind of rhythm you can establish when typing in long import statements. Suppose you want to type in "import com.elvenware.codebox.FilePath." To enter this line, you first type in **import com.** Don't forget the period at the end of the statement. Then wait a moment, and CodeInsight will give you a list similar to the one in Figure 7-5. Pick the item you want from the list. Now your code should read "import com.elvenware." Put a period after this, and again JBuilder will put up a list similar to the one in Figure 7-5 but filtered for the new package you are searching. Pick the item you need from the list so that your code reads "import com.elvenware.codebox." Now type in another period, and proceed as before. As I say, this process has something of a rhythm to it, and if you get in time with JBuilder's beat, then you can fill in even long and complex import statements very quickly.

The code template mechanism provides an easy means to insert most of the import sections you will ever need in your program. Simply type **imp**, and press **Ctrl+J** to insert the following items in your program:

```
import javax.swing.*;
import javax.swing.event.*;
import javax.swing.text.*;
```

```
import java.awt.*;
import java.awt.event.*;
import java.util.*;
import java.text.*;
import java.beans.*;
```

When you are through designing your program, right-click and choose **Optimize Imports** to get rid of the import statements that you no longer need. The Optimize Imports option is described in more depth later in this chapter.

This technology is really part of the CodeInsight feature called MemberInsight, but I present it here in its own section because I personally think of it as belonging in its own category. If you want to turn this feature off, read the relevant paragraphs from the "MemberInsight" section of this chapter.

More on Import Statements

JBuilder 7 and above provide support for automatically inserting import statements into your source files. If you type in a statement that JBuilder cannot parse, it will be underlined in red. Left-click on a type that is shown in red, and the small ClassInsight one-line dialog will pop up. Click on the magnifying class icon, and the ClassInsight dialog will appear. Often it will contain the one item you need to add to your import statement. Click **OK** to add it. Sometimes, there will be multiple items, or you may even have to browse to find your import statement. In any case, it can help you quickly add import statements to your project.

NOTE: If necessary, you may need to add a library to your project to expand your class path. This is discussed in Chapter 27 in the section called "Setting Your ClassPath: JBuilder Library Files."

To test this feature, start a new application, as described in Chapter 3. Move to the top of the Frame1 class and add a new field that looks like this:

```
ArrayList list;
```

By default, JBuilder will not recognize the ArrayList class. To add the necessary import statement, left-click on the word **ArrayList**. A small dialog will appear. Click on the magnifying class icon to bring up the ClassInsight dialog. The import statement you need, java.util.ArrayList, should be visible in the dialog. You will have three options:

- Insert an import statement that looks like this: import java.util.ArrayList.
- Insert an import statement that looks like this: import java.util.*.
- Qualify the variable that you declared: java.util.ArrayList list.

Pick the option you want and click the **OK** button.

Optimizing Imports

The JBuilder SE and Enterprise level products have a tool to help you optimize your import section. In particular, this tool will help you discard unused import statements and help you find your preferred combination of wildcard and explicit class references in your import statements.

To get started optimizing your import section, open up your java file and right-click on it. Choose **Optimize Imports** from the pop-up menu. By default, all the unused import statements will be eliminated. Consider this import statement, which appears by default at the top of an applet produced by the JBuilder Applet Wizard:

```
import java.awt.*;
import java.awt.event.*;
import java.applet.*;
```

If you add no code to the java file produced by the wizard, and then choose **Optimize Imports**, the import section will be culled by the Optimize Imports tool and end up looking like this:

```
import java.applet.*;
```

Two of the three import statements were deleted, since they were not needed in your file.

NOTE: You might ask why the JBuilder Applet Wizard inserted the statements if they were not needed. The reasoning on the part of the JBuilder team was simply that you would probably need those statements, so they are inserted as a courtesy to you, the programmer. The ability to automatically cull out the unused portions of this import block makes the team's decision less susceptible to criticism.

When you use the Optimize Imports tool, any references to multiple classes from the same package will, by default, be reduced to a single statement. Consider this import statement, which I will refer to as option 1:

```
import java.applet.Applet;
import java.applet.AppletContext;
```

By choosing Optimize Imports with the default settings, your code will be changed to this statement, which I will refer to as option 2:

```
import java.applet.*;
```

Some people don't want this kind of optimization to take place automatically. For instance, you might prefer to work with some heuristic which states that up to three explicit class references are okay, but if you get four of them, you want to switch to using a wildcard. Fortunately, JBuilder allows you to fine-tune the import optimization tool.

Choose **Project | Project Properties**, and turn to the **Import Style** page. If you select Always import classes, the first form of the two options discussed above will always be used. If you do not select Always import classes, you can define the threshold at which the import statement will switch from importing individual classes and begin importing the entire package. For instance, if you set the threshold at 2, option 1 would be used if you import one or two classes from the java.applet package. However, if you imported a third class, the import statement would automatically be converted to the option 2 format, which uses a wildcard. For instance, if you set the threshold to two, this import statement would be converted:

```
import java.applet.Applet;


import java.applet.AppletContext;
import java.applet.AppletStub;
```

With the threshold set to 2, after choosing Optimize Imports, the statement would look like this:

```
import java.applet.*;
```

Consider this import statement:

```
import java.awt.event.*;
import java.awt.Point;
import javax.swing.*;
import gridworlds.entities.*;
import gridworld.utils.*;
```

If you have Always import classes selected, choosing Optimize Imports will, under certain circumstances, convert the code to this:

```
import java.awt.Point;
import java.awt.event.KeyEvent;
import gridworlds.entities.EntityBase;
import gridworlds.entities.EntityList;
import gridworlds.entities.Hero;
import gridworlds.utils.TCoordinateConversion;
```

If you did not have Always import classes selected, and you set the threshold to 0 or 1, the statement would look like this after choosing Optimize Imports:

```
import java.awt.*;
import java.awt.event.*;
import gridworlds.entities.*;
import gridworlds.utils.*;
```

All of this is not really as complex as it might seem when reading about it. Just get in there and start experimenting with this tool, and you should soon be able to find settings that meet your style of programming.

CodeInsight

The next section of this chapter will be dedicated to an exploration of CodeInsight. This extremely powerful feature will give you hints as to what you should type next in the current context. As a rule, CodeInsight depends on JBuilder's remarkable ability to compile your code on the fly. The complete scope of this multifaceted feature will not, however, become apparent until you have read this entire section.

NOTE: I have had trouble with CodeInsight on Linux under KDE 2.0. If CodeInsight does not appear to be working at all for you, try switching to GNOME, updating your Linux build, or switching to KDE 3.0. This is not a difficult feature to use. It should just pop right up, and if it doesn't do that, then something could be wrong. The most likely fix is to upgrade to KDE 3.0.

CodeInsight is quite snappy on even a 500 MHz machine. If it is slow for you, consider getting more memory.

MemberInsight

MemberInsight, a feature of all editions of JBuilder, shows you all the methods you can call on a particular object. For instance, it will show you all the methods that belong to the JButton class. In some cases, it will filter the methods it shows you to fit the current circumstances. For instance, if you are assigning some value to a string, MemberInsight will sometimes show you only the methods of an object that return a string.

To use MemberInsight, first type in the name of a class instance used in your program, such as jButton1. Follow the identifier with a period. JBuilder should now automatically pop up a list of class members that can be used in this context. Alternatively, you can press Ctrl+Space or Ctrl+H to pop up the list manually. (You must be working with valid variables for this feature to work properly. Errors near your current insertion point can cause this feature to fail. The solution, needless to say, is to fix the errors. Then MemberInsight should work properly. Syntax errors in your code can also cause MemberInsight to fail to properly filter your available options.)

If you want to turn MemberInsight off, select **Tools | Editor Options** from the JBuilder menu. Turn to the **CodeInsight page**. Here you can turn off the option called Auto popup MemberInsight. This will disable the feature described in this section unless you explicitly summon it by pressing the appropriate hot key.

You can use the same dialog to have the system pause a longer or shorter period of time before popping up to help you fill in your code. The period of time you will want to wait before this option pops up depends a little on your skills as a typist and a little on your knowledge of Java. If you are a very fast typist, and you know Java cold, then you may find that MemberInsight just gets in your way. If you are a fast typist but don't always know which method you want on an object, then you might want this feature to pop up after you have delayed long enough to show you are not certain of your next choice. And so on. This is a configurable feature, and you can make it do what you want. However, the defaults will probably seem about right to most users.

MemberInsight is aware of the methods you type in. This is not a hard-coded set of rules that only apply to the JDK or registered files. Any code you include in your program will appear in MemberInsight the moment you type it in correctly. You do not need to first build or make your project.

Sometimes, however, MemberInsight will appear to not be working. This usually occurs because you have entered invalid syntax either in the current line or somewhere near the current line. If you have invalid syntax in one method, it is unlikely to cause troubles with CodeInsight in a second method. The problem is usually confined to the area near where you made the mistake.

ClassInsight

ClassInsight is available in all versions of JBuilder. To access it, you need to use **Ctrl+Alt+Space** or **Ctrl+Alt+H**.

In the JBuilder Personal edition, these keys will pop up the Class Browser. In the Class Browser dialog, you can browse to an object you want to add and then press **OK**. JBuilder will then add the import statement for the object's class to your program and insert the name of the object at your cursor. For instance, if you browse to java | io | BufferedReader, JBuilder will create the following import statement:

```
import java.io.BufferedReader;
```

and BufferedReader will appear at the insertion point marked by your cursor.

In the JBuilder SE and Enterprise versions, **Ctrl+Alt+Space** or **Ctrl+Alt+H** will pop up a different dialog, labeled ClassInsight, as shown in Figure 7-6. As you type information in the Search for text field at the top of the dialog, JBuilder will find classes on the classpath that correspond to your input.

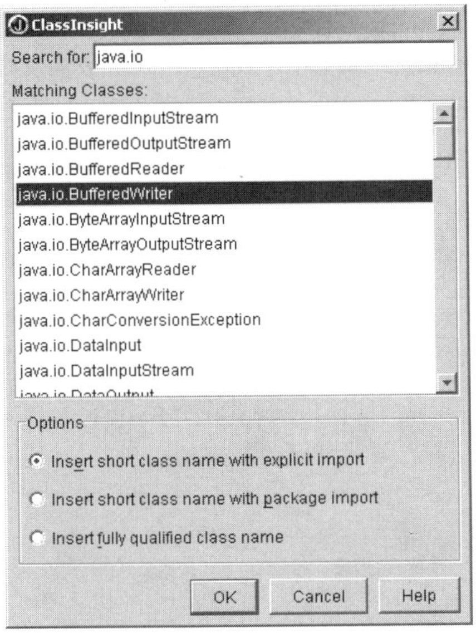

Figure 7-6: The ClassInsight dialog

You have several options in the dialog. Choosing the first option creates the same result as using the Class Browser dialog in the JBuilder Personal edition: JBuilder will create the import statement, import java.io.BufferedWriter, and the name of your class, BufferedWriter, will appear at the insertion point marked by your cursor. The second choice, Insert short class name with package import, imports the package in which your object resides. For instance, if you choose BufferedWriter, the import statement will read:

```
import java.io.*;
```

BufferedWriter will appear at your insertion point. If you choose Insert fully qualified class name, JBuilder does not generate an import statement, but the full class name for your object will appear at the insertion point:

```
java.io.BufferedWriter
```

ParameterInsight

ParameterInsight is a feature in all editions of JBuilder. If you type the name of an existing method in the editor, ParameterInsight will appear when you type the left parenthesis of the method. To test this, open up Application1.java in a default JBuilder application. Find the Application1 constructor method. (This method begins right under the comment "//Construct the application.") If you go to the end of that method, you will see a line of code that reads:

```
frame.setVisible(true);
```

Right under that line of code, type:

```
frame.setBounds(
```

Once you have typed the left parenthesis, you will see a pop-up box with the possible parameters for this method, as shown in Figure 7-7. Because this is an overloaded method, there are two versions of the parameters.

Figure 7-7: ParameterInsight should pop up automatically when you press Ctrl+Shift+Space or when you place an open parenthesis after a variable name.

Each line of the box represents a different set of parameters, which could be appropriate given the method you are calling. On the top line, int p0 is highlighted. Once you enter an integer, JBuilder highlights int p1, indicating that it is now the parameter in play. That will continue until you have filled in all of your parameters for this method call.

Find Definition

Find Definition will take you to the definition for a code element. You can easily test this with the default application you opened. Compile the project, and then in Frame1, find this line of code in the jbInit() section:

```
contentPane.setLayout(borderLayout1);
```

Place your cursor over the word **contentPane**, and then press **Ctrl+Enter**. The cursor will move to the line of code that reads:

```
JPanel contentPane;
```

Now move your cursor to the line of code that reads:

```
System.exit(0);
```

Place your cursor over the word **System** and press **Ctrl+Enter**. JBuilder will open a new tab labeled System and provide the documentation and source for the exit method in the System class. You can also access this tool by right-clicking on the variable you want to explore and choosing **Find Definition** from the menu.

Find References

There are several different ways to find out the object from which a class such as Frame1 is descended. For instance, this information can easily be retrieved from the help file associated with JFrame itself, if the project has already been compiled.

To find this information in a help file, go to the opening line in the declaration for Frame1, which looks like this:

```
public class Frame1 extends JFrame
```

Just as you did earlier in the chapter, place your mouse over the word **JFrame** and right-click. A pop-up menu will appear. From this menu, choose **Find Definition.** This will take you to the source for JFrame. Select **Doc** from the file view tabs. This will take you to the source for the Javadoc for JFrame. At the top of this Javadoc, you will find the hierarchy for JFrame.

In JBuilder SE and Enterprise, there is a second way to find the hierarchy for Frame1. Once again, move to the top of Frame1.java and right-click, this time on the word **Frame1**. From the pop-up menu, select **Find References**. When you do this, information about Frame1 will appear in the message pane, as shown in Figure 7-8. Among the information will be a list of all the ancestors of Frame1.

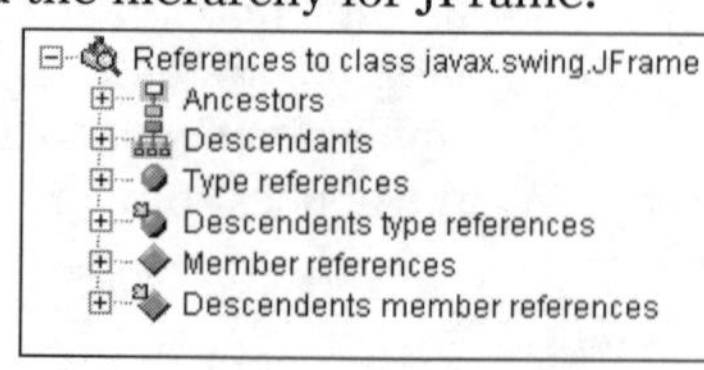

Figure 7-8: The nodes in the message pane after selecting Find References

You can then expand the References node to see a little about the "history" of this object, as shown in Figure 7-9.

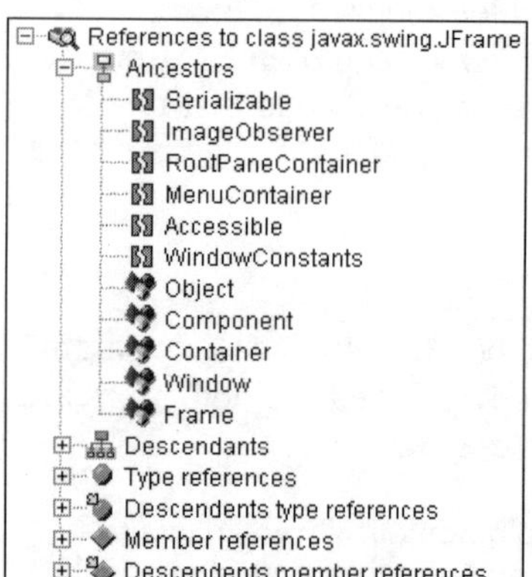

Figure 7-9: The Ancestors nodes

Integration with the Structure Pane

Perhaps one of the JBuilder editor's most powerful features is its integration with the structure pane. If you add a data member or method to a class, it will automatically appear in the structure pane. Conversely, if you click on a data member or method in the structure pane, you will be taken to the declaration for that method or variable in your source.

If you are typing in code in the editor and you write something that will not compile, usually an error node will appear at the top of the structure pane. If you open up the error node, you can often see the nature of the mistake you have made. This process can save you the trouble of having to compile before you can see your errors.

You can also add todo items into your JBuilder source and have them appear as nodes at the top of your structure pane. You can then click on the various todo nodes in the structure pane and be taken immediately to the area of your code that needs to be updated. To add a ToDo note to the structure pane, type something like the following code in your source file:

```
/** @todo This is a todo item. */
```

Overall, I would consider the editor's integration with the structure pane to be one of its most powerful and useful features. In particular, I find myself quite often glancing at the structure pane to make sure that little error node has not insinuated itself into my life. If you have written a line of code that is not quite right, it is best to know about it at the time you write it, rather than at compile time.

NOTE: If I type in this bit of drivel: jButton1.asdf(); JBuilder notes that the syntax looks valid, and it knows that there is no asdf() method on jButton1. It will thus underline it in red and then add an error node to the structure pane.

Resource Strings

The Resource Strings Wizard helps you to create *resource bundles*, which contain strings and other code elements. One purpose of these bundles is to help you internationalize or localize your code. Instead of messages being hard coded into your project, translations of the messages in different languages could be included in the resource bundles. In addition, the bundles may contain other code elements, such as icons. This allows you to further customize your project for different audiences. If you are interested in resource bundles, look at the database chapters in Part VIII, where they are used to store SQL strings.

The Resource Strings Wizard is a feature of JBuilder SE and Enterprise.

Override Methods

The Override Method Wizard in JBuilder SE and Enterprise provides a simple way for you to override a method in a superclass. Before you choose this wizard, you need to choose the class in which you want to insert the method. In the project pane, select the class by clicking on it.

Once the class you want to alter is highlighted, choose **Wizards | Override Methods** in the menu. After the wizard appears, you will not be able to change your choice of class unless you close the wizard and choose another file in the project pane.

The wizard gives you a check box option to override all unimplemented abstract methods. By default, this is checked. In my opinion, you usually don't want to override all the methods in your inheritance tree. This could end up inserting dozens of new methods into your code. As a result, you usually begin by unchecking this option.

If you have unchecked the Override all option, the next step is to select the methods you do want to override. The wizard will show you a list of the inherited classes. When you expand the list, you will see all the available methods that can be overridden for that class. Simply select the method you wish to override and click OK. JBuilder will create a code stub for that method and add an item to the todo list, reminding you to write the code to implement the override of the method. For example, if you wanted to override the setBounds() method in Frame1 of an application, you could select **java.awt.Component**, open up the tree, and then select **setBounds(int,int,int,int)** in the wizard, as shown in Figure 7-10.

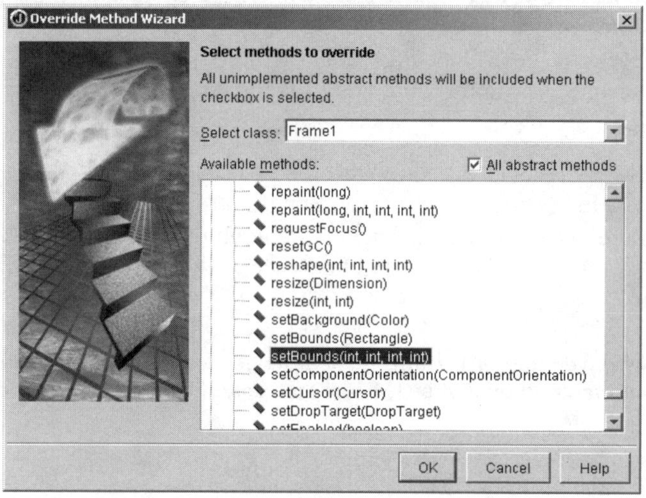

Figure 7-10: The Override Method Wizard

The code JBuilder created would look like this:

```
public void setBounds(int parm1, int parm2, int parm3, int parm4)
{
    /**@todo Override this java.awt.Component method*/
    super.setBounds( parm1,  parm2,  parm3,  parm4);
}
```

Implementing Interfaces

The Implement Interface Wizard, a feature of JBuilder SE and Enterprise, helps you insert an interface into your code. If you wanted to add an interface to your code by typing it in yourself, you would need to add **implements** and the name of the interface to the beginning of the class definition, right after the class name. Once an interface has been added to your class, you are required to define all the methods that are part of that interface, using the return types and parameters specified by that interface. This can be a very tedious task. The Implement Interface Wizard removes a lot of the grunt work from this process.

Starting from within a default application, choose **Frame1** in the project pane. Once it is highlighted, choose **Wizards | Implement Interface**. In the list of available interfaces, choose **java | awt | shape**, and then click **OK**.

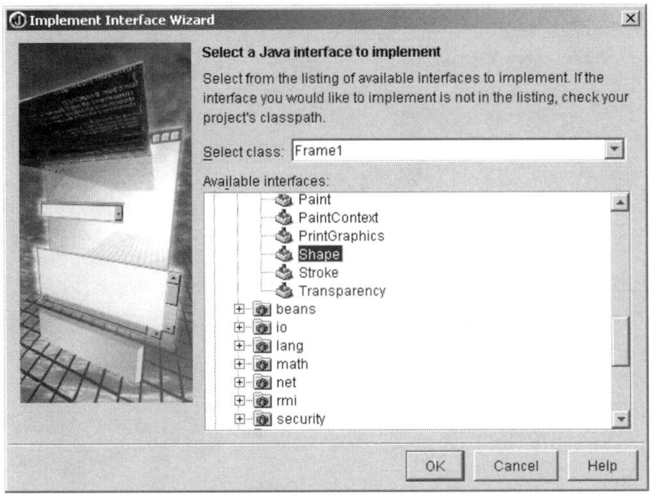

Figure 7-11: The Implement Interface Wizard

JBuilder will supply the entire skeleton of the interface, ready for your definitions, as shown in Listing 7-1. This is a default application after the wizard has inserted the interface code.

Listing 7-1: Generating skeleton code for an interface's methods with the Implement Interface Wizard

```
package untitled83;

import java.awt.*;
import java.awt.event.*;
import javax.swing.*;
import java.awt.geom.Rectangle2D;
import java.awt.geom.Point2D;
import java.awt.geom.PathIterator;
import java.awt.geom.AffineTransform;

public class Frame1 extends JFrame implements Shape {
    JPanel contentPane;
    BorderLayout borderLayout1 = new BorderLayout();

    //Construct the frame
    public Frame1() {
        enableEvents(AWTEvent.WINDOW_EVENT_MASK);
        try {
            jbInit();
        }
        catch(Exception e) {
            e.printStackTrace();
        }
    }
    //Component initialization
    private void jbInit() throws Exception  {
        contentPane = (JPanel) this.getContentPane();
        contentPane.setLayout(borderLayout1);
        this.setSize(new Dimension(400, 300));
```

```
        this.setTitle("Frame Title");
    }
    //Overridden so we can exit when window is closed
    protected void processWindowEvent(WindowEvent e) {
        super.processWindowEvent(e);
        if (e.getID() == WindowEvent.WINDOW_CLOSING) {
            System.exit(0);
        }
    }
    public Rectangle2D getBounds2D() {
        /**@todo Implement this java.awt.Shape method*/
        throw new java.lang.UnsupportedOperationException(
            "Method getBounds2D() not yet implemented.");
    }
    public boolean contains(double parm1, double parm2) {
        /**@todo Implement this java.awt.Shape method*/
        throw new java.lang.UnsupportedOperationException(
            "Method contains() not yet implemented.");
    }
    public boolean contains(Point2D parm1) {
        /**@todo Implement this java.awt.Shape method*/
        throw new java.lang.UnsupportedOperationException(
            "Method contains() not yet implemented.");
    }
    public boolean intersects(double parm1, double parm2,
                              double parm3, double parm4) {
        /**@todo Implement this java.awt.Shape method*/
        throw new java.lang.UnsupportedOperationException(
            "Method intersects() not yet implemented.");
    }
    public boolean intersects(Rectangle2D parm1) {
        /**@todo Implement this java.awt.Shape method*/
        throw new java.lang.UnsupportedOperationException(
            "Method intersects() not yet implemented.");
    }
    public boolean contains(double parm1, double parm2,
                            double parm3, double parm4) {
        /**@todo Implement this java.awt.Shape method*/
        throw new java.lang.UnsupportedOperationException(
            "Method contains() not yet implemented.");
    }
    public boolean contains(Rectangle2D parm1) {
        /**@todo Implement this java.awt.Shape method*/
        throw new java.lang.UnsupportedOperationException(
            "Method contains() not yet implemented.");
    }
    public PathIterator getPathIterator(AffineTransform parm1) {
        /**@todo Implement this java.awt.Shape method*/
        throw new java.lang.UnsupportedOperationException(
            "Method getPathIterator() not yet implemented.");
    }
```

```
    public PathIterator getPathIterator(AffineTransform parm1, double parm2) {
        /**@todo Implement this java.awt.Shape method*/
        throw new java.lang.UnsupportedOperationException(
            "Method getPathIterator() not yet implemented.");
    }
}
```

Note that the wizard generated import statements as well as the method stubs.

Integration with emacs and Other Editors

You can use the Configure Tools menu item from the Tools menu to fairly effectively integrate a third-party editor into your JBuilder editing process. Turn to the section titled "Adding a Third-Party Tool to the JBuilder Menu System" from Chapter 5.

Using the techniques described in that section, I have been able to greatly enhance the power of JBuilder. For instance, I just pop up Homesite or Dreamweaver whenever I want to edit an HTML document. I use JBuilder to help me select the document and view the document, but I actually edit it in Homesite. I also use Visual Slick Edit quite often when inside of JBuilder. When I close the third-party editor, JBuilder has automatically updated my source file to reflect the changes I have made. (Or at least it always does in Windows. In Linux, this feature works on some distros and does not work on others.)

Using Bookmarks

You can use a bookmark to mark lines of code in your program. Once they are marked, you can return to them with a simple keystroke combination. You can set up to ten bookmarks at a time.

To set a bookmark, choose **Ctrl+Shift+***x*, where *x* is a number between 0 and 9. To go to the bookmark, choose **Ctrl+***x*, where *x* is a number between 0 and 9.

Access to Javadoc

Javadoc is a mechanism created by Sun for documenting a class. It is the primary means used for documenting the SDK. Techniques for using and configuring Javadoc will be discussed in detail in Chapter 21. Here I will only talk about the way that Javadoc is integrated into your code.

Viewing Javadoc with the F1 Key

One of the most powerful aspects of the JBuilder editor is its ability to give you nearly instant access to the java class libraries. To understand this, create a default application. See Chapter 3 for instructions on creating a default application if you need help with this. Now find the line in Frame1.java that states **public class Frame1 extends JFrame**. Place your cursor over the word **JFrame** and hit the **F1** key. The Javadoc documentation for the JFrame class will appear in a pop-up window. Notice that the documentation is in the form of an HTML document, which has links through which you can drill down farther into the areas of your interest.

If you place your cursor over other words, such as public, class, or extends, help files with documentation will pop up for these code elements as well. Generally speaking, if you have a question about how to work with a component, you can probably get your answer by including the component in your project and then pressing F1 to browse the documentation.

Viewing Javadoc with the File View Tabs

If you have JBuilder SE or Enterprise, you can use the Javadoc Wizard to create Javadoc html files that will display in the Doc pane. Chapter 21 describes the use of this wizard in detail. However, if you want to just get a feeling for this, go to the menu and choose **Wizards | Javadoc**. Once you are in the Javadoc Wizard, click **Finish**. Then right-click on the standard doclet that appears in your project pane and choose **Make**. Javadoc documentation will appear in the Doc pane.

If you have JBuilder Personal, you can still use the Doc pane, but you will not have access to the wizard. Because Javadoc is part of the Java JDK, you can run the Javadoc utility from the command line to create documentation. You will find instructions for doing this in Chapter 21. The main thing to remember is to run Javadoc so that its output ends up in the directory, which is specified on the Documentation page of the Project Properties dialog for your project. If your project were called untitled39, then you would go to the root directory for your project and type this at the command prompt:

```
Javadoc -d doc –sourcepath src untitled39
```

Once you have created the documentation, it should display in the Doc pane.

You can automatically view the Javadoc files for the JDK classes in the Doc pane. For instance, go to the top of a Frame1 instance and place the cursor over the word **JFrame** in the declaration for your object. Right-click and select **Find Definition** from the menu. You will be taken to the source for JFrame. Click the **Doc** tab to view the Javadoc documentation. The technique described here is a variation on the one described in the previous section of this chapter. The advantage of this second system is that it lets you view the source for JFrame or view the Javadoc for JFrame. The previous system really only showed you the Javadoc.

Viewing Javadoc by Unzipping a JAR File

At times you may find that it is easier to work with documentation that is displayed outside of JBuilder rather than in the JBuilder help. Chapter 21 describes how to automatically use JBuilder to view Javadoc in a browser rather than inside the IDE.

Finding Errors after a Compile

The final subject I want to touch on is discovering the errors or warnings in your code after you have compiled your source. On some occasions, which are, of course, extremely rare, we might find that the code we have entered into a source file is invalid. After compilation, JBuilder will use the message pane to list the errors and warnings found in your source file. You can click on any of these errors and be taken directly to the offending line of code.

You can also select one of the errors or warnings in the message pane and press F1 to be taken to help on all error messages. From that help screen, you can quickly move to the individual error that you encountered. To be frank, the help is not always as detailed as you might want, but it at least gives you a sense of what has gone wrong. There are some cases, however, where the help can be quite illuminating.

Summary

The JBuilder editor provides you with many tools that are extremely helpful in writing code. Among the features we examined were CodeInsight, Javadoc, several powerful wizards, and various options that give you the ability to customize your environment's appearance and keystrokes. JBuilder was developed by programmers who were able to envision what features would be most helpful to other programmers. It is an environment that puts the Java JDK at your fingertips. Time you spend learning to use it properly is time well spent.

It was not possible to cover all the features of the editor in this short chapter. However, I have covered most of them.

Oh! One more thing — perhaps the most amazing thing about JBuilder is that it is written entirely in Java. If there is anyone left who still doesn't believe that Java is ready for prime time, then about ten minutes using this product should set them straight. It is a beautiful piece of code, and the editor's flawless performance and fast response time is a tribute to the Java language. Many of the tricks that the editor performs amaze me, though the debugger is no less of a masterpiece.

Part II

Java Language

Chapter 8

Java Basics: Classes, Methods, and Interfaces

Charlie Calvert

It's time to start digging into some of the details of the Java syntax. The process begins in this chapter and continues over the next three chapters.

Overall, Java is an admirably clean and logical language. If you have some experience programming, it's easy to pick up most of the syntax of the language. However, there are a few peculiarities in Java, and it is easy to be thrown by them if you don't know what to look for.

It happens that most of these peculiarities have to do with the way Java sets up the scope of the various regions of the code you write and the way that it allows you to package your code when you want to save it to file or share it with others. In short, you have to understand the role that classes, packages, and JAR files play in Java or you won't be able to understand the structure of the programs you create.

The purpose of the next three chapters is to get these basic syntactical elements out of the way so that we can proceed to look at the language and JBuilder itself in more depth. I want to try to put most of the curves that the language is likely to throw at you in these chapters, thereby opening up the road ahead.

In particular, this chapter covers classes and methods and the next chapter covers types. The third chapter covers statements and expressions, and the final chapter in Part II is on looping and math operators. Most of the tricky stuff is in this chapter.

By the time you finish reading this chapter, you should be able to do the following:

- Create a simple Java class with either default or public scope.
- Add a method to the class.
- Create an instance of your class.
- Call the method that you added to your class from a standard JBuilder application.

The Governing Analogy of the Next Three Chapters

Analogies are not meant to be rigorously logical. Instead, they are a mental trick that we can play to help understand new concepts by setting up parallels between the elements of a familiar idea and the elements of an unfamiliar idea. In this case, I want to develop some analogies between the act of writing code and the act of writing a book.

The basic elements in a written work are, from smallest to largest: words, sentences, paragraphs, chapter sections, chapters, and books. Likewise, code is made up of identifiers, statements, methods, classes, packages, and JAR files. My analogy, which is quite rough, even somewhat arbitrary, sets up the following parallels:

Written Word	Code
Sentences	Statements
Paragraphs	Methods
Chapter sections	Classes
Chapters	Packages
Books	JAR files

Analogies like this can be tricky. Don't take them too literally, particularly if you are relatively new to programming.

For instance, I don't mean to imply that a statement in code and a sentence in a book are the same thing. I mean only to suggest that they share some things in common.

A programming statement has the same relative importance to an entire program as a sentence does to an entire book. A statement is a relatively small and detail-oriented syntactical element in a program. A sentence plays the same relative role in a book. Certainly the syntax for a sentence and the syntax for a statement are quite different. I'm only suggesting that there are some rough similarities between the relative importance of sentences and statements.

NOTE: We can usually hold all the specifics of a simple programming statement in our mind at one time. Similarly, we can usually hold all the specifics of a single sentence in our mind at one time. Very bright people can hold the specifics of even relatively complex paragraphs in their mind at one time, just as bright people can think or imagine a complete method all at one time. But larger chunks, such as a complete class or a complete section of a chapter, are grasped only in a rather general sense by most people.

It's actually interesting to note that you can literally see the limits of the average human mind when you read quotations from extemporaneous public speakers in a magazine or newspaper. Several recent U.S. presidents, for instance, spoke in sentence fragments. When speaking off the cuff, they usually couldn't quite manage to put a whole sentence together without losing their way. Other U.S. presidents, on the other hand, speak off the cuff in not only complete sentences, but complete paragraphs. A facility like this is quite unusual. It is equally unusual to find programmers who can really think clearly and specifically in terms of entire classes. In fact, most programmers have trouble holding the entire contents of a 10- or 15-line method in their head at one time. One of the major reasons we break programs into sections is to help overcome this problem. Most of us can't keep a large number of complex ideas in our heads at one time. As a result, we attempt to conquer the problem by dividing our code into relatively small syntactical elements.

Classes are as integral a part of good programming as sections of a chapter are of good technical writing. Some people write code that is, in effect, nothing more than one long paragraph or, at best, a series of paragraphs that have no subheadings to aid the reader in finding the text's structure. These programmers make the mistake of failing to use classes to break up their code into coherent and reasonable sections. Code that looks like this will still work, just as you could still understand my text if I wrote it all in one long paragraph or didn't use subtitles to break up the various sections of my text. However, code without classes is usually poorly structured and hard to understand!

Adding section titles to my text helps me, as an author, to organize my text. In the same way, adding classes to a program helps us, as programmers, add structure to our programs. Classes benefit both the writer and the reader of a program.

Object-oriented programming has many benefits. However, the primary benefit that it gives you is simply to help you break your code into manageable chunks. Though hopefully better off than the politicians who can't quite manage to speak in complete sentences, we programmers are nonetheless struggling with a similar problem. Writing code is complex, and our minds have limited abilities. By dividing up our code into discrete syntactical elements, we can help overcome that complexity.

You can view the history of programming as little more than a struggle to discover the correct syntax for dividing programs into manageable bits. Structured programming gave us functions, procedures, and modules. Object-oriented programming has brought us classes. Later in this text, we will look at an even more sophisticated tool called a component, or JavaBean.

Java fully embraces object-oriented programming. In particular, it uses classes to help us divide our code into meaningful chunks. These chunks have the same relative significance to an entire program as the sections of a chapter have to a larger work, such as a chapter or a book. Syntactically, they are quite different from the sections of a chapter, but in terms of their relationship to a larger work, they have a similar importance and play a similar role.

Understanding Java Classes

For the sake of clarity and readability, I will not make this examination of classes exhaustive. Instead, I will cover only the basic facts that you need to know. Other texts tend to cover the entire subject of classes in one chapter or two or three contiguous chapters. The problem with this approach, from my point of view, is that it mixes up beginning level programming issues with advanced programming issues. That can be useful for advanced programmers who just want a quick primer on a new language, but it is not helpful to the newcomer who is trying to understand the basic facts he or she needs to know to start writing code. As a result, I will selectively choose to cover only the key facts about classes in this chapter.

Almost everything in Java is a class. The exceptions to this rule are for a few operators, a few basic types such as integers, booleans, characters, and floating-point numbers, and a few stray elements such as the package and import statements. But overall, classes play a very big role in Java programming. Java's heavy reliance on classes is a very good thing. It's one of the great strengths of the language.

Clearly, if we are going to get anywhere with Java, the first thing we need to understand is classes. In fact, it is difficult to talk sensibly, even about simple types, until we first understand the basic facts about the setting in which the types are placed. It's my contention that you can't effectively use Java types until you understand the classes in which they must reside. So I cover classes first, then types.

Classes are usually considered a relatively advanced feature. In the case of Java, however, they are fundamental to the language. Classes simply must be understood from the beginning, or it is impossible to write even the simplest example programs.

Basic Class Syntax

At this stage, it's time to start drilling down into some specifics. Here is the basic syntax for declaring a class:

```
class MyClass
{
}
```

This class doesn't do anything, but it is syntactically correct. It is the minimum code you need to write to declare a class. You need to write more code to use the class, but the declaration I show here will compile on its own without error.

Some people prefer to put the first brace at the end of the first line of a class declaration:

```
class MyClass{
}
```

Others prefer the style I show in my first example. Both syntaxes are correct. I use the first technique simply because I find it easiest to read. If you find the other technique simpler to read, then you should use it. Good editors, such as Visual SlickEdit, contain *source beautifiers* that will switch your code back and forth between the two styles at the press of a button. There are a number of free tools on the web that perform this task for you.

The Scope of a Class: Default vs. Public

The *scope* of a piece of code determines its visibility. A class with very wide scope can be seen throughout an entire program. A class with more limited scope can be seen only within a particular package. When I say that a class can be "seen," I mean that it can be called. If you can't "see" a class because it has too narrow a scope, then you will not be able to use the class. You will not be able to create an instance of it or call its methods.

The class I have named MyClass has a default scope; in other words, it is not declared private or public. By default, classes can be seen only inside the current package.

I will talk more about packages later, but in general, you can think of a package and a directory as being synonymous. Classes with default scope are visible throughout a single package. That means any other source file in the current directory will be able to see classes declared in this manner. If you have a source file in another directory, it will not be able to see a class declared in a second directory if that class is declared with default scope.

Here is another declaration for a class:

```
public class MyClass
{
}
```

This class has the word "public" preceding it. Classes declared this way can be seen by files in the current package and in other packages. Once again, I'm aware that I haven't defined the word package yet, but recall that it is roughly synonymous with the word directory. If you are in directory A, you can see public classes declared not only in your current directory, but also in directories B, C, D, etc. You can also see any methods in those classes that are declared public.

Public classes must go in their own Java source file, and that file must have the same name as the class. For instance, the class we have declared, MyClass, must go in a source file called MyClass.java.

You can't have two public classes in the same source file. You can, however, have more than one class in the same source file. If you have one public class and one class with default scope in the same file, and you compile that source file, the result will be two compiled files with a .class extension. There is one .class file for each class you declare, even though they are both declared in the same java source file.

Nested Class: Not Covered in this Chapter

Java allows you to nest classes within other classes:

```
class Foo
{
        int i;
        static class Nested
        {
                int j;
        }
}
```

Several variations on this type of syntax are available, each having its own fine shade of meaning. However, I use this syntax rarely in this book. In particular, I use it when talking about pseudo-enumerated types defined as a class.

There are certain advanced programming situations in which a nested class syntax might be useful in the hands of a talented programmer, but beginning and intermediate level programmers will probably find few occasions when it will prove useful to them. As a result, I cover this subject only in the more advanced chapters of this text.

Creating and Destroying Classes

Like Delphi, but unlike C++, Java insists that you create an instance of most classes before you use them. Here is the syntax for creating a class:

```
MyClass myClass = new MyClass();
```

With one notable exception, you are never going to be able to do much with a class unless you first create it with the operator new. What you are really doing in cases like this is creating an object on the heap; that is, you are allocating memory for your object. But just as in Delphi, but unlike C++, you don't have to use pointer syntax when addressing this object. Instead, you use dot syntax:

```
myClass.doSomething;
```

Unlike Delphi programmers, Java programmers usually don't have to free the instances of the classes they create. Instead, the system will automatically free them. In fact, Java will automatically free nearly all memory allocations. This admirable system is called garbage collection.

Sometimes, when you are running a Java program, it will seem to "go away for a second;" in other words, it will appear to pause. In a standard Windows program written in C or Pascal, that usually means that the Window's swap file is busy. In a Java program, that often means that the garbage collector is running. Of course, on Java programs running on Windows, it could mean either the swap file is busy or the garbage collector is busy. Take your pick!

Declaring Methods in a Class

In Java, there is no such thing as a stand-alone function, procedure, or subroutine. All the code you write must be part of a class. These elements inside a class are called *methods*. Here is what that looks like in practice:

```
class MyClass
{
        String getString()
        {
                return "This is a string";
        }
}
```

Here you can see the standard declaration for a class with default scope. Remember, a class with default scope can be seen from anywhere inside our current directory.

The new declaration for MyClass contains one method called getString. If you call this method, it will return a string containing the words "This is a string." In other words, the method getString is a little machine whose purpose is to return four words. More explicitly, the words that it returns are: "This is a string." The syntactical element return tells the compiler that you are about to state the value that a function "returns" to the user.

Working with Strings

In the last paragraph, I used the word string. What is a string? In general terms, a *string* is a piece of text embedded in a program. If you want to use the written word to say something to the user, then you create a string.

Of course, the string you create could contain not only written words, but numbers, nonsense syllables, or other content, all of which makes strings seem a bit amorphous. To help you get a better grip on what a string is, it might help to talk purely in terms of the syntax of the Java language.

Any time you put two double quotation marks together in a java source file, you are creating a string. Even if you put two pairs of quotes together with nothing between them, you are still creating a string. It just happens to be an empty string. Whenever you write one quote, you must also include the closing quote. The pairs of quotes you create must be on the same line of code. If you need to go to a second line, use the plus operator to concatenate your strings:

```
String getString()
{
    return "She walks in beauty, like the night\n" +
    " Of cloudless climes and starry skies";
}
```

Note how I was careful to append a "\n" character, known as carriage return or linefeed, to the end of the string on the first line. This ensures that the second line I wrote does not appear on the same line as the first. In the same spirit, sometimes you must add a space at the end of one line so the beginning of the next line does not run up against the end of the first:

```
String getString()
{
    return "This is a string. " +
```

```
        "Yes it is.";
}
```

Without the space, your string will look like this: "This is a string.Yes it is." If you put the space in, the string is printed as we expect: "This is a string. Yes it is."

Declaring the Type of a Method

We know the getString method returns a String because it is declared to do so:

```
String getString()
```

If we had written the method to return an integer, it would have looked like this:

```
int getString()
```

In this example I have removed the word String and put in its place the word int. This means the function returns an integer rather than a string.

I capitalize the word String because it is a class, and I don't capitalize the word int because it is a simple type. I will talk more about simple types and the String class in the next chapter.

I capitalize the word MyClass because by convention the names of all classes start with a capital letter in Java. If you create a name for a class by combining multiple words, then by convention you capitalize the first letter in each word: MyClass. This is often called camel caps.

The word getString starts with a small letter because, by convention, all the names for methods in Java start with a small letter. If the name you choose for your method or variable contains more than one word, then the second and all subsequent words should begin with a capital letter: myMethod, myVariable, myFancyVariable. If you are unclear as to what variables are, don't worry, as I will explain the subject in more depth in the next chapter.

One last point needs to be made about the getString method. Consider the following class declaration:

```
public class MyClass
{
        public String getString()
        {
                return "This is a string";
        }
}
```

As you can see, I declare this method to be public. That means it can be seen in both this directory and in other directories. In other words, it can be seen in both this package and in other packages. I also declare the method getString to be public. If I did not declare it to be public, then I could not call it from a class in another directory. I could create an instance of the class, because the class is declared public. But if the method getString was declared with default scope, then I could not call it from a class in another directory. In other words, if MyClass had public scope and getString had default scope, then I could create an instance of MyClass, but I could not call the method getString. By declaring getString public, I make it possible to call the method from a class that resides outside the current directory — that is, from a class in another package.

Using a Class in an Application

Suppose that we have a class with a method that does something useful, such as return a string. What can we do with that class?

Listing 8-1 shows the frame (also known as a form or a window) from a simple JBuilder application that uses the class we have created. Take a look at the listing, and then I will explain how to create it.

Listing 8-1: The Frame1.java source file from the MethodTest program

```
package methodtest;
import java.awt.*;
import java.awt.event.*;
import javax.swing.*;

public class Frame1 extends JFrame
{
  JPanel contentPane;
  JButton jButton1 = new JButton();
  MyClass myClass = new MyClass();
  JTextArea jTextArea1 = new JTextArea();

  //Construct the frame
  public Frame1()
  {
    enableEvents(AWTEvent.WINDOW_EVENT_MASK);
    try
    {
      jbInit();
    }
    catch(Exception e)
    {
      e.printStackTrace();
    }
  }

  //Component initialization
  private void jbInit() throws Exception
  {
    jButton1.setText("jButton1");
    jButton1.setBounds(new Rectangle(113, 124, 155, 29));
    jButton1.addActionListener(new
      Frame1_jButton1_actionAdapter(this));
    contentPane = (JPanel) this.getContentPane();
    contentPane.setLayout(null);
    this.setSize(new Dimension(400, 300));
    this.setTitle("Frame Title");
    jTextArea1.setText("jTextArea1");
    jTextArea1.setBounds(new Rectangle(70, 27, 248, 88));
    contentPane.add(jButton1, null);
    contentPane.add(jTextArea1, null);
  }
```

```
  //Overridden so we can exit when window is closed
  protected void processWindowEvent(WindowEvent e)
  {
    super.processWindowEvent(e);
    if (e.getID() == WindowEvent.WINDOW_CLOSING)
    {
      System.exit(0);
    }
  }

  void jButton1_actionPerformed(ActionEvent e)
  {
    jTextArea1.setText(myClass.getString());
  }
}

class MyClass
{
  public String getString()
  {
    return "She walks in beauty like the night\n" +
      "Of cloudless climes and starry skies";
  }
}

//Recall that in my JBuilder environment I chose Project | Default
//Options, turned to the code style page, and chose Standard adapters
//for event handling

class Frame1_jButton1_actionAdapter implements java.awt.event.ActionListener
{
  Frame1 adaptee;

  Frame1_jButton1_actionAdapter(Frame1 adaptee)
  {
    this.adaptee = adaptee;
  }

  public void actionPerformed(ActionEvent e)
  {
    adaptee.jButton1_actionPerformed(e);
  }
}
```

For help creating the boilerplate outline of this project, turn to Chapter 3. Once you have created the project, return to this point in the text.

Scroll down to the bottom of Frame1.java, and insert the declaration for MyClass:

```
class MyClass
{
    String getString()
    {
```

```
        return "She walks in beauty like the night\n" +
            "Of cloudless climes and starry skies";
    }
}
```

You also need to add code to your project to declare an instance of your class and initialize it. Go to the beginning of the declaration for Frame1 and add the declaration for your class:

```
public class Frame1 extends JFrame
{
    JPanel contentPane;
    MyClass myClass = new MyClass();
    // lots of code omitted here
```

In this code fragment I want you to focus on the last line. The other lines are included so you can see where in your program you should insert the line.

The code I show you first declares an instance of your object:

```
MyClass myClass
```

It then creates the instance:

```
myClass = new MyClass();
```

If you put it all together, you have this:

```
MyClass myClass = new MyClass();
```

The act of using the new operator allocates memory for your class. So the process involves two steps: First declare your instance of the class, and then create it.

Compile the project once to make sure you have typed in the class declaration correctly. To do this, open the Project menu and select either **Make project methodtest** or **Make frame1.java.** In the first case you will make the entire application; in the second, you will make only frame1.java. Either action suits our current needs.

If your code compiles correctly, click on the Design page at the bottom of the editor. You will be placed in design mode. Be careful not to turn to the AWT page. We are creating an application, not an applet. As a result, we don't need to worry about compatibility with some older versions of the JDK. Instead, you can select your controls from the Swing page of the component palette. (You can, of course, use Swing controls in an applet. The only problem is that you might not be able to use that applet with some contemporary HTML browsers.)

In this particular case, you want to select a JButton and a JTextArea. Arrange them as shown in Figure 8-1.

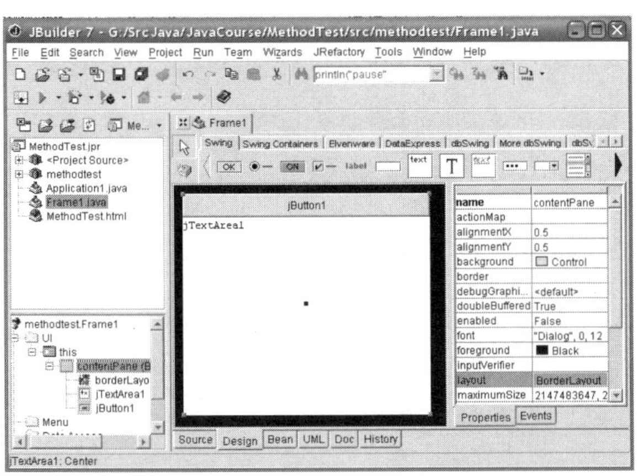

Figure 8-1: The main frame for your application as it appears at design time

In order to get your controls to look like the ones shown in the figure, you should first be sure you are using BorderLayout. To do this, click on **contentPane** in the JBuilder structure pane, and then use the Inspector to set layout to **BorderLayout**. (The structure pane is the second (lower) of the two windows on the left of your screen. As you can see in Figure 8-1, the contentPane is the highlighted item in the hierarchical list of items shown in the structure pane.)

Click on jButton1 and use the JBuilder Inspector to set its constraints to either **North** or **South**, depending on your tastes. Set the constraints for the text area to **Center**.

I discuss layouts in more depth in several chapters in Part III: JBuilder Fundamentals. In those chapters, I show how to avoid using the limited null layout in your final code.

Now double-click on the button to create an event handler. When you are done, the following code, or something like it, should have been added to your program:

```
void jButton1_actionPerformed(ActionEvent e)
{
}
```

Change the code so that it looks like this:

```
void jButton1_actionPerformed(ActionEvent e)
{
    jTextArea1.setText(myClass.getString());
}
```

That's it! Your program is finally done. Now you should be able to select the green "run" arrow to compile and launch your program. When it is loaded, press the button you created, and you should see the text from your class in the JTextArea component.

Constructors

If you can stand swallowing one last bit of syntactical jargon in this chapter, I would like to add a quick explanation of constructors. *Constructors* are methods added to your class that will be called automatically when the class is created.

Consider the following declaration:

```
package sammy;

public class MyClass
{
    String myString;
    public MyClass()
    {
        myString = "She walks in beauty like the night\n" +
            "  Of cloudless climes and starry skies\n" +
            "And all that's best of dark and bright\n" +
            "  Meet in her aspect and her eyes:\n" +
            "Thus mellowed to that tender light\n" +
            "  Which heaven to gaudy day denies.\n";
    }

    public String getString()
    {
```

```
            return myString;
        }
    }
```

This class contains a constructor called MyClass. The constructor for your class should always have the same name as the class itself.

The constructor will be called automatically when you create an instance of your class. As a result, it is a great place for you to perform initialization for a class.

In this case, note that I have declared a variable called myString. I initialize that string in my constructor. Then in the getString method, all I need to do is return my initialized string.

In Java, any variables that you do not initialize in your constructor will be zeroed out. Thus, if you declare an int as a field of your class, and you do not explicitly assign it a value, it will automatically be set to zero when the class is created. Strings, on the other hand, are not set to an empty string but to null. All classes that have not been explicitly initialized are said to contain the value null, which is really a fancy way of saying that they are not initialized.

Since Java automatically initializes all the variables in your class to zero, null, or some similar default value, you need not bother initializing variables in your constructor if you just want to "zero them out." Only initialize the variable explicitly in your constructor if you want to set it to some explicit value other than zero, null, etc. In our case, we indeed want to do that, so I have created a constructor.

Public Classes, Your First Package

Notice also that I have declared MyClass to be public. Furthermore, I have declared both the constructor and the getString method to be public. As a result, you can place this file in a separate directory and call it from your current directory.

As you saw in the last section, I have declared the package for this file to be "Sammy." Package names are almost always in lowercase. This means that this file (which has to be called MyClass.java) must be placed in a directory called Sammy. For instance, you could create a directory beneath the directory where Frame1.java is stored and call it Sammy. You could then copy this file into that directory. Now add the file to your current project by choosing the **Add to the project** button in the IDE. This speed button shows a picture of a folder with a green cross on it ( ). (Or, if you prefer, choose **Project | Add to Project** from the menu.

Now you need to make some changes to your Frame1.java source file. At the very top of this file, add an import statement for the Sammy package:

```
package untitled7;

import java.awt.*;
import java.awt.event.*;
import javax.swing.*;
import untitled7.sammy.*;
```

Now remove the initial declaration for MyClass that you had written near the bottom of Frame1.java:

```
class MyClass
{
    public String getString()
    {
```

```
        return "She walks in beauty like the night\n" +<
            "Of cloudless climes and starry skies";
    }
}
```

You no longer need this declaration because the class is now declared in MyClass.java, which is stored in the Sammy directory.

Now you can save your work and run the program. You may find that with the new, larger string returned by the getString method, you will have to resize the jTextArea while in design mode to make the program look right at run time.

Don't worry if you had trouble understanding some of the concepts mentioned in this last section of the chapter. I will talk more about variables and packages in the next two chapters. I pushed the envelope a bit here in this last section in order to give you a foretaste of some of the subjects being covered in the next two chapters.

Inheritance

Let's talk briefly about inheritance before leaving this chapter. In the discussion that follows, I assume that you already understand the basics of object-oriented programming. I am going to show you how to apply those basic principles to the Java language.

Consider the following declarations:

```
class Foo
{
        void foobar()
        {
                System.err.println("To see the world in a grain of sand");
        }
}

class Goober extends Foo
{
        void foobar()
        {
                System.err.println("And a heaven in a wild flower");
        }
}
```

The class Goober is said to *extend* class Foo. We know this because the word "extends" appears in its declaration:

```
class Goober extends Foo
```

In this example, Foo is the parent class, and Goober is the child class. As a result, Goober is said to *inherit* the capabilities of class Foo.

What makes this particular example interesting is that both Goober and Foo have a method called foobar. Over the next few paragraphs, you will learn a little about how Java decides to cope with situations like this. In short, you will learn which of these two methods will be called under various different sets of circumstances.

In this example, if you create an instance of class Foo, a call to foobar will print out the message "To see the world in a grain of sand." If, however, you create an instance of class Goober, a call to the method foobar will print out the words "And a heaven in a wild flower." The second instance of the method foobar is said to override the first instance. The instance of the method foobar from class Goober is called in place of the instance of method foobar that appears in class Foo.

NOTE: The example you have just seen illustrates the fact that all Java methods are declared to be virtual by default. We call a method virtual if it can either be overridden by another method of the same name or override another method with the same name. In the Java language, and indeed in all object-oriented languages, the methods in a child object will override the methods in a parent object if they have the same name. Thus, Goober.foobar() overrides Foo.foobar() because Goober is the child of Foo.

Consider this rewrite of class Goober:

```
class Goober extends Foo
{
        void foobar()
        {
                super.foobar();
                System.err.println("And a heaven in a wild flower");
        }
}
```

Instantiate an instance of Goober and call its foobar() method. The output from this program will now include calls to both instances of the method foobar():

```
To see the world in a grain of sand.
And a heaven in a wild flower.
```

The call to super.foobar() from Goober.foobar() calls the method foobar() that resides in class Foo. Using the word "super" in this way registers a request to call a function in the ancestor class.

Consider this declaration:

```
class Foo
{
        final void foobar()
        {
                System.err.println("To see the world in a grain of sand");
        }
}

class Goober extends Foo
{
        void foobar()
        {
                System.err.println("And a heaven in a wild flower");
        }
}
```

The second class is said to descend from, or extend, the first one. Class Goober is a child of class Foo. Both classes have a method called foobar. As shown here, there is an error in the program. Class Foo declares foobar to be final. This means that class Goober cannot override it. You declare a method as final if you want to make explicit the idea that a child class cannot override it.

These are examples of inheritance and overriding methods. Inheritance is an important part of Java programming, but you need not fully understand it in order to write simple Java programs. The other material in this chapter, however, you must understand.

Here is something else you don't need to understand:

```
class Foo
{
       void foobar()
       {
              System.err.println("To see the world in a grain of sand");
       }
}

final class Goober extends Foo
{
       void foobar()
       {
              System.err.println("And a heaven in a wild flower");
       }
}
```

Class Goober descends from class Foo. You cannot create a descendant of class Goober because it is declared final. If you don't want to make it possible for a class to have any children, you can effectively neuter it by declaring it as final.

Interfaces

An interface allows you to declare a *standard*, a specification for how a class will behave. In particular, interfaces allow you to declare the methods that will appear in a class without having to declare an implementation for those methods.

At heart, interfaces are an extremely simple concept. Nonetheless, they occasionally cause trouble for newcomers because they are an abstract concept and because of some of the rather complex ways in which they can be used. First, I'll show you the simple syntax for interfaces and then explain how to use them.

Here is a simple interface and a class that implements the interface:

```
interface Foo
{
       void foobar();
}

class Goober implements Foo
{
       public void foobar()
       {
              System.err.println("To see the world in a grain of sand");
       }
}
```

This looks very much like the classes we were looking at in the previous section on inheritance. The difference is threefold:

1. Foo is declared with the keyword interface rather than the keyword class.

2. There is no implementation for the foobar() method in the Foo interface. This is the defining feature of an interface: Its methods are not implemented. Notice that Goober.foobar() is declared public. All methods in an interface are declared public by default. When you implement these methods, you should therefore declare your methods to be public. The point here is that interface Foo declares a public standard that class Goober must implement. I'll explain this concept in more depth in just a moment.
3. Class Goober uses the keyword implements rather than the keyword extends. If a class implements an interface, it will define the methods that were declared in the interface. In particular, Goober.foobar() is an implementation of the foobar() method declared in interface Foo.

Clearly the syntax for interfaces is straightforward. If there is confusion in some people's minds about interfaces, it usually does not stem from a misunderstanding about how to declare or implement an interface. That part of the story is simple. The only real question is why interfaces were created in the first place.

One major use of an interface is simply to define a standard. If a class implements an "interface," then at least you know something about how it will behave; it will behave in accordance with the methods declared in the "interface" that it implements.

An analogy might be helpful here. Almost all cars have a steering wheel, a gas pedal, and brakes. One could therefore say that cars implement the steering wheel, gas pedal, brake "interface." We all know how to drive cars because they all behave in a predictable fashion; that is, they all implement the steering wheel, gas pedal, brake interface. This is a standard to which most cars adhere.

Cars also tend to implement either the automatic transmission or the stick-shift transmission "interfaces." It didn't have to be this way. We could have steered our cars with a stick and used a wheel to shift gears. It might seem strange to us, but it would have worked. The worst-case scenario would have been to have some cars use a stick to steer and others a wheel to steer. Then there would be confusion. We are grateful for the standards that make cars behave in predictable ways.

A Java interface does the same thing for a class. If a class defines an interface, it will behave in a predictable way. Consider a set of classes that all implement this interface:

```
interface FileType
{
      int read();
      void write(int data);
}
```

Any class that implements this interface is guaranteed to support the read and write methods defined in the FileType interface. It would not matter if the class wrote to a file, an FTP server, a block of memory, or a wormhole. In all cases, we would understand how to read and write int values using that class, regardless of the details of how the class was implemented. (Okay, the bit about the wormhole is conceptually a bit difficult, but I'm sure you get my point.)

By now you should have a pretty good idea of what an interface is and why it is useful. There is, however, legitimate reason for there to be some confusion surrounding this subject. In particular, it turns out that you can do some tricky but very useful things with interfaces. For instance, if you want to declare a plug-and-play architecture for your program, interfaces could be a big help. You could say that any one class that implements a particular interface could be plugged into your program at a particular location. As a result, you could create a program in which many of your classes never directly call any other classes; instead, they call a set of interfaces that are implemented by a particular class or set of classes. Thus, you could remove whole sections of your program and test them separately or plug in new modules that define the same interface. The actual syntax for doing this is not complex, but creating an architecture of this type can take some careful planning.

When groups of programmers are working together on a project, they could give each other assignments by asking their fellow programmers to create a class that implemented a particular interface. This can be useful because it can allow you to compile and run a program containing classes that are not yet implemented. The interface is declared, so you can create a dummy class that mocks up an implementation for a particular interface. You can then use the class in your program. Even though the class does not yet do anything, it nonetheless can act as a placeholder and allow you to continue development while you are waiting for a particular feature to appear.

The uses for interfaces described in the last two paragraphs are not really so terribly complex. Nevertheless, understanding them takes a certain ability to master abstract concepts. If you understand the simple syntax for using interfaces, you should not have too much trouble wrestling these ideas to the mat. For me to take this subject much further would be to step too far outside the bounds of this book.

To sum up, let me say that interfaces are very simple at heart. However, they can be used in some rather complex ways. If, however, you can master the concepts involved with using interfaces, you will find them to be one of the most important tools in your skill set. Interfaces are one of the foundations on which modern object-oriented computer languages rest. Learn to use them correctly, and you will be able to create large, complex programs that are remarkably easy to maintain.

NOTE: C++ programmers can think of interfaces as classes that contain nothing but virtual abstract methods. You can learn about JBuilder's tools for automatically implementing interfaces in Chapter 7, "Using the Editor."

Summary

In this chapter you learned the basic facts about classes, methods, and interfaces. You should now know enough to begin using classes in your programs. Additional important information about classes will be presented in the next two chapters. You also learned about interfaces, which are one of the most important features of the Java language.

Chapter 9

Simple Types

Charlie Calvert

This chapter covers the basic facts about working with Java types. You will read about all eight simple types — or primitive types, as they are sometimes called — in the Java language. You will also find examples of how to work with each of these types.

A *simple type* in Java is a type that is not encapsulated inside a class. As you know, almost everything in Java is a class — except these eight simple types.

There are, however, classes that wrap each of these types. The class names all begin with capital letters (Boolean, Integer, Float, Double, and so on). It is a bit more expensive to use the class types rather than the simple types. However, classes in Java are so well optimized that you need not fear this overhead in many circumstances. The advantage that class types have over the simple types is that they have built-in methods for performing useful tasks associated with a class. The most obvious example is the ability to convert an integer or floating-point type to a string.

The example program from this chapter will give you plenty of opportunity to set up event handlers that respond to the visual controls in your application. You can find it on the book CD under the name CallMyTypes. Finally, this chapter continues the discussion of classes and methods that was begun in the last chapter.

In general, the subject matter of this chapter covers not only types, but also many general programming issues. So, without further ado, let's begin our exploration of the basic Java types.

The Basic Java Types

Java, being a well-defined, strongly typed language, handles the whole subject of types with remarkable aplomb. There are only eight types, and each one is admirably simple in conception. Table 9-1 provides an overview of the types that are discussed in this chapter.

Table 9-1: The eight types, their sizes, and their ranges

Type	**Size**	**Range or Comment**
boolean	NA; usually 32	Only false or true
byte	8 bits	–127 to 127
char	16 bits	Any Unicode or standard character
short	16 bits	–32,768 to 32,767
int	32 bits	–2,147,483,648 to 2,147,483,647
long	64 bits	–9,223,372,036,854,775,808 to 9,223,372,036,854,775,807
float	32 bits	–3.4E38 to 3.4E38 (six to seven significant digits)
double	64 bits	–1.7E308 to 1.7E308 (15 to 16 significant digits)

Each of these types is always set to a certain immutable number of bits. You have none of the monkey business that you get in C++ or Pascal, where an int (or integer) is 16 bits in one set of circumstances, 32 bits in another, and perhaps 64 in yet a third set of circumstances. A Java int has 32 bits in all instances on all platforms. Neither do you have to worry about whether a particular value is signed or not. All types are signed; that is, they can be either negative or positive numbers. There is no such thing as an unsigned integer type in Java. Oh frabjous day! Callooh! Collay! What an admirable design!

As you can see by looking at the table, there are simple types for 8-, 16-, 32-, and 64-bit integers, or *scalar numbers*, as they are sometimes called. The integer types (byte, short, int, and long) hold whole numbers such as 1, 5, 25, –15, or 0. The types with the larger number of bits hold larger numbers.

The floating-point types (float and double) differ from the integer types (byte, short, int, and long) in that they can have decimal places. For instance, the number 3.2 is a floating-point number, and the number 16 is an integer.

The char type is not 8, but 16 bits. This means that it is Unicode ready. Unicode characters are important because they capture foreign language sets, such as the kanji characters used in the Far East. In the old world of DOS programming, kanji characters were difficult to encode because the char type had only 8 bits and therefore could contain only 256 characters. There are thousands of kanji characters, and to capture them all, a new standard needed to be developed. That standard is called Unicode, and Java fully supports it.

The boolean type only needs to capture one of two values: true or false. Nevertheless, the type usually takes up 32 bits, since that is the default size for a word on most modern computers. However, the subject of how much space a boolean takes up is purely academic, since it literally can contain only two values and cannot be coerced into containing any other values. Later in the chapter I will take up this subject again, covering it in more depth and in plainer English.

A Class that Uses All the Types

Now that you have been introduced to the Java types, the next step is to look at them in more detail. To begin that process, let's examine a class that exercises the most fundamental properties of each type. The class in question is shown in Listing 9-1.

Listing 9-1: The MyTypes class shows how to use all the basic Java types.

```
package foo;

public class MyTypes
{

  // Boolean: This is a simple type, and can only be true or
  // false. It can't be coerced into being an int or a char.
  boolean myBool;

  // Characters such as 'A' 'B' 'C'. For strings use the String class instead.
  char myChar;

  // Integers
  byte myByte;      // 8 bit
  short myShort;    // 16 bit
```

```
int myInt;        // 32 bit
long myLong;      // 64 bit, use L in assignments of literals: MyLong = 2L;

// Floating Point
float myFloat;    // 32 bit, use F in assignments of literals: myFloat = 2.0F
double myDouble; // 64 bit

public MyTypes()
{
  myBool = true;
  myChar = 'A';
  myByte = Byte.MAX_VALUE;          // 127;
  myShort = Short.MAX_VALUE;        // 32767;
  myInt = Integer.MAX_VALUE;        // 2147483647;
  myLong = 9223372036854775807L;    // Add an l or L for literals
  myFloat = 1.0f;                   // Add an f or F to declare literal
  myDouble = Double.MAX_VALUE;
}

public byte getMyByte()
{
  return myByte;
}

public String getMinByteAsString()
{
  return Byte.toString(Byte.MIN_VALUE);
}

public int getMyInt()
{
  return myInt;
}

public String getMinIntegerAsString()
{
  return Integer.toString(Integer.MIN_VALUE);
}

public long getMyLong()
{
  return myLong;
}

public String getMinLongAsString()
{
  return Long.toString(Long.MIN_VALUE);
}

public short getMyShort()
{
```

```
    return myShort;
  }

  public String getMinShortAsString()
  {
    return Integer.toString(Short.MIN_VALUE);
  }

  public float getMyFloat()
  {
    return myFloat;
  }

  public String getMinFloatAsString()
  {
    return Float.toString(Float.MIN_VALUE);
  }

  public double getMyDouble()
  {
    return myDouble;
  }

  public String getMinDoubleAsString()
  {
    return Double.toString(Double.MIN_VALUE);
  }
}
```

The purpose of the class is to show how to use all the simple types in Java. The code also gives us practice working with the syntax of classes and methods. Let's take a look at this code and see if we can make some sense out of it.

Declaring the Simple Types

The class begins by declaring a few variables:

```
// Boolean: A simple type, which can only be true or false. It can't
// be coerced into being an int or a char.
boolean myBool;

// Characters such as 'A' 'B' 'C'. For strings use the String class instead.
char myChar;

// Integers
byte myByte;      // 8 bit
short myShort;    // 16 bit
int myInt;        // 32 bit
long myLong;      // 64 bit, use L in assignments of literals: MyLong = 2L;

// Floating Point
```

```
float myFloat;   // 32 bit, use F in assignments of literals: myFloat = 2.0F
double myDouble; // 64 bit
```

The first value is a boolean, the second a char, the third a byte, the fourth a short, the fifth an int, the sixth a long, the seventh a float, and the eighth a double. There they are — all the simple types available in Java.

Now that we've declared all the simple Java types, what do we do with them? The answer to that question is actually fairly complex and takes up the majority of the rest of this chapter. I begin the examination in the next section, where you can take a look at the constructor for the MyTypes class.

Initializing the Simple Types

The first significant code in this class initializes all the values in the class's constructor:

```
public MyTypes()
{
  myBool = true;
  myChar = 'A';
  myByte = Byte.MAX_VALUE;            // 127;
  myShort = Short.MAX_VALUE;          // 32767;
  myInt = Integer.MAX_VALUE;          // 2147483647;
  myLong = 9223372036854775807L;      // Add an l or L for literals
  myFloat = 1.0f;                     // Add an f or F to declare literal
  myDouble = Double.MAX_VALUE;
}
```

The variables myBool and myChar are assigned literal values. A *literal* is simply a raw declaration of some value such as a string, a character, or a number. You can't assign a value to a literal, as they are not variables. myBool is a variable; the value true is a literal value. myChar is a variable; 'A' is a literal. myByte is a variable; the number 127 is a literal. String is a class type, while a string literal is written like this: "This is a string literal."

The code in the MyTypes class initializes the byte variable to the largest possible byte value, which is 127:

```
myByte = Byte.MAX_VALUE;          // 127;
```

I could, of course, have written: myByte = 127. Assigning myByte to the literal value 127 would have had exactly the same result as the code I wrote here. Instead, I used the MAX_VALUE field of the Byte class, which returns a constant equal to the maximum legal value for a byte. Needless to say, the class can also return a MIN_VALUE. The only reason to use MAX_VALUE is that it will help you remember a way to easily obtain the maximum value for a byte. In C++ or Pascal, you use similar functions in part because some types, such as integers, vary in size depending on the platform you are using. But here you don't have to worry about that, and you use the tool simply as a mnemonic.

You are allowed to write myByte = Byte.MAX_VALUE without using new to create an instance of the Byte class. This is legal because MAX_VALUE is declared to be static. In particular, here is the way the values are declared in the Java source code:

```
public final class Byte extends Number implements Comparable
{
    /**
     * The minimum value a Byte can have.
```

```
     */
    public static final byte   MIN_VALUE = -128;

    /**
     * The maximum value a Byte can have.
     */
    public static final byte   MAX_VALUE = 127;
```

The extends keyword in the class header is explained in the previous chapter. The idea of implementing an interface is discussed briefly in Chapter 7. I include that line simply so you can see that you are looking at the declaration for the Byte class.

As you can see, MIN_VALUE is declared to be a simple variable of type byte:

```
byte MIN_VALUE = -128;
```

That's as simple as programming gets. But what about the "public static final" business? What's that all about?

You saw in the previous chapter that the word public means that the variable can be accessed from outside of the package in which the class is declared. This is, of course, crucial in this case, since the Java source code is not declared in the same directory as your program.

The word static means that you can access this variable without creating an instance of the class. In other words, you don't have to write this:

```
Byte myByte = new Byte();
byte myVariable = myByte.MAX_VALUE;
```

Instead, you can write:

```
byte myVariable = Byte.MAX_VALUE;
```

Normally you can't access the fields or methods of a class without first creating an instance of the class. You can only do it when you are accessing a method or field that is declared static.

Note yet again the perhaps too subtle interplay between the byte type and the Byte class. Classes should always begin with a capital letter and simple types begin with a small letter. It's madness — definitely part of the dark side of the Java language — but it is how the game is played. Whether a letter is capitalized or not can make a lot of difference in Java (perhaps a bit too much difference for my tastes)!

And what about final? What is that all about? The keyword final is used when you want to declare a value that will not and cannot change. Many other languages use the word const to designate the same thing. Java chose final for reasons that are not entirely clear to me.

NOTE: The rules about the word final are fairly simple:

- A class declared final cannot be extended. You cannot create a subclass of a class declared to be final. You cannot descend from it. It can have no children.
- A method declared to be final cannot be overridden. In this sense Java is opposite of languages like Pacal or C/C++. All methods are implicitly declared to be virtual unless they are explicitly marked as final. A final method is not just a method stripped of its virtualness. It is illegal to declare a method of the same name in a descendant class. A compile-time error results from any such attempt. See Chapter 8 for an example.
- A final variable is what other languages call a constant. It cannot be changed. If you do not assign anything to a final variable, it is called a blank variable. It will never have a value.

Though mentioned earlier in this text, let me remind you how to find the declaration for the Byte class. JBuilder makes this process easy. In the source code for your program, find the variable or type that you want to explore. For instance, find a place in your code that reads

Byte.MAX_VALUE. Highlight the word **Byte** with the mouse, right-click on it, and choose **Find Definition** (called Browse Symbol in older versions of the product) from the pop-up menu. The appropriate source file will be loaded automatically, and you will be taken to the proper place in that source.

When you are browsing the source from the JDK, you will see a tab in the JBuilder IDE called Doc. If you click on the Doc tab, you will see the docs for the class you are currently viewing. As a rule, there are doc files for all the classes in the JDK. However, the classes that you create will not have docs unless you explicitly create them. There is a technology called Javadoc discussed at length later in the book for creating these documents.

The previous paragraphs highlight two important facts:

- JBuilder gives you a powerful ability to browse your source code.
- Java comes with source. There are no black boxes in Java. There is source code for everything, and you get it all for free just by downloading the JDK.

Besides MAX_VALUE and MIN_VALUE, the Byte class has other useful features such as the ubiquitous method toString(), which converts a byte to String. For instance, it would convert the number 127 to the string "127." I will show exactly how to do this later in the chapter.

JBuilder provides a powerful tool called CodeInsight that can help you explore the Byte class. In fact, it can help you explore any Java source code — or any other source code, including your own. In particular, you can find all the methods of the Byte class by using CodeInsight.

To use CodeInsight, type in an instance of a class or the name of a class followed by a period. For instance, write the letters **Byte** followed by a period in your source code. Now press **Ctrl+Alt+H** or **Ctrl+Space**, depending on the type of keyboard emulation you are using. (To find out which strokes to use, select **Tools | Editor Options** from the menu. On the editor page, press the **Customize** button. The keystrokes are arranged by category, so CodeInsight would be in the C section.) After pressing the right keys, a window will pop up showing all the methods of your class, as shown in Figure 9-1. This list is created dynamically, so it will be available for the SDK and classes that you declare. It will always reflect the current state of the object.

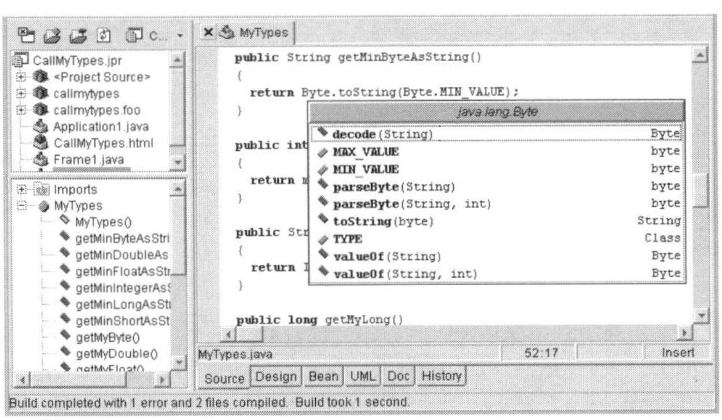

Figure 9-1: The JBuilder IDE supports CodeInsight. Here you can see the fields and methods of the Byte class in the pop-up window.

We've covered a lot of ground in this section of the chapter, but there is still a point I want to mention before moving on to the next subject. Consider these two lines from the MyTypes constructor:

```
myLong = 9223372036854775807L;  // Add an l or L for literals
myFloat = 1.0f;                 // Add an f or F to declare literal
```

Notice that I have appended an L to the end of the number assigned to myLong. Though not necessary, it is often a good idea to do this when assigning a literal to a long. A similar pattern is in effect for floats. When you assign a literal to a float, it is a good idea, and often necessary, to append an f to the number. In particular, you can get rid of the "loss of precision" error from the compiler by appending an F or f to a float.

In the two lines under discussion, I could have written code that paralleled the other examples in the constructor:

```
myLong = Long.MAX_VALUE;
myFloat = Float.MAX_VALUE;
```

I didn't take this approach simply because I wanted to show you that you often need to add l's and f's to literals that are assigned to these types.

We're through now with the subject of initializing types. In the next few sections I will say a few more words about the Java simple types and then move on to a discussion of a program that demonstrates the types.

Thinking about booleans

I initialized the boolean type to true.

```
myBool = true
```

I could have set it to false. There are no other values to which you can set a boolean.

In C/C++ and Object Pascal, you can treat a boolean variable as a numeric value if you want. You can't do that in Java. The only thing you can do with a boolean is set it to true or false.

In Java you cannot typecast an integer value to treat it as a boolean. In Pascal or C++, you can draw parallels between the number zero and the value false and any other scalar number and the value true. You can't do this in Java, unless you want to write code that looks like this:

```
void jMenuItem2_actionPerformed(ActionEvent e)
{
  int Num = Integer.parseInt(jTextField1.getText());

  boolean myBool = (Num == 0 ? false:true);

  if (myBool == false)
    jTextField1.setText("false");
  else
    jTextField1.setText("true");
}
```

This code checks to see whether a scalar number is zero. If it is zero, it sets myBool equal to false; if it is non-zero, it sets myBool equal to true. It's a long way around, but the end effect is the same as typecasting the number as a boolean. The if statement here is discussed in more depth in Chapter 10.

Thinking about chars

chars are character values; that is, they are letters such as 'A,' 'B,' or 'C.' You can also set chars equal to basic syntactical elements of a string, such as a space, a tab character, or an exclamation point. A char can also be set equal to a number, such as '1' or '2.' However, you have to realize that the character '1' is fundamentally different from the number 1. You always define characters by putting single quotes around them, while you define strings by putting double quotes around them. This is a char: 'a,' and this is a string: "My String."

I initialize the char value to the letter A. In Java, you typically don't use chars as strings. Instead, you use the String class, or sometimes the StringBuffer class, when you want to work with strings. In other words, there is no simple type for a string in Java. As I will show in a later chapter, you can create an array of char, but don't try to use an array of char as a string. Trying to treat an array of char as a string in Java is simply too complicated. The language isn't designed to support that kind of syntax.

You can perform basic arithmetic operations on chars. Consider the following code:

```
void AddCharMenu_actionPerformed(ActionEvent e)
{
    char temp = 'A';
    String S;

    jTextField1.setText("");

    for (int i = 0; i < 26; i++)
    {
      S = jTextField1.getText();
      S = S + temp + ' ';
      jTextField1.setText(S);
      temp++;
    }
}
```

As you can see, this method is an event handler. In particular, it will be called in response to a menu selection, but it could just as well occur in response to a button press. (Later in this chapter, I will show how to set up menus; for now, just concentrate on the core code in the body of the method.)

I declare two variables, one of type char and the other of type String. I initialize the char to the letter A but do not initialize the String to anything. On the frame for this application, I have dropped down a JTextField. After declaring my variables, the first thing I do in the method is empty any text in the JTextField.

I then begin a for loop. Most readers will probably know what for loops are, but don't worry if they are unfamiliar to you. I will talk about them in more depth in Chapter 11 when I cover looping. For now, you need to merely know that any code between the beginning of the for loop and the curly brace that closes the for loop will be repeated 26 times. In particular, the following code will be repeated 26 times:

```
      S = jTextField1.getText();
      S = S + temp + ' ';
      jTextField1.setText(S);
      temp++;
```

I begin by retrieving the string from the JTextField. The first time through the loop, the string will be empty. I then set it equal to itself, plus the current value of Temp, plus a space character. The first time through the loop, the end result is this:

```
A
```

I show the user the value of the string by calling the setText method of the JTextField object. (Remember that Java programmers write JTextField with a capital J when they are talking about the JTextField class, but they write jTextField1 with a small j when creating a default variable name to point at an instance of this object. You can, of course, give the variable any name you want, but jTextField1 is the default name assigned by the IDE to the first instance of this type of object that you drop on a form. The second instance gets the name jTextField2, etc.)

The last line of the code in the loop increments the value of temp by using the ++ operator. In other words, it adds 1 to the value of temp, which is 'A.' What is A plus 1, you might ask? The mathematicians in the crowd already have the answer, while readers with a background in the humanities are probably wondering what I could possibly be talking about. A is a letter, and what sense does it make to add a number to a letter? Well, it happens that A + 1 equals, naturally enough, B!

How can this be?, you ask. Good question. The thing to remember about computers is that numbers underlie everything you see on the screen. Internally, the letter A is represented by a number. The letter B is represented by the next number in that sequence, the letter C by the next number, and so on. So if you add 1 to A, you get the next item in the sequence, which is B. You can usually count on computers being very logical. (They are not so hot on intuition, but they understand logic!) If the number 65 stands for A, then the number 66 will stand for B, 67 for C, and so on.

It happens that not only are computers logical, but in this rare case, so is your author. In particular, it happens that the letter A is in fact represented by the number 65, B by 66, C by 67, etc. As a result, the first two lines of our method could have looked like this:

```
    char Temp = 65; // Same thing as Temp = 'A';
    String S;
```

When you are working with chars, there is no difference between writing char Temp = 'A'; and writing char Temp = 65;. If all this sounds confusing, don't be disturbed; it's just an example of the way computers like to operate.

Consider the following two lines from Shakespeare's Sonnet 22:

```
My glass shall not persuade me I am old,
So long as youth and thou are of one date;
```

People with a background in the humanities understand that Shakespeare is saying that he does not feel old so long as his love remains young. A necessary corollary of this idea explains a lot of irrational behavior that men engage in while traversing their middle years. Shakespeare doesn't speak as plainly as he could because he wants to:

- Create something aesthetically pleasing.
- Devise a puzzle that is pleasing to unravel.
- Give his words added weight, thereby encouraging the reader to engage in that most rewarding of all human arts: contemplation.

Artists have their reasons for doing things, and computer programmers have their own reasons for doing things. Each discipline has its own mysteries, its own charms, its own reasons for going about things in a particular way. chars in Java have a special relationship to numbers. It's the way of the world for programmers.

All of this makes possible an explanation of a fact I mentioned at the beginning of this section. I said that the character '1' is not the same thing as the number 1. The issue here is that the character '1' is almost always represented on computers by the number 49, '2' by 50, and so on. I say almost always because the value of a char depends a little on the character set you are using, I will take up this subject again at the end of this chapter. Clearly the character '1' is very different from the number 1. Computers think of the number 1 as being a 1. There is no translation necessary.

It is time to return now to the subject at hand, which was incrementing char values with the ++ operator. As you recall, the loop in our method is going to repeat 26 times. So now the code jumps back to the beginning of the loop and uses the getText method of JTextField to retrieve the current value of the string in the text field. It then appends the current value of temp plus one space to this string:

```
S = jTextField1.getText();
S = S + Temp + ' ';
```

When the string is first retrieved from the JTextField, it equals "A." After executing the second line in the loop, it equals "A B." The code then increments temp again by calling temp++. Now temp is equal to 67 or 'B.'

Needless to say, the loop continues on in this fashion, executing 26 times. By the time it is done, our little method has taught Java to say its ABCs, as shown at the bottom of Figure 9-2.

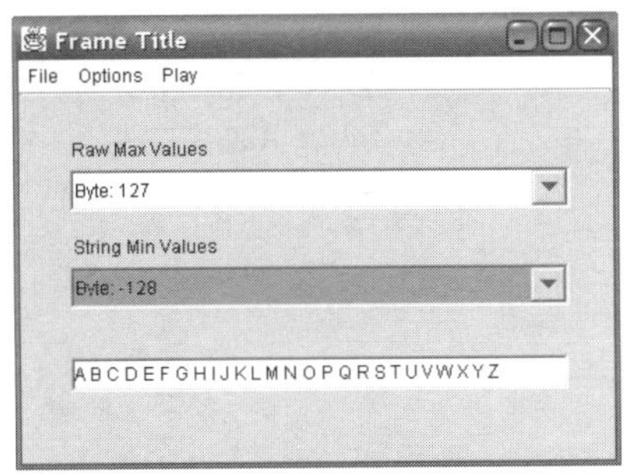

Figure 9-2: Driven by the power of a loop and the relationship between chars and numbers, Java learns its ABCs.

I mentioned earlier that the character '1' is usually equal to 49. I say usually because the actual values printed by a particular font can vary. You know that some fonts are called Times Roman, others Courier, and others Arial, while other fonts take on even more exotic characteristics such as gothic letters or characters that look like written script. These different font sets nearly always follow the standard that the 65th character in the set will be the letter A, and the 49th character in the set will be the number 1, etc. However, there is nothing that says that a particular character set cannot do something ever so logical such as setting the first character to the number 1, the second to 2, etc. In practice, this is not going to happen, as it would cause chaos in the computer world. The font would not work on any standard editor. But there is no theoretical reason why fonts of this type could not be made. Furthermore, some character sets don't show numbers or letters at all. For instance, the Wingdings character set, common on Windows installations, shows only a series of iconic pictures, never any numbers or letters at all. You can see an example of this character set in the third line of Figure 9-3. Character sets of this latter type are fairly common. They should not cause confusion as long as the user understands that they cannot be used to depict the letters of the alphabet.

Figure 9-3: The same four characters shown in several different character sets. Note the third character set does not show any letters at all.

The tenth character in most character sets is the linefeed character, which can be written like this: '\n.' The following table shows how to work with some other characters of this type:

Character	Number	Name
'\b'	8	backspace
'\t'	9	tab
'\n'	10	linefeed
'\f'	12	formfeed
'\r'	13	carriage return
'\"'	34	double quote
'\''	39	single quote
'\\'	92	backslash

That's all I want to say about characters. Later in the book we can chat some about character arrays, but that is really a different subject.

Working with bytes

bytes represent whole numbers between –128 and 127. They take up 8 bits.

Why is it that a byte ranges from –128 to 127? Why doesn't it range from some nice round number like –250 to 250. Or why must it have a range at all?

The issue here is that you can only hold a number of a certain size in 8 bits. A bit is a binary number that can hold either 0 or 1. A one-bit number can therefore hold only the values 0 and 1. A two-bit number allows you to count up to 3.

Binary	Base Ten
00	0
01	1
10	2
11	3

With three bits you can count up to 7.

Binary	Base Ten
000	0
001	1
010	2
011	3
100	4
101	5
110	6
111	7

With 4 bits you can get to 15, with 5 bits you can get to 31, 6 bits gets you 63, 7 bits to 127, and 8 bits to 256.

All that is simple enough. The question then becomes, if 8 bits allows you to count up to 256, why does the 8-bit byte type go up to only 127? The reason is that the eighth bit, the highest bit, is considered the sign of the number. If the eighth bit is a 1, the number is negative; if it is 0, the number is positive. This means that the eighth bit is already spoken for, meaning that you only have seven bits to work with, and the highest number you can depict with 7 bits is 127.

Working with shorts, ints, and longs

The previous section ended with a discussion of bits. One of the interesting corollaries of all you read about bits is that it is not legal to write the following code:

```
byte a = 1, b = 2, c;
c = a + b;
```

Instead, you must write:

```
byte a = 1, b = 2, c;
c = (byte)(a + b);
```

What you are doing in the second case is typecasting the value (a + b) to a byte. You must perform this typecast because the value a + b could be larger than 127. As a result, the compiler assumes that the result of the addition will be larger than a byte. It is expecting a type larger than a byte. In particular, according to the *type promotion* rules of Java, the compiler will convert the result to an int. The only way to keep it from doing this is to explicitly use a typecast.

In the previous example, if a were equal to 100 and b were equal to 100, then a + b would equal 200, which cannot be captured in seven bits. As a result, the result of the addition would not be 200, but –56. There are reasons why the number –56 emerges here, and many of you can probably figure them out, but for our purposes, it's simplest to say that the result of such an addition would be undefined.

The governing rule in this case is that whenever you want to assign a smaller type to a larger type, you have to use a typecast. A typecast coerces the compiler into doing something it would normally consider illogical. You are saying, in effect: "Hey, I know that adding two bytes together can be problematic, but in this case I promise you that it will work out." Note that you must perform the typecast even if you explicitly set the values a and b to values that will not exceed 127. The computer is too busy with other matters to bother checking whether the addition will proceed safely. Instead, it insists that you take responsibility for the code.

Here is another way to state the same thing. You can assign smaller numerical values to large numerical values. For instance, you can assign a byte to a short:

```
byte MyByte = 3;
short MyShort;
MyShort = MyByte;
```

To go the opposite way, you must use an explicit cast:

```
byte MyByte = 3;
short MyShort;
MyByte = (byte)MyShort;
```

The following code is legal:

```
byte a = 100, b = 100;
int c;

c = a + b;
```

Even if a were set to Byte.MAX_VALUE and b to Byte.MAX_VALUE, the value of the two numbers added together would not exceed Integer.MAX_VALUE. As a result, you do not need to perform a typecast. In other words, you are trying to assign from a larger type to a smaller type, so you can proceed with normal code.

It is legal to assign a char to a short, int, or long, so long as you use a typecast:

```
short x;
char y = 'A';
x = (short)(y);
```

In this case, x would, of course, be set equal to 65.

What Should I Use: A byte, short, int, or long?

By now you have probably heard more than you wanted to hear about bytes, ints, shorts, and longs. The only topic I haven't addressed is probably the one uppermost in your mind: "What type should I use by default in my code?" Fortunately, the answer to this question is very simple: Use the int type!

Most computers these days use 32-bit operating systems and 32-bit chips. For instance, the Intel Pentium chips are all 32-bit chips. Windows 2000 and Windows 98 are both 32-bit operating systems. This means that they work most readily with 32-bit values. As a result, it usually takes a computer longer to work with a byte than it does to work with an int. We might find numbers in the range –128 to 127 easier to work with than numbers in the range –2,147,483,648 to 2,147,483,647. Computers, however, don't think that way. They don't find it any easier to work with the number 1 than the number 2,147,483,647. It's all the same to them, as these are both numbers that fit neatly into 32 bits.

Furthermore, a computer has to go out of its way to work with a value that is explicitly cast to be less than 32 bits. It's harder for a 32-bit Intel chip to work with a byte than to work with an int! It's not necessarily a lot harder, and sometimes it all amounts to the same thing, but it certainly is never, or at least very rarely, easier or faster for the chip to work with 8-bit values rather than 32-bit values.

Given these facts, why should we even bother with bytes and shorts? It happens that there are some occasions when they are useful. Sometimes when you are performing bit manipulations, it really matters how many bits there are in a particular value. Or if you want to declare an array of 10,000 numbers, an array of 10,000 bytes will take up 10,000 bytes of memory, while an array of 10,000 ints will take up 40,000 bytes of memory. Most of the time, however, these kinds of issues are not worth your consideration, and you should just use ints.

The sad fact of the matter is that most beginning and intermediate level programmers never really get anywhere when they try to optimize their code. Attempts to use bytes instead of ints in order to save space or speed up code will backfire as often as not for any but the most expert programmer. Furthermore, expert programmers wrote the compilers and JDKs that you use. As a result, they often automatically put in optimizations that speed up your code. In other words, they often see when it is useful to automatically convert an int to a byte, or vice versa, and they perform the chore for you automatically in the background in a totally safe and highly efficient manner.

All of which is not to say that really good programmers can't optimize their code effectively. They can. But optimizing code is a lot more complicated than most programmers think. As a result, most of our efforts to optimize our code are wasted efforts.

Working with floats and doubles

Just as bytes, shorts, ints, and longs are all considered integer types, floats and doubles are both considered to be floating-point types. The words "floating point" are just a generic way of referring to any number that contains a decimal point.

A floating-point literal is assumed to be a value of type double. In other words, if you write 5.5 or 0.2, the compiler automatically converts that number to a double. Therefore, it is illegal to write the following:

```
float a = 5.6;
```

This code assigns a float to a double, which is illegal, since you can't assign a smaller type to a larger type. As a result, you must write:

```
float a = (float)(5.6)
```

or

```
float a = 5.6f
```

or

```
float a = 5.6F
```

All of these statements are different ways of saying the same thing. In other words, appending an f or an F to a floating-point number is the same as typecasting it to a float.

Here is how to assign a float to an int:

```
float a = (float)(1.2);
int b = (int)(a);
```

The typecast is all you need.

If you multiply an int and a double, the rules of Java say that the result will be a double unless you explicitly typecast it to some other type. As mentioned earlier, this is known as type promotion. If you add or multiply two bytes or shorts together, the result is automatically promoted to an int. If you add or multiply an integer type with a floating-point type, the result will always be a double, unless you typecast it to coerce the compiler into treating it as some other type.

A Program to Test the MyTypes Class

It is at last time to start using the simple, or primitive, types in a Java program. The example program in Listing 9-2 is not very practical, but hopefully you will find it helps you understand what the simple types are about and what kinds of operations you usually perform with them.

The code in Listing 9-2 demonstrates how to use the MyTypes class. As in the previous chapter, I assume that you have created a directory called foo beneath your project and dropped the MyTypes class into that directory. You must also add a statement to import the package foo into your current project. (If you wanted, you could put MyTypes.java into the same directory as your Frame1.java and then change the package name to correspond to the package where your project is listed.

Listing 9-2: The source to the Frame1.java file from the CallMyTypes project found on the CD

```
package callmytypes;

import java.awt.*;
import java.awt.event.*;
import javax.swing.*;
import callmytypes.foo.MyTypes;

public class Frame1 extends JFrame
{
  JPanel contentPane;
  JMenuBar jMenuBar1 = new JMenuBar();
  JMenu jMenu1 = new JMenu();
  JMenuItem jMenuItem1 = new JMenuItem();
  JMenu jMenu2 = new JMenu();
  JMenu jMenu3 = new JMenu();
  JMenuItem rawMyIntegerMenu = new JMenuItem();
  JMenuItem rawMyByteMenu = new JMenuItem();
  JMenuItem rawMyLongMenu = new JMenuItem();
  JMenuItem rawMyFloatMenu = new JMenuItem();
  JMenuItem rawMyDoubleMenu = new JMenuItem();
  JMenu jMenu4 = new JMenu();
  JMenuItem stringMyByteMenu = new JMenuItem();
  JMenuItem stringMyShortMenu = new JMenuItem();
  JMenuItem stringMyIntegerMenu = new JMenuItem();
  JMenuItem stringMyLongMenu = new JMenuItem();
  JMenuItem stringMyFloatMenu = new JMenuItem();
  JMenuItem stringMyDoubleMenu = new JMenuItem();
  MyTypes myTypes = new MyTypes();
  JComboBox jComboBox1 = new JComboBox();
  JComboBox jComboBox2 = new JComboBox();
  JLabel jLabel1 = new JLabel();
  JLabel jLabel2 = new JLabel();
  JMenuItem allRawMenu = new JMenuItem();
  JMenuItem AllStringMenu = new JMenuItem();
  JMenuItem rawMyShortMenu = new JMenuItem();
  JTextField jTextField1 = new JTextField();
  JMenu jMenu5 = new JMenu();
  JMenuItem AddCharMenu = new JMenuItem();
  JMenuItem jMenuItem2 = new JMenuItem();

  //Construct the frame
  public Frame1()
  {
      enableEvents(AWTEvent.WINDOW_EVENT_MASK);
      try
      {
        jbInit();
```

```
    }
    catch(Exception e)
    {
      e.printStackTrace();
    }
  }

  //Component initialization
  private void jbInit() throws Exception
  {
    contentPane = (JPanel) this.getContentPane();
    contentPane.setLayout(null);
    this.setSize(new Dimension(400, 300));
    this.setTitle("Frame Title");
    jMenu1.setText("File");
    jMenuItem1.setText("Exit");
    jMenu2.setText("Options");
    jMenu3.setText("Raw");
    rawMyIntegerMenu.setText("myInteger");
    rawMyIntegerMenu.addActionListener(new Frame1_rawMyIntegerMenu_actionAdapter(this));
    rawMyByteMenu.setText("myByte");
    rawMyByteMenu.addActionListener(new Frame1_rawMyByteMenu_actionAdapter(this));
    rawMyLongMenu.setText("myLong");
    rawMyLongMenu.addActionListener(new Frame1_rawMyLongMenu_actionAdapter(this));
    rawMyFloatMenu.setText("myFloat");
    rawMyFloatMenu.addActionListener(new Frame1_rawMyFloatMenu_actionAdapter(this));
    rawMyDoubleMenu.setText("myDouble");
    rawMyDoubleMenu.addActionListener(new Frame1_rawMyDoubleMenu_actionAdapter(this));
    jMenu4.setText("AsString");
    stringMyByteMenu.setText("myByte");
    stringMyByteMenu.addActionListener(new Frame1_stringMyByteMenu_actionAdapter(this));
    stringMyShortMenu.setText("myShort");
    stringMyShortMenu.addActionListener(new Frame1_stringMyShortMenu_actionAdapter(this));
    stringMyIntegerMenu.setText("myInteger");
    stringMyIntegerMenu.addActionListener(new Frame1_stringMyIntegerMenu_actionAdapter(this));
    stringMyLongMenu.setText("myLong");
    stringMyLongMenu.addActionListener(new Frame1_stringMyLongMenu_actionAdapter(this));
    stringMyFloatMenu.setText("myFloat");
    stringMyFloatMenu.addActionListener(new Frame1_stringMyFloatMenu_actionAdapter(this));
    stringMyDoubleMenu.setText("myDouble");
    stringMyDoubleMenu.addActionListener(new Frame1_stringMyDoubleMenu_actionAdapter(this));
    jComboBox1.setBounds(new Rectangle(33, 50, 331, 27));
    jComboBox2.setBounds(new Rectangle(33, 114, 330, 27));
    jLabel1.setText("Raw Max Values");
    jLabel1.setBounds(new Rectangle(34, 27, 188, 18));
    jLabel2.setText("String Min Values");
    jLabel2.setBounds(new Rectangle(35, 91, 178, 18));
    allRawMenu.setText("All Raw");
    allRawMenu.addActionListener(new Frame1_allRawMenu_actionAdapter(this));
    AllStringMenu.setText("All AsString");
    AllStringMenu.addActionListener(new Frame1_AllStringMenu_actionAdapter(this));
```

```
    rawMyShortMenu.setText("myShort");
    rawMyShortMenu.addActionListener(new Frame1_rawMyShortMenu_actionAdapter(this));
    jTextField1.setText("jTextField1");
    jTextField1.setBounds(new Rectangle(33, 174, 329, 22));
    jMenu5.setText("Play");
    AddCharMenu.setText("Add Char");
    AddCharMenu.addActionListener(new Frame1_AddCharMenu_actionAdapter(this));
    jMenuItem2.setText("Bool Test");
    jMenuItem2.addActionListener(new Frame1_jMenuItem2_actionAdapter(this));
    jMenuBar1.add(jMenu1);
    jMenuBar1.add(jMenu2);
    jMenuBar1.add(jMenu5);
    jMenu1.add(jMenuItem1);
    jMenu2.add(jMenu3);
    jMenu2.add(jMenu4);
    jMenu3.add(rawMyByteMenu);
    jMenu3.add(rawMyShortMenu);
    jMenu3.add(rawMyIntegerMenu);
    jMenu3.add(rawMyLongMenu);
    jMenu3.add(rawMyFloatMenu);
    jMenu3.add(rawMyDoubleMenu);
    jMenu3.add(allRawMenu);
    jMenu4.add(stringMyByteMenu);
    jMenu4.add(stringMyShortMenu);
    jMenu4.add(stringMyIntegerMenu);
    jMenu4.add(stringMyLongMenu);
    jMenu4.add(stringMyFloatMenu);
    jMenu4.add(stringMyDoubleMenu);
    jMenu4.add(AllStringMenu);
    contentPane.add(jLabel1, null);
    contentPane.add(jComboBox1, null);
    contentPane.add(jLabel2, null);
    contentPane.add(jComboBox2, null);
    contentPane.add(jTextField1, null);
    jMenu5.add(AddCharMenu);
    jMenu5.add(jMenuItem2);
    this.setJMenuBar(jMenuBar1);
}

//Overridden so we can exit when window is closed
protected void processWindowEvent(WindowEvent e)
{
    super.processWindowEvent(e);
    if (e.getID() == WindowEvent.WINDOW_CLOSING)
    {
      System.exit(0);
    }
}

void rawMyIntegerMenu_actionPerformed(ActionEvent e)
{
```

```
        jComboBox1.addItem("Integer: " + Integer.toString(myTypes.getMyInt()));
    }

    void rawMyLongMenu_actionPerformed(ActionEvent e)
    {
        jComboBox1.addItem("Long : " + Long.toString(myTypes.getMyLong()));
    }

    void rawMyFloatMenu_actionPerformed(ActionEvent e)
    {
        jComboBox1.addItem("Float: " + Float.toString(myTypes.getMyFloat()));
    }

    void rawMyByteMenu_actionPerformed(ActionEvent e)
    {
        jComboBox1.addItem("Byte: " + Byte.toString(myTypes.getMyByte()));
    }

    void rawMyShortMenu_actionPerformed(ActionEvent e)
    {
        jComboBox1.addItem("Short: " + Short.toString(myTypes.getMyShort()));
    }

    void rawMyDoubleMenu_actionPerformed(ActionEvent e)
    {
        jComboBox1.addItem("Double: " + Double.toString(myTypes.getMyDouble()));
    }

    void stringMyByteMenu_actionPerformed(ActionEvent e)
    {
        jComboBox2.addItem("Byte: " + myTypes.getMinByteAsString());
    }

    void stringMyShortMenu_actionPerformed(ActionEvent e)
    {
        jComboBox2.addItem("Short: " + myTypes.getMinShortAsString());
    }

    void stringMyIntegerMenu_actionPerformed(ActionEvent e)
    {
        jComboBox2.addItem("Integer: " + myTypes.getMinIntegerAsString());
    }

    void stringMyLongMenu_actionPerformed(ActionEvent e)
    {
        jComboBox2.addItem("Long: " + myTypes.getMinLongAsString());
    }

    void stringMyFloatMenu_actionPerformed(ActionEvent e)
    {
        jComboBox2.addItem("Float: " + myTypes.getMinFloatAsString());
```

```
}

void stringMyDoubleMenu_actionPerformed(ActionEvent e)
{
     jComboBox2.addItem("Double: " + myTypes.getMinDoubleAsString());
}

void AllStringMenu_actionPerformed(ActionEvent e)
{
     this.stringMyByteMenu_actionPerformed(null);
     stringMyShortMenu_actionPerformed(null);
     stringMyIntegerMenu_actionPerformed(null);
     stringMyLongMenu_actionPerformed(null);
     stringMyFloatMenu_actionPerformed(null);
     stringMyDoubleMenu_actionPerformed(null);
}

void allRawMenu_actionPerformed(ActionEvent e)
{
     rawMyByteMenu_actionPerformed(null);
     rawMyShortMenu_actionPerformed(null);
     rawMyIntegerMenu_actionPerformed(null);
     rawMyLongMenu_actionPerformed(null);
     rawMyDoubleMenu_actionPerformed(null);
     rawMyFloatMenu_actionPerformed(null);
}

void AddCharMenu_actionPerformed(ActionEvent e)
{
     char temp = 65;
     String S;

     jTextField1.setText("");

     for (int i = 0; i < 26; i++)
     {
       S = jTextField1.getText();
       S = S + temp + ' ';
       jTextField1.setText(S);
       temp++;
     }
}

void jMenuItem2_actionPerformed(ActionEvent e)
{
    int Num = Integer.parseInt(jTextField1.getText());

    boolean myBool = (Num == 25 ? true:false);

    if (myBool == false)
      jTextField1.setText("false");
```

```
      else
        jTextField1.setText("true");
  }


}

class Frame1_rawMyIntegerMenu_actionAdapter implements java.awt.event.ActionListener
{
  Frame1 adaptee;

  Frame1_rawMyIntegerMenu_actionAdapter(Frame1 adaptee)
  {
      this.adaptee = adaptee;
  }

  public void actionPerformed(ActionEvent e)
  {
      adaptee.rawMyIntegerMenu_actionPerformed(e);
  }
}

class Frame1_rawMyLongMenu_actionAdapter implements java.awt.event.ActionListener
{
  Frame1 adaptee;

  Frame1_rawMyLongMenu_actionAdapter(Frame1 adaptee)
  {
      this.adaptee = adaptee;
  }

  public void actionPerformed(ActionEvent e)
  {
      adaptee.rawMyLongMenu_actionPerformed(e);
  }
}

class Frame1_rawMyFloatMenu_actionAdapter implements java.awt.event.ActionListener
{
  Frame1 adaptee;

  Frame1_rawMyFloatMenu_actionAdapter(Frame1 adaptee)
  {
      this.adaptee = adaptee;
  }

  public void actionPerformed(ActionEvent e)
  {
      adaptee.rawMyFloatMenu_actionPerformed(e);
  }
```

```
}

class Frame1_rawMyByteMenu_actionAdapter implements java.awt.event.ActionListener
{
  Frame1 adaptee;

  Frame1_rawMyByteMenu_actionAdapter(Frame1 adaptee)
  {
      this.adaptee = adaptee;
  }

  public void actionPerformed(ActionEvent e)
  {
      adaptee.rawMyByteMenu_actionPerformed(e);
  }
}

class Frame1_rawMyDoubleMenu_actionAdapter implements java.awt.event.ActionListener
{
  Frame1 adaptee;

  Frame1_rawMyDoubleMenu_actionAdapter(Frame1 adaptee)
  {
      this.adaptee = adaptee;
  }

  public void actionPerformed(ActionEvent e)
  {
      adaptee.rawMyDoubleMenu_actionPerformed(e);
  }
}

class Frame1_stringMyByteMenu_actionAdapter implements java.awt.event.ActionListener
{
  Frame1 adaptee;

  Frame1_stringMyByteMenu_actionAdapter(Frame1 adaptee)
  {
      this.adaptee = adaptee;
  }

  public void actionPerformed(ActionEvent e)
  {
      adaptee.stringMyByteMenu_actionPerformed(e);
  }
}

class Frame1_stringMyShortMenu_actionAdapter implements java.awt.event.ActionListener
{
  Frame1 adaptee;
```

```
  Frame1_stringMyShortMenu_actionAdapter(Frame1 adaptee)
  {
      this.adaptee = adaptee;
  }

  public void actionPerformed(ActionEvent e)
  {
      adaptee.stringMyShortMenu_actionPerformed(e);
  }
}

class Frame1_stringMyIntegerMenu_actionAdapter implements java.awt.event.ActionListener
{
  Frame1 adaptee;

  Frame1_stringMyIntegerMenu_actionAdapter(Frame1 adaptee)
  {
      this.adaptee = adaptee;
  }

  public void actionPerformed(ActionEvent e)
  {
      adaptee.stringMyIntegerMenu_actionPerformed(e);
  }
}

class Frame1_stringMyLongMenu_actionAdapter implements java.awt.event.ActionListener
{
  Frame1 adaptee;

  Frame1_stringMyLongMenu_actionAdapter(Frame1 adaptee)
  {
      this.adaptee = adaptee;
  }

  public void actionPerformed(ActionEvent e)
  {
      adaptee.stringMyLongMenu_actionPerformed(e);
  }
}

class Frame1_stringMyFloatMenu_actionAdapter implements java.awt.event.ActionListener
{
  Frame1 adaptee;

  Frame1_stringMyFloatMenu_actionAdapter(Frame1 adaptee)
  {
      this.adaptee = adaptee;
  }

  public void actionPerformed(ActionEvent e)
```

```
  {
      adaptee.stringMyFloatMenu_actionPerformed(e);
  }
}

class Frame1_stringMyDoubleMenu_actionAdapter implements java.awt.event.ActionListener
{
  Frame1 adaptee;

  Frame1_stringMyDoubleMenu_actionAdapter(Frame1 adaptee)
  {
      this.adaptee = adaptee;
  }

  public void actionPerformed(ActionEvent e)
  {
      adaptee.stringMyDoubleMenu_actionPerformed(e);
  }
}

class Frame1_AllStringMenu_actionAdapter implements java.awt.event.ActionListener
{
  Frame1 adaptee;

  Frame1_AllStringMenu_actionAdapter(Frame1 adaptee)
  {
      this.adaptee = adaptee;
  }

  public void actionPerformed(ActionEvent e)
  {
      adaptee.AllStringMenu_actionPerformed(e);
  }
}

class Frame1_allRawMenu_actionAdapter implements java.awt.event.ActionListener
{
  Frame1 adaptee;

  Frame1_allRawMenu_actionAdapter(Frame1 adaptee)
  {
      this.adaptee = adaptee;
  }

  public void actionPerformed(ActionEvent e)
  {
      adaptee.allRawMenu_actionPerformed(e);
  }
}

class Frame1_rawMyShortMenu_actionAdapter implements java.awt.event.ActionListener
```

```
{
  Frame1 adaptee;

  Frame1_rawMyShortMenu_actionAdapter(Frame1 adaptee)
  {
     this.adaptee = adaptee;
  }

  public void actionPerformed(ActionEvent e)
  {
     adaptee.rawMyShortMenu_actionPerformed(e);
  }
}

class Frame1_AddCharMenu_actionAdapter implements java.awt.event.ActionListener
{
  Frame1 adaptee;

  Frame1_AddCharMenu_actionAdapter(Frame1 adaptee)
  {
     this.adaptee = adaptee;
  }

  public void actionPerformed(ActionEvent e)
  {
     adaptee.AddCharMenu_actionPerformed(e);
  }
}

class Frame1_jMenuItem2_actionAdapter implements java.awt.event.ActionListener
{
  Frame1 adaptee;

  Frame1_jMenuItem2_actionAdapter(Frame1 adaptee)
  {
     this.adaptee = adaptee;
  }

  public void actionPerformed(ActionEvent e)
  {
     adaptee.jMenuItem2_actionPerformed(e);
  }
}
```

There is a lot of code in this program, but most of it is very simple. If you had to write all this code yourself, you would soon become exhausted. But JBuilder makes the process of creating a program of this type very simple. Ninety-eight percent of the code you see here was generated automatically by the IDE. All you have to do is type in the body of a few methods.

Before I can describe the code, however, I need to spend a few moments talking about menus.

Working with Menus

Menus are also covered in Chapter 13, "More Layouts and Menus." I will give you another example of using them here, so you can have a second chance to see how they work.

The simplest way to add menus to your program is to include them from the very beginning by requesting them from the Application Wizard. When you choose File | New | Application, the wizard will ask if you want to add menus to your main form. If you answer yes to this question, your program will automatically contain a few basic menu items that you can edit to suit your purposes. However, we don't always remember or think to add menus when creating a project.

If you want to add menus to an existing form that does not have menus, turn to the Swing Containers page of the component palette and drop down a JMenuBar. Then add the following line of code to the end of your jbInit method:

```
this.setJMenuBar(menuBar);
```

If you want to add menus to an existing JFrame descendant in an entirely manual fashion, you can do so by adding a few simple lines of code to your program. Start by adding this code at the top of your declaration for Frame1:

```
public class Frame1 extends JFrame
{
  JPanel contentPane;
  JMenuBar menuBar = new JMenuBar();
  JMenu menu = new JMenu();
  ... // Code ommitted here
```

I've included the declaration for Frame1 and the contentPane to give you enough code to get oriented.

Now add the following code to your jbInit method:

```
menuBar.add(menu);
this.setJMenuBar(menuBar);
```

The fact that you can create visual items either in code or by using the visual tools is a technology that Borland calls *two-way tools*. Two-way tools are glorious because they ensure that you are not working with any black boxes. You can use either the source code or the visual tools to create your program; it's up to you. In practice, most people use a combination of the two approaches. The key point, however, is that JBuilder is not locking you into some visual tool which creates code you can't understand. Instead, JBuilder just uses standard Java code.

In the structure pane for Frame1, you can find a place to edit menus, as shown in Figure 9-4. To get a similar view, right-click on **Menu** in the structure pane, and choose **Activate Designer** from the menu.

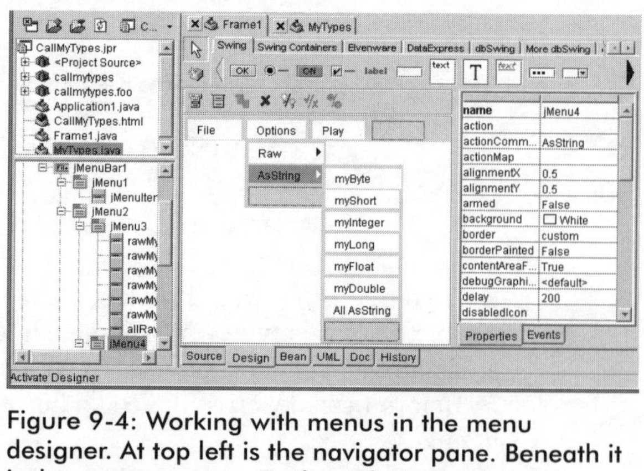

Figure 9-4: Working with menus in the menu designer. At top left is the navigator pane. Beneath it is the structure pane. To the right is the menu designer. On the far right is the Inspector.

To edit any of the items, you can use either the designer itself or the Inspector, which is shown to the right of the designer. In Figure 9-4, if you look to the right of the word Play, you can see a little area with a dotted outline. If you double-clicked on this area, it would turn into an edit control. There you could type in the caption for a new JMenu. Adding this caption will automatically create the menu itself. You can use the same process to add a JMenuItem to the bottom of an existing drop-down menu. For instance, if you double-clicked on the area beneath the words **AsString** or the words **All Raw**, you would get a chance to type in the caption for your menu, and the JMenuItem itself would be appended to the menu.

To further edit the menus, you can work in the Inspector. The key fields you need to use for now are the text property on the Properties page and the actionPerformed event on the Events page. You can flip back and forth between the Properties page and the Events page by clicking on the tabs at the bottom of the Inspector, as shown in Figures 9-5 and 9-6.

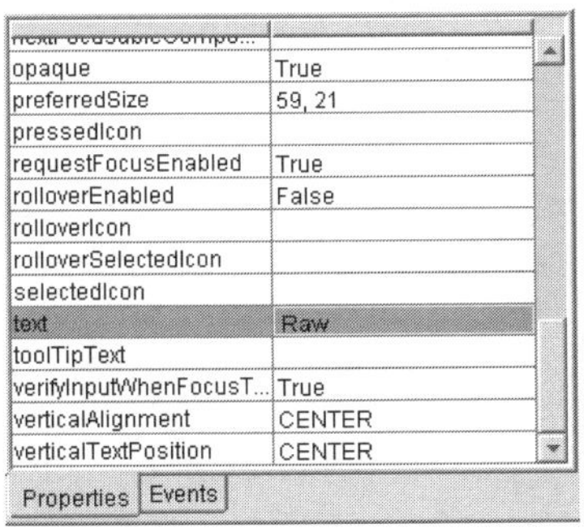

Figure 9-5: The Properties page of the Inspector

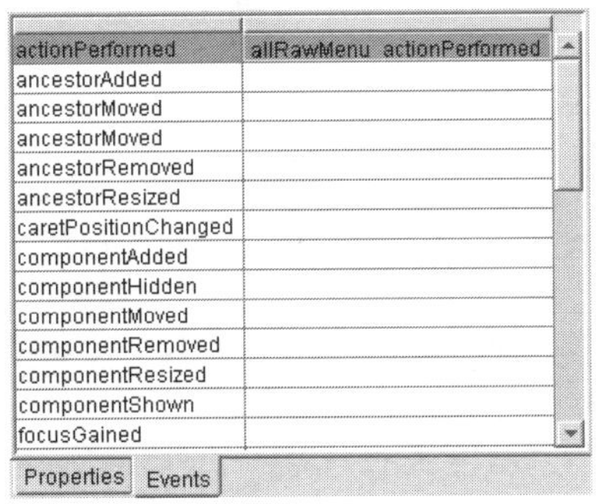

Figure 9-6: The Events page of the Inspector

If you look at Figure 9-5, you can see that I have changed the default name of this JMenuItem from jMenuItemX to AllRawMenu. I have made this change because the name AllRawMenu tells me something about what the menu item does, while jMenuItemX does not tell me anything.

On the Events page, shown in Figure 9-6, you can see that I have associated an event with this menu item. To do this, I simply turned to the Events page, highlighted the actionPerformed event, and pressed the Enter key. The words allRawMenu_actionPerformed were typed in for me automatically by the IDE, and the following code was added to my program:

```
  // Code omitted here
  void allRawMenu_actionPerformed(ActionEvent e)
  {
  }
}

class Frame1_allRawMenu_actionAdapter implements java.awt.event.ActionListener
{
  Frame1 adaptee;

  Frame1_allRawMenu_actionAdapter(Frame1 adaptee)
  {
    this.adaptee = adaptee;
  }
```

```
  public void actionPerformed(ActionEvent e)
  {
    adaptee.allRawMenu_actionPerformed(e);
  }
}
```

You've seen code like this before. The class at the bottom of the code fragment is the adapter, which will automatically handle events for me. In particular, whenever the AllRawMenu is selected by the user, the Frame1_AllRawMenu_actionAdapter class will automatically call the allRawMenu_actionPerformed method. Events are discussed in more depth in Chapter 15, "Firing Events."

This program uses some nested menus, as shown in Figure 9-4. The nomenclature for menus runs as follows. The bar along the top of the program that contains the menus is called a JMenuBar. The individual words appearing on the JMenuBar are each held by an instance of the Java JMenu class. When you drop down a JMenu, you get a list of words such as Raw and AsString. Each of these are JMenuItems.

If you drill down one layer further so that the Raw JMenuItem has another menu in it, you have created a nested menu. The JMenuItems with captions that read myByte, myInt, etc., are all part of a nested menu. I created this nested menu by right-clicking on the word Raw and selecting Insert Nested Menu from the JBuilder pop-up menu.

The Code in the CallMyTypes Application

Most of the methods that handle clicks on the menu items in the CallMyTypes program are very simple. All they do is call methods in the MyTypes class and display the results of the call to the user.

The calls in the program demonstrate how to use each of the numeric types. (The program also shows how to use booleans and chars, but I showed you the code for those methods earlier in this chapter in the "Thinking about chars" and "Thinking about booleans" sections.)

Here is the code for working with the int type:

```
void rawMyIntegerMenu_actionPerformed(ActionEvent e)
{
  jComboBox1.addItem("Integer: " + Integer.toString(myTypes.getMyInt()));
}
```

As shown in Figure 9-2, the main form for this program contains two JComboBoxes. You can find the JComboBoxes on the Swing page of the component palette. The code in this method places some text in the first of these combo boxes. It does this by calling the addItem method of the JComboBox class.

The MyTypes class has a method called getMyInt, which returns the value to which we initialized the variable myInt in the MyTypes constructor:

```
myInt = Integer.MAX_VALUE;       // 2147483647;

// Code omitted here

public int getMyInt()
{
  return myInt;
}
```

It should be clear to you that getMyInt will return the value 2147483647. I use the toString method of the Integer class to convert this number into a String. After doing this, the program is holding the string value "2147483647" in memory. I then use the + operator to concatenate the string "Integer:" to the string "2147483647." The end result is "Integer: 2147483647." (I will talk more about operators in Chapter 11, "Looping, Operators, and Currency.") This is the value that is placed in the JComboBox.

Another JMenuItem actionPerformed response method looks like this:

```
void stringMyIntegerMenu_actionPerformed(ActionEvent e)
{
   jComboBox2.addItem("Integer: " + myTypes.getMinIntegerAsString());
}
```

The code shown here calls the getMinIntegerAsString method of the MyTypes class. Here is what that method looks like:

```
public String getMinIntegerAsString()
{
  return Integer.toString(Integer.MIN_VALUE);
}
```

By now you should be starting to understand the rhythm of this program. It consists of a series of menu items, each of which calls a method from the MyTypes class. Once I have called all the methods in the class, the program is done.

I'm not going to step through each of those methods, since the process is repetitive and relatively simple to understand. Instead, I suggest that you spend time examining Listing 9-2, going over it until it all makes sense to you. Furthermore, you should spend time running the program in the JBuilder IDE, experimenting with it as you see fit. The best possible course of action would be to create the program yourself in the IDE, rather than just running my copy of it.

When you are working with the program, please note that I show you standard Java class types used to wrap each of the simple types.

Simple Type	Class Type
byte	Byte
short	Short
int	Integer
long	Long
float	Float
double	Double

I use each of the class types at least once in the program. Usually I just call the toString method of the class or use the MAX_VALUE or MIN_VALUE fields of the class. In fact, there isn't a whole lot more to the classes than these few features, but you can use the online help or browse the source to find out more if you wish.

There are two methods in the CallMyTypes application that deserve perhaps a moment's comment. If you are working your way through the nested menus in this program, it can take quite a while to fill in the JComboBoxes with the results from all the methods in the MyTypes class. For instance, you have to individually click on the myByte, myShort, myInt, etc., JMenuItems. While it's not a daunting task, this process still gets a bit trying at times. As a result, I created a menu item with the label "All Raw" that will call all the nested JMenuItems at once. Here is the method that is called in response to a click on the "All Raw" JMenuItem:

```
void allRawMenu_actionPerformed(ActionEvent e)
{
   rawMyByteMenu_actionPerformed(null);
   rawMyShortMenu_actionPerformed(null);
   rawMyIntegerMenu_actionPerformed(null);
   rawMyLongMenu_actionPerformed(null);
   rawMyDoubleMenu_actionPerformed(null);
   rawMyFloatMenu_actionPerformed(null);
}
```

This code calls each of the response methods for the other nested JMenuItems in this group. As result, a single click on the All Raw menu item has the effect of calling all the other methods in that group of menu items.

Each of the response methods called in this event takes a parameter of type ActionEvent:

```
void stringMyIntegerMenu_actionPerformed(ActionEvent e)
```

ActionEvents are discussed in Chapters 14 and 15. In this case, we can ignore the parameter altogether and pass in null in its place.

You can think of the value null as pointing to a class that has not been initialized. Normally we reference the address of a class by writing the name of a variable that points to it:

```
MyTypes myTypes = new TMyTypes();
```

In this code, myTypes references an actual instance of a class of type MyTypes. It is, for all intents and purposes, a pointer to the place in memory where an initialized instance of the class MyTypes resides. If we set myTypes equal to null, we are saying that this variable does not point to an initialized instance of the MyTypes class. It points at nothing; it references nothing. It is just a variable, and you can't do much with it other than say its name. Its value is nil, nothing, null!

A class that doesn't point at anything isn't much good to you most of the time. But in this one case, there is some value in it. In particular, it allows you to call your method handlers without having to come up with an initialized variable of type ActionEvent. Since you are not going to use the ActionEvent object, there is no harm in omitting it in this case.

Summary

That is all I'm going to say about the Java simple, or primitive, types. Hopefully this chapter has given you a sense of what they are all about.

This chapter also gave you a look at an example application called CallMyTypes, which showed you how to use the simple types. Perhaps of equal importance is the fact that the application makes heavy use of menus and events. Creating menus and events in Java is normally a time-consuming process that involves a lot of typing. JBuilder eliminates the need for you to do any typing of all that repetitive menu and event handler code. It literally saves you hours, if not days, of time.

Creating a program like CallMyTypes would be a major undertaking without the help of visual tools like those found in JBuilder. That's a pity because the program is conceptually very simple. The code in the program isn't difficult, just long and repetitive. JBuilder eliminates all that typing and repetition. It's one of the many good reasons to use this tool.

Chapter 10

Statements, Expressions, and Keywords

Charlie Calvert

In this chapter you will get a look at some of the basic syntactical elements used in a Java program. Topics covered include such fundamental elements as keywords, expressions, and statements. I am covering these subjects so that I can use these terms meaningfully throughout the rest of the book.

It is, of course, very important to have a sense of how the basics of a language fit together. If you have a solid base in a language, you can always build on it when searching for ways to enhance your knowledge. However, if you don't have a solid base, your attempts to enhance your knowledge can lead to the construction of rickety edifices that are not reliable.

In order to talk intelligently about operators, branching, and looping, I'm going to have to use terms such as "statement" and "expression." As a result, I'm going to make a stab at defining these hard-to-pin-down terms. Then in the next chapters, I will be able to use them when talking about other Java programming concepts.

Statements

Statements are the basic building blocks out of which programs are created. An application or applet begins by executing the first statement in your code and proceeds in a linear fashion executing each statement that you wrote, one at a time.

NOTE: What is said in the last paragraph is really something of an oversimplification. The JVM actually implements an event loop. Your program is called when an event such as a mouse click or keyboard click occurs. At that time, a call is made to a method in your program. The statements in that method are then executed in a linear fashion. When the method is through, the focus moves back to the message loop until a new message is sent. The presence of multiple threads in your program or in the Java VM can complicate this model even further, but the basic idea holds true in even the most complex programs.

There are many types of commonly used statements in Java. They include while, if, for, switch, do, break, continue, throw, catch, and synchronized statements. A line of code in which one value is set equal to another is an *assignment statement*. Java has no goto statement, but it does have labels. When you are using a label, you write a label statement. There is also something called an empty statement, and the declaration of a variable is also considered a statement. It is called, appropriately enough, a *declaration statement*. Finally, there is something called a block statement. A *block statement* begins with a curly brace and ends with a curly brace. Anything between the two curly braces, including other statements, can be considered part of one large statement called a *compound statement*.

The previous paragraph contains a fairly complete list of all the statements available for you when you want to build a program in Java. As such, this list is probably a relatively precise definition of what a statement is, but I don't expect that it will mean much to most readers, since I haven't yet defined what all these statements are or why they exist. In the next section of the text, however, I will give a few examples of statements, and hopefully the ideas expressed in the last paragraph will start to make some sense to you. I will, of course, more formally define each of these elements of the language in later portions of this text.

Before I begin, I will try to give you a second, less precise way to think about statements. Please understand that it is difficult to come up with a general definition of the term "statement" that will still be meaningful to people who are relatively new to programming. When language lawyers really decide to pin this subject down, the resulting discussion can go on for pages, and much of it will be hard for any but the most advanced programmer to fully understand. Fortunately, I don't need that kind of precision in order to communicate the ideas that I want to express in this chapter or elsewhere in this book. As a result, I will talk in much more general terms.

Speaking very loosely, a statement is to a program much as a sentence is to a book. With the exception of compound statements, a statement is usually a relatively small syntactical element. It is, however, large enough to contain a complete thought or discrete logical entity.

Most statements end with a semicolon or are bracketed by a pair of curly braces. A pair of curly braces denote a block of code. As explained in the section of this chapter called "Compound Statements," a block of code can itself contain multiple statements.

In a sense, when you add a semicolon to a bit of code or set it off in curly braces, you are usually saying that you have come to the end of a thought. You have expressed a complete idea that can, given the addition of some variable declarations, stand on its own. As such, it is similar to, but by no means identical to, a sentence in prose. I should hasten to add, however, that not all syntactical elements in the Java language that stand on their own and end with a semicolon are statements. I am merely saying that a large percentage of the elements in your code that stand on their own and end with a semicolon happen to be statements.

Examples of Statements

It is time to move past a metaphorical or abstract description of statements and start seeing some of the details of how they actually work.

Here is a classic, and very simple, statement:

```
c = a + b;      // assignment statement.
```

The example shown here is known as an *assignment statement*. As such, it is built around the assignment operator, which in Java is an equals sign.

Note that there are no declarations in this statement. Somewhere else in the code you need to declare the type of the variables a, b, and c. For instance, they might all be of type int. (The declaration for your local variables will itself be a statement.)

Nevertheless, despite the absence of the type declarations, the statement represents what I call a complete thought. That is, it's a discrete bit of code that stands on its own. From a grammatical point of view, what makes it a statement is the fact that it ends with a semicolon, but from a more semantic point of view, it does represent a relatively complete thought that the compiler can, given the presence of some type declarations, treat as a discrete entity.

Basic syntactical elements such as for, if, and while statements will probably be familiar to most readers who have had experience with another computer language. I will show you a few examples of these kinds of statements. Once again, if they make no sense to you, don't worry, as I will describe these kinds of statements in more depth in the next chapter.

Consider the following statement:

```
if (x == 1)
  i = 2;
```

The code shown here is an if statement. It is one complete statement, even though it appears on two lines.

Consider the following code:

```
while (x < 5)
  x++;
```

Again, this is one single statement, even though it appears on two lines. For now, it is not important that you understand what the statement means or how it works, but only that you recognize it as a statement. The reason you know it is a statement is that it ends with a semicolon.

Consider this statement:

```
if (a > b)
  b = 0;
else
  a = 0;
```

This is an example of a single statement that consists of two parts, an if statement and an else clause. It happens that the code up to the first semicolon can stand on its own as a single statement. The code in the else clause cannot stand on its own; it makes sense only when taken as part of the larger statement. Again, it is not important that you understand what the statement means, only that you see that some statements work this way.

The reason the else clause is not a statement is that it will not stand on its own without the support of the main body of the if statement itself. Statements need to have a certain autonomy, or they are not really statements. It is, to revive the analogy used earlier, the same principle we find in sentences. A sentence represents a whole thought. In the same way, a statement represents a complete autonomous chunk of code, except for the missing declarations or possible references in the statement to other functions or objects.

NOTE: At this point you can begin to grasp why it is that statements are hard to define and understand as anything other than a list of syntactical elements such as I presented at the beginning of this chapter. You could justifiably say at this point: "Hey, Charlie, you just told us that statements end with a semicolon, yet now you are saying that here is an example of something that ends with a semicolon that is not a statement." If you look back, you will see that my definition is actually qualified by the word "usually," but nonetheless, it is frustrating to find these exceptions to such a nice clean rule. It happens that the vast majority of the time my rule does hold, and I believe it gives you a place to start when trying to find the statements in your code. In some languages, the if statement shown here would not include a semicolon after the line b = 0. These languages argue that the statement is not over yet, and so no semicolon should be inserted.

Consider the following method:

```
int foo()
{
  return 2;
}
```

The single line of code in this method, return 2, is a full statement. It is known, naturally enough, as a *return statement*. There are many other statements of this type, such as the break statement and the continue statement. (Again, my point here is not to try to define return statements or break statements, but only to show them to you as examples of the kind of code that is called a statement.) In this case, you can recognize the piece of code as a statement in part from the presence of the semicolon and simply memorizing the fact that the keyword return is part of a statement. (I would not necessarily bother trying to memorize facts like that but simply be guided by the general rule about semicolons instead.)

Compound Statements

Here is another type of statement called a compound statement:

```
{
   int a, b, c;
   c = a + b;
   double b = a * c;
}
```

In this example there are several statements inside one set of curly braces. Each individual statement is a full statement, but all of them together are part of a compound statement, or block statement, as it is sometimes called. The block statement is defined by a set of matching curly braces.

Note that the declaration int a, b, c; is itself a statement. It is called a local variable declaration statement. The second statement in the compound statement is a simple assignment statement. The last statement is both an assignment statement and a declaration statement.

Language lawyers take justifiable delight in odd cases, such as the *empty statement*, which consists of a single semicolon with nothing attached to it. I won't, however, try to pursue this subject any further, as we don't really need such a technical definition of statements in order to use the term in this book. All I'm really trying to do is give you a reasonably usable working definition of the term and enough examples so that you will have some idea of what I'm talking about when I use the word "statement."

Once again, we can follow two very loosely defined rules: Most statements end with a semicolon or else they are contained between two matching curly braces. That definition is not technical enough to pass muster with a language lawyer, but it should help you get a general feeling for the term. A more technical definition might simply end up listing all the possible kinds of statements, such as assignment statements, if statements, while statements, switch statements, empty statements, etc. Eventually, you might want to memorize such a list of statements, but you don't need that degree of rigor while you are still just getting a feeling for how the language works.

Expressions

Expressions are a bit more abstract than statements, but ultimately I think they are easier to understand. This is largely due to the fact that it is easier to find rules that pin down exactly what an expression does.

Expressions yield results; that is, they return some kind of value. Most expressions involve at least one operator.

Speaking more generally, one can say that expressions are usually smaller than statements, and in fact, they are often subsets of statements. It is not true, however, that all expressions need to be a subset of a statement. In short, there is something known as an expression statement. It is simultaneously both an expression and a statement.

Here are a few examples of expressions:

```
a + b;          // Add a + b to yield a result
doSomething();  // Method invocation
```

The first expression shown above will not stand on its own. Like all expressions, it yields a result. Language lawyers will sometimes call this *denoting* a variable or value. When we look at the statement c = a + b, the a + b part is known as an expression because it yields a result, which in this case is c. By itself, c is not an expression, since it yields no result. It is just a code fragment.

The second example is a method invocation: doSomething(). It might appear that this is not an expression, since it does not appear to yield a result. It is just a method call. Most methods, however, return a value. Even if the method doSomething is declared to be of type void, calling it is still considered an expression, since it yields the type void. In Pascal, a procedure "yields the type void." In VB, a sub usually yields the type void. In C++ or Java, there is no such thing as a procedure or a sub, and they have functions or methods instead. All methods in Java either return a type such as an int or return nothing, which means they return the type void.

Here is a function that returns int:

```
int foo()
{
  return 2;
}
```

Here is a function that returns void:

```
void foo()
{
  int a, b, c;
  c = a + b;
}
```

A simple call to a method of type void or a method that returns a value is called an *expression statement*. It is both an expression and a statement at the same time. The method itself is not an expression; it is only the call to the method that is an expression. It fits the definition of an expression because a call to a method yields a result — the only difficulty here is simply understanding that the result returned is sometimes of type void.

If this last bit makes little sense to you, I would not worry. There are more important things to think about if you are new to the language. However, you should try to reach the point where you can at least understand that a + b is an expression because it yields a result.

In this section you have learned that expressions are syntactical elements in your code that return a value. It would be an oversimplification to say that the two simple examples I show in this chapter embody all you need to know about expressions, but they do in fact capture many of the key points.

At this stage you hopefully have a general sense of what statements and expressions are all about. A full understanding of these terms will probably only become clear as you read the next few chapters. However, the explanations I've given here should get you started down the road to comprehending expressions and statements.

Keywords

All of this discussion of expressions and statements is meant merely to set the scene for the next chapters, such as the one on operators, Chapter 11. However, I want to get one more topic out of the way before closing this short chapter. In particular, I want to talk briefly about keywords. This subject is not as intimately connected to understanding operators as the subject of statements and expressions, but it is nonetheless good to understand this concept before talking in too much depth about the syntax of a language. Unlike statements and expressions, keywords are very simple to understand.

Every language has a certain number of keywords. These are words that the language uses for its own purposes. For instance, the simple types are all designated by keywords such as char, int, long, etc. These words are reserved for the language itself, so you cannot use keywords as variable names. Keywords cannot be used as identifiers that you create for your own use in your programs.

The following declarations are illegal:

```
int return;
int void;
int else;
long public;
short int;
```

The problem with all of these declarations is that they declare variables with names that are keywords — return, void, else, public, and int.

The following declarations are legal:

```
int i;
int numHouses;
long acornCount;
String myNameString;
```

These statement declarations are legal because the variable names are not keywords. In particular, the identifiers numHouses, acornCount, and myNameString are not keywords.

There is no good way to figure out whether or not a word is a keyword. You simply have to memorize the keywords or else look them up in the online help. It is not, however, really necessary to memorize all the keywords in the language. Instead, you are probably okay if you simply understand what keywords are so that you can recognize what the compiler is complaining about if you accidentally try to use a keyword as a variable name. In particular, misusing a keyword will probably get you an error about "malformed declarations." If you see that error, one possible explanation for why you got it is simply that you are trying to use a keyword as a variable name.

Another way to spot a keyword is by watching the syntax highlighter. If a word appears in bold inside the JBuilder editor, it is probably a keyword.

The following is a list of the keywords in the Java language at the time JDK 1.2 shipped. More have been added since then. It is not important that you know what all the keywords mean but only that you know they exist, so you don't try to use them as variable names in your own programs.

abstract	default	goto*	operator*	synchronized
boolean	do	if	outer*	this
break	double	implements	package	throw
byte	else	import	private	throws
byvalue*	extends	inner*	protected	transient
case	false	instanceof	public	true
cast*	final	int	rest*	try
catch	finally	interface	return	var*
char	float	long	short	void
class	for	native	static	volatile
const*	future*	new	super	while
continue	generic*	null	switch	

The words with an asterisk after them are reserved but not currently in use. For instance, there is no goto statement in Java, but the word is reserved nonetheless on the odd chance that it might be required later.

Assertions

Assertions are a key new feature of JDK 1.4. They are discussed in Chapter 29, "The Debugger."

Summary

In this chapter you have learned about statements, expressions, and keywords.

Statements are the building blocks out of which you assemble programs. You saw that there are two kinds of statements, simple statements and compound statements. Simple statements express a complete thought, much like a sentence in a piece of prose. You also saw that the best way to get a more precise definition of statements is simply to list all the possible statements available in the Java language, such as assignment statements, if statements, while statements, etc. Compound statements contain a list of simple statements set off between two matching curly braces.

Expressions return a value. The only odd case is a method call that returns void. This is considered an expression since such a method can — if you are willing to stretch a bit — be considered as returning the type void. Most expressions are not complete thoughts but are instead parts of a statement. One exception to this rule is the expression statement. An example of an expression statement is the call to a method.

Keywords are nothing more than a list of words reserved for the use of the creators of the Java language. As such, keywords are not allowed as identifier names for the variables you declare in your programs. The only way to know for sure whether or not a word is a keyword is to look it up in the online help or memorize the list of all keywords. When using JBuilder, however, you can usually spot a keyword because it will be highlighted in bold.

This chapter has been a bit abstract, and you haven't really learned to write any new code by reading it. This material will, nevertheless, hopefully fill in some holes left in earlier discussions and lay the groundwork for the remaining chapters in this book.

Chapter 11

Looping, Operators, and Currency

Charlie Calvert

In this chapter you will learn how to work with while and for loops. In addition, I will show the math operators that govern basic operations such as addition, subtraction, multiplication, and division. These operators work more or less exactly like the operators that you saw in grade school math courses.

Material on working with floating-point numbers and currency is also included in this chapter, where you will learn about rounding errors and the BigDecimal type.

It's time now to forge ahead and see what actually lies in store for us. The MathOpsSimple, BigDecimalTest, and WhileLoops example programs shown in this chapter are found on the CD and on www.elvenware.com. Another example program called floatops, found on the CD, includes a lengthy HTML document that expands on some of the material found in this chapter.

Loops

As you learned in the previous chapter, for loops and while loops are both statements. Computer programs are assembled out of statements much as houses are made out of bricks or novels out of sentences. There are several kinds of important statements, but two of the most important of all are the for loop and while loop. Not much code could be written without these essential elements.

Both for loops and while loops allow the programmer to repeat a certain block of code multiple times. In short, loops are all about repetition.

Repetition is a bit of a dirty word for most people. We usually don't like to be involved in repetition. For instance, many repetitious jobs are considered unattractive, and everyone hated the repetition that was involved in certain kinds of schoolwork.

It happens, however, that many creative acts are repetitious. As a tree grows, it continues to do the same thing over and over and over again, slowly adding bulk to its size. Music also involves a great deal of repetition, with certain chord patterns or rhythmic structures being repeated numerous times. This is true even in relatively sophisticated forms of musical expression, such as jazz or a piece by J.S. Bach.

Computers allow us to take some of the strain out of repetition by automating it. In particular, the for and while statements allow us to automate many repetitious acts.

for Loops

for loops in Java look almost exactly like for loops in C/C++. The syntax is the same, and their semantic significance is the same.

Consider the following simple piece of code:

```
int j;

for (int i = 0; i < 10; i++)
{
  j = (i * i) + 1;
}
```

This code declares two integers, one called j and the other called i. Notice that i is declared inside the for statement itself. This is perfectly legal and is in fact considered the proper way to name the *control variable* in a for loop.

This loop says that it will repeat ten times, incrementing the variable i each time the repetition occurs. Thus, the variable i will start out as 0 and will be incremented ten times, until it reaches the value 9. At that point the loop will end. The code that increments the variable i looks like this: i++. I will talk about the effect of the ++ unary operator later in this text.

NOTE: The variable i has scope only within the for loop. Outside of the loop, Java will claim complete ignorance of its existence:

```
int j;

for (int i = 0; i < 10; i++)
{
  j = (i * i) + 1;
}

j = i; // No good. The variable i does not exist out here.
```

You should also notice the curly braces around the heart of the for loop. They are not necessary in a for statement with a body that is one line long. Nevertheless, I consider it good programming practice to include them. Here is an example of what the loop would look like without them:

```
for (int i = 0; i < 10; i++)
  j = (i * i) + 1;
```

Here is a pseudocode description of the syntax for the for loop:

```
for (initialization; test; increment)
  statement
```

Looking back at our example, you can see that the code fragment int i = 0 is the initialization, the test or condition is i < 10, and the increment looks like this: i++. The increment section is poorly named, as you can either increment or decrement a variable in this part of your code.

In the general form of the for statement shown here, you might want to call the first line the header and the second line the body. Thus, the body consists of the part called *statement*.

In the body of the for statement, you can have one or more statements, which are usually set off by curly braces. As mentioned earlier, you need not include the curly braces if you only include one statement in the iteration portion of the loop.

When a for loop is executed, the initialization expression is processed first. Furthermore, it is processed only one time. The test, or condition part of the statement, is then examined. If this expression evaluates to true, execution of the for loop continues; if not, the code exits the loop. At this stage, the body of the statement is executed. Whether the increment element is executed before or after the body depends a bit on the way it is written.

Here is an example of a for loop that you can try out in a JBuilder application:

```
void jButton1_actionPerformed(ActionEvent e)
{
  int j;
  for (int i = 0; i < 10; i++)
  {
    j = (i * i) + 1;
    jComboBox1.addItem(Integer.toString(j));
  }
}
```

To run this code, you need to first open up JBuilder, create an application as explained in Chapter 3, and then drop a button and a combo box on the main form. If you leave the JComboBox with its default name, you can create an event handler for the button that looks exactly like the one shown here. As you recall, you can create an event handler by going into design mode, selecting the JButton, turning to the Events page in the Inspector, selecting the actionPerformed event, and pressing the Enter key.

It happens that you can do all sorts of insane things with for loops. This license to be crazy occurs in large part because of the extreme syntactical flexibility of Java language's for loop architecture. For instance, the following two examples are perfectly legal:

```
for (;;)
for (int x=3, y=10; x < 100; x++, y-=3)
```

The first example starts an infinite loop, which you can exit by using a break or return statement:

```
int x = 3;
for (;;)
{
  x++;
  if (x > 5)
    break;
}
```

This code is not, I'll confess, particularly sensible, but it is legal. It says, in effect, break out of this for loop only when x is larger than 5. There are simpler ways to write this code. Indeed, I very rarely find a need for such esoteric constructs. That is, however, merely a matter of personal taste, and I have met many excellent programmers who clearly luxuriate in the lush syntax made possible by the flexibility of the Java for statement. In general, I would say that this kind of flexibility is a boon to a small percentage of the most highly skilled and experienced programmers. For beginners, intermediate level programmers, programmers with only modest skill sets, and sensible people everywhere, it is probably little more than an invitation to trouble.

None of this is meant to imply that the basic syntax of the for statement is complex or difficult to understand. In fact, once you start to understand for loops, they are really quite remarkably simple beasts. But as simple as this syntax may be, it is nonetheless one of the fundamental engines that drives much of the software in use today. for loops are used everywhere in programming in almost every language. They are one of the cornerstones on which most computer languages are built.

There are additional examples of for loops spread throughout much of the remaining code in this chapter. Before we get to that code, however, I want to take a moment to discuss while loops.

while Loops

Like the for loop, the while loop is a fairly simple, yet nonetheless remarkably powerful, syntactical construct. The general syntax for a while loop looks like this:

```
while (expression)
  statement
```

Here is an example while statement that you can compile inside of JBuilder:

```
void whileLoopBtn_actionPerformed(ActionEvent e)
{
  int i = 0;

  while (i < 10)
  {
    i++;
    jComboBox1.addItem(Integer.toString(i));
  }
}
```

This method begins by declaring a variable i. It then enters a while loop. The expression in the loop is evaluated. If it evaluates to true, the body of the loop is executed. After execution, the expression is again evaluated, and the code in the body of the loop will be executed again, so long as the expression yields true. If it yields false, the program breaks out of the while loop and the body of code in the loop is skipped. Note that you must explicitly increment the variable i. If you do not increment the control variable in this example, the program will enter an infinite loop.

NOTE: In the old days of Turbo Pascal, there was an entry in the index for that product's documentation that read something like "infinite loop: see loop, infinite." Needless to say, if you looked up "loop, infinite," it said "see infinite loop." This is a fine example of hacker humor and is also as good an explanation of infinite loops as one is ever likely to need. In short, the writers of the documentation had found a way to fully document a relatively complex subject without ever asking the reader to leave the index. As far as I know, this is the only example I know of where the index of a book performs the same task as the text of a book without needing to refer to the text of the book itself!

Java also provides a do-while loop, which is the opposite of the while loop.

```
do
{
  i--;
  jComboBox1.addItem(Integer.toString(i));
}
while(i > 0);
```

The do-while statement differs from the while statement because it will be executed at least once, regardless of the initial value of the variable i. In short, if you want to be sure a loop is executed at least once, use the do-while syntax; otherwise, use the while syntax.

Compulsive optimizers might like to rewrite the previous statement in this form:

```
do
{
  jComboBox1.addItem(Integer.toString(i));
}
while(i-- > 0);
```

Whether or not this code executes any more quickly than the code in the previous example, I do not know. However, it is a valid alternative to the first example.

It is perhaps interesting to note that the following code does something slightly different than the code in the two previous examples:

```
do
{
  jComboBox1.addItem(Integer.toString(i));
}
while(--i > 0);
```

The code in this example will count down to one and then break out of the loop. The code in the previous example counts down to zero before breaking out of the loop. The difference between the two examples is the use of the -- operator. In the first case, the variable is decremented after the boolean expression in the while loop is evaluated, and in the second case, it is decremented before the expression is evaluated. I say all this not to drive you crazy with nit-picking details, but to begin to change the focus of the text away from looping and onto the subject of operators and their usage in the Java language.

An example program on the CD called WhileLoops demonstrates how to use most of the code discussed so far in this chapter. Explanations of how to build programs like this are found in Part III: JBuilder Fundamentals. For now, I would just run the program and experiment with it a bit. You will have plenty of other chances to learn how to build a program like this in other sections of the book.

Understanding Math Operators

It is at last time to start exploring operators.

This section covers the basic math operators: +, –, *,%, and /. These are the operators used for addition, subtraction, multiplication, getting the remainder of a division, and simple division.

Name	Operator	Example
Addition	+	1 + 1
Subtraction	–	1 – 1
Multiplication	*	1 * 1
Division	/	1 / 1
Modulus	%	1 % 1

Note that you can think of the modulus operator as the remainder operator if you so wish. It returns the remainder of the division of two numbers. For instance, 10 % 3 yields 1. But I am getting ahead of myself, as I will explain much of this in detail as the rest of this chapter unfolds.

Using the Math Operators

The basic math operators are simple to use. For instance, here is how to add two numbers together:

```
int a = 10, b = 5; c;
c = a + b;
```

All this is more or less completely intuitive. In this particular case, it is perhaps more interesting to see how I show that code inside of a JBuilder application. In other words, it is not difficult to understand how the + operator works, but it takes a moment to explain how I demonstrate these simple math operators. The explanation is important because it demonstrates the string concatenation operator.

The example program for this section of the chapter is called MathOpsSimple. The output from the program looks like this:

```
addition
c = a + b
13 = 10 + 3
-----------
multiplication
c = a * b
30 = 10 * 3
-----------
subtraction
c = a - b
7 = 10 - 3
-----------
division
c = a / b
3 = 10 / 3
-----------
remainder (modulus)
c = a % b
1 = 10 % 3
-----------
```

To create this program, first create a new project called MathOpsSimple. Then create a new class using the **File | New Class** menu item, as shown in Figure 11-1. Notice that the class derives from java.lang.object, and it has a main method.

Fill in the class so that it looks like the source shown in Listing 11-1. This class relies on a second class that you will create called Adder. Thus, it harks back to the lessons on classes that we learned in Chapter 8.

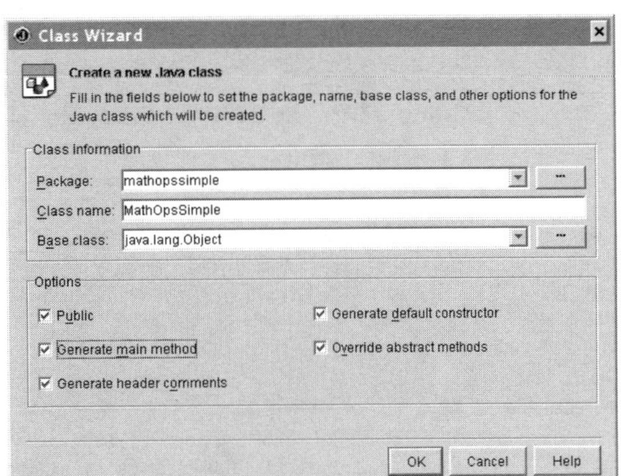

Figure 11-1: Creating the main class for the MathOpsSimple program

Listing 11-1: The main class for the MathOpsSimple program

```
package mathopssimple;

public class MathOpsSimple
{
      public static void main(String[] args)
      {
            int a = 10, b = 3;

            Adder adder = new Adder();
            adder.add(a,b);
            adder.multiply(a, b);
            adder.subtract(a, b);
            adder.divide(a, b);
            adder.modulus(a, b);
      }
}
```

Choose **File | New Class** again, and create a second class called **Adder**, as shown in Figure 11-2. This class also derives from java.lang.object, but it has no main method.

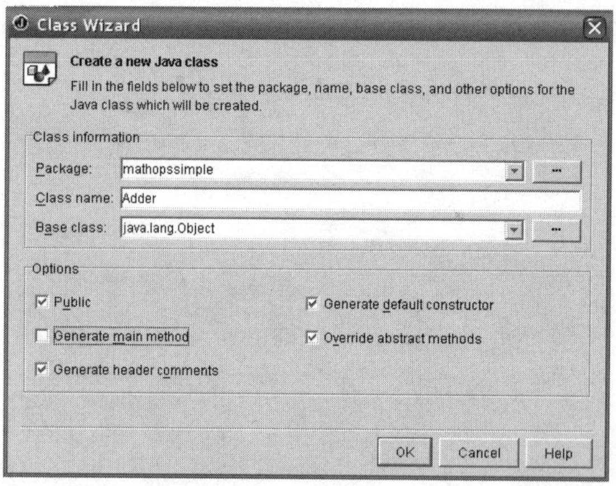

Figure 11-2: Create a second class called Adder with no main method that descends from java.lang.object.

Create code for this second class so that it looks like the class shown in Listing 11-2. This is the class that is called from the main class shown in Listing 11-1.

Listing 11-2: The code for the Adder class performs simple math.

```
package mathopssimple;

import java.awt.*;
import java.awt.event.*;
import javax.swing.*;

/**
 * <p>Title: </p>
 * <p>Description: </p>
 * <p>Copyright: Copyright (c) 2002</p>
 * <p>Company: </p>
 * @author unascribed
```

```
 * @version 1.0
 */

public class Adder extends JFrame
{
      private void addSpace(String opName)
      {
            System.out.println("-----------");
            System.out.println(opName);
      }

      void add(int a, int b)
      {
            int c;
            addSpace("addition");
            System.out.println("c = a + b");
            c = a + b;
            System.out.println(c + " = " + a + " + " + b);
      }

      void multiply(int a, int b)
      {
            int c;
            addSpace("multiplication");
            System.out.println("c = a * b");
            c = a * b;
            System.out.println(c + " = " + a + " * " + b);
      }

      public void divide(int a, int b)
      {
            int c;
            addSpace("division");
            System.out.println("c = a / b");
            c = a / b;
            System.out.println(c + " = " + a + " / " + b);
      }

      public void modulus(int a, int b)
      {
            int c;
            addSpace("remainder (modulus)");
            System.out.println("c = a % b");
            c = a % b;
            System.out.println(c + " = " + a + " % " + b);
      }

      public void subtract(int a, int b)
      {
            int c;
            addSpace("subtraction");
```

```
            System.out.println("c = a - b");
            c = a - b;
            System.out.println(c + " = " + a + " - " + b);
        }
}
```

The add method in the Adder class looks like this:

```
void add(int a, int b)
{
        int c;
        addSpace("addition");
        System.out.println("c = a + b");
        c = a + b;
        System.out.println(c + " = " + a + " + " + b);
}
```

The code in this method takes two variables of type integer. It declares a local variable of type int called c. The first real code in the method calls a method named addSpace:

```
private void addSpace(String opName)
{
        System.out.println("-----------");
        System.out.println(opName);
}
```

I have added this method to the program in order to provide some spacing between the elements that I print to standard out using the Java System.out.println method.

The addSpace method is very simple. It merely prints out a dotted line and then whatever string you pass to the method. You will find that I call this method over and over. If you don't like the output that this program produces, you can change this one method, and those changes will be reflected in each part of the program that calls this method.

The code in this method gets called from many different places in this program. I could have simply hard-coded these strings into each of those locations. Instead, I opted to have them call this method. Now, if I change the way this one method works, all the methods that call it will behave differently, in that they will print out data to the list box in a new way. If I had not done things this way, I would have had to make changes to each method just to change the way they wrote the separator that divided them from the previous output in the list box. Chapter 22, "Modularity," discusses this point in more detail.

After calling the addSpace method, the program next displays for the user the code that is about to be executed:

```
System.out.println("c = a + b");
```

The final step is to perform the actual math operation and show the user the values that were actually added together and their result:

```
c = a + b;
System.out.println(c + " = " + a + " + " + b);
```

Notice the last line of code. It "strings" the variables and quoted strings together into a single string by using the + operator. The relevant code starts by listing the variable c, which is, by this time, set to 13. Then I concatenate onto that value the string " = ". Doing this yields the output "13 = ", which is indeed what gets printed in the list box. I then use the plus operator to concatenate the value of a to the string and a simple string that looks like this: " + ". After doing this, the result printed to the screen looks like this: "13 = 10 + ". The final step is to add in the value of b, so the string printed to the screen looks like this: "13 = 10 + 3". You can look at Figures 11-3 and 11-4, or run the program for yourself, to confirm this value for the string.

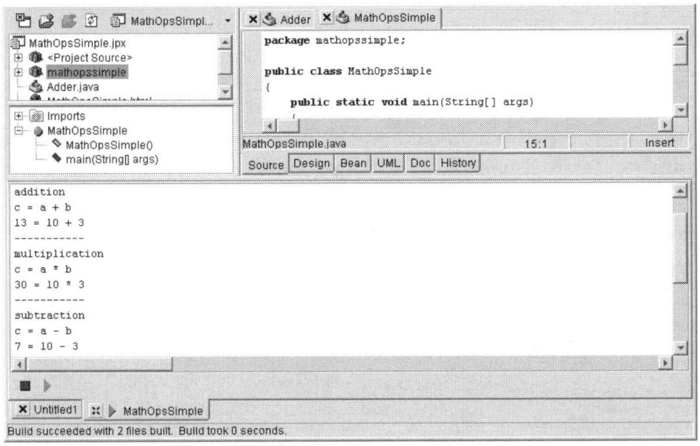

Figure 11-3: The output for a run of the MathOpsSimple program appears in the message window at the bottom of the IDE.

In the previous paragraph I show two different uses for the plus operator. In one case I am using it for addition, and in another case I am using it to concatenate two strings together. You have to look at the context in which the + operator is used in order to understand whether it is meant to be an addition operator or a string concatenation operator.

The code shown here is complicated further by the fact that the raw variables a, b, and c are being promoted to strings automatically. This is an artifact of the way the String class is handled.

In practice, behind the scenes, it involves the use of another class called a StringBuffer. The actual code that gets executed looks like this:

```
x = new StringBuffer().append("15").append(" = ").
      append("10").append(" + ").append(5).toString();
```

Multiplication Operators and Integers

The hard part of this section of the text is behind us. Now we can look at another example, say, one for multiplication, and understand it very quickly:

```
void multiply(int a, int b)
{
      int c;
      addSpace("multiplication");
      System.out.println("c = a * b");
      c = a * b;
      System.out.println(c + " = " + a + " * " + b);
}
```

As in the previous example, the code shown here begins by declaring some variables and initializing them to simple integer values. The method then calls the addSpace method, shows the user what operation is about to take place, performs the operation, and displays the results of the operation to the user. Again, the only really tricky code here is the lengthy string concatenation that shows the values “30 = 10 * 3” to the user.

Here is the code demonstrating how to divide two integer values in Java:

```
public void divide(int a, int b)
{
        int c;
        addSpace("division");
        System.out.println("c = a / b");
        c = a / b;
        System.out.println(c + " = " + a + " / " + b);
}
```

This code divides the number 10 by 3, which yields a result of 3. Any remainder is thrown away by the operation.

Here is the code that shows how to work with the modulus operator:

```
public void modulus(int a, int b)
{
        int c;
        addSpace("remainder (modulus)");
        System.out.println("c = a % b");
        c = a % b;
        System.out.println(c + " = " + a + " % " + b);
}
```

The modulus operator is the opposite of the division operator: It returns the remainder of a division operation. The expression 10 / 3 yields 3, and the expression 10 % 3 yields 1, since 10 divided by 3 yields 3 with 1 left over. The expression 10 % 3 is usually pronounced 10 mod 3 or 10 modulus 3. My preference is the first of the two options.

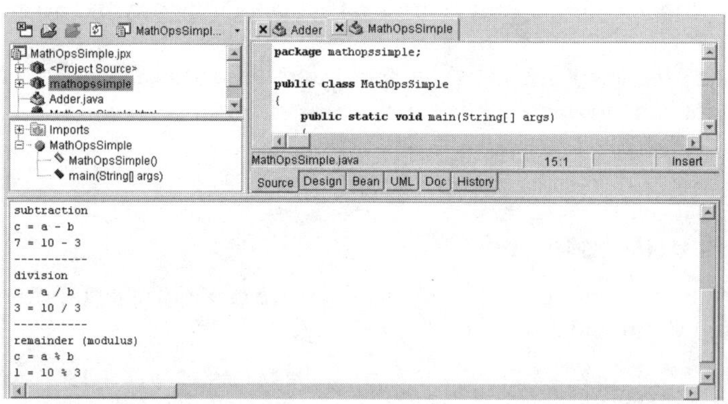

Figure 11-4: Here you can see the output for the division and modulus methods in the MathOpsSimple program.

At this stage you should have a fairly good grasp on the simple subject of using the basic math operators with integers and the + operator to concatenate strings. The next section, sensibly enough, shows how to work with math operators and floating-point numbers.

Floating-Point Operations and Accuracy

It is probably worth emphasizing that floating-point addition, subtraction, multiplication, and division on computers is not a precise science. If you assign a variable of type float to the value .05 and add it to itself three times, the result is not necessarily going to be .15. In fact, it is highly unlikely that you will get precisely that number. Instead, you will probably return a value that is close to that value but not exactly right on the money.

Consider the following code:

```
double a = 0.05;
double b = 0;
for (x = 0; x < 5; x++)
{
  b = b + a;
  jComboBox1.addItem(Double.toString(b));
}
```

On my computer, it produces these results:

```
0.05
0.1
0.15000000000000002
0.2
0.25
```

Though it is a small error, the third item in this list is nonetheless not entirely accurate. The error, as you can see, is so small that it's virtually meaningless to most of us, yet it is an error. That's not a problem with Java; that's just the way it goes when you use floating-point types on a computer. As a result, you should convert your dollar values to pennies and use integer values or a specially prepared set of tools if you want to use a computer to track money.

Floating-Point Types and Money: BigDecimal

Another solution to the problems with money and floating-point types discussed in the last section is the java.math.BigDecimal type. Consider the following code:

```
import java.math.*;

      void jButton1_actionPerformed(ActionEvent e)
      {
            BigDecimal a = new BigDecimal(0.05);
            BigDecimal b = new BigDecimal(0.0);
            for (int x = 0; x < 25; x++)
            {
              b = b.add(a);
              b = b.setScale(2, BigDecimal.ROUND_HALF_EVEN);
              System.out.println(b.toString());
            }
      }
```

Notice the import statement included in this code fragment. Notice also that there are two instances of the BigDecimal type used in this method. I use their constructors to initialize these values.

The BigDecimal type has methods like add, divide, multiply, abs, timesTenToThe, and compareTo for performing actual operations with these types. In other words, you don't use operators with these types. Instead, you call methods like the add routine shown in this code fragment. The call to setScale defines how many decimal places you want to preserve and how you want to handle rounding values up and down. The rounding constants include:

```
ROUND_UP
ROUND_DOWN
ROUND_CEILING
ROUND_FLOOR
ROUND_HALF_UP
ROUND_HALF_DOWN
ROUND_HALF_EVEN
ROUND_UNNECESSARY
```

The code shown in this example produces the following output:

```
0.05
0.10
0.15
0.20
0.25
0.30
0.35
0.40
0.45
0.50
0.55
0.60
0.65
0.70
0.75
0.80
0.85
0.90
0.95
1.00
1.05
1.10
1.15
1.20
1.25
```

Ah. That's more like it. For more information, see the "Representing Currencies" tech tip on the Sun site. At the time of publication, it could be found here: http://developer.java.sun.com/developer/JDCTechTips/2002/tt0409.html#tip2.

This tip includes an explanation of the handy Currency type that is part of JDK 1.4.0.

A program called BigDecimalTest on the CD gives you a working example of how to use this code. Again, you will have plenty of chances to build programs like this in other parts of the book. For now, you might simply run the program and experiment with it.

NOTE: Another type called BigInteger can be used for working very accurately with large numbers.

Review of Promoting and Converting Types

We are nearly at the end of this long chapter, but before closing, I'm going to review some material covered in the previous chapters. As you recall, math operators, as a rule, preserve the type that you are using. If you use integers in your code, you will get an integer as a result:

```
int b, c;              // declare integers
int  a = b + c;        // result will be an integer
```

Conversely, if you declared all your variables as a double, you would get a double as a result.

If you use both a double and an int in an expression, the result of a basic math operation will be a double.

```
int a;
double b;
double c = a + b;
```

If you tried to do things the other way around, you would get an error:

```
int a;
double b;
int c = a + b;
```

In particular, the attempt to assign the addition of a double and an integer to an integer would give you a loss of precision error. You can force the compiler to cooperate by using a typecast:

```
int a;
double b;
int c = (int)(a + b);
```

What we are really doing here is telling the compiler to ignore the rule and believe that we know what we are doing. This is not a figure of speech; it is literally what we are saying to the compiler. The code says: "I know you would normally complain about this kind of error, but I know what I'm doing, trust me!"

To sum up: If you want to assign a smaller type to a larger type, you must use a typecast. If you use two different types in an expression, the result will be at least as large as the larger of the two types.

If you add two bytes, two shorts, or some combination of bytes and shorts together, the result will be promoted to an int. This is done in part to ensure that there is no loss of information when the operation is performed. In particular, you don't want to overflow the bounds of the type that receives the result of the expression.

Assignment Operators

Another type of operator is the assignment operator, which looks like this: =. We have seen many examples of using the assignment operator throughout this text. Its use is entirely intuitive and needs no commentary.

Consider this code, which you saw earlier in this chapter:

```
double a = 0.05;
double b = 0;
for (x = 0; x < 5; x++)
{
```

Part II

```
        b = b + a;
        jComboBox1.addItem(Double.toString(b));
    }
```

Without changing its meaning, it can be altered to look like this:

```
double a = 0.05;
double b = 0;
for (int x = 0; x < 5; x++)
{
  b += a;
  jComboBox1.addItem(Double.toString(b));
}
```

This code uses the standard assignment operator in the first few statements, but in the midst of the for loop, it uses the += operator. The += operator is just a shorthand way of b = b + a. In other words, there is no significant difference between writing b = b + a and writing b += a. Other operators of this type include *=, /=, %=, and –=.

There is no particular reason, other than peer pressure, to use either the a = a + 1 or the a += 1 syntax. It all amounts to the same thing, and you can use the coding style that best suits your tastes.

These kinds of shorthand assignment operators are inherited directly from the C/C++ language. Once upon a time, compiler writers found it simpler to optimize code written in the second style, but those days are long gone. Code of either type now executes exactly the same.

Summary

Quite a bit of material was covered in this chapter. In particular, you saw how to work with for statements, while statements, and do-while statements.

The text then explored the subject of basic math operators as they behave when working with both floating-point numbers and integers. You also got a good look at the string concatenation operator.

You saw how to work with pre and post increment and decrement operators, which allow you to write code that looks like this: i++, ––j. I also briefly discussed assignment operators.

An example program, called floatops, found on the CD, includes a lengthy HTML document that expands on some of the material found in this chapter.

Part III

JBuilder Fundamentals

Chapter 12

Layout Managers

Margie and Charlie Calvert

This chapter tackles the complicated but very important world of layout managers. Layout managers dictate much about the appearance of a Java program at run time. The purpose of this chapter is to first explain layouts and then show how JBuilder makes it easy for you to use them.

The primary rationale for layout managers stems from the cross-platform nature of Java. Code meant to run on many different platforms can make very few assumptions about how a window will behave.

In a product like Delphi or Visual Basic, components are usually placed at specific x and y coordinates on a form. In Java, components are instead placed in relationship to one another. The various layout managers help you decide the nature of the relationships between the components.

Describing the relationship between controls provides more flexibility than specifying the coordinates of controls. For instance, if the coordinate system is radically different on one platform than it is on another platform, you have a problem if you have used coordinates to describe the position of components. However, if you say that one component is above, to the right of, or 30 percent bigger than another component, you have a system that can be made portable.

There are many layout managers, and they operate by defining general rules for the placement and sizing of components. In several example programs shown so far in this book, the main panel for a program had BorderLayout. You probably noticed that as you added components to the panel, they followed a pattern in their placement. In particular, they went to the North, South, East, West, or Center of the panel. This pattern was dictated by the layout manager, which is an object that determines how components are displayed.

Not all layout managers are as easy to understand as BorderLayout. Some, such as GridBagLayout, are extremely complicated. Others, such as GridLayout, are relatively straightforward, as long as you understand a few simple tricks. Many of them lie somewhere in between.

Layout Theory

Before discussing the details of how layouts work, it is probably helpful to begin with a little theory. If you understand something of the context in which layouts exist, you should find the whole process of working with them greatly simplified.

Some Theory on Containers

Layouts live inside of containers. A container is not only a technical term in Java, it is also the name of a specific class.

A *container* is a Java class that can contain other components. Examples of container classes are JPanel, JFrame, and JApplet.

If you have SE or Enterprise, go to the top of a typical Frame1 class for a standard JBuilder application. Right-click on the word **JFrame** in the class declaration. Choose **Find References** from the pop-up menu. You will see a great deal of information about the JFrame class. Included in this information is the list of the JFrame's ancestors. If you have JBuilder Personal, you can get the list of ancestors by moving your cursor to the word JFrame and pressing F1. In the Javadoc file that appears, you will see the following hierarchy:

```
java.lang.Object
  |
  +-java.awt.Component
        |
        +-java.awt.Container
              |
              +-java.awt.Window
                    |
                    +-java.awt.Frame
                          |
                          +-javax.swing.JFrame
```

One of the glories of Java is the sensible naming conventions used by the developers at Sun. Just a glance at this hierarchy tells you that a JFrame is a both a component and a container. These words are, in and of themselves, fairly informative. Nevertheless, it might be helpful to define them a bit more explicitly:

- A *component* is a visible class that can interact with a user.
- A *container* is a component that can contain other components.

A container has two very important methods called add and setLayout.

Use the container's add method to add a component to a container. Use the setLayout method to specify the layout for a particular container:

```
contentPane = (JPanel) this.getContentPane();
contentPane.setLayout(gridLayout1);
contentPane.add(jButton1, null);
```

The relationship between components, containers, and layouts is very clearly defined and very intuitive. This is what good design is all about.

GridBagLayout vs. the World

You will find that GridBagLayout is probably the most flexible of the layout managers. If you come to understand it, it can be used to solve almost any layout problem you might confront. It is, however, a bit tricky to use. Without a clever tool like JBuilder, many programmers have found it virtually impossible to use. I recommend taking the time to tackle this tool. Once you master it, you can quickly use it to create Java programs with the kind of look and feel that you want to create.

NOTE: GridBagLayout belongs to that elite set of Java components that are not deprecated but considered uncool by a very vocal set of critics. Other well-known members of this club are the Applet and JApplet classes. The arguments against GridBagLayout boil down to claiming that it is more trouble than it is worth. Though I too have struggled with the class at times, I have found that ultimately it is manageable. As a result, I will continue to treat it as a first-class component.

GridBagLayout can often be replaced by a combination of several different layouts. For instance, you can combine GridLayout or BorderLayout with one or two other layouts, such as BoxLayout, to produce a relatively flexible interface.

Needless to say, all of this requires some serious study on the developer's part. GridBagLayout is a challenge, and learning to use multiple different layouts requires that you master several different tools. I say this by way of preparing you for a task that is nontrivial but not overwhelmingly complicated.

JBuilder, of course, uses its visual tools to greatly simplify the task of creating well-designed layouts. If, however, you want to start coding your layouts by hand, you can simply switch to source mode and start typing. If you remember to enter all your layout code in the jbInit method, you can switch back and forth between design and source mode as often as you want.

A Layout is Just a Class

A layout manager is just a Java class. Each class implements a layout policy. The policy might be to place a component on a container's left side, top side, right side, bottom side, or center. Or you might want to arrange a set of components in a grid pattern, as if they were being placed on a chessboard. Or possibly you would want the components stacked from the top to the bottom of a container or laid out horizontally from left to right. Each of these schemes is called a *policy*, and *layout managers* are simply classes that implement these policies. For instance, BorderLayout implements the first of the policies described in this paragraph, the second is implemented by GridLayout, and the third by BoxLayout.

Since a layout is just a class, it is possible to add new layout managers to the language. Borland has done this in several cases. Some of these classes are very useful, such as VerticalFlowLayout.

Another Borland class, called XYLayout, behaves a lot like a Delphi or VB form. It does not, however, necessarily behave well in a cross-platform application. As a result, it is generally not very useful, except for mocking up the layout for a container. I suggest that you avoid XYLayout unless you know exactly why you are using it. Instead, read through this chapter and see if you can learn to do things the Java way. Layout managers take a bit of getting used to, but once you understand how they are put together, I think you will find them a usable technology.

Using Borland Classes in Your Program

I have frequently mentioned that the developers at Sun did not always think of all the tools that a developer of a program like JBuilder might need. In this chapter, that problem will quickly come to the fore. There are times when it is difficult to design even simple interfaces in the JBuilder designer using only the tools that Sun provides.

In some cases, Sun did not even provide bean wrappers for key layout classes such as BoxLayout. Without a bean wrapper for a class, it is difficult or impossible to use the class as a visual component that can be dragged from the component palette or easily manipulated by Borland's visual tools. In short, without a bean wrapper, you can't use the class inside a visual design tool such as JBuilder. Instead, you must switch to JBuilder's source mode and type in your code by hand. This takes away many of the important advantages supplied by JBuilder and forces you to work in much the way you would if you were using a simple text editor, such as Notepad or Kate.

Fortunately, Borland has come to the rescue with a few new layout managers. For instance, there is a bean wrapper for BoxLayout called BoxLayout2. In the previous section, I mentioned another useful Borland layout manager called VerticalFlowLayout.

These Borland classes are kept in a directory in the JBuilder install called redist. This is where Borland keeps files intended for redistribution with your application. It appears you can distribute them any way you want, as long as you don't include the actual source files. For instance, you can include all the Borland files in their native JAR file, called JBCL.jar. Or you can just link in individual class files either by themselves or by using the Archive Builder. The Archive Builder is described in Chapter 28, "Deploying Applets, Applications, and Java Executables."

NOTE: Please read the legal notices for yourself, and do not attempt to use this book as a legal guide. To learn more about the legal aspects of using Borland code in your program, read the license.html file that ships in the JBuilder root directory, and read the following file from the JBuilder 7 redist directory:

```
2. JBCL Redistributables
========================
For the purpose of the license(s) included with this product,
the redistributables for the JavaBeans Component Library (JBCL)
is defined as the jbcl.jar file in the /jbuilder6/redist directory,
and/or the individual files in that archive.

To the extent that you are allowed to redistribute these files under
the terms of your license, you may redistribute these classes in
any of the following formats:

a) As individual class files
b) As the entire jbcl.jar file
c) As class files included in your archive files, for example by
   use of the Archive Builder
```

My point here is that it is simple and easy to use the Borland classes in your programs. If you have further questions, go to forums.borland.com, and check out the newsgroup borland.public.jbuilder.jbcl.

This is the end of the theoretical part of this chapter. You are now ready to begin a study of the individual layout classes.

BorderLayout

This is purely a matter of taste, but for me, BorderLayout is the default layout manager of choice. It is easy to use and understand, and it is flexible enough to allow you to create reasonably logical layouts for test applications. Whenever I want to start dropping things on a container, with no sure feeling of where I am heading, I start out by asking the container to use BorderLayout.

Ultimately, however, BorderLayout will rarely be enough, in and of itself, to allow you to design a good-looking application. It is part of many applications and works well for test applications, but it usually comes up short as a single solution for any but the simplest applications. Nonetheless, it is indispensable, and all Java UI programmers should be comfortable with it.

The BorderLayout manager divides a visual component into five zones, as shown in Figure 12-1. You can create one zone in the Center and align others along the four edges. The edges are labeled North, South, East, and West. In Figure 12-1, jButton3 is in the North zone, jButton1 to the West, etc.

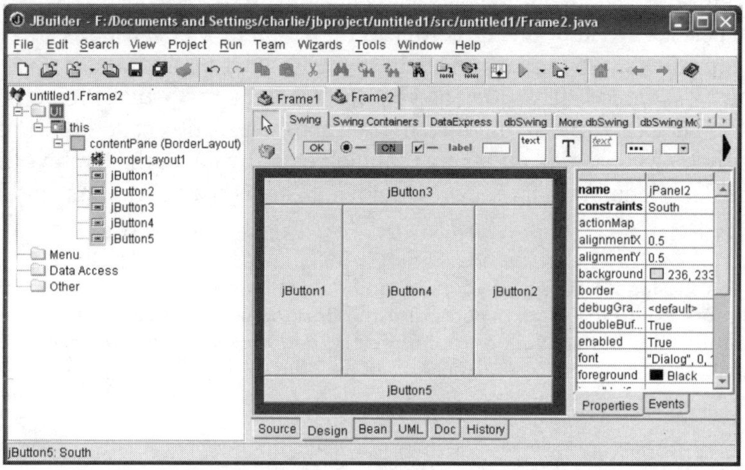

Figure 12-1: BorderLayout divides the screen into five zones labeled North, South, East, West, and Center. In this figure, each of the buttons occupies one of the zones.

BorderLayout is the default layout of the JPanel contentPane on which you drop your components when working with JFrame descendants. To get a feel for how this layout works, start a new default application and put Frame1 into design mode.

Add five JButtons to Frame1. The first component you place on the panel will be at the top of the UI designer. As you add buttons, they will illustrate the size and placement rules of BorderLayout as it functions inside JBuilder. Figure 12-1 shows the UI designer with five buttons in border layout.

NOTE: There are a couple of things that can go wrong when dropping components onto a BorderLayout.

If, by some odd chance, the components do not end up as you wish, try setting their constraints property to North, South, East, West, or Center, depending on your needs.

When you drop components that are also active containers onto a container, it is sometimes possible to drop one component on top of another, rather than on the underlying panel to which it should belong. For instance, if you drop five JPanels onto a JFrame, it is easy to make one a child of another JPanel rather than a child of the JFrame. To avoid this problem, try working in the structure pane rather than in the content pane. Just drag and drop the JPanel onto the place in the structure pane where you want them to appear. For me, this can be a more intuitive way to work with not only BorderLayout but many other layouts.

JButtons are also descendants of the Container class. They will not, however, act as containers by default inside of JBuilder. As a result, you can usually drop them onto the content pane rather than the structure pane. (You can, however, manually add one button to another button if you can ever think of a rationale for doing such a confusing thing to your users! But fortunately, JBuilder does not exhibit this behavior by default in the content pane.)

In Figure 12-1, notice that the structure pane shows Frame2, which is referenced as this. The sole child of Frame2 is the contentPane. All of the buttons, as well as the BorderLayout object, are all children of the contentPane. Becoming familiar with the way components look in the structure pane is one of the most important skills you can master if you want to become familiar with JBuilder.

Let's look at the code for Frame2. The source for this JFrame descendant is shown in Listing 12-1.

Listing 12-1: The source for a JFrame object with five buttons arranged on it

```
package untitled1;

import java.awt.*;
import java.awt.event.*;
import javax.swing.*;

public class Frame2 extends JFrame
{
    JPanel contentPane;
    BorderLayout borderLayout1 = new BorderLayout();
    JButton jButton1 = new JButton();
    JButton jButton2 = new JButton();
    JButton jButton3 = new JButton();
    JButton jButton4 = new JButton();
    JButton jButton5 = new JButton();

    //Construct the frame
    public Frame2()
    {
        enableEvents(AWTEvent.WINDOW_EVENT_MASK);
        try
        {
            jbInit();
        }
        catch(Exception e)
        {
            e.printStackTrace();
        }
    }

    //Component initialization
    private void jbInit() throws Exception
    {
        contentPane = (JPanel) this.getContentPane();
        contentPane.setLayout(borderLayout1);
        this.setSize(new Dimension(291, 227));
        this.setTitle("Frame Title");
        jButton1.setText("jButton1");
        jButton2.setText("jButton2");
        jButton3.setText("jButton3");
        jButton4.setText("jButton4");
        jButton5.setText("jButton5");
        contentPane.add(jButton1, BorderLayout.WEST);
        contentPane.add(jButton2, BorderLayout.EAST);
        contentPane.add(jButton3, BorderLayout.NORTH);
        contentPane.add(jButton4, BorderLayout.CENTER);
        contentPane.add(jButton5, BorderLayout.SOUTH);
    }
    //Overridden so we can exit when window is closed
    protected void processWindowEvent(WindowEvent e)
```

```
        {
            super.processWindowEvent(e);
            if (e.getID() == WindowEvent.WINDOW_CLOSING)
            {
                System.exit(0);
            }
        }
    }
```

Concentrate for a moment on the data for the Frame2 object:

```
public class Frame2 extends JFrame
{
    JPanel contentPane;
    BorderLayout borderLayout1 = new BorderLayout();
    JButton jButton1 = new JButton();
    JButton jButton2 = new JButton();
    JButton jButton3 = new JButton();
    JButton jButton4 = new JButton();
    JButton jButton5 = new JButton();
```

Here you can see each of the children for the JFrame. In reality, the contentPane ends up owning the layout and the buttons. This is hard to see in this part of the code, but you can see it in jbInit, and you can see it in the structure pane of Figure 12-1:

```
        contentPane.setLayout(borderLayout1);
        contentPane.add(jButton1, BorderLayout.WEST);
        contentPane.add(jButton2, BorderLayout.EAST);
        contentPane.add(jButton3, BorderLayout.NORTH);
        contentPane.add(jButton4, BorderLayout.CENTER);
        contentPane.add(jButton5, BorderLayout.SOUTH);
```

Remember that the contentPane is in turn owned by Frame1. As a result, these buttons are ultimately owned by the frame itself.

Look at jbInit for a moment, and see the simple Java statements generated by JBuilder when you dropped your components on Frame2. This is pretty much exactly the same code that any knowledgeable Java programmer would have created when designing an interface like that shown in Figure 12-1. It is the only reasonable way to design this kind of JFrame descendant.

You can, of course, tweak the source code itself if you want to change the layout of Frame2. However, it is usually simpler to make these kinds of changes in design mode. In particular, design mode has the ability to give you immediate feedback to confirm that the changes you are making are appropriate.

For instance, you can use the constraints property in the Inspector to choose the placement of your component, as shown in Figure 12-2. In BorderLayout, you can choose North, South, East, West, or Center as the constraint for placement. By changing the constraint for jButton1 to North, for instance, you will ensure that it displays along the top of the panel.

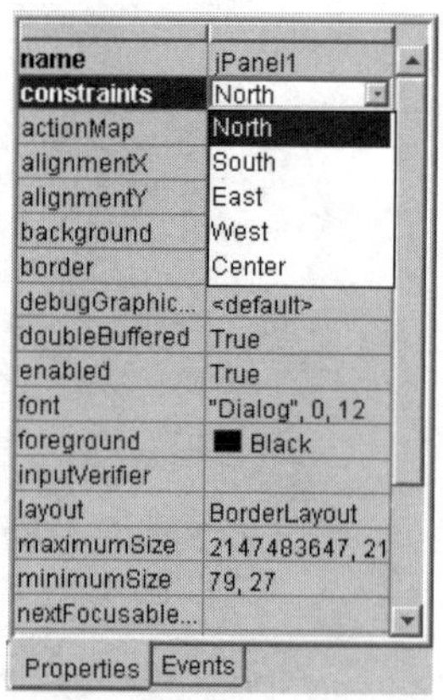

Figure 12-2: Set the button's constraints property in the Inspector.

GridLayout

GridLayout allows you to create a set of evenly spaced rows and columns arranged in a checkerboard pattern. The simplest GridLayout might be a rectangle divided evenly into two sections, a bit like a ping-pong table divided by a net. A more complex GridLayout might look like a chessboard.

In the Inspector, you can configure GridLayout by choosing the number of rows and the number of columns, as well as the horizontal and vertical gaps. This is a great layout to use when you need even spacing, such as when you are generating a keyboard display or a board for a game. It can also be useful for controlling components on a nested panel. Like the BorderLayout, it can often be used as the home on which other panels containing their own layouts will be placed.

Create a default JBuilder application and set the layout for Frame1 to **GridLayout**. Drop five or six buttons on Frame1. When you run your program, it should look something like what you see in Figure 12-3.

In design mode, select **gridLayout1** by clicking on it in the structure pane. Change the rows field from 1 to **2** and the columns field to **3**. Frame1 should now look like the image shown in Figure 12-4.

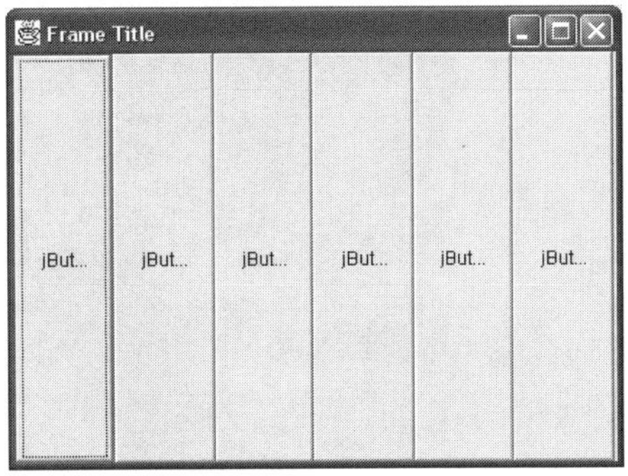

Figure 12-3: A GridLayout with one row and six columns

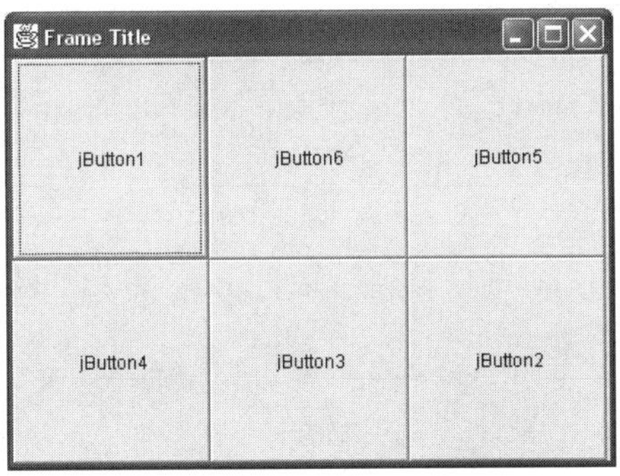

Figure 12-4: A GridLayout with two rows and three columns

The Inspector, shown in Figure 12-5, displays simple controls for setting the values used in GridLayout.

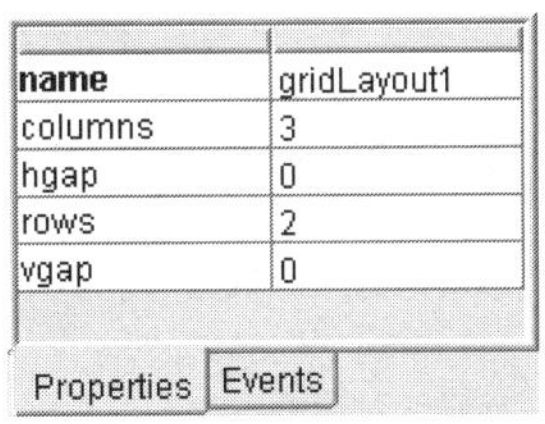

Figure 12-5: The Inspector displaying the fields of the GridLayout class

Listing 12-2 gives the source for the program shown in Figure 12-4.

Listing 12-2: The source for a simple program using GridLayout. A set of buttons is arranged in two rows and three columns.

```
package untitled1;

import java.awt.*;
import java.awt.event.*;
import javax.swing.*;
import java.applet.AppletContext;

public class Frame1 extends JFrame
{
```

```
JPanel contentPane;
JButton jButton1 = new JButton();
JButton jButton3 = new JButton();
JButton jButton4 = new JButton();
JButton jButton6 = new JButton();
JButton jButton2 = new JButton();
JButton jButton5 = new JButton();
GridLayout gridLayout1 = new GridLayout();

//Construct the frame
public Frame1()
{
    enableEvents(AWTEvent.WINDOW_EVENT_MASK);
    try
    {
        jbInit();
    }
    catch(Exception e)
    {
        e.printStackTrace();
    }
}

//Component initialization
private void jbInit() throws Exception
{
    contentPane = (JPanel) this.getContentPane();
    contentPane.setLayout(gridLayout1);
    gridLayout1.setColumns(3);
    gridLayout1.setRows(2);
    this.setSize(new Dimension(400, 300));
    this.setTitle("Frame Title");
    jButton1.setText("jButton1");
    jButton3.setText("jButton3");
    jButton4.setText("jButton4");
    jButton6.setText("jButton6");
    jButton2.setText("jButton2");
    jButton5.setText("jButton5");
    contentPane.add(jButton1, null);
    contentPane.add(jButton5, null);
    contentPane.add(jButton2, null);
    contentPane.add(jButton4, null);
    contentPane.add(jButton6, null);
    contentPane.add(jButton3, null);
}

//Overridden so we can exit when window is closed
protected void processWindowEvent(WindowEvent e)
{
    super.processWindowEvent(e);
    if (e.getID() == WindowEvent.WINDOW_CLOSING)
```

```
        {
            System.exit(0);
        }
    }
}
```

Here is the code that creates and sets up an instance of GridLayout:

```
GridLayout gridLayout1 = new GridLayout();
contentPane.setLayout(gridLayout1);
gridLayout1.setColumns(3);
gridLayout1.setRows(2);
```

As you can see, this is a very simple layout to use, even if you have to write out the code by hand. But using the JBuilder visual tools, the component becomes even easier to use. More importantly, you get visual feedback about your code instantly, as you make the changes in the designer.

NOTE: You may have noticed that I have been showing you essentially the same program over and over again, but with a different layout each time. This allows you to see the way a JFrame descendant looks with five or six buttons on its surface and one of various different layouts. Opening JBuilder and switching back and forth between these different layouts might help you get a sense of what it is they do. You should also try running the programs and resizing Frame1 just to see how the different layouts behave.

FlowLayout

FlowLayout is used as the default layout for JPanel instances. It is a simple layout. The first component you drop appears in the center on the top row. Add another component, and the two components you have dropped will be centered in the top row. If you add enough components, the components you are creating will wrap around to the center of a second row. You can configure the layout in various ways, such as setting the alignment to the right or left rather than in the center.

NOTE: When using JBuilder to work with FlowLayout in a JPanel, you may run across a strange anomaly. In particular, you may not be able to use the Inspector to see the properties of the default FlowLayout class used by the JPanel. To fix the problem, use the Inspector to make sure that the layout property is set to something like flowLayout1 and not to a string that looks like this: <FlowLayout>.

Here is a more in-depth explanation of the problem: When you first drop down a JPanel, the layout property in the Inspector will read <default layout>, and the words <FlowLayout> will appear in the structure pane. If you click on <FlowLayout> in the structure pane, nothing will happen in the Inspector. This is not good. To improve the situation, use the Inspector to drop down the list of items in the layout property. From the list, choose **FlowLayout**. Now the layout property in the Inspector will read FlowLayout, and you will see FlowLayout1 in the structure pane. When you select FlowLayout1 in the structure pane, you will see the properties of the object in the Inspector. I will discuss this issue in a bit more detail in the next section.

The components you place in FlowLayout will assume their natural size. For instance, if you drop a set of buttons onto a flow layout, the one with the longest caption will be the biggest and the others will be smaller. FlowLayout will not automatically make all the components conform to a single size.

To use FlowLayout, you can simply drop a JPanel on top of a JFrame descendant. Or, if you wish, you can set the layout for a Frame1 instance to FlowLayout instead of BorderLayout.

For our example, let's create a new application and focus Frame1. Make sure that the contentPane is selected in the structure pane. In the Inspector, click on the layout property and select **FlowLayout** in the drop-down list, as shown in Figure 12-6. Drop down five JButtons on Frame1.

You will now probably see four buttons arranged along the top of the panel, with one centered underneath them. Add four more buttons. The buttons will arrange themselves in rows, centered horizontally on the panel, as shown in Figure 12-7.

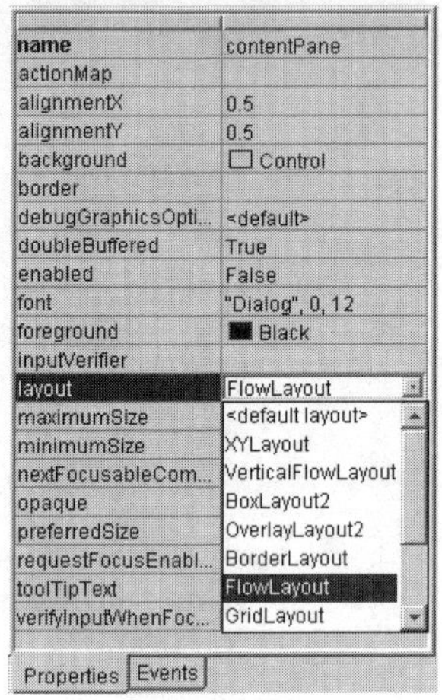

Figure 12-6: Choose FlowLayout in the Inspector.

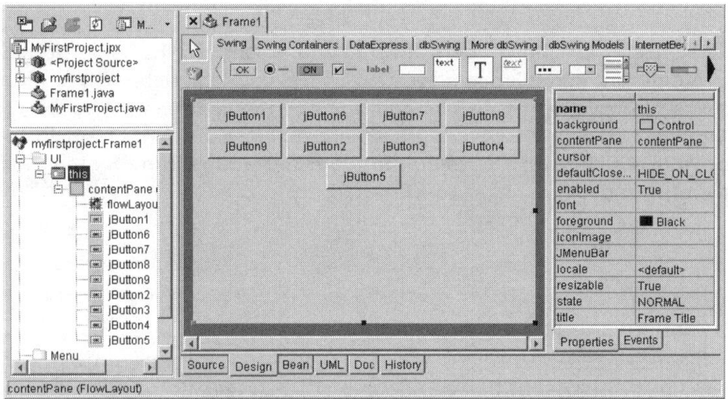

Figure 12-7: FlowLayout in JBuilder's UI designer

Click on **flowLayout1** in the structure pane to select it. The Inspector will shift focus to the flow layout object. Now you can use the Inspector to change the default alignment to left or right and adjust the horizontal and vertical gaps.

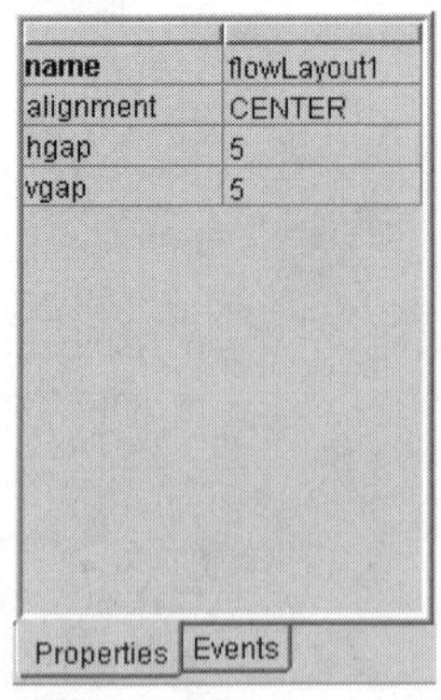

Figure 12-8: Choosing settings for FlowLayout

By playing with the settings of FlowLayout, you can create different looks for an interface such as a panel of buttons. The program in Figure 12-9 uses right alignment, a horizontal gap of 20, and a vertical gap of 30.

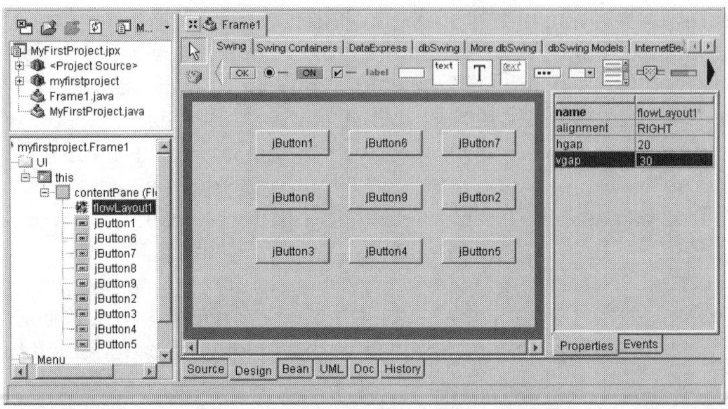

Figure 12-9: Button placement was adjusted using the Inspector.

Basic Dialog Look with FlowLayout

Now that you understand how FlowLayout works, let's take a quick look at how to use it to build a simple interface for a real-world application. The example program you are about to create, shown in Figure 12-10, is found in the program FlowLayoutButtons on the CD. This program will be recreated several different times in this chapter using a slightly different layout scheme each time.

Begin by creating a new application. On Frame 1, drop down two JPanels, one oriented in the center and the second oriented to the south. Drop two buttons on the JPanel that is oriented to the south. In the Inspector, change the background property of jPanel1 to LightGray.

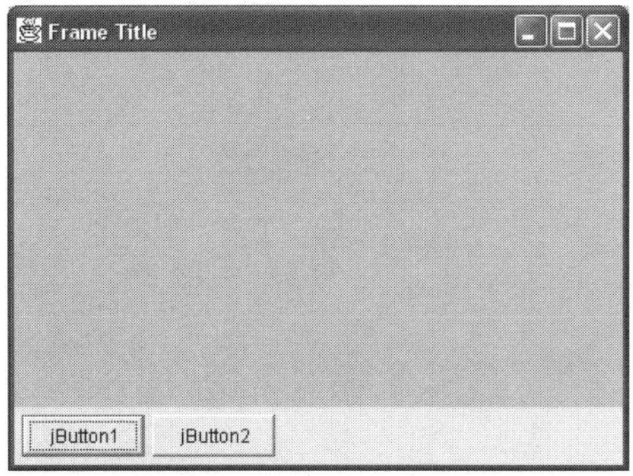

Figure 12-10: A simple layout with a wide display area and two buttons on the bottom left of the screen.

At this stage, the interface looks almost like the one shown in Figure 12-10. The only problem is that the buttons are displayed in the center of the second JPanel and not over to the left. To fix this problem, you need to take two steps:

1. Explicitly set the layout for jPanel2 (the one with the buttons on it) to **FlowLayout**. By default, it is set to the default layout, which happens to be FlowLayout. However, this is really just a variable declared at the top of FlowLayout.java and not an actual instance of FlowLayout. As a result, it will not display correctly in the Inspector. To get things to look right in the Inspector, you must explicitly set the layout property for the panel with the buttons on it to FlowLayout. When you are done, the layout property will look something like this: flowLayout1, and not like this: <FlowLayout>.
2. Set the alignment property for the FlowLayout to **LEFT**.

At this stage, you have things set up the way they appear in Figure 12-10. This is probably the simplest and cleanest way to achieve this particular look. The source for this program is shown in Listing 12-3.

Listing 12-3: The source for Frame1 from the FlowLayoutButtons program

```
package flowlayoutbuttons;

import java.awt.*;
import java.awt.event.*;
import javax.swing.*;

public class Frame1 extends JFrame
{
      JPanel contentPane;
      BorderLayout borderLayout1 = new BorderLayout();
      JPanel jPanel1 = new JPanel();
      JPanel jPanel2 = new JPanel();
      JButton jButton1 = new JButton();
      JButton jButton2 = new JButton();
      FlowLayout flowLayout1 = new FlowLayout();

      //Construct the frame
```

```
    public Frame1()
    {
        enableEvents(AWTEvent.WINDOW_EVENT_MASK);
        try
        {
            jbInit();
        }
        catch(Exception e)
        {
            e.printStackTrace();
        }
    }

    //Component initialization
    private void jbInit() throws Exception
    {
        contentPane = (JPanel) this.getContentPane();
        contentPane.setLayout(borderLayout1);
        this.setSize(new Dimension(400, 300));
        this.setTitle("Frame Title");
        jPanel1.setBackground(Color.lightGray);
        jButton1.setText("jButton1");
        jButton2.setText("jButton2");
        jPanel2.setLayout(flowLayout1);
        flowLayout1.setAlignment(FlowLayout.LEFT);
        contentPane.add(jPanel1,  BorderLayout.CENTER);
        contentPane.add(jPanel2,  BorderLayout.SOUTH);
        jPanel2.add(jButton1, null);
        jPanel2.add(jButton2, null);
    }

    //Overridden so we can exit when window is closed
    protected void processWindowEvent(WindowEvent e)
    {
        super.processWindowEvent(e);
        if (e.getID() == WindowEvent.WINDOW_CLOSING)
        {
            System.exit(0);
        }
    }

}
```

When looking over the source, notice that two panels are added to the contentPane of Frame1, which has BorderLayout:

```
        contentPane = (JPanel) this.getContentPane();
        contentPane.setLayout(borderLayout1);
        contentPane.add(jPanel1,  BorderLayout.CENTER);
        contentPane.add(jPanel2,  BorderLayout.SOUTH);
```

The panels are aligned to the CENTER and the SOUTH.

jPanel2 has FlowLayout, with the alignment set to the left. It also sports two buttons:

```
jPanel2.setLayout(flowLayout1);
flowLayout1.setAlignment(FlowLayout.LEFT);
jPanel2.add(jButton1, null);
jPanel2.add(jButton2, null);
```

Again, you can see that JBuilder is doing little more than generating the code that you would inevitably end up typing by hand were you not working in a visual development environment. Why in the world would anyone want to type all this messy syntax by hand when they can create it so easily in a free tool like JBuilder Personal?

NOTE: In some school situations, you may be asked to take a test in which you are not allowed to use JBuilder. Even in those cases, I think JBuilder is still useful because it can show you how to use a particular layout. For instance, if you need to create a program with the layout shown in Figure 12-10, you can create it in JBuilder, and then look at the code JBuilder created for you. This is the code you need to memorize so you can pass your test. (Of course, it would make more sense if your teacher had you memorize something you couldn't so easily generate in a free product, but that is an entirely different matter.)

Basic Dialog Look with VerticalFlowLayout

The system described in the previous section works fine if you want to align your buttons along the bottom of a container. But what if you want to place them on the right? For that case, it is simplest to use a Borland class called VerticalFlowLayout. This layout manager is available in the SE and Enterprise versions of JBuilder.

NOTE: If you use VerticalFlowLayout, BoxLayout2, or any other JBCL class, you need to include the JBCL library in your project. If you add these Borland layouts from the JBuilder Inspector, you will automatically have the JBCL classes added to your project. Trouble may occur, however, if you create the code some other way. For instance, if you paste or type code that uses the JBCL directly into the editor, you will have to manually add the JBCL library to your project. To do this, go to Project | Project Properties, and turn to the Required Libraries page. Press the Add button. Scroll down until you see the JBCL library, and click OK.

In Figure 12-11, you can see the FlowLayoutRight program, which is included on the CD. It demonstrates the look and feel that we are seeking. The source for the program is found in Listing 12-4.

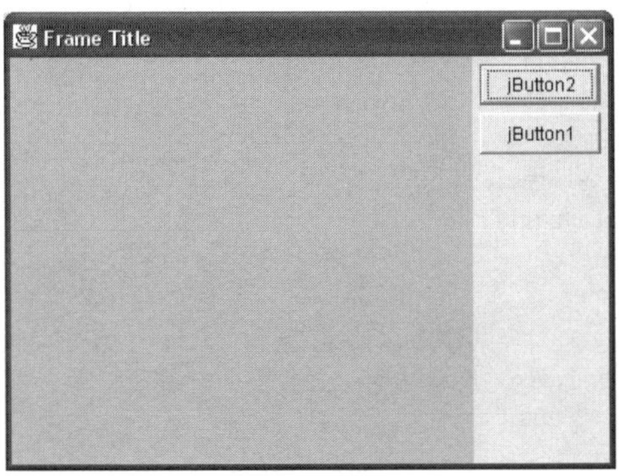

Figure 12-11: A simple program with buttons arranged on the right.

Listing 12-4: The source for Frame1 in FlowLayoutRight. The key to this program is the use of the JBCL class called VerticalFlowLayout.

```
package flowlayoutright;

import java.awt.*;
import java.awt.event.*;
import javax.swing.*;
import com.borland.jbcl.layout.*;

public class Frame1 extends JFrame
{
      JPanel contentPane;
      BorderLayout borderLayout1 = new BorderLayout();
      JPanel jPanel1 = new JPanel();
      JPanel jPanel2 = new JPanel();
      VerticalFlowLayout verticalFlowLayout1 = new VerticalFlowLayout();
      JButton jButton1 = new JButton();
      JButton jButton2 = new JButton();

      //Construct the frame
      public Frame1()
      {
            enableEvents(AWTEvent.WINDOW_EVENT_MASK);
            try
            {
                  jbInit();
            }
            catch(Exception e)
            {
                  e.printStackTrace();
            }
      }

      //Component initialization
      private void jbInit() throws Exception
      {
            contentPane = (JPanel) this.getContentPane();
            contentPane.setLayout(borderLayout1);
            this.setSize(new Dimension(400, 300));
            this.setTitle("Frame Title");
            jPanel1.setBackground(Color.lightGray);
            jPanel2.setLayout(verticalFlowLayout1);
            jButton1.setText("jButton1");
            jButton2.setText("jButton2");
            contentPane.add(jPanel1,  BorderLayout.CENTER);
            contentPane.add(jPanel2,  BorderLayout.EAST);
            jPanel2.add(jButton2, null);
            jPanel2.add(jButton1, null);
      }

      //Overridden so we can exit when window is closed
```

```
    protected void processWindowEvent(WindowEvent e)
    {
        super.processWindowEvent(e);
        if (e.getID() == WindowEvent.WINDOW_CLOSING)
        {
            System.exit(0);
        }
    }
}
```

Begin this program as you did the previous program. Create a new application, and drop down two JPanels in Frame1. Align the first to **CENTER** and the second to **EAST**. You will do this using the visual tools, but here is what it looks like in code:

```
        contentPane = (JPanel) this.getContentPane();
        contentPane.setLayout(borderLayout1);
        contentPane.add(jPanel1,  BorderLayout.CENTER);
        contentPane.add(jPanel2,  BorderLayout.EAST);
```

Use the Inspector to set the layout for the JPanel in the east to **VerticalFlowLayout**. Click on **VerticalFlowLayout** in the structure pane, and then use the Inspector to set the alignment for verticalFlowLayout1 to **TOP**, which is the default.

Finish the task by dropping down two JButtons on the JPanel that uses VerticalFlowLayout. (Again, you will probably find it easiest to drop these components on the word jPanel2 in the structure pane. Sometimes working in the content pane is more trouble than it is worth. Or rather, the structure pane is the perfect tool to use when you are configuring a complex container.)

Boxes, More Boxes, and Box Layouts

In the next few sections of the text, you will read about the Box class, the BoxLayout class, and the BoxLayout2 class. I am going to start by focusing on the Box class, since it is probably the easiest to use inside of JBuilder.

Using the Box Container Component

This is a chapter on layout policies, but I am going to suggest that in many cases, you should use a container class called Box in the place of a layout class. You can find this component on the Swing Containers page of the component palette.

Box is actually a fairly versatile class and can do a number of things not shown here. I'm not going to discuss it in depth, as this is a book on JBuilder, not on the JDK. I will, however, show you several different ways to use this class.

Let's begin by creating a first version of the application shown in Figure 12-12. You can find this program on the CD in the directory called BoxLayout02.

Get started by creating a new application. On the UI Designer, drop down a horizontal Box class from the component palette. Set its orientation to **SOUTH**. Now drop down a JPanel on the structure

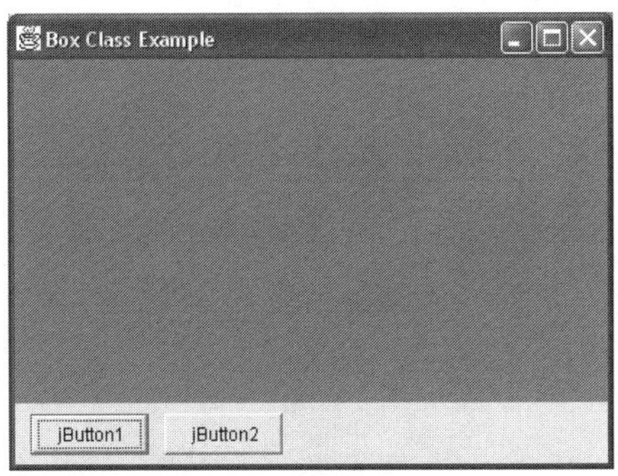

Figure 12-12: A design that has buttons properly spaced inside their container

pane, and orient it toward **CENTER**. Set its color to **dark gray** or some other shade of your choice, so you can distinguish it easily. The JPanel class should be a sibling of box1, not a child of it.

Use the structure pane to drop two buttons on the Box component. When you are done, the buttons should be children of the Box component. Frame1 should now look as it does in Figure 12-13. Notice that the two buttons are squished together on the left. This is not very attractive. Our goal is to get the buttons to look as they do in Figure 12-12, where they are set off by borders on both their sides and top.

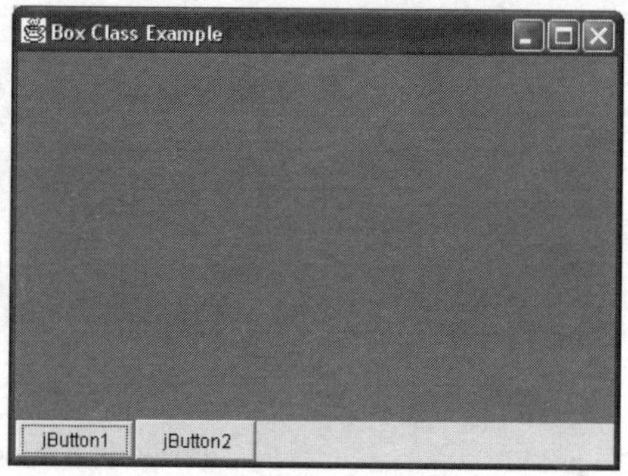

Figure 12-13: A design that has buttons squished over on the left side of the Box container in which they live

A simple way to get the borders around our buttons is to again use the Box class. Only this time, we will code the class by hand rather than use the visual designer. The final result is the code shown in Listing 12-5. Take a look at it, and then we can spend a few moments discussing it.

Listing 12-5: The Box container component can be a good substitute for the BoxLayout2 class.

```
package boxlayout02;

import java.awt.*;
import java.awt.event.*;
import javax.swing.*;

/**
 * <p>Title: </p>
 * <p>Description: </p>
 * <p>Copyright: Copyright (c) 2002 by Charlie Calvert</p>
 * <p>Company: Elvenware</p>
 * @author Charlie Calvert
 * @version 1.0
 */

public class Frame1 extends JFrame
{
      JPanel contentPane;
      BorderLayout borderLayout1 = new BorderLayout();
      JPanel jPanel1 = new JPanel();
      Box box1;
      JButton jButton1 = new JButton();
      JButton jButton2 = new JButton();
      Component boxHorzSpace01;
      Component boxHorzSpace02;
      Component boxVertSpace;

      //Construct the frame
      public Frame1()
      {
```

```
        enableEvents(AWTEvent.WINDOW_EVENT_MASK);
        try
        {
            jbInit();
        }
        catch(Exception e)
        {
            e.printStackTrace();
        }
    }
    //Component initialization
    private void jbInit() throws Exception
    {
        contentPane = (JPanel) this.getContentPane();
        box1 = Box.createHorizontalBox();
        boxHorzSpace01 = Box.createHorizontalStrut(10);
        boxHorzSpace02 = Box.createHorizontalStrut(10);
        boxVertSpace = Box.createVerticalStrut(40);
        contentPane.setLayout(borderLayout1);
        this.setSize(new Dimension(400, 300));
        this.setTitle("Box Class Example");
        jPanel1.setBackground(Color.gray);
        jButton1.setText("jButton1");
        jButton2.setText("jButton2");
        contentPane.add(jPanel1,  BorderLayout.CENTER);
        contentPane.add(box1,  BorderLayout.SOUTH);
        box1.add(boxHorzSpace01);
        box1.add(jButton1, null);
        box1.add(boxHorzSpace02);
        box1.add(jButton2, null);
        box1.add(boxVertSpace);
    }
    //Overridden so we can exit when window is closed
    protected void processWindowEvent(WindowEvent e)
    {
        super.processWindowEvent(e);
        if (e.getID() == WindowEvent.WINDOW_CLOSING)
        {
            System.exit(0);
        }
    }
}
```

The key code in this object is shown in the data section at the top:

```
    Component boxHorzSpace01;
    Component boxHorzSpace02;
    Component boxVertSpace;
```

These three Component classes will be used to provide spaces between the buttons. A judicious use of these spaces will change the appearance of the application from what you see in Figure 12-13 to what you see in Figure 12-12.

Here is how the components are created:

```
boxHorzSpace01 = Box.createHorizontalStrut(10);
boxHorzSpace02 = Box.createHorizontalStrut(10);
boxVertSpace = Box.createVerticalStrut(40);
```

As you can see, static methods of the Box class create these components with certain declared sizes. For instance, the horizontal struts will have a width of 10 and the vertical strut will have a height of 40.

The horizontal struts will provide spaces between the left and right sides of the buttons, while the vertical strut will make the Box container tall enough to give the buttons some breathing room:

```
box1.add(boxHorzSpace01);
box1.add(jButton1, null);
box1.add(boxHorzSpace02);
box1.add(jButton2, null);
box1.add(boxVertSpace);
```

Please note that the order in which these Component instances are added to the form is very important. boxHorzSpace01 provides space between the left edge of the Box class and the left edge of the first button. boxHorzSpace02, on the other hand, separates jButton01 from jButton02.

Clearly you can achieve the same effect more easily using the FlowLayout class. However, there are certain cases where the struts from a Box class can solve complex problems for you quite easily. What I have done here is give you a simple example of how to use the class.

BoxLayout2

Perhaps the simplest of all layouts is BoxLayout2, which is available in the SE and Enterprise versions of JBuilder. This class gives you two options:

1. You can arrange components on the x-axis.
2. Or you can arrange components on the y-axis.

The simplicity of this class is mitigated by the fact that Sun never wrapped it in a bean. As a result, you should use a Borland class called BoxLayout2 if you want to use BoxLayout in the visual designer.

BoxLayout2 is actually a Borland bean that wraps the BoxLayout class that ships with the JDK. The issue here is that Sun has not released BoxLayout as a bean, and so Borland did the job for them. This is yet another example of the mismatch that results when one company builds an API and the other the development environment.

BoxLayout2 is a very small class, and including it in your programs would be a trivial procedure. It is part of the JBCL, which is a JAR file that ships with some versions of JBuilder. The source is also available in some JBuilder releases.

You don't have to ship all of JBCL.jar with your project if all you want is this one tiny class. Instead, you can simply place the BoxLayout2 class on your source path and then compile it directly into your own program. Alternatively, you can design your program using BoxLayout2 and then switch instances of BoxLayout2 to BoxLayout when you ship, as shown by the comments in Listing 12-6. Yet a third alternative would be to create a "clean room" wrapper of this class yourself. It is extremely trivial to write and involves simply wrapping the methods in the BoxLayout class with your own methods. If you have never written a bean before, see Part VII.

BoxLayout is a great tool to use when you want to create simple dialogs that look a lot like something you might see in a standard Windows application. An example of using the BoxLayout class is shown in the following section.

NOTE: What I take as a humorous note is included in the Borland source file for BoxLayout2:

```
/**
 *  A Bean wrapper class for javax.swing.BoxLayout
 *  (Sun - the company that invented java beans)
 */
```

One can't be certain, but I believe I detect a slight touch of sarcasm in this note, as the writer wonders exactly why Sun (of all companies) did not create a bean wrapper for this class!

Using the Box Class with BoxLayout2

My example for the BoxLayout2 class is very similar to the previous example. In fact, it is basically the same code but uses the BoxLayout2 class as a container, rather than the Box class.

NOTE: If you can't achieve your goals with one of the simpler layouts in combination with the Box class, then often your only alternative is to rely on GridBagLayout. Since GridBagLayout is regarded by many as a challenge, you might want to pay special attention to the techniques for using the Box class.

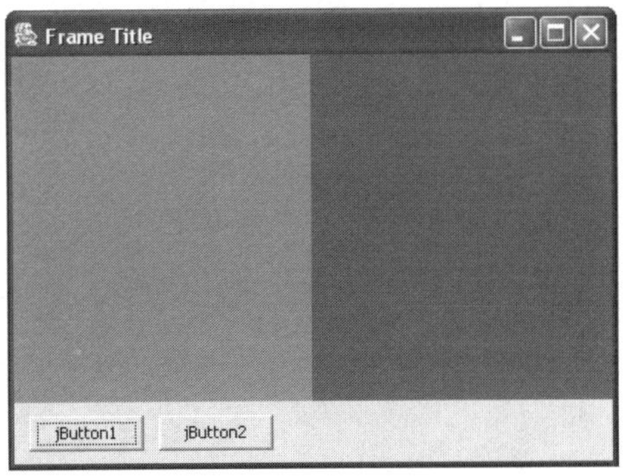

Figure 12-14: The RenumFile program on the CD shows how to use the BoxLayout02 class.

Suppose you have two buttons arranged on a JPanel, which is placed to the south of a BorderLayout. If you place both buttons on a BoxLayout aligned on the x-axis, the buttons will be flush with the left side and immediately adjacent to one another, as shown in Figure 12-13. You can use the Box class to separate these components so that they have a more pleasing look, as shown in Figure 12-14. As I said, this example is very much like the previous one. As a result, I'm asking you to just reference a screenshot for the previous example.

The code in Listing 12-6 gives an example of how to accomplish this goal. As mentioned earlier in the chapter, if you use BoxLayout2 from the JBuilder Inspector, you will automatically have the JBCL classes added to your project. Otherwise, you will have to explicitly add the class to your project using Project | Project Properties.

Listing 12-6: Using the Box class to properly space buttons on a form. Notice the comments that allow you to switch between BoxLayout2 and BoxLayout.

```
package renumfile;

import java.awt.*;
import java.awt.event.*;
```

```
import javax.swing.*;
import com.borland.jbcl.layout.BoxLayout2;
import javax.swing.border.*;

public class Frame1 extends JFrame
{
      JPanel contentPane;
      BorderLayout borderLayout1 = new BorderLayout();
      JPanel jPanel1 = new JPanel();
      JButton jButton1 = new JButton();
      JButton jButton2 = new JButton();
      JPanel jPanel2 = new JPanel();
      JPanel jPanel3 = new JPanel();
      JPanel jPanel4 = new JPanel();
      GridLayout gridLayout1 = new GridLayout();
      BoxLayout2 boxLayout = new BoxLayout2();
      //BoxLayout boxLayout;
      Component box1;
      Component box2;
      Component box3;

      //Construct the frame
      public Frame1()
      {
            enableEvents(AWTEvent.WINDOW_EVENT_MASK);
            try
            {
                  jbInit();
            }
            catch(Exception e)
            {
                  e.printStackTrace();
            }
      }
      //Component initialization
      private void jbInit() throws Exception
      {
            contentPane = (JPanel) this.getContentPane();
            box1 = Box.createHorizontalStrut(10);
            box2 = Box.createHorizontalStrut(10);
            box3 = Box.createVerticalStrut(16);
            contentPane.setLayout(borderLayout1);
            this.setSize(new Dimension(400, 300));
            this.setTitle("Frame Title");
            jButton1.setAlignmentY((float) 0.1);
            jButton1.setHorizontalAlignment(SwingConstants.LEFT);
            jButton1.setText("jButton1");
            jButton2.setAlignmentY((float) 0.1);
            jButton2.setHorizontalAlignment(SwingConstants.LEFT);
            jButton2.setText("jButton2");
            jPanel2.setLayout(gridLayout1);
```

```
        jPanel3.setBackground(SystemColor.inactiveCaption);
        jPanel4.setBackground(Color.magenta);
        //boxLayout = new BoxLayout(jPanel1, BoxLayout.X_AXIS);
        jPanel1.setLayout(boxLayout);
        jPanel1.setMinimumSize(new Dimension(188, 27));
        jPanel1.setPreferredSize(new Dimension(188, 40));
        contentPane.add(jPanel1,  BorderLayout.SOUTH);
        jPanel1.add(box1, null);
        jPanel1.add(jButton1, null);
        jPanel1.add(box2, null);
        jPanel1.add(jButton2, null);
        jPanel1.add(box3, null);
        contentPane.add(jPanel2,  BorderLayout.CENTER);
        jPanel2.add(jPanel3, null);
        jPanel2.add(jPanel4, null);
    }
    //Overridden so we can exit when window is closed
    protected void processWindowEvent(WindowEvent e)
    {
        super.processWindowEvent(e);
        if (e.getID() == WindowEvent.WINDOW_CLOSING)
        {
            System.exit(0);
        }
    }
}
```

The program shown in Listing 12-6 starts out with a simple BorderLayout for Frame1:

```
    contentPane = (JPanel) this.getContentPane();
    contentPane.setLayout(borderLayout1);
```

On top of this, two panels are placed, jPanel1 and jPanel2. One is oriented toward the center, and the other is oriented toward the south. The one with center orientation is set to GridLayout and has two additional panels placed on it called jPanel3 and jPanel4, as shown in Figure 12-14. I have set each of these panels to different colors, so they are easy to identify. jPanel1 is set to BoxLayout and has two buttons placed on it:

```
    contentPane.add(jPanel1,  BorderLayout.SOUTH);
    jPanel1.add(jButton1, null);
    jPanel1.add(jButton2, null);
    contentPane.add(jPanel2,  BorderLayout.CENTER);
    jPanel2.add(jPanel3, null);
    jPanel2.add(jPanel4, null);
```

This is similar to the way things stand in Figure 12-13. Everything is as we want it, except the buttons are squished on the left side. To fix this problem, go to source mode and type in the code to use the Box class to create two components. Insert these components at the appropriate place between the two buttons on jPanel1:

```
    Component box1;
    Component box2;
    Component box3;
```

Part III

```
// … Code omitted here for clarity's sake

box1 = Box.createHorizontalStrut(10);
box2 = Box.createHorizontalStrut(10);
box3 = Box.createVerticalStrut(16);

// … Code omitted here for clarity's sake

contentPane.add(jPanel1,  BorderLayout.SOUTH);
jPanel1.add(box1, null);
jPanel1.add(jButton1, null);
jPanel1.add(box2, null);
jPanel1.add(jButton2, null);
jPanel1.add(box3, null);
```

Remember, you must manually type in the code for the Box class. This is not something you can do with the visual tools, at least as JBuilder ships.

BoxLayout Dialog Buttons on Right

Getting the BoxLayout to place buttons on the right, as shown in Figure 12-15, is a bit tricky. However, learning how to do this can help you see the various combinations of tools that you might employ to accomplish a particular goal. Again, I would suggest using VerticalFlowLayout to achieve the particular effects shown here. I am showing you this code only to give you a sense of what you can do with BoxLayout2 and the Box class. There are times when VerticalFlowLayout is not the solution to your problem, and code like this might work for you.

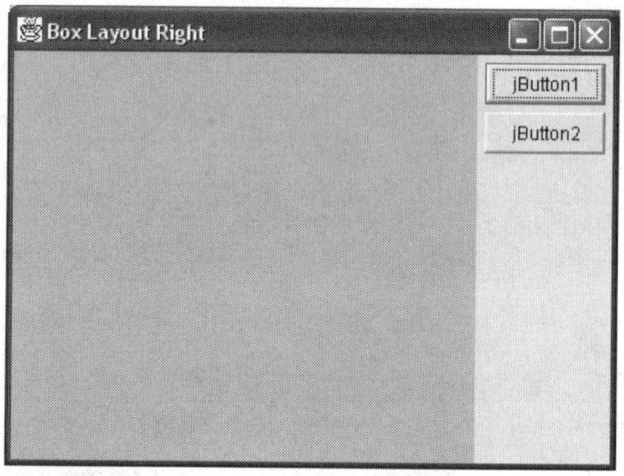

Figure 12-15: The BoxLayoutRight program from the CD

Begin by creating our standard application with two JPanels, one in the center and the other to the east. Set the layout for the one in the east to **BoxLayout2**. Drop two buttons onto this latter JPanel. Select **boxLayout21** in the structure pane, and then, in the Inspector, set the axis to **y-axis**.

At first, you will find our old nemesis: The buttons are squished up on the top and have no borders to their east and west. By now, the solution for getting the vertical gap between the two buttons should be fairly obvious. One simply switches to source mode and types code that uses Box.createVerticalStrut to create two components that can be inserted in the proper locations:

```
spaceHeight = Box.createVerticalStrut(5);
jPanel2.add(spaceHeight);
jPanel2.add(jButton1, null);
spaceHeight2 = Box.createVerticalStrut(5);
jPanel2.add(spaceHeight2);
jPanel2.add(jButton2, null);
```

In Listing 12-6 you will notice that the spaceHeight and spaceHeight2 components are actually declared earlier in the top section of the program. You can, if you wish, create the struts and add them to the panel with a single statement:

```
jPanel2.add(Box.createVerticalStrut(5));
```

This is totally correct code, but for better or worse, the JBuilder UI designer does not let you select components created in this fashion. That may not matter to you, but it is probably better to proceed as I do here. Then, when you go into design mode, you can select the struts you created and see exactly how they fit into your scene.

NOTE: Many compilers will optimize code like that under discussion so that there is no difference between creating an object as part of an argument or creating it as a separate variable. Even if the compiler were not smart enough to fix the problem, you would have to be in a quite unusual situation before an issue of this type would significantly affect your program. For instance, if you were using C or C++ to create a game and were in the middle of a loop that got executed thousands of times, this kind of optimization might be useful. In normal programs, however, it's just not something to worry about.

At this stage, you are almost set, but you need to create a border on the left and right of the button. The simplest way to do this is not with the Box class. Instead, select the panel and click the ellipsis on the far right of its Border property. The dialog shown in Figure 12-16 will appear. In this dialog, set the Border Type to **Empty**, and set the Left and Right insets to **5**. When you are done, you will have the look and feel shown in Figure 12-15.

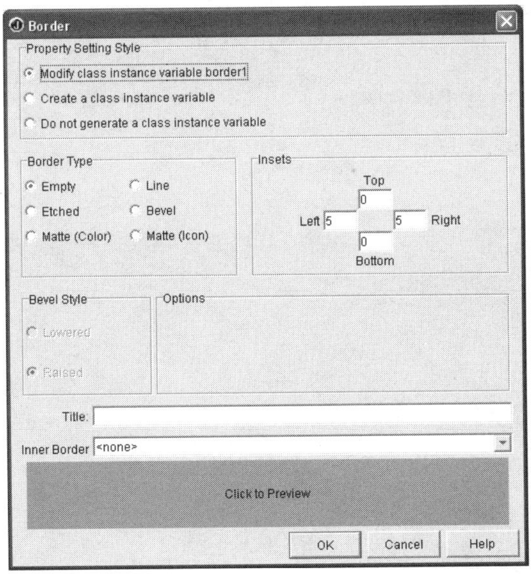

Figure 12-16: Using JBuilder to configure the size of a border

Listing 12-7: BoxLayoutRight, which has buttons aligned in a JPanel on the right of the dialog, is on the CD.

```
package boxlayoutright;

import java.awt.*;
import java.awt.event.*;
import javax.swing.*;
```

```
import com.borland.jbcl.layout.*;
import javax.swing.border.*;

/**
 * <p>Title: </p>
 * <p>Description: </p>
 * <p>Copyright: Copyright (c) 2002 by Charlie Calvert</p>
 * <p>Company: Elvenware</p>
 * @author Charlie Calvert
 * @version 1.0
 */

public class Frame1 extends JFrame
{
      JPanel contentPane;
      BorderLayout borderLayout1 = new BorderLayout();
      JPanel jPanel1 = new JPanel();
      JPanel jPanel2 = new JPanel();
      BoxLayout2 boxLayout21 = new BoxLayout2();
      JButton jButton1 = new JButton();
      JButton jButton2 = new JButton();
      Component spaceHeight, spaceHeight2;

      //Construct the frame
      public Frame1()
      {
            enableEvents(AWTEvent.WINDOW_EVENT_MASK);
            try
            {
                  jbInit();
            }
            catch(Exception e)
            {
                  e.printStackTrace();
            }
      }
      //Component initialization
      private void jbInit() throws Exception
      {
            contentPane = (JPanel) this.getContentPane();
            border1 = BorderFactory.createEmptyBorder(0,5,0,5);
            contentPane.setLayout(borderLayout1);
            this.setSize(new Dimension(400, 300));
            this.setTitle("Box Layout Right");
            jPanel2.setLayout(boxLayout21);
            jButton1.setText("jButton1");
            boxLayout21.setAxis(BoxLayout.Y_AXIS);
            jButton2.setText("jButton2");
            jPanel1.setBackground(Color.lightGray);
            jPanel2.setBorder(border1);
            contentPane.add(jPanel1,  BorderLayout.CENTER);
```

```
            contentPane.add(jPanel2,  BorderLayout.EAST);
            spaceHeight = Box.createVerticalStrut(5);
            jPanel2.add(spaceHeight);
            jPanel2.add(jButton1, null);
            spaceHeight2 = Box.createVerticalStrut(5);
            jPanel2.add(spaceHeight2);
            jPanel2.add(jButton2, null);
      }
      //Overridden so we can exit when window is closed
      protected void processWindowEvent(WindowEvent e)
      {
            super.processWindowEvent(e);
            if (e.getID() == WindowEvent.WINDOW_CLOSING)
            {
                  System.exit(0);
            }
      }
      Border border1;
}
```


Summary

In this chapter you have learned about layout managers. You have seen the relationship between layout classes and the containers that own them. You have seen simple layouts such as BorderLayout and GridLayout and also learned about more complex techniques, such as combining BoxLayout2 and the Box class. Most importantly, you learned that most successful layouts end up being a combination of several different layouts.

In the next chapter, you will read about GridBagLayout, Null and XYLayout, and CardLayout. That will wind up the discussion of layouts. Ultimately, however, the only way to really understand layouts is to see many different applications and applets in action and study their design. This book contains many such example programs, and hopefully you will learn from them as you read about them in the rest of this book.

The next chapter will also contain a discussion of the menu designer. It turns out that the menu designer is very easy to use. However, it is not always obvious to some developers how to bring up the menu designer and start using it in applications. As a result, the menu designer discussion should prove very useful to newcomers who have not yet mastered this powerful JBuilder feature.

Chapter 13

More Layouts and Menus

Margie and Charlie Calvert

In this chapter you will hear more about layout managers and then learn something about the tools for building menus. These are both fundamental skills that will be needed in many programs.

Perhaps the major topic encountered in the chapter will be GridBagLayout, which is a subject Java interface programmers simply have to master at some point. It is a bit difficult to understand, but there are many, many Java programs that depend on it. Furthermore, once you master it, you will find it provides the simplest and least confusing way to solve many layout problems.

The new layout classes provided by Java 1.4 will not be discussed in this text since JBuilder did not support them at the time of publication. You can still use them in your programs, but out of the box, JBuilder will not help you set them up.

The end of the chapter focuses on the menu designer. Once you learn a few simple tricks, you will find that this is an easy tool to use that can save you many hours of boring coding. It is, however, a very important skill that you simply have to master if you want to build the interface for your programs. Menus will be used in many of the programs you see in this book.

Null and XYLayout

Let's take a look at the layout managers called Null and XYLayout. Neither of these layout managers should be used very often in your programs. However, they provide a simple means of setting up a complex GridBagLayout. As a result, they are worth understanding. They can also be used when you are developing prototypes for your program.

Null layout is exactly what it sounds like: no layout. That means that your application might not display at all as it looked in the UI designer. Furthermore, the components are not likely to respond well to resizing. The worst layout problems associated with Null layout may not show up on the Windows platform or even on Linux, but it could start to plague you on other platforms.

XYLayout allows you to place components at X and Y locations, much as you would in Delphi or Visual Basic. XYLayout is available only in the SE and Enterprise versions of JBuilder. For our purposes, either Null or XYLayout will work.

When you are working with the UI designer, using Null or XYLayout allows you to manually size and place your components. This makes either Null or XYLayout very useful for setting up a GUI.

Create a new standard application. Refer to Chapter 3 if you need instructions for doing this.

Focus Frame1 by clicking on it in the project pane. Then change to design view. Move to the Swing Containers page of the component palette and drop a JPanel down onto the designer. Check the Inspector to ensure that its constraints property is set to Center. Set its layout property to either **Null** or **XYLayout**. Change the color to blue by going to the background property and choosing **blue** from the drop-down list.

In the component palette, click on the **JPanel**, and then click in the **UI designer**. Now drop down a second JPanel below the first one. Use the sizing handles to adjust their size, shape, and placement. If you want them to be the same size, press the **Shift** key and left-click on both JPanels to select them both. Right-click on one of the panels and choose **Same Size Horizontal** and **Same Size Vertical** in the context menu. The panel you left-clicked on first when you were selecting the panels will determine the width and height of both components.

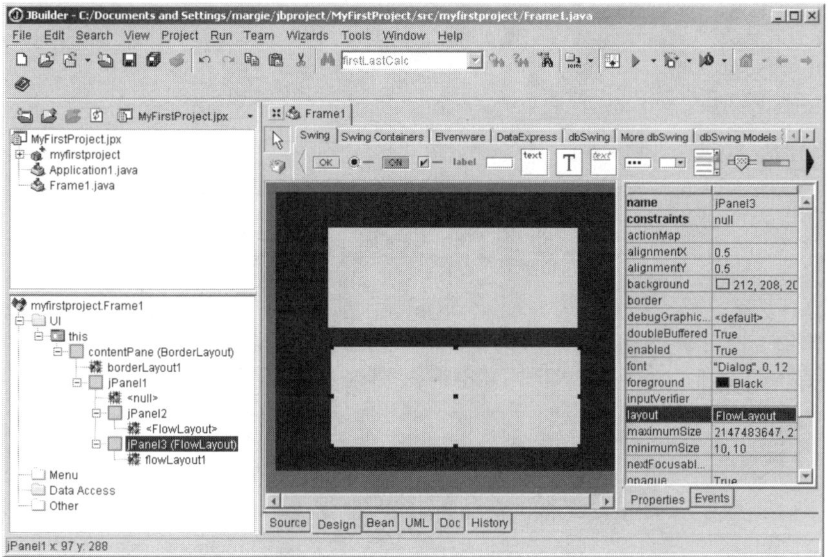

Figure 13-1: Two JPanels lie on top of a third JPanel

By default, the two JPanels you have dropped down will use FlowLayout. Change the layout for the bottom JPanel to BorderLayout.

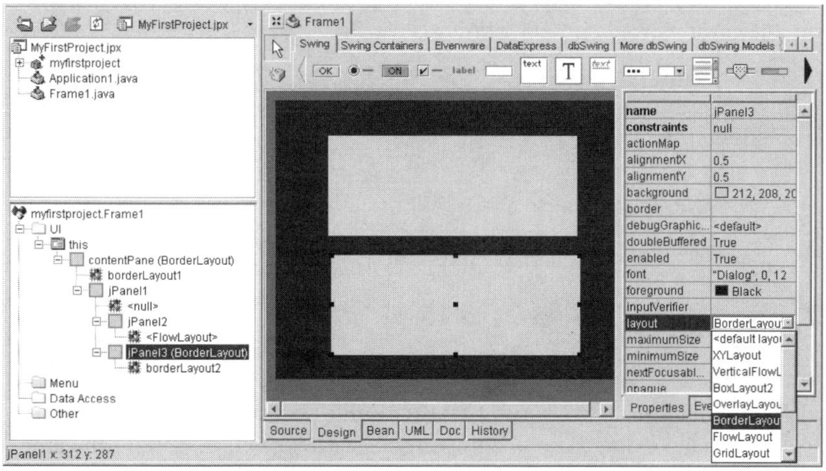

Figure 13-2: Change the layout of the bottom JPanel to BorderLayout.

Now drop down two buttons on the bottom JPanel. Name the first button **jButtonSlideLeft** and set its caption to "**Slide to Start**." Name the second button **jButtonSlideRight** and set its caption to "**Slide to End**." Make sure that one of the buttons on the bottom JPanel has a constraint of NORTH and that one of them has a constraint of SOUTH, as shown in Figure 13-3.

On the top JPanel, drop down a JSlider component ( ). Using the Inspector, set the majorTickSpacing for the component to **10** and set the minorTickSpacing to **5**. Set both paintLabels and paintTicks to **true**. When you are done, switch to code view and note that the following code has been generated:

```
JSlider1.setMajorTickSpacing(10);
JSlider1.setMinorTickSpacing(5);
JSlider1.setPaintLabels(true);
JSlider1.setPaintTicks(true);
```

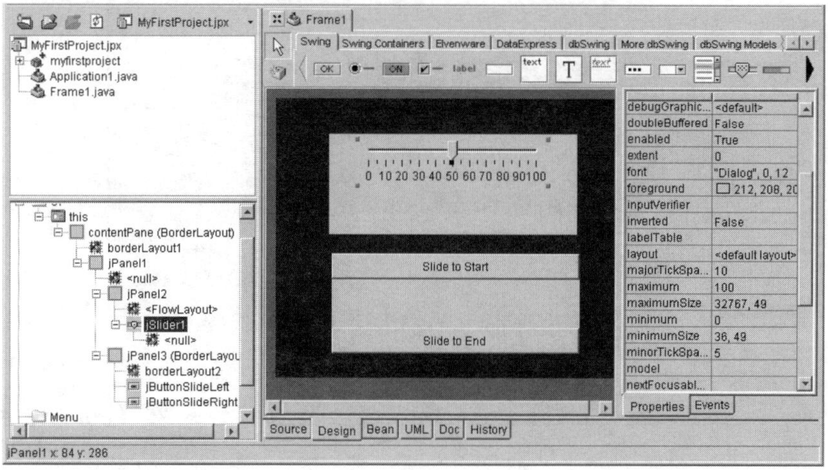

Figure 13-3: Panels help to control the look of the GUI.

Double-click on each of the buttons to associate an event handler with them. If necessary, turn to the Events page in the Inspector and use the actionPerformed property to set up the events. Now fill in the two events as follows:

```
void jButtonSlideLeft_actionPerformed(ActionEvent e)
{
      JSlider1.setValue(0);
      JSlider1.setPaintTicks(true);
}

void jButtonSlideRight_actionPerformed(ActionEvent e)
{
      JSlider1.setValue(JSlider1.getMaximum());
      JSlider1.setPaintTicks(false);
}
```

It is fairly obvious that you can achieve a fair amount of control over the appearance of your graphical user interface using various components with various layouts. But how do you convert the XY or Null layout to something you can deploy?

Change the focus to the base JPanel and choose **GridBagLayout** as the layout manager in the Inspector. JBuilder will automatically make the conversion to GridBagLayout for you.

With a little luck, the arrangement you have made will appear when you test it by running the application. However, it is possible that you may need to tweak the settings. For this, you will need to enter into the complexities of GridBagLayout.

NOTE: If you used XYLayout, then you have included a Borland class in your program. This means you need to include Borland's jbcl.jar file when you distribute your application or else link the appropriate files into your project using the Archive Manager. Some versions of JBuilder ship with the source to JBCL, and in those cases, you have more flexibility with regard to your usage of the code. The Archive Manager is discussed in the chapters on distributing applications and applets, as well as in the database chapters.

If you have converted your program to use GridBagLayout, you can manually remove the import statement com.borland.jbcl.layout.* from your source file. Once you've done this, you no longer have any reliance on Borland code, and you can simply compile your program with any standard Java JDK.

As I mentioned earlier, there is nothing wrong with using third-party code in your programs. In fact, it is often the intelligent thing to do, since you don't want to waste time reinventing the wheel.

There is one final change you should make to the program. In source view, look in jbInit for the caption for your frame. Change it so that it reads as follows:

```
this.setTitle("Mission Critical Enterprise Application");
```

When you run the program, it appears as shown in Figure 13-4. A copy of the program you have just created is available on the companion CD as GridBagSlider. It demonstrates how you can use Null layout and GridBagLayout to quickly assemble a Java application with a very non-standard interface that nonetheless is well behaved. Try resizing the main form, and notice that — within limits — it behaves well whether you make it large or small, tall or narrow.

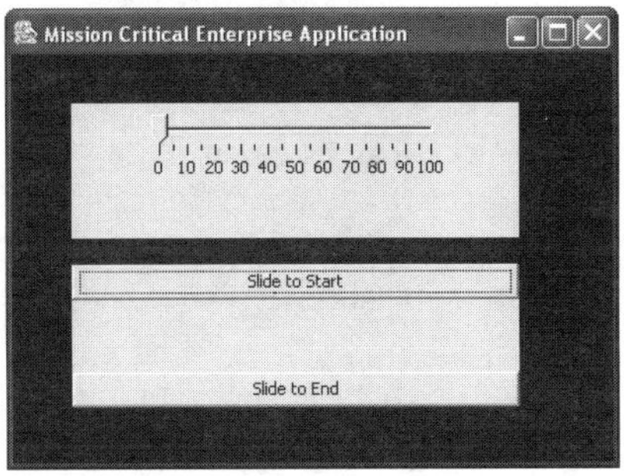

Figure 13-4: The GridBagSlider component has a flexible interface that handles being resized by the user.

GridBagLayout

GridBagLayout is probably the most complicated layout to learn. It is also the most powerful layout because it provides flexible and decisive tools for defining the layout rules that will be affecting the appearance of your components. With GridBagLayout, you can have quite a lot of control over how your GUI will actually look, and you can create fairly complex layouts.

NOTE: GridBagLayout is a hard technology to love, but it is also a hard technology to live without. If you learn to treat GridBagLayout as a game, it can really be rather a pleasure to use. When you play FreeCell, you don't really think about getting a job done; you just know that you are enjoying moving all the cards around and trying to solve a puzzle. Treat GridBagLayout the same way. Don't think of it as a tool, but as a fun little puzzle with lots of neat rules. GridBagLayout has a useful purpose, but you will probably get the most out of it if you let the playful side of your personality take over when you are working with it.

For our discussion of GridBagLayout, we will be creating a JPanel descendant on which we will paint our design. Because we will be working within the discrete container provided by a

JPanel, we will be able to reuse the code in various projects. In short, we will be creating a reusable component, which in the Java world is often simply referred to as a bean.

NOTE: There are several chapters in this book dedicated to the JavaBeans specification. In those chapters, you will hear a more rigorous definition of a bean. However, the term is frequently used in Java circles fairly loosely to designate any kind of reusable component.

Create a new standard project and application. See the instructions in Chapter 3 if you need some help with this. Name the project **MyGridBagDemo**. Once you have a new project and application, choose **File | New Class** or choose **File | New** and select **Class** from the General page of the Object Gallery. This will bring up the Class Wizard. On the first page of the Class Wizard, call the class **MyGUI**. Click on the ellipsis button next to the Base class field. This will bring you to the Select a Base Class dialog. In that dialog, choose **javax**, then **swing**, and then **JPanel**.

Once you have selected javax.swing.JPanel as your base class, the Class Wizard will look like Figure 13-6.

Figure 13-5: The Select a Base Class dialog

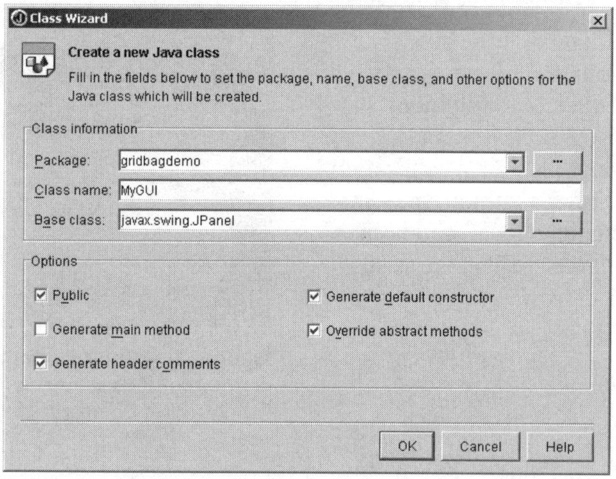

Figure 13-6: The Class Wizard set up to use JPanel as the base class and the gridbagdemo package.

Click **OK** to return to the JBuilder AppBrowser. The MyGUI class will be open in the editor. Click on the **Design** tab to move to design view. Change the layout of this in the UI folder to **BorderLayout**. (In this case, the variable called this references your JPanel descendant.)

Click on the **Swing Containers** page and pick a JPanel and drop it onto the designer. Set the constraint of the JPanel to **Center** in the Inspector. Use the Inspector to set the background color to **blue** and the layout to **GridBagLayout**.

We are ready to explore the basics of GridBagLayout. Move to the Swing page of the component palette and drop down a JButton on the designer. The button will appear in the center of the designer. Now drop down two more JButtons, each time clicking immediately to the left of the first JButton. The new JButtons will display just to the left of the first one. Drop one more button down, clicking this time above the middle JButton. Notice that as you add components to the designer, a grid begins to form that incorporates these components. If you wanted to, you could drag, drop, and resize components within the grid. For instance, you could move JButton4 into the cell to its right or left, and you could adjust it so that it was larger or smaller. Return it to its original position, however, before continuing.

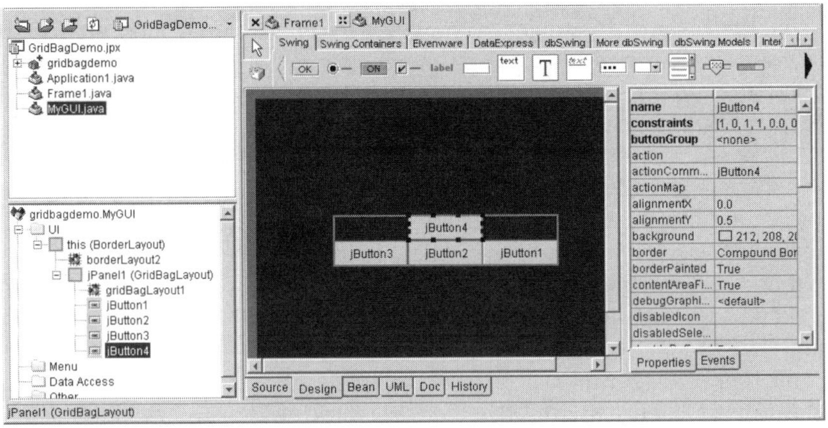

Figure 13-7: The designer with four buttons confined within a GridBagLayout.

Now we have an opportunity to edit the constraints that will determine how our buttons display. Right-click on jButton4 and choose **Constraints** from the pop-up menu.

You will see the GridBagConstraints Editor. An alternative way to reach the GridBagConstraints Editor is to use the ellipsis button on the constraints property for jButton4 in the Inspector. As you change the constraint values in the GridBagConstraints Editor, numbers corresponding to your settings will appear in the constraints property field.

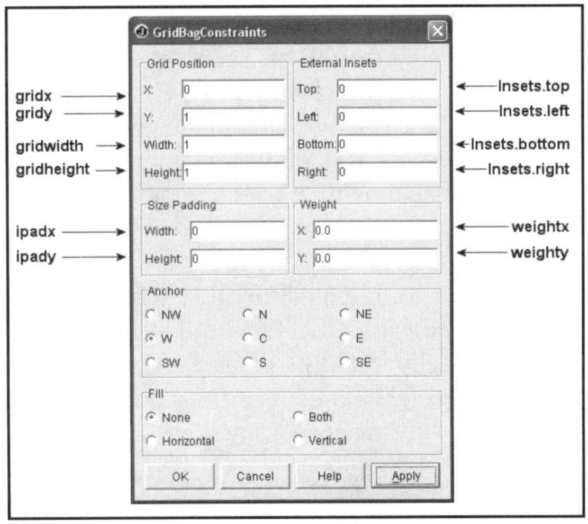

Figure 13-8: The GridBagConstraints Editor is the key to gaining mastery over GridBagLayout.

NOTE: In most cases, you will be able to pop up the GridBagConstraints Editor dialog either from the constraints property of the Inspector or from the pop-up menu just referenced. However, there are some situations in which you will have to access this dialog from the pop-up menu. For instance, this is the case when you are multi-selecting components. You should be sure you know both methods of getting at this important dialog.

In the editor, under Grid Position, set X to **1** and Y to **0**. These variables refer to the grid that is being created as you drop components on the form. The X position (the gridx constraint) refers to the column and the Y position (the gridy constraint) refers to the row, using a zero-based counting system. The cells of the grid increment from left to right and from top to bottom, with the top-left cell at position 0. If you have trouble visualizing this, take a moment to click on the other buttons in the grid. As you click on each button, the GridBagConstraints Editor will give the constraints for that button and you will be able to see the button's row and column position.

The Width (the gridwidth constraint) and Height (the gridheight constraint) are both listed as 1. The gridwidth and gridheight refer to the number of cells that the component can, but not necessarily will, fill. gridheight refers to the number of rows in the component's display area, and gridwidth refers to the number of columns in the component's display area.

To help you understand this subject, I am going to refer to the display area for a cell as its kingdom, its dominion. If gridwidth and gridheight are 1, the component owns only one cell.

Take a look at Figure 13-7. The top button is currently occupying one cell in the middle of the grid. If you set the gridwidth to 3, the top button could — at least in theory — occupy all three cells in the top row. Whether it actually will fill those cells depends on other properties that you set. But the point here is that gridwidth and gridheight define the range of cells over which a component can wander. The cells are in its dominion, as it were.

The anchor constraint comes into play when the dominion for a component is larger than the component itself. In other words, if the component owns more than one cell, the anchor constraint becomes relevant. It will tell JBuilder where in the dominion to show your component.

To see how this works, click on **jButton4**, bring up the constraints editor, and set X to **0** and the gridwidth to **3**. That will tell JBuilder that three cells are allotted to the component, starting with the far left column (X is set to 0).

Skip down to the area of the editor labeled Anchor. Click **W** and then **Apply** to set the anchor to West. Zoom, off goes the cell to visit the west part of his kingdom. Now click **C** for Center and **Apply** and **E** for East and **Apply**. As you make each assignment, the button will move to a new cell in his dominion. jButton4 will move horizontally in the three cells assigned to it, based on the anchor setting. In short, you are keeping the button the same size, but you are moving it over the range of cells in its dominion. You are asking it to visit each cell in its dominion in turn.

Suppose that you want to have jButton4 fill all three cells in its dominion. Go to the Fill area of the editor and choose **Horizontal**. jButton4 will expand to fill the three cells in its row that are allotted to it. The horizontal setting specifies that the component can expand horizontally to fill the display area or dominion it has assigned to it, but there will be no change in its height. The fill settings are constants, and when you check your code, you will notice that they are in all capital letters (e.g., HORIZONTAL).

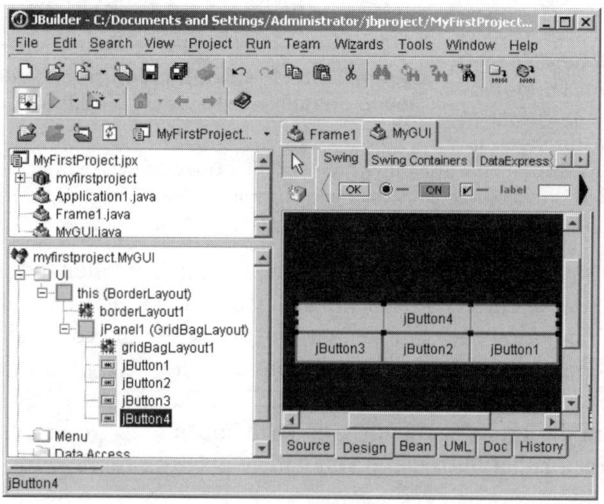

Figure 13-9: Because its width is set to 3 and its Fill property is set to horizontal, jButton4 occupies three cells. It has expanded to fill all the cells in its dominion.

So far, we have changed the number of cells that are in the button's dominion but not the size of the cells themselves. So how do we grow the dominion by not adding cells to it but by changing the size of the cells themselves?

Let's make jButton4 a little taller. Go to the Size Padding area of the editor and set the Height to **20**. When you do this, you will be setting the ipady constraint. The way that the padding works is that when you set padding for the height, the component will be at least its minimum height, plus the ipady constraint * 2. That is because the padding is on both sides of the component. If you had set the ipadx constraint, which controls width, the same rule would apply: The component would be at least its minimum width plus the ipadx constraint * 2. You set ipadx by putting a number in the Width field in the Size Padding part of the GridBagConstraints Editor.

Once you have clicked Apply, you will see jButton4 expanded by 40 pixels.

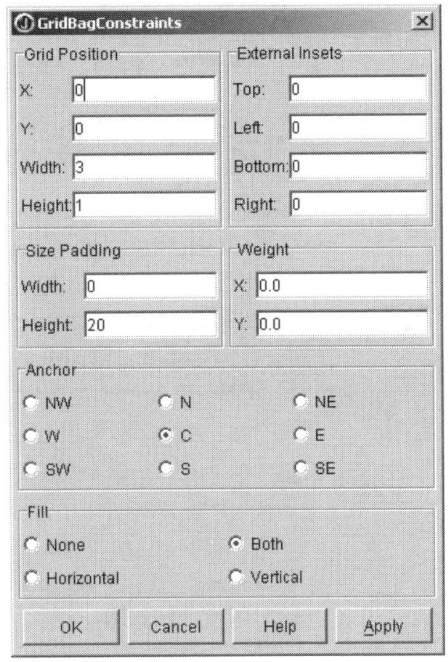

Figure 13-10: The GridBagConstraints Editor with Height in the Size Padding set to 20

NOTE: A way to help you remember this is to think about the ipadx and ipady properties as padding the account of the component that uses it. CEOs in today's world always say things like, "I only get paid $250,000 a year." Struggling along they are, on that meager salary. What they don't tell you is that they also got $1,000,000 in stock options as padding to help tide them through their frugal existence. In the same way, ipadx and ipady factors make a component's domain larger without actually adding to the number of cells in it: "Oh, I only own two cells." What they don't tell you is that they have padded the cells to make them huge. Or, to shift the metaphor slightly, it is like padding an expense account to make it look larger than it really is. Use whatever mental or mnemonic tricks you can come up with to help you remember what this brutal array of properties can actually do for you.

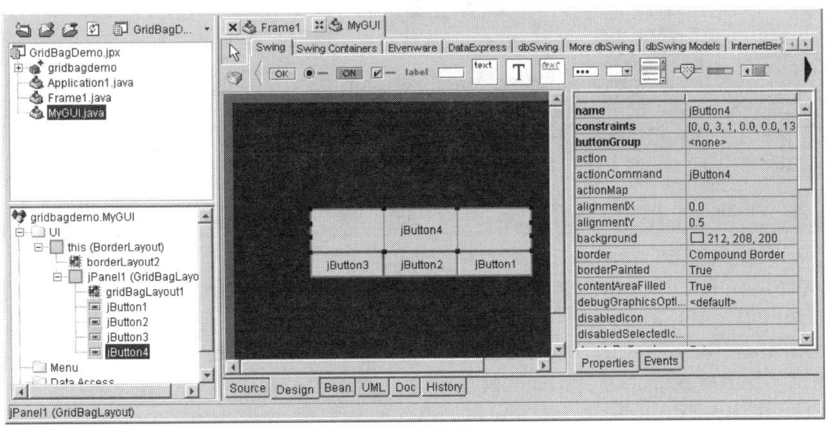

Figure 13-11: If you set the ipady property of jButton4 to 20, the component is expanded by 40 pixels: 20 on top, 20 on the bottom.

Our next step is to set the external border of the components, or the insets. The insets determine the minimum amount of space between the component and the borders of its display area, which is the cell or cells allotted to it.

> **NOTE:** The border area around the edge of a cell is often referred to as "padding." In this case, we want to avoid that word because we are already talking about the ipadx and ipady properties. So think of the insets as an empty border around a component.

By default, the inset of any component will be set to 0. The External Insets are located at the top-right of the GridBagConstraints Editor. We will set the external insets for all of the buttons to five pixels in all four fields (Top, Left, Bottom, and Right). To do this, exit the GridBagConstraints dialog, and use the Shift key and the mouse to select all four of the buttons in the structure pane. Now right-click on one of the buttons in the designer, and choose **Constraints** from the pop-up menu. Then enter **5** in each of the four External Insets fields.

Once you have clicked OK, the buttons will be in the configuration in which we want them.

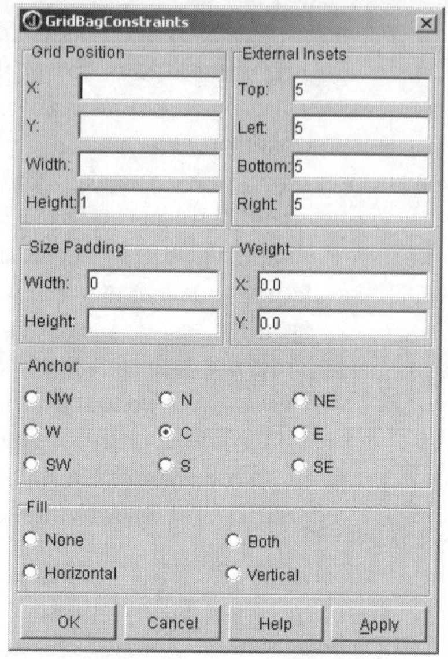

Figure 13-12: The GridBagConstraints editor with all the External Inset fields set to 5

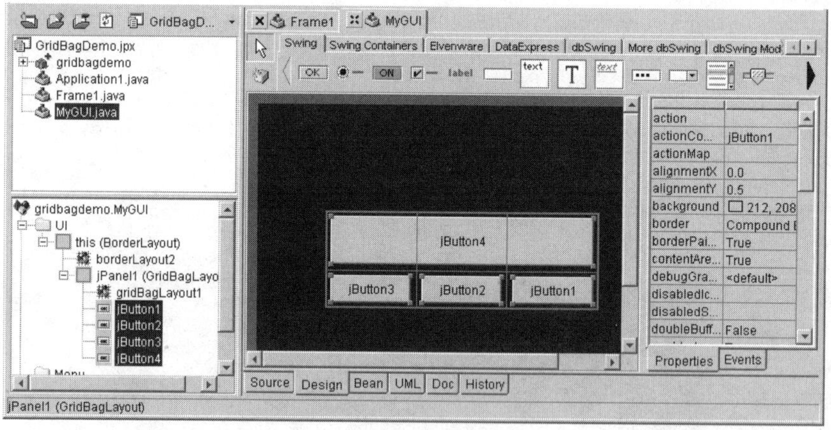

Figure 13-13: All of the buttons now have their External Insets set to 5.

Now that we have created our component, we need to make a final adjustment, which is to set the weight constraints, known as weightx and weighty. The weight constraints control the way in which the components react to the empty space around them. In particular, it changes the way they fill in the empty space that might appear if the window they are in is resized. It guarantees that the component will always own a certain percentage of the available space whenever the window is made larger or smaller.

The weight is like a magical property in a game or those holes in the tax laws that let fat cats make lots of money in good times while doing nothing to help out the little guys who live next to them. If you have a lot of weight, and the window in which your kingdom is located expands, you will fill in that extra space automatically. Components that don't have any weight, the featherweights, will not expand to take in any extra area. If your weight is one-fifth of the weight of all the cells in your row, you will expand to fill one-fifth of the row no matter how big the row might get. If you own three-quarters of the combined weight of your row, you will expand to fill in three-quarters of the width of the row. So if you at least have some weight, you will grow and shrink as the window grows and shrinks. If you have no weight, you do not grow and shrink, but you also won't ever go beneath a certain minimum size.

If the weight constraints are set at the default, 0, resizing will not affect the size of the components' display area. Instead, the area around the grid will increase in size, leaving the components clustered near the center of the display area. The components will tend to stay at their "preferred" size, which is the size they are when dropped down on the designer, the size you made by changing the number of cells they occupied, or the size of the cells themselves. These values are all constants. The weight is the wild card that grows proportionately to the size of the entire window.

The weights are doubles and range from 0 to 1. A zero weight means that if the container is resized, none of the extra space will go to the component's cell. If a weight is set, the amount of the extra space that will go to the component's cell will be a percentage of the total weights that are assigned. For example, focus on the X weight (weightx), which will determine how space is portioned out horizontally among the columns in the grid. Assign jButton1 and jButton3 each a weight of 0.2, and give jButton2 a weight of 0.6. The total weights in the row add up to 1.0. The column containing jButton1 and the column containing jButton2 will each have 0.2/1.0, or one-fifth, of the additional horizontal space in the window added to it, and the column containing jButton3 will have 0.6/1.0, or sixth-tenths, of the additional horizontal space assigned to its cell. If you want the components to grow to fill the cells, you will need to set the fill property to Horizontal or Both.

As you assign these values, you will notice that the grid expands to take in the whole width of the JPanel horizontally, and the cells have changed in size to reflect the values that you put in. The display area for jButton4 will have grown as well. That is because, for each column, the weight of the column is related to the highest weightx assigned to any component in the column. Just to be sure that jButton4 spreads across the whole area, assign it an X weight of 1. An X weight of 1 will allow the cell to fill all of the available horizontal space.

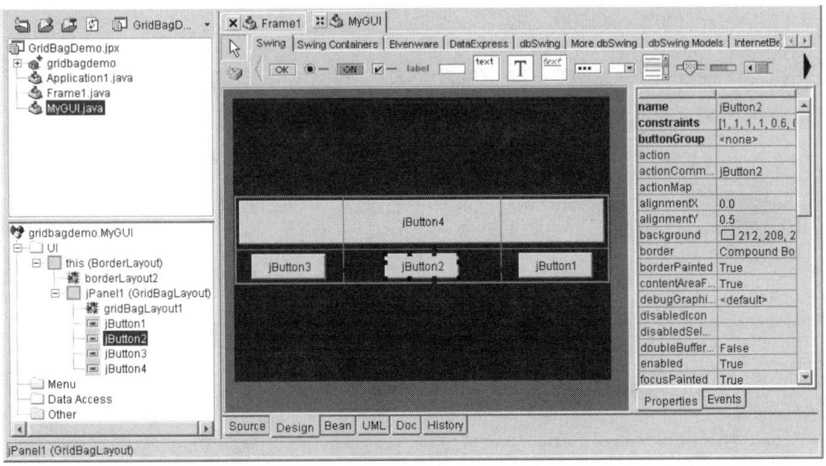

Figure 13-14: The buttons after X weights have been added

The Y weight operates on the same principles. In the GridBagConstraints Editor, change the Y weight of jButton3 to 0.5, and choose Both as the fill constraint. Then change the Y weight of jButton4 to 0.5. You will see that jButton3 has expanded to fill its cell except for the 5-pixel external insets. The jButton3 cell has expanded to include half of the free vertical space, and the cells of jButton4 have expanded to fill the remaining half of the free vertical space.

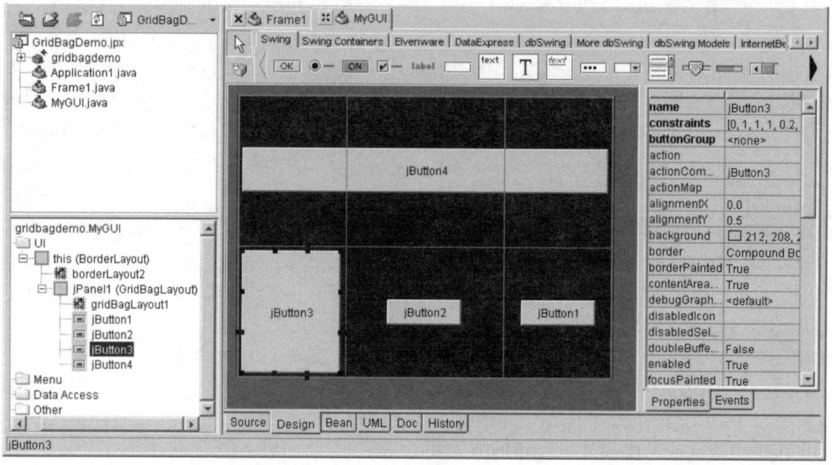

Figure 13-15: Y weights of 0.5 have been added to jButton3 and jButton4.

If you look at the source code, you will see the results of your selections in the GridBagConstraints Editor in the jbInit() section.

Listing 13-1: The code shows your choices.

```
private void jbInit() throws Exception
  {
    this.setLayout(borderLayout1);
    JPanel1.setBackground(Color.blue);
    JPanel1.setLayout(GridBagLayout1);
    JButton1.setText("JButton1");
    JButton2.setText("JButton2");
    JButton3.setText("JButton3");
    JButton4.setText("JButton4");

    JPanel1.add(JButton1, new GridBagConstraints(2, 1, 1, 1, 0.2, 0.0,
      GridBagConstraints.CENTER, GridBagConstraints.NONE,
      new Insets(5, 5, 5, 5), 0, 0));

    JPanel1.add(JButton2, new GridBagConstraints(1, 1, 1, 1, 0.8, 0.0,
      GridBagConstraints.CENTER, GridBagConstraints.NONE,
      new Insets(5, 5, 5, 5), 0, 0));

    JPanel1.add(JButton3, new GridBagConstraints(0, 1, 1, 1, 0.2, 0.5,
      GridBagConstraints.CENTER, GridBagConstraints.BOTH,
      new Insets(5, 5, 5, 5), 0, 0));

    JPanel1.add(JButton4, new GridBagConstraints(0, 0, 3, 1, 1.0, 0.5,
      GridBagConstraints.CENTER, GridBagConstraints.HORIZONTAL,
      new Insets(5, 5, 5, 5), 0, 20));
    this.add(JPanel1, BorderLayout.CENTER);

  }
```

Probably the most instructive JButton to look at is jButton4.

```
JPanel1.add(JButton4, new GridBagConstraints(0, 0, 3, 1, 1.0, 0.5,
      GridBagConstraints.CENTER, GridBagConstraints.HORIZONTAL,
      new Insets(5, 5, 5, 5), 0, 20));
```

The first six numbers listed after the parenthesis following new GridBagConstraints show gridx, gridy, gridwidth, gridheight, weightx, and weighty. The anchor parameter is GridBagConstraints.CENTER. The fill parameter is gridBagConstraints.HORIZONTAL. The part of the code that states new Insets(5, 5, 5, 5), 0, 20) gives the four inset settings, followed by ipadx, which is the Size Padding Width constraint (that we did not set), and ipady, which is the Size Padding Height Constraint, set to 20.

Of course, it is possible to make the changes we have discussed in the source view of the AppBrowser. Try this by changing the snippet of code for jButton3 that reads GridBagConstraints.BOTH to GridBagConstraints.NONE. Then click the **File |Save All** icon and move to the design view. You will see that jButton3 no longer fills its cell. If you check in the GridBagConstraints Editor, you will see that Fill has been set to None. However, even though you can manually code in the constraints, it is much easier for most people to change them in the GridBagConstraints Editor.

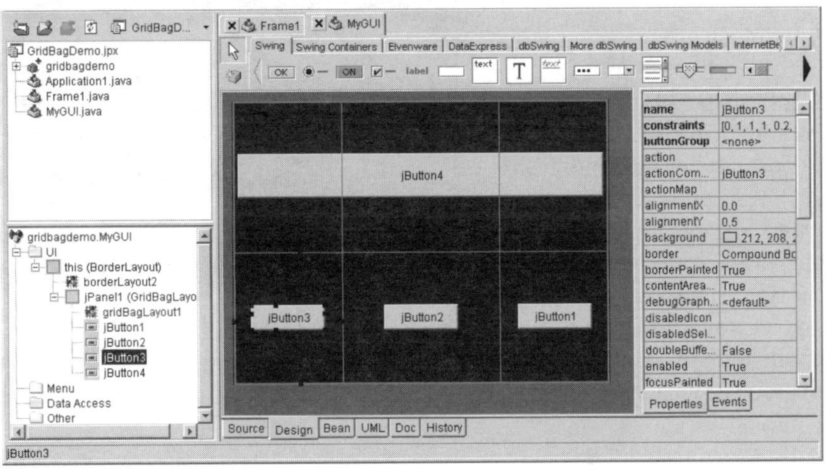

Figure 13-16: The Fill parameter for jButton3 was changed in source view.

Now it's time to test our work. First, choose **File | Save All** to be sure that you have saved your code. Double-click on **Frame1.java** in the project pane to select it. You should see a blank panel (the UI designer) in the content pane in design view. Click on the **Bean Chooser** ( )in the component palette. Choose **Select…** and find gridbagdemo in the Bean Chooser dialog. Click on the plus sign to the left of gridbagdemo, select **MyGUI** from the list, and click **OK**. Place your cursor on the upper left of the designer, drag down and right, and then release. Your GUI will appear.

Run the program, and try making it bigger, smaller, maximized, etc. Notice that the dialog performs fairly well in most shapes and sizes that the user is ever likely to choose. The rules that you set up with the GridBagConstraints will hold, no matter what the size. Once you have played with the GUI you have created, you may want to make some adjustments.

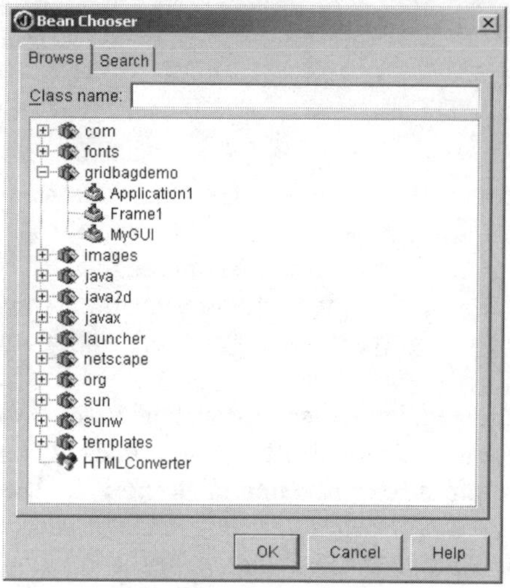

Figure 13-17: The Bean Chooser dialog

Our discussion of the GridBagConstraints Editor and GridBagLayout has not been exhaustive, but with a little bit of effort, you should now be able to get started. You will probably have to use trial and error for a while until you get used to how your choices appear in the designer. However, your efforts with this layout manager will be richly repaid, as it allows you to achieve most reasonable design goals of a window. The site http://java.sun.com and JBuilder Help both have additional information if you wish to pursue this subject in more depth. You can view the complete source for the GridBagConstraints class by moving your cursor over GridBagConstraints in the editor and pressing the F1 key. The application we built in this section is on the CD as GridBagDemo.

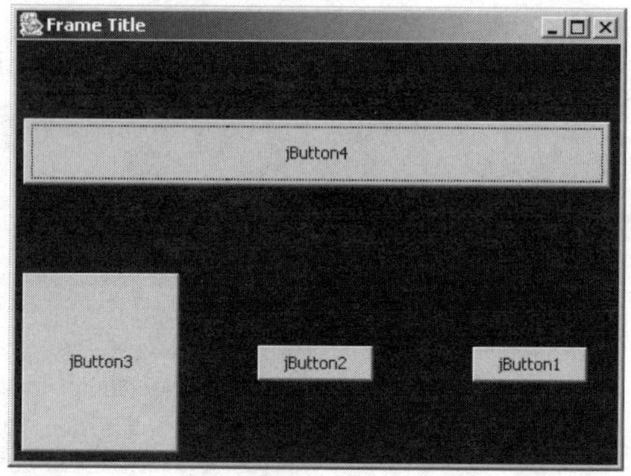

Figure 13-18: The GUI at run time

Ultimately, using GridBagLayout is a matter of attitude. It's the ultimate techie tool, a bit like a stereo that has more knobs and switches on it than anyone can possibly understand. It's complicated not because it needs to be so complicated but for the sake of being complicated. When you've finished laying something out with GridBagLayout, you know that you have accomplished something that is beyond the reach of normal people. You have reached some kind of technological nirvana.

CardLayout

CardLayout places components on top of each other so that you can see only one of them at a time. The analogy is to a deck of cards, only one of which is visible at a time. CardLayout needs to be used with another component, such as a check box, radio button, or TabSetControl, that can control which component will display when. It is useful when two or more components need to occupy the same space, as when building a wizard.

NOTE: CardLayout is not particularly difficult to understand, but in many cases it has been effectively replaced by the Swing JTabbedPane component. You need a bit of knowledge to understand that CardLayout is probably something you don't want to use in most Swing programs, unless you are building a wizard.

CardLayout is actually fairly simple to use. An example program on the CD called MyCardLayout shows you how to proceed.

Create a new default application in a project named MyCardLayout. See Chapter 3 if you have any questions about how to do this. In your new project, focus Frame1.java and move to design view.

Move to the Swing Containers page and drop a JPanel down onto the designer. In the Inspector, make sure that the constraints property is set to Center and rename it to **basePanel**. Set its layout property to **Null**. Drop a button onto basePanel and place it in the upper left-hand corner. Drop a JPanel onto basePanel below the button. Set its name to **cardPanel**, its background color to **black**, and its layout property to **CardLayout**.

In the structure pane, click on the plus sign to the left of cardPanel to display cardLayout1. Click on **cardLayout1** to focus it and rename it **myCardLayout** in the Inspector.

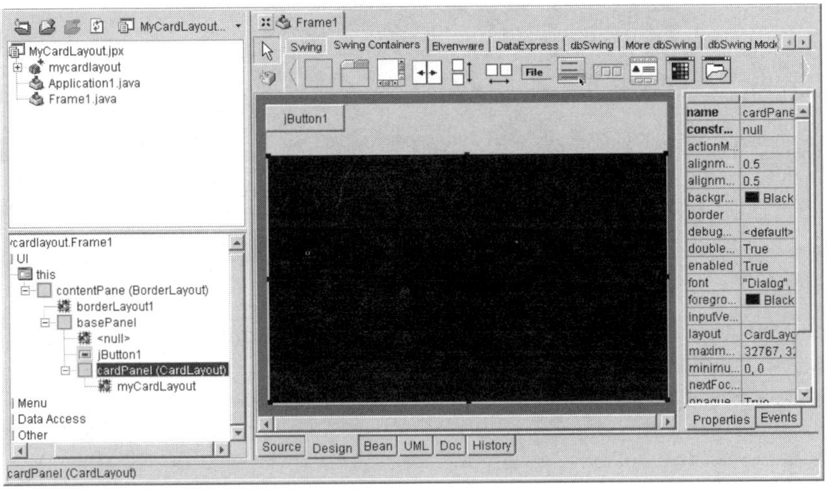

Figure 13-19: The GUI begins to take shape.

CardLayout has five methods that we will be exploring in this tutorial. They are:

- void first(Container parent)
- void last(Container parent)
- void next(Container parent)
- void previous(Container parent)
- void show(Container parent, String name)

NOTE: To obtain a complete list of the methods, position your cursor on myCardLayout in the structure pane and hit F1. You will see the information on the CardLayout class, including all of the methods available to you.

To see how these methods work, we will add more buttons and more panels to our GUI and use the events for the buttons to trigger the methods. We will give each panel a distinct background color so that we can tell them apart.

First, we will add more panels. The container or parent referred to in the methods is cardPanel, the panel whose layout we just set to CardLayout. The panels we add will be like cards in a deck of cards. cardPanel is like the deck itself, the container for the cards.

In this tutorial, we will use four JPanels for our deck of cards. Turn to the Swing Containers page, and press the **Shift** key. Then click on the **JPanel**. Click four times on the word **cardPanel** in the structure pane. jPanels 1, 2, 3, and 4 should now be visible in the structure pane. Be sure to click on the white selection tool arrow once you have finished adding your panels.

Click on **jPanel1** to focus it. In the Inspector, change its background color to red and its name to redPanel. Notice that the constraints property will continue to read jPanel1 after you have changed the name. Change the constraint property to redPanel as well.

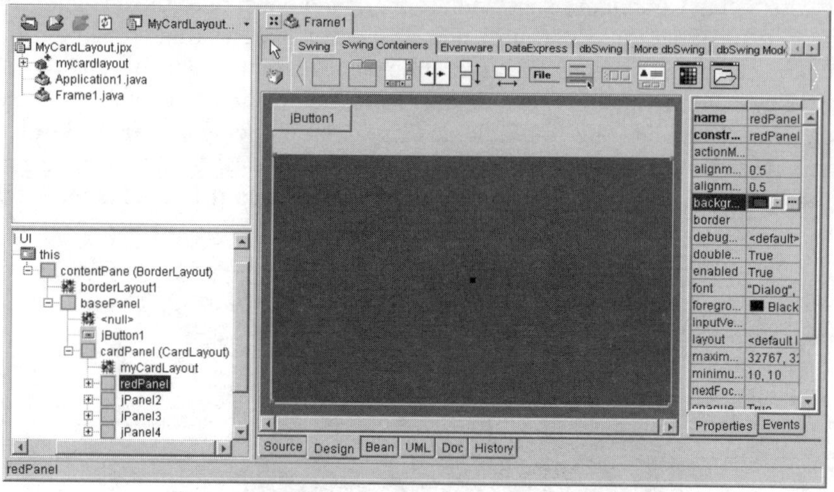

Figure 13-20: Four JPanels have been added to the Container for CardLayout.

Change the name and constraints properties of jPanels 2, 3, and 4 as well, giving each its own background color and a name that reflects the color. In the example, jPanel2 is orangePanel, jPanel3 is greenPanel, and jPanel4 is bluePanel.

Drop down four additional buttons along the top of basePanel. Change their text properties, from left to right, to **First**, **Last**, **Next**, **Previous**, and **Orange**. You will find it helpful to change the names of the buttons to reflect the text property (e.g., firstButton). You will probably have to enlarge previousButton a little bit to show the entire word "Previous."

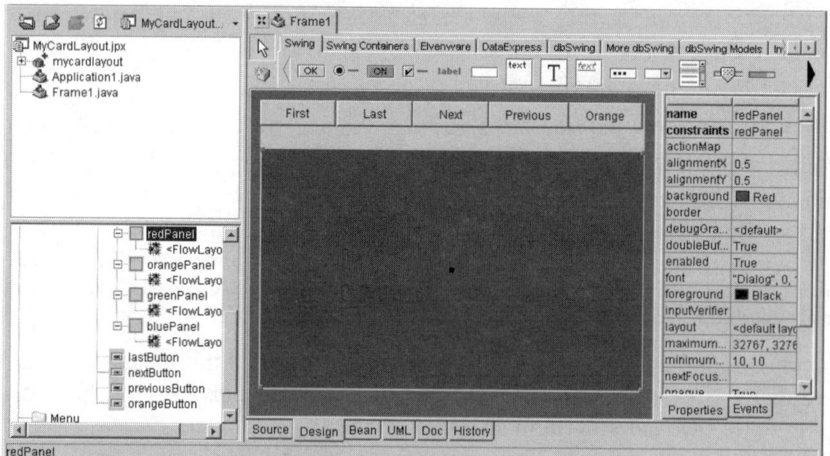

Figure 13-21: The buttons have been added and renamed.

Now we are ready to add events to the buttons. Double-click on **firstButton** and add code to the event code stub so that the event reads like this:

```
void firstButton_actionPerformed(ActionEvent e)
{
      myCardLayout.first(cardPanel);
}
```

This will place the first panel in the deck "on top" — in other words, redPanel will display when the button is clicked.

The event code for lastButton is just as simple:

```
void lastButton_actionPerformed(ActionEvent e)
{
      myCardLayout.last(cardPanel);
}
```

The blue panel will display, as it is the last JPanel that was added to the deck (that is, to the container for the panels, which is the JPanel cardPanel).

The code for nextButton will probably be no surprise at this point:

```
void nextButton_actionPerformed(ActionEvent e)
{
      myCardLayout.next(cardPanel);
}
```

This will surface the next "card" in the deck. The previous card is equally straightforward to reach:

```
void previousButton_actionPerformed(ActionEvent e)
{
      myCardLayout.previous(cardPanel);
}
```

The orangeButton event is slightly more complicated:

```
void orangeButton_actionPerformed(ActionEvent e)
{
      myCardLayout.show(cardPanel, "orangePanel");
}
```

The myCardLayout.show method takes two parameters, the Container parent, which is cardPanel, and a string, which is the name of the "card" you wish to show. In this case, we are using this method to show orangePanel.

NOTE: If you have trouble with this method, double-check to be sure that you changed the constraints property to orangePanel in the Inspector. This method will not work until you do that.

If you understand how to use these methods, you are well on your way to being able to create your own wizards. When you run this project, notice that the cardPanel, the container for the deck, which we colored black, never displays. This project is on the CD under the name MyCardLayout.

NOTE: If you use an approach like this to create your wizard, you should be sure to convert the layout for basePanel from Null layout to GridBagLayout when you are finished. This process is covered earlier in this chapter.

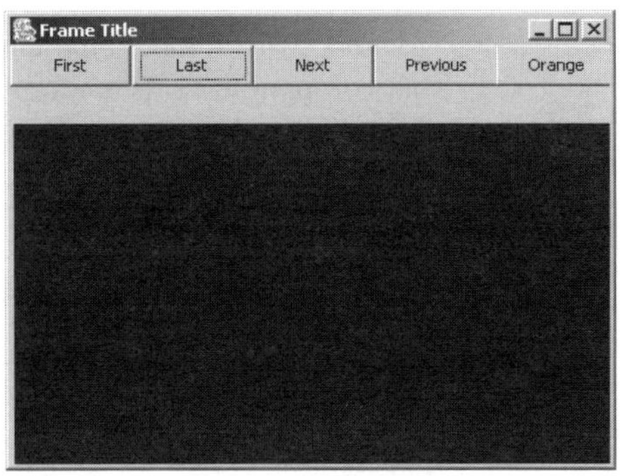

Figure 13-22: The application running

SE and Enterprise Level Layout Managers

In addition to XYLayout, which we have already discussed, JBuilder SE and Enterprise versions also come with PaneLayout, which allows you to set the percentage of the container space that a component will take. VerticalFlowLayout was discussed in the previous chapter, as well as BoxLayout2. An additional layout, called OverlayLayout2, is a bean wrapper class similar to BoxLayout2.

By now, you should have some sense of how layout managers work. As a result, I will leave it up to you to discover these additional layouts and find out how to use them in your programs.

The Menu Designer

The easiest way to generate a menu in an application is to check Generate menu bar in Step 2 of the Application Wizard as you are creating the application. This would automatically generate a menu bar with two items, File and Help. Each of those menus has one item: File | Exit and Help | About.

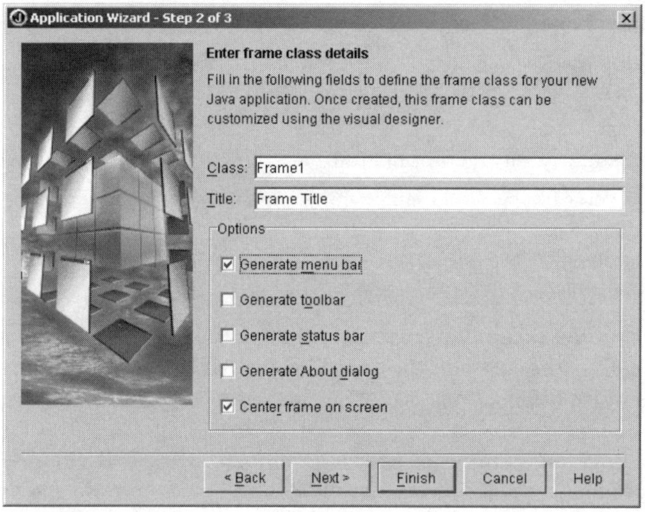

Figure 13-23: Step 2 of the Application Wizard

However, if you have an application that is open and wish to add a menu bar to it, you can pick this component off the component palette. Open up the Swing Containers page of the component palette. Near the middle you will see an icon bearing the word File. If you move your cursor over it, it will be identified as a JMenuBar. Click on the icon, and then click on the Menu folder in the structure pane. jMenuBar1 will appear in the structure pane.

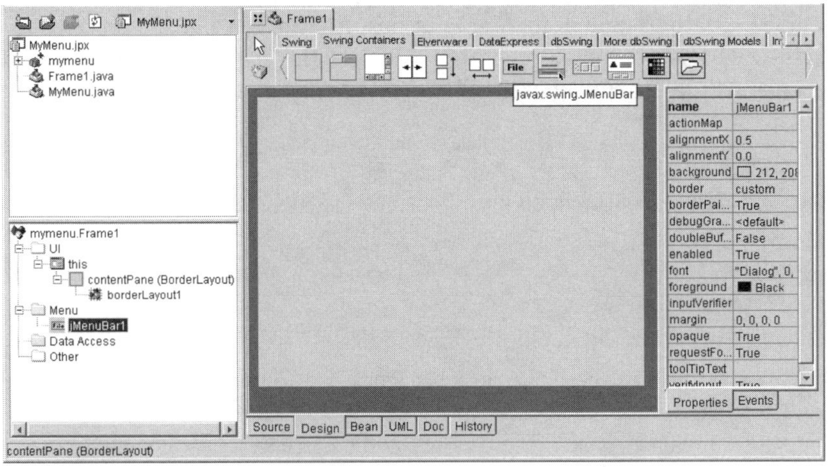

Figure 13-24: The JMenuBar in the component palette

Please pay attention to this next step. Your menu will not appear in the application without it! Go to the source view of the content pane. In the editor, find the end of the jbInit() method and add this line of code:

```
this.setJMenuBar(jMenuBar1);
```

Now go back to the design view. In the structure pane, right-click on **jMenuBar1** and choose **Activate Designer** from the pop-up menu. Again, please pay special attention to this step. You have to right-click on jMenuBar1 and select Activate Designer!

Bring your cursor to the left side of the menu that has appeared in the UI designer to the spot where the File menu usually is. Click on that spot and type **File**, and then press **Enter**. When you do, a spot for the first item in the File menu will appear. Type **Close** and press **Enter**. If you open up the component tree in the structure pane, you will be able to see jMenu1 and jMenuItem1 in addition to jMenuBar1, as shown in Figure 13-25.

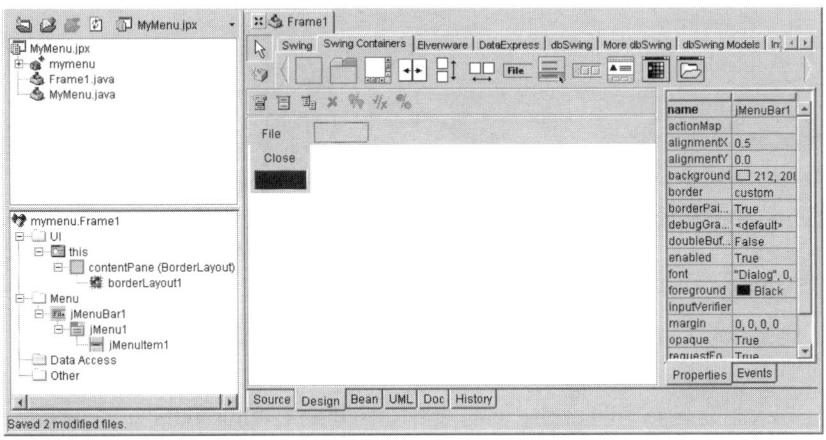

Figure 13-25: jMenuItem1 is visible in the designer and structure pane.

To add event code to the menu item, highlight **jMenuItem1** in the structure pane. In the Inspector, click the **Events** tab at the bottom. Click in the actionPerformed property editor and press **Enter**. JBuilder will generate all the event code and a code stub for you. In the editor, type:

```
System.exit(0);
```

between the curly braces of the code stub. The result will look like this:

```
voidjMenuItem1_actionPerformed(ActionEvent e)
 {
   System.exit(0);
 }
```

Now run your application to see if the menu is working. You will find this project listed as MyMenu on the CD.

Note that you can easily expand the menu you have created by right-clicking. For instance, set up the menu designer as it appears in Figure 13-25. Now select the word **Close** in the menu designer and right-click on it. You will see the options Insert a Menu Item, Insert a Separator, and Insert a Nested Menu. A nested menu is shown in Figure 13-26.

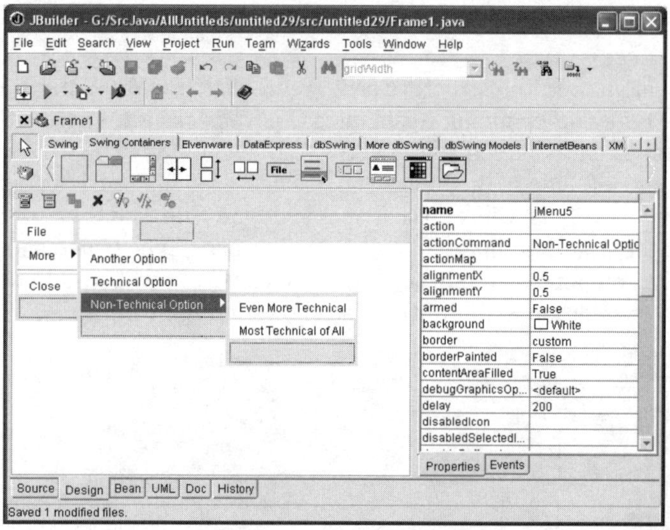

Figure 13-26: Use the right mouse button to access advanced options such as nested menus.

Overall, the menu designer is simple to use. Most of the time, you just find the place in the designer where you want add an item, and then start typing. When in doubt, right-click and look for any additional options.

Summary

In this chapter we have looked at the uses of Null and XYLayout and explored GridBagLayout and CardLayout. The chapter ended with an examination of the JBuilder menu designer. This tool can help you quickly and easily design even the most complex menus. As a result, it can save you literally hours of time and a significant amount of typing.

Chapter 14

Event Handling

Charlie Calvert

In this chapter and the next you are going to learn the basic facts about handling events. The text will cover four major topics, the first two in this chapter and the last two in the next:

- Basic event handling: Learn the mechanism that JBuilder employs to allow you to handle the most basic events generated by a particular class. For instance, you will learn how to respond to a click on a JButton. More importantly, you learn how the code that supports this kind of simple event handler is constructed and the various options you will have when implementing it. In particular, you will have a chance to examine the syntax for both anonymous and standard adapter classes.
- Supporting listener interfaces: Learn to create a class that supports an interface such as MouseListener, KeyListener, or a JDK 1.4 class called MouseWheelListener. These interfaces can enable a class to respond to a wide range of events.
- Generating events: Create a class that cannot only receive events but also fire events. This technology can be used as a form of loosely coupled communication between the classes in your program. Loose coupling of this kind is highly respected in the OOP programming world because it promotes reuse and helps develop robust architectures.
- Custom events: Look at how to create custom events that are tailor-made to convey a particular type of information.

JBuilder provides easy-to-use mechanisms for handling most of these technologies. This chapter will explore these techniques and give you some tips on how to expedite event-based development.

Java events are not always an easy subject, especially for people new to the Java language. The level of complexity involved is significant but not mind-boggling. A modest level of effort in this area will yield big results in the long run. Furthermore, JBuilder makes this topic much simpler than it would be were you trying to write event-handling code by hand.

NOTE: Not all of the techniques shown in this chapter are supported in the Personal version of JBuilder. However, I will show all the code that the JBuilder wizards generate. If necessary, you can simply type the code in by hand. The MouseWheelListener class is found only in JDK 1.4.

Basic Event Handling

You already know the simplest way to handle events in JBuilder. However, we should go over it one more time to be sure that we understand exactly how this code is structured.

NOTE: In this chapter you are going to learn how to make a JButton object respond to events. You will also learn about the ActionEvent object. I will not, however, include descriptions of how to make a JButton respond to keypresses or how to make it respond to a key combination, such as Alt+X. I will also not cover changing the text of the button, using HTML with the button, or adding

icons to the button. All of these latter subjects are discussed later in this section of the book. In particular, see Chapter 18, "The Art of the Button."

Create a new project and place inside it a new application that includes a JMenuBar. The ability to create a menu bar as part of the application is built into the JBuilder Application Wizard, which was described in Chapter 3.

Make sure Frame1 has its layout set to the default BorderLayout. Drop a JButton down on Frame1. Make sure the constraints for the button are set to Center. At this stage, your application is all button. When you run it, it should look like Figure 14-1.

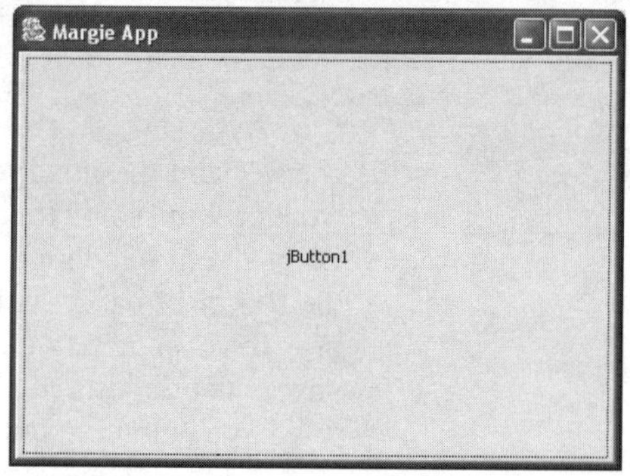

Figure 14-1: A default JBuilder project with a button dropped down onto Frame1

What we want to do now is create a simple event that can be associated with this button. More specifically, when the user presses this button, we want our event to be called and some associated action to take place. For instance, we might pop up a dialog that will allow the user to choose a new application.

There are two ways to associate an event with the button:

1. Double-click on the button. This will automatically take you to the source for your program and create a method handler stub for you.
2. Turn to the Events page of the Inspector and click on the actionPerformed property. A single click should give you an editable suggested name for your property. Use this single-click technology to specify the name for the event handler you are about to create. You can go with the default if you want, but you can use this opportunity to give your event handler a more meaningful name. A double-click or a press of the Enter key will take you to source view and create the method stub for you.

Regardless of which course you take, the method stub that was created should look something like this, though the actual name of the method will vary:

```
void JButton1_actionPerformed(ActionEvent e)
{

}
```

Fill in the method with some simple code so that you can see it in action:

```
void JButton1_actionPerformed(ActionEvent e)
{
      JOptionPane.showMessageDialog(this,
            "Hate is not conquered by hate, hate is conquered by love!");
}
```

The JButton1_actionPerformed method will be called automatically when jButton1 is selected by the user.

NOTE: The JOptionPane class is designed to help you build pop-up dialogs of various types. It has methods such as showMessageDialog, showInputDialog, showConfirmDialog, and so on. This book is about JBuilder, not about the JDK, so I will ask that you read the help or visit Sun's web

site if you want to learn more about this class. There are many examples of using the class in the source code on the CD, so you can grep through that code if you want to see the class in action.

NOTE: Before moving on to the next subject, I should perhaps mention that there are occasions when you will get error messages when trying to create an event handler. For instance, you might double-click on jButton1 and receive a seemingly nonsensical error saying that a parenthesis was not found. If something like this happens to you, try closing the file you are working on and then opening it again from the recently used files list. This usually fixes the problem for me.

How Events Get Called

The JButton1_actionPerformed method in the previous section is not called directly by the JDK. Instead, it is called by a class embedded inside of Frame1. It is now time to spend a moment thinking about that class.

The class that calls JButton1_actionPerformed can appear in one of two places in your source code. Where it resides depends on the settings you selected in the Project Properties dialog reached by selecting Project | Project Properties | Code Style from the JBuilder menu. The dialog, which was mentioned in Chapter 5, is shown in Figure 14-2.

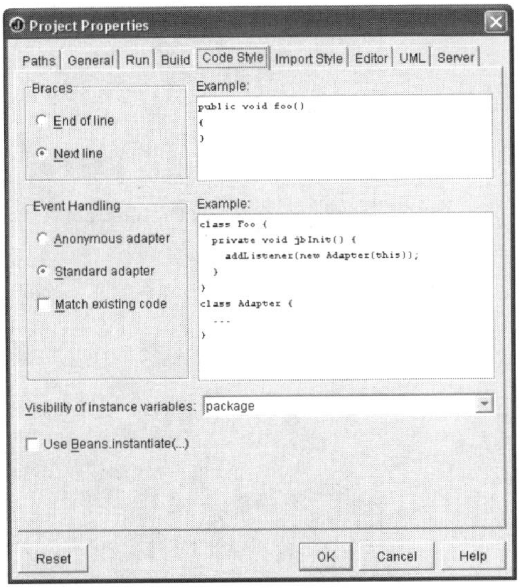

Figure 14-2: Selecting the style for event-handling adapters in the Project Properties dialog

To understand exactly what is happening now, you need to take a look at two copies of the complete source code for a JFrame with a button on it and one response method. The first version is found in Listing 14-1 and the second in Listing 14-2.

Listing 14-1: The source for Frame1 as it appears when you use standard adapters

```
package untitled32;

import java.awt.*;
import javax.swing.*;
import java.awt.event.*;

public class Frame2 extends JFrame
{
    JButton JButton1 = new JButton();

    public Frame2()
    {
        try
        {
            jbInit();
        }
        catch(Exception e)
        {
            e.printStackTrace();
```

```
        }
    }
    private void jbInit() throws Exception
    {
        JButton1.setText("JButton1");
        JButton1.addActionListener(new Frame2_JButton1_actionAdapter(this));
        this.getContentPane().add(JButton1, BorderLayout.CENTER);
    }

    void JButton1_actionPerformed(ActionEvent e)
    {

    }
}

class Frame2_JButton1_actionAdapter implements java.awt.event.ActionListener
{
    Frame2 adaptee;

    Frame2_JButton1_actionAdapter(Frame2 adaptee)
    {
        this.adaptee = adaptee;
    }
    public void actionPerformed(ActionEvent e)
    {
        adaptee.JButton1_actionPerformed(e);
    }
}
```

Listing 14-2: The source for Frame1 as it appears when you use anonymous adapters

```
package margieapp;

import java.awt.*;
import javax.swing.*;
import java.awt.event.*;

/**
 * <p>Title: </p>
 * <p>Description: </p>
 * <p>Copyright: Copyright (c) 2002</p>
 * <p>Company: </p>
 * @author unascribed
 * @version 1.0
 */

public class Frame2 extends JFrame
{
      JButton JButton1 = new JButton();

      public Frame2()
      {
```

```
        try
        {
            jbInit();
        }
        catch(Exception e)
        {
            e.printStackTrace();
        }
    }
    private void jbInit() throws Exception
    {
        JButton1.setText("JButton1");
        JButton1.addActionListener(new java.awt.event.ActionListener()
        {
            public void actionPerformed(ActionEvent e)
            {
                JButton1_actionPerformed(e);
            }
        });
        this.getContentPane().add(JButton1, BorderLayout.CENTER);
    }

    void JButton1_actionPerformed(ActionEvent e)
    {

    }
}
```

I created these two source files by first choosing File | New from the JBuilder menu. In the General page of the Object Browser, I then chose Frame, which created a new instance of the JFrame class. In Listing 14-1, the Code Style for Event Handling in the project was set to Standard Adapter, and in Listing 14-2, it was set to Anonymous Adapter. I then dropped a button on each frame and created a handler for it.

The reason I created new JFrame descendants rather than working with a Frame1 instance was so these examples would not include irrelevant code, such as the processWindowEvent method. This code is stripped down so that it shows little detail other than the code we want to focus on.

In Listing 14-1, notice that there is a class called Frame2_JButton1_actionAdapter:

```
class Frame2_JButton1_actionAdapter implements java.awt.event.ActionListener
{
   Frame2 adaptee;

   Frame2_JButton1_actionAdapter(Frame2 adaptee)
   {
      this.adaptee = adaptee;
   }
   public void actionPerformed(ActionEvent e)
   {
      adaptee.JButton1_actionPerformed(e);
   }
}
```

Part III

Look further and you will see that this class calls the JButton1_actionPerformed method that we had created earlier:

```
adaptee.JButton1_actionPerformed(e);
```

What we have established so far is that there is a class called an adapter included in your source code that calls the button handler. The button handler is where you place the code you want to have called when the button is pressed.

So how does the JDK know to call your adapter when the button is pressed? The following code in jbInit supplies part of the answer to that question:

```
JButton1.addActionListener(new Frame2_JButton1_actionAdapter(this));
```

The addActionListener method exists deep inside the JDK. This method calls it and assigns the Frame2_JButton1_actionAdapter class to this instance of the JButton class. The jButton1 class maintains a list of all the actionAdapters that have been registered with it. When the button itself is pressed, it looks at that list and calls the actionPerformed method of that class:

```
public void actionPerformed(ActionEvent e)
{
    adaptee.JButton1_actionPerformed(e);
}
```

So now the mystery is no longer a mystery. We have established that the JDK knows to call the adapter class because you called addActionListener, and we have seen that the adapter class calls our JButton1_actionPerformed method. So far so good.

NOTE: You will, in fact, learn more about this process in the next chapter. There you will create your own custom instances of the addActionListener method. But for now, you have enough information to see how the system works.

You might also be interested in viewing the first method of the adapter:

```
Frame2 adaptee;

Frame2_JButton1_actionAdapter(Frame2 adaptee)
{
    this.adaptee = adaptee;
}
```

This method is the constructor. It is passed an instance of the main frame for your application back in jbInit:

```
JButton1.addActionListener(new Frame2_JButton1_actionAdapter(this));
```

The word "this" is the reference to Frame2 that gets passed to the adapter's constructor.

The frame is then assigned to the variable adaptee. The adaptee variable is used in the actionPerformed method to call JButton1_actionPerformed.

NOTE: In case you are curious, I believe that adaptee is not an English word. It is, however, a proper French word. I'm sure that the JBuilder developers were in fact thinking in French when they came up with this variable name.

At this stage, you now know the whole story of how events work when you use standard adapters in a JBuilder application. I believe that all of the code in this book uses standard adapters.

Anonymous Adapters

Anonymous adapters, shown in Listing 14-2, use an anonymous class instead of a standard Java class. The anonymous class is created in jbInit:

```
JButton1.addActionListener(new java.awt.event.ActionListener()
{
        public void actionPerformed(ActionEvent e)
        {
                JButton1_actionPerformed(e);
        }
});
```

Anonymous classes are created, declared, and implemented inside the parameter of another method. The method in this case looks like this:

```
JButton1.addActionListener( - class inserted here - )
```

The class that has been inserted into the parameter for this method looks like this:

```
new java.awt.event.ActionListener()
{
        public void actionPerformed(ActionEvent e)
        {
                JButton1_actionPerformed(e);
        }
}
```

Note the existence of the word new before the class declaration, and note further that the ancestor class name is given, but the class itself has no name: It is anonymous. The class is derived from ActionListener, but the child class has no name.

As you can see, this class is very similar to the adapter class from Listing 14-1. It has no constructor and no Francophile adaptee variable. Nevertheless, its structure should be very familiar. The adaptee variable is not needed since this class lives inside the scope of Frame2, and hence can call its methods directly. In fact, this class has an actionPerformed method that directly calls JButton1_actionPerformed:

```
public void actionPerformed(ActionEvent e)
{
        JButton1_actionPerformed(e);
}
```

Once again, the JButton1.addActionListener method inserts a handle to this anonymous class into a list maintained by jButton1. When jButton1 is pressed, all the classes in that list have their actionPerformed method called. What happens inside that method is up to us. In this case, we have that method call JButton1_actionPerformed. Or rather, JBuilder automatically generates code that will call JButton1_actionPerformed.

Anonymous Adapters vs. Standard Adapters

When writing this book and developing the example programs, I had to decide whether I wanted to use anonymous adapters or standard adapters. As you already know, I chose to use standard adapters.

Why did I make that decision? To me, standard adapters are easy to parse visually. Furthermore, the use of standard adapters helps to keep my jbInit methods free of clutter.

I make absolutely no claim that my choice here is better than its opposite. To my mind, this is simply a matter of taste, and my taste tends toward standard adapters. You should examine your own mind and use the technique that you prefer. In the long run, it is all pretty much six of one, half a dozen of the other. You should just pick your favorite technology and go along with it as happily as possible.

The ActionEvent Class

As you know, ActionPerformed methods get passed a parameter of type ActionEvent:

```
void JButton1_actionPerformed(ActionEvent e)
```

The ActionEvent class contains a good bit of information about the state of the mouse and keyboard when this event was triggered. You will get a chance to explore many of the more important features of this class in the next chapter, "Firing Events." In that chapter, you will learn how to create instances of this class and how to use many of its methods. For now, however, there are still a few basic things you ought to know about the class.

Consider the methods of the ActionEvent class shown in Table 14-1.

Table 14-1

Method	Description
e.getActionCommand();	Retrieve a string associated with the command.
e.getModifiers();	Retrieve the state of the Alt and Ctrl keys.
e.getID();	Retrieve an integer associated with the command.
e.getWhen();	Find out when the command was issued.
e.getSource();	Which control caused the event? In our case, jButton1.

NOTE: The e.getWhen() method is a new feature in JDK 1.4. That means that unless you switch the JDK to 1.4.0, you will not be able to use this portion of the code. If you need to switch your JDK, you will find instructions for this in Chapter 1 and in the ReadMe file on the CD, which is called index.html. If you are using JBuilder Personal, you may not be able to switch the JDK, so comment out the code that relates to this method. See Chapter 1 and the ReadMe file.

A program called ActionEventMadness, found on the CD that accompanies this book, demonstrates many of the important methods supported by the ActionEvent class. The key parts of that program are examined over the course of the next few paragraphs.

Consider the following button response method:

```
void JButton1_actionPerformed(ActionEvent e)
{
        System.out.println("ParamString: " + e.paramString());
        System.out.println("Action Command:" + e.getActionCommand());
        int modifiers = e.getModifiers();
        System.out.println("Modifiers: " +
                KeyEvent.getKeyModifiersText(modifiers));
        System.out.println("ID: " + e.getID());
        long a = e.getWhen();
        Date d = new Date(a);
        System.out.println("When: " + d);
        System.out.println("Source: " + e.getSource().getClass().getName());
}
```

This method outputs the following information:

```
ParamString: ACTION_PERFORMED,cmd=JButton1,when=1019943559903,modifiers=
            Alt+Shift+Button1
Action Command:JButton1
Modifiers: Alt+Shift+Button1
ID: 1001
When: Sat Apr 27 14:39:19 PDT 2002
Souce: javax.swing.JButton
```

The paramString() method of the action event gives you some general information about the state of the button used to trigger the event. Action Command is a string associated with the button. You can change this string in the Inspector at design time.

The modifiers define which special keys were selected at the time the button was pressed. Here I used the KeyEvent.getKeyModifiersText method to find out the state of the buttons. You could do so yourself with code that looks like this:

```
void JButtonBitMasks_actionPerformed(ActionEvent e)
    {
        String stateStr = "";
        int keyState = e.getModifiers();
        if ((keyState & InputEvent.ALT_MASK) != 0) {
            stateStr += "Alt is down\n";
        }
        if ((keyState & InputEvent.SHIFT_MASK) != 0) {
            stateStr += "Shift is down\n";
        }
        if ((keyState & InputEvent.CTRL_MASK) != 0) {
            stateStr += "Ctrl is down\n";
        }
        if (stateStr.length() == 0) {
            stateStr = "You did not hold down Alt, Shift, or Ctrl";
        }

        jTextArea1.setText(stateStr);
    }
```

This code uses the logical & operator to perform bitwise operations revealing the state of the pressed keys. For instance, this code will reveal whether or not the Alt key was selected at the time the button that triggered the event was pressed:

```
int keyState = e.getModifiers();
if ((keyState & InputEvent.ALT_MASK) != 0)
```

The ID returned by a call to ActionEvent.getID() represents a unique number associated with a particular event.

A call to ActionEvent.getWhen() reveals the time when the event occurred. Here is code for translating the returned long integer into a string:

```
        long a = e.getWhen();
        Date d = new Date(a);
        System.out.println("When: " + d);
```

The result might look something like this:

```
When: Sat Apr 27 14:39:19 PDT 2002
```

Finally, the getSource method returns an instance of the control that triggered the call to this event handler. Call getSource.getClass.getName to get the type of class that caused the event. Here is code to retrieve the caption of the button that was pressed:

```
jTextArea1.append("\nButton caption: " + ((JButton)(e.getSource())).getText());
```

Using Other Standard Events

It should be obvious that JBuilder supports more than the actionPerformed event. When you select a particular component, and turn to the Events page in the Inspector, you are likely to see a range of event handlers that JBuilder will create for you. For instance, JButton supports the ancestorAdded, ancestorRemoved, itemStateChanged, stateChanged, etc., events. Exploring all of these event handlers is a major undertaking and is really the task of a book on the JDK, not a book on JBuilder. So I will leave it up to you to explore these various event handlers and see what you can do with them.

Customizing the JBuilder Event-Handling Mechanism

You have seen the technique that JBuilder uses to handle events. In most cases, I suggest going with the flow and allowing JBuilder to create your event handlers for you, using the techniques just described. However, I want to take a moment to point out two things:

- There are other ways to handle events than those shown so far in this chapter.
- JBuilder may not help you create these alternative kinds of event handlers, but it will not prevent you from using them if you want.

The StringTest01 program, found in the ComplexProject subdirectory on this book's CD, shows an alternative way to handle events. The event code in that program was partially created by JBuilder and partially created by hand.

At the very bottom of Frame1.java, you will find a class that looks like this:

```
/** I am using the same ActionListener for all of my menu items in this
 *  application. Furthermore, I am sending most of them to the same
 *  event handler back in the main program.
 */
class MainListener implements ActionListener
{
  Frame1 adaptee;

  MainListener(Frame1 adaptee)
  {
    this.adaptee = adaptee;
  }

  public void actionPerformed(ActionEvent e)
  {
      if (e.getSource() == adaptee.jMenuFileExit)
      {
        adaptee.jMenuFileExit_actionPerformed(e);
      }
```

```
        else if (e.getSource() == adaptee.jMenuHelpAbout)
        {
          adaptee.jMenuHelpAbout_actionPerformed(e);
        }
        else if (e.getSource() == adaptee.jMenuItemReverse)
        {
          adaptee.jMenuItemReverse_actionPerformed(e);
        }
        else if (e.getSource() == adaptee.jMenuItemGetFirstWord)
        {
          adaptee.jMenuItemReverse_actionPerformed(e);
        }
        else if (e.getSource() == adaptee.jMenuItemStripFirstWord)
        {
          adaptee.jMenuItemReverse_actionPerformed(e);
        }
    }
  }
```


This class is like the Frame2_JButton1_actionAdapter class you saw earlier in this chapter:

```
class Frame2_JButton1_actionAdapter implements java.awt.event.ActionListener
```

It is of the same type, and it is declared in the same location. The only difference is that it has a shorter name and calls not one event handler back in class Frame1 but a whole series of them.

If you have been using Java for a while, I'm sure you have seen code similar to this. It uses a method of the ActionEvent object passed to the handler to sort out which control in Frame1 actually called the class. The method it uses is called getSource, and it returns the instance of the class that called MainListener.

After the class decides which object called it, it uses that information to call the appropriate method back in Frame1:

```
        else if (e.getSource() == adaptee.jMenuItemStripFirstWord)
        {
          adaptee.jMenuItemReverse_actionPerformed(e);
        }
```

There were several different ways to associate the MainListener class with the various event-generating components in Frame1. The technique this program uses looks like this:

```
MainListener listen = new MainListener(this);
jMenuFileExit.addActionListener(listen);
jMenuItemReverse.addActionListener(listen);
jMenuItemGetFirstWord.addActionListener(listen);
etc…
```

There is no way to make JBuilder generate code of this type automatically. You have to write it yourself. I simply created one event handler using the JBuilder tools and then wrote the rest of the code by hand.

The technique shown here clearly uses fewer resources than the technique that JBuilder uses. In particular, it uses only one adapter class, while JBuilder code for handling this kind of situation would generate several adapter classes. On the other hand, a pure OOP-based language like Java is optimized to have very little overhead when creating classes. The overhead created by the adaptor classes is small enough to have no significant impact on the vast majority of programs. So wasting a lot of time doing things as I do here is usually not worth it. However, the option is available.

In the long run, perhaps the most important point is to see that JBuilder will allow you to customize your code to whatever extent you want. Do things the JBuilder way if you want, or go off in another direction if you prefer. JBuilder gives you the freedom to do what you want.

Listener Interfaces and Adapter Classes

Very few classes get raw mouse events automatically. In those few classes, if you turn to the Events page of the JBuilder Inspector, you will be able to create event handlers for mouse events just as you create event handlers for the actionEvent that occurs when the user clicks on a button.

NOTE: A JButton ActionPerformed event is clearly caused by a button click, but it is not a button event in the strict sense of the word. It tells you that the button was selected, and if you explore the ActionEvent parameter passed to this method, you can find out about the state of the mouse and keyboard when the button was selected. But still, the purpose of the event is not to tell you about the mouse itself, but only that the user wanted to access the functionality encapsulated in your response handler.

Sometimes you will see that a class does not receive events that you might want it to receive. For instance, you might want to allow a JFrame descendant to receive mouse events. This last section of the chapter shows how to add mouse events to a class that does not already provide support for mouse events in the Events page of the Inspector.

So far in this chapter you have had a chance to look at both firing and receiving events. The events we have been looking at are fairly straightforward. Some events, like those associated with the MouseListener interface, are a bit more complex:

```
public interface MouseListener extends EventListener
{
    public void mouseClicked(MouseEvent e);
    public void mousePressed(MouseEvent e);
    public void mouseReleased(MouseEvent e);
    public void mouseEntered(MouseEvent e);
    public void mouseExited(MouseEvent e);
}
```

By this point in the chapter, it should be relatively clear what is going on in this interface. We have a single event called a MouseEvent that gets sent to you on five different occasions: when the mouse is clicked, pressed, or released, and when the mouse enters or leaves the current window. You will get an even deeper understanding of how all this occurs when you read the next chapter and start creating your own events and listener interfaces.

NOTE: A clicked event occurs when the mouse has been pressed and released in one motion, while the pressed event occurs when the mouse has been pressed.

KeyListener, MouseListener, MouseWheelListener, and MouseMotionListener

I'm going to show you a program found on the CD called MouseKey that demonstrates how to set up a JFrame descendant that supports the KeyListener, MouseListener, MouseWheel-Listener, and MouseMotionListener interfaces. The program is shown in Figure 14-3.

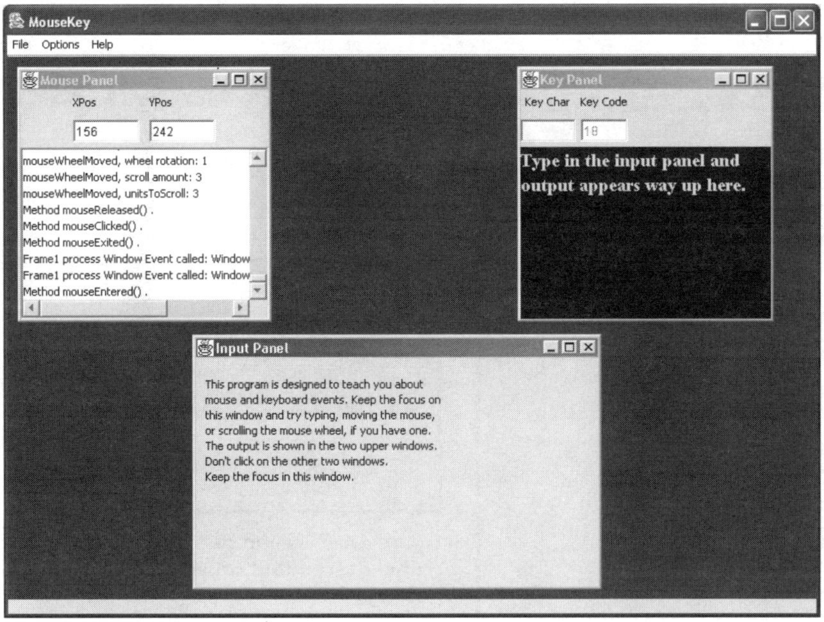

Figure 14-3: The MouseKey program supports the MDI interface. It demonstrates techniques for accepting mouse and keyboard input.

NOTE: The MouseWheelListener interface described in this chapter is part of JDK 1.4. If you need to switch your JDK, you will find instructions for this in Chapter 1 and in the ReadMe file on the CD, which is called index.html. If you are using JBuilder Personal, you may not be able to use the MouseWheelListener interface inside of JBuilder. See Chapter1 and the ReadMe file.

The MouseKey program uses an MDI interface. Near the end of the chapter, I will explain exactly how to create a program that uses this kind of interface. For now, you need only know that there is a main window in the program. Residing on top of this main window are three JPanel descendants. The lower of the three panels is the InputPanel. You can type on this panel. The top two panels will be used to display the input that occurs in the InputPanel. In particular, when the user clicks in the InputPanel, a report of that mouse event is shown in the MousePanel. When the user types on the InputPanel, a report of the user's keypresses is shown in the KeyPanel.

Understanding the MouseKey Program

You may want to follow along here and try to create your own copy of the MouseKey program. I will not give you detailed instructions on how to proceed, but I will try to give you enough information so you should not find it hard to fill in the blanks by yourself. The glue that holds the program together is MDI, or virtual desktop. I will explain how that glue works at the very end of this chapter.

If building the program feels a bit too daunting, then simply open the copy found on the CD that accompanies this book. Run the program a few times, and examine the code included in it so that you can see how the text in the book relates to a real world program.

To create the program yourself, first create a new project and new application, as described in Chapter 3. Choose **File | New Class** from the JBuilder menu and create a JPanel descendant called InputPanel.java. Figure 14-4 shows how to pick the base class, and Figure 14-5 shows the correctly filled out Class Wizard. Click **OK** to close the wizard, and then focus this class in the editor.

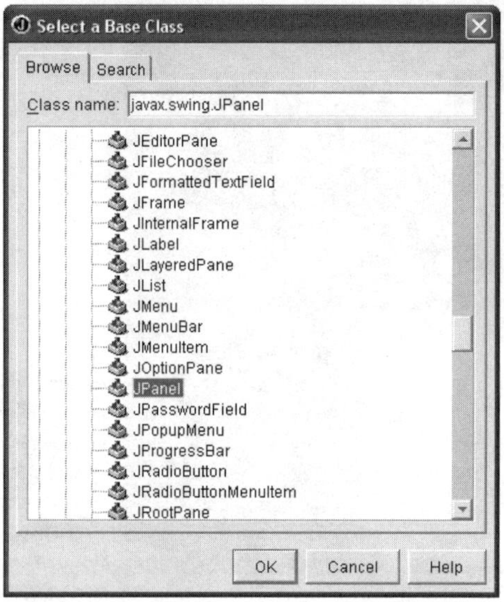

Figure 14-4: Browsing to select the class from which the InputPanel will descend

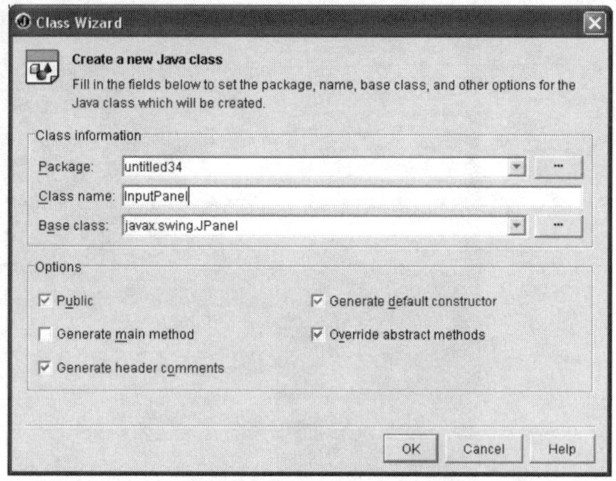

Figure 14-5: Filling out the Class Wizard to put a new JPanel descendant called InputPanel in the untitled34 package

If you are using the SE or Enterprise versions of JBuilder, choose **Wizards | Implement Interface**. Browse to java.awt.event, and select the **MouseMotionListener**, **MouseListener**, **KeyListener**, and (if you have JDK 1.4) **MouseWheelListener** interfaces, as shown in Figure 14-6.

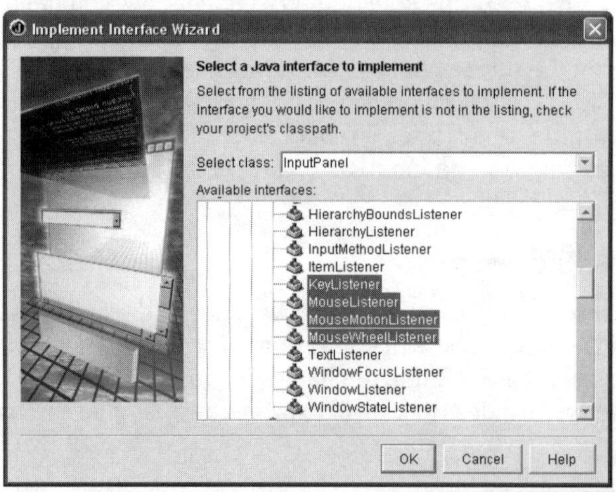

Figure 14-6: Selecting interfaces in the Implement Interface Wizard

The following code will be added near the top of your InputPanel.java file:

```
public class InputPanel extends JFrame
      implements MouseListener, MouseMotionListener, MouseWheelListener,
                 KeyListener
```

If you don't have the Implement Interface Wizard in your version of the product, you will have to type in this code manually.

In the implementation of your class, code similar to that shown in Listing 14-3 will be added by the Interface Wizard. If you are using the Personal edition of JBuilder, you will have to type in this code manually. The code is a little lengthier than this, in that it includes more methods and provides the name of the method that failed if an exception is raised. I've pared it down just a bit here so that it will be easier to read.

Listing 14-3: The default implementation of the MouseListener, MouseMotionListener, and MouseWheelListener that is provided by the Interface Wizard

```
public void mouseClicked(MouseEvent e)
{
  /**@todo Implement this java.awt.event.MouseListener method*/
  throw new java.lang.UnsupportedOperationException("not yet implemented.");
}
public void mousePressed(MouseEvent e)
{
  /**@todo Implement this java.awt.event.MouseListener method*/
  throw new java.lang.UnsupportedOperationException("not yet implemented.");
}
public void mouseReleased(MouseEvent e)
{
  /**@todo Implement this java.awt.event.MouseListener method*/
  throw new java.lang.UnsupportedOperationException("not yet implemented.");
}
public void mouseEntered(MouseEvent e)
{
  /**@todo Implement this java.awt.event.MouseListener method*/
  throw new java.lang.UnsupportedOperationException("not yet implemented.");
}
public void mouseExited(MouseEvent e)
{
  /**@todo Implement this java.awt.event.MouseListener method*/
  throw new java.lang.UnsupportedOperationException("not yet implemented.");
}
public void mouseDragged(MouseEvent e)
{
  /**@todo Implement this java.awt.event.MouseMotionListener method*/
  throw new java.lang.UnsupportedOperationException("not yet implemented.");
}
public void mouseMoved(MouseEvent e)
{
  /**@todo Implement this java.awt.event.MouseMotionListener method*/
  throw new java.lang.UnsupportedOperationException("not yet implemented.");
}
public void mouseWheelMoved(MouseWheelEvent e)
```

```
{
   /**@todo Implement this java.awt.event.MouseWheelListener method*/
   throw new java.lang.UnsupportedOperationException("not yet implemented.");
}
```

All of the @todo items will show up at the top of the structure pane under the node called To Do, as shown in Figure 14-7.

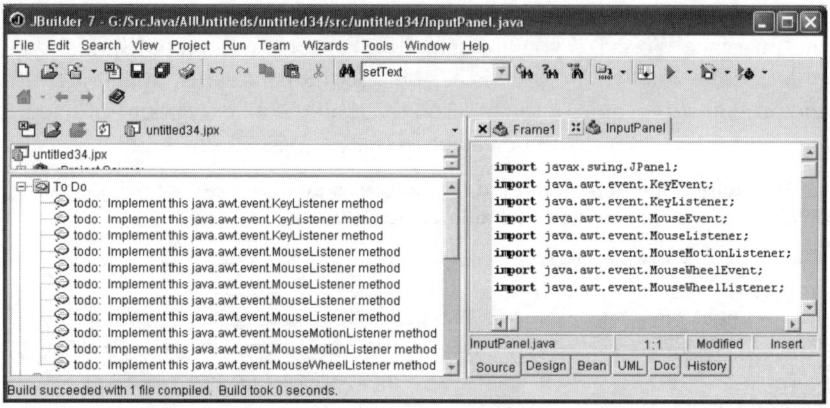

Figure 14-7: The todo items and import statements generated by the Interface Wizard all show up in the structure pane.

KeyListener Interface

Though it is not shown in Listing 14-1, the KeyListener interface is also supported by the MouseKey program. The KeyListener interface looks like this:

```
public interface KeyListener extends EventListener
{
   public void keyTyped(KeyEvent e);
   public void keyPressed(KeyEvent e);
   public void keyReleased(KeyEvent e);
}
```

You won't see this interface in the MouseKey exactly as shown here. However, the InputPanel class implements each of these methods in order to fulfill the contract implied by having a class implement the interface.

keyTyped events do not provide as much detailed information about the key event as keyPressed events. They only tell you what key was pressed and not the key code. You will learn more about key codes later in the chapter. The Sun documentation suggests that you consider keyPressed events as the preferred way to get character input since they are more completely platform independent. On the other hand, if you want to know a bit more about which key was pressed on a Windows or Linux platform, then use keyTyped.

Creating the KeyPanel and MousePanel

After setting up the InputPanel, you should create two more JPanel descendants called KeyPanel and MousePanel. Give them the appearance of the two top windows shown in Figure 14-3. Because of space considerations, I don't want to explain these classes in too much detail. If you need help building them, look at the code for the MouseKey program found on the CD, but you should be able to recreate their general appearance by basing your code on what you see in Figure 14-3.

These two panels will be used to display the input that occurs in the InputPanel. In particular, when the user clicks in the InputPanel, a report of that mouse event is shown in the MousePanel. When the user types on the InputPanel, a report of the user's keypresses is shown in the KeyPanel. I will explain later in the chapter exactly how the code to display the information should look. For now, just create the interface.

Registering a Listener

Let's take a moment here to contemplate what has happened. You have stated that your class, InputPanel, supports interfaces designed to handle mouse input and keyboard input. Declaring all these interfaces gives you the potential to receive events.

To switch from being a potential listener to being an actual recipient of events, you need to register yourself with the class that will generate the events. You will probably do this in the jbInit method of the InputPanel:

```
this.addKeyListener(this);
this.addMouseListener(this);
this.addMouseMotionListener(this);
this.addMouseWheelListener(this);
```


After adding these methods, the only thing you have left to do is fill in the code in the methods that receive the events. In this case, all we really want to do is record that we are receiving the events. So you could write something like this:

```
System.out.println("Mouse clicked pressed.");
```

However, we want to do something a little bit more interesting. In particular, we want to show the output in the KeyPanel and MousePanel classes that you created. In the next section, you will see how to proceed.

Using the KeyPanel and MousePanel

As you know, the mouse and keyboard input recorded by the InputPanel is displayed on the interface for the KeyPanel and MousePanel classes. In the InputPanel's constructor, pass in the instances of the mousePanel and keyPanel so that it will have access to them:

```
MousePanel mousePanel;
KeyPanel keyPanel;

public InputPanel(MousePanel mousePanel, KeyPanel keyPanel)
{
      this.mousePanel = mousePanel;
      this.keyPanel = keyPanel;
      this.addKeyListener(this);
      this.addMouseListener(this);
      this.addMouseMotionListener(this);
      this.addMouseWheelListener(this);
}
```

Now the InputPanel will be able to send messages to these panels when it receives input:

```
      public void keyPressed(KeyEvent e)
      {
            keyPanel.keyTyped(e.getKeyChar(), e.getKeyCode());
            Frame1.say("Method keyPressed() .");
```

```
    }

    public void mouseMoved(MouseEvent e)
    {
          mousePanel.setMouseX(e.getX());
          mousePanel.setMouseY(e.getY());
    }
```

The methods keyPanel.keyTyped, mousePanel.setMouseX, and mousePanel.setMouseY simply display the data that is passed to them. Here is the keyTyped method from KeyPanel.java:

```
    public void keyTyped(char key, int code)
    {
          jTextField1.setText(new String() + key);
          jTextField2.setText(new String () + code);
          if (code == 8)
          {
                String s = jTextArea1.getText();
                s = s.substring(0, s.length() -1);
                jTextArea1.setText(s);
          }
          else
          {
                jTextArea1.append(new String() + key);
          }
    }
```

And here is the method setMouseX from MousePanel.java:

```
    public void setMouseX(int mouseX)
    {
          this.mouseX = mouseX;
          jTextField2.setText(String.valueOf(mouseX));
    }
```

The JTextFields and JTextAreas that display data in the MousePanel and KeyPanel get the data that they will display from these calls to setMouseX, setMouseY, and keyTyped. Look at Figure 14-3 if you need clarification about what these methods do.

You should also note how the methods of the KeyEvent and MouseEvent classes are used to acquire specific information about the state of the keyboard or the mouse. For instance, the MouseEvent.getX() method tells the current X position of the mouse. The KeyEvent.getKeyChar() method reveals the key that the user pressed, such as the "A" or "B" key. More detailed information, such as the ASCII code of the key, can be found by calling getKeyCode. There are, of course, additional methods on all of these objects that you can use.

Finally, you should add a method to the InputPanel that sends more generic information to the MousePanel:

```
    protected void say(String outString)
    {
          mousePanel.addString(outString);
    }
```

Using the say method, you can quickly output a good deal of detailed information. For instance, these three lines of code use the MouseWheelEvent class, declared here as the variable e, to talk about the state of the wheel found in the middle of most modern mice:

```
say("mouseWheelMoved, wheel rotation: " + e.getWheelRotation());
Frame1.say("mouseWheelMoved, scroll amount: " + e.getScrollAmount());
Frame1.say("mouseWheelMoved, unitsToScroll: " + e.getUnitsToScroll());
```

NOTE: The mouse wheel classes are part of JDK 1.4.

The end result of all this passing around of information is to produce the program called MouseKey that is shown in Figure 14-3. When using the program, as long as you focus the bottom window, any mouse or keyboard input that you produce will be shown in the two upper windows.

Virtual Desktops: JDesktop, JInternalFrame, and MDI Programs

As you may have noticed, the MouseKey program has an unusual interface. It accepts mouse and keyboard input in one window and allows you to see the mouse events in a second window and the keyboard events in a third window, as shown in Figure 14-3. To do this, I used a JDesktopPane and JInternalFrame to create a virtual desktop. In the Windows world, this is called an MDI, Multiple Document Interface.

In Figure 14-3, you can see that three windows are shown as children of the main window. In particular, Frame1 owns three other windows called InputPanel, MousePanel, and KeyPanel. These windows are not dialogs that float on top of Frame1; instead they are children of Frame1 that live on its surface, much as a JButton or JTextField lives on the surface of a JFrame. The big difference is that a JButton stays in one place and never changes size, while these windows are moveable and resizeable. You cannot, however, move them outside the boundaries of Frame1.

To support the MDI interface, you should first declare a class called JDesktopPane:

```
JDesktopPane desktop;
```

Declare this class at the top of Frame1, up where JBuilder places the declarations for JButtons, JTextFields, and other data members of the class. In your jbInit method, you will declare that the JDesktopPane instance you create will live on the surface of Frame1:

```
    desktop = new JDesktopPane();
    contentPane.add(desktop);
```

The desktop will be the surface on which the MDI windows will live.

You can actually place one of the JPanel descendants we have created on the desktop by using the following code:

```
    private void createFrame(int x, int y, JPanel panel, int width,
            String caption)
    {
        JInternalFrame j = new JInternalFrame(caption,
            true,  // Window is resizable
            true,  // Window has a close icon
```

```
                true,  // Window has a maximizable icon
                true); // Window can be minimized to an icon
        j.setBounds(x, y, width, 250);
        j.setContentPane(panel);
        desktop.add(j);
        j.show();
    }
```

A JInternalFrame is a lightweight container for the windows that will be residing on the JDesktopPane instance. The first parameter in the JInternalFrame constructor is the name you want to give the window. This name will appear in the Windows caption bar. The next four parameters are Boolean values. Use them to decide whether the window can be resized, closed, maximized, minimized, and shown as an icon.

The code then goes on to set the bounds of the window. The next step is to place the JPanel instance that we are working with inside the JInternalFrame and add it to the JDesktopPane instance:

```
    j.setContentPane(panel);
    desktop.add(j);
```

In your jbInit, add the following code, which calls the createFrame method that we have just finished exploring:

```
        desktop = new JDesktopPane();
        contentPane.add(desktop);
        createFrame(10, 10, mousePanel, 250, "Mouse Panel");
        createFrame(500, 10, keyPanel, 250, "Key Panel");
        inputPanel = new InputPanel(mousePanel, keyPanel, "Input Panel);
        createFrame(150, 275, inputPanel, 400);
```

Mouse Adapters

An interface like MouseListener can be a bit intimidating at times. If all you want to do is find out when the mouse was clicked, it seems like quite a bit of trouble to have to implement five methods. (Of course, the Interface Wizard makes your task simpler, but there is still the sheer bulk of all those methods.)

A possible solution to this problem is a JDK class called java.awt.event.MouseAdapter:

```
public abstract class MouseAdapter implements MouseListener
{
    public void mouseClicked(MouseEvent e) {}
    public void mousePressed(MouseEvent e) {}
    public void mouseReleased(MouseEvent e) {}
    public void mouseEntered(MouseEvent e) {}
    public void mouseExited(MouseEvent e) {}
}
```

This class provides a very minimal implementation of the MouseListener interface. All of the methods are entirely empty, but they do in fact exist. Given this class, you can implement your mouseClicked event very simply:

```
class MyClass extends MouseAdapter
{
      public void mouseClicked(MouseEvent e)
      {
```

```
                // Do your stuff here.
        }
}
```

Summary

In this chapter you learned several different ways that a class can receive events. The chapter started out with a simple explanation of using the Inspector to pick up on the most common events, such as a click on a button. You learned that there are several different ways to handle these events, including the use of anonymous and standard adaptors.

The text then went on to explore event listener interfaces, which can be used to enable a class to receive various events that are not listed in the JBuilder Inspector. This section of the text focused on learning about MouseListeners, MouseMotionListeners, MouseWheel-Listeners, and KeyListeners.

As an aside, you also learned how to use JDesktopPane and JInternalFrame to produce MDI applications, or virtual desktops. This proved to be a very easy subject to understand.

In the next chapter, you are going to turn the whole subject on its head and learn how a class can fire events. In that chapter, you will also learn how to create custom events.

Chapter 15

Firing Events

Charlie Calvert

In the previous chapter you learned how a class can be taught to receive events. The next step is to learn how your class can generate events. The classes in the previous chapter sat passively by and waited for events to come to them. It is time for our objects to start taking a more active role.

Because the events you have seen have come seemingly out of nowhere, they may have taken on an aura of mystery. Mysterious subjects can often seem deep and complex. Let me assure you that the mechanism Java uses for generating events is not at all mysterious. It has a very logical structure that is easy to understand.

In this chapter you will learn how a class can fire standard events built into the JDK. You will also learn how to create your own custom events that are tailor-made for special situations.

NOTE: In this chapter, you will find that I use the words "event" and "message" synonymously.

A Send Event Example Program

Let's take a look at a very simple program with two windows, one of which sends an event to the other. You can find this program on the CD under the name SendSimpleMessage.

To build the program yourself, create a new project and place a default JBuilder application inside it, as explained in Chapter 3. After creating the application, choose **File | New Class** and add a new JDialog to the project called **MessageSender**.

MessageSender is going to send a simple message back to Frame1, and Frame1 is going to show the message to the user in a JTextArea. In a sense, MessageSender is a server, serving up data, and Frame1 is a client that consumes the data generated by MessageSender.

To give MessageSender the ability to send messages to Frame1, you should first select the **Bean** tab from the file view tabs along the bottom of the editor. There are five tabs in the Bean tools. Choose the **Events** tab.

NOTE: If you don't have a version of JBuilder that supports BeansExpress, you will have to type in this event code by hand. In that case, you might consider using a tool that can store these kinds of code snippets so that you can easily access them and paste them into your classes.

The Events page is divided up into two sections, as shown in Figure 15-1. On the left are events that this class is going to send. On the right are events that this class will receive or listen for.

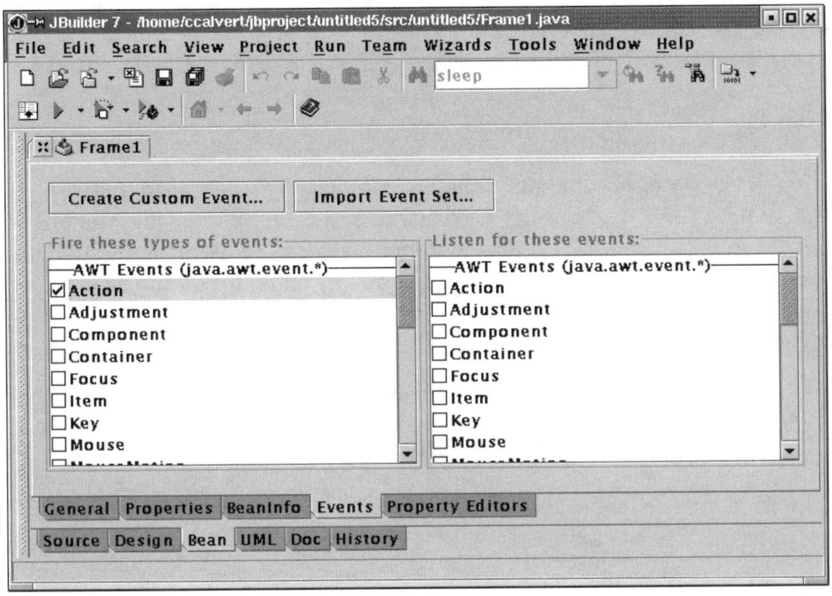

Figure 15-1: Tools for helping a class send and receive messages are found in the BeansExpress windows that come with JBuilder SE and Enterprise.

Choose the top event on the left, electing to have this class send an Action event. The following code will be added to MessageSender.java:

```
public synchronized void addActionListener(ActionListener l)
{
      Vector v = actionListeners == null ? new Vector(2) :
                 (Vector) actionListeners.clone();
      if (!v.contains(l))
      {
            v.addElement(l);
            actionListeners = v;
      }
}

public synchronized void removeActionListener(ActionListener l)
{
      if (actionListeners != null && actionListeners.contains(l))
      {
            Vector v = (Vector) actionListeners.clone();
            v.removeElement(l);
            actionListeners = v;
      }
}

protected void fireActionPerformed(ActionEvent e)
{
      if (actionListeners != null)
      {
            Vector listeners = actionListeners;
            int count = listeners.size();
            for (int i = 0; i < count; i++)
```

```
            {
                ((ActionListener) listeners.elementAt(i)).actionPerformed(e);
            }
        }
    }
```

This is quite a lot of code, but it is not difficult to understand. The first method, addActionListener, is one that you have already called many times. Now you are seeing how to implement it. It is the method that the listener class calls when it wants to list itself as a recipient of messages. As you can see, the code simply adds the calling class to an internal vector, or list of classes:

```
v.addElement(l);
```

All the other code is little more than syntactical sugar. This one line is the heart of the matter. Nothing could be much simpler.

The next method, removeActionListener, allows a class to unregister itself:

```
v.removeElement(l);
```

Once again, there may be several lines of code here, but it all boils down to something extremely simple.

The final method, fireActionPerformed, is in some ways the most important and most interesting. It is the method you will call when it is time to send a message to the listeners. There is nothing at all magical about the act of actually sending the message. The method simply iterates through all the classes in its list of listeners and calls the actionPerformed method of each class:

```
((ActionListener) listeners.elementAt(i)).actionPerformed(e);
```

This is why each listener class must support the ActionListener interface. If it did not support that interface, it would not be possible to typecast the class as an ActionListener, and it therefore would not be possible to call its actionPerformed method. Here is the complete declaration for the ActionListener interface:

```
public interface ActionListener extends EventListener
{
    public void actionPerformed(ActionEvent e);
}
```

This interface states that any class that supports it must have a method in it called actionPerformed that takes an ActionEvent as its sole parameter. When you start to put all the pieces together, you can see that the system is really simplicity itself. There is nothing complicated about it at all — so long as you really understand OOP and how it works. If you don't know about interface and typecasts and polymorphism, then it can all seem a bit mysterious. But if you understand OOP, this is really a very simple and instructive example of how it all works. It is as if the developers had set out as their goal to create the simplest possible demo that illustrated the basic principles of interfaces and polymorphism.

The Method that Sends the Message

The final question on the firing side of the equation is how to actually send a message. Here is the relevant code:

```
void jButton1_actionPerformed(ActionEvent e)
{
```

```
        String message = "The more ripe a cluster of rice becomes,\n" +
           "the lower it bows down its head.";
        ActionEvent event = new ActionEvent(this, 1, message);
        fireActionPerformed(event);
    }
```

As you can tell from looking at the method header, this is a simple handler for a button click. The method begins by declaring the String-based message that it wants to send to the client. The next step is to create an instance of the ActionEvent class. This is the class that will actually be passed from the server to the client when you call fireActionPerformed:

```
protected void fireActionPerformed(ActionEvent e)
{
        ... code omitted here
        ((ActionListener) listeners.elementAt(i)).actionPerformed(e);
        ... code omitted here
}
```

There are three constructors for ActionEvent. The one most commonly called is the one shown here. It takes three parameters:

```
public ActionEvent(Object source, int id, String command)
```

The first parameter is the instance of the object that is sending the message. As you recall, ActionEvent supports a method called getSource. We used the getSource method in the previous chapter in the StringTest01 program when trying to discover which component sent the message. ActionEvent.getSource() simply returns the method we include in this first parameter.

The second parameter is an ID that you assign to the event. This ID provides a way of discovering the source and the intent of the message that was sent. Just as we used getSource to find which component sent a message, you can use this id parameter to discover what type of message a particular component is sending. If a component only sends one type of message, which is the case in this example, this parameter is not particularly useful. Of course, if the message you want to send is itself an integer, you could use this parameter as the content of your message.

The final parameter, command, is a String specifying the message that you want to send. In this case, we want to send an old Japanese proverb about the value of humility. So that is what we place in the command parameter.

As I mentioned previously, there are two other constructors for the ActionEvent class. These constructors allow you to add the time that the message was sent and which keys were held down when the message was sent. In most cases, these latter parameters are not necessary, so you can just use the constructor I show here.

When the message is fully prepared, it can be sent to the client class via a call to fireActionPerformed:

```
        ActionEvent event = new ActionEvent(this, 1, message);
        fireActionPerformed(event);
```

In the various button response methods that you saw in the previous chapter, you learned one way that a client class can listen for messages sent by a class like MessageSender.java. This technique involves the creation of an adapter class, a call to the addActionListener method of the "server" class, and finally, the creation of a method to handle the call.

There is, however, a second way to receive messages: Frame1 itself can support the ActionListener interface. It is easy to write the code that will give Frame1 this ability. However, you can use the BeansExpress tools to create the event handler. Figure 15-2 shows the Events page in BeansExpress.

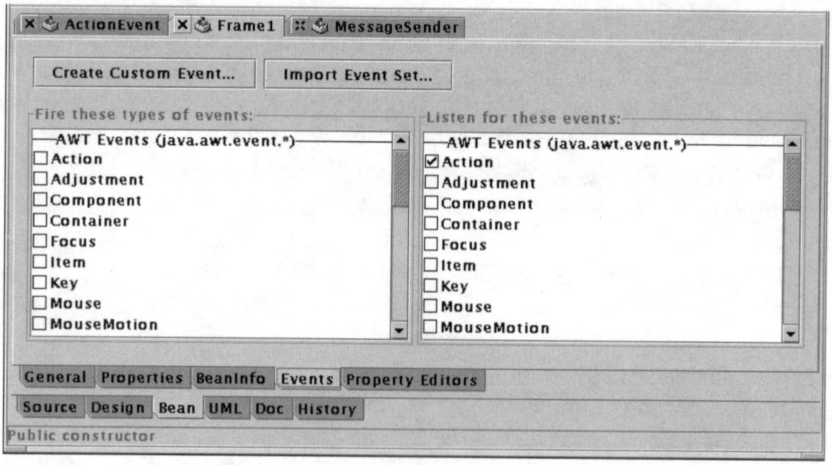

Figure 15-2: Using BeansExpress to ask a class to listen for a particular kind of event

Instead of having Frame1 generate an event, we are asking it to listen for events. After checking the Action box in the right-hand column, the following code is inserted into Frame1:

```
public class Frame1 extends JFrame implements ActionListener
{
      ... code omitted here

      public void actionPerformed(ActionEvent e)
      {
      }
}
```

As you can see, this code does nothing more than implement the ActionListener interface. As a result, one could just as easily have added this code to the class by using the Interface Wizard. If you had done that, the actionPerformed method would have looked like this:

```
public void actionPerformed(ActionEvent e)
{
  /**@todo Implement this java.awt.event.ActionListener method*/
  throw new java.lang.UnsupportedOperationException("Method actionPerformed() " +
      " not yet implemented.");
}
```

NOTE: Because the name actionPerformed is not very descriptive or specific, I am often tempted to give actionPerformed a new name. It should be clear to you that it would be a rather serious error to rename actionPerformed. We know that the ActionPerformed interface specifies that a class descended from it must implement a method called actionPerformed. If you rename the method, the class will no longer support the interface, and hence it 1) will no longer compile and 2) would not receive messages properly even if it could compile. If this is unclear to you, go back and look at the ActionListener interface:

```
public interface ActionListener extends EventListener
{
```

```
    public void actionPerformed(ActionEvent e);
}
```

To say that a class implements this interface is simply to say that it will have a method called actionPerformed. That is the full and total extent of the contract between a class that implements an interface and the interface itself. Implementing an interface is useful because it guarantees that a particular class will contain a particular set of methods. If this guarantee could not be established, the fireActionPerformed method would not work.

Simply supporting the ActionListener interface is not enough. You must also register the Frame1 class with the MessageSender class by calling addActionListener. In Frame1 of the SendSimpleMessage program, that task is accomplished as follows:

```
void jButton1_actionPerformed(ActionEvent e)
{
    MessageSender messageSender = new MessageSender(this);

    // Register this class as a recipient of ActionPerformed events
    messageSender.addActionListener(this);

    Dimension dimension = this.getSize();
    messageSender.setBounds(0, 0,
        (int)dimension.getWidth(), (int)dimension.getHeight());
    messageSender.show();
}
```

This method first creates an instance of the MessageSender class. It then calls the addActionListener method. Finally, it displays the MessageSender class as a dialog. After doing these things, the scene is set to allow the MessageSender class to call back into Frame1 and send it messages. These messages are displayed in the JTextArea found in the interface for Frame1:

```
public void actionPerformed(ActionEvent e)
{
    jTextArea1.append(e.getActionCommand() + "\n");
}
```

Notice that the string associated with the ActionEvent when you called its constructor is retrieved by calling getActionCommand. It doesn't take a lot of insight to guess that you can also retrieve the ID you passed into the constructor by calling a method named getID(). Once again, here is the most commonly used constructor for ActionEvent:

```
public ActionEvent(
    Object source,   // retrieved by calling getSource
    int id,          // retrieved by calling getID
    String command)  // retrieved by calling getActionCommand
```

Hopefully you now know all that you need to know to start sending simple messages back and forth between two classes. There is, however, a bit more to this topic. As a result, the discussion of this subject will continue in the next section.

Sending Custom Messages

If you look at Figures 15-4 and 15-5, you can see that there are several different kinds of messages that can be sent between objects. You should spend time becoming at least passingly familiar with these different kinds of events.

There may, however, come a time when none of the built-in message types will work for you. In such a case, you will want to send a custom message. The CustomMessageSender program, shown in Figure 15-3, demonstrates how to create a custom message and use it in a program.

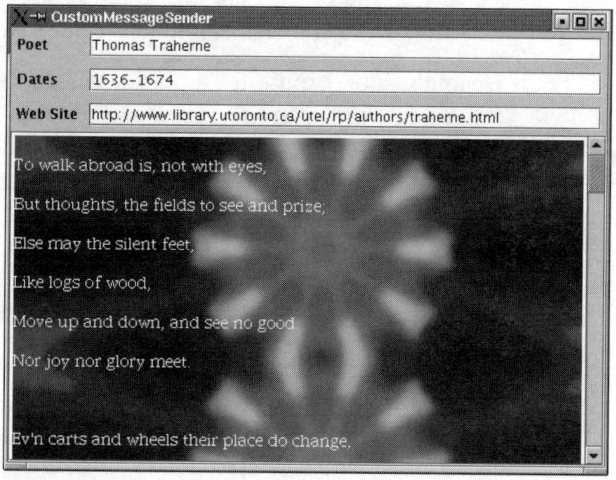

Figure 15-3: A sample view of the CustomMessage-Sender program

To create the program, first start a new project and insert a new application into it, as described in Chapter 3. As shown in Figure 15-4, use the File | New Class option to add a new class to your application called PoetMessageSender.java. The class should descend from java.lang.Object and be placed in a package called custommessagesender.poet.

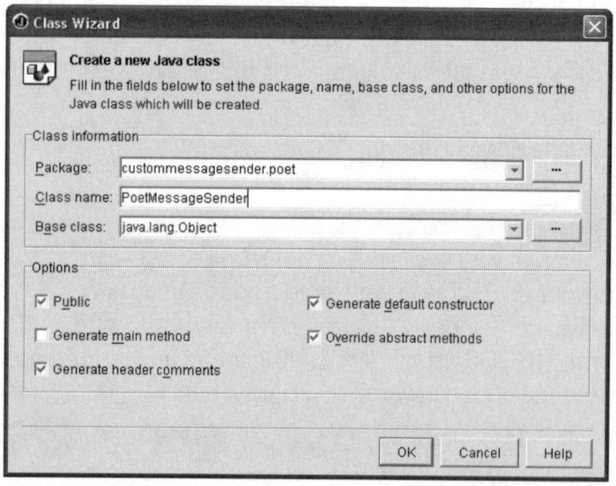

Figure 15-4: The new class you are creating should reside in a subdirectory of your main package called poet.

NOTE: A more in-depth discussion of packages is included in Part V: Project Management.

Focus your new class in the content pane. From the file view tabs beneath the editor, choose **Bean** and then the **Events** page. At the top of the page, you will see a button called Create Custom Event. Select the button. In the New Event Set dialog, create a new event called **Poet**, as shown in Figure 15-5. The class you are creating needs to fire two events. You can stay with dataChanged, which is the default name assigned to the first event. The second event should have the name percentDone. More than any other single thing, it is the existence of this second method that makes your event a unique custom event.

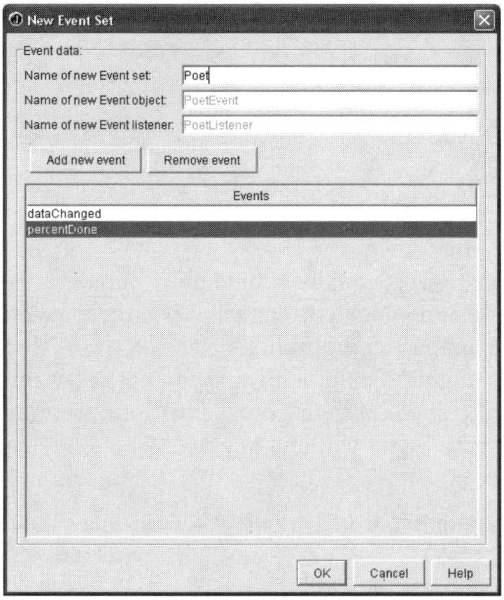

Figure 15-5: Fill out at least two fields in the New Event Set dialog. At the top, add the name of the event set. Use the bottom half of the dialog to add one or more method names.

Click **OK** in the dialog shown in Figure 15-5. You will be taken back to the BeansExpress Events page. As shown in Figure 15-6, put a check mark in the left-hand column of the page next to the event you have created.

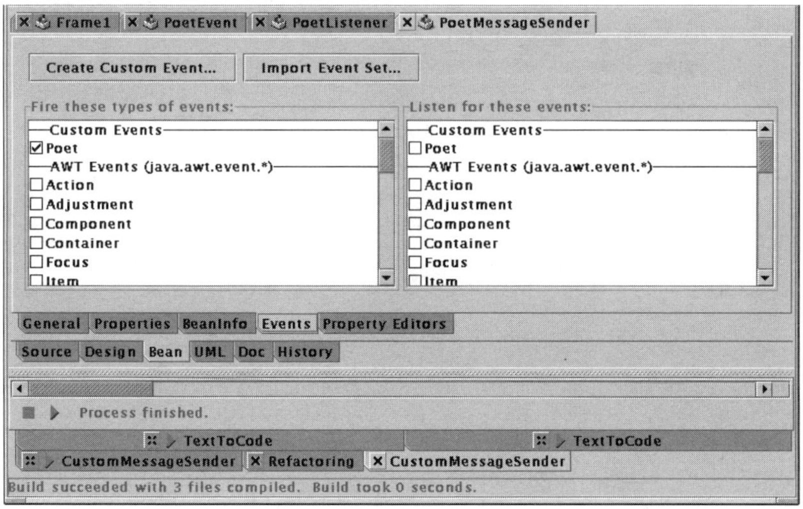

Figure 15-6: To use BeansExpress to create code for firing your new event, all you need to do is put a check mark by the new event you created.

After you put a check mark in front of the word Poet, the code for handling the event will be generated by JBuilder. The event itself will be stored in PoetEvent.java, and its listener interface will be stored in PoetListener.java. When you first see it, the PoetEvent class will look like this:

```
package custommessagesender.poet;

import java.util.*;
```

```
public class Poet1Event extends EventObject
{

    public Poet1Event(Object source)
    {
        super(source);
    }
}
```

The PoetListener class, shown in Listing 15-1, is equally simple in its initial incarnation. In essence, these two classes are blank slates on which you can paint whatever you please.

Knowing the high value that modern computer corporations place on the 17th century Metaphysical English poets, I thought it might be helpful if I turned PoetEvent into a small class that allowed you to easily incorporate some of their poems into your programs. The result is shown in Listing 15-2. In Listing 15-3 you will find PoetMessageSender.java, updated to fire PoetEvent messages.

Listing 15-1: A custom listener interface designed to work with the PoetEvent class shown in Listing 15-2

```
package custommessagesender.poet;

import java.util.*;

public interface PoetListener extends EventListener
{
      public void dataChanged(PoetEvent e);
      public void percentDone(int percent);
}
```

Listing 15-2: The custom event class that can be sent to a listener

```
package custommessagesender.poet;

import java.util.*;
import com.elvenware.codebox.FileBox;
import java.net.*;

/**
 * <p> A class for serving up data about the Metaphysical poets.</p>
 * <p>To use this class, first call getURL, then getPoet, getSite, and
 * getDate.<p>
 *
 * <p>Copyright: Copyright (c) 2002 Charlie Calvert</p>
 * <p>Company: Elvenware</p>
 * @author Charlie Calvert
 * @version 1.0
 */

public class PoetEvent extends EventObject
{

      Random random = new Random();
      private int poetIndex = 0;
```

```
private int percentDone = 0;

private String sites[] = new String[] {
      "http://www.luminarium.org/sevenlit/donne/",
      "http://www.luminarium.org/sevenlit/herbert/",
      "http://www.luminarium.org/sevenlit/vaughan/",
      "http://www.library.utoronto.ca/utel/rp/authors/traherne.html",
      "http://www.luminarium.org/sevenlit/cowley/",
      "http://www.luminarium.org/sevenlit/crashaw/",
      "http://www.luminarium.org/sevenlit/marvell/",
      "http://www.library.utoronto.ca/utel/rp/authors/coleridg.html"};

private String poets[] = new String[] {"John Donne",
      "George Herbert", "Henry Vaughan", "Thomas Traherne",
      "Abraham Cowley", "Richard Crashaw", "Andrew Marvell",
      "Samuel Taylor Coleridge"};

private String dates[] = new String[] {"1572-1631",
      "1593-1633", "1622-1695", "1636-1674", "1618-1667",
      "1612-1649", " 1621-1678", "1772-1834"};

private String poems[] = new String[] {
      "John_Donne-Song.html",
      "George_Herbert-Love_III.html",
      "Henry_Vaughan-The_Shower.html",
      "Traherne.html",
      "Abraham_Cowley-The_Spring.html",
      "Richard_Crashaw-Song.html",
      "Andrew_Marvell-The_Mower_to_the_Glo-Worms.html",
      "samuel_taylor_coleridge-songs_of_the_pixies.html"};

public PoetEvent(Object source)
{
      super(source);
}

public PoetEvent(Object source, int percentDone)
{
      super(source);
      this.percentDone = percentDone;
}

private int getNewPoetIndex()
{
      return random.nextInt(poems.length);
}

public String getFileName()
{
      return FileBox.getCurrentDirectory() +
            "poems" + FileBox.fileSeparator + poems[poetIndex];
```

```
        //return "rohan/temp/" + poems[poetIndex];
    }

    public URL getURL()
    {
        poetIndex = getNewPoetIndex();
        String opening = "file://";
        String currentFile = getFileName();
        URL url = null;
        try
        {
            url = new URL(opening + currentFile);
        }
        catch (MalformedURLException ex)
        {
            ex.printStackTrace();
        }

        return url;
    }

    public String getPoet()
    {
        return poets[poetIndex];
    }

    public String[] getPoets()
    {
        return poets;
    }

    public int getPoetIndex()
    {
        return poetIndex;
    }

    public String getDate()
    {
        return dates[poetIndex];
    }

    public String[] getDates()
    {
        return dates;
    }

    public String[] getSites()
    {
        return sites;
    }
```

```
        public String getSite()
        {
            return sites[poetIndex];
        }
        public int getPercentDone()
        {
            return percentDone;
        }
}
```

Listing 15-3: A class designed to fire PoetEvents

```
package custommessagesender.poet;

import java.lang.*;
import java.util.*;
import java.awt.event.*;

/**
 * <p>Title: </p>
 * <p>Description: </p>
 * <p>Copyright: Copyright (c) 2002 Charlie Calvert</p>
 * <p>Company: Elvenware</p>
 * @author Charlie Calvert
 * @version 1.0
 */

public class PoetMessageSender
            //extends Thread
            implements Runnable
{
        private long saveTime;
        private long switchTime;
        private transient Vector poetListeners;
        private boolean firstTime = true;

        public PoetMessageSender(long switchTime)
        {
            Date saveDate = new Date();
            saveTime = saveDate.getTime();
            this.switchTime = switchTime;
        }

        private void runApp()
        {
            Date d = new Date();
            long time = d.getTime() - saveTime;
            System.out.println("Time: " + time);
            try
            {
                Thread.sleep(1000);
            }
```

```
        catch (InterruptedException ex)
        {
            ex.printStackTrace();
        }

        float percentLeft = ((float)time / switchTime) * 100;
        PoetEvent pe = new PoetEvent(this, (int)percentLeft);
        if ((time > switchTime) || (firstTime))
        {
            firstTime = false;
            System.out.println("sending message");
            Date newDate = new Date();
            saveTime = newDate.getTime();
            fireDataChanged(pe);
            firePercentDone(pe);
        }
        else
        {
            firePercentDone(pe);
        }
    }

    public void run()
    {
        while(true)
        {
            runApp();
        }
    }

    public synchronized void removePoetListener(PoetListener l)
    {
        if (poetListeners != null && poetListeners.contains(l))
        {
            Vector v = (Vector) poetListeners.clone();
            v.removeElement(l);
            poetListeners = v;
        }
    }
    public synchronized void addPoetListener(PoetListener l)
    {
        Vector v = poetListeners == null ? new Vector(2) :
                (Vector) poetListeners.clone();
        if (!v.contains(l))
        {
            v.addElement(l);
            poetListeners = v;
        }
    }

    protected void fireDataChanged(PoetEvent e)
```

```
    {
        if (poetListeners != null)
        {
            Vector listeners = poetListeners;
            int count = listeners.size();
            for (int i = 0; i < count; i++)
            {
                ((PoetListener) listeners.elementAt(i)).dataChanged(e);
            }
        }
    }

    protected void firePercentDone(PoetEvent e)
    {
        if (poetListeners != null)
        {
            Vector listeners = poetListeners;
            int count = listeners.size();
            for (int i = 0; i < count; i++)
            {
                ((PoetListener) listeners.elementAt(i)).percentDone(e);
            }
        }
    }

}
```

Take a moment to glance over this code. Each of the classes shown here will be discussed in the next few sections of the text.

Understanding the Custom PoetEvent Class

Besides providing mission-critical functionality for Enterprise development teams, the PoetEvent class also illustrates how to create a custom event. The code shown in Listing 15-3 provides a number of methods for discovering information about the Metaphysical poets. It serves up poems, the names of poets, the dates when poets lived, and URLs on the web where you can find information about these poets.

NOTE: Coleridge is the odd man out in this collection. He lived some hundred years after the Metaphysical poets and wrote a very different kind of verse. But the poems of his that I include in this program harken back to the world of the Metaphysical poets.

I don't want to spend a lot of time discussing the specifics of the PoetEvent class. You might note, however, that if you call its getURL method, you will be given the URL of a randomly chosen poem. The poems are found on the CD in the directory called poems. This directory is a subdirectory of the CustomMessageSender program.

In the PoetEvent class, a randomly chosen number is used to select the next poem to be shown to the user. Given this random number, you can also discover the name of the poet who wrote the poem, the dates he lived, and a URL on the web that discusses him in some detail.

In short, the syntax used in the PoetEvent class is really quite simple. Furthermore, it is the act of sending this class as an event, not the class itself, that really interests us in this chapter.

Firing a Custom Event in a Thread

The class called PoetMessageSender.java fires PoetEvents. Most of the code for this class was created when you put a check mark in front of the Poet event, as shown in Figure 15-6. To understand the rest of the code in the method, you need some background information about the purpose of the CustomMessageSender program.

The CustomMessageSender program requires no interaction from the user. Instead, it shows a frequently changing display of information that the user can sit back and watch. In particular, every *x* seconds a new poem will be shown to the user. Accompanying the poem is information about the poet who wrote it.

The purpose of the PoetMessageSender class is to send a new poem event every *x* seconds. You specify the time between messages in the object's constructor. Every second, the program will also send an update on how long it will be until the next poet message is sent. Frame1 does nothing more than receive the events and display their content to the user.

It is important to understand that the fact this class sends two distinct messages is what made it necessary for me to create a custom class. If the class only sent PoetEvents, then I could have used some typecasting and one of the standard Java events to send this message. But because this class sends two bits of information, I needed to create a custom message specifically designed to handle this particular situation.

NOTE: I should add that it is not a bad idea to create a custom message whenever you create your own class like PoetEvent that you want to send as a message. If you create your own listener interface for your class, you can be sure that it will be typesafe. If you don't create the custom listener, you will be forced to use typecasts to make the code work. The typecasts are efficient, but they are not typesafe.

Using Threads to Create a Timer

There are a number of different ways to get the PoetMessageSender class to fire off events at specified intervals. The technique I chose involves running the PoetMessageSender class in a thread. This thread is designed to fire off Poet events every *x* number of seconds.

Classes that are run on threads often support the Runnable interface. This is another very simple interface, consisting of only one method:

```
Public interface Runnable
{
    public abstract void run();
}
```

For PoetMessageSender to support this interface, you must proceed much as you did when handling the ActionListener interface. In particular, you change the header for the class and add in a method called run:

```
public class PoetMessageSender implements Runnable

.../ Lots of code ommited here
public void run()
{
}
```

To get PoetMessageSender to support the Runnable interface, you can either use the Interface Wizard or type in the code by hand. I have already described the Interface Wizard, and typing the code in is easy, so I'll leave this step up to you.

The idea behind the Runnable interface is very simple. First create an instance of the JDK Thread class, passing in PoetMessageSender as a parameter to its constructor:

```
PoetMessageSender poetSender = new PoetMessageSender();

Thread t = new Thread(poetSender);
t.start();
```

Then call the start method of your thread. After you do this, your thread will call the PoetMessageSender.run() method for you automatically. Needless to say, the call will be made inside a separate thread.

NOTE: An alternative technique would be to descend PoetMessageSender from java.lang.Thread. If you took this choice, the PoetMessageSender run() method would look exactly the same as it does in a class that implements Runnable. In fact, Thread itself implements Runnable. The header for the class you create would look like this:

```
public class PoetMessageSender extends Thread
```

When you launch the class, the code would look like this:

```
PoetMessageSender poetMessageSender = new poetMessageSender();
poetMessageSender.start();
```

The advantage of implementing Runnable rather than descending from Thread is simply that your class does not have to carry around the extra weight inherent in any class descending from Thread, and it is also free to descend from some other class. Therefore, you should descend from Thread only if you need to override some of the Thread's methods other than run(). In most cases, simply implement Runnable, as shown in the current example program.

Here is the implementation for the run method of the PoetMessageSender class:

```
    public void run()
    {
        while(true)
        {
            runApp();
        }

    }

    private void runApp()
    {
        Date d = new Date();
        long time = d.getTime() - saveTime;
        System.out.println("Time: " + time);
        try
        {
            Thread.sleep(1000);
        }
        catch (InterruptedException ex)
        {
            ex.printStackTrace();
        }

        float percentLeft = ((float)time / switchTime) * 100;
```

Part III

```
            PoetEvent pe = new PoetEvent(this, (int)percentLeft);
            if ((time > switchTime) || (firstTime))
            {
                firstTime = false;
                System.out.println("sending message");
                Date newDate = new Date();
                saveTime = newDate.getTime();
                fireDataChanged(pe);
                firePercentDone(pe);
            }
            else
            {
                firePercentDone(pe);
            }
        }
```

The run() method calls runApp() from inside of an infinite loop. This does not cause any trouble because this class is on its own thread, and the only thing this class is supposed to do is call the runApp() method. In short, it may be stuck in an infinite loop, but it's stuck in the right infinite loop! Needless to say, the loop is stopped when the program is closed.

The call to the Thread.sleep method inside the loop puts the thread offline for one second at a time. This means the thread is sound asleep almost all the time, doing absolutely nothing. In other words, it is not wasting clock cycles spinning on the infinite loop. When it wakes up, it checks to see how much time has gone by. If it is the first time through the loop or if the appropriate amount of time has elapsed, it sends a PoetEvent message and an update saying that we are at the 100 percent mark:

```
            if ((time > switchTime) || (firstTime))
            {
                firstTime = false;
                System.out.println("sending message");
                Date newDate = new Date();
                saveTime = newDate.getTime();
                fireDataChanged(pe);
                firePercentDone(pe);
            }
            else
            {
                firePercentDone(pe);
            }
```

Our custom event supports not one method, but two methods. The first method is dataChanged, and the second is percentDone. As you know, the dataChanged method holds a fully loaded and newly initialized PoetEvent, while the percentDone method tells how long it will be until the next updated PoetEvent is sent.

NOTE: Besides creating and firing a poet event, notice that the runApp() method also sets the time counter back to the current time. The method will then check every second to see if *x* seconds have elapsed since the last time the method was called. If it has, it sends another PoetEvent message.

DataChanged messages are sent every *x* seconds. PercentDone methods are sent every second. This program also sleeps for one second between iterations of the loop. Therefore, even if it is not time to call the dataChanged event, it is nonetheless time to tell the main program how long it will be until the next poet event is fired. To do that, the runApp code calls firePercentDone with the poetEvent initialized to contain the percentage of time that has elapsed since the last call to fireDataChanged.

```
protected void fireDataChanged(PoetEvent e)
{
        if (poetListeners != null)
        {
                Vector listeners = poetListeners;
                int count = listeners.size();
                for (int i = 0; i < count; i++)
                {
                        ((PoetListener) listeners.elementAt(i)).dataChanged(e);
                }
        }
}

protected void firePercentDone(PoetEvent e)
{
        if (poetListeners != null)
        {
                Vector listeners = poetListeners;
                int count = listeners.size();
                for (int i = 0; i < count; i++)
                {
                        ((PoetListener) listeners.elementAt(i)).percentDone(e);
                }
        }
}
```

NOTE: If you start looking through the events fired on all the available Java listener interfaces, you will see that they always take the same parameters. In this case, all the methods shown in the PoetListener interface take a PoetEvent as a parameter:

```
public void dataChanged(PoetEvent e);
public void percentDone(PoetEvent e);
```

One could imagine passing in different parameters. For instance, it would be legal to create a fireDataChanged method that looked like this:

```
protected void fireDataChanged(PoetEvent e, int percent)
{
        if (poetListeners != null)
        {
                Vector listeners = poetListeners;
                int count = listeners.size();
                for (int i = 0; i < count; i++)
                {
                        ((PoetListener) listeners.elementAt(i)).dataChanged(e,
                                    percent);
                }
        }
}
```

As you can see, I have slightly altered the fireDataChanged method so that it can accommodate not one parameter, but two.

In this case, the one method, dataChanged, could perform the same task that is accomplished in our interface by dataChanged and percentDone. As I said, this is totally legal syntactically. However, it is not the way things are done in Javaland. Instead, you should proceed as we do in our example program. Standards are important, and the standard in the Java world is to work as we do in the CustomMessageSender program.

Architectural Traits of the Poet Event

You now hopefully understand everything you need to know about creating and firing the custom poet event. But there are a couple of points that should be made before moving on:

- The PoetEvent, PoetListener, and PoetMessageSender classes work together to form a single chunk of functionality. As a result, they really belong in their own package. That is why I asked you to place the PoetMessageSender class in its own package. The PoetEvent and PoetListener classes should both automatically have been created in this same package. The presence of this package helps make it clear that these three classes work together as a single unit. If you wanted to make reusing them even easier, you could also place them in their own JAR file. In effect, you would be creating a JavaBean, a topic that will be discussed later in the book.
- The second important point is that the PoetMessageSender class fires events, but it has no public methods other than its constructor, the run method, and the event listening mechanism. That may sound like a lot of public functionality, but really, all you ever do with this class is construct it, put it in a thread, and register another class as its listener. All these things take place at one time, and then you let the class run. The flow of information is from the PoetMessageSender to the listener class. There is no flow going back the other way. You do call some get methods on the PoetEvent class, but you never call any set methods on the class. I'm emphasizing this because it makes for a very robust architecture. Because the flow is all in one direction, there is some limit on the number of things that can go wrong once you have the class up and running. When you start sending a message back to the class that sent you a message, trouble can arise. There is nothing wrong with doing that, and it is not illegal. But it has a tendency to cause trouble. Issues like this will be discussed in Part IV: Project Architecture. There you will find another program, called FileRename, that further illustrates some of the principles discussed here.

Listening for Custom Events

To help a class listen for PoetEvents, and only for PoetEvents, JBuilder created an interface called PoetListener. As you know, PoetListener.java has only one job: It is intended to declare the method or methods that must be supported by any class that wants to listen for PoetEvents. How can you most easily use this interface to give Frame1 the ability to listen for PoetEvents?

The simplest solution is to use the Interface Wizard, as described earlier in the chapter. You can also simply type in the code by hand:

```
public class Frame1 extends JFrame implements  PoetListener

… Lots of code omitted here

public void dataChanged(PoetEvent e)
```

```
{

}

public void percentDone(PoetEvent e)
{

}
```

A third technique would be to use BeansExpress, if it is available in your version of the product. Choose the **Bean** tab from the file view tabs beneath the editor. When you switch to the Events page for Frame1, you will not see the new custom event you created. Instead, you need to click the **Import Event Set** button. When you do, a dialog will pop up requesting the class that you want to import. Browse for the PoetListener class found in the custommessagesender.poet package, as shown in Figure 15-7. Click **OK** twice to return to the Bean Events page. It should now look as it does in Figure 15-8, with the new event added at the top. On the right-hand column, the listen column, click **Poet**. As you know, you could also use the Interface Wizard to give Frame1 support for the PoetListener interface.

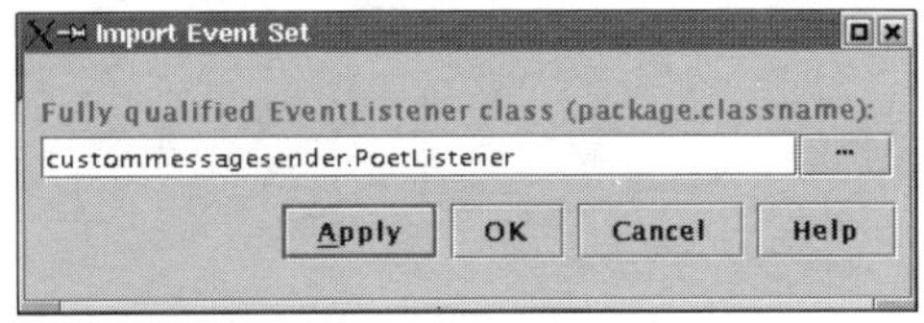

Figure 15-7: Selecting the custom Poet Listener class so that Frame1 can listen for events of this type

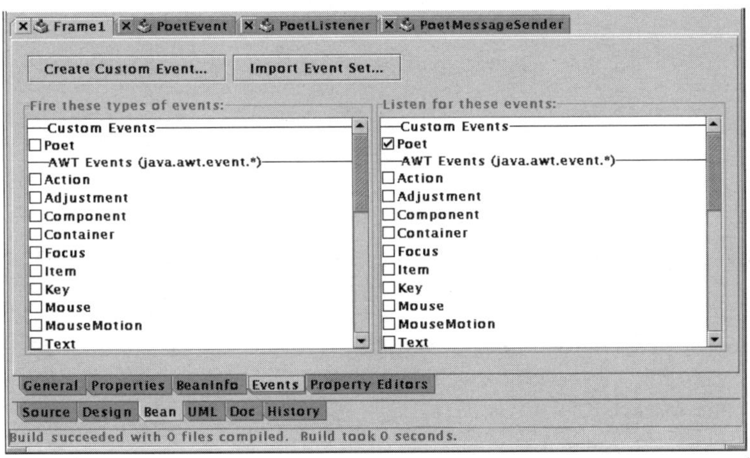

Figure 15-8: The new custom event added to the Frame1 Bean Events page

Whether you typed in the code yourself, used the Interface Wizard, or used BeansExpress, Frame1 should now have two new methods that can listen for PoetEvents. It is also marked as implementing the PoetListener interface, as shown in the code fragment at the beginning of this section of the chapter.

You should now add code to Frame1 that will create an instance of the PoetMessageSender class, register Frame1 as a listener, and then start the new class on a thread. Furthermore, you need to fill in the code that will respond to PoetEvents:

```
// Send messages once every 5000 milleseconds, or once every 5 seconds
PoetMessageSender poetSender = new PoetMessageSender(5000);

... code omitted here
public Frame1()
```

```
    {
        ... code omitted here

        poetSender.addPoetListener(this);
        Thread t = new Thread(poetSender);
        t.start();
    }

    ... code omitted here

    private void setPoetPage(PoetEvent e)
    {
        URL url = e.getURL();
        System.out.println("Got message: " + url);
        jTextFieldPoet.setText(e.getPoet());
        jTextFieldDates.setText(e.getDate());
        jTextFieldWebSite.setText(e.getSite());
        try
        {
            if (jEditorPane1 != null)
            {
                jEditorPane1.setPage(url);
            }
        }
        catch (IOException ex)
        {
            System.err.println("Exception setting page");
            ex.printStackTrace();
        }
    }

    public void dataChanged(PoetEvent e)
    {
        java.net.URL url = e.getURL();
        System.out.println("Got message: " + url);
        jTextFieldPoet.setText(e.getPoet());
        jTextFieldDates.setText(e.getDate());
        jTextFieldWebSite.setText(e.getSite());

        try
        {
            jEditorPane1.setPage(url);
        }
        catch (IOException ex)
        {
        }
    }

    public void percentDone(PoetEvent poetEvent)
    {
        int percent = poetEvent.getPercentDone();
```

```
            System.out.println("Percent: " + percent);
            jProgressBar1.setValue(percent);
    }
```

The code that creates the thread appears in the constructor for Frame1. The dataChanged method is the place where PoetEvents will come to rest, once every 5 seconds. (If you are wondering where the 5 seconds comes from, look at the call to the constructor for the PoetMessageSender class at the top of this listing.) The percentDone method is called once a second to update the user on how long it will be until the next event is sent.

The interface for the CustomMessageSender program features three JTextFields and a JEditorPane, as shown back in Figure 15-3. The text fields are used to display a poet's name, dates, and the URL of his web site. The JEditorPane is used to display a poem or piece of text associated with the poet. In our case the poems are stored as HTML files. Fortunately, JEditorPane can display moderately complex HTML, so we are able to build some interesting-looking pages for the user to peruse. I pass in the name of the file to display in a java.net.URL object. This class is very flexible and can be used not only to work with text files but also to allow the JEditorPane to display pages pulled down off the web.

That is all I'm going to say about creating custom messages. I suggest that you take time to examine the code on the CD and experiment with creating your own custom messages.

Summary

In this chapter you learned about firing events and creating custom events. The first example program fired a simple ActionEvent. While looking at that program, you learned how to use the JBuilder BeansExpress to create the methods used to register or unregister classes that want to listen for your events, as well as the method used to fire the events themselves. You also saw how to create code that constructs an ActionEvent and then calls the fireActionEvent interface.

The next section of the text showed how to create a program that fired not ActionEvents, but your own custom event. You saw how to write a simple class called PoetEvent that can be sent as an event. You learned that many custom events support not one, but two or more methods. The PoetListener interface defined the two methods that define PoetEvents. One contained the event itself, and the next told how long it would be until the next PoetEvent was fired. The chapter then went on to explain what was involved in handling these two methods when it came time to fire the events.

This completes the sections of this book that are dedicated to event handling. However, many of the other programs found on the CD or discussed in the rest of this text use event handling. As a result, you will probably pick up additional information on this subject simply by working through the other chapters in this book.

It should be clear that event handling is one of the most important parts of the Java language. Events play a key role in many Java tools, such as the Swing classes. But that is not the whole story. As I suggested in this chapter, events can be used to help you construct robust and easily reusable components. It is not always easy to design programs that use events, but once they are constructed, they are easy to maintain. This whole subject will be covered again in Part IV: Project Architecture, particularly in Chapter 22, "Modularity."

Chapter 16

Radio Buttons and Check Boxes

Charlie Calvert

In this chapter you are going to read about using radio buttons and check boxes. This is not a difficult subject, but there are a few simple tricks you need to master before you can use the components in your own programs.

Using radio buttons and check boxes is really all about handling events. Events have played a big role in the last few chapters, so you should not have much trouble with this subject.

The end of the chapter includes a very brief overview of a way to add a kind of ersatz enumerated type to the Java language. The technique is a bit difficult to understand, but it is easy to use in your programs. I have found it particularly useful when working with radio buttons, and that is why I have included it in this chapter.

This is the first of a series of chapters to feature a lot of hands-on work in the JBuilder designer. If you are new to Java or JBuilder, there is a lot to be said for recreating the programs that I describe from memory. I'll confess that such work is not much fun, but if you get to the point where you can build some of these example programs without referencing this book, you will have added some valuable skills to your resume.

I am deliberately trying to show you the features that you will use most often. If you can get to the point where doing many of these things is second nature, those talents will stand you in good stead in the long run. I know that most of the time you have some specific goal that you are trying to achieve. But if you can take the time to get really good at using the core Java components, you will find that programming in Java with JBuilder is a much more pleasant experience than it would be if you always had to think about or look up each step that you take.

Creating an Application that Uses Radio Buttons and Check Boxes

Let's start by building a simple application, as shown in Figure 16-1. This project will introduce you to the basic techniques to use when working with check boxes and radio buttons. The check boxes and radio buttons used in this program will allow the user to set the colors of the controls in the graphical user interface.

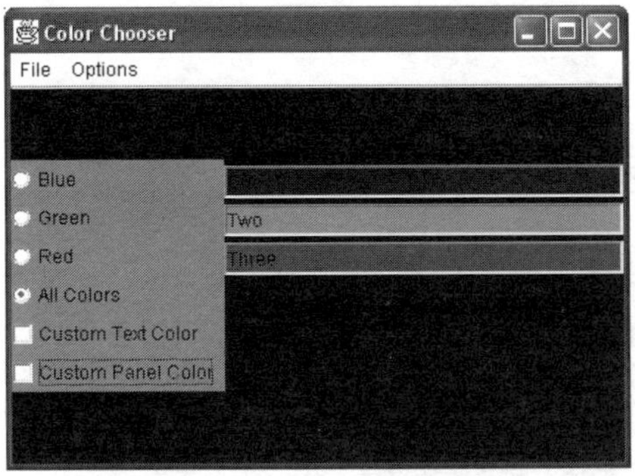

Figure 16-1: A simple application that demonstrates how to use check boxes and radio buttons

The program we are about to build is called ColorChooser. You can find a copy of it on the CD and on www.elvenware.com.

Start by creating a standard JBuilder application, using the approach laid out in Chapter 3. After creating the application, focus Frame1.java in the content pane. Click the **Design** tab at the bottom of the content pane to move to design view.

Click on the **Swing Containers** tab of the component palette. Select the **JPanel** component and click in the center of the designer. In the Inspector, set the JPanel's background property to **Black** and the layout property to **null**. Make sure that the constraints property is set to **Center**, as shown in Figure 16-2.

NOTE: Generally speaking, the Null layout is very useful when you are in the process of designing a GUI. However, once you have completed your design, you will need to change to a different layout before deploying your application or applet. Your options for doing that are discussed in Chapters 12 and 13. In this particular case, you will have to switch to GridBagLayout once you have used the null layout to discover the basic look and feel of your application.

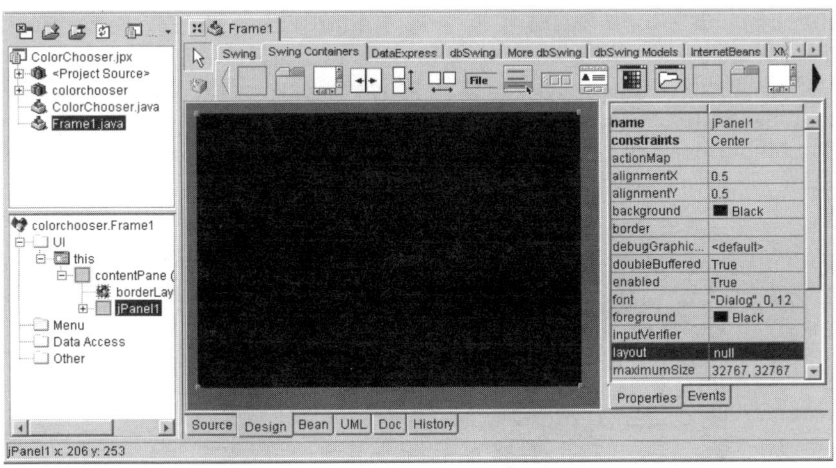

Figure 16-2: In the structure pane, you can see the JPanel resting on the contentPane. The layout is set to null.

The component palette should still be open to the Swing Containers page. Pick the **JColorChooser** component (to the left of the folder icon) by clicking on it. Then click on the **UI** folder in the structure pane. If the JColorChooser appears in the designer, delete it and try again. The structure pane should show a dotted line from the UI folder to the JColorChooser component, as shown in Figure 16-3.

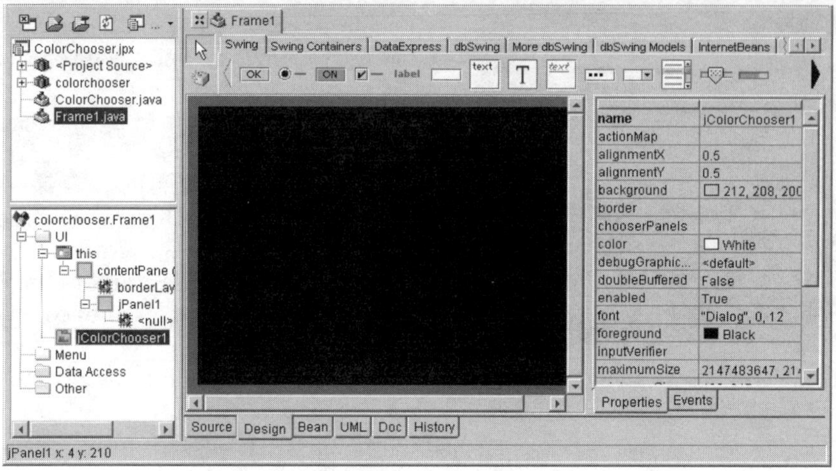

Figure 16-3: The JColorChooser should be dropped not on the contentPane, but on the UI node itself. You want to use it as a non-visual component.

The next step is to place four radio buttons on the JPanel. The radio buttons are located on the Swing page of the component palette. Hold down the **Shift** key and click on the **JRadioButton** component. Now click on the designer. Each time you click in the designer, you will add a new radio button. Move your cursor down the screen a little between clicks so that the buttons are arranged in a column. Click the selection tool (the white arrow at the left of the component palette) to end this operation. Name the components **jRadioButtonBlue**, **jRadioButtonGreen**, **jRadioButtonRed**, and **jRadioButtonAll**. The text property for the four buttons should be set to **Blue**, **Green**, **Red**, and **All Colors**.

To line up the radio buttons, press **Ctrl** and click on each of them in turn. The resizing handles for the radio buttons will change color, indicating that they are selected. Right-click on one of the radio buttons and choose **Align Left** and **Even Space Vertical** in the pop-up menu. The result should look a little like Figure 16-4.

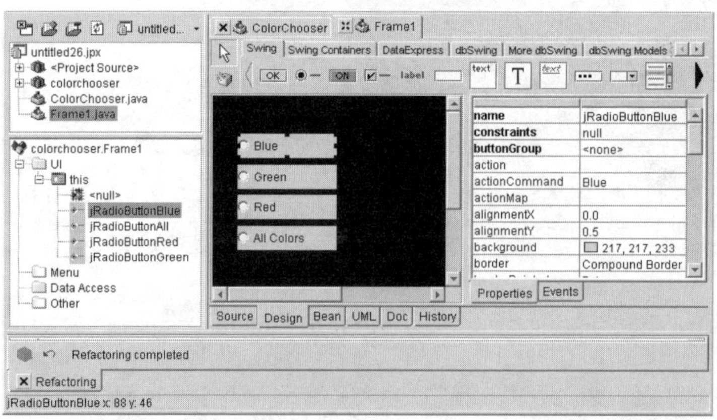

Figure 16-4: The radio buttons are arranged in a column.

On each end of the component palette are arrows that you can use to scroll the palette left or right. If necessary, click on the arrow on the right side of the palette to move the palette until you see the button group icon. Click on the button group icon, and then click in the designer. The button group is not a visual component, so you will not see it appear on the designer, but you will see it listed in the structure pane as buttonGroup1. Now that you have added the button group, buttonGroup1 will appear on the drop-down list next to the buttonGroup property in the Inspector. Set the buttonGroup property of each radio button to **buttonGroup1,** as shown in Figure 16-5.

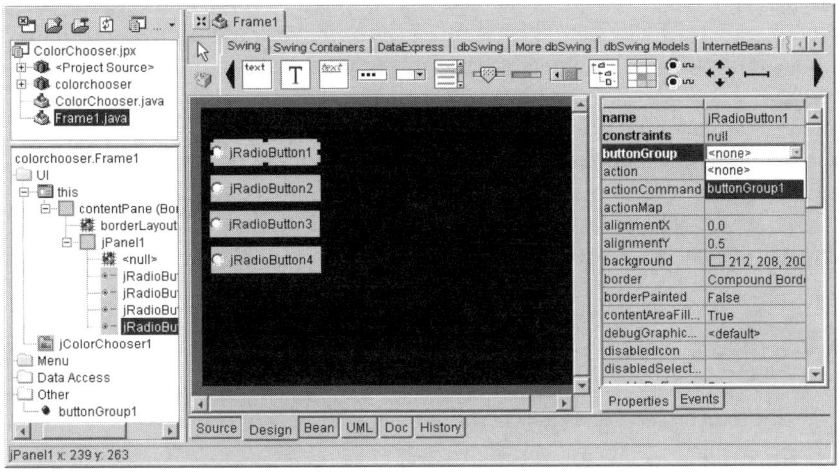

Figure 16-5: Setting the buttonGroup property

Setting the buttonGroup property ensures that at run time, one, and only one, of the radio buttons added to the group can be selected. If you did not do this, the user could select all four radio buttons at one time. The purpose of radio buttons is to give the user an exclusive choice between options. Letting him or her select all the buttons at one time would, to put it mildly, undermine the basic goal of the program.

In this particular program, it would not be appropriate to have a radio button selected by default. However, you can do so by choosing one of the radio buttons and setting its selected property to True in the Inspector. An example of this is shown in the demo at the end of this chapter.

The next step is to drop down three JTextField components. You will find them on the Swing page of the component palette. In the designer, line up the text fields with the radio buttons, as shown in Figure 16-1. Use **Ctrl+Click** to select both a radio button and a text area, and then right-click to access the pop-up menu. Align bottom will line up the components horizontally, using the component you click first as a guide.

Once you have the components positioned, change their text property. Set the text property of the JTextField components in the first row to **One**, in the second row to **Two**, and in the third row to **Three.** If you have not already done so, set the text property for the four radio buttons to **Blue, Green, Red**, and **All Colors**.

NOTE: Here is a tip that you might find useful in some cases: If you select both a radio button and a text field, you will be able to change the text property for both simultaneously. In general, you will find that you can multi-select components in order to change the same property on multiple components at one time.

The JCheckBox components are also located on the Swing page. Drop down two of them in the designer below your other components and line them up. Change the text property on the top check box to **Custom Text Color** and on the lower check box to **Custom Panel Color**. To allow the text to display completely, you will need to adjust the size of the check boxes. Because you are in null layout, you can just use the resize handles to increase the width. You should also change the names of the components to **jCheckBoxTextColor** and **jCheckBoxPanelColor**.

Your interface is almost complete. As a finishing touch, select all the radio buttons and both check boxes using **Ctrl+Click**, and then reset their background property to **Blue**. This is another instance of multi-selecting components in order to change a series of properties in one fell swoop.

Now comes the tricky part. Switch the layout for the panel to **GridBagLayout**. Hopefully the controls will stay lined up just as you wanted them. If necessary, you may have to play with GridBagLayout some to make the buttons line up just as you prefer. You might also look at Listing 16-1, where you can see the GridBagConstraints properties as they are set in my version of the program. The interface should now begin to look a little like what you see in Figure 16-1.

NOTE: When you are working with GridBagLayout, the following line must occur before you begin constructing the GridBagConstraint objects:

```
jPanel1.setLayout(gridBagLayout1);
```

Listing 16-1: The GridBagConstraints for the components in the ColorChooser program

```
        jPanel1.setLayout(gridBagLayout1);

        jPanel1.add(jRadioButtonGreen,
            new GridBagConstraints(1, 1, 1, 1, 0.0, 0.0,
            GridBagConstraints.CENTER, GridBagConstraints.HORIZONTAL,
            new Insets(0, 0, 0, 0), 0, 0));

        jPanel1.add(jRadioButtonRed,
            new GridBagConstraints(1, 2, 1, 1, 0.0, 0.0,
            GridBagConstraints.CENTER, GridBagConstraints.HORIZONTAL,
            new Insets(0, 0, 0, 0), 0, 0));

        jPanel1.add(jRadioButtonBlue,
            new GridBagConstraints(1, 0, 1, 1, 0.0, 0.0,
            GridBagConstraints.CENTER, GridBagConstraints.HORIZONTAL,
            new Insets(0, 0, 0, 0), 0, 0));

        jPanel1.add(jTextField3,
            new GridBagConstraints(2, 2, 1, 1, 0.0, 0.0,
            GridBagConstraints.SOUTHWEST, GridBagConstraints.HORIZONTAL,
            new Insets(0, 0, 0, 0), 0, 0));

        jPanel1.add(jTextField2,
            new GridBagConstraints(2, 1, 1, 1, 0.0, 0.0,
            GridBagConstraints.SOUTHWEST, GridBagConstraints.HORIZONTAL,
            new Insets(0, 0, 0, 0), 0, 0));

        jPanel1.add(jTextField1,
            new GridBagConstraints(2, 0, 1, 1, 1.0, 0.0,
            GridBagConstraints.SOUTHWEST, GridBagConstraints.HORIZONTAL,
            new Insets(0, 0, 0, 0), 0, 0));
```

```
        jPanel1.add(jCheckBoxTextColor,
              new GridBagConstraints(1, 5, 1, 1, 0.0, 0.0,
              GridBagConstraints.CENTER, GridBagConstraints.HORIZONTAL,
              new Insets(0, 0, 0, 0), 0, 0));

        jPanel1.add(jCheckBoxPanelColor,
              new GridBagConstraints(1, 6, 1, 1, 0.0, 0.0,
              GridBagConstraints.CENTER, GridBagConstraints.HORIZONTAL,
              new Insets(0, 0, 0, 0), 0, 0));

        jPanel1.add(jRadioButtonAll,
              new GridBagConstraints(1, 4, 1, 1, 0.0, 0.0,
              GridBagConstraints.CENTER, GridBagConstraints.HORIZONTAL,
              new Insets(0, 0, 0, 0), 0, 0));
```

This listing for these GridBagConstraints objects is fairly long. However, the visual effects you are trying to achieve are straightforward. As a result, you should have little trouble getting the controls to line up as you want.

In this case, almost all the work is done by using the gridx and gridy properties of GridBagConstraints. The only other GridBagConstraint parameter that really comes into play is the anchor argument, which is set to GridBagConstraints.SOUTHWEST for the JTextField components.

Adding Menus

At this stage you want to add a menu for the program. The menu will allow you to easily exit the program and change the default colors that will be associated with each of the components.

As you recall from Chapter 13, you can create a menu by first dropping the JMenuBar component onto the structure pane. You will find this component on the Swing Containers page of the component palette. To make the menu visible at run time, add the following line to the end of your jbInit method:

```
this.setJMenuBar(jMenuBar1);
```

NOTE: It goes without saying that it is best if you remember to add a menu bar to your program when you first run the Application Wizard. If the truth be told, I rarely think to do it on that occasion. As a result, I usually add the menu following the directions laid out here. However, those who plan their work ahead of time are definitely ahead of the game on this one.

Once you have the JMenuBar in place and properly initialized, right-click it in the structure pane to bring up the menu designer. Add a File | Exit menu item and then five more menu items, as shown in Figure 16-6. The menu items shown here allow the user to set the color for the program's text, its panel, and the three JTextFields.

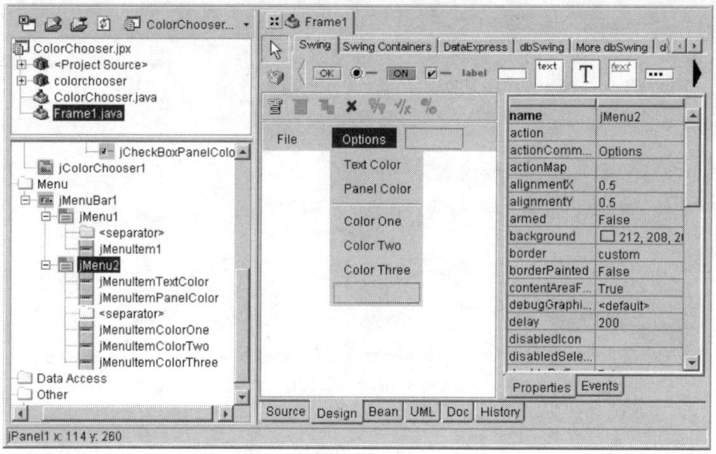

Figure 16-6: Creating a menu for the ColorChooser program

Adding Events

Now that the interface is complete, the next step is to add events. Before you do that, take a moment to look at the code that JBuilder generated behind the scenes based on your actions in the visual design environment. In source view, you will see standard Java code, declaring and instantiating the components you have dropped down, and setting their properties. If you are learning Java, this code provides a good example for you to follow.

At the very top of the class, you should add in some data fields with default values that will be used throughout this program:

```
private Color textColor = Color.magenta;
private Color panelColor = Color.cyan;
private Color textFieldColor1 = Color.blue;
private Color textFieldColor2 = Color.green;
private Color textFieldColor3 = Color.red;
```

The goal of this program is to allow the user to set the colors associated with the various components on the main form. The private variables listed above declare the default colors for each component. Each instance of the Color class is initialized using one of the constants declared in the Color class itself. For instance, textColor is set to Color.magenta.

It is now time to add our first events. As we add each event, you will be switching back and forth between source and design view.

Switch back to design view, and select **jRadioButtonBlue** by clicking on it. Choose the **Events** page of the Inspector, and click in the column next to the **actionPerformed** event. A suggested name for this action, such as jRadioButtonBlue_actionPerformed, will appear in that column. If you want, you can edit this name to something a bit more manageable, or you can just stick with the defaults.

NOTE: The advantage of changing the name for an event handler is that your code might be a little easier to read. The advantage of sticking with the default is that you can easily recreate the event should your code become damaged at some point. The need doesn't arise often, but sometimes you might want to recreate the adapter classes used to call your method. This might occur if you accidentally deleted some code or attempted to make some changes that you want to roll back. If you stick with the default names, it can be very easy to recreate your event handlers and the adapters that call them.

Double-click on the word **jRadioButtonBlue_actionPerformed** in the property editor, and JBuilder will bring you back to the source view. Your cursor will be positioned between the curly braces of an actionPerformed method stub for jRadioButtonBlue. At this point, JBuilder has created the event code for the radio button, with an empty method that is waiting for your input:

```
void jRadioButtonBlue_actionPerformed(ActionEvent e)
{
}
```

Create a new method called **setTextFields** and call it from inside your newly created actionPerformed method:

```
void setTextFields(Color color)
{
      jTextField1.setBackground(color);
      jTextField2.setBackground(color);
      jTextField3.setBackground(color);
}

void jRadioButtonBlue_actionPerformed(ActionEvent e)
{
      setTextFields(textFieldColor1);
}
```

This code sets the color of all the JTextFields to the color that is currently assigned to the data field textAreaColor1.

Return to the design view and double-click on **radioButtonGreen** in the designer. JBuilder will bring you back to the source view and will have created the actionPerformed method for radioButtonGreen. In JBuilder, any time you wish to use a simple actionPerformed method, you have the option of double-clicking on the component in the designer. In the actionPerformed method for radioButtonGreen, you will add a slightly modified version of the code you used for jRadioButtonBlue:

```
void jRadioButtonGreen_actionPerformed(ActionEvent e)
{
      setTextFields(textFieldColor2);
}
```

Go back to the design view, double-click on **radioButtonRed**, and place this code in its event:

```
void jRadioButtonRed_actionPerformed(ActionEvent e)
{
      setTextFields(textFieldColor3);
}
```

Finally, you should create an event handler for jRadioButtonAll:

```
void jRadioButtonAll_actionPerformed(ActionEvent e)
{
      jTextField1.setBackground(textFieldColor1);
      jTextField2.setBackground(textFieldColor2);
      jTextField3.setBackground(textFieldColor3);
}
```

This method differs slightly from the others in that it sets each JTextField to a different color.

At this point, you will probably want to test out the code you have entered by compiling and running the application. Click the green triangle on the toolbar. It is usually located just below and to the right of the Help menu item.

Handling Check Box Events

The next step is to add event code for the check boxes. This time, we will not be using the generic actionPerformed method. The reason for this is that we want to have different settings for the selected and deselected states of the check box and we can't get information about these states from an ActionEvent. Instead, we will use the ItemStateChanged event.

Return to the design view, select **jCheckBoxTextColor**, and choose the **Events** page in the Inspector. The events are listed in alphabetical order. Click in the column to the right of itemStateChanged, as shown in Figure 16-7.

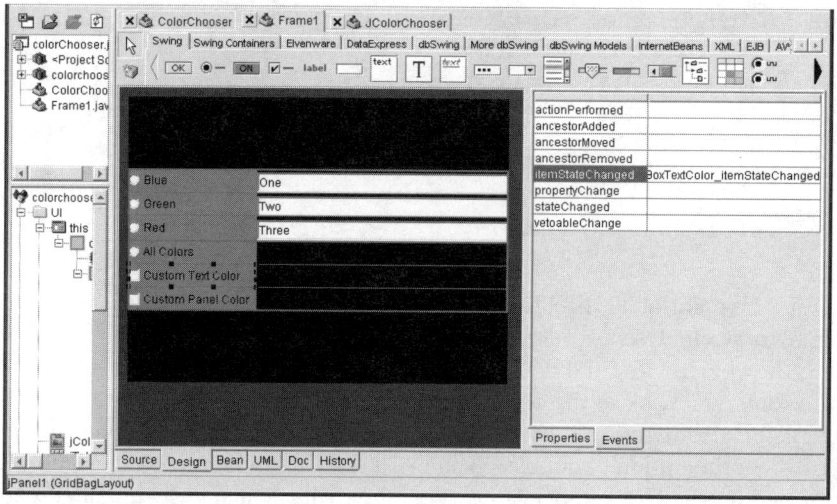

Figure 16-7: The itemStateChanged event in the Events page of the Inspector

Double-click on the word **jCheckBoxTextColor_itemStateChanged** in the column next to the itemStateChanged method in the Inspector. You will be placed back in source view in the itemStateChanged method for this component. (Pressing Enter rather than double-clicking should have the same effect.) Insert this code into the method handler:

```
void jCheckBoxTextColor_itemStateChanged(ItemEvent e)
{
      if(e.getStateChange()==ItemEvent.DESELECTED)
      {
      jTextField1.setForeground(Color.black);
      jTextField2.setForeground(Color.black);
      jTextField3.setForeground(Color.black);
    }
    else
    {
      jTextField1.setForeground(textColor);
      jTextField2.setForeground(textColor);
      jTextField3.setForeground(textColor);
    }
}
```

This code states that if the check box is deselected, the text color will be black. If the check box is selected, the color will be set to the value assigned to textColor. Needless to say, the key line of code is the first one:

```
        if(e.getStateChange()==ItemEvent.DESELECTED)
```

The key point to grasp here is that the ItemEvent has some fields not available in an ActionEvent. In particular, it lets you know whether the current component has a check in it or not. If it has a check, ItemEvent.getStateChange equals ItemEvent.SELECTED. If it does not have a check, it equals ItemEvent.DESELECTED.

Return to design view, select **jCheckBoxPanelColor**, and create an itemStateChanged method stub for it the same way you just did for jCheckBoxTextColor. The code for this method stub is as follows:

```
if(e.getStateChange()==ItemEvent.DESELECTED)
{
  jPanel1.setBackground(Color.black);
}
else
{
  jPanel1.setBackground(panelColor);
}
```

That's it! You now know how to handle check boxes. Run your application again to test how it works.

Event Handlers for the Menu Items

The final step in the program will give the user the option of changing the colors associated with each of the visual components shown in the application. This step involves using the JColorChooser that you dropped down near the beginning of this chapter.

You should now build event handlers for each of the menu items you created. Focus Frame1.java in the editor and switch to design mode. Right-click on the menu node in the structure pane and select **Activate Designer**. Select the first menu item for which you want an event. Turn to the **Events** page in the JBuilder Inspector. Select the **actionPerformed method** and double-click or press **Enter** to create the event handler. If you need more help with menus, turn to Chapter 13.

The code for these response methods is shown in Listing 16-2. Notice that at the top of this code excerpt, you can see the set of java.awt.Color class objects declared as data members of the Frame1 class.

Listing 16-2: The event handlers for the menu items in your program set the colors for the components.

```
        private Color textColor = Color.magenta;
        private Color panelColor = Color.cyan;
        private Color textFieldColor1 = Color.blue;
        private Color textFieldColor2 = Color.green;
        private Color textFieldColor3 = Color.red;

        void jMenuItemTextColor_actionPerformed(ActionEvent e)
        {
              textColor = jColorChooser1.showDialog(this, "Text Color",
                          textColor);
```

```
    }

    void jMenuItemPanelColor_actionPerformed(ActionEvent e)
    {
        panelColor = jColorChooser1.showDialog(this, "Panel Color",
                panelColor);
    }

    void jMenuItemColorOne_actionPerformed(ActionEvent e)
    {
        textFieldColor1 = jColorChooser1.showDialog(
            this, "Color One", textFieldColor1);
    }

    void jMenuItemColorTwo_actionPerformed(ActionEvent e)
    {
        textFieldColor2 = jColorChooser1.showDialog(
            this, "Color Two", textFieldColor2);
    }

    void jMenuItemColorThree_actionPerformed(ActionEvent e)
    {
        textFieldColor3 = jColorChooser1.showDialog(
                this, "Color three", textFieldColor3);
    }

    void jMenuItemExit_actionPerformed(ActionEvent e)
    {
        System.exit(0);
    }
```

The code shown here is quite simple. In most cases, it simply applies new colors to the variables declared at the top of the program. Notice the last method, which will cause the program to exit when the user chooses the File | Exit button.

When you call the JColorChooser showDialog method, you pass in three parameters. The first is the instance of the class that acts as the parent of the dialog. This parent class defines where the dialog will be shown. In particular, this is a modal dialog. *Modal dialogs* appear on top of some window specified by the programmer. The window on top of which a modal dialog appears is called the *parent window*. A modal dialog prevents the user from going back to that parent window until the OK or Cancel button in the dialog is clicked. The question is which window should lie beneath the dialog, and the answer is supplied by this parent variable passed in the first parameter to showDialog.

The second parameter to showDialog defines the caption shown on top of the JColorChooser dialog. For instance, in Figure 16-8, you can see the JColorChooser dialog. Notice that it has the caption supplied by the response to the Panel Color menu item:

```
void jMenuItemPanelColor_actionPerformed(ActionEvent e)
{
    panelColor = jColorChooser1.showDialog(this, "Panel Color", panelColor);
}
```

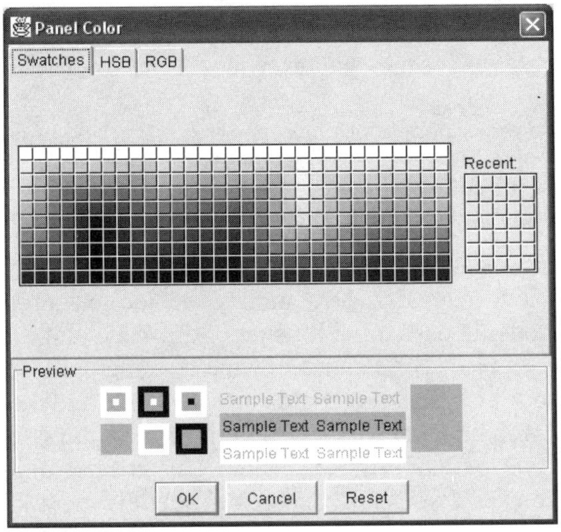

Figure 16-8: The JColorChooser dialog in all its glory. Notice the programmer-supplied caption at the top of the form.

The final parameter passed to JColorChooser is the default color to be selected when the dialog appears. This will always be one of the Color data members declared at the top of the Frame1 class.

The final point to bring up in regard to this code involves the way we initialized the JColorChooser object. As you recall, it was dropped down from the component palette onto the structure pane. It turns out that it is not difficult for you to create an instance of the JColorChooser dialog by hand:

```
JColorChooser j = new JColorChooser();
```

Since this call is so easy, what real advantage is there in pulling the JColorChooser off the component palette? What is JBuilder's contribution in a case like this?

The answer to this question is twofold:

1. By dropping down the control from the component palette, you create a single instance of the control that can be used globally throughout the program. Yes, you could do that by hand, but it really is convenient to have JBuilder declare this instance for you. By using the same instance over and over, you spare the garbage collector a lot of work, and the consequent wasted time.
2. More importantly, if you can access the JColorChooser object in design mode, you can see its properties in the Inspector. If you look back at Figure 16-3, you can see the JColorChooser's properties in the Inspector. If you want to tweak these properties, they are all easily accessible. This can be particularly useful when you are working with one of the FileChooser dialogs.

This marks the end of the section of the text on using radio buttons and check boxes. Hopefully you now see how to put these components to work in your own programs. You should also know a little bit more about how to use the JBuilder visual tools to create an interface for your program.

Radio Buttons and Enumerated Types

Radio buttons tend to go well with enumerated types. If you have three radio buttons, one standing for red, one for blue, and one for green, it is helpful to use an enumerated type with members RED, BLUE, and GREEN in conjunction with the radio buttons.

Unfortunately, Java does not support enumerated types. There is, however, a workaround that can resolve this problem. In this section of the chapter, you will explore that solution.

NOTE: In the Java programming world many people use integer constants in lieu of enumerated types. This solution is reasonably effective. However, it is not completely typesafe and can lead to errors. After you have a chance to see the solution provided here, I will come back to this subject and show why integer constants are not quite as safe a solution as the one I am about to present.

The code I am about to show you is quite easy to implement and use. It is, however, difficult to fully understand if you do not have a very good understanding of object-oriented programming in general and the Java object model in particular. If some of this code just flies over your head, you might try to see if you can just get a sense of what is going on. Hopefully you will be able to pick up enough information so that you could copy this code and modify it slightly to use in your own programs. You should be able to do this even if you don't fully understand it. If that fails, I would not become overly concerned. This is a useful technique if you can understand it, but it is by no means something that you absolutely must know if you want to use radio buttons in your program.

It's time to begin our exploration of this technique. To get started, we are going to look at a program that makes use of it.

The RadioButtonApplet program found on the CD shows a different picture for each of the four radio buttons in the program's interface. As you can see from Figure 16-9, the radio buttons allow you to choose a picture of a lighthouse, some rocks, a mountain range, and a stretch of rocky coastline called West Cliff.

Figure 16-9: The RadioButtonApplet allows the user to view four different pictures of the California coast.

The program uses a class-based enumerated type to keep track of which picture the user wants to view:

```
private final static class PictureChoice
{
```

```
        private final String name;

        private PictureChoice(String name)
        {
            this.name = name;
        }

        public String toString()
        {
            return name;
        }

        static final PictureChoice LIGHT_HOUSE = new
                PictureChoice("LIGHT_HOUSE");
        static final PictureChoice ROCKS = new PictureChoice("ROCKS");
        static final PictureChoice WEST_CLIFF = new PictureChoice("WEST_CLIFF");
        static final PictureChoice MOUNTAINS = new PictureChoice("MOUNTAINS");
    }
```

This is a private, static, final, inner class that is part of the applet class itself. Besides the private constructor and the toString method, this class has four static methods, which are the only legal means of creating instances of this class. Because the constructor is private, you can't use it to create an instance of the class. Instead, you must use one of the four static methods that appear at the end of the class.

If you have never seen this kind of class before, you are probably a bit taken aback by the description you found in the previous paragraph. Let's take a moment or two to consider what is happening here.

Our ultimate goal is to use this class in much the same way that we would use an enumerated type. Consider the following perfectly legal syntax, which takes advantage of this class:

```
        PictureChoice pictureChoice = PictureChoice.LIGHT_HOUSE;
```

Here is a declaration of a variable of type PictureChoice that is set to the value PictureChoice.LIGHT_HOUSE. This is very close to the syntax one would use if pictureChoice were not a class instance, but instead an enumerated type such as you would find in Object Pascal or C/C++.

Furthermore, you can write code that looks like this:

```
            if (pictureChoice == PictureChoice.LIGHT_HOUSE)
            {
                picture = lightHouse;
            }
            else if(pictureChoice == PictureChoice.MOUNTAINS)
            {
                picture = mountains;
            }
            else if (pictureChoice == PictureChoice.WEST_CLIFF)
            {
                picture = westCliff;
            }
            else if (pictureChoice == PictureChoice.ROCKS)
            {
```

```
                    picture = rock;
            }
```

Again, this is very similar to code you might use if pictureChoice were an enumerated type. If you want to change the type of pictureChoice, you can write code that looks like this:

```
pictureChoice = PictureChoice.ROCKS;
```

This code makes pictureChoice no longer of type LIGHT_HOUSE but instead of type ROCKS.

By now, you should be getting a sense of what is going on here. The PictureChoice class, as odd as it might be, serves as a kind of substitute for an enumerated type.

If you understand that much, it becomes easier to make sense of the class's declaration. The constructor is declared private because you don't want the user to ever create an instance of the class through the standard means of calling new on a constructor. It's not that it would be wrong to do so, but this class is not intended to be used that way. Its purpose is to act as an enumerated type, and it can only fulfill that function if created through the static methods listed at the end of the class.

The class is also declared as static and final because classes declared that way can be highly optimized by the VM. Furthermore, there is never going to be a need to create a descendant of the class or change any of the data members of the class once it is created. Additionally, there will only be one instance of this class in your program. As a result, it is safe to declare the class as both final and static. The *final* part of the declaration says that the class cannot be extended, and the *static* part says that its members cannot be changed after it has been created.

The last important idea that you must grasp is what is going on in the few statements included at the end of the class:

```
static final PictureChoice LIGHT_HOUSE = new PictureChoice("LIGHT_HOUSE");
```

LIGHT_HOUSE is a variable, a data member, of the PictureChoice class. It is set equal to an instance of the PictureChoice class that has its name set to the string "LIGHT_HOUSE."

A single instance of the PictureChoice class is going to be created when the applet starts up. When that class is created, its data members will automatically be initialized. That is simply one of the rules of Java. As a result, each of the four static access methods will be called in turn:

```
static final PictureChoice LIGHT_HOUSE = new PictureChoice("LIGHT_HOUSE");
static final PictureChoice ROCKS = new PictureChoice("ROCKS");
static final PictureChoice WEST_CLIFF = new PictureChoice("WEST_CLIFF");
static final PictureChoice MOUNTAINS = new PictureChoice("MOUNTAINS");
```

After they are all called, the class will contain four copies of itself, each initialized in a slightly different way. It is still true that there is only one instance of the class; it just happens that that one instance contains four more instances inside itself. However, none of these instances are mutable. They are all static and cannot and will not be changed.

After the initialization, the class will not be constructed again during the life of the program. All the heavy lifting is out of the way. Consider this code once again:

```
pictureChoice = PictureChoice.ROCKS;
```

At run time, after the initialization, an assignment like this does not call a constructor of PictureChoice. It merely points the variable pictureChoice at a different data member of the PictureChoice class.

TypeSafe and Unlikely to be Abused

The glory of this system is that it is absolutely typesafe. Think what would happen if LIGHT_HOUSE, ROCKS, WEST_CLIFF, and MOUNTAINS were simply integer types declared like this:

```
LIGHT_HOUSE=0;
ROCKS=1;
WEST_CLIFF=2;
MOUNTAINS=3;
pictureChoice = ROCKS;
```

In the program, it would be legal to write code like this when one wanted to reference the MOUNTAIN type:

```
if (pictureChoice == 3) doThis();
```

The problem with this type of code is that it is not absolutely safe. One could later change what MOUNTAINS is equal to, thereby making the code no longer work. But if you declare these variables as an instance of type PictureChoice, you could not ever compare pictureChoice to anything else other than an instance of the PictureChoice class:

```
if (pictureChoice == PictureChoice.MOUNTAINS) doThis();
```

In short, you would completely eliminate one potential source of error from your program.

NOTE: If you know the JDK fairly well, it would not be hard to find many examples of cases where Sun uses an integer type rather than an "enumerated" class like I have shown you here. If this technique is so good, why doesn't Sun use it more often? This is a good question, and in part it leads back to my opening statement on this subject: This is just a useful technique, and you don't have to employ it if you don't want to or if you don't understand it. I would add, however, that there are important members of the Java team at Sun who now believe that enumerated classes of the type I have shown here are not only representative of good programming technique, but also the preferred way to handle situations that can make use of enumerated types. See, for instance, item 21 in *Effective Java* by Joshua Bloch. At the time of publication you can find this excellent book online at http://java.sun.com/docs/books/effective/.

Making Your Enumerated Type Public

The last point that I would make about this code is that there will be many cases when you would want to declare PictureChoice as a public class so that other people could get at it. Exposing a class like this can be helpful if other people will use your object and need access to this enumerated type.

What I am proposing is that you declare PictureChoice not as a private inner class, but instead as a public class that resides in its own source file. It would still be declared final and static, and it would still have a private constructor, but the class itself would no longer be declared private. Then you could export your enumerated type so that users of your class could benefit from it. That makes no sense in our current example, so I declared PictureChoice as a private inner class. If you are supplying a component or class to other users, and you wanted to expose an enumerated type to those users, you would want to use a public instance of one of the "enumerated" classes.

The Source for the RadioButtonApplet Example

Because this is a fairly complicated idea, I'm going to show you the complete source to the whole example program. You can find it in Listing 16-3. Study this code for awhile and see if you can figure out what is going on. If you can get it all straight, you will have learned some valuable things about the Java language, including a technique that can help you write robust, error-free programs.

Listing 16-3: The RadioButtonApplet program provides an example of how to use an "enumerated class" in one of your programs.

```
package radiocheckbuttondemos;

import java.awt.event.*;
import java.applet.*;
import javax.swing.*;
import java.awt.*;

/**
 * <p>Title: RadioCheckButtonDemo</p>
 * <p>Description: RadioButton and CheckButton Demos</p>
 * <p>Copyright: Copyright (c) 2002 Charlie Calvert</p>
 * <p>Company: Elvenware (www.elvenware.com)</p>
 * @author Charlie Calvert
 * @version 1.0
 */

public class RadioButtonApplet extends JApplet
{
    PictureChoice pictureChoice = PictureChoice.LIGHT_HOUSE;
    ImageIcon lightHouse;
    ImageIcon rock;
    ImageIcon westCliff;
    ImageIcon mountains;

    boolean isStandalone = false;
    BorderLayout borderLayout1 = new BorderLayout();
    ButtonGroup buttonGroup1 = new ButtonGroup();
    GridLayout gridLayout2 = new GridLayout();
    JPanel jPanel1 = new JPanel();
    JPanel jPanel2 = new JPanel();
    JRadioButton jRadioButtonLightHouse = new JRadioButton();
    JRadioButton jRadioButtonRocks = new JRadioButton();
    JRadioButton jRadioButtonMountains = new JRadioButton();
    JRadioButton jRadioButtonWestCliff = new JRadioButton();
    JTextField jTextField1 = new JTextField();
    JPanel jPanel3 = new JPanel();
    GridBagLayout gridBagLayout1 = new GridBagLayout();

    //Get a parameter value
    public String getParameter(String key, String def)
    {
```

```
        return isStandalone ? System.getProperty(key, def) :
            (getParameter(key) != null ? getParameter(key) : def);
    }

    //Construct the applet
    public RadioButtonApplet()
    {
        init();
    }

    //Initialize the applet
    public void init()
    {
        try
        {
            jbInit();
        }
        catch(Exception e)
        {
            e.printStackTrace();
        }
    }

    //Component initialization
    private void jbInit() throws Exception
    {
        JPanel pane = (JPanel)this.getContentPane();
        jPanel2.setLayout(gridLayout2);
        DefaultHandler defaultHandler = new DefaultHandler(this);
        jRadioButtonLightHouse.addActionListener(defaultHandler);
        jRadioButtonRocks.addActionListener(defaultHandler);
        jRadioButtonMountains.addActionListener(defaultHandler);
        jRadioButtonWestCliff.addActionListener(defaultHandler);
        gridLayout2.setRows(2);
        gridLayout2.setColumns(2);
        jRadioButtonLightHouse.setSelected(true);
        jRadioButtonLightHouse.setText("Light House");
        jRadioButtonMountains.setText("Santa Cruz Mountains");
        jRadioButtonWestCliff.setText("West Cliff");
        jRadioButtonRocks.setText("Rocks");
        pane.setLayout(borderLayout1);
        jPanel1.setLayout(gridBagLayout1);
        jPanel3.setBackground(Color.yellow);
        jPanel1.add(jPanel3,
            new GridBagConstraints(0, 1, 1, 1, 1.0, 1.0,
            GridBagConstraints.CENTER, GridBagConstraints.BOTH,
            new Insets(0, 0, 0, 0), 123, 123));
        buttonGroup1.add(jRadioButtonLightHouse);
        buttonGroup1.add(jRadioButtonRocks);
        buttonGroup1.add(jRadioButtonMountains);
        buttonGroup1.add(jRadioButtonWestCliff);
```

Part III

```
        jPanel1.add(jTextField1,
              new GridBagConstraints(0, 0, 1, 1, 1.0, 0.0,
              GridBagConstraints.CENTER, GridBagConstraints.HORIZONTAL,
              new Insets(0, 0, 0, 0), 0, 0));
        jPanel2.add(jRadioButtonLightHouse, null);
        jPanel2.add(jRadioButtonRocks, null);
        jPanel2.add(jRadioButtonMountains, null);
        jPanel2.add(jRadioButtonWestCliff, null);
        jTextField1.setText("jTextField1");
        pane.add(jPanel1,  BorderLayout.CENTER);
        pane.add(jPanel2,  BorderLayout.NORTH);
        lightHouse = new ImageIcon(
              this.getClass().getResource("light-house.png"));
        rock = new ImageIcon(this.getClass().getResource("rocks.png"));
        mountains = new ImageIcon(
              this.getClass().getResource("santa-cruz-mountains.png"));
        westCliff = new ImageIcon(
              this.getClass().getResource("west-cliff.png"));
  }

  //Get Applet information
  public String getAppletInfo()
  {
        return "Applet Information";
  }

  //Get parameter info
  public String[][] getParameterInfo()
  {
        return null;
  }

  //Main method
  public static void main(String[] args)
  {
        RadioButtonApplet applet = new RadioButtonApplet();
        applet.isStandalone = true;
        Frame frame;
        frame = new Frame()
        {
              protected void processWindowEvent(WindowEvent e)
              {
                    super.processWindowEvent(e);
                    if (e.getID() == WindowEvent.WINDOW_CLOSING)
                    {
                          System.exit(0);
                    }
              }
              public synchronized void setTitle(String title)
              {
                    super.setTitle(title);
```

```
                enableEvents(AWTEvent.WINDOW_EVENT_MASK);
            }
        };
        frame.setTitle("Applet Frame");
        frame.add(applet, BorderLayout.CENTER);
        applet.init();
        applet.start();
        frame.setSize(620,540);
        Dimension d = Toolkit.getDefaultToolkit().getScreenSize();
        frame.setLocation((d.width - frame.getSize().width) / 2,
            (d.height - frame.getSize().height) / 2);
        frame.setVisible(true);
    }

    void jRadioButtonMountains_itemStateChanged(ActionEvent e)
    {
        jTextField1.setText("Mountains");
        pictureChoice = PictureChoice.MOUNTAINS;
        repaint();
    }

    void jRadioButtonRocks_itemStateChanged(ActionEvent e)
    {
        jTextField1.setText("Rocks");
        pictureChoice = PictureChoice.ROCKS;
        repaint();
    }

    void jRadioButtonLightHouse_itemStateChanged(ActionEvent e)
    {
        jTextField1.setText("Light House");
        pictureChoice = PictureChoice.LIGHT_HOUSE;
        repaint();
    }

    void jRadioButtonWestCliff_itemStateChanged(ActionEvent e)
    {
        jTextField1.setText("West Cliff");
        pictureChoice = PictureChoice.WEST_CLIFF;
        repaint();
    }

    public void paint(Graphics g)
    {
        super.paint(g);
        ImageIcon picture = lightHouse;
        if (pictureChoice == PictureChoice.LIGHT_HOUSE)
        {
            picture = lightHouse;
        }
        else if(pictureChoice == PictureChoice.MOUNTAINS)
```

```
            {
                picture = mountains;
            }
            else if (pictureChoice == PictureChoice.WEST_CLIFF)
            {
                picture = westCliff;
            }
            else if (pictureChoice == PictureChoice.ROCKS)
            {
                picture = rock;
            }

            Graphics g3 = jPanel3.getGraphics();
            int width = jPanel3.getWidth();
            int height = jPanel3.getHeight();
            g3.drawImage(picture.getImage(), 0, 0, width, height, 0, 0, 620, 465, this);
        }

        private final static class PictureChoice
        {
            private final String name;

            private PictureChoice(String name)
            {
                this.name = name;
            }

            public String toString()
            {
                return name;
            }

            static final PictureChoice LIGHT_HOUSE = new PictureChoice("LIGHT_HOUSE");
            static final PictureChoice ROCKS = new PictureChoice("ROCKS");
            static final PictureChoice WEST_CLIFF = new PictureChoice("WEST_CLIFF");
            static final PictureChoice MOUNTAINS = new PictureChoice("MOUNTAINS");
        }
    }

    class DefaultHandler implements java.awt.event.ActionListener
    {
        RadioButtonApplet adaptee;

        DefaultHandler(RadioButtonApplet adaptee)
        {
            this.adaptee = adaptee;
        }
        public void actionPerformed(ActionEvent e)
        {
            if (e.getSource() == adaptee.jRadioButtonLightHouse)
            {
```

```
                System.out.println("light house");
                adaptee.jRadioButtonLightHouse_itemStateChanged(e);
            }
            else if (e.getSource() == adaptee.jRadioButtonMountains)
            {
                System.out.println("mountains");
                adaptee.jRadioButtonMountains_itemStateChanged(e);
            }
            else if (e.getSource() == adaptee.jRadioButtonWestCliff)
            {
                System.out.println("west cliff");
                adaptee.jRadioButtonWestCliff_itemStateChanged(e);
            }
            else if (e.getSource() == adaptee.jRadioButtonRocks)
            {
                System.out.println("Rocks");
                adaptee.jRadioButtonRocks_itemStateChanged(e);
            }
        }
}
```


NOTE: I had mentioned earlier in this chapter that this example program has a radio button selected by default. If you look in jbInit, you will find the following code: jRadioButtonLight-House.setSelected(true). It is this line that ensures that the top-left radio button is selected when the program is launched.

The Event Handlers

Besides the enumerated type itself, you might notice that the code shown here uses a different kind of event handler than is commonly used in JBuilder programs. I discussed this kind of event handling mechanism in Chapter 14. However, I will go over it again quickly so that you will be reminded of how it works. I have used it here because it takes up less code than the default JBuilder event handling mechanism. I wanted to show you the whole program, but I also wanted to take up the least possible amount of space in the book.

If you look in jbInit, you will find code that looks like this:

```
    DefaultAdapter defaultAdapter = new DefaultAdapter(this);
    jRadioButton1.addItemListener(defaultAdapter);
    jRadioButton2.addItemListener(defaultAdapter);
    jRadioButton3.addItemListener(defaultAdapter);
    jRadioButton4.addItemListener(defaultAdapter);
```

This code creates an instance of the DefaultAdapter class and then reuses the class as the handler for each of the radio buttons in this program:

```
class DefaultHandler implements java.awt.event.ActionListener
{
    RadioButtonApplet adaptee;

    DefaultHandler(RadioButtonApplet adaptee)
    {
        this.adaptee = adaptee;
```

```
        }
        public void actionPerformed(ActionEvent e)
        {
            if (e.getSource() == adaptee.jRadioButtonLightHouse)
            {
                System.out.println("light house");
                adaptee.jRadioButtonLightHouse_itemStateChanged(e);
            }
            else if (e.getSource() == adaptee.jRadioButtonMountains)
            {
                System.out.println("mountains");
                adaptee.jRadioButtonMountains_itemStateChanged(e);
            }
            else if (e.getSource() == adaptee.jRadioButtonWestCliff)
            {
                System.out.println("west cliff");
                adaptee.jRadioButtonWestCliff_itemStateChanged(e);
            }
            else if (e.getSource() == adaptee.jRadioButtonRocks)
            {
                System.out.println("Rocks");
                adaptee.jRadioButtonRocks_itemStateChanged(e);
            }
        }
    }
```

This code will handle the events for all the radio buttons found in the program. It uses the getSource method of the ActionEvent to sort out which radio button called the adapter. Once it knows who called it, the adapter can use that information, and its knowledge of the French word adaptee, to call the appropriate method back in the English-speaking main program.

You have to type in this code by hand, as JBuilder will not generate it for you automatically. It does, however, take up a bit less space than the code that JBuilder generates for you. As I said in Chapter 14, in most circumstances, this type of code is more trouble than it is worth. Here I have employed it only to avoid wasting space in this book and perhaps also as a reminder that you can use this kind of code if you want.

Summary

In this chapter you have learned how to use radio buttons and check boxes. These controls can appear a bit tricky to use when you first encounter them. However, once you understand the "secret" to their construction, they become very easy to use. In particular you have seen that ActionPerformed events are central to the use of JRadioButtons, and ItemStateChanged events are crucial when you want to use a JCheckBox.

At the very end of the chapter, you saw an example of how to use a kind of ersatz enumerated type that can be very helpful when you are using radio buttons. Indeed, this method of adding an enumerated type to the Java language can be quite useful in many places throughout your programs. It is a little tricky to understand, but it is not hard to implement in your own programs.

Chapter 17

Visual Design and Reuse

Margie and Charlie Calvert

In this chapter you are going to learn about creating list boxes with the JList component, using the JSlider component, and creating your own reusable interface components. The section on the JList class will show how to put bitmaps in your list boxes. You will also learn a few more tricks to use when working with JTextArea controls.

In addition, you will learn a number of techniques for handling events. For instance, you will see how to hook up multiple controls to the same event handler. Other subjects covered include converting applet descendants into JApplet descendants.

Perhaps one of the most important features shown in this chapter is how to build the interface for your program on a JPanel. You can then use the JavaBeans technology to insert the JPanel into the main window of your application or applet. This kind of architecture makes it easy for you to reuse the components that you create while developing a program.

This chapter is part of the "JBuilder Fundamentals" section of the book. Overall, these chapters are simply meant to help make you as familiar as possible with working inside the IDE and the visual designer. I have found that when it comes to this kind of knowledge, there is nothing like plenty of hands-on experience. The number one goal of this chapter is to give you experience using the JBuilder IDE. To help facilitate this process, I suggest that you read through the chapter, and then close the book and try to recreate the program described here from memory or with only the screen shots in the text to guide you.

Using the JSlider Component in an Applet

You are now going to build a color chooser component, much like the one shown in Figure 17-1. The program you are going to build is called MyColorSlider, which is available on the CD.

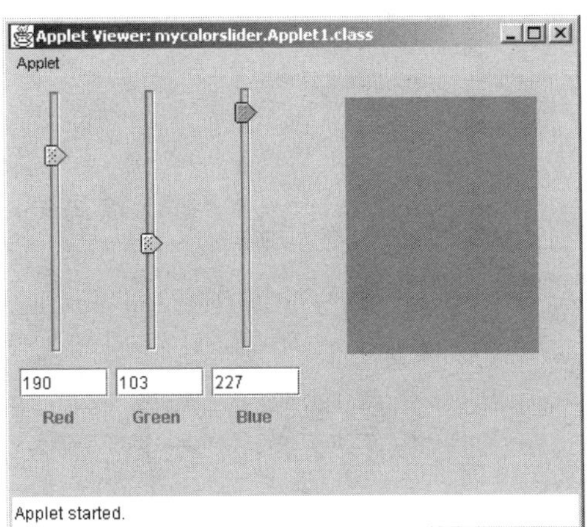

Figure 17-1: The MyColorSlider program allows you to play with mixes of red, green, and blue to create splendiferous colors of many shades.

To get started, first create a new applet, as described in Chapter 3. In step 1 of the Project Wizard, name the project **MyColorSlider** and click **Finish**. This will bring you to the Applet Wizard. In the Applet Wizard, accept the default settings by clicking **Finish** to generate your applet.

Creating the Interface

The interface for this program will be built on top of a JPanel component. After you create the interface, you will insert it into the applet using very simple JavaBeans technology. The end result is the production of a reusable color slider component.

To get started, choose **File | New Class** from the JBuilder menu. Create a new javax.swing.JPanel descendant called **MyColorSlider**, as shown in Figure 17-2. Click the **OK** button to complete the process.

Focus MyColorSlider.java in the editor and switch to design view. Your first task is to make sure the layout for this JPanel descendant in the structure pane is FlowLayout, as shown in Figure 17-2. In the structure pane of this project, the node labeled "this" refers to your JPanel descendant. You can confirm that by running your cursor over the word "this" in the structure pane. A tool tip message will appear stating "this: javax.swing.JPanel."

The JSlider component is on the right-hand side of the Swing page of the component palette. You may have to scroll the component palette to see it. Press the **Shift** key, click once on the JSlider in the component palette, and click three times on the designer to drop three JSliders down onto MyColorSlider. Be sure to click the white arrow (selection tool) to return your cursor to normal functioning.

Hold down the **Ctrl** key and click on all three sliders to select them. In the Inspector, change the orientation property of all three sliders to **VERTICAL**, and change the maximum property to **255**. Figure 17-2 shows you how to proceed.

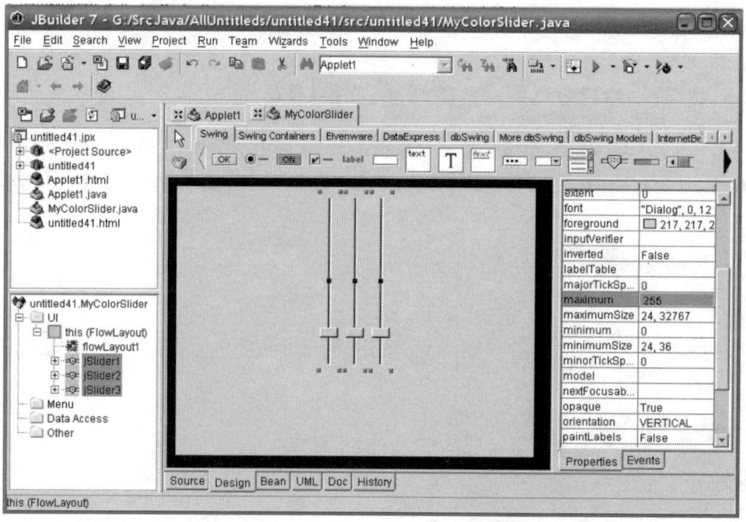

Figure 17-2: Three JSliders on the designer with their orientation set to VERTICAL and the maximum property in the act of being modified

Now change the layout of MyColorSlider to **null**, as shown in Figure 17-3. This may cause the JSlider components to appear to vanish. If this happens, close MyColorSlider and then reopen it again using the **File | Reopen** menu item.

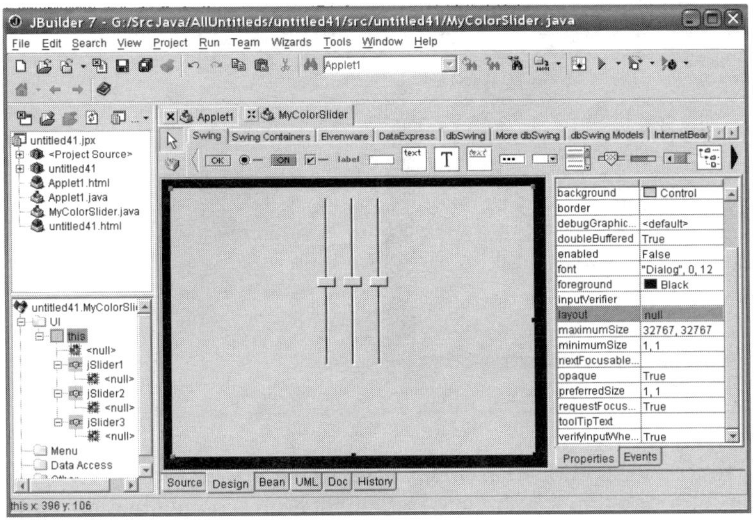

Figure 17-3: Setting the layout of the new JPanel descendant that you created to null

Select all three sliders again and move them to the left side of the designer. They should remain perfectly aligned, as they were in FlowLayout. Change the name property of each JSlider in the Inspector so that they are called, from left to right, **sliderRed**, **sliderGreen**, and **sliderBlue**.

You will probably want to increase the horizontal space between the sliders to make room for the labels you will be adding later. Because you are in Null layout, you can use your mouse to reposition them. Or, if you prefer, hold down the **Ctrl** key and use the arrow keys to move the component one pixel at a time. This latter method can be very helpful when you want to move a component to the right or left without accidentally moving it up and down.

Use the **Ctrl** key to select multiple components, just as you have been doing, and right-click on a component to access the pop-up menu to adjust the alignment. Either Align Bottom or Align Top will be useful in this process. You might also want to choose **Even Space Horizontal**.

NOTE: In Null layout, there are a number of useful tools in the right-click pop-up menu for aligning your components. If you multi-select several components, you can align them to the right, top, left, or bottom. You can make them all the same size or space them evenly. Remember also the trick for using the Ctrl and Arrow keys to move the component one pixel at a time. These technologies can save you a lot of effort if you remember to use them.

Drop a JTextArea down on the right side of the designer. Set the text property for the control to an empty string. To do this, click on the **text** property in the Inspector. Use the Backspace key to clear the field next to the word "text," and then press **Enter**. The text area will now be blank.

Adjust the JTextArea so that it covers a fair proportion of the right side of the designer. The result should look something like what you see in Figure 17-4.

As you are engaged in this process, you may wish to view your applet. To do this, first save all your files and then build your project by clicking on the **Make** icon. Then click **Applet1.html** in your project pane, and choose the **View** page.

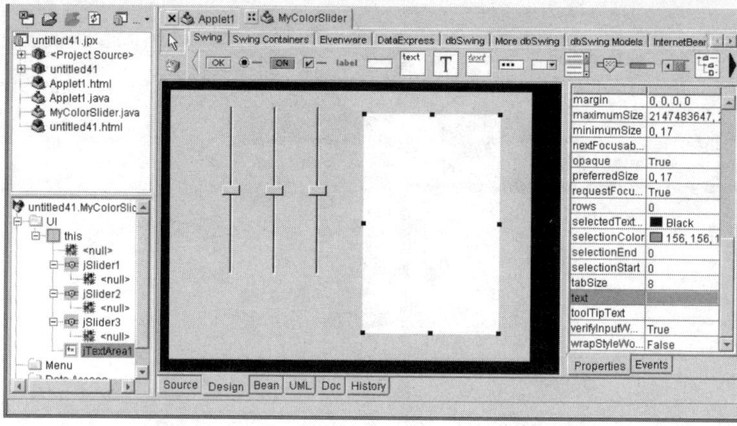

Figure 17-4: The JSliders and the JTextArea are on the designer.

Drop down three JTextFields and three JLabels, and place a JTextField and a JLabel at the base of each JSlider. You may find it helpful to initially line up the middle resizing handles of the JTextField and the JLabel with the bottom of the JSlider. Again, use the skills you have already learned to adjust the alignment and spacing.

Change the text on the three JLabels to read, from left to right, **Red**, **Green**, and **Blue**. Clear all three JTextFields of text and change their names, using the Inspector, to **textFieldRed**, **textFieldGreen**, and **textFieldBlue**. The name changes may seem to be extra work, but you would be surprised how descriptive names can simplify your life as you write code.

The only thing left to do at this stage is to switch from Null layout to GridBagLayout. Once again, select the this node in the structure pane. In the Inspector, change the layout from null to **GridBagLayout**. With a little luck, the conversion will go smoothly and your program will look exactly right. Figure 17-5 shows the current state of the program.

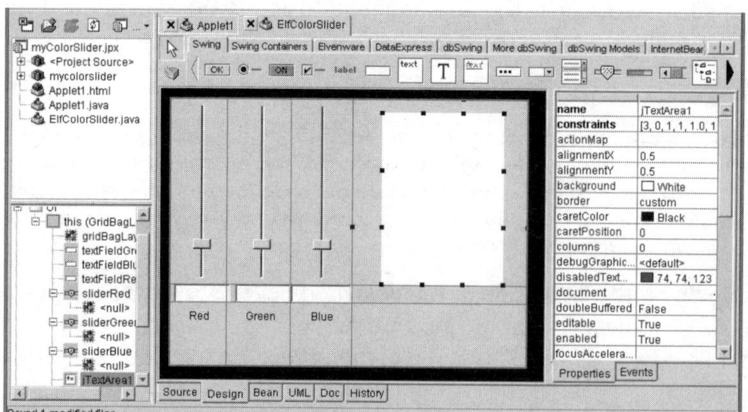

Figure 17-5: The interface for the MyColorSlider component is finished.

In this particular case, the conversion from Null to GridBagLayout went very smoothly for me. I did not need to make any further changes to the program's UI. If you are having problems with this step, you might find it helpful to study the code on the CD.

Adding Events

The next thing you need to do is hook up some events so that the program actually does something.

Click on **sliderRed** to select it, and then turn to the **Events** page of the Inspector. There you will see, in alphabetical order, the events that are available to you. You will want to use the mouseReleased event. To do this, click in the property editor field to the right of the word mouseReleased, and then press **Enter** when text appears in the field. Figure 17-6 illustrates this operation.

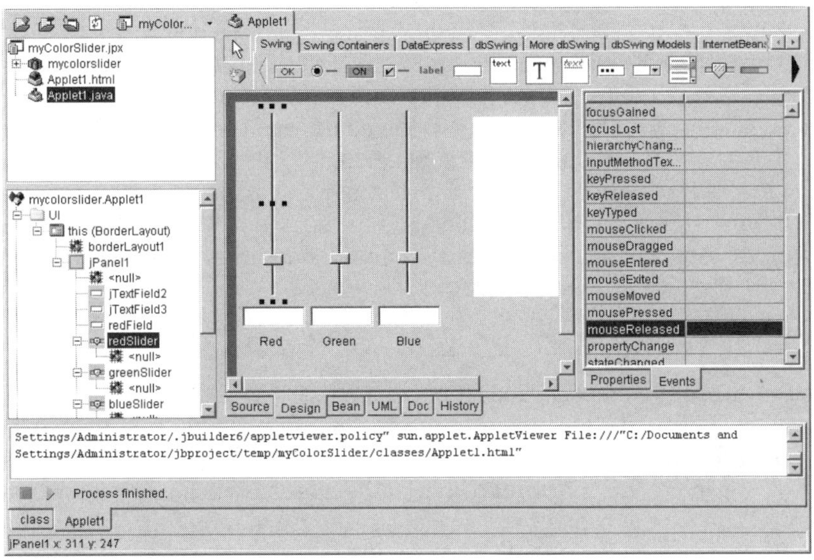

Figure 17-6: The mouseReleased event in the Inspector

JBuilder will bring you to the editor and create an event code stub. All the necessary code for your event will be generated for you. Place the following code in the event:

```
void sliderRed_mouseReleased(MouseEvent e)
{
  int redInt = redSlider.getValue();
  int blueInt = blueSlider.getValue();
  int greenInt = greenSlider.getValue();
  redField.setText(Integer.toString(redInt));
  greenField.setText(Integer.toString(greenInt));
  blueField.setText(Integer.toString(blueInt));
  jTextArea1.setBackground(new Color(redInt,greenInt, blueInt));
}
```

This code retrieves the current value of the redSlider, blueSlider, and greenSlider:

```
int redInt = redSlider.getValue();
int blueInt = blueSlider.getValue();
int greenInt = greenSlider.getValue();
```

Because of the range you set up for the sliders, this value will be an integer value between 0 and 255. We now use these numbers to change the color of the JTextArea:

```
jTextArea1.setBackground(new Color(redInt,greenInt, blueInt));
```

This one call mixes the current red, green, and blue values into the appropriate shade, much as a painter would mix colors on a palette board.

We also show the numbers used to make up the colors in the JTextFields:

```
redField.setText(Integer.toString(redInt));
greenField.setText(Integer.toString(greenInt));
blueField.setText(Integer.toString(blueInt));
```

Hooking Up Multiple Controls to the Same Event

We want all three sliders to access the same event. As a result, we will be hooking all of the sliders to the sliderRed_mouseReleased event. Turn back to the design view. Click on **sliderGreen**, turn to the **Events** page in the Inspector, and click in the text field next to mouseReleased. Change the text to read **sliderRed_mouseReleased**.

Press **Enter**. The view will switch again to the editor, and the cursor will appear in the same code stub you just programmed for the SliderRed_mouseReleased event. Change back to the design view, click on **sliderBlue**, and go through the same process. By doing this, you are hooking all three sliders to the same code and the same event. When you move any of the sliders, this one method will be called. It takes into consideration the state of all three sliders and shows the resulting color in the JTextArea.

Adding MyColorSlider to the Main Window of the Applet

It is now time to add the JPanel descendant component that you have created to the main window of your applet. This is the step that can teach you much of what you need to know to reuse a component in multiple applications.

Use the project pane to focus **Applet1.java** in the editor. Switch to design mode. Make sure the contentPane for the applet has its layout set to **BorderLayout**.

Select the **Bean Chooser** from its location on the far left of the component palette. It is directly beneath the white selection tool arrow, as shown in Figure 17-7.

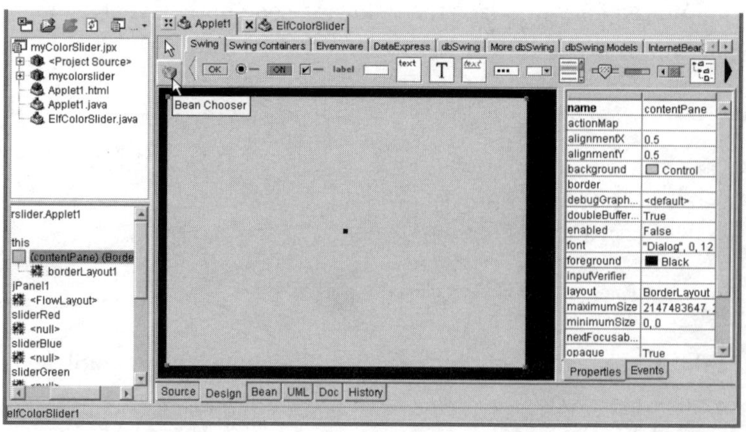

Figure 17-7: You can use the Bean Chooser to add components that you created to the interface of your applet.

Choose the item labeled **Select** from the pop-up menu enabled by the Bean Chooser. Use the BeanChooser dialog to browse for and select the MyColorSlider class, as shown in Figure 17-8.

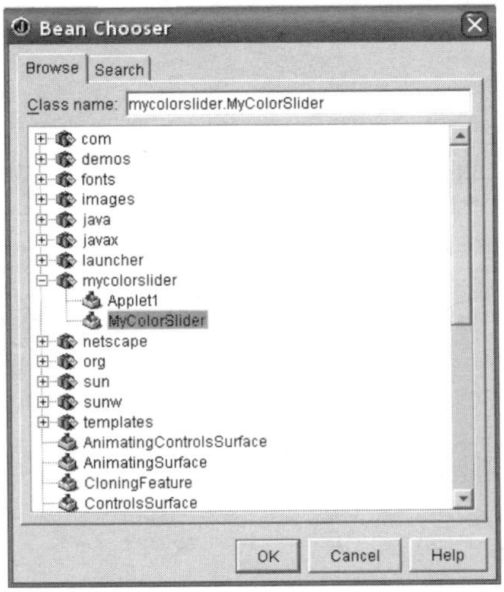

Figure 17-8: Using the Bean Chooser to select the JPanel descendant class that you just finished creating

After choosing MyColorSlider, the cursor will change to a cross, just as it would had you selected the component from the component palette. Now paint your new control onto the surface of the applet, just as you would were you adding a new JPanel to it. Set the constraints property for your new control to **Center**, as shown in Figure 17-9.

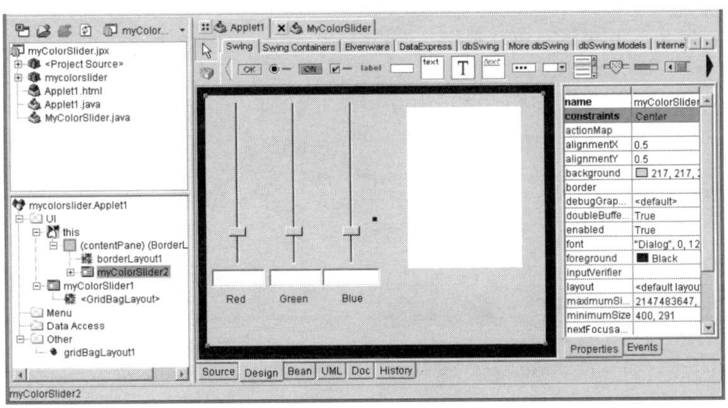

Figure 17-9: The MyColorSlider JPanel descendant resting on top of a JApplet instance. The constraints for MyColorSlider are set to Center.

You have just finished creating a JavaBean and adding it to your application. For now, however, you don't have to think of this whole process as being part of the JavaBeans technology. Instead, you can simply think of it as an easy way to create reusable components. I will, however, discuss JavaBeans technology in depth in Part VII: JavaBeans.

It should be fairly obvious to you that you could easily move the MyColorSlider file to another project and reuse it. The only real change you would have to make is to the package statement at the top of the file. While reading Part VII: JavaBeans, you will learn that even that small change will not be necessary if you set things up correctly. For now, however, you should be content with seeing how easy it was to start treating the relatively complex bundle of components that make up MyColorSlider.java as a single, reusable entity.

Testing the Applet

Be sure to save your work by choosing **File | Save All**. Now run the applet. You can test to be sure you got everything right by setting each slider in turn to the maximum (the top of the slider), while the other two are at the minimum (the bottom of the slider). If all is working as it should, the red slider at its maximum will create a red display, the green slider will create a green display, and the blue slider will create a blue display. The JTextArea will change its color to any combination of red, green, or blue, depending on the slider settings. The text field below each slider will show the RGB settings you are creating. Figure 17-10 is a sample of the applet's appearance as it is running.

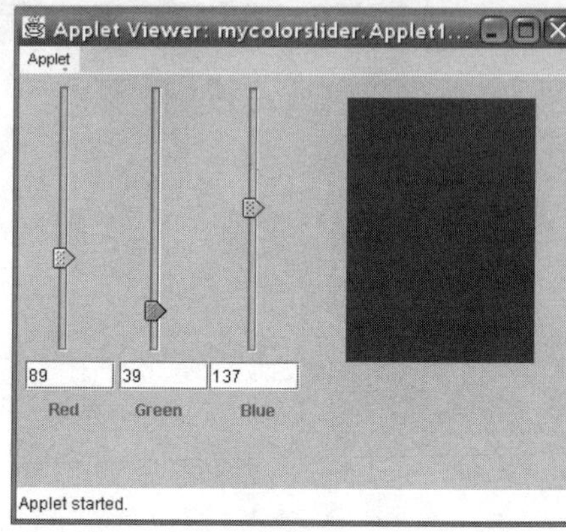

Figure 17-10: The MyColorSlider applet running (the color shown is purple)

Building Your Applet out of Multiple Components

Now that you understand how to add one custom bean to your applet, you might want to see how you can build a more complex program out of a series of such beans. In particular, we are going to add a new panel to the bottom of the MyColorSlider program that contains a button used to close the project. This addition will blend in seamlessly with your current applet, as shown in Figure 17-11.

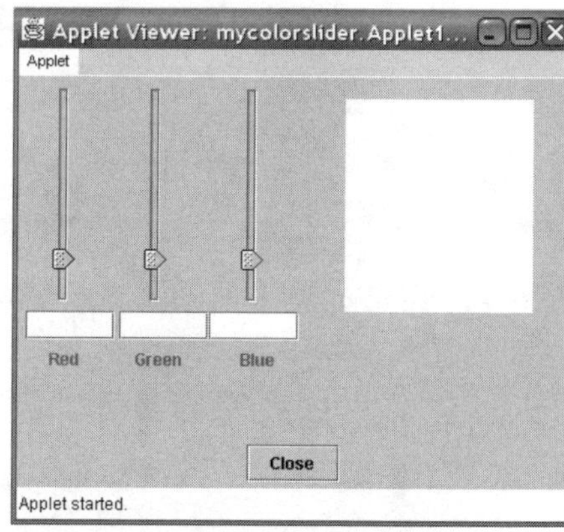

Figure 17-11: A second JPanel descendant has been added to the bottom of the program, making the interface to the whole applet a composite of two custom components.

To get started, choose **File | New Class** from the JBuilder menu. Create a new JPanel descendant called **ClosePanel**, as shown in Figure 17-12.

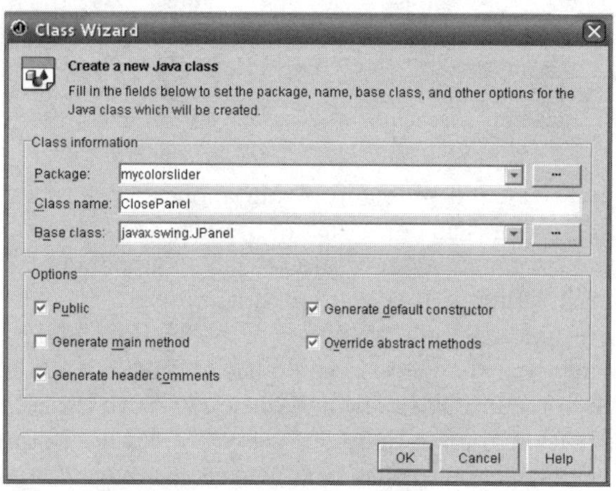

Figure 17-12: Creating a descendant of javax.swing.JPanel called ClosePanel

As shown in Figure 17-13, you should design this simple component to contain a single button, called jButtonClose, that has its text property set to the word **Close**.

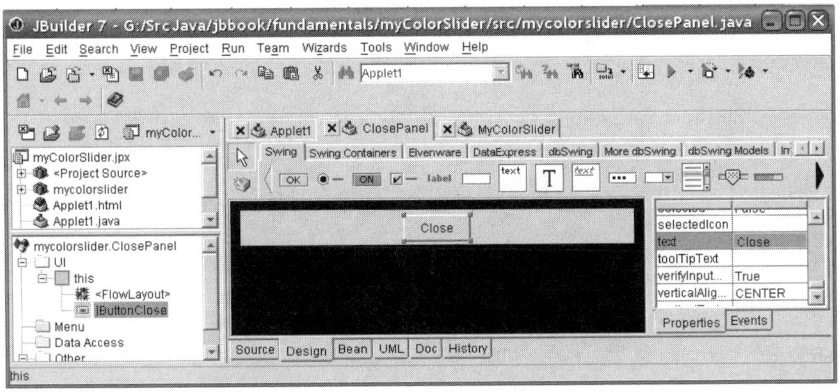

Figure 17-13: Designing the simple ClosePanel component that will be added to the interface of the applet

Clearly we want to use the ClosePanel component to close the main applet on which it will rest. To achieve this goal, we could have the ClosePanel component call a method of Applet1.java. The problem with this solution, however, is that it would link ClosePanel and Applet1.java in a very specific way. As a result, ClosePanel would no longer be a truly reusable component that could be plugged into another program.

To avoid this problem, you can have the ClosePanel fire an event when the user selects the Close button. The applet can then listen for this event and close itself when it receives it.

In Chapter 15 you learned how to teach a component to send a message to another component. If you have the SE or Enterprise versions of JBuilder, you can do this with the BeansExpress technology. Otherwise, you will have to type in the code by hand.

If you have the technology available, select the **Bean** tab from the file view tabs. Turn to the **Events** page and give the ClosePanel the ability to fire an ActionEvent, as shown in Figure 17-14. Fill in the ActionEvent handler for the Close button with this code, which is designed to fire an event each time the user presses the Close button:

```
void jButtonClose_actionPerformed(ActionEvent e)
{
      ActionEvent closeEvent = new ActionEvent(this, 1, "Close");
      fireActionPerformed(closeEvent);
}
```

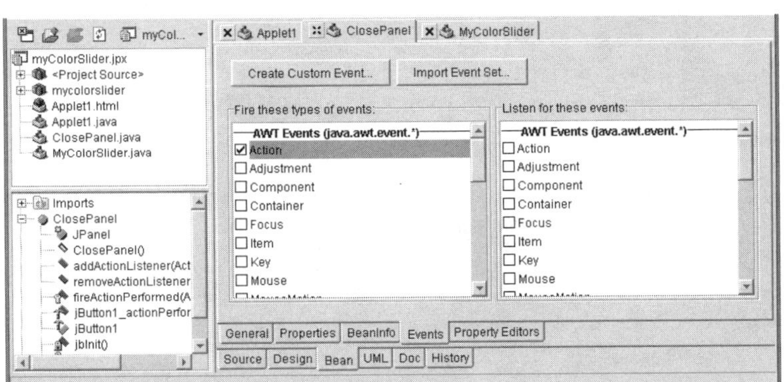

Figure 17-14: Using BeansExpress to give the ClosePanel the ability to fire ActionEvents

The entire source for the ClosePanel is shown in Listing 17-1. You can use this as a guide if you are working with the Personal edition of JBuilder.

Listing 17-1: The source for the simple ClosePanel bean

```
package mycolorslider;

import javax.swing.*;
import java.awt.event.*;
import java.util.*;


/**
 * <p>Title: </p>
 * <p>Description: </p>
 * <p>Copyright: Copyright (c) 2002</p>
 * <p>Company: </p>
 * @author unascribed
 * @version 1.0
 */

public class ClosePanel extends JPanel
{
      JButton jButtonClose = new JButton();
      private transient Vector actionListeners;

      public ClosePanel()
      {
            try
            {
                  jbInit();
            }
            catch(Exception e)
            {
                  e.printStackTrace();
            }
      }
      private void jbInit() throws Exception
      {
            jButtonClose.setText("Close");
            jButtonClose.addActionListener(
                  new ClosePanel_jButtonClose_actionAdapter(this));
            this.add(jButtonClose, null);
      }

      void jButtonClose_actionPerformed(ActionEvent e)
      {
            ActionEvent closeEvent = new ActionEvent(this, 1, "Close");
            fireActionPerformed(closeEvent);
      }

      public synchronized void removeActionListener(ActionListener l)
```

```
    {
        if (actionListeners != null && actionListeners.contains(l))
        {
            Vector v = (Vector) actionListeners.clone();
            v.removeElement(l);
            actionListeners = v;
        }
    }
    public synchronized void addActionListener(ActionListener l)
    {
        Vector v = actionListeners ==
            null ? new Vector(2) : (Vector) actionListeners.clone();
        if (!v.contains(l))
        {
            v.addElement(l);
            actionListeners = v;
        }
    }
    protected void fireActionPerformed(ActionEvent e)
    {
        if (actionListeners != null)
        {
            Vector listeners = actionListeners;
            int count = listeners.size();
            for (int i = 0; i < count; i++)
            {
                ((ActionListener) listeners.elementAt(i)).actionPerformed(e);
            }
        }
    }
}

class ClosePanel_jButtonClose_actionAdapter implements java.awt.event.ActionListener
{
    ClosePanel adaptee;

    ClosePanel_jButtonClose_actionAdapter(ClosePanel adaptee)
    {
        this.adaptee = adaptee;
    }
    public void actionPerformed(ActionEvent e)
    {
        adaptee.jButtonClose_actionPerformed(e);
    }
}
```

You should now use the Bean Chooser to add the CloseBean to Applet1.java. Simply follow the same steps you used when adding the MyColorSlider component. Only this time, you should drop the component down not on the designer, but on the structure pane. Set its constraints property to **South**, as shown in Figure 17-15.

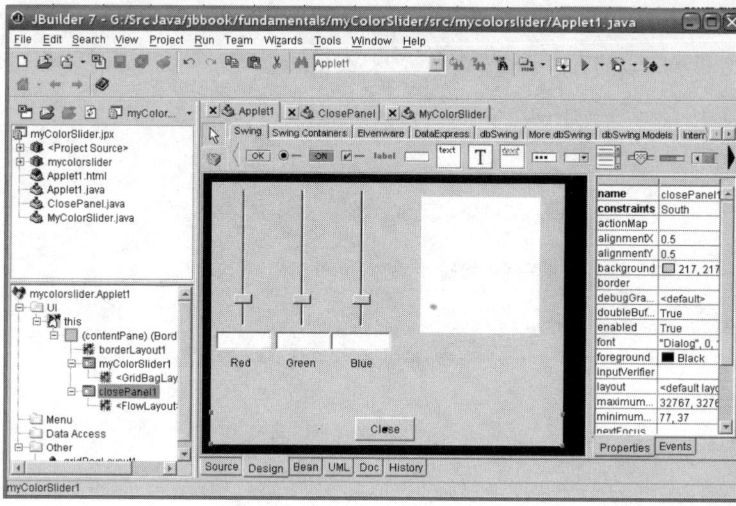

Figure 17-15: The newly created ClosePanel added to the MyColorSlider applet

The final step in this process is to teach Applet1.java to listen for, and respond to, close events fired from the ClosePanel. If you have the tools, you can finish the task fairly easily by focusing Applet1.java in the editor, bringing up BeansExpress, turning to the Events page, and giving the applet the ability to listen for ActionEvents, as shown in Figure 17-16.

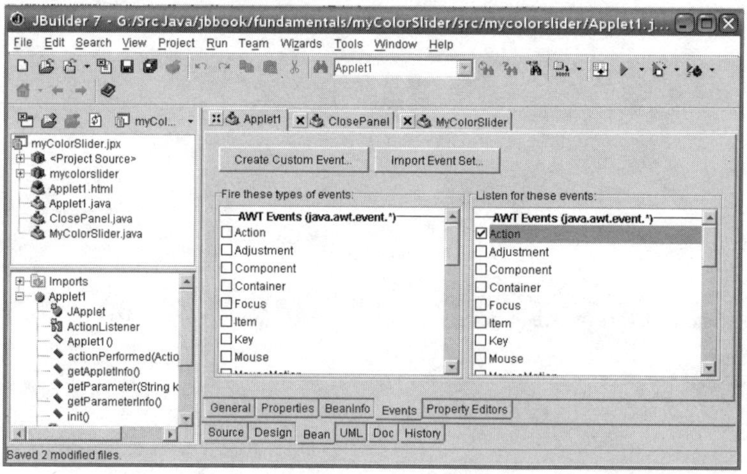

Figure 17-16: Using BeansExpress to train the applet to listen for ActionEvents

The code needed to get Applet1 to listen for ActionEvents is shown here:

```
public class Applet1 extends JApplet implements ActionListener
{
      … Code omitted here.

      public void actionPerformed(ActionEvent e)
      {
      }
}
```

You should also be sure to add code to jbInit that explicitly asks the ClosePanel to send you events:

```
//Component initialization
private void jbInit() throws Exception
{
        … Code omitted here

        closePanel1.addActionListener(this);
}
```

To make the applet actually close when it receives this event, edit the actionPerformed event as follows:

```
public void actionPerformed(ActionEvent e)
{
        System.exit(0);
}
```

You can now run the application to test it and see if this new feature works. If you have any problems, turn to the CD or www.elvenware.com to work with a completed version of the MyColorSlider program.

NOTE: Now that you have assembled your program, you should remember to always make changes to MyColorSlider.java and ClosePanel.java directly. Don't try to visually edit these components while they are in place inside Applet1.java. Instead, focus ClosePanel.java or MyColorSlider.java and make your changes to the components themselves. For instance, if you wanted to add a Cancel button to the ClosePanel, you should first focus ClosePanel.java in the project pane, and then switch into design mode and make the changes there. When you then run the applet, or put Applet1.java into design mode, you should automatically see the changes you made to ClosePanel. If you don't see the changes you made to ClosePanel.java reflected in Applet1.java, try closing and reopening your project. Particularly on Linux, there can be some problems with the buffers that prevent the JBuilder designer from updating itself as quickly as you might like.

The technology shown in this part of the chapter is very important. The ability to easily create small, reusable visual components such as MyColorSlider or ClosePanel is one of the great virtues of the Java language. You will read much more about this kind of technology in Part VII: JavaBeans.

Interlude: Applets, JApplets, and Swing

JBuilder allows you to create applets based on the old 1.x Applet class or create them based on the Swing-based JApplet class. If you use the Applet class and the AWT controls in your project, you can run on some very old JREs. Having this backward compatibility is sometimes convenient. However, it deprives you of the ability to use the new features found in Swing.

The moment you drop a component from the Swing page onto an Applet descendant, you might as well have built the whole thing using JApplet and the Swing classes. If you have even one JTextField on your applet, there is no going back to the old JRE 1.x way of doing things. You have crossed the Rubicon and entered Swingland. If that is what you meant to do, you might as well upgrade the whole program to Swing.

I often need to upgrade old applets to JApplets. And sometimes, in my haste, I will accidentally create an Applet when I meant to create a JApplet. If I get far enough down the road creating my new applet, I don't want to start again from scratch.

Here is how to proceed if you want to convert an Applet descendant into a JApplet descendant. First import the Swing package and then change the name of the class from which you descend to JApplet:

```
import javax.swing.*;

public class Applet1 extends JApplet
```

Now go to jbInit and find the references to the variable this:

```
this.setLayout(borderLayout1);
this.add(jPanel1, BorderLayout.CENTER);
```

You will want to get a handle to the JApplet content pane and then change the references quoted above, and any similar references, so that they read as follows:

```
JPanel contentPane = (JPanel)this.getContentPane();
contentPane.setLayout(borderLayout1);
contentPane.add(jPanel1, BorderLayout.CENTER);
```

In most cases, that's all you need to do. Now your Applet class has been upgraded to run as a JApplet.

List Boxes

The list box component is one of the most commonly used Swing tools. In this section of the chapter, you will learn how to build a simple application that features a list box containing a series of bitmaps. The sample application, called simply ListBox, is shown in Figure 17-17.

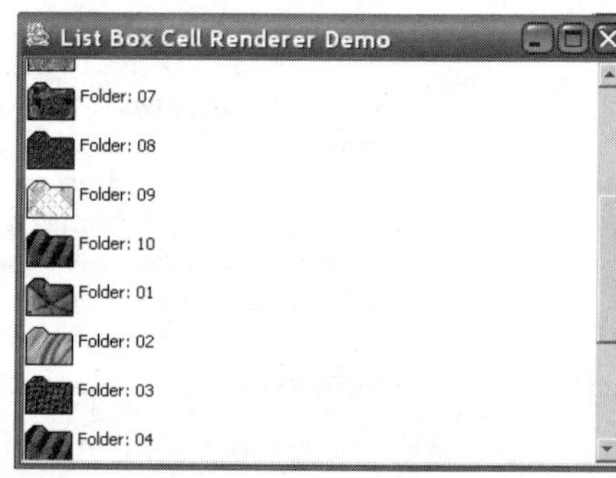

Figure 17-17: A simple list box application. On the far left of the list box, you can see a series of bitmaps that scroll up and down as you move through the list.

Building the List Box Sample

To get started, create a default JBuilder application, as outlined in Chapter 3. Focus **Frame1** in the editor and switch to design mode. Make sure the layout for the contentPane is set to **BorderLayout**. Drop down a JScrollPane from the Swing Containers page on the contentPane. Set its constraints property to **Center**. Turn to the Swing page and drop down a JList on top of the JScrollPane.

At this stage the interface for the application is completed. It should look much as it does in Figure 17-17, except the JList will be empty of content.

The question now is how to get content into the JList. One technique would be to go to the top of Frame1 and edit the constructor for the JList object. Before you make any edits, the constructor will look like the last line in this code fragment:

```
public class Frame1 extends JFrame
{
      JPanel contentPane;
      BorderLayout borderLayout1 = new BorderLayout();
      JScrollPane jScrollPane1 = new JScrollPane();
      JList jList1 = new JList();
```

The only line that matters here is the last one. I'm including the others only to give you context.

To place some simple String items in the JList, you could write something like this:

```
JList jList1 = new JList(new String[] {"Sam", "Joe", "Paul"});
```

This line of code constructs and initializes the JList object so that it includes several strings, as shown in Figure 17-18.

Figure 17-18: The JList with a few simple strings inserted in it

In a few cases, code like this will meet your needs. However, in most cases, you will want to add and delete items from the list not at design time, but at run time. To do that, you will want to work with an object called a DefaultListModel:

```
public class Frame1 extends JFrame
{
      JPanel contentPane;
      BorderLayout borderLayout1 = new BorderLayout();
      JScrollPane jScrollPane1 = new JScrollPane();
      JList jList1 = new JList();
      DefaultListModel model = new DefaultListModel();

      … Code omitted here.

      private void jbInit() throws Exception
      {
            … Code omitted here
            jList1.setModel(model);
      }
```

The last data field in this code fragment initializes an instance of the DefaultListModel class. The last line in jbInit associates the DefaultListModel with the JList. After writing this code, the JList will use the DefaultListModel to manage the list of items that it displays.

DefaultListModels allow you to add and insert items, such as Strings, that you want to display in a JList. For instance, if you wrote the following code, the list box would contain the data shown in Figure 17-19:

```
for (int i = 0; i < 25; i++)
{
      model.addElement("Information" + String.valueOf(i));
}
```

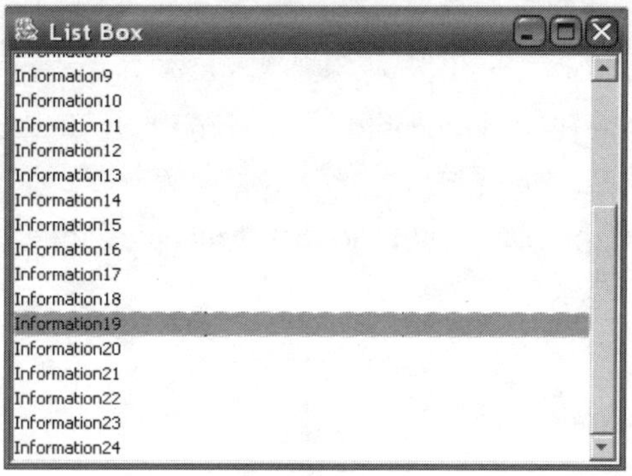

Figure 17-19: A series of strings added into a JList with the aid of the DefaultListModel class

To retrieve items from this list, you might write code that looks like this:

```
void jButton1_actionPerformed(ActionEvent e)
{
      DefaultListModel list = (DefaultListModel)jList1.getModel();
      int selectedIndex = jList1.getSelectedIndex();
      if (selectedIndex != -1)
      {
            String s = (String)list.get(selectedIndex);
            System.out.println("List: " + s);
      }
      else
      {
            System.out.println("You must select an item");
      }
}
```

This code first retrieves the DefaultListModel inserted earlier into the JList object. It then uses the JList.getSelectedIndex() method to retrieve the index of the currently selected item from the list box. If no item is selected in the list box, getSelectedIndex returns –1. Otherwise, you can use this index to retrieve the selected item from the list itself using the get method:

```
String s = (String)list.get(selectedIndex);
```

There are other useful methods of DefaultListModel, such as clear, contains, firstElement, getSize, indexOf, lastElement, remove, isEmpty, removeAllElements, and removeRange. The names of these methods are fairly descriptive, and their use is generally fairly intuitive, so I will not bother exploring them in depth here.

Adding Objects to a JList

You can store items other than strings in a JList. Consider the following code fragment from jbInit:

```
jList1.setModel(model);
model.addElement(jScrollPane1);
model.addElement(jButton1);
model.addElement(jPanel1);
```

In this code sample, standard Java classes are being added to the JList rather than Strings. At run time, the results of this action appear as in Figure 17-20.

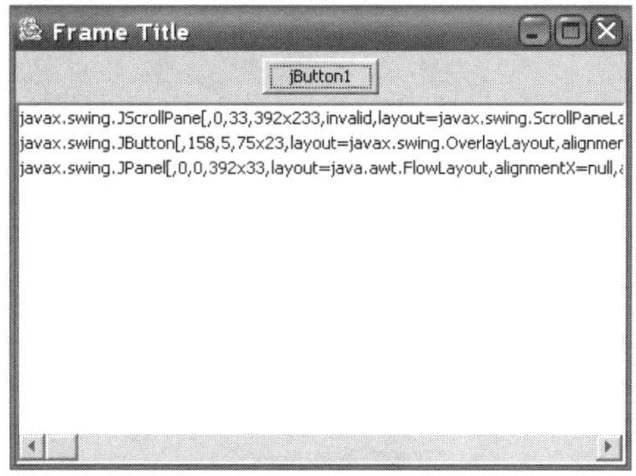

Figure 17-20: If you add objects other than Strings to a JList, their toString method is called when it comes time for them to be displayed.

In Figure 17-20 you can see that jScrollPane1.toString(), jButton1.toString(), and jPanel1.toString() were automatically called by the JDK to produce the output shown in the JList. It doesn't take much imagination to see that you could create your own custom objects that had more aesthetically pleasing output from their toString methods. You could then store the objects in a JList, have the user select them, and then do some fancy things with the object behind the scenes.

Adding Graphics to a JList

Now that you know how to manage items in a JList, the final step is to learn how to associate graphics with each line in the list. To do this, you use the interface called javax.swing.ListCellRenderer. In most cases, you will create a descendant of the JLabel class that implements the ListCellRenderer interface. The idea is that you will fill in the label with a bitmap and text, and then the label will be shown in the appropriate row of the JList. The JLabel descendant used to produce the output shown in Figure 17-17 is displayed in Listing 17-2.

Listing 17-2: A ListCellRenderer object that assigns bitmaps to the items in a JList

```
package listbox;

import javax.swing.ListCellRenderer;
import java.awt.*;
import javax.swing.*;
import java.util.*;

public class FolderRenderer extends JLabel implements ListCellRenderer
{
     ArrayList folderIcons;

     public FolderRenderer(ArrayList folderIcons)
     {
          this.folderIcons = folderIcons;
     }

     public Component getListCellRendererComponent(JList list, Object value,
               int index, boolean isSelected, boolean cellHasFocus)
     {
          if (value != null)
          {
               ListModel model = list.getModel();
               String text = (String)model.getElementAt(index);
               System.out.println("Text: " + text + " " + value.toString());

               setText(text);
               setOpaque(true);
```

```
            }

            if (folderIcons != null)
            {
                  setIcon((Icon)folderIcons.get(index));
            }


            if (isSelected)
            {
                  setBackground(list.getSelectionBackground());
                  setForeground(list.getSelectionForeground());
            }
            else
            {
                  setBackground(list.getBackground());
                  setForeground(list.getForeground());
            }
            return this;
      }
}
```

I don't mean to sound like a broken record, but I want to remind you one more time that this class extends JLabel. You have to remember that or this code won't really make sense to you.

The constructor for this object accepts an array of icons:

```
      ArrayList folderIcons;

      public FolderRenderer(ArrayList folderIcons)
      {
            this.folderIcons = folderIcons;
      }
```

The array of icons is initialized and constructed back in Frame1, along with the DefaultListModel:

```
ArrayList list = new ArrayList();
DefaultListModel model = new DefaultListModel();

for (int i = 1; i < 20; i++)
{
      int num = i;
      if (num > 10) num -= 10;
      String value = StringBox.intToStrPad0(num, 2);
      model.addElement("Folder: " + value);
      list.add(new ImageIcon("Folder" + value + ".png"));
}
jList1.setModel(model);
jList1.setCellRenderer(new FolderRenderer(list));
```

The intToStrPad0 method shown here takes a string such as 2 and converts it into a string padded with zeros: 02. It is the kind of routine you would use to ensure that a time display for two minutes after two looked like this: 2:02, and not like this: 2:2. Here is the code for the method:

```
public static final String intToStrPad0(int value, int paddings)
{
      String rawString = String.valueOf(value);
      StringBuffer paddedString = new StringBuffer(rawString);
      while (paddedString.length() < paddings)
      {
            paddedString.insert(0, '0');
      }
      return paddedString.toString();
}
```

You can pass in both the value you want to pad and the number of digits you want to see. For instance, intToStrPad0(5, 4) would yield the string 0005, and intToStrPad0(25, 2) would yield the string 25. Note that a StringBuffer is used rather than a String object. String objects are immutable, hence they need to be created over and over in loops like the one used in intToStrPad0. StringBuffer objects are better suited to use in this kind of code and should not make the garbage collector work quite as hard.

The IntToStrPad0 method is important because the bitmaps to be displayed in the list box are saved to disk in this format:


```
Folder01.png
Folder02.png
Etc…
```

To generate these strings on the fly, I want to create strings that look like Folder01.png, not like Folder1.png.

The following lines of code load each bitmap from disk, store it in an instance of the ImageIcon object, and then add the object to the ArrayList:

```
String value = StringBox.intToStrPad0(num, 2);
list.add(new ImageIcon("Folder" + value + ".png"));
```

Cell Renderers: Creating the Components to be Displayed in a JList

Once you have passed in the array of icons to the ListCellRenderer implementation, the cell renderer class is fully initialized. When it comes time to draw the bitmaps in the list box, the following method of our ListCellRenderer implementation class is called:

```
public Component getListCellRendererComponent(JList list, Object value,
      int index, boolean isSelected, boolean cellHasFocus)
```

This method returns the current instance of the JLabel component that we are in the process of creating. In response to the method call, we are expected to fill out our JLabel instance and return it back to the system. In an oversimplified and entirely theoretical form, the call would look like this:

```
public Component getListCellRendererComponent(JList list, Object value,
      int index, boolean isSelected, boolean cellHasFocus)
{
      setText("My Text");
      return this;
}
```

Recall that we are inside an instance of a JLabel descendant. The call to setText, therefore, sets the text of the JLabel. The code then returns the JLabel to the system, which displays it as a row in the list box.

At any rate, that is the theory behind the system. In practice, things are a little more complicated. Not really all that much more, but still a bit more complicated.

NOTE: One complication that you need to keep in mind is that you are not creating a whole series of JLabels, but really only using one JLabel component that keeps mutating to fit the needs of the current line in the list box. In this section of the text, I will sometimes — for the sake of syntactical simplicity — speak as if a series of JLabels were being created. But that is not the case. There is only one JLabel, but you keep redefining how it behaves so that it appears correctly each time it is painted.

The JList that we are working with is passed to us by the system in the first parameter of the call to getListCellRendererComponent. The second parameter contains the currently selected item in the list. In our case, that will be a string. You have seen, however, that it could be almost any type of object. (That would make it possible for you to include the icon you want to associate with an object inside the object itself!) The third parameter is the selectedIndex of the item in the list. The fourth is whether or not this is the currently selected item. Remember, you are going to be called to draw all the visible rows, not just the currently selected row. So you will need to know whether or not to draw the current row passed to this method as if it were selected. Finally, the last parameter lets you know whether or not the cell you are drawing is not only selected but also currently focused. We will not use this last parameter.

The first chunk of code in our implementation of getListCellRendererComponent gives you the chance to set the text you want to display:

```
setOpaque(true);
if (value != null)
{
      ListModel model = list.getModel();
      String text = (String)model.getElementAt(index);
      System.out.println("Text: " + text + " " + value.toString());

      setText(text);
}
```

You have already seen code almost exactly like this, so you should have no trouble understanding what it is all about. Note that in this case, I don't have to worry about index being –1, as the system very kindly will not ask me to draw a cell that does not exist.

```
The next step is to draw the bitmap that we want to display:
if (folderIcons != null)
{
      setIcon((Icon)folderIcons.get(index));
}
```

This is clearly the most important step in this process. Nonetheless, it is extremely simple — so simple, in fact, that I can't think of anything intelligent to say about it.

The last chunk of code in getListCellRendererComponent paints the background of the area of the list box that we are filling:

```
if (isSelected)
{
      setBackground(list.getSelectionBackground());
      setForeground(list.getSelectionForeground());
}
else
{
      setBackground(list.getBackground());
      setForeground(list.getForeground());
}
```

As you can see, all we are doing is asking the JList itself to supply us with the default selected or non-selected background colors and then using them to paint the controls. I suppose one could do something more complicated, but the code shown here is pretty much boilerplate for most implementations of this object that I have seen. The key point here is that we need to draw the item one way if it is selected and a second way if it is not selected.

If you forget to take this last step of drawing the selected row properly, everything in your list box will render more or less correctly, and it will act more or less correctly, only you will be given no visual clue as to which item is currently selected. This usually gives the impression that the list box is not reacting to mouse clicks. In fact, it is reacting, but there is no change in the appearance of the object to let us know that the mouse clicks are getting through. Fill in the code properly, and the correct items in the list box will be visibly selected and deselected. That will make both you and the user much happier.

The final line of code in the getListCellRendererComponent method simply returns the completed JLabel descendant:

```
return this;
```

The system then displays the item in the list box, giving the rest of the world the impression that something quite wonderful is going on. Only the struggling programmer who created the code knows that the user is seeing little more than a single JLabel descendant being displayed over and over inside a little boxed-off rectangle of the screen. It's the Wizard of Oz phenomenon played out for us in living color, with live bitmaps.

Summary

In this chapter, you have used some of JBuilder's visual design tools to create a few simple programs. You have gotten practice in using the designer, the Inspector, the structure pane, the project pane, and the editor. You have also learned a little about the events that are available to you through the Events page of the Inspector.

One of the most important passages in the chapter showed how to build the interface for your application on two reusable JPanel objects. You can easily reuse these components in other applications. Another great benefit of constructing your application out of a series of JPanels is that you break up the complexity of the code in your main window. In particular, all the components that would have appeared in one jbInit are instead spread out over several jbInits, thereby greatly enhancing the manageability of your code.

The last section of the chapter gave you a chance to have some fun with bitmaps and the JList object. There is no way to explain just how deeply a few simple bitmaps can impact the users of your program. If you are one of the lucky computer programmers who have gotten outdoors recently during daylight hours, you may have noticed certain colorful objects such as the sky, trees, and flower beds. These objects are actually not rendered by computers. They are natural objects. Nonetheless, they can have a huge impact on the human mind. Computer developers can share a little of this magic if they place some appealing bitmaps in their programs. Differentiators like this are becoming increasingly important as users grow in sophistication and the number of applications that they can choose from increases.

Now might be a good time to close the book, fire up JBuilder, and see if you can recreate the programs described in this chapter. If possible, try to use only the screen shots as hints. See if you can get to the point where you can build the programs without looking at the text in the book or the code on the CD. If you can get that far, you know you have internalized the information found in this chapter. Remember that you can find the example programs on the CD and on www.elvenware.com. The programs are called MyColorSlider and ListBox.

Chapter 18

The Art of the Button

Charlie Calvert

In this chapter you will step through the process of learning how to use the button component. That may seem like an overly simple goal for a chapter, but most readers should be able to find a number of useful tips here.

The real goal of this chapter is to act as an introduction to the more advanced uses of the Swing components included on the first page of the component palette. When you finish this chapter, you should be somewhat proficient at using some of the intermediate level features of the visual designer and the Inspector.

This chapter contains a number of general programming tips that have to do with building the interface for your application, including a discussion of how to set the icon that appears in the caption bar, which is associated with your application. You also will learn how to use the IconImage component to load a bitmap from disk.

The latter half of the chapter will show you how to create an ersatz button that looks and acts like a button but isn't really a button. This latter section of the chapter will also show how you can use GridBagLayout and buttons to radically change the interface for your program.

In short, this chapter includes material on building the interface for your program using Swing components. This information will be leavened with a generous helping of tips and strategies. Some of the coverage will be of simple graphics techniques, and some will be hints on fancy things you can do with layout managers. To learn about all the issues covered, the best thing to do is to simply read on.

Working with Buttons

The first step is to learn the basic facts you need to know to configure the JButton component. This includes learning how to make it respond to a key combination, such as Alt+X. I will also talk about changing the text of the button, using HTML with the button, and adding icons to the button.

In this chapter, we are going to look at two programs. The first, called WorkingButtons, shows some of the basic things you can do with buttons. The second program, called TheCompleteButton, shows some very fancy things you can do with buttons. The programs are shown in Figures 18-1 and 18-2.

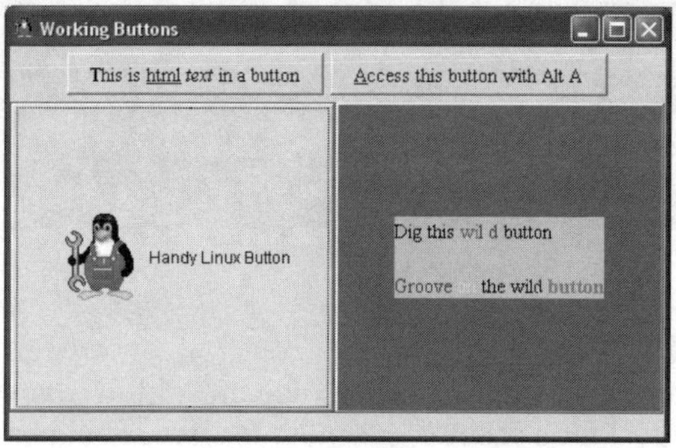

Figure 18-1: The WorkingButtons program does some interesting things with HTML and buttons. You need to run the program to see all the colors on the buttons.

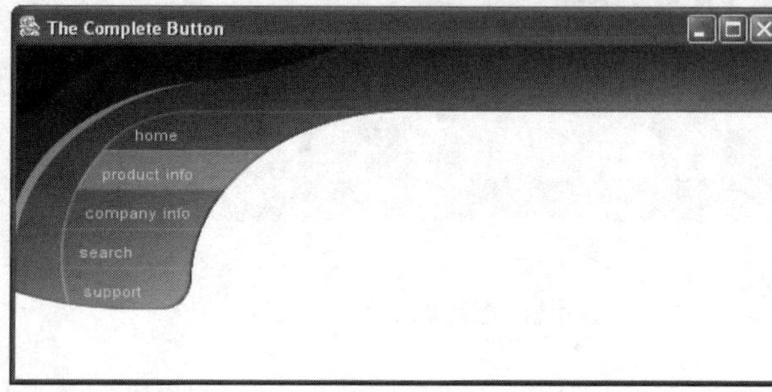

Figure 18-2: TheCompleteButton program shows the kind of fancy user interface you can create with some bitmaps, GridBagLayout, and a little ingenuity.

HTML, Mnemonics, and Responding to the Alt Key

One of the fundamental features of a useful user interface is a hot key. You want to be able to put labels on buttons such as Exit, with the x underlined, and allow the user to press the button not only by using the mouse, but also by using the Alt+X key combination.

One way to proceed is to use HTML to create the underline beneath the letter x, and then use the mnemonic property to specify the hot key. To round things out, you can set the tool tip text:

```
jButtonAltA.setText("<html><u>A</u>ccess this button with Alt A</html>");
jButtonAltA.setMnemonic(KeyEvent.VK_A);
jButtonAltA.setToolTipText("Here is the tool tip text");
```

The call to JButton.setText() may look a bit funny at first glance. That's HTML being placed directly inside of a call to setText. The key to making this work is simply to remember to begin your HTML statement with an <html> tag:

```
"<html><u>A</u>ccess this button with Alt A</html>"
```

The setMnemonic method assures Linux and Windows users that an Alt+A combination will have the same effect as actually clicking the button. As you can see from the setText call, the "A" in the word Access is underlined: <u>A</u>. This is the clue most users expect when they are trying to figure out which hot key to use. Calling setMnemonic with the character "A" as a parameter tells Java to listen for Alt+A key presses and to then call our button if the key combination is pressed.

The Java documentation suggests that you call setMnemonic with an integer value. In particular, you should use the VK_XXX constants declared in java.awt.event.KeyEvent:

```
jButtonAltA.setMnemonic(java.awt.event.KeyEvent.VK_A);
```

You can also call the method with a char:

```
jButtonAltA.setMnemonic('A');
```

This can sometimes be useful, particularly when you are working with the JBuilder Inspector. You should note that the JDK documentation states that calling this method with a char is now obsolete. It is not, however, marked as deprecated.

NOTE: In this text I am assuming that the Alt key will be the combination that you will want to use to trigger this mnemonic. However, this is really talking about the action key, which just happens to be an Alt key on Windows and Linux. I'm not a Mac user, but I know that there is a special key for this purpose on that system.

The last call in the series sets the tool tip text that will show up if the user holds the mouse over the control:

```
jButtonAltA.setToolTipText("Here is the tool tip text");
```

Of course, you can — and should — enter all this code through the JBuilder Inspector. Each of these properties is surfaced in the Inspector, and you can simply paste in the HTML, and fill in the other property editors, to end up producing this code. Figure 18-3 shows what the Inspector looks like when it is properly filled out.

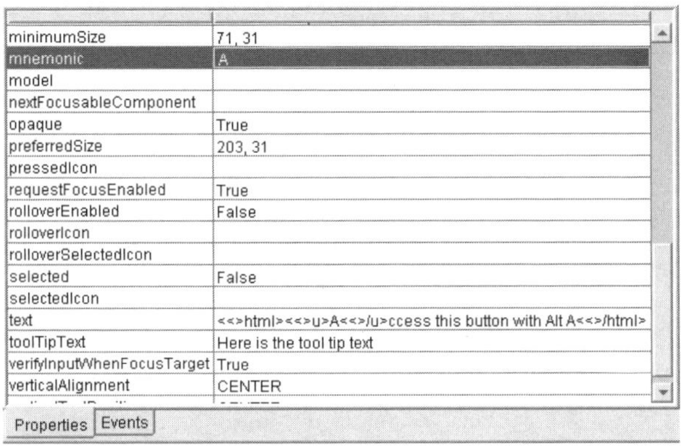

Figure 18-3: Use the Inspector to see the properties for a JButton.

NOTE: Because of the peculiar syntax involved, you may have trouble typing the HTML directly into the Inspector. If you get confused, either compose the HTML elsewhere and paste it in or switch to source mode and type the HTML directly into the setText statement in jbInit.

There are some limits to what you can do with the HTML inside a button. However, the following sample, which works for me on Windows and Linux, shows that you can push the envelope a bit if you want:

```
String text =  "<html><body text=\"#000000\" bgcolor=\"#ccccff\""+
               " link=\"#0000ee\" vlink=\"#551a8b\" alink=\"#0000ee\">" +
               "<p>Dig this <font color=\"#cc33cc\">w</font>"+
               "<font color=\"#33cc00\">i</font>" +
               "<font color=\"#3333ff\" #6600cc=\"\">" +
               "l</font><font color=\"#ff0000\"> d</font> button<br></p>" +
               "<p><font color=\"#ff0000\">Groove</font> " +
               "<font color=\"#ffff00\">on</font> the" +
               "<font color=\"#0000ff\"> wild</font> <b>" +
               "<font color=\"#cc66cc\">button</font></b>" +
               "</p></body></html>";
jButtonHtmlComplex.setText(text);
```

To create this example, I composed the HTML in Dreamweaver, and then just pasted it into the source file. Because there were many embedded quotes, I had to put in a number of escape characters. For instance, Dreamweaver produced this syntax: "#000000." To make that work in a Java I string, I had to escape it: \"#000000\". The backslashes before the quotation marks tell Java that I am not trying to end the string, but rather I want to include a literal quotation mark inside the string itself.

NOTE: You might want to call jButtonHtmlComplex.setContentAreaFilled(false) and jButtonHtmlComplex.setBorderPainted(false) just to get a sense of what these calls do. There you will be able to clearly see what happens when a button's border is drawn and its contentArea is filled. The contentAreaFilled property can sometimes be useful when you want to use a bitmap to render the surface of a button. A discussion of rendering a button with a bitmap is included in the second half of this chapter.

I'm not really suggesting that you would want to include such complex HTML in a real-world program. Nonetheless, it is interesting to see that it works. I should perhaps add that I had a bit of trouble with this syntax when I tried to format the button in GridBagLayout. The problem went away when I switched to a simpler layout. Needless to say, both the credit and the blame for the handling of HTML belongs to Java developers at Sun. JBuilder has no effect on how these things are handled.

Bitmaps in Buttons

You probably noticed that there was a bitmap in one of the buttons in Figure 18-1. The Java language makes it very simple for you to add an icon of this type. To get started, declare an instance of the ImageIcon class as a data member of your Frame1 class:

```
ImageIcon buttonIcon;
```

In the jbInit for Frame1, load a bitmap into an instance of the ImageIcon class:

```
buttonIcon = new ImageIcon(this.getClass().getResource("tux_config.png"));
```

This code is not quite as complex as it might seem. The call to ImageIcon's constructor uses the getResource method of the JFrame to load in the bitmap.

When loading a bitmap, it is important to look for the bitmap in the right directory. Therefore, the crucial part of this call is the part that defines where Java is going to look for your bitmap. The code shown here specifies that Java will look for the bitmap in the package/directory where the Frame1 class file is stored.

Here is another way to look at the same issue. We are asking Frame1 to load the bitmap. As a result, the Frame1 class is going to look in its current package for the bitmap that it wants to load. This means that you should store the bitmap in the same directory in which Frame1.java is stored. In this case, that is the WorkingButton/src/workingbutton/directory. At compile time, JBuilder will copy the bitmap to the WorkingButton/classes/workingbutton/ directory. Then at run time, the Frame1 class will look for the bitmap in its current directory, which is WorkingButton/classes/workingbutton.

The long and short of it is that this syntax asks that you store the bitmap in the same directory where you store the source file that will load it. That's all you really need to know.

Once you have the bitmap, you can call the setIcon method to have the button process the image and display it:

```
jButton5.setIcon(buttonIcon);
```

Needless to say, you don't have to type in this code by hand. Instead, you can just use the icon property in the Inspector. If you have declared a valid instance of the ImageIcon class in your source file, you can pick this value from a drop-down list in the Inspector. There is no need for typing; just pick the item you want from a list.

You might notice that this same icon appears in the simple dialog that pops up when you click on one of the buttons. This effect is shown in Figure 18-4.

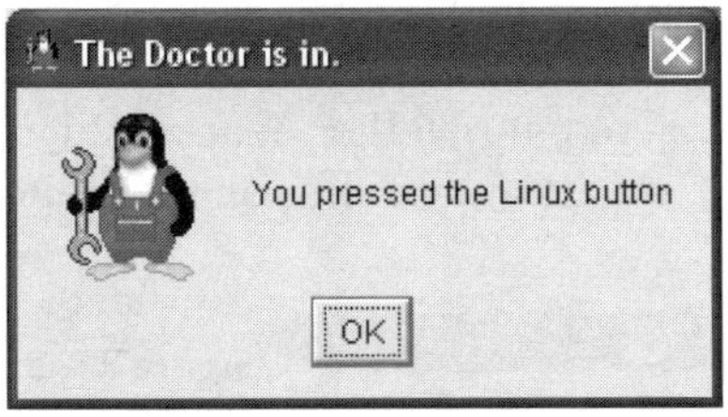

Figure 18-4: Placing an icon in a JOptionPane

The code for achieving this effect is very simple; I just reuse the same icon that appears in the buttons:

```
JOptionPane.showMessageDialog(this, "You pressed the Linux button",
  "The Doctor is in.", 0, buttonIcon);
```

Setting an IconImage for your Application

If you use the WorkingButtons program, you will notice that the icon on the caption bar and the icon that you see when you Alt+Tab between different programs in Linux or Windows, as well as the icon that you see when you minimize the program, is not the standard Java coffee cup. Instead, it is the same Tux icon that is shown in the button in Figure 18-4. Here is how to get that effect:

```
setIconImage(Toolkit.getDefaultToolkit().createImage(
      Frame1.class.getResource("tux_config.png")));
```

If you look at this code for a bit, it might look familiar. In every Frame1 instance that you create, JBuilder will include a commented-out instance of this code. To use it, just remove the comments and put in the name of the bitmap that you want to display. The bitmap should be located in the same directory as the Frame1.java class, per the discussion in the previous section of this chapter.

Using GridBagLayout to Push the Button Envelope

If you look at Figure 18-2, you might well think that it is not a Java program, but a web page. In fact, it is a Java program — a Java program with live buttons in irregular patterns that respond by changing hue when you wave the mouse over them. Within reasonable parameters, the program will respond correctly when you resize it.

NOTE: Trouble will develop if you try to make the program too small. In that case, the buttons appear as a jumble of bitmaps. You could fix this by setting the Resizable property of the JFrame instance that hosts the buttons to false. I don't choose to do this here because I want you to see both that this arrangement of buttons will handle most resizing options and what goes wrong if you make the application too small. It might be an interesting exercise to try to use the weight parameters to fix this problem.

One simple way to create a program with this look would be to have one big bitmap on the surface that looked like what you see in Figure 18-2. That would take care of the look all right, but it would not help with the "feel" part of the equation. The interface needs to respond to the user's input by changing colors when the mouse is moved over a button and by giving the appropriate feedback when a button is pressed. To do that, you need to make up the interface out of a series of smaller bitmaps displayed on separate components. In some cases, one component will need to display a different bitmap, depending on its state.

The key to making the whole thing work is GridBagLayout. As you can perhaps surmise from looking at Figure 18-5, this layout is non-trivial to put together. When studying the code, you might want to go back and reread Chapter 13, which contains tips on the sleight of hand necessary to work the GridBagConstraints object.

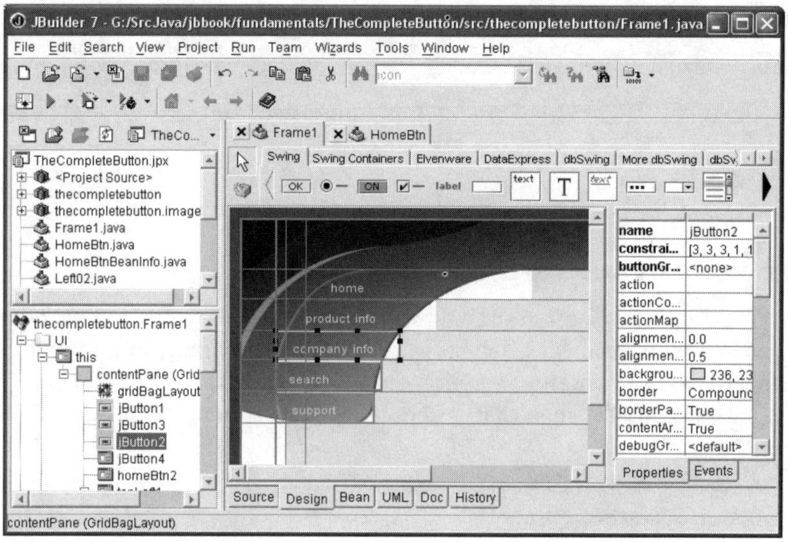

Figure 18-5: In this screen shot you can get a sense for the complexity inherent in the layout components used in the program TheCompleteButton.

Take a look at Listing 18-1, which shows the GridBagLayout code from TheCompleteButton program.

Listing 18-1: The GridBagLayout code from TheCompleteButton program

```
contentPane.add(jButton1,
      new GridBagConstraints(2, 4, 4, 1, 1.0, 0.0,
      GridBagConstraints.WEST, GridBagConstraints.NONE,
      new Insets(0, 0, 0, 0), 0, 0));

contentPane.add(jButton3,
      new GridBagConstraints(1, 5, 5, 1, 1.0, 0.0,
      GridBagConstraints.WEST, GridBagConstraints.NONE,
      new Insets(0, 0, 0, 0), 0, 0));

contentPane.add(jButton2,
      new GridBagConstraints(3, 3, 3, 1, 1.0, 0.0,
      GridBagConstraints.WEST, GridBagConstraints.NONE,
      new Insets(0, 0, 0, 0), 0, 0));

contentPane.add(jButton4,
      new GridBagConstraints(4, 2, 2, 1, 1.0, 0.0,
      GridBagConstraints.WEST, GridBagConstraints.NONE,
      new Insets(0, 0, 0, 0), 0, 0));
```

```
        contentPane.add(homeBtn2,
            new GridBagConstraints(0, 1, 6, 1, 1.0, 0.0,
            GridBagConstraints.WEST, GridBagConstraints.NONE,
            new Insets(0, 62, 0, 0), 0, 0));

        contentPane.add(topLeft1,
            new GridBagConstraints(0, 1, 5, 1, 0.0, 0.0,
            GridBagConstraints.CENTER, GridBagConstraints.NONE,
            new Insets(0, 0, 0, 0), 0, 0));

        contentPane.add(topPanel1,
            new GridBagConstraints(0, 0, 6, 1, 1.0, 0.0,
            GridBagConstraints.WEST, GridBagConstraints.NONE,
            new Insets(0, 0, 0, 0), 0, 0));

        contentPane.add(left021,
            new GridBagConstraints(0, 2, 4, 1, 0.0, 0.0,
            GridBagConstraints.CENTER, GridBagConstraints.HORIZONTAL,
            new Insets(0, 0, 0, 0), 0, 0));

        contentPane.add(left031,
            new GridBagConstraints(0, 3, 3, 1, 0.0, 0.0,
            GridBagConstraints.CENTER, GridBagConstraints.NONE,
            new Insets(0, 0, 0, 0), 0, 0));

        contentPane.add(left041,
            new GridBagConstraints(0, 4, 2, 1, 0.0, 0.0,
            GridBagConstraints.CENTER, GridBagConstraints.NONE,
            new Insets(0, 0, 0, 0), 0, 0));

        contentPane.add(left051,
            new GridBagConstraints(0, 5, 1, 1, 0.0, 0.0,
            GridBagConstraints.CENTER, GridBagConstraints.NONE,
            new Insets(0, 0, 0, 0), 0, 0));

        contentPane.add(jPanel1,
            new GridBagConstraints(0, 6, 4, 1, 0.0, 1.0,
            GridBagConstraints.CENTER, GridBagConstraints.BOTH,
            new Insets(0, 0, 0, 0), 0, 0));
```

This code is too convoluted to discuss in any depth without reducing your author to tears. However, a few simple comments can be made that might prove useful. Notice that the Insets class is never used. Instead, the real work is done by simply getting the component in the right part of the grid, giving it the right weight, and then aligning it properly with the fill and anchor properties. It is really more a question of what you don't do, rather than what you do do.

In particular, study the first six parameters passed to the GridBagConstraints constructor:

```
    new GridBagConstraints(0, 6, 4, 1, 0.0, 1.0,
```

Notice the first two arguments, which are the gridx and gridy values. These tell you which part of the grid the control calls home. The next two parameters, the gridwidth and gridheight, tell how many cells of the grid are occupied by this control. Once you have these values down correctly, everything else tends to fall in place.

The point here is that once you have the control in the correct square of the grid, you can usually just experiment with the weight, anchor, and fill properties until things look right. Of course, the deeper your understanding of the weight, anchor, and fill properties, the more quickly you will be able to find the right settings for these properties.

Configuring Your Bitmap Buttons

The buttons used in TheCompleteButton program have been tweaked fairly heavily to make them cooperate. Take a look at the code for jButton1:

```
searchUp = new ImageIcon(this.getClass().getResource("search-up.png"));
searchDn = new ImageIcon(this.getClass().getResource("search-dn.png"));

jButton1.setBackground(Color.white);
jButton1.setBorder(null);
jButton1.setMaximumSize(new Dimension(102, 29));
jButton1.setMinimumSize(new Dimension(102, 29));
jButton1.setPreferredSize(new Dimension(102, 29));
jButton1.setIcon(searchUp);
jButton1.setRolloverIcon(searchDn);
jButton1.setSelectedIcon(searchDn);
jButton1.setFocusPainted(false);
jButton1.setContentAreaFilled(false);
// jButton1.setBorderPainted(false);
```

Here you can see I used the border property in the JBuilder Inspector to set the border to none, which translates into a call to setBorder(null). The usual shadowed edges around the border of a button are not needed in this program because we intend to paint the button with a bitmap. You can also call setBorderPainted to false to make sure the component does not waste time painting the border. If setBorder is called with the null parameter, the border will not be painted whether or not you call setBorderPainted. As a result, this call is probably not necessary.

I also found that I derived little benefit from calling setContentAreaFilled with an argument of false. This call did little to change the appearance of my application. However, I assume that filling in the background of the button when that part of the button will never be shown is a waste of time. As a result, I request that the button not fill the content area.

NOTE: You might find that you can better understand what setContentAreaFilled does if you use it with the JButtonHtmlComplex button found in the WorkingButtons example shown earlier in the chapter. There you will be able to graphically see the effect of this call.

I've also set the background of the bitmap to white. This is necessary because the bitmaps that I am using are meant to blend into a white surface. In this case, it is the art that dictates what must be done. In particular, the anti-aliasing included in the bitmaps will never look right if you don't use a white bitmap. Don't worry if you don't know what anti-aliasing is all about. It is a graphics term and not germane to a discussion of buttons.

On the other hand, the calls to setting the maximum, minimum, and preferred size of the buttons are crucial to our current endeavor. Each button will display a bitmap that has a very specific size. I want to make sure that the button has exactly the same number of pixels in it as the bitmap it will display. If this is not the case, there will be unsightly gaps or overlaps in the interface of the program.

NOTE: When looking at this code, you would be right to wonder how portable it is. I have, of course, tested this code on both Linux and Windows. I can't test it on all platforms because I don't have access to that wide a range of machines. But as far as I can tell, this interface truly is portable. The key, of course, is the lamentable GridBagLayout code, which is designed to create portable interfaces.

The last lines in this code fragment include code that tells the VM which bitmap to paint when the button is in a particular state. By changing the shading and hues of the bitmaps, you can create very interesting effects that morph back and forth as the user moves the button over the controls. Certainly you can get into even more detailed artwork than I do here, but this should be enough to give you a sense of what can be done. Again, you can and should set all these icons for the various properties of the button in the JBuilder Inspector.

NOTE: The artwork for these buttons comes from my distribution of Paint Shop Pro. The license there states that I can use a limited amount of the art in my own works, which is exactly what I have done here. As you might surmise, the bitmaps were originally intended for use in a web page. The whole point of this exercise is to show that you can make Java code conform to the rigorous rules enforced by a set of HTML TABLE tags.

The final bit of code shown makes sure that the JDK does not draw that little dotted rectangle that specifies that a control is selected. When you are creating a fancy interface like this, you usually want to use an aesthetically pleasing bitmap to give that kind of information to the user.

Turning a JPanel into a Button

If you dig into the code for TheCompleteButton program, you'll notice that not all of the buttons in the program are really buttons. In fact, the top two buttons are actually JPanels.

What's going on? Well, I found that despite all my labors, the buttons still didn't look quite right when pressed down by the mouse. They looked okay if you just waved the mouse over the button for a rollover effect, but there was dirtiness around the button edges when pressed with the mouse. If my button shapes had been absolutely square, this probably would not have mattered, but since I was using irregular shapes, problems did surface.

The actual problems, minor as they may have been, differed on Windows and Linux. As a result, I thought I might need a bit more control, so I used a JPanel instead. If you look at Listings 18-1 and 18-2, you can see the code creating the panels that are acting like buttons in TheCompleteButton program.

Listing 18-2: The code for an abstract JPanel descendant called BasePanelButton that acts like a button. You must override the loadBitmaps method.

```
package thecompletebutton;

import javax.swing.JPanel;
import java.awt.*;
import java.awt.event.*;
import javax.swing.*;
import java.util.*;

/**
```

```
 * <p>This is the base class for an imitation button made out of a panel.
 * Notice that the class is abstract. You must override the loadBitmaps
 * method. </p>
 *
 * <p>Copyright: Copyright (c) 2002 by Charlie Calvert</p>
 * <p>Company: Elvenware </p>
 * @author Charlie Calvert
 * @version 1.0
 */

public abstract class BasePanelButton extends JPanel implements MouseListener
{
    ImageIcon homeUp;
    ImageIcon homeDn;
    boolean buttonUp = true;
    private transient Vector actionListeners;

    public BasePanelButton()
    {
        this.addMouseListener(this);
        loadBitmaps();
    }

    // Load the bitmaps in this method
    public abstract void loadBitmaps();

    public void paint(Graphics g)
    {
        super.paint(g);
        if (buttonUp)
        {
            g.drawImage(homeUp.getImage(), 0, 0, this);
        }
        else
        {
            System.out.println("Painting down");

            g.drawImage(homeDn.getImage(), 0, 0, this);
        }

    }

    public void mouseClicked(MouseEvent e)
    {
        System.out.println("Mouse Clicked");
    }

    public void mousePressed(MouseEvent e)
    {
        System.out.println("Mouse Pressed");
        ActionEvent actionEvent = new ActionEvent(this, 1, "mouse pressed");
```

```
        fireActionPerformed(actionEvent);
    }

    public void mouseReleased(MouseEvent e)
    {
        System.out.println("Mouse Released");

    }

    public void mouseEntered(MouseEvent e)
    {
        buttonUp = false;
        this.repaint();
    }

    public void mouseExited(MouseEvent e)
    {
        buttonUp = true;
        this.repaint();
    }

    public synchronized void removeActionListener(ActionListener l)
    {
        if (actionListeners != null && actionListeners.contains(l))
        {
            Vector v = (Vector) actionListeners.clone();
            v.removeElement(l);
            actionListeners = v;
        }
    }

    public synchronized void addActionListener(ActionListener l)
    {
        Vector v = actionListeners ==
            null ? new Vector(2) : (Vector) actionListeners.clone();
        if (!v.contains(l))
        {
            v.addElement(l);
            actionListeners = v;
        }
    }

    protected void fireActionPerformed(ActionEvent e)
    {
        if (actionListeners != null)
        {
            Vector listeners = actionListeners;
            int count = listeners.size();
            for (int i = 0; i < count; i++)
            {
                ((ActionListener) listeners.elementAt(i)).action-
```

```
                                        Performed(e);
                            }
                    }
            }
    }
```

Listing 18-3: Code for a second descendant BasePanelButton object that acts like a button

```
package thecompletebutton;

import java.awt.*;
import java.awt.event.*;
import javax.swing.*;
import java.util.*;

public class ProductBtn extends BasePanelButton
{
        public ProductBtn()
        {
        }

        public void loadBitmaps()
        {
                homeUp = new ImageIcon(this.getClass().getResource("product-up.png"));
                homeDn = new ImageIcon(this.getClass().getResource("product-dn.png"));
        }
}
```

Notice the declaration for the header of the BasePanelButton class and the loadBitmaps method:

```
public abstract class BasePanelButton extends JPanel implements MouseListener

// Load the bitmaps in this method
public abstract void loadBitmaps();
```

As you can see, BasePanelButton is declared abstract. This is one of those words that can cause the hearts of people new to Java to beat a little bit more quickly with anxiety. There is, however, no need for concern.

An abstract class has one or more methods in it that all child classes must implement. In particular, this class has a method called loadBitmaps that is declared abstract. As you can see, its declaration ends with a semicolon. It has no implementation:

```
public abstract void loadBitmaps();
```

Any class that descends from BasePanelButton must implement this method or the compiler will emit an error. This is exactly the effect I want to produce. I want to force the descendants of this class to implement one very simple method that will load the bitmaps they want to use.

NOTE: In a sense, an abstract class makes a regular class act a little bit like an interface. An interface requires that implementing classes implement every single method listed in the interface. An abstract class requires that descendant classes implement only the abstract methods that they declare. So an abstract class lives in a world that is halfway between an interface and a regular class. If you need more help with this subject, see Chapter 8. You might also learn from reviewing the discussion of listener interfaces in Chapters 14 and 15.

In Listing 18-2, you can see an implementation of the loadBitmaps method:

```
public class ProductBtn extends BasePanelButton

      public void loadBitmaps()
      {
            homeUp = new ImageIcon(this.getClass().getResource("product-up.png"));
            homeDn = new ImageIcon(this.getClass().getResource("product-dn.png"));
      }
```

The ProductBtn class extends, or descends from, BasePanelButton. As a result, it must implement the loadBitmaps method. The implementation that it provides simply assures that the homeUp and homeDn data members of the BasePanelButton class are properly initialized.

That is all you need to do to create a descendant of BasePanelButton. This one simple method does the trick.

You can create lots of different buttons by descending from BasePanelButton and then filling in this one simple method. It's not quite as easy as using a button, but it certainly has a manageable level of complexity.

Event Handling in a JPanel Button

In this section of the chapter, you will see how to get our panel button components to respond to mouse clicks. They need to do this if they are going to act like buttons.

The first step in this process is to make sure the BasePanelButton class fires Action events. You learned all about this process in Chapters 14 and 15. As a result, I'll just touch on the subject quickly. If you have the SE or Enterprise versions of JBuilder, you can implement this code by choosing the Bean page from the file view tabs beneath the editor. Turn to the **Events** page in BeansExpress and check the **Action** check box, as shown in Figure 18-6.

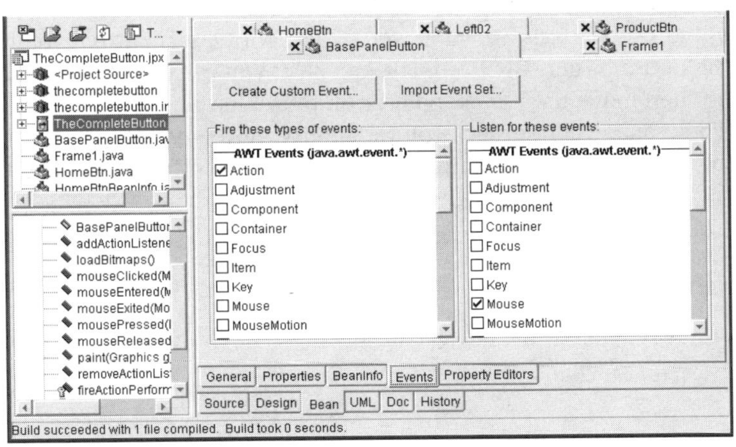

Figure 18-6: Check the Action option in BeansExpress to automatically generate firstActionPerformed, removeActionListener, and addActionListener methods.

If you have the Personal edition of JBuilder, you will have to write the event firing code by hand, following the example shown in Listing 18-2. In particular, you will need to implement the fireActionPerformed, removeActionListener, and addActionListener methods.

The BasePanelButton also implements the MouseListener interface:

```
public abstract class BasePanelButton extends JPanel implements MouseListener
```

After reading Chapters 14 and 15, it should be clear to you what it means to implement the MouseListener interface. In particular, the MouseListener technology is just a means of making the BasePanelButton respond to mouse clicks.

You will notice that I don't do anything inside most of the MouseListener methods:

```
public void mousePressed(MouseEvent e)
{
      System.out.println("Mouse Pressed");
}

public void mouseReleased(MouseEvent e)
{
      System.out.println("Mouse Released");
}
```

There is, however, one method that I do fully implement:

```
public void mouseClicked(MouseEvent e)
{
      System.out.println("Mouse Clicked");
      ActionEvent actionEvent = new ActionEvent(this, 1, "mouse clicked");
      fireActionPerformed(actionEvent);
}
```

This is the method that fires off ActionPerformed events when the user clicks on the panel. It is really the key element of the control, since it is the one that makes the JPanel act like a button. That is, it is the method that makes this JPanel descendant respond to clicks of the mouse.

If this method were called in response to a mousePressed event, rather than to a mouseClicked event, it would fire immediately the moment the user clicked on the panel. As you know, that is not the way buttons are supposed to act. With a real button, you have some control over when the button is actually fired. For instance, you can select the button, hold the mouse down, and then move the mouse pointer off to the left or right without releasing the mouse button. Then, once your cursor is off the mouse button, you can release the mouse button, and the event will not be triggered. If you let the mouse button up while still over the button, the event will be triggered. To get this effect, respond to mouseClicked events, not to mousePressed events.

Painting the JPanel Button

It turns out to be very easy to paint the surface of this new faux button that we have created:

```
public void paint(Graphics g)
{
      super.paint(g);
      if (buttonUp)
      {
            g.drawImage(homeUp.getImage(), 0, 0, this);
      }
      else
      {
            g.drawImage(homeDn.getImage(), 0, 0, this);
```

```
        }
    }
```

This code is based on the state of the boolean buttonUp data member, which is set in the mouseEntered and mouseExited methods from the MouseListener interface:

```
    public void mouseEntered(MouseEvent e)
    {
          buttonUp = false;
          this.repaint();
    }

    public void mouseExited(MouseEvent e)
    {
          buttonUp = true;
          this.repaint();
    }
```

Both the mouseEntered and mouseExited events set the value of the buttonUp variable and then call repaint. Repaint forces a call to the paint method shown at the beginning of this section.

You will notice that paint is declared like this:

```
    public void paint(Graphics g)
```

This is the signature of the paint method inherited by the JPanel class, which in turn inherits the method from JComponent. Whenever a component needs to have its interface painted, this method will automatically be called. That is why you usually want to call the base implementation of this method:

```
    super.paint(g);
```

This makes sure that the ancestors of this class have a chance to paint themselves properly.

Finally, the call uses either the homeUp or homeDn IconImage component to paint the appropriate bitmap so that the user can see it:

```
    g.drawImage(homeUp.getImage(), 0, 0, this);
```

The call uses the parameter g, which is of type Graphics. The Graphics class is built into the JDK. The drawImage method takes as parameters the bitmap you want to paint, the x and y location where you want to paint it, and optionally the control that is responsible for loading it. There are, in fact, many different versions of the drawImage method that take a wide variety of parameters. But this is one that is called quite frequently.

Using Your Own JavaBeans in Your Program

If you are new to JavaBeans, I have good news for you. The very brief ProductBtn class shown in Listing 18-3 is a small but perfectly serviceable bean. I will, in fact, discuss this subject in more depth in Part VII: JavaBeans. But for now, this one little class will serve as a kind of abbreviated introduction to the subject.

The main reason that ProductBtn can act as a bean is because it is declared as a public class with a public constructor that takes no parameters. As I said, this will be explained in more depth later in the book. But for now, you can just appreciate the fact that the bar for creating a bean is extremely low.

To use your bean in the UI designer, simply switch **Frame1** into design mode and select the **Bean Chooser** ( ).

If you choose the Select option in the menu that the Bean Chooser pops up, you can bring up the Bean Chooser dialog, shown in Figure 18-7. Open up the node for your current project, which in this case is called thecompletebutton. Find the bean class that you want to select. In this case, it is called ProductBtn.

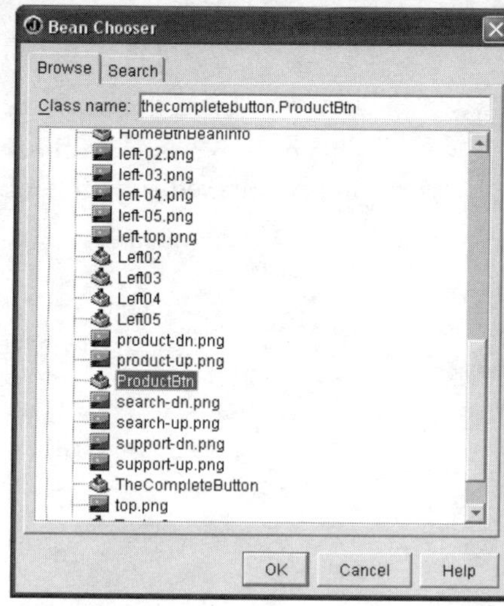

Figure 18-7: Selecting a bean from the Bean Chooser

After you close the Bean Chooser dialog, your cursor will be shaped like a cross. This is the same cursor you get after you have selected a bean from the component palette. You can now "paint" the control into the UI designer just as you would any other component. In practice, this usually means that you want to drop the control down onto the structure pane.

Once you have placed the control on Frame1, you need to use the GridBagConstraints class to get it lined up correctly. As I stated earlier, this is not a trivial procedure, but it is one that you can master if you work at it.

The important thing here is the finished product. If you click the Search or Support buttons in the applications, you will see some artifacts produced by the fact that they are buttons. If you click the Home or Product buttons, which are both descendants of BasePanelButton, everything looks clean on both Linux and Windows.

So now you know how you can create your own buttons if the JButton class is not quite suiting your needs. Code like this helps to give you a chance to dig down beneath the surface of the Swing world and discover how Java really works. As I have said, you will learn much more about JavaBeans technology in Part VII.

Summary

In this chapter you have had a chance to learn a little about the way the JButton component works. You saw that you can use HTML to gussy up the text shown in the button. Using HTML you can underline certain characters in the buttons, thereby marking them hot keys. You can use the mnemonic property of the JButton component to specify the hot key that you want to use.

IconImages were used to display bitmaps in buttons. You saw that there were a number of properties of buttons, such as the icon property, the rolloverIcon property, and the selectedIcon property that could be used to display various different bitmaps when the button was in different states.

You also learned how to use the setBorderPainted and setFocusPainted methods to turn on and off the drawing of the selection rectangle and the border of a button. Many similar functions were discussed.

Finally, at the end of the chapter, you had a brief look at creating your own button from the JPanel component. This exercise taught you a little bit about JavaBeans and gave you some sense of how to go about making Java do what you want it to do.

Chapter 19

Creating Dialogs

Charlie Calvert

In this chapter you will learn some of the ways you can create a dialog. Dialogs are windows that pop up over the current window and allow the user to view information, enter data, or make a selection.

Most dialogs are modal. A *modal dialog* pops up over its parent window and will not allow the user to go back to the parent until he or she has finished using the dialog. This can be a very convenient way of leading the user to complete certain steps in an order that the programmer finds convenient.

Most of the code you will be seeing appears in a program called DialogDemo, found on the CD that accompanies this book and on www.elvenware.com. You can run that program or follow the steps outlined below to create it yourself.

Starting the DialogDemo Application

To build the DialogDemo program, begin by creating a simple application that includes a menu bar and an About dialog, as outlined in Chapter 3. When stepping through the Application Wizard, use the second page of the wizard to include both a menu bar and an About dialog.

Run the program once and select **Help | About** from its menu. A dialog will appear, as shown in Figure 19-1. The key thing to notice about this dialog is that it is modal. You will not be able to use any of the features of the main frame of the dialog demo until you close this dialog.

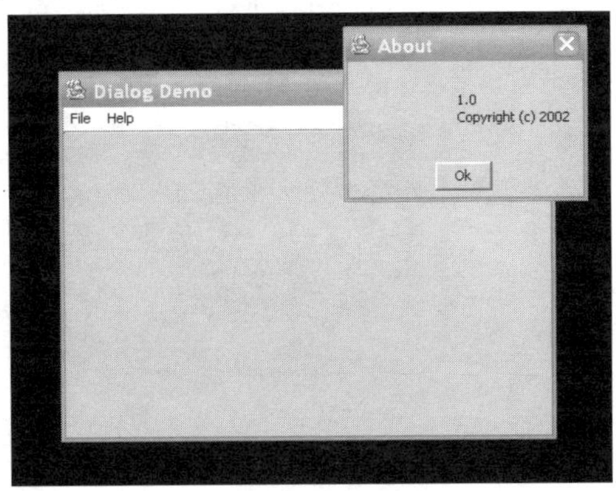

Figure 19-1: A default JBuilder modal About dialog displayed on top of a JFrame

Using the JBuilder About Dialog

Looking at Figure 19-1, you might notice that the dialog is a bit plain looking. One of the quickest ways to polish the appearance of this tool is to add a bitmap to it, as shown in Figure 19-2.

To convert what you see in Figure 19-1 to the dialog shown in Figure 19-2, you need only to supply a bitmap and change one word in your application.

Figure 19-2: A default JBuilder About dialog with a bitmap in it

The first step is to find the bitmap that you want to display. If you have a digital camera or some artistic ability, you can probably create the image yourself. Your company may also have many free images that you can download from the company web site.

If these options don't pan out, there are thousands, possibly millions, of free images on the web. Many computer stores have, for less than $10, disks full of free images that you can use in your programs. In short, there is not much reason why you can't put some kind of bitmap in your dialogs to make them look a little better.

Make sure the bitmap you select is a JPG, GIF, or PNG file. The first and the last are the preferred choices in this day and age. Copy the bitmap into the same directory where you store the About box source file, called, by default, Frame1_AboutBox.java.

Focus **Frame1_AboutBox.java** in the editor. Find the first line in jbInit, which should look something like this:

```
//imageLabel.setIcon(new ImageIcon(
      Frame1_AboutBox.class.getResource("[Your Image]")));
```

Remove the comments and type in the name of the bitmap that you want to load, being sure to pay attention to case sensitivity:

```
imageLabel.setIcon(new ImageIcon(
      Frame1_AboutBox.class.getResource("ElvenwareLogo.png")));
```

Now you are in business. Your dialog has a logo!

Other simple changes that you might make include moving the panel where the text controls in your dialog reside beneath the bitmap. This is simply a matter of changing its constraints property from Center to **South**. Now fill in the rest of the fields in the dialog. The completed About box should resemble Figure 19-3.

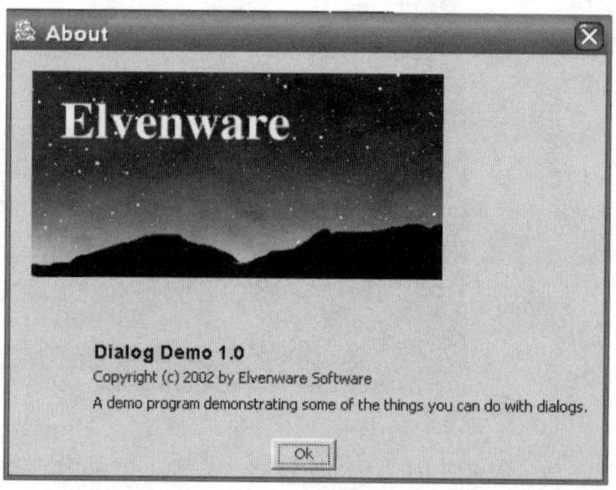

Figure 19-3: The completed About dialog for the DialogDemo program

You might notice that in Figure 19-3 the name of your program is shown in large, bold letters. To create this effect, select the JLabel component that contains your product name. In the JBuilder Inspector, select the font property and use the ellipsis button to pop up the Font dialog, as shown in Figure 19-4. Set the size of the font to **14** and select the **Bold** attribute.

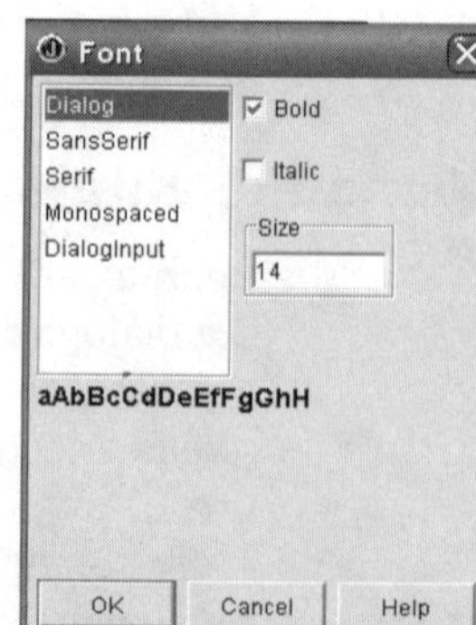

Figure 19-4: Configuring the font used to display text in an About dialog

Using JOptionPane to Create Input Dialogs

In this section, you are going to see several quick ways to create dialogs using JOptionPane. The dialogs that we create will be popped up from the menu of the DialogDemo program. As a result, you will need to edit the menu that you added to the program when you first created it with the wizard.

NOTE: If you forgot to add the menu while running the Application Wizard, just grab a JMenuBar from the Swing Containers page of the component palette and drop it on the structure pane. Then add this code to the end of your jbInit method: this.setJMenuBar(jMenuBar1);.

Right-click on the menu node in the structure pane and choose **Activate Designer** from the pop-up menu. Now edit the menu so that it looks like the image shown in Figure 19-5.

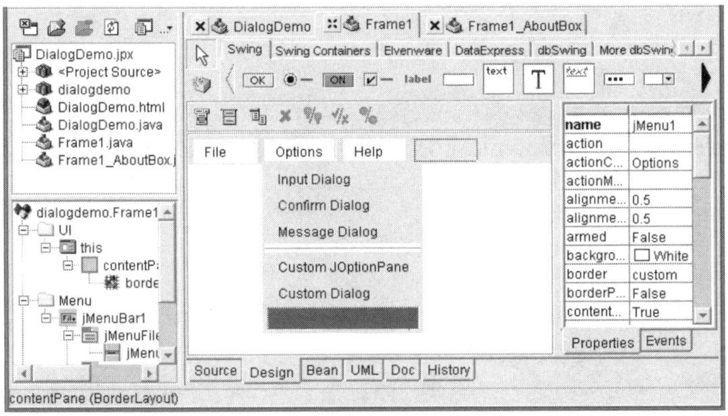

Figure 19-5: The menu for the DialogDemo program as it appears in design mode

When using the menu designer, you can insert menu items and menu separators by right-clicking on the designer and selecting the appropriate items from a pop-up menu. If you need help doing this, refer to Chapter 14.

Input and Message Dialogs

After you create the menu, select the **Input Dialog** menu item and turn to the **Events** page in the Inspector. Select the **actionPerformed** event and either double-click in the property editor, or select the property editor and press the **Enter** key. You will be taken to source view. Edit the response handler so that it looks like one of the following three options:

```
void jMenuItem1_actionPerformed(ActionEvent e)
  {
       String input = (String)JOptionPane.showInputDialog(this, null,
            null, JOptionPane.QUESTION_MESSAGE,
            null, new String[] {"Sam", "Tom"}, null);
       if (input != null)
       {
            JOptionPane.showMessageDialog(this, "You entered: " + input);
       }
}

void jMenuItem1_actionPerformed(ActionEvent e)
  {
       String input = (String)JOptionPane.showInputDialog(this, null,
```

```
                null, JOptionPane.QUESTION_MESSAGE,
                null , null, "Tux");
            if (input != null)
            {
                JOptionPane.showMessageDialog(this, "You entered: " + input);
            }
    }

    // This simpler option will only work in JDK 1.4.0 or higher
    void jMenuItem1_actionPerformed(ActionEvent e)
    {
            String input = JOptionPane.showInputDialog(this, "Enter Name", "Tux");
            if (input != null)
            {
                JOptionPane.showMessageDialog(this, "You entered: " + input);
            }
    }
```

The first call shown here is to the static method of JOptionPane that pops up a showInputDialog. Please note that this call will not compile unless you have imported javax.swing.JOptionPane or javax.swing.* at the top of your source file. The second of these import statements will usually be included by default by JBuilder.

NOTE: A static method of an object is a method that can be called without first having to initialize the object. There is no code that looks like this:

```
JOptionPane myDialog = new JOptionPane();  // Not needed when you use JOptionPane
myDialog.showInputDialog(this, "Enter Name", "Tux");
```

In particular, you don't need to construct an instance of the JOptionPane. Instead, the program calls the showInputDialog directly off the class name itself. This is possible because showInputDialog is a static method. The whole point of static methods is that you do not have to create an instance of their object in order to use them.

The first two options shown here work in at least JDK 1.3.1 or higher. Here is the declaration for the call:

```
public static Object showInputDialog(
  Component parentComponent,   // The parent window on which the dialog is shown
  Object message,              // The string to prompt the user for input
  String title,                // The title to display at the top of dialog
  int messageType,             // A constant such as WARNING_MESSAGE or
                                  QUESTION_MESSAGE
  Icon icon,                   // An icon like that shown in WorkingButtons
                                  project on CD
  Object[] selectionValues,    // Usually a String Array from which the user
                                  can choose
  Object initialSelectionValue)// Usually a suggested default string value
```

Pass in the JFrame descendant or other component on top of which the dialog will appear in the first parameter. As you will see later in the chapter, the second parameter can be a JPanel or other JComponent descendant, but it is usually just a string to prompt the user for input. The third parameter is a title, and the fourth is a constant specifying one of the default icons. The fifth parameter can be a custom icon that you create, such as the one shown in the

WorkingButtons project discussed in the previous chapter. The last two parameters are usually either an uneditable list of strings from which the user can choose or a default string that the user can edit.

The third option is a JDK 1.4.0 version of showInputDialog that can take a wide range of parameters. The most useful, however, are the ones shown here:

```
public static String showInputDialog(
        Component parentComponent,
        Object message,
        Object initialSelectionValue)
```

Pass in the name of the parent of the dialog in the first parameter. This is helpful because a modal dialog can most easily be displayed properly when you specify its parent. In many cases, it is okay to pass in null in this parameter, but pass in the parent if you possibly can. In this case, passing in the parent ensures that the dialog will be modal in respect to Frame1. The next parameter is the prompt to show the user. The final parameter is a default value that the user can either edit or accept. The end effect is shown in Figure 19-6.

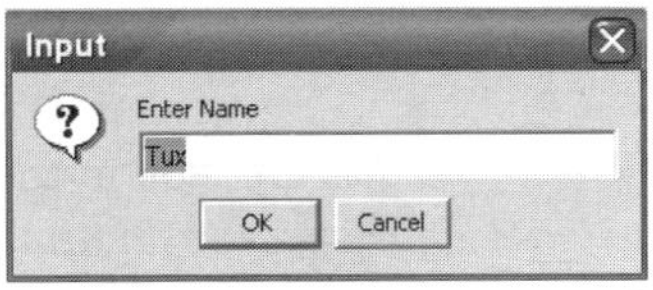

Figure 19-6: A simple InputDialog with the Linux mascot Tux entered as the default value

The JDK 1.4.0 showInputDialog returns the string that the user typed in. If the user presses the Cancel button, the dialog returns null. As a result, you should check for the null value any time you use the showInputDialog.

Assuming the return value is not null, the code uses the JOptionPane.showMessageDialog call to display this string to the user. Like showInputDialog, showMessageDialog can take a wide range of parameters. The most common are the ones shown here. The first parameter is the parent window, and the second is the string that you want to display.

NOTE: It would not be an error to attempt to display a null string in a showMessageDialog. Instead, the dialog would appear as normal, and the string that it would display would be the most famous four-letter word in the Java language: null.

Using JOptionPane to Display a Confirmation Dialog

Go back into design mode on Frame1. If necessary, activate the menu designer. Select the **Confirm Dialog** menu item, turn to the **Events** page in the JBuilder Inspector, and create the following event handler:

```
void jMenuItemConfirm_actionPerformed(ActionEvent e)
{
        int returnValue = JOptionPane.showConfirmDialog(this,
                "Are you sure?", "Confirm this for me",
                JOptionPane.OK_CANCEL_OPTION,
                JOptionPane.WARNING_MESSAGE);
}
```

This example shows off some of the more advanced features in the JOptionPane's repertoire. The fruits of the call are shown in Figure 19-7.

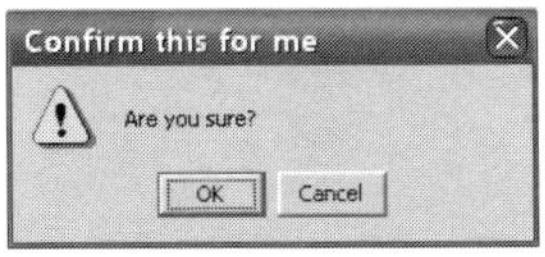

Figure 19-7: Popping up a confirm dialog that displays an exclamation icon

Here is the declaration for our particular variant of the heavily overloaded showConfirmDialog method:

```
public static int showConfirmDialog(Component parentComponent,
        Object message, String title, int optionType, int messageType)
```

Here you can see that the first parameter of the method is the parent window that will own the modal confirm dialog. The second parameter is usually a string value containing the message you want to display. It can, however, be other types of objects. You will find out more about this subject later in this chapter in the section titled "Custom JOptionPane Dialogs."

The last two parameters to this variant of showConfirmDialog are constants that define features of the dialog. The first constant, OK_CANCEL_OPTION, tells the VM to display a dialog with an OK and Cancel button in it. The second option specifies that we want an exclamation icon in the dialog. Normally, a confirm dialog would show a question icon, but I have displayed an unusual icon in order to drive home the point that such features are configurable.

NOTE: I should warn you that some managers are very fussy about what icons are shown in dialogs. For instance, they might insist that all confirm dialogs use a question mark icon. To me, demands such as these are a bit too precious, but I suppose it is simplest to just go with the flow in such cases.

CodeInsight Rides in on a White Horse

I have stated that there are a number of variants of the methods used to pop up these various JOptionPane dialogs. Remember that JBuilder can always show you all these variants through the ParameterInsight tool shown in Figure 19-8. You can invoke ParameterInsight by holding down the Ctrl+Shift+Space keys simultaneously.

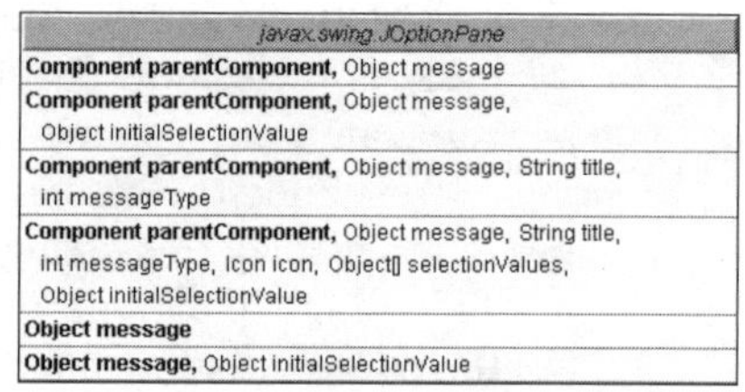

Figure 19-8: Parameter insight will let you see all the variants of an overloaded method.

A Fancy Message Dialog

You should now create an event handler for the Message Dialog menu item from the menu in Frame1. Edit the handler so that it looks like this:

```
void jMenuItemMessage_actionPerformed(ActionEvent e)
{
      JOptionPane.showMessageDialog(this,
            "Brahman is life, Brahman is joy, Brahman is the void",
            "Satyakama Jabala",
            JOptionPane.PLAIN_MESSAGE);
}
```

This version of the showMessageDialog method uses the JOptionPane.PLAIN_MESSAGE constant to completely suppress the icon, as shown in Figure 19-9. Alternatively, you can specify a custom icon, such as the one shown in Figure 19-10, which is an image from the example program WorkingButtons, described in the previous chapter.

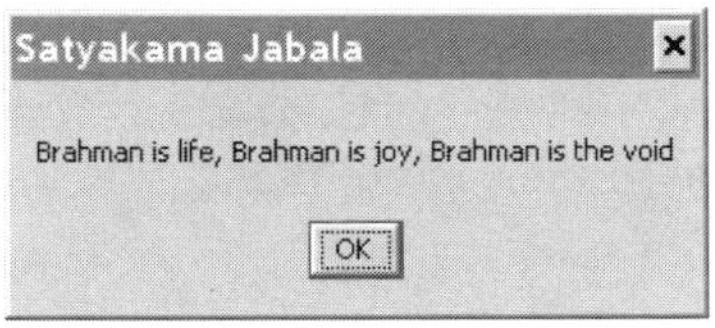

Figure 19-9: A message dialog with no icon

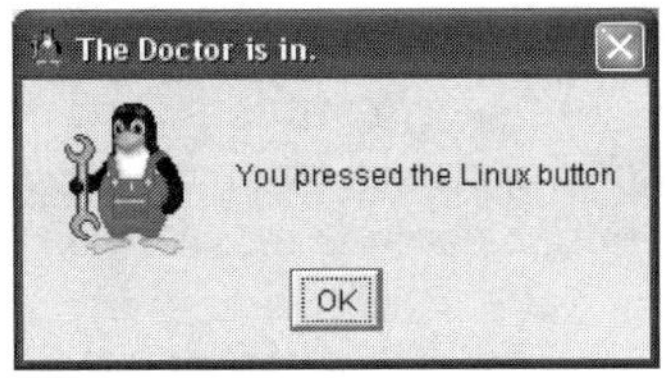

Figure 19-10: A message dialog with a custom icon

Here is the code from the WorkingButtons program that generated the dialog shown in Figure 19-10:

```
// Data field
ImageIcon buttonIcon;

// From jbInit
buttonIcon = new ImageIcon(this.getClass().getResource("tux_
                              config.png"));

// Event handler
void jButton5_actionPerformed(ActionEvent e)
{
      JOptionPane.showMessageDialog(this, "You pressed the Linux button",
        "The Doctor is in.", 0, buttonIcon);
}
```

The code shown here is explained in more depth in the previous chapter. For now, you need notice only the declaration for the ImageIcon, the code that constructs an instance of the ImageIcon, and the way the icon is used in the last parameter of the call to showMessageDialog.

Custom JOptionPane Dialogs

The final JOptionPane that I want to show you will take advantage of that strange parameter of showMessageDialog I mentioned earlier that can handle either a String or some kind of custom class. The trick here is to create a component, usually a JPanel descendant, that contains all the elements you want to show in your dialog. You then pass in this JPanel in lieu of the message string in a call to showMessageDialog or showConfirmDialog. The end result is that you see a dialog with your JPanel displayed inside it.

To get started, add a new JPanel descendant to the DialogDemo example program. To do this, choose **File | New Class** from the JBuilder menu. Fill in the New Class dialog, as shown in Figure 19-11, and click the **OK** button.

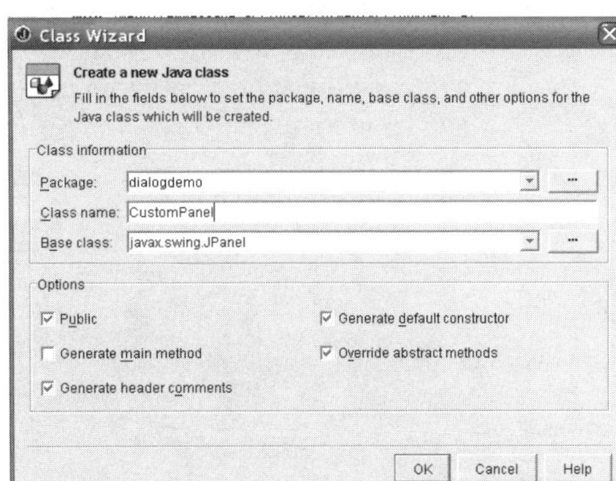

Figure 19-11: Creating a JPanel descendant called CustomPanel

Set the layout property of CustomPanel to **BorderLayout**. Drop down a JTextArea from the Swing page. Set the constraints property for the JTextArea to **Center**.

Type the following stanza from a poem by Thomas Traherne into the text property of the JTextArea (the entire poem is included on the CD):

```
Wonder

Thomas Traherne

How like an angel came I down!
How bright are all things here!
When first among his works I did appear
O how their glory me did crown!
The world resembled his eternity,
In which my soul did walk;
And ev'ry thing that I did see
Did with me talk.
```

When entering this poem, the preferred method is to use a text editor to create the poem and then paste the text you created into the text property of the JTextArea. I will discuss this subject at more length later in this chapter.

Now create an event handler for the Custom JOptionPane menu item:

```
void jMenuItemCustomOption_actionPerformed(ActionEvent e)
{
      CustomPanel customPanel = new CustomPanel();
      JOptionPane.showMessageDialog(this,
            customPanel,
            "Thomas Traherne",
            JOptionPane.PLAIN_MESSAGE);
}
```

This code first creates an instance of the CustomPanel object that we just finished building. It then passes that instance of our JPanel descendant as the second parameter of the JOptionPane.showMessageDialog. The program also uses the JOptionPane.PLAIN_MESSAGE constant to ensure that there are no icons on the dialog. When you run the program and click the appropriate menu item, the end result is as shown in Figure 19-12.

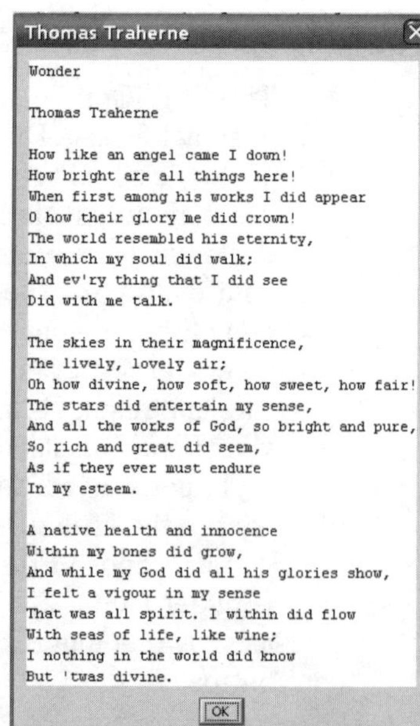

Figure 19-12: The first three stanzas from a poem by Thomas Traherne shown in a JOptionPane dialog instance

Creating a Custom Dialog

When I first tried to create the dialog shown in Figure 19-12, I included all eight stanzas from the poem by 17th century poet Thomas Traherne. In hopes that so much text could be handled properly, I included a JScrollPane to place scroll bars in the JTextArea. However, I found that this did not work out as I hoped when I tried to display my dialog. In particular, the scroll bars did not show up and the dialog was taller than my screen, obscuring the OK button at the bottom. When things like that happen, you may need to create a custom dialog.

NOTE: I want to emphasize that in many cases, JOptionPane will work very well as a host for your JPanel descendants. The objects that you insert into the second parameter of a call to showMesssageDialog can, in fact, be quite complex. They may contain numerous JTextFields, buttons, and other controls. In short, the technique usually works quite well with a wide range of coding options. But sometimes you can't quite make it work. In those cases, you will want to use the method I am about to explain. In most cases, having to switch from a custom JOptionPane to a custom JDialog should not cost you any time. After all, the JPanel or JComponent descendant that you inserted into the JOptionPane is a reusable visual component that can just as easily be inserted into a JDialog. For more help creating reusable components, see Chapter 17.

To create this dialog, choose **File | New** from the JBuilder menu and select the **Dialog Wizard** from the General page. Fill out the Dialog Wizard, as shown in Figure 19-13.

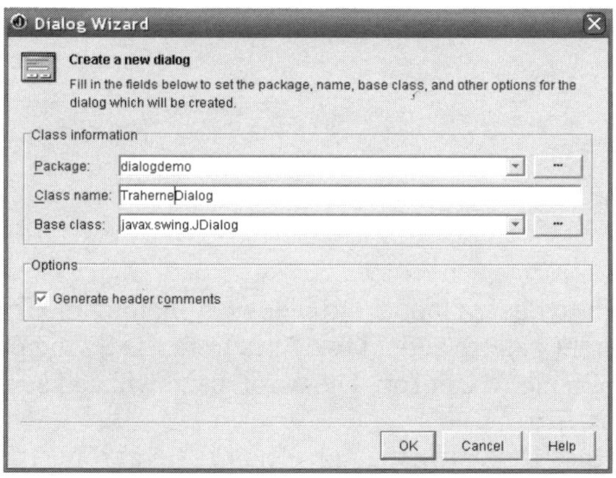

Figure 19-13: Creating a custom JDialog descendant using the Dialog Wizard

NOTE: Unless you have good reason to do otherwise, it is better to use the Dialog Wizard than to use the Class Wizard when creating dialogs. The Dialog Wizard creates a JDialog descendant that contains useful initialization code, while the Class Wizard just gives you a bare-bones descendant of JDialog that looks like this:

```
public class ClassDialog extends JDialog
{
    public ClassDialog()
    {
    }
}
```

Compare that to the code that the Dialog Wizard produces:

```
import java.awt.*;
import javax.swing.*;
```

```
public class Dialog2 extends JDialog
{
    JPanel panel1 = new JPanel();
    BorderLayout borderLayout1 = new BorderLayout();

    public Dialog2(Frame frame, String title, boolean modal)
    {
        super(frame, title, modal);
        try
        {
            jbInit();
            pack();
        }
        catch(Exception ex)
        {
            ex.printStackTrace();
        }
    }

    public Dialog2()
    {
        this(null, "", false);
    }
    void jbInit() throws Exception
    {
        panel1.setLayout(borderLayout1);
        getContentPane().add(panel1);
    }
}
```

Click **OK** in the Dialog Wizard. Switch to design mode. Drop down a JScrollPane from the Swing Containers page of the component palette and a JTextArea from the Swing page. Set the constraints property for the JScrollPane to **Center**. The scroll pane will add scroll bars to the bottom and right edges of the JTextArea.

Select the **JTextArea** and turn to the JBuilder Inspector. Find the text property and select the associated property editor. Select a large chunk of text from some other source and paste it into the property editor. Don't worry that the property editor is small and your text is long. Just compose the text elsewhere, and then paste it in. JBuilder will take care of the rest for you.

Drop a JPanel onto the structure pane for the new dialog you have created. Set its constraints property to **South**, so it shows up beneath the JTextArea. Place a button on the JPanel object. Name it **jButtonOk** and set its caption to **OK**. The end result should look something like what you see in Figure 19-14.

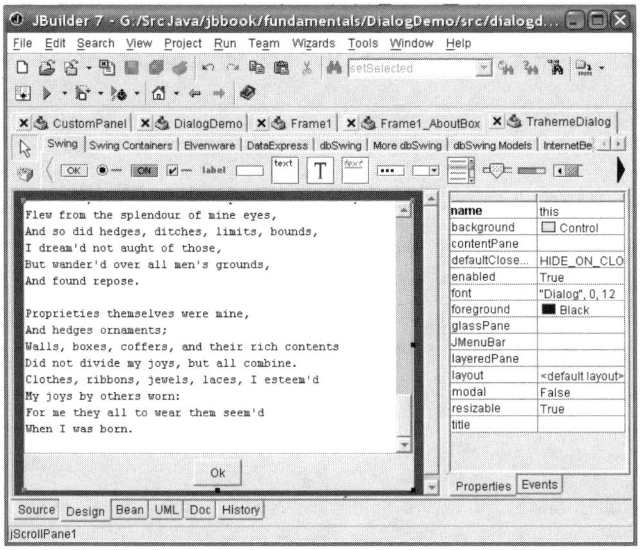

Figure 19-14: Designing a custom dialog that contains scroll bars, a JTextArea, a JPanel, and a JButton

Create an event handler for the JButton that looks like this:

```
void jButtonOk_actionPerformed(ActionEvent e)
{
    this.dispose();
}
```

This call will be used to close the dialog when you are done.

Now go back to Frame1 and create an event handler for the final menu item that you created. Enter two additional lines of code so that the handler looks like this:

```
void jMenuItemCustomDialog_actionPerformed(ActionEvent e)
{
    TraherneDialog dlg = new TraherneDialog();
    dlg.show();
}
```

Now run the program and select the Custom Dialog menu item. The results, while fairly impressive, are not quite right. This dialog contains the scroll bars that we want and does not stretch outside the bounds of the screen. However, it is fairly narrow and exactly as tall as the entire screen, as shown in Figure 19-15. This is better than before but still less than perfect.

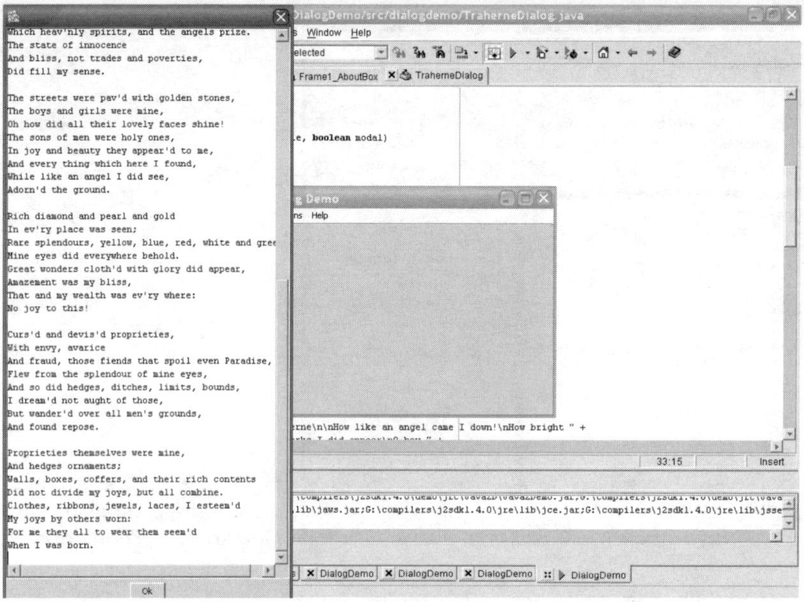

Figure 19-15: The Traherne dialog is usable now, but it is an awkward shape and size.

One quick fix for this situation is to switch back to source view for the JDialog descendant. Find the constructor, and add a single line to it that sets the size of the dialog:

```
public TraherneDialog(Frame frame, String title, boolean modal)
{
      super(frame, title, modal);
      try
      {
            jbInit();
            pack();

            // This is the new line that we have added to set the size
               of the dialog.
            this.setSize(640, 480);
      }
      catch(Exception ex)
      {
            ex.printStackTrace();
      }
}
```

If we run the program now, it is much closer to what we want. The dialog is the right size, and it has pleasing dimensions, as you can see from Figure 19-16.

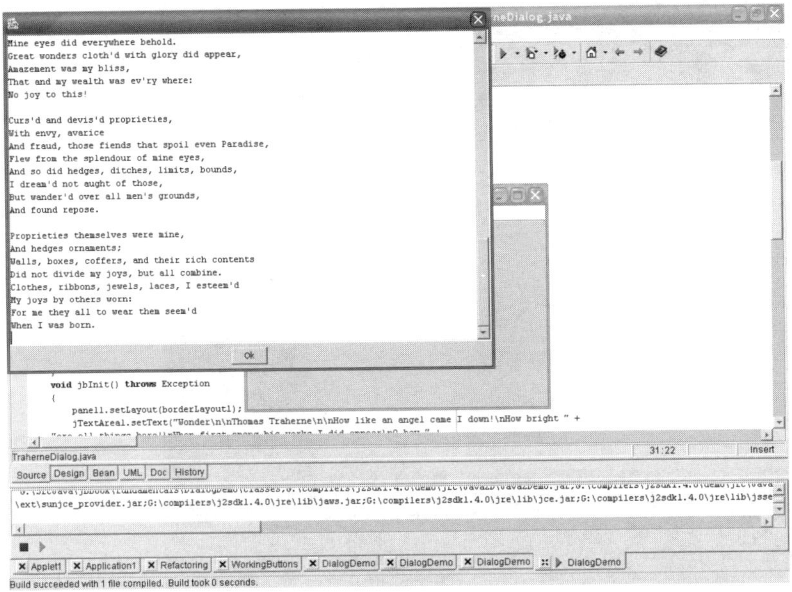

Figure 19-16: The dialog as it appears after we insert code to define its size and shape

Yet still the dialog is not entirely satisfactory. What we need is code that will also center the dialog. This need is so frequent that I have created a method that handles the task for us. Before using the method, you should comment out the code that you used to set the size of the dialog in its constructor. Now go back to Frame1, add in a new method called showDialogSize, and alter the code that launches the dialog:

```
public void showDialogSize(Component parent, JDialog dlg,
        int width, int height)
{
      Dimension dlgSize = new Dimension(width, height);
      Dimension ownerSize = parent.getSize();
      Point loc = parent.getLocation();
      dlg.setSize(dlgSize);
      dlg.setLocation((ownerSize.width - dlgSize.width) / 2 +
            loc.x, (ownerSize.height - dlgSize.height) / 2 + loc.y);
      dlg.show();
}

void jMenuItemCustomDialog_actionPerformed(ActionEvent e)
{
      TraherneDialog dlg = new TraherneDialog();
      showDialogSize(this, dlg, 640, 480);
}
```

The method called showDialogSize takes as parameters the parent of the dialog, the dialog itself, and the preferred size of the dialog. The method will then display the dialog in the center of the screen, as shown in Figure 19-17.

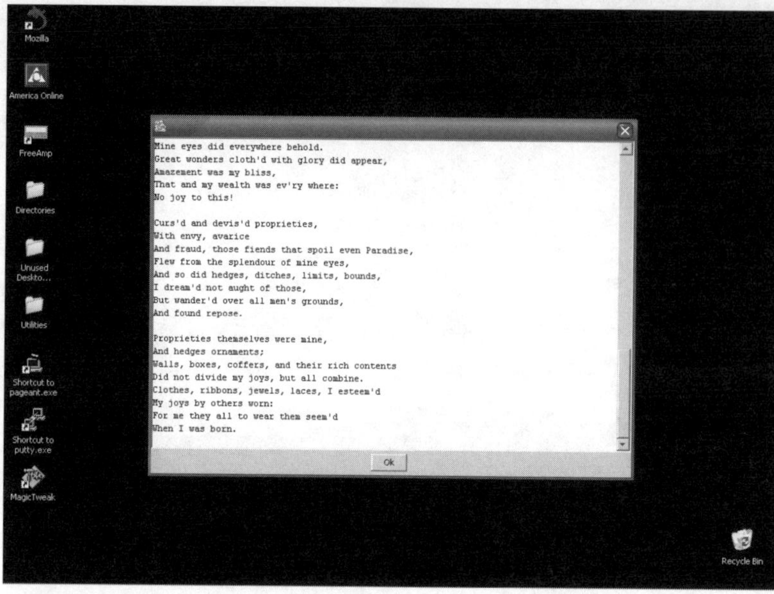

Figure 19-17: The dialog as it appears with its size set and its location centered in the middle of the screen

NOTE: In the com.elvenware.codebox package, there is a file called GuiBox.java. It contains the showDialogSize routine and a number of similar methods that display dialogs in a variety of different ways. I include that code so that you can use these methods in your own programs.

One would like to believe that all is now well, but there is yet one more nagging problem. If you look carefully at Figures 19-15 through 19-17, you might notice that we are looking at the end of the Thomas Traherne poem, not at the beginning. I am afraid that I can't fully explain exactly why the JDK should act this way, but I do know how to solve the problem.

The following code, if inserted into the Traherne dialog, ensures that the JTextArea is scrolled up to the top a moment before the dialog is displayed on the screen:

```
public void show()
{
      super.show();

      // Scroll to the top of the text area
      jTextArea1.setCaretPosition(0);
}
```

The show method, as you know, is one that is inherited from an ancestor of JDialog. In Java, all methods are automatically declared as virtual. Here we are overriding the show method and changing — ever so slightly — the way it behaves. Note first the call to the ancestor show method:

```
      super.show();
```

Without this call, the dialog would not draw itself correctly. Then examine the simple call to jTextArea1.setCaretPosition. This call forces the JTextArea to scroll to the top. The final result is shown in Figure 19-18.

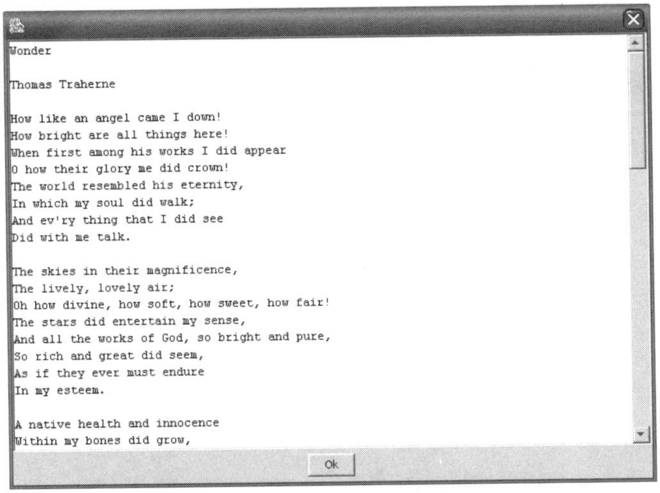

Figure 19-18: The Traherne dialog with the text scrolled all the way to the top position

I have not spent a great deal of time discussing the boilerplate code that the JBuilder Dialog Wizard produces. Most of it is not very interesting, but I show it to you in Listing 19-1 so you can see how to declare such a dialog.

Listing 19-1: The code for the Traherne dialog

```
package dialogdemo;

import java.awt.*;
import javax.swing.*;
import java.awt.event.*;

/**
 * <p>Title: </p>
 * <p>Description: </p>
 * <p>Copyright: Copyright (c) 2002</p>
 * <p>Company: </p>
 * @author unascribed
 * @version 1.0
 */

public class TraherneDialog extends JDialog
{
      JPanel panel1 = new JPanel();
      BorderLayout borderLayout1 = new BorderLayout();
      JScrollPane jScrollPane1 = new JScrollPane();
      JTextArea jTextArea1 = new JTextArea();
      JPanel jPanel1 = new JPanel();
      JButton jButtonOk = new JButton();
      FlowLayout flowLayout1 = new FlowLayout();

      public TraherneDialog(Frame frame, String title, boolean modal)
      {
            super(frame, title, modal);
```

```
        try
        {
            jbInit();
            pack();
            //this.setSize(640, 480);
        }
        catch(Exception ex)
        {
            ex.printStackTrace();
        }
    }

    public TraherneDialog()
    {
        this(null, "", false);
    }
    void jbInit() throws Exception
    {
        panel1.setLayout(borderLayout1);
        jTextArea1.setText(
    "Wonder\n\nThomas Traherne\n\nHow like an angel came I down!\nHow bright " +
    "are all things here!\nWhen first among his works I did appear\nO how " +
    "their glory me did crown!\nThe world resembled his eternity,\nIn which " +
    "my soul did walk;\nAnd ev\'ry thing that I did see\nDid with me talk.\n" +
    "\nThe skies in their magnificence,\nThe lively, lovely air;\nOh how " +
    "divine, how soft, how sweet, how fair!\nThe stars did entertain my " +
    "sense,\nAnd all the works of God, so bright and pure,\nSo rich and " +
    "great did seem,\nAs if they ever must endure\nIn my esteem.\n\nA native " +
    "health and innocence\nWithin my bones did grow,\nAnd while my God did " +
    "all his glories show,\nI felt a vigour in my sense\nThat was all spirit. " +
    "I within did flow\nWith seas of life, like wine;\nI nothing in the " +
    "world did know\nBut\'twas divine.\n\nHarsh ragged objects were conceal\'d,\n" +
    "Oppressions tears and cries,\nSins, griefs, complaints, dissensions, " +
    "weeping eyes\nWere hid, and only things reveal\'d\nWhich heav\'nly spirits, " +
    "and the angels prize.\nThe state of innocence\nAnd bliss, not trades " +
    "and poverties,\nDid fill my sense.\n\nThe streets were pav\'d with golden " +
    "stones,\nThe boys and girls were mine,\nOh how did all their lovely " +
    "faces shine!\nThe sons of men were holy ones,\nIn joy and beauty they " +
    "appear\'d to me,\nAnd every thing which here I found,\nWhile like an " +
    "angel I did see,\nAdorn\'d the ground.\n\nRich diamond and pearl and " +
    "gold\nIn ev\'ry place was seen;\nRare splendours, yellow, blue, red, " +
    "white and green,\nMine eyes did everywhere behold.\nGreat wonders cloth\'d " +
    "with glory did appear,\nAmazement was my bliss,\nThat and my wealth " +
    "was ev\'ry where:\nNo joy to this!\n\nCurs\'d and devis\'d proprieties,\n" +
    "With envy, avarice\nAnd fraud, those fiends that spoil even Paradise,\n" +
    "Flew from the splendour of mine eyes,\nAnd so did hedges, ditches, " +
    "limits, bounds,\nI dream\'d not aught of those,\nBut wander\'d over all " +
    "men\'s grounds,\nAnd found repose.\n\nProprieties themselves were mine,\n" +
    "And hedges ornaments;\nWalls, boxes, coffers, and their rich contents\n" +
    "Did not divide my joys, but all combine.\nClothes, ribbons, jewels, " +
```

```
    "laces, I esteem\'d\nMy joys by others worn:\nFor me they all to wear " +
    "them seem\'d\nWhen I was born. \n");

        jButtonOk.setText("Ok");
        jButtonOk.addActionListener(
            new TraherneDialog_jButtonOk_actionAdapter(this));
        jPanel1.setLayout(flowLayout1);
        getContentPane().add(panel1);
        panel1.add(jScrollPane1, BorderLayout.CENTER);
        panel1.add(jPanel1,  BorderLayout.SOUTH);
        jPanel1.add(jButtonOk, null);
        jScrollPane1.getViewport().add(jTextArea1, null);
    }

    void jButtonOk_actionPerformed(ActionEvent e)
    {
        this.dispose();
    }

    public void show()
    {
        super.show();
        // Scroll to the top of the text area
        jTextArea1.setCaretPosition(0);
    }

}

class TraherneDialog_jButtonOk_actionAdapter implements java.awt.event.ActionListener
{
    TraherneDialog adaptee;

    TraherneDialog_jButtonOk_actionAdapter(TraherneDialog adaptee)
    {
        this.adaptee = adaptee;
    }
    public void actionPerformed(ActionEvent e)
    {
        adaptee.jButtonOk_actionPerformed(e);
    }
}
```

When you are examining this code, you might pay special attention to the way the Traherne poem is formatted. When I pasted the code into the property editor for the JTextArea's text property, it was formatted as it appears in Figure 19-18. It was JBuilder that went through the work of converting standard text into something that can be stored in a Java file. This conversion saves you a good deal of time, which is why I made such a point of describing how to paste the poem into the source file.

Part III

Summary

This chapter concentrated on various techniques for displaying dialogs. You saw how to create your own dialogs and use the built-in dialogs that come with the JOptionPane class. Most of these technologies are simple to use, though we did find that there were a few tricks you might want to use when working with custom dialogs. The JBuilder Dialog Wizard, however, takes care of most of the hard work for us.

Once again, I suggest that you now close the book, fire up JBuilder, and see if you can recreate the programs described in this chapter. If possible, try to use only the screen shots as hints. See if you can get to the point where you can build the programs without looking at the text in the book. If you can get that far, you know you have internalized the information found in this chapter. If you need more help, you can find both example programs on the CD and on www.elvenware.com. The program shown in this chapter is called DialogDemo.

Part IV

Project Architecture

Chapter 20

Composing Java

Charlie Calvert

This chapter begins Part IV: Project Architecture. Each of the three chapters in this part will be a fairly short commentary on how to use JBuilder to help you write clean code.

In this chapter in particular, but throughout the next chapters, you will also learn how to use JBuilder to unscramble poorly written code. If you have inherited a poorly written project, this chapter can help you make sense of it.

I don't want this book to just cover a series of isolated features found in JBuilder. Instead, I want to show how to use JBuilder to create well-written code. JBuilder was designed to facilitate not only the production of code but the production of good code. This chapter, and the next two, define what it means to write reusable code that is easy to maintain. Along the way, I will show you as often as possible how to use JBuilder to help you achieve these ends.

Cold Mountain Code

There is a famous series of Japanese poems called Cold Mountain. The poems are supposedly written by a Japanese hermit who started out with a simple, very ordinary life but ended his days as a visionary hermit in a place called Cold Mountain.

Here is my version of one of the last poems in the Cold Mountain series:

```
So Hanshan writes these words
These words that no one will believe
Honey is sweet, we like its taste
Medicine is bitter and hard to swallow
What soothes the senses brings contentment
What opposes the will calls forth anger.
But I ask you to look at the wooden puppets
Worn out by their moment at play on the stage.
```

At first glance, this poem may appear a bit opaque, but I take it to be an extremely simple work, one that anyone can understand. Hanshan says that we sometimes feel good, and we sometimes feel bad. We sometimes get what we want, and we sometimes have to accept bad news. When all is said and done, the poet believes that these are the basic facts that describe our day-to-day life. And yet, he says, we always end up overwrought, overly excited, whenever we get something we want or whenever we are deprived of a hoped-for gift or reward. He believes that we should stop wearing ourselves out over the inevitable ups and downs of life.

Of course, the poet starts out by saying that no matter how simple his message may be, no one is going to believe him. Back in the world of Java programming, there are a number of people who speak on the virtues of good program architecture and design who perhaps feel a little like Hanshan. Most of their suggestions are very simple, sometimes even very obvious, and yet most programmers go on their merry way, totally ignoring this good advice. As a result, these wayward programmers encounter untold difficulties and confusion. It is ironic that advice so simple and commonplace is so frequently ignored.

Topics Covered in this Chapter

This chapter covers the following topics:

- Naming conventions: The skill of properly naming a variable, method, object, or package is more complex than it seems at first. Difficulties are encountered not because of laziness, but through a misunderstanding of the nature of the subject.
- This chapter also covers the art of discovering and exploring variables with JBuilder tools, such as Find Resources, Find Definition, and Find In Path. These tools have been mentioned in earlier portions of the book, but here you will see them being used in a practical context.

The next chapters cover the following topics:

- Commenting code: Again, this is a subject that many programmers think they understand, yet in practice they fail to deliver even the most basic functionality in this area. Most programmers claim laziness or lack of time as their excuse for their failure to write comments. Yet a closer look reveals that there is more to this subject than first meets the eye. It is a failure to grasp the nature of the task that leads many programmers astray when it comes to writing comments. Chapter 21 also covers creating Javadoc.
- Modularity and reuse: Finding the proper architecture for a program is a difficult skill to master. At the core of the problem is the art of discovering the methods, objects, and packages inherent in any particular problem. You can use any version of JBuilder to help you restructure your program. However, if you have the SE or Enterprise versions, the refactoring tools inside JBuilder can greatly simplify this process.
- In this book I also include an examination of several technologies that can help you write robust code. Among the subjects examined are patterns, unit testing, extreme programming, and Hungarian notation. I don't just rubber-stamp approval on these technologies, but instead I examine their pros and cons. Some of these technologies are explored in more depth in their own chapters. In particular, both refactoring and testing your code are covered in later chapters.

NOTE: I want to do something a little unusual in this section of the book and dedicate it to myself. All of the mistakes covered in these chapters are mistakes I have made in my own programs. Some of them I keep making right to this day.

If we are fortunate, we learn from our mistakes. If I hadn't been such a careless programmer, I never would have made so many mistakes. If I hadn't made so many mistakes, I wouldn't have known what to write. As a result, I dedicate this chapter to myself, in thanks for the lessons I have learned from my own mistakes and in the hope that I won't make them again!

Simplify, Simplify, Simplify

The main theme of this section of the book is the need to simplify your code. I will show how you can do this by creating good naming conventions; by dividing your code into discrete methods, objects, and packages; by writing good comments; and using utilities such as JUnit or the JBuilder refactoring tools.

Regardless of what specific technique I am using, the overall purpose of this chapter is to sing the virtues of writing code that is simple and easy to read. In my opinion, code that is simple and easy to read is more elegant, more aesthetically pleasing, and easier to maintain than even the most skillfully wrought complex code.

This is the Earnest Hemingway school of programming that I am advocating. Hemingway was famous for writing beautifully structured prose based on short, simple sentences. I advocate using the same techniques to create good code. Work with simple, easy-to-read methods and simple, easy-to-read objects. In the long run, that technique will help you produce the best programs.

A programmer isn't cool because he or she can write hard-to-read code. That programmer is failing to find a way to write code in a simple, easy-to-read manner.

Such are the rules being advocated in this chapter. You may disagree with them, but hopefully my point is easy to understand.

Java to the Rescue

I believe that Java itself is one of the best advocates I can have for the "simple is best" approach to programming. The majority of the JDK consists of simple, easy-to-use objects. Think of how much simpler it is to use the Java list containers than it is to use the C++ STL containers. The STL is a fabulous and interesting piece of code, but it can take years to thoroughly understand. Many programmers are obviously frightened of it and avoid it like the plague. Most programmers, on the other hand, can understand the Java list containers after a few hours of study.

The Java object model, the JavaBeans specification, the networking classes, and the String class are all further examples of how Java succeeds in making difficult subjects appear simple. There are areas where Java is difficult, but overall it is a remarkably simple specification.

The simplicity and clarity of the JDK helps programmers be productive. Its methods and classes have good naming conventions and a good sense of modularity and are well documented. The JDK itself is a real-world example of the kind of programming I am advocating in this chapter.

Naming Conventions

The act of properly naming variables, methods, and objects is one of the most important things you can do if you want to write clean, easy-to-read programs. Of course, programmers already know that they are supposed to create good names for their identifiers. We have all heard as much.

Yet many, perhaps even most, programmers never follow through on these simple principles. Why is that?

Despite what you may hear, the problem is usually not a lack of time. The problem is that it is hard to come up with good variable names.

Naming something well is a difficult skill to master. Some programmers simply don't have the innate talents necessary to excel at this skill. However, they can avoid certain painfully obvious mistakes if they really put their minds to it.

Bear with me while I cover this topic in some detail. It is more complex than it first appears, and its importance is much greater than most programmers, in their heart of hearts, have actually come to believe.

Abstract Language vs. Specific Language

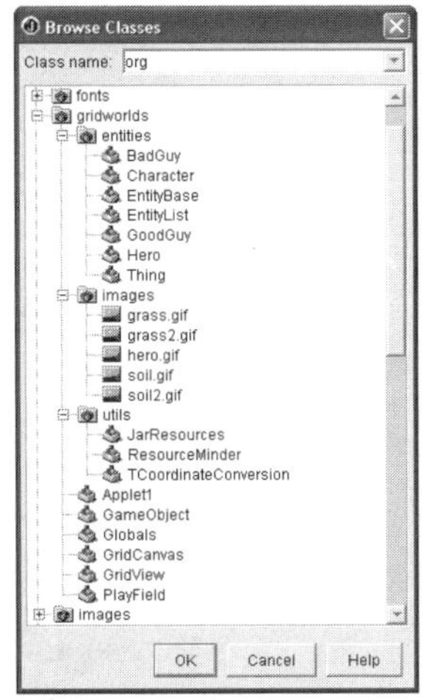

Figure 20-1: Viewing all the classes in a medium size project using the Browse Classes tool

This section offers a meditation on the need to use precise naming conventions. The basic theme of the section is simple and easy to understand: Use easily identifiable, and very specific, nouns and verbs for identifiers.

Don't use variable names like num, item, list, value, or strItem. These names are not specific enough. Instead, use names like bookList, numPencils, strPencilDescription, or salaryTotal. It's all very simple — at least on paper. But in practice, we find that this is more difficult than it first appears. Let's find out why.

Suppose a programmer named Victoria is assigned to fix a bug in a big program that contains a piece of code that encapsulates a list of books. It's the code that deals with this list that is broken. When Victoria begins the assignment, the first thing she needs to do is locate that list inside the body of code she has inherited.

Perhaps her first stop will be the Browse Classes tool in the JBuilder Search menu. This tool can show all the classes in the current project, as shown in Figure 20-1.

NOTE: Please understand that in Figure 20-1 and other screen shots in this chapter, I am not showing you the actual files that Victoria was working on when she got in her fix. These are just files from a project that comes with this book. I'm using them merely to illustrate a point. A project the size of Victoria's would take up several screens full of information, while here you can see a whole project in one window.

Part IV

After viewing the classes and packages in the project, the next thing Victoria might do is use the UML view. This is only available to developers who are using the Enterprise version of the product. It can, however, help a programmer like Victoria understand the scope of a project.

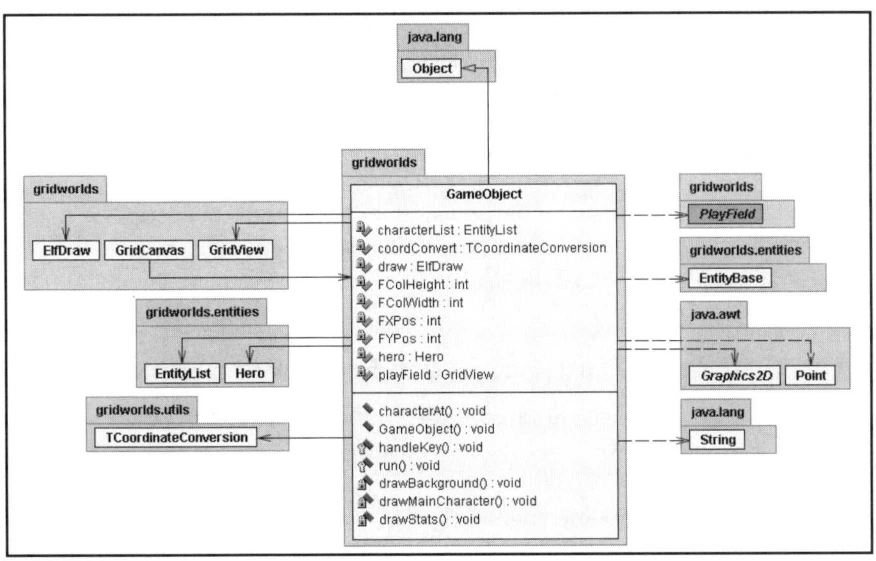

Figure 20-2: A UML view of a portion of the same program shown in Figure 20-1

This diagram can reveal a good deal about the structure, particularly the dependencies, of the various classes that make up a project. (UML will be covered in more depth in Chapter 31.)

By now Victoria will have some sense of how her project is put together. But she needs to get down to business and locate that darn list.

She is told that the list is approximately 250 members long. For a list this size, the program does not need to use a database. Instead, Victoria can guess that the developers of the code probably used a less expensive data structure, such as an array or linked list.

While Victoria is looking for the code that holds this list of books, she stumbles across a variable called cAll, which is of type ArrayList. "I wonder what this variable does?" Victoria asks herself.

Victoria considers whether or not this variable could possibly hold her list of books. She doesn't know how this list is maintained. Is it in a hash table? A linked list? An array? Maybe it is kept in a text file. She doesn't even know for sure if the variable she is looking for exists. Maybe the books are kept in some other kind of data structure entirely.

She looks again at the variable called cAll. By looking at that variable, there isn't much she can tell about it.

Is it the word "call" with strange capitalization? Well, that's not likely, but it is difficult to rule that option out. Perhaps there is some form of Hungarian notation going on here. Maybe the "c" stands for container, and All is a word that lives on its own. That sounds a bit more reasonable, but again, it is not definite. For instance, the c might stand for char, or for currency, for cache or for calc, for calendar or caption, for certificate or class, for check box or client. Quite frankly, it could stand for just about anything.

Frustrated, Victoria decides to move on. The next question, of course, is what does the word "All" refer to? Does it refer to all the widgets in the program? All the strings in the program? Or maybe it refers to all the books in the program?

Given the context of this discussion, you probably are inclined to go with the last option. It must mean all the books in the program.

But think for a moment. Suppose the code for this program is 50,000 lines long. And suppose that the class Victoria is looking at is 1,200 lines long, and suppose it has 35 variables at the top, all of which have names like cAll. For instance, there is another variable hMask, and another one called cStuff, and a third one called cList. Perhaps there are other variables named cArray and cLinkedList. After looking at these other variables, how sure can Victoria be that cAll contains the list of books that she is trying to locate?

Some programmers might suggest that Victoria is just lazy and that she should start looking through the code, trying to discover how the variable is used. They advocate a brute force technique to figure out the meaning of the variable by seeing it in context. It's not their job to name the variable correctly; it's Victoria's job to be smart enough to figure out what it means!

Working with people who think like this is not ideal. However, it is common. Many programmers think this way. If you are stuck in such a morass, JBuilder can help.

Using JBuilder to Soften the Blow of Brute Force Programming

To try to get out of her fix, Victoria can use the JBuilder Find References tool. She can go to the top of the file where her variable is declared and place the mouse cursor on the code element in question. Right-click and choose **Find References** from the pop-up menu. The message pane will then open up, and a display like the one shown in Figure 20-3 will become visible. Here you can see all the places in your program where a particular variable is used. If she clicks on any of the elements in the message pane, Victoria will be taken immediately to the code she wants to find.

If this technique does not work, another tool that might be helpful is the Find in Path utility from the Search menu. If Victoria uses this utility to find all the references to this variable, she will end up with a listing like that shown in Figure 20-4. As you can see, Figures 20-3 and 20-4 are very similar in appearance. Perhaps the one advantage that the Find in Path tool has is that the code need not compile for it to work correctly.

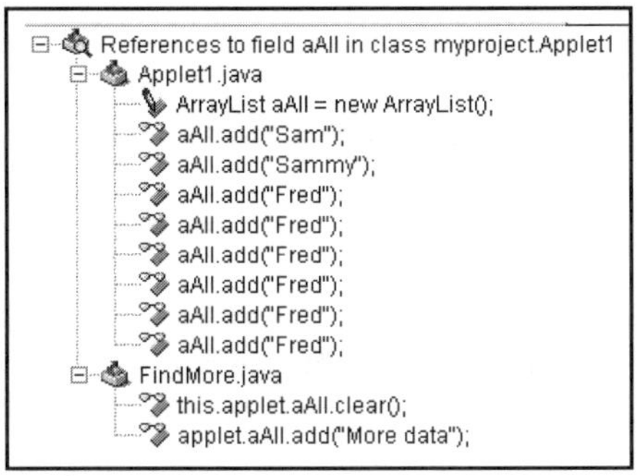

Figure 20-3: Using Find References to track down the references for all the variables in your program

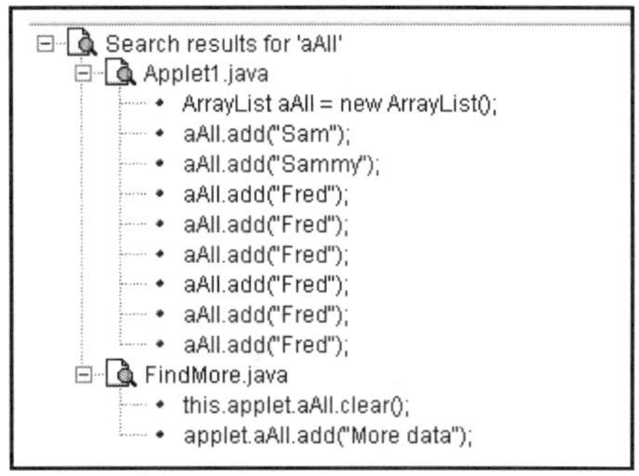

Figure 20-4: Using the Find in Path tool to track down references to a variable across multiple files

NOTE: The Find in Path tool can be very helpful when you want to make sure that you have been using good variable naming conventions. For instance, you can use it to look for all instances of the word "item" or the word "list" or "value." These are all very abstract names of the kind that cause trouble in programs. If you find instances of these variables using the Find in Path tool, you can click on each one and use your imagination to come up with better names.

In JBuilder 7, you can use the Find in Path tool to perform global search and replaces. This tool is useful when you want to replace all the instances of a poorly named variable with a better name.

There is yet another JBuilder tool that Victoria might find useful. In her explorations of the source, she has found that there are multiple declarations for the variable cAll in multiple classes and in multiple scopes within a single class. At times, it might not be clear to her which variable instance is being referenced. Again, this is an example of terrible programming practice. But Victoria is stuck with the code, and she has to try to make sense of it. To help resolve this issue, she can right-click on the variable she is confused about and choose Find Definition from the JBuilder pop-up menu. She will then be taken immediately to the declaration of the variable.

Finding a Remedy

Victoria has now used many powerful JBuilder tools to explore the code she inherited. But even with lots of help, bad programming practices can be difficult to overcome.

Suppose Victoria finds five variables that are good candidates. She now has to parse the code for each of those variables in order to find the one she needs. After she does find it, she will inevitably be asked to spend time on another project, or perhaps Christmas break will come along. Two weeks later she comes back. She finds that she has forgotten whether the books are stored in the variable called cAll rather than the variable called cArray. Or is it maybe in cList? Well, the only thing to do is start parsing the code again and figuring it out the hard way one more time.

At this stage we are back to Hanshan's problem. The solution here is really very obvious. One should call the variable something like booklist, or perhaps aBookList to designate that it is an array containing a list of books. Victoria is forced to throw a great deal of complicated technology at the code to try to solve the problem. But the best solution is very low tech indeed: Just give the variable a good name.

The point here is that one never saves time by hurrying through the process of naming a variable. In the long run, that oversight will cause you a much greater loss of time than any that could have accrued from taking the time to properly name it in the first place.

One should also add a comment to the variable, describing how it is used in the program. For instance, "List of books automatically initialized on program startup" or "Call fillBookList() to initialize this variable." The subject of commenting your code is addressed in the next chapter.

Yes, we all know what the programmer who wrote this code should have done. The variable should have been given a good name. Only, using Hanshan's rule, we know that many programmers won't actually use that solution, even though it is so obvious! In real life, many programmers are actually going to name the variable cAll! In doing so, they are creating ugly, unnecessarily complex code.

Mistakes like this lie right at the heart of what it means to write code that I find unappealing. I don't care how fast, small, or elegant the code the original programmers wrote might have been. In my opinion, it is bad code, in and of itself, by definition, because it is hard to read!

Epilogue

Some readers might want to hear the end of Victoria's story. It goes like this. Victoria finally figured out what variable held the list. It was, of course, not the cAll variable, but cList. So she changed its name to bookList.

Strangely enough, after she checked in her code, the next day she found that the variable had been changed back to cList. She used her version control system to find out the name of the person who made the change. It turned out to be someone named Dave. She wrote Dave an email, explaining why she changed the variable name to bookList and asking him to be reasonable. He wrote back and said that he wrote the code, and he thought her name for the variable "stunk," and he wanted it to be cList. He had other code that depended on that variable, and he didn't want to have to edit that other code just because of her whims. End of topic.

That might have been the end of the story. Only it turned out that Victoria was not only good at naming variables, but she also happened to be a very attractive young woman. And when Dave finally got the nerve to ask that hot redhead down the hall out for a date, he never could figure out why she suddenly turned such a cold shoulder to him after she learned his name.

Variable Names and Access Methods

As you probably know, in Java, you should not usually directly access a data element from a second object. For instance, the cList object in Victoria's program should not be called directly from another source file. Instead, the data referenced by the object should be accessed via getter and setter methods. These access methods are simply wrappers around a variable:

```
public ArrayList getBookList()
```

```
{
        return bookList;
}
```

You may have noticed that the name getBookList is very easy to read and simple to understand. Compare that name with the name getAAll(). This latter name is one that would be generated from one of the variable names used by the programmer who created Victoria's program. A method with a name like getAAll() is ugly, hard to read, hard to understand, and perhaps even somewhat repulsive.

Good variable naming conventions help you write good data access methods. If the names for the getters and setters in a program look slightly ridiculous, that is often a sign that something is amiss.

Method Arguments: Bad, Average, and Good Naming Conventions

If you are a professional programmer, it is likely that on this very day you had the misfortune of looking at a method with a declaration similar to this:

```
String parseString(String name, String data, int value)
```

Try, for just a moment, to guess what such a method might do. If you are like me, you probably won't be able to get very far. This method is hard to read. Even if its implementation is only three or four lines long, and even if it is very fast and very efficient, this method is still hard to read! It is hard to read not because of the quality of the code in its method body but because of the naming conventions it uses.

Now, look at this rewrite of the parseString method declaration:

```
String findLastName(String userName, String delimiter, int maxChars)
```

This latter method is much easier to understand. It might not answer all your questions, but it at least gives you a sense of what it is that this method is all about. It is still not clear what maxChars does, and there is at least some doubt as to the purpose of delimiter. But overall, this is a big improvement. It is not great code, but it is acceptable. Looking at it, you can guess that it is likely a method for retrieving the last name from a string that contains both a first and last name. For instance, you pass in Linus Torvalds, and you get back out Torvalds.

Take a moment to consider this variation on the same method:

```
String getLastNameFromUserName(String userName,
        String userNameDelimiter, int MaxCharsInLastName)
```

I believe this code is better than the second example because it is more specific. In fact, your understanding of one or more of the identifiers in this method may have changed after you saw this third declaration. It is more concise and therefore easier to read.

Take a look at Figure 20-5. It shows ParameterInsight helping a developer discover the parameters to the getLastNameFromUserName method. If you take time in creating the argument names for your methods, and if you use ParameterInsight, there is little need for either help files or documentation. Your code really does become self documenting, and you can find out all the information you need by simply typing an open parenthesis and pressing Ctrl+Shift+Space to bring up ParameterInsight.

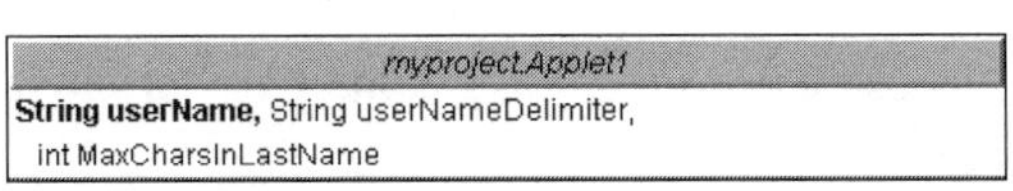

Figure 20-5: The parameters to getLastNameFromUserName as they appear in ParameterInsight

> **NOTE:** It is possible to understand the purpose and usage of this function just by reading its declaration. I do not mean to suggest that you should not comment your code, only that if you do fail to comment your code, at least you can provide decent variable names.

Why Do Programmers Use Bad Naming Conventions?

Why do programmers (including myself) often create bad variable names even when they know better?

The problems we are confronting in this situation are threefold:

- **Management doesn't have the right priorities.** Managers should not push a programmer so hard that he or she really doesn't have time to create good variable names. Doing so will only cause unnecessary delays during maintenance or debug phases of development.
- **Programmers don't have the right priorities.** No matter how much time pressure we are under, the truth is that getting our declarations at least to the second stage of the three options shown above is vitally important. It is more important than making deadlines, getting home for dinner 15 minutes early, or getting back to the more interesting parts of the problem we are currently writing. Why is it more important than these things? Because in the long run, good naming conventions will help us get our projects in on time, help us get home from work early, and free us up so that we can concentrate on the interesting parts of our programs. In other words, we only think we are saving time when we make a declaration like the first one shown above. In truth, we are wasting time, and we are wasting not only our own time, but the time of anyone else who reads our code!
- **Some programmers aren't very good with words.** Let's face it: Programmers don't get hired because they have great communication skills. Most programmers are good at logic and working with abstractions and symbols, and many of them are good at problem solving. If they don't have at least some of these skills, they can't write code. But you don't have to be good with words to write code that works. You do, however, have to be good with words if you want to create good variable names. In truth, it is often harder to come up with good names for your identifiers than it is to get your program to compile or run correctly. Sadly enough, good naming conventions are in part the result of an innate skill that you were either born with or acquired through many years of hard work.

If these are the problems, then what are the solutions? Well, that's a hard question to answer, but here are my guidelines:

- When it comes to naming variables, don't let your attention flag. Work hard at this important part of your program. It is okay to be lazy when you are programming. The point is not to be lazy at the wrong time. <u>If there is any chance that the purpose of a variable can be misunderstood by a reasonably competent programmer, then give it a precise name!</u>
- Realize that few things that you do have as much importance as declaring your variables correctly. In the long run, it will save you time, make your job more pleasant, and free you up to work on interesting problems. <u>Get your priorities straight. Few things are more important than properly naming the identifiers in your program!</u>
- You may not be the next Shakespeare, but you can get past stage one. Don't ever use variables that are excessively imprecise. Don't call something "list" when it is really a

bookList. Don't call a variable "name" when it is really a firstName. Be as precise as you can, and don't worry if you can't achieve perfection.

- Set aside time to clean up hastily written code. This is a job that can be done when you are too tired to work on harder problems, when you have a small chunk of time that needs to be filled with a task that can be broken up into small pieces, or when you are stuck in a boring meeting.

In short, the art of naming a variable properly requires hard work, patience, a good set of priorities, and a fair amount of creativity. Maybe this task isn't quite as simple as it seemed at first. The trick here is to realize the importance of this subject and start taking pride in handling it correctly. If you can understand the importance of the task, you will start giving it a higher priority.

Is it Ever Okay to Use Imprecise Variable Names?

As has been said many times, programming is an art, not a science. In many cases, there is no one variable name that is best. There might be ten possible names, and maybe three or four of them are bad, three of them are good, and three of them are excellent choices. Picking any of these options is better than using an imprecise option, such as num, value, or item. But deciding which is best is an art, not a science.

In the imprecise world of programming, rules are made to be broken. So yes, naming variables precisely is important in most cases. But are there cases when it is just a waste of time to do the hard, artful work of coming up with the right name for a variable?

Consider the following method:

```
void setFirstName(String value)
{
      this.firstName = value;
}
```

Some might argue that this method declaration violates the rule against using imprecise variables. In particular, the variable value has no specific meaning. It is as imprecise a name as one can imagine.

However, I would argue that in a case like this, there is no harm done in using a variable name of this type. Why is such blatant imprecision acceptable in this case? The answer, in my opinion, looks like this:

- **The method is very short and very simple**. As a result, there is not much room for confusion. If the method were more complex, there would be more opportunities for confusion and more need for precision.
- **The purpose of the method is very obvious, and therefore there is little chance that confusion will arise**. The method is obviously a setter method, which fits into a well-known Java scheme of getters and setters. Furthermore, it has a very clear and easy-to-understand method name. It is simply obvious to any but the most rank beginner that the purpose of this method is to assign the variable value to a String with object scope that is called firstName. There just isn't much room for confusion.
- **There is only one variable declared in the method**. If the method had the same name and the same simple purpose but took two parameters, there would be a need for more precision. For instance, if it took two parameters called String value and String data, it would not be immediately obvious what you are supposed to do with them. In such a case, you would need more precise variable names, such as String aFirstName and String aMilitaryRank.

The final point to be made here is that precision in variable names is meant to be an aid to programmers, not an annoyance. It takes work to come up with good variable names. In a case like this one, there is no need for precision, so it is okay to use abstract and imprecise names that are easy to invent and the production of which can even be automated. (In fact, when you read about BeanInsight, you will see that JBuilder does automate the production of variable names, such as the one shown here.)

Well, that is the end of the section of this chapter that focuses on naming variables. I have gone on at some length, but I felt that I needed to in order to emphasize the extreme importance of this topic and to make clear that it is not an easy problem to solve.

Summary

If you give your variables good names, you might find yourself finishing your work way before smarter programmers who pay no attention to such details. Anyone can comment their code and come up with at least reasonably specific variable names. Use these "secret coding techniques" to jump ahead of others who can't be bothered with such mundane tasks.

This chapter also showed you how to use some of JBuilder's tools to untangle code that is poorly written, hard to read, or extremely complex. In short, it shows how to use JBuilder to untangle the kind of code you are likely to inherit from other programmers if you work in a corporate environment.

In the next chapter you will read about commenting your code and using Javadoc. The chapter after that discusses dividing your code up into discrete methods and objects. The techniques for doing this can greatly simplify your code.

In Chapter 30, "Unit Testing with JUnit," you will read about "good coding practice" technologies, such as extreme programming and unit testing. Material related to our current subject matter is also covered in Chapter 31, "Refactoring and UML."

Chapter 21

Comments and Javadoc

Margie and Charlie Calvert

This chapter is about writing and producing documentation for your project. The opening sections of the text will discuss the task of commenting your code from a theoretical point of view. The latter sections will be more technical, explaining exactly how to convert your comments into Javadoc. Don't be fooled by the theoretical material in the first pages of the chapter; it also contains a lot of hard technical material about JBuilder.

Javadoc is a series of auto-generated HTML files that go a long way toward outlining the structure of your program. Simply comment your code properly, and Javadoc will automatically convert those comments into well-laid-out documentation for your product.

Writing the best possible documentation involves more than just commenting your code. You will also need to add a few extra files to the mix. These files give an overview of your whole project and your packages. Adding these extra overview and package files is optional. However, I recommend using them. As you will see, you can automatically integrate them into your Javadoc output.

The text also shows how JBuilder can help you write comments that are thorough and well structured. It can't write the comments for you, but it can help you properly format your comments, help you comment each parameter, and make the task of writing them a bit easier.

See Chapter 7 for details about how JBuilder makes it easy for you to view Javadoc in the IDE. This chapter will show you how to create Javadoc.

Commenting Your Code

Why are programmers so lax when it comes to commenting their code? Perhaps the problem is simply that many programmers have a background in mathematics and not in writing. Few people are good at both writing and math. Perhaps another piece of the puzzle is that leaders in the community tend not to emphasize this part of their task. For instance, the creator of Linux, Linus Torvalds, writes this on his home page:

```
"If you're looking for Linux information, you'll find more of it somewhere else, because
I'm hopeless when it comes to documentation."
```

Anders Hejlsberg, creator of Turbo Pascal, recipient of Dr. Dobb's Journal's 2001 Excellence in Programming Award, and the Microsoft chief architect for C#, was famous during his tenure at Borland for never once commenting even his most egregiously complex assembly language code.

And so there it is in a nutshell: Most programmers don't like to write documentation. And the great programmers, who we all want to emulate, don't always set the best example.

But I am not Anders or Linus, and most of the programmers I have met don't work on their level. For the vast majority of us, comments are one of the most useful and important tools available to us as programmers.

Nearly the entire Java JDK is beautifully commented. I use the comments in the actual JDK source file as a primary source of information about Java programming. When it comes to commenting my code, I personally try to follow the example set by the developers at Sun.

NOTE: Lest I sound too self righteous, I can assure you that I too often fail to comment my code properly. When I do so, I hurt no one so much as myself. I have spent long hours trying to piece together the current state of old projects that I failed to comment properly. So this entire chapter is in part simply a long exhortation to myself to improve my errant ways.

Man vs. the Machine

Very few programmers enjoy commenting their code. As a result, I'm going to talk a little bit about what you can do to get some decent comments in your code with the least possible amount of work.

To understand how to shape your comments, you must make an attempt to understand what it is you are trying to achieve. This quest is not as easy as some might think.

Computer languages are designed to make sense to computers, while your native language is designed to make sense to human beings. Our minds are not as precise or reliable as a computer, but they are much more flexible and sophisticated. As a result, the tightly structured, logical patterns found in computer code do not provide the best means for communicating ideas to a human reader. Our minds are not as detail oriented or logical as a CPU, but we have a capacity for generalizing and for reaching common-sense conclusions that a computer can't even begin to match.

My point here is that computer languages and human languages perform quite different tasks. When I comment my code, I try to bridge the gap between the human way of thinking and the way that computers process information.

When writing code, we lay things out step by step in very specific language. When commenting our code, we make generalizations. For instance, we say, "This object allows you to retrieve patient data from a database." Most of the time, these generalizations will mean nothing to a computer, but a person will understand what you mean.

NOTE: Don't be fooled by people who claim that generalizations or analogies are symptomatic of sloppy thinking. It is precisely our ability to generalize and draw analogies that makes humans such versatile and resourceful thinkers. Computers are not better than us because they are always specific and never generalize. Instead, their inability to perform abstract thinking severely limits their usefulness.

Computers can only parse code. They can make no sense of a sophisticated language like English. People, on the other hand, can both read English and parse code. It is just that most of us are better at reading English than we are at parsing code.

The goal of documentation is frequently to see past the details to the general tasks that are being performed. Find the abstractions that lie behind the details, and you can quickly and easily comment your code.

The Three Levels of Completeness when Commenting Code

In the following sections of the text, I will show you three different levels of code documentation. I am, at least to some degree, advocating the use of the third of these three technologies. However, as you will see, that represents something of an ideal. In the real world, I think most programmers will be lucky if they can do even a fair job of reaching the second level of commenting expertise that I am about to describe.

Code without Comments

The worst possible thing you can do is to not comment your code at all. This is also the most common state of affairs. You should avoid this barren repast at all costs. However, if you simply can't find time to comment your code, there are three things you can do to improve the situation:

- Be especially carefully with your naming conventions.
- Be careful to create objects, methods, and packages for each task in your project. Don't create one method that does three different things. The same with objects. If you discover major tasks in your project that take several objects to implement, place these related objects into their own package with a descriptive name.
- Add todo notes for every incomplete or hacked part of your code. Tell anyone who has to maintain your code what it is you have left undone.

Once again, I'm not recommending that you leave your code completely uncommented. However, taking the three steps listed above will at least help those who need to work with your code. Doing these things will also lighten the burden of reaching the second level of documentation.

Commenting Each Object and Method

If you decide you are going to comment your code, start from the outside and work toward the middle. First comment the packages, then each object, and finally each method that you create. A huge amount of good is done by even the simplest comments at the package level.

For instance, you might proceed in this order:

1. Create an overview HTML file that describes each package in your project.
2. Comment each package in a separate HTML file.
3. Open up the source files, and comment each class in your packages.
4. If there is still time left, move on to the public methods and perhaps a few of the protected methods in your objects. If you still have time, comment the data and even the private methods in your classes.

NOTE: Javadoc has a well-defined system for creating the overview, package, class, and method documentation for your projects. I will explain this entire system in the second half of this chapter.

The point here is to remember your goal: You are not trying to document the details; rather you are trying to give an overview of the code you have written. If you have time, you can get to the details, but start with the overview.

The first task is to help someone who is totally new to your code become familiar with its basic structure. To do this, write a two- or three-sentence summary of each of your packages and classes. If possible, summarize them in a single sentence. The point is to make your intent clear in the smallest number of words possible. After writing your summary, you can add more detail, but start with the summary.

Most programmers can guess at the details once they understand the structure of your program. If, for instance, you know that a data structure is a binary tree of some sort, then you don't really need an explanation of what happens when a node is added or deleted from the tree. Most programmers can figure that part out. What they need is an overview of the object itself so they don't have to parse each method in order to figure out the overall intent of your code!

By this stage, you have an understanding of how to document your project. In my opinion, this is all that most people ever need to do. However, there is a step beyond this to which you can go if you want to really make your code readable.

Fully Commenting Your Code

Fully commented code is fully comprehensible without the reader ever being forced to parse a single line of code for themselves. Consider this simple method:

```
/**
 * This method returns the first word from a string
 *
 * @param value The string to be parsed
 * @return The first word from the string passed to the method
 */
public static final String getFirstWord(String value)
{
      // remove any white space
      String cleanValue = value.trim();

      // Get the index of the first space
      int indexOfFirstSpace = cleanValue.indexOf(' ');

      // if there is only one word in the string, return it

      if ((indexOfFirstSpace == 0) || (indexOfFirstSpace == -1))
      {
            return cleanValue;
      }

      // return the first word from the string
      return cleanValue.substring(0, indexOfFirstSpace);
}
```

Read through the comments to this method without even glancing at the code. By the time you get to the end, you should have a very good sense of what this method does. You can get an in-depth knowledge of the method without reading any of the code.

There is almost a one-to-one relationship between each line of code and each comment. Instead of reading the line of code, one can simply read the comment. This is one simple way of checking your logic and ensuring that the code is well documented.

In some methods, however, there is no need to comment every single line. Instead, you can often comment a block of code, and then leave it to the user to decide how deeply they want to examine it. For instance, consider this code fragment:

```
// Copy the string one char at a time in reverse order
for(int i = 1; i < (len + 1); i++)
{
      result += stringToReverse.substring(len - i, (len - i) + 1);
}
```

Here, one comment explains four lines of code. This works out fine, since any reasonably experienced programmer can read the comment, then just glance at the mere presence of the for loop and guess what is going on.

The Technology Behind the Theory

It is now time to stop talking about commenting code and instead show how JBuilder and the Java SDK can help you create the best possible set of documentation with the least amount of work. First, this section will discuss how JBuilder helps you add comments to your code, and the next section explains how it helps you create Javadoc from those comments.

JBuilder and Comments

JBuilder can help you write well-structured comments that can be translated into Javadoc. Javadoc comments should begin with a forward slash and two asterisks: /**. The comments end with a single asterisk and forward slash: */. In between you will find comments, tags that begin with the @ symbol, and sometimes HTML tags such as <p>. All this will be explained in more depth later in the chapter. For now, let's see how JBuilder SE and Enterprise can help you write code that follows this kind of syntax.

Consider the following method declaration:

```
public static final String getFirstWord(String value)
```

After writing this declaration, place your cursor before the word public and enter a forward slash and two asterisks:

```
/**public static final String getFirstWord(String value)
```

At this stage, your cursor should be after the third character, that is, after the asterisk and before the p. Press **Enter**. JBuilder will insert the following code automatically:

```
/**
 *
 * @param value
 * @return
 */
public static final String getFirstWord(String value)
```

JBuilder inserted the additional asterisks, the closing comment, and the @param and @return tags. The commented code that has been inserted here is custom made to help you create good Javadoc files. It is now up to you to round out the comments with something like this:

```
/**
 * This is a method that returns the first word from a string.
 *
 * @param value String from which you want to retrieve the first word.
 *
 * @return The first word from the string passed in the value
 * parameter. If the string contains only one word, then the value is
 * returned. If the string is empty or null, then an empty string is
 * returned.
 */
public static final String getFirstWord(String value)
```

In the upcoming sections of the chapter, you will see that the Sun Javadoc utility will parse a comment like this and translate it into the HTML code shown in Figure 21-1.

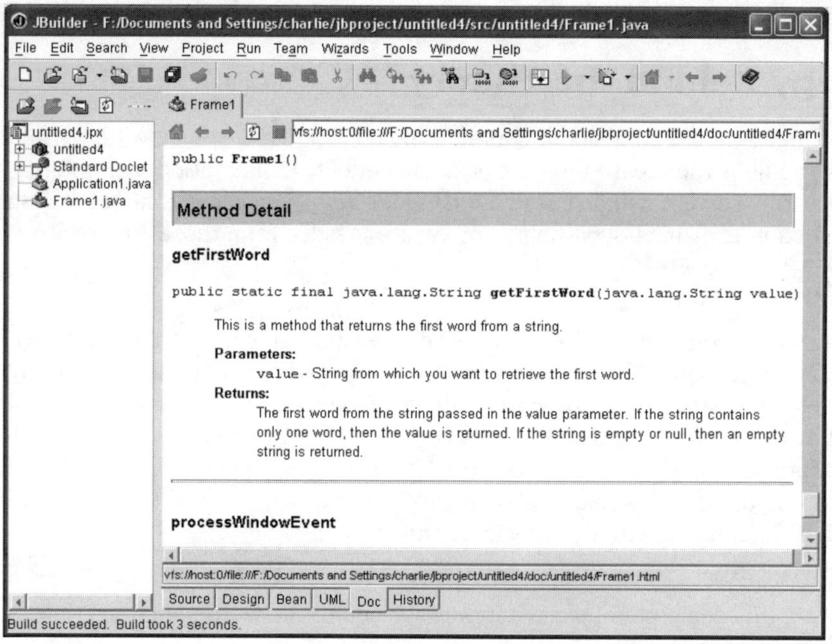

Figure 21-1: Javadoc translation of simple comments

While you are typing, all editions of JBuilder will help you write your description. For instance, if you are in the middle of a block of comments, JBuilder will automatically place a space and an asterisk at the beginning of each line you create. For instance, consider this comment:

```
/**
 * A method that returns the first word from a string.
 */
```

If you place your cursor after the second line, and then press Enter, JBuilder will write the following code for you:

```
/**
 * A method that returns the first word from a string.
 * |
 */
```

The pipe symbol on the third line of this code fragment shows where JBuilder will place your cursor. It seems like a little thing, but it can make the task of writing comments much simpler.

Additional information on creating comments is found later in this chapter in the section called "Javadoc Tags and Syntax Highlighting."

Using Javadoc

JBuilder simplifies the use of Javadoc, a tool that is part of the JDK. Javadoc pulls out the comments from your code and displays them in separate files where you can easily look at them. You can also view Javadoc files in the Doc pane of the file view tabs. For instance, if you browse to JFrame, JApplet, or any other JDK source file, and then turn to the Doc pane, you should see the Javadoc for that file.

Javadoc also allows you to document your packages and create an overview file for your entire project.

If you properly comment your code and add in the package and overview files, Javadoc can in effect document your project on the fly. Because Javadoc focuses on declarations and comments, it can be run on an early stage of a project that has code stubs standing in for completed code. As you add more methods and more comments, you can regenerate the Javadoc, thereby continually and automatically updating the documentation for your project.

Doclets

The class that contains instructions for the content and format of the output of the Javadoc tool is called a *doclet*. In the Javadoc Wizard, JBuilder will give you a choice between using the standard doclet, which is the current default, or the older JDK 1.1 doclet. Either class will generate HTML files from your comments, but the newer standard will allow you to achieve a greater level of detail.

Javadoc can be run on a package or on individual source files (files ending in .java). However, JBuilder has a strong bias toward documenting packages.

Javadoc is part of the family of Sun command-line utilities such as Jar, Javac, and Java. JBuilder has wizards in the SE and Enterprise versions of the product that really simplify the use of Javadoc.

Part IV

NOTE: If you have the Personal version of JBuilder, you might be interested in the following tools:

- Javadoc Wizard Free. This tool was developed by Gillmer Derge, whose email account is spam@gillmerderge.com. This is a free download. You can find it on http://codecentral.borland.com, as entry 15540. Here is the URL: http://codecentral.borland.com/codecentral/ccweb.exe/listing?id=15540.
- Javadoctool Personal OpenTool. It was developed by Valentino Kyriakides, who can be emailed at vkyr@lavielle.com. This shareware download is supposed to work a bit like the Javadoc Wizard. You can find the download on http://codecentral.borland.com, as entry number 17606. Here is the URL: http://codecentral.borland.com/codecentral/ccweb.exe/listing?id=17606.

You will first see how to create Javadoc files using JBuilder's tools. After that, you will look at how to work with Javadoc from the command line. Further sections of the text will show how to work with comment tags you create yourself.

If you are interested in pursuing this subject beyond the scope of this book, Sun has many pages of documentation on the Javadoc tool on its web site. At the time of publication, you could access this complete documentation by going to java.sun.com and typing javadoc into the search engine.

The Javadoc Wizard

This section describes how to use JBuilder's tools to create documentation. Begin by creating an application, as described in Chapter 3.

After creating your application, the JBuilder project pane will contain three files:

- Your project file, which has a .jpr or .jpx extension
- Application1.java
- Frame1.java

NOTE: If you chose to create a project notes file, you will see four files in the project pane.

Use the Javadoc Wizard to add a new node to this window. Go to the file view tabs on the bottom of the content pane and click on **Doc**. For now, you will see a nearly blank file.

From the main menu, choose **Wizards | Javadoc**. The Javadoc Wizard will appear. In Step 1 of the wizard, choose **Standard Doclet**, as shown in Figure 21-2.

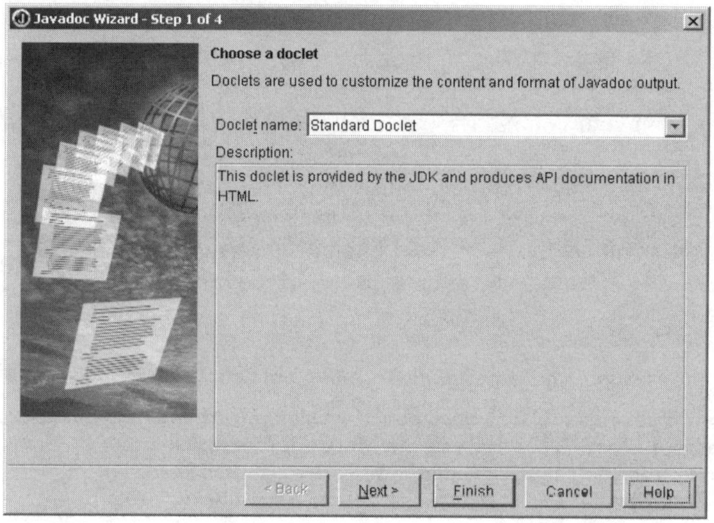

Figure 21-2: Step 1 of the Javadoc Wizard

Click **Next** to move to Step 2 of the Javadoc Wizard, as shown in Figure 21-3. Here you can change the name of your doclet and choose a directory in which to store your output. Leave the settings for these as the defaults for now. However, check **Show console output**, and deselect **Always run Javadoc when building the project**. Viewing console output will allow you to see any warnings. However, always running Javadoc on building will slow down your compile times and probably is not necessary for most people. Javadoc often improves with each version of the JDK, so select **Use project JDK when running Javadoc** if you are running your app against a newer version of the JDK than the one JBuilder uses.

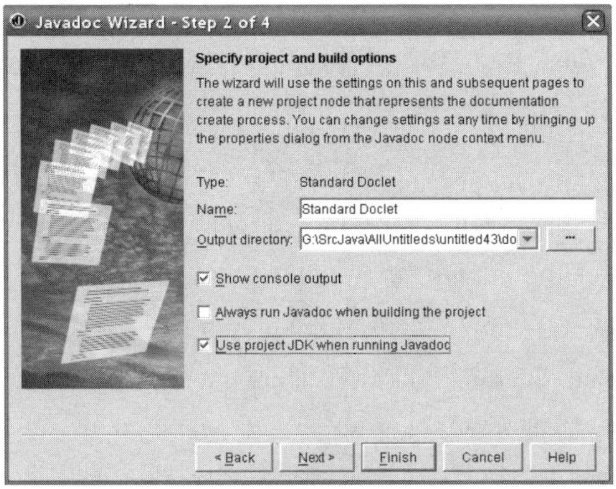

Figure 21-3: Step 2 of the Javadoc Wizard

Step 3 of the wizard allows you to pick specific packages in your project to document, as shown in Figure 21-4. The default setting is to document the entire project. If you deselect the check box for documenting the whole project, a list of the packages in the project will appear and you can add or remove packages from the list.

The radio buttons at the bottom of the Step 3 window allow you to determine the completeness of the documentation you produce. Select Public to see only public classes and members. Select Protected to document protected as well as public classes and members. Selecting Private will produce documentation on all classes and members in your project.

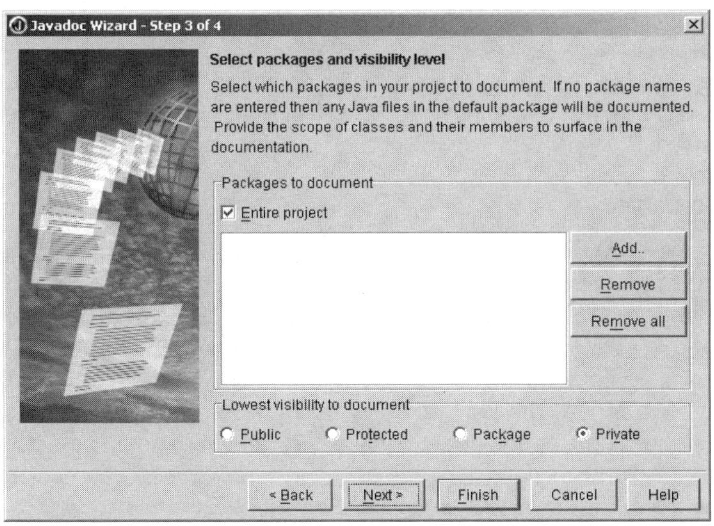

Figure 21-4: Step 3 of the Javadoc Wizard

Looking at Figure 21-4, you will notice that there is another visibility option. If you choose Package, a special file in each package will be parsed and translated into Javadoc. This is in addition to the public and protected classes in your project. The point of the Package option is to give you a way to document the packages in your project. I regard this as a very important feature and will explain it later in the chapter in the section called "Package Level Comments."

For now, select **Private**. This will give you the most complete overview of the application you have created.

When you click **Next** and move to Step 4, the process of setting the content of your documentation continues, as shown in Figure 21-5. For this example, check all the standard options and tags listed in the wizard, except for Separate index per letter.

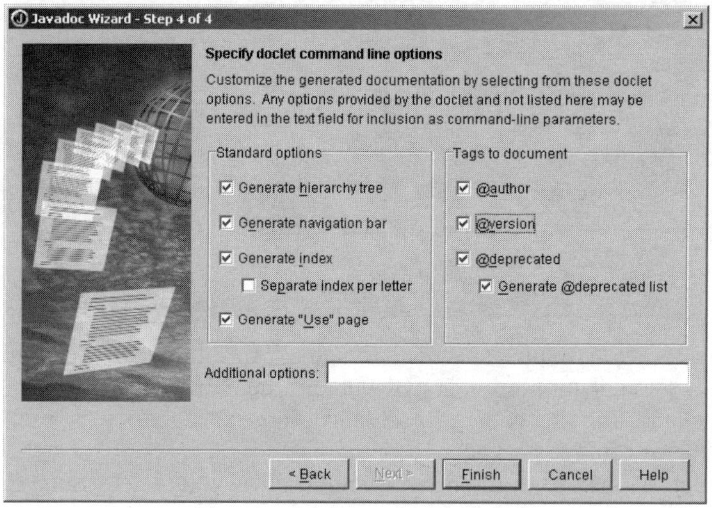

Figure 21-5: Step 4 of the Javadoc Wizard

There is a text field where you can specify additional options. Examples of using this field are found in the "Overview Comments" and "Javadoc Options" sections later in this chapter.

Click **Finish.** As soon as you exit the Javadoc Wizard, you will see a new node called Standard Doclet in your project pane.

It is possible at any time to change the decisions you made in the Javadoc Wizard. Right-click on **Standard Doclet**, and choose **Properties.** You will again have access to the pages you have just used.

Generating Documentation

Use the Windows Explorer, KDE Konqueror, or some other file browser to examine the directory where your project is stored. You will see a classes directory and a src directory. If you have not yet run the Javadoc Wizard, there will be no directory called doc. (For the sake of this discussion, delete the directory if it does exist. The entire contents of the directory can be recreated by the Javadoc Wizard.)

Go back to JBuilder and choose the **Doc** file view tab in the AppBrowser. Now switch back to your file browser, and note that a doc directory has been added to your project.

NOTE: If you deleted the doc file from your project directory and then choose the Doc file view tab, you may see an alert stating that there is a problem. If you do, choose another file view tab and then refocus on the Doc file view tab. The problem should resolve itself when you do this. The doc directory will be created when you focus on the Doc tab the second time.

This new directory will contain an HTML file. This same file will appear in your JBuilder content pane when the Doc tab is selected, as shown in Figure 21-6. This file was generated by JBuilder and is not part of the standard doclet.

Make sure that the Doc file view tab on the content pane is selected now, so that you will be able to see what happens next.

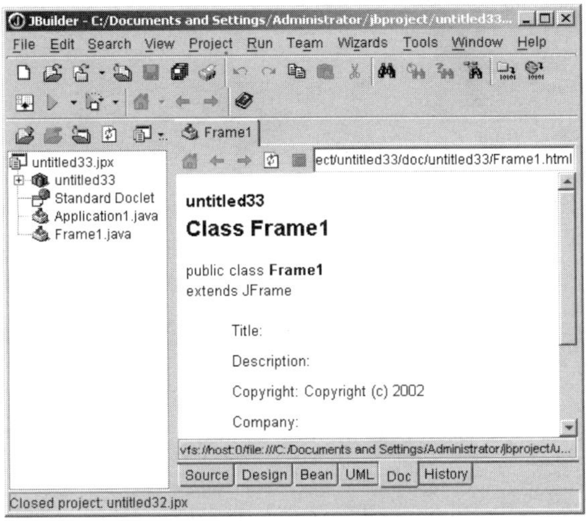

Figure 21-6: The Doc pane before running the doclet

Right-click on **Standard Doclet**. In the pop-up menu, choose **Make.** The comments and code in your source files will be automatically converted into HTML documentation stored in the doc directory. Open up the doclet node in the project pane. Select **index.html**. You will see the official Javadoc documentation for your project appear in the content pane, as shown in Figure 21-7.

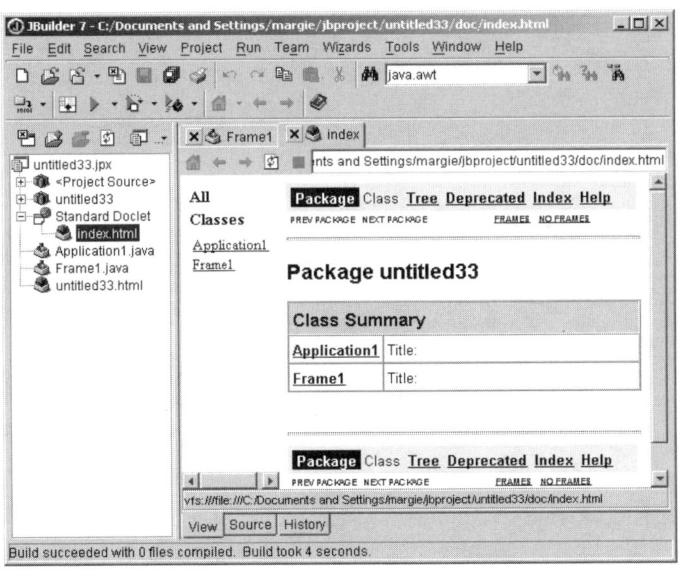

Figure 21-7: The Doc pane after running the doclet and selecting index.html from the doclet node in the project pane

If you check on the files in the doc directory, you will now see quite a few new files, as shown in Figure 21-8. You can open them directly from your file browser if you wish to see them; they can be viewed like any other files of their type. For instance, you can view the HTML files from your Internet browser. To do this, just double-click on **index.html**.

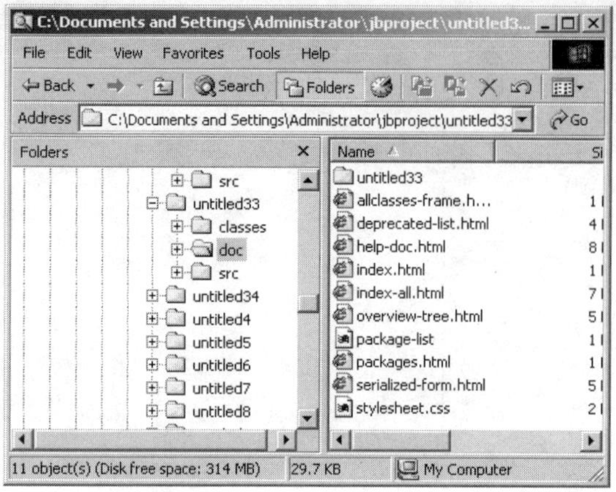

Figure 21-8: The Doc directory contains new documentation files.

NOTE: For more information on viewing the Javadoc files, see the section near the end of this chapter titled "Viewing the Javadoc Files in a Browser."

Understanding the Javadoc Files

View the index.html file, which is the Package or overview page. You can see it in the doc pane, as shown in Figure 21-9. From there you can choose links to the classes in your package, in this case, Application1 and Frame1.

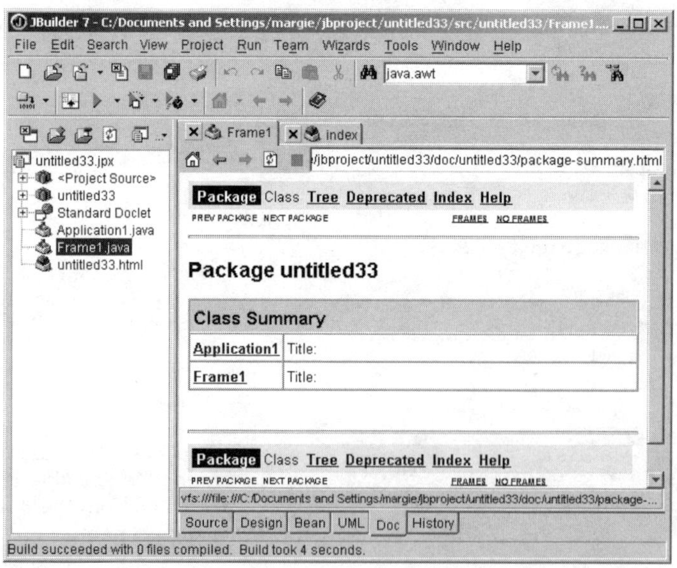

Figure 21-9: The overview or Package page

NOTE: Select Ctrl+Alt+Z to get more viewing area by closing the message, project, and structure panes.

From the Package page you can access the rest of the documentation. Click **Application1**. You will move to the Class page, shown in Figure 21-10. Here you can see that Application1 inherits from java.lang.Object. This page contains a description of the class, and documents all of its fields, methods, and constructors. A list of all inherited methods is included. Notice that when you are in the Class page, the links to the other documentation pages are all active.

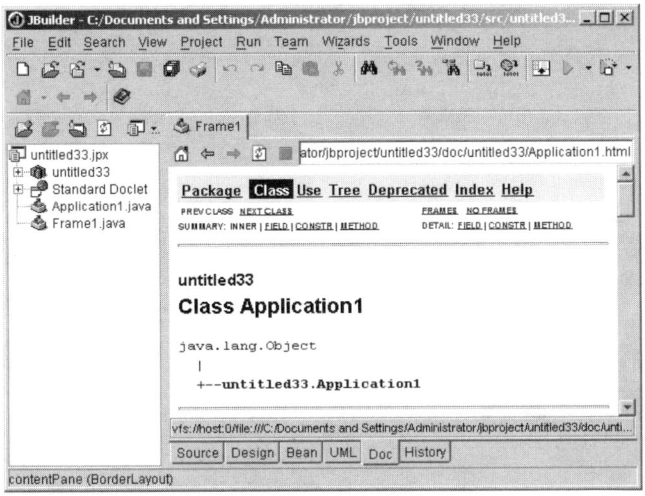

Figure 21-10: The Class page

Now move to the Tree page, which will show the class hierarchy for your package, as shown in Figure 21-11.

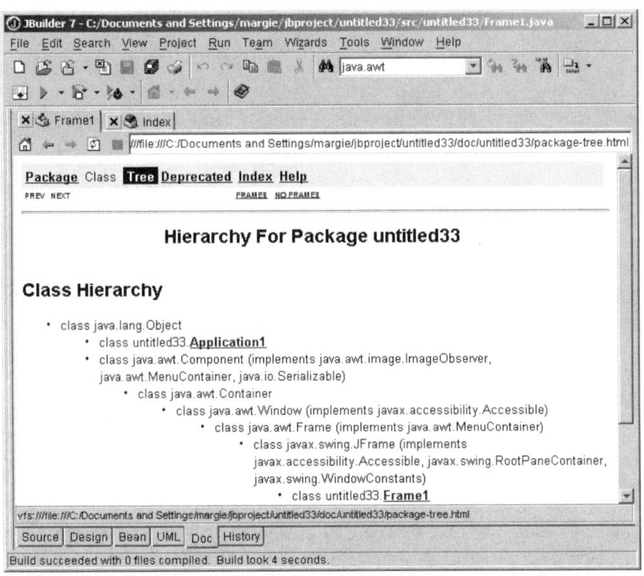

Figure 21-11: The Class hierarchy

If you click on Index in the navigation bar, you will be able to access information about all the component parts of the package, as shown in Figure 21-12. For instance, find **Application1** in the Index page. The Index page identifies it as a class. If you click on it, JBuilder will bring you to the Class page for Frame1.

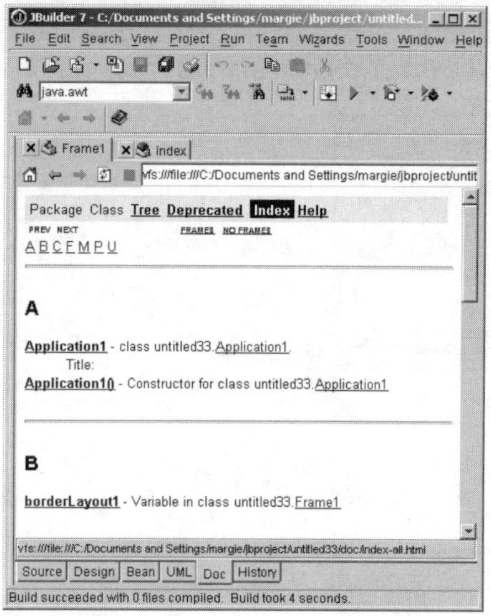

Figure 21-12: The Index page

In addition to the pages we have looked at, the Use page lists the code elements that use any part of the package, class, or interface you are exploring. The Deprecated page would indicate any use of deprecated code. Be aware that these pages are not always generated. They will appear only if you checked that you wanted to document the @use and @deprecated tags in Page 4 of the Javadoc Wizard. The Help page gives you an overview of all of the pages, and is well worth perusing.

It is often useful to view the documentation generated by Javadoc through a browser that is open and directed at the index.html file of the docs directory, instead of using the content pane. If you are regenerating pages, try this approach, as JBuilder can have refresh problems. See the section near the end of this chapter called "Viewing the Javadoc Files in a Browser" for hints on how to do this.

Package Level Comments

I mentioned earlier that there is a way to generate Javadoc that includes comments about your packages. These comments show up in the Javadoc files if you choose Package or Private from the Javadoc Wizard, as shown in Figure 21-4.

The basic technique to employ is very simple. In each package that you create, you should include a file called package.html. The source for this file might be based on the official Sun template for package files, shown in Listing 21-1.

Listing 21-1: The official template from Sun for generating Javadoc comments for each package that you create. Delete the sections enclosed in #### symbols.

```
<!DOCTYPE HTML PUBLIC "-//W3C//DTD HTML 3.2 Final//EN">
<html>
<head>
<!–

  @(#)package.html 1.60 98/01/27

  Copyright 1998 Sun Microsystems, Inc. 901 San Antonio Road,
```

```
    Palo Alto, California, 94303, U.S.A.  All Rights Reserved.

    This software is the confidential and proprietary information of Sun
    Microsystems, Inc. ("Confidential Information").  You shall not
    disclose such Confidential Information and shall use it only in
    accordance with the terms of the license agreement you entered into
    with Sun.

    CopyrightVersion 1.2

  -->
  </head>
  <body bgcolor="white">

  ##### THIS IS THE TEMPLATE FOR THE PACKAGE DOC COMMENTS. #####
  ##### TYPE YOUR PACKAGE COMMENTS HERE.  BEGIN WITH A      #####
  ##### ONE-SENTENCE SUMMARY STARTING WITH A VERB LIKE:     #####
  Provides for....


  <h2>Package Specification</h2>

  ##### FILL IN ANY SPECS NEEDED BY JAVA COMPATIBILITY KIT #####
  <ul>
    <li><a href="">##### REFER TO ANY FRAMEMAKER SPECIFICATION HERE #####</a>
  </ul>

  <h2>Related Documentation</h2>

  For overviews, tutorials, examples, guides, and tool documentation, please see:
  <ul>
    <li><a href="">##### REFER TO NON-SPEC DOCUMENTATION HERE #####</a>
  </ul>

  <!-- Put @see and @since tags down here. -->

  </body>
  </html>
```

The source code between the body tags of your package.html files will be inserted into the package pages of your Javadoc source files. By providing this kind of information, you are on the way to providing quite complete documentation for your project.

In the source code included on the CD for this book, you will find examples of this kind of file for the more complex projects. For instance, the GridWorld and Breakout programs have package files.

Please note that the package.html file should be placed in the same directory as your java source files. Furthermore, you won't see the file included in your Javadoc unless you choose Package in the Javadoc Wizard, as shown in Figure 21-4.

If you are working from the command line, append the command -package to the end of your list of arguments to the Javadoc utility. Techniques for working from the command line are explained in the section titled "Working with Javadoc from the Command Line."

Overview Comments

By this time you have had a chance to comment most aspects of your project. The only thing that is missing is the overview of the entire program. Unfortunately, JBuilder's support for this particular feature is not the best, although you can make it work just fine if you are willing to put up with a small inconvenience.

Javadoc automatically creates an overview page for each project it creates, as shown in Figure 21-9. This file is called index.html, and it is the first page in all Javadoc projects.

Fortunately, Javadoc provides a means for letting you add text to the overview page. By convention, you should create a file called overview.html and place it in the root of your project. When running Javadoc from the command line, pass in a parameter called -overview that points at this file. Javadoc will parse your overview file and place the first sentence from it at the top of the overview file. It will then append the entirety of the document, including your first sentence, to the end of the overview file.

It turns out that JBuilder provides a field on the last page of the Javadoc Wizard that lets you pass in any arbitrary commands you want to Javadoc. The field, called Additional Options, is visible in Figure 21-5. In theory, we could just pass in the following to this field:

```
-overview overview.html
```

Unfortunately, this won't work because the system won't be able to find overview.html unless you specify the path to it in more detail.

The problem comes in specifying the path to your file without hard-coding in the drive and directory where your project is stored. If you hard-code in the drive or directory, you will have problems if you try to move the project to a new location.

I finally gave up trying to find a way around this issue and just hard-coded the information:

```
-overview G:/SrcJava/jbbook/Games/Breakout/Breakout.html
```

Obviously, you should edit the code to reflect the name and location of the project with which you are working.

To edit a standard doclet, go to the Standard Doclet node you placed in the project pane. Right-click and select **Properties.**

NOTE: When you create a project in JBuilder, it will generate an HTML file in your project's root directory. The file will usually have the same name as your project. If you edit this file properly it can serve as the file that Javadoc will insert into the overview file for your Javadoc project. The advantage to doing this is that it will be easily found by other developers who open your project, and also by people who reference your Javadoc.

One final word is necessary here. A few of the projects on the CD that accompanies this book have overview files that are best read as part of the Javadoc output. These files will ship on the CD. However, if you want to update them, I will usually have a batch file or a Jakarta Ant build.xml file that can be run from the command line. By using these tools you can automatically regenerate the Javadoc for my projects without concern for the paths of my original project. In other words, the command-line version of Javadoc allows me to use relative paths to this file, even if JBuilder does not.

Javadoc Tags and Syntax Highlighting

If you use a Java language keyword or name, you should enclose it in <code></code> tags to give it the appropriate "syntax highlighted" look in your HTML file. The elements covered by this include:

- Java keywords
- Package names
- Class names
- Method names
- Interface names
- Field names
- Argument names
- Code examples

The complete set of rules and suggestions for writing Javadoc comments lies beyond the scope of this book. However, the Sun site has great documentation on this.

After you have written your description, the next part of the comment often includes one or more tags. There are actually two kinds of tags. These tags begin with an @ symbol and are translated into some form of attractive HTML inside of your Javadoc files.

A stand-alone tag, such as @param, must be placed after a blank space following the asterisk at the beginning of the comment line. If you place it somewhere else in the text, Javadoc will not recognize it. The stand-alone tags include @author, @deprecated, @exception, @link, @param, @return, @see, @serial, @serialData, @serialField, @since, @throws, and @version.

An inline tag is set off by curly braces. The curly braces alert Javadoc that the inline tag is a tag and can be parsed from anywhere in the comment. The inline tags include: {@docRoot}, {@inheritDoc}, {@link}, {@linkplain}, and {@value}. Several of the inline tags, including {@inheritDoc}, {@linkplain}, and {@value}, are new with Java 1.4.

For an up-to-date list of tags and their uses, go to the java.sun.com site and search under javadoc for the javadoc documentation. Currently the information for java version 1.4 is at http://java.sun.com/j2se/1.4/docs/tooldocs/win32/javadoc.html#javadoctags.

Part IV

Javadoc Options

For more information on the Additional Options field, consult the JBuilder Help index page and find "javadoc documentation viewing, for entire project" and under it "command line options." Scroll down and you will find a list of options not set in the wizard. Another way to get a list of command-line options is to go to your command prompt and type **javadoc –help**. A third way to access the command-line options is to go to java.sun.com. The information is currently at http://java.sun.com/j2se/1.3/docs/tooldocs/win32/javadoc.html#javadocoptions.

Here is the list of command-line options which, according to JBuilder Help, are not set in the wizard. The explanations here are truncated versions of the information available at java.sun.com and are taken directly from Sun's documentation. Please refer to the documentation at java.sun.com for further information about using command-line options.

Option	Description
-overview *path\filename*	Specifies that javadoc should retrieve the text for the overview documentation from the "source" file specified by *path\filename* and place it on the overview page (overview-summary.html). The *path\filename* is relative to the -sourcepath.
-help	Displays the online help, which lists these Javadoc and doclet command-line options.
-J*flag*	Passes *flag* directly to the runtime JDK that runs Javadoc. (For example, this could be used for memory allocation.)
-locale *language_country_variant*	Specifies the locale that Javadoc uses when generating documentation. Options include en_US (English, United States) or en_US_WIN (Windows variant).
-doctitle *title*	Specifies the title to be placed near the top of the overview summary file.
-windowtitle *title*	Specifies the title to be placed in the HTML <title> tag.
-header *header*	Specifies the header text to be placed at the top of each output file. The header will be placed to the right of the upper navigation bar.
-footer *footer*	Specifies the footer text to be placed at the bottom of each output file. The footer will be placed to the right of the lower navigation bar.
-bottom *text*	Specifies the text to be placed at the bottom of each output file. The text will be placed at the bottom of the page, below the lower navigation bar.
-link *extdocURL*	Creates links to already existing Javadoc-generated documentation of external referenced classes. The argument *extdocURL* is the URL for the external documentation you want to link to.
-linkoffline *extdocURL packagelistLoc*	You must use this option instead of -link if, at the time you run Javadoc, the external document's package-list file does not exist at the *extdocURL* location (is "offline") but exists at a different location *packagelistLoc* (typically local).
-group *groupheading packagepattern:packagepattern:...*	Separates packages on the overview page into whatever groups you specify, one group per table.
-nosince	Omits from the generated docs the "Since" sections associated with the @since tags.
-nohelp	Omits the Help link in the navigation bars at the top and bottom of each page of output.
-helpfile *path\filename*	Specifies the path of an alternate help file *path\filename* that the Help links in the top and bottom navigation bars link to. Without this option, Javadoc automatically creates a help file help-doc.html that is hard-coded in Javadoc.
-stylesheetfile *path\filename*	Specifies the path of an alternate HTML stylesheet file. Without this option, Javadoc automatically creates a stylesheet file stylesheet.css that is hard-coded in Javadoc.
-serialwarn	Generates compile-time warnings for missing @serial tags. By default, Javadoc 1.2.2 (and later versions) generates no serial warnings.

-charset *name*	Specifies the HTML character set for this document.
-doencoding *name*	Specifies the encoding of the generated HTML files.

If you are tempted to set an option in the Additional Options field that is not listed above, be aware that setting an option here will override any other choices you made about that option in the wizard.

Viewing the Javadoc Files in a Browser

Depending on your goals, JBuilder is not always the best way to view Javadoc. If you want help on a particular class, JBuilder is great. However, I find it a bit restricting when I want to browse through a whole set of Javadoc files.

One solution is to add Internet Explorer or some other browser to the JBuilder Tools menu. Then you will be able to launch the browser, with your source files displayed in it, from inside JBuilder.

Select **Tools | Configure Tools** from the JBuilder menu to bring up the Configure Tools dialog. Click the **Add** button to bring up the Add Tool dialog.

In the Add Tool dialog, type in the name of your browser in the Title field. In the Program field, use the ellipsis button to browse for your browser's main file. In the case of Internet Explorer, that is usually C:\Program Files\Internet Explorer\IEXPLORE.EXE. In the Parameters field, add the **($FilePath)** macro. Press **OK** to close the Add Tool dialog and **Close** to close the Configure Tools dialog. Go to **Standard Doclet** in the project pane and expand its nodes. Use the mouse to focus Index.html from Standard Doclet in the content pane. Now you can select your newly added browser option from the Tools menu and your Javadoc source will appear inside of it.

While we are on this topic, I should mention that JBuilder keeps its help files and JDK help files in JAR files in the JBuilder installation. Go to the JBuilder7/doc directory and pick a JAR file. For instance, you might select jdk13docs.jar. Use a standard extractor program such as the jar utility or WinZip to decompress the files. You can then view them in the Windows Explorer or the KDE Konqueror. This can sometimes be more convenient than accessing the help files through the menu, as the file is completely independent of what you are doing in the JBuilder GUI.

It should be obvious that you can combine the two technologies discussed in this section to automatically access the JDK help in Internet Explorer or KDE Konqueror with only one click of the mouse on the Tools menu. Use the technology explained above for adding a second listing for your browser to the Tools menu. Instead of placing ($FilePath) in the Parameters field, place the path to where you decompressed the JDK help files. Make sure you reference the index.html file that is the start page for the whole JDK help system. When you launch Internet Explorer or KDE Konqueror from the JBuilder menu, these browsers will now come up with the JDK docs selected and ready to browse. You can Alt+Tab back and forth between the browser and JBuilder.

NOTE: If you are working with JBuilder 7 but are using JDK switching to support Java 1.4 as your development platform, you can use this technique to easily "integrate" the Java 1.4 docs into the IDE.

Working with Javadoc from the Command Line

JBuilder helps you document your code with Javadoc quickly. If you operate from the command line, you have to do a little more typing, but you are still able to generate appropriate comments through Javadoc. You could use this technique to help you automate a build process with batch files or scripts. You might also work from the command line to generate Javadoc if you have the Personal version of JBuilder.

All of the options you used inside of JBuilder are available from the command line. In fact, if you look at the output from Javadoc in the message pane, you will see that JBuilder simply runs the Sun Javadoc tools.

When working from the command line, here is the basic formula to follow:

```
javadoc –d [destination directory] –sourcepath [source directory] packagename.
```

The destination directory is the directory where you want your Javadoc files to be stored. The source directory is the name of the directory where your java source files are stored. The packagename is the root package directory where you want documentation to begin.

To identify the source directory for your Javadoc documentation, you could either change to the appropriate directory or type -sourcepath to give the path to the package or class you wish to document. For instance, if you were in the C drive and you wanted to document a package called myproject located in e:\personal\test\src and put the output HTML files in e:\personal\test\docs, the command line would look like this:

```
javadoc -d e:\personal\test\docs -sourcepath e:\personal\test\src myproject
```

If you were in the directory [e:\personal\test] and wanted to put the document files in a docs directory, you could use a relative rather than an absolute path. For instance, the command line would look like this:

```
[e:\personal\test] javadoc -d docs -sourcepath src myproject
```

It is possible to document a single file in a package. In that case, you would not need the -sourcepath command. Instead, you would give the relative or absolute path to the file you wish to document:

```
javadoc -d docs src\myproject\Application1.java
```

If you wanted to document more than one file, you would just append the name of the additional file to your existing command line.

In step 3 of the Javadoc Wizard, you were choosing other command-line options, including the lowest visibility to document — public, package, protected, or private. These radio buttons corresponded to options which could be written from the command line as -public, -package, -protected, and -private. Step 4 of the wizard gives you additional options for tags and command-line options. To select one of these using the command line, you would just list it after your other entered information. For example:

```
javadoc -d docs src\myproject\Frame1.java -package
```

Here is an example of a command that uses an overview file:

```
javadoc -d doc -package -sourcepath src -overview src/overview.html breakouts
```

Summary

In this chapter you have learned about commenting your code and automatically creating documentation with Javadoc. I have spent a considerable period of time covering this subject for two reasons:

- I believe documenting your code is important. All across the world there are thousands of programmers who inherit code from other developers. These programmers are performing a very difficult task. Every day that they are delayed in completing their work costs their employers hundreds, and usually thousands, of dollars. Few things can help ease this situation more than proper documentation of source code.
- The Javadoc utility provides a very powerful means for documenting your code. If you understand how to use it, you can save yourself and others a great deal of time and trouble.

Getting programmers to document their code is a bit like getting a child to take a bad-tasting medicine; most of them don't like to do it. Javadoc, however, is actually a very pleasing system. If you understand how it works, it can be a pleasure to use.

Chapter 22

Modularity

Charlie Calvert

This chapter is about package, class, and method composition. The major theme is the need to simplify code by dividing and conquering.

In most cases, programming should not be difficult. If it is difficult, that is usually due to a fault in the design of a program.

When you are writing code, your major goal should be to be as clear and straightforward as possible. If you have completed your project, find that everything is working perfectly, and then discover that there is some area where performance is a serious issue, you should start thinking about optimizing your code. But in most cases, optimization is a secondary consideration. It's not a non-issue, but in most cases it is not a primary concern.

The primary cause of concern in most programs is handling the sheer bulk of code required to get serious work done. Serious programs require large volumes of code. As a result, your emphasis has to be on reducing the complexity as much as possible. Keep things simple and architect your program so that it is easy to maintain and as modular as possible.

The Aesthetics of Programming

In this chapter, I will make very few absolute statements. Instead, most of my comments will be prefaced by words such as "most of the time" or "whenever possible." The point is that this chapter deals in the aesthetics of programming, not in facts that can be scientifically proved.

There are no hard facts when it comes to aesthetics. Most of the time it is a mistake to create a book that is not divided into chapters. Yet there may be occasions when it is appropriate. Most of the time it is a mistake to create a single paragraph that runs on for 20 pages, yet there are times when it is appropriate. Most of the time it is wrong to include nude children in a painting, yet sometimes it is appropriate. For instance, Michelangelo was not creating an aesthetic or moral blunder by including cherubs or other nude figures in his paintings. There are many poems and even some novels that lack capital letters. Some great novels don't have quotation marks around spoken words.

It is, of course, a mistake to assume that because no hard rules can be established in an area, then no rules should be created at all. For instance, the fact that there is no hard rule as to when to divide material into paragraphs doesn't mean that paragraphs should be abandoned. The fact that there is nudity in the Bible doesn't mean that all books can or should contain nudity. The fact that e.e. cummings, a respected poet, didn't capitalize any of the words in his poems doesn't mean that capitalization should be abandoned in poetry.

In this chapter the talk is about ways to create code that is easy to read and easy to understand. This is not a hard science. Yet it is possible to establish guidelines that most programmers should follow in most situations.

It is okay to break a rule once you are sure you understand it. No one doubts that e.e. cummings knew how to properly capitalize the words in a sentence. Molly Bloom's soliloquy at the end of *Ulysses* does not follow the standard rules of English grammar, but no one doubts that James Joyce knew how to write proper English when required. As a result, it's okay for these authors to break some generally accepted rules. If you know how to follow the rules in this chapter and you have actually followed them in many large programs, then you can begin to think about breaking them under certain circumstances. Most, of the time, however, I would like to think of them as helpful guidelines that are worth following.

The Divide and Conquer Aesthetic

The packages and classes in a project should to some degree "tell the story" of a program. You should be able to understand a project not only by reading its code, but also by reading the names of its classes and packages.

If you have a long complex object that performs several discrete tasks, it may need to be broken out into several objects. If you have a long complex method that performs several discrete tasks, it may need to be broken out into several methods. If you have a lot of classes in one package, they may need to be broken out into several packages.

There are times when you must create big classes, long methods, or complex packages. But it should not happen very often. If a particular programmer's projects are always appearing in one large package, something is almost certainly wrong. If someone writes a lot of big objects that perform several totally discrete tasks, something is usually very wrong. If someone writes a series of long methods, and especially if many of those methods contain repetitive code, something is almost certainly wrong.

Repetition will creep into code. It should at least be recognized as an error. The repeated code should be parsed out into discrete methods or objects that can be easily called.

The presence of repetitive code in a project is a sign that the code needs to be factored into discrete methods or classes. Another common clue is simply that the code is difficult to reuse. If you say, "Oh heck, it will be easier to rewrite it than to try to reuse it," you know something has gone wrong.

The trick, of course, is to discover when you should divide things up and when you really need to engage a lot of complexity in a single package, method, or class.

In a sense, there are two battles that need to be fought:

- The first battle is between chaos and order. If you have one class, method, or package that is performing five different tasks, most of the time that code will be poorly organized, hard to understand, and generally chaotic. So the first battle is to create order out of chaos by properly segmenting the different parts of your program.
- The second battle is between order and size. In some cases, the simplest, most orderly way to arrange things is to put a lot of code in one method or class, or to put a lot of different classes in one package. The problem comes when this sense of order forces you to create classes that are just too big to understand. At some point, many programmers will want to break up a method, class, or package just because it is too large. At the same time, there are cases when a sense of order will indicate that large passages of code belong in one package, class, or method. It is not always easy to make such decisions. In these difficult cases, there is a struggle between order and size. Most of the time, a big class, package, or method is trying to do too much. But sometimes a big

method really does focus on one discrete idea. If it contains no repetitive code and it is easy to reuse, why break it up? There should be an ongoing battle between the desire to simplify your code by segmenting it and the desire to encapsulate related code in one method, class, or package.

The goal of this chapter is to try to reconcile these opposing forces. This is not a simple task.

Usable, Extensible, and Abstract

In his book *Delphi Component Design*, Danny Thorpe talks about the importance of creating classes that are usable, extensible, and abstract.

The main point Mr. Thorpe emphasizes is that classes should be designed to be reusable: "...the component writer's highest priority at all times is to make components that are useful to the application writer, that are easy to use, and that have clear and bulletproof public interfaces." Here he is talking about building classes specifically designed to be used by other programmers. But in this day and age, who writes code that will not be read by other people? We are all writing code that will be used by others, and so we should all follow Mr. Thorpe's guidelines whenever possible.

Even if we are likely to be the only person who will use the code, still there is the problem of code that sticks around year, after year, after year. Code that you wrote five or ten years ago might as well have been written by someone else. Hardly anyone remembers details over that long a period of time. As a result, you will do yourself a favor if you create code that is easy to maintain and reuse.

Objects and Scope: Hide as Much as Possible

Making it possible to extend an object is in part a question of properly manipulating the private, protected, and public sections of a class. It is not easy to decide which segments of a class will be visible only to other classes inside one source file (private) or one package (protected) and which sections of a class will be public to all comers.

Probably every Java programmer knows the experience of moving a class from one package to another and suddenly finding that the code no longer compiles because of scoping issues. In particular, the class that you moved may call protected methods of classes in the package where it formally resided.

If two classes are so closely linked that they need to call each other's protected methods, they belong in the same class. If it becomes clear that they belong in separate packages, they never should have been calling each other's protected methods. There should be a clear, simple, public interface that exposes only the necessary portions of each class.

Again, we are looking at a battle with no clear path to victory. We should hide all the data and every possible method behind the strongest possible scoping rules. Many of the best objects expose only one public method as an entry point, along with a constructor or a method that follows the singleton pattern. But which methods should be public, and which objects can afford to have only the sparsest interface?

NOTE: In this section of the text, I am mostly using the word "interface" in an abstract sense. I am not necessarily referring to the Java type called an Interface. When I do, I will capitalize it.

There is a need to abstract the interface of a class. One class should not know very much about another class. Instead, the interface between them should be as abstract and generalized as possible. Often the best means of doing this is by creating an Interface.

When thinking about scope, the lessons are simple:

- Batten down the hatches. Hide everything that can possibly be hidden behind private methods in a discrete class that resides in its own source file.
- Never expose any of the data from your class other than immutable constants.
- Revisit the public methods for your class again and again and see if there is some way to change them into private methods.
- Make the public interface to your class as simple as possible. A single access point to a class is ideal.

At several points in this book I talk about tasks that you can do on those days when you are too tired to do any real work. Changing public methods to private is one of those "busy work" tasks that you can do while waiting for a phone call or when you only have 20 minutes after a meeting before you go out to lunch.

Performance Issues

Though it might not be obvious at first, simple code usually helps developers create the fastest, most robust programs. Code that is divided into discrete objects encourages reuse. As it turns out, reuse is usually the easiest of all possible ways to create small, fast programs.

When I first pursued the techniques described in this chapter, I feared my efforts at dividing up code into smaller methods and objects would add bulk to my program. In the end, it had the opposite effect. I reused the code in the small methods and small objects that I created, thus avoiding repetition. My programs were smaller and faster than they would have been had I used my original, and supposedly more efficient, code.

I feared that the overhead of creating objects or making method calls was going to be prohibitively expensive. Ten or fifteen years ago, there might have been some truth to that kind of argument. But modern compilers and CPUs have pretty much put that kind of concern to rest. On a 2 GHz processor, a method call is now so inexpensive as to have virtually no impact on your program.

Looked at in another way, a 30-line method is likely to have at least 20 method calls to the JDK in it. Suppose you divide up that method into two 15-line methods. Add in the extra call to the new method, and you now have not 20 method calls but 21. Do you really think that having 21 method calls rather than 20 method calls is going to significantly impact the performance of your program? Unless the method call is in the middle of a huge, extremely time-sensitive loop, the answer is absolutely no: It is not going to make the least difference. One single pass of the garbage collector will have a much bigger impact on your program. The point is that many developers have an irrational concern about calling their own methods, even though they are busily calling the JDK in every three out of four lines of their code.

Code broken out into discrete classes and methods is also much easier to reuse. The goal here is to reuse your code.

Remember a point I made earlier in the text: In real-world programs, when creating JPanel or JFrame descendants, you should either be creating a completely reusable class or have almost zero potentially reusable code in the class. If you create an event handler for a JButton, that actionPerformed method should do little other than call into some other discrete object that does the real work. Unless you can reuse the entire panel or frame, don't put any serious code in the event handlers for the panel or frame. Simply include code that references a second object that does the real work.

For instance, if you write code for transferring files using HTTP, don't put that code inside a JPanel or JFrame descendant unless you intend for people to always reuse your entire class. Instead, put the code inside a class called HTTPTransfer. Then your current JFrame or JPanel descendant can call that class, as can any other JPanel or JFrame descendants. The code is reusable. Code sitting inside a jButton1_ActionPerformed method for a JFrame descendant is usually impossible to reuse. Don't put anything important in those methods.

Simple, easy-to-read code is good in and of itself. An actionPerformed method that contains a one- or two-line call to a class that transfers a file via HTTP is a lot easier to read than an actionPerformed method that contains the 20 or 30 lines of code dedicated to making the transfer.

The golden rule here is to remember to give each class only one major function. If the JPanel descendant is going to have one button on it and that one button calls a 20-line piece of code to transfer a file, then everything is probably okay. But if the JPanel descendant has 20 buttons on it and each button calls a separate 20-line ActionPerformed method, then you don't have a class, you have chaos. In this latter case, you should dedicate the JPanel to getting input from the user, and then delegate the handling of those user requests to separate, easily reusable objects.

How Much Complexity is Enough Complexity?

All hundred thousand line programs are complex. That statement is true by definition. So you are going to encounter plenty of complexity if you write serious programs. The choice you have is whether you want to write a hundred thousand line program that is complex and impossible to debug and maintain or whether you want to write a hundred thousand line program that is complex but still maintainable.

The benefit you derive from simplicity, modularity, and reusability is that you will make your deadlines and can maintain your code more easily. You can find and fix the bugs in code that is modular and easy to read. If necessary, you can hopefully break out the various chunks of your larger program and test them in smaller, easier to understand programs.

The tide in big programs doesn't ebb and flow. It is always flooding in. The urge will always be to write code that is not reusable. The urge will always be to have lots of repetition in your programs. It is a constant battle to try to defeat these forces.

At first, it takes more time to write an object that you can reuse than it does to stuff a bunch of code into the current method or class of your program. But if you do make your code modular, you will save time in the long run.

Just as importantly, you will save your fellow workers a lot of headaches. Simple, modular, easy-to-read code is good for no other reason than that it is simple and easy to read.

It is best if you get to the point where you like simple and easy-to-read code. Simple code is elegant code. It has its own aesthetic charm, which is greater than the charm of other code, no matter how complex it might be.

Java the Exemplar to the Rescue

When Java first came out, thousands of programmers who had labored long in the world of C++ regarded it as something of a miracle. Projects that took years to write in C++ could be completed in Java in a matter of a few months. A six-month project in C++ could be completed in Java in two months.

What was the big difference? Why was Java so much easier to use than C++?

There are a number of answers to that question, but perhaps the most important was that the Java language provided a rich set of simple, easy-to-use objects that got real work done fast. Java itself is the best possible advocate I could have for the techniques I stress in this chapter.

Look at the standards in the Java world that have really caught on. Classic examples include JUnit, Ant, the Java networking classes, and the Applet and JApplet classes. These are all examples of simple, easy-to-use code that has burned a swath through the developer community.

Planning Your Code

The next section of the text is divided into three subsections, some of which have in turn their own subsections. The first topic taken up will be techniques for discovering objects. I then talk about composing methods and wind up with a brief discussion of discovering packages.

Discovering the Objects in a Problem

There is no single concept that can save you more time or trouble than the simple idea of dividing your code into discrete, reusable classes.

Let's go back for a moment to a problem discussed in Chapter 6. In that chapter I discussed the problem of creating a Java grep tool. A grep tool allows you to look through multiple files for a particular string. For instance, you might want to look through all the source files in your project for instances of the word "DefaultModel." In JBuilder, if you choose Search | Find In Path, you will encounter a tool of this type. However, in this chapter I am discussing a stand-alone version of this type of program.

A tool of this kind should present users with an interface that allows them to define what directories they want to search, a place to enter the string they want to search on, and most likely an extension that will allow them to filter out files that need not be searched. For instance, if you want to search through your source files, you will want to look in files with the extension .java and ignore files with the extensions .exe or .class.

Given this problem, what is the worst possible solution that a programmer could find in terms of design? The worst case would be a single class, with a single method, that was some 10,000 lines in length. The problem is that one method, called main, is performing multiple discrete tasks. It is searching through directories, opening and closing files, searching through files, displaying information to the user, and accepting information from the user. That is way too much activity for any one method.

The next worst case would be a program with a single class and many methods. This single class is again bearing too much of a burden. It has no single discrete task but instead is performing all the tasks listed in the previous paragraph. Furthermore, it is impossible to reuse. It has only one purpose, which is the program for which it was created.

Imagining the Solution

Mary Caroline Richards says, "The imagination equips us to perceive reality when it is not fully materialized." We have a single problem; in this case it is to write a grep program. So we begin by imagining a program with a single method called grep.

It should become obvious that a program of this type is going to need several classes to properly divide and conquer the problem it wishes to solve. It is clear that there need to be at least three classes to solve this problem:

- A class such as a JPanel or JFrame descendant that can be used to get input from the user and to display output from the search to the user.
- A class to iterate over a series of directories and find a set of files with a particular extension. In fact, in the Java world, this might be two classes, one for iterating over directories and a second one for filtering out unneeded files.
- A third class to iterate over all the bytes in a particular file, looking for instances of the string the user wants to find.

You are now ready to start writing some code. In saying this, I do not mean to imply that you are through planning your program. Instead, you are entering a cycle that will be repeated many times. The cycle looks like this:

- First you do some planning.
- Then you write some code.
- Then you test your code to make sure it works. This process may involve using the JUnit tools that are integrated into JBuilder and are discussed in Chapter 30, "Unit Testing with JUnit." You will probably do some refactoring even at this early stage.
- Then you show your code to someone and ask if it performs the task in the proper manner.

By now you have undoubtedly learned a lot about the problem domain for your program. You see solutions to problems that you did not see before, and you see new problems.

A little real-world experience might teach you the following things:

- Iterating through directories on Windows is different than on Linux, because the system for handling drives and partitions is different on each system.
- When iterating over files, you may encounter particular files that are being used by another program. As a result, you are going to have to find a way to handle locked files.
- Some users are going to want to search for words in a case-sensitive manner, and others will want to search in a case-insensitive manner.

With all this information in mind, you do some planning on how to solve your new problems. Then you write some code, do a little refactoring, and run your old test programs to make sure you didn't break anything. Then you write some test programs to test the new functionality in your program. Finally, you show the program to someone, and ask if it works for them.

They will undoubtedly report problems and ask for new features. Maybe they want the program to run on multiple threads so they can examine found files while the program is still searching. And so on....

These are the tasks involved in creating a program that will really work. It is a repetitive job that involves iterating over the same three or four steps again and again. If your program is big enough and complex enough, you might iterate over these steps many different times.

The lessons you learn from creating programs like this grep example is that each object ought to have one, and only one, task. If you try to put too much of a burden on any one class, the weight of constantly changing your program, constantly improving it, and constantly refactoring it becomes insupportable.

Creating the Public Methods for a Class

A very delicate time is the moment when you create the interface for a particular object. The interface for a class should be as abstract as possible. To the greatest extent possible, this interface should hide the actual implementation of the object it encapsulates. For instance, it should not expose any of the arrays it encapsulates directly to the user.

Composing Methods

It is now time to shift the focus from writing objects to writing individual methods. This subject is closely linked to the discussion in the previous section, so I will move right into it without further ado.

Never Copy Code

Ah, the evils of the block copy command! As useful as it can be, sometimes there is no command more insidious than the seemingly innocent block copy command.

The problem with block copying the code from one place to another is that you end up with two copies of code that perform the same task. This adds bulk to your program. Worse, it means that bug fixes in one object need to be performed on a second object. It is the exception, and not the rule, when we have the discipline to make fixes of that kind to both objects rather than to just one object. And if you are a new programmer on the project and you don't know that a second copy of the bug even exists, you will not know to make your fixes in two places.

NOTE: Some people have an extraordinary capacity for recalling even the tiniest details. Being blessed with such a talent is not an excuse for writing sloppy code. Just because you can remember for several weeks at a time all the places where you have block copied one particular chunk of code does not make it okay to indulge in that practice. Instead, you should be putting your skills to some useful purpose, such as devising a means for reusing code rather than block copying it. Isn't it more interesting to discover ways to reuse the code than to simply use brute force memorization to handle the problem? If all else fails, go back and watch the Alfred Hitchcock film *The 39 Steps*. Maybe being Mr. Memory isn't quite as exciting as it might seem at first.

Isolate Discrete Tasks

Suppose you have a method that parses a sentence into individual words and then sorts the words in alphabetical order. This seems like one task to you when you first write the code. But later, in a different part of your program, you find you need to parse all the words in a sentence into an array and then reverse the order of the words. Clearly, there is one task, namely parsing the words in a sentence into discrete objects, that is shared by both tasks. In such cases, immediately stop what you are doing, and create and test a method that parses the words of a sentence into an array. Both of your previous methods can first call this method, and then go on to party in their own way on the resulting array.

A good programmer would do as I describe in the previous paragraph. A great programmer would have detected the presence of a discrete task in the first method and separated it out into its own method or class. He would then have no extra work to do when it came time to create the second method.

About Long Methods

I suppose there is nothing wrong, in and of itself, with a long method. However, I believe there is probably a problem if you have a large number of long methods.

The problem with long methods is not that they are long but that they might contain code that could be reused if it stood on its own.

How can you recognize a method that needs to be long when you encounter it? Well, there are two things to look for in particular:

- It contains a big case statement. Case statements lead to big methods. Such is life. The only danger in such situations is allowing each section of the case statement to become its own mini-method. If one particular case in your case statement is longer than two or three lines, and it could possibly be reused, then you should consider treating it in its own method which you call from the case statement.
- Simple if-else statements also can lead to big methods. Again, if any particular part of the if-else statement gets overly long, you should consider handling it in its own method which is called from within the if-else statement.

A more controversial case is an embedded if-else statement of the type shown in Listing 22-1.

Listing 22-1: The complex method called handleOptions contains several embedded if statements.

```
void say(String s)
{
      System.out.println(s);
}

// The quotes in this method are from the poet William Blake.
void handleOptions(boolean a, boolean b, boolean c, boolean d,
      boolean e, boolean f, boolean g)
{
      if (a == true)
      {
            if (b == true)
            {
                  say("Joys impregnate. Sorrows bring forth.");
            }
            else if (c == false)
            {
                  if (d == true)
                  {
                        say("Shame is pride's cloak");
                  }
                  else
                  {
                        say("Expect poison from the standing water.");
                  }
            }
      }
      else if (e == false)
      {
            if (f == true)
            {
```

```
                say("Excess of sorrow laughs, excess of joy weeps.");
            }
            else
            {
                if (g==true)
                {
                    say("Listen to the fools reproach, it is a kingly title!");
                }
                else
                {
                    say("To create a little flower is the labor of ages");
                }
            }
        }
}
```

It is arguable that in its current form, a method like this is acceptable. It is, after all, well organized and neatly laid out. But it could be broken up. Consider the easy-to-create alternative shown in Listing 22-2.

Listing 22-2: Breaking up a complex if statement into sub methods

```
void say(String s)
{
    System.out.println(s);
}

void doOptionA(boolean b, boolean c, boolean d)
{
    if (b == true)
    {
        say("Joys impregnate. Sorrows bring forth.");
    }
    else if (c == false)
    {
        if (d == true)
        {
            say("Shame is pride's cloak");
        }
        else
        {
            say("Expect poison from the standing water.");
        }
    }
}

void doOptionB(boolean e, boolean f, boolean g)
{
    if (f == true)
    {
        say("Excess of sorrow laughs, excess of joy weeps.");
    }
    else
```

Part IV

```
        {
            if (g==true)
            {
                say("Listen to the fools reproach, it is a kingly title!");
            }
            else
            {
                say("To create a little flower is the labor of ages");
            }
        }
    }

    void handleOptions(boolean a, boolean b, boolean c, boolean d,
        boolean e, boolean f, boolean g)
    {
        if (a == true)
        {
            doOptionA(b, c, d);
        }
        else if (e == false)
        {
            doOptionB(f, d, g);
        }
    }
```

The first thing you are likely to notice when comparing Listings 22-1 and 22-2 is that Listing 22-1 is nine lines shorter. Perhaps the second thing you would notice is that handleOptions is relatively difficult to parse in Listing 22-1 and exceedingly easy to parse in Listing 22-2. If you look further, you can see that both doOptionA and doOptionB are also relatively manageable methods.

By dividing and conquering, you are able to simplify the code shown in Listing 22-1. This may or may not be worthwhile depending on whether or not you can reuse the two new methods you created.

Use Packages for Major Subtasks

If you discover a task that requires five or six objects to complete, you should move those objects into their package. For instance, if you are creating a control that is used to retrieve a file over the Internet, parse the file, and mail it to a destination, then almost certainly you should create at least one package to house that part of your program. If you place all those methods and objects inside the same directory as the rest of your program, you have gone beyond the pale. (For further information on going beyond the pale, please see Joseph Conrad's *The Heart of Darkness*.)

Event Madness

I want to spend a few minutes discussing in general terms the FileRename program, found in the Utilities directory on the CD. This program shows an interesting approach to creating modular, easy-to-reuse code.

The FileRename program relies entirely on events and interfaces. After program initialization, none of the objects ever directly call one another. There is no shared data between the main objects in the program other than the data needed by Frame1 at startup to create instances of the objects that will be in play. But Frame1 itself is not in play. All it does is instantiate other objects, then play host to them.

This model adds robustness to your program, and it makes each object a truly discrete entity. When developing this kind of program, you need to think about creating objects that know how to live on their own. If you want to create a truly plug-and-play architecture, you have to break the dependencies that the objects in a program have upon one another. You are creating simple little machines that know how to run on their own.

This model takes more work, and often it takes more thought to create. But it ends up producing very robust programs. Furthermore, it is easy to reuse the elements in your program.

To grasp some of the complexities involved, consider the following issue: If the user changes any data in the program, all interested parties need to be notified via events. One object can't simply ask another object for its current state via a method call. Instead, if one object changes, it needs to tell the other objects that it has changed. Any object that needs to know about changes to the state of one object should support the appropriate event listening interface and then register itself as an event listener.

Am I suggesting that this is the best way to write true OOP-based programs? Well, I probably would not go that far. Using getter and setter methods is so much simpler that I can't help but feel it is appropriate in many cases. Still, this model is compelling in some cases.

The FileRename Program

The example program for this section of the chapter grew out of a need I had to massage files that I was downloading from a web site called www.emusic.com. For a monthly fee, subscribers can download MP3 files from this site. The filenames for the songs retrieved from the site come in the following format:

```
ArtistName-Album-TrackNo-SongTitle.mp3
```

This format can lead to some very long filenames, some of which exceeded the length that my CD-ROM burning software was able to support. So I wrote a program that would break these names up into a directory called ArtistName, a subdirectory called AlbumName, and then a series of files called TrackNo-SongTitle. For instance, a download might end up in a directory called Tom_Waits/Mule_Variations, and the songs might be called 01-Big_In_Japan.mp3, 02-Lowside_Of_The_Road.mp3, and so on.

A utility of this kind was not hard to write, but it involved several different classes. Each of these classes needed to communicate with at least one other class. As an exercise, I decided to have most of the classes talk to one another using messages rather than using getter and setter methods.

For instance, a class in the FileRename program sends an ActionEvent to classes called ControlPanel and DisplayData when the user selects a new directory, as shown in Figure 22-1. The only way that ControlPanel and DisplayData can find out the current directory is by receiving this message. They never check the current directory themselves, and they do not use a getter method to ask FileHandler the name of the current directory.

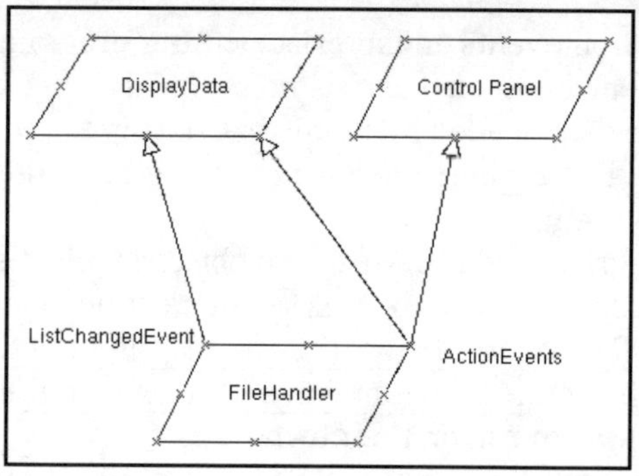

Figure 22-1: A visual representation of the FileRename program shows events flowing from the FileHandler class to the ControlPanel and DisplayData classes.

To make this work, it is necessary to ensure that neither ControlPanel nor DisplayData have the ability to change this data. Only one object should be able to change the data, and it should tell other objects when that data has changed. If you don't obey these rules, you will have chaos. On the other hand, if you do obey these rules, there is a very clear delegation of tasks and an orderly structure to the whole program.

One way to check your logic when designing this kind of program is to ensure that data flows in only one direction. For instance, you could draw a diagram of the objects in your program. If messages flow from Class A to Class B, put an arrow pointing from A to B in your diagram. Trouble arises if Class A points at Class B, and Class B points at Class A. That kind of situation can get dicey very fast. It is best if information flows in only one direction.

Summary

This chapter was something of an odd duck in this book in that it featured little code. Instead, it tried to express a few simple ideas, most of which can be encapsulated in short sentences:

- Divide and conquer.
- The presence of repetitive code in a project is a sign that the code needs to be factored into discrete methods or classes.
- Another common clue that something is amiss is that reuse is difficult.
- Each method ought to have one, and only one, task. The only possible exception is when you are sure the tasks will never be reused.
- Each class ought to have one, and only one, task. There is no single concept that can save you more time or trouble than the simple idea of dividing your code into discrete, reusable classes.
- Use packages to encapsulate major tasks embodied in several classes.
- If you want to create a truly plug-and-play architecture, you have to break the dependencies that the objects in a program have upon one another.
- Reuse is usually the easiest of all possible ways to create small, fast programs.
- Create reusable methods. Don't allow repetitious code to creep into your programs.
- Hide everything that can possibly be hidden behind private methods in a discrete class that resides in its own source file.
- Never expose any of the data from your class other than immutable constants.
- Revisit the public methods for your class again and again and see if there is some way to change them into private methods.

- Make the public interface to your class as simple as possible. A single access point to a class is ideal.
- When it comes to creating classes, simplicity trumps complexity.
- Rules are meant to be broken.

Use your brainpower to find the objects and the methods in your code that need to be separated into their own little fiefdoms. Unlike commenting your code or naming variables, this is a task that can daunt even the most intelligent programmers. It can take real brainpower to find the unique or reusable objects hidden in a complicated program. But if you can find them, you can write code that is smaller, faster, and easier to maintain than anyone else's code in the shop.

Part V

Project Management

Chapter 23

Building Simple Applications

Charlie Calvert

This chapter explains how to run the simplest possible Java programs in JBuilder. The goals of the chapter are fivefold:

- To aid beginning level Java programmers who want to create very simple programs.
- To familiarize all users with the basics of using the JBuilder project manager.
- To explain how to build simple command-line utilities in JBuilder of the type that you might use for maintenance in an IS facility.
- To begin talking about running programs from the command line.
- To show how to convert and run relatively simple non-JBuilder projects such as the samples that come with the JDK.

I will intentionally not use packages in any of the sample projects shown in this chapter. Almost all the rest of the programs seen in this book will use packages. I am avoiding packages in this chapter not to simplify the code I am creating, but in order to show you how to make JBuilder work with projects that don't use packages.

NOTE: It would be a total misunderstanding of my intentions were you to walk away from this chapter thinking that I don't like the idea of using packages. By all means use packages in all but the simplest of your projects. Even then, it is probably still best to use them. Using packages is good programming practice. My goal in this chapter is to show you how to use JBuilder with very simple projects, not to encourage bad programming practices.

JBuilder is a very powerful tool, designed to help you create both simple projects and very complex projects. In a somewhat ironic twist of fate, it happens that it is easier to build and run a relatively complex project in JBuilder than it is to build and run a simple project.

Don't be fooled by the fact that this chapter focuses on simple projects. There is quite a bit of information in this chapter that will appeal to intermediate and advanced Java developers.

What are JPR and JPX Files?

A JPR or JPX file is a JBuilder project file. You can't compile anything in the JBuilder IDE without first creating a project. If you want to edit and debug an applet or application inside of JBuilder, this file must exist.

A JPR file is just a text file. A JPX file is an XML-based text file. In JBuilder 7, JPR and JPX files work in all editions of JBuilder. There is no advantage that I can see to using either JPR or JPX files, but I think JPX files are currently the preferred model and JPR files are simply there to support legacy applications. All other factors being equal, you should therefore choose JPX files as your default.

When you open up a JBuilder project, this is the file you open. When you first open a project, don't browse for files with a .java extension; instead browse for files with a .jpr or .jpx extension.

As you know, JBuilder does not require any special form of Java code. If the code you have created compiles at the command prompt with some existing JDK, you should not have any trouble compiling it inside JBuilder. In my experience, there is no such thing as a standard Java application or applet that will not compile and run inside JBuilder. The reverse is also true. If you can compile it inside of JBuilder, you should have no trouble compiling your code from the command line.

Adding a JPR or JPX file to your project does not require any changes to the java source files that are part of your project. Nor does the existence of this file alter the ability of your code to compile at the command prompt or inside some other Java IDE. In fact, JBuilder project files can greatly simplify the act of compiling from the command line. All a JPR or JPX file does is help JBuilder manage your project.

In some cases you may want to have multiple JPX/JPR files for one project. You would do this in order to quickly and easily work with the same project under multiple configurations.

NOTE: I have had trouble opening or running Java projects in JBuilder under two circumstances:

- If there are invalid java source files in a package. These files may never be used by other files in the package. Such projects can be made to compile and link successfully from the command line. However, in JBuilder, you should remove any invalid java source files from packages included in your project. In short, all the source files in all the packages that are part of your project must compile.
- For reasons I do not fully comprehend, some people store projects in absolutely absurd directories that have nothing to do with the packages that will eventually contain the files. Some sort of complex makefile is then used to copy the files into a valid package and compile the files there. This type of structure will not work inside of JBuilder. You will need to start storing the files in valid packages if you want the project to run inside of JBuilder.

Simple Applications without Packages

Part V

Suppose you have been handed or have been working on an applet or application that has no packages. How do you open such a project and begin debugging it in the JBuilder IDE?

NOTE: It turns out that there are two ways to perform this task. One involves using a wizard called Project for Existing Code. You reach the wizard by choosing File | New, then turning to the Project page. This wizard does not come with the Personal version of JBuilder, nor does it really save you very much time. In fact, the process of using it is nearly identical to the steps I will outline in the next few paragraphs. As a result, I will discuss it later in the chapter, and only rather briefly.

Consider the very short application shown in Listing 23-1. You can find it on the CD in the directory called SimpleClass.

This is the type of project you might construct in a beginning level Java course. The question, of course, is what to do with a pre-existing instance of this kind of project from inside of JBuilder.

Listing 23-1: A very simple Java project

```
class SimpleClass
{
  public static void main(String arg[])
  {
```

```
        System.out.println("Hi, ho the wind and the rain");
    }
}
```

If the project does not already exist, and you are simply following along with the logic of this chapter, use a text editor to create the project and save it into its own directory. For the purposes of this discussion, we will assume that you have created a file called SimpleClass.java, stored in the SimpleClass directory. If the file already exists, copy it into its own directory. Place nothing else inside the directory where this file exists. (Later in this chapter I will show you how to put multiple projects in one directory.)

In this chapter I am assuming that all your code is in one directory. Furthermore, I assume that directory is not the root directory of your drive. For instance, it is not the C:\ directory, or even a UNIX-based \ directory, or your Linux \home\MyUserName\ directory.

In Windows, I would suggest putting your file in a directory called c:\srcjava\SimpleClass. If you are in Linux, you might place it in /home/MyUserDir/srcjava/SimpleClass. I find it best to avoid putting spaces in the path that leads to your project.

Now that you have the directory set up and the file placed in it, it is time to begin setting up your JBuilder project. This will take several steps. The overall goal, however, is simply to place a JBuilder project file in your working directory.

1. Launch JBuilder, and choose **File | Close Projects** to close all your existing projects. (Again, this is not a necessity, but in this case it will be simplest to start with a blank slate.)
2. Choose **File | New Project**. Click on the ellipsis button next to the Directory field and browse for the directory above the one where you placed your source file. For instance, if you placed your program in c:\srcjava\SimpleClass, then browse for the directory c:\srcjava.
3. In the Name field, type in the name of the directory where you placed your source file. For instance, type in **SimpleClass**. The Template field should be set to the default value.

A correctly filled out dialog is shown in Figure 23-1.

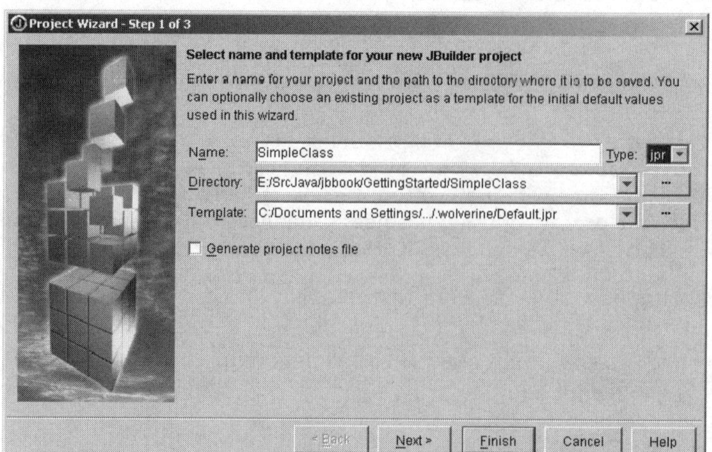

Figure 23-1: The first step in filling out the Project Wizard for a simple project that does not use packages

Click **Next** to go to the second page of the Project Wizard. Edit the Output Path field so that it does not have the word "classes" appended to it. This line defines where JBuilder places the class files it makes at compile time. It is the equivalent of the -d option in the command-line javac.exe utility. Our goal is to put the class files in the same directory as the source file.

On the Source page of the tabbed notebook near the bottom of the dialog, click on the entry that has the word "src" appended to it. Choose the **Edit** button, and set the source directory for your project to the directory where you stored your SimpleClass.java file.

When you are done, the dialog should look as it does in Figure 23-2.

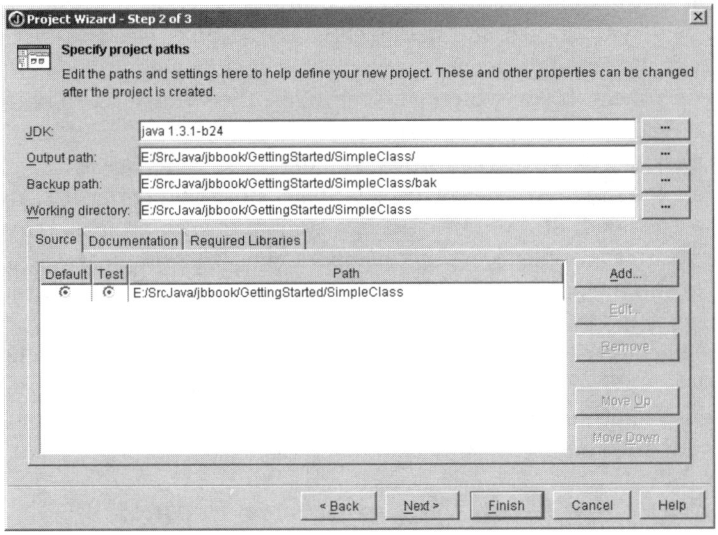

Figure 23-2: The second step in the Project Wizard. The changes you made were to the Output Path field and the Source page of the tabbed notebook at the bottom of the dialog.

Click **Next** to go to the third page of the Project Wizard. Accept the defaults by clicking the **Finish** button.

When you are done, the JBuilder IDE should look as it does in Figure 23-3. (If Figure 23-3 looks a bit strange to you, the reason is that I have the IDE as small as possible so as to show you lots of detail without wasting space.)

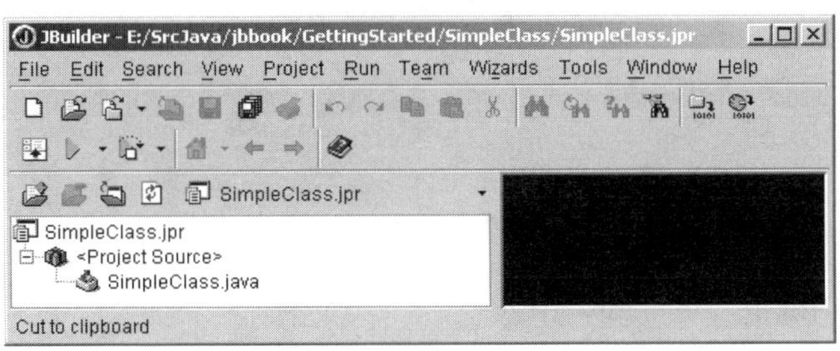

Figure 23-3: The JBuilder IDE after you have run the Project Wizard

Exploring Your New Project

There are three key points to notice in Figure 23-3:

- The path to your JPR/JPX file is visible at the top of the IDE.
- The name of the project is the same as the directory it's stored in.
- The blue icon next to the words "<Project Source>."

The first of these topics is self explanatory. The latter two need a bit of explanation.

The project file in this project is called SimpleClass.jpr. If we had chosen to save the file in XML format, it would have been called SimpleClass.jpx.

In large part, the project got this name because you saved it into a directory called SimpleClass. You can see the SimpleClass.jpr file in the project pane at the left of Figure 23-3. If you right-click on this node, and choose Properties from the popup menu, you could edit the properties for your project. You could, for instance, make changes to all the actions you made after completing the first page in the Project Wizard.

The little blue package with the words "<Project Source>" after it represents the main package for your project. It has no name, since you are not really using packages in the construction of this simple project. If you were using packages, the words "<Project Source>" would be replaced with the name of your package.

If you opened the package, however, you would see that it contains the file SimpleClass.java, as shown in Figure 23-3. This is perhaps a little bit confusing. You are not using packages, and yet JBuilder still put the package symbol in your project! What you are seeing is JBuilder's bias in favor of projects that use packages. The simplest way to think of the matter is simply to see the package as a directory symbol. This is not really much of a stretch, since a package is in fact a directory.

The next step is to click on the green plus symbol shown in Figure 23-3 just above the navigation pane. This will bring up a dialog that will allow you to officially add SimpleClass.java to your project. Doing this is not required, and in big projects I don't like to do this with all the files in an application. But in a simple project like this, it makes sense.

Running Your Code: Setting the Main Class for Your Project

The final step is setting the main class for your project. In this step you tell JBuilder which class contains the method called main that is the entry point for your project. If you were running an applet, you would follow nearly identical steps but point JBuilder at the JApplet or Applet descendant that is the main class for your project. Alternatively, you could point JBuilder at the HTML file that is used to launch your applet.

To get started, choose **Project | Project Properties** to open the Project Properties dialog. This is the same dialog you can access by right-clicking on your JPR file.

1. Turn to the Run page.
2. Click on the **New...** button on the right side of the dialog. This will take you to the Runtime Properties dialog. The Application Page will be open by default. Make sure that the application page is selected.
3. Click on the ellipsis button to the right of the Main Class field, and browse for **SimpleClass**, which is listed near the bottom of the Select Main Class for Project dialog. Note that the class is not in any of the packages listed at the top of the dialog. It is not in one of the packages because you are not using the package directive in your source code.

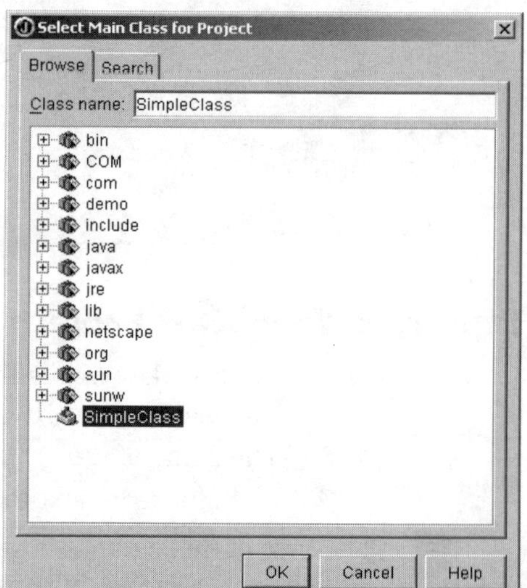

Figure 23-4: The dialog you use for selecting the main class for your project

4. As an optional step, you can go to the Configuration Name field at the top of the Runtime Properties dialog and type in the name **Simple Class**. This can help if you decide to have more than one runtime configuration. Click **OK.**
5. Back in the Project Properties dialog, click the appropriate check box to select Simple Class as the default main class for the project. This is not necessary if you have only one configuration, but it is still good practice.
6. Click the **OK** button. The Project Properties dialog should now look as it does in Figure 23-6.

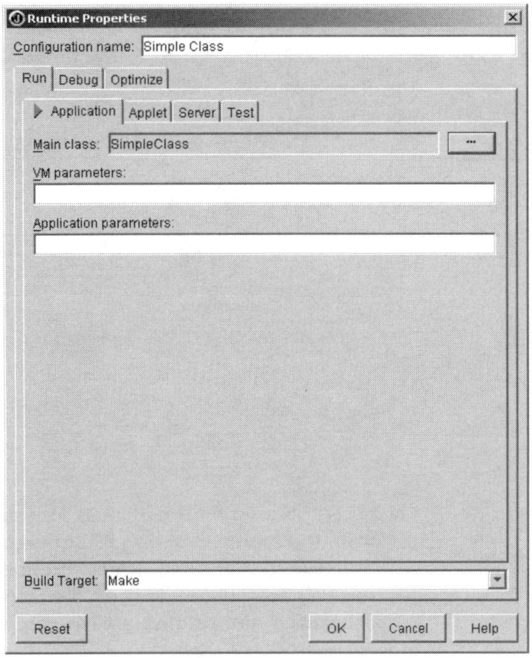

Figure 23-5: The Runtime Properties dialog

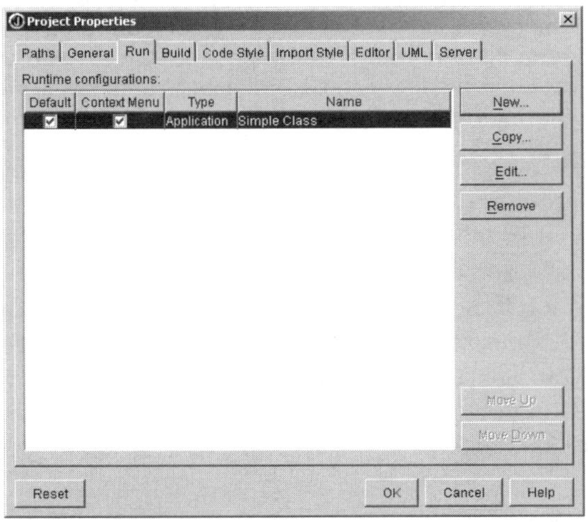

Figure 23-6: The Project Properties dialog as it looks after you have selected the main class for your project

NOTE: The Run page of the Project Properties dialog changed between JBuilder 6 and JBuilder 7. The new features added in JBuilder 7 allow you to have multiple configurations. As a result, step 4 is potentially important. It gives you a chance to properly name a particular configuration.

A second way to provide yourself with multiple configurations for a single project is to have multiple JPX/JPR files for the same project. The JBuilder team quite consciously decided that it would be simpler for you to have multiple JPX/JPR files rather than having multiple configuration options inside a single project file. This latter option is the route taken by Microsoft in Visual Studio, where you can choose between the debug and release version of your project. Instead, in JBuilder, you should have a debug and release JPX file. You might, for instance, use multiple JPX files to set up multiple sets of breakpoints for debugging different parts of your application.

If you have an existing project, and you want to create a second JPX file for it, choose File | New from the JBuilder menu and turn to the Project page. Select the option called Project for Existing code. This wizard will help you create a new JPX file for your existing source, as described below.

After you click **OK** in the Project Properties dialog, you are at last free to compile and run your JBuilder application. Click the green **Run** icon or choose **Run | Run Project** from the menu. The results should look something like what you see in Figure 23-7.

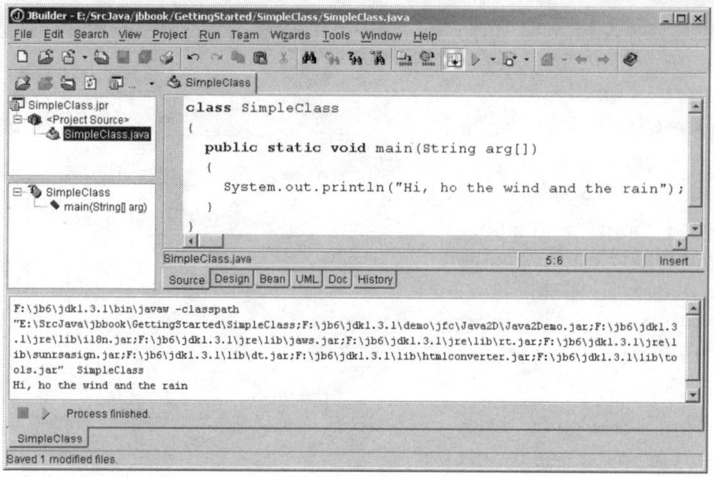

Figure 23-7: The IDE after a run of the SimpleClass project

NOTE: Picking the main class for your project makes it possible to run your project by selecting Run from the menu, pressing F9, or pressing the green run button. However, you can run a file by right-clicking it in the project pane and choosing Run from the popup menu. Only files that can be run will have a Run item on the pop-up menu. A file that can be run would be an application that contains a main statement, the main file for an applet, or an HTML file that references an applet.

Notice in Figure 23-7 that you can see the output from your project near the bottom of the IDE in the message pane, below the printout of the classpath. You can also see the sole method of your class in the structure pane. In this case, the structure is very simple, since you only have one class, called SimpleClass, and one method in the class, called main.

If you go to the command prompt or open Windows Explorer, you will see that all the files for your project are in one directory. Well, almost all the files. There is a still a bak directory where JBuilder keeps backup copies of your source. But overall, JBuilder has set things up to work exactly as you would were you creating the project with no packages inside a text editor. The only real difference is that JBuilder has created a JPR or JPX file to accompany your source.

There is no denying that it was a bit tricky to explain how to import even a simple project into JBuilder. If this complexity seems daunting to you, there are three things to keep in mind:

- Importing a project into JBuilder somehow gets simpler each time you do it. The first time, it might take you as long as ten or fifteen minutes. The second time, it might take you five. After you have done it a few times, you can complete the process in less than a minute. It is just a question of becoming familiar with the tools.
- The work of setting up a project in JBuilder is well worth the effort. Once you have a project imported in JBuilder, you get all the benefits of working inside the IDE. For instance, CodeInsight is available to you, the debugger is available to you, and you can see the hierarchy of your project and any possible errors in your code in the structure pane.
- Finally, as I mentioned earlier, it is more difficult to set up a simple project like this than it is to set up the more complex default JBuilder project that will be discussed in the next chapter.

NOTE: Later in this chapter, in the section called "Compiling from the Command Line," I will explain how to run this program from the command line.

The "Project for Existing Code" Wizard

As I mentioned earlier, the SE and Enterprise versions of JBuilder have a tool called "Project for Existing Code." You reach this dialog by choosing **File | New**, then turning to the Project page, and selecting **Project for Existing Code** from the Object Repository.

The Project for Existing Code (PEC) Wizard works in almost exactly the same way as the Project Wizard described earlier in this chapter. The only real difference is that the first page of the PEC wizard allows you to select the directory in which your project will reside rather than the directory beneath the directory in which your project will reside. Here is another way to make the same point: The PEC Wizard assumes that you have already created the root directory for your project, while the Project Wizard assumes that you want it to create the root directory for your project.

All the other steps in the PEC Wizard are nearly identical to the steps in the Project Wizard. In particular, you need to properly configure the paths for your project, as shown in Figure 23-2, and then properly configure the main class for your project, as shown in Figures 23-4, 23-5, and 23-6.

Moving a Project

Keeping in mind the needs of beginning level students, I want to take a moment to describe how to move this project, or any other valid JBuilder project, from one location to another.

Though it might appear daunting at first, it turns out to be easy to move the entire project from one area of your hard drive to another. This is one task, however, that I would not do from inside of JBuilder. Instead, I would close JBuilder and move things around with the Windows Explorer or some equivalent tool. For instance, you could open the Windows Explorer, right-click on the root node for your project, and choose Cut from the Windows menu. Now find the place on your hard drive where you want to move the project. Right-click in the Windows Explorer and choose Paste. Now you can open the project in JBuilder from the new location, and everything should work fine.

By the same measure, you can zip up an entire project and email it to someone, then they could unzip it and load it directly into JBuilder.

Finally, a teacher might want to see only your java source file and not care about your JPX file, the class files you produced, or the files in the JBuilder bak directory. If such is the case, there is no need to worry. Just send your teacher the SimpleClass.java file, and it will rest on its own as a valid Java program. Nothing bad happened to the file just because it was opened or edited in JBuilder.

Creating a Simple Project with No Packages

Earlier in this chapter you opened an existing project that contains no packages in the JBuilder IDE. The next step is creating such a simple project in the IDE from scratch. This is the process you would follow were you using JBuilder to help you work your way through a simple Java 101 course. For instance, if you were trying to create the application shown in Listing 23-1 from scratch, this is the approach you would take.

The process you are about to go through is very similar to the one you went through in an earlier section of this chapter. As a result, I will keep the explanations as short as possible. If you want more detail, see "Simple Applications without Packages" earlier in this chapter.

1. Choose **File | Close Projects** to close and save any existing work.
2. Choose **File | New Project**. In the first page of the Project Wizard, click on the ellipsis button to the right of the Directory field and browse to the directory beneath the location where you want to place your project. For instance, if you want your project to be in the directory c:\srcjava\Java101, you should browse to the c:\srcjava directory.
3. Fill in the Name field with the name of the directory where you want your project to be located. For instance, if you have set the Directory field to the c:\srcjava directory, and you want your project to be in the c:\srcjava\Java101 directory, type **Java101** in this field. Keep the Template field set to the default value, as shown in Figure 23-8. Press **Next**.

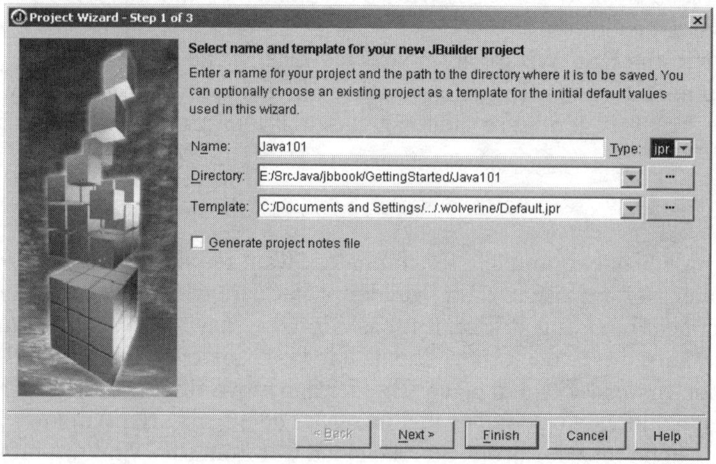

Figure 23-8: Setting up a project for a simple JBuilder application that uses no packages

On the next page, delete the word "classes" from the Output Path field, and edit the source path so that it no longer points at the src directory. When you are done, the dialog should look as it does in Figure 23-9. Press **Next**.

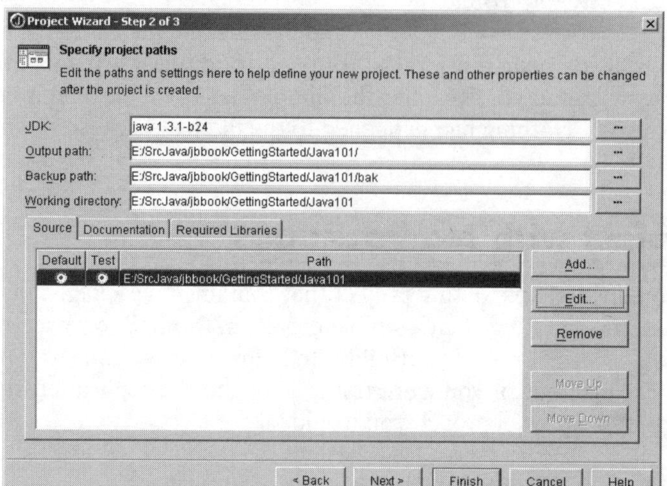

Figure 23-9: The Project Wizard's second page as it should look when you are using JBuilder to create very simple Java projects

You need make no changes on the third page of the Project Wizard.

You now have the project directory and JPR file set up for your application. This is the part where it is easy to make a mistake. Logic might lead you to choose File | New Application at this stage. However, the JBuilder Application Wizard will create a project more complex than you need as the basis for a simple utility or as the basis for an assignment in a simple beginning level Java course. As a result, I suggest you choose **File | New Class**, rather than File | New Application.

In the Class Wizard, set the Package field to an empty string. Set the Class Name field to **BasicJavaApp**. The base class should be **java.lang.Object**.

In the Options section, choose **Public**, **Generate main method**, and **Generate header comments**.

When you are done, the dialog should appear as it does in Figure 23-10.

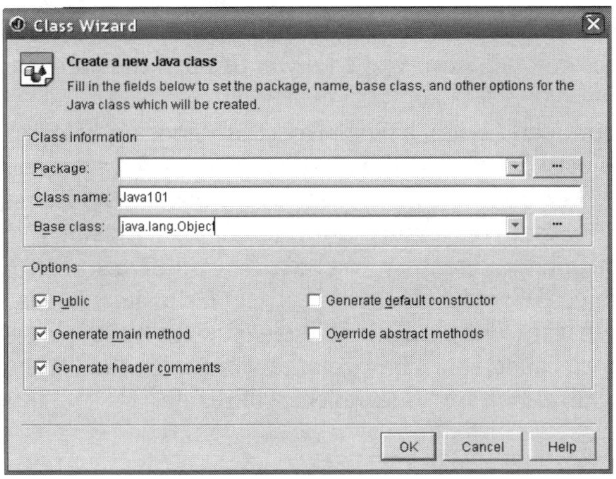

Figure 23-10: Creating the main class for a simple Java application. Notice that the Package field is blank.

Click the **OK** button in the Class Wizard. The source code produced by this process is shown in Listing 23-2.

Listing 23-2: The auto-generated source for a very simple Java application

```
public class Java101
{
  public static void main(String[] args)
  {
    System.out.println("Turn, turn, to the wind and the rain.");
  }
}
```

At this stage, all you need to do is edit the main method so it looks as it does in Listing 23-1. Then choose **Project | Project Properties**, turn to the Run page, and set the main class to **BasicJavaApp**, as described earlier.

Bravo, you are all done! You can begin editing and debugging your project. Later in this chapter, in the section called "Compiling from the Command Line," I will explain how to run this program from the command line.

Creating a JBuilder Type Project with No Packages

The last two projects had no packages but kept all their files in one directory. As you know, this is not the default JBuilder behavior. Instead, JBuilder prefers to put all your source files in one directory or hierarchy of directories and all your class files in another directory or hierarchy of directories. By default, the source files go beneath a directory called src, and the class files go beneath a directory called classes.

In this section of the chapter, I show you how to build JBuilder projects that have no packages but still put the source and class files in separate directories. Following this technique will provide a simple means for you to separate the class files that you want to distribute to others from the Java source files, which you may not wish or need to distribute. Or, conversely, it will help you easily delete your .class files while not risking an accidental loss of your java source files.

I'm not going to detail all the steps involved in this process, as they are very similar to the steps you saw earlier in this chapter. I will, however, take you through the steps in a brisk manner.

Start by closing any previous projects. Begin a new project by choosing **File | New Project**. On the first page of the Project Wizard, find the place on your hard drive beneath the directory that you want to create. For instance, go to c:\srcjava. Now use the Name field to designate the name of the directory that you want to work in, much as you did in Figures 23-1 and 23-8. In this case, however, name the directory you create **SimpleDirs**.

On the second page of the Project Wizard, you should accept all the defaults, as shown in Figure 23-11. In particular, note that the Output Path field is set to the classes directory and the source path is set to a directory called src. When you are done, click the **OK** button to create your JPR file and the directories where your project will reside.

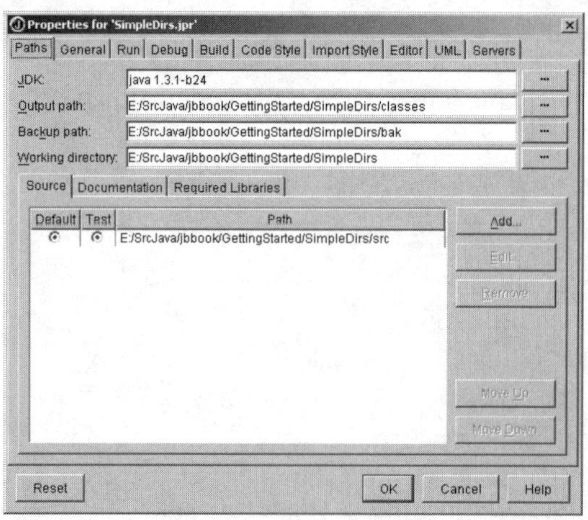

Figure 23-11: A view from the JBuilder Project Properties dialog showing how to fill out the second page of the Project Wizard

NOTE: In Figure 23-11, you might notice that there is a column with a radio button in it labeled "Test." This option is useful if you want to use a tool called JUnit to help you build code for testing your application or applet. I will describe this process in Chapter 30.

Once you have created your project, the next step is to add a class to it. Choose **File | New Class**, and fill in the dialog as shown in Figure 23-12. The most important point is that you should not include a package when creating your class. Click **OK** in the Class Wizard to create your class.

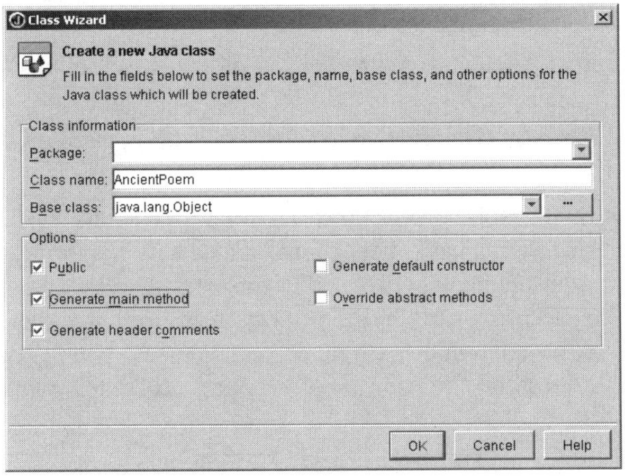

Figure 23-12: Creating a simple Java application with a single class and no packages. Notice that the Generate main method option is checked.

You should fill in your class as shown in Listing 23-3. This listing includes an excerpt from a poem by the 13th century Afghan poet Rumi.

Listing 23-3: A simple Java program that prints out a poem at the command line

```
public class AncientPoem
{
  public static void main(String[] args)
  {
    String S = "Don't worry about saving these songs!\n" +
      "And if one of our instruments breaks,\n" +
      "it doesn't matter.\n\n" +
      "We have fallen into the place\n" +
      "where everything is music.\n\n...\n" +
      "Stop the words now.\n" +
      "Open the window in the center of your chest,\n" +
      "and let the spirits fly in and out.\n\n" +
      "by the Afghan poet Rumi, writing in the 13th century.";
    System.out.print(S);
  }
}
```

If you open up the Windows Explorer or some equivalent tool, you will find that your project is divided into four main directories as shown in Figure 23-13.

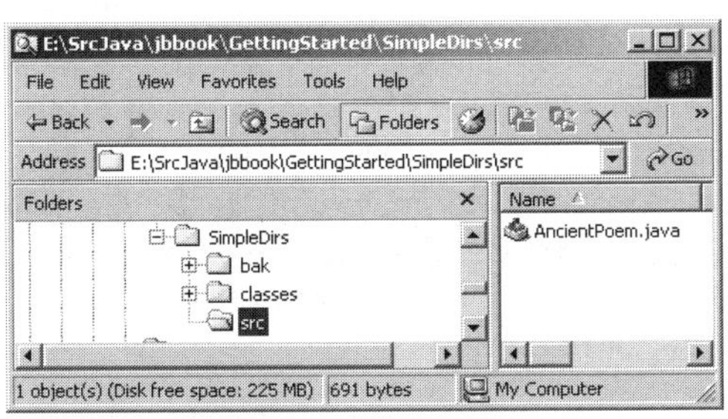

Figure 23-13: Using the Windows Explorer to see the core directories found in a simple JBuilder application

Here is an explication of the four main directories for your project:

- SimpleDirs is the root directory for your project. The other three main directories in your project are subdirectories of this directory.

- The src directory contains the AncientPoem.java file.
- After you compile your project, the classes directory contains the AncientPoem.class file.
- The bak directory contains backup copies of your source files. You can view these files in the History page from the file view tabs.

If you want to share your work with someone else, you can simple give them the file AncientPoem.java. Since it is not stored in a package, others will be able to compile it easily. The fact that we gave this project a bit more structure did not materially change the nature of the source files being created. The structure only helps you organize your work and leads us all toward a better understanding of how JBuilder sets up project files. As you begin creating more complex projects, you will understand the wisdom of properly structuring your applications.

You can find an example program of this type on the CD in the SimpleDirs directory.

Compiling from the Command Line

Now that you have built a few simple projects inside JBuilder, you might want to see for yourself that you can still compile them from the command line if you so desire. For many people, this will be an essential component of JBuilder development. For instance, if you are taking a Java course, your teacher will almost certainly want you to compile your projects from the command line. If you are an experienced Java programmer writing utilities for a corporation, you will also need to know how to compile and run your project from the command line.

Compiling the first two projects we created is very simple. Here is a batch file that you can use to create and run the SimpleClass program using any standard JDK:

```
javac SimpleClass.java
java SimpleClass
```

You need only add the line **#! /bin/bash** to the top of this file to convert it into a script for use on Linux or Solaris.

As you can see, this is exactly the same code that you would use to create the program had you built it inside of emacs or Notepad. JBuilder does not force you to adopt any non-standard programming techniques. All it does is provide a powerful debugger and a flexible set of tools to help you create your application.

There are three other ways to compile this project from the command line.

- You can use the Borland utility bcj.exe, which will perform the same task as javac.exe.
- You can use the Borland utility bmj.exe, which will perform a make rather than a build. In short, it will only compile a java file to a class file if there is no existing .class file or if that .class file is out of date. If the .class is up to date, it does nothing. This can help speed up compile time on large projects that contain many .java files.
- The third way to compile your project from the command line is to type **JBuilder -build SimpleClass.jpx**. This technique is particularly useful when you start creating complex projects that would be difficult to compile because of the complexity of their package structure.

Consider for a moment the AncientPoem program called SimpleDirs. This project has its source files in one directory and its class files in a separate directory. When compiling from the command line, you could, of course, just change to the src directory and compile it exactly as you did the SimpleClass program. But just for the sake of argument, let's assume you want to compile from the root directory of your project, and let's assume you want to put the class files you create in the class directory. Here is how to do that with a batch file:

```
javac -d classes src\AncientPoem.java
java -classpath classes AncientPoem
```

This batch file passes the -d switch to javac to force the compiler to place the output from your project in the classes directory. The second argument is the file you want to compile.

When it comes time to run the program, you need to pass Java.exe the -classpath directive so that you can tell it the location of your .class files. In this case, your .class file is in the classes directory. The second argument is the name of the main class in your project. (In this case, it's also the only class in your project, but that is neither here nor there.)

As you know, there is a second way to compile this project from the command line: Just go to the root directory for the project and type **jbuilder -build SimpleDirs.jpr**. After you have compiled the project, you will still have to run it using the java command with the -classpath directive.

It is obvious that using JBuilder -build is going to be the simplest way to compile your projects from the command line. Given that fact, why don't I simply tell you to compile your programs that way and ignore the other options?

In most cases, I think you should use JBuilder -build whenever possible. That is indeed the simplest way to proceed. However, in this chapter I want to emphasize that JBuilder is not locking you into any one particular option. You can create your projects in JBuilder, and then still build them from the command line using the same techniques that all other Java programmers use.

NOTE: If JBuilder.exe is not on your path, you won't be able to execute so simply from the command line. In such cases, either place jbuilder on your path, or type the full path to the JBuilder executable: c:\JBuilder7\bin\jbuilder.exe -build SimpleDirs.jpr.

If you are having trouble compiling the project, you can get additional debug information by typing **c:\JBuilder7\bin\jbuilder.exe -build -verbose SimpleDirs.jpr**. Detailed information about what classes are being used by your project will then be displayed on the command line.

Placing Multiple Projects in One Directory

In this section of the chapter, I will quickly show you how to put multiple applications in a JBuilder project. This is a very simple process, and many readers can probably guess how to proceed. But just in case there is any confusion, I'll outline the steps in a few short paragraphs.

NOTE: In my opinion, it is good programming practice to put each of your applications in its own directory. However, if you are creating very simple programs for a beginning level Java course or you are writing a series of simple command-line utilities, you may not see the need to put all your applications in different directories. In fact, it might be convenient to put a set of utilities or sample programs in a directory called Java101 or SystemMaintenanceUtilities. In general, if your project consists of more than one source file, you probably want to put it in its own directory. But if you have five simple applications, each of which is contained in its own single file, then you could place all five application source files in a single directory. (Don't try to put more than one application in a single file. I mean only that you can put five applications, each of which consists of a single file, in a single directory.)

By this stage in the chapter, there should be little need for me to explain how to proceed in any great depth. Simply create a project directory with its own JPR or JPX file, as shown in several previous sections of this chapter. Take a look at Figure 23-1 or Figure 23-8 if you need a reminder as to how to proceed.

Choose **File | New** and use the Class Wizard to add two new class files to that directory, making sure that each one includes a main method. Call the first one **ApplicationOne** and the second **ApplicationTwo**. In keeping with the theme of this chapter, you should opt not to place those files in a package. If you need a reminder about how to proceed, take a look at Figure 23-10.

When you are done you will have one new project file and one new directory. Inside the directory there will be a series of smaller applications. To switch from one application to the next, simply choose **Project | Project Properties** and turn to the Run page.

In JBuilder 7 and above, you have the option of running multiple projects from a single JPX file. Simply add two items to the Runtime configurations dialog shown in Figure 23-14. To do this, press the **New** button, then browse for the class you want, as shown in Figure 23-15. Once you have set up both configurations, you can then simply open the dialog and select one or the other project as the default. Then close the dialog and press the **Run** button. To run the other project, repeat the process, this time selecting the other configuration as the default.

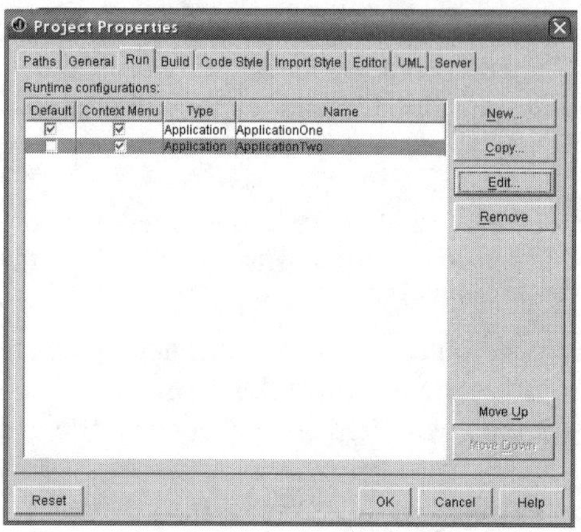

Figure 23-14: The Project Properties dialog as it appears if you decide to run ApplicationOne rather than ApplicationTwo

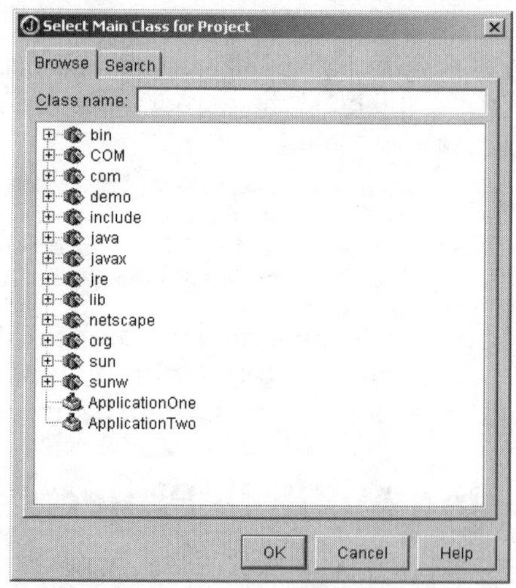

Figure 23-15: Browsing for a class file. Notice that you can see both ApplicationOne and ApplicationTwo in the list of files from which you can choose.

You can find an example program of this type on the CD in the directory called MultiProj.

Running the Simpler JDK Demos from JBuilder

At first, you may have the impression that JBuilder demands that you set up projects in a certain way in order to run them. This is not true. To help emphasize that point, I want to step you through the process of running a few of the demos that come with the JDK from inside of JBuilder.

Running the Animator Demo

The Animator demo is in the jdk1.3.1/demo/applets directory. This demo has shipped with most versions of the JDK.

- Open JBuilder and choose **File | Close Projects** to close any existing projects.
- Choose **File | New Project.**
- Press the ellipses (browse) button next to the Directory field.
- Browse for the jb7/jdk1.3.1/demo directory. With the word **applets** highlighted, press the **OK** button, as shown in Figure 23-16.

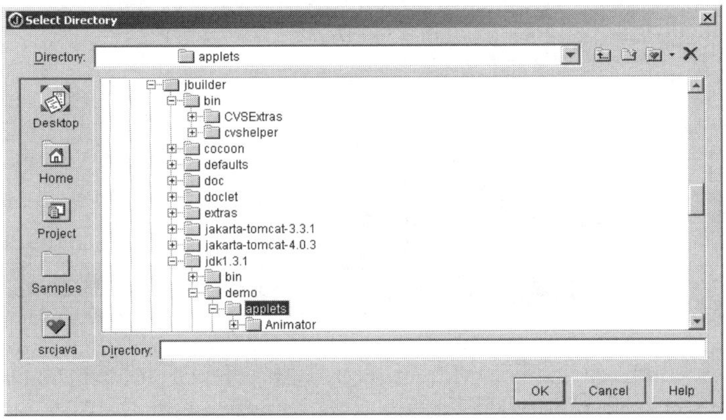

Figure 23-16: Browsing for the jdk1.3.1/demo/applets directory

- In the Name field of the first page of the Project Wizard, type in the name of the project you want to run. This is Animator, as shown in Figure 23-17. In Figure 23-16, you can see that Animator is the first project in the applets directory.

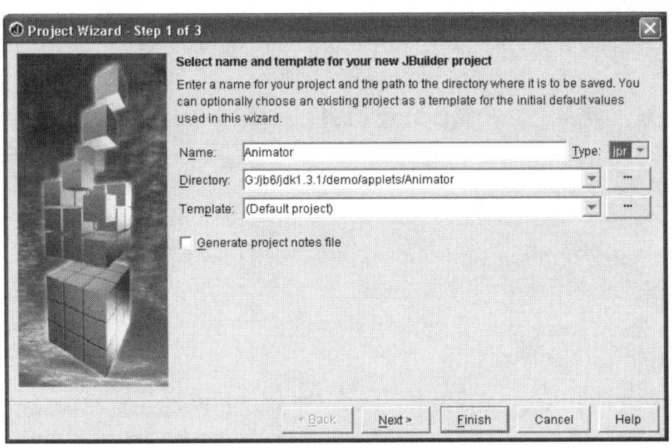

Figure 23-17: Identifying the demo project that you want to run

- There is no need to go through Steps 2 and 3 of the Project Wizard, so simple click **Finish.**
- Inside JBuilder, click the green **Add to project** symbol. It is located just above the project name, as shown in Figure 23-18. Alternatively, you can choose **Project | Add Files/Packages** from the JBuilder menu.

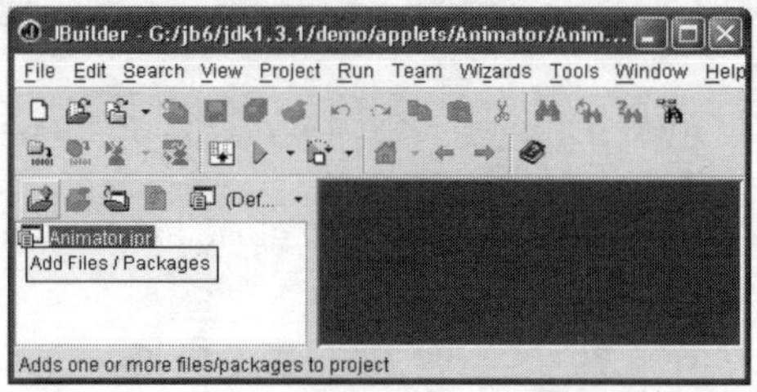

Figure 23-18: The hint for the Add Files to a Project button, which appears as an open folder and a plus symbol

- Add all the HTML files from the Animator package. When you are done, the IDE should look as it does in Figure 23-19.

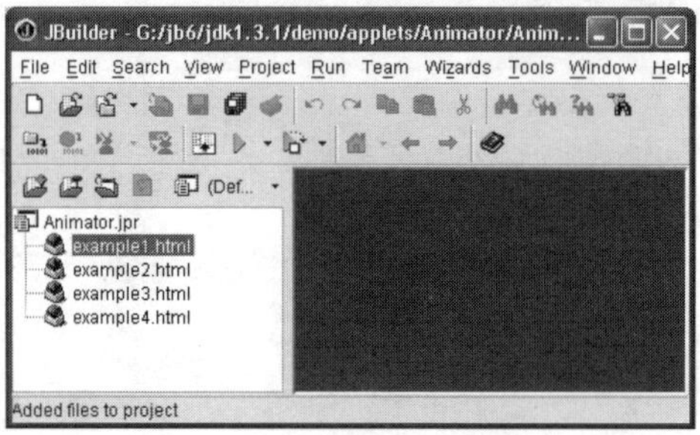

Figure 23-19: The IDE after you have added four HTML files to the project

The HTML files you have added to the project are the ones that load the applet. To run the applet, simply right-click on the HTML file titles shown in Figure 23-19, and then choose **Run** from the menu shown in Figure 23-20.

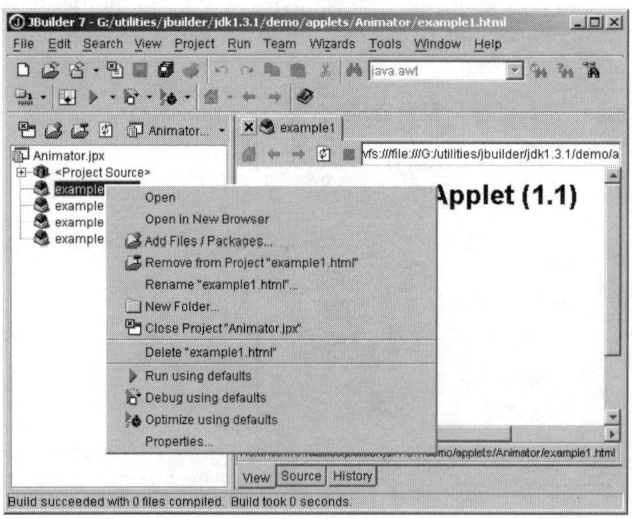

Figure 23-20: Right-click on an HTML file to get this menu. Select Run to launch the applet.

The running applet is shown in Figure 23-21.

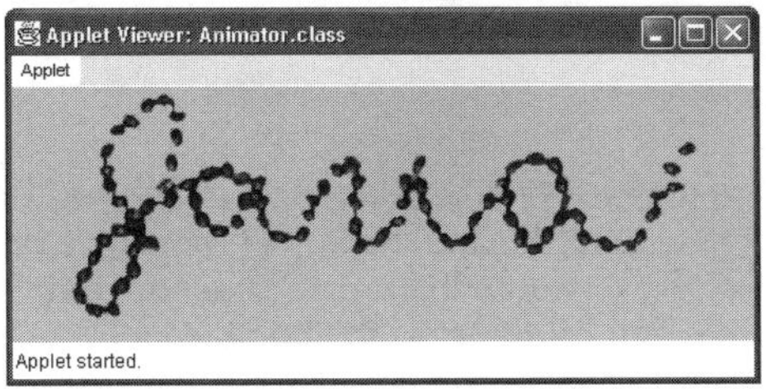

Figure 23-21: The applet once it is launched from the JBuilder IDE

The process shown here may seem a bit complex when you read about it. However, once you get the hang of it, you should be able to do it in just a few seconds.

Running the ArcTest Applet

The ArcTest applet is the second demo in the applets directory. To run it, choose **File | New Project**. Browse to the jdk1.3.1/demo/applets directory and press **OK**. In the Name field of the Project Wizard, type **ArcTest**. In both these steps you should be modeling your actions after the steps shown in Figures 23-16 and 23-17.

Press the **Add Files/Packages** button and add the example1.html file from the ArcTest directory, much as you did in Figures 23-18 and 23-19. Now right-click on the HTML file, and choose **Run** from the menu. The result is the applet shown in Figure 23-22.

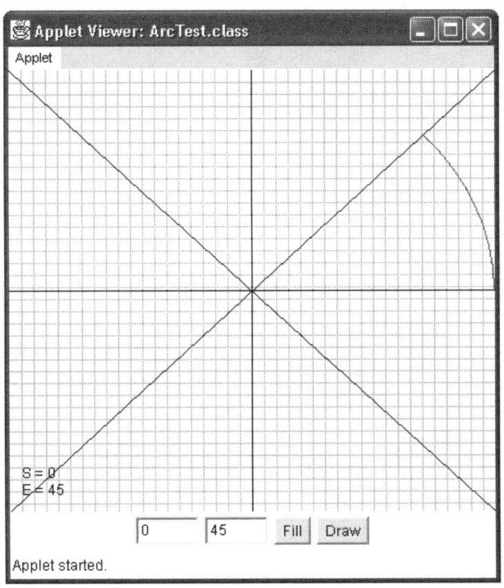

Figure 23-22: The ArcTest applet run from inside of JBuilder

If you want, you can choose **Project | Project Properties**, then turn to the Run page. Set the main class to one of the HTML files. Now you will be able to run the project by choosing Run from the menu.

Of course, the simple act of running an applet from inside of JBuilder is not what is important. The real power here lies in the fact that you can now use JBuilder's debugger and editor to examine and modify the demo program. This, however, is not the right time to get into those features of the product.

For now, the main point is that it is easy to load existing projects into the JBuilder IDE. This is true even for projects like these demos, which were clearly never designed explicitly to be run in JBuilder. Of course, these are simple projects, but the point is that JBuilder can open random projects and run them.

NOTE: I timed myself on loading and running the next project in the applets directory. It took me 40 seconds to go from a complete standstill to actually having the applet running. I started with the IDE open, then browsed for the right directory to create the project, added the right file to the project, and ran it. I'm sure that if you practice, you could get to the point where you load and run the project even faster than this. Again, the point is that — once you know what you are doing — it is easy to start new projects in JBuilder and run them.

Running Applications from the JDK

Let's take a moment to run two applications from the JDK. One is simple to run, while the other is a bit more of a challenge.

Close any existing projects and prepare to create a new one. Choose **File | New Project**, and browse to the jb7/jdk1.3.1/demo/jfc directory, following the pattern shown in Figure 23-16. Type in the name of one of the applications, which in this case is called **SimpleExample**. The end result is shown in Figure 23-23.

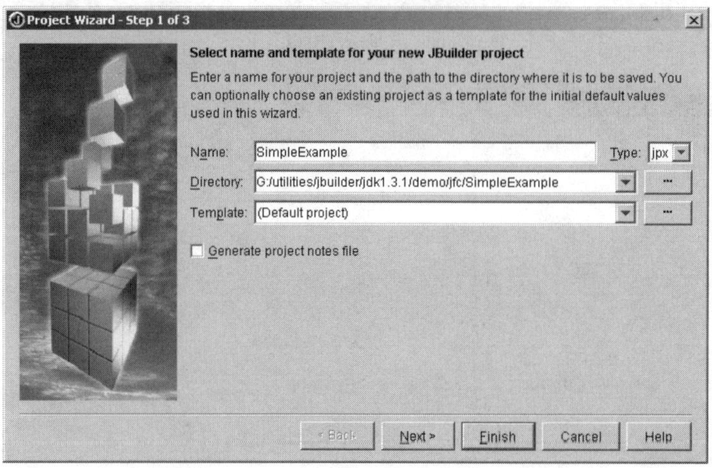

Figure 23-23: Setting up a JBuilder project for the SimpleExample program that ships with JDK

Note that when you are done, your directory field looks something like this:

```
G:/compilers/j2sdk1.4.0/demo/jfc/SimpleExample
```

Click the **Finish** button shown in Figure 23-23, and then use the **Add Files/Packages** button to browse for and add to your project the SimpleExample.java file from the SimpleExample/src directory. Right-click on the file in the IDE and choose **Run** from the menu. This is very much like what you did in Figure 23-20, but this time you are clicking on a Java file rather than an HTML file.

NOTE: You may find yourself asking: How do I make the menus show all the options? In particular, if you have chosen a file that does not have a main method, is not the main file for an applet or is not an HTML file that wraps an applet, the Run option will be missing from the menu. In such a case, simply choose another file, repeating the process until you find one you can run.

If you have the SE or Enterprise version of JBuilder, you can use the Project for Existing Code (PEC) Wizard to help with this process. Choose **File | New** from the JBuilder menu, turn to the Projects page, and run the PEC wizard. Browse for the SimpleExample directory, as shown in Figure 23-24.

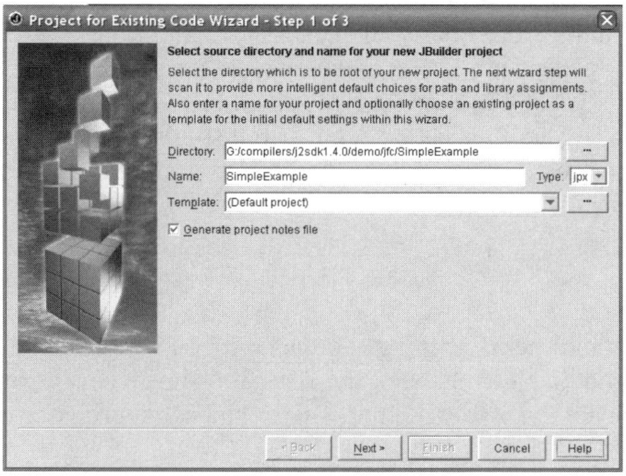

Figure 23-24: Importing a project into JBuilder using the Project for Existing Code Wizard

In the second page of the dialog you can just accept the defaults. This is possible because the source code is indeed in a directory called src. If this were not the case, you might have to edit this dialog.

Now close the dialog, open up the Project Source node in the project pane, right-click on **SimpleExample.java**, and choose **Run** from the menu. You could also set up a run configuration from the Project | Project Properties | Run page as shown in Figures 23-6 and 23-14.

You can run much more complex third-party applications and applets from JBuilder than the ones I have talked about in this examination of the JDK demos. As I said earlier, if you can compile it from the command line, you should be able to compile it from JBuilder. But in this chapter I have concentrated on working with simple examples.

Making Sense of the Options

I've given you a number of different options in this chapter. For instance, I showed how you could write your code first in a text editor and then bring it in to JBuilder for debugging. I also showed how you could build the project in JBuilder but override its default behavior of using packages. I showed how you could place all your files in the root directory for your project, or place your source files in the src directory and your class files in the classes directory. By now you should see that there are even more possible combinations, such as placing the source files in the project root directory and the class files in the classes directory, or calling the src directory Source, etc., etc., etc.

Certainly one of my points is that JBuilder is a very flexible tool, and you can set it up to behave in pretty much any way you want. You are not locked into any particular format.

As to which choice is best, that really is up to you. I suppose that placing all your files in one directory, and even placing multiple applications in one directory, makes sense if you are building simple projects. However, as you begin working with more complex projects, it makes sense to follow the JBuilder default options of using packages and working with the src and classes directories.

However, you should do what feels most comfortable to you. If you have lots of experience programming, then you should feel free to adopt the style that has worked best for you in the past. If you are working with a team, you need to work together to establish standards. If you are new to Java or new to programming, you might want to use JBuilder's default options, particularly as you start to build more complex programs.

The people who designed JBuilder were nearly all excellent programmers with many years of experience behind them. If they decided to have JBuilder work a particular way, they certainly had good reason for doing so. But don't let their reputation push you around. If you have some good reason for following another path, then just tell JBuilder to do what you want, not what the developers of the product built in as its defaults. After all, the act of experimenting can often be the best teacher of all.

Summary

At this stage, you should understand the basic things you need to know to compile and run simple projects from the command line and inside of the IDE. You should also be aware of the many options available to you inside the IDE. JBuilder will let you configure your projects pretty much any way you want.

In the next chapter, I will continue a discussion of how to create and run projects in JBuilder and from the command line. However, the programs shown in the next chapter will be more complex than those shown in this chapter. In particular, they will be stored in packages, and most of them will be GUI based. In succeeding chapters, I will push the subject toward its limits, showing you how to work with complex projects that have multiple packages and that include multiple libraries that are stored in JAR files.

After you understand project management, I will talk about deployment of applications. In particular, I will show how to deploy your applications or applets in a JAR file.

Chapter 24

The Structure of a Default JBuilder Project

Charlie Calvert

This chapter covers working with default JBuilder projects. These projects are created by the JBuilder Application wizard. By the time you have finished reading the chapter, you should understand everything you need to know to work with the most commonly encountered type of JBuilder application.

This is a short chapter, and the material it covers is not particularly complex. However, the structure of JBuilder projects is essential to your understanding of JBuilder itself. Further, it is a subject that can cause considerable confusion for newcomers to either JBuilder or Java. As a result, I will make a sincere effort to cover the subject in a clear and definitive fashion. In the next chapter, you will see how to build on this default structure to create complex JBuilder projects.

You may recall that the previous chapter focused on project management concepts that ended up being fairly simple to understand. The key was coming to terms with the theory behind the JBuilder project management wizards. You will find the same is true of this chapter. JBuilder provides sensible means for working with complex projects. To get started, you just need to understand a few basic concepts.

At the end of this chapter I have included a few short tips and techniques for working with key parts of the JBuilder IDE. Subjects covered include:

- Turning off the sound effects
- Switching between an applet and an application
- Telling JBuilder the main file for the project
- JDK switching

Default JBuilder Projects

I will begin by defining what a default JBuilder project looks like. Most of the projects in this book start with this default format, so it is important that you understand its structure.

The default application produced by the JBuilder wizard has a very robust and flexible structure. It is not necessarily the simplest way to create a Java application, but it is perhaps the best way to create a foundation on which medium and large Java applications can be built. In short, its virtues may not be apparent to you at first, but when you create more complex applications you should begin to see the wisdom behind this architecture.

Creating a Default Application

To create a default project in JBuilder you follow a set of easy-to-use wizards. I describe this process in some depth in Chapter 3. If you need help creating a default application, please review that chapter. Figures 24-1 and 24-2 show the key steps in the process of creating an application.

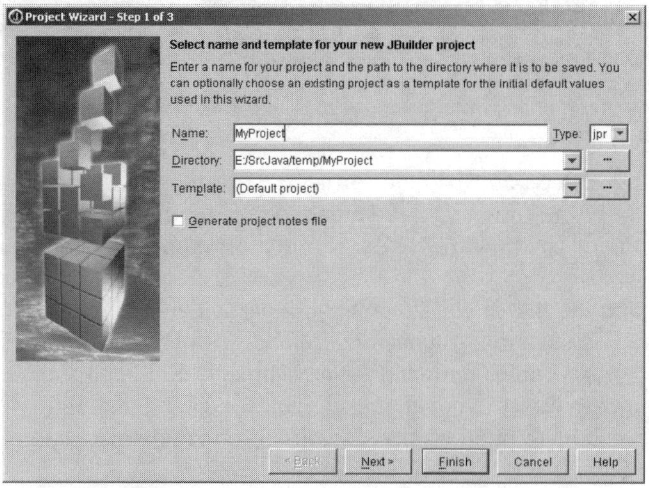

Figure 24-1: Using the first page of the Project Wizard to change the default name of a project from untitledx to MyProject

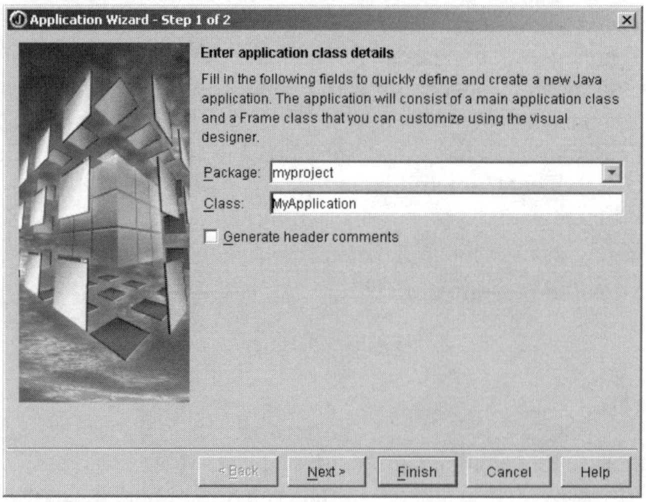

Figure 24-2: Changing the name of the main class of an application from Application1 to MyApplication on the first page of the Application Wizard

Remember that JBuilder does not contain any black boxes. If you set the name of a directory or the name of a class, you are not writing your changes in stone. Even if you exit JBuilder, you can still change the name of that directory or the name of that class exactly as you would when working with any other directory on your system or any other piece of Java source code. The JBuilder wizards are just Borland's way of helping you fill in the parts of your code that you would have to type out or create for yourself anyway. The developers of JBuilder are religious about ensuring that development in the environment involves no black boxes or deep secrets. After all, they are developers themselves, and they want exactly the same kinds of flexibility in project development that you would want.

Later in the book, in Chapter 31, you will learn how to automatically change package or class names in your project. Refactoring changes not only the name of a single directory or a single class but also all references to that class or package throughout your project.

Locating Your Files on the Hard Drive

I want to now spend a few pages discussing the meaning and function of the files that JBuilder generates when you create a new project. This discussion is broken up into two sections. The first will cover where your source and class files reside relative to the root directory for your project. The second section will discuss how to change the default root directory for your project.

Default Paths for Files

Having created a default JBuilder project, the next step is to understand what that project looks like from the point of view of the local file system. What files and directories were created?

In what follows I am assuming you are creating a project called MyProject and that it resides in a package called myproject.

Your source code ends up, by default, in a directory with this signature:

```
../MyProject/src/myproject
```

In a typical default JBuilder application, there will be two files in this directory. The first file, by default, will be called Application1.java. The second file will be called Frame1.java. This chapter is not the place to discuss the contents of those files. All you need to know is that Application1 contains the startup code for your application, and Frame1 is a container that holds the components in your user interface. For instance, Frame1 might contain buttons, list boxes, menus, and other tools with which the user can interact.

In a default JBuilder project, the compiled class files end up in this directory:

```
../MyProject/classes/myproject
```

Needless to say, a compilation of your default project would place two files in classes/myproject, one called Application1.class and the second called Frame1.class. As your project grows in complexity, additional files will be added to this directory.

JBuilder will also create a directory called ../MyProject/bak, which will contain backup copies of your source files. You can view these files in the History window found on the file view tabs beneath the content pane. In particular, notice the Diff page in the History window. Use this page to view the differences between versions of your current file. There is also typically a directory called doc, which you can use for Javadoc files. Javadoc files were discussed in Chapter 21.

Changing the Default Location for Your Projects

On Windows, JBuilder, by default, puts your project files in the awkward, and in my opinion ill-conceived, Microsoft Documents and Settings directory. In doing so, it is simply following the illogical recommendations put forward by Chairman Bill. Both following Microsoft's advice and using the Documents and Settings directory is, of course, both in principle and in practice, a bad policy. In particular, Java has a hard time working with long filenames that have spaces in them.

NOTE: The JBuilder team didn't have much choice in this matter. Java, by default, only knows of a few directories on a system. One of them is the user's home directory, which is, by default, in Documents and Settings. The blame here really rests with Microsoft, which never should have created this awkward name.

Because the directory Documents and Settings has spaces in its path, you probably don't want to stick with the defaults employed by JBuilder. Instead, you may want to create a directory of your own for storing projects. You will, of course, want to ensure that there are no spaces in the path leading to this directory.

The process of telling JBuilder to use a new directory is really very simple, once you understand the relevant tools provided by JBuilder. However, understanding these tools is a bit of a challenge. Please pay close attention to the text in the next few paragraphs. There is one key concept you need to grasp to make sense of this JBuilder tool, but you may need to read these paragraphs a few times and experiment once or twice with JBuilder itself before you feel comfortable with this concept. So pay close attention, and you will soon understand how to tell JBuilder where to place your projects.

You can change the default location for your projects by choosing **Project | Default Project Properties** from the JBuilder menu. Select the **Paths** page, which should be focused automatically. Edit the values in the fields on the Paths page to suit your tastes, as shown in Figure 24-3. I will spend the next few paragraphs explaining the text entered into the dialog shown in the figure.

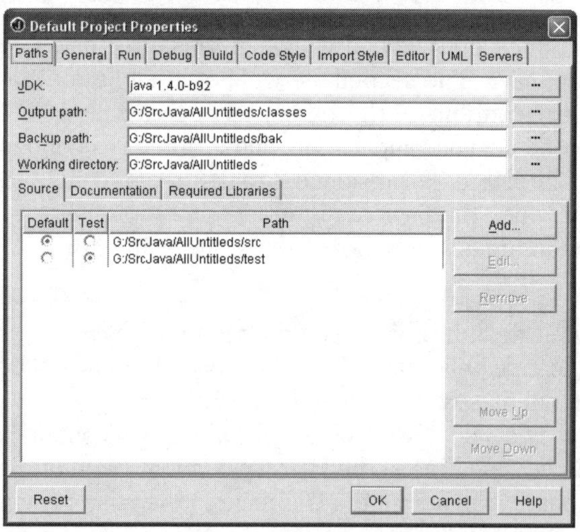

Figure 24-3: A properly filled out Paths page from the Default Project Properties dialog. Here I have elected to put my projects in a directory called AllUntitleds.

In the Default Project Properties dialog shown above, you are really specifying the *pattern* for the directories you want to create and not the actual directories themselves. Notice that I set the classes directory to G:/SrcJava/AllUntitleds/classes. This does not mean that you want JBuilder to put the files in a directory called G:/SrcJava/AllUntitleds/classes. Instead, it tells JBuilder the pattern you want it to follow when it is creating the new directory for your projects. In particular, you are telling JBuilder that when you create a new project, it will have a path like this for the classes directory: G:/SrcJava/AllUntitleds/untitled1/classes. For instance, when you create a new project with the Project Wizard, then it should by default now have values similar to those shown in Figure 24-4.

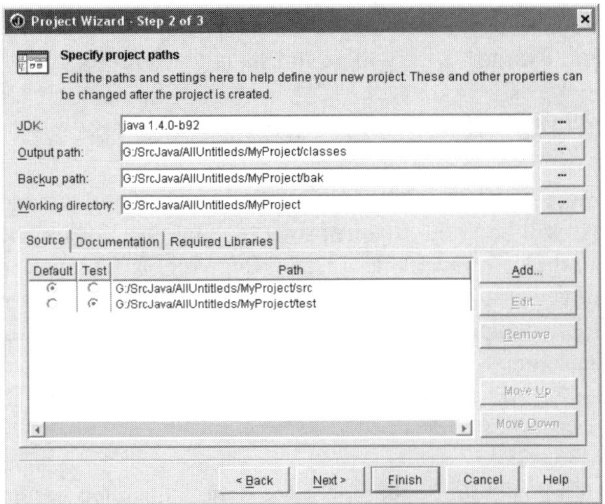

Figure 24-4: Given the default values shown in Figure 24-3, this is how the second page of the New Project Wizard will look.

Notice the insertion of the word MyProject, which is the name of your project. So the pattern is to take the directory you specify as your default classes directory, in this case AllUntitleds, and then add the name of your project, which might be something like untitled1 or MyProject. The first line that follows shows the pattern you give, and the next two lines show examples of actual project directories based on this pattern:

```
G:/SrcJava/AllUntitleds/classes
G:/SrcJava/AllUntitleds/untitled1/classes
G:/SrcJava/AllUntitleds/MyProject/classes
```

I have always found the Paths page of the Default Project Properties dialog to be somewhat confusing. As a result, it might help if I restate what I have said above in slightly different terms. In Figure 24-3, I am not asking JBuilder to actually put files in a directory called E:\SrcJava\AllUntitleds\src. Instead, I am asking JBuilder to put it in E:\SrcJava\AllUntitleds\MyProject\src\myproject, where MyProject is the name of the project you are creating. For instance, it might be called untitled1 or whatever name you choose to give it. Then JBuilder inserts the src directory. Inside the src directory is the package called myproject used by the project.

In the code fragments following this paragraph, first I show you what you enter in the Default Project Properties dialog, and then I show you the results that this input produces when you create a new project. Here is what happens when you specify the default directory for your source files:

```
G:\SrcJava\AllUntitleds\src
G:\SrcJava\AllUntitleds\MyProject\src\myproject
```

Here is what happens when you specify the default directory for your classes files:

```
G:\SrcJava\AllUntitleds\classes
G:\SrcJava\AllUntitleds\MyProject\classes\myproject
```

As you can see, there is a very clear pattern here. First you list the name of the subdirectory where you want to place your source or class files. Files with a .java extension will go in the src directory; those with a .class extension will go in the classes directory. When you actually create a project, JBuilder first inserts the name of your project directory, then the name of the directory you specified, then the name of the default package for your project. The source files, such as Application1.java and Frame1.java, will go in this latter directory.

NOTE: You can, of course, give directories such as src and classes any name you want. For instance, you could call them source and output if you wanted.

You simply have to intuit that JBuilder is not asking you to work with literal directories in this dialog but only with a pattern that will be used in your projects. The directories such as G:\SrcJava\AllUntitleds\classes and G:\SrcJava\AllUntitleds\src, which are shown in Figure 24-3, are not real directories. They are more like hints for the pattern JBuilder should follow when it creates your projects. In particular, the E:\SrcJava\AllUntitleds directory is the default root directory for my temporary projects. The classes part of the formula just shows the directory that should be appended on to G:\SrcJava\AllUntitleds\MyProject when it comes time to specify the path to your class files.

NOTE: I cannot even pretend that I think the JBuilder team has done a good job designing the Paths page of the Default Project Properties dialog. However, once you understand the developers' intent, the dialog is very easy to use.

Speaking of things that are hard to understand, I should perhaps add a word of explanation as to why I specify a directory called AllUntitleds as the default location of my files. I never put any real projects that I want to keep in the AllUntitleds directory but instead in directories that branch off of g:/srcjava/ itself. The AllUntitleds directory is where I put all my untitledx projects that are really nothing more than minor experiments or tests of certain ideas. I tend to generate a lot of these files. Then, when I come up with something I really need, I pare the relevant code out of the untitled directory and place it in a more permanent location.

When you are creating a JBuilder project, you do not need to place your files in the default directory you set up in the Default Project Properties dialog. Turn back a few pages and take a look at the Directory field in Figure 24-1. You can use this field to place the root directory for your project on any location on your hard drive that you desire. JBuilder will have no trouble understanding what you have done.

If all of this seems somewhat overly complex and confusing, the silver lining is that it is all part of a system with enormous flexibility and also an inherent sense of structure. JBuilder will let you structure your projects in virtually any way you want. And the default structure it provides is a good one. You simply need to understand how the system works. Understanding the system may be somewhat challenging, but once you understand it, the system is easy to use. More importantly, it is very flexible.

Notes on Projects

I mentioned in the last chapter the technique for moving a project. Let's review that process as quickly as possible. If you have stored a project in one place on your hard drive and want to move it to another place, you can usually accomplish this task by simply moving the root directory for your project. All the other paths that are stored in the JPX file for your project should usually be relative paths, and so your project should move from one location to another with little fuss. I will say a few more words on this subject in the next section, which covers JPX files.

By now you should have a good sense of how JBuilder structures a default project and how you can specify the location where that default project resides. You can change this structure in almost any way you want. You should note, however, that in this book I do not care about the default root directory for your project, but I do care about the structure of your project.

For instance, I don't care if you use Documents and Settings, e:\srcjava, or somewhere else as the root for your projects. But I generally do focus on building projects that use the classes and src directories created in a default JBuilder project.

Thinking about JPX and JPR Files

The closest thing that JBuilder has to a black box is the JPR and JPX files that it uses to manage your project. In fact, these files are not black boxes. They are simple text files. But they definitely have a vaguely threatening aura about them, and so it is worth taking a moment to demystify them.

NOTE: As you know from the last chapter, in all versions of JBuilder you have a choice between using JPR and JPX files. For simplicity's sake, I will refer to both files as JPR files throughout the next few paragraphs. I do this because the mnemonic of JPR standing for JBuilder Project file is easy to remember and understand. Note, however, that JPX files, with their easy-to-understand and -parse XML syntax, will probably be the preferred format for many developers.

Though JPR files are tightly integrated with the IDE, nonetheless they play much the same role in a JBuilder project that a makefile plays in a C++ project. In fact, you can compile a JPR file from the command line by typing **jbuilder -build MyProject.jpr**. I am not aware of a tool for converting a JPR file to a makefile or to a batch file. There are tools from third parties that automatically create Ant files from JBuilder projects.

As you already know, the code in the JPR file has nothing to do with Java per se. It is simply a tool used by JBuilder to help manage your project. Your code will compile fine under any standard JDK regardless of whether or not the JPR file is present. The JPR file is needed by JBuilder but not by the JDK.

Listing 24-1 shows the complete JPR file for the project created with the dialogs shown in Figures 24-1 and 24-2.

Listing 24-1: A simple JBuilder project file

```
;JBuilder - PROJECT FILE VERSION {2.00} - do not alter this line!
#0=MyProject.jpr
#1=src\myproject\Frame1.java
#2=src\myproject\MyApplication.java
runtime.0[0].RunnableType=com.borland.jbuilder.runtime.ApplicationRunner
runtime.0[0].application.class=myproject.MyApplication
sys[0].AuthorLabel=@author
sys[0].BackupPath=bak
sys[0].BeansInstantiate=false
sys[0].BraceStyle=1
sys[0].CheckStable=1
sys[0].Company=Elvenware
sys[0].CompanyLabel=Company:
sys[0].Copyright=Copyright (c) 2001
sys[0].CopyrightLabel=Copyright:
sys[0].DefaultPath=src
sys[0].Description=
sys[0].DescriptionLabel=Description:
sys[0].DocPath=doc
sys[0].EventMatch=false
sys[0].EventStyle=0
```

Part V

```
sys[0].ExcludeClassEnabled=0
sys[0].IncludeTestPath=1
sys[0].InstanceVisibility=0
sys[0].JDK=java 1.3.1-b24
sys[0].LastTag=2
sys[0].Libraries=
sys[0].MakeStable=0
sys[0].OutPath=classes
sys[0].SourcePath=src
sys[0].TestPath=src
sys[0].Title=
sys[0].TitleLabel=Title:
sys[0].Version=1.0
sys[0].VersionLabel=@version
sys[0].WorkingDirectory=.
sys[1].Parent=0
sys[2].Parent=0
```

The first and most obvious thing to note about the project file is that it is a text file, not a binary file. In the normal course of things, you would have no reason to edit a JPR file directly. However, if you want to edit it, you can feel free to do so.

In general, you can use the tools in JBuilder to change the contents of a JPR file. However, there are rare occasions when it seems simplest to open the file in a text editor, and perform search and replaces to alter the code. This might be helpful if you are renaming a file or package referenced throughout the JPR file.

Most of the entries in the JPR file are quite easy to understand. For instance, these lines tell JBuilder what files are part of the project itself:

```
#0=MyProject.jpr
#1=src\myproject\Frame1.java
#2=src\myproject\MyApplication.java
```

That is about the simplest syntax the Borland engineers could have found for performing this particular task. Obviously you could edit this list yourself, though of course you wouldn't want to do so without first closing the project. You can also see that this kind of code is generated automatically when stepping through the JBuilder project and application wizards, and when using the JBuilder tools for adding and removing files from a project.

I mentioned in the previous section that you can usually move a project around on your hard drive by simply moving the location of the root directory for your project. You can even use this technique for moving projects from one machine to another. As a rule, the project will compile unchanged after you move it. However, if you do have problems moving a project, looking for the location of your files in the JPR code is obviously a good place to start tracking down any problems you might encounter.

Pursuing the JPR listing further, you can see that it contains information that is appended to the top of your files if you ask to include *header comments* when creating a new class. Other parts reflect the braces and event styles you can change by choosing **Project | Project Properties | Code Style** from the JBuilder menu, as shown in Figure 24-5.

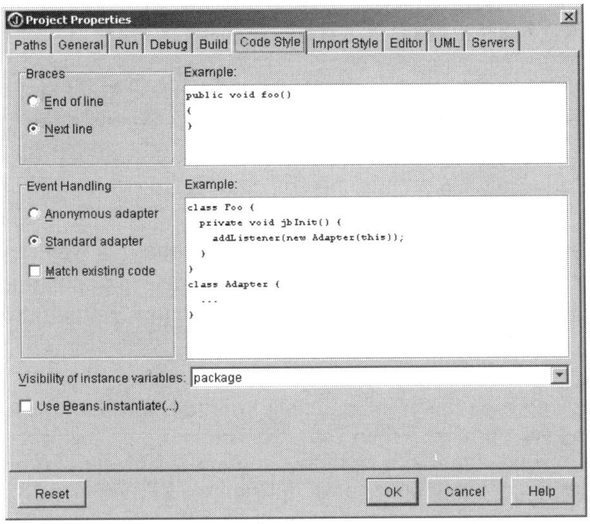

Figure 24-5: The decisions you make in the Code Style page of the Project Properties dialog are ultimately recorded in the JPR file.

It is a fairly straightforward process to see how some of the elements in the Code Style dialog translate into JPR code such as the following:

```
sys[0].BraceStyle=1
sys[0].EventMatch=false
sys[0].BeansInstantiate=false
sys[0].EventStyle=0
```

Please understand that I am not suggesting you make changes to these types of features in the JPR file itself. It is much easier to use the JBuilder dialogs. My point is simply to make sure you are not afraid of or mystified by something as simple as the JPR file.

The code for JPX files is usually nothing more than a simple port of a JPR file into XML syntax. For instance, here are the lines for designating the source and classes directories:

```
<property category="sys" name="OutPath" value="classes"/>
<property category="sys" name="SourcePath" value="src;test"/>
```

Here is the same code for a JPR file:

```
sys[0].OutPath=classes
sys[0].SourcePath=src;test
```

It's pretty much six of one, half a dozen of the other. As usual, the XML code is a bit more verbose, but it does have the advantage of following a well-defined and very flexible standard.

In closing I want to stress two points:

- In general, you don't need to think much about JPR files until something has gone wrong with your project, which should happen very infrequently. However, when it does happen it can pose a serious problem. Then you will be glad that you understand a little something about JPR files.
- JPR files are saved in text format. This means you can place them under source control with a tool like CVS. If you want to share files via source control, try to avoid hard-coding any specific paths into your project files. Instead, always work with relative paths. JBuilder will always try to place relative paths in your JPR/JPX files. You have to go out of your way to get it to do anything else.

Compiling Default Projects from the Command Line

We are almost through with this discussion of default JBuilder projects. All I want to do now is discuss compiling them from the command line, and then we will be free to move on to the next chapter where you will find a discussion of how to create more complex projects.

In the normal course of development, you would have no reason to compile from the command line. After all, you can easily compile, run, and debug your applications from inside the IDE. However, you can automate certain tasks from the command line in a way that you can't easily automate them inside an IDE. So coverage of the command line is important, both because it is a valuable convenience and because it gives us the warm fuzzies to know that we are not locked into the GUI.

NOTE: In this discussion of compiling from the command line, I am talking about the kind of compiling you will do while deploying your project. When you have finished a project, you want to package it up in some way, often by placing it in a JAR file. Creating JAR files and running projects stored in JAR files are separate topics and will be covered in Chapters 27, 37, and 43.

As always, the simplest way to proceed is to just type **jbuilder -build MyProject.jpr**. Then use a standard java or appletviewer statement to launch your application, as explained below.

Many people still want to know how to build the application without using any JBuilder tools. Here is a batch file that you can modify for compiling and running a default application from the command line:

```
javac -d classes -sourcepath src src\untitled6\Application1.java
java -classpath classes;. untitled6.Application1
```

The javac statement uses the -d switch to tell the compiler to put the generated files in the classes directory. Since the project lives in a package called untitled6, the actual directory where your class files reside will be classes/untitled6. The -sourcepath directive tells javac to look for any needed source files in the src/untitled6 directory. This is necessary because a standard Java application uses two files, Application1.java and Frame1.java. javac won't know where to find Frame1.java unless you tell it explicitly with the -sourcepath switch. Finally, you end the javac command by explicitly pointing at the main file for your application: src\untitled6\Application1.java.

The java statement includes the -classpath switch to remind the jvm to look in the classes directory for our package. Though it is not strictly necessary in this case, I also tell it to look in the current directory by adding a semicolon and a period. This latter step has no effect in a simple project, but it is a good habit to develop when you are building more complex projects. Finally, you state the name of your package followed by the name of your main class file for the project, untitled6.Application1. People who are new to Java should remember never to append the .class extension to the listing for the main class file. Java will very impolitely choke on statements such as java -classpath classes untitled6.Application1.class.

Here is a batch file that you can modify for compiling any default applet from the command line:

```
javac -d classes src/minesweeper/*.java
appletviewer classes/MineSweeper.html
```

Finally, some people will want to compile JBuilder projects from inside a Jakarta Ant build file. Here is a sample of the syntax to use:

```
<target name="init">
    <!- Create the time stamp ->
    <tstamp/>
    <!- set global properties for this build ->
    <property name="src" value="src"/>
    <property name="build" value="classes"/>
    <!- Create the build directory structure used by compile ->
    <mkdir dir="${build}"/>
</target>

<target name="compile" depends="init">
    <!- Compile the java code from ${src} into ${build} ->
    <javac srcdir="${src}" destdir="${build}"/>
</target>
```

I'm not going to spend any time discussing this syntax, as it is not the topic of this book and there are many examples on this book's CD. I use Ant heavily. As a result, the source files for this book are a cornucopia of Ant tips and techniques.

Configuration Issues

This section covers basic configuration issues. Some of these issues are exceedingly straightforward; others are a bit more complex. None of them are terribly important, but they seemed worthy of a brief mention, and this was the best home I could find for them.

How Do I Save a File?

Choose **Ctrl+S** to save a file, and **Ctrl+Shift+A** to save your project. If you are a Delphi and CBuilder developer, you may be used to choosing Alt+F+S to save. This does not work very well in JBuilder. It is simplest just to get used to choosing Ctrl+S to save.

JBuilder and Linefeeds

One of the common problems with Java applications involves working with the characters placed at the end of a file. In the UNIX world, one typically ends a line with \n, or the 13th character. In the Mac world, the linefeed character is \r, or the 10th character. In the Windows world, the winner is \r\n.

Clearly, this is an area where problems can arise. The key point to emphasize here is that JBuilder will support whatever type of line endings you prefer to use.

By default, JBuilder simply continues using the current type of linefeeds in the file it has opened. However, by choosing Project | Default Project Properties | Editor from the menu, you can choose to explicitly use Windows style, UNIX style, or Mac style line endings.

NOTE: The subject of linefeeds is one that can, surprisingly enough, cause tempers to flare. Don't let people accuse JBuilder itself of messing up the linefeeds in a file. If trouble arises, it is not likely that JBuilder is the culprit. Instead, I would double-check to make sure that the problem doesn't come from your version control system. In particular, my favorite version control system, CVS, will, when run under Windows, add \r\n to files if you do not explicitly tell it to cease and desist. Other version control systems might cause similar problems.

How Do I Turn Off the Sound Effects?

By default, the JBuilder IDE can be a bit noisy. Choose **Tools | IDE Options** from the menu and turn to the Audio page. Turn off the items you don't want to make sounds.

How Do I Tell JBuilder the Main File for My Project?

If you have more than one file with a main statement in the source for your application, you can switch between them using the Project | Project Properties | Run page to reach the Runtime Properties dialog. This subject was discussed in some depth in the previous chapter.

Another solution is to right-click on the file in the structure pane and choose **Run**. If you right-click on a file and there is no option to run, then the file you have clicked does not have a main method in it, is not the main file for an applet or JApplet, or is not an HTML file that includes the Applet tag. The three options here are the primary types of files that can be run from the JBuilder IDE.

Applet and Application Hybrids

A default JBuilder applet can be run as either an application or an applet. To switch between the two, simply:

- Choose **Project | Project Properties** from the menu.
- Turn to the Run page in the Project Properties dialog and choose either the Application page or the Applet page. The choice you make will dictate whether your program will be run from the IDE as an application or an applet.
- Be sure that you set the main class for the project by setting the appropriate field in either the application or applet project. To do this, select the ellipsis button at the upper-right corner of the Application or Applet page. JBuilder will let you browse for the Java source file for your project that contains either your JApplet class or your main method. By default, this will be Applet1.java or Application1.java.

You can tell that an applet has the capability to run as an application or an applet if it contains a method called main. You can toggle this feature with the Can run standalone option on the first page of the applet wizard.

Examine Figures 24-6 and 24-7 for examples of how to proceed when you want to set either an application or an applet as the main class to run when you launch your application from inside the JBuilder IDE.

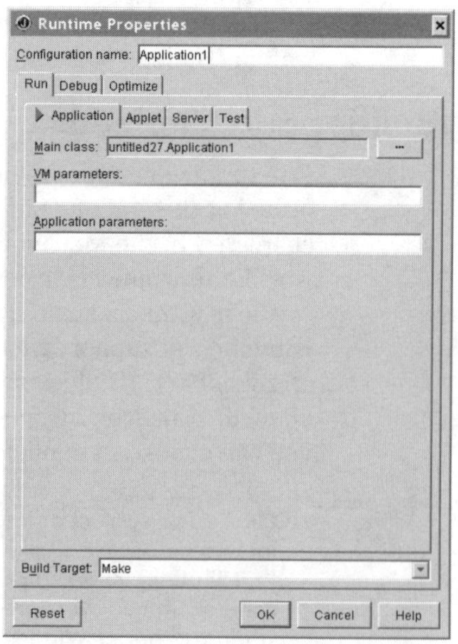

Figure 24-6: The Runtime Properties dialog of JBuilder can be set up to run either an applet or application. Here it is set to run an application.

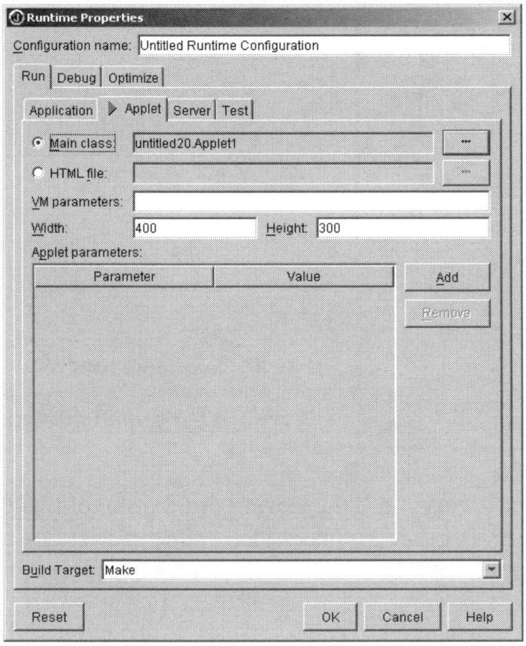

Figure 24-7: This is the page to use to set up JBuilder to run an applet. Notice that you can run the applet inside JBuilder's applet viewer or choose to use an HTML file when you launch your applet.

The key point to grasp here is that JBuilder will attempt to run a file as an application if you focus the Application page in the dialog, and it will attempt to run it as an applet if you focus the Applet page in the dialog. Look carefully at the images in Figures 24-6 and 24-7, and you will see that in one figure the Application page of the Run dialog is focused, while in the other figure the Applet page is focused.

NOTE: You can also specify an HTML file that contains a valid applet tag as the main class for an applet. To do this, choose the HTML File radio button shown in Figure 24-7. In the edit control next to the radio button, type in or browse for the name of the HTML file for your applet. When you select the Run button, JBuilder will launch your applet inside of the HTML file rather than inside an applet viewer.

What about JDK Switching?

JBuilder allows you to work with multiple JDKs. However, most of the time, you can use the default JDK that ships with the product.

If you have the SE or Enterprise edition of the product, choose **Project | Project Properties** from the JBuilder menu. On the Paths page, click the ellipsis button next to the JDK field. You will see a dialog that gives you a choice of one or more JDKs. This is the JDK that your program will use after it is launched from the JBuilder IDE.

If you click on the New button, you will be able to browse for a directory in which you have installed a JDK, as shown in Figure 24-8. You don't need to browse for the bin directory; instead browse for the root directory for the JDK.

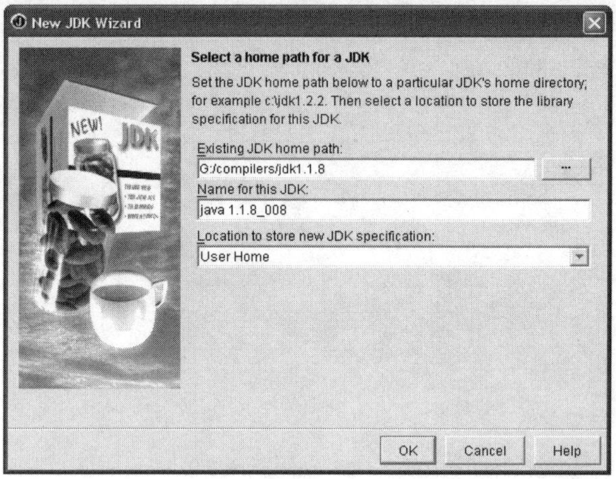

Figure 24-8: Getting ready to run JBuilder under an ancient JDK. This particular JDK was created back when the earth's crust was still cooling.

Figure 24-8 shows an example of using a very old JDK. During the writing of this book, I primarily used either a beta or, in the later stages of composition, a shipping version of JDK 1.4. JBuilder ships with JDK 1.3.1, but I focus instead on JDK 1.4, as it was the latest and greatest at the time I was writing.

If you have the Personal edition, you will need to change the JDK through the Tools menu. Choose **Tools | Configure JDKs.** Figure 24-9 shows the Configure JDKs dialog. Use the Change button to browse for your JDK.

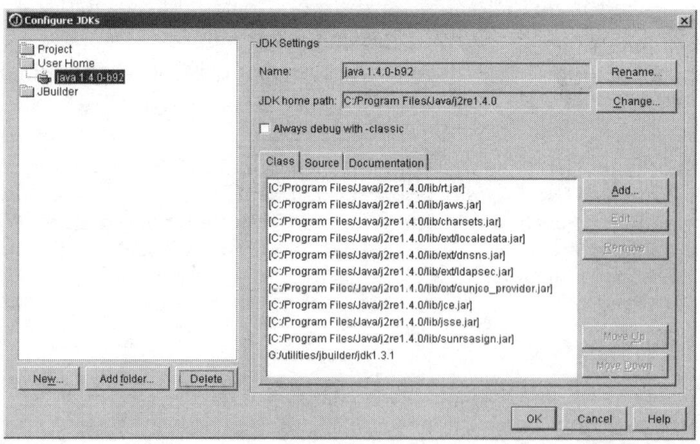

Figure 24-9: The Configure JDKs dialog allows you to choose your JDK.

Summary

In this chapter you have learned about the fundamental structure of a JBuilder application. This is foundation material on which your understanding of JBuilder itself must rest. You will never really be comfortable with JBuilder until you understand how it structures its projects. This subject appears a bit daunting at first, but once you have it nailed down, you can quickly and easily get JBuilder to do what you want.

Chapter 25

Creating Complex Projects

Charlie Calvert

This chapter focuses on projects that contain complex classpaths, extra class files, and similar features. Most serious Java projects have complexities of this type. Here you will learn how to use JBuilder's tools to make it as easy as possible to deal with these kinds of projects.

In the previous two chapters you saw how to work with default JBuilder projects and projects that are even simpler than the default. This chapter helps fill out the picture by showing projects that are more complex than standard JBuilder projects.

In the next chapter you will learn about CVS and team development. That will be the last chapter on the subject of creating and managing projects in JBuilder. After that, the text will move on to an in-depth examination of deployment issues.

There are two thoughts I want to add before digging into more technical matters:

- In this chapter you will see at least one project that has a fairly complex UI. I am not, however, going to spend much time talking about the technical aspects of that program. Instead, I will simply ask you to run the project and see how it performs. The focus in this chapter is on creating projects and handling packages. I don't want to distract you from that subject by focusing too much on Java syntax and how it is handled in JBuilder.
- Some of the subjects in this chapter are relatively advanced. If you are very new to Java and just want to get started creating applications, there probably is not a whole lot in this chapter for you. On the other hand, if you want to understand how to structure more complex Java applications or if you want to see how to use JBuilder to manage complex applications, then you have come to the right place.

Complex Projects

I'm going to show you several different types of applications in this chapter. Here is an overview of what you can expect to see:

- Projects that have complex classpaths. In these applications, not all the source files go into a single directory.
- Applications containing packages local to the current project. That is, packages that are subdirectories of the project's main directory.
- Other examples will show how to use packages that are not part of the current project per se but which are brought in as utilities. These utilities are intended for use in multiple projects. They are therefore not part of the directory tree that forms the structure for the main application. Instead, they reside elsewhere on your hard drive.

Throughout most of this chapter we are going to be developing the very beginnings of a set of utility routines that will become part of other projects developed in this book. Utility routines are a classic example of the kind of file that needs to be added to a project without being explicitly considered an integral part of the project itself. In short, they are the kind of file that will complicate the structure of your project.

Ultimately, all the routines developed in this chapter and throughout other portions of this book will be stored in a file called codebox.jar. codebox.jar is included in source and binary form on the CD that accompanies this book. It will be released under the Mozilla license and will be freely available to developers everywhere. As such, these utility routines will give you a view of how to not only create reusable packages but also how to install and use them.

NOTE: I am using the Mozilla license as a means of making sure that you feel free to use the code as you want. My intention is simply to be sure you can do whatever you want with the code except release it under your own copyright. You are free to use the code in your own projects and to make money with that project without having any financial obligations to me whatsoever. The code should be available through my web site at www.elvenware.com in such a way that you and I both can add updates to it. Once again, my intention is to ensure that you can do anything you want with the code except release it in its current form as your own code. In particular, you should not create another book, put my code in that book, claim it is your own, and try to make money off of it. But you can use the code in your development projects in any way you want without having any obligations to me. Needless to say, the license also ensures that I cannot be held legally or financially responsible for anything that might go wrong with the code if you use it in your programs.

There is a huge amount of code floating around on the web, and much of it is not just good but of superb quality. Learning how to use these third-party tools is an important part of every Java developer's toolbox. An important addition to this information will be the material on JAR files that is found in Chapter 28 and elsewhere in the book.

Adding, Deleting, and Refreshing Project Files

In Chapter 4, you were introduced to the project pane. I want to re-emphasize a few points about the project pane, as they are particularly relevant to the current discussion.

When working with complex projects, there inevitably comes a time when you need to add, delete, or refresh the list of files you see in your project pane. You can use the Project menu to perform these actions. To do so, use the toolbar located directly above the project pane or right-click on the project pane.

There isn't much to say about adding files to a project. It is an intuitive process that acts exactly as you would expect. Just click on the green plus button in the toolbar and select the file you want to create.

NOTE: If you right-click on the top node in the project pane, you might notice that there is an option to create a new folder. This folder will be a "virtual" folder that is part of your project file, and not an OS-based folder that is part of your directory structure. You can use these folders to help you organize your code inside of JBuilder, but they do not help you create Java packages.

There are two options for deleting files. One is called removing the file and the other deleting a file. If you remove a file from the project, the file is still part of the project; it just is no longer visible in the project pane unless you open the package icon in which it resides. Removing a file does not physically delete the file from disk. A file is part of your project if it is in a package that is part of your project. Listing it in the project pane just makes it more accessible to you and does not give it any other significance.

If, however, you elect not to remove but to delete a file from the project pane, that file will be deleted from your hard drive. Thus, deleting a file from your project is a very significant act.

There can be times when the listing for a project in the project pane might not match what is actually stored on disk. For instance, you might see packages listed that you know you deleted from your hard drive. In such circumstances, use the Refresh button or Refresh on the toolbar or the Project | Refresh menu item. If, for instance, you have changed the structure of your packages with Windows Explorer, KDE Konquerer, or some other file manager, you might need to refresh your project before continuing work inside JBuilder.

NOTE: If you make changes to the directories or files in your src packages, JBuilder will not always update the same information in your classes directories. When this happens, you will sometimes get very nonsensical error messages from JBuilder or else old code that you have deleted will continue to appear in your program. If that happens, or if you suspect it might be happening, try deleting all the directories beneath your classes directory. Don't just delete your .class files; go ahead and delete the whole directory structure! Be especially careful to delete the package cache directories.

JBuilder and Packages

The first step is to create an application that contains code for developing and testing our utility routines. In a case like this, you do not want to place all the files in the same directory as your current application. Instead, you want to place the utility routines in a separate directory where they can be separated from your test bed application.

Let's take a moment to think about what it means to put a file in a package other than the main package for your project. This theoretical knowledge will make it easier to understand the material in this chapter.

The primary goal behind the creation of a package is to help you organize your code. Packages are a form of encapsulation. Encapsulation helps you reuse code, thereby saving you time. It can also help you maintain large projects and create robust projects from pre-designed modules of well-tested code.

You can see a list of all the classes in a particular package by choosing **Search | Find Classes** from the JBuilder menu. Alternatively, you can begin typing in an import statement and then press **Ctrl+Alt+Space** to pop up a dialog. If you then select a class in the dialog, and press **OK**, the class name will automatically be inserted into your source code. A view produced by this dialog is shown in Figure 25-1.

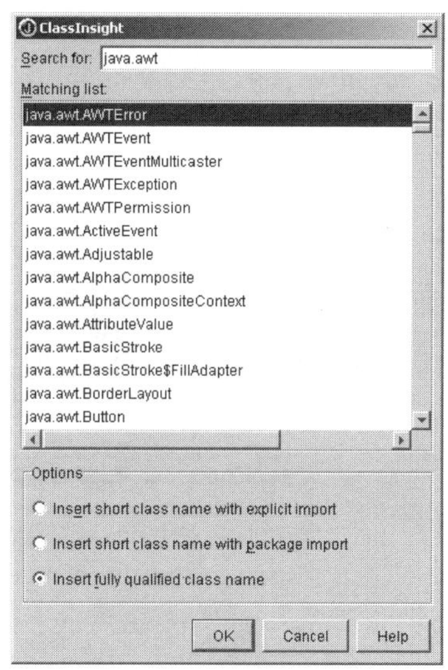

Figure 25-1: Using JBuilder to browse the classes available to a Java programmer

Automatically Importing Packages in JBuilder

If you add a new variable to your program, you sometimes have to add import statements before Java will recognize the type of your variable. For instance, if you create a default JBuilder application and add a variable of type ArrayList to your program, you will also have to add java.util.ArrayList or java.util.* to your list of imports at the top of the file. This is necessary because the code defining the ArrayList class is stored in the class called java.util.ArrayList.

The ClassInsight dialog shown in Figure 25-1 is very useful when you need to add imports to your project. In particular, it can be used to find the import statement that you want to include and to automatically insert it.

Suppose you add the following method to a default JFrame descendant called Frame1:

```
void jButton1_actionPerformed(ActionEvent e)
{
      ArrayList list;
}
```

This code will not automatically compile unless you have added the proper import statement at the top of the program. The problem, of course, is that you often can't remember which Java package contains the ArrayList class.

JBuilder can find the package for you. Press **Ctrl+Alt+Space** to pop up the ClassInsight dialog shown in Figure 25-1. Type the word **ArrayList** in the Search For field. The Matching List field will display the reference that you want, as shown in Figure 25-2.

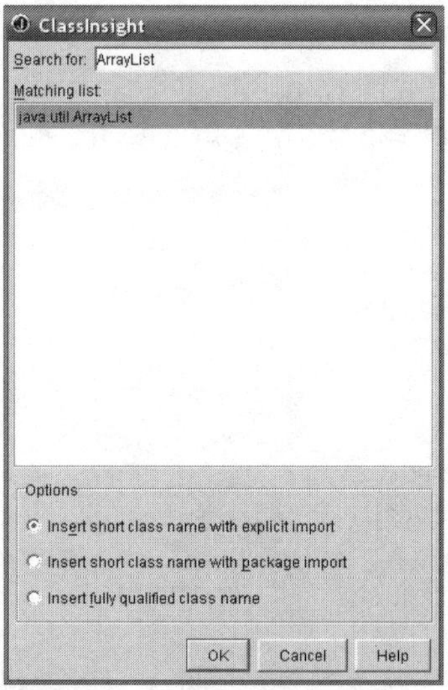

Figure 25-2: Using JBuilder to automatically find the package that contains the ArrayList class

At the bottom of Figure 25-2 you can see that there is an option to insert a fully qualified class name directly into your code:

```
void jButton1_actionPerformed(ActionEvent e)
{
      java.util.ArrayList list;
}
```

The other options add either an explicit or a package import for the ArrayList class to the top of your current file. Here is a short class name and an explicit import:

```
import java.util.ArrayList;

void jButton1_actionPerformed(ActionEvent e)
{
```

```
    ArrayList list;
}
```

Here is a package import and a short class name:

```
import java.util.*;

void jButton1_actionPerformed(ActionEvent e)
{
    java.util.ArrayList list;
}
```

Understanding Packages

Consider the following common import statements:

```
import java.awt.*;
import java.awt.event.*;
import javax.swing.*;
```

Though built into the JDK, these imports nonetheless reference packages of the type that will be discussed in this chapter. Here you can see references to three different packages. The first two begin with the word "java," which means that they are part of the core Java API. All you have to do is look at the word "java," and you already know something about that package. In particular, you know that it is built into the Java JDK and will probably be part of any default Java platform.

Both the first and the second statements reference the awt package. "awt" stands for the Abstract Window Toolkit, which is used to help you create the user interface, or UI, for your program. Core Java classes such as Button, Font, Check Box, Dialog, Label, and Menu are found in this package.

The event package is referenced in the second of the three import statements above. It contains code related to events, such as ActionEvent, ActionListener, FocusEvent, and MouseListener.

The third of the import statements is javax.swing.*. The javax package contains a set of extensions to Java made by Sun, and the swing package contains a second set of UI controls such as buttons, list boxes, etc. The swing controls all begin with the letter J: JButton, JListBox, JTree, etc. As a rule, the buttons and other controls in the swing package are said to supercede the older controls in java.awt.

The point here is that packages provide a means of logically dividing up sets of routines into related categories. In essence, they are a kind of database of objects. You browse the database by thinking logically about the names of the packages and their intended significance. This is one of the core concepts in the Java language.

Introducing CodeBox

The utilities routines created in this chapter will be laid out in a similar manner to the routines in java.awt, java.awt.event, and java.swing. In particular, they will be stored in a package called com.elvenware.*. For instance, they have names like com.elvenware.codebox.* and com.elvenware.comp.*. The first package contains simple utility routines and the second contains components.

The first word in the package list is "com," which means that these routines were developed by a company. The second word is "Elvenware," which is the name of my company. The third word is "codebox," which is the name of this set of routines.

To use this set of routines, you must add an import com.elvenware.codebox.* statement to your Java source file. Or, if you wanted, you could specify the name of a particular class, such as com.elvenware.codebox.StringBox. The latter syntax references a particular class inside the codebox package.

The question that remains, then, is how to set up a project that contains these kinds of files. Just what does the path structure of the project look like, and what do you need to tell JBuilder to get it to understand the project? These questions will be answered in the next section, where you examine a program that illustrates the principles involved in creating this kind of project.

Creating Complex Projects

The name of the project created in this section is StringTest01. Its purpose is simply to show you how to create a project that can aid you in developing a set of utility routines. In particular, this example is meant to illustrate how to set up a unique package for your utility routines.

To create the kind of project outlined in the last section you should still place all your files in the default JBuilder src directory. But now, your src directory will have two subdirectories, one for the main code in your project and one for the utility routines we are developing. Figure 25-3 shows the directory layout as it appears in the KDE Konquerer on a Linux Red Hat 7.2 installation.

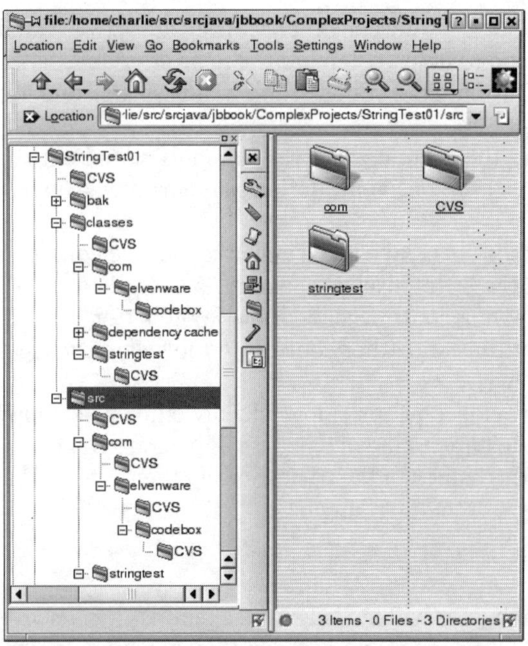

Figure 25-3: The Linux file browser showing the directory structure of the StringTest01 project

NOTE: You might notice some directories called CVS in Figure 25-3. These are created by the open source version control system called CVS. They do not contain any Java code and do not have much relevance to the subject matter of this chapter. CVS, however, is a very useful and relatively well-made program. It will be discussed in the next chapter.

The main source for your application will go in the StringTest01/src/stringtest directory. The source for the utilities routines will go in the StringTest01/src/com/elvenware/codebox directory. Take a second look at Figure 25-3 if you are at all unclear about how this looks on disk. Here is what the package statement looks like for the StringBox.java file in the codebox directory:

```
package com.elvenware.codebox;
```

Here is how that code is referenced from inside the stringtest directory where the main program resides:

```
import com.elvenware.codebox.StringBox;
```

Once you have set up a directory structure, you do not need to give JBuilder any special commands. It will automatically know what to do as long as you place your source files in the right directory and add the proper import and package statements to your project. In short, the mere act of placing your files in these directories and adding these important statements to your code is enough to inform JBuilder (and the Java JDK) where your classes are and what you want to do with them.

In particular, remember that a default JBuilder project puts the src directory shown in Figure 25-3 on your JBuilder classpath. You can configure this by going to **Project | Project Properties** in the JBuilder menu and looking at the Source section of the Paths page.

You do, however, have to tell JBuilder how to produce the com.elvenware.codebox.StringBox.java file. There is nothing to prevent you from creating this file by hand, but it happens that JBuilder will create it for you if you ask it to. Take a look at Figure 25-4.

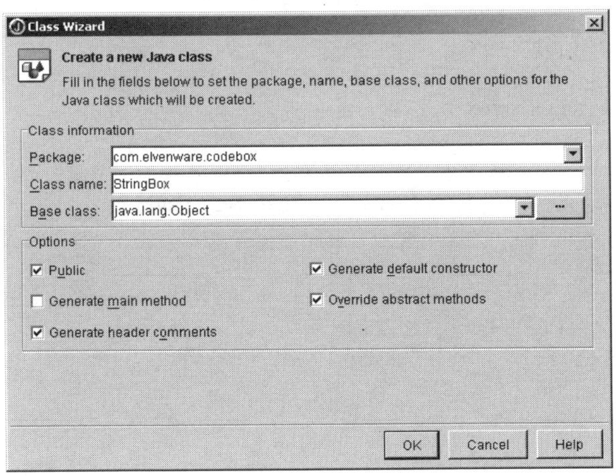

Figure 25-4: Creating a new class file in a new package

You access the dialog shown in Figure 25-4 by selecting **File | New Class** from the JBuilder menu. Then simply type in the name of the new package you want to create in the Package field. In the Class Name field, type in the name of the class you want to create. When you are done, press **OK**. JBuilder will automatically create all the new directories that are part of the \StringTest01\src\com\elvenware\codebox path statement and automatically generate the framework for your StringBox.java file.

That is all there is to it. Now you can simply fill in the methods of the StringBox.java file, add an import statement to Frame1.java, and you are ready to go. Nothing could be simpler — as long as you know how to proceed!

For now, just leave StringBox.java as an empty class. I want to focus on using JBuilder to create packages and classes, not on writing code.

Examining StringTest01

The main things you need to know about the StringTest01 project have now been presented. However, let's take a quick look at the source for the project so we can understand what it is all about.

The source for the utilities routines is shown in Listing 25-1, while the source for the frame of the main program is shown in Listing 25-2. I am not showing you the code for the main application itself, as it is simply boilerplate code that would be generated by default in any JBuilder project of the type described in Chapter 3.

Listing 25-1: The source for a preliminary version of the utility routines.

```
package com.elvenware.codebox;

/**
 * Title:        String Test
 * Description:  String utilities
 * Copyright:    Copyright (c) 2001 by Charlie Calvert
 * Company:      Elvenware
 * @author Charlie Calvert
 * @version 1.0
 */

import java.lang.String;

/** <p>A class for performing various String related utility functions.
 *
 *  <p>We can't do this by inheriting from String because string is declared final.
 *  An alternative would be to create our own string class, but that would mean
 *  we might introduce bugs, or miss out on updates to String.
 *
 *  <p>Because we have declared this class final, and have made all the methods
 *  static and final, the compiler will inline all these methods, making them
 *  much faster than if they were part of a regular object. */
public final class StringBox
{

    /**
     * Empty constructor
     */
     public StringBox()
     {
     }

    /**
     * This is a method that returns the first word from a string.
     *
     * @param value String from which you want to retrieve the first word.
     *
```

```
    * @return The first word from the string passed in the value
    * parameter. If the string contains only one word, then the value is
    * returned. If the string is empty or null, then an empty string is
    * returned.
    */
   public static final String getFirstWord(String value)
   {
        // remove any white space
        String cleanValue = value.trim();

        // Get the index of the first space
        int indexOfFirstSpace = cleanValue.indexOf(' ');

        // if there is only one word in the string, return it
        if (indexOfFirstSpace == 0)
        {
            return cleanValue;
        }

        // return the first word from the string
        return cleanValue.substring(0, indexOfFirstSpace);
        }

   /**
    * Remove the first word from a string. If the string is empty, return an
    * empty string. If it contains one word, return that word.
    *
    * @param value The source string
    * @return The first word from the source string
    * @see getFirstWord()
    */
   public static final String stripFirstWord(String value)
   {
        // remove any white space
        String cleanString = value.trim();

        // Get the index of the first space
        int indexOfFirstWhiteSpace = temp.indexOf(' ');

        // if there is only one word in the string, return it
        if (indexOfFirstWhiteSpace == -1)
            return value;

        // find the length of the string
        int stringLength = temp.length();

        // return all but the first word of the string
        return temp.substring(indexOfFirstWhiteSpace, stringLength).trim();
   }

   /**
```

```
         * Returns the reverse of the string passed in
         * @param value The source string
         * @return the reverse of the source string
         */
        public static final String reverse(String value)
        {
              // Create memory for the string we will return
              StringBuffer result = new StringBuffer(value);
              return result.reverse().toString();
        }
}
```

Listing 25-2: The source for the project's main frame

```
package stringtest;

import java.awt.*;
import java.awt.event.*;
import javax.swing.*;
import com.elvenware.codebox.StringBox;

public class Main extends JFrame
{
  JPanel contentPane;
  JMenuBar jMenuBar1 = new JMenuBar();
  JMenu jMenuFile = new JMenu();
  JMenuItem jMenuFileExit = new JMenuItem();
  JMenu jMenuHelp = new JMenu();
  JMenuItem jMenuHelpAbout = new JMenuItem();
  JToolBar jToolBar = new JToolBar();
  JButton jButton1 = new JButton();
  JButton jButton2 = new JButton();
  JButton jButton3 = new JButton();
  ImageIcon image1;
  ImageIcon image2;
  ImageIcon image3;
  JLabel statusBar = new JLabel();
  BorderLayout borderLayout1 = new BorderLayout();
  JMenu jMenu1 = new JMenu();
  JMenuItem jMenuItemReverse = new JMenuItem();
  JMenuItem jMenuItemGetFirstWord = new JMenuItem();
  JMenuItem jMenuItemStripFirstWord = new JMenuItem();

  /**Construct the frame*/
  public Main()
  {
    enableEvents(AWTEvent.WINDOW_EVENT_MASK);
    try
    {
      jbInit();
    }
    catch(Exception e)
```

```
    {
      e.printStackTrace();
    }
  }
  /**Component initialization*/
  private void jbInit() throws Exception
  {
    image1 = new ImageIcon(stringtest.Main.class.getResource("openFile.gif"));
    image2 = new ImageIcon(stringtest.Main.class.getResource("closeFile.gif"));
    image3 = new ImageIcon(stringtest.Main.class.getResource("help.gif"));
    contentPane = (JPanel) this.getContentPane();
    contentPane.setLayout(borderLayout1);
    this.setSize(new Dimension(400, 300));
    this.setTitle("String Test");
    statusBar.setText(" ");
    jMenuFile.setText("File");
    jMenuFileExit.setText("Exit");
    MainListener listen = new MainListener(this);
    jMenuFileExit.addActionListener(listen);
    jMenuHelp.setText("Help");
    jMenuHelpAbout.setText("About");
    jMenuHelpAbout.addActionListener(listen);
    jButton1.setIcon(image1);
    jButton1.setToolTipText("Open File");
    jButton2.setIcon(image2);
    jButton2.setToolTipText("Close File");
    jButton3.setIcon(image3);
    jButton3.setToolTipText("Help");
    jMenu1.setText("Options");
    jMenuItemReverse.setText("Reverse");
    jMenuItemReverse.addActionListener(listen);
    jMenuItemGetFirstWord.setText("GetFirstWord");
    jMenuItemGetFirstWord.addActionListener(listen);
    jMenuItemStripFirstWord.setText("StripFirstWord");
    jMenuItemStripFirstWord.addActionListener(listen);
    jToolBar.add(jButton1);
    jToolBar.add(jButton2);
    jToolBar.add(jButton3);
    jMenuFile.add(jMenuFileExit);
    jMenuHelp.add(jMenuHelpAbout);
    jMenuBar1.add(jMenuFile);
    jMenuBar1.add(jMenu1);
    jMenuBar1.add(jMenuHelp);
    this.setJMenuBar(jMenuBar1);
    contentPane.add(jToolBar, BorderLayout.NORTH);
    contentPane.add(statusBar, BorderLayout.SOUTH);
    jMenu1.add(jMenuItemReverse);
    jMenu1.add(jMenuItemGetFirstWord);
    jMenu1.add(jMenuItemStripFirstWord);
  }
```

```
/**File | Exit action performed*/
public void jMenuFileExit_actionPerformed(ActionEvent e)
{
  System.exit(0);
}

/**Help | About action performed*/
public void jMenuHelpAbout_actionPerformed(ActionEvent e)
{
  Main_AboutBox dlg = new Main_AboutBox(this);
  Dimension dlgSize = dlg.getPreferredSize();
  Dimension frmSize = getSize();
  Point loc = getLocation();
  dlg.setLocation((frmSize.width - dlgSize.width) / 2 +
    loc.x, (frmSize.height - dlgSize.height) / 2 + loc.y);
  dlg.setModal(true);
  dlg.show();
}

/**Overridden so we can exit when window is closed*/
protected void processWindowEvent(WindowEvent e)
{
  super.processWindowEvent(e);
  if (e.getID() == WindowEvent.WINDOW_CLOSING)
  {
    jMenuFileExit_actionPerformed(null);
  }
}

void jMenuItemReverse_actionPerformed(ActionEvent e)
{
  String data = "Able was I ere I saw Elba";
  // String reverse example
  if (e.getSource() == jMenuItemReverse)
  {
    data = StringBox.reverse(data);
  }

  // getFirstWord example
  if (e.getSource() == jMenuItemGetFirstWord)
  {
    data = StringBox.getFirstWord(data);
  }

  // stripFirstWord example
  if (e.getSource() == jMenuItemStripFirstWord)
  {
    data = StringBox.stripFirstWord(data);
  }
```

```
    JOptionPane.showMessageDialog(this, data);
  }
}

/** I am using the same ActionListener for all of my menu items
 *  in this application. Furthermore, I am sending most of them
 *  to the same event handler back in the main program.
 */
class MainListener implements ActionListener
{
  Main adaptee;

  MainListener(Main adaptee)
  {
    this.adaptee = adaptee;
  }

  public void actionPerformed(ActionEvent e)
  {
    if (e.getSource() == adaptee.jMenuFileExit)
    {
      adaptee.jMenuFileExit_actionPerformed(e);
    }

    if (e.getSource() == adaptee.jMenuHelpAbout)
    {
      adaptee.jMenuHelpAbout_actionPerformed(e);
    }

    if (e.getSource() == adaptee.jMenuItemReverse)
    {
      adaptee.jMenuItemReverse_actionPerformed(e);
    }

    if (e.getSource() == adaptee.jMenuItemGetFirstWord)
    {
      adaptee.jMenuItemReverse_actionPerformed(e);
    }

    if (e.getSource() == adaptee.jMenuItemStripFirstWord)
    {
      adaptee.jMenuItemReverse_actionPerformed(e);
    }
  }
}
```

If you run this project, you will see that it presents the user with a few simple menu items that allow you to reverse a string, and delete or extract the first word from a string. It is, in short, a test bed for utility routines that might be useful in a real-world application.

NOTE: The kind of string parsing shown in StringBox.java is often performed with regular expressions. Regular expressions are a part of JDK 1.4, but I elected not to use them since this book is focused primarily on JDK 1.3.1. The routines I have created here are designed to be small, fast, and easy to understand.

This is perhaps also a good place to point out that JUnit is a good technology to use when testing code of the type found in StringBox.java. I will discuss JUnit in Chapter 30.

There are two things to note when looking at the source for this project. The first has to do with the way I declare the object and methods in the StringBox.java file, and the second has to do with the way events are handled in the Main.java file.

When creating a set of utility routines for working with strings, one's natural inclination would be to create a descendant of the String class. Then one could write syntax such as MyString.reverse(); to reverse the string. Unfortunately, this approach is not possible in this case because the Java String class is declared final:

```
public final class String implements java.io.Serializable, Comparable {
```

Classes that are declared final cannot be extended. So that's the end of that. There is no way to pursue the project from that angle.

Instead, I have declared the StringBox class itself to be final, and I have declared all the methods in the class to be static final. This has two advantages. First, it allows the developer to write a fairly simple syntax:

```
myString = StringBox.reverse(myString);
```

The second advantage is that Java will inline each of the methods in the StringBox class. In particular, if you declare a class to be final and then make each of its methods static final, Java will produce very fast inline code for each of the methods in your object. Inline code is inserted directly into your program, thereby avoiding the overhead of a method call. It will, on the other hand, take up more space in your program than a method call would. In short, you are gaining speed in your program but increasing its size. In most cases, that will prove to be a reasonable trade-off.

NOTE: There was actually a third alternative open to me in this case. Rather than inheritance or static final methods, I could have chosen to go with delegation. In delegation, one class is made a field of a second class. In particular, the String class would be encapsulated as a field of a wrapper object. This provides much the same result as simple inheritance, but it is more flexible and is not limited by the fact that the String class is declared as final. I chose not to use that technique because I believe inlining would generate, in most cases, small amounts of code and use small amounts of memory. However, if I needed to create code that will be used in loops or in other cases where saving space is important, I might have opted for delegation. Some concrete discussion about how to optimize your code will appear later in this chapter, when we take a look at producing an object that times how long chunks of code take to execute.

The reverse method is implemented as follows:

```
public static final String reverse(String value)
{
      // Create memory for the string we will return
      StringBuffer result = new StringBuffer(value);
      return result.reverse().toString();
}
```

I could have written the reverse function like this:

```
public static final String reverse(String value)
```

```
    {
        // Create memory for the string we will return
        String result = new String();

        // Get the length of the string to reverse
        int len = value.length();

        // Copy the string one char at a time in reverse order
        for(int i = 1; i < (len + 1); i++)
        {
            result += value.substring(len - i, (len - i) + 1);
        }

        // Return the reversed string
        return result;
    }
```

Here, the variable result is declared as a String. A better version of the same method looks like this:

```
    public static final String reverse(String value)
    {
        // Create memory for the string we will return
        StringBuffer result = new StringBuffer(256);

        // Get the length of the string to reverse
        int len = value.length();

        // Copy the string one char at a time in reverse order
        for(int i = 1; i < (len + 1); i++)
        {
            result.append(value.substring(len - i, (len - i) + 1));
        }

        // Return the reversed string
        return result.toString();
    }
```

The second version uses result.append, rather than result +=. The String class, being immutable, is not the right tool to use when you need to continually adjust the size of a string. The problem is that code of the type found in the for loop will cause a String class variable's constructor to be called over and over again. Every time you change an instance of String class, its constructor is called. A StringBuffer, on the other hand, need only be created once to be used in a case like this.

NOTE: When you use the String concatenation symbol, which is a plus sign, the compiler implements your code using a StringBuffer. See the introduction to the Javadoc file shipped by Sun for the StringBuffer class for more details. Inside the JBuilder IDE you should be able to view this file by bringing up the StringBuffer class in the editor and selecting the Doc tab from the file view tabs seen along the bottom of the editor. You can also find or type in a declaration for a StringBuffer variable in JBuilder by placing your cursor over the word and pressing F1 to find the appropriate Javadoc file. Finally, you should be able to locate the Javadoc files for the StringBuffer class at this web site: http://java.sun.com/j2se/1.4.1/docs/api/java/lang/StringBuffer.html.

StringTest01 Events

I discussed events in Chapters 14 and 15. However, I want to resurrect the subject in order to briefly mention the event mechanism employed in the StringBox01 program.

The code in the Main.java source file goes out of its way to limit the number of ActionListener classes that it contains. The program has a number of menu items. Rather than create an ActionListener for each menu item, I have instead sent all the messages to a single, albeit rather lengthy, ActionListener:

```
class MainListener implements ActionListener
{
  Main adaptee;

  MainListener(Main adaptee)
  {
    this.adaptee = adaptee;
  }

  public void actionPerformed(ActionEvent e)
  {
    if (e.getSource() == adaptee.jMenuFileExit)
    {
      adaptee.jMenuFileExit_actionPerformed(e);
    }

    if (e.getSource() == adaptee.jMenuHelpAbout)
    {
      adaptee.jMenuHelpAbout_actionPerformed(e);
    }

    if (e.getSource() == adaptee.jMenuItemReverse)
    {
      adaptee.jMenuItemReverse_actionPerformed(e);
    }

    if (e.getSource() == adaptee.jMenuItemGetFirstWord)
    {
      adaptee.jMenuItemReverse_actionPerformed(e);
    }

    if (e.getSource() == adaptee.jMenuItemStripFirstWord)
    {
      adaptee.jMenuItemReverse_actionPerformed(e);
    }
  }
}
```

As you can see, I check the source of each item that calls the ActionListener and then call the method that is associated with that object:

```
    // this line determines which menu called the actionlistener
    if (e.getSource() == adaptee.jMenuItemStripFirstWord)
    {
```

```
    // This line calls your event handler
    adaptee.jMenuItemReverse_actionPerformed(e);
  }
```

When setting up the ActionListeners in the jbInit method, I simply create one listener object and then assign it to each of the menu items:

```
MainListener listen = new MainListener(this);
jMenuFileExit.addActionListener(listen);
jMenuHelpAbout.addActionListener(listen);
etc...
```

Coding this way forces you to do a little extra work. In fact, it is simpler to allow JBuilder to create a new ActionListener for each MenuItem you create. The method shown here, however, may strike some people as being useful when it comes time to maintain your code. In particular, the code is relatively short and easy to read. Furthermore, it encapsulates all your event handling in one method, thereby making it easy to track down problems with the event mechanism. You can study this technique in more depth in Chapter 14.

The StringTest01 program uses menus to generate events. I discussed creating and using menus in Chapter 13.

More Complex Paths

The theory of encapsulation asserts that large projects are easier to maintain if broken up into small subsections. Creating multiple packages in one project can help you achieve this goal.

In the previous section, you saw how to add a new set of files to a project. The files you added, in the com.elvenware.codebox package, had nothing to do with the original package, which was called stringtest. They were two entirely different packages.

In this section, you will see how to add packages that become an integral part of a project. These new packages will be subdirectories of the main package for the project. This technique is useful when you are creating a very large application that has many intricate parts.

In this project, found on the CD as TimeIt, we will create a Timer class. The class will be used to measure the length of certain events.

As programmers, and particularly as Java programmers, we are always wondering what is the fastest way to do something. Rarely, however, do we ever actually bother to take the simple steps necessary to ascertain some verifiable data about performance. Instead, we tend to rely on guesswork, as if we were ancient druids mumbling incantations over a fire in the night.

In this program, I will add a Timer class to a simple Java applet. However, I will not place the class in the same directory as the main file for the application. Instead, I will place it in a directory beneath the main package for the project. Consider this example:

```
MyProject/src/myproject/mynewpackage/MyNewPackage.java.
```

In this example, a package called mynewpackage has been entered beneath the myproject directory. The myproject directory was created by default by JBuilder. The mynewpackage directory is one that we are adding on to the project. By way of comparison, let me remind you of the structure of the last program you studied:

```
MyProject/src/myproject/
MyProject/src/com/elvenware/codebox/
```

Later I will show you yet a third way to arrange things that might look something like this:

```
MyProject/src/myproject/
MyProject/src/com/elvenware/codebox/
/com/elvenware/codebox
```

In all cases we are able to add a new package to our project. However, the style and semantics of each package are really quite different. My point here is not that one technique is better than another. All three are valid, and all are likely to play roles in your JBuilder applications. The point is merely to be sure that you know how to handle each type of situation.

NOTE: In a program this simple, separating out files into a new directory is not at all necessary. These projects are too simple to derive benefits from these techniques. But I need to show you simple examples so that you do not waste time wrestling with code that is not germane to the topic at hand. This program is really just a simulation of what you would do if you were working on a complex project that needed to be broken up into separate packages.

The source for the project is shown in Listings 25-3 and 25-4. This time the first listing is the frame for the application and the second is the source for the Timer class. You can find the source on the CD in the TimeIt directory.

Listing 25-3: The source for the application frame

```
package timeit;

import java.awt.*;
import java.awt.event.*;
import javax.swing.*;
import timeit.elftimer.ElfTimer;
import com.borland.jbcl.layout.*;

public class Frame1 extends JFrame
{
  JPanel contentPane;
  BorderLayout borderLayout1 = new BorderLayout();
  DefaultListModel listModel = new DefaultListModel();
  JPanel jPanel1 = new JPanel();
  JButton jButtonListBox = new JButton();
  JButton jButtonStandardOut = new JButton();
  JScrollPane jScrollPane1 = new JScrollPane();
  JList jList1 = new JList();
  ElfTimer timer = new ElfTimer();
  JTextField jTextFieldTime = new JTextField();
  VerticalFlowLayout verticalFlowLayout1 = new VerticalFlowLayout();

  /**Construct the frame*/
  public Frame1()
  {
    enableEvents(AWTEvent.WINDOW_EVENT_MASK);
    try
    {
      jbInit();
    }
    catch(Exception e)
```

```
  {
    e.printStackTrace();
  }
}
/**Component initialization*/
private void jbInit() throws Exception
{
  contentPane = (JPanel) this.getContentPane();
  contentPane.setLayout(borderLayout1);
  this.setSize(new Dimension(400, 300));
  this.setTitle("Frame Title");
  jButtonListBox.setText("List Box");
  jButtonListBox.addActionListener(new Frame1_jButtonListBox_actionAdapter(this));
  jButtonStandardOut.setText("Standard Out");
  jButtonStandardOut.addActionListener(new Frame1_jButtonStandardOut_actionAdapter(this));
  jList1.setModel(listModel);
  jPanel1.setLayout(verticalFlowLayout1);
  contentPane.add(jPanel1,  BorderLayout.SOUTH);
  jPanel1.add(jTextFieldTime, null);
  jPanel1.add(jButtonStandardOut, null);
  jPanel1.add(jButtonListBox, null);
  contentPane.add(jScrollPane1,  BorderLayout.CENTER);
  jScrollPane1.getViewport().add(jList1, null);
}

/**Overridden so we can exit when window is closed*/
protected void processWindowEvent(WindowEvent e)
{
  super.processWindowEvent(e);
  if (e.getID() == WindowEvent.WINDOW_CLOSING)
  {
    System.exit(0);
  }
}

    void jButtonListBox_actionPerformed(ActionEvent e)
    {
          timer.start();
          StringBuffer S = new StringBuffer(256);
          for(int i = 0; i < 150; i++)
          {
                S.setLength(0);
                S.append("Sam: " + String.valueOf(i));
                listModel.addElement(S);
          }
          timer.stop();
          jTextFieldTime.setText("Elapsed time: " + timer.getTimeStr());
    }

    void jButtonStandardOut_actionPerformed(ActionEvent e)
    {
```

```
            timer.start();
            StringBuffer S = new StringBuffer(256);
            for(int i = 0; i < 15000; i++)
            {
                  S.setLength(0);
                  S.append("Sam: " + String.valueOf(i));
                  System.out.println(S);
            }
            timer.stop();
            jTextFieldTime.setText("Elapsed time: " + timer.getTimeStr());
      }
}

class Frame1_jButtonListBox_actionAdapter
  implements java.awt.event.ActionListener
{
  Frame1 adaptee;

  Frame1_jButtonListBox_actionAdapter(Frame1 adaptee)
  {
    this.adaptee = adaptee;
  }
  public void actionPerformed(ActionEvent e)
  {
    adaptee.jButtonListBox_actionPerformed(e);
  }
}

class Frame1_jButtonStandardOut_actionAdapter
  implements java.awt.event.ActionListener
{
  Frame1 adaptee;

  Frame1_jButtonStandardOut_actionAdapter(Frame1 adaptee)
  {
    this.adaptee = adaptee;
  }
  public void actionPerformed(ActionEvent e)
  {
    adaptee.jButtonStandardOut_actionPerformed(e);
  }
}
```

Listing 25-4: The ElfTimer class makes it easy for you to time events in your Java programs.

```
package timeit.elftimer;

/**
 * Title:        Time It
 * Description:
 * Copyright:    Copyright (c) 2001 by Charlie Calvert
 * Company:      Elvenware
```

```
 * @author Charlie Calvert
 * @version 1.0
 */

public class ElfTimer
{
  private long startTime;
  private long stopTime;
  private boolean running;

  public ElfTimer()
  {
    startTime = -1;
  }

  public long getTime()
  {
    return stopTime - startTime;
  }

  public String getTimeStr()
  {
    return String.valueOf(getTime());
  }

  public boolean getRunning()
  {
    return running;
  }

  public long getStartTime()
  {
    return startTime;
  }

  public void start()
  {
    startTime = System.currentTimeMillis();
    running = true;
  }

  public void stop()
  {
    stopTime = System.currentTimeMillis();
    running = false;
  }
}
```

When I ran this program, I was surprised to see the results it produced. The program calculates the length of time required to write a string 15,000 times to standard out and 15,000 times to a list box. I thought that writing to standard out would be faster than writing to a list box. Furthermore, I expected to find that the Java list box might have a hard time holding 15,000 strings. I was wrong on both counts, which shows why we should always test our theories rather than merely proceed by guesswork.

Below you can see the heart of the code I used to generate the output. The first method writes to a list box and the second to standard out.

```
void jButtonListBox_actionPerformed(ActionEvent e)
{
      timer.start();
      StringBuffer S = new StringBuffer(256);
      for(int i = 0; i < 150; i++)
      {
            S.setLength(0);
            S.append("Sam: " + String.valueOf(i));
            listModel.addElement(S);
      }
      timer.stop();
      jTextFieldTime.setText("Elapsed time: " + timer.getTimeStr());
}

void jButtonStandardOut_actionPerformed(ActionEvent e)
{
      timer.start();
      StringBuffer S = new StringBuffer(256);
      for(int i = 0; i < 15000; i++)
      {
            S.setLength(0);
            S.append("Sam: " + String.valueOf(i));
            System.out.println(S);
      }
      timer.stop();
      jTextFieldTime.setText("Elapsed time: " + timer.getTimeStr());
}
```

You can see that both methods are based on simple loops. One loop generates strings for standard out, and the other generates identical strings to be sent to a list box.

It took between one-quarter and one-eighth the amount of time to write to the list box as it did to write to standard out. Furthermore, it took only about one-quarter of a second to write all 15,000 strings to the Java list box. When making the timings, I was working on an 800 MHz Red Hat Linux 7.2 box with what proc/meminfo reported as 448 MB of RAM.

These statistics would have to give pause to those people who are convinced that the Java GUI is hopelessly slow and clunky. The simple truth is that Java is a lot more powerful than one might suspect! This doesn't mean that Java isn't slow in some areas. But clearly there are tasks that it handles with remarkable aplomb. All of which goes to show that much of what passes for wisdom in the computer world is — at best — wild speculation.

Classpaths in the Timer Application

Let's talk for a moment about how I created the Timer class. It is this discussion that will emphasize the techniques necessary for getting JBuilder to properly handle classpaths.

When creating the Timer class, you want to make sure that it is placed in a new directory. We do this in order to show how to properly partition a program to promote reuse.

The Timer class belongs in the directory beneath the main package for the project. Figure 25-5 illustrates this, showing how the file ElfTimer.java is located in the /src/timeit/elftimer directory. The main files for the project, of course, are located in /src/timeit/.

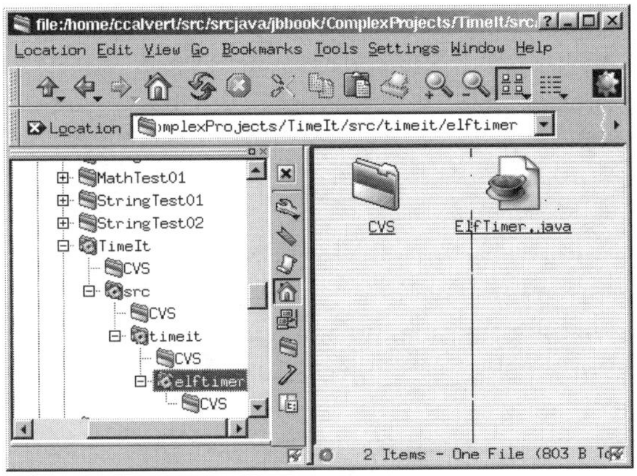

Figure 25-5: The KDE file browser shows how the ElfTimer.java file resides in the directory beneath the project's main package.

To place your files this way, choose **File | New Class** from the JBuilder menu. When you fill in the name and package of the class, simply type in the name of the new package using dot notation. Figure 25-6 shows how this works. You type in the name of the current package where your files reside, add a period, then add the name of the new package you want to create. In this case, the current package is timeit, and the new package is called elftimer. When you are done, the new directory will be created for you automatically and your new class file will be placed inside it. This example is similar to the one in the previous program, but it provides a few new twists of logic. Ultimately, you will need to use both techniques depending on your circumstances.

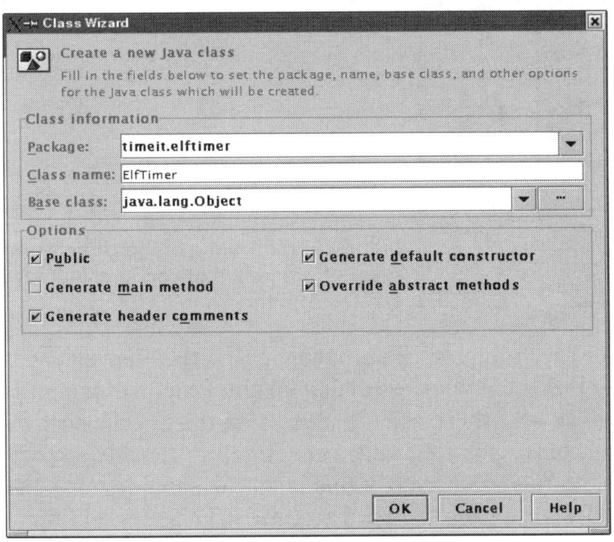

Figure 25-6: Using the Class Wizard to create a new package for a new class

At this stage, all you need to do is add the appropriate import statement at the top of your package, and then you will be able to access the classes you place in the elftimer package. In particular, notice both the package statement at the top of the ElfTimer.java file and the import statement in the main program:

```
package timeit.elftimer;          // From ElfTimer.java
import timeit.elftimer.ElfTimer; // From Frame1.java
```

With your code set up this way, you do not need to change the class path or ask JBuilder to do anything special. All you need to do is write your code and press the green compile button. Everything else happens automatically.

Paths Outside Your Project

The examples presented so far in this chapter show how to share code inside one project that contains complex class paths. Given that information, it should not be hard to see how to share code between multiple applications inside one project. But what can you do if you want to share code between multiple projects?

Consider the window shown in Figure 25-7. Here you can see that the StringTest01, StringTest02, TimeIt, and TimeIt02 projects are all on the same level as a directory called src. In the src directory are the com.elvenware.codebox and timeit.elftimer packages. What we will examine now is how to have the code inside the TimeIt02 program access the utility packages in this new src directory.

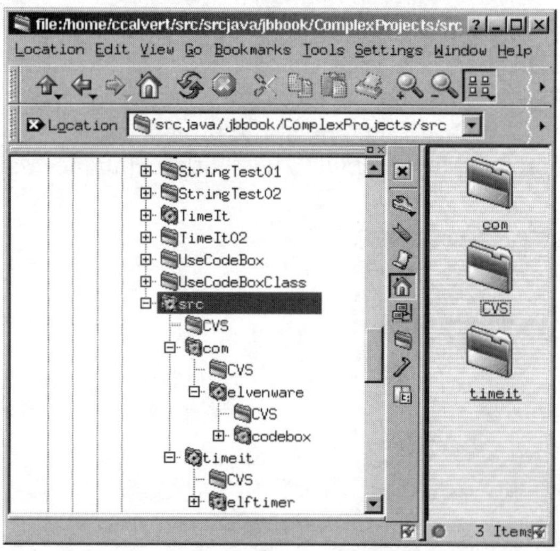

Figure 25-7: A view of the directory structure for a set of projects that can share utility routines in the src directory

If you read the previous chapter carefully, you can probably guess the answer to this question. In Figure 25-8, you can see the Project Properties dialog for the Linux version of JBuilder open to the Paths page. As you can see, there are two entries in the Source section of the page. The first line is the default entry pointing to the src directory for this project. The second entry, however, points back to the src directory that is on the same level as the StringTest01, StringTest02, and TimeIt project root directories. This second entry was added to the dialog by selecting the Add button and browsing for the directory using JBuilder's tools.

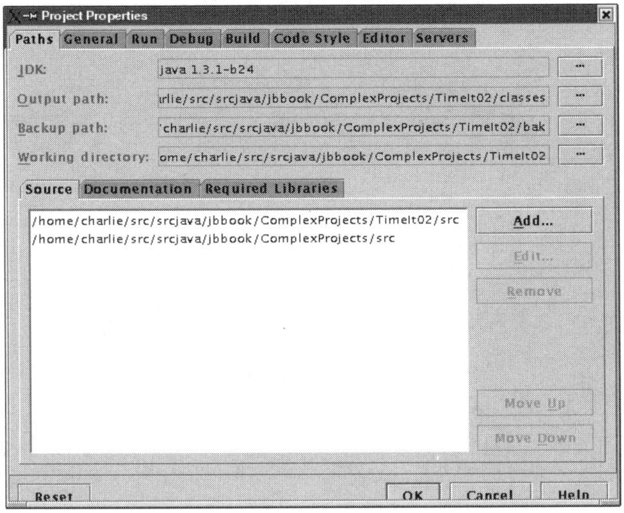

Figure 25-8: The Project Properties dialog can be used to tell JBuilder to access code located outside of your project.

The source for the TimeIt02 project is shown in Listing 25-5. It contains a reference to the timeit.elftimer package. This version of the package is not in the TimeIt project but rather in the src directory that appears on the same level as the TimeIt and TimeIt02 projects. Look at Figure 25-7 once again if you are having trouble visualizing exactly how the directory structure looks.

The Project Properties dialog allowed us to tell JBuilder where to look for the source for this project. It performs the same task as the -sourcepath switch that you can pass to javac.

By making this one change to your Project Properties dialog, you are able to easily share code between multiple projects. This way you can have one project dedicated to testing the code and multiple other projects that use the code. (Once again, I will explain how to deploy all this code in a later chapter. For now we are only concerned with the act of creating and debugging your projects.)

Spend a few more moments looking over the source for the TimeIt02 project. As I said earlier, this is not the time to study how the project works or how to create it inside JBuilder. Instead, you should focus solely on the issue of understanding how JBuilder handles paths and packages.

Listing 25-5: The source for a project that compares the speed and capabilities of the JListBox and JTree components

```
package timeit02;

import java.awt.*;
import java.awt.event.*;
import javax.swing.*;
import javax.swing.tree.TreePath;
import javax.swing.tree.DefaultMutableTreeNode;
import timeit.elftimer.ElfTimer;
import com.borland.jbcl.layout.*;

/**
 * Title:        TimeIt02
```

```
 * Description:
 * Copyright:    Copyright (c) 2001 by Charlie Calvert
 * Company:      Elvenware
 * @author Charlie Calvert
 * @version 1.0
 */

public class Frame1 extends JFrame
{
  JPanel contentPane;
  BorderLayout borderLayout1 = new BorderLayout();
  JPanel jPanel1 = new JPanel();
  JPanel jPanel2 = new JPanel();
  DefaultMutableTreeNode rootNode = new DefaultMutableTreeNode("My Root Node");
  DefaultListModel model = new DefaultListModel();
  JScrollPane jScrollPane1 = new JScrollPane();
  JTree jTree1 = new JTree(rootNode);
  ElfTimer timer = new ElfTimer();
  JScrollPane jScrollPane2 = new JScrollPane();
  GridLayout gridLayout1 = new GridLayout();
  JList jList1 = new JList();
  GridLayout gridLayout2 = new GridLayout();
  JPanel jPanel3 = new JPanel();
  JLabel jLabel1 = new JLabel();
  JTextField jTextField1 = new JTextField();
  BorderLayout borderLayout2 = new BorderLayout();
  JPanel jPanel4 = new JPanel();
  JButton jButtonAddToTree = new JButton();
  JButton jButtonCount = new JButton();
  JButton jButtonClearAll = new JButton();
  JButton jButtonAddToListBox = new JButton();
  GridLayout gridLayout3 = new GridLayout();

  /**Construct the frame*/
  public Frame1()
  {
    enableEvents(AWTEvent.WINDOW_EVENT_MASK);
    try
    {
      jbInit();
    }
    catch(Exception e)
    {
      e.printStackTrace();
    }
  }
  /**Component initialization*/
  private void jbInit() throws Exception
  {
    contentPane = (JPanel) this.getContentPane();
    contentPane.setLayout(borderLayout1);
```

```
    this.setSize(new Dimension(611, 413));
    this.setTitle("Frame Title");
    jPanel1.setLayout(gridLayout1);
    gridLayout1.setColumns(2);
    jList1.setModel(model);
    jPanel2.setLayout(gridLayout2);
    gridLayout2.setRows(2);
    gridLayout2.setColumns(1);
    jPanel2.setPreferredSize(new Dimension(725, 75));
    jLabel1.setText("Elapsed Time");
    jPanel3.setLayout(borderLayout2);
    jButtonAddToTree.setText("Add to Tree");
    jButtonCount.setText("Count");
    jButtonClearAll.setText("ClearAll");
    jButtonAddToListBox.setText("Add to List Box");
    MyAdapter listener = new MyAdapter(this);
    jButtonClearAll.addActionListener(listener);
    jButtonAddToTree.addActionListener(listener);
    jButtonAddToListBox.addActionListener(listener);
    jButtonCount.addActionListener(listener);
    jPanel4.setLayout(gridLayout3);
    contentPane.add(jPanel1, BorderLayout.CENTER);
    jPanel1.add(jScrollPane2, null);
    jScrollPane2.getViewport().add(jList1, null);
    jPanel1.add(jScrollPane1, null);
    jScrollPane1.getViewport().add(jTree1, null);
    contentPane.add(jPanel2,  BorderLayout.NORTH);
    jPanel2.add(jPanel3, null);
    jPanel3.add(jTextField1,  BorderLayout.CENTER);
    jPanel3.add(jLabel1,  BorderLayout.WEST);
    jPanel2.add(jPanel4, null);
    jPanel4.add(jButtonAddToListBox, null);
    jPanel4.add(jButtonAddToTree, null);
    jPanel4.add(jButtonCount, null);
    jPanel4.add(jButtonClearAll, null);
  }

  /**Overridden so we can exit when window is closed*/
  protected void processWindowEvent(WindowEvent e)
  {
    super.processWindowEvent(e);
    if (e.getID() == WindowEvent.WINDOW_CLOSING)
    {
      System.exit(0);
    }
  }

  void clearTree()
  {
    model.clear();
     rootNode.removeAllChildren();
```

```
    jTree1.updateUI();
  }

  void jButtonAddToTree_actionPerformed(ActionEvent e)
  {
    timer.start();

    for (int i = 0; i < 5000; i++)
    {
      DefaultMutableTreeNode node =
        new DefaultMutableTreeNode("Data: " + String.valueOf(i));
      rootNode.add(node);
    }
    jTree1.expandPath(new TreePath(rootNode));
    jTree1.updateUI();
    timer.stop();
    jTextField1.setText(timer.getTimeStr());
  }

  void jButtonAddToListBox_actionPerformed(ActionEvent e)
  {
    timer.start();

    for (int i = 0; i < 5000; i++)
    {
      model.addElement("Data: " + String.valueOf(i));
    }
    timer.stop();
    jTextField1.setText(timer.getTimeStr());
  }

  void jButtonClearAll_actionPerformed(ActionEvent e)
  {
    clearTree();
  }

  void jButtonCount_actionPerformed(ActionEvent e)
  {
    String S = "ListBox: " + String.valueOf(model.getSize());
    S += " Tree: " + String.valueOf(rootNode.getChildCount());
    JOptionPane.showMessageDialog(this, S);
  }
}

class MyAdapter implements java.awt.event.ActionListener
{
  Frame1 adaptee;

  MyAdapter(Frame1 adaptee)
  {
    this.adaptee = adaptee;
```

```
    }

    public void actionPerformed(ActionEvent e)
    {
      if (e.getSource() == adaptee.jButtonAddToTree)
      {
        adaptee.jButtonAddToTree_actionPerformed(e);
      }
      else if (e.getSource() == adaptee.jButtonAddToListBox)
      {
        adaptee.jButtonAddToListBox_actionPerformed(e);
      }
      else if (e.getSource() == adaptee.jButtonClearAll)
      {
        adaptee.jButtonClearAll_actionPerformed(e);
      }
      else if (e.getSource() == adaptee.jButtonCount)
      {
        adaptee.jButtonCount_actionPerformed(e);
      }
    }
  }
```

The TimeIt02 program is very much like TimeIt01. Rather than standard out and list boxes, this second project compares JTrees and list boxes. In this case you will find that list boxes also outperform JTrees, which certainly doesn't come as a big surprise. My results showed that if you are dealing with relatively small numbers of items, say less than 10,000, the differences are relatively small. However, when you start putting 50,000 or 100,000 items in these controls, JTree takes up to a couple of seconds to respond, while the JListBox still snaps to attention in under a second.

NOTE: 100,000 items in one list box! These are very powerful tools that come with the JDK.

If you take a look at Figure 25-9, you can see that the UI for this project is considerably more complex than the UI for the TimeIt project. As you saw in Part III: JBuilder Fundamentals, creating a project like this is not terribly difficult. You do, however, have to know a few tricks to make it all work correctly. In particular, you need to remember to use the structure pane for all but the most trivial operations. The visual designer itself is mostly there so you can check your work.

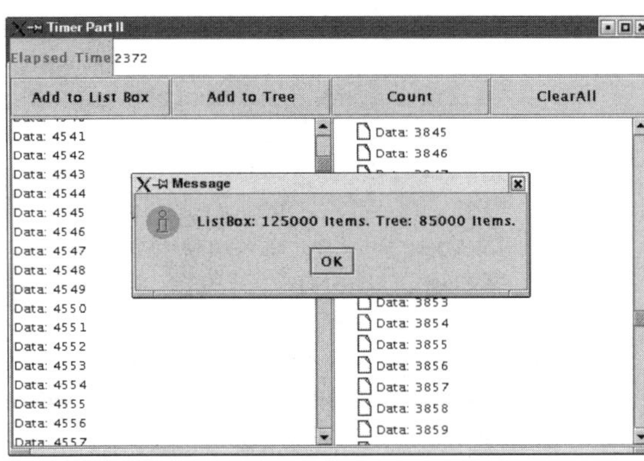

Figure 25-9: The UI for the TimeIt02 project involves working with multiple JPanels and multiple layout managers.

NOTE: One of the more confusing aspects of the CD is that files like com.elvenware.codebox.StringBox.java appear in several different locations. You will find it, for instances, in the StringTest01 program, in the src directory off the root of the ComplexProjects directory, and in the root directory for all the source files for this book. It is this latter version of the Elvenware files that is complete and contains my final versions of this code. The other directories are merely created for the purpose of illustrating subjects covered in this chapter and the next. You will, of course, be able to get updates to these files on the http://www.elvenware.com web site.

Creating Classes in Directories Outside Your Current Project

The final piece you need to understand is how to move classes into a directory outside your current project. One technique is to simply move them with the Konqueror or Windows Explorer. However, JBuilder will allow you to create new classes in directories outside your current project.

Notice in Figure 25-10 that the G:\SrcJava\jbbook\ComplexProjects\src directory is listed before the G:\SrcJava\jbbook\ComplexProjects\TimeIt02\src directory. Furthermore, it is designated as the default directory. As a result, if you create a new class, it will be placed in the ComplexProjects\src directory, and not the \TimeIt02\src directory.

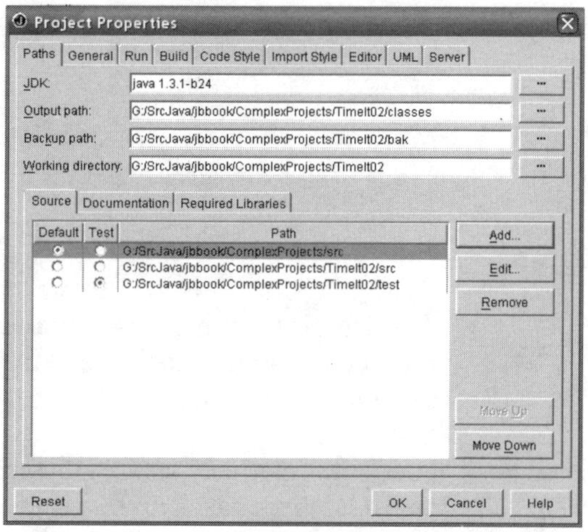

Figure 25-10: Use the default setting in the Project Properties | Paths page to designate where you want new source files that you create to be placed.

If you want to move existing files around, you can use either the refactoring tools or the rename option, which you can reach by right-clicking on the files in the project pane. I have found that the refactoring tools do not obey the settings you make in the Project Properties | Paths page, but that is possibly a bug that will be fixed in your version of JBuilder.

Summary

In this chapter you have learned a good deal about how to work with projects that have relatively complex paths. By necessity, all of the projects I have shown you in this chapter have been quite simple. However, if you start building serious Java applications, you will find that your projects have dozens, and often hundreds, of files in them. Managing all those files can be quite a complex chore. The tools you have learned about in this chapter can help you with that operation by allowing you to divide the project up into multiple packages. As always, the theme is "divide and conquer."

One important question that was not addressed in this chapter was how to package up source directories such as those shown in Time02 into JAR files. That subject will be addressed in the chapter on deployment, and in various other places in the book, such as Part VII: JavaBeans and Part VIII: Databases.

Chapter 26

Team Development

Margie Calvert and Charlie Calvert

Another name for team development is version control. The team development part of JBuilder is where you work with version control.

JBuilder gives you several choices of version control systems. CVS, which stands for "Concurrent Versions System," is an open source application that has been integrated with the SE and Enterprise versions of JBuilder. I'm a big user of CVS, and this section of the chapter is all about how to use CVS in the JBuilder environment. For those who have the Personal version of JBuilder, the text will briefly cover how to use CVS from your command line at the end of this chapter.

I will explain how to log onto a CVS server twice in this text. The first example will show how to log onto a local server. The second example, found in the section on working from the command line, explains how to log onto a PServer. The PServer option is used frequently when you want to connect to a remote machine. It stands for "password server," and it is useful because it grants you at least a reasonable degree of security.

Why Use CVS

To use CVS, you must first allocate a directory that can serve as a repository for your projects. CVS allows you to check projects out of the repository, make changes to them, and then check them back in. Each time you make changes and return a project to the repository, CVS will create and name a new version of your project. However, the version that existed before you checked it out will also remain in the repository. That way, as you keep working on your project, you will have all the versions that ever existed of your project, preserved intact.

The major reason to use CVS is to allow a team of people to work on a project at the same time. For instance, if two people are working on a project, it is important for each of them to be aware of the changes the other person is making. If one person stays late at night working on a project, and the other person goes home and then wants to work on the project, how would the person who went home remain aware of the most recent changes? If they both use CVS, the person who is working at the office can commit his or her changes to the repository. The person at home would then access the most recent version by using the CVS update command, and would be working with the latest revisions.

A second reason is to allow a single person to maintain multiple versions of a single project across multiple machines. For instance, if you work on a project at the office and also work at home, you could use CVS to keep the two projects in sync. If you sometimes do development on Windows and would like to maintain the same project on a Linux machine, you could use CVS to make sure the Windows and Linux versions of the project are identical.

CVS can also help you keep versions of your project. For instance, you can use CVS to mark the 1.0 version of your product. If you do this, you can begin work on version 2.0, knowing that you can always go back to the version 1.0 source code whenever you need it. Obviously, this is helpful when you take a wrong turn with a project.

The JBuilder team development tools have become quite sophisticated in recent versions of the product. Finding a good front end for CVS is not easy, particularly on the Windows platform. I have found that the JBuilder version control front end provides a great way to manage not only Java projects but all my CVS projects. I have used JBuilder to manage projects that are not built in Java. For instance, I used JBuilder to manage the development of the text for this book.

Terminology

Perhaps the biggest single piece of terminology that you need to learn is the difference between a commit and an update. The commit command puts data into the repository, and the update command checks it out of the repository. It is unlikely that you will get confused about the word "commit." That word is well chosen and implies the idea of committing the local copy of your work to the repository. The word "update," however, can be confusing. Are you updating the repository, or are you updating your local system? By now you know that the answer is that you are updating your local system. Probably the best way to remember this is to focus on the word "commit" and to then recall that update is the opposite of commit.

Adding a Project and Files to CVS

To use the team development portion of JBuilder, you will first need to create a project. Be sure to close any existing projects, and then choose **File | New**. On the Project page in the Object Gallery, choose **Project** and click **OK**. On the Step 1 page of the Project Wizard, name the project **cvsProject** and click **Finish**. JBuilder will create a default project. Even though at this time the project is essentially blank, you can place it in a CVS repository. Choose **Team | Select Project VCS...** on the menu bar. In the dialog that pops up, choose **CVS**.

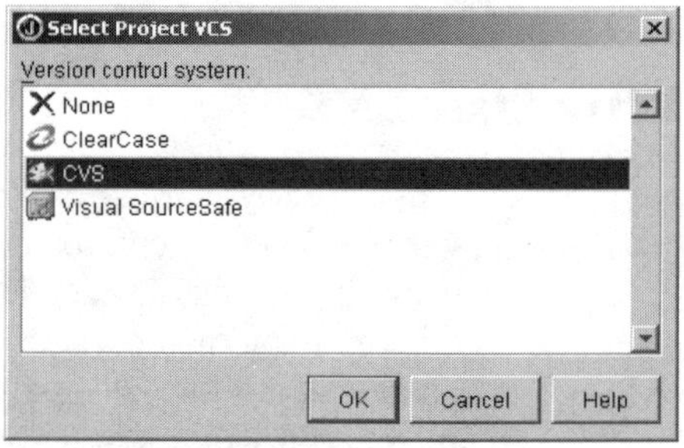

Figure 26-1: Selecting CVS in the Select Project VCS dialog

When you accessed the Team menu, you probably noticed that your only viable choice on the menu was Select Project VCS. Now go back to the Team menu. At this time, you have several choices. Choose **Create Local Repository...** to designate an empty directory to serve as the repository for the project. Use the ellipsis button to browse to the directory you would like to use, as shown in Figure 26-2. Once you click **OK**, you will see a message stating that the repository has been created successfully.

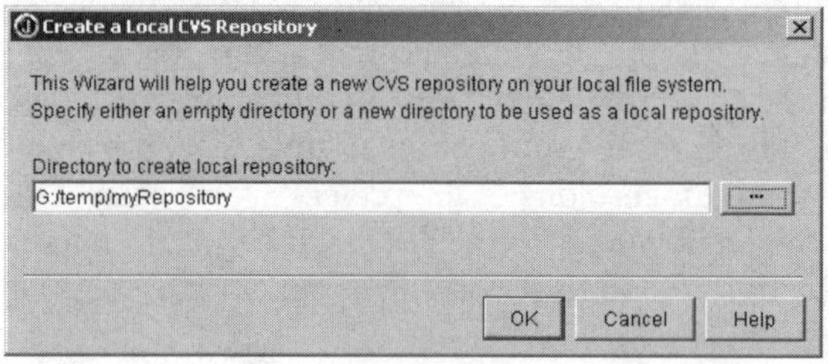

Figure 26-2: Creating a repository

In the Project pane, you will see cvsProject.jpx. Right-click on **cvsProject.jpx** and choose **CVS | Place Project into CVS...** from the menu that appears, as shown in Figure 26-3. If you wanted to, you could also access this command from the Team menu.

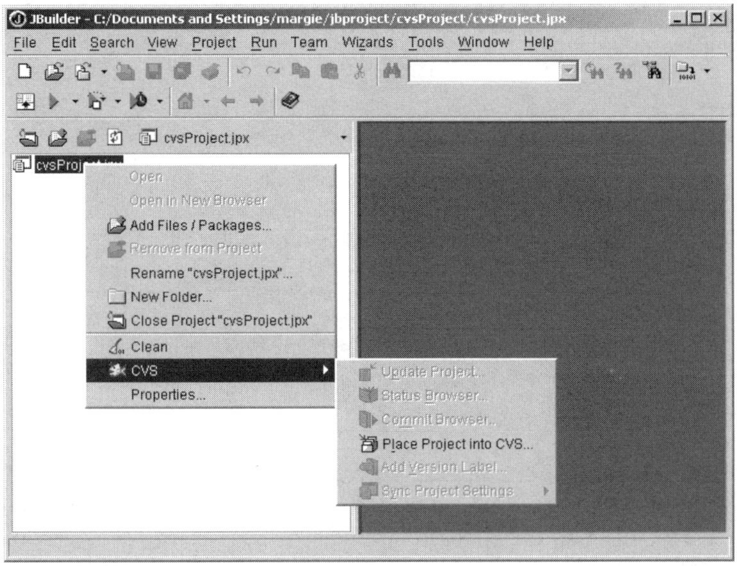

Figure 26-3: Accessing the context menu

JBuilder will guide you through the three-step CVS Wizard, which will allow you to add the project to the CVS repository you designated. In Step 1, choose **Local** as the connect type. When you do this, the repository directory you created will appear in the Repository Path field, as shown in Figure 26-4.

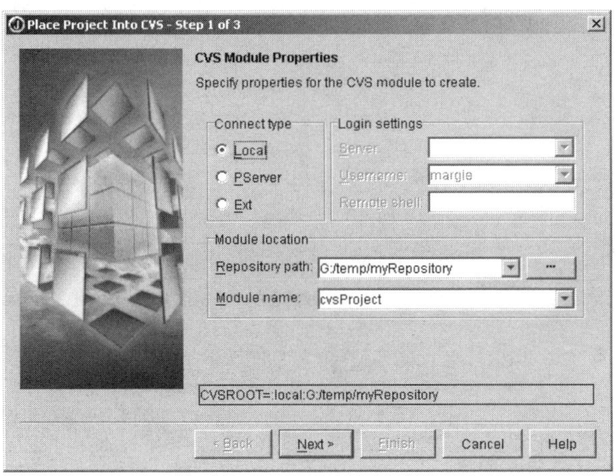

Figure 26-4: Step 1 of the CVS Wizard

Click **Next** to move to the next page, shown in Figure 26-5. Accept the default description and click **Next**.

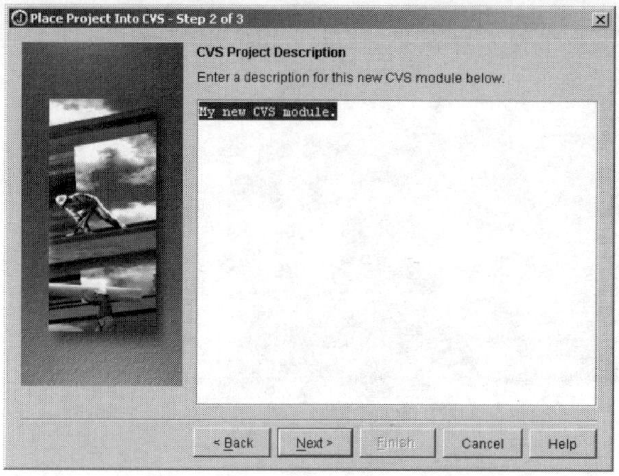

Figure 26-5: Step 2 of the wizard

Step 3 allows you to choose which files and directories will be placed in the repository, as shown in Figure 26-6. Leave the defaults and click **Finish**. You normally do not want to put your bak and classes directories in the repository.

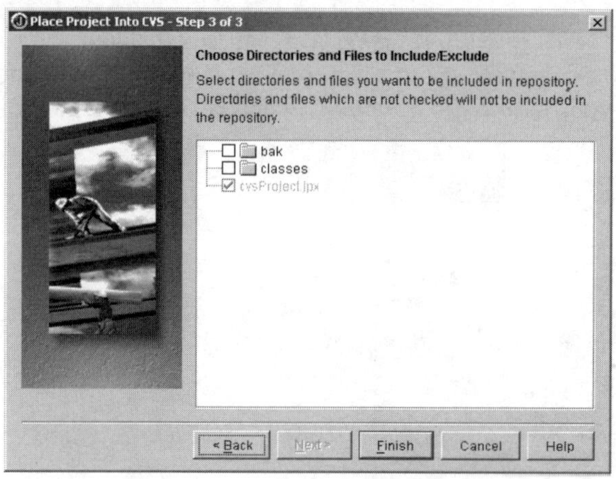

Figure 26-6: Step 3 of the wizard

Once you have clicked Finish, CVS will check to make sure that the project you are placing in the directory does not already exist in the directory. You will receive a message that CVS has successfully placed your project in the directory, as shown in Figure 26-7.

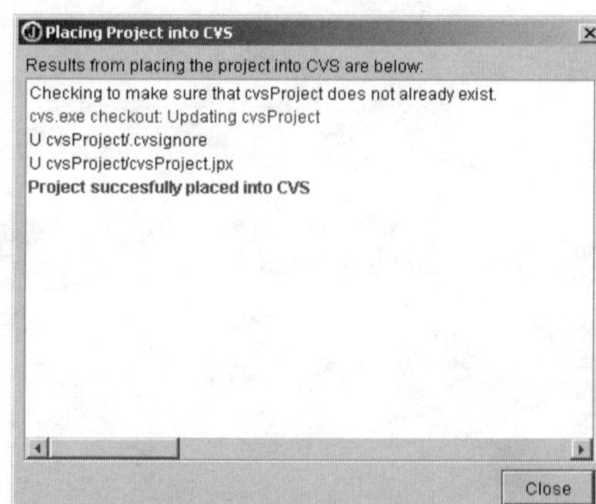

Figure 26-7: The Placing Project into CVS feedback dialog box

If you look carefully at Figure 26-7, you will see that some of the commands are prefixed with a U. The U stands for update. As you know, you commit files into the repository and update the files that are stored on your system. Why would there be an update involved in placing a new project in the repository?

The answer is that JBuilder and CVS are actually doing quite a bit in the background.

First, your new project is committed to the repository, then the directory in which it resides is renamed cvsProject.precvs. This directory will hold your old project in the state it was in before you entered it into CVS. Then your project is checked out of CVS and placed in a directory called cvsProject.

If you look at your hard drive, you can see both directories — the old one called cvsProject.precvs and the new one called cvsProject. The new one will contain a series of directories called CVS. In these directories you will find files called Entries, Repository, and Root. Do not delete files, as they are important to maintaining your project and its connection to CVS.

While you are looking at the hard drive, you might browse over to the directory that you designated as your repository. There you will find the files from your project stored as text in a series of directories that mirror the structure of your project. If I want to delete a directory from the repository, I have found that one of the simplest ways to do it is to simply physically remove the directory from the repository.

Adding an Application

Now add an application to your project. Go to **File | New** and choose **Application** from the General page of the Object Gallery, then click **OK**. When the Application Wizard pops up, accept the default settings and choose **Finish**. JBuilder will create an application and place it in your project.

NOTE: It is not important whether you created the project before or after you checked it into the repository. If you have a huge project that you have been working on for months, you can go ahead and check it into the repository at any time using the techniques described in the last section.

Although you have just added the application to your project, you have not added the application files to CVS. Right-click on Application1.java and choose **CVS | Status for Application1.java....** A dialog will pop up stating "This file is not currently under CVS." Right-click on Frame1.java and choose **CVS | Status for Frame1.java...** you will get the same result. Click on **Application1.java**, then press the Shift key and click on **Frame1.java.** They will both be highlighted, indicating that they are selected. Right-click and choose **CVS | Add Files....** A dialog will appear that allows you to add a comment. Type **Added Frame1.java and Application1.java**, as shown in Figure 26-8. It is not necessary to enclose it in angle brackets.

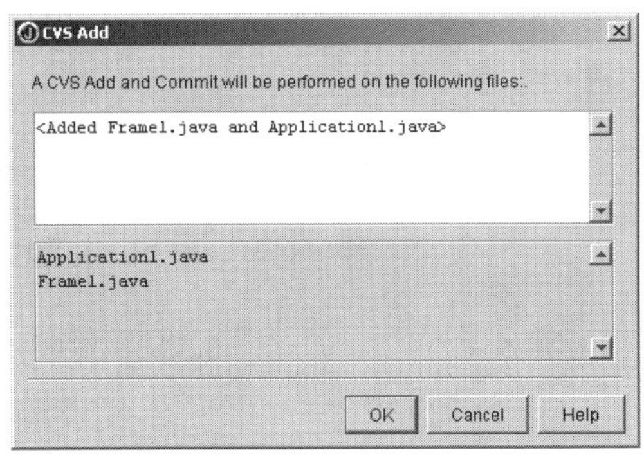

Figure 26-8: Adding a comment when you add files

Once you click **OK**, JBuilder will add the files to the CVS repository and give you a message confirming this.

Part V

The Status Browser

Now let's make some changes to both of these files. Change to the design view and drop a button down on the designer. This changes the code in Frame1.java. Click on **Application1.java** in the project pane to select it, change to the editor view, and add the following import statement:

```
import java.math.*;
```

It does not matter what changes you make — the slightest change will be sufficient for our purposes, as any change to the files will be picked up by JBuilder.

Just to make things a little more interesting, we will add two classes to the project as well. Choose **File | New Class**, click **OK**, and then repeat the process. You will have two additional classes named Untitled1.java and Untitled2.java in your project. Choose **File | Save All** to save your changes.

Choose **Team | Status Browser**, and select the **Changes** page. The Status Browser should look like Figure 26-9.

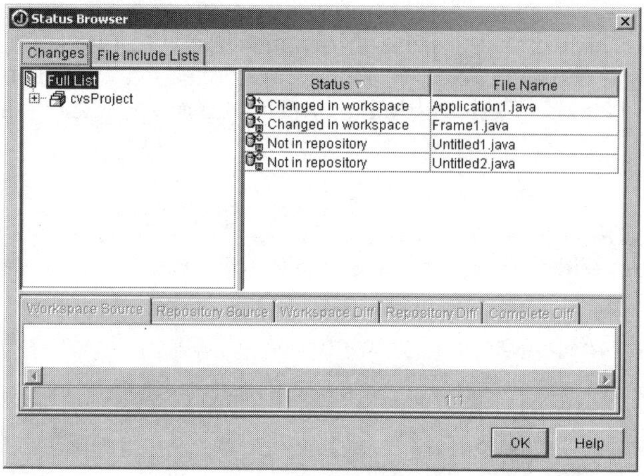

Figure 26-9: The Status Browser

The Status Browser alerts you to the fact that Application1.java and Frame1.java have changed. It also lets you know that Untitled1.java and Untitled2.java are not in the repository. Click **OK** to close the Status Browser.

NOTE: The Status Browser may appear to be absolutely blank if you have a completely up-to-date project. This can be a bit confusing, as it may appear that JBuilder is telling you nothing about the status of your projects. The obvious fix is to make some small change to one of your files, load the Status Browser again, and see if things are a bit more interesting.

The purpose of the Status Browser is to allow you to check on the state of your project in the repository without necessarily making any changes. Later in the chapter you will see that you can use the Status Browser to tell CVS to ignore certain files that you don't want to check in to the repository.

The Commit Browser

In the menu, choose **Team | Commit Browser.** On the Commits page you will see the name of each file that has been changed or added, the status of the file, and a recommended action, as shown in Figure 26-10.

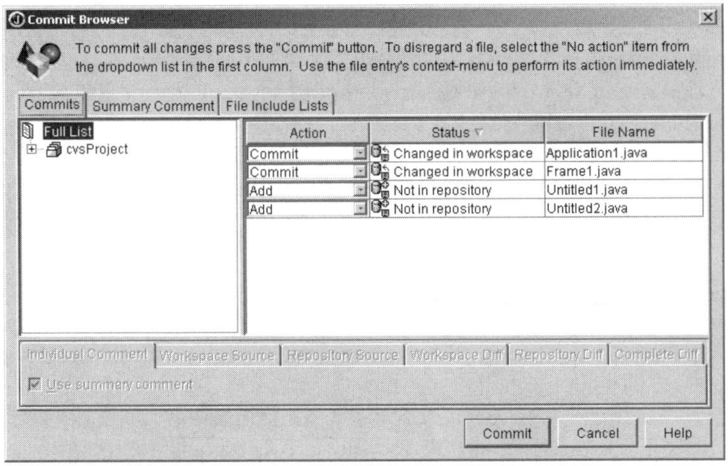

Figure 26-10: The Commit Browser

To commit the changes in the two files that were previously added to the repository (Application1.java and Frame1.java) and to add the files that are not in the repository (Untitled1.java and Untitled2.java), all you need to do is click the Commit button. If you would like to attach a comment describing these changes, go to the Summary Comment page of the Commit Browser before you click Commit, and type in a comment. Once you have committed your changes, JBuilder will show a Version Control Operations dialog box that lists what was accomplished with the commit and confirms that the commit was successful.

Sometimes the default actions suggested by JBuilder are not appropriate for a given file. The combo boxes in the Action column of the Commit Browser give you additional options, as shown in Figure 26-11. You could choose No action for any of the files, which would leave that file unchanged in its status. You could also choose Revert for the two files already in the CVS repository. This would bring the last version in the repository into your project. In this project, using Revert for these files would mean that you would then have the original version of Application1.java without the import statement and the original version of Frame1.java without the button.

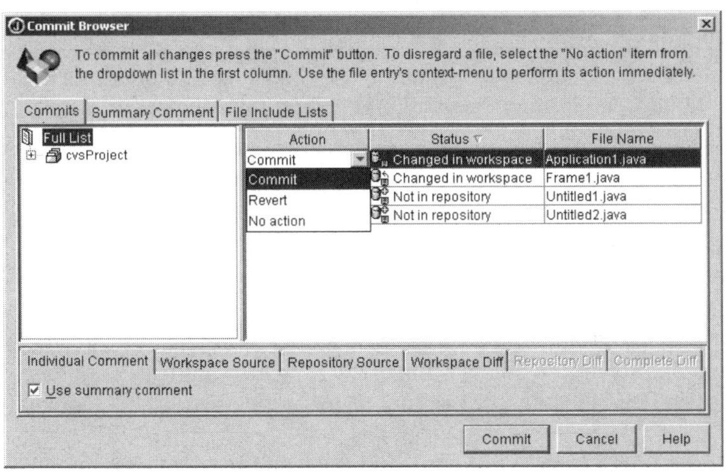

Figure 26-11: Combo boxes show additional options.

Occasionally you will find items in the Commit Browser that won't go away no matter how many times you try to commit them. In particular, you might see a single file that appears to simultaneously need to be committed and updated. This file will be listed twice, once for the update and once for the commit. This usually means that there is a file on your local system that is "in the way." Usually, if you delete the file on your local system that is "in the way" and then run a CVS update, you will find that the problem committing files will go away. Of course, I recommend that you first back up the file to a temp directory, delete it from your local system, and then try the update. If all goes well, you can delete the file from your temp directory or leave it in the temp directory until some other process goes and cleans it up.

More on Using the Status Browser

As you have seen, you can use the Status Browser to check on the current status of all the files in your project.

Often, when you are looking in the Status Browser, you can see that a lot of files are scheduled to be added to CVS that you would prefer to ignore. It is easy to fix this problem. Click on the File Include Lists tab and choose either the Team Include List or the Personal Include List, depending on whether you want to make settings for the whole team or just for yourself. Find the directory or package that includes the files that you want to include or exclude. Uncheck the items that you want to exclude from CVS and check the items that you want to include. Now go back to the Changes page. You will see that the items from the list that you wanted to exclude or include have been either deleted from or added to the Changes list, depending on your choices.

If you exclude some files, go to the command prompt and change to the directory where you were excluding files. Note that there is a file in your directory called .cvsignore. This is a simple text file listing all the files or directories in the current directory that you want CVS to ignore. You can edit this file by hand, and JBuilder will pick up on your changes. But in most cases, you will find it easiest to edit the file using the JBuilder team development tools.

JBuilder allows two levels for ignoring files. There are files that you want to ignore on a personal basis and, as described in the previous paragraph, those that everyone who checks files out from the repository will ignore. I believe that the local ignore files are stored in the .jpx.local file for your project.

NOTE: When working in the Status Browser, it is not necessary to actually commit or update your files in order to change the contents of a .cvsignore file. Simply moving back and forth between the File Include Lists and Changes pages seems to be enough to write your changes to the .cvsignore file and post those changes to the repository.

At the bottom of the Changes page in the Status Browser you will see several tabs. You can use these tabs to view the current state of your file in your project and in the repository. You can also see views that show the differences between two versions of your files. This technology will be discussed in more depth later in the chapter.

Once you start to get the rhythm of working with the Status Browser, you can bring even very large projects under control fairly quickly. For instance, I keep all the projects for this book in CVS under one single entry in the repository. Beneath that entry is a very large tree, but neither CVS nor the JBuilder team development tools have any trouble working with such a large number of files.

Removing a File

To remove a file from your project, double-click on the file in the project pane to select it. For instance, double-click on **Untitled1.java** in the project pane. Then choose **Team | Remove Untitled1.java.** You will be given an opportunity to write a comment. Accept the default, which is <No comment entered>, and click **OK.** You will receive a message that the file has been removed from your workspace and also from the repository.

NOTE: If you did not add Untitled1.java to the repository when you were using the Commit Browser, you will not have the option of removing it from the repository when you double-click on it. You will, however, see "Add Untitled1.java" as an option in the Team menu.

Version Labels

You will see an option in the Team menu to add a version label to a project. In CVS, this is called tagging a build of a project.

The goal of a version label is to draw a line in the sand that marks a stage in the development of your project. You can then retrieve the project using that particular version label and get the exact state of the project at the time you added the label.

The most obvious use for a version label would be to state that a project has reached version 1.0 or version 2.0. But you might also find it useful to add version labels at odd times that include a date: version_march_12_2002. Then you can retrieve your project as it appeared on that particular date.

There are two different ways to pull a particular version from CVS. Both of them involve working from the command line. I will therefore explain that process later in this chapter.

Checking Out and Updating a Project

To simulate two users working simultaneously on the project, we will open a new browser, check out the project, and make some changes to the project. We will then update the original project with the changes that were made.

In the JBuilder menu, choose **Window | New Browser**. When the new copy of the browser opens, choose **File | Close Projects** and close all open projects. Now choose **File | New** to access the Object Gallery and then choose the **Project** page. On the Project page, click on **Pull Project from CVS** and click **OK.**

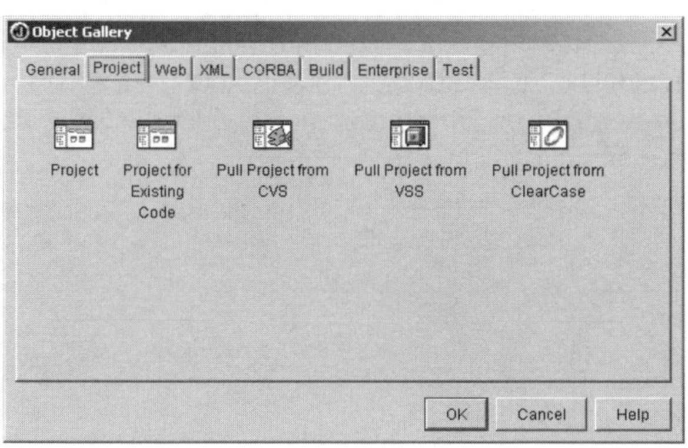

Figure 26-12: The Project page of the Object Gallery

The Pull Project from CVS Wizard will appear. In Step 1 of the wizard, you will set the directory where your copy of the project will reside. The only thing to remember when setting the directory is that the new directory must be empty at this stage. It can often be helpful to standardize the directory structure between members of the team. In this example, we will use the name myDirectory. Browse to the directory where you want to place your copy of the project, and click **Next**.

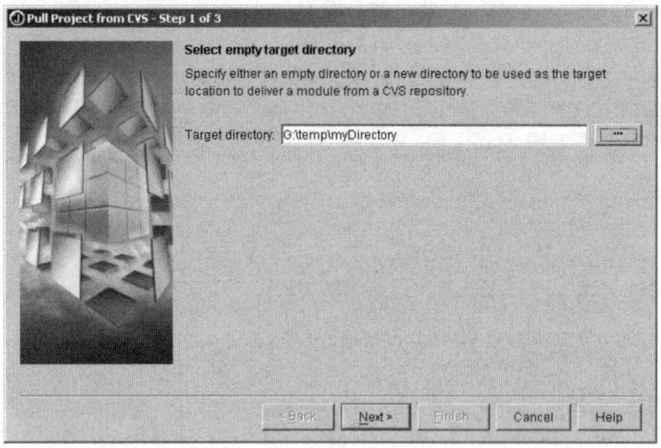

Figure 26-13: Step 1 of the wizard

In Step 2 of the wizard, choose **Local** as your connect type and click **Next**.

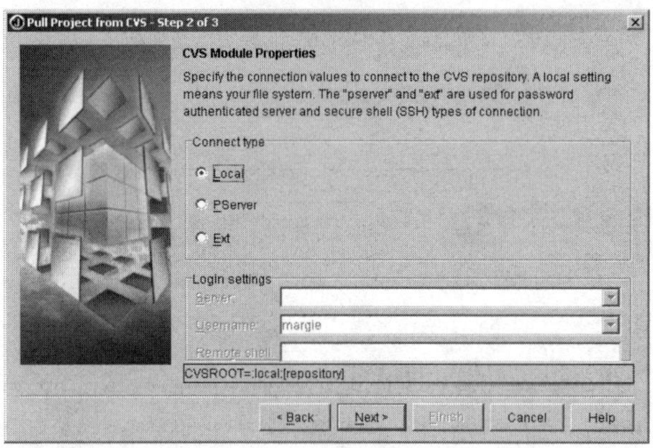

Figure 26-14: Step 2 of the wizard

In the next step of the wizard, shown in Figure 26-15, leave the default settings, which should identify cvsProject and the path to the repository you created. If the project you want is not displaying, you can browse to the repository and then type in the name of your project, which in this case is cvsProject. You should also be able to pick your project from a list that appears in the Module Name combo box. You might find it interesting to select the Show console messages option, particularly if you are familiar with CVS.

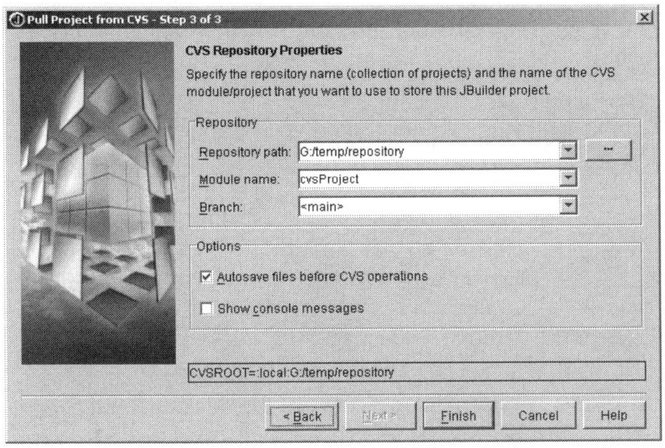

Figure 26-15: Step 3 of the wizard

After you click Finish, JBuilder will indicate whether or not you have successfully checked the project out, as shown in Figure 26-16.

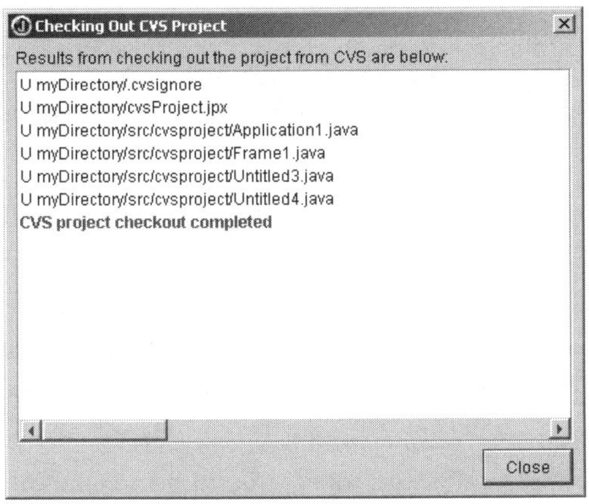

Figure 26-16: The CVS project checkout was successful.

At this time, you have two copies of the project active. Look at the path information at the top of your project and you will see that the copies of the project are in different directories.

On the new version of the project, drop down an additional button on Frame1.java in design view and add this import statement to Application1.java:

```
import java.io.*;
```

Save your work and choose **Team | Commit Browser**. Commit your changes to the repository by clicking on the **Commit** button. (If you have questions about this step, look at the previous example of using the Commit Browser.)

Move to the other open copy of the project. At this point, it will not have the new information you just added. Choose **Team | Update Project**. JBuilder will show you a message indicating that it will update your project from the repository, as shown in Figure 26-17.

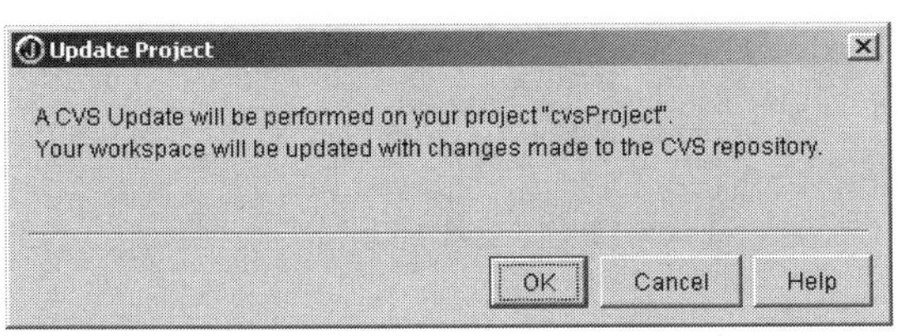

Figure 26-17: An update alert

Click **OK**. You will see additional messages, with the last one indicating that your update was successful, as shown in Figure 26-18.

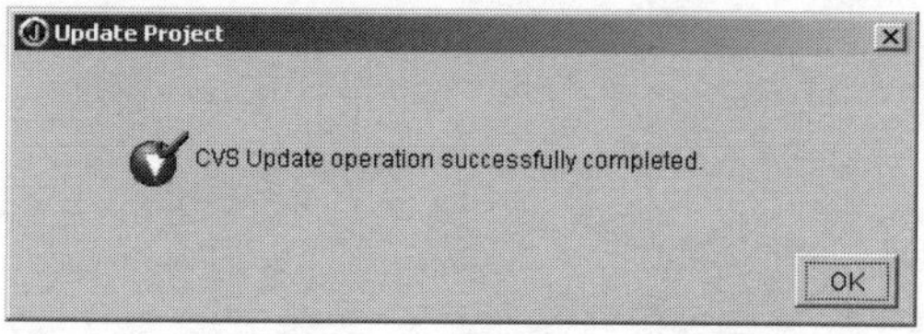

Figure 26-18: The update is complete.

Take a moment to compare your copies of the project. They are identical to each other and to the files in the repository.

For better or worse, you can also use the Commit Browser to update your project. If you choose this option, the drop-down list shown in Figure 26-11 will give you the choice of either updating your project or taking no action.

NOTE: Probably the most important thing to remember when you are using CVS is to update your project before you start working on it. That way, you can incorporate any changes that were made in your code. Make it a habit to update before you do anything else, and your life will go a lot smoother. It is also helpful to update before you commit. That way you can avoid situations in which there are conflicts between your version of the product and the version in the repository.

Resolving Conflicts

In this next section of our discussion, we will first create a conflict and then use JBuilder's tools to resolve it. Start with the first copy of the project that we created. Imagine that this copy of the project is checked out to someone named Jane. In Application1.java, place your cursor on the line directly under the package statement at the top of the editor and type:

```
//Mary had a little lamb
```

Save your work, but do not do a commit. At this point, Jane has made some changes in the file but has not changed the file in the repository.

Imagine that another person named Bob has checked out the copy of the project we created by pulling it from CVS. In the copy we pulled from CVS, go to Application1.java, place your cursor on the line directly under the package statement and type:

```
//Its fleece was white as snow
```

Save your work here as well. Now the situation is that both Jane and Bob have changed the same line of the file, but neither of them has changed the copy that is in the repository. (Don't ask yourself why they are typing nursery rhymes into their code; you don't want to know.)

In the copy of the project that we pulled from CVS, choose **Team | Commit Browser** and commit your changes. The process will go smoothly. Now the copy of the file in the repository will read Its fleece was white as snow. This situation reflects what would happen if Bob committed his changes to the repository. Meanwhile, Jane is happily working away on her version of the file.

In the copy that you originally created, choose **Team | Update Project**. JBuilder will give you a message, shown in Figure 26-19, that indicates there are conflicts. At this point, Jane has just updated her files and has found that the copy of Application1.java in the repository does not match her copy of the file. The editor will explain the conflicts, as illustrated in Figure 26-20.

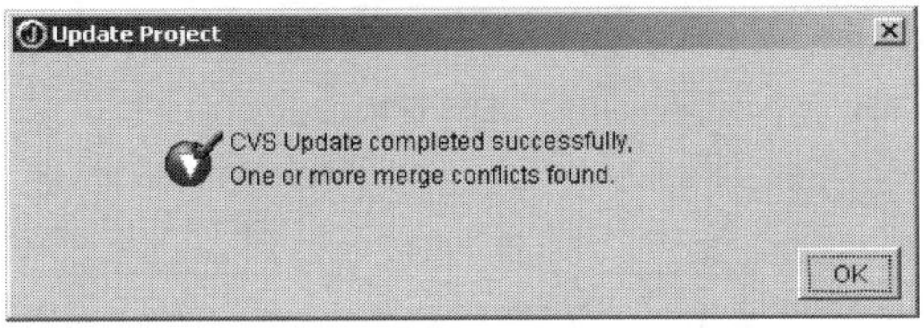

Figure 26-19: JBuilder alert regarding conflicts

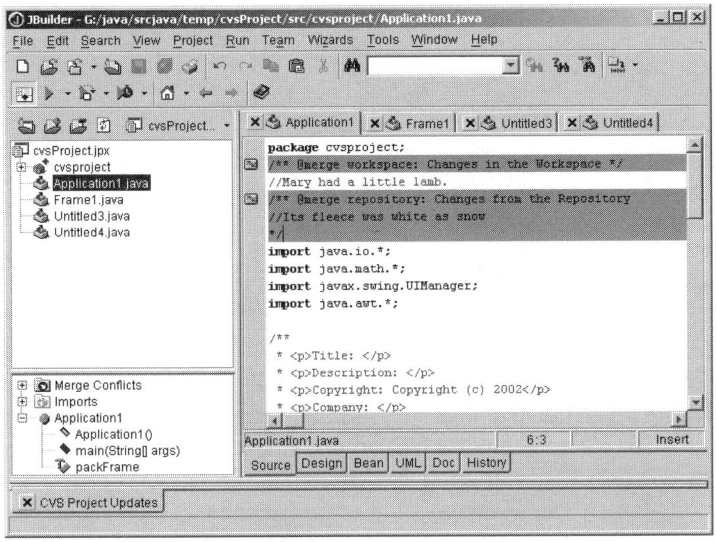

Figure 26-20: JBuilder explains the conflicts in the editor.

You can use the little tabs visible in the gutter to resolve the conflict, but I first want to show you some interesting features of the Status Browser.

Choose **Team | Status Browser** to bring up the Status Browser. In the Status field of the Browser, you will see Has conflicts listed as the status, as shown near the top right of Figure 26-21. Click on **Application1.java** in the File Name field of the Status Browser. The file tabs in the middle of the browser will no longer be grayed out. These tabs give you the tools you need to track down the conflict and see how the versions of your file differ. You may need to expand the space beneath the tabs to get a view of the file. To do this, place your cursor on the boundary between the file tabs and the top portion of the browser. When you see a double-headed arrow, left-click and drag upward.

NOTE: The Commit Browser has a similar interface for scrutinizing merge conflicts.

The Workspace Source tab shows the current local version of the file, including unsaved changes. The Repository Source tab shows the version that is in the repository. Repository Diff shows any changes that were made to the repository version of the file since you checked it out. If someone else has made changes to the file after you checked it out from the repository, Repository Diff would highlight the changes. Workspace Diff shows the changes you made since you checked the file out. It compares the version of the file you checked out to the version you have in your workspace now. Complete Diff displays the difference between the most recent workspace version of the file and the most recent version in the repository. Complete Diff will have the most complete information about any merge conflict. As Figure 26-21 shows, the change in the workspace, which in this case is Mary had a little lamb, and the change from the repository, Its fleece was white as snow, are both identified for you.

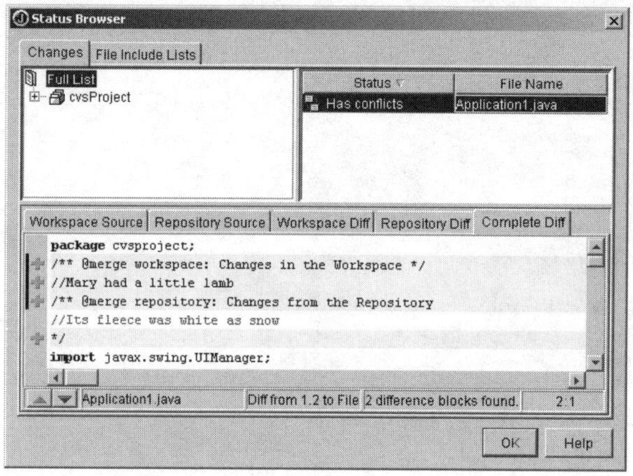

Figure 26-21: The Complete Diff page

Cancel out of the Status Browser and return to the editor, where your conflicts will continue to be highlighted, as shown in Figure 26-22. Notice the small buttons in the gutter on the left side of the editor. Clicking on either will pop up a message. One reads Keep Workspace Changes and the other reads Keep Repository Changes. Click on the message of your choice to resolve the conflict.

If you prefer, you can identify the source of conflict in the message pane and resolve it manually, being careful to delete the comments that JBuilder created in the editor as well. However, I prefer a slightly different technique. Double-click on the message in the message pane to bring the cursor to the source of the conflict. Small buttons will appear in the gutter to the left of your source. These buttons are partially visible in Figure 26-22, beneath the edge of the pop-up dialog. One button will pop up a dialog allowing you to use the source found in the repository to resolve the conflict. The other button will pop up the dialog shown in Figure 26-22, which allows you to keep the workspace changes. This dialog allows you to use the source found in your project to resolve the conflict. Just use the appropriate JBuilder dialog to select the resolution that you prefer. Then commit your work. You might at this time pick up the phone and tell the other person working on the file that they should do an update.

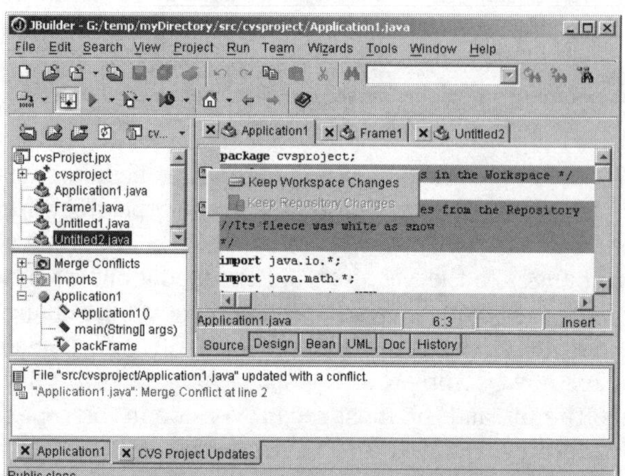

Figure 26-22: Clicking on the message you agree with resolves the conflicts.

Using CVS with JBuilder Personal and SE Editions

Those of you who have JBuilder Personal edition can work with CVS from the command line or by using one of the several graphical user interfaces that have been developed for CVS. CVS is an open source project, and therefore it and most of the client-side graphical user interfaces for it are free.

Basic Information and Resources

If you need to download CVS, it is available through the Internet. The home site for CVS is http://cvshome.org/. If you are running a Linux box, you will want to access http://cvshome.org/dev/codelinux.html. Most distributions of Linux come with CVS already installed. If you are using Windows, the appropriate site is http://cvshome.org/dev/codewindow.html. If you use a Mac, you can find some versions of CVS clients for the Mac at http://www.loria.fr/cgi-bin/molli/wilma.cgi/rel. This site is also a very good resource for finding other CVS tools.

The initial setup for CVS can vary depending on the platform on which you are going to install it. Most Linux machines have a copy of CVS already installed. The Windows version of CVS consists of a single executable called cvs.exe. It is usual, if you need to link more than one machine in a network, to have a Linux machine as the server, with clients that are either Windows or Linux machines. You could use NFS or SAMBA to connect to the server, which would share a drive with all the machines on the network. Most of the time, however, you will want to use a PServer, as explained later in this chapter. Each client would have a copy of CVS on it. At this time, the Windows version of CVS cannot be the server.

If you want to use CVS to keep two machines in sync with each other, you might use a third machine as an intermediary between them. The third machine would contain the repository. You could also have one machine act as both a CVS server and a development machine.

Front-End Tools

Front-end tools for Windows include:

- TKCVS: http://cvshome.org/dev/addontkcvs.html
- JCVS: http://cvshome.org/dev/addonjcvs.html
- WinCVS: http://cvshome.org/dev/addonmaccvs.html

I am familiar with TKCVS and find that it definitely makes CVS easier to use. It requires recent versions of tcl to run, but, for instance, a standard install of Red Hat includes everything you need.

While not a fancy app by Windows standards, it is nonetheless sophisticated enough to be useful to most developers. In particular, it can help you learn all the options CVS has available. Furthermore, it makes it easy for you to experiment with these options, so see what they can do for you.

On those occasions when TKCVS lets you down, you still have the option of dropping back to the command prompt and running your old commands. In fact, you can combine the GUI interface with a command-line approach in any way you want. That way you can get the best from both worlds: the chance to write scripts at the command prompt and the chance to browse your project and run reports inside the TKCVS GUI. (The sad truth is that I do a lot of CVS work from the command line. It's fast, efficient, and easy.)

On TKCVS, in the Options menu, there is a Checkout with Options item that will allow you to check out directories. You need to specifically mark the Checkout with Options item, or this will not work.

TkDiff is an excellent diff engine that can be used to compare two files. It is really meant to be part of the TKCVS suite, but you can use it as a stand-alone tool.

Working with CVS from the Command Line

In this portion of the chapter, we will review some of the main commands that you will need if you are working with CVS from the command line. If you seriously start to work with CVS, you will probably want to access the official online manual, which has all the latest information in it. It is called "Version Management with CVS" but is commonly known as "the Cederqvist" after its original author, Per Cederqvist. You can find it at http://www.cvs-home.org/docs/manual. I also recommend the book *Open Source Development with CVS* by Karl Fogel (Coriolis Group). The author has done an excellent job writing a book that is both informative and interesting to read.

You will probably notice as you go along that cvs commands take the following form:

```
cvs command
```

They will always start with cvs and then will give the information needed for the operation that you wish to do (command).

Initializing a CVS Repository for PServer

In this section you will read a little bit about setting up CVS on a Linux box so that you can use it with the PServer option. This is not a detailed explanation, but hopefully what you find here will help you over the rough spots that are not explained well in the available documentation.

If you have installed CVS, you still have to initialize the directory from which you want to serve files. The code to do that is as follows:

```
cvs -d /usr/local/cvsrep init
```

The cvs part of the code is a mandatory part of the syntax for using CVS. -d stands for directory, which in this case is the repository. /usr/local/cvsrep gives the location for the repository.

Though it's probably there already, make sure /etc/services contains:

```
cvspserver 2401/tcp
```

Add the information shown in Listing 26-1 to /etc/xinetd.d, in a file called cvs. The whole path to the file will therefore look like this: /etc/xinetd.d/cvs.

Listing 26-1: The tiny cvs file that you add to the xinetd.d directory

```
service cvspserver
{
      disable = no
   socket_type     = stream
   protocol        = tcp
   wait            = no
   user            = root
   server          = /usr/bin/cvs
   server_args     = -allow-root=/usr/local/cvsrep -f pserver
}
```

You should then reboot the system or reinitialize xinetd. You can find xinetd in the /etc/init.d directory. It has options to restart or reload:

```
/etc/init.d/xinetd restart
```

If you get an error message to the effect that "can't chdir..." when you try to access CVS, the problem is you forgot the -f from this line in xinetd:

```
server_args     = –allow-root=/usr/local/cvsfred -f pserver
```

Logging into a CVS PServer

It is now time to talk about logging onto the server from a remote machine. You may find writing a batch file useful for initializing CVS. Here is the batch file I run before accessing the project:

```
@echo off
set HOME=G:\utils\cvsPassFiles\bree
set HOMEPATH=\utils\cvsPassFiles\bree
set HOMEDRIVE=G:
set USER=charlie
set CVSROOT=:pserver:charlie@MyServer:/usr/local/cvsrep
```

The HOME and HOMEPATH environment variables point to a place where CVS can store some information about your connections, such as an encrypted version of your password. I put all this in a batch file and run it automatically when I log on to my development machine.

You will probably have to sign on to CVS on the server once before you start. If so, here is the command:

```
cvs -d :pserver:UserName@Server:/usr/local/cvsrep login
```

You will be prompted for your password. If all goes well, the command will return with no comment. In typical UNIX style, you will not get a "Success" notification. You are just returned to the prompt. If you get any feedback at all, that probably means something has gone wrong.

In the command above, -d stands for directory. In this context, the directory in question is the repository. If the repository had been on a local machine, then you could have just typed:

```
cvs –d /usr/local/cvsrep
```


Creating a CVS Project

Creating a CVS project is a process of importing it into the repository. Before you place the project into the repository, be sure to clean it up, as CVS will import everything in the directory tree. The code you will want is:

```
cvs import -m "initial import into cvs" cacheguide charlie start
```

The word import indicates that the project is being imported into the repository. The -m part of the code indicates that there will be a short message following it. In this case the message is "initial import into cvs." The next argument, cacheguide, is the name of the project. The following two tags are the vendortag and the releasetag. These tags help in tracking third-party sources. Generally speaking, they are not important, and you can use a username and the word start for filler. You saw the releasetag earlier, when you learned how to tag a point in your development process with a version label.

If you add a new project to the repository, you should not continue to work in the directory you just imported. Instead, you should rename that directory and then perform a checkout, as described in the following section. For instance, if you stored the code in a directory called MyProject, you should rename MyProject to MyProject.precvs. Then when you perform a checkout of the project, it will automatically be placed in a directory called MyProject.

Checking out a CVS Project

The command to get a project from CVS is:

```
cvs checkout MediaPlayer
```

You want to issue the command from the directory beneath where you want your project to reside. For instance, if your project were called MediaPlayer and it was in the c:\src directory, issuing the command from the c:\src directory would put the files in the c:\src\MediaPlayer directory.

NOTE: You might want to spend some time making sure that all the files have regular capitalization. That is, there are no files called MYFILE.JAVA or myfile.java or MYFILE.java. They should probably all follow standard camelcaps, such as MyFile.java, or else they should all be in small letters. If you add new files to the project, it would help to get the caps right before adding them to CVS. It is probably best to keep projects off Windows 98 during development, as Win98 is bad about caps. But if you get it set up right once and do the checkout to Win98, it should be okay.

Committing Your Work

Here is the command to commit your work at the end of the day:

```
cvs commit -m "Here is my work for today"
```

By this time, you will probably recognize the cvs command format. -m is a flag indicating that a message follows, just as you saw in the section on creating a new project. Committing your work will place it in the repository.

Getting Updates

To get updates from the repository, for example, to update one machine if you have done a commit from another machine, you will use this command:

```
cvs update
```

To get new directories from the repository, issue this command:

```
cvs update -d
```

If you enter cvs update -P, then any empty directories should be pruned from the directory tree.

Adding Files

Adding a file is simple to do:

```
cvs add MyFile.pas
```

This command would add MyFile.pas to your project only after you issue a cvs update. To add a binary file, type this:

```
cvs add -kb MyPicture.png
```

Removing Files

To remove a file, first delete it from the hard drive and then use this command:

```
cvs remove MyFile.pas
```

Backup copies of your file will remain in CVS, so you could restore it later if you wished.

Getting the Status of a File

Here is the command to check on the status of a file:

```
cvs status MyFile.pas
```

NOTE: When the commands are this simple, you may find that you have a tendency to forget to put in the cvs part of the command. If you are trying to perform an operation like this and it isn't working, check to be sure that you did not overlook this crucial part of the command.

Look for the -kb symbol in the status report to confirm that a file is binary.

Getting the Status of a Directory or Entire Project

You can get the status of a directory or project by typing cvs status with no parameters. This will usually send you more information than you want. The solution is to type the following:

```
cvs status > status.txt
```

You should then open status.txt in a text editor. In particular, you will want to focus on the beginning of the file, which lists all the files that are not included. If you get tired of seeing some of these files, simply place their name in a file called .cvsignore, which is stored in the same directory as the file you want CVS to ignore.

Making a File Binary after It Has Been Checked In

CVS is very bad about handling binary files. Essentially, it only keeps the most recent copy of your binary files such as JPGs. If you put a binary file such as a PNG or JPG in the repository and forget to mark it as binary, you will have trouble. At times you may want to make a file binary if it is not listed as binary in the repository.

```
cvs admin -kb MyFile.gif
```

The -kb part of the code tells CVS to disable keyword expansion and line-ending conversion for the file. These are features that are helpful in text files but would not be useful at all in a binary file. admin is a command that allows you to change something in the repository. After giving this command, you should then commit a valid version of the binary file.

Retrieving a Tagged Version Label

You can tag a version of CVS with this command:

```
cvs tag version-1-jan-1-1956
```

You can retrieve that version into a new, empty directory with this command:

```
cvs checkout -r version-1-jan-1-1956
```

You can replace the version in the current directory with an older version by issuing this command:

```
cvs update -r version-1-jan-1-1956
```

You do not have to use dates as part of the name, but I have found it to be useful.

NOTE: There is also an easy-to-use option in the JBuilder Team menu for tagging a version of your source.

Summary

In this chapter you have learned at least a little bit about working with CVS and the team development tools in JBuilder. I am a big supporter of CVS and have used it extensively for years. It has a few quirks, but it has proved to be absolutely rock solid. Right now I can't remember ever having serious trouble with it. One nice feature of CVS is that you can take a whole repository, burn it on to a CD, and save it as backup. You can then just copy it off the CD to restore it. You will, of course, probably have to change the file permissions after copying it off the CD.

Chapter 27

Working with JAR Files

Charlie Calvert

This chapter and the next show how to build and use JAR files. This chapter focuses on JAR file basics, while Chapter 28 discusses deploying applications in JAR files and executables.

In this chapter you will see:

- What role JAR files play in many Java projects. Understanding JAR files is key to your ability to create complex projects that are easy to maintain. This section of the chapter focuses on general Java programming issues and not exclusively on JBuilder. I am including it simply because so many Java books skip over the subject. The "learn-to-program" Java books think the subject too advanced, and the advanced books think it too fundamental. The result is that much too little has been said about the subject.
- How to create JAR files that contain utility routines you want to share between multiple projects.
- How to integrate JAR files into a JBuilder project with library files. This is an important skill, since JAR files are used heavily in Java development. This subject is covered near the end of the chapter. If you are not interested in creating JAR files, please skip right to that section and learn how to integrate JAR files into your programs.
- How to construct projects that contain .class files that are not accompanied by source files. This case is easy to handle, but you first need to understand JBuilder library files.
- How to compile projects from the command line that rely on JAR files.

Probably the most important concept that you will explore in this chapter is that of the JBuilder library. Libraries in JBuilder perform the same task that the classpath does when you compile from the command line using the JDK tools. In particular, you can use library files to tell JBuilder about the classpath on your system.

This chapter is closely related to the following chapter, which discusses deployment. Both chapters discuss the creation of JAR files. The intention of this chapter is to explain how to integrate JAR files into JBuilder development. The intention of Chapter 28 is to show how to wrap up an entire application in a JAR file. JAR files will also be discussed in Part VII: JavaBeans, where you will learn how to place a component in a JAR file. And finally, JAR files will be discussed near the end of Chapter 43, where you will learn how to deploy large applications that depend on multiple JAR files. In short, JAR files are an important part of Java development, so they are getting heavy play in this book.

The directory structure of the projects on your disk will be very important when studying the examples in this chapter. In particular, you need to have files called MathBox.java and StringBox.java in a particular directory on your hard drive. These files are part of the CodeBox JAR file discussed in Chapter 25. In this chapter I will give instructions on placing these files properly. However, if you have been following along through the last few chapters, your computer should be set up properly. If not, you might want to install the sample files from the CD that accompanies this book or download them from the Internet. You can find a reference to the files to download on my web site at http://www.elvenware.com. They are also discussed in depth in the index.html file on the CD.

Understanding JAR Files

JAR files are a technology based on the zip format that allows you to bundle directories and files into a single container. For all practical purposes, they are simply another form of tar or zip file customized for Java development. In fact, most programs that handle multiple file compression technologies will also handle JAR files. For instance, the well-known Windows program WinZip can open not only zip files and tar files but also JAR files.

JAR files, however, do not have the same primary purpose as tar and zip files. In particular, you generally run code directly out of a JAR file. Zip files, on the other hand, are usually just a mechanism for storage of files. So even if the technology for JAR files and zip files is nearly identical, the intended use of the files is quite different.

In this chapter, we are examining JAR files that contain multiple .class files that will be used by your main program. In Chapter 28, you will look at JAR files that contain your main program and any files on which it relies.

JAR files can track not only the .class files you place inside them, but also the directory structure in which those class files reside and any resources on which your project depends. As a result, JAR files can house packages and bitmaps as well as class files.

Here is a summary of the nature of the connection between JAR files and Java programs:

- Since the JDK and JRE are stored in JAR files, all Java programs depend on JAR files in order to run. Sometimes, however, your program will depend on other JAR files besides the ones distributed by Sun. If you use a class that is stored in a JAR file, on some occasions you will need to pin down the directory — that is, the package — in which that JAR file resides. In particular, you need to make sure it is on your classpath. In JBuilder, you will usually do this by setting up a library file. Library files will be explained later in this chapter. (In all the recent JDKs and JREs, you don't need to worry about putting the Sun JAR files on your classpath. That will be taken care of for you automatically.)
- JAR files themselves can contain packages. In fact, most JAR files will include not only Java class files but also a directory structure to house those class files. It is, in fact, often simplest to think of a JAR file as a housing for a set of packages.

Why Use Packages?

Packages have the following benefits:

- They help you organize your code.
- They help avoid name collisions. A class named MyPackage.MyClass can be distinguished from a class called YourPackage.MyClass.
- They help with reuse. Once you create a package, you can often easily share it among multiple projects.
- They work on all platforms. All computers support the idea of directories. When the Java developers were creating the language, they needed a means of distinguishing one file from another so that projects could link. The technique they were searching

for had to be platform neutral. The solution decided upon by the engineers at Sun was to use packages.

- Java dependency on packages was significantly increased by the decision to insist that each public class reside in its own source file. This greatly increased the number of files that make up both the JDK and our projects. Packages were needed to help sort out this wide range of files.

When using packages, you need to remember that the actual location on the hard drive of a package is not always important to Java. Consider the following directory structure:

```
c:\temp\MyPackage\sam.java
f:\goober\MyPackage\tom.java
```

In this particular scenario, if both c:\temp and f:\goober are on your classpath, Java regards both c:\temp\MyPackage and f:\goober\MyPackage as the same package. This can cause confusion if you are not careful.

NOTE: Though theoretically possible, I have found it unwise to put a package inside a directory with the same name. For instance, I avoid structures such as c:\goober\MyPackage\MyPackage\MyPackage.jpr. Though it is not certain that this will lead to trouble, it can, nevertheless, cause considerable confusion when working in JBuilder. I would correct the above directory structure to read c:\goober\MyPackage\MyPackage.jpr.

JAR Files and Classpaths

People new to Java might not at first understand the direct connection between JAR files and classpaths. But, in fact, the two subjects are closely linked. The exact nature of that relationship, however, is less than intuitive to the uninitiated.

Each JAR file contains class files usually arranged inside packages. The end result is that the directory structure you care about exists in two places:

- You are concerned about the packages, or directories, found on your hard drive.
- You are also concerned about the packages, or directories, found inside a JAR file.

You need to think about both sets of packages in order to make successful use of JAR files.

Here is how to proceed:

You first point your global environment's classpath, or a JBuilder library file, at a particular JAR file. After completing this task, the packages inside that JAR file can be treated like normal paths found on your hard drive.

It might help to consider a particular example. Consider the case where you have placed a JAR file called MyCode.jar in the c:\src\classes directory. Inside MyCode.jar you can find the following package:

```
com.mycompany.utils
```

If you want to reference the files in the utils directory that is part of the JAR file, first put MyCode.jar on your classpath. Here is a Linux script for achieving that goal:

```
export CLASSPATH=$CLASSPATH:/home/UserName/src/classes/MyCode.jar
```

Here is the same script for Windows:

```
set CLASSPATH=%CLASSPATH%;c:\src\classes\MyCode.jar
```

NOTE: In Windows, you put % marks around an environment variable when you want to reference its contents. For instance, %PATH% is another way of referencing the contents of your current path as it is stored in the path environment variable. In Linux, you get the same effect by using a $. As a result, $CLASSPATH references the classpath environment variable in Linux. So the two statements above are asking to set the CLASSPATH to the existing CLASSPATH, plus a new segment of the path that includes a JAR file. You can always see the contents of your environment by typing set at the command prompt. You can see the contents of a particular variable in the environment by typing echo $PATH or echo %PATH.

After setting up your classpath this way, you can simply add the following statement to your source files to access the code in your utils package:

```
import com.mycompany.utils.*
```

Here is one way to begin to make sense of the situation: You can access a JAR file by putting it on your classpath or referencing it from a JBuilder library file. After you place MyCode.jar where it can be accessed, you can forget that MyCode.jar is a file and pretend instead that it is a directory called MyCode.

When you added MyCode.jar to your classpath, you essentially added a new set of directories to your hard drive. The situation is now exactly the same as it would be were there a directory structure on your hard drive that looked like this:

```
c:\src\classes\MyCode\com\mycompany\utils
/home/UserName/src/classes/MyCode/com/mycompany/utils/
```

In the two examples shown here, the first line is for Windows and the second for Linux. The important point in these examples is that I'm pretending that MyCode is a directory and not a JAR file. That is the way Java thinks about JAR files: It sees their contents as an extension to your hard drive.

Let's review what we have just said. Whether the packages you want to reach are in a JAR file or not, you need to understand that the path to your package has three parts:

- One part is the path on your hard drive that leads to your JAR file. This part should be on your classpath or referenced by a JBuilder library file.
- The second part is the JAR file itself.
- The third part of the equation is the contents of the JAR file itself, particularly the packages that are stored in the JAR file. You access the files in these packages via an import statement.

The part that is on your hard drive looks like this:

```
c:\src\classes\MyCode.jar
```

It is divided up into two sections, the path to the JAR file and the JAR file itself.

The part that is in a JAR file might look like this:

```
com.mycompany.utils
```

From inside your program, that part will look like this:

```
import com.mycompany.utils.*;
```

To get at the files in c:\src\classes\MyCode.jar\com.mycompany.utils, you must think about all parts of the equation. Setting up your classpath correctly takes care of the first two parts of the equation. But to take care of the third part, you must add the proper import statement to your code.

All of this is difficult to understand the first time, and difficult to explain in simple language. However, if you get it just once, then you will soon reach the stage where classpaths lose their mystery. Few subjects in computing (actually only a very few) are difficult once you understand how they work. This subject, however, can be hard to understand but relatively simple to put into practice once you know the trick. It is definitely a case where you need to have your epiphany, your "ah-ha" moment, and from then on you should no longer have much trouble.

In the remainder of this chapter you are going to learn about the relationship between Java, JBuilder, library files, your classpath, and JAR files. In particular, I will now illustrate with examples what I have just said in words. I will also introduce you to JBuilder library files. As stated earlier, JBuilder library files are probably the single most important topic in this chapter.

Creating and Using JAR Files

We are at last prepared to scramble to the top of a peak that we have been scaling for the last several chapters. From the top, we can get a clear overview of how to use JAR files inside a JBuilder project. From this vantage point, you should be able to quickly see how you can structure even the most complex JBuilder projects.

It is now time to create a simple JAR file and to access it from inside JBuilder. Once you have mastered that technique, you should be able to easily include other third-party JAR files, such as Xerces.jar or Soap.jar. Files such as these play a key role in many types of modern Java development.

This part of the chapter is divided into three sections.

- The first part will show how to set up and test the files that will become part of your JAR file.
- In the second part you will learn two different ways to create a JAR file.
- The third part will show how to use that JAR file. You will use the JAR file alone and not reference the original class and source files that were used to create the JAR file.

Setting up the Test Program

In this section I will create a standard Java program for testing the various parts of the CodeBox JAR file that we are about to create. This JAR file will contain the compiled source for the StringBox.java file that we have been developing over the last few chapters. I have also included two additional files called MathBox.java and FileBox.java. These files contain additional utility routines that you might want to use in your programs.

NOTE: It is important to understand that I am not going to use the JUnit tool that will be introduced later in this book. JUnit allows you to construct and easily run tests on a Java class that you have created. The purpose of the tests is to ensure that your code works as you intended. JUnit is the right way to test your code, but I want to discuss that very important code in its own chapter.

JUnit cannot, however, be easily used to test the UI of a program. Therefore, you usually need two kinds of tests for your code. One will be the kind shown in this chapter and the other will be the kind you develop with JUnit.

The project you are going to create is called ManageCodeBoxSimple. Like all the examples discussed in this book, it is available on the CD and from www.elvenware.com. It will allow you to compile the MathBox, StringBox, and FileBox files, and to run some rudimentary tests on them. Start by creating a new project called ManageCodeBoxSimple in the ComplexProjects directory, as explained in Chapter 3. Add an application into that project. Fill out the Paths page as shown in Figure 27-1.

NOTE: There are actually two projects called ManageCodeBox on the CD that accompanies this book. One is called ManageCodeBoxSimple and the other is ManageCodeBox. Because this book is aimed at multiple editions of JBuilder, I ended up needing to create a complex directory structure for the CodeBox files that includes subdirectories for the Personal, SE, and Enterprise editions. I don't want you to have to wrestle with that kind of problem in this chapter, so I have created a simplified project called ManageCodeBoxSimple. It will run in all editions of JBuilder. The ManageCodeBox project, on the other hand, will run only in JBuilder Enterprise. The final version of codebox is in the src directory off the root directory for the examples on the CD. It will contain scripts for compiling a final version of codebox.jar under each edition of JBuilder.

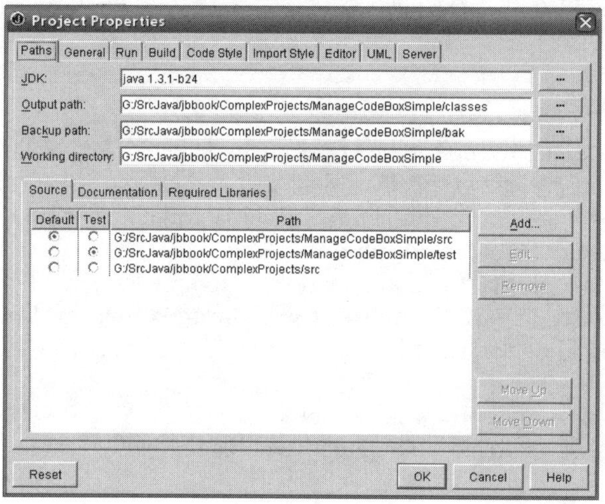

Figure 27-1: Choose Project | Project Properties to configure JBuilder so it knows where to find the src directory that contains the codebox files.

Everything on the Project Properties page shown in Figure 27-1 is fairly straightforward except for the addition of the ComplexProjects/src directory in the Source pane. This is the directory where the source for the codebox units is located. The structure for that directory will look something like this:

```
../ComplexProjects/src/com/elvenware/codebox
```

In the ComplexProjects directory, there are numerous projects, all of which are discussed in this section of the book. Many of those projects use the source code from the codebox package. As a result, I have placed that code in the src directory, where it will easily be shared by all these projects. There are many real-world cases where you might want to do something similar.

Focus Frame1 in the content pane, and switch to design view. Drop down a JButton and JTextArea, as shown in Figure 27-2.

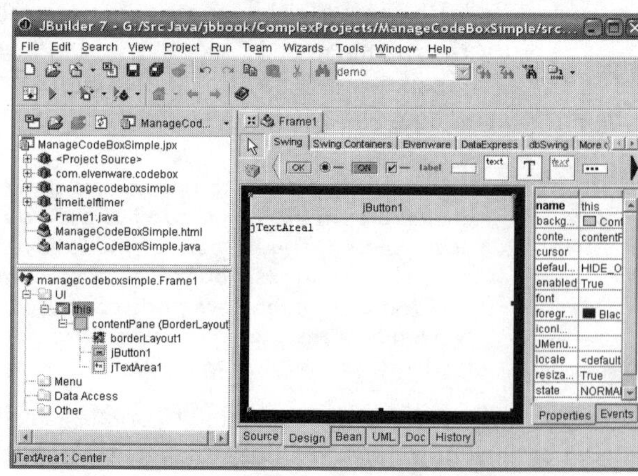

Figure 27-2: Examine the structure pane in this screen shot if you have any questions about the structure of the visual components in this application.

In Listing 27-1 you will find the source code for the main unit of this project. It provides a simple method for testing at least a portion of the code found in the codebox directory. As mentioned earlier, later in the book I will show you how to use JUnit to test many more of the methods in this source file.

To create the file shown in Listing 27-1, first add an **import com.elvenware.codebox.*** statement to the top of the file. Then go into design mode and double-click on the button to create an event handler. Fill in the code for the button as follows:

```
void jButton1_actionPerformed(ActionEvent e)
{
  String S = StringBox.reverse("Sam");
  jTextArea1.setText(S);
}
```

This will give you a simple way to begin testing the codebox units.

Listing 27-1: An excerpt from the source code for the ManageCodeBoxSimple program

```
package managecodeboxsimple;

import java.awt.*;
import java.awt.event.*;
import javax.swing.*;
import com.elvenware.codebox.*;

public class Frame1 extends JFrame
{
  JPanel contentPane;
  BorderLayout borderLayout1 = new BorderLayout();
  JButton jButton1 = new JButton();
  JTextArea jTextArea1 = new JTextArea();

  //Construct the frame
  public Frame1()
  {
    enableEvents(AWTEvent.WINDOW_EVENT_MASK);
    try
    {
      jbInit();
    }
    catch(Exception e)
    {
      e.printStackTrace();
    }
  }
  //Component initialization
  private void jbInit() throws Exception
  {
    contentPane = (JPanel) this.getContentPane();
    jButton1.setText("jButton1");
    jButton1.addActionListener(new
      Frame1_jButton1_actionAdapter(this));
    contentPane.setLayout(borderLayout1);
```

```
        this.setSize(new Dimension(400, 300));
        this.setTitle("Frame Title");
        jTextArea1.setText("jTextArea1");
        contentPane.add(jButton1, BorderLayout.WEST);
        contentPane.add(jTextArea1,  BorderLayout.CENTER);
    }
    //Overridden so we can exit when window is closed
    protected void processWindowEvent(WindowEvent e)
    {
      super.processWindowEvent(e);
      if (e.getID() == WindowEvent.WINDOW_CLOSING)
      {
        System.exit(0);
      }
    }

    void jButton1_actionPerformed(ActionEvent e)
    {
      String S = StringBox.reverse("Sam");
      jTextArea1.setText(S);
    }
}

class Frame1_jButton1_actionAdapter implements
    java.awt.event.ActionListener
{
    Frame1 adaptee;

    Frame1_jButton1_actionAdapter(Frame1 adaptee)
    {
      this.adaptee = adaptee;
    }
    public void actionPerformed(ActionEvent e)
    {
      adaptee.jButton1_actionPerformed(e);
    }
}
```

When you run this project, you will see that it tests the various portions of the codebox classes. However, for our purposes, its most important trait is simply to compile the source files used by this project.

NOTE: When attempting to run this project, you may get errors about the *import com.elvenware.codebox.** statement. If so, you need to make changes to the Project Properties dialog shown in Figure 27-1. Teaching you how to make those kinds of changes has been the burden of the last several chapters of this book. The source for the codebox units such as StringBox.java and MathBox.java are on the CD that accompanies this book or accessible from my web site at http://www.elvenware.com.

Creating the CodeBox JAR File

Here is how to create a JAR file from inside of JBuilder. This option is not available in the Personal version of JBuilder, but it is in the SE version. If you don't have the feature, don't worry, as it is not at all difficult to create JAR files from the command line. In fact, there are many people who will probably prefer to create JAR files from the command line since you can automate the process from inside a script.

We will visit the subject of creating JAR files again in the next chapter when deployment is discussed. But this time we want to create a small JAR file that contains not a whole project but only the files in the codebox unit. Here are the steps:

1. Choose **Wizards | Archive Builder** from the menu.
2. Set the Archive type to **Basic**, and select the **Next** button.
3. In Step 2 of the wizard, name your archive **CodeBoxSimple**. This is the name the archive will have inside of JBuilder, not the name of your JAR file on disk.
4. Click the ellipsis button next to the File text field, and choose the location where you want to place your JAR file. This can be anywhere convenient on your hard drive. If you want, you can place it inside this project. Or perhaps you will want to create a directory on your hard drive where globally accessed Java files and classes can be kept. This might be your /home/UserName/classes directory, or c:\utils\classes directory, or some other place that makes sense to you.
5. While you have this dialog open, set the name of your output file to **CodeBoxSimple.jar**. When you are done, Step 2 of the wizard should look as it does in Figure 27-3. When you have it set up right, hit the **Next** button.
6. In Step 3, select **Include required classes and known resources**. Choose the **Add Classes** button and browse for the root of the CodeBox package, as shown in Figure 27-4. The root will be called com, as in com.elvenware.codebox. Add it to the archive. Explicitly add the StringBox and MathBox classes to your archive as shown in Figure 27-5. If choosing these packages and files is not an option on your system, then you did not set up your source path correctly. Go back and look at Figure 27-1 and the discussion about it to help correct the problem. Click the **Next** button.
7. There are no dependencies in this project, so you can just toggle through Step 4, accepting the defaults.
8. In Step 5, you can again accept the defaults, leaving a check mark before **Include a manifest in the archive** and a selection mark in front of **Create a manifest**.
9. When you are all done, right-click on the archive in the project pane and choose **Make** from the menu. After you have done this, a plus sign will appear next to the archive. Click on it to open it up and double-click on the JAR file to open it up. You should then be able to view the contents of your archive in the structure pane. Figure 27-6 shows how this should look to you on screen. When examining this screen shot, note that I have compressed the IDE as much as possible to allow you to focus in on the relevant parts of the product's interface. If the ManageCodeBoxSimple or TimeIt packages are included in the archive, go back to Step 3 of the wizard and make sure you are following the directions as precisely as possible.

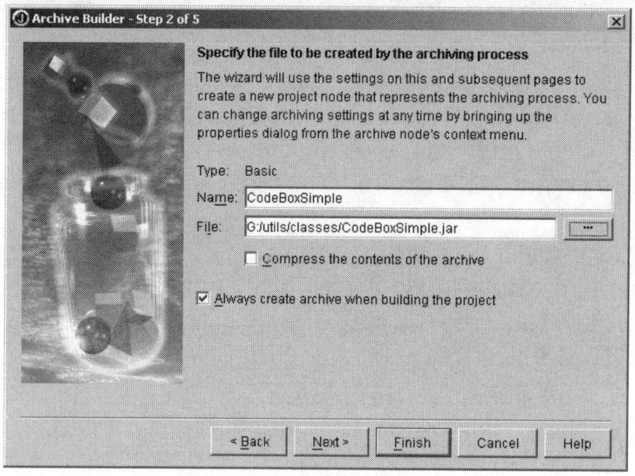

Figure 27-3: Step 2 of the Archive Builder allows you to set the name of your archive as it appears in JBuilder and the name of the output file that you want to create.

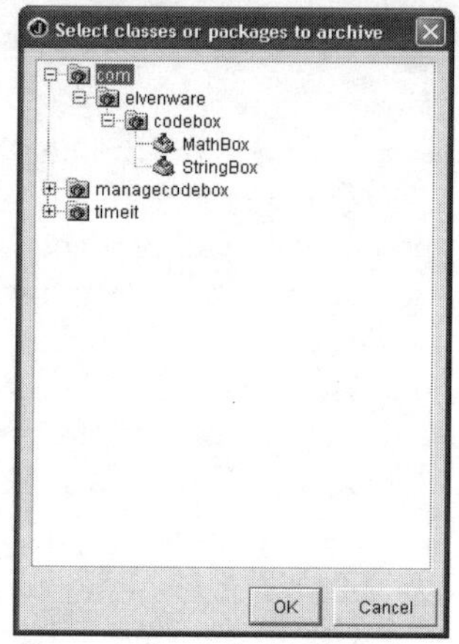

Figure 27-4: Selecting the packages and files that you want to place in your archive

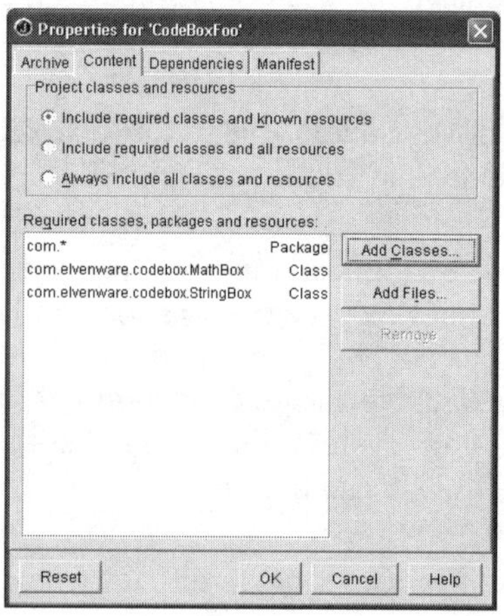

Figure 27-5: To populate your JAR file, you should select the package you want to include and the class files that you want your users to access.

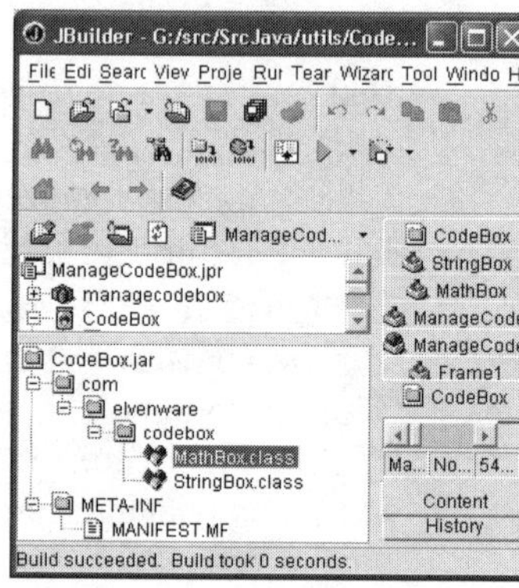

Figure 27-6: Viewing the content of a JAR file inside the JBuilder IDE

You might notice that your JAR file includes something called a manifest. I will describe manifests immediately after the section on compiling from the command line.

Building CodeBoxSimple.jar from the Command Line

In the previous section you learned how to build a JAR file from inside the IDE. You need the SE or Enterprise version of JBuilder to do this. If you have the Personal version, you will need to build the JAR file from the command line. This section of the chapter explains how to proceed with this relatively simple task.

Move into the ComplexProjects directory. This directory should be the root directory for the src and classes directories. The src directory should contain the source to the codebox files:

```
/ComplexProjects/src/com/elvenware/codebox/MathBox.java
/ComplexProjects/classes/com/elvenware/codebox/MathBox.class
```

Make sure that the bin directory for the JDK is on your path:

```
path=%path%;c:\jbuilder7\jdk1.3.1\bin
```

You should be able to type java -version and get back some kind of meaningful reply if the proper directory is on your path:

```
[g:\srcjava\jbbook\complexprojects]java -version
java version "1.3.1"
Java(TM) 2 Runtime Environment, Standard Edition (build 1.3.1-b24)
Java HotSpot(TM) Client VM (build 1.3.1-b24, mixed mode)
```

Here is the command you can use at the shell prompt from the ComplexProjects directory for first compiling the source files and then creating a JAR file that contains the StringBox and MathBox classes:

```
javac -d classes -sourcepath src src\com\elvenware\codebox\*.java
mkdir classes
jar cvf codeboxsimple.jar -C classes com
```

The call to javac compiles all the java source files in the codebox directory and places them in the classes directory. (Make sure the classes directory exists: mkdir classes.) The third command creates an archive from the compiled class files.

The first word in the third line invokes the jar utility. The second word contains three flags passed to the jar utility:

- c: Create the JAR file
- v: Produce verbose output
- f: Specify the name of the JAR file to create

Here are the other parts of the command:

- codeboxsimple.jar is the name of the file to create.
- -C classes tells the jar utility to switch to a new directory called classes. This command is fussy; if you type -C classes/ you won't get what you want.
- The final word in the command tells the jar utility to zip up the contents of the com directory.

When examing a JAR file from the command prompt, you can check out its contents by typing **jar tf codeboxsimple.jar**. The t asks the jar utility to list the contents of the file, and the f informs JBuilder that you are going to specify the name of the JAR file that you want to examine. The output from the command should look something like this:

```
META-INF/
META-INF/MANIFEST.MF
com/
com/elvenware/
com/elvenware/codebox/
com/elvenware/codebox/FileBox.class
com/elvenware/codebox/Finance.class
com/elvenware/codebox/MathBox.class
com/elvenware/codebox/StringBox.class
```

Note the third, fourth, and fifth lines, which show the existence of three important packages in the archive. Also, be sure that you don't end up getting the classes directory in the archive: classes/com/elvenware.

The Manifest File

If you build your JAR file using either of the techniques shown in the last two sections, it will automatically contain something called a manifest. A *manifest* is simply a text file that describes the contents of your JAR file. The manifest is usually of more use to programs that want to use your JAR file than to humans who want to read about your JAR file.

In this particular very basic JAR file, your manifest contains only the following line of text: Manifest-Version: 1.0. This text and the manifest itself are inserted into the file automatically; you need do nothing to create them.

Manifests will be discussed in more depth in Chapters 28 and 32 and in Part VII: JavaBeans. For now, you don't really need to think about them very much.

At this stage, you have created a JAR file that you can use from inside the JBuilder IDE. The next section explains how to use it.

Testing Your Jar File

Once you have created the JAR file, the next step is to test it. To do this, you must make sure that you remove any references to the class files placed in your JAR file. The point here is that you want to access StringBox.class from the JAR file, not from a copy of the class file stored on your system. The first step is to make sure that your project cannot find the com.elvenware.codebox.* package.

The simplest way to do this is to completely delete your classes directory for the ManageCodeBoxSimple project, and then choose **Project | Project Properties** and make sure that the ComplexProject/src directory is not listed, as shown in Figure 27-7. Compare this screen shot with the one shown in Figure 27-1. In Figure 27-1, the source directory is listed.

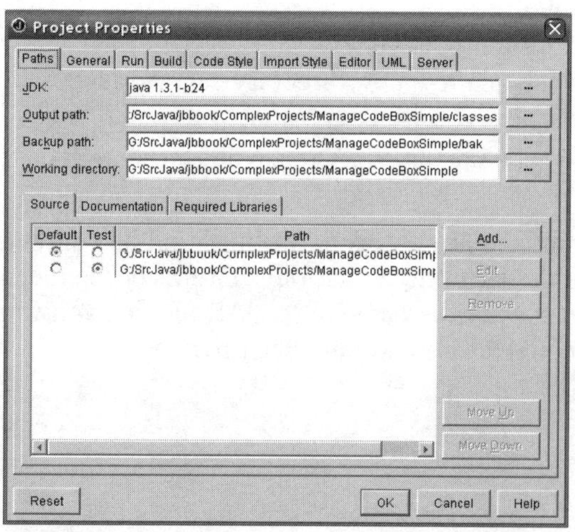

Figure 27-7: Make sure there are no references to the directories that hold StringBox.java.

If you have done everything correctly, then your project will not compile. In particular, you will get an error pointing at the import com.elvenware.codebox.* line and saying that JBuilder cannot access the directory.

Now you want to create a library that points at your JAR file. That process is described in the next sections of the text.

Setting Your Classpath: JBuilder Library Files

One of the core concepts in JBuilder development is the library file. If you want to get something on the classpath for your JBuilder project, the accepted way to do it is with a JBuilder library file. Library files are XML files that end with the extension .library. In all editions of JBuilder, they can be stored in the .jbuilder7 directory off of your home directory. (If you are using another version of the product, this directory might be called .jbuilder6 or .jbuilder8, etc.) Advanced editions give you additional locations to store your library files.

You do not normally have to know the syntax for a JBuilder library file. The IDE creates and manages them for you automatically. To use them, all you have to do is push a few buttons in the IDE. Nevertheless, I'm going to show you the actual syntax for a library file, in part to help demystify them and in part to make sure you fully understand what it is these files do for you.

Here is what a typical .library file looks like:

```
<?xml version="1.0" encoding="UTF-8"?>
<library>
  <!--JBuilder Library Definition File-->
  <fullname>JavaHelp</fullname>
  <class>
    <path>[G%|/src/srcjava/classes/jh.jar]</path>
  </class>
</library>
```

The key part is the class section. As you can see, it lists the path to the JAR file that you want to include in your project. This is JBuilder's way of defining a classpath for you when you are inside the IDE. Few concepts in this book are more important than this one: JBuilder uses libraries to help you define your classpath!

NOTE: The library encoding provides substitutes for some characters. For instance, the colon character in the path is replaced by %|. Thus, the path G:/src/srcjava, becomes G%|/src/srcjava. You might know that this same kind of encoding is used in cookies.

Most library files that you care about reside in your home directory inside a directory called .jbuilderx, where x is the version of JBuilder that you are using. Note the period before the word jbuilderx. In Linux, that will usually be /home/UserName/.jbuilderx, and in Windows, that will usually be c:\Documents and Settings\UserName\.jbuilderx\. On the SE and Enterprise versions of JBuilder, you can store these files as part of your project or as part of the JBuilder installation directories.

You can configure the libraries in one of two places:

- Choose **Tools | Configure Libraries** from the JBuilder menu.
- Choose **Project | Project Properties | Paths** from the JBuilder menu. In the tabs in the lower half of this dialog, turn to the Required Libraries page and choose the **Add** button.

I will explain more about this configuration process in the next section.

Using Your JAR File in the JBuilder IDE

In this section of the text you are going to create a library file that references your JAR file. To create a library file, choose **Tools | Configure Libraries** from the JBuilder menu. Select the **New** button from the Configure Libraries dialog. Name your library **CodeBoxSimple** and set its location to **User Home**. Click the **Add** button and browse for your JAR file, which should be called codeboxsimple.jar. It might be located in the c:\utils\classes directory, or wherever you placed it. When you are done, the New Library Wizard should look something like what you see in Figure 27-8.

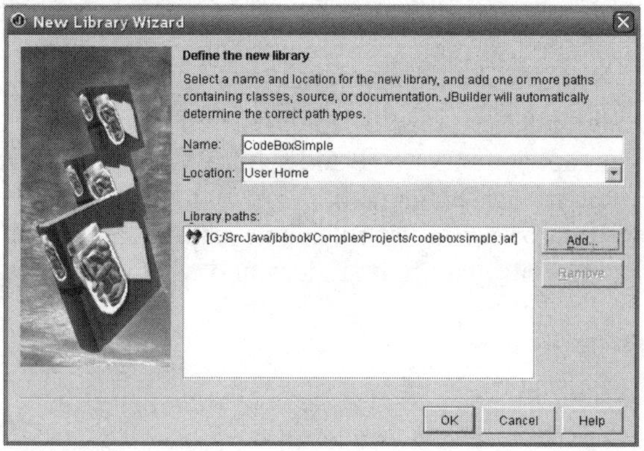

Figure 27-8: The New Library Wizard showing a library called CodeBoxSimple, stored in the .jbuilderx directory beneath the user's home directory, and pointing at a file called codeboxsimple.jar located in the G:\srcjava\jbbook\ComplexProjects directory

When you press OK in the New Library Wizard you are returned to the Configure Libraries dialog. It should now appear something like the screen shot shown in Figure 27-9. Figure 27-9 contains more libraries in User Home than you probably have on your system, but the general appearance should be the same.

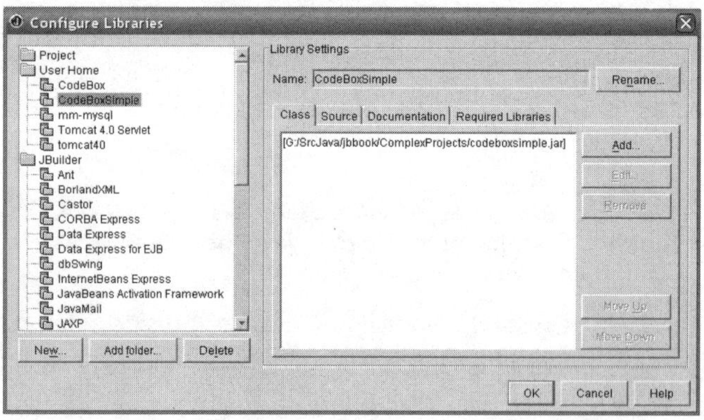

Figure 27-9: Viewing the CodeBox library in the Configure Libraries dialog

At this stage, you have the CodeBox library set up and ready to be used inside one or more of your projects. To actually add it to your project, choose **Project | Project Properties** from the JBuilder menu. Turn to the Required Libraries page and click the **Add** button. You should then be able to select your library from a dialog that looks like the JTreeView seen on the left-hand side of the dialog shown in Figure 27-9.

The end result is that CodeBoxSimple is listed in your required libraries, as shown in Figure 27-10. Once the library is part of your project, you should be able to compile and run your project. If you have trouble with any of these steps, just open up the project that accompanies this book and compare it to what you have on your system.

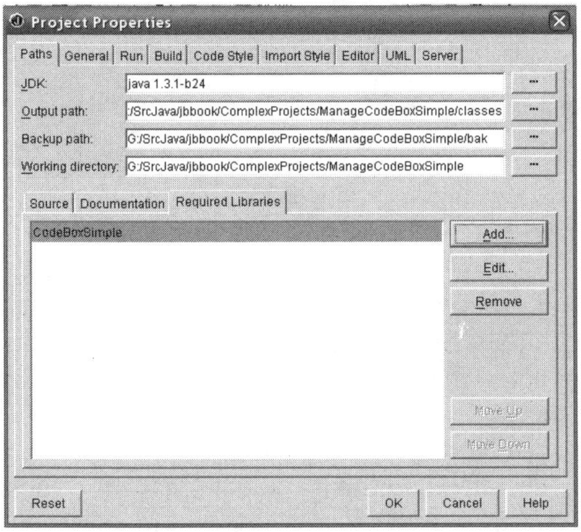

Figure 27-10: Adding the CodeBoxSimple library to the Required Libraries section of the Project Properties dialog

You should now be able to run your project, and the error regarding the com.elvenware.codebox directory should be cleared up. The point is that you are now accessing the StringBox class from the JAR file, not from some class file on your system. This may seem like a small accomplishment, but it really means that you can use the many open source JAR files that you find on the Internet.

Libraries that Contain Only Class Files

Just as you can create a library that points at a JAR file, so can you create a library that points at a package containing a series of class files. If you then include that library in your project, you can automatically include raw class files in your project. This can be very helpful if somebody sends you one or more class files with no accompanying source.

NOTE: Though results can differ depending on the version of JBuilder that you are running, as a rule I would not try to place these class files directly in your project. For instance, I would not place them in the default classes directory created by JBuilder. In some versions of JBuilder, doing something like that can lead to weird errors, and in other versions, JBuilder simply summarily deletes the class file on general principles. Instead, if someone hands you a set of class files, I would suggest doing what I recommend here — that is, point to them with a library file.

I'm mentioning this late in the chapter because it is not something you would normally have to do. However, there are occasions when someone will hand you a bunch of raw class files and ask you to include them in your project. You could, of course, wrap the class files in a JAR file. But there are times when that might not be expedient. In such cases, you want to create a library file.

To create such a library file, proceed exactly as you did in the previous section. But when it comes time to select a JAR file from the New Library Wizard, instead you should select the directory that contains the /com/elvenware/codebox directories.

Consider a directory tree that looks like this:

```
g:\src\srcjava\classes\com\elvenware\codebox
```

In this case, you want to add the "g:\src\srcjava\classes" directory to your library, just as you added codeboxsimple.jar to your library in the previous example. When you are done, if you go to your User Home directory, you should be able to find the .library file that you created. In my case, that library file looked like this:

```
<?xml version="1.0" encoding="UTF-8"?>
<library>
```

```
    <!--JBuilder Library Definition File-->
    <fullname>CodeBoxClasses</fullname>
    <class>
      <path>G%|/src/SrcJava/jbbook/classes</path>
    </class>
    <source>
      <path>G%|/src/SrcJava/jbbook/ComplexProjects/src</path>
    </source>
  </library>
```

As you can see, the library contains both the classes directory and the directory where the source for the files is located. To insert both pieces of information, I needed to only point at the location of the classes directory. The classes directory would have been sufficient to allow me to compile the project, but knowing the location of the source helps when you do a build on your project. Of course, that section should be empty if you don't have the source. You do not need to include the source directory; it is merely a convenience that helps you build your project.

This section of the text on library files that point at packages containing classes is short, but it is not unimportant. There are occasions when a library of this type can be extremely useful to you. These occasions do not arise very often, but when they do come up, the library files can be crucial to the success of a project.

Compiling TimeIt from the Command Line

To help round out this chapter, I'm going to review how to use a JAR file created by Borland when compiling from the command line without using any JBuilder tools. This section of the chapter applies only to those using JBuilder SE or Enterprise.

NOTE: I don't tell you how to do these things from inside of JBuilder because JBuilder will automatically add the appropriate library files to your project if you use one of their tools in your program.

There are times when you are working in the JBuilder IDE when you might accidentally add proprietary Borland classes to your project. In particular, this can happen when working with layouts. If you do this, you can always remove the code from your project. But if you want to keep the code, and if you want to compile it from the command line before deploying the project, you will need to know the material I discuss in this section.

As you recall, in Chapter 25 we created a program called TimeIt that compiled and ran effortlessly from inside the JBuilder IDE. That program helped to illustrate how to handle complex paths inside of JBuilder.

There is, however, one catch in the program I created. In particular, it uses the VerticalFlowLayout class. VerticalFlowLayout is not part of the standard Sun JDK. Instead, it is a class explicitly created by Borland that resides in a JAR file created and maintained by Borland. As such, references to VerticalFlowLayout compile fine inside the JBuilder IDE. But what happens if you want to run the TimeIt program from the command line? How do you tell javac and java about a Borland JAR file?

In this discussion, I am addressing how to compile and run the program on a machine that already hosts JBuilder. See the next chapter for a discussion of how to deploy the program to other machines. Many readers, however, will probably begin to understand at least one crude way to deploy the project to another machine once they see how to get it to compile on their development machine. Nevertheless, the main purpose of this discussion is to tell you what to do if you are using JBuilder and suddenly want to switch development out of the IDE and to the command line. (As mentioned earlier, you can use the JBuilder.exe -build switch to handle these problems automatically, but right now, I don't want to go down that path. Instead, I want to show you how to compile the project using the JDK itself.)

The following line from near the top of Frame1.java hints at the nature of the problem we are currently discussing:

```
import com.borland.jbcl.layout.*;
```

Clearly a file housed in a package called com.borland is not likely to ship with the Java SDK. So, one might now ask: How do I compile such a program from the command line without using any custom Borland tools? By now, you should be able to figure out the answer without too much sweat, but I want to explain this example anyway for two different reasons:

- It will help emphasize the key points made in this chapter.
- Some people will need to use the Borland-specific class files in their projects, and this section in conjunction with Chapter 28 will tell you much about how to proceed.

Though it is not strictly necessary in order to show how to proceed, I am going to throw a little wrinkle into this example. In particular, I want to show you a bash script.

Here are some excerpts from the script that I run:

```
#! /bin/bash

JBUILDER_HOME=$HOME/jb7
JBUILDER_LIBS=$JBUILDER_HOME/lib
JAVA_HOME=$JBUILDER_HOME/jdk1.3.1

export JAVA_HOME JBUILDER_HOME JBUILDER_LIBS
```

The same file in Windows might look something like this:

```
set JBUILDER_HOME=d:\jb7
set JBUILDER_LIBS=%JBUILDER_HOME%\lib
set JAVA_HOME=%JBUILDER_HOME\jdk1.3.1
```

As you can see, these scripts define a few environment variables that might be of use to Java programmers. In particular, notice that I define a variable that points at the JBuilder 7 lib directory. This directory contains a number of JAR files that might be of interest to us. In particular, this is where the JBCL.jar file lives. JBCL.jar contains the classes that define VerticalFlowLayout.

Here is the bash script for compiling the TimeIt program from the command line:

```
#! /bin/bash
#-----------------------------------------------------------

# Define the environment variable JBUILDER_LIBS before running
# this script. It should point to your JBuilderX/lib directory.
#-----------------------------------------------------------

javac -d classes -sourcepath src -classpath $JBUILDER_LIBS/jbcl.jar \
  src/timeit/TimeIt.java
java -classpath .:classes:$JBUILDER_LIBS/jbcl.jar timeit.TimeIt
```

And here is the same script in a batch file for use under Windows:

```
rem -----------------------------------------------------------
rem Define the environment variable JBUILDER_LIBS before running
rem this script. It should point to your JBuilderX/lib directory.
rem -----------------------------------------------------------
javac -d classes -sourcepath src -classpath %JBUILDER_LIBS%/jbcl.jar \
  src/timeit/TimeIt.java
java -classpath .;classes;%JBUILDER_LIBS%/jbcl.jar timeit.TimeIt
```

These scripts are much like the ones you saw in Chapters 23 and 24. However, notice that they explicitly place JBCL.jar on your class path. Once Java is made aware of JBCL.jar, it can find the class files that define VerticalFlowLayout. Equipped with that knowledge, Java can both compile and run the TimeIt program.

Summary

In this chapter you have learned about JAR files and JBuilder libraries, and how you can use them to help organize your projects. If you want to become an intermediate or advanced level Java programmer, you have to understand the material found in this chapter. Furthermore, you will never really understand how to use JBuilder unless you understand how to manipulate and use JAR files and library files from inside the JBuilder IDE.

Certainly some of the material found in this chapter can be a bit difficult to grasp at first. However, once you get the hang of working with JAR files, you will find that they are a tremendous aid in project development. In particular, they provide a great means of encapsulating portions of your project in a discrete and easy-to-use "package" of code. They help you achieve two key goals of good programmers:

- Reuse code as often as possible.
- Encapsulate code in discrete "packages," called JAR files, so that it is easy to understand and maintain.

Chapter 28

Deploying Applets, Applications, and Java Executables

Margie and Charlie Calvert

Archive Builder is a JBuilder wizard that simplifies deployment by helping you gather all the files you need in a single JAR (Java archive) file. You can also create JAR files from the command line using the jar utility that comes with the JDK. This latter subject will be discussed briefly in this chapter.

We will be using a very simple application to illustrate the construction of JAR files. The application will use a button image to customize a JBuilder button. This is an important addition because you will often need to bundle resources with your class files. Generally speaking, a JAR file bundles all of the class files and auxiliary resources needed by an applet or application into one file.

In JBuilder 7, you have the ability to create either a JAR file or an executable. The executable is really a glorified JAR file that contains a true Windows, Linux, or Solaris executable that will automatically launch the JAR file. From the user's point of view, this file will look and act exactly like an executable. Discussion of how to create an executable of this type is included in this chapter.

Creating a Resource

The chapter begins with a brief discussion of how to create a button image to be used as a resource in your program. After all, if you are going to use the resource, you need to know how to create it. If you have artists at your company who can create the art for you, then simply skip ahead to the section called "Creating the Application."

Once the button image is created, the application to host the button will be created. Then you will see how to wrap the whole works in a JAR file or executable.

Many of the common paint programs make it easy to create buttons. The image I am using was created using Paint Shop Pro, which is a fairly low-cost shareware paint program available for download on the Web. For those using Linux, I also include instructions on how to create buttons in the GIMP. The GIMP is an open source program available on the web. Making your own buttons is very simple once you get the hang of it and allows you to have more control over how your interface looks.

Creating a Button in Paint Shop Pro

Choose **File | New.** That will bring up the New Image dialog. Set Width to **79** and Height to **27**, and ensure that **Pixels** is chosen in the field to the right of the height and width text fields. This size — 79 pixels by 27 pixels — is the default size of a button in JBuilder. Click **OK** to create an image.

A toolbar known as the Tool Palette should be visible on the left side of your screen. If it is not, choose **View | Toolbars | Tool Palette.** On the Tool Palette is an icon showing a tipped paint can with a drop falling from its lip. This is the Flood Fill. A small label will pop up to identify it when you run your cursor over it. Click on **Flood Fill** to select it.

On the right side of your screen, you should see the Color Palette. Again, if it is not visible, choose **View | Toolbars | Color Palette.** You will see a rectangle filled with many colors, which is called the Available Colors Panel. Below it are two boxes. The top box is your foreground color and the bottom one is your background color. Click on the top box, and choose a color you like in the dialog that pops up. Click **OK** and then click on your image. The image will turn to the color you picked.

Now click on the other box to set the background color. Use the dialog to pick a color that you think harmonizes well with the first color you picked, and click **OK.**

Choose **Effects | 3D Effects | Buttonize.** Paint Shop Pro will create a button that blends the foreground and the background colors. Right at the center of the button you will probably see an area that is purely the foreground color. If you like the way this looks, fine. Otherwise, proceed with the next step.

Look on the Tool Palette for a dropper icon. It will probably appear just a little above the halfway mark on the Palette. Select the **Dropper** and click on your image to select the color that you would like to have for the top of your button. You will probably want the top of the button to be all one color, so click in the area just surrounding the solid-colored area at the center.

The next step is to select the Paint Brush icon, which is right below the Dropper. Once you have clicked on it to select it, move your cursor back and forth over the solid colored area to paint it the color you chose with the dropper.

At this point, your button is ready for text. Click on the large **A** on the Tool Palette, which is the Text tool, and then click on your image. A dialog that gives you options for setting the text will pop up. A font size of 16, set to bold, can look good on this size of button. Notice that you can choose the color for the fill, and you can also choose to have a different color for a stroke, which would outline the text. Click **OK.** Click on the image and move the text around until you think it is positioned in the right place. When it seems to be positioned correctly, click the **Object Selector** icon, which is in the very bottom position on the Tool Palette. Click back on the image outside the text. If you don't like the result, use **Ctrl+X** to delete the text and start over, or **Ctrl+Z** to undo. When you have a button you like, choose **File | Save As** and save the image to the directory of your choice.

Creating a Button in the GIMP

Choose **File | New.** The New Image dialog will appear. Set Height to **27** pixels and Width to **79** pixels, choose **Background** as the fill type, and click **OK** to create a new image.

At the bottom left of the GIMP toolbox are two squares. You will use the top square to set the foreground color and the bottom square to set the background color. Double-click in either box to access the Color Selection dialog. In that dialog, you will see a large square containing various shades of a color. To the right of the square is a thin rectangle containing many colors.

Click in the multicolored rectangle to select a color, click in the square to choose its shade, and finally close the dialog once you have made your selection. Choose both a background and a foreground color in this way.

In the toolbox, click on the **Bucket Fill** tool (which is marked with a bucket) to select it, and then click on the image to paint it the foreground color. If at this point you realize that you really want to paint with the color you chose as a background, simply click on the curved double arrow located to the right of the foreground color square to switch the colors.

Next, double-click on the **Blend(Gradient) Fill** tool, which you will probably find to the right of the Bucket Fill tool. Double-clicking on the Blend Fill tool will open up its Tool Options dialog. In the Tool Options dialog, set Blend to **FG to BG(RGB)** and Gradient to **Shapeburst(Spherical)**, and then close the dialog. Click on the left side of the image and drag to the right, then release. This will create a button effect.

To add text, double-click on the capital **T** icon in the toolbox to access the Tool Options dialog for the Text tool. In the dialog, click to place a check mark next to **Use Dynamic Text** and close the dialog. Click on the image; a dialog will appear that allows you to set your font's color, size, style and other attributes. Once you have made your selections, click **OK**. The text will appear on the button. If you don't like the placement, use **Ctrl+X** and **Ctrl+V** to delete the text and then again place it on your image as a floating selection. Move the text to position it correctly, then right-click on the image and choose **Layers | Anchor Layers** to anchor the text to the image. Use **Ctrl+Z** if you wish to make any last-minute adjustments, and then again anchor the text. Right-click again to access the **File | Save As** option.

Creating the Application

To get started, we will create a default application, using the steps described in Chapter 3. Name the project **ExitApplication**. Name your application **ExitApplication** and put it in a package called **exitapplication.**

Click the **Design** file tab to change to design view. Click on **contentPane** in the structure pane to select it. In the Inspector, change the layout property of contentPane to **FlowLayout.** Click on the **JButton** on the component palette, and then click in the designer to drop a button down.

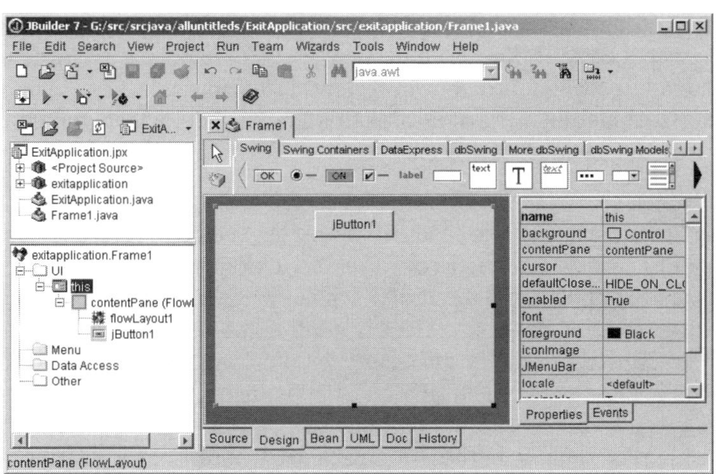

Figure 28-1: A JButton on the UI designer. "this" is selected in the structure pane, and the resize handles are visible.

NOTE: Because we are only using one component in the UI designer, you may wish to change the size of contentPane. To do this, click on "this" in the structure pane. Resize handles will appear, and you can adjust the size. When the application runs, it will keep the new dimensions you have created.

Change to source view, and add this import statement:

```
import java.net.URL;
```

Go down a few lines and place this code after the declaration for jButton1.

```
URL location = this.getClass().getResource("exit.png");
ImageIcon exitIcon = new ImageIcon(location, "Foo");
```

This code, shown in Figure 28-2, gives the URL location for your image and creates a new ImageIcon.

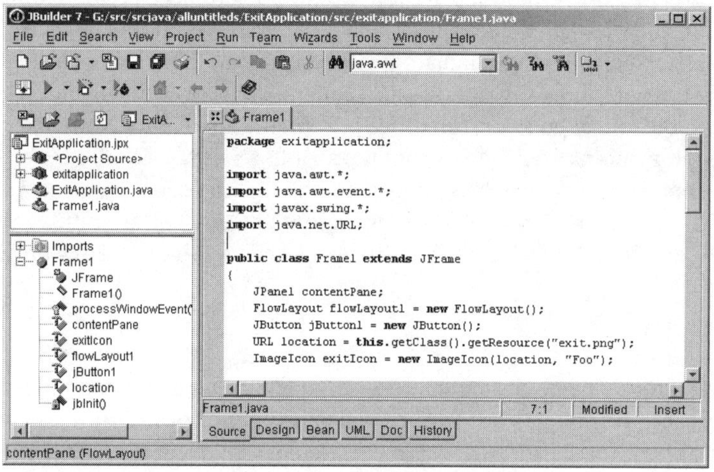

Figure 28-2: The editor after adding the code

Integrating a Resource into Your Application

You need to place your image in the src/exitapplication directory for your project. This is the same folder that holds your application1.java and frame1.java files. When you compile your project, JBuilder will place a copy of the image in the classes/exitapplication directory for your project. From there, it can be loaded into your program at run time.

To understand what is happening here, consider this line of code, which you entered into your program in the previous section of this chapter:

```
URL location = this.getClass().getResource("exit.png");
```

In this code, "exit.png" is the name of the image. Notice that the code references this, which is the current instance of Frame1. Frame1 lives in the src/exitapplication directory and is deployed into the classes/exitapplication directory. This is why you put the button image resource in the src/exitapplication directory. Here is another way to think of the same issue: By calling this.getClass().getResource(), you are explicitly asking the Frame1 object to load the resource. Frame1 is happy to oblige, but it won't find your resource unless the path to the resource is described in terms relative to the package where Frame1.class lives. The simplest way to handle that problem is to put it in the same package where Frame1.class is stored.

Configuring the Button

Change to design view, be sure that jButton1 is active, and change some of its properties in the Inspector. Change the border property to **RaisedBevel**, change the text property so that there is no text, and set the focusPainted property to **false.** Compile the project at this time and then set the icon property to **exitIcon.** After you have done this, your button should carry the image you are using. Double-click on it to create an event, and type the following code in the event stub:

```
System.exit(0);
```

Use **File | Save All** to save your work. Your code will look like this:

```
package exitapplication;

import java.awt.*;
import java.awt.event.*;
import javax.swing.*;
import java.net.URL;
import javax.swing.border.*;

public class Frame1 extends JFrame
{
  JPanel contentPane;
  FlowLayout flowLayout1 = new FlowLayout();
  JButton jButton1 = new JButton();
  URL location = this.getClass().getResource("exit.png");
  ImageIcon exitIcon = new ImageIcon(location, "Foo");

  //Construct the frame
  public Frame1()
  {
    enableEvents(AWTEvent.WINDOW_EVENT_MASK);
    try
    {
      jbInit();
    }
    catch(Exception e)
    {
      e.printStackTrace();
    }
  }

  //Component initialization
  private void jbInit() throws Exception
  {
    contentPane = (JPanel) this.getContentPane();
    jButton1.setBorder(BorderFactory.createRaisedBevelBorder());
    jButton1.setFocusPainted(false);
    jButton1.setIcon(exitIcon);
    jButton1.addActionListener(new Frame1_jButton1_actionAdapter(this));
    contentPane.setLayout(flowLayout1);
    this.setSize(new Dimension(400, 300));
```

```
    this.setTitle("Frame Title");
    contentPane.add(jButton1, null);
  }

  //Overridden so we can exit when window is closed
  protected void processWindowEvent(WindowEvent e)
  {
    super.processWindowEvent(e);
    if (e.getID() == WindowEvent.WINDOW_CLOSING)
    {
      System.exit(0);
    }
  }

  void jButton1_actionPerformed(ActionEvent e)
  {
    System.exit(0);
  }
}

class Frame1_jButton1_actionAdapter implements java.awt.event.ActionListener
{
  Frame1 adaptee;

  Frame1_jButton1_actionAdapter(Frame1 adaptee)
  {
    this.adaptee = adaptee;
  }
  public void actionPerformed(ActionEvent e)
  {
    adaptee.jButton1_actionPerformed(e);
  }
}
```

When you run the application, it will look something like Figure 28-3.

Figure 28-3: The application running

Deploying the Application

The next step is to bundle the application files, including exit.png, for deployment. In the JBuilder menu, choose **Wizards | Archive Builder.** The first of the wizard's seven steps allows you to choose what kind of archive you wish to create. The dialog gives you a drop-down list that includes, among other options, Applet JAR, Applet zip, and Application. As you browse through these file types, you will see a short description of each. Choose **Application**, and go to the next page of the wizard.

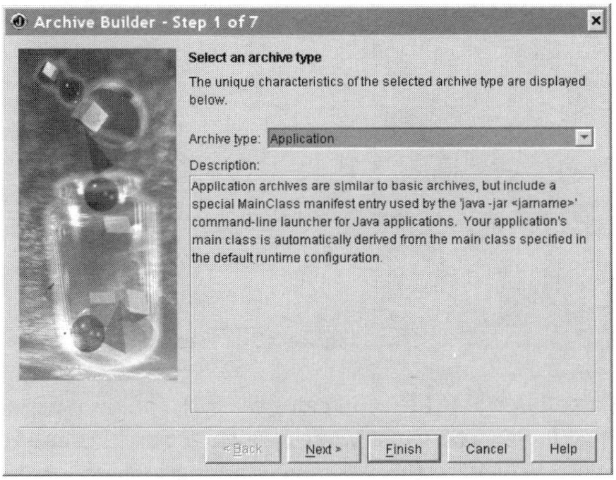

Figure 28-4: Step 1 of the Archive Builder

Step 2 of the Archive Builder allows you to create a name for your JAR file. Set the name to **ExitApplication.** In the File field, make sure that the JAR file you create will be called **ExitApplication.jar.** Clicking the ellipsis button will allow you to confirm this and to set the location for your archive. In most cases, you will just want to leave the default settings. You may want to check **Compress the contents of the archive.** You also have the option of requiring JBuilder to create an archive whenever it builds the project. I prefer to select the compression option and to deselect the option of creating an archive with each build.

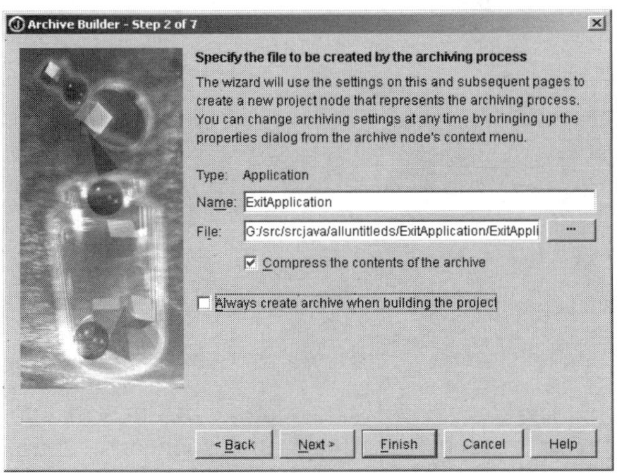

Figure 28-5: Step 2 of the Archive Builder

In Step 3 of the wizard, be sure that **Always include all classes and resources** is selected. If you do have it selected, there is no need to add "exit.png" to the project files; it will automatically be included with the rest of the project.

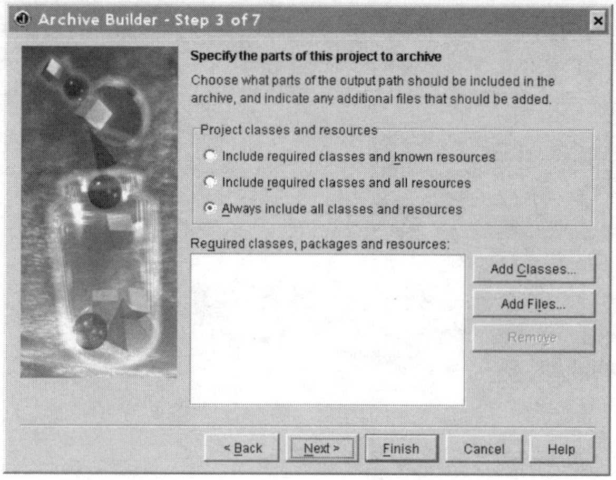

Figure 28-6: Step 3 of the Archive Builder

If you want to attempt to create a smaller JAR file, you can play with the options in Steps 3 and 4 of the Archive Builder. In particular, you can try paring away class files and resources, seeing how small you can make your project without losing any functionality.

Step 4 allows you to make decisions about library dependencies. That is not an issue with this project. Because there are no libraries used in the project, you will not need to make any choices here. In Part VIII: Databases you will need to build JAR files that contain the contents of other JAR files. There is more information on this subject at the end of Chapter 43.

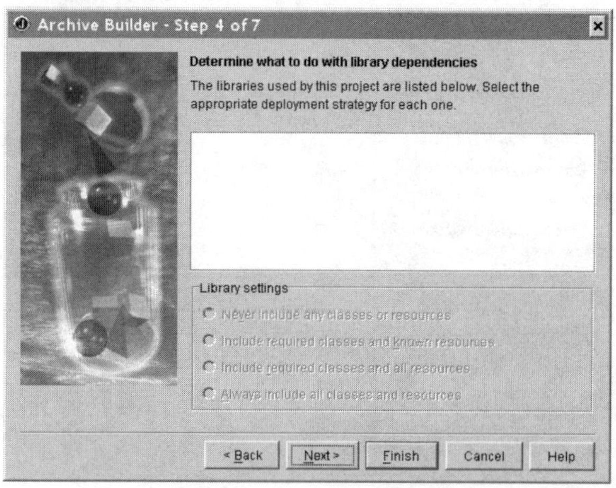

Figure 28-7: Step 4 of the Archive Builder

It is, however, important that you understand how JBuilder treats JAR files that your project depends upon. If you add a JAR file to the archive in Step 4, then some or all of the class files from that JAR file will be added in to the JAR file that you are creating. This whole process is entirely automatic. All you have to do is list the JAR file as a library dependency, and its contents will automatically be integrated with your current JAR file. Behind the scenes, the JAR file that you depend on will be "un-jarred" and the class files from inside it will be added to your JAR file.

NOTE: You add JAR files to your project before you enter the Archive Builder. Go to Project Properties and add the JAR file as explained in the previous chapter.

You might now begin to understand why there are so many options at the bottom of the dialog for Step 4 of the Archive Builder. You would choose the first option if you want to ship a particular JAR file separately. The middle two options give you a chance to integrate some portion of a JAR file with your project. For instance, you might want to link in only the SAX portions of the large Xerxes.jar file from www.apache.org. If, on the other hand, you wanted to include the entire Xerxes.jar file into your current JAR file, you would choose the last option. In the long run, you simply have to experiment, testing the JAR file you created to see how small you can make it without breaking your code.

Needless to say, Step 4 of the Archive Builder can be, for some projects, one of the most important features that JBuilder has to offer. By using the middle two options in Step 4 of the Archive Builder, you can ask JBuilder to discover exactly what dependencies your project has on a particular JAR file. It will then include the necessary class files automatically. This can help make your final JAR file much smaller in size and can save you hours, and probably days, of painstaking work.

Step 5 focuses on the project manifest. Leave the default options, which are **Include a manifest in the archive** and **Create a manifest**. I will talk more about the significance of this step when you complete Step 6 of the Archive Builder.

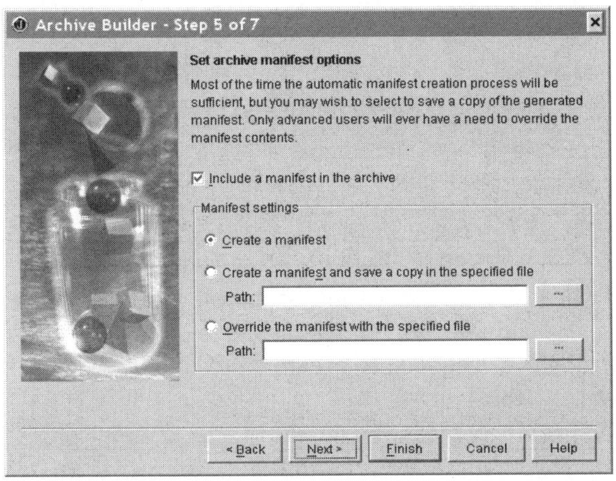

Figure 28-8: Step 5 of the Archive Builder

Step 6 allows you to choose your main class. Leave the default setting of **Determine main class from runtime configurations**.

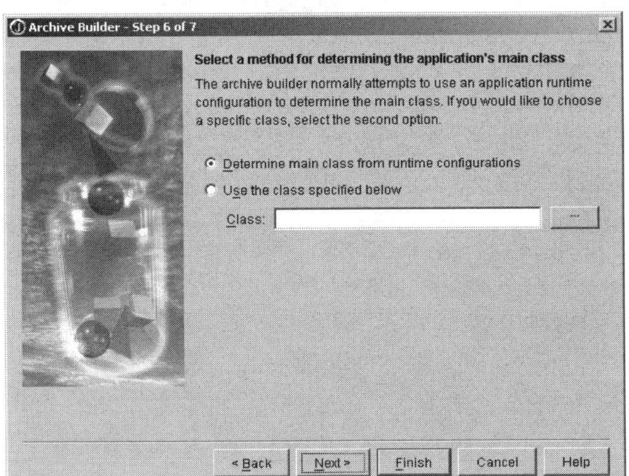

Figure 28-9: Step 6 of the Archive Builder

Manifests are small text files inserted into JAR files in order to automate certain tasks that involve the JAR file. For instance, a JAR file that contains an application is useless unless you know the class that contains the main method for that application. In our case, that main class will be either exitapplication.Application1 or exitapplication.ExitApplication, depending on how you constructed your application. (There are two files in this project, one called Frame1.java. The other java source file is the main file for this application.)

If you have followed the steps outlined above, the manifest for this application will look like this:

```
Manifest-Version: 1.0
Main-Class: exitapplication.ExitApplication
```

The first line tells the version of the manifest. The second line tells the main class for this application. Because the name of the main class is stored in the JAR file, there is no need for the user to explicitly specify the main class when he or she uses the JAR file. As a result, you can simply type the following line in Windows to run the application from the created JAR file:

```
javaw -jar ExitApplication.jar
```

The javaw command, when combined with the -jar argument, will be smart enough to find your manifest and start the application automatically. On Linux, you would call java instead of javaw.

But I am getting ahead of myself. Please read the next section of the text to learn more about creating a JAR file.

Creating the JAR File

At this stage you have two choices:

- You can click Finish and exit the Archive Builder with the capacity to create a JAR file.
- You can continue on to the last step and leave the Archive Builder with the capacity to build both a JAR file and an executable. (Actually, this decision is not final. At any time you can opt to edit your archive and choose to create an executable, even if you did not select that option the first time through.)

Let's suppose you decide to exit the wizard without creating an executable. In other words, let's suppose you skipped the last step in the Archive Builder and clicked Finish while in the middle of Step 6.

Once you have clicked Finish, you will see a new entry in the project pane, entitled ExitApplication. You have not at this time, however, created the JAR file. If you have doubts about that, look for it in the root directory of your project.

To actually create the JAR file, right-click on the new **ExitApplication** file that has appeared in your project pane and choose **Make**. Now bring up your command prompt and go to the ExitApplication directory where all of your project files are stored. Type:

```
javaw -jar ExitApplication.jar
```

Very shortly, you should see your application running. This demonstrates that you have all you need to run your application in the JAR file.

Viewing the Archive You Have Created

Not every JAR file that you create will run correctly the first time. This is not due to deficiencies in the Archive Builder but due to the fact that you might not have included all the files and resources needed to run your program. In particular, you should be sure to move your archive out of the directory in which it was created, preferably to a machine that is not used for development, and make sure that it runs correctly. If it does not, you have probably left certain files out of the archive. In that case, you will want to explore the archive and see what is in it.

NOTE: The point here is that almost any archive built from a valid project will run correctly if it is in the root directory of that project. From there it can easily access the resources and class files from your project and will run like a charm regardless of whether or not the files it is using are actually in the archive itself. As a result, you must test the archive from a completely different drive and directory, preferably from a completely different machine that is not used for development.

If you double-click the archive node in the project pane, you will be able to see the contents of the archive in the structure pane, as shown in Figure 28-10.

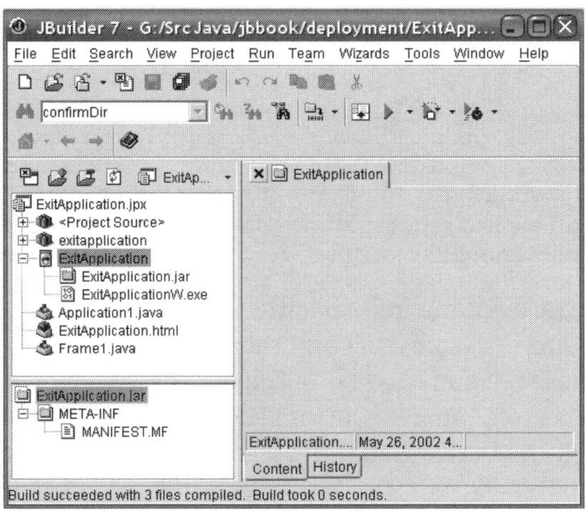

Figure 28-10: An incomplete archive displayed in the structure pane

Figure 28-10 is instructive, since it shows an incomplete archive. In particular, you might want to compare it with Figure 28-11, which shows the exitapplication package along with the Frame1.class and ExitApplication.class files inside the archive. Notice that exit.png is also clearly visible.

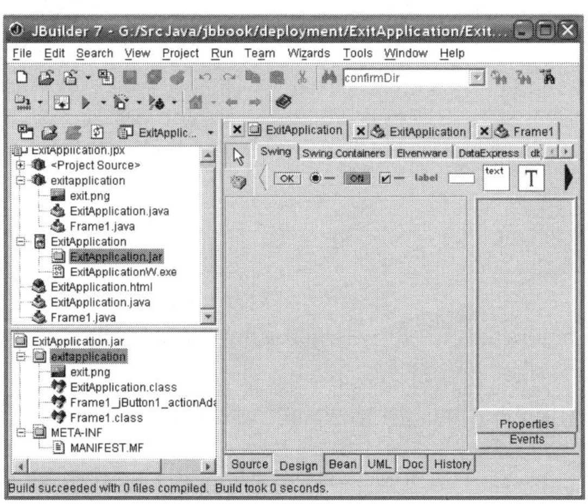

Figure 28-11: A complete archive showing the presence of the exitapplication package in the archive

If you end up with an archive like the one in Figure 28-10, you can encourage JBuilder to actually include your packages in the archive by explicitly listing them in the Archive Builder. In particular, you can right-click on the archive node in the project pane, choose Properties, and turn to the Content page, as shown in Figure 28-12.

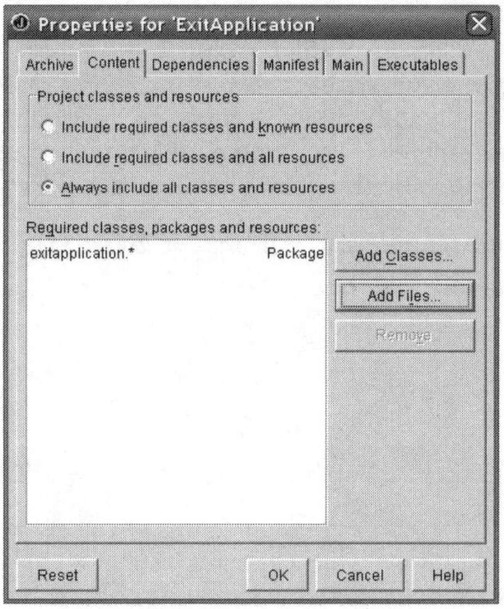

Figure 28-12: The Content page of the Archive Builder with an explicit request to include the entire exitapplication package in the archive

In Figure 28-12, you can see that there are options to explicitly add either a class or a file to the list of required classes, packages, and resources. Clearly there was not enough room on the button in this dialog to list both packages and classes on the first button. Nevertheless, rest assured that you can add not just classes but also entire packages to the archive with the button labeled "Add Classes." Just click the button and browse for the package that you want to add, as shown in Figure 28-13.

Figure 28-13: Browsing for the package that you want to add to your archive

Another trick you can use to determine what has gone wrong with an archive is to launch it with the verbose option:

```
java -jar -verbose ExitApplication.jar
```

If you do this, you will see a great deal of output as you launch the application. Sometimes this information can help you determine what has gone wrong.

Creating an Executable

Actually creating an executable in JBuilder is an extremely simple process. Simply turn to the last page of the Archive Builder as shown in Figure 28-14 and elect to build an executable for one or more of the following platforms:

- Windows GUI
- Windows Console
- Linux
- Solaris
- Mac

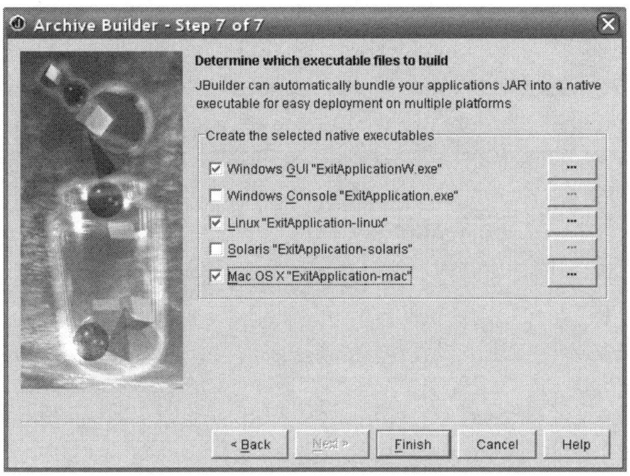

Figure 28-14: Asking the Archive Builder to create an application

If you did not decide to do this the first time through the wizard, you can always right-click the new archive node in the project pane that you just created. Select Properties from the pop-up menu. You will then be given access to most of the pages from the wizard. Turn to the last page and decide to create an executable for one or more platforms.

Understanding JBuilder Executables

Let's talk for a moment about the executable you are creating. As you perhaps know, JAR files use the zip format. This format for compressing and bundling files is available on Windows, Linux, and many other platforms.

You have perhaps also seen zip files that are distributed as executables. This is an option in some zip programs. You simply request that the archive you are creating not have a zip extension but instead be an executable. When the computer runs this program, it will automatically unpack itself, just as if it were opened by WinZip, UnZip, PKZIPC, or some other archive program.

This whole scheme is really just sleight of hand. A small executable is placed in the beginning of the archive. When the user runs the program, it knows enough to reach back into the file from which it was spawned and find the archive appended onto the end of the executable.

The same thing is happening in a JBuilder executable. What you really have is a simple JAR file with an executable for a Solaris, Windows, Linux, or Mac platform appended to the front of it. If you want to confirm this, try opening one of these files in WinZip. It may complain and issue errors, but at least on my system it is able to read the JAR file appended on to the executable.

Creating a JAR File from the Command Line

If you do not have JBuilder SE or Enterprise, you will have to create JAR files from the command line. Even if you have SE or Enterprise, you may prefer to create a JAR file from the command line because you can easily automate the process.

Here is a simple command to build a JAR file from the command line. Run it from the root directory for the project:

```
jar cvfm ExitApplication.jar MANIFEST.MF -C classes.
```

The above command assumes that the following file, called MANIFEST.MF, is in the root directory:

```
Manifest-Version: 1.0
Main-Class: exitapplication.ExitApplication
```

The jar command is built into the JDK. On Windows, it is stored in the x:\JBuilder7\jdk1.3.1\bin directory as jar.exe. On Linux, it would be called /home/userDir/JBuilder7/jdk1.3.1/bin/jar.

The jar utility takes a number of parameters. In this case we are passing in cvfm:

- c stands for create JAR file.
- v asks for verbose output while the JAR file is being created.
- f states that you will specify the name of the file you want to create.
- m states that you will supply your own manifest file.

The -C classes bit tells the jar utility to switch to the classes directory before archiving the files.

Had you not included the manifest, the JAR file would still have been valid. However, you would have had to start the JAR file by specifying the name of your main class:

```
java -classpath ExitApplication.jar exitapplication.ExitApplication
```

In this statement, you specify the classpath to point to ExitApplication.jar and end the command by specifying the name of the class that you want to run.

To verify the contents of a JAR file, type the following:

```
jar ft ExitApplication.jar
```

This gives you a view much like the one shown in Figures 28-10 and 28-11, only you are simply seeing the output on the command line:

```
[g:\srcjava\jbbook\deployment\exitapplication\classes]jar ft ExitApplication.jar
META-INF/
META-INF/MANIFEST.MF
exitapplication/
exitapplication/exit.png
exitapplication/ExitApplication.class
exitapplication/Frame1.class
exitapplication/Frame1_jButton1_actionAdapter.class
package cache/
package cache/exitapplication.dep2
```

Here you can see that the archive includes not only the expected files but also the JBuilder effluvia found in the unsightly package cache directory. This extra information needlessly adds to the size of your package but does it no real harm. You might want to create a script that will delete these directories before creating the archive or you might delete them from the archive after creating it. You could delete the files using a tool like WinZip.

Creating an Archive with Ant

You have probably noticed the many build.xml files found on the CD that accompanies this book. These are files used by the open source utility called Ant. The Apache Jakarta Ant project is a tool that duplicates and exceeds the functionality of the make utility used by many C/C++ programmers.

If you are familiar with Ant, you can add nodes like this to your Ant file to create a JAR file:

```
<target name="init">
      <!-- set global properties for this build -->
      <property name="build" value="classes"/>
      <property name="dist"  value="lib"/>
      <!-- In the ideal situation, you should only have to edit these -->
  <property name="small-name" value="exitapplication"/>
      <property name="camel-name" value="exitApplication"/>
      <property name="caps-name" value="ExitApplication"/>
      <!-- End edit section -->
      <property name="project-jar" value="${dist}\${small-name}.jar"/>
      <echo message="project jar = ${project-jar}"/>
</target>

<target name="dist" depends="compile">
      <!-- Create the distribution directory -->
      <mkdir dir="${dist}"/>
  <jar jarfile="${project-jar}" basedir="${build}"/>
</target>
```

The jar command seen at the bottom of this file will create a JAR file called lib\exitapplication.jar. Here is how to extend the jar task to handle the creation of a manifest:

```
<target name="dist" depends="compile">
      <!-- Create the distribution directory -->
      <mkdir dir="${dist}"/>
  <jar jarfile="${project-jar}" basedir="${build}">
            <manifest>
                  <attribute name="Built-By" value="${user.name}"/>
                  <attribute name="Main-Class" value="exitapplication/ExitApplication"/>
                  <attribute name="Date-Built" value="${TODAY}" />
            </manifest>
      </jar>
</target>
```

The manifest resulting from this input looks like this:

```
Manifest-Version: 1.0
Built-By: charlie
Main-Class: exitapplication/ExitApplication
Created-By: Ant 1.4.1
Date-Built: May 26 2002
```

The extra information in the JAR file is useful and does not cause any harm.

Placing an Applet in a JAR File

It is just as easy to place an applet in a JAR file as it is to place an application in a JAR file. In fact, it is probably easier.

I should add that applets really should be placed in JAR files, particularly if they consist of more than one class. When you access an applet, each class that is part of the application needs to be pulled down over the wire. It only makes sense that it will be simplest and fastest to pull down all the classes in one go, rather than starting a series of Internet transactions. If not all the classes are needed at one time, you might consider wrapping the ones that are needed first in one JAR file and the other classes in one or more JAR files that can be pulled down after the first file is in place.

On the CD that accompanies this book you will find a java applet called ExitApplet. You can use this project as an example of how to wrap an applet in a JAR file. ExitApplet, which borrows some code for the JDK demos, is shown in Figure 28-15.

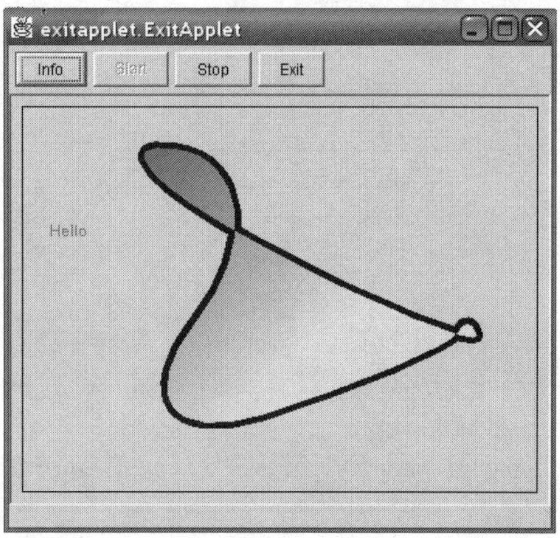

Figure 28-15: The ExitApplet program gives some hints as to how to perform smooth animation in an applet.

I'm not going to talk you through the creation of this applet, as its content is not really germane to the subject matter of this book. In fact, you would do just as well to create a default JBuilder applet as described in Chapter 3. You could then wrap your simple applet up in a JAR file, as described in the next section. The applet I have created on the CD in the ExitApplet directory is more fun than a default applet, but it is interesting primarily as an exploration of Java2D. It does little to further your knowledge of JBuilder itself.

Creating the JAR File for an Applet

The code for ExitApplet consists of two files. The main file, called ExitApplet.java, contains the JApplet descendant that is the heart of the program. The second file, called BezierAnim.java, is a modified version of a file from the JDK. When creating the JAR file for this program, we must include both source files. Since they are both in the same package, this is not difficult.

In fact, it turns out that creating the JAR file for this project is an almost mindless activity. Get started by selecting **Wizards | Archive Builder** from the JBuilder menu. On the first page of the wizard, set Archive Type to **Applet JAR**, as shown in Figure 28-16.

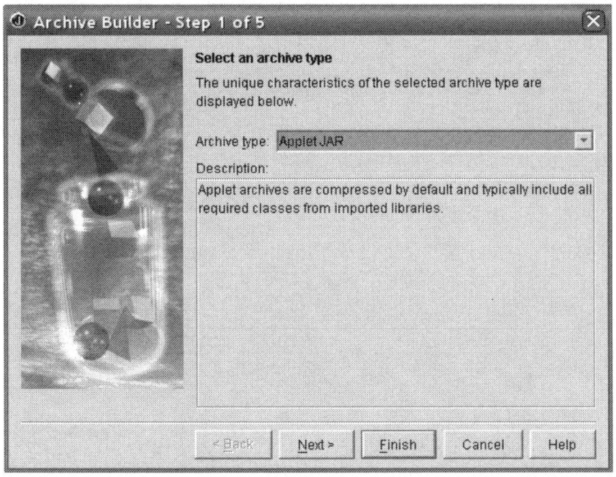

Figure 28-16: The first page of the Archive Builder gives you the chance to define the type of JAR file that you want to create.

You can accept the default values on all the other pages of the Archive Builder. When you are done, a new node should be added to your project. This node represents the archive that you created. If you double-click on it, you can see the content of your archive, as shown in Figure 28-17.

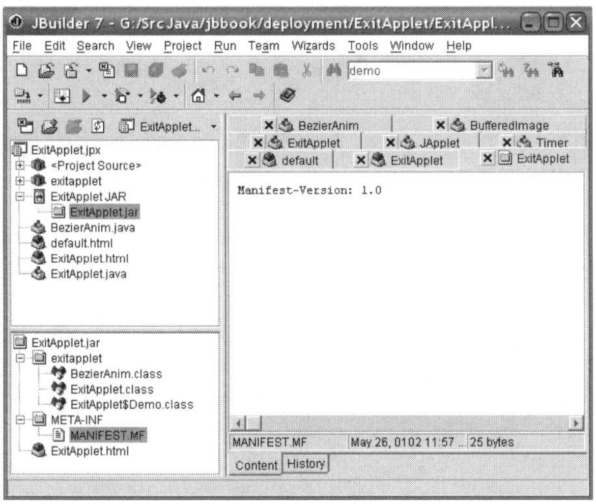

Figure 28-17: A complete archive for a simple Java applet. The new node is visible in the project pane and the contents of the archive are shown in the structure pane.

As you can see, the manifest for this file does not contain information about the main class. When dealing with applets, this information is not needed. Instead, you must create an HTML file that contains the proper tags for launching your applet.

Using the Archive in a Browser

Before you can use your newly created archive, you must make some minor changes to the HTML file automatically generated by JBuilder. Listing 28-1 shows the newly minted file.

Listing 28-1: Add an Archive tag to your HTML file if you want to launch an applet from an archive

```
<html>
<head>
<title>
HTML Test Page
</title>
```

```
</head>
<body>
exitapplet.ExitApplet will appear below in a Java enabled browser.<br>
<applet
  codebase = "."
  code     = "exitapplet.ExitApplet.class"
  name     = "TestApplet"
  archive  = "ExitApplet.jar"
  width    = "400"
  height   = "300"
  hspace   = "0"
  vspace   = "0"
  align    = "middle"
>
</applet>
</body>
</html>
```

The key line in this HTML file is the one that references your newly created JAR file:

```
  archive  = "ExitApplet.jar"
```

With this line included, the JRE will know to look for your JAR file in ExitApplet.jar. It then references your code line to see which class to launch:

```
  code     = "exitapplet.ExitApplet.class"
```

When testing your code, make sure you copy both your HTML file and the JAR file to a remote directory or, preferably, to a remote machine that is not used for development. You need to make sure that you have really bundled all the necessary files into your JAR file. When working with applets it is usually a bit simpler to isolate an applet so that you are sure that no files that just happen to be on your classpath are being referenced.

NOTE: If your project consists of multiple JAR files, you can list them all on the archive line, separating each jar with a semicolon:

```
  archive  = "certify.jar;version/pod.jar"
```

The ExitApplet

Despite the fact that I borrowed the heart of it from the JDK demo examples, you still might find the ExitApplet program interesting since it illustrates how to create smooth animation in a Java2D application. In particular, the code in the main file is almost a template for any applet you create that needs to perform smooth animation. You can see the code in Listing 28-2. The other file for the program is the one that I borrowed from the JDK. It draws the fancy graphic that is being animated. In this text, however, I will concentrate on the code that performs the animation, rather than the code that is animated.

Listing 28-2: Code for performing animation in a JBuilder applet

```
package exitapplet;

import java.awt.*;
import java.awt.event.*;
import java.applet.*;
import javax.swing.*;
```

```
import java.awt.image.BufferedImage;

/**
 * <p>Title: </p>
 * <p>Description: </p>
 * <p>Copyright: Copyright (c) 2002</p>
 * <p>Company: </p>
 * @author unascribed
 * @version 1.0
 */

public class ExitApplet extends JApplet
{

      SmoothAnimate smoothAnimate;

      //Get Applet information
      public String getAppletInfo()
      {
            return "Applet Information";
      }

      //Get parameter info
      public String[][] getParameterInfo()
      {
            return null;
      }

      //Initialize the applet
      public void init()
      {
            try
            {
                  jbInit();
            }
            catch(Exception e)
            {
                  e.printStackTrace();
            }
      }

      //Component initialization
      private void jbInit() throws Exception
      {
            getContentPane().add(smoothAnimate = new SmoothAnimate());
      }

      public void start()
      {
            smoothAnimate.start();
      }
```

```
public void stop()
{
      smoothAnimate.stop();
}

static class SmoothAnimate extends JPanel implements Runnable
{
      BufferedImage backSurface;
      int xPos = 0;
      int newSize = 2;
      boolean clearDemo = false;
      BezierAnim bezierAnim = new BezierAnim();
      private Thread thread;

      //Construct the applet
      public SmoothAnimate()
      {
      }

      public Graphics2D createGraphics2D(int w, int h)
      {
            Graphics2D g2 = null;
            if(backSurface == null || backSurface.getWidth() != w ||
                  backSurface.getHeight() != h)
            {
                  backSurface = (BufferedImage) createImage(w, h);
            }
            g2 = backSurface.createGraphics();
            if(clearDemo)
            {
                  g2.setBackground(getBackground());
                  g2.clearRect(0, 0, w, h);
            }
            return g2;
      }

      public void paint(Graphics g)
      {
            super.paint(g);
            clearDemo = true;
            Dimension d = getSize();
            bezierAnim.step(d.width, d.height);

            Graphics2D g2 = createGraphics2D(d.width, d.height);
            bezierAnim.render(d.width, d.height, g2);
            g2.drawString("Hello", xPos + 10, 100);
            g2.dispose();
            g.drawImage(backSurface, 0, 0, this);
            if(xPos > d.width - 30)
            {
                  newSize = -2;
```

```
            }
            if(xPos < 0)
            {
                newSize = 2;
            }
            xPos += newSize;
        }

        public void start()
        {
            thread = new Thread(this);
            thread.setPriority(Thread.MIN_PRIORITY);
            thread.start();
        }

        public synchronized void stop()
        {
            thread = null;
        }

        public void run()
        {
            Thread me = Thread.currentThread();
            while(thread == me)
            {
                repaint();
                try
                {
                    thread.sleep(10);
                }
                catch(InterruptedException e)
                {
                    break;
                }
            }
            thread = null;
        }

    }
}
```

The JApplet descendant shown here does not do any drawing. Instead, it creates a JPanel descendant called SmoothAnimate. This latter class, which is run on a thread, performs the actual animation. Here is the main loop for the thread:

```
        public void run()
        {
            Thread me = Thread.currentThread();
            while(thread == me)
            {
                repaint();
                try
```

```
                {
                        thread.sleep(10);
                }
                catch(InterruptedException e)
                {
                        break;
                }
        }
        thread = null;
}
```

The code does nothing more than call repaint, go to sleep for a bit, call repaint again, go back to sleep, etc.

The heart of the program is therefore the paint method for the SmoothAnimation class. This method calls the CreateGraphics2D method, which in turn creates a buffered image:

```
backSurface = (BufferedImage) createImage(w, h);
```

This image, called backSurface, is used in a double buffering scheme. All the painting is done to this back surface. When it comes time to show the user the painting, the graphics drawn on backSurface are blitted to the screen in this key call from the paint method:

```
g.drawImage(backSurface, 0, 0, this);
```

Double buffering schemes of this type are very effective at hiding the artifacts of drawing from the user. In particular, the drawing is always done to a back buffer that is hidden from the user. Once the picture is complete, it is shown to the user. If this pattern can be repeated more than 25 times a second, the user will never see any of the individual frames being drawn. Instead, the animation will appear like a fluid and constantly morphing image.

Think of the animators at Disney when they created a film like *Snow White*. To make the film, they drew a series of pictures. Each picture was placed on a separate frame of the final movie. When you watch all the pictures zooming by at 24 frames per second, they appear not to be individual frames but a constantly morphing world.

The same thing is happening here. The drawing is done to backSurface. As soon as the drawing is ready, the image on backSurface is shown to the user. Then a new backSurface is created and drawn upon. As soon as it is ready, it is shown to the user. Each backSurface is destroyed as soon as it is no longer needed. The animators at Disney were good, but they could not produce images in real time, which is what we are doing here.

Web Start Applications

JBuilder 7 Enterprise edition has the capacity to generate Web Start applications. The Web Start technology enables you to launch any application or applet just by navigating to a particular web page. The application, applet, and required JRE do not need to be present on your current system at the time you navigate to the web page. All the required files will be downloaded to your system automatically if you have Web Start installed on your system and navigate to the correct page.

I am fascinated by this technology but have not had great success using it myself. As a result, I do not cover it in this book.

My personal recommendation would be to start by using the Borland technology for creating executables with the Archive Builder. I have found that to be the simplest possible way to deploy a Java program. Simple JAR files are also quite powerful in many circumstances.

Roadblocks

The most difficult challenge I have faced when deploying Java applications has not been creating JAR files or executables. Rather, trouble stems from mismatches between my application and the JRE or JDK on the target system. To be utterly frank, Sun has not been as careful as they should have been about providing backward compatibility in their JDKs. For instance, even Java programs created by Sun itself to run under Java 1.2 will not necessarily run correctly under Java 1.4.

As a result, you might want to check the version of Java that your program is running under:

```
public static final String version = System.getProperty("java.version");
```

You can access this information by using the System class or by using the constants stored in com.elvenware.codebox.FileBox.java.

Summary

In this chapter you have learned how to create JAR files and executables from the source to your programs. The explanation has been a bit lengthy, but in practice I have found the Archive Builder to be an extremely simple tool to use. In many cases I have been able to create an archive or executable in just a few seconds using this tool.

I also discuss JAR files in Part VII: JavaBeans and in Part VIII: Databases. You will also find that most of the applications on the CD that accompanies this book use Ant scripts to create JAR files. I also have archive nodes for many of the example programs on the CD.

Part VI

Testing, Debugging, and Maintenance

Chapter 29

The Debugger

Charlie Calvert

This chapter covers various debugging strategies. The heart of the chapter covers the JBuilder debugger itself. However, there are other less technically compelling, but nonetheless powerful, strategies that need to be discussed.

Topics covered in this chapter include:

- Stepping through code
- Setting breakpoints, conditional breakpoints, and breakpoints that output the status of variables in your program
- Setting watches
- Debugging threads
- Using call stacks to find out which functions called the function where you have set a breakpoint
- Writing to standard out
- Using the logging classes found in JDK 1.4.0 and higher
- Disabling debugging for some classes
- Viewing the loaded classes and static data in your program at run time

The JBuilder debugger is one of the most useful parts of the IDE. I use it every day, usually many times a day. Understanding how it works is a key part of learning to take advantage of JBuilder itself.

Tough Guys Don't Use Debuggers

There are those who feel that debuggers are for intellectual lightweights or that they are some form of cheating. There are few statements that could possibly be further from the truth. Let's take these objections one at a time:

- **Debuggers are for intellectual lightweights.** During my time at Borland, I worked with some of the great programmers in this industry, and I assure you, they nearly all used debuggers. The difference between the good programmers and the great programmers wasn't that one used a debugger and the other did not. On the contrary, the difference was that the great programmer used the debugger with consummate skill, while the good or average programmers used the debugger with less skill.
- **Debuggers are some form of cheating.** I am sure that when horses and carts were first discovered, the best runners in the tribe all denigrated this new technology. After all, a fast horse was faster than a fast runner. The runner was about to lose status, and so he told people not to use horses. The same kind of thing happened when people first created automated looms, trains, and cars or when they first created calculators, word processors and, yes, debuggers. To be able to debug a program without the help

> of a debugger is definitely a very admirable skill. I also have great admiration for fast runners and people who can do long division in their head. For now, however, I am going to continue to use bicycles and cars when I need to get somewhere quickly, and I will use a calculator or computer to help me with math. Following the same logic, I will use a debugger to help me debug applications.

I strongly believe that the JBuilder debugger is one of the most powerful and useful parts of the product. There are few enterprises that can more readily reward your efforts to become a great Java programmer than a steady and serious study of the JBuilder debugger. It will help you write better code in less time. What else could you possibly want?

Simple Debugging Techniques

Before exploring the debugger itself, there are three very simple strategies for debugging that deserve serious mention:

- Using System.out.println and System.err.println
- Logging
- Assertions

These are old strategies, but the latter two have a new twist in that they were added to the language with the advent of Java 1.4.0.

Writing to Standard Out

When you send debug messages to System.out.println, you are usually sending the message to standard out. Thus, it is quite similar to using WriteLn statements in Pascal or printf statements in C/C++.

When I write to standard out as a means of debugging, I often declare a final static boolean variable at the top of my current class:

```
private final static boolean debug = true;
```

I can use this variable to determine whether or not to write error messages:

```
if (DEBUG)
{
      System.out.println("Value of dataDetails in MyClass: " + dataDetails);
}
```

In this case, dataDetails could be any sort of variable that might help you report the status of your program. It might be a return value from another function, a string, anything that could help you get a handle on what went wrong. If there are no local variables that help you report the nature of the error or the status of your program, you can just skip that part of the report:

```
if (DEBUG)
{
      System.out.println("An error occurred");
}
```

NOTE: Because DEBUG is declared as final and static, most Java compilers will be very smart about optimizing your code if you set DEBUG to false at the top of your file. For all practical purposes, if you set DEBUG to false, the code that you place in these DEBUG blocks is ignored completely by the compiler and does not add to the bulk of your program. Set DEBUG to true, and the code in the DEBUG block once again becomes part of your program. It is perhaps not quite as

effective as using conditional compilation in Object Pascal or C/C++, but it is quite close. If you want a deeper understanding of this technique, read the Java Language Specification, item 14.20, called Unreachable Statements. At the time of publication, it is found at: http://java.sun.com/docs/books/jls/second_edition/html/statements.doc.html.

Consider the following simple function:

```
public static final String intToStrPad0(int value, int paddings)
{
      String rawString = String.valueOf(value);
      StringBuffer paddedString = new StringBuffer(rawString);
      while (paddedString.length() < paddings)
      {
            paddedString.insert(0, '0');
      }
      return paddedString.toString();
}
```

This routine, as you may recall, is designed to convert an integer into a string and pad the beginning of the string with zeros. For instance, you might pass in 7 and 3 and expect to get back James Bond himself: 007. If you pass in 3 and a 4, you would get back 0003.

If you add a System.out.println statement, you can get a pretty good sense of what is happening inside the method. For instance, suppose you altered the method in this fashion:

```
public static final String intToStrPad0(int value, int paddings)
{
      String rawString = String.valueOf(value);
      StringBuffer paddedString = new StringBuffer(rawString);
      while (paddedString.length() < paddings)
      {
            paddedString.insert(0, '0');
            if (DEBUG)
            {
                  System.out.println("Call: " + paddedString);
            }
      }
      return paddedString.toString();
}
```

If DEBUG is set to true, and you call the method with parameters of 25 and 8, you will see the following output on the command line:

```
Call: 025
Call: 0025
Call: 00025
Call: 000025
Call: 0000025
Call: 00000025
```

For some reason, a number of people denigrate programmers who write to standard out as a debugging technique. I suppose it is regarded as old-fashioned. I have noticed, however, that a number of excellent professional programmers with many years of experience use the technique quite heavily. My suggestion is that you use the technique if you find it useful, and let others worry about whether or not it's cool.

It is sometimes also useful to declare a function through which all your error messages are sent:

```
if (DEBUG)
{
      reportError(this, : " + errorDetails);
}
```

You can then set up the reportError function to state the name of the class that sent the error message, the time the error occurred, and perhaps some other relevant information. The reportError function can be designed to write to standard out, or it can be altered so that you write to a log file.

If you just want to send messages to yourself for debugging purposes, use System.out.println. If you want to report error conditions, use System.err.println. The code that you send to System.err.println will usually come out in a different color, such as red. This makes it easy for you to find amidst the standard debug output that you may be producing.

It should be obvious that I use writing to System.out.println heavily in GUI applications. The point is that the GUI continues to behave as normal, but the message pane of JBuilder can fill up with debug information that you wrote to standard out. Then, when you want to ship, just set your DEBUG variable to false, and all that output in the message pane will go away.

Writing to Log Files

Starting with Java 1.4.0, Java has built-in logging facilities. These new logging classes can be an excellent means of tracking what is happening in your program. The TestLogger program from the Utilities directory on the CD can show you how to proceed.

At the top of your class, include the following import statement:

```
import java.util.logging.*;
```

You also need to declare a field of your object that will hold an instance of the Logger class that you are about to create:

```
Logger log;
```

Then in one of the methods of your program, you can open up a log using the Logger variable you declared as global to your class:

```
Logger log;

      private String getHomeDir()
      {
            String homeDir = System.getProperty("user.home") +
            System.getProperty("file.separator") + "elvenware";
            com.elvenware.codebox.FileBox.confirmDir(homeDir);
            System.err.println("homeDir: " + homeDir);
            return homeDir + System.getProperty("file.separator");
      }

      void jButton1_actionPerformed(ActionEvent e)
      {
            try
            {
                  Handler fh = new FileHandler(getHomeDir() + "elvenware.log");
```

```
                Logger.getLogger("com.elvenware").addHandler(fh);
                log = Logger.getLogger("com.elvenware");
                log.setLevel(Level.ALL);
            }
            catch (java.io.IOException ioe)
            {
                System.err.println(ioe);
            }
            log.fine("sam");
            log.log(Level.WARNING, "Tim");
            jButton1.setText("Wrote to: " + getHomeDir());
        }
```

The getHomeDir method discovers the user's home directory and creates a directory called Elvenware inside of it. The codebox routine confirmDir ensures that the directory will exist. If it does not exist, the directory is created:

```
        public static final boolean confirmDir(String aPath)
        {
            boolean result = true;

            File appDir = new File(aPath);
            if(appDir.exists())
            {
                if(!appDir.isDirectory())
                {
                    System.out.println("The directory, " + aPath + ", is not a directory");
                    result = false;
                }
            } else if(!appDir.mkdir())
            {
                System.out.println("The directory, " + aPath + ", cannot be created.");
                result = false;
            }
            return result;
        }
```

After creating the home directory where the log file will be stored, the next step is to open a file in that directory:

```
        Handler fh = new FileHandler(getHomeDir() + "elvenware.log");
```

The FileHandler class is part of the new logging facilities. It extends the abstract class called Handler. FileHandler can be used to write to either a particular file or a series of files, changing file handles whenever any one file reaches a particular size.

You then pass the FileHandler instance that you created to the JDK logging facility in order to register your handler:

```
        Logger.getLogger("testlogger").addHandler(fh);
```

In return, you can retrieve an instance of the logging tools that you can write to:

```
        log = Logger.getLogger("testlogger");
```

The name we are passing in here should be based on the package or class that is outputting the information. You can use dot-separated names if you wish, such as "testlogger.Frame1."

Logging Levels

Before writing any messages to the log, you can set the level of messages that you want to report:

```
log.setLevel(Level.ALL);
```

If you look at the Java source, you will see that the Level class is a pseudo-enumerated type of the kind that I have shown you in other parts of the book, such as in Chapter 16.

The following levels are available:

SEVERE (highest value)
WARNING
INFO
CONFIG
FINE
FINER
FINEST (lowest value)
ALL — Report all error messages
OFF — Turn error messages off

Here are two different ways to write an error message at a particular level:

```
log.fine("This is a very detailed bit of information about my program");
log.log(Level.WARNING, "Something may have gone wrong");
```

The output from this code in the user's home/elvenware directory looks like this:

```
<?xml version="1.0" encoding="windows-1252" standalone="no"?>
<!DOCTYPE log SYSTEM "logger.dtd">
<log>
<record>
  <date>2002-05-10T17:06:30</date>
  <millis>1021075590984</millis>
  <sequence>0</sequence>
  <logger>com.elvenware</logger>
  <level>FINE</level>
  <class>testlogger.Frame1</class>
  <method>jButton1_actionPerformed</method>
  <thread>10</thread>
  <message>sam</message>
</record>
<record>
  <date>2002-05-10T17:06:31</date>
  <millis>1021075591000</millis>
  <sequence>1</sequence>
  <logger>com.elvenware</logger>
  <level>WARNING</level>
  <class>testlogger.Frame1</class>
  <method>jButton1_actionPerformed</method>
  <thread>10</thread>
  <message>Tim</message>
</record>
```

If you look in the middle of the two large XML statements generated here, you can see that one marks the error level as FINE and the other as a WARNING. If you set the level of your log to WARNING, the first of these two messages would not be recorded:

```
Handler fh = new FileHandler(getHomeDir() + "elvenware.log");
Logger.getLogger("com.elvenware").addHandler(fh);
log = Logger.getLogger("com.elvenware");
log.setLevel(Level.WARNING);
```

If you set the level to SEVERE, neither message would be recorded. In this latter case, the log file would look like this:

```
<?xml version="1.0" encoding="windows-1252" standalone="no"?>
<!DOCTYPE log SYSTEM "logger.dtd">
<log>
</log>
```

It should not be hard to see how this technique can be used to create debug reports of all kinds. Simply by changing the level of the messages generated, you can scan your code for only severe errors or even the most trivial reports on its status.

I have only touched the surface of the capabilities available with this logging facility. There are, for instance, tools for reading the log files and generating HTML reports based on their content. You could have users in the field turn the logging facility on when they are having trouble with your program and then send you the log reports.

Again, I can imagine that some people might find such a simple technology a bit old-fashioned. However, I have found that creating log files can be an enormous time saver when creating complex projects. They can often help you spot bugs even before common users of your program know there is something wrong.

Assertions

Assertions are available in JBuilder whether you are using the JDK 1.3.1 that ships with the product or whether you are running your application against JDK 1.4.0 or higher. The Java language only added assertions in JDK 1.4.0, but JBuilder provides a means of giving you the same functionality even if you are using JDK 1.3.1. The examples shown below are found on disk in the directory called AssertTest.

Assertions are designed to test Boolean functions to confirm that they are true. For instance, here is the simplest possible test, confirming that you are really living on Earth and not on some far planet:

```
void jButton1_actionPerformed(ActionEvent e)
{
      int i = 2 + 2;
      assert i == 4;
}
```

If the assert statement does not evaluate to true, something is terribly wrong. For instance, you might be living on a planet where 2 + 2 equals 5. For most people, this will be bad news.

Consider the following method:

```
void jButton2_actionPerformed(ActionEvent e)
{
      String paddedInteger = intToStrPad0(4, 3);
```

```
        assert (paddedInteger.equals("004"));
    }
```

This function provides a simple means of testing that the intToStrPad0 method we were looking at earlier really performs as expected. If the method returned anything other than 004, something is wrong and the assert method will raise an exception.

If you are using JBuilder with JDK 1.3.1, you can turn on Assertions by choosing **Project | Project Properties** and turning to the **General** page. At the top of the page is the Enable the assert keyword option. Place a check mark in front of this option to use assertions in your program. The assertions will raise a java.lang.error exception.

If you are using JDK 1.4.0 with JBuilder 7, you do not need to check the Enable the assert keyword option. Instead, you can turn on assertions by choosing **Project | Project Properties**, turning to the **Run** page, pressing the **Edit** button for your current run-time configuration, and passing in **-enableassertions** as a VM parameter. The errors raised in this case will be a java.lang.AssertionError. In either case, you can click on the blue highlighted filename in the message pane to be taken directly to the cause of the problem.

NOTE: If you are familiar with the very popular JUnit project, you will note that there are strong similarities between JUnit and what you find with the assertion facility. JUnit, however, provides a deeper level of support than you get from assertions.

There is much more to learn about assertions than the simple introduction I have provided here. A good way to begin increasing your knowledge of this subject is by reading the excellent introduction to the topic found at: http://java.sun.com/j2se/1.4/docs/guide/lang/assert.html.

In JDK 1.4.0 or above, you can turn off assertions just by removing the -enableassertions switch from the Project Properties dialog. If you want further support, use the "conditional compilation" trick discussed earlier in regard to the final static DEBUG variable.

The JBuilder Debugger

The real purpose of this chapter, of course, is not to study standard out, the logging facilities, or even assertions. Instead, the main focus of the chapter is on the JBuilder debugger. Needless to say, one of the great advantages of the debugger is that it does not force you to change your code at all. All the methods shown so far involve manually inserting information into your code.

The JBuilder debugger is an enormously powerful tool. I suppose one could write an entire book on the subject. But there are a few basic facts that all developers should know, and I will attempt to cover them in the next few pages.

Turning On the Debugger

Create a new application, as explained in Chapter 3. Name the application **SimpleDebug**.

Focus **Frame1** in the editor and switch to design view. Drop a button on the window. Create a handler for the button and insert the following code into it:

```
void jButton1_actionPerformed(ActionEvent e)
{
    String message = "This is my message";
    System.err.println(message);
}
```

This is the entire program that we are about to explore. You can be forgiven if you think that this is an unusually simple program, and therefore, what you are about to read must be quite straightforward. In fact, we are going to find an almost unlimited degree of complexity as we begin to explore this simple program with the debugger.

To get the debugger running, first set a breakpoint on the System.err.println statement that you just created. To set a breakpoint, switch to source view and left-click in the gutter beside the println statement. You can also press the **F5** key to toggle the breakpoint on and off. A red bar should appear through your code, as shown in Figure 29-1. In the figure, the gutter appears directly to the left of the println statement and directly below the X in the tab for the Frame1 source file.

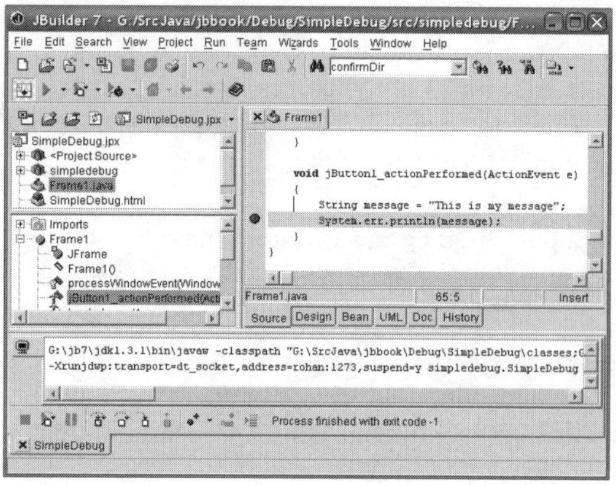

Figure 29-1: Click in the gutter to the left of the editor to create a breakpoint. The F5 key can also be used to toggle a breakpoint on and off.

Now that you have the breakpoint set up, choose **Run | Debug Project** from the JBuilder menu. You can also start the debugger by pressing **Shift+F9**. Another way to start the debugger is to press the green arrow with the white box on it that is located to the right of the green arrow you normally use to run a program. As if all these options weren't enough, you could also right-click on the main source file for your application in the project pane and choose **Debug using "SimpleDebug"** from the pop-up menu.

However you start the debugger, it will begin by loading your application just as if you were running the program normally. In the running application, press the button you created. Your program will become unresponsive, as if it has frozen up. This occurs because you have hit the breakpoint you set up on your println statement. If you switch to the IDE, you will see the scene shown in Figure 29-2.

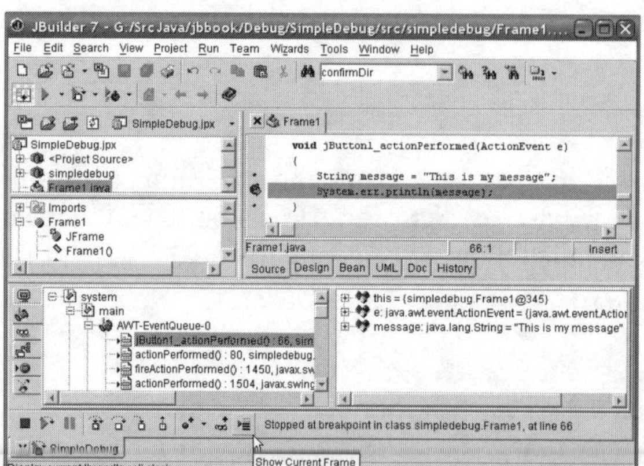

Figure 29-2: The JBuilder debugger appears in the message pane beneath the editor and the structure pane.

NOTE: The debugger takes up quite a bit of memory. If you find it very slow and unresponsive, you should seriously consider adding more memory to your machine. 256 MB is a good starting point for JBuilder development. I have just shy of 512 MB on my machine and find that the JBuilder debugger runs beautifully.

If you are not already familiar with the scene shown in Figure 29-2, this is one of those moments when you should exclaim with the immortal John Keats:

Then I felt like some watcher of the skies
  When a new planet swims into his ken;
Or like stout Cortez, when with eagle eyes
  He star'd at the Pacific - and all his men
  Look'd at each other with a wild surmise -
Silent, upon a peak in Darien.

The breakpoint you hit stopped the flow of events in your program. It has suspended your program in time, allowing you to peer into its depths.

For now, don't try to step through your code or try to get the debugger to do anything. Instead, let's just take a few minutes to absorb what you are looking at.

It turns out that there is a good deal of information for you to absorb. I will start by showing how the debugger can give you a snapshot of your program from the perspective of a particular location. After that I will show you how to control the debugger and, finally, how to explore the different views of your program available in the debugger.

Finding Your Place in the Debugger

At the bottom of Figure 29-2, you will see a line of text that reads Stopped at breakpoint in class simpledebug.Frame1, at line 66. To the left of this line is a series of icons. Click the icon on the far right. The mouse in Figure 29-2 is pointing at the button, and you can see the tool tip message associated with it.

You just clicked the Show Current Frame button. (This is also the default view that you get in the debugger, so nothing much may appear to happen when you first click the button.) This view will, in the words of the IDE, display the current thread's call stack. In plain English, the button takes you to a place where you can easily examine the current state of your program.

More particularly, it gives you a view on the right side of the debugger of the variables that are currently accessible. On the left side of the debugger, it shows you the list of methods that were called just before the action_performed method where your breakpoint was set. This is known as the *call stack*. The methods called previously are all *stacked* up in a row for you to examine. If you click on one of them, you will be taken to that method.

For now, however, you should just look at the three variables shown on the right-hand side of the debugger. The top one is called this. It references the currently instantiated instance of Frame1. The second variable is the ActionEvent that was passed to the actionPerformed method where you set the breakpoint. The third variable is the String called message that you declared. As you can see from looking at Figure 29-2, it currently contains the value "This is my message."

In Figure 29-3, I have enlarged the debugger so that it takes up most of the IDE. On the left you can see the long stack of methods that were called previous to the moment when your breakpoint was hit. If you look down at the bottom of the list, you can see the method run, which launched the thread you are currently viewing.

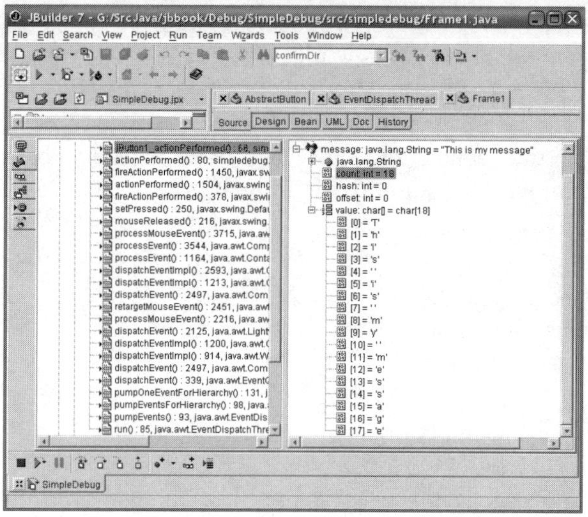

Figure 29-3: A close-up view of the debugger, showing the stack of methods on the left and a String object on the right

On the right side of Figure 29-3, you can see that I have clicked the plus sign to the immediate left of message string. This allows us to open up our view of this String object. Inside the object, we can see that the count variable is set to 18. This is the number of characters in the string. All 18 characters that hold the char array are then displayed, in order, running down to the end of the string.

If you look carefully at Figure 29-3, you might notice that there is an unopened plus symbol on the second line of visible information about the message string. If you click that plus symbol, you will see the information displayed in Figure 29-4.

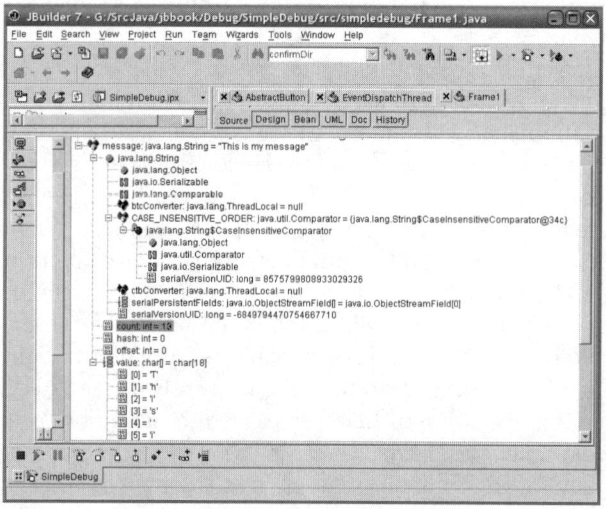

Figure 29-4: Viewing considerably more than you ever wanted to know about the instance of the String class used in the actionPerformed method

You may notice that there are icons to the left of most of the elements shown in Figure 29-4. The round ones represent classes. The one on the top line represents an object. The one next to java.io.Serializable represents an interface. The icons about two-thirds of the way down the window and next to the words count, hash, and offset represent primitive types. The one next to ctbConverter, which is a darkened version of the icon at the top of the window, represents a null object. The help for JBuilder provides a complete listing of all the icons used in the IDE.

About this time it is probably dawning on you, if it did not dawn on you earlier, that the JBuilder debugger is an incredibly powerful tool. The simple truth is that it gives you more information about your program than you could ever possibly consume at one time. In fact, the left-hand pane shown in Figure 29-3 is currently only depicting one of the several threads that you can examine in the debugger.

This chapter is not, however, intended to be an in-depth exploration of all of these complex features. In fact, our goal is not to explore every nook and cranny of the debugger, but rather to pull back and find some way to get a handle on all this information. What we need now is not a magnifying glass, but a filter. How can you find the important pieces that you will use to solve the most commonly faced debugging problems?

The best method is to see how to control the flow of events in the debugger. In particular, you will learn how to run and stop and step through the code. A later section will give you a general overview of the views that the debugger gives you of your program.

Controlling the Debugger

Figure 29-5 gives you a close-up view of the icons used to control the flow of events in the debugger. These icons are located along the bottom of the debugger, just to the left of where the icon points in Figure 29-2.

Figure 29-5: The icons used to control the flow of events in your program

On the left is a square button that you can use to stop and close your program. The next button, a green arrow, will allow you to continue running your program after you have stopped at a breakpoint. To restart your program after you hit a breakpoint, do not hit the green buttons on the toolbar at the top of the IDE. Those buttons will start a second copy of your program running. Instead, use this green arrow, which allows you to restart the flow of events in your program. The third button in Figure 29-5 allows you to pause your program at any time without actually setting a breakpoint. As shown in Figure 29-5, it is grayed out. After all, your program is already at a breakpoint, so it would make no sense to pause it when it is already paused.

The next four buttons are used to help you step through your code. When you step through your code, you can move through it one line at a time, checking the state of your program as each line of code executes.

Let me say that one more time: The debugger allows you to step through your program, one line at a time, while you examine the state of the variables in your program. When you are doing your day-to-day grunt work, this is, in my opinion, the most important debugging tool you have at your disposal.

In all the fancy new movies, such as *The Matrix* or *Spider-Man*, the audience always oohs and ahhs when the camera goes into slow motion to depict the way the hero sees events around him taking place. At these slowed-down speeds, it is possible for the hero to dodge fists, hurled objects, and even bullets. The point is not so much that the hero's reflexes are fast as that he is able to slow down time and dodge the oncoming projectile aimed at his vulnerable heart. In one particularly illuminating sequence in *Spider-Man*, Peter Parker looks around him at the people in the room while he is in the process of dodging a punch. For him, time is moving so slowly that he not only has time to dodge the punch but also to look around him and take in the surrounding scene.

The debugger lets you do the same thing. As you step through your program, events are slowed down so that you can see everything that is happening in your program. The debugger gives you superpowers. Now you can perhaps begin to understand why some people don't want you to use the debugger. It makes you way too powerful and robs other people of the advantage they have over you. It is, as they say in a different type of movie, an equalizer.

There are four buttons used to help you step through your code. The first of these allows you to toggle something called *smart step* on and off. Smart step allows the debugger to intelligently prevent you from stepping into JDK or Borland code that is not part of your program and that you probably don't want to see while you are debugging your own code. If you turn smart step off, you can step into these disabled classes. Most of the time, I would suggest keeping smart step turned on.

NOTE: In JBuilder SE and Enterprise, you can get complete control over which classes are enabled and disabled for smart stepping by using the bottom icon at the left of the debugger, as shown in Figure 29-8. I will explain how the tools associated with this icon work later in the chapter.

The next two buttons allow you to step into the current method or step over it. In Figure 29-6, I have used the step over button (hot key F8) to step over the method where our breakpoint is set and land on the curly brace at the end of this method. If I press the F8 key one more time, I end up in the method that called the actionPerformed method.

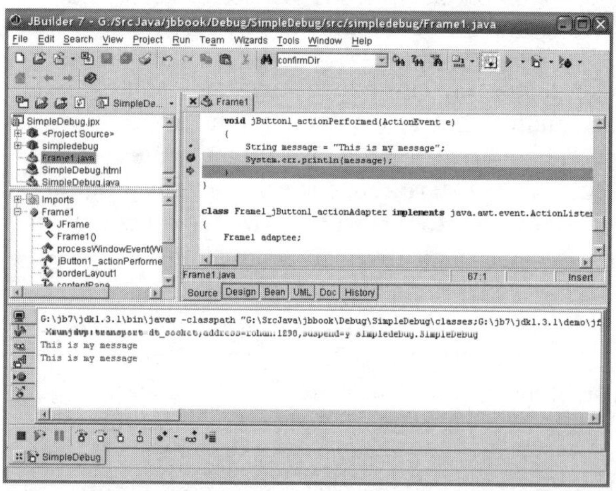

Figure 29-6: Using the debugger to step over a line of code to reach the end of the actionPerformed method

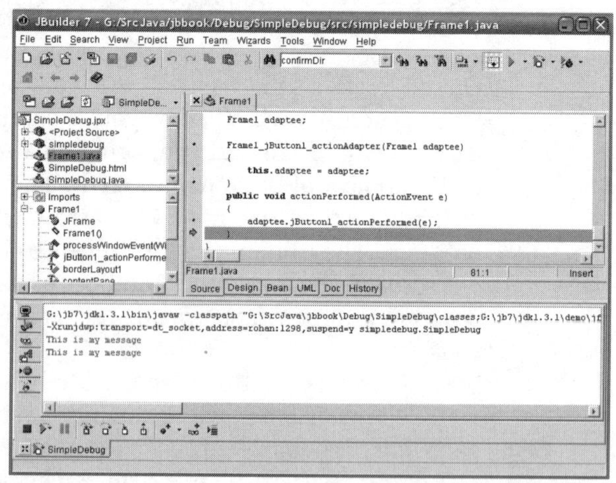

Figure 29-7: Stepping through another line of code to enter the method that called the actionPerformed method

The third of the three buttons under discussion, step out, would have immediately taken us out of the actionPerformed method and into the calling method, as shown in Figure 29-7.

NOTE: Unfortunately, both methods shown in Figures 29-6 and 29-7 have the words actionPerformed in them. If you look carefully, however, you will see that they are two different methods. In particular, the latter method is part of an adapter object, while the former is the jButton1_actionPerformed method.

The step out method is a quick exit button, like a pilot who wants to bail out of a plane. You usually press this button when you want to hurry up and move on to the next method in your program's chain of execution.

Hopefully, you now have a sense of what it means to step through your program with the debugger. I could go on talking about it for some time, but you will learn more easily if you simply use the debugger yourself.

The last three buttons at the bottom of the debugger allow you to add a breakpoint, add a watch, and move to a view of the current execution point. Earlier in the chapter you learned about the last button, and you now know about breakpoints. Adding a watch will be covered later in the chapter.

The Debugger Views

You have now examined all but one of the icons that run along the bottom of the debugger. The second important set runs along the left-hand edge. Each of the icons on the left represents one of the views of your project that the debugger can give you. You can see an illustration of the icons in Figure 29-8.

Figure 29-8: The icons that allow you to switch between the different views available in the debugger

NOTE: It is possible to change the order of the icons shown in Figure 29-8. I assume this is a feature. If, however, you want to restore the order of the icons, right-click on the debugger and choose Restore default view order.

The Message View

The top icon gives you a view of the command line that JBuilder used to start your program, along with any output produced by your program. You can see this view in Figure 29-7. At the bottom of that screen shot, you can see the output sent by the program to standard error.

The next icon down is the threads icon. More officially, it is the Threads, Call Stacks and Data view. This is the view of your program that you had earlier in the chapter when you were examining the state of your program as it appeared when you hit your breakpoint. In this view, you can examine the current state of variables, such as the string message, and the stack of methods that were piled up as the program moved inexorably to your breakpoint.

Part VI

The Watch View

The next icon down is the watch icon. Watches used to be the most important part of a debugger. In modern debuggers like JBuilder's, they are less important because you can see the state of most of the variables of your program in the Threads view.

If you want to add a watch to the watch window, you can do so by right-clicking on the variable you want to view. A lengthy pop-up menu appears. Near the bottom is an option to add watches to the debugger. Selecting that option brings up the dialog shown in Figure 29-9. In Figure 29-9, you are examing the variable e from an actionPerformed method: actionPerformed(ActionEvent e).

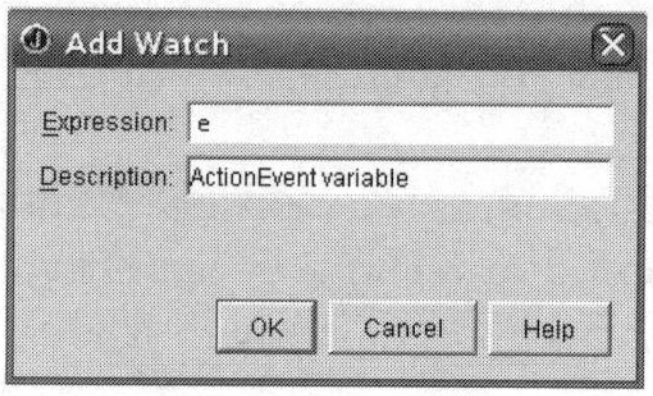

Figure 29-9: Setting up a watch for the ActionEvent variable, called e, that was passed to an event handler: actionPerformed(ActionEvent e)

NOTE: You can also add a watch by using the watch icon shown in Figure 29-5. This is the icon that is second from the right, the only icon in that series not discussed in the previous section of the text. I encourage you not to use that icon, but instead to right-click on the variable you want to view and then choose the watch option from the pop-up menu. The advantage of this latter technique is that the variable will automatically be inserted into the watch dialog, as shown in Figure 29-9. In either case, you will have to type in the description of the variable.

After you close the Add Watch window, you can see the variable you examined in the debugger, as shown in Figure 29-10. Right-clicking on the watch window will give you other options, such as creating a free-floating window containing your current view of the debugger.

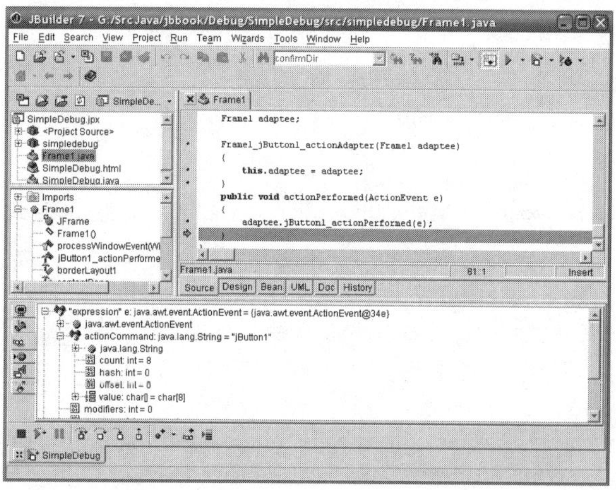

Figure 29-10: Examining a watched variable in the JBuilder debugger. In this case you are looking at the ActionEvent variable e that was passed to the actionPerformed method.

Notice in Figure 29-10 that you can see the ActionCommand associated with the ActionEvent you are currently examining. This variable is set to the value "jButton1." This is a useful bit of information, as it makes clear what component called this action event handler. In other words, this method was called because the user clicked on jButton1.

I said earlier that the difference between a good programmer and a great programmer is not that one uses the debugger and the other does not. All programmers should use the debugger. But a beginning level programmer might not understand what the actionCommand output in Figure 29-10 means. A more experienced programmer, on the other hand, will understand that this information reveals what component was used to call the actionPerformed method. You should not feel bad about using the debugger; instead, you should work hard to increase your understanding of how the debugger works and what it can tell you about your program.

The Breakpoint View

Beneath the watch window icon on the left of the debugger is another icon that lets you see all your current breakpoints, as shown in Figure 29-11. If you right-click in the Breakpoint view on the breakpoint you set at line 66, you can pop up the breakpoint dialog, shown in Figure 29-12.

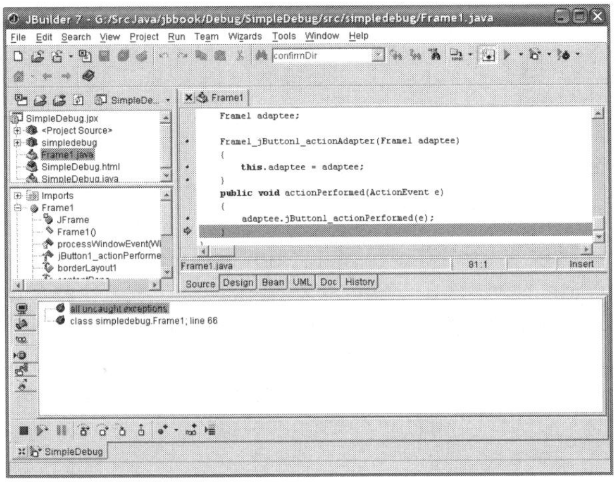

Figure 29-11: In this view of the breakpoints in a program, you can see the breakpoint set on line 66 of the SimpleDebug project.

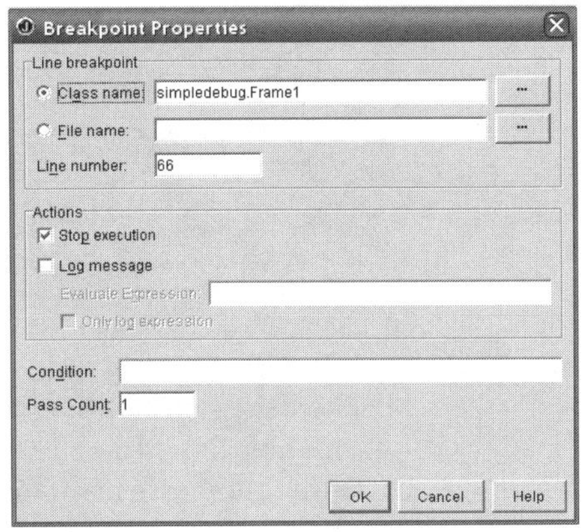

Figure 29-12: The Breakpoint Properties dialog

The view in Figure 29-11 identifies the sole breakpoint found in our program as residing on line 66 of your code. Because we have only one breakpoint, this may not seem like very useful information. But if you have 10 or 20 breakpoints set in your code, this view can be very helpful.

NOTE: Having 10 or 20 breakpoints set at one time is not at all an unusual situation. In fact, it is common. Sometimes a single developer will be responsible for many different areas in a single program. This can cause problems because the developer might have one set of breakpoints for debugging one area of the code and another set for debugging a second area. It is annoying to hit a breakpoint in a part of your program that you are not currently trying to debug. One trick you can use to help manage your breakpoints is to have multiple JPX files for your project. In one JPX file, you can set all the breakpoints for one particular view of your program, such as the part that handles Internet traffic. Use that JPX file when you want to debug the Internet portion of your code. In another JPX file, have another set of breakpoints that allows you to debug the UI portion of your code for getting input from the user. You can create a new JPX for your project by choosing File | New | Project | Project for Existing Code from the JBuilder menu.

Breakpoints that Don't Stop Execution of Your Program

Let's take a moment to understand the very important Breakpoint Properties dialog you reached by right-clicking on the breakpoint you set on line 66. Consider the view of the breakpoints dialog that you get in Figure 29-13. Here you can see that the option to stop execution at a breakpoint has been turned off. Why would you want to do this? Isn't the whole point of a breakpoint that it stops you at a particular point in your program and lets you examine the state of your program? Well, yes, that is the most common thing to do with breakpoints. But they can be used for other purposes, such as exporting log information.

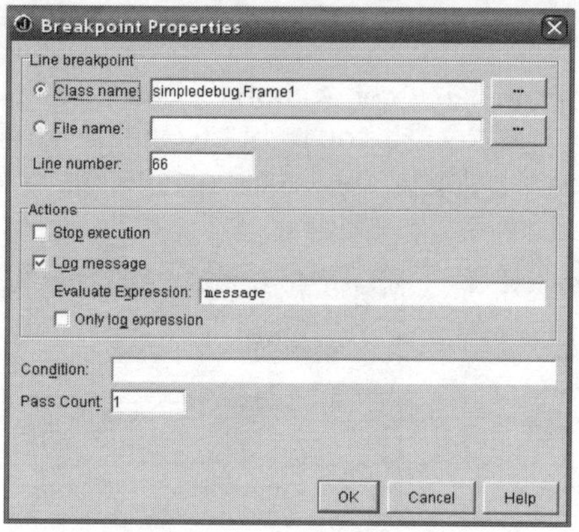

Figure 29-13: Setting up the Breakpoint Properties dialog so that your program does not stop at a breakpoint but instead outputs data to standard out

In the Evaluate Expression control shown in Figure 29-13, the debugger has been told to report on the current state of the String variable called message. In effect, these commands tell the debugger not to stop your program when it hits the breakpoint, but instead to output information about the current state of the variable message.

To see this state of affairs in action, hit the green continue button at the bottom of the debugger, the one discussed in the "Controlling the Debugger" section. When the program resumes running, tap the button in your program two or three times. Now the breakpoint won't stop you on line 66. Instead, it will spew information to the message pane, as shown in Figure 29-14.

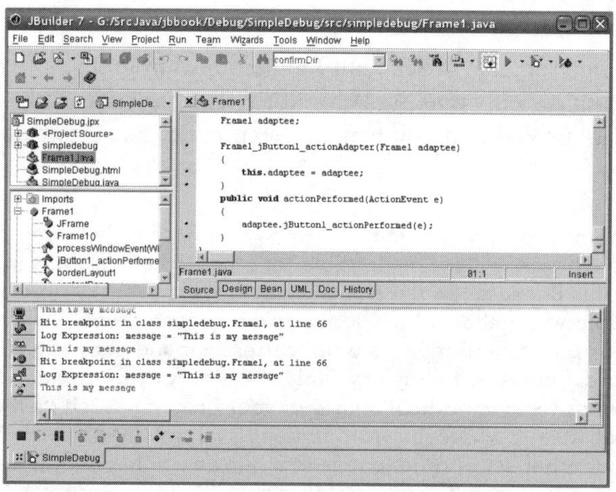

Figure 29-14: The debugger as it appears when you have hit a breakpoint designed to log information to standard out

The messages sent to the debugger look like this:

```
This is my message
Hit breakpoint in class simpledebug.Frame1, at line 66
Log Expression: message = "This is my message"
```

The first line is the message output by the call that we wrote to System.out.println. The next line is a message from the debugger telling you that your breakpoint has been reached. The last line gives the current state of the variable message. Of course, in this program, the message variable will never change, but you don't need much imagination to see how useful this feature can be. In effect, it gives you a quick way to start logging information to the screen, much like we did at the beginning of the chapter when using System.out.println. The difference is that this technique works without your having to modify your code.

Disabling Breakpoints

You can enable and disable breakpoints without deleting them. To do this, turn to the Breakpoint view shown in Figure 29-11. Right-click on a breakpoint and deselect the **Enable breakpoint** option. This will enable you to ignore a breakpoint for a time without having to delete it. If you delete it, you will have to recreate it if you want to see it again. That can be a boring and frustrating task, particularly if you want to make a lot of changes to the breakpoint dialog.

Conditional Breakpoints

A conditional breakpoint is a breakpoint that will fire only if certain conditions are true. Consider the following method:

```
void jButtonConditional_actionPerformed(ActionEvent e)
{
        double j;
        for (int i = 0; i < 10; i++)
        {
                j = Math.pow(i, 2.0);
                System.out.println("Value of j: " + j);
        }

}
```

This method has a loop that executes ten times. Stepping through this loop all ten times can be repetitive and boring. Using conditional breakpoints, you can stop only when the value of the variable i has a particular value (for instance, the value 5).

Figure 29-15 shows the Breakpoint Properties dialog set up to output data to the message window only if the variable i is set to 5. In particular, the output in the message pane will look like this:

```
Value of j: 0.0
Value of j: 1.0
Value of j: 4.0
Value of j: 9.0
Value of j: 16.0
Hit breakpoint in class simpledebug.Frame1, at line 109
Log Expression: j = 25.0
Value of j: 25.0
Value of j: 36.0
Value of j: 49.0
```

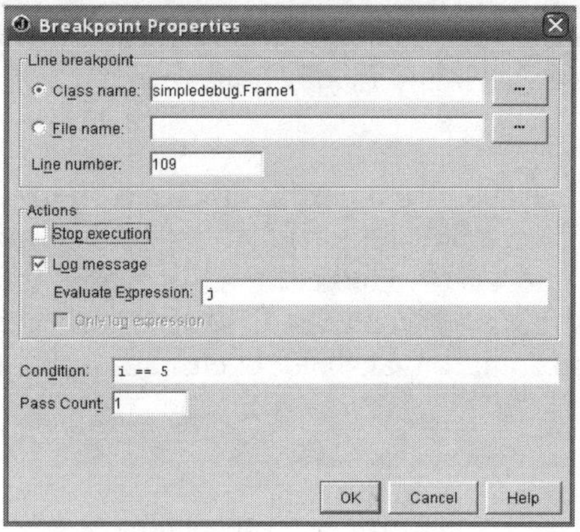

Figure 29-15: Setting a conditional breakpoint that will fire when the variable i has a value of 5

Note that Stop execution is not checked, Log message is checked, the Evaluate Expression field is set simply to the variable j, and the Condition field is set to i == 5.

I find that conditional breakpoints can be a bit slow to fire not only in JBuilder but also in Delphi and C++Builder. As a result, I use this feature sparingly. Nevertheless, when I need it, it is well worth the few extra seconds necessary to use this powerful tool.

NOTE: Remember that conditional breakpoints won't work unless you start debugging your application. If you hit the Run button instead of the Debug button, the breakpoints will not fire.

The Loaded Classes View

The next to last view that you can have of the debugger allows you to see which classes have been loaded in this run of your program, as well as any static data associated with a particular class. Remember, this is not C/C++ and Java has no preprocessor. As a result, you can see the value associated with a constant in your program at run time.

The Classes with Tracing Disabled View

The final view of the debugger, the last icon shown in Figure 29-8, allows you to see which classes have been disabled for use with the smart step feature discussed earlier in this chapter. In JBuilder SE and Enterprise, you can right-click on this view to either add or delete classes to the smart step list.

Taking Stock

You have now had an overview of all the major features in the debugger. At this point, however, your knowledge of the debugger is really more theoretical than practical. In the next two sections of the text, you will get a chance to use the debugger to solve a problem and explore a program that uses threads.

Finding the Bug in a Program

Consider this method, which is designed to return the first word from a string:

```
public static final String getFirstWord(String value)
{
      // remove any white space
```

```
        String cleanValue = value.trim();

        // Get the index of the first space
        int indexOfFirstSpace = cleanValue.indexOf(' ');

        // if there is only one word in the string, return it
        if (indexOfFirstSpace == 0)
        {
            return cleanValue;
        }

        // return the first word from the string
        return cleanValue.substring(0, indexOfFirstSpace);
    }
```

If you pass in the string " Much have I travell'd in the realms of gold," this method would return the word "Much."

Or at least that is the theory. In practice, the routine has a bug in it. Some people would say that the best way to find the bug is to read the code over and over until you see what is wrong with it. Indeed, many people might find that task quite simple. Others might not see the problem so readily, and they would be likely to find the debugger helpful.

For the sake of argument, however, let's use the debugger to find the bug. Add the method to the SimpleDebug program, and add a second button and a JTextArea to the program, as shown in Figure 29-16.

Figure 29-16: The interface to the SimpleDebug program found on the CD that accompanies this book

In response to a click on the First Word Bug button, add this code:

```
    void jButtonFirstWord_actionPerformed(ActionEvent e)
    {
        getFirstWord("Sam");
    }
```

If you run the program and click on the actionPerformed button, you will get the following error:

```
Exception occurred during event dispatching:
java.lang.StringIndexOutOfBoundsException: String index out of range: -1
    at java.lang.String.substring(String.java:1525)
    at simpledebug.Frame1.getFirstWord(Frame1.java:89)
    at simpledebug.Frame1.jButtonFirstWord_actionPerformed(Frame1.java:94)
    at simpledebug.Frame1_jButtonFirstWord_actionAdapter.actionPerformed(Frame1.java:122)
    at javax.swing.AbstractButton.fireActionPerformed(AbstractButton.java:1450)
    etc…
```

To figure out what went wrong, set a breakpoint on the call to getFirstWord and rerun the program. Click on the **First Word Bug** button. You will be taken to the call to getFirstWord, as shown in Figure 29-17. Press **F7** or the **Step Into** icon to step into the GetFirstWord method, as shown in Figure 29-18.

NOTE: When you press the F7 or F8 keys to step through your code, you have to make sure that the debugger has the focus, or it will not catch your keypress. One way to ensure that all is well is to use the mouse to click directly on the current line that is executing. Then press the F7 or F8 key.

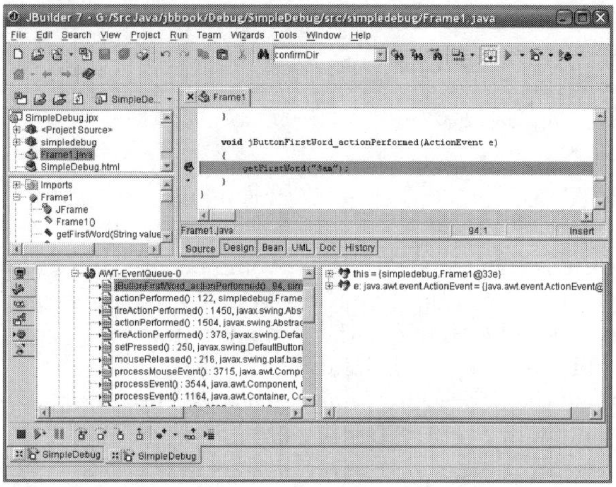

Figure 29-17: Stopping at a breakpoint in the debugger

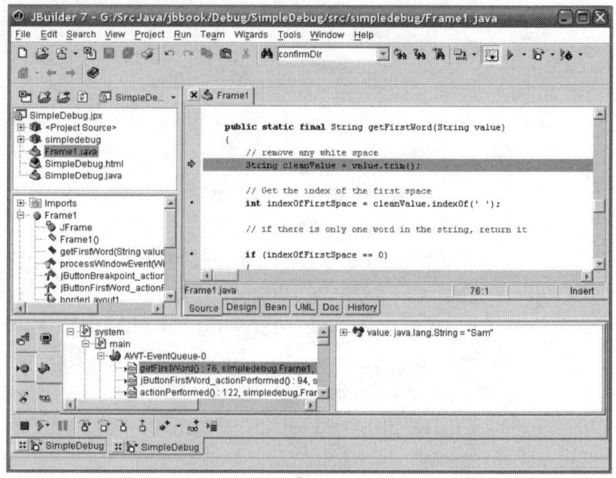

Figure 29-18: Stepping into a buggy method

When you reach the beginning of the method shown in Figure 29-18, all is still well. You can see the value that was passed into the method. At this time it is set to the string "Sam."

In Figure 29-19, however, you might begin to see what has gone wrong. In this view of the program, I have stepped forward three more lines. In the variable view on the bottom right, you can now see three variables:

```
value  = "Sam"
cleanValue = "Sam"
indexOfFirstSpace = -1
```

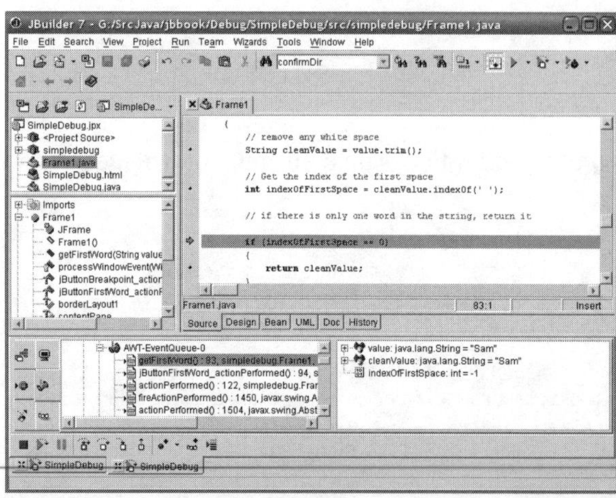

Figure 29-19: Getting warm! Zeroing in on the bug in our program.

Now that we can see it, it is this last line that should set off warning bells in our heads. Remember the error message generated by the SDK:

```
java.lang.StringIndexOutOfBoundsException: String index out of range: -1
```

Hmmm. indexOfFirstSpace is set to –1, and the error message said something about a String index being out of range with a value of –1.

The next few lines in the method look like this:

```
        // if there is only one word in the string, return it
        if (indexOfFirstSpace == 0)
        {
            return cleanValue;
        }
```

This code is supposed to force us to exit the method if there is only one word in the string. Well, that is the case for us now, and yet we can see that indexOfFirstString is not set to 0, but to –1. The fix should be clear. We can change the next line to either of the following options to solve the problem:

```
if ((indexOfFirstSpace == 0) || (indexOfFirstSpace == -1))
```

Or perhaps on further consideration we can see that it is unlikely that indexOfFirstSpace will ever equal 0, since there was an earlier call to the trim method. So the following call would probably solve the problem equally well:

```
if (indexOfFirstSpace == -1)
```

Or, you could write:

```
if (indexOfFirstSpace <= 0)
```

The point here is that the debugger helped us find what was wrong. The anti-debugger crowd could perhaps argue that you might have found the problem just as easily by thinking carefully about the method. And perhaps that is true, but I find that the debugger actually helps me think carefully about my code.

And yet there is an argument here on both sides. I suppose the ideal solution is both to read your code through carefully and also step through it with the debugger. Black and white solutions are rarely the best. There are, as so often happens, good arguments on both sides of the fence.

NOTE: You could also have used the techniques discussed in the beginning of this chapter to help you track down this bug. For instance, you could write a test routine for this method that looks like this:

```
String s = getFirstWord("Sam is red hot");
assert (s.equals("Sam"));
s = getFirstWord("Sam");
assert (s.equals("Sam"));
s = getFirstWord("");
assert (s.equals(""));
```

If your method can run this gauntlet, then you can be fairly sure it is bug free. If a user finds a case that causes the method to fail, simply add the test to your string of assertions. Once again, this is more or less the technique used in JUnit, so you can learn more about this technology by reading the next chapter.

Debugging Threads

The final step in our journey through the land of Debug is to see how the JBuilder tools can help you find problems in code that has multiple threads.

The DebugThread program found on the CD contains a class that is run on a separate thread. The code that calls the thread looks like this:

```
void jButton1_actionPerformed(ActionEvent e)
{
      MyThread myThread = new MyThread();
      myThread.addActionListener(this);
      myThread.start();
}
```

NOTE: The Frame1 class to which this code belongs is designated as the ActionListener for this thread. That means that Frame1 must have implements ActionListener added to its header. Then add code to handle the event:

```
public void actionPerformed(ActionEvent parm1)
{
      // Do something here with the event
}
```

You can use either BeansExpress or the Interface Wizard to help you write this code, or you can easily type it in by hand since it is so brief. See the code on the CD if you have further questions.

The code in the ActionPerformed method first creates a class called myThread that descends from class Thread.

NOTE: Earlier in the book I showed you another class that ran on a thread. That class implemented the Runnable interface instead of descending from class Thread. I told you at the time that it was usually better to have a class you want to run on a thread implement Runnable rather than descend from class Thread. That still holds true. Your code will be needlessly bulkier if you descend from Thread in a case like this. But in this case, I am showing you how to follow the other course of action just so you can see both sides of the coin. The other program was called CustomMessageSender and was discussed in Part III: JBuilder Fundamentals. The discussion of that program explored threads in more depth than I will in this section of the text.

After creating an instance of the Thread class, the code adds the current class as an ActionListener. It then starts the thread.

The Thread descendant class has a very simple run method that creates an ArrayList. The run method then fires off a series of ActionEvents, each of which encapsulates a single member of the ArrayList. Frame1 receives the list and displays its content to the user. You can see the Thread class in Listing 29-1 and the JFrame descendant class that listens to it in Listing 29-2.

Listing 29-1: The Thread descendant that creates a list of strings and then sends them back to the main class as part of an event

```
package debugthread;

import java.util.*;
import java.awt.event.*;

public class MyThread extends Thread
```

```
{
    public MyThread()
    {
    }

    public void run()
    {
        ArrayList list = new ArrayList();
        list.add("Sam");
        list.add("foo");
        list.add("tom");
        Iterator itr = list.iterator();
        while (itr.hasNext())
        {
            String data = (String)itr.next();
            ActionEvent myEvent = new ActionEvent(this, 1, data);
            fireActionPerformed(myEvent);
        }
    }

    public synchronized void removeActionListener(ActionListener l)
    {
        if (actionListeners != null && actionListeners.contains(l))
        {
            Vector v = (Vector) actionListeners.clone();
            v.removeElement(l);
            actionListeners = v;
        }
    }
    public synchronized void addActionListener(ActionListener l)
    {
        Vector v = actionListeners ==
            null ? new Vector(2) : (Vector) actionListeners.clone();
        if (!v.contains(l))
        {
            v.addElement(l);
            actionListeners = v;
        }
    }
    private transient Vector actionListeners;
    protected void fireActionPerformed(ActionEvent e)
    {
        if (actionListeners != null)
        {
            Vector listeners = actionListeners;
            int count = listeners.size();
            for (int i = 0; i < count; i++)
            {
                ((ActionListener) listeners.elementAt(i)).actionPerformed(e);
            }
```

```
            }
        }
    }
```

Listing 29-2: The Frame1 instance that listens for a report from the MyThread class

```
package debugthread;

import java.awt.*;
import java.awt.event.*;
import javax.swing.*;
import java.util.*;
import com.elvenware.comp.*;

public class Frame1 extends JFrame implements ActionListener
{
      JPanel contentPane;
      BorderLayout borderLayout1 = new BorderLayout();
      JButton jButton1 = new JButton();
      JPanel jPanel1 = new JPanel();
      ElfListBox elfListBox1 = new ElfListBox();
      BorderLayout borderLayout2 = new BorderLayout();

      //Construct the frame
      public Frame1()
      {
            enableEvents(AWTEvent.WINDOW_EVENT_MASK);
            try
            {
                  jbInit();
            }
            catch (Exception e)
            {
                  e.printStackTrace();
            }

      }
      //Component initialization
      private void jbInit() throws Exception
      {
            contentPane = (JPanel) this.getContentPane();
            jButton1.setText("jButton1");
            jButton1.addActionListener(new java.awt.event.ActionListener()
            {
                  public void actionPerformed(ActionEvent e)
                  {
                        jButton1_actionPerformed(e);
                  }
            });
            contentPane.setLayout(borderLayout1);
            this.setSize(new Dimension(400, 300));
            this.setTitle("Frame Title");
```

```
        jPanel1.setLayout(borderLayout2);
        contentPane.add(jButton1,  BorderLayout.SOUTH);
        contentPane.add(jPanel1,  BorderLayout.CENTER);
        jPanel1.add(elfListBox1,  BorderLayout.CENTER);
    }
    //Overridden so we can exit when window is closed
    protected void processWindowEvent(WindowEvent e)
    {
        super.processWindowEvent(e);
        if (e.getID() == WindowEvent.WINDOW_CLOSING)
        {
            System.exit(0);
        }
    }

    void jButton1_actionPerformed(ActionEvent e)
    {
        MyThread myThread = new MyThread();
        myThread.addActionListener(this);
        myThread.start();
    }
    public void actionPerformed(ActionEvent e)
    {
        elfListBox1.setString(e.getActionCommand());
    }
}
```

You should add two breakpoints to the DebugThread program. The first is in the actionPerformed method above, which creates and calls an instance of the thread. This is line 74 of Frame1:

```
    void jButton1_actionPerformed(ActionEvent e)
    {
        MyThread myThread = new MyThread(); // Set the breakpoint here
        myThread.addActionListener(this);
        myThread.start();
    }
```

The second breakpoint should be on the first executable line of the run method for the MyThread class:

```
    public void run()
    {
        ArrayList list = new ArrayList(); // Set the breakpoint here
        list.add("Sam");
        list.add("foo");
        list.add("tom");
        Iterator itr = list.iterator();
        while (itr.hasNext())
        {
            String data = (String)itr.next();
            ActionEvent myEvent = new ActionEvent(this, 1, data);
            fireActionPerformed(myEvent);
```

```
        }
    }
```

Figure 29-20 shows what the Threads view of the debugger looks like when the program hits the first breakpoint. Figure 29-21 shows the state of affairs when the breakpoint on the run method of the MyThread class is executed.

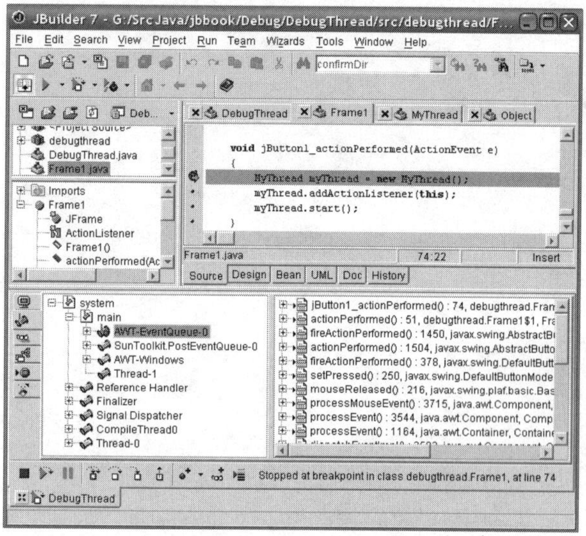

Figure 29-20: Before the new thread is created, you can see four nodes on the main branch of the left-hand part of the thread window.

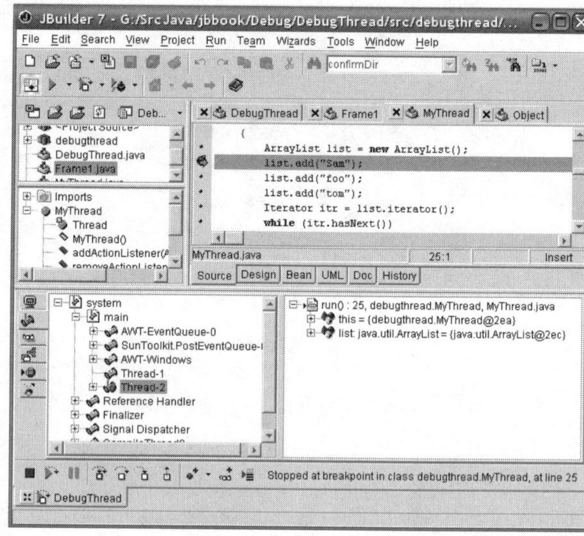

Figure 29-21: Once the new thread is created, you can see that new nodes have been added to the Threads view of the debugger.

In Figure 29-20, you may be able to see that the currently active thread has a tiny little red dot on it. I know you can't see the color in the screen shot, but perhaps you can see the dot on the top thread. The dot means the thread is active. In Figure 29-21, you can see that a new thread has been added to the list of threads. It is called Thread-2, and it now has the red dot on it. It is this second thread, Thread-2, that is now the current thread in the program.

The threads with yellow spools in front of them are blocked threads. Those in blue are active. A black spool represents a dead thread.

Notice that in Figure 29-21, you can see all the currently active variables in the active thread in the right-hand window. You can inspect these variables just as we did the variable called message earlier in this chapter.

At this stage you really know all the key facts you need to understand to start debugging your threads in JBuilder. The simple miraculous truth of the matter is that JBuilder will let you see each of the threads running in your program. If you set breakpoints judiciously, you can step right into your threads and see their state while they are executing.

If you are new to programming, this tour of debugging threads might not seem like such a big deal. But it is really a small miracle. The people on the JBuilder team that created the debugger deserve considerable praise for their efforts. I suppose the folks back at Sun deserve a pat on the back also. When you see technology like this, with all the code — including the debugger — written in Java, you suddenly start to see that Java is fast becoming a first-class, premier language.

Reminders and Hints

Before closing the chapter, let me remind you that there are (at least) two green run buttons at the top of the JBuilder IDE. The first one runs your program, and the second allows you to debug your program.

It is easy to start multiple copies of your programmer in the debugger. For instance, you might be finding and fixing a bug and then hit the green Run button to test your program. At this stage you have two programs launched, one in the debugger and the second just running normally. After awhile, the bottom of the IDE can have numerous tabs on it for each of the debug and run instances that you have started. (Mostly, I start them accidentally, but you may have started them on purpose.) Figure 29-22 shows an example of what can happen if you start a number of programs at once in the IDE.

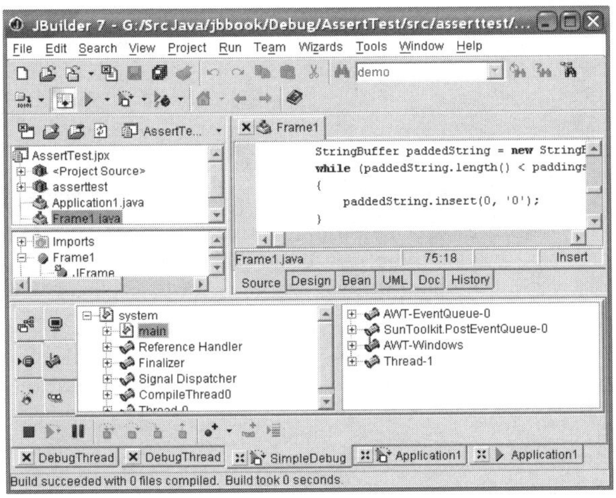

Figure 29-22: Notice all the tabs lined up at the bottom of the IDE. Here I have two copies of DebugThread, one copy of SimpleDebug, and two copies of Application1 open.

NOTE: Elsewhere in the text, I have encouraged you not to name all the main classes of your programs Application1. A glimpse at Figure 29-22 can help you see one of the reasons why this might be a bad practice: If you are working on multiple projects at once, you can more easily sort the various programs out if you name their main classes intelligently.

You can right-click on these tabs to close them. In JBuilder 7, there is also an X on the tabs that you can hit to close the tab. However, I find that the simplest way to handle this proliferation of tabs is often to right-click on any one of the tabs and choose **Remove all tabs**. All the tabs will then disappear. If some of the programs are loaded at the time you choose this, you will be prompted to close them. I have had no trouble closing programs through this technique and then continuing to work in the IDE. If there is a memory loss that occurs in such situations, it is not apparent to me on my machine. On older builds of JBuilder, however, I did encounter memory loss from time to time. I fixed it by closing and restarting the IDE.

Garbage Collection

The Borland tool called OptimizeIt can help you study garbage collection in your program in depth. There is, however, a simple technique that everyone can use to view much of what is happening when the Java garbage collector sweeps through your program. The trick is simply to pass this switch to the JDK when you launch your program: -verbose:gc.

In particular, open up **Project | Project Properties** from the JBuilder menu and turn to the **Run** page. Edit your current run-time configuration and add the **-verbose:gc** switch to your VM parameters, as shown in Figure 29-23.

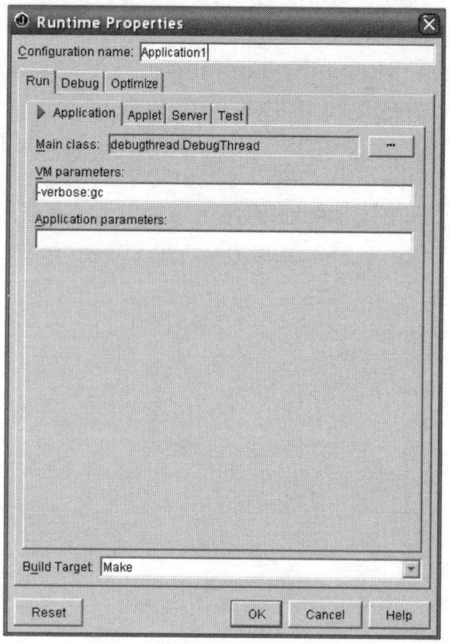

Figure 29-23: Passing in a switch to the Java VM that will help you see just when garbage collection is taking place, how long the action takes, and how much memory is collected

The output for using this switch can be seen in the message pane:

```
[GC 1254K->745K(1984K), 0.0051940 secs]
[GC 1257K->746K(1984K), 0.0013247 secs]
[GC 789K->746K(1984K), 0.0006990 secs]
[Full GC 746K->746K(1984K), 0.0808960 secs]
```

There are three small passes of the garbage collector in this listing, and then one major pass shown on the last line.

The -Xms and -Xmx options that you can pass to the VM can be used to tweak the way Java handles garbage collection. At the time of publication, there was more information about this at: http://java.sun.com/docs/hotspot/gc/.

Summary

In this chapter you had a chance to learn about debugging Java programs. The chapter started out by showing some conventional but still very powerful means of debugging through writing to standard out or creating log files. A short section on assertions was also included.

The text then moved on to show you how to set breakpoints in a JBuilder program and how to then examine the current state of your application or applet. Next came an overview of the various views found in the debugger. This included views of the current variables and threads in your program, views of the loaded classes and their static data, a watch view, a breakpoint view, and finally a view for enabling and disabling the classes you wish to step through.

Near the end of the chapter you saw an example of how to find and fix a simple bug in a program. Then finally, at the very end, you had a peek at how to debug a program that contains multiple threads.

I did not discuss remote debugging or using the OptimizeIt tool to help you debug. OptimizeIt is particularly useful if you want to study the way garbage collection works in your program.

This chapter comes late in the book, and it is not particularly long, but it is still one of the more important chapters in the text. If you are new to the powerful debugger found in JBuilder, then hopefully you now have enough information to begin a serious exploration of one of the most useful, enlightening, and truly amazing features in the entire product.

Chapter 30

Unit Testing with JUnit

Charlie Calvert

This chapter is about a technology called *unit testing*. The idea behind the kind of unit testing explored in this chapter is that you should create Boolean methods for testing as many features of your code as possible. Using a tool called JUnit, these methods will be called automatically and a report generated to confirm that they all passed correctly or that one or more of the tests failed.

Unit testing is a way of life. It is part of a philosophy of development called "extreme programming." One of the core concepts of extreme programming is that you should always be producing code that compiles and runs correctly. Even if you only have one feature completed out of a project that will include hundreds of features, you should still start with a version of your product that fully supports that one feature.

To confirm that your product is working correctly, you should write a series of Boolean tests that demonstrate the correctness of the code you have written. As you begin to add more code to your project, you will continue to add tests and write new tests. You should run the tests at least once a day, preferably many times each day. They will prove not only that your new features work, but that they do not break any of your already established code base.

To help make this process as simple as possible, an open source project called JUnit was created. The sole purpose of JUnit is to make it as easy as possible for you to write and run tests of the kind described in the last few paragraphs.

NOTE: Most of the features for integrating JUnit into JBuilder are included only in the Enterprise version of JBuilder. However, JUnit is an open source project. So don't fear, you can and should use JUnit regardless of which version of JBuilder you are using. I will show you first how to integrate the tools into JBuilder Enterprise and then spend a little time showing how to proceed even if you are working with JBuilder Personal. Everyone ought to use JUnit, not just those with the Enterprise edition. You might want to read this chapter through from the beginning, regardless of which edition you have, as there are many hints scattered throughout about using JUnit.

Unit Testing in the Enterprise Version

In this section I will show you how to use JUnit with the Enterprise version of JBuilder. Later in the chapter I will show you how to proceed if you have the Personal edition. The code shown in this chapter is drawn mostly from an example program called UnitTesting, found on the CD that accompanies this book.

NOTE: The code generated by JBuilder Enterprise is nothing more than simply Java source code for use with the JUnit open source project. Thus, you can download JUnit from www.junit.org and use it to run the scripts that I describe in this chapter. The scripts themselves are easy to understand, and you should have no problem generating them by hand. The JUnit site also includes code for automatically generating tests, so you can use the open source code in lieu of the code in the

Enterprise version of JBuilder. In short, this chapter really is for everyone, not just users of the Enterprise edition of JBuilder.

Start a new application using the techniques described in Chapter 3, and add the following two methods to the Frame1.java:

```
public int add(int a, int b)
{
      return a + b;
}

public int multiply(int a, int b)
{
      return a * b;
}
```

Don't bother to call the methods. For now, all that matters is that the two methods are included in Frame1.java.

Make sure Frame1 is focused in the content pane. Now choose **File | New** from the JBuilder menu and turn to the **Test** page in the Object Gallery. Click on the **Test Case** option. The dialog shown in Figure 30-1 will appear. Highlight the two public methods that you see in the dialog, and press the **Finish** button. Don't bother stepping through the whole wizard; just press Finish after filling out the first page.

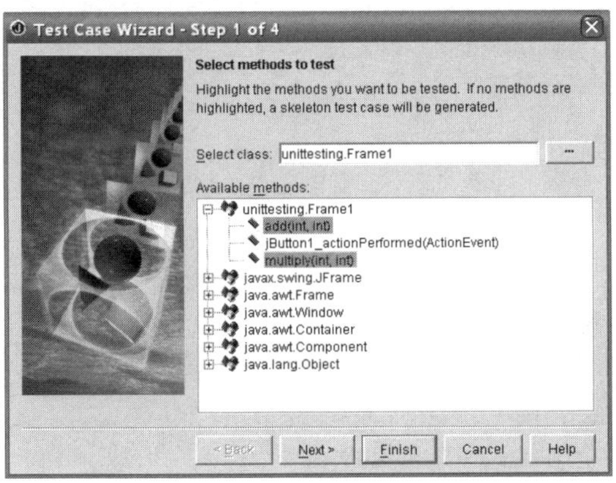

Figure 30-1: Selecting the add and multiply methods from Frame1 so that you can test them with JUnit

After you press Finish, the code shown in Listing 30-1 will be generated automatically. This is the test code used to confirm that the functions we have written work correctly. Notice the presence of the import junit.framework.* statement at the top of the source file. Notice further that TestFrame1 extends a class from the JUnit framework called TestCase. You are extending this class solely so that you can add the functionality for testing your two methods to it. All the other features necessary to automatically call your methods and give you a graphical report on the success of your methods are built into JUnit itself.

Listing 30-1: A class generated by JBuilder and designed to automatically test the methods found in Frame1. You need only add the assert statements to this code.

```
package unittesting;

import junit.framework.*;
import java.awt.event.*;
```

```
import unittesting.*;

public class TestFrame1 extends TestCase
{
  public TestFrame1(String s)
  {
    super(s);
  }

  protected void setUp()
  {
  }

  protected void tearDown()
  {
  }

  public void testAdd()
  {
    Frame1 frame1 = new Frame1();
    int a1=  2;
    int b2=  2;
       int intRet = frame1.add(a1, b2);
  }

  public void testMultiply()
  {
    Frame1 frame1 = new Frame1();
    int a1=  2;
    int b2=  3;
    int intRet = frame1.multiply(a1, b2);
  }
}
```

The code for setting up and tearing down the class is not needed in our case, so you can delete it or ignore it. You should also add code for actually performing tests in the testAdd and testMultiply methods, as described immediately after Listing 2. The end result is the class shown in Listing 30-2.

Listing 30-2: A valid test case for the Frame1 class

```
package unittesting;

import junit.framework.*;
import unittesting.*;

public class TestFrame1 extends TestCase
{
  public TestFrame1(String s)
  {
      super(s);
  }
```

```
    public void testAdd()
    {
        Frame1 frame1 = new Frame1();
        int a1=  2;
        int b2=  2;
        int intRet = frame1.add(a1, b2);
        assertEquals( intRet, 4);
    }

    public void testMultiply()
    {
        Frame1 frame1 = new Frame1();
        int a1=  2;
        int b2=  3;
        int intRet = frame1.multiply(a1, b2);
        assertEquals( intRet, 6);
    }
}
```

Take a look at the testAdd method. It uses code generated by JBuilder to set up the test. Then a method called assertEquals is called. This method tests to make sure that the return value from the Frame1.add method is equal to 4. If it is equal to 4, the test succeeds. If it is not equal to 4, the test fails. The same principle is applied to the testMultiply method.

Now that you have your test case set up, the next step is to run the test case and see if it works. Perhaps the simplest way to do that is to pick **TestFrame1.java** out of the list in the project pane. Right-click on it and choose **Run**. You do not want to run your main application; instead you want to run the test case that was generated by the JBuilder Wizard. The results of a successful run are shown in Figure 30-2.

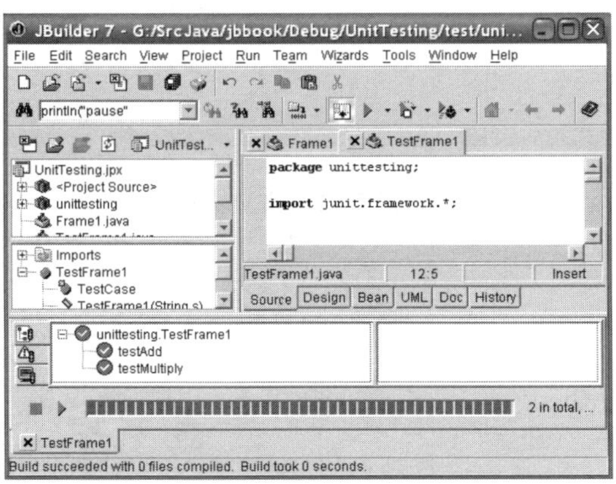

Figure 30-2: A successful JUnit test run in the JBuilder IDE. Notice the check marks in the circles shown in the message pane.

Part VI

The JBuilder IDE gives you visual feedback so you can verify the results of these tests. Figure 30-2 shows the case where both tests succeed, while Figure 30-3 shows the case where the second test fails. The failures and successes are clearly visible on a color screen. Successful calls are shown in green and failures in red.

The second test might fail if you changed the testMultiply method to look like this:

```
    public void testMultiply()
    {
```

```
        Frame1 frame1 = new Frame1();
        int a1=  3;
        int b2=  3;
        int intRet = frame1.multiply(a1, b2);
        assertEquals( intRet, 6);
    }
```

This test will fail because 3 times 3 does not equal 6. The call to assertEquals states that the variable intRet should be equal to 6. If it is equal to 6, the call succeeds; otherwise, an error state is recorded by JUnit.

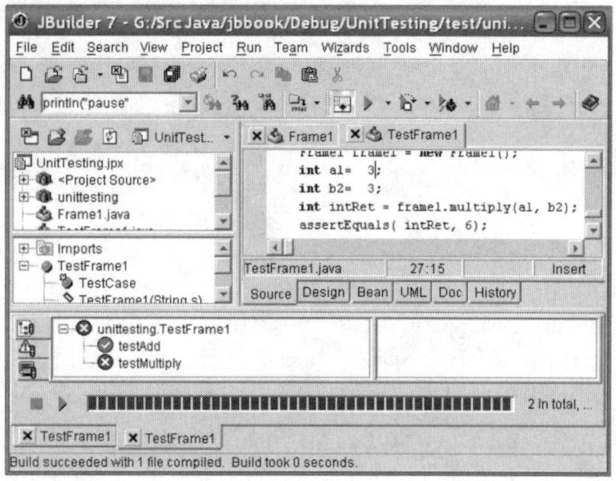

Figure 30-3: A failed JUnit test run in the JBuilder IDE. Notice the X marks found in the circles shown in the message pane. These will show up in red on your screen.

assertEquals is one of a series of methods supplied by the developers of JUnit for testing your code. The other methods are called assertNotNull, assertNull, assertSame, and assertTrue. There is also a method called assert, but it has been deprecated now that the JDK has a method of the same name built into it. The assertTrue method was written to replace the old JUnit call to assert.

Adding Tests of the CodeBox Class

Now that you have a feeling for how JUnit works, the next step is to create a more complex test. In particular, we will build tests for the StringBox unit found in the free Elvenware CodeBox JAR file that ships on the CD for this book.

Add the Elvenware code to the Paths page of the Project Properties dialog, as shown in Figure 30-4. After you install the code for this book, you should have a directory called something like jbbook\src\personal on your system. It is this directory that you want to add to your source path.

After you click OK in the Project Properties dialog, you will probably need to press the Refresh button (fourth from the left) in the toolbar above the project pane so that you can see the com.elvenware.* packages, as shown in Figure 30-5.

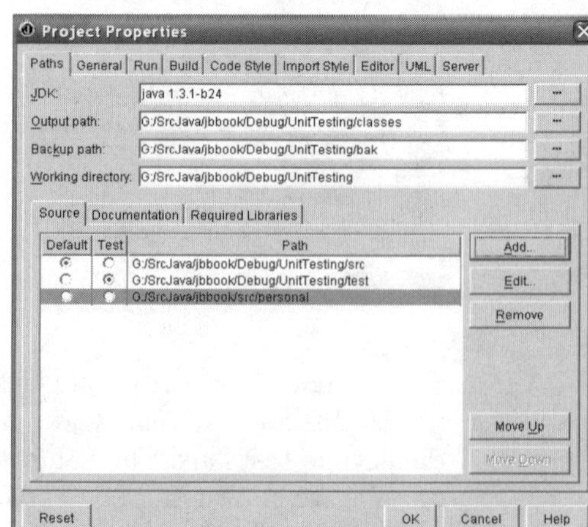

Figure 30-4: Setting up the source path for your JBuilder project so that you can access the code in the Elvenware packages

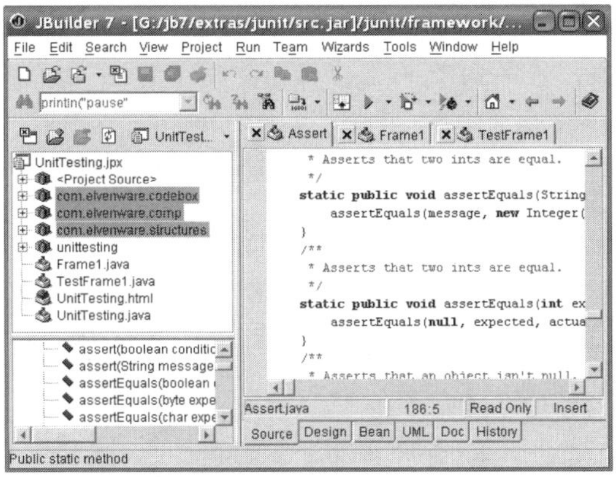

Figure 30-5: When you press the Refresh button over the project pane, you should be able to see the new packages you have added to your source path.

Open up the StringBox class from the com.elvenware.codebox package. Make sure it is focused in the content pane of the IDE. From the JBuilder menu, select **File | New**, and turn to the **Test** page. Run the first item, called Test Case.

On the first page of the Test Case Wizard, select all the methods from StringBox.java except sayMouse, as shown in Figure 30-6. Press the **Next** button.

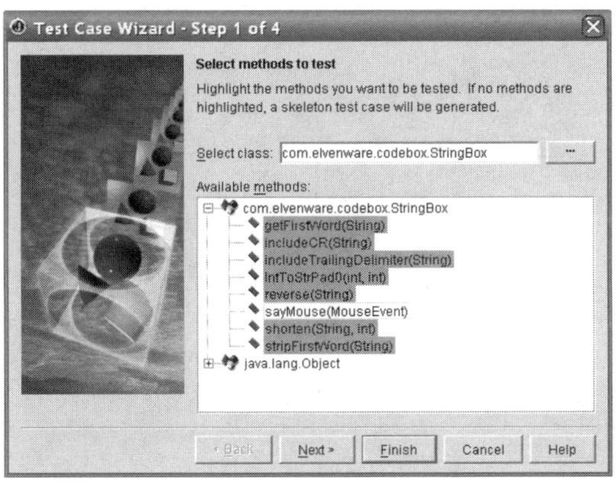

Figure 30-6: Selecting the methods from the StringBox class that you want to test

On the second page of the Test Case Wizard, make sure that the TestStringBox class ends up in the unittesting package, as shown in Figure 30-7, and not in com.elvenware.codebox. This is determined by the top field in the dialog, labeled Package. Everything in the codebox package is likely to end up in CodeBox.jar. The test programs, however, do not belong in the JAR file. As a result, you probably want to keep them out of the codebox package lest they end up in the JAR file by mistake. To do this, just use the Package field to put them in the unittesting package. When you press the Finish button, the code shown in Listing 30-3 will be created.

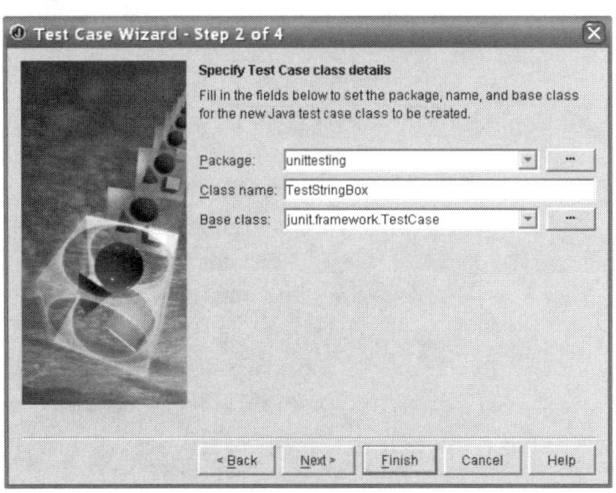

Figure 30-7: Use the Package field to determine the package where your test case will be stored.

Listing 30-3: The code generated by JBuilder for testing your class

```
package com.elvenware.codebox;

import junit.framework.*;

public class TestStringBox extends TestCase
{

  public TestStringBox(String s)
  {
    super(s);
  }

  protected void setUp()
  {
  }

  protected void tearDown()
  {
  }

  public void testGetFirstWord() {
    String value1=  "STRINGO";
    String stringRet = StringBox.getFirstWord(value1);
  /** @todo:  Insert test code here.  Use assertEquals(), for example. */
  }
  public void testIncludeCR() {
    String value1=  "STRINGO";
    String stringRet = StringBox.includeCR(value1);
  /** @todo:  Insert test code here.  Use assertEquals(), for example. */
  }
  public void testIncludeTrailingDelimiter() {
    String fileName1=  "STRINGO";
    String stringRet = StringBox.includeTrailingDelimiter(fileName1);
  /** @todo:  Insert test code here.  Use assertEquals(), for example. */
  }
  public void testIntToStrPad0() {
    int value1=  0;
    int paddings2=  0;
    String stringRet = StringBox.intToStrPad0(value1, paddings2);
  /** @todo:  Insert test code here.  Use assertEquals(), for example. */
  }
  public void testReverse() {
    String stringToReverse1=  "STRINGO";
    String stringRet = StringBox.reverse(stringToReverse1);
  /** @todo:  Insert test code here.  Use assertEquals(), for example. */
  }
  public void testShorten() {
    String s1=  "STRINGO";
    int charsToCut2=  0;
    String stringRet = StringBox.shorten(s1, charsToCut2);
```

```
   /** @todo:  Insert test code here.  Use assertEquals(), for example. */
   }
   public void testStripFirstWord() {
     String value1=  "STRINGO";
     String stringRet = StringBox.stripFirstWord(value1);
   /** @todo:  Insert test code here.  Use assertEquals(), for example. */
   }
}
```

You can see that there is one test method generated for each method in the StringBox class. All that is left for us to do is tweak some variables and compose the assertEquals or assertTrue method that will prove that the generated tests work. The test case that I came up with is shown in Listing 30-4.

Listing 30-4: A JUnit test case for the StringBox class

```
package unittesting;

import junit.framework.*;
import com.elvenware.codebox.*;

public class TestStringBox extends TestCase
{

      public TestStringBox(String s)
      {
            super(s);
      }

      protected void setUp()
      {
      }

      protected void tearDown()
      {
      }

      public void testGetFirstWord()
      {
            int value = 1;
            String theWord = "OneWord";
            String result = StringBox.getFirstWord(theWord);
            System.out.println("GetFirstWord: " + result);
            assertTrue(result.equals(theWord));
      }

      public void testGetFirstWord2()
      {
            int value = 1;
            String theWord = "";
            String result = StringBox.getFirstWord(theWord);
            System.out.println("GetFirstWord: " + result);
            assertTrue(result.equals(theWord));
```

```
}

public void testGetFirstWord3()
{
      int value = 1;
      String theWord = "Two words";
      String result = StringBox.getFirstWord(theWord);
      System.out.println("GetFirstWord: " + result);
      assertTrue(result.equals("Two"));
}

public void testGetFirstWord4()
{
      int value = 1;
      String theWord = " A then this is another test";
      String result = StringBox.getFirstWord(theWord);
      System.out.println("GetFirstWord: " + result);
      assertTrue(result.equals("A"));
}

public void testIncludeCR()
{
      String value1=  "STRINGO";
      String stringRet = StringBox.includeCR(value1);
      assertTrue(stringRet.endsWith("\n"));
}

public void testIncludeTrailingDelimiter()
{
      String fileName1=  "STRINGO";
      String stringRet = StringBox.includeTrailingDelimiter(fileName1);
      assertTrue( (stringRet.endsWith("\\")) || (stringRet.endsWith("/")) );
}

public void testInToStrPad0()
{
      int value = 1;
      int paddings2=  3;
      String result = StringBox.intToStrPad0(value, paddings2);
      System.out.println("IntToStrPad0: " + result);
      assertTrue(result.equals("001"));
}

public void testIntToStrPad0()
{
      int value1=  0;
      int paddings2=  0;
      String stringRet = StringBox.intToStrPad0(value1, paddings2);
      assertTrue(stringRet.equals("0"));
}
```

```
    public void testReverse()
    {
        String stringToReverse1=  "STRINGO";
        String stringRet = StringBox.reverse(stringToReverse1);
        assertEquals(stringRet, "OGNIRTS");
    }

    public void testShorten()
    {
        String s1=  "STRINGO";
        int charsToCut2= 4;
        String stringRet = StringBox.shorten(s1, charsToCut2);
        assertEquals(stringRet, "STR");
    }

    public void testStripFirstWord()
    {
        String value1=  "STRINGO";
        String stringRet = StringBox.stripFirstWord(value1);
        assertEquals(stringRet, "");
    }

    public void testStripFirstWord2()
    {
        String value1=  "";
        String stringRet = StringBox.stripFirstWord(value1);
        assertEquals(stringRet, "");
    }

    public void testStripFirstWord3()
    {
        String value1=  "This time";
        String stringRet = StringBox.stripFirstWord(value1);
        assertEquals(stringRet, "time");
    }

    public void testStripFirstWord4()
    {
        String value1=  "This time is true";
        String stringRet = StringBox.stripFirstWord(value1);
        assertEquals(stringRet, "time is true");
    }
}
```


Perhaps the most interesting thing about this code is the amount of repetition in it. For instance, there are four test cases for both the stripFirstWord and getFirstWord methods. The tests include making sure the methods work correctly when passed a multi-word string, a stringwithonewordinit, and an empty string. The more inventive you are in coming up with tests, the more likely it is that your code will be bug free. Needless to say, you should add new tests the moment you find a bug in any of these routines. The extreme programming people would say that you should add the test even before you try to fix the bug. The first step is to produce a test to check for error conditions, while the second step is to fix the bug itself.

NOTE: It is quite literally true that many extreme programming advocates would recommend that the first thing you do when starting a new project is write a test. As soon as you have the test in place, you can begin attempting to write a program that will pass the test. All of this is explained in more depth on http://www.extremeprogramming.org. Another interesting extreme programming resource is found at: http://ootips.org/xp.html.

These tests can help you define exactly what a method should do. For instance, I had not really made up my mind if the stripFirstWord method should return one word or an empty string if you pass in a string that contains only one word. Creating test cases forced me to come to terms with this method and define how it should behave. (I decided that it should return an empty string.)

Another important feature of tests like this is that they give you confidence when it comes time to fix bugs in your code or enhance the performance of your code. If I need to improve the getFirstWord method, I can proceed with confidence because I know that these tests will catch at least the most obvious bugs I might introduce while attempting to enhance the code.

One of the key ideas behind extreme programming is that it is actually fun to write tests. You do just a little bit of work, and then almost instantly you begin to get feedback. For once, you don't have to worry that the code you are writing might slow down your program. Instead, you should just exercise your creativity to the fullest extent possible and generate as many tests as possible. This is something you should integrate into your daily work habits. It is, however, also something useful that you can do when you just don't have the energy for more complex tasks. Have fun with it!

Testing Methods that Return Strings

For those times when you are not feeling very creative, you should try to come up with some rules that can help you compose tests. For instance, when testing a string routine, you should always generate code for at least two methods:

- Test the method when passing in a normal string.
- Test the method when passing in an empty string.

From the StringBox class, here are two examples of what I mean:

```
public void testReverse()
{
  String value1=  "abc";
  String stringRet = StringBox.reverse(value1);
  assertEquals(stringRet, "cba");
}

public void testReverseEmpty()
{
  String value1=  "";
  String stringRet = StringBox.reverse(value1);
  assertEquals(stringRet, "");
}
```

There are simple rules like these for mathematical methods as well. For instance, always test your code with 0 as a parameter and with both negative and positive parameters.

Test Fixtures

You have now seen the first two pages in the Test Case Wizard. The final page in the wizard is for creating something called *fixtures*. Fixtures are used to help you set up and tear down test cases. The fixture in question can be any class or set of variables that you want to use in the setup and teardown methods to help you run your tests. These fixtures might do nothing more than initialize variables.

Note that the setup and teardown methods will be called between each test that makes up your test case. That way you can be sure that all the tests are run against an object that is correctly initialized. For instance, if you are running tests against a remote server, your fixture code might connect you to that server. Then you can safely run tests against all of the methods on that server.

For more information on fixtures, visit the well-documented www.junit.org web site.

Test Suites

After creating tests for the methods in Frame1 and StringBox classes, we end up with two test cases, one called TestFrame1 and the other called TestStringBox. A test suite enables you to write code that will run both sets of tests at one time. The result is what you see in the message pane shown in Figure 30-8.

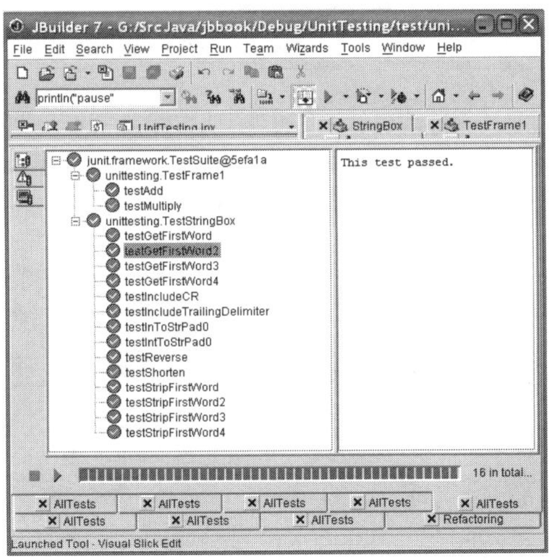

Figure 30-8: Running tests on both Frame1 and StringBox yields a hierarchy with two sets of tests.

It is easy to create a test suite in JBuilder Enterprise. Indeed, it is easy to create a test suite by hand. In JBuilder, just choose **File | New** from the menu. Turn to the **Test** page of the Object Gallery and select the **Test Suite Wizard.** On the first page of the wizard, use the **Add** button to add both the TestFrame1 and TestStringBox classes to your test suite, as shown in Figure 30-9. Move to the next page and make sure that the Package field is set to **unittesting.** This is the same drill that you went through with the TestStringBox class, so just follow the same procedure outlined earlier in the chapter.

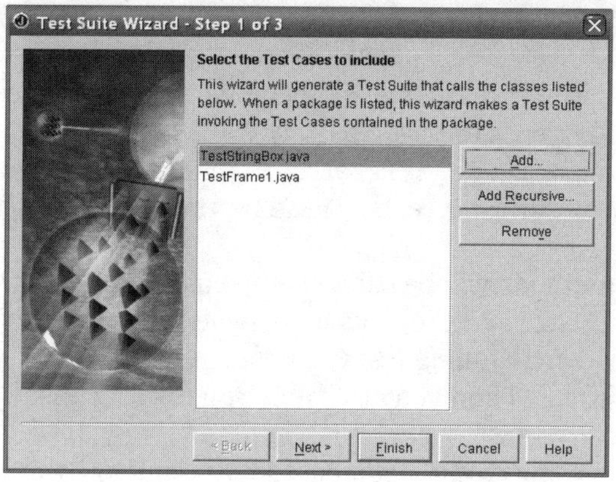

Figure 30-9: Use the Add button to add to your test suite the test cases that you want to run.

Press the **Finish** button to close the Test Suite Wizard. The code that is generated looks like that shown in Listing 30-5.

Listing 30-5: A simple JUnit test suite

```
package unittesting;

import junit.framework.*;

public class AllTests extends TestCase
{

  public AllTests(String s)
  {
      super(s);
  }

  public static Test suite() {
      TestSuite suite = new TestSuite();
      suite.addTestSuite(unittesting.TestFrame1.class);
      suite.addTestSuite(unittesting.TestStringBox.class);
      return suite;
  }
}
```

You can see that a TestSuite object is created in the suite method of this class. Calls to addTestSuite on the suite object register with JUnit the test cases that we created. The end result is that all the tests in the TestFrame1 and TestStringBox classes end up being automatically called by this test suite, as shown in Figure 30-8.

NOTE: In other parts of the text, I talked about the virtues of writing simple, easy-to-use classes. JUnit is an excellent example of the right way to architect a relatively complex set of classes.

Running JUnit Tests from the Command Line

In this section, you will learn how to run test suites from the command line. Needless to say, this is the part of the chapter where those who use the Personal version of JBuilder can learn how to run JUnit tests. As I said earlier, being able to automate tests from the command line is perhaps the preferred way to use JUnit, so you really are not missing much if you do not have the built-in JBuilder tools.

NOTE: As mentioned earlier, the code in Listing 30-5 is simply standard JUnit test code of the type that all users of this open source project would use. JBuilder helps you generate the code automatically, but the generated code is just standard code for use with JUnit. You can therefore create a default JBuilder project as described at the beginning of this chapter. Insert the add and multiply methods shown at the beginning of this chapter into Frame1.java. Type in the JUnit code shown in Listings 30-2, 30-4, and 30-5, or just find the same source files on the CD. Save the JUnit code in the same directory as Frame1.java, and then use it as described in the remaining sections of the chapter.

The open source JUnit code is stored in a file called junit.jar. This JAR file ships with JBuilder in the /JBuilder7/lib directory. You can download up-to-date versions of that JAR file from www.junit.org. The code found on junit.org is open source, so it is a free download with few strings attached.

NOTE: There is a license associated with JUnit source code, but it is not unduly restrictive. The code is meant to be used freely by developers in their day-to-day work. JUnit is released under IBM's Common Public License Version 0.5. If you are brave, you can read about the license at: http://oss.software.ibm.com/developerworks/oss/licensecpl.html. Here is one excerpt from this license: "Subject to the terms of this Agreement, each Contributor hereby grants Recipient a non-exclusive, worldwide, royalty-free copyright license to reproduce, prepare derivative works of, publicly display, publicly perform, distribute and sublicense the Contribution of such Contributor, if any, and such derivative works, in source code and object code form." I have no idea what this means, but it sounds like it might be something good.

The JUnit JAR file comes with both a GUI interface to the test suites and a command-line version. The GUI interface is good when you want to run the tests interactively, and the command-line version is good if you want to integrate the tests into your build process. The output from the GUI interface to JUnit is shown in Figure 30-10.

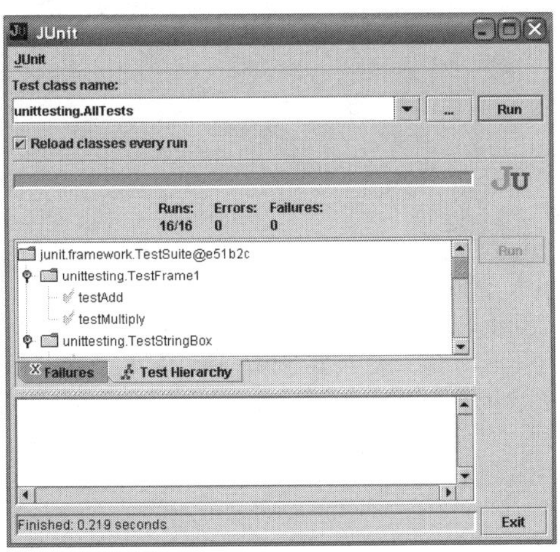

Figure 30-10: A successful run of 16 tests against the StringBox class developed earlier in this book, as well as the Frame1 class created earlier in this chapter

A sensible way to run the GUI tests is to ensure that codebox.jar and junit.jar are on your classpath. As you recall, codebox.jar comes on the CD for this book. You can also download it from www.elvenware.com. Change to the root directory for the UnitTesting project, which we have developed in this chapter. Now issue this command:

```
java -cp .;%CLASSPATH%;classes junit.swingui.TestRunner unittesting.AllTests
```

Though perhaps less sensible, the following code shows a bit more explicitly what is going on in the previous call:

```
java -cp .;g:/utils/classes/codebox.jar;g:/jb7/lib/junit.jar;classes \
      junit.swingui.TestRunner unittesting.AllTests
```

The variable %CLASSPATH% resolves at run time to the contents of your current classpath. My classpath is more complicated (or is it cluttered?) than the second example suggests, but I have pared it down so that you can see the important parts of the call.

Running Tests in Text Mode

If you want to run the tests in text mode, you can issue the following command:

```
java -cp .;%CLASSPATH%;classes junit.textui.TestRunner unittesting.AllTests
```

This command is nearly identical to the one for launching the GUI version of JUnit. In this case, however, you call junit.textui.TestRunner rather than junit.swingui.TestRunner. For those who want to work with older Java code, there is junit.awtui.TestRunner.

Here is a run of the text-based version of JUnit:

```
[g:\srcjava\jbbook\debug\unittesting]runTextTests.bat
java -cp .;g:/utils/classes/jaxp.jar;g:/utils/classes/codebox.jar;g:/jb7/lib/dx.
jar;g:/jb7/lib/dbswing.jar;g:/jb7/lib/jbcl.jar;g:/jb7/lib/junit.jar;g:/utils/cla
sses/mm.mysql-2.0.11-bin.jar;g:/Compilers/interbase/InterClient/interclient.jar;
classes junit.textui.TestRunner unittesting.AllTests
...GetFirstWord: OneWord
.GetFirstWord:
.GetFirstWord: Two
.GetFirstWord: A
...Data
Call: 01
Call: 001
IntToStrPad0: 001
.Data
......
Time: 0.5

OK (16 tests)
```

On the first line, you can see the call to the batch file where I store the command shown at the beginning of this section. The next chunk of code simply echoes the command back at us. In particular, you see the whole classpath, followed by the call junit.textui.TestRunner. Finally, you see the name of the class that holds the tests we want to run: unittesting.AllTests.

The references to GetFirstWord and IntToStrPad0, etc., are the output from various calls to System.out.println that I have scattered in my code. The next to last line with text on it shows how long the run of JUnit took, and the final line shows that all 16 tests passed.

JUnit and Ant

A synergy has developed between an open source project called Ant and the JUnit project. The Apache Jakarta Ant project is a Java version of the make utility. Ant is much easier to use than make, and at least for Java development, it is much more powerful. In particular, it is easy to extend the functionality found in Ant.

Ant allows you to automate the process of building your applications. The synergy between Ant and JUnit stems from the fact that you can use Ant to automatically run the test scripts that you build with JUnit. In particular, you can make your daily build process include a run through JUnit test suites.

The developers at Borland recognize that both Ant and JUnit have made significant contributions to the development process. As a result, both tools are integrated into the JBuilder 7 IDE.

The JBuilder Ant and JUnit tools are mostly enterprise level development tools. However, you can and should use these tools with all editions of JBuilder. In particular, there are open source projects for integrating Ant into even the Personal edition of JBuilder. The name of one tool for integrating Ant into JBuilder is AntRunner. You can find it at: http://antrunner.sourceforge.net/.

Once you have Ant integrated into JBuilder, you can also integrate JUnit into your development process via Ant scripts. Or, if you want, go to codecentral.borland.com and retrieve the unit testing tool. It should be available for download at: http://codecentral.borland.com/codecentral/ccweb.exe/listing?id=17168.

For a more in-depth exploration of Ant and JUnit, please see the useful book titled *Java Tools for Extreme Programming* by Hightower and Lesiecki (John Wiley & Sons). Its emphasis on J2EE development is unfortunate, but it is nevertheless well written and contains plenty of useful information.

Summary

In this chapter you have had a brief look at unit testing with the tool called JUnit. You have seen that this tool is well integrated into the JBuilder IDE. However, you can just as easily use JUnit from the command prompt.

Particularly if you are using the SE or Personal version of JBuilder, you should visit www.junit.org. That site has many tips on using JUnit. Included on the site are tools that will help you automatically generate test cases using tools similar to those included with the Enterprise version of JBuilder. You will also find some unique tools that can help you test the GUI portions of your applications.

Chapter 31

Refactoring and UML

Margie Calvert

In Java, renaming a class or package involves a fairly complex process called *refactoring*. Refactoring refers to the act of changing the name or location of the elements of your program in all of the places in your program where they are referenced.

Refactoring solves a number of related problems that you may already have experienced. It is most commonly used to move files or rename classes and packages. Even the act of renaming a single method or variable is part of refactoring. Often, a programmer generates many experimental tries at solving a problem. Occasionally one of these tries works out. At this point, the project may need a new name. The act of renaming a project is also part of refactoring.

In this chapter, we will first refactor using the UML Browser, which is an enterprise level tool. In the SE version, you can refactor just as readily without the use of the UML browser. We will also examine other JBuilder refactoring tools. Later in the chapter we will discuss how to refactor in the Personal version of the product using a powerful open source tool called JRefactory. This tool also provides UML support and pretty printing. The ability to rename a class or package while viewing UML diagrams is also part of JRefactory.

Please don't be intimidated by the presence of UML drawings or the sound of a fancy word like refactoring. This is an easy subject to understand. All you are doing is using some fancy-sounding tools to rename a class or a package. Don't get me wrong: These tools perform a very useful function, and they must have been quite difficult to write. However, using them is not difficult.

Refactoring Packages

The term "refactoring" sounds complicated. Yet, refactoring a package involves nothing more than renaming it.

Suppose you created a default project with a name like untitled27. You start experimenting with the project and suddenly realize that you have come up with something interesting that you want to keep. But you don't want to stick with the default package name of untitled27. Instead, you want to call it myfancycode. The problem you face is that there may be numerous references throughout your project to the term untitled27. The refactoring tools allow you to easily rename all the references in your project that refer to untitled27. The process involves not only changing your code, but actually moving the files on disk from the directory called untitled27 to your new directory called myfancycode.

Refactoring is a chore that must be performed at some point in virtually every computer language. However, Java's heavy dependence on packages makes this an especially important task that needs to be performed frequently.

The extreme programming school of development places a heavy emphasis on refactoring. As described in the previous chapter, extreme programming adherents believe that your code should be in an almost constant state of change, always evolving toward a more perfect state. Unit testing is part of the process, but another big part of the process is refactoring.

Whether you subscribe to the tenets of extreme programming or not, you will still likely encounter many occasions when you need to rename a package, a class, or some variable in your program. The JBuilder refactoring tools come to the rescue in such cases.

Getting Ready to Refactor

Our first step will be to create a default program. First, close any open projects in JBuilder. Then choose **File | New** and click on **Application** on the General page of the Object Gallery. This will open the Project Wizard. In Step 1 of the Project Wizard, name the project **myTrialProject** and click **Finish.** This will open up the Application Wizard. Leave the default settings and click **Finish.**

In the following sections, I'm going to show you how to rename packages in the Enterprise and SE editions of JBuilder. Both processes are very similar. The Enterprise version allows you to view your project in UML while you are refactoring. This is a very useful luxury but hardly a necessity.

Renaming a package, or a class for that matter, is a two-phase process. You first choose the element you want to rename, and then you actually rename it. The first step can be done two ways in the Enterprise product but only one way in the SE product. Users of the Enterprise edition can use either technique, while users of the SE edition must use the second technique.

Renaming in the Enterprise Edition

If you are using the Enterprise version of JBuilder, click on the **UML** file tab at the bottom of the content pane to view the UML Browser. From here you can get an overview of the major features of your project.

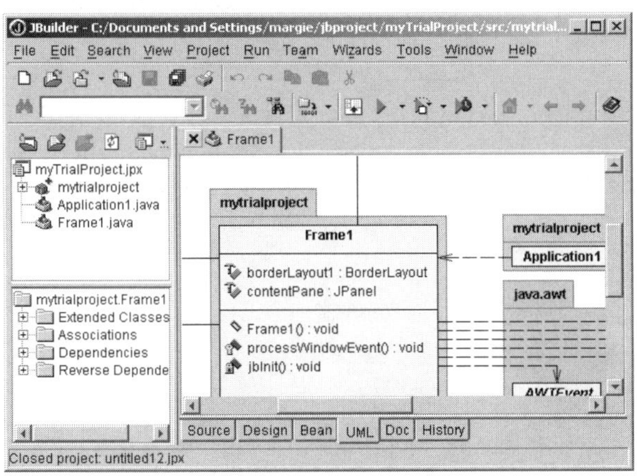

Figure 31-1: The UML Browser lets you see the relationships between the classes in your project.

In the UML Browser, right-click on the word **mytrialproject** where it appears above the UML diagram of Frame1. A context menu will appear. Choose **Rename...** by clicking on it.

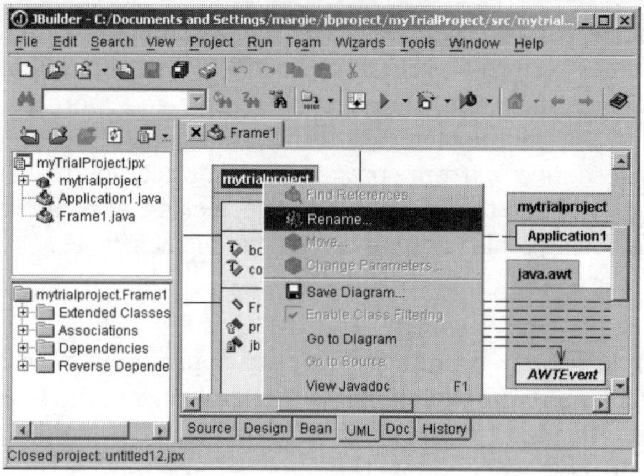

Figure 31-2: Choosing Rename... from the context menu

The next section describes a second way to start renaming a package. Since this second technique also works in the Enterprise edition, users of that product should continue reading.

NOTE: Tools similar to the ones described here are also available in JRefactory.

Renaming in the SE Edition

If you are using the SE version of JBuilder, you do not have the UML Browser. However, you can still rename your packages using the same technology found in the Enterprise version. Instead of opening the UML Browser, simply open the editor. Move to the top of Frame1 and locate the package statement:

```
package mytrialproject;
```

Right-click on the word **mytrialproject**. A pop-up menu similar to the one shown in Figure 31-2 will appear. Choose **Rename Package mytrialproject** from the menu.

Refactoring Continued

From here to the end of this section, the text applies to both the Enterprise and SE editions.

After you have clicked on **Rename...** you will see a dialog that allows you to rename the package. In the text field provided, change the name of the project to **myfinalproject** and click **OK**.

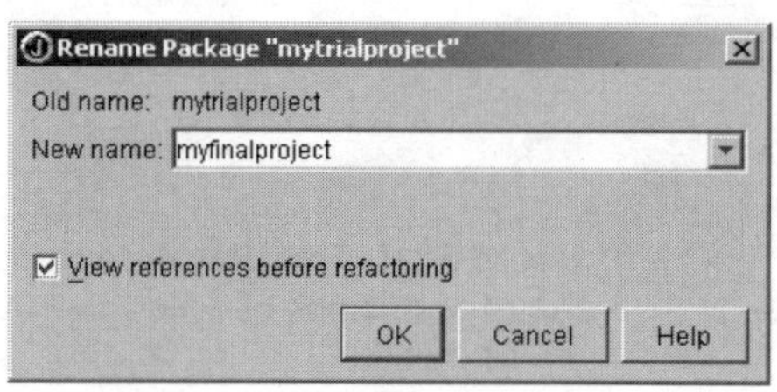

Figure 31-3: Renaming the package

At this time, the package has not yet been renamed. You will see a message in the message pane stating that the package is being renamed. Below the message pane you will see the Refactor button ( ). Once you click on this button, JBuilder will rename the package.

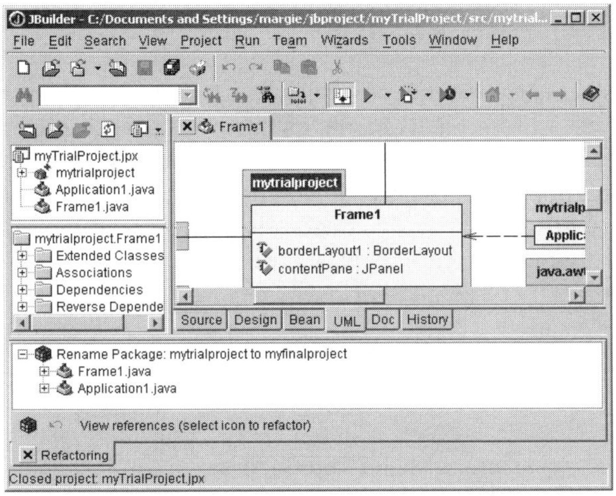

Figure 31-4: The message pane with the Refactor button below it on the Refactoring tab

At this time, if you go to the directory myTrialProject where your file was, you will see that the src directory for the project now contains a folder called myfinalproject. The source for the project is now inside of that folder. You may also see a folder called mytrialproject. That folder is now empty and can be deleted. The UML Browser now shows the package name as myfinalproject.

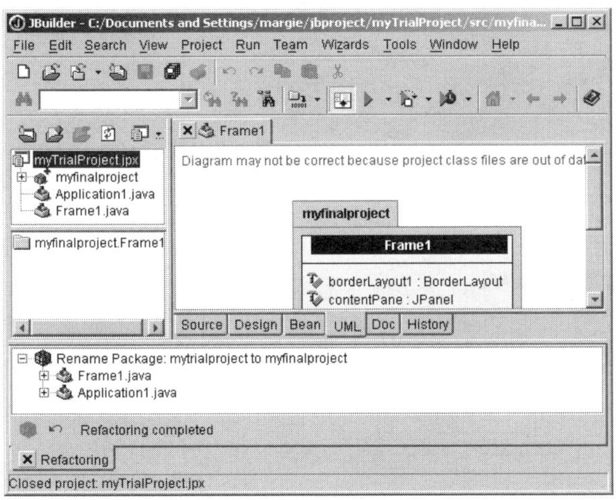

Figure 31-5: The project after refactoring

NOTE: If you are working in the Windows environment and wish to change a name from something like MyFinalProject to myFinalProject, you will need to use another name temporarily to perform the swap. Windows does not always properly recognize capitalization differences for file names and package names.

You have now successfully performed a refactoring operation. You may find, however, that your project does not run correctly after the refactoring. This is due to the fact that the main class for your project specified in the Run page of the Project Properties dialog is no longer correct. I will explain how to fix this problem in the section called "Using the Package Browser to Set Your Main Class."

Renaming Classes, Methods, and Fields

The process of renaming a class is nearly identical to the process of renaming a package. The only difference is that you right-click on the class name instead of on the package name in order to access the menu with the Rename option on it. The same applies to variables or methods inside a class. The point, of course, is that you will not be renaming only this one reference to a class, variable, or method. Instead, you will rename the identifier you are working with and all references to that identifier throughout your project.

I will discuss renaming classes in more detail later in the chapter. In particular, see the section called "The Wrong Way to Rename a Class."

Renaming the .jpx File

Refactoring is a technology aimed at renaming the elements found in the Java source code you are creating. The JBuilder JPX file is not part of your project proper. Rather, it is simply a utility used by JBuilder to aid with the management of your project. As a result, you do not use the refactoring tools to rename a JPX file. You can still, however, easily rename a JPX file from inside the JBuilder IDE.

You can rename myTrialProject.jpx to myFinalProject.jpx in the project pane. To do this, right-click on **myTrialProject.jpx** and choose **Rename** from the context menu, as shown in Figure 31-6.

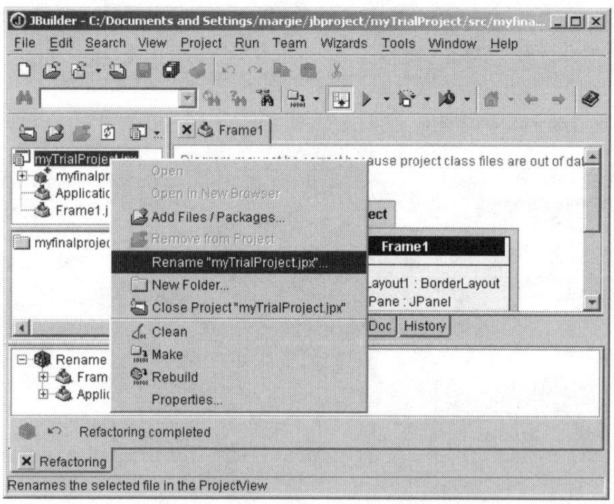

Figure 31-6: Renaming the .jpx file in the project pane

This is all you have to do. The JPX file is very self contained and should include only relative paths to the elements of your project. As a result, the simple act of renaming the JPX file as described here should be sufficient to meet your needs.

Renaming the Root Directory for Your Project

Sometimes you will want to rename the root directory for your project. For instance, if you created a project in a directory called untitled27 and wanted to keep the project, you would want to change the name of not only the packages in the project and the JPX file for the project, but also the root directory for the project itself. To perform this last step, you will have to exit from the project and then rename the directory to **MyFinalProject**. Now reopen JBuilder, browse for your JPX file, and resume work.

Undoing a Refactoring

If you have not made any changes in the source, you can undo a refactoring by clicking on the Undo button ( ).

Using the Package Browser to Set Your Main Class

If you were to run your project after renaming the main class of your project or after renaming the package that holds the main class of your project, you would receive a java.lang.NoClassDefFoundError: mytrialproject Application1 message in the message pane. JBuilder would at this time still be looking for Application1.java in the old, now empty, directory ..\myTrialProject\src\mytrialproject. To fix this, choose **Project | Project Properties** and choose the **Run** page.

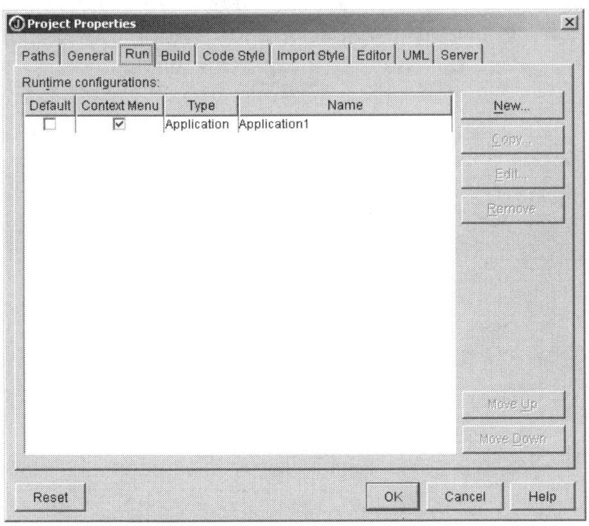

Figure 31-7: The Run page of the Project Properties dialog

Everything looks as if it is in order, but the path to Application1 is aimed at the old directory. Choose the **Edit** or the **New...** button. This will bring you to the Runtime Properties dialog shown in Figure 31-8.

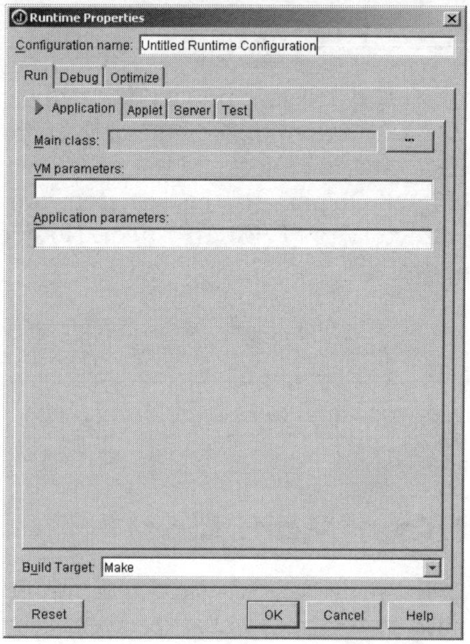

Figure 31-8: The Runtime Properties dialog

The problem is that the main class for your project, shown at the top of the dialog in Figure 31-8, is either empty or not properly set. Use the ellipsis button to browse for the main class. Once you click on the ellipsis button, you will see the Package Browser dialog box. Both mytrialproject and myfinalproject will be listed. Choose **myfinalproject** and open it by clicking on the plus sign to the left of it. Choose **Application1**, shown in Figure 31-9. Click **OK** to exit the Package Browser and **OK** to exit the Runtime Properties dialog.

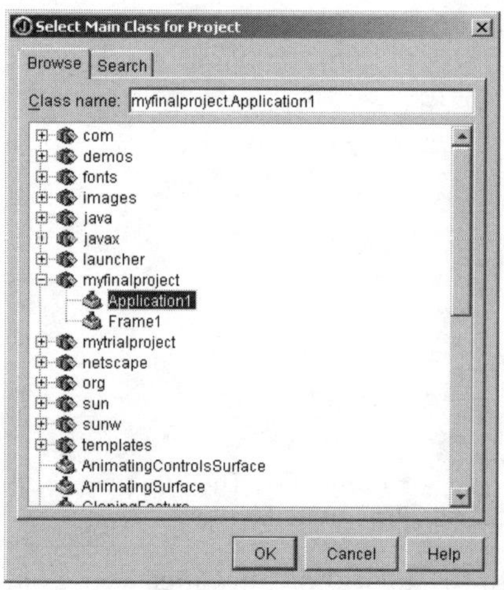

Figure 31-9: Choosing myfinalproject | Application1 in the Class Browser

If you choose New rather than Edit, you will now see a new entry in the Project Properties dialog box. If necessary, mark the check box to select the configuration that points to the default location for the correct main class.

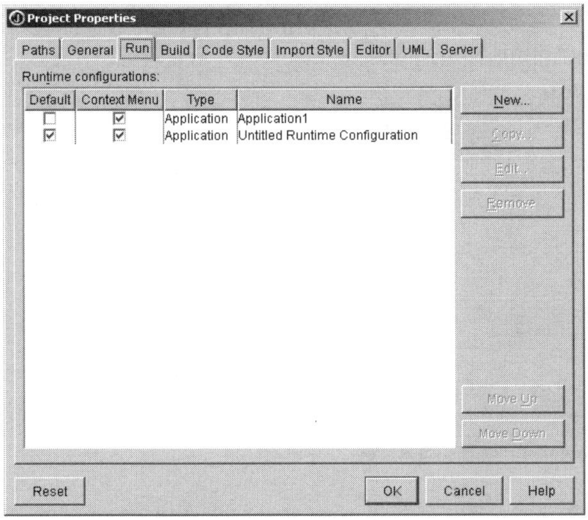

Figure 31-10: The Project Properties dialog as it looks after you have added a second run-time configuration

Click **OK** to accept the changes, and run the application. You should not see any error messages this time.

The Need to Rebuild

After performing a refactoring operation, you may have trouble running your project. In the previous section you saw how trouble with the settings for your main class can get in your way. But even after you fix that problem, you may still have trouble compiling. The solution is frequently as simple as choosing Rebuild rather than Make from the Project menu.

In extreme cases, you can choose Project | Project Properties and bring up the dialog shown in Figure 31-8. At the bottom of the dialog you will see options to set the build target. If you drop down this list, you will see, at a minimum, options to clean, make, or rebuild your project. Choose **Clean**. Close the dialog and press the green run button. This should result in completely deleting your classes directory. In short, it provides a means of getting a complete restart on the act of building your project. Now go back to the Runtime Properties dialog and set the target back to **Make**. Try running your project and see if it doesn't build correctly this time.

The Wrong Way to Rename a Class

At this point, let's suppose that you have decided that you want to change the name of your main class from Application1.java to something a little more descriptive, such as the title of the project. You would be tempted to go to the project pane, right-click, and choose Rename Application1.java... from the context menu. If you did this and then ran your project, you would get the following message in the message pane:

```
"MyFinalProject.java": Error #: 475 : class Application1 is public; must be declared in a file
named Application1.java at line 15, column 8
```

If you change the name of the file to MyFinalProject.java by right-clicking and using the context menu in the project pane, the file tab and the project pane will reflect the change. However, internally the file will still have the same code as it did before. Figure 31-11 displays this rather mixed-up state of affairs. Obviously, your project will not work correctly if you leave it in this state, so if you have renamed Application1 in the project pane, reverse the operation by renaming it back to Application1.java.

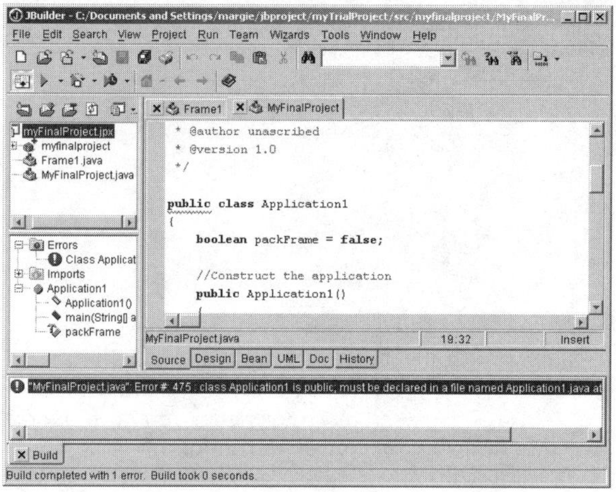

Figure 31-11: The wrong way: The source code is still referencing Application1.

The Right Way to Rename a Class

Move to the source view and make sure that Application1.java is showing in the editor. In the editor, right-click on the first reference to Application1 in the source code:

```
public class Application1
```

A context menu will appear that includes the option Rename Application1… preceded by the refactoring symbol.

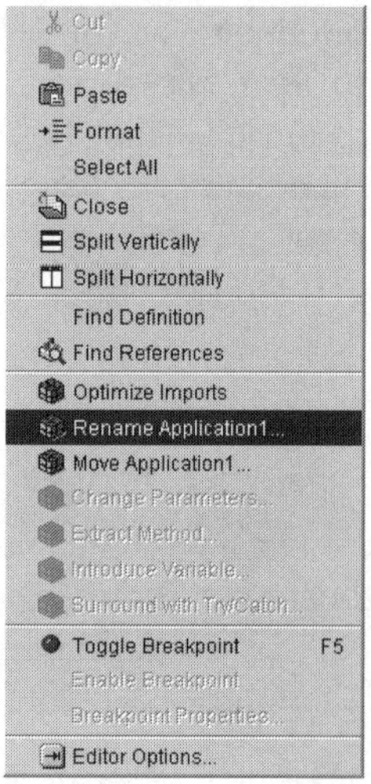

Figure 31-12: The context menu shows the refactoring symbol and a rename option.

If you click on Rename Application1… you will see a dialog that prompts you to rename the application. When you enter the new name, do not include the .java suffix. Click **OK** to start the refactoring process.

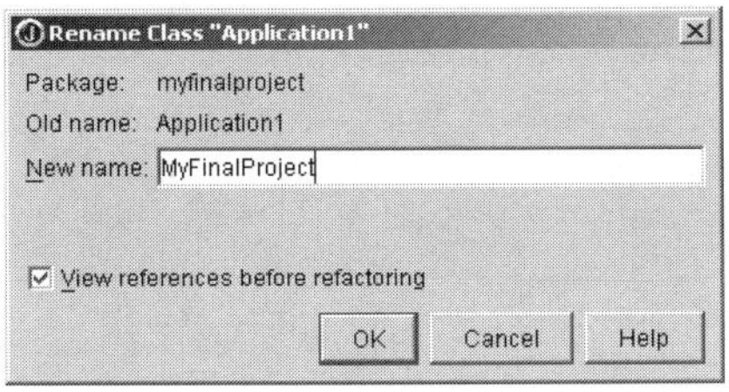

Figure 31-13: The Rename Class dialog

NOTE: The Rename Class dialog is a feature of both JBuilder Enterprise and JBuilder SE. If you have the Enterprise version of the product, you can also reach this dialog from the UML Browser.

Once you have clicked OK, the Refactor button will appear below your message pane. Left-click on it to rename the class. Once you have done that, JBuilder will change all the references to Application1 in the code to MyFinalProject.

If you save and run the project at this point, you will see a dialog box stating "Could not find the main Class. Program will exit!" You have already stepped through the process of redirecting JBuilder toward the appropriate main class, and you will need to repeat those steps. Choose **Project | Project Properties**, choose the **New...** button, and browse in the Package Browser for your newly titled main class, MyFinalProject. Choose that as the default configuration, and then run the project. It should compile beautifully. If you have any problems with these steps, review the directions earlier in the chapter for setting a main class through the Package Browser.

Refactoring Using JBuilder Personal

Except for the UML Browser, all of the tools that we used to do refactoring in the Enterprise version also work in the SE version. You could rename the package manually, but it isn't much fun. In JBuilder Personal, none of the refactoring tools of JBuilder are installed. Fortunately, there is an open source tool, called JRefactory, which is available at http://sourceforge.net/projects/jrefactory.

The instructions for installing it are found at http://jrefactory.sourceforge.net/csr-jbuilder.html. I will go through those instructions in this section. However, this is a JBuilder OpenTool, so if you are familiar with installing OpenTools, you should have no trouble with this process.

Your first task is to download the program from the Internet. At the time of publication, it was accessible by clicking on Download, right-clicking on the .zip file for the latest version, and choosing **Save Target As....** You will be able to choose if you want the binary version or the full version of the program. The full version includes the source code for the product.

Once you have the download, you will need to extract the files using a standard utility such as WinZip. The file that you will need to add to JBuilder is called jrefactory.jar. You can probably extract it directly to the appropriate location in JBuilder, as described in the next paragraph.

Use your directory browsing system to go to the directory where you stored JBuilder on your machine. Inside the JBuilder directory, you need to find the lib directory. Inside of the lib directory is the ext directory. Place the jrefactory.jar file in the ext directory. JAR files with OpenTool extensions that are placed in the ext directory will automatically load when JBuilder starts up.

Now start your copy of JBuilder. You will see the following:

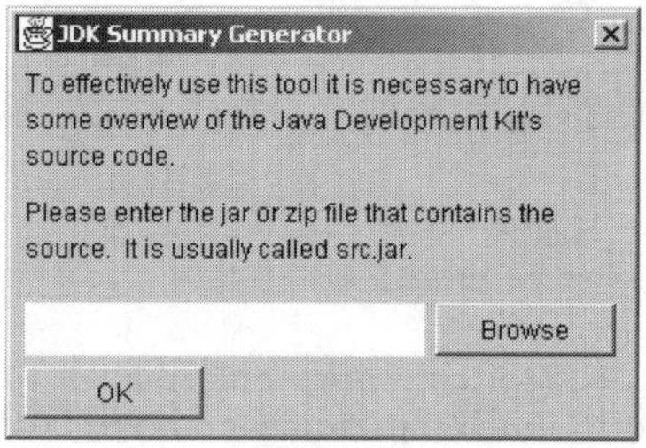

Figure 31-14: This dialog will pop up when you load JBuilder.

Use the Browse button to locate the file in JBuilder where the JDK is stored. This file is located in the JBuilder7/jdk1.3.1 directory. On my system the path to the file looks like this: G:\jb7\jdk1.3.1\src.jar. After you have browsed to the appropriate place, click **OK**.

Once JBuilder has booted up, you will see JRefactory on the menu bar. Go ahead and create a default project and default application. (If you are unclear on how to do this, check the section earlier in this chapter or look at Chapter 3.) Name your project **MyFirstProject**.

Click on **JRefactory**, and you will see the menu items shown in Figure 31-15.

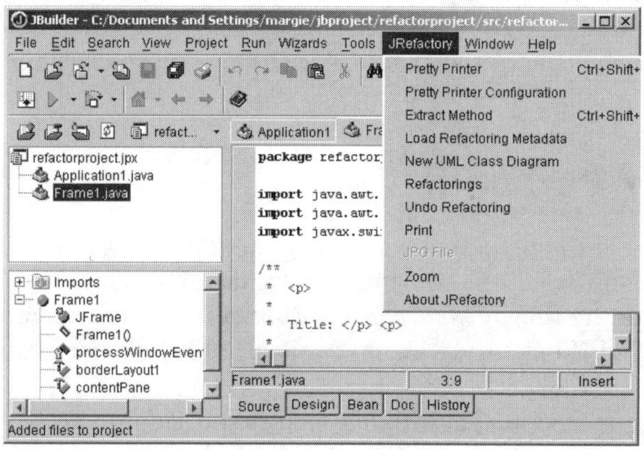

Figure 31-15: JRefactory has been added to the JBuilder menu.

Changing a Package Name Using JRefactory

When using JRefactory, you can do all your work inside of JBuilder except for actually renaming the root folder that contains the project. This limitation is also part of the tools built into JBuilder. We might as well get past that, so save all your files, close the project in JBuilder, and then browse to the directory that contains your project. Change the name of the directory to **MySecondProject**.

NOTE: If your project has been compiled, there will be a classes folder in your project directory. Delete this folder, as it may contain some references that will no longer be accurate.

Now open the project again by browsing to the MySecondProject directory and opening the .jpx file. The .jpx file will still read MyFirstProject.jpx.

Before renaming anything using JRefactory, you should first compile your project. It is probably safest to also run it first, just to make sure everything is working properly.

In the project pane, right-click on **myFirstProject.jpx** and rename it **mySecondProject.jpx**. This tool is built into JBuilder and is not part of JRefactory.

At last it is time to do some refactoring. Double-click on **Application1.java** in the project pane to select it, and then choose **JRefactory | Refactorings | Type Refactorings | Move Class**. In the Move class to new package dialog, type in the name of your new package, **mysecondproject**, and press **OK**.

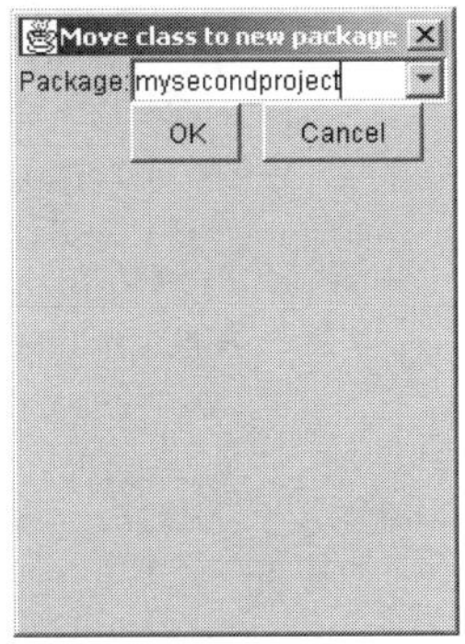

Figure 31-16: The Move class to new package dialog

Once you have clicked on OK, you will be prompted to save the project. Choose **OK**.

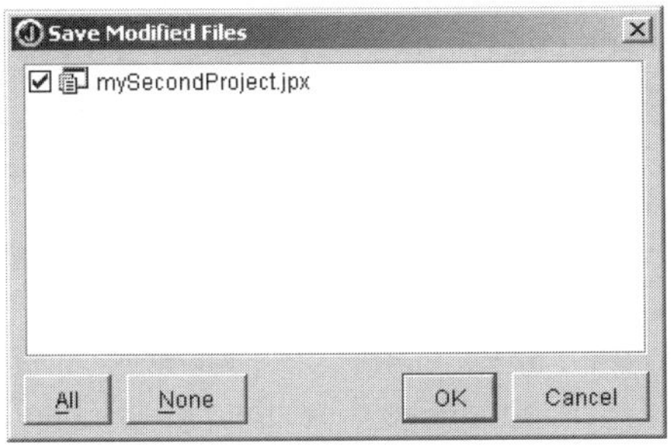

Figure 31-17: The Save Modified Files dialog

At this time, you should right-click on **Application1.java** in the project pane and choose **Remove from Project**. In doing this, you are simply removing any references in your JPX file to the old location of Application1.java. JRefactory will have copied it and moved it to another directory, and so your JPX file is out of date. You will notice, however, the presence of a new icon for your new package in the project pane. If you open that icon, you will see Application1.java inside the mysecondproject package.

Go through the same steps with Frame1.java, first moving the file with the JRefactory tool and then removing the old reference that is still showing in the project pane.

The next step is to add the new files you have generated to your project. You don't have to do this, but it may be convenient to do so. Click on the **Add Files** icon on the toolbar above the project pane and browse to **MySecondProject\Src\mysecondproject** to find and add first Application1.java and then Frame1.java. At this point, you will have renamed the package, and your program will run.

Changing a Class Name Using JRefactory

Changing a class name is easy. Because Frame1 is referenced in Application1, it makes a good test case. First, double-click on **Frame1.java** in the project pane. This should open it up in the editor. Choose **JRefactory | Refactorings | Type Refactorings | Rename Class**. The Rename class dialog is shown in Figure 31-18. Use it to type in the new class name, which in this case is **MyFrame**.

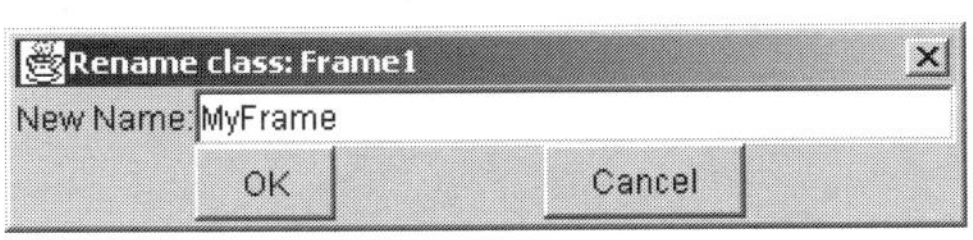

Figure 31-18: The Rename class dialog

A dialog will pop up prompting you to save your modified files (see Figure 31-17). Click **OK**.

Once you have clicked OK, Frame1.java source code will no longer be visible in the editor. If you double-click on Frame1.java in the project pane, the file should be blank. (Sometimes there is a little buffer latency, but the file should in fact really be moved.) Right-click on **Frame1.java** and remove it from your project. Just above the project pane is an icon showing a folder with a green plus sign. Double-click on this icon and browse to the folder where your project is. Inside of that folder, you may need to move down the directory tree to src\mysecondproject and open the source files for your project. There you will see MyFrame.java. Click on it to select it, and click **OK.** In the JBuilder editor, look at MyFrame.java and Application1.java, and you will see that the refactoring is completed.

JRefactory will also create UML diagrams, as well as performing many other refactoring operations. The full capabilities of this product are outside the scope of this book but would be worth exploring.

NOTE: Because you actually delete the old file and add the new file, you will not have to step through the process of aiming JBuilder at a new main class if you choose to change the name of Application1.java. This process was described in depth in the section called "Using the Package Browser to Set Your Main Class." Needless to say, I would not have included that section in the chapter were the failure to reset the class name not also a limitation of the tools built into JBuilder. Some of the tools inside of JBuilder are in fact a bit more powerful than JRefactory, but the differences are not large.

I have really only touched on the capabilities found in JRefactory. For instance, it can also be used to rename classes and packages while in UML mode, as described at the beginning of this chapter. The UML features in JRefactory, shown in Figure 31-19, are not quite as complete or powerful as those in JBuilder Enterprise, but they are nonetheless useful.

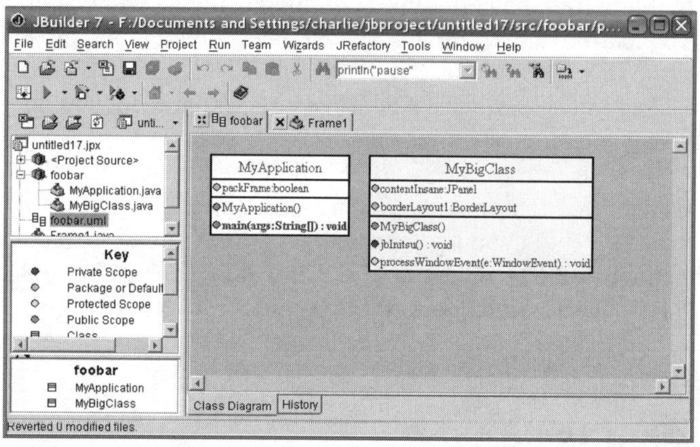

Figure 31-19: Like the Enterprise version of JBuilder, JRefactory can be used to view UML and rename the elements of your program while in UML mode.

Summary

In this chapter you have learned to use JBuilder to refactor code. You have stepped through some of the basic operations of refactoring and have learned to use the JBuilder tools that are available to you. You have explored some of the possibilities of using an open source plug-in as well and have learned to download and install that program. There is more discussion of OpenTools in the following chapter.

Chapter 32

Introduction to the OpenTools API

Charlie Calvert

The OpenTools API allows you to make changes to the behavior of JBuilder itself. By creating an OpenTool, you are, in effect, becoming a member of the JBuilder development team. The product no longer does only what Borland wants it to do, but it also has new features that you have created yourself.

As you will learn in this chapter, adding an OpenTool to the IDE is very simple. All you need to do is place a single JAR file in the right directory. In most cases, the correct directory is /jb7/lib/ext.

Furthermore, there is a widespread network of developers who are creating OpenTool extensions to the IDE. As a result, there is an ever-growing set of OpenTools that can be called upon to add features to the JBuilder IDE. Many of these OpenTools are free.

In earlier chapters of this book, I have stressed how JBuilder, by default, encourages you to write absolutely standard Java code that compiles unchanged from the command line with the Java JDK. This chapter shows an entirely different side of the product. Not only is JBuilder not forcing you to work with black boxes in your code, but you can actually change, on the programmatic level, the way that JBuilder behaves.

What You Can Do with the OpenTools API

Perhaps an example will help you understand the significance of the OpenTools API. One of the first components that I saw that excited my interest in the OpenTools API (OTA) is called the GetSetCreator. This OpenTool allows you to automatically create getters and setters for a particular variable. For instance, consider the following simple class:

```
public class SampleClass
{
  int Foo;

  public SampleClass()
  {
  }
}
```

After installing the GetSetCreator, you can place your cursor over the identifier Foo, press Alt+G, and see automatic insertion of the getters and setters. The result is a near instantaneous transformation of SampleClass into code that looks like this:

```
package untitled4;
```

```
public class SampleClass extends Object
{
  int Foo;

  public SampleClass()
  {

  }

  public int getFoo()
  {
    return this.Foo;
  }

  public void setFoo(int foo)
  {
    this.Foo = foo;
  }
}
```

Needless to say, this is a very useful tool and a significant extension to the IDE. For more information on this OpenTool, see Ron Hodgin's source on CodeCentral: http://codecentral.borland.com/codecentral/ccweb.exe/author?authorid=63550.

Creating a Simple OpenTools Project

It is now time to learn how to go about creating your own OpenTool. The basic syntax for creating an OpenTool is very straightforward. However, there are a few concepts you must learn before you begin adding the features that you want to the JBuilder IDE. This chapter shows you the basic steps you must master to add code to JBuilder.

Implementing a Simple Command Line-Based OpenTool

To help you get started, I will show you how to create a fairly simple OpenTool. This tool will run from the command line when you start JBuilder. In particular, if you invoke a special parameter that you define, JBuilder will not start up the Borland IDE but will instead print a stanza of verse, as shown in Listing 32-1.

Listing 32-1: See the output from our OpenTool by invoking it with the -MyOpenTool parameter.

```
[e:\jb7\bin]JBuilder.exe -MyOpenTool

JBuilder 7 Enterprise
Licensed to Charlie Calvert, Elvenware
Copyright (c) 1996-2001 Borland Software Corporation.  All rights reserved.

She walks in beauty, like the night
Of cloudless climes and starry skies,
And all that's best of dark and bright
Meets in her aspect and her eyes;
Thus mellow'd to that tender light
Which Heaven to gaudy day denies.
```

The developers of JBuilder can be forgiven for not realizing that some people might want to use the product as a means of printing out dog-eared and long-yellowed verses written by Lord Byron. Nevertheless, we can thank them for making it possible for us to add such a feature, if we desire it, through the good graces of the OpenTools API.

Working with the Command Interface

To create the command line-based, Lord Byron inspired OpenTool, the first thing you need to do is implement an instance of the com.borland.primetime.Command interface:

```
package com.borland.primetime;

// Imports
import java.io.PrintStream;

public interface Command
{
  // Methods
  void printCommandHelp(PrintStream parm1);
  String getCommandDescription();
  void invokeCommand(String[] parm1);
  boolean takesCommandArguments();
}
```

This interface is the key to getting a command line-based OpenTool integrated into JBuilder. You will not usually use these methods in most GUI-based OpenTools. In fact, you will find the syntax for creating GUI-based OpenTools even easier than the syntax for creating command-line OpenTools. However, there are other complications involved in making GUI-based tools that led me to decide that it would be simplest to start with a command line example.

The methods in the Command interface are designed primarily to help you perform simple tasks common to command line-based tools. For instance, they allow you to print help strings and a short description of your OpenTool. The next few paragraphs will show you each of these command-line options.

The method invokeCommand actually runs your OpenTool. Once your project is compiled, you invoke the command by passing JBuilder the parameter MyOpenTool, as shown in Listing 32-1:

```
JBuilder.exe -MyOpenTool
```

The command MyOpenTool is configurable and must be defined by the developer. I will show you how to define this word later in the chapter in the section called "Registering Your OpenTool."

As shown in Listing 32-2, getCommandDescription is called when you pass JBuilder the -help parameter:

```
JBuilder.exe -help
```

Listing 32-2: See the output from getCommandDescription by invoking our OpenTool with the -help parameter and examining the first of the "Available command line options."

```
e:\jb7\bin\JBuilder.exe -help

JBuilder 7 Enterprise
Licensed to Charlie Calvert, Elvenware
```

```
Copyright (c) 1996-2001 Borland Software Corporation.  All rights reserved.

Available command line options:

  -MyOpenTool: Say some lines from Lord Byron.
  -build: Build JBuilder projects
  -hello: Displays a greeting
  -help: Display help on command line options
  -info: Display configuration information
  -license: Displays the license manager
  -nosplash: Disable splash screen
  -treefont: Sets the font size used in trees in the IDE
  -verbose: Display OpenTools loading diagnostics
```

printCommandHelp shows the help for our new JBuilder tool, as shown in Listing 32-3:

```
JBuilder.exe -help MyOpenTool
```

Listing 32-3: See the output from printCommandHelp by invoking our OpenTool from the command line with the -help MyOpenTool parameter.

```
e:\jb7\bin\JBuilder.exe -help MyOpenTool.

JBuilder 7 Enterprise
Licensed to Charlie Calvert, Elvenware
Copyright (c) 1996-2001 Borland Software Corporation.  All rights reserved.

-MyOpenTool Hear from Lord Byron.
```

The fourth method in the Command interface is a Boolean value designating whether or not your OpenTool takes parameters. This result of this function will be set to false in all the examples shown in this chapter.

As you have seen, there are four methods in the Command interface. You will find that each of these methods is extremely simple to implement. Furthermore, the methods are well named. As a result, I believe that they need little explanation beyond what I have provided here. You will find a complete implementation for the interface in Listing 32-4. A description of how to create the code is found later in this chapter.

Listing 32-4: A simple implementation of the Command interface

```
import com.borland.primetime.*;
import java.io.PrintStream;

public class NewCommand implements Command {
/**

  Boolean function specifying whether this takes arguments */
  public boolean takesCommandArguments()
  {
    return false;
  }

  /** The implementation of the open tool */
  public void invokeCommand(String[] args)
  {
```

```
      String S =
      "She walks in beauty, like the night\n" +
      "Of cloudless climes and starry skies,\n" +
      "And all that's best of dark and bright\n" +
      "Meets in her aspect and her eyes;\n" +
      "Thus mellow'd to that tender light\n" +
      "Which Heaven to gaudy day denies.\n";
      System.out.println(S);
    System.exit(0);
  }

  /** Invoked by type JBuilder - help */ public
  String getCommandDescription() {
  return
    "Say some lines from Lord Byron."; }
  /**

  Invoked by type JBuilder -help MyOpenTool */
  public void printCommandHelp(PrintStream printStream)
  {
    printStream.println("Hear from Lord Byron.");
  }
}
```

Listing 32-4 shows the nearly complete source code for the OpenTool. To make it part of the IDE, you need only write one additional two-line method that registers your code, which is explained in the next section.

Registering Your OpenTool

Now that you have created the class for your OpenTools project, the next step is to create code that will register it with JBuilder. Place your new class in the current package and have the class itself extend the default Object class.

You will need to add a single method to this class called initOpenTool. This method creates an instance of the class that defines your OpenTool and then passes that class to a static method called PrimeTime.registerCommand.

NOTE: PrimeTime was the code name for the first all-Java version of JBuilder. The name has been memorialized inside the JBuilder project object hierarchy.

As shown in Listing 32-5, registerCommand takes two parameters. The first parameter is the name that you want to give your command. This name will be the word you pass to JBuilder when you want to invoke your command from the command line. The second parameter is the class that defines your OpenTool. Note that your class is a descendant of class Command, and that is why the method we are calling is named register Command.

Listing 32-5: The class RunOpenTool contains a method called initOpenTool, which is required for the creation of this type of command line-based OpenTool.

```
package myopentools;

/**
 * Title:        My Open Tools
```

```
 * Description:  Basic Open Tools Framework
 * Copyright:    Copyright (c) 2001
 * Company:      Elvenware
 * @author Charlie Calvert
 * @version 1.0
 */

import com.borland.primetime.*;

public class RunOpenTool
{
  /** All OpenTools addins must implement a method called initOpenTool. */
  public static void initOpenTool( byte majorVersion, byte minorVersion )
  {
    // Create an instance of the class that implements the open tool
    MyOpenTool command = new MyOpenTool();
      //  Register the open tool with JBuilder itself.
    PrimeTime.registerCommand("MyOpenTool", command);
  }
}
```

The name you give the class in the first parameter of registerCommand can be defined according to your personal whims. However, you do need to remember this name, as it will play a role in the creation of the JAR file that contains your OpenTool. Furthermore, it is the name used to invoke the OpenTool from the command line.

Notice that in your entire OpenTool project there is no main method, no applet code — nothing but two simple classes. The application to which these classes belong is JBuilder itself. What you are doing is simply writing an extension to JBuilder. All of JBuilder is written in Java, and all you are doing is adding your own Java code to the product. You are becoming a de facto member of the JBuilder development team. (I would, however, recommend exercising some restraint when it comes time to write out your next resume.)

At this stage you know all you need to know about writing the core code for a simple OpenTools application that runs from the command line. Let's now take a look at OpenTool development inside the JBuilder IDE.

Using the JBuilder IDE to Create an OpenTool

I have shown you the code for creating an OpenTool, but I have not really outlined the steps necessary to make the OpenTool inside of JBuilder. Many of these steps should be fairly obvious to you by this stage in the book, but nevertheless, I want to detail them, as they differ from the steps taken when creating an applet or application.

1. Choose **File | New** from the menu and create a new project named **MyOpenTools**. Accept all the other defaults on the first page of the wizard.
2. On the second page of the Project Wizard, choose **Required Libraries | Add.** A dialog will appear. In the dialog, choose **JBuilder | Open Tools SDK**, and click the **OK** button. Open Tools SDK should now be listed under the Required Libraries section. You are now through with the Project Wizard, so you can click the **Finish** button.
3. It is now time to implement the class that will be the heart of your OpenTool. Choose **File | New** from the menu and create not a new application or applet but rather a new class. Give it the name **MyOpenTool**. It should extend com.borland.primetime.Command.

You can type this class name into the Base class combo box in the JBuilder dialog or else browse through the class lists for the name. To browse for the class name, press the ellipsis button for the Base class and browse to **Com | Borland | primetime | Command**. Click the **OK** button. When you are done, the dialog should appear as it does in Figure 32-1. (The option to browse for the Command class will not be available if you did not add the Open Tools SDK to your Required Libraries, as explained in Step 2.)

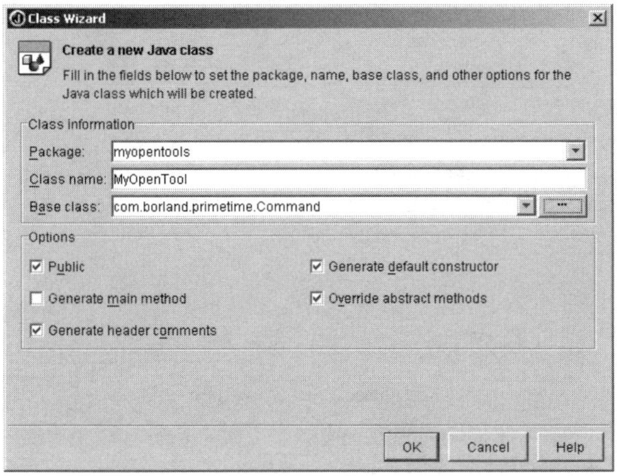

Figure 32-1: Creating the main class for an OpenTools project

4. Press the **OK** button. The code shown in Listing 32-6 should be inserted automatically into your editor.

Listing 32-6: The code for an OpenTools project as it is automatically generated for you by the JBuilder IDE

```
package myopentools;

import com.borland.primetime.Command;
import java.io.PrintStream;

/**
 * Title: MyOpenTools
 * Description: Demo
 * Copyright: Copyright (c) 2001
 * Company: Elvenware
 * @author Charlie Calvert
 * @version 1.0
 */

public class MyOpenTool implements Command {

  public MyOpenTool()
  {
  }

  public void printCommandHelp(PrintStream parm1)
  {
    /**@todo: Implement this com.borland.primetime.Command method*/
    throw new java.lang.UnsupportedOperationException(
```

```
        "Method printCommandHelp() not yet implemented.");
  }

  public String getCommandDescription()
  {
    /**@todo: Implement this com.borland.primetime.Command method*/
    throw new java.lang.UnsupportedOperationException(
      "Method getCommandDescription() not yet implemented.");
  }

  public void invokeCommand(String[] parm1)
  {
    /**@todo: Implement this com.borland.primetime.Command method*/
    throw new java.lang.UnsupportedOperationException(
      "Method invokeCommand() not yet implemented.");
  }

  public boolean takesCommandArguments()
  {
    /**@todo: Implement this com.borland.primetime.Command method*/
    throw new java.lang.UnsupportedOperationException(
      "Method takesCommandArguments() not yet implemented.");
  }
}
```

Once you have everything set up like this, it is relatively simple to type in your code so that it looks like Listing 32-4. Notice that absolutely everything else has been set up for you by JBuilder.

NOTE: Recall that the @todo symbols in the JBuilder-generated code show up at the top of the structure pane in the IDE. todo messages are a mainstay of my day-to-day development under the JBuilder IDE.

You will also need to add a class to your project for registering your OpenTool in an initOpenTool method. This second class was explained earlier in the section called "Registering Your OpenTool." To create this class, choose **File | New Class** from the menu. The class should be placed in your current package and implemented as shown in Listing 32-5.

Running a Simple OpenTools Project

Now that you have created all the code for your project inside the IDE, the next step is to run your finished code. It turns out that there are three different ways to do this, all of which I have found useful at one time or another:

- Use the JBuilder Archive Builder to create a JAR file, which you can then place in the jb7/lib/ext directory.
- If you do not have a version of JBuilder that includes the Archive Builder, you can create the JAR file on your own from the command line. When you are done, place your JAR file in the jb7/lib/ext directory.

- The third technique is to run the OpenTool from the raw class files in the directory in which it was created. This option is not a good choice for deployment, but it can be useful during the development of your OpenTool.

Each of the options listed here are explained in depth over the course of the next four subsections. I suggest that you read through all these sections, as there is information revealed in each section that may be helpful to you. Furthermore, I find that each technique has its pluses and minuses. As a result, I tend to use all three methods, switching back and forth depending on the exigencies of my current task. Regardless of which method you choose, be sure to read the first of the next four sections, called "The classes.opentools File." This section explains the most complicated part of creating an OpenTool. It is relevant to all three of the succeeding sections.

> **NOTE:** An archive is just a JAR file. JAR files are a method of gathering multiple files together into one file. The file can be, and usually is, compressed. A JAR file is a variant on the zip file, tar file, cab file, and other compression technologies that have blinked in and out of fashion over the years. The popular program WinZip, and many other compression utilities, will open a JAR file.

The classes.opentools File

The process of running an OpenTool is quite straightforward with one exception. The sole tricky part is the creation and deployment of the mysterious classes.opentools file. You will need to create this file regardless of which of the three methods you choose for deploying your OpenTool.

classes.opentools is a manifest file. Manifests are simple text files placed inside a JAR file for the purpose of describing the contents of the file. Usually, a manifest describes which file in a JAR file should be invoked in order to start the application stored in the JAR file. It defines the name and location of the main class file in the library.

You need to fill in the content of the manifest file by hand. Here is the single line that you type into this file:

```
OpenTools-Core: myopentools.RunOpenTool
```

Be sure to include a linefeed at the end of this line.

> **NOTE:** After entering text into classes.opentools, you may get a warning about the line "missing a terminator." This simply means that you need to hit the Enter key once at the end of the line so that it is terminated with a linefeed.

The line of code in classes.opentools specifies that the registration method for your OpenTool is in the myopentools package in a class called RunOpenTool. Please note that this line invokes the class file that registers your OpenTool and not the actual implementation of your OpenTool. In particular, it references RunOpenTool.class, not MyOpenTool.class. Of course, you do not include the ".class" part in the manifest file, just as you do not pass the ".class" part to the Java.exe command-line utility.

A few words now need to be said about the name of the classes.opentools file:

- The opentools part of the name is defined by JBuilder and must be the same in all your OpenTool projects. It is the flag that JBuilder checks to see if this is indeed an OpenTool that it has encountered.
- The classes part of the name for this file defines the directory in which your OpenTool resides. Recall that in a default installation of JBuilder, your OpenTool will reside in a directory called classes. In particular, your code resides inside the classes directory in

a package/directory called myopentools. The myopentools part of the equation, as you recall, is specified in the text of the classes.opentools file.

OpenTools and the Archive Builder

To create a JAR file for an OpenTools project with the Archive Builder, first open your OpenTools project in JBuilder. Select **Wizards | Archive Builder** from the menu. (This feature is not available in all versions of JBuilder.)

Set the Archive Type to **OpenTool**, and choose the **Next** button to turn to Step 2 of the wizard. You can accept all the defaults for this page if you want, or type in a name for your JAR file, such as **MyOpenTool**. A correctly filled out dialog is shown in Figure 32-2.

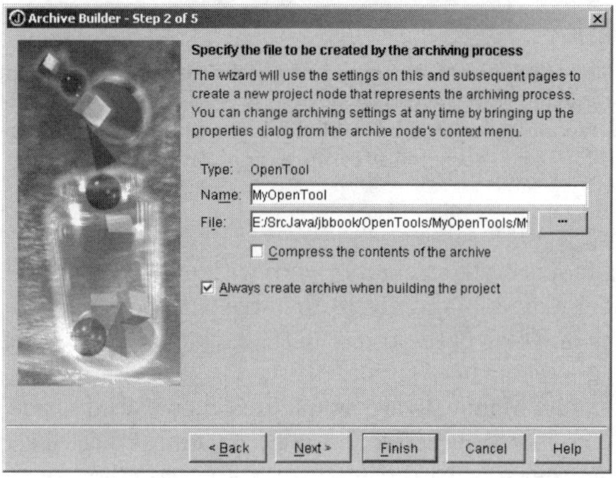

Figure 32-2: Optionally, you can specify your preferred name for your archive.

Accept the defaults for all the other pages, taking special care that Step 4 of the wizard lists **Exclude All** for the OpenTools SDK, as shown in Figure 32-3. In Step 5, check **Include a manifest in the archive** and select **Override the manifest with the specified file**, as shown in Figure 32-4. Click the **Finish** button.

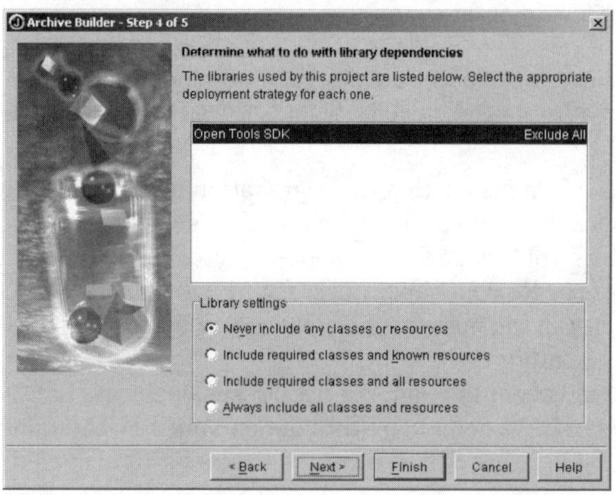

Figure 32-3: Make sure you select Never include any classes or resources.

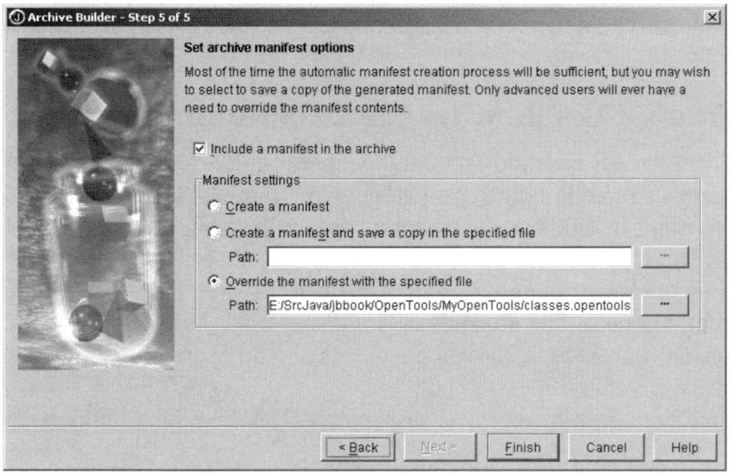

Figure 32-4: Be sure to include a manifest file and override the manifest with your own version of classes.opentools.

When you are done creating your archive, your project will automatically have a blank file in it called classes.opentools. You will need to fill this file out, as explained earlier.

Now that all of the dirty work is out of the way, you can build your project once to ensure that the JAR file was created. By default, your JAR file will be recreated each time you choose Build. Copy the JAR file to the ../jb7/lib/ext directory, or its equivalent, on your system. Go into the ../jb7/bin directory. Now start JBuilder from the command line, passing it the -help parameter. The command you type will read **JBuilder.exe –help.** You should see the output from your implementation of the getCommandDescription method, as shown in Listing 32-2. You do not need to exit your current version of JBuilder in order to run this test.

NOTE: JBuilder may be using your JAR file if it existed when the IDE was launched, and so you may need to close the IDE to avoid file usage conflicts when trying to delete or replace the JAR file. This is the cure for the "cannot access this file because it is being used by another process" message.

If you do not see your text when you invoke the JBuilder help, try running JBuilder with the verbose option turned on: **JBuilder.exe -help -verbose**. This should give you a more detailed explanation of what has gone wrong.

Other debugging techniques involve studying the several different OpenTools projects that come on the CD for this book or on the JBuilder CD itself. You can compare the work found in them to your own work. In particular, see the project called MyOpenTools included with the code for this book and make sure that everything in your project agrees with it — at least in principle!

When debugging your code, note that in the IDE you can double-click on the archive you created. When you do so, it will open up. Double-click on the JAR file itself to see the class files and the manifest in the structure pane. Examine the files to make sure they are correct. For instance, you should see two class files, MyOpenTool.class and RunOpenTool.class. They should both be in the package myopentools. The manifest should look like this:

```
Manifest-Version: 1.0
OpenTools-Core: myopentools.RunOpenTool
```

NOTE: If you feel that you got any of the settings wrong inside the Archive Builder, you can edit the choices you made by right-clicking on the Archive node in the project pane on your archive and choosing Properties from the pop-up menu.

In the next section of this chapter, you will learn about a second way to view the contents of a JAR file.

Developing an OpenTools JAR File from the Command Line

If you do not have JBuilder SE or Enterprise, the Archive Builder will not be a part of the IDE. This is not a serious impediment to project development. All you need to do is create the JAR file by hand. I find that this is a very useful way to create a JAR file, since I can automate it in a script or batch file.

First, create a copy of classes.opentools and place it in the root directory for your project. That is, place it directly beneath the src and classes directories. As you recall from reading the previous section, the contents of classes.opentools should contain this line of code, followed by a linefeed:

```
OpenTools-Core: myopentools.RunOpenTool
```

Here is the code you can type at the command prompt to create your JAR file:

```
jar -cfm MyOpenTools.jar classes.opentools -C classes myopentools
```

The first word in the command invokes jar.exe. jar.exe is located in the bin directory of Java SDK. Needless to say, this directory must be on your path or you will not be able to invoke the command. Run jar.exe with no parameters to learn about the various "tar-like" switches you can pass to this utility. For instance, the c stands for create, f designates that you are going to pass in a filename for your JAR file, and m refers to the manifest file that you want to include in the package.

When you are done, you can check the contents of your JAR file by typing:

```
jar tf MyOpenTools.jar
```

The t switch tells jar to list the contents of your archive. The output from this command should look like this:

```
META-INF/
META-INF/MANIFEST.MF
myopentools/
myopentools/MyOpenTool.class
myopentools/RunOpenTool.class
```

Now copy the JAR file to the jb7/lib/ext directory and invoke JBuilder with the -help parameter: jbuilder.exe -help. You should see a new item added to the list of help commands.

NOTE: If you get stuck at this stage, see the text at the end of the previous section, where I go into more detail about how to debug problems with JAR files.

Running an OpenTool from Its Project Directory

You do not have to run an OpenTool from inside a JAR file. In fact, it is very easy to run it from the .class files created from your source code.

To get started, simply create the classes.opentools file as described in the previous subsections of this chapter. Make sure the file is in the root directory of your project.

Now list the root directory for your project in the JBuilder.config file found in the /jb7/bin directory created when JBuilder was installed. Edit a portion of the JBuilder.config file so that it reads as follows:

```
# Add all the configuration files located in the lib/ext directory
```

```
includedir ../lib/ext
addpath E:/SrcJava/jbbook/OpenTools/OpenToolsBasic/classes
```

The comment and the includedir directive found on the first two lines are unchanged from the way they appear after a default install of JBuilder. I'm showing you these lines so you can find the correct place to make changes to JBuilder.config. The line that you add is the third one, which lists the location of the classes file for your project. You will, undoubtedly, wish to edit the line so that it conforms to the location of the file on your system.

Given the information you provided in its config file, JBuilder will locate the classes.opentools file located in the E:/SrcJava/jbbook/OpenTools/OpenToolsBasic directory and, hence, be able to load your OpenTool.

Now type **JBuilder.exe -help** at the command prompt; you should be able to see information about your OpenTool. Try also typing in **JBuilder.exe -help MyOpenTool** and **JBuilder.exe -MyOpenTool**.

This is the end of the first section of the chapter. At this point, you should know how to create a simple OpenTool, how to register it with JBuilder, and how to invoke it from the command line.

Creating a GUI Tools Project

In this section, you will learn how to add a new menu item to the IDE. The menu item will allow you to invoke a dialog that you created. Given the information you already have about creating OpenTools, you will find this to be an extremely simple operation.

The project we want to create will print out a poem by Lord Byron, as shown in Figure 32-5. Once it is installed, you will be able to access this dialog by selecting Tools | Byron from inside the JBuilder IDE.

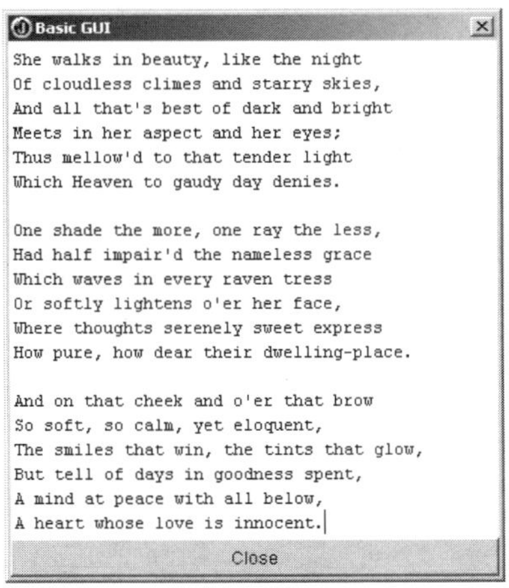

Figure 32-5: The BasicGUI OpenTool consists of a dialog displaying the text of a poem by Lord Byron.

Using the JBuilder IDE to Create an OpenTool

To set up JBuilder for creating an OpenTool, such as our BasicGUI project in the IDE, first choose **File | New** from the menu and create a new project, giving it the name **BasicGUI**. Accept all the other defaults on the first page of the wizard.

On the second page of the Project Wizard, choose **Required Libraries | Add**. A dialog will appear. In the dialog, choose **JBuilder | Open Tools SDK**. Click the **OK** button. Open

Tools SDK should now be listed under the Required Libraries section. You are now through with the Project Wizard, so you can click the **Finish** button.

It is now time to implement the class that will be the heart of your OpenTool. Choose **File | New** from the menu and create not a new application or applet, but rather a new class. Give it the name **BasicGUI**. It should extend java.lang.Object. Now create a second class called **BasicGUIDialog.** It should extend the class JDialog.

The Code for the GUI OpenTool

The BasicGUI application is divided into two sections, shown in Listings 32-7 and 32-8. The code in Listing 32-7 shows how to integrate your OpenTool into the IDE. The code in Listing 32-8 is nothing more than a simple JDialog that uses a JTextPane to display a few stanzas of immortal poetry. Since dialogs and text panes are not the topic of this chapter, I am going to say little more about Listing 32-8 other than to assert that it is perfectly ordinary code of the type that could appear in any project, whether it is an OpenTool or not. If you desire more information about dialogs, you might want to look at Chapter 19.

NOTE: When debugging the dialog part of your application, it might be simplest to call it from a standard Java application that you build for testing purposes. Once you have the dialog working correctly, then you can link it into your OpenTools project. This can help you get around some of the problems you might encounter when debugging an OpenTools project.

As you have learned, the important code in the BasicGUI application is found in Listing 32-7. I'll give you a moment to peruse that code, then we can resume what will prove to be a very simple and brief discussion of its key features.

Listing 32-7: This is the main module for the BasicGUI Tools project.

```
package basicgui;

/**
 * Title:        Open Tools Basic GUI App
 * Description:  Simple Open Tools project running in the GUI
 * Copyright:    Copyright (c) 2001
 * Company:      Elvenware
 * @author Charlie Calvert
 * @version 1.0
 */

import com.borland.jbuilder.JBuilderMenu;
import com.borland.primetime.ide.Browser;
import com.borland.primetime.ide.BrowserIcons;
import com.borland.primetime.ide.BrowserAction;
import com.borland.primetime.PrimeTime;
import java.awt.Rectangle;
import java.awt.Dimension;
import java.awt.Toolkit;

public class BasicGUITool
{
```

```
  public BasicGUITool()
  {

  }

  /**
   *
   * Add a menu item to the Tools menu in the IDE
   *
   * @param   majorVersion  The major version number of OpenTools
   * @param   minorVersion  The minor version number of OpenTools
   */
  public static void initOpenTool(byte majorVersion, byte minorVersion)
  {
    if (majorVersion == PrimeTime.CURRENT_MAJOR_VERSION)
    {
      MyBrowserAction ba =
          new MyBrowserAction("Byron", 'B', "Lord Byron poem");
      JBuilderMenu.GROUP_Tools.add(ba);
    }
  }
}

class MyBrowserAction extends BrowserAction
{
  public MyBrowserAction(String p0, char p1, String p2)
  {
    super(p0, p1, p2);
  }

  public void actionPerformed(Browser browser)
  {
      // Create the modal dialog box and center it on the screen
    BasicGUIDialog dialog =
        new BasicGUIDialog(browser, "Basic GUI", true);
    Rectangle screenBounds =
        new Rectangle(Toolkit.getDefaultToolkit().getScreenSize());
    dialog.setSize(350, 400);
    Dimension dialogSize = dialog.getSize();
    dialog.setLocation(
      screenBounds.x + (screenBounds.width - dialogSize.width) / 2,
      screenBounds.y + (screenBounds.height - dialogSize.height) / 2);

    dialog.setVisible(true);
  }
}
```

Listing 32-8: This is the dialog for the BasicGUI Tools project.

```
package basicgui;

import java.awt.*;
```

```
import javax.swing.*;

/**
 * Title:        Open Tools Basic GUI App
 * Description:
 * Copyright:    Copyright (c) 2001
 * Company:      Elvenware
 * @author Charlie Calvert
 * @version 1.0
 */

public class BasicGUIDialog extends JDialog
{
  JPanel panel1 = new JPanel();
  BorderLayout borderLayout1 = new BorderLayout();
  JTextPane jTextPane1 = new JTextPane();
  JButton jButton1 = new JButton();

  public BasicGUIDialog(Frame frame, String title, boolean modal)
  {
    super(frame, title, modal);
    try
    {
      jbInit();
      pack();
    }
    catch(Exception ex)
    {
      ex.printStackTrace();
    }
  }

  public BasicGUIDialog()
  {
    this(null, "", false);
  }

  void jbInit() throws Exception
  {
    String S =
      "She walks in beauty, like the night\n" +
      "Of cloudless climes and starry skies,\n" +
      "And all that\'s best of dark and bright\n" +
      "Meets in her aspect and her eyes;\n" +
      "Thus mellow\'d to that tender light\n" +
      "Which Heaven to gaudy day denies.\n\n" +

      "One shade the more, one ray the less,\n" +
      "Had half impair\'d the nameless grace\n" +
      "Which waves in every raven tress\n" +
```

```
        "Or softly lightens o\'er her face,\n" +
        "Where thoughts serenely sweet express\n" +
        "How pure, how dear their dwelling-place.\n\n" +

        "And on that cheek and o\'er that brow\n" +
        "So soft, so calm, yet eloquent,\n" +
        "The smiles that win, the tints that glow,\n" +
        "But tell of days in goodness spent,\n" +
        "A mind at peace with all below,\n" +
        "A heart whose love is innocent.";

      panel1.setLayout(borderLayout1);
      jTextPane1.setText(S);
      jButton1.setText("jButton1");
      getContentPane().add(panel1);
      panel1.add(jTextPane1,  BorderLayout.CENTER);
      panel1.add(jButton1, BorderLayout.SOUTH);
    }
  }
```

The core method employed in creating an OpenTool is called initOpenTool. Here is what it looks like in Listing 32-7 of the BasicGUI project:

```
    public static void initOpenTool(byte majorVersion, byte minorVersion)
    {
      if (majorVersion == PrimeTime.CURRENT_MAJOR_VERSION)
      {
        MyBrowserAction ba =
            new MyBrowserAction("Byron", 'B', "Lord Byron poem");
        JBuilderMenu.GROUP_Tools.add(ba);
      }
    }
```

This code begins by checking that our current version of JBuilder is the same as that used to compile the OpenTool. If it is, the code creates a user-defined object called MyBrowserAction. This object contains an event handler that will be used to create an instance of our dialog. When the user selects a menu item in the IDE, the event handler will be called and an instance of the dialog will be instantiated for the user's personal delectation.

The program uses the predefined JBuilderMenu object to add our OpenTool to the menu. The line of code referencing this object takes care of a registration process for you. All you have to do is add your OpenTool to the JBuilder menu, and the rest of the integration process will be taken care of for you "automagically."

MyBrowserAction is a descendant of a Borland class called BrowserAction, which is in turn an implementation of the AbstractAction class that is part of the Java SDK. AbstractAction implementations are meant to make it easy for users to instantiate valid ActionListeners. In other words, the AbstractAction interface defines a way to implement most of the hard parts of the action listener for us, leaving us the simple task of creating an ActionPerformed handler, as shown in Listing 32-7. The actual code for the implementation of AbstractAction is hidden from us, since it is part of the proprietary sections of the JBuilder IDE. More information on ActionListeners is found in Chapter 14. Notice that the constructor for MyBrowserAction takes three parameters:

```
MyBrowserAction ba =
        new MyBrowserAction("Byron", 'B', "Lord Byron poem");
```

The first is the text that will appear in the menu, the second is the hot key for that text, and the third parameter appears in the JBuilder status bar as a hint. The hint only appears if the user moves the mouse over the new menu item.

Once you have typed in the code for your implementation of the BasicGUI object, you should compile it. Wrap your compiled code and a classes.opentools manifest in a JAR file, as described previously. Now copy the JAR file to your /jb7/lib/ext directory, and restart JBuilder. The new menu item should appear under the Tools menu.

That is all there is to creating a GUI extension to the JBuilder IDE. As I mentioned before, you will find that this process is a bit simpler than adding a command line extension to JBuilder. However, there is a bit more handwaving going on in the GUI example, and it contains more actual lines of code than the command line example.

Summary

At this point, you should know how to create a simple OpenTool, how to register it with JBuilder, and how to invoke it from the command line or the IDE.

Part VII

JavaBeans

Chapter 33

JavaBean Basics

Charlie Calvert

JBuilder SE and Enterprise provide a number of timesaving tools to help you create JavaBeans. Even with these tools, the act of creating a bean is still complex enough to offer some interesting challenges.

NOTE: If you are using the Personal Edition of JBuilder, please see the section called "Beans and the Personal Edition."

There is a classic distinction between people who create visual components and people who use visual components. In languages such as Delphi, C++, or Visual Basic, the act of creating a good component is often sufficiently complex that it can safely be said that component creation is not for everyone. The same is not really true in Java, where the creation of a bean is relatively trivial.

NOTE: In the Java world, there is at least a theoretical difference between the word "component" and the word "bean," but for now, I am using the words interchangeably. Almost any reusable object is a component, but a bean has certain specific traits that define it. All of these matters will be discussed in more depth later in this chapter.

A bean is both easy to use and easy to understand. More specifically, a bean is easier to understand, easier to use, and easier to maintain than a standard Java object. In particular, a bean usually provides a well-tested and easy-to-use visual interface, while a Java object is just raw source code. Beans are particularly easy to use in JBuilder, where the Borland visual tools can help you visualize and edit the significant features of a bean with just a few clicks of the mouse.

Hopefully I've whetted your appetite for this interesting and rewarding subject. It's now time to dig into the JavaBean technology itself.

Overview

The key to JavaBean development in JBuilder is a feature called BeansExpress. BeansExpress provides support for JavaBean designers in four different ways:

- It helps you create properties and property editors. You will find that most of the component properties and their related getters and setters can be generated for you automatically by JBuilder. BeansExpress can help you visualize and maintain the properties supported by your component, and it can also help you quickly generate the properties themselves.
- BeansExpress helps you create BeanInfo files. BeanInfo files allow a visual tool such as JBuilder to query a bean and provide users with a visual interface to the bean. In particular, a BeanInfo file helps JBuilder expose properties in the Inspector. (You can

find out about a bean using traditional Java introspection, but a BeanInfo file can help fine-tune the interface a bean presents to the world.)

- BeansExpress also helps you create events and event handlers.
- BeansExpress helps you test your bean via BeansInsight.

In the next few pages I will spend a little time examining each of these aspects of JBuilder BeansExpress. I will also spend a little bit of time discussing the JavaBeans specification from a technical perspective.

What is BeansExpress?

I tend to think of BeansExpress as consisting of the following features:

- The JavaBean Wizard you access by selecting File | New | JavaBean from the JBuilder menu.
- The BeanInsight dialog found on the Tools menu.
- The tabs you access via the file view tab labeled Bean, which appears at the bottom of the editor, as shown in Figure 33-1. In particular, note the tabs labeled General, Properties, BeanInfo, Events, and Property Editors. The tools found on these tabs are the heart of BeansExpress.

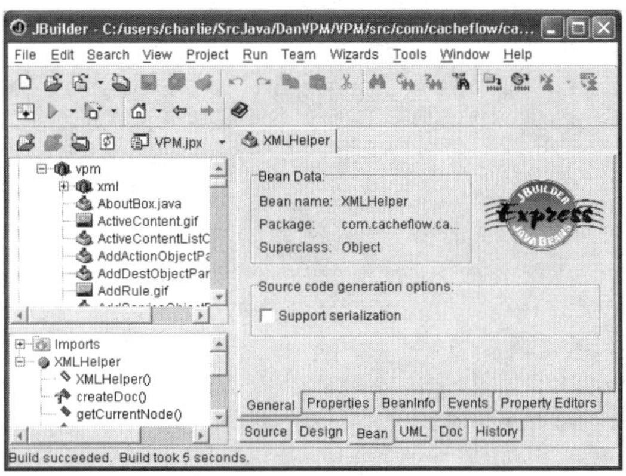

Figure 33-1: Access the heart of BeansExpress from the file view tabs at the bottom of the editor.

Beans and the Personal Edition

BeansExpress and the JavaBean Wizard are both missing from the Personal edition of JBuilder. For most developers, these will probably be two of the most significant omissions from the Personal edition.

If you are using the Personal edition, all is not lost. None of the code in this chapter is tied to a particular edition of the product. Only the utilities that help you automatically generate the code are missing.

Since I show you all the code that the JavaBean Wizard produces, there is no reason why you can't simply type in the code that you find in this chapter. And the programs you find on the CD should also run fine in your edition of the product.

When using a bean, you want to be able to do one of two things with it:

- Use the Bean Chooser dialog to select a bean from your current project so you can use the bean in your program.
- Place a custom-made bean stored in a JAR file on your component palette so you can select it as you would any other component.

These two features allow you to significantly enhance the power of JBuilder. Fortunately, both tasks can be performed in the Personal edition. You will read about the first task in this chapter and the second in Chapter 37.

Defining Our Terms

Sun usually calls an individual JavaBeans component a bean, while it refers to the entire concept as the JavaBeans architecture. I will not be quite so formal. You will find me calling an individual component either a bean or a JavaBean.

The JavaBeans component architecture was first created in February 1997 as part of the Java JDK 1.1. A bean is little more than a glorified standard Java class or a collection of classes. Beans are usually stored inside of JAR files.

The key requirements for making a normal class a bean are as follows:

- It must be declared public.
- It must have a default constructor. A default constructor is a constructor that takes no parameters. This is necessary because JBuilder (and similar tools) need to create the bean on the fly. They would not know what parameters to pass to the constructor of the object if such parameters existed. As a result, beans need to have a simple constructor that does not require parameters.

Given this definition, the following class would qualify as a bean:

```
public class MyBean
{
      public MyBean()
      {
      }
}
```

A component architecture can't get much simpler than that!

The following are common features of most beans:

- A bean usually has properties and events associated with it. The properties are simple access methods that let you get at a bean's data. Events are the mechanism a bean uses to notify another object that some change has occurred.
- A bean should also have an accompanying BeanInfo file. BeanInfo files, which provide support for what Sun calls introspection, will be discussed later in this chapter and in more depth in Chapter 35.

As you can see, there is really very little difference between a standard Java class and a bean. The simplicity of the JavaBeans specification stands in stark contrast to the relative complexity of Delphi components and the mind-boggling complexity of ActiveX controls.

Beans are easy to create and easy to understand. Like many programmers, I like what is simple and straightforward and distrust complexity. There is elegance in the simple design of the JavaBeans architecture that wins my admiration and respect.

NOTE: The one part of the JavaBeans specification that is perhaps a bit more complex than necessary is the event mechanism. The Java event specification is powerful and flexible, but it is also verbose and at times somewhat convoluted. Be that as it may, all Java programmers must eventually spend a few hours really focusing their attention on Java events before fully understanding them. Fortunately, the complexity of the specification is ultimately relatively manageable, and JBuilder does a lot to help smooth over the rough spots. Once you have the hang of them, Java events are a simple enough tool to use, one that can be easily employed to enhance your beans. See Chapter 14 for more information about events.

Given these facts about the JavaBeans specification, it is likely that many of the classes you have already created would qualify as valid beans. This is in fact the case. Many classes could be treated as beans if you so desired. The only further additions you might want to add to them would be a default constructor and a BeanInfo file. This latter feature will be discussed later in this chapter.

Creating a Simple Bean

Let's create a simple bean so that we will have something concrete to refer to during this discussion. Begin by creating a new project, and start a new application inside the project. You can accept the default names for the project and the application.

Choose **File | New | JavaBean** from the JBuilder menu. A dialog will appear that looks and behaves very much like the New Class dialog. You can see this dialog, called the JavaBean Wizard, in Figure 33-2.

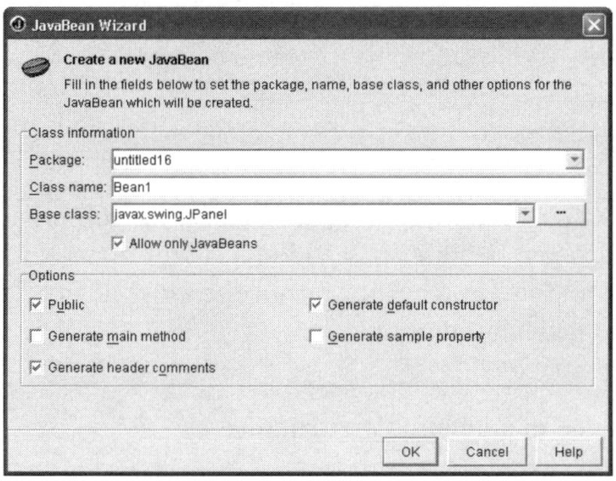

Figure 33-2: The JavaBean Wizard is very similar both in appearance and in functionality to the New Class Wizard.

Inside the JavaBean Wizard, you need to select the package, class name, and base class for your bean. For now, you can just go with the default package and class names. Make sure the base class is set to **JPanel**. If necessary, click the ellipsis button at the right of the Base Class field and browse for javax.swing.JPanel. Select **Public**, **Generate header comments**, and **Generate default constructor** in the Options area. There is no need for a main method, and there is no need for a sample property, as we will soon be creating our own.

NOTE: In most cases there is little difference between choosing JPanel or JComponent as the ancestor of a visual JavaBean. I am starting you out using JPanel, as you are already familiar with that component. However, a JComponent is lighter weight and is probably a better choice in production applications.

After you click the OK button, your bean will be generated automatically. The resulting code should look something like what you see in Listing 33-1.

Listing 33-1: A sample bean created with the JavaBean Wizard

```
package untitled7;

import java.awt.*;
import javax.swing.JPanel;
```

```
public class Bean1 extends JPanel
{
  BorderLayout borderLayout1 = new BorderLayout();

  public Bean1()
  {
    try
    {
      jbInit();
    }
    catch(Exception ex)
    {
      ex.printStackTrace();
    }
  }

  private void jbInit() throws Exception
  {
    this.setLayout(borderLayout1);
  }
}
```

As you can see, this bean looks very much like an ordinary Java class. In fact, it is nothing more than the most ordinary of Java classes. JBuilder has added a layout manager for you, but this is just a courtesy and has nothing to do with whether or not the class is a real bean or not. One important feature is that the class is declared public:

```
public class Bean1 extends JPanel
```

The other crucial feature is the existence of a default constructor:

```
  public Bean1()
  {
    try
    {
      jbInit();
    }
    catch(Exception ex)
    {
      ex.printStackTrace();
    }
  }
```

Testing Your Bean with BeanInsight

JBuilder SE and Enterprise provide a tool called BeanInsight that can examine your bean and report on its status. To use BeanInsight, first select your bean in the JBuilder content pane (aka the editor). Select **Tools | BeanInsight** from the menu. JBuilder will launch a dialog, shown in Figure 33-3, that has two buttons near the top. The top field, labeled **Select a bean to examine**, allows you to choose the source file you want to test. Since we started this operation by focusing our bean in the content pane, there is no need to use this button. Instead, select the second button, **Examine Bean**. The text shown in Figure 33-3, in the BeanInsight results section, appears after you select this button.

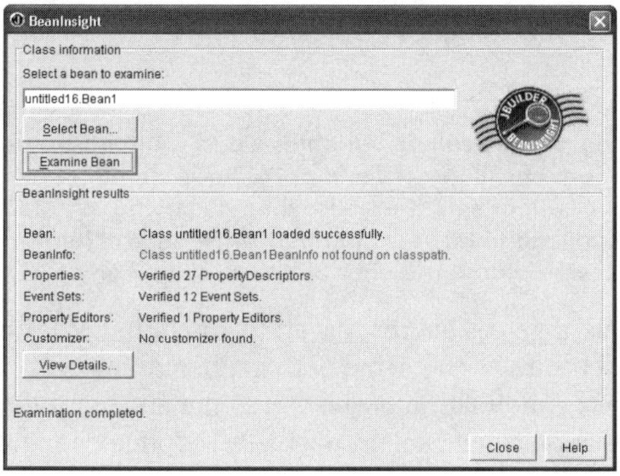

Figure 33-3: Examining your bean in the BeanInsight tool

As you can see, the BeanInsight tool likes everything about our bean, except the fact that it has no BeanInfo file associated with it. We will add that feature after discussing a few more preliminary issues.

NOTE: You may get an error from BeanInsight saying "class X not found on classpath." This usually means you haven't properly compiled your bean. To fix this problem, choose Project | Rebuild Project from the JBuilder menu. (A make will probably work just as well as a build.) After your bean is compiled, the BeanInsight tool should begin giving you more useful information. If this does not solve the problem, you probably have a classpath problem. Fix this by moving your bean into a package that you know is part of your project or by choosing Project | Project Properties and adding a new library to your project. Issues of this kind were discussed in some depth in Part V: Project Management.

Notice the View Details button at the bottom of Figure 33-3. Selecting this button brings up several tabbed pages describing the details of how your bean is constructed. In particular, the pages are named Bean, BeanInfo, Properties, Event Sets, Property Editors, Customizer, and Attributes. During the discussion of BeanInfo files, I will take you through these pages in more detail.

Adding a Property to Your Bean

At this stage you have a perfectly respectable bean that doesn't do anything very interesting. Needless to say, you add features to your bean by associating methods and data with it.

Properties in Java don't have the same syntax as properties in a product such as Delphi. To define a Java property, all you do is define an access method. An access method is just a getter and/or setter for the variable you have declared. For instance:

```
private int xPos;

public int getXPos()
{
    return xPos;
}

public void setXPos(int value)
{
    xPos = value;
}
```

Here the data is an integer called xPos. To convert this data into a property, you give it getter and setter methods.

NOTE: I have produced bugs in my programs by calling variables x and y. Incredible as it might seem, Sun declares methods of JComponent called getX and getY. Since all methods in Java are virtual, the JDK can end up calling your getX or setX methods when it is trying to determine the boundaries of your component. This can lead to all kinds of nasty drawing problems. As a result, I strongly suggest that you do not ever name a data member of a Java class x or y.

The important thing to note here is that a getter begins, naturally enough, with the word get followed by the property name. A setter follows the same pattern, beginning with the word set followed by the property name. This combination of the words get and set followed by a property name is the way Java defines something as a property. In Delphi, programmers use the keyword property. In Java, you don't use a keyword; instead you create a syntactic pattern.

NOTE: To complicate matters just a bit, the getter for a Boolean value begins not with the word get, but the word is. For instance, if you had a variable declared as Boolean bigOne, its getter and setter would be isBigOne and setBigOne. This may or may not be a good thing, but it certainly forces us to stay on our toes.

It seems a bit painful to have to write all this code just to create a property. Fortunately, JBuilder can create most of the code for you automatically. To understand how this works, let's try two different scenarios.

First, go into the content pane in source mode and add a variable at the top of your class. For instance, write **private int yPos;** just above the constructor for your class. Now click on **Bean | Properties** in the pages at the bottom of the content pane. In the Properties page, you should now see your variable in a grid, as shown in Figure 33-4.

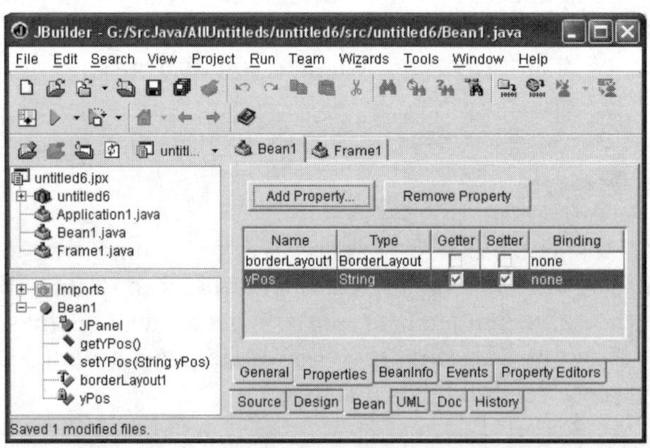

Figure 33-4: A property displayed in BeansExpress

In Figure 33-4, you can see that I have checked the Getter and Setter columns for variable y. Doing so automatically generated the following code:

```
public int getYPos()
{
      return yPos;
}

public void setYPos(int yPos)
{
```

```
            this.yPos = yPos;
        }
```

This is very simple code that you could easily have written yourself. However, the act of writing the code is tedious, and it is nice to let JBuilder automate the task. It is particularly helpful if you are working with several variables at one time. With just a few clicks of the mouse, you can generate or erase 20 or 30 lines of code, which is definitely a big time saver.

Go back to JBuilder and stay on the same pane shown in Figure 33-4. This time choose the **Add Property** button. A dialog called New Property will appear, as shown in Figure 33-5. Type in a new property name, such as **myString**.

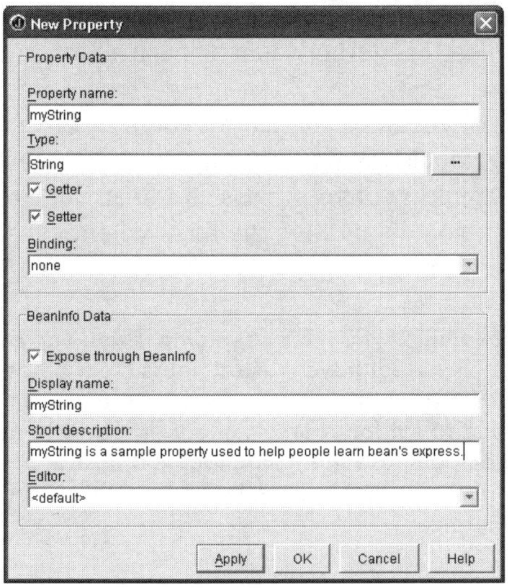

Figure 33-5: Creating a property in JBuilder

As you can see, I have given my property a name, defined its type, and asked JBuilder to implement a getter and setter. I also provided a display name and short description for my property.

After you click OK in the New Property dialog, go back to the editor. You will find the following code has been added to your program:

```
private String myString;

        public void setMyString(String myString)
        {
            this.myString = myString;
        }

        public String getMyString()
        {
            return myString;
        }
```

If you now want to rename your property, go back to the Properties page shown in Figure 33-4. Click the left-hand column where the name of your property appears. Type in a new name, such as **yourString**. Now go back to your source, and you will see that all the appropriate changes have been made to your code:

```
private String yourString;

      public void setYourString(String yourString)
      {
            this.yourString = yourString;
      }

      public String getYourString()
      {
            return yourString;
      }
```

You can remove a property and its getter and setter methods just as easily. Simply choose the Remove Property button in BeansExpress.

The tools I'm showing you here are quite powerful. If you have a complex object with many variables, you can use BeansExpress to quickly and easily rename many of its key properties. These tools work even if you are not thinking of your class as a bean but as just another component in your program. In short, you should use the tools whenever you want to add properties to a class or rename properties in a class.

NOTE: The key point here is remembering that JBuilder has this capability. There can be little doubt that thousands of JBuilder users (myself included) have wasted hours creating and/or renaming properties and their getters and setters the hard way. If you have a powerful tool like JBuilder on your side, one of the tasks you need to set for yourself is learning how to use its advanced features — and then remember to actually use them. JBuilder is a best of breed tool. There is no other Java editor and compiler of its caliber. However, its real worth is dependent on each developer's ability to utilize its intricacies.

BeanInfo Files

Simply defining a property is enough to make the property show up in the JBuilder Inspector. However, you can gain more control over the properties for your bean if you also add a BeanInfo file.

A BeanInfo file is a standard defined by Sun that allows you to explicitly surface and highlight features of your bean. The Java introspection technologies (i.e., its RTTI) will allow you to find out much about the structure and contents of a class. But a BeanInfo file gives you more control over the interface for your class. In particular it allows you to:

- Expose or hide the properties and other features of your bean.
- Associate an icon with your bean.
- Provide custom display names and descriptions for the properties and other features of your bean. Specifically, you can use BeanInfo to associate a help string with a property of your bean.
- Create categories for the features of your bean, such as Enterprise vs. Standard properties, expert vs. intermediate level properties, etc.

It is simple to create a BeanInfo file in JBuilder. First, select your bean in the project pane, as seen in Figure 33-6. Choose **Bean** from the file view tabs at the bottom of the content pane, and turn to the **BeanInfo** page. Choose to expose the properties of your bean by selecting the check boxes in the Expose column. Select the **Generate BeanInfo** button. This will create a new file, called something like Bean1BeanInfo.java. The actual filename will be the name of your bean followed by the words BeanInfo.java: xxxBeanInfo.java. The name of a generated BeanInfo file is visible in the project pane shown in Figure 33-6.

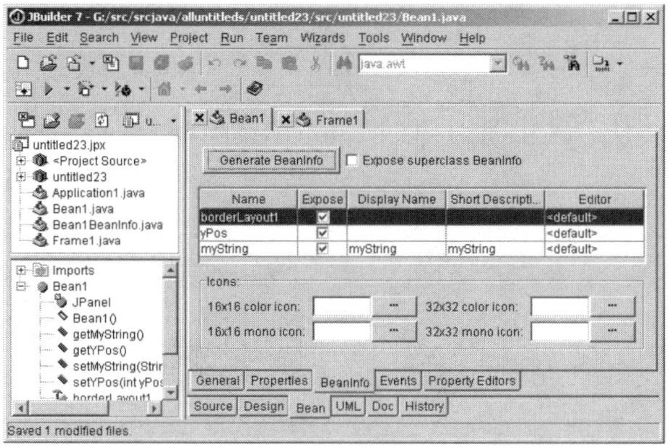

Figure 33-6: Generating BeanInfo. Note the checks in the Expose column, as well as the Bean1BeanInfo.java node visible in the project pane.

As stated above, the name of a BeanInfo file must follow a specific pattern. This pattern is part of the Java specification for beans. In particular, Bean1 is the name of your bean, and BeanInfo is the type of the Java source file. Combine the two, and you have the BeanInfo filename for your bean: Bean1BeanInfo.java. If the name of your bean was MyListBox.java, the BeanInfo file for your bean would be called MyListBoxBeanInfo.java.

Recognizing this pattern is how JBuilder and other Java development environments know to find the BeanInfo file for your bean. These patterns are as much a part of the specification for the language as a keyword like property is part of the Object Pascal language or a keyword like void is part of the C/C++ language.

NOTE: By now you have seen two cases in Java where the pattern of words in a name is significant. First you saw that the names for getters and setters follow the pattern getX, setX. Now you have seen that the name for BeanInfo files follows the pattern xxxBeanInfo.java. Like it or hate it, love it or leave it, this is the way things are done in the Java world. For what it's worth, my personal opinion is that there doesn't seem to be much harm in this kind of pattern matching, and it does help establish naming conventions, which is undoubtedly a good thing. In public talks that the creator of Java, James Gosling, has given, he has strongly implied that if he had the chance to do it all over again, he might have gone with the Delphi method of handling properties instead of using pattern matching.

After running the BeanInfo tool, you can examine Bean2BeanInfo.java and see what it contains. Let's take a look at the file you have created, which is shown in Listing 33-2.

Listing 33-2: A simple BeanInfo file

```
package untitled6;

import java.beans.*;

/**
 * <p>Title: </p>
 * <p>Description: </p>
 * <p>Copyright: Copyright (c) 2002 by Charlie Calvert</p>
 * <p>Company: Elvenware</p>
 * @author Charlie Calvert
 * @version 1.0
```

Part VII

```
 */

public class Bean1BeanInfo extends SimpleBeanInfo
{
    Class beanClass = Bean1.class;
    String iconColor16x16Filename;
    String iconColor32x32Filename;
    String iconMono16x16Filename;
    String iconMono32x32Filename;

    public Bean1BeanInfo()
    {
    }
    public PropertyDescriptor[] getPropertyDescriptors()
    {
        try
        {
            PropertyDescriptor _yPos = new PropertyDescriptor("yPos",
                                  beanClass, "getYPos", "setYPos");
            _yPos.setDisplayName("yPos");
            _yPos.setShortDescription("yPos");
            PropertyDescriptor _myString = new
                        PropertyDescriptor("myString", beanClass,
                              "getMyString", "setMyString");
            _myString.setDisplayName("myString");
            _myString.setShortDescription("myString");
            PropertyDescriptor[] pds = new PropertyDescriptor[] {
                  _yPos,
                  _myString};
            return pds;
        }
        catch(IntrospectionException ex)
        {
            ex.printStackTrace();
            return null;
        }
    }
    public java.awt.Image getIcon(int iconKind)
    {
        switch (iconKind) {
        case BeanInfo.ICON_COLOR_16x16:
              return iconColor16x16Filename != null ?
                        loadImage(iconColor16x16Filename) : null;
        case BeanInfo.ICON_COLOR_32x32:
              return iconColor32x32Filename != null ?
                        loadImage(iconColor32x32Filename) : null;
        case BeanInfo.ICON_MONO_16x16:
              return iconMono16x16Filename != null ?
                        loadImage(iconMono16x16Filename) : null;
        case BeanInfo.ICON_MONO_32x32:
```

```
                return iconMono32x32Filename != null ?
                        loadImage(iconMono32x32Filename) : null;
                            }
            return null;
        }
    }
```

A quick look at this code should help you understand its purpose. The class contains an empty default constructor and two methods:

- getIcon: This method returns the icons to be associated with your bean.
- getPropertyDescriptors: This method returns basic information about the properties of your bean.

Here is the description of one property:

```
PropertyDescriptor _myString = new PropertyDescriptor("myString",
      beanClass, "getMyString", "setMyString");
_myString.setDisplayName("myString");
_myString.setShortDescription("myString");
```

You can see that the property is described via a class called a PropertyDescriptor. Some of the methods of a PropertyDescriptor are very straightforward, such as the setDisplayName and setShortDescription routines. However, a bean can have more complex features, such as a custom property editor. This editor will pop up automatically when you use the JBuilder Inspector. Its purpose is to allow the user to edit the property.

Understanding SimpleBeanInfo

JBuilder's BeanInfo classes descend from a JDK class called SimpleBeanInfo. Here is the declaration for that class, with the lengthy implementation of the final method stripped out:

```
package java.beans;

public class SimpleBeanInfo implements BeanInfo
{

    public BeanDescriptor getBeanDescriptor()
      {
            return null;
    }

    public PropertyDescriptor[] getPropertyDescriptors()
      {
            return null;
    }

    public int getDefaultPropertyIndex()
      {
            return -1;
    }

    public EventSetDescriptor[] getEventSetDescriptors()
      {
```

Part VII

```
            return null;
    }

    public int getDefaultEventIndex()
      {
            return -1;
    }

    public MethodDescriptor[] getMethodDescriptors()
      {
            return null;
    }

    public BeanInfo[] getAdditionalBeanInfo()
      {
            return null;
    }

    public java.awt.Image getIcon(int iconKind)
      {
            return null;
    }

    public java.awt.Image loadImage(final String resourceName)
      {
            // I've deleted the implmentation of this method
    }

}
```

If a method of BeanInfo class returns null or –1, it is in effect saying that it has no information to expose about that particular feature. This might mean that the bean should hide that feature altogether, or it might mean that it should use traditional Java introspection to discover that feature of the bean. Introspection, sometimes called Run Time Type Information, or RTTI, is a means of directly querying an object in order to discover its features. For instance, you can find out the type of a field that is part of a class via introspection.

Because JBuilder BeanInfo classes descend from this class, by default, a BeanInfo class reveals absolutely nothing about the beans with which it is associated. Whenever the JBuilder Inspector asks for information by calling one of these methods, all it gets in return is null or –1. Depending on the method involved, this means that JBuilder or similar tools will show no information at all, or else will use introspection to find out what it can by studying the patterns implemented in the class. For instance, if you provide no information at all about events, JBuilder will use introspection to discover the events available on the class.

As you have seen, JBuilder overrides some of these methods when you ask it to expose information about your bean. In particular, you have seen that it overrides the getPropertyDescriptors method. By doing this, you begin to tell the outside would about the properties in your bean.

Exposing and Hiding Ancestor Properties

A BeanInfo class is used to expose the properties of your control. One of the questions you need to answer is whether you want to expose the properties of an ancestor class or to hide those properties.

If you have no BeanInfo class at all, JBuilder will use the Java introspection services to discover the properties available on your class. It will search the class for getter and setter methods and then expose them to the outside world as properties in the Inspector.

If you create a BeanInfo class that descends from SimpleBeanInfo, then by default, the introspection mechanism for properties is turned off. Instead, you see only the properties explicitly exposed by your BeanInfo class. This gives you complete control over the interface your component presents to the outside world.

NOTE: If you really wanted to protect a class from exposure in a tool like the JBuilder Inspector, you could refuse to use the getter and setter naming patterns. Instead, you could supply a BeanInfo class that would expose only those properties you wanted to expose. Your class would only be usable in the JBuilder Inspector or in similar tools if you provided the BeanInfo class. This could, perhaps, provide a degree of copy protection for your work.

If you want to expose all the properties that you inherited from your ancestor class, add this code to your BeanInfo class:

```
public BeanInfo[] getAdditionalBeanInfo()
{
        Class superclass = beanClass.getSuperclass();
        try
        {
                BeanInfo superBeanInfo = Introspector.getBeanInfo(superclass);
                return new BeanInfo[] { superBeanInfo };
        }
        catch(IntrospectionException ex)
        {
                ex.printStackTrace();
                return null;
        }
}
```

This is one of the methods of the SimpleBeanInfo class that was given earlier in this chapter. In overriding this method, JBuilder provides code that exposes the BeanInfo information available from ancestor classes.

NOTE: The name of the getBeanInfo method called in the getAdditionalBeanInfo method shown here is perhaps a bit misleading. When you call getBeanInfo, Java will first look for explicitly declared BeanInfo classes. But it will also look for any derived information it can glean by searching for such things as getter and setter patterns.

The documentation for the Introspector class in the Sun Javadoc files is so well written that it almost brings tears to my eyes. Here, for instance, are the very enlightening last sentences of the overview for this class: "If we don't find explicit BeanInfo on a class, we use low-level reflection to study the methods of the class and apply standard design patterns to identify property accessors, event sources, or public methods. We then proceed to analyze the class's superclass and add in the information from it (and possibly on up the superclass chain)." When they write this clearly and articulately, it is criminal not to take the time to actually read the Sun Javadocs for some of these classes.

Inside of JBuilder, you generate the code shown in the getAdditionalBeanInfo method by going into BeansExpress and selecting **Bean** from the file view tabs. Turn to the **BeanInfo** page, and check **Expose superclass BeanInfo.** When you click the **Generate BeanInfo** button, the getAdditionalBeanInfo method will be generated automatically.

NOTE: Sometimes, when I am deleting and adding properties to a component, the only way I can make them disappear from JBuilder's Inspector is to delete the entire directory and all the directories found inside it, including the package cache. I have also seen instances in which the getAdditionalBeanInfo code was not deleted when I unchecked it. If necessary, go in there and delete the method by hand.

There is more to say about BeanInfo files. However, I want to end the current discussion of BeanInfo here, as this chapter is meant to be an introduction to the basic facts about JavaBeans. More advanced information on BeanInfo files, and on all aspects of JavaBean creation, will be found in the next few chapters. There you will find specific examples of more complex beans that exercise all of the features of the JavaBean specification. In particular, see the section called "Exposing Properties for the New Clock" and "Exposing Events for the New Clock" in Chapter 35.

Using Your Bean

Now that you have created a simple bean, the only thing left to do is actually use it in your program. Before doing that, however, we should do something to give it a distinctive look and feel. Right now, the interface for our bean is blank, and therefore it is not particularly interesting to look at.

Select **Bean1.java** in the project pane. Click the **Design** tab from the file view tabs visible at the bottom of the editor. Make sure that the layout for the bean is set to **BorderLayout**. Now drop a JButton and JTextArea onto your bean, as shown in Figure 33-7.

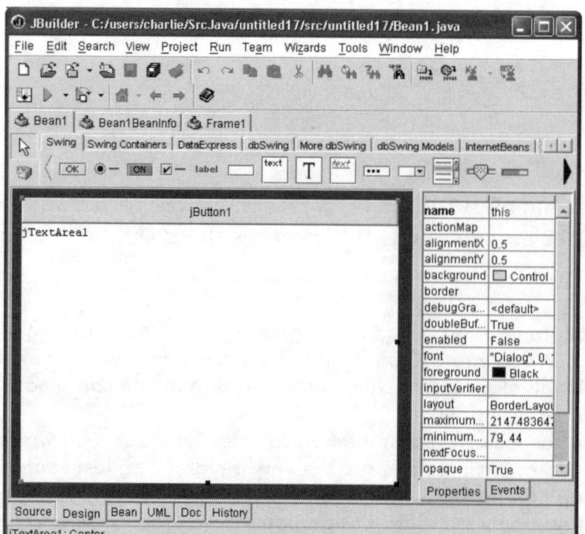

Figure 33-7: The interface for a simple bean

Double-click once on **jButton1**, and add a simple event handler that looks like this:

```
void jButton1_actionPerformed(ActionEvent e)
{
      jTextArea1.setText("This is a simple bean.");
}
```

Now use the project pane to focus **Frame1.java** in the content pane. Switch to design mode. Make sure the layout for Frame1 is set to **BorderLayout**. (A JFrame descendant, such as Frame1, will be set to BorderLayout by default. An applet, however, will be set to FlowLayout.)

Click on the **BeanChooser**, which appears as a silver box with a yellow star at the far left of the component palette, as shown in Figure 33-8.

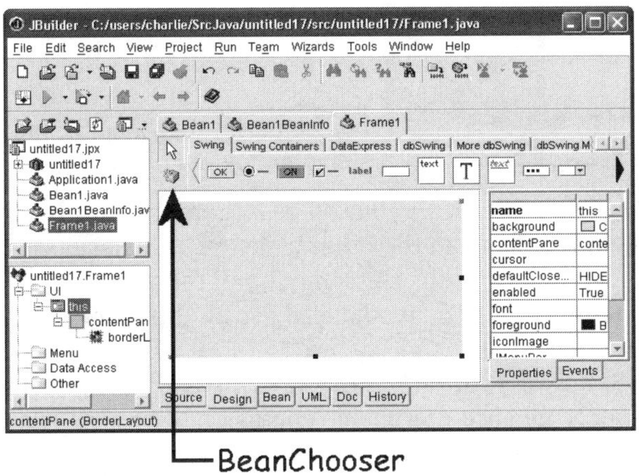

Figure 33-8: The BeanChooser is located to the right of the project pane, on the far left of the component palette, and just below the Selection tool.

The BeanChooser pops open the Bean Chooser dialog, which allows you to select your bean from the packages available to your project. In Figure 33-9, I have highlighted Bean1 from a project called untitled17. Needless to say, your project may have a different name.

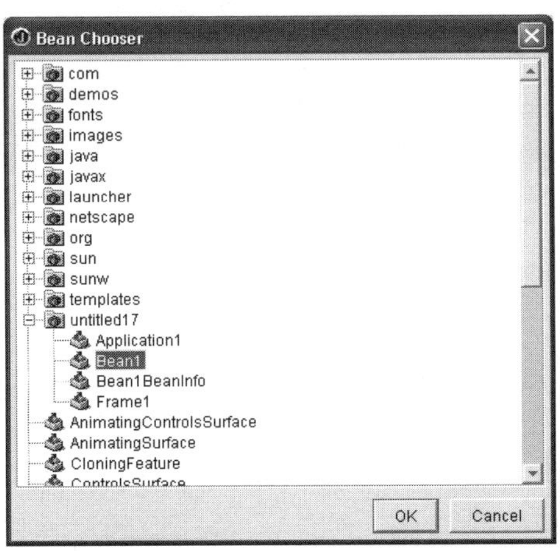

Figure 33-9: Selecting a bean in the Bean Chooser dialog

After choosing your bean, the JBuilder cursor will turn into a plus symbol, just as it does when you select a component from the component palette. Use your mouse to "paint" the component onto Frame1, as shown in Figure 33-10. When you are done, Frame1.java will look very much like Bean1.java. This is because its entire surface is now covered with your bean. However, if you look in the structure pane, you will see that the bean is now sitting on top of the contentPane for Frame1. (In some cases, you may have to set the constraints for the bean itself to Center.)

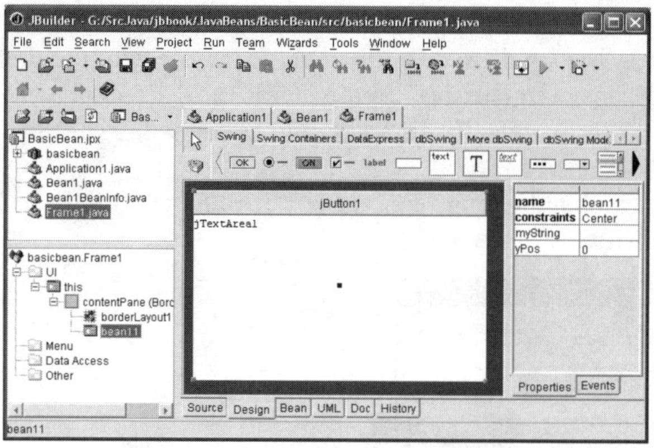

Figure 33-10: An instance of Bean1.java sitting on top of Frame1

Take a glance at the Inspector in Figure 33-10. As you can see, there are now two properties visible in the Inspector, one called myString and the other called yPos. These properties are visible because we explicitly exposed them in our BeanInfo file. If there were no BeanInfo file, you might still see these properties, but you would also see all the properties inherited from JPanel.

If you now run the project and click on jButton1, the text in the text area will change to the string "This is a simple bean." Just to be sure there is no confusion over what has happened, I have included this project on the CD under the title BasicBean. Listing 33-3 shows the code for the bean itself, and Listing 33-4 shows the code for Frame1.java after you have dropped the bean onto it.

Listing 33-3: The code for a simple bean

```
package basicbean;

import java.awt.*;
import javax.swing.*;
import java.awt.event.*;

public class Bean1 extends JPanel
{
      BorderLayout borderLayout1 = new BorderLayout();
      JTextArea jTextArea1 = new JTextArea();
      JButton jButton1 = new JButton();
      private String myString;
      private int yPos;

      public Bean1()
      {
            try
            {
                  jbInit();
```

```
        }
        catch(Exception e)
        {
            e.printStackTrace();
        }
    }

    private void jbInit() throws Exception
    {
        jTextArea1.setText("jTextArea1");
        jButton1.setText("jButton1");
        jButton1.addActionListener(new Bean1_jButton1_actionAdapter(this));
        this.setLayout(borderLayout1);
        this.add(jTextArea1,  BorderLayout.CENTER);
        this.add(jButton1, BorderLayout.NORTH);
    }

    void jButton1_actionPerformed(ActionEvent e)
    {
        jTextArea1.setText("This is a simple bean");
    }

    public void setMyString(String myString)
    {
        this.myString = myString;
    }

    public String getMyString()
    {
        return myString;
    }

    public void setYPos(int yPos)
    {
        this.yPos = yPos;
    }

    public int getYPos()
    {
        return yPos;
    }
}

class Bean1_jButton1_actionAdapter implements java.awt.event.ActionListener
{
    Bean1 adaptee;

    Bean1_jButton1_actionAdapter(Bean1 adaptee)
    {
        this.adaptee = adaptee;
```

```
        }
        public void actionPerformed(ActionEvent e)
        {
                adaptee.jButton1_actionPerformed(e);
        }
}
```

Listing 33-4: A JFrame descendant that hosts a simple bean

```
package basicbean;

import java.awt.*;
import java.awt.event.*;
import javax.swing.*;

public class Frame1 extends JFrame
{
        JPanel contentPane;
        BorderLayout borderLayout1 = new BorderLayout();
        Bean1 bean11 = new Bean1();

        //Construct the frame
        public Frame1()
        {
                enableEvents(AWTEvent.WINDOW_EVENT_MASK);
                try
                {
                        jbInit();
                }
                catch(Exception e)
                {
                        e.printStackTrace();
                }
        }

        //Component initialization
        private void jbInit() throws Exception
        {
                contentPane = (JPanel) this.getContentPane();
                contentPane.setLayout(borderLayout1);
                this.setSize(new Dimension(400, 300));
                this.setTitle("Frame Title");
                contentPane.add(bean11, BorderLayout.CENTER);
        }

        //Overridden so we can exit when window is closed
        protected void processWindowEvent(WindowEvent e)
        {
                super.processWindowEvent(e);
                if (e.getID() == WindowEvent.WINDOW_CLOSING)
                {
```

```
                        System.exit(0);
                    }
            }
    }
```

Enhancing Your Bean

If you want to edit the bean further, you have to resist the temptation to focus Frame1.java. Instead, you should focus Bean1.java and make your changes to the bean itself. Then, when you recompile, Frame1.java will pick up the changes you made to the bean. In short, don't try to edit the instance of the Bean1 class that is embedded in Frame1.java. You might have some success doing this, but it is not the right approach.

Before closing the chapter, I want to mention that I have not yet covered two of the most important features of beans — wrapping the bean in a JAR file and placing a bean on the component palette.

Don't worry; both of these features are covered in Chapter 37. Many other features of beans will be covered over the next few chapters.

Exercises

Some books have a regular set of exercises at the end of each chapter. Though that is not a feature of this text, in this particular case the exercise format gives me an opportunity to stress some important features of the JavaBeans specification.

If you take the time to work through these three simple exercises, your knowledge of beans and what they can do for you should be significantly improved.

1. Add an applet or a second application to the last project developed in this chapter. Don't start a new project; add it to the current project. Use the BeanChooser to add the bean we've created to your new application or applet. Notice that you can use this one bean simultaneously in more than one Java program. (If you are working with an applet or JApplet, be sure to set the layout property to BorderLayout.)
2. Make additional changes to your bean, such as changing the name of the button from jButton1 to myButton. Recompile your project and run it. Notice that the program picks up on the changes you made to your bean. The point here is to make changes to the bean itself, not to the bean embedded into Frame1.
3. Delete your bean from Frame1.java by clicking directly on the bean and pressing the Delete button. Drop down a panel on Frame1.java and set its constraints to Center. Set the layout for this panel to GridLayout, and give it two rows and one column. Now use the BeanChooser to drop down two instances of your bean, one in the top row of your panel and one in the bottom row. Run your application and test each instance of the bean.

On the CD, you will find the solutions to questions 1 and 3 in the BasicExercises directory. In the directory, to get the answer to question 1, go to the BasicBean01 directory and open the project you find there. Right-click in the project pane on **Application1** or **Applet1.html** and choose **Run** from the pop-up menu. You will see that the same bean appears in both the applet and the application.

To get the answer to question 3, go to the BasicExercises directory and open the project in BasicBean02. Right-click on **Application1** and choose **Run** from the menu.

Bound and Constrained Properties

A bound property is a property that will send out notifications if it is changed. For instance, if two classes called A and B are using a third class called C, class A might want to be notified if B changes a particular property in class C. Properties that can provide this service are called *bound properties*. They use a class called java.beans.PropertyChangeEvent.

A constrained property is similar to a bound property. Consider the example just mentioned when A and B are using a third class called C. If A and B are both using a constrained property of class C, class A, for instance, could veto a change that class B might want to make to the property in question. Classes of this type use a fourth class called a VetoableChangeListener, which is related to the PropertyChangeListener mentioned in the previous paragraph.

I do not present a specific example of using bound and constrained properties in this book. JBuilder, however, will automatically generate the necessary code for handling these kinds of properties. Simply select the **Bean** page from the file view tabs at the bottom of the editor, and turn to the **Properties** page. Create at least one property. On the far right of this page you will see a column called Binding, as shown in Figure 33-11. From this drop-down list you can select bound, constrained, or none. After making the selection, the necessary code will be generated for you automatically.

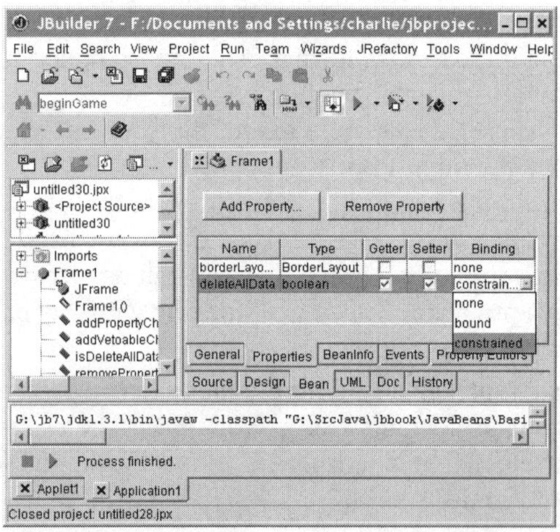

Figure 33-11: Setting the bindings to bound, constrained, or none. Here you can see the drop-down list from which you can choose the option you prefer.

When you add a new property to a class using BeansExpress, you also have the option of selecting the kind of binding you want to use, as shown in Figure 33-12.

You can read an in-depth explanation of bound and constrained properties in *Developing JavaBeans* by Robert Englander.

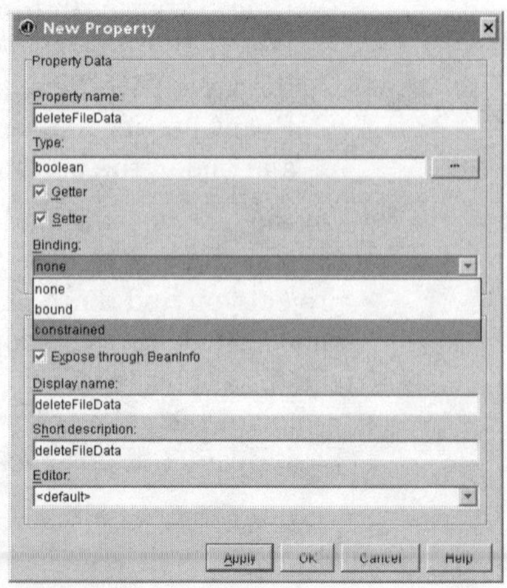

Figure 33-12: If you use BeansExpress, you can decide whether or not to bind or constrain a property at the time you create it.

Summary

In this chapter you have learned how to create simple JavaBeans. You have also learned how to use all the key features of JBuilder BeansExpress, including BeanInsight, the JavaBean Wizard, and creating, renaming, and exposing properties.

Subjects that still need to be covered include advanced features of BeanInfo and creating and using event handlers. Another important subject not covered in this chapter is how to wrap your bean in a JAR file and place icons for it on the component palette. That subject will be covered in depth when we begin creating sample beans.

One of the most important features of this chapter was the discussion of how to use the property editor tools in BeansExpress. Java developers spend a lot of time creating properties, and this tool can ease your job, whether or not you are trying to create a JavaBean.

Chapter 34

JavaBean Harvest

Charlie Calvert

It is time at last to begin to harvest the fruits of our labors. In this chapter, you will see how to create some very simple beans that can enhance your programming life.

Knowing how to create the controls shown in this chapter is a large part of what it means to know how to build JavaBeans. Java is designed to allow you to simply and easily create visual components. In this chapter you will see just how easy that task can be and just how much you have to gain from learning how the technology works.

In particular, you will build two beans, both of them based on a JList component. Both of them add functionality to the built-in JList class. In the chapters following this one, you will see how to build a component from scratch rather than enhancing an existing component. In those chapters, you will be doing all the drawing of the component yourself.

Wrapping Swing

If you have been running the programs on the CD included with this book, you have no doubt encountered a component called ElfListBox. It is stored in the comp package of the codebox JAR file, along with the ElfClock that you will be developing in the next chapters. In this chapter you are going to build a local copy of the ElfListBox component. By local, I mean that this copy of the component will not reside in codebox.jar or in the com.elvenware package.

If you come from the Delphi or VB world, you may have noticed that some of the Swing controls behave differently from many popular visual components used in other languages. The primary reason for this is the Swing model-view-event architecture. For instance, you can't just test a property of a check box to get its current state. Instead, you respond to events and check the parameters of messages to discover the control's state. When working with a JList, you can't automatically add and delete items to the list unless you first create your own DefaultListModel class or something like it. In Swing, components are all about models and events. In VB or Delphi, components are not partitioned into a model-view-event architecture. Instead, they exist as one whole, fully integrated component.

If you prefer the Delphi or VB way of doing things, it is not at all hard to change the behavior of existing Java components to conform with your expectations. The developers of Java have gone to great lengths to make it possible for you to make these kinds of changes.

The ElfListBox

On the CD, you will find an applet in the ElfListBox directory. This program is the test bed used while developing the simple ElfListBox component.

To create the test program and the component yourself, you need to first create a standard Java applet, as described in Chapter 3.

The code you are going to develop depends on files stored in the codebox JAR file on the CD. As a result, you will need to either include the codebox JAR file as a library in your project or have your project's sourcepath point at my codebox sourcecode. The former method is preferred in this case.

As you recall, a library adds a JAR file or package to JBuilder's view of your classpath. If necessary, choose **Tools | Configure Libraries** in JBuilder to set up the library. The key part of this process is locating codebox.jar, as shown in Figure 34-1. The process of adding a library to JBuilder is described in Part V: Project Management and in the index.html file on the CD. You would then use Project | Project Properties to add the codebox library to your current project, as shown in Figure 34-2. By adding the library, you put the specified JAR file or package on the classpath for your current project.

NOTE: It may be confusing to you to use codebox.jar while you are recreating a local copy of one of the components stored in codebox.jar. The com.elvenware tree stored in codebox.jar has a branch called codebox, where utility routines are stored, and a branch called comp, where components are stored. The component you are about to build depends on the utility routines found in the com.elvenware.codebox utility package. So you need access to codebox.jar to access those utility routines. For now you can just ignore the comp part of the JAR file. In other words, you will import com.elvenware.codebox.*, but you will not import com.elvenware.comp.*.

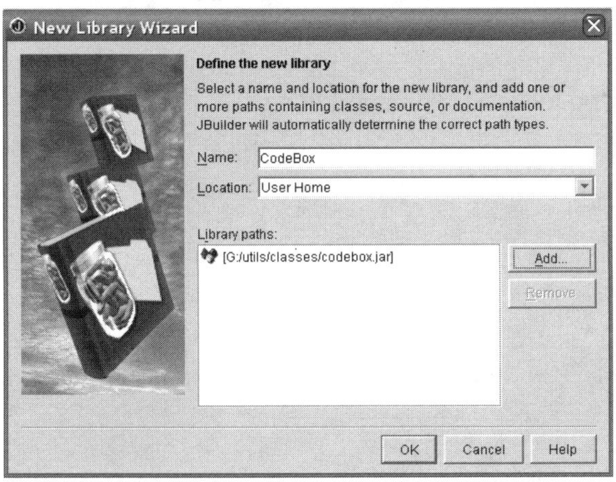

Figure 34-1: Setting up the codebox library. Notice that the location is set to User Home and library path points at the JAR file.

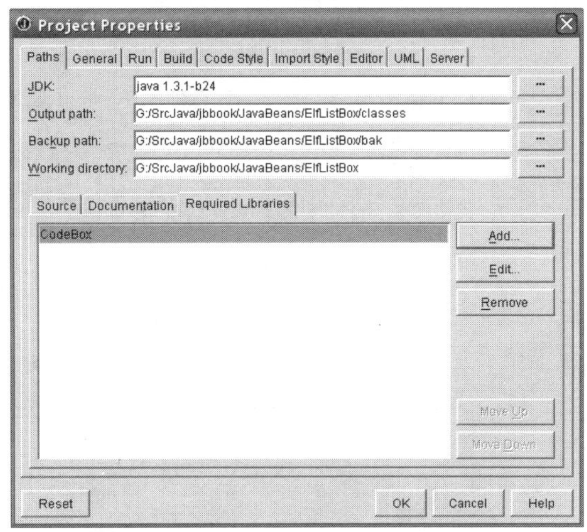

Figure 34-2: Setting up JBuilder so that it knows where to find the com.elvenware.codebox package and knows to put new components in that package by default

You are now ready to add the ElfListBox to your test project. To keep this version totally distinct from the version in CodeBox.jar, call it MyElfListBox.

Choose **File | New | JavaBean** and add the bean to your current package. If you press the ellipsis button to the right of the Package field, as shown in Figure 34-3, you can bring up the Select a Package dialog, which lets you pick the package where your control will reside. There should be only one option in this case, elflistbox. When you are done, the JavaBean Wizard appears, as shown in Figure 34-3. Notice that the package selected in the figure is called elflistbox and the component descends from javax.swing.JList and has the name MyElfListBox.

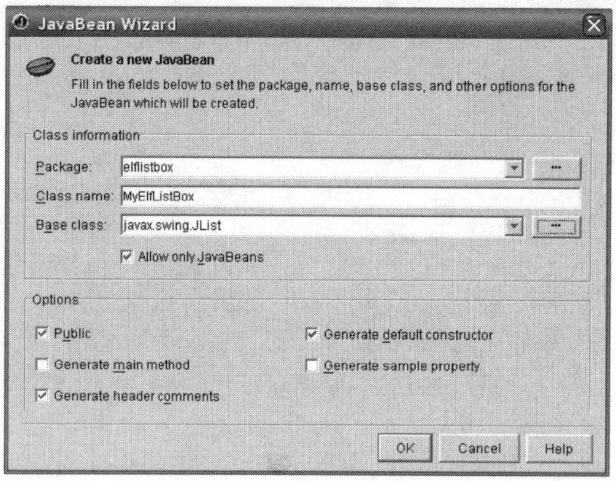

Figure 34-3: The JavaBean Wizard as it appears when you are creating a bean

NOTE: One of the things that makes programming so much fun is that there are many different ways to accomplish the same goal. I have chosen to descend MyElfListBox from JList. An alternative technique would have been to descend from JComponent and make JList a field of my component. Then I could have used BeanInfo and wrapper properties to expose some of the underlying fields of the JList. This latter technique is more difficult, but it gives you more flexibility. Exploring subjects of this kind would have been an option in a book dedicated to building visual controls. But in this book I have to limit my scope and keep things as simple as possible. You, however, should explore such possibilities for your own controls.

The source that JBuilder generates for you looks something like this:

```
public class MyElfListBox extends JList
{
    BorderLayout borderLayout1 = new BorderLayout();

    public MyElfListBox()
    {
        try
        {
            jbInit();
        }
        catch(Exception ex)
        {
            ex.printStackTrace();
        }
    }
    private void jbInit() throws Exception
    {
        this.setLayout(borderLayout1);
    }
}
```

This is the basis on which you can build your component. The component itself is shown in Listing 34-1.

Listing 34-1: ElfListBox does little more than bind a DefaultListModel and a JList into one component.

```
package elflistbox;
```

```
import java.awt.*;
import java.util.*;

import javax.swing.*;

import com.elvenware.codebox.*;

public class MyElfListBox extends JList
{
      private BorderLayout borderLayout1 = new BorderLayout();
      private DefaultListModel list = new DefaultListModel();

      public MyElfListBox()
      {
            super();
            try
            {
                  jbInit();
            }
            catch(Exception e)
            {
                  e.printStackTrace();
            }
            this.setModel(list);
      }

      private void jbInit() throws Exception
      {
      }

      public void addString(String value)
      {
            list.addElement(value);
            this.repaint();
      }

      public void addString(String value, boolean scrollToEnd)
      {
            addString(value);
            Rectangle r= getCellBounds(list.size() - 1, list.size() -1);
            scrollRectToVisible(r);
      }

      public void clear()
      {
            list.clear();
      }

      public void deleteCurrentItem()
      {
            int selectedItem = getSelectedIndex();
```

```
        list.remove(selectedItem);
    }

    public String getSelectedString()
    {
        int selectedIndex = getSelectedIndex();
        if (selectedIndex != -1)
            return (String)list.get(selectedIndex);
        else
            return "";
    }

    public void remove(int value)
    {
        list.remove(value);
    }

    /**
     * @deprecated Use getString instead
     *
     * @param value Add this string to the list box.
     */
    public void setString(String value)
    {
        addString(value);
    }

    public String getString(int i)
    {
        return (String)list.get(i);
    }

    public ArrayListStream getArrayList()
    {
        ArrayListStream arrayList = new ArrayListStream();
        for (int i = 0; i < list.size(); i++)
            arrayList.add(list.get(i));
        return arrayList;
    }

    public DefaultListModel getList()
    {
        return list;
    }

    public void setList(DefaultListModel list)
    {
        this.list = list;
    }

    public void setVisible(boolean visible)
```

```
        {
            super.setVisible(visible);
        }

        public void setArrayList(ArrayList list)
        {
            String value;
            Iterator itr = list.iterator();
            while (itr.hasNext())
            {
                Object obj = itr.next();

                if (obj instanceof String)
                {
                    value = (String)obj;
                }
                else
                {
                    value = obj.toString();
                }
                this.list.addElement(value);
            }
        }
    }
```

The key lines of code here are the ones that add a DefaultListModel to the JList:

```
        private DefaultListModel list = new DefaultListModel();

        public ElfListBox()
        {
            this.setModel(list);
        }
```

Once you have a copy of a DefaultListModel attached to a list box, you can start creating a list box that acts the same way a Delphi list box would act:

```
        public void addString(String value)
        {
            list.addElement(value);
            this.repaint();
        }

        public void addString(String value, boolean scrollToEnd)
        {
            addString(value);
            Rectangle r= getCellBounds(list.size() - 1, list.size() -1);
            scrollRectToVisible(r);
        }
```

These two methods of ElfListBox allow you to easily add a string to the list box or add a string and then scroll to the end of the list box.

To see exactly how they work, you need to set up the test program properly. Focus the main class of your applet, or Frame1 of your application, in the editor and switch to design mode. Paint a JScrollPane from the Swing Containers page of the component palette onto the main window of your program. Use the **BeanChooser** to browse for the ElfListBox, as shown in Figure 34-4.

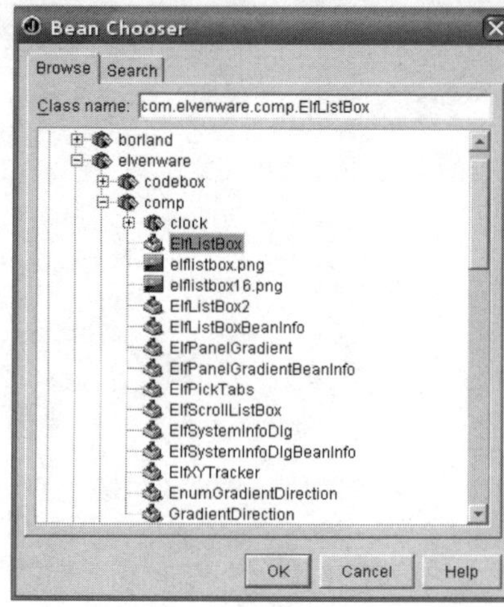

Figure 34-4: Using the Bean Chooser dialog to select a bean

After you have located the bean and clicked **OK** in the Bean Chooser dialog, you can simply paint your control on top of the JScrollPane as you would any other component. Now add a JPanel to the content pane of your main window and drop a few buttons on the control. Ultimately, you are trying to create the interface shown in the applet in Figure 34-5. If you have trouble building this interface, read the chapters in Part III: JBuilder Fundamentals or look at the source code to the example program found in the ElfListBox directory on the CD.

In response to a click on the AssignStrings button shown in Figure 34-5, create this event handler:

```
void jButtonAssignStrings_actionPerformed(ActionEvent e)
{
      for (int i = 0; i < 100; i++)
      {
            elfListBox1.addString("Elf-" + String.valueOf(i));
      }
}
```

The code shown here will allow you to quickly add 100 strings to the ElfListBox, as shown in Figure 34-5. Bingo! This is very close to the way a Delphi programmer would expect a list box to work. Just drop the control on a window and use one call, with a name like addString, to start adding strings to the list box. The ElfListBox is just as easy to use as a System.out.println — perhaps even a bit easier. When you consider that list boxes are much faster than standard out in Java programs, you can start to see that tools like this open some doors for developers.

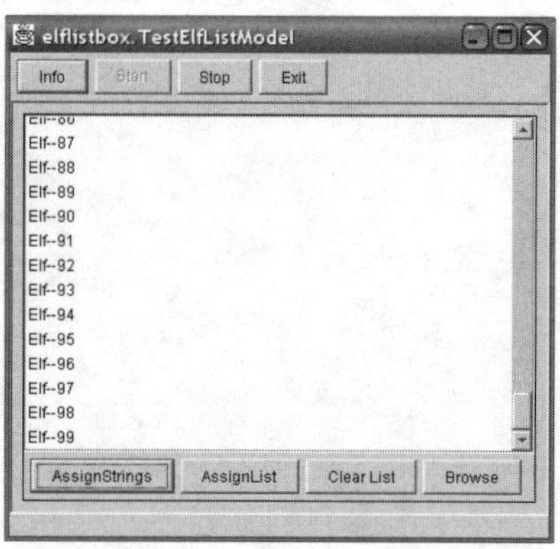

Figure 34-5: The ElfListBox after the AssignStrings button has been clicked

List Boxes, ArrayList, and Streams

Another thing you will want to do with a list box is add an array of strings to it quickly and easily at run time. I've added list support to ElfListBox to give you this kind of easy-to-use functionality:

```
public ArrayListStream getArrayList()
{
      ArrayListStream arrayList = new ArrayListStream();
      for (int i = 0; i < list.size(); i++)
            arrayList.add(list.get(i));
      return arrayList;
}

public void setArrayList(ArrayList list)
{
      String value;
      Iterator itr = list.iterator();
      while (itr.hasNext())
      {
            Object obj = itr.next();

            if (obj instanceof String)
            {
                  value = (String)obj;
            }
            else
            {
                  value = obj.toString();
            }
            this.list.addElement(value);
      }
}
```

NOTE: The ArrayListStream class is part of the codebox JAR file. As described above, this code won't compile unless you have included codebox.jar in the Required Libraries page of your Project Properties dialog. A library is the technology JBuilder uses to place files on your classpath. You can set up a library using Tools | Configure Libraries from the JBuilder menu. You can use a library in your current project by choosing Project | Project Properties from the JBuilder menu and then turning to the Required Libraries page and pressing the Add button. If you need help working with libraries, see Part V: Project Management. You will need to add two import statements at the top of your class. They should read:

```
import com.elvenware.codebox.*;
import java.io.*;
```

The setArrayList and getArrayList methods allow you to easily add an ArrayList of strings or other items to the list box and easily convert the list associated with the list box into an ArrayList.

As a result, you can now write code that looks like this:

```
void jButtonAssignList_actionPerformed(ActionEvent e)
{
      ArrayListStream list = new ArrayListStream();
```

```
            list.add("Beorn");
            elfListBox1.setArrayList(list);
        }
```

Of course, you would never have occasion to write code exactly like this in a production application, but you can see how easily ArrayLists can be made to work with an ElfListBox.

The one piece of functionality that is now missing is the ability to easily read in a text file and display it in the list box. That is a task that I have to perform quite frequently when programming, and so I created the ArrayListStream class to help out. This class, found in codebox.jar and in the com.elvenware.codebox package on the CD, is a descendant of ArrayList, much as ElfListBox is a descendant of JList. The entire class is shown in Listing 34-2.

Listing 34-2: ArrayListStream class

```
package com.elvenware.codebox;

import java.util.ArrayList;
import java.util.Iterator;
import java.io.PrintWriter;
import java.io.FileWriter;
import java.io.FileReader;
import java.io.IOException;
import java.io.BufferedReader;
import javax.swing.*;

/**
 * Title:
 * Description: An Array of strings that can be written and read from a text file
 * Copyright:    Copyright (c) 2001
 * Company:
 * @author Charlie Calvert
 * @version 0.2
 */

public class ArrayListStream extends ArrayList
{

    public ArrayListStream()
    {
    }

    public void store(String fileName)
    {
        FileWriter fw = null;
        PrintWriter pw = null;
        try
        {
            fw = new FileWriter(fileName);
            pw = new PrintWriter(fw);

            Iterator itr = this.iterator();
            while (itr.hasNext())
```

```
                {
                        String s = (String)itr.next();
                        pw.println(s);
                }
        }
        catch(IOException e)
        {
                System.out.println(e);
        }
        finally
        {
                try
                {
                        //pw.close();
                        fw.close();
                }
                catch(IOException e)
                {
                        System.out.println(e);
                }
        }
}

public boolean load(String fileName)
{
        if (!FileBox.fileExists(fileName))
        {
                JOptionPane.showMessageDialog(null, "File does not exist");
                return false;
        }
        FileReader fr = null;
        BufferedReader br = null;
        String inString;
        try
        {
                fr = new FileReader(fileName);
                br = new BufferedReader(fr);
                while ((inString = br.readLine()) != null)
                {
                        this.add(inString);
                }
        }
        catch(IOException e)
        {
                System.out.println(e);
        }
        finally
        {
                try
                {
                        fr.close();
```

```
                    br.close();
                }
                catch(IOException e)
                {
                    System.out.println(e);
                }
            }
            return true;
        }
    }
```

The primary features of the ArrayListStream class are simple load and save methods that use basic Java stream functionality to read a text file from disk or save a text file to disk. The point, of course, is that the text file is automatically wrapped inside an ArrayList.

The end result of all this is that you can write code that looks like the following:

```
void jButtonBrowse_actionPerformed(ActionEvent e)
{
    JFileChooser fileChooser = new JFileChooser(FileBox.getCurrentDirectory());
    if (fileChooser.showOpenDialog(this) == JFileChooser.APPROVE_OPTION)
    {
        ArrayListStream listStream = new ArrayListStream();

        try
        {
            listStream.load(fileChooser.getSelectedFile().getCanonicalPath());
        }
        catch (IOException ex)
        {
            ex.printStackTrace();
        }
        elfListBox1.setArrayList(listStream);
    }
}
```

NOTE: In JBuilder 7, you don't have to manually type in the try..catch block or add the import java.io.* statement at the top of your file. Instead, right-click on the statement that needs to be surrounded by a try block and choose Surround with try/catch from the pop-up menu. The try..catch block will automatically be inserted in your program and any necessary import statements will be inserted at the top of your file.

If you strip the try..catch block out of this method, you can see that it consists of a very few lines of code that pop up a JFileChooser, allowing the user to select a text file. It then uses the ArrayListStream class to load the file from disk and display it in the ElfListBox:

```
ArrayListStream listStream = new ArrayListStream();
listStream.load(fileName);
elfListBox1.setArrayList(listStream);
```

The end result of loading a poem from disk and displaying it in the ElfListBox is shown in Figure 34-6. This kind of functionality is what modern visual developers expect from a development tool. It is amazing to see how simple it is to convert the Java Swing classes into components that behave in such an intuitive and simple manner.

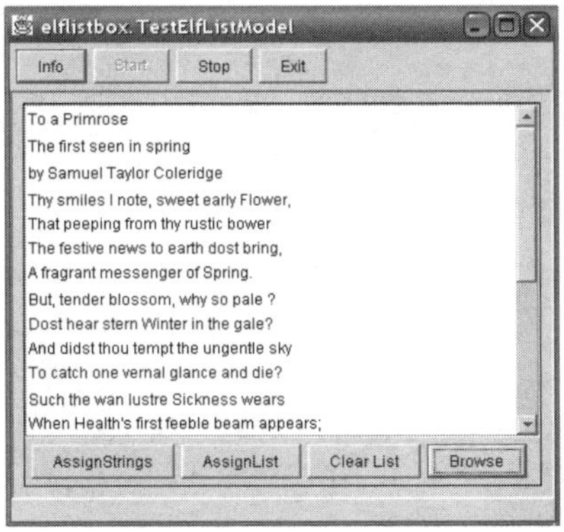

Figure 34-6: Displaying a poem in an ElfListBox with the aid of the ArrayListStream class

In saying this, I'm not trying to imply that I'm smarter than the developers at Sun. To the contrary, I'm saying that Sun designed these classes so that it is very easy to extend them exactly as I show in this chapter. If you are a Java programmer, then for Pete's sake, pick up the tools that Sun gave you and put them to work using the simple techniques shown here!

The ElfScrollListBox

Perhaps the greatest shortcoming of the ElfListBox is that it still forces you to add in a JScrollPane. After all, when are you going to create a list box and not need it to scroll?

The simplest solution to this problem is not to further extend ElfListBox itself but rather to extend the JScrollPane class. An example of how to do this is shown in Listing 34-3. An example program showing how to use the component is found in the ElfScrollList directory on the CD.

Listing 34-3: An ElfScrollListBox combines a JList and a JScrollPane.

```
package elfscrolllist;

import java.awt.*;
import javax.swing.*;

public class MyElfScrollListBox extends JScrollPane
{
      BorderLayout borderLayout1 = new BorderLayout();
      JList jList1 = new JList();
      private DefaultListModel list = new DefaultListModel();

      public MyElfScrollListBox()
      {
            try
            {
                  jbInit();
            }
            catch(Exception ex)
            {
                  ex.printStackTrace();
            }
```

```
        }

        private void jbInit() throws Exception
        {
              // Commenting out next line so as not to change the JScrollPane layout
              //this.setLayout(borderLayout1);
              this.getViewport().add(jList1, BorderLayout.CENTER);
              jList1.setModel(list);
        }

        public void addString(String value)
        {
              list.addElement(value);
              this.repaint();
        }
  }
```

Listing 34-3 shows a very stripped-down version of the ElfListControl. You can see that the component descends from JScrollPane and contains a JList and DefaultListModel:

```
  public class ElfScrollListBox extends JScrollPane
  {
        BorderLayout borderLayout1 = new BorderLayout();
        JList jList1 = new JList();
        private DefaultListModel list = new DefaultListModel();
```

The jbInit method has been modified to not change the default layout of the JScrollPane and to initialize the ListModel of the JList:

```
        private void jbInit() throws Exception
        {
              // Commenting out next line so as not to change the JScrollPane layout
              // this.setLayout(borderLayout1);
              this.getViewport().add(jList1, BorderLayout.CENTER);
              jList1.setModel(list);
        }
```

Finally, an addString method has been inserted into the control so that you can quickly and easily drop down an instance of this component and put it to work:

```
        public void addString(String value)
        {
              list.addElement(value);
              this.repaint();
        }
```

Using the component is simplicity itself. Here is the same sort of method you found for testing the ElfListBox. Only this time it is put to work testing the ElfScrollListBox:

```
        void jButton1_actionPerformed(ActionEvent e)
        {
              for (int i = 0; i < 100; i++)
              {
                    elfScrollListBox1.addString("ListBox Mania " + i);
              }
        }
```

Marking Code as Deprecated

One thing that I ought to mention before closing this chapter is the proper way to mark a method as deprecated. This is something you will need to do if you begin creating components.

When I first created ElfListBox, I used the method setString for adding a string to the list box. That was not exactly the right name, as what I am really doing is adding the string to the list box. Unfortunately, I already had a lot of code out there using the old setString method. Rather than break that code, I simply marked the method as deprecated. To do so, I only had to use the @deprecated symbol in a comment before the method.

```
/**
 * @deprecated Use getString instead
 *
 * @param value Add this string to the list box.
 */
public void setString(String value)
{
     addString(value);
}
```

After doing this, I got a deprecation warning every time I used setString instead of addString. For a situation like this, that was about exactly what I wanted: It reminded me to change the code but did not actually force me to fix anything until I had time to get around to it.

Ext Directories

If you create a JAR file, you normally can't use it unless you place it on your classpath or in a JBuilder library. One simple way around this is to place the JAR file in the jre/lib/ext directory for your JDK. The directory should exist by default. If it does not, you can make the directory, and the JDK will know to look inside it. You will probably have to restart JBuilder before it will recognize that you placed the library in the ext directory.

NOTE: On Windows, one semi-reliable way to check that JBuilder has found your JAR file in an ext directory is to try to delete it. You can assume JBuilder has a hold of it if Windows stops you by giving you this message: "The process cannot access the file because it is being used by another process." Needless to say, you should back up the file before running this little test.

The Future of Visual Development

For some reason, some people get the idea that there is something wrong with using alternative controls from third parties rather than sticking to the raw Swing API. There are few things in this world that could be further from the truth. The whole point of Java architecture and a tool like JBuilder is that they allow you to create and easily use a wide variety of components.

Besides the fact that I find it useful, one of the reasons I have made such heavy use of the ElfListBox in the example programs for this book is because I want to get you used to the idea of using third-party components. I view Swing as a starting point on which the really great Java visual controls can be built.

The chapters you have been reading about JavaBeans, along with Part V: Project Management, are designed to make you intimately familiar with Java packages, JAR files, classpaths, and components. I want you to feel very comfortable using components that are not part of the JDK itself.

If you have bought a copy of JBuilder from Borland, you should have the Companion Tools CD; which contains a whole series of beautifully written third-party controls. It is simply madness not to explore those controls and see what they can do for you.

The developers of Java made a huge effort to give you a tool that can easily create and consume components. JavaBeans are very much a part of what Java is all about.

The powerful new processors, video cards, and plentiful fast memory found on even low-cost modern computers have at last brought Java GUI applications into the mainstream. I can still detect a difference in performance between a tool such as JBuilder, which is written in Java, and native tools such as Delphi or Visual C++, which are written in Object Pascal or C++. But the difference is becoming increasingly academic.

The Java community needs to fully embrace visual tools and component-based architectures and begin distributing their powerful applications based on the very fancy available third-party tools. Spend time exploring what is available for free over the web and what you can buy relatively cheaply from third parties. The results may well surprise you.

Summary

Now that you have a sense of what can be done with JavaBeans, you should begin to understand just how flexible a tool we have in the Java language. Building components like ElfListBox or ElfScrollListBox is what JavaBeans programming is all about. There is no reason ever to waste time futzing around with JLists, JScrollPanes, and DefaultListModels when you can so quickly and easily create an ElfScrollListBox and then reuse it over and over again in your own programs.

Don't stop here. The controls I supply are primarily teaching tools. You can easily extend them to have much more functionality. You can find ideas for extending your versions of the controls by exploring the many Java visual tools found on the web or on the JBuilder Companion CD.

Chapter 35

JavaBeans and Properties

Charlie Calvert

In this chapter you will learn more about building beans. The main learning mechanism will be an examination of a bean that can be used to display the time.

Subjects covered in this chapter include:

- Choosing the ancestor of your bean
- Adding properties to your bean
- More on working with BeanInfo
- Filtering the view the user has of the properties of your bean
- Exposing or hiding properties inherited from an ancestor component
- Overriding existing properties
- Working with timers
- Overriding the paint method for your control

There will also be a brief discussion of how to architect beans so that they are easy to maintain.

The example program used in this chapter is found in the Clock directory on the CD. This chapter uses BeansExpress, which is a feature of the SE and Enterprise versions of JBuilder. For those with the Personal edition, an effort is made to supply the code that would be created by BeansExpress.

NOTE: Though its appearance was perhaps a bit premature, you nonetheless saw a bean earlier in this book in Chapter 18. If you reexamine that chapter, you will find a small bean that descends from a class called BasePanelButton. Reading over the description of that class will teach you a good deal about JavaBeans and also about creating beans that respond to events.

A Clock Bean

It is now time to begin building a clock bean. Start a new project and add an application to it called **Clock.** If you need help building default JBuilder applications, see Chapter 3.

Use **File | New | JavaBean** to create a new JComponent descendant called **ElfClock.** You could also use JPanel as the ancestor, but JComponent is probably preferable since it is a bit more lightweight.

Switch the ElfClock object into design mode and drop a JTextField control onto it. Make sure the Clock component is using the **BorderLayout**, and set the constraints property for the JTextField to **Center.** When you are done, the JTextField should take up the entire width and breadth of your control.

Adding Properties to a Bean

With the ElfClock object focused, go to the file view tabs beneath the editor and open up BeansExpress. Choose the **Properties** page. Add two new properties to your project called timer and running:

- To create the timer property, choose the **Add Property** button. Set the name field to **timer** and the type to **javax.swing.Timer**. Add neither a getter nor a setter, and do not expose this property through BeanInfo. See Figure 35-1 for an example.
- To create the running property, choose the **Add Property** button. Set the name field to **running** and the type to **boolean**. Use both a getter and setter and expose the property through BeanInfo, as shown in Figure 35-2.

NOTE: The ellipsis button beside the Type field allows you to browse for complex types. Simple types like int or boolean need to be typed in by hand.

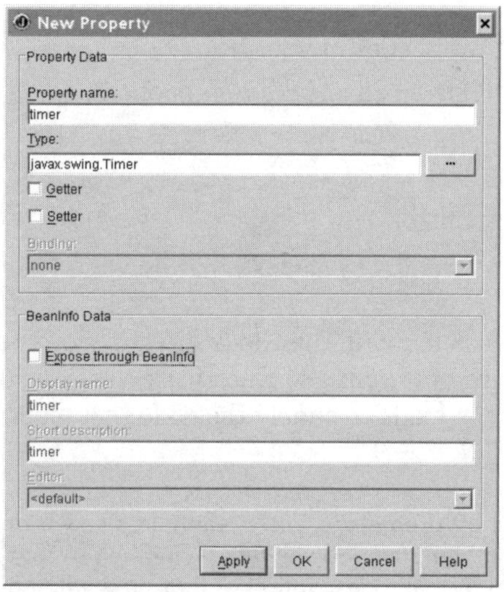

Figure 35-1: Using BeansExpress to add a property of type Timer to a component

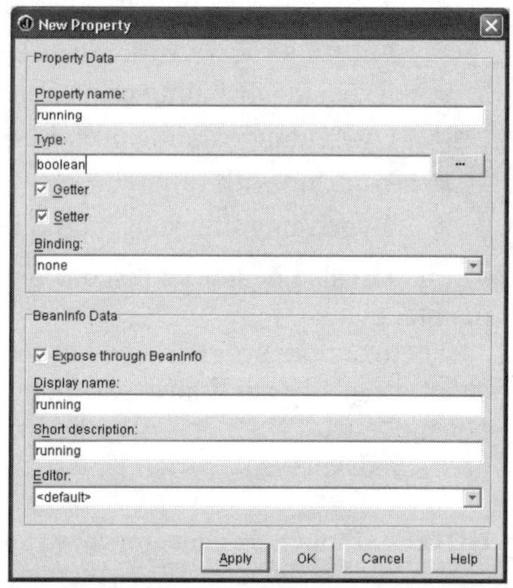

Figure 35-2: Using BeansExpress to add a Boolean property to a component. This property has both a getter and setter, as well as being exposed through BeanInfo.

Turn to source view and notice that the running property, when created, uses a set method called setRunning and a get method called isRunning. This follows the standard Java convention for Boolean properties:

```
public void setRunning(boolean running)
{
  this.running = running;
}

public boolean isRunning()
{
  return running;
}
```

Initializing the Timer

Go to the jbInit section, and type the following:

```
timer = timer
```

Keep the cursor on or next to the second instance of the word "timer." Now press **Ctrl+J**. The following code should be inserted into your program automatically:

```
timer = new javax.swing.Timer(, new ActionListener()
{
      public void actionPerformed(ActionEvent e)
      {

      }
});
```

When you press Ctrl+J, you invoke the JBuilder Code Template mechanism. It will leave the cursor after the open parenthesis in the call to the Timer constructor: Timer(. You should type in the interval at which you want the timer to call your code at this point: Timer(250, new ActionListener()....

Now enter the following code into the actionPerformed method:

```
            timer = new javax.swing.Timer(250, new ActionListener()
            {
                  public void actionPerformed(ActionEvent e)
                  {
                        Date d = new Date();
                        jTextField1.setText(d.toString());
                  }
            });
```

Edit the setRunning method so that it looks like this:

```
public void setRunning(boolean running)
{
      this.running = running;
      if (this.running)
            timer.start();
      else
            timer.stop();
      }
```

Compile your code. If you have trouble, check the top of your file and ensure that the following import statements are present:

```
import java.awt.event.*;
import java.util.*;
```

NOTE: Through a tool called ClassInsight, JBuilder 7 and above provide support for automatically inserting import statements into your source files. If you type in a statement that JBuilder cannot parse, it will be underlined in red. Click on a type that is shown in red, and the small ClassInsight one-line dialog will pop up. Click on the magnifying class icon, and the ClassInsight dialog will appear. Often it will contain the one item you need to add to your import statement. Click OK to add it. Sometimes there will be multiple items, or you may even have to browse to find your import statement. In any case, it can help you quickly add import statements to your project. This subject is discussed in more depth in Chapter 7.

Switch to the Frame1 component and move into design mode. Select the **Bean Chooser** from the little icon beneath the arrow on the component palette, as shown in Figure 35-3.

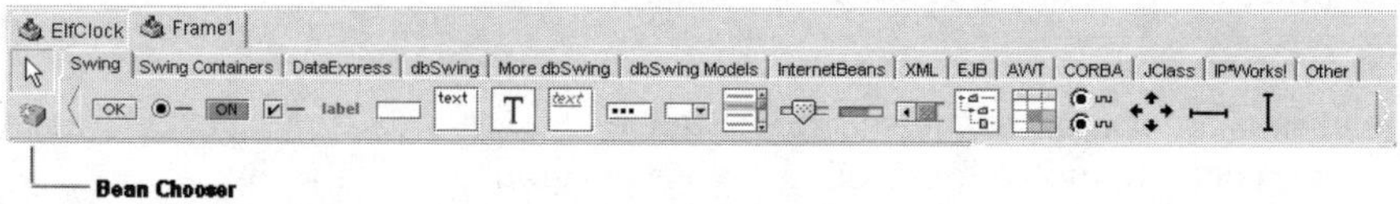

Figure 35-3: Selecting the Bean Chooser from the component palette

With the Bean Chooser open, you can browse for the class that you want to insert into your project, as shown in Figure 35-4. When you select the class, your cursor changes into a cross. Use the cursor to insert the component into Frame1 just as you would insert any other component.

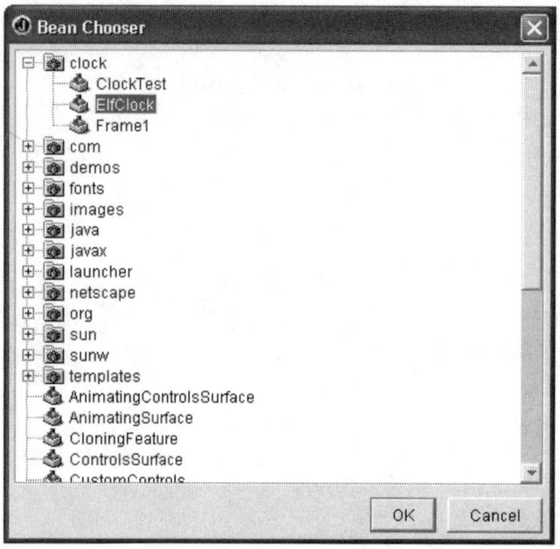

Figure 35-4: Using the Bean Chooser to select a class from the current project

At this stage, you have a rough mockup of your clock. To use it, select the new component you have created and turn to the Inspector. Set the running property to **True**. When you are done, your clock should be ticking away inside JBuilder's UI designer, as shown in Figure 35-5.

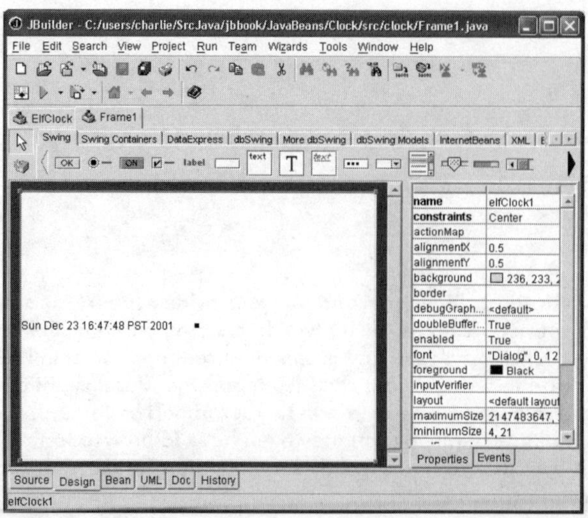

Figure 35-5: A rough cut of the Clock component running inside of the JBuilder development environment

NOTE: In the screen shot shown in Figure 35-5, you might notice that the project pane, structure pane, and message pane are all hidden. This has been mentioned before, but it might be helpful to remind you that you can toggle these panels on and off with the Ctrl+Alt+P, Ctrl+Alt+S, and Ctrl+Alt+M keys. Press Ctrl+Alt+Z to close them all at once.

Enhancing the Clock Component

JBuilder makes it amazingly simple to create a tool like the Clock component. However, just creating the core of the component is really only a small portion of the work involved in finishing the component. As it stands, no one would really want to use this component. It is too ugly to look at, and it doesn't have many features.

One of the first problems you might notice with the component is that its font property doesn't work correctly. In particular, changes that you make to the font property via the Inspector have no impact on your control.

A moment's thought reveals the nature of the problem. The currently exposed font property is the font of the underlying JComponent or JPanel control on which the component is based. The text that you see in the component, however, is displayed in a JTextField control that sits on top of the panel.

There are two solutions to this problem:

- Expose the font property of the JTextField in place of the font property of the JPanel.
- Remove the JTextField and completely take over the drawing of text for our component.

Overriding an Existing Property

Let's take the options one at a time. To implement the first solution, open up BeansExpress for the Clock component. Make sure you have ElfClock.java focused and not Frame1.java. Turn to the Properties page and create a new property called **font**, of type **java.awt.Font.**

Fill it out as shown in Figure 35-6, being sure to add a getter and setter for the property and to expose the property via BeanInfo. When you click the OK button, you will see the message shown in Figure 35-7, stating "Property font exists in superclass. Override?" That is indeed exactly what we want to do, so we click the **Yes** button. Doing so effectively replaces the old font property from the JPanel class with the new font property that we create.

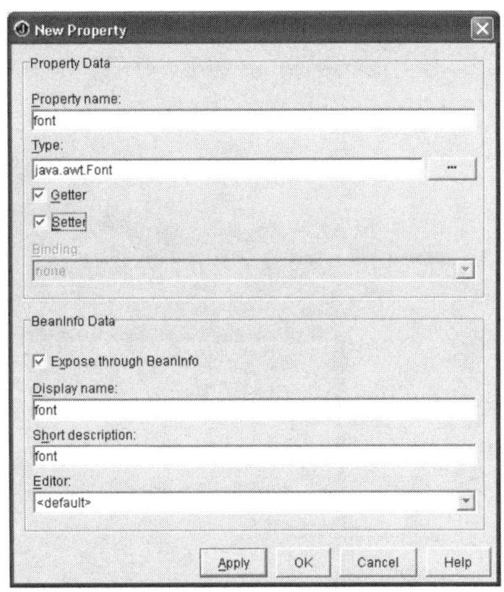

Figure 35-6: Creating the font property

Figure 35-7: Overriding an existing property

By default, the code inserted in your application by BeansExpress looks like this:

```
    public void setFont(java.awt.Font font)
  {
    this.font = font;
  }
  public java.awt.Font getFont()
  {
    return font;
  }
```

You want to change it so that it looks like this:

```
    public java.awt.Font getFont()
    {
          if (jTextField1 != null)
                return jTextField1.getFont();
          else
                return null;
    }

    public void setFont(java.awt.Font font)
    {
          if (jTextField1 != null)
                jTextField1.setFont(font);
    }
```

Now the changes that you make to the font property in the Inspector for the ElfClock control will be as you expect. See Figure 35-8 for an example of the Clock component with a new font.

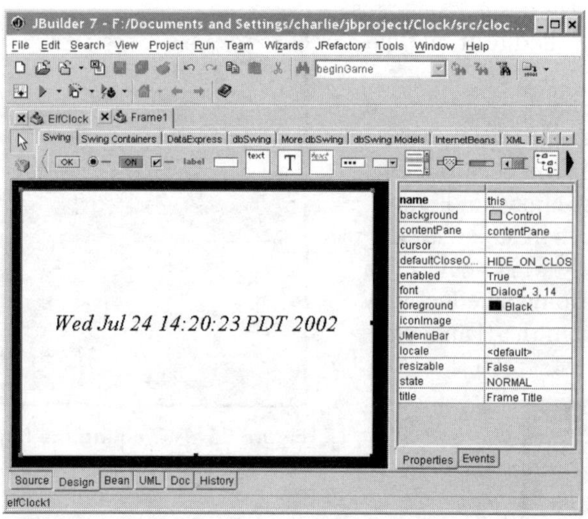

Figure 35-8: The ElfClock control residing in the IDE with its font set to a new value

In Figure 35-8, you can see that text is centered in the window. I accomplished that by adding this code to my jbInit for the Clock component:

```
jTextField1.setHorizontalAlignment(SwingConstants.CENTER);
jTextField1.setRequestFocusEnabled(false);
```

The second line of code shown here effectively makes the control read only. The user will not be able to focus the control, and hence will be unable to edit the text that it shows.

At this stage, our component code for one version of the Clock component is complete. You can see the complete source in Listing 35-1.

Listing 35-1: The source for the first version of the Clock component

```
package clock;

import java.awt.*;
import java.awt.event.*;
import java.util.*;
import javax.swing.*;
import javax.swing.Timer;

/**
 * <p>A simple clock component</p>
 * @author Charlie Calvert
 * @version 1.0
 */
public class ElfClock extends JPanel
{
      BorderLayout borderLayout1 = new BorderLayout();
      /** The timer that drives the clock */
      Timer timer = null;
      /** Whether the clock is running or not */
      private boolean running;
      /** Control for displaying the time and date */
      JTextField jTextField1 = new JTextField();

      /**
       * Constructor
       */
      public ElfClock()
      {
            try
            {
                  jbInit();
            }
            catch(Exception ex)
            {
                  ex.printStackTrace();
            }
      }

      /**
       * Custom method for JBuilder initialization of visual components
       *
       * @throws Exception
       */
      private void jbInit() throws Exception
```

```
{
      jTextField1.setText("jTextField1");
      jTextField1.setHorizontalAlignment(SwingConstants.CENTER);
      jTextField1.setRequestFocusEnabled(false);
      this.setLayout(borderLayout1);
      timer = new javax.swing.Timer(250, new ActionListener()
      {
            public void actionPerformed(ActionEvent e)
            {
                  Date d = new Date();
                  jTextField1.setText(d.toString());
            }
      });
      this.add(jTextField1, BorderLayout.CENTER);
}

/**
 * Property to turn the clock on or off
 *
 * @param running Whether to stop or start the clock
 */
public void setRunning(boolean running)
{
      this.running = running;
      if (this.running)
            timer.start();
      else
            timer.stop();
}

/**
 * Determines if the clock is active or not.
 *
 * @return Whether or not the clock is running
 */
public boolean getRunning()
{
      return running;
}

/**
 * The get portion returns the font property for the JTextField
 *
 * @return The font the user requested
 */
public java.awt.Font getFont()
{
      if (jTextField1 != null)
            return jTextField1.getFont();
      else
            return null;
```

```
    }

    /**
     * The set part of the custom font property.
     *
     * @param font The font to display to the user
     */
    public void setFont(java.awt.Font font)
    {
        if (jTextField1 != null)
            jTextField1.setFont(font);
    }
}
```

Directly Painting the Text on the Control

We are now going to rewrite the ElfClock control in such a way as to give us more control over its appearance. The first stage of this process is to delete the JTextField.

If you understand how JBuilder works, you know that the simplest way to delete the JTextField is to focus ElfClock.java, go into design mode, click once on the JTextField in the UI designer, and then hit the Delete key. Doing this deletes the component and most of the references to the component that appear in your code. In particular, JBuilder finds the references to JTextField in the jbInit method, but it will miss the one in the anonymous ActionListener for the Timer and the ones in the getter and setter for the font. You can, however, clean up the getter and setter code for the font by going into BeansExpress, turning to the Properties page, selecting the font property, and pressing the Remove Property button. This is okay to do, since the font property was associated with the JTextField, which has already been deleted.

NOTE: I suppose I'm being a bit glib in suggesting that you delete the get and set methods for the font property in BeansExpress. In practice, you would probably just delete the code in the editor. However, if you had ten properties that you needed to remove and several more that you wanted to keep, BeansExpress would probably be the simplest way to solve the problem.

The only reference left to the JTextField is in the anonymous listener. You can delete that reference, but you might keep the code that creates the Date object:

```
    timer = new javax.swing.Timer(250, new ActionListener()
    {
        public void actionPerformed(ActionEvent e)
        {
            Date d = new Date();
            //jTextField1.setText(d.toString());
        }
    });
```

Overriding the Paint Method

It's now time to override the paint method for the component and start the process of drawing the clock ourselves:

```
    public void paint(Graphics g)
    {
        super.paint(g);
```

```
        Date d = new Date();
        g.drawString(d.toString(), 10, 30);
    }
```

This code will be called automatically since it overrides the regular paint method for the JComponent or JPanel component. The contract with the system inherent in this code states that it will be called automatically whenever the surface of the component needs to be redrawn.

This much code allows us to output the current time, as shown in Figure 35-9.

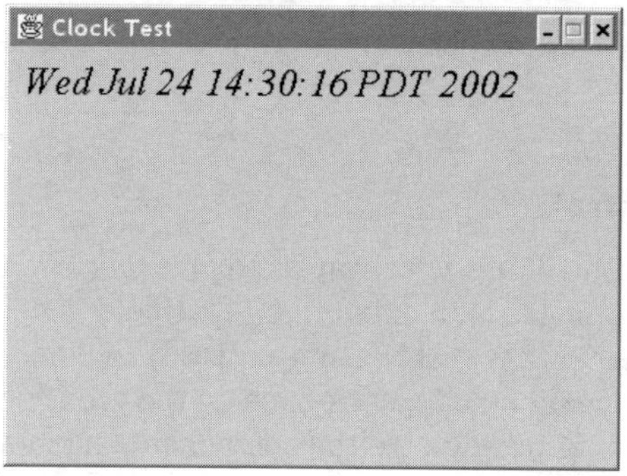

Figure 35-9: The output from the paint method at run time; the component looks much the same at design time.

If we hook up the timer so that the paint method gets called over and over, we get back to the stage that we were in for the first version of this component. Here is the code to get the timer to call the paint method every quarter second:

```
    timer = new javax.swing.Timer(250, new ActionListener()
    {
        public void actionPerformed(ActionEvent e)
        {
            repaint();
        }
    });
```

It turns out that this method of painting the clock control was not as difficult to implement as it might have at first appeared. But of course, one rarely finds the best way to do things on the first try. Instead, the process of writing good code is iterative. You come out with a first version that works at least a little bit. In the worst-case scenario, it at least compiles and runs. The process of writing that code helps you think about what you are doing and helps you learn a little about the technology involved. So perhaps the second time through your code will be a little better, and the third time through will perhaps be a little better again. And so on. The goal is to keep your code in a state where it can be compiled and tested.

Improving the Control

At this stage, we can begin asking ourselves a good number of questions. The first might be whether we want our control to descend from JPanel or JComponent.

As we begin to think of getting more control over the clock, one thing that I like to do is break the complex or discrete portions of the code out of the existing object and put them into a world of their own. In particular, the act of painting the surface of the clock is really a discrete task that can be easily isolated. As a result, I plug it into its own separate object, called DrawClock, which is shown in Listing 35-2.

Listing 35-2: The simplest possible way to paint the clock object

```
package clock;

import java.awt.*;
import java.util.*;

public class DrawClock
{

      public DrawClock()
      {
      }

      public void draw(Graphics g)
      {
            Date d = new Date();
            g.drawString(d.toString(), 10, 30);
      }
}
```

To create this file, choose **File | New Class** from the JBuilder menu. Call the class **DrawClock**. The ancestor, or base class, should be java.lang.Object. Place it in the same clock package as the ElfClock component. Select all the options in the New Class Wizard, except Generate main method.

In the first version of the new class, all the work is done in a single method called draw. In Listing 35-2 you can see that the draw method simply creates an instance of the Date class and then draws the current time to the screen using an instance of the Graphics2D class. Don't forget to add the two import statements shown at the top of Listing 35-2.

You could make the draw method static or else create an instance of the DrawClock class in the initialization section of the ElfClock component:

```
public class ElfClock extends JComponent
{
      DrawClock drawClock = new DrawClock();
      BorderLayout borderLayout1 = new BorderLayout();
      private javax.swing.Timer timer;
      etc...
}
```

The new class is called like this from the ElfClock component:

```
      public void paint(Graphics g)
      {
            super.paint(g);
            drawClock.draw(g);
      }
```

The code first calls the ancestor's paint method. It then passes the responsibility for painting the object to a second class.

The reason this architecture is useful is that it allows us to plug in various different clocks into the main object by simply instantiating a different kind of DrawClock object. For instance, the DrawPieceClock, which we will build in the next chapter, can look like the image shown in Figure 35-10.

Figure 35-10: The DrawPieceClock looks like it has an LED interface.

Exposing Properties for the New Clock

In the ElfClock component, we don't want to expose the ancestor class properties in the JBuilder Inspector. This is a very simple component, and there is no need to overwhelm the user with a lot of information that they are never going to need.

NOTE: Well, okay. Maybe some developers will need it. But for the sake of argument, let's pretend they won't. There are occasions when you really will want to hide properties or events, and this is a good chance for you to see how the system works.

To hide the ancestor properties, create a BeanInfo class. Do this by using the file view tabs to turn to the Bean tab. Inside BeansExpress, turn to the BeanInfo page.

Make sure the Expose superclass BeanInfo option in the BeanInfo page of BeansExpress is not checked. Click the **Generate BeanInfo** button. To be sure that the right code is being generated, look inside the generated BeanInfo file and make sure there is no method called getAdditionalBeanInfo. If there is such a method, delete it or comment it out.

In Figure 35-11 you can see what the Inspector looks like if the ancestor properties are exposed. In Figure 35-12, you can see what the Inspector looks like when the ancestor properties are hidden. If you need more information, see the sections that discuss BeanInfo in Chapters 33 and 34.

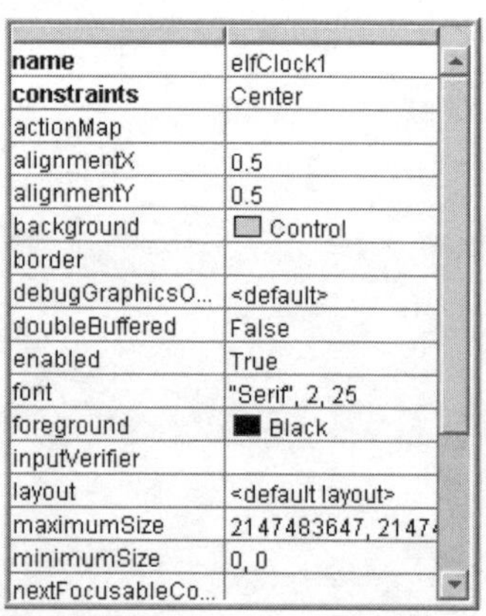

Figure 35-11: The ancestor property information for the ElfClock is exposed.

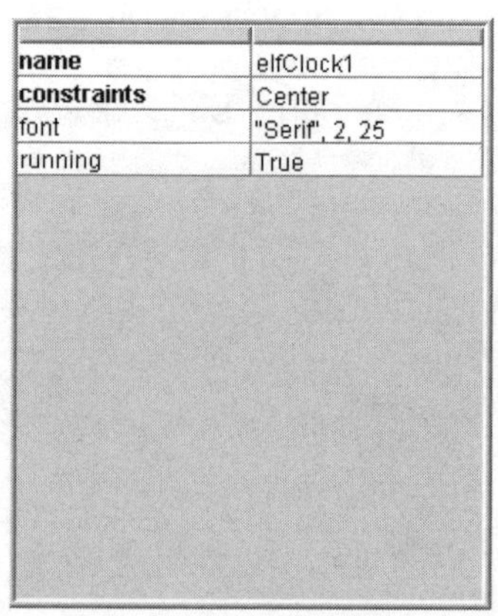

Figure 35-12: The ancestor property information is hidden.

Having successfully hidden the properties of the ancestor component that you do not want to expose, you may find that there are some that you do want to expose. This is a common situation. You want to hide most of the information from ancestor classes, but there are some methods that you want to expose.

In particular, there are two properties from the ancestor class that we want to expose in the clock. One is the text color or foreground property of the numbers that appear in the clock. The other is the color of the background. Use BeansExpress to add these two properties.

The first is the text color. Focus **ElfClock.java** in the content pane. Switch to BeansExpress, and bring up the Properties page. Create a new property called **foreground**, of type **java.awt.Color**. Create both a getter and setter for the property, and expose the property through BeanInfo. When creating the properties, JBuilder will ask whether you want to override existing properties with these same names. Answer **Yes**.

NOTE: It is best to follow the convention of most Swing components by sticking with the words foreground and background. There will be a temptation to choose more descriptive names, such as textColor and backgroundColor. But I've decided to stick with Sun's convention.

Do the same for a second property called **background**. Add a property of type **int** called **textWidth**. After creating the properties, don't forget to go to the BeanInfo page to regenerate the BeanInfo.

NOTE: The textWidth property will be used in later chapters.

You may not be entirely happy with JBuilder's implementation of these methods. For instance, I find it easiest to implement them by simply calling through to their ancestor. Here is the code that I entered along with the generated code that I have commented out:

```
//private java.awt.Color foreground;
//private java.awt.Color background;

    public void setForeground(java.awt.Color foreground)
    {
        super.setForeground(foreground);
        //this.foreground = foreground;
    }

    public java.awt.Color getForeground()
    {
        return super.getForeground();
        // return foreground;
    }

    public void setBackground(java.awt.Color background)
    {
        super.setBackground(background);
        //this.background = background;
    }

    public java.awt.Color getBackground()
    {
        return super.getBackground();
        //return background;
    }
```

You can stick with generated code for the getter and setter, as shown in Listing 35-2. However, there is a little controversy surrounding the best way to declare the ElfClock paint method:

```
public void paint(Graphics g)
{
        //super.paint(g);
        g.setColor(this.getBackground());
        g.fillRect(0, 0, this.getWidth(), this.getHeight());
        g.setColor(this.getForeground());
        drawClock.draw(g);
}
```

As you can see, I have opted to comment out the call to the super.paint method, since we are going to take over painting the entire control. I then set the color of the component and paint its surface with a call to fillRect.

The ElfClock code shown here ends up acting very much as if it were still drawing the clock using the JTextField component. The new version of the ElfClock component is, however, architected in such a way that it will be fairly easy to extend and improve its functionality.

Exposing Events for the New Clock

Focus the ElfClock component in the design mode view of Frame1 and turn to the Events page in the Inspector. By default, your bean will expose all the events it inherited from its ancestor, as shown in Figure 35-13. The logic here is the opposite of what it was with SimpleBeanClass.getAdditionalBeanInfo. In Chapter 33, you saw that if getAdditionalBeanInfo returns null, then knowledge about ancestor classes would be suppressed. Here the situation is reversed. If the getEventSetDescriptors method returns null, all the event information that can be culled from ancestor classes will be not hidden, but exposed.

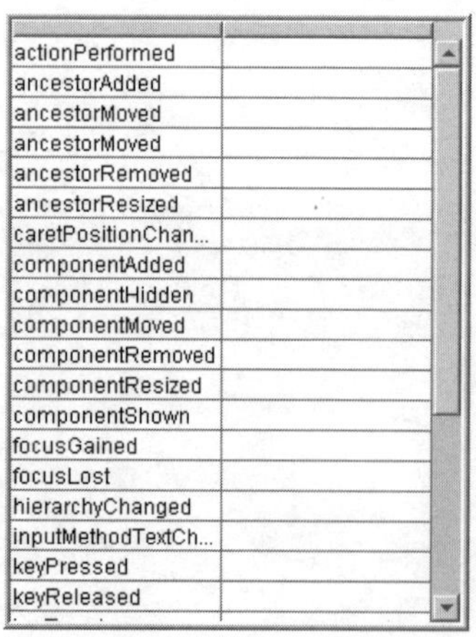

Figure 35-13: The Inspector for the ElfClock class as it appears if you have no BeanInfo or you use the default implementation of getEventSetDescriptors

Before you proceed, open up your ElfClockBeanInfor.java file and add the following import statement:

```
import java.awt.event.*;
```

To suppress most of the information about ancestor classes, focus your ElfClockBeanInfo.java source file in the JBuilder editor, and type in the following implementation of the getEventSetDescriptors method:

```
public EventSetDescriptor[] getEventSetDescriptors()
{
      try
      {
          EventSetDescriptor mouse = new EventSetDescriptor(
                ElfClock.class,
                "MouseListener",
                MouseListener.class,
                new String[] {"mousePressed", "mouseClicked",
                  "mouseReleased", "mouseEntered", "mouseExited"},
             "addMouseListener",
                "removeMouseListener");

            EventSetDescriptor eda[] = { mouse };
            return eda;
      }
      catch (IntrospectionException e)
      {
            e.printStackTrace();
      }
      return null;
}
```

This code says that all events except MouseListener should be suppressed. The first call to the constructor for the EventSetDescriptor class is unchanged. In the second call, the first parameter is the class you are working with, the second is the name of the event set, and the third is the event interface you want to expose. The fourth parameter is the names of the methods on that interface. You can find this list by looking at the source for the MouseListener interface. The fifth and sixth arguments are the methods used to add or remove the listener interface.

The end result of your work is that only the MouseListener interface is supported, as shown in Figure 35-14.

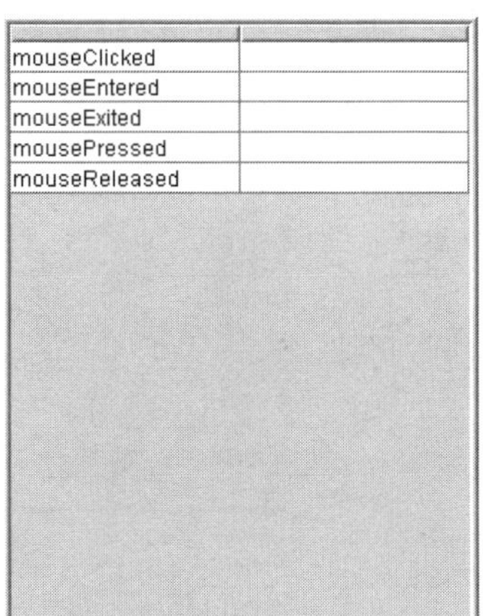

Figure 35-14: The Inspector for a class when you use BeanInfo to suppress all but MouseListener events

Consider the following code, but do not yet enter it into JBuilder:

```
public EventSetDescriptor[] getEventSetDescriptors()
{
      try
      {
          EventSetDescriptor action = new EventSetDescriptor(
                ElfClock.class, "ActionListener",
                ActionListener.class, "actionPerformed");

          EventSetDescriptor edArray[] = { action };
          return edArray;
      }
      catch (IntrospectionException e)
      {
            e.printStackTrace();
      }
      return null;
}
```

This is a simpler version of the getEventSetDescriptors method. It is tailor-made for working with simple events. This code says that all events, except ActionListener events, should be suppressed. Here is the lowdown on the constructor for the EventSetDescriptor class:

- The first parameter of the EventSetDescriptor constructor is a reference to the class you are working with: ElfClock.class.
- The second parameter is the name of the event set: "ActionListener".
- The third is the event interface you want to expose: ActionListener.class.
- The fourth is the name of the sole method on that interface: "actionPerformed".

Near the end of the getEventSetDescriptors method you set up the return value, which is an array of EventSetDescriptors. In this case, there is only one member in the array.

NOTE: The simple constructor used in the ActionEvent example should only be used for event interfaces that have a single method and add and remove listener methods that follow the standard pattern of addXXX and removeXXX, where XXX is the name of the event listener interface. The MouseListener interface shown above follows this pattern correctly. The MouseListener class itself, however, would not fit correctly into the pattern of this constructor because there are too many methods on it. I'm not saying that you won't be able to get your code to work with this simpler constructor, only that you really shouldn't use it because the MouseListener class has too many methods. Instead, you should use the first version of the getEventSetDescriptors constructor, as shown above.

Figure 35-15: The Inspector for a class when you use BeanInfo to suppress all but ActionListener events

Figure 35-15 shows what things look like after you insert the getEventDescriptors method shown above that works with ActionListeners.

There is, however, one significant problem with the ActionListener code shown here. Our component, ElfClock, does not handle ActionEvents. If you did try to insert the code shown here into your BeanInfo file, JBuilder would simply ignore the method and go back to the state of affairs shown in

Figure 35-13. That is, it would show you all the events on your current class and its ancestor. This is an indication that you are in an error state. The problem is figuring out what went wrong.

If you started JBuilder from the KDE, GNOME, or Windows Start menus, you would have no way of knowing what was wrong. However, if you went to the command prompt and started JBuilder from a shell or DOS window, you could see JBuilder spewing exceptions into the shell or command window when it tried to work with your BeanInfo class that contains the errant ActionEvent code. The lesson here is simple: If you are having trouble getting your BeanInfo code to work, start JBuilder from the command prompt and look for exceptions in the command prompt window at compile time.

There is, of course, a way to get the ActionPerformed instance of getEventSetDescriptors to work. All you need to do is add an ActionEvent to the ElfClock component, as shown in Figure 35-16 and as discussed in the chapters on event handling in Part III: JBuilder Fundamentals.

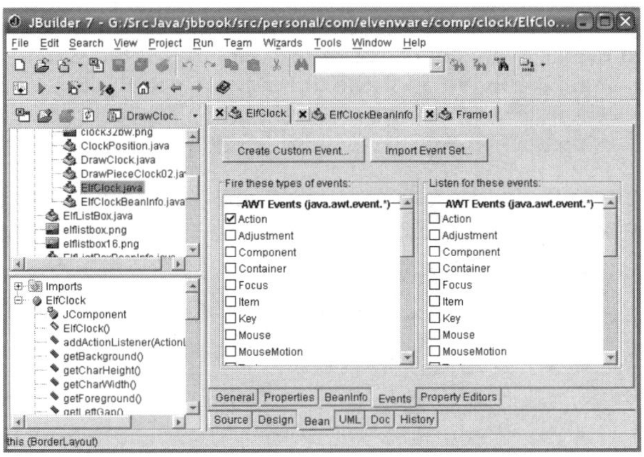

Figure 35-16: Using BeansExpress to add an ActionPerformed event handler to the ElfClock component

If you are using the Personal version of JBuilder, you would have to type in the generated code by hand:

```
public synchronized void removeActionListener(ActionListener l)
{
    if (actionListeners != null && actionListeners.contains(l))
    {
      Vector v = (Vector) actionListeners.clone();
      v.removeElement(l);
      actionListeners = v;
    }
}
public synchronized void addActionListener(ActionListener l)
{
    Vector v = actionListeners == null ? new Vector(2) : (Vector) actionListeners.clone();
    if (!v.contains(l))
    {
      v.addElement(l);
      actionListeners = v;
    }
}
```

```
protected void fireActionPerformed(ActionEvent e)
{
    if (actionListeners != null)
    {
      Vector listeners = actionListeners;
      int count = listeners.size();
      for (int i = 0; i < count; i++)
      {
          ((ActionListener) listeners.elementAt(i)).actionPerformed(e);
      }
    }
}
```

NOTE: As the component currently stands, there is no good reason to have ElfClock emit ActionPerformed events. In this particular case, I'm doing so only so you can better understand how the whole subject of events, event descriptors, and BeanInfo files fit together. If you wanted, however, you could extend the ElfClock component to fire ActionEvents at some predefined interval. For instance, it could fire the events every minute or at some interval requested by the user of the component. All that sounds to me like fun to implement, but I won't clutter the text of this book with that kind of code, as it is not essential to the current topic. I did, however, do something like that in the chapters on event handling back in Part III: JBuilder Fundamentals.

If you have more than one set of events that you want to expose on a component, use the following implementation of getEventSetDescriptors:

```
public EventSetDescriptor[] getEventSetDescriptors()
{
      try
      {
          EventSetDescriptor action = new EventSetDescriptor(
                ElfClock.class, "ActionListener",
                ActionListener.class, "actionPerformed");

          EventSetDescriptor mouse = new EventSetDescriptor(
                ElfClock.class,
                "MouseListener",
                MouseListener.class,
                new String[] {"mousePressed", "mouseClicked",
                  "mouseReleased", "mouseEntered", "mouseExited"},
             "addMouseListener",
                "removeMouseListener");

            EventSetDescriptor edArray[] = { action, mouse };
            return edArray;
      }
      catch (IntrospectionException e)
      {
            e.printStackTrace();
      }
      return null;
}
```

This code says that all events except MouseListener and ActionListener should be suppressed.

Notice the call near the bottom of the method that sets up an array of EventSetDescriptors:

```
EventSetDescriptor edArray[] = { action, mouse };
return edArray;
```

This is the value returned by the method. You can see the impact of all this on the Inspector by looking at Figure 35-17.

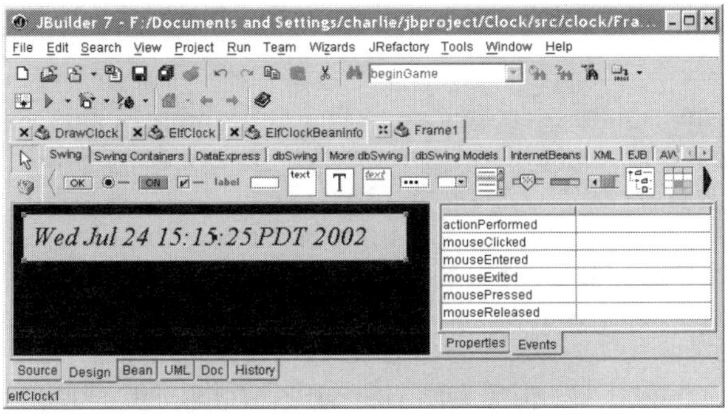

Figure 35-17: The Inspector for a class when you use BeanInfo to suppress all but ActionListener and MouseListener events

There is actually a bit more to be said about handling actionListeners. You will read about it in Chapter 37 in the section on BeanInsight.

Summary

I'm going to end the chapter here not because I am through talking about the Clock component but because the chapter is getting a bit long. You will want a break and a chance to experiment with the code you have seen before learning what more can be done with the Clock component.

In this chapter you have learned about working with bean properties. In particular, you saw how to use BeanInfo to hide and expose the properties of your bean. You also learned about the Timer object and paint methods.

In the next chapter, you will see how to add more features to the clock and how to convert it into a completely reusable component that resides in a JAR file.

Chapter 36

JavaBeans, Packages, and Java 2D

Charlie Calvert

This chapter continues the examination of the clock bean begun in the previous chapter. Here you will learn more about creating and manipulating properties. There will also be information on enhancing your components with Java2D.

Perhaps the most important sections of the chapter involve moving the files for the Clock component into an appropriate package. Conceptually, this task is quite simple, but you need to have a good understanding of JBuilder to make it work smoothly. The opening pages of the chapter address this issue.

The program explored in this chapter is called DrawClock02, which is included on the CD. This program depends on the src directory that is also on the CD. As a result, you will not be able to run this one program unless you install the code from the DrawClock02 directory structure and the src directory structure. Needless to say, the program will not run without modification unless you keep the relationship between the two directories the same. The install program on the CD should preserve that relationship for you.

Creating Version 1.0 of the Clock

By now we are ready to create a version of the clock that might be semi-useful in a real program. The primary difference between this version and the previous versions is threefold:

- The drawing of the letters will use Graphics2D to create an LCD appearance with the edges of the numbers rounded.
- Control will be given over the placement and appearance of the clock. It will be possible to resize the LCD numbers and establish the position of the clock inside control.
- The clock has been moved into its own package, com.elvenware.comp.clock.

Bringing the control to version 1.0 doesn't really mean that it can't be improved. It is more a matter of saying that the control is good enough for now.

Moving Files to a New Package

Let's begin by putting the component in a package where it can be accessed by other programs. This step is complicated but very important. Java is all about creating reusable components. If you don't store the components in a directory where all of your projects can get at them, they aren't reusable. What you are about to read may be complex, but once you get it straight, you will have the key to reusing components in your programs.

In this book, we are putting all the globally visible classes in a package that is part of the com.elvenware.* tree. If the idea of placing a component in a package does not make sense to you, then reread the chapters in Part V: Project Management. In particular, see Chapter 25.

If the root directory for the source code for this book is called jbbook, here is where we want to place these files:

```
/src/com/elvenware/comp/clock
```

The current location of our source files might be in a directory that looks like this:

```
/src/DrawClock/src/drawclock
```

Here you would find the files ElfClock.java and DrawClock.java, which were created in the previous chapter. These are the files you want to move.

NOTE: The actual directories where you currently store ElfClock.java and DrawClock.java are not important. Nor is it terribly important exactly where you move them. The point here is that sometimes you have code that you want to access from multiple programs. To make this work, it is often simplest to get the source files out of the directory tree for your current project and move them to a directory that you can make globally accessible to one or more projects. It is this general task that is important, and specific directory names are not important.

The code for the Clock component should go in a package called com.elvenware.comp.clock. Use the JBuilder tools to move your existing classes into the package called clock. On your system, the path to this directory might look like this:

```
/src/com/elvenware/comp/clock
```

Again, the specific directory that you put it in is not important. Just be sure that the com, elvenware, comp, and clock directories exist.

In particular, you can start by moving ElfClock.java and DrawClock.java into com/elvenware/comp/clock. Inside your source files, you will reference this with the following package statement:

```
package com.elvenware.comp.clock
```

The simplest way to move the source for a single class from one location to another is to go to the project pane, right-click on the file you want to move, and choose **Rename** from the pop-up menu. The Rename dialog pops up, as shown in Figure 36-1.

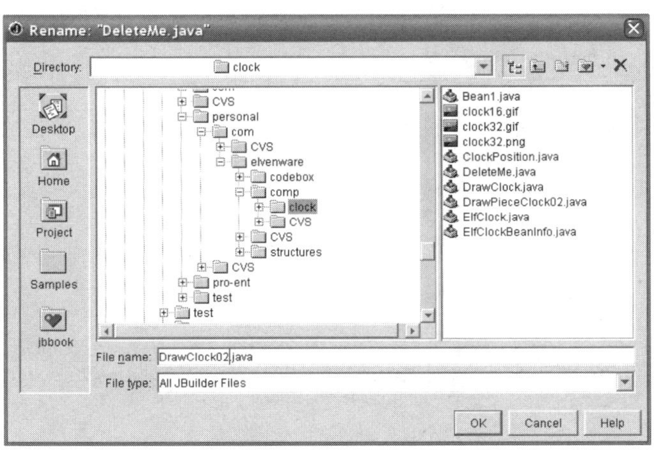

Figure 36-1: The Rename dialog allows you to not only rename a file but to move it from one location to another.

In this case, if you want to move a file from one directory to another, don't bother with the File Name and File Type text field controls shown at the bottom of Figure 36-1. Instead, use the directory tree shown above them to browse to the place where you want to move the file. If you need to create new directories, use the icon designated for that purpose at the top-right corner of the Rename dialog. When you have created the directories you need and navigated to the correct location, press the **OK** button, and your code will be moved.

At this stage, you will probably need to edit the package statement at the top of each file. In particular, they should now read com.elvenware.comp.clock.

NOTE: I have found that the refactoring utilities in JBuilder SE and Enterprise editions are not the right tools for moving files in the way suggested here. If you can get it to work, fine, but I found that refactoring does not work well when you want to move files to directories outside the scope of the current project. Instead, I would use the simple technique outlined above.

NOTE: I should add that there are several other ways to solve the problem I have explored in this section of the chapter. For instance, in Java, it is possible to have the package called com.elvenware.* in multiple locations across your hard drive. All you really need to do is put the base directory for all these different locations on your classpath, and Java will solve the rest of the problem for you. Or you could store the source in multiple directories and ask Java to put the compiled .class files in a single directory.

I do not mean to say that such systems are completely useless. There are times when they might be the perfect solution for you, particularly if you are working with a big team, but it is not the right solution for me in this case.

Path Issues: Creating Files in a New Directory

Once you have moved your files, there are two issues you need to confront:

- How can you get the new directory on the classpath for your current project?
- How can you ensure that any new files you want to add to the Clock component will end up in the correct directory?

As you know from Part V: Project Management, you can place packages on your JBuilder source path by using the Project Properties dialog shown in Figure 36-2.

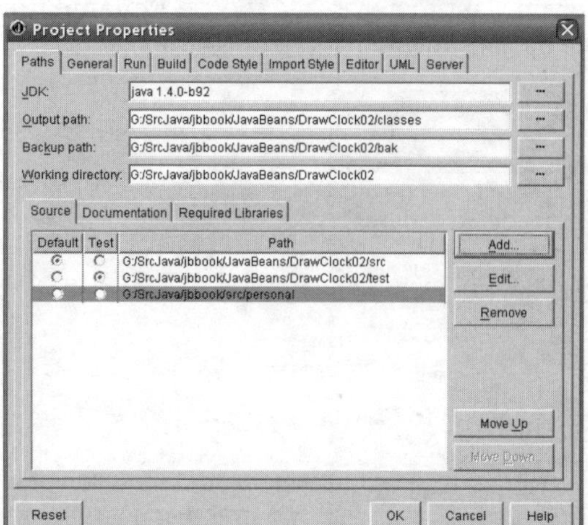

Figure 36-2: Referencing the directory where the source for the com.elvenware.* source tree is stored

In Figure 36-2, the directory to which I moved DrawClock.java and ElfClock.java is now listed on the source path. The next step is to add the proper import statement into Frame1.java:

```
import com.elvenware.comp.clock.*;
```

As a result, I can access the source just as easily as I could if it were in the same directory as the rest of my code. In particular, see Figure 36-3, which shows what the project pane should look like if everything is set up correctly.

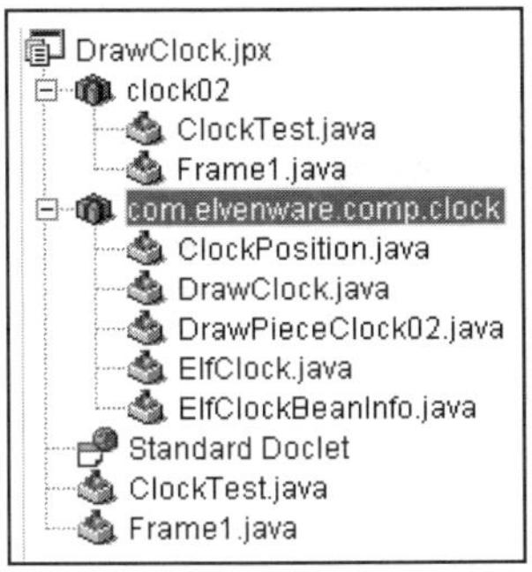

Figure 36-3: The project pane for the DrawClock program after you have moved the pieces of the Clock component into the com.elvenware.comp.clock package

NOTE: Unfortunately, the paths shown in Figure 36-2 won't be exactly the same as the ones on your system. On my system, the two classes are now in this directory: G:\srcjava\jbbook\src\personal\com\elvenware\comp\clock

The important part is that I have added the com.elvenware.comp.clock package to my path. To do this, I placed G:\srcjava\jbbook\src\personal in the dialog shown in Figure 36-2.

Figure 36-3 shows that the com.elvenware.comp.clock source package is now recognized as being part of your project. I should emphasize that it is the source files and not the class files that are being sorted out here. At this stage we are not trying to sort out where the class files will end up. In fact, they will end up as part of your local project. But that is not important to us. When the matter does become important, I will show you how to sort things out using JAR files.

NOTE: Your head may be spinning from trying to understand what is happening with all these source paths and classpaths. I believe that I mentioned earlier that packages are to Java a little bit the way pointers are to C and C++. It is a hurdle you have to get over. But once you understand what you can do with paths in Java, you may find that packages, like pointers, end up being a very useful tool.

There are several things to say about what you see in Figure 36-2. The good part of it is that you can see the code pointing at the jbbook/src/personal directory. This is the place where I store the Elvenware components on my machine:

```
/jbbook/src/personal/com/elvenware/codebox
/jbbook/src/personal/com/elvenware/comp/clock
```

NOTE: On the CD for this book, there are two sets of directories under /jbbook/src/. The first one, called personal, contains code that will compile in the Personal edition of JBuilder. The second one, called pro, will compile in the SE or Enterprise versions of JBuilder. I needed to do this so that I could provide source for all editions of the product. There is more information on this subject in the file on the CD called index.html.

If your system is set up like what is shown in Figure 36-2, JBuilder will be able to find any classes stored in the /src/personal directory and use them in your project. In effect, it puts the packages you point at on your source path. At the same time, it will solve your classpath problems for you, at least in terms of the current project.

However, JBuilder will not necessarily place or move new classes into the src/personal directory. The problem is that src/personal is not the default directory. As a result, if you select File | New Class and ask to put a file in the com.elvenware.comp.clock directory, your code might end up in:

```
/jbbook/JavaBeans/DrawClock/src/com/elvenware/comp/clock.
```

That is not what you wanted. You were hoping to place the code in:

```
/jbbook/src/personal/com/Elvenware/comp/clock.
```

To force the code into the proper directory, set the /src/personal directory as the default directory and locate it at the top of the list, as shown in Figure 36-4.

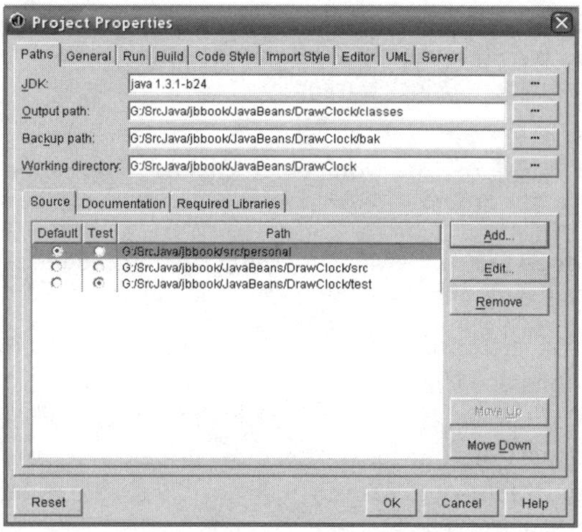

Figure 36-4: Making the /src/personal directory the default location where code will be created or moved

I know that all of this moving pieces around into their own directories and setting up all these packages adds a layer of complication to the task of building the clock bean. However, the point of this book is not really to teach you how to build JavaBeans. That is explained in other books. This book is focusing on JBuilder itself, and all of this shuffling of code and packages forces you to learn how it really works.

I want to emphasize that this kind of shuffling of packages is something that can definitely happen quite often in Java project development. In fact, there is one school of development, called extreme programming, that puts a huge emphasis on exactly the kind of refactoring that I have been describing in the last few pages. Moving classes around from package to package is a skill that most developers need to master.

The rest of this chapter discusses how to create the interface for the new clock bean. The information found there will show you how to create the heart of the bean. However, that job is really just a Java programming task and as such, has only peripheral interest to readers of this book. If you are anxious to move on, you can skip to the next chapter and learn how to examine the bean you have created and how to wrap it in a JAR file. If you would prefer to explore the whole subject of creating the properties and interface for a bean in more depth, then read on.

Upgrading the Interface of the Clock

At last you are ready to begin working on phase two of the development of the Clock component. The goal here is to upgrade the interface of the component so that it appears as it does in Figure 36-5.

Figure 36-5: The new interface for the Clock component looks like it has an LCD display.

As you can see from Figure 36-5, the component now looks as though it has an LCD display. This version of the component lets you change the color, size, and location of the characters being displayed.

You will find that the source code for ElfClock.java is nearly identical to what it was in the first version of this program. The difference comes from the addition of a new class, called DrawPieceClock02.java, which derives from the simple DrawClock class we saw earlier. You can see portions of the source for this class in Listing 36-1. Listing 36-2 shows the new source for ElfClock.java.

Listing 36-1: The source for the DrawPieceClock02 class shows how to create LCD numbers using Java2D.

```
package com.elvenware.comp.clock;

import java.awt.*;
import java.awt.geom.*;
import java.util.*;

/**
 * <p>Title: </p>
 * <p>Description: Draws a clock using military time </p>
 * <p>Copyright: Copyright (c) 2001 by Charlie Calvert</p>
 * <p>Company: Elvenware</p>
 * @author Charlie Calvert
 * @version 1.0
 */

public class DrawPieceClock02 extends DrawClock
{
      private Graphics2D g2;
      /** left is the gap between letters */
      private int leftGap = 2;
      /** How far should the whole clock display be moved in from the left */
      private int leftOffSet;
      /** How far from the top should the clock display be offset? */
      private int topOffSet = 0;
      /** How wide is each char. Real value is this value minus left offset */
      private int charWidth = 25;
      /** How high is the character. Real value is this value minus top offset */
      private int charHeight = 25;
      /** The permanent gap at the top of the clock. See topOffSet. */
```

```
private int HORZ_Y_TOP = 5;
/** The position of the middle bar */
private int HORZ_Y_MIDDLE = HORZ_Y_TOP + charHeight;
/** The position of the bottom bar */
private int HORZ_Y_BOTTOM = HORZ_Y_MIDDLE + charHeight;
/** The text color */
private Color foreGround = Color.green;
/** The width of lines in the letters */
private int textWidth;
/** Go from left to right */
private     com.elvenware.comp.clock.ClockPosition H_TOP =
      com.elvenware.comp.clock.ClockPosition.H_TOP;
/** Go from right to left */
private     com.elvenware.comp.clock.ClockPosition H_TOP_BACK =
      com.elvenware.comp.clock.ClockPosition.H_TOP_BACK;
/** A middle bar from left to right */
private     com.elvenware.comp.clock.ClockPosition H_MIDDLE =
      com.elvenware.comp.clock.ClockPosition.H_MIDDLE;

// A number of lines of very repetitive code like the previous three statements
// are omitted here. See the source on the CD for the complete listing.

/** The Shape object used when drawing a letter */
private GeneralPath gp;

/** Default constructor creates the GeneralPath */
public DrawPieceClock02()
{
      gp = new GeneralPath(GeneralPath.WIND_EVEN_ODD);
}

/**
 * Draw the letter and reset (empty) the path for the next letter
 *
 */
private void doDraw()
{
      g2.draw(gp);
      gp.reset();
}

/**
 * Give this command to draw the clock. Other than the constructor and
 * getters and setters, this is the only public command on the object.
 *
 * @param initG2 The graphics object to paint with.
 */
public void draw(Graphics2D initG2)
{
      Calendar c = new GregorianCalendar();
```

```
        // We need to get each number in the time to be drawn.
        // For instance, in 12:34:56, 1 is big hour, 2 is small hour, etc
        int seconds = c.get(Calendar.SECOND);
        int smallSec = seconds % 10;
        int bigSec = seconds / 10;

        int minutes = c.get(Calendar.MINUTE);
        int smallMin = minutes % 10;
        int bigMin = minutes / 10;

        int hours = c.get(Calendar.HOUR_OF_DAY);
        int smallHour = hours % 10;
        int bigHour = hours / 10;

        g2 = initG2;
        g2.setColor(foreGround);
        // Set width of the lines in the numbers and appearance of their ends
        g2.setStroke(new BasicStroke(textWidth, BasicStroke.CAP_ROUND,
          BasicStroke.JOIN_ROUND));

        printNum(bigHour, 0);
        printNum(smallHour, 1);
        colon(2);
        printNum(bigMin, 3);
        printNum(smallMin, 4);
        colon(5);
        printNum(bigSec, 6);
        printNum(smallSec, 7);
    }

    /**
     * Calculate the coordinates in pixels of the lines to be drawn to make
     * up each letter. Each part of the letter is a different bar, and
     * a generalPath is used to append all the different parts together
     * and draw a whole letter.
     *
     * @param position: Which bar in the letter is it.
     * @param place: Place in number, in 12:34:56, 3 is in the 4th place.
     */
    private void drawBar(ClockPosition position, int place)
    {
        int addIn = getSpace(place); // place * (charWidth + textWidth + 2);
        int xPosStart = leftGap + addIn;
        int xPosEnd = charWidth + addIn;
        int yPosTop = HORZ_Y_TOP + topOffSet;
        int yPosMiddle = HORZ_Y_MIDDLE + topOffSet;
        int yPosBottom = HORZ_Y_BOTTOM + topOffSet;

        if (position == H_TOP)
        {
            Line2D l = new Line2D.Double(xPosStart, yPosTop, xPosEnd, yPosTop);
```

```
            gp.append(l, true);

        }
        else if (position == H_TOP_BACK)
        {
            Line2D l = new Line2D.Double(xPosEnd, yPosTop, xPosStart, yPosTop);
            gp.append(l, true);
        }
        else if (position == H_MIDDLE)
        {
            Line2D l = new Line2D.Double(xPosStart, yPosMiddle,
                xPosEnd, yPosMiddle);
            gp.append(l, true);
        }
        else if (position == H_MIDDLE_BACK)
        {
            Line2D l = new Line2D.Double(xPosEnd, yPosMiddle,
                xPosStart, yPosMiddle);
            gp.append(l, true);
        }
        else if (position == H_BOTTOM)
        {
            Line2D l = new Line2D.Double(xPosStart, yPosBottom,
                xPosEnd, yPosBottom);
            gp.append(l, true);
        }
        else if (position == V_LEFT_TOP)
        {
            Line2D l = new Line2D.Double(xPosStart, yPosTop,
                xPosStart, yPosMiddle);
            gp.append(l, true);
        }
        else if (position == V_LEFT_BOTTOM)
        {
            Line2D l = new Line2D.Double(xPosStart, yPosMiddle, xPosStart,
                yPosBottom);
            gp.append(l, true);
        }
        else if (position == V_MIDDLE)
        {
            Line2D l = new Line2D.Double(xPosEnd - (charWidth / 2),
                yPosTop, xPosEnd - (charWidth / 2) , yPosBottom);
            gp.append(l, true);
        }
        else if (position == V_RIGHT_TOP)
        {
            Line2D l = new Line2D.Double(xPosEnd, yPosTop, xPosEnd, yPosMiddle);
            gp.append(l, true);
        }
        else if (position == V_RIGHT_SIDE)
        {
```

```
            Line2D l = new Line2D.Double(xPosEnd, yPosTop, xPosEnd, yPosBottom);
            gp.append(l, true);
        }
        else if (position == V_RIGHT_BOTTOM)
        {
            Line2D l = new Line2D.Double(xPosEnd, yPosMiddle,
                xPosEnd, yPosBottom);
            gp.append(l, true);
        }
    }

    /**
     *  Draw an individual number to the screen. For instance, in
     *  12:34:56, draw the number 1, or the number 6.
     *  @param num The number to draw
     *  @param place Position in the time. Is it the BigHour, Little Hour, etc?
     */
    private void printNum(int num, int place)
    {
        switch (num)
        {
            case 0:
                zero(place);
                break;
            case 1:
                one(place);
                break;

            // Repetitive code omitted for cases 3-9. See the CD for a complete listing

            default:
                System.err.println("Error");
                break;
        }
        doDraw();
    }

    /**
     * When offsetting a number to the third or fourth place, this calculates
     * how far to offset it.
     *
     * @param place The place in the number. In 12:34:56, 2 is in the second
     * place
     *
     * @return The offset in pixels
     */
    private int getSpace(int place)
    {
        return ((charWidth + textWidth + 2) * place) + leftOffSet;
    }
```

Part VII

```
/**
 * Draw the colon
 *
 * @param place Position of number.
 */
private void colon(int place)
{
      int pos = getSpace(place);
      int space = 2;
      int x = (charWidth / 2) + pos;
      int y1 = HORZ_Y_TOP + 10 + topOffSet;
      int y2 = HORZ_Y_BOTTOM - space + topOffSet;
      g2.drawRect(x - space, y1 - 5, space, space);
      g2.drawRect(x - space, y2 - 5, space, space);
      doDraw();
}

/**
 * Calculate the lines in a zero.
 *
 * @param place The place in the number, in 12:34:56, 3 is in the 4th place
 */
private void zero(int place)
{
      drawBar(V_LEFT_BOTTOM, place);
      drawBar(V_LEFT_TOP, place);
      drawBar(H_TOP, place);
      drawBar(V_RIGHT_TOP, place);
      drawBar(V_RIGHT_BOTTOM, place);
      drawBar(H_BOTTOM, place);
}

/**
 * Calculate the lines in a one
 *
 * @param place The place in the number, in 12:34:56, 3 is in the 4th place
 */
private void one(int place)
{
      drawBar(V_MIDDLE, place);
}

// In the text of this book, I omit the code implementing the remaining methods.
// See the source on the CD for complete listing.
private void two(int place)
private void three(int place)
private void four(int place)
private void five(int place)
private void six(int place)
private void seven(int place)
private void eight(int place)
```

```
    private void nine(int place)
    public Color getForeGround()
    public void setForeGround(Color foreGround)
    public int getTextWidth()
    public void setTextWidth(int textWidth)
    public int getCharWidth()
    public void setCharWidth(int charWidth)
    public int getCharHeight()

    /**
     * When setting the height of a character, we need to make sure
     * that the settings for the top, middle and bottom of the character
     * are adjusted accordingly.
     *
     * @param charHeight The height of the character
     */
    public void setCharHeight(int charHeight)
    {
        this.charHeight = charHeight;
        HORZ_Y_MIDDLE = HORZ_Y_TOP + this.charHeight;
        HORZ_Y_BOTTOM = HORZ_Y_MIDDLE + this.charHeight;
    }

    public int getTopOffSet()
    public void setTopOffSet(int top)
    public void setLeftOffSet(int leftOffSet)
    public int getLeftOffSet()
    public int getLeftGap()
    public void setLeftGap(int leftGap)
}
```

Listing 36-2: The source for ElfClock.java has been modified slightly since the previous chapter to give you access to the DrawPieceClock02 class.

```
package com.elvenware.comp.clock;

import java.awt.*;
import java.awt.event.*;
import java.util.*;
import javax.swing.*;
import javax.swing.Timer;

/**
 * <p>Title: ElfClock</p>
 * <p>Description: A simple clock component</p>
 * <p>Copyright: Copyright (c) 2001</p>
 * <p>Company: Elvenware </p>
 * @author Charlie Calvert
 * @version 1.0
 */
public class ElfClock extends JComponent
{
```

```
BorderLayout borderLayout1 = new BorderLayout();
/** The timer that drives the clock */
Timer clockTimer = null;
/** Whether the clock is running or not */
private boolean running;
/** Control for displaying the time and date */
private DrawPieceClock02 drawClock = new DrawPieceClock02();
/** The width of the lines in the clock */
private int textWidth;
/** The width of the numbers in the clock */
private int charWidth = 25;
/** The height of the numbers on the clock */
private int charHeight = 25;
private int leftOffSet = 2;
private int topOffSet = 2;
private int leftGap = 2;
/** The color of the numbers on the clock */
// private java.awt.Color foreground=Color.green;
/** The background color */
//private java.awt.Color background=Color.black;

/**
 * Constructor
 */
public ElfClock()
{
      try
      {
            jbInit();
      }
      catch(Exception ex)
      {
            ex.printStackTrace();
      }
}

/**
 * Custom method for JBuilder initialization of visual components
 *
 * @throws Exception
 */
private void jbInit() throws Exception
{
      this.setLayout(borderLayout1);
      clockTimer = new javax.swing.Timer(250, new ActionListener()
      {
            public void actionPerformed(ActionEvent e)
            {
                  repaint();
            }
      });
```

```
    }

    /**
     * Property to turn the clock on or off
     *
     * @param running Whether to stop or start the clock
     */
    public void setRunning(boolean running)
    {
        this.running = running;
        if (this.running)
            clockTimer.start();
        else
            clockTimer.stop();
    }

    /**
     * Determines if the clock is active or not.
     *
     * @return Whether or not the clock is running
     */
    public boolean isRunning()
    {
        return running;
    }

    public void paint(Graphics g)
    {
        super.paint(g);
        g.setColor(getBackground());
        g.fillRect(0, 0, this.getWidth(), this.getHeight());
        drawClock.setForeGround(getForeground());
        drawClock.setTextWidth(textWidth);
        drawClock.setCharWidth(charWidth);
        drawClock.setCharHeight(charHeight);
        drawClock.setTopOffSet(topOffSet);
        drawClock.setLeftOffSet(leftOffSet);
        drawClock.setLeftGap(leftGap);
        drawClock.draw((Graphics2D)g);
    }

    public void setTextWidth(int textWidth)
    {
        this.textWidth = textWidth;
    }

    public int getTextWidth()
    {
        return textWidth;
    }
```

```
public void setCharWidth(int charWidth)
{
      this.charWidth = charWidth;
}

public int getCharWidth()
{
      return charWidth;
}

public void setCharHeight(int charHeight)
{
      this.charHeight = charHeight;
}

public int getCharHeight()
{
      return charHeight;
}
public void setLeftOffSet(int left)
{
      this.leftOffSet = left;
}
public int getLeftOffSet()
{
      return leftOffSet;
}
public void setTopOffSet(int top)
{
      this.topOffSet = top;
}
public int getTopOffSet()
{
      return topOffSet;
}
public void setLeftGap(int leftGap)
{
      this.leftGap = leftGap;
}
public int getLeftGap()
{
      return leftGap;
}
public void setForeground(java.awt.Color foreground)
{
      super.setForeground(foreground);
}
public java.awt.Color getForeground()
{
      return super.getForeground();
}
```

```
        public void setBackground(java.awt.Color background)
        {
            super.setBackground(background);
        }
        public java.awt.Color getBackground()
        {
            return super.getBackground();
        }
    }
```

When looking at Listing 36-2, notice that the variable that previously pointed at the class called DrawClock now points at DrawPieceClock:

```
    private DrawPieceClock02 drawClock = new DrawPieceClock02();
```

A few new properties have also been added to the ElfClock class. Most of these new properties are used in the updated paint method:

```
        public void paint(Graphics g)
        {
            super.paint(g);
            g.setColor(getBackground());
            g.fillRect(0, 0, this.getWidth(), this.getHeight());
            drawClock.setForeGround(getForeground());
            drawClock.setTextWidth(textWidth);
            drawClock.setCharWidth(charWidth);
            drawClock.setCharHeight(charHeight);
            drawClock.setTopOffSet(topOffSet);
            drawClock.setLeftOffSet(leftOffSet);
            drawClock.setLeftGap(leftGap);
            drawClock.draw((Graphics2D)g);
        }
```

As you can see, most of the properties are actually implemented in DrawPieceClock. I create wrapper methods for them in ElfClock so that they can be surfaced as properties in the JBuilder Inspector. In particular, look at Figure 36-6, which shows the exposed properties of the new version of the ElfClock component.

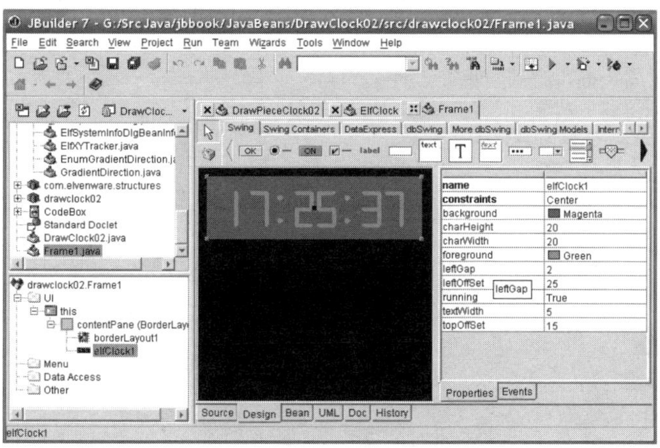

Figure 36-6: In its new incarnation, the ElfClock component now has a number of different properties that allow the user to fine-tune its appearance.

In Figure 36-6, you see the ElfClock bean resting inside a JFrame descendant. The ElfClock component is selected in the structure pane, and the Inspector shows the public properties of the component. I have suppressed all the ancestor properties by not overriding the SimpleBeanInfo implementation of getAdditionalBeanInfo. As you recall, this method returns null by default. A value of null returned by this method of the BeanInfo object tells the Inspector not to perform any further introspection on the bean but to surface the public properties exposed by the BeanInfo class itself.

Drawing LCD Numbers with Graphics2D

In this section I describe how to draw the letters of the improved clock. This is a complex process that I isolate in a separate object called DrawPieceClock02.java. I pay a very small price in terms of memory usage for breaking off a part of the ElfClock into this separate drawing object. I believe, however, that it makes the code more readable and isolates a certain degree of complexity. In particular, all the drawing of the clock takes place in that one object, while any other maintenance tasks, such as constructing the timer that drives the clock, are taken care of in ElfClock. It's a typical divide and conquer strategy.

When drawing the letters, I use the General Path object that is part of Java2D. I first create the GeneralPath in the constructor:

```
gp = new GeneralPath(GeneralPath.WIND_EVEN_ODD);
```

The real work is then done inside the draw method, which ends up controlling the object:

```
public void draw(Graphics2D initG2)
{
    Calendar c = new GregorianCalendar();

    // We need to get each number in the time to be drawn.
    // For instance, in 12:34:56, 1 is big hour, 2 is small hour, etc
    int seconds = c.get(Calendar.SECOND);
    int smallSec = seconds % 10;
    int bigSec = seconds / 10;

    int minutes = c.get(Calendar.MINUTE);
    int smallMin = minutes % 10;
    int bigMin = minutes / 10;

    int hours = c.get(Calendar.HOUR_OF_DAY);
    int smallHour = hours % 10;
    int bigHour = hours / 10;

    g2 = initG2;
    g2.setColor(foreGround);
    // Set width of the lines in the numbers and appearance of their ends
    g2.setStroke(new BasicStroke(textWidth, BasicStroke.CAP_ROUND,
      BasicStroke.JOIN_ROUND));

    printNum(bigHour, 0);
    printNum(smallHour, 1);
    colon(2);
    printNum(bigMin, 3);
```

```
            printNum(smallMin, 4);
            colon(5);
            printNum(bigSec, 6);
            printNum(smallSec, 7);
        }
```

The code first creates a calendar object. It then retrieves the seconds, minutes, and hours from the calendar. Note that it retrieves the military time using Calendar.HOUR_OF_DAY rather than Calendar.HOUR. The latter constant retrieves the time for the two 12-hour segments of the day, rather than one 24-hour segment.

The next step is to convert the seconds, minutes, and hours into individual digits. For instance, if it is 23 minutes after the hour, the program needs to divide that number up into two digits, a 3 and a 2. It then draws each digit individually, as shown earlier in Figure 36-5.

If you look at Figure 36-5, you can see the soft, or rounded, edges noticeable at the top of the 1, at the beginnings and ends of the 2's, and at the edges of the 0. These effects were achieved through Graphics2D calls. In particular, the stroke for the instance of Graphics2D we are using is set up with the CAP_ROUND and JOIN_ROUND constants:

```
            g2.setStroke(new BasicStroke(textWidth, BasicStroke.CAP_ROUND,
              BasicStroke.JOIN_ROUND));
```

The stroke will now have rounded edges, as shown in Figure 36-5.

NOTE: There is a second version of this component, found in the DrawClock directory on the CD, that uses the old Java graphics classes to draw the component. As a result, the edges of the clock are flat rather than rounded. You can run that program if you would like to compare the two versions of the code.

All that is left to do at this stage is create the individual numbers and then draw them. Each number enters the world in a separate method. For instance, the number 0 is created in this method:

```
        private void zero(int place)
        {
            drawBar(V_LEFT_BOTTOM, place);
            drawBar(V_LEFT_TOP, place);
            drawBar(H_TOP, place);
            drawBar(V_RIGHT_TOP, place);
            drawBar(V_RIGHT_BOTTOM, place);
            drawBar(H_BOTTOM, place);
        }
```

The pseudo-enumerated types, such as V_LEFT_BOTTOM, designate each of the different lines out of which a number is made. To create a letter, you must combine one or more of these lines, as shown in Figure 36-7.

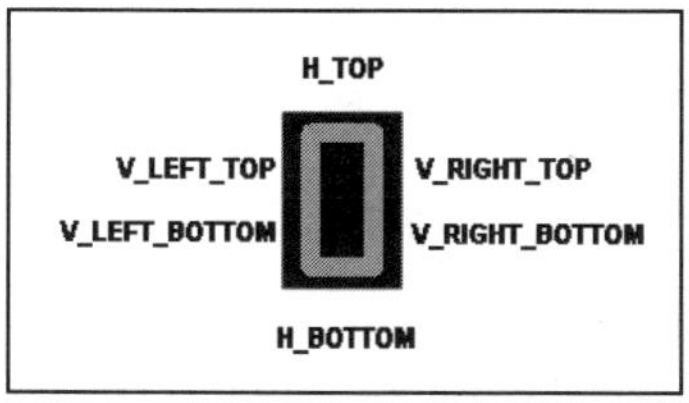

Figure 36-7 : The six lines out of which the number zero is made

Each call to drawBar ends up placing a new line into the GeneralPath:

```
private void drawBar(Position position, int place)
{
      int addIn = getSpace(place); // place * (charWidth + textWidth + 2);
      int xPosStart = leftGap + addIn;
      int xPosEnd = charWidth + addIn;
      int yPosTop = HORZ_Y_TOP + topOffSet;
      int yPosMiddle = HORZ_Y_MIDDLE + topOffSet;
      int yPosBottom = HORZ_Y_BOTTOM + topOffSet;

      if (position == H_TOP)
      {
            Line2D l = new Line2D.Double(xPosStart, yPosTop,
                  xPosEnd, yPosTop);
            gp.append(l, true);

      }
      else if (position == H_TOP_BACK)
      {
            Line2D l = new Line2D.Double(xPosEnd, yPosTop,
                  xPosStart, yPosTop);
            gp.append(l, true);
      }
      else if (position == H_MIDDLE)

      etc...
```

In this code fragment, you can see that each new line is created using the Line2D object from the java.awt.geom package. In some cases, it will matter whether the line is drawn from left to right or from right to left. In such cases, I have designated two enumerated constants. For instance, in this code you can see H_TOP and H_TOP_BACK. One goes from right to left and the other from left to right. Other constants go from top to bottom and bottom to top. I also have a special line for drawing the number one.

The drawBar method begins with some simple calculations that determine the proper location for each letter. There are several different considerations in this matter. Consider the time 12:34:56. In this moment of time, the 2 should be drawn to the right of the 1, and the 3 to the right of the colon, 1, and 2. These offsets are calculated at the beginning of drawBar. The user of the component also has the option of placing an offset, or margin, around the entire clock. The topOffSet and addIn variables help account for this factor.

Once all the lines making up a number have been appended to the general path, the only thing left to do is draw it:

```
private void doDraw()
{
      g2.draw(gp);
      gp.reset();
}
```

This exceedingly simple call first uses the Graphics2D object to draw the GeneralPath. The call works because GeneralPath is a descendant of the Shape object, and all Shape objects can be drawn by the Graphics2D.draw method. Furthermore, all Graphics2D geometry objects, including a Line2D, are also descendants of Shape. Therefore, you can draw any Graphics2D object with the Shape method.

I will not go into any detail describing the various properties that I have added to the Clock component. However, when you are using the component, you should note the topOffSet, leftOffSet, textWidth, charHeight, and charWidth properties. Each of these properties give you some control over the appearance of the clock. For instance, the textWidth property lets you define the thickness of the lines that are used to draw the numbers of the clock. The charWidth and charHeight properties define the height and width of the numbers that are drawn.

The best way to learn about these properties is to use them interactively inside the JBuilder IDE. Just try plugging different values into them, and you will soon see what each one is about. You might also look at the code in the paint method for the ElfClock where the user's settings for these values are passed off to the DrawPieceClock02 object, which actually does the hard work of drawing the clock.

The Enumerated Type

You might be interested in the constants, such as H_TOP and H_MIDDLE, that I use in this program. As you know, Java does not have an enumerated type. As a result, I use a little trick that creates something that acts like an enumerated type. My explanation of this syntax appears in Chapter 16.

Here is the class that is used to declare the pseudo-enumerated type:

```
public final class ClockPosition
{
      private ClockPosition() {}
      public static final ClockPosition H_TOP = new ClockPosition();
      public static final ClockPosition H_TOP_BACK = new ClockPosition();
      public static final ClockPosition H_MIDDLE = new ClockPosition();
      public static final ClockPosition H_MIDDLE_BACK = new ClockPosition();
      public static final ClockPosition H_BOTTOM = new ClockPosition();
      public static final ClockPosition V_LEFT_TOP = new ClockPosition();
      public static final ClockPosition V_LEFT_BOTTOM = new ClockPosition();
      public static final ClockPosition V_MIDDLE = new ClockPosition();
      public static final ClockPosition V_RIGHT_TOP = new ClockPosition();
      public static final ClockPosition V_RIGHT_SIDE = new ClockPosition();
      public static final ClockPosition V_RIGHT_BOTTOM = new ClockPosition();
}
```

Here is an example of how to use the class:

```
      private     com.elvenware.comp.clock.ClockPosition V_RIGHT_SIDE =
            com.elvenware.comp.clock.ClockPosition.V_RIGHT_SIDE;
      private     com.elvenware.comp.clock.ClockPosition V_RIGHT_BOTTOM =
            com.elvenware.comp.clock.ClockPosition.V_RIGHT_BOTTOM;

      // Code ommitted here

      private void drawBar(ClockPosition position, int place)
      {
            // Code ommitted here
```

```
            if (position == V_RIGHT_SIDE)
            {
                Line2D l = new Line2D.Double(xPosEnd, yPosTop, xPosEnd, yPosBottom);
                gp.append(l, true);
            }
            else if (position == V_RIGHT_BOTTOM)
            {
                Line2D l = new Line2D.Double(xPosEnd, yPosMiddle,
                    xPosEnd, yPosBottom);
                gp.append(l, true);
            }
        }

        drawBar(V_RIGHT_BOTTOM, place);
```

The call to drawBar at the bottom of this code fragment sets the position variable to one of the "enumerated" types. Based on that setting, one particular branch of the drawBar method is called. The advantage of this system over integer constants is that it is type safe.

Summary

In this chapter you saw how to move the components you created in the previous chapter into their own directory. This maneuver allows you to use the files easily from multiple projects. It also helps set the scene for the next chapter, in which you will learn how to wrap the bean in a JAR file.

You have also seen all the important code involved in drawing the clock. Most of the task involved learning how to use Java2D.

The last sections of the chapter offered another example of how to use a pseudo-enumerated type in a Java program. This topic was discussed in Chapter 16.

Chapter 37

BeanInsight and JAR Files

Charlie Calvert

In this chapter we will continue to examine the Clock component. There will be three particular areas of study:

- Examining the bean with BeanInsight
- Wrapping the bean in a JAR file
- Placing the bean on the component palette

By now you should feel as though you have a fairly good sense of how to put together a JavaBean. In fact, much of the work you have been doing throughout the book should now be beginning to bear fruit.

In this chapter you will learn how to put the finishing touches on your control so that you can easily share it with others.

Using BeanInsight

BeanInsight is a tool used to confirm the validity of your bean and examine its properties. In many ways, the JBuilder Inspector does an adequate job of handling these tasks. However, there are a few new things you can learn if you put BeanInsight on the job. BeanInsight is an SE and Enterprise level tool.

To use BeanInsight, choose **Tools | BeanInsight**. Click on the ellipsis to the right of the Select a bean to examine input field to bring up the Bean Chooser dialog shown in Figure 37-1. Search for the ElfClock class. Alternatively, focus the class you want to examine in the editor or designer before you bring up BeanInsight. Then you won't need to browse for it.

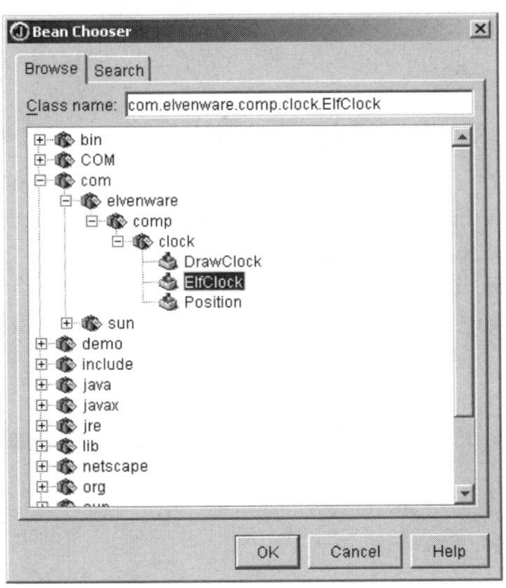

Figure 37-1: Using the Bean Chooser from BeanInsight to search for the ElfClock class that you want to examine

Click **OK** to return to the BeanInsight dialog. Press the **Examine Bean** button. BeanInsight should now look as it does in Figure 37-2.

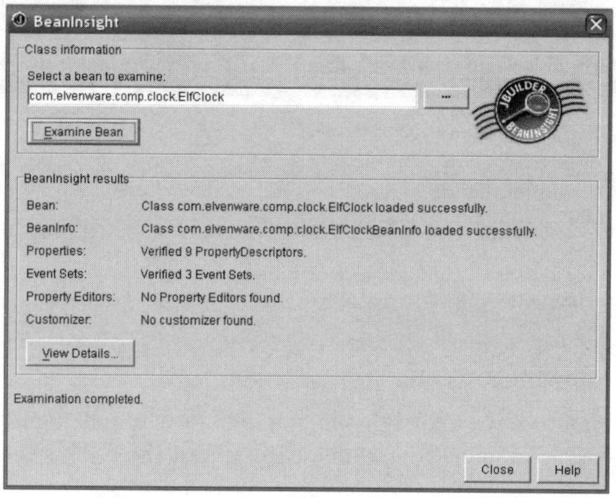

Figure 37-2: Examining your bean with BeanInsight

You can see that the bean is valid and has nine property descriptors, three event descriptors, and so on. If something is terribly wrong with your bean, one of the items in the results section would turn up in red. For instance, if you did not include a BeanInfo file, there would be a message to that effect written in red in the results section of the dialog.

The nine property descriptors correspond to the background, charHeight, charWidth, foreground, leftGap, leftOffSet, running, textWidth, and topOffSet properties you created in the last two chapters. You can also find these descriptors listed in the ElfClockBeanInfo class:

```
PropertyDescriptor[] pds = new PropertyDescriptor[] {
    _background,
    _charHeight,
    _charWidth,
    _foreground,
    _leftGap,
    _leftOffSet,
    _running,
    _textWidth,
    _topOffSet};
```

If you click the View Details buttons, you can find out more about your bean, as shown in Figure 37-3. There you can see that this class meets the basic requirements for a bean in that it has a default constructor and is stored in a public class. You can also see the inheritance tree for the bean and the implemented interfaces. The ElfClock class did not implement these interfaces; rather, it inherited their implementation.

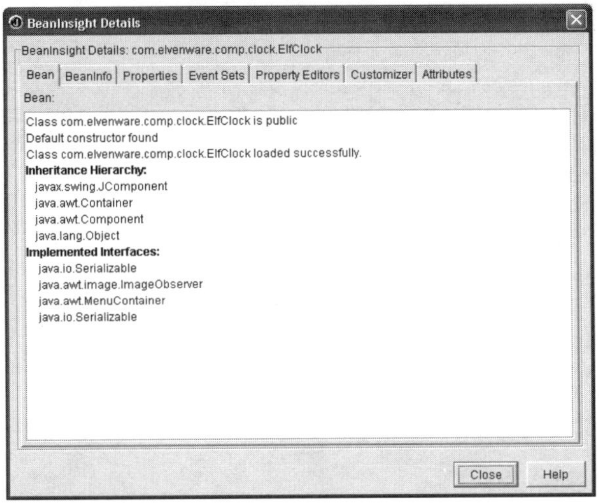

Figure 37-3: Using BeanInsight to learn about the inheritance tree for a bean

In Figure 37-4 you can see all of the events associated with your bean. These were the events explicitly surfaced in the previous chapter by overriding the getEventSetDescriptors method of SimpleBeanInfo.

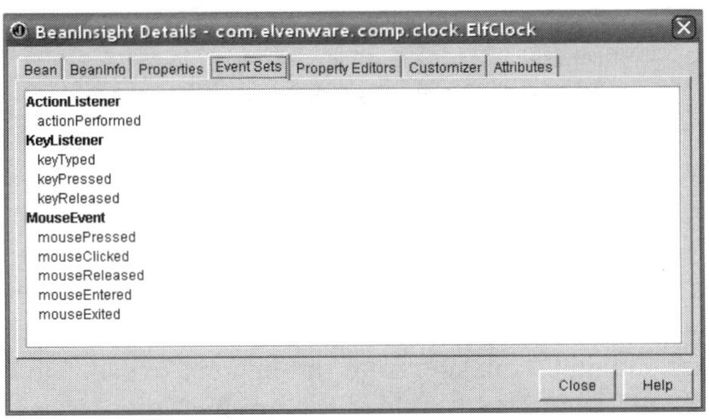

Figure 37-4: Using BeanInsight to view the events associated with your bean

In BeanInsight, your connection to the code you wrote in ElfClockBeanInfo is somewhat closer than it is in the Inspector. Here, once again, is the method in the BeanInfo file that exposes the events — and only the events — that the component wants to make available to the user.

```
public EventSetDescriptor[] getEventSetDescriptors()
{
    try
    {
        EventSetDescriptor action = new EventSetDescriptor(
            ElfClock.class, "ActionListener",
            ActionListener.class, "actionPerformed");

       EventSetDescriptor key = new EventSetDescriptor(
           ElfClock.class, "KeyListener",
           KeyListener.class,
           new String[] {"keyTyped", "keyPressed", "keyReleased"},
           "addKeyListener",
```

Part VII

```
                  "removeKeyListener");

            EventSetDescriptor mouse = new EventSetDescriptor(
                  ElfClock.class, "MouseEvent", MouseListener.class,
                  new String[] {"mousePressed", "mouseClicked",
                        "mouseReleased", "mouseEntered", "mouseExited"},
                  "addMouseListener",
                  "removeMouseListener");

            EventSetDescriptor edArray[] = { action, key, mouse };
            return edArray;
      }
      catch (IntrospectionException e)
      {
            e.printStackTrace();
      }
      return null;
}
```

Suppose one were to change the listing for the MouseListener section of this method by removing some of the methods:

```
      EventSetDescriptor mouse = new EventSetDescriptor(
                  ElfClock.class, "MouseEvent", MouseListener.class,
                  new String[] {"mouseReleased", "mouseEntered", "mouseExited"},
                  "addMouseListener",
                  "removeMouseListener");
```

Here, the mouseClicked and mousePressed methods have been deleted. If you did this, the view you would see in Figure 37-4 would be modified accordingly. That is, the mouseClicked and mousePressed methods would disappear from BeanInsight. However, these changes would not be reflected in the Inspector, or at least, they are not reflected in my version of JBuilder. I rather believe that they should be missing from the Inspector also. But they are not. Perhaps this is a bug that will be fixed in your build of the product.

I suppose I could go on at some length about BeanInsight. However, you should by now have a good sense of what it is all about and why you might find it useful. I would think it would be particularly helpful if you were trying to target a range of development tools with your bean. It looks beyond the needs of JBuilder and tells you as much as possible about the state of your bean. In effect, it is an attempt to expose as much information as possible about your bean via the Java introspection facilities.

Understanding JAR Files

We talked about JAR files in some depth in Part V. However, let's have a little review, just to help you better understand the complex subject matter that lies ahead.

Placing code in a JAR file allows it to be easily reused. Just give someone the JAR file, and they can use our components. If JAR files didn't exist, developers would have to distribute all the many raw class files that make up a component. Furthermore, they would have to ensure that each class file was in the proper package after distribution. JAR files relieve us of that wearisome burden.

Java treats JAR files as if they are another directory on your system. Suppose you have a directory called c:\src. Now suppose you put a JAR file in c:\src:

```
c:\src\codebox.jar
```

As far as Java is concerned, codebox.jar is just another directory located inside of c:\src. To use the contents of the new "directory," put the JAR file on your classpath.

To get JBuilder to know about this JAR file, you must create a JBuilder library that points at it. You learned about creating libraries in Part V. After you have added the library to JBuilder, JBuilder treats your JAR file as if it were a directory on your classpath.

Inside this directory/jar file, you can place the classes that you want other users to access. The JAR file contains not only the classes, but also the directories that lead to the classes. So if you want to give the user access to com.elvenware.comp.clock.ElfClock.class, you must create the directory structure com/elvenware/comp/clock in the JAR file. Once the directory structure is in place, you can place the class file in the appropriate directory of the JAR file. The JBuilder Archive Builder helps to automate this process. You can also easily create JAR files from the command line using the JDK jar utility or facilities provided by the open source Apache Jakarta Ant project.

NOTE: Why are we placing our classes in a directory called com.elvenware.comp? Remember first that there is a natural correspondence between package names ("com.elvenware.comp") and directories (com/elvenware/comp) for src and class files; while this is not always enforced, it does avoid problems and confusion that arise when building or running a Java project. Certain elements of this particular package name are purely a matter of convention. In the Java world, there are dozens, or even hundreds, of classes in nearly every project. As a result, there needs to be a considerable amount of order in the structure of these packages. One way of imposing order is to ensure that each company has its own clearly marked package. All the companies that create components place their components in a package called com. Inside this package they create a directory with their company name: com.elvenware. Then inside of that they create directories that properly categorize their components: com.elvenware.comp.clock. All of this is just a convention. It imposes order on the many tens of thousands of existing packages available to Java developers. In that sense, it is similar to the Dewey decimal system used in a library: It is just a way of organizing a plethora of individual items.

Creating a JAR File for Your Bean

In this section you are going to build a JAR file for your new bean. This is a crucial step because it makes the bean reusable by a wide variety of developers.

In the previous chapter, I showed you techniques for getting your bean in a directory where multiple programs can reach the source. Here we are not concerned with sharing the source but only the .class files. This might seem like a lesser accomplishment, but ultimately a JAR file full of class files is what other developers need if they want to use your components. It is the standard format used to distribute beans to the outside world. Other developers probably don't want to see your source; they just want to use your component. JAR files are the simplest and best way to give it to them.

I am going to put the code for this bean in the same archive as the codebox code developed in Part V: Project Management: codebox.jar. All of the code from that section went into a package called codebox. After you read this chapter, the code for the JAR file will contain two packages, com.elvenware.codebox and com.elvenware.comp. Here, comp is an abbreviation for "component."

As it happens, there is some overlap between the two trees, so you have to include the codebox code in order to build a useful archive. Furthermore, it is more convenient to place all the code from the examples in this book in one archive, so I recommend that you place both the codebox and comp code in the same JAR file, which is the process I describe in this section of the text.

NOTE: I'm actually oversimplifying matters a bit. On the CD that comes with this book, you will see that the codebox source is further broken down into a Personal branch and a branch called pro-ent, which contains SE or Enterprise code. The vast majority of the code developed for the codebox JAR file will work in the Personal edition, but the database code requires the Enterprise edition of JBuilder. Please read the index.html file on the CD for final updates on how I ended up breaking out the code so that everyone can use it. For now, just ignore the pro-ent branch, as it has no bearing on this part of the code development.

Creating JAR Files from the Command Line

One simple way to create a JAR file for your bean is to work from the command line. In particular, you can update the buildcodebox.bat file that was developed in Part V. A BuildCodeBox.sh file for Linux is found on the CD. Ant files are also available. The new Windows batch file is shown in Listing 37-1:

Listing 37-1: The batch file for creating the new CodeBox.jar archive

```
@echo off

rem $Id: index.html,v 1.9 2002/01/02 03:32:51 ccalvert Exp $
echo -----------------------------------------------------------------
echo The last line in this script copies the jar file to a specific directory.
echo You may need to edit that line for compatibility with your system.
echo -----------------------------------------------------------------
echo Building codebox.jar

javac -sourcepath src\personal\com\elvenware\codebox\ -d \
      classes src\com\elvenware\codebox\*.java
javac -sourcepath src\personal\com\elvenware\comp\clock\ -d \
      classes src\com\elvenware\comp\clock\*.java

jar -cvf codebox.jar -C classes com
copy codebox.jar g:\utils\classes
```

This batch file is designed to be run from the root directory of the install for this book's code. Your version of this file may differ slightly to accommodate your path structure. Notice also that I have wrapped some lines with the backslash character so they would fit properly in the text of this book. In your version, that code should probably appear all on one line.

The two statements that call javac simply ensure that the source files are properly compiled. The jar statement near the end of the script creates the JAR file. The final statement copies the JAR file to the place where your classpath, and your JBuilder library file, expects it to be located.

NOTE: Choose Tools | Configure libraries in JBuilder to set up a library. A library adds a JAR file or package to JBuilder's view of your classpath. You would then use Project | Project Properties to add a library to your current project. By adding the library, you put the specified JAR file or package on the classpath for your current project. If you ever got a message saying that your project can't find com.elvenware.XXX, one possible solution to the problem is to add codebox.jar to your project's classpath, as specified in this note.

Using the Archive Builder to Create a JAR File

If you have the SE or Enterprise version of JBuilder, you can use the Archive Builder to create the JAR file.

Choose **Wizard | Archive Builder** from the menu. Set the Archive Type to **Basic** and click **Next.**

Set the Name to **CodeBox**. Set File to the location where you want to place codebox.jar, as shown in Figure 37-5. In general, I find it simplest to place all my JAR files in the same directory. I prefer not to build the jar each time I compile the project. Select the **Next** button to move to Step 3 of the Archive Builder.

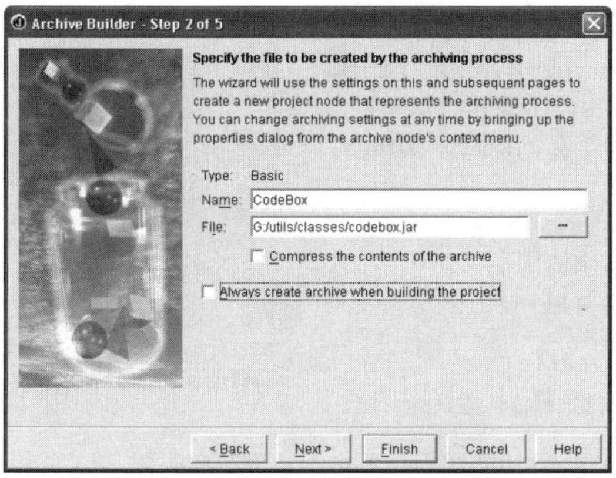

Figure 37-5: Setting up the Archive Builder filename and path

Choose the **Add Classes** button to add the com.elvenware.codebox.* and com.elvenware.comp.clock.* class tree to your archive, as shown in Figure 37-6. You might also want to add com.elvenware.comp.*, as that package contains several components that I have not had the time or room to discuss in this text. The end result should be something like what you see in Figure 37-7.

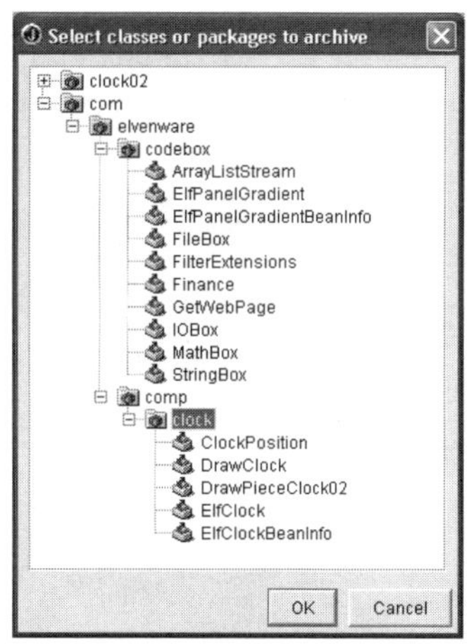

Figure 37-6: Adding the elvenware codebox and clock classes to your JAR file

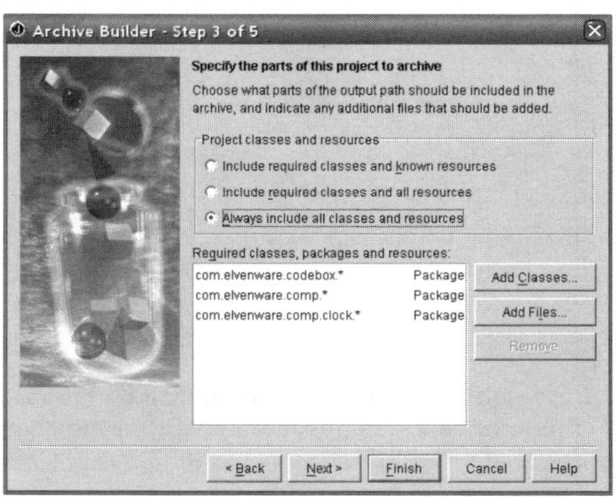

Figure 37-7: Three branches of your code added to the archive

In Step 3 of the wizard, choose to include all classes and all resources. This is a part of the wizard that you might want to experiment with. The goal is to have the fewest possible classes and resources in your JAR file without actually causing any loss of functionality. Try building the archive in several different ways and see how small you can make it without breaking your code. Often I have found that the Include required classes and all resources option works best for me.

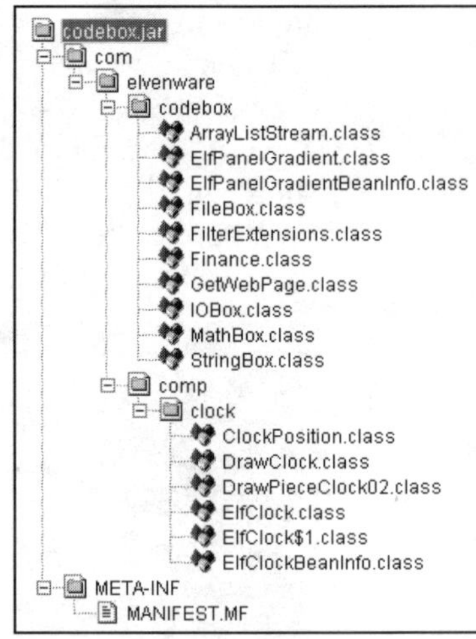

Figure 37-8: The structure pane after you have clicked on the new archive to open up its nodes

In Step 4 you can decide to include any classes from other JAR files on which your code might be dependent. For instance, if we wanted to create a version of codebox that included the Borland database code, this would be the place to do it. JBuilder can be very smart about opening up those other JAR files, finding only the classes you need, and placing those classes in your JAR file. Be careful, as you may not have the rights to distribute other people's classes.

Choose **Include a manifest in the archive** and set the Manifest settings to **Create a manifest**. (Manifests are described in more depth in Chapter 28.) Click the **Finish** button.

You can now close the Archive Builder and build your JAR file by right-clicking on the new node in the project pane. When you are done, the structure pane, when fully expanded, should look as it does in Figure 37-8.

Placing the Bean on the Component Palette

It is now time to place the bean on the component palette. When you are done, our new component will act just like any other bean that you select from the JBuilder IDE and drop onto the UI designer.

To begin, choose **Tools | Configure Palette** from the JBuilder menu. Alternatively, you can go into design mode, right-click on the component palette itself, and choose **Properties**. In either case, you will bring up the Palette Properties dialog shown in Figure 37-9.

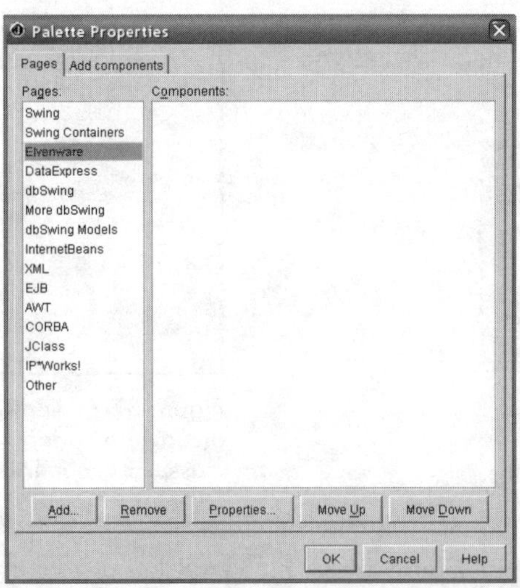

Figure 37-9: You can use the Palette Properties dialog to configure the beans that appear on the component palette.

In Figure 37-9 you can see that I have used the Add button at the bottom of the dialog to add a new page to the component palette. The page is called Elvenware. I have moved this page up the list, using the Move Up and Move Down buttons. I make heavy use of the components I create, so I like to move the page where they live up near the top so I can get at them easily.

Click on the **Add Components** tab at the top of the dialog. Click on the **Select Library** page and browse for CodeBox library, as shown in Figure 37-10. Click to close the browse dialog.

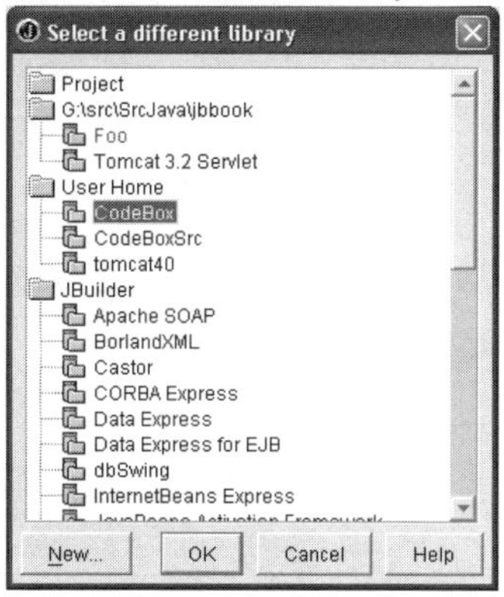

Figure 37-10: Browsing for the CodeBox library

NOTE: You should already have the CodeBox library set up from earlier chapters in the book. If you do not, you should click the New button seen at the bottom of the dialog in Figure 37-10. Alternatively, you could select Tools | Configure Libraries and click the New button in that dialog. The New Library Wizard dialog will appear. Set the location for your library to User Home. Type in the name of the library, which is CodeBox. Select the Add button and browse for codebox.jar. When you are done, close the dialog and continue working. If you had trouble with this process, you can read the detailed sections on libraries found in Part V.

After closing the Select a different library dialog, you should set Component Filtering to **JavaBeans only**, as shown in Figure 37-11.

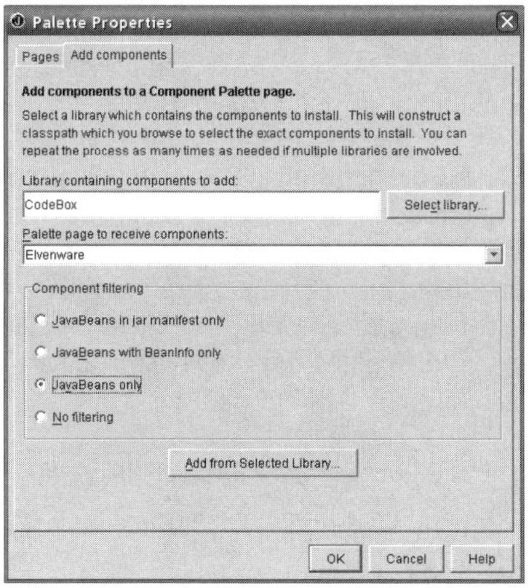

Figure 37-11: The Palette Properties dialog as it should appear just before you begin adding beans to the component palette

The next step is to add beans from the CodeBox library to the component palette. Choose **Add from Selected Library** and browse for the ElfClock bean, as shown in Figure 37-12.

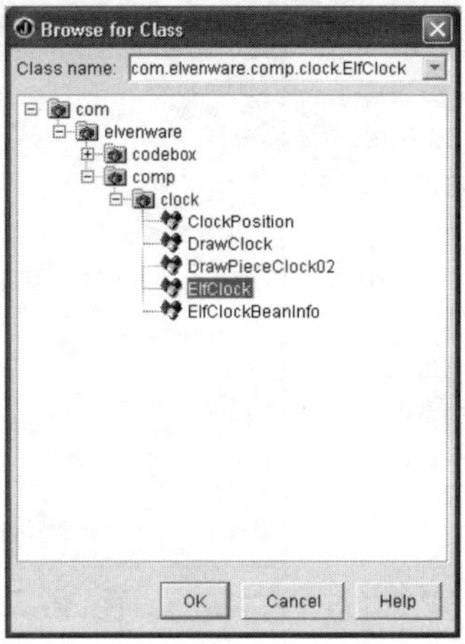

Figure 37-12: Browsing for the ElfClock bean

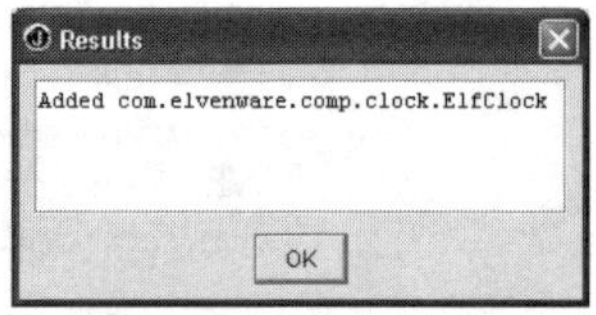

Figure 37-13: The message that JBuilder sends to you if your component has been successfully added to the component palette

To confirm that the bean was selected correctly, JBuilder pops up a Results dialog, as shown in Figure 37-13. If something has gone wrong, you will see an empty dialog or a dialog with an error message.

If all has gone well, you should be able to see your component on the component palette itself. At this stage, it would simply have the default icon associated with it. But it should appropriately identify itself in a tool tip message if you leave your mouse on it for a moment.

Building a Test Applet

You have now done all the hard work. To make sure everything is working correctly, you need only to start a new project, add a JApplet to it, and use the Inspector to set the properties to the values you desire. When you are done, run the applet to test it.

The only tricky part of this process is to make sure you create a JApplet rather than an Applet. As you are well aware, this component uses a lot of fancy Graphics2D calls. As a result, there is no point in trying to use it in an old Applet from the java.awt days. This component is wedded to Swing.

NOTE: It does not matter if you place your control on an applet or an application. If you need help building either, see Chapter 3.

Adding Component Palette Icons to Your Bean

One nice thing you can do to make your bean appear more professional, or just to make it more fun to use, is to add an icon to it. You have no doubt noticed that there are fields for doing this in BeansExpress, as shown in Figure 37-14.

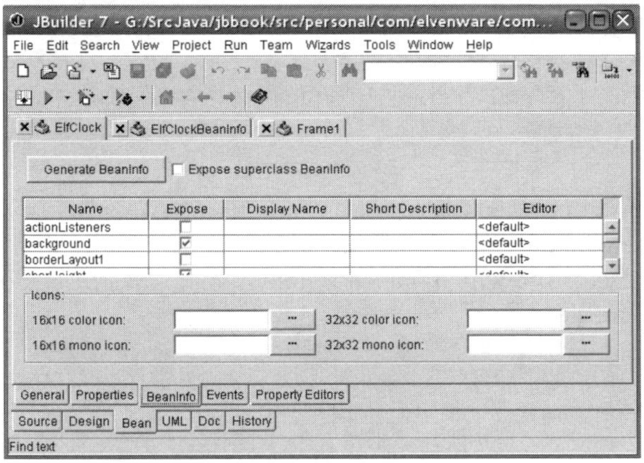

Figure 37-14: Use the fields at the bottom of the BeanInfo page in BeansExpress to add icons to your component. The icons appear in the component palette.

The changes made to your BeanInfo file look like this:

```
String iconColor16x16Filename = "clock16.png";
String iconColor32x32Filename = "clock32.png";
String iconMono16x16Filename = "clock16bw.png";
String iconMono32x32Filename = "clock32bw.png";
```

This code is then used in the getIcon method at the bottom of the BeanInfo file:

```
public java.awt.Image getIcon(int iconKind)
{
      switch (iconKind)
      {
            case BeanInfo.ICON_COLOR_16x16:
                  return iconColor16x16Filename !=
                        null ? loadImage(iconColor16x16Filename) : null;
            case BeanInfo.ICON_COLOR_32x32:
                  return iconColor32x32Filename !=
                        null ? loadImage(iconColor32x32Filename) : null;
            case BeanInfo.ICON_MONO_16x16:
                  return iconMono16x16Filename !=
                  null ? loadImage(iconMono16x16Filename) : null;
            case BeanInfo.ICON_MONO_32x32:
                  return iconMono32x32Filename !=
                  null ? loadImage(iconMono32x32Filename) : null;
      }
      return null;
}
```

It is usually best to put the icons directly in the same package with your source files. For instance, in this case you would put them in this directory:

```
/src/com/elvenware/comp/clock
```

Of course, the actual path might be somewhat different on your system.

The PNG graphics format is the one I prefer, but GIF files and JPG files will also work. If you cannot create your own icons, you should have little trouble finding a free one by browsing the web.

NOTE: I prefer PNG files for two reasons:

- The GIF file format has copyright restrictions.
- The JPG format introduces slight, but noticeable, compression artifacts.

Creating a Fancy Manifest File

If you look at Figure 37-11, you might notice that there is an option for JavaBeans in jar manifest only. This option provides a means for you to specify which files in your JAR file are actually the main class for a JavaBean and which ones are just support files or utility files.

Consider the following manifest file:

```
Manifest-Version: 1.0
Built-By: charlie
Created-By: Ant 1.4.1

Name: com/elvenware/comp/ElfListBox.class
Java-Bean: True

Name: com/elvenware/comp/clock/ElfClock.class
Java-Bean: True
```

This file selects the ElfListBox and ElfClock components and specifies that they are JavaBeans. If you include this manifest file in your project, the JavaBeans in jar manifest option will suddenly begin working for you. If you select that option, and then click the Add from Selected Library button, you will not be prompted to browse for your beans. Instead, the beans will be found automatically, and you will see the dialog shown in Figure 37-15.

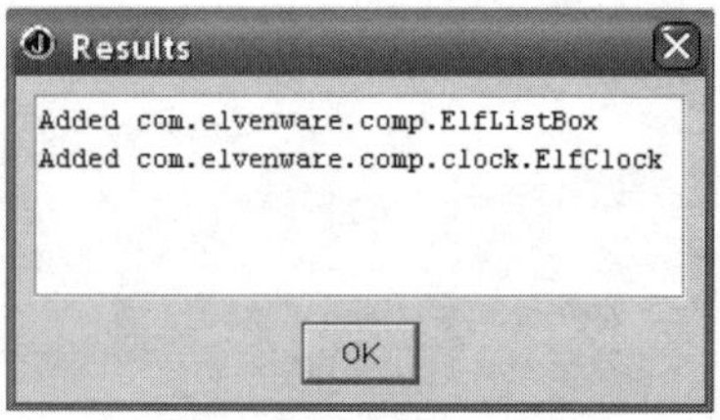

Figure 37-15: If you set up your jar manifest correctly, JBuilder can automatically find the classes you have marked as beans.

To add the manifest to your JAR file, first right-click on the archive node from the project pane. You created this archive earlier in the chapter by stepping through the Archive Wizard. Select the **Properties** dialog from the pop-up menu.

The Manifest page of the Properties dialog is shown in Figure 37-16. You can see that JBuilder has automatically found the right place for you to put the manifest file that you create. You should build one like the one shown earlier in this section of the text and then place it where JBuilder recommends.

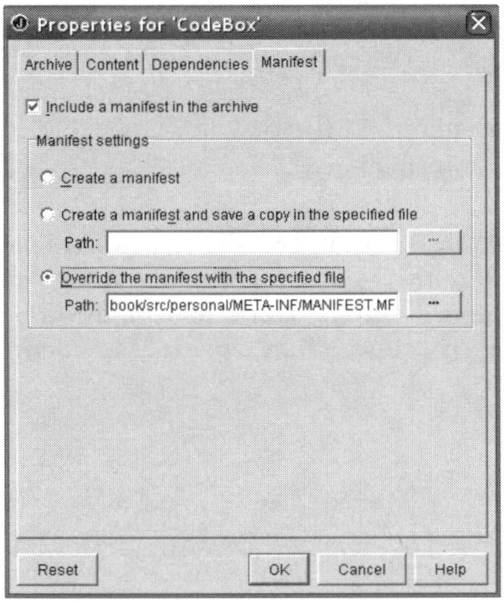

Figure 37-16: If you select the right option in the archive Properties dialog, JBuilder will automatically show you where to place your manifest file.

After you have set up the archive node correctly, right-click on it one more time, and this time choose to rebuild your JAR file. Now exit and restart JBuilder. If you do not, JBuilder will not properly read in your new JAR file. Now bring up the Palette Properties dialog shown in Figure 37-11, choose **JavaBeans in jar manifest**, and press the **Add from Selected Library** button. You should see a dialog like that found in Figure 37-15.

Working with Ant Files

There is, in fact, one other way to create a JAR file for your bean. This is perhaps the way I do it most often. It is not, however, nearly as easy to set up as the Archive Builder. I use it only because it provides a quick means of managing projects from the command line.

Here is the relevant section of my Ant file for creating the personal branch of the codebox JAR file:

```
<target name="package" depends="compile">
      <echo message="Building personal jar file"/>
    <jar jarfile="${jar-file}" basedir="${build}">
            <manifest>
                  <attribute name="Built-By" value="${user.name}"/>
                  <section name="com/elvenware/comp/ElfListBox.class">
                        <attribute name="Java-Bean" value="True"/>
                  </section>
                  <section name="com/elvenware/comp/clock/ElfClock.class">
                        <attribute name="Java-Bean" value="True"/>
                  </section>
            </manifest>
      </jar>
    <copy file="${jar-file}" todir="${jar-home}" />
</target>
```

When looking at this file, notice the section that creates the JAR file itself:

```
<jar jarfile="${jar-file}" basedir="${build}">
```

Beneath that, you will find syntax for creating the manifest file on the fly. You can see the entire build.xml ant file on the CD that accompanies this book.

NOTE: build.xml is the default name for an Ant file. As a result, you can run the Ant file simply by moving to the directory where it is stored and typing the word ant. For this to work, Ant must be installed properly on your system. The Ant web site is at http://jakarta.apache.org/ant/index.html. You can add Ant files to JBuilder 7 Enterprise projects or use a free OpenTool to integrate them with JBuilder.

Summary

In this chapter, you learned to use BeanInsight. You also learned ways to create a JAR file and add a bean and icon to the component palette.

I want to remind you to read over the section on the BasePanelButton found in Chapter 18. There you will have a chance to learn more about working with JavaBeans technology. I quite strongly recommend that you look at the BasePanelButton example, as it is short, easy to understand, and contains a good deal of very useful information.

Part VIII

Databases

Chapter 38

Introduction to Database Programming

Charlie Calvert

This is the first of several chapters on database access in JBuilder. When you are done reading these chapters, you should have a good sense of all the basic tasks necessary to create a powerful database application.

The purpose of this chapter is to provide introductory material on databases for people who are new to the technology or want a quick review. In these pages you will read about:

- The target audience for this section of the book
- The definition of a JDBC database and its purpose
- The difference between true SQL databases, such as Oracle or MySQL, and local databases, such as Paradox or Access
- The definition and purpose of relational and SQL databases
- The role of a database driver

Target Audience

Most of this section of the book requires that you have the Enterprise version of JBuilder. (In JBuilder 6 or earlier, you can use the Pro version.) In saying this, I don't mean to imply that you can't access databases from JBuilder Personal or SE. There is absolutely nothing involving databases that you can do in the Enterprise version that you could not also do in the Personal version. The catch, of course, is that JBuilder will do nothing to help you in that endeavor, unless you own the Enterprise version.

In the Personal or SE version, you must do everything involving databases by hand. The Enterprise versions provide tools that help you automatically generate high-quality database code. That is the value you get for paying the higher price for the more advanced versions.

There is some discussion of the JDBC database programming scattered throughout these chapters. The main purpose of Part VIII: Databases, however, is to show you how to build tools using Borland DataExpress.

Finally, I want to emphasize a point I made in the introduction. I believe in IDEs like JBuilder and think that it is well worth the effort to learn how to use them. The fact that you can write a database application by hand does not mean you should do so if you have an alternative. It's a bit like walking across the country when you could take an airplane. Yes, you'll get there if you walk, but if time is a factor, it just makes more sense to fly. None of this, however, should become an excuse for writing sloppy code. If JBuilder helps you save time, pay a little of it back by taking extra care in designing and implementing your ideas.

What is JDBC and What Does DataExpress Have to Do with It?

JDBC stands for Java Database Connectivity. It is a Sun API designed to give a uniform interface to databases in Java. Furthermore, JDBC is written in Java, so it is a portable tool.

The JDBC API is well designed and fairly easy to use. The advantage of Borland tools is that they make it possible for you to automatically generate your database code or visually manipulate the pieces of your database code.

DataExpress is Borland's wrapper around JDBC. It is often abbreviated as dx, and it is stored in a single JAR file: /JBuilder7/lib/dx.jar.

The DataExpress wrappers are needed in order to provide a means of creating the kind of powerful database tools necessary to help automate database access in JBuilder. The code that implements these tasks is stored in the DataExpress JAR file and another file in the same directory called dbswing.jar.

DataExpress exposes the underlying JDBC code that it wraps. If you are familiar with JDBC, you can usually access the key JDBC objects by calling the appropriate methods of the DataExpress library. I will show you how to do that in this book, but it is usually not necessary.

NOTE: DataExpress involves a certain amount of code that must be included with your application. Using the Archive Builder included in the SE and Enterprise versions, you can automatically build a JAR file that includes the DataExpress code. I will show how to do that in Chapter 43.

What is a Database Server?

A *database server* is a tool for storing and accessing data. There are many database servers available for you to use. Perhaps the most popular one is Oracle. Oracle is very fast, very scalable, and very expensive.

NOTE: A scalable database is one that can handle many users. If a database can scale up from ten users to 10,000 users without coming to a stuttering halt, it is a very scalable database.

MySQL is almost exactly as fast as Oracle, and it scales beautifully. It is an open source database that is free for personal use and very inexpensive for businesses to use. Oracle has better tools than MySQL, but sometimes I fear Oracle is so popular simply because it is so expensive. Managers who don't know technology have a tendency to believe in a product if it costs a lot of money.

In saying this, I don't mean to imply that MySQL is not popular. It is very widely used all across the Internet. If you use the Internet regularly, you are almost certainly viewing data stored in MySQL databases on a regular basis.

Another very popular database is Microsoft SQL Server (MSSQL). MSSQL is not as fast as MySQL or Oracle, but it has beautiful tools and comes at a mid-level price range. Microsoft also makes a local database called Access, which I will discuss later in this chapter.

InterBase is a database that Borland creates. It comes in both a free open source version and in a very moderately priced version. It was originally created for, and is still often used as, an embedded database. As a result, one of its virtues is its small size.

JDataStore is another database from Borland. JDataStore is an ANSI-92 compliant database written entirely in Java. It is portable to all Java platforms and is extremely easy to deploy. There are fees involved in distributing the code you build with JDataStore.

SQL Servers and Local Databases

Most databases are designed to be used remotely. Your program will usually run on one machine, and the database will usually reside on a second machine. These are called SQL servers, file servers, or client-server databases.

Some databases, such as Access, dBASE, or Paradox, are local databases, or desktop databases, designed to be run from the machine on which they reside. It is possible to access these databases remotely, but that is not their standard mode of operation.

Applications that use local databases usually talk directly to the database. A real SQL database, on the other hand, is usually accessed via TCP/IP. In some cases, the client and the server part of an SQL server will be located on the same machine. However, the two parts of the application will still talk to one another using a wire protocol.

If you are building a database that will only be accessed by one person at a time or that will only be used by a handful of people, you could use a local database. If you are writing a program that will have many simultaneous users, you should use a database like Oracle, MSSQL, MySQL, or InterBase. Regardless of the number of users, a true SQL database will usually be more reliable and less prone to data loss than a local database.

Oracle, MySQL, InterBase, and MSSQL are all true SQL databases. dBASE, Paradox, and Access are local databases. This doesn't mean that local databases are not powerful tools with complex features but only that they have limitations when it comes to securing your data.

What is a Relational Database?

Relational databases are innately complex. However, if you have never dealt with them before, there are a few simple things that can be said about them to help you understand what they are all about. If you want a serious discussion of this topic, you should buy a book on the subject.

A relational database is designed to avoid duplication by storing your data in multiple, related tables. Both the local and SQL server databases discussed in this chapter are relational databases.

Suppose you are trying to keep track of the sales receipts for a company. If you used a non-relational database, you might end up creating a table with fields that look like this:

```
MyCompany, MyCompanyAddress, MyPhoneNumber, ItemSold, QuantitySold, Cost
```

For each item sold, you would simply add a new row to the table:

```
Elvenware, Santa Cruz, 333-333-3333, Java Book, 1, $2,000.00
Elvenware, Santa Cruz, 333-333-3333, C++ Book, 1, $2.00
Elvenware, Santa Cruz, 333-333-3333, Delphi Book, 1, $2,000
Elvenware, Santa Cruz, 333-333-3333, Java Book, 1, $2,000
Microsoft, Redmond, 666-666-6666, Visual Basic Book, 1, $0.25
Microsoft, Redmond, 666-666-6666, Visual Basic Book, 1, -$1.25
```

The problem with this system is that most of the data in your database is being repeated over and over again. In particular, the name, city, and phone number of each company is repeated many times.

A relational database breaks up this kind of data into two tables:

```
Company Table
Company ID = 1
Company Name = Elvenware
```

```
Company Address = Santa Cruz
Company Phone = 333-333-3333

Sales Table
Sale ID = 22054
Item Sold = Java Book
Quantity = 1
Cost = $2,000
Company ID = 1
```

The most important field in this declaration is the Company ID. Elvenware has a company ID of 1. As a result, you can simply include this single number in each row of the SALES table to designate the company that made the sale:

```
22054, Java Book, 1, $2,000, 1
22055, C++ Book, 1, $2.00, 1
22056, Visual Basic Book, 1, $0.10, 2
22057, Visual Basic Book, 1, -$5.00, 2
```

In this example, we can see in the last field that the first two books were sold by Elvenware, which has an ID of 1. The third book was sold by some other company with an ID of 2.

A relational database makes it easy for you to create associations between these two tables. For instance, you can ask, "What are all the items in the SALES table that have a Company ID of 1?" The answer to the question is a dataset containing all the sales made by the Elvenware company.

In the next few chapters, we are going to spend a lot of time exploring relational databases. In fact, one of the main purposes of these chapters is to show how JBuilder makes it easy for you to work with the sometimes rather complex relationships between the many tables that reside in a typical relational database.

What is SQL?

Most client-server databases are SQL databases. SQL is a language for querying databases. The acronym SQL stands for Structured Query Language. (And what, one might ask, is an Unstructured Query Language?)

Let's think for a moment about some of the different kinds of languages that exist. Java is a general-purpose programming language. JavaScript is a language for programming web pages. Batch files use a simple language for executing lists of commands in a DOS window. The Bash Shell language is a more powerful tool for performing actions at the Unix command prompt. And the language we are currently discussing, the SQL language, is a language for querying databases.

SQL brings unity to a diverse field. A core set of SQL commands work equally well on almost any SQL compliant database. SQL is not an OS. Nevertheless, SQL plays much the same role in database development that Java does in cross-platform development: It is a standard designed to work on all platforms. SQL is a standard designed to work with all databases.

In this day and age, nearly every serious database product on the market supports SQL. It is the standard for database development in the computer world. Thinking about databases without SQL is a bit like trying to think about cars without roads. The two subjects are intimately tied together.

A full description of the SQL language is beyond the scope of this book. However, the most common commands look like this:

```
CREATE DATABASE MyDatabase;
USE DATABASE MyDatabase;
DROP DATABASE MyDatabase;
CREATE TABLE  MyTable (id int, data VarChar(128));
DROP TABLE MyTable;
CREATE INDEX MyIndex ON MyTable (id);
SELECT * FROM MyTable;
INSERT INTO MyTable (id, data) values (1, "MyData");
UPDATE MyTable SET data = "NewData" WHERE id = 1;
DELETE FROM MyTable WHERE id = 1;
```

Needless to say, these commands demonstrate how to create a database, select a database, delete (drop) a database, create a table, delete a table, create an index on a table, select data from a table, add a new row to a table, update an existing row in a table, and delete a row from a table. These are the basic things you do with a database.

SQL is not always as terse a language as it might appear from this brief introduction. It is possible, in fact, to create very long SQL statements that go on for thousands of lines.

What is a Dataset?

A *dataset* is a collection of rows pulled from a database via an SQL query. The following is a view of a small dataset:

```
Elvenware, Santa Cruz, 333-333-3333, JavaBook, 1, $2,000
Microsoft, Redmond, 666-666-6666, Visual Basic Book, 1, $0.25
```

If the data were still in the database, it would be called a table or part of a table. You can think of a dataset as being the result of a query. If you query a table for a certain set of rows, the thing you get back from the database is not a table, but a dataset or resultset.

In most cases your client is going to be running on one machine and your server on another. When you want to view data, you move it from the server to the client via TCP/IP or some other Internet-based protocol.

SQL databases are incredibly powerful. There is, however, one rule you have to remember if you want to work with them successfully: Keep your datasets as small as possible.

If you create a query that yields ten megabytes of data, in most cases you are going to be in trouble. Your client program won't be able to handle all that data, and it will become bogged down, unresponsive, and might well appear to have locked up. It therefore follows that one of the rules of the database game is that you have to make requests for a limited number of rows of data.

It is ultimately up to you to devise strategies that will prevent you from getting into trouble when requesting datasets. For instance, you will often want to ask for all the people listed in the database whose name begins with A, rather than for all the people in an entire table.

Preserving a Relational Database's Integrity

Relational databases have rules that can be automatically enforced to make sure you are not entering data that makes no sense whatsoever. For instance, it would not make sense to delete Elvenware from the COMPANY table if there were still records in the SALES table that referenced it. Consider this situation:

```
22054, Java Book, 1, $2,000, 1
22055, C++ Book, 1, $2.00, 1
```

As you recall, these are two records from the SALES table. The last field in the record, a 1, references the item in the COMPANY table that has an ID of 1. In other words, it references the Elvenware record from the COMPANY table:

```
1, Elvenware, Santa Cruz, 333-333-3333
2, Microsoft, Redmond, 666-666-6666
```

If you delete Elvenware from the COMPANY table, the 1 in the SALES table no longer has any meaning. The records that used this ID would be orphaned. If you later added a new record to the company table and gave it an ID of 1, the records in the SALES table would contain invalid data.

To prevent this, it is possible to put a constraint on the COMPANY table such that it is illegal to delete Elvenware from the table so long as there are any records in the SALES table that reference it.

You create constraints and validity checks at the time you define a table in a database. In general, defining a pair of related primary and foreign keys is enough to establish this kind of integrity constraint. I will talk about primary and foreign keys later in this chapter.

Special SQL statements such as CHECK, CONSTRAINT, and CREATE RULE can also cause database rules to come into effect. Enforcing these rules should be the job of the database, not the job of a Java developer. However, there is debate over whether it is a good idea for developers to also attempt to enforce such rules on the client side.

Cascading Deletes

There will, of course, be times when you will want to delete a company from the COMPANY table. At the same time, you will want to also delete all the related records from the SALES table. This kind of action is called a *cascading delete*. It cascades from the COMPANY table down to the SALES table. In practice, it could also cascade to tables that are linked to the SALES table, and so on, through several layers.

Later in the book we will look at how to automatically perform cascading deletes. The point for now, however, is simply to realize that relational databases often come equipped with a set of rules that can be vigorously enforced to help you maintain the integrity of your data.

Keys and Indices

Most SQL statements of the kind we have been looking at have a kind of intuitive logic to them that is easy to understand. The one exception is the concept of an index, which in certain cases is closely related to the concept of a key.

In a relational database, you are constantly using certain fields in order to relate tables. The fields you choose to use to define the relationship are known as *keys*. An index, on the other hand, can help you quickly sort or find data in a table. Keys relate tables; indices help you sort and search a table.

A primary key is usually made on the first field or fields of a table. These fields usually have a unique index and cannot be set to null. A unique index specifies that each element in a particular field must be unique. For instance, if you put a unique index on the CompanyID field in the COMPANY table, you could be sure that no two companies would have the same ID. It is also possible to specify that a field cannot be empty. For instance, you might want to specify that the Company ID field must have a value. You do this by saying that it cannot be null.

NOTE: Unfortunately, there is a certain amount of variation from database to database on exactly what results from specifying a primary key. Indeed, many of the rules for working with databases change from server to server. In most cases, a primary key will do just what I say here: It will create a unique indexed value. If you are uncertain what your database does, you can usually open the table in question in a tool like the JBuilder Database Pilot and look to see if your primary key is also indexed. The Database Pilot is covered in Chapter 40. To sum up: It is possible to think of a primary key field that is not indexed. In practice, however, most primary key fields are indexed. Foreign keys, on the other hand, are not always automatically indexed.

The primary purpose of an index is to help you sort and search through data. A key helps you establish relationships between two tables that share a common field. To understand this better, let's take a look at two tables related through a foreign and primary key.

Validity Checks, Keys, and Differences between Databases

You might recall the COMPANY and SALES tables from earlier in the chapter:

```
Company Table
Company ID = 1
Company Name = Elvenware
Company Address = Santa Cruz
Company Phone = 333-333-3333

Sales Table
Sale ID = 22054
Item Sold = Java Book
Quantity = 1
Cost = $2,000
Company ID = 1
```

The instance of Company ID in the COMPANY table would be a good candidate for a primary key, while the instance of Company ID in the SALES table would be a good candidate for a foreign key.

An index that is just used to sort data or to speed access during a search is known simply as an index. An index field is also a key field when it involves linkage between multiple tables.

Put all these concepts together and what you have is an indexed primary key on the CompanyID field that specifies that it cannot be null. In SQL, that would look like this:

```
CREATE TABLE Company
(
      CompanyID INT not null,
      CompanyName VARCHAR(128),
      CompanyAddress VARCHAR(128),
      CompanyPhone VARCHAR(15),
      PRIMARY KEY(CompanyID)
);
```

Notice the not null statement near the beginning of the declaration and the primary key statement near the end of the declaration.

If you are working with MySQL, you will want to declare your tables to be of type InnoDB. InnoDB tables can support foreign keys and have other advantages. I will talk more about setting up InnoDB in the next chapter. Here is how to add InnoDB support in a CREATE TABLE statement:

```
CREATE TABLE Company
(
      CompanyID INT not null,
      CompanyName VARCHAR(128),
      CompanyAddress VARCHAR(128),
      CompanyPhone VARCHAR(15),
      PRIMARY KEY(CompanyID)
) TYPE=INNODB;
```

Or you could execute this line after creating the table:

```
ALTER TABLE Company TYPE=INNODB;
```

The CompanyID field is declared to be of type integer, and the other fields are strings of varying lengths. CompanyID is declared such that it must contain a value, must be unique, and will be indexed. Because it is indexed, it will be possible to perform very fast searches on this field and quickly sort the table on this field. Because it is a key, it can be used in relationships between this table and another table, such as the SALES table. Because it is a primary key, you can usually assume that the values in it will be unique. You can, if you want, specify that more than one field will be part of the primary key.

Here is how to create the SALES table in MySQL:

```
CREATE TABLE Sales
(
      SaleID INT not null,
      ItemSold VARCHAR(128),
      Quantity INT,
      Cost FLOAT,
      CompanyID INT,
      PRIMARY KEY(SaleID),
      INDEX compid (CompanyID),
      FOREIGN KEY(CompanyID) references Company(CompanyID)
) TYPE=INNODB
```

Notice the use of InnoDB and the explicit creation of an index called compid on the CompanyID field.

NOTE: If you see the error code 150 when submitting this kind of statement to MySQL, there is probably something wrong with your syntax or your logic. The rest of the error may not make any sense; it's the number 150 that you are looking for.

In InterBase or Access, however, the INDEX statement will not work. Instead, you should write this:

```
CREATE TABLE Sales
(
      SaleID INT not null,
      ItemSold VARCHAR(128),
      Quantity INT,
      Cost FLOAT,
      CompanyID INT,
      PRIMARY KEY(SaleID),
```

```
        FOREIGN KEY(CompanyID) references Company(CompanyID)
)
CREATE INDEX compid ON sales(CompanyID);
```

If you didn't do so at the time you created the table, you can add a foreign key to either an InterBase or a MySQL table like this:

```
ALTER TABLE Sales ADD CONSTRAINT SalesInteg FOREIGN KEY(COMPANYID)
        REFERENCES Company(CompanyID);
```

Let's take a look at these tables in a JBuilder tool called the Database Pilot. For now, just accept the presence of this tool. In later chapters, I will explain it in more depth. In the first example, shown in Figure 38-1, we are in an InterBase database. In Figure 38-2, we are looking at a MySQL database.

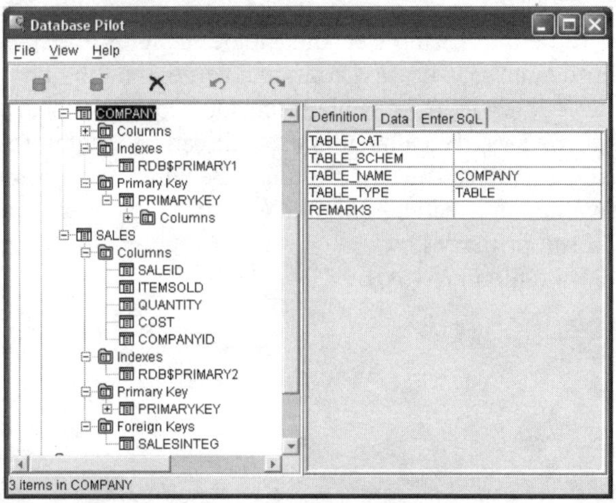

Figure 38-1: Viewing the primary and foreign key of InterBase tables in the Database Pilot

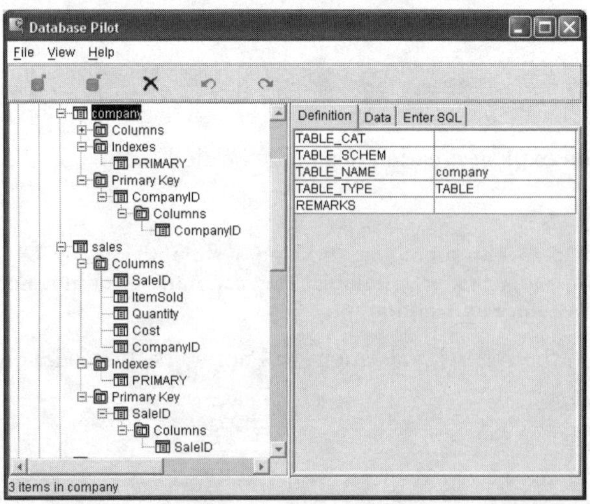

Figure 38-2: Viewing the structure of the COMPANY and SALES tables in MySQL

Why is there a difference between the two tables? Well, it turns out that in MySQL, creating a foreign key does not automatically create an index. But MySQL requires indices on foreign keys, and you will have to create them explicitly.

Let's test what we have done in the real world:

```
insert into Company  values (1, 'Elvenware', 'Santa Cruz', '555-555-5555');
insert into Sales values (1, 'Book', 1, 2000, 1);
delete from Company where CompanyName = 'Elvenware';
```

After entering the first two lines, any attempt to delete the Elvenware record should fail with an exception. The exception occurs because the SALES table contains a record with its CompanyID field set to 1.

NOTE: When using the Database Pilot, exceptions might appear in the message pane. In the example programs we will build over the next few chapters, you will find that such exceptions are raised more explicitly.

The rules we have laid out really should specify that it is impossible to enter a value into the SALES table unless its CompanyID field matches a record in the COMPANY table. For instance, given the current state of our tables, the insert statement should fail:

```
insert into Sales values (1, 'Book', 1, 25, 2);
```

The issue here is that there is no record in the COMPANY table that has a CompanyID of 2.

Unfortunately, not all databases will enforce this rule about not entering invalid records into the SALES table. For instance, MySQL and Interbase will enforce the rule, but Access will not.

A good primer on SQL is an invaluable companion when making database applications. There are many available, most of them fairly equal in quality. I have found *The Practical SQL Handbook* from Addison-Wesley to be a useful reference.

JBuilder, however, is designed to shield you from SQL and generate it automatically whenever possible. As a result, a passing understanding of SQL will probably be sufficient for understanding this text.

What is a Database Driver?

In the Java world, a database driver provides a means for JDBC to be able to talk to a database. The problem, of course, is that each database is implemented in slightly different ways. As a result, it is up to each database vendor to write a driver that connects JDBC to their particular database. In the case of open source databases, it is up to the open source community to provide this driver.

When looked at from this perspective, it looks almost as if JDBC provides a standard, while the drivers provide the implementation. There is some truth to this point of view, but JDBC is more than just a standard in that it provides a number of utility functions for developers.

The point here is that JDBC is a standard that provides a single, unified, and easy-to-use interface to developers. This standard is very valuable to developers, and they will naturally be attracted to databases that can use this standard. Otherwise, the developer would have to write his or her own custom code for accessing the database. And the developer would have to keep rewriting the code each time he or she changed platforms.

The driver is the glue that holds this system together. Each driver provides a bridge between the JDBC standard and a particular database. Obviously, there are different drivers for MySQL, Oracle, MSSQL, Access, dBASE, Paradox, and InterBase.

JDBC vs. ODBC

There are at least two different kinds of drivers you can install. One is a JDBC driver, which is written in Java and works on multiple platforms. A second kind of driver is called an ODBC driver.

ODBC is also a cross-platform standard, but it is used most often on Windows. ODBC drivers are usually not written in Java; hence you need to have a different version of your driver for each operating system. I will discuss installing drivers later in Chapter 40, "Connecting to Databases from JBuilder."

A tool that ships with the Sun JDK called the JDBC-ODBC Bridge provides a link between the ODBC drivers out there in the world and the JDBC code used in Java programs. You will see how to use this bridge in Chapter 40.

The difference between an ODBC driver and a JDBC driver is that a single JDBC binary JAR file can contain a driver that will work on multiple platforms. ODBC drivers are usually written in C/C++ and therefore need to at least be recompiled for each platform.

Summary

In this chapter you have been introduced to the basic concepts you need to understand in order to program databases in Java. In the next chapter, you will read about installing and using specific database drivers and how to set up a connection to a few of these databases.

Chapter 39

Database Setup

Charlie Calvert

The database servers and database tables used in this book's example programs are examined in this chapter. The text will explain how to set up the servers and create the databases and tables used in the example programs on the CD.

Most of the database programs in this book should work with little effort on your part if you have Access, MySQL, or InterBase installed on your system and the necessary libraries set up inside of JBuilder. If you don't have any of these databases installed, use the information in this chapter to help you set them up. If you are not sure which way to go, I would choose MySQL first, then InterBase, and finally Access. Various examples on the CD use all of these options, so if you want to run all the programs without modifying them, you will need to set up all three databases. If you prefer to use one database, you should be able to get all the programs working by simply modifying the driver for programs that are set to use a database not installed on your system. As explained in the next section of this chapter, the CD for this book contains three sets of identical data, one each for MySQL, InterBase, and Access.

In writing this book, I chose to emphasize the MySQL database. I picked this product because it is freely available, reliable, fast, powerful, and a widely used standard. I will try to provide enough information so that you can use InterBase or Access as alternatives if you prefer. However, the text itself will use MySQL as the primary database. I have tried to make sure that all the example programs work with any of the database servers.

NOTE: Because it is so popular and the install is so simple, I will not explain setting up Access in this chapter. In the next chapter, however, I will show you how to connect to it from JBuilder. I'm supporting Access as an aid to readers who would like to try a little database programming without having to get too serious about setting up a server.

Most of the commands I will show you will work equally well with any major database product. The whole point of the JBuilder and Java database tools is to abstract the code away from the specifics of any one kind of database.

If you already have MySQL, InterBase, or Access installed, you can skip much of this chapter. The sections that everyone should focus on are "Working with Different Databases," "Creating Data for Use with this Book," and the final sections of the chapter on setting up your environment and setting up Ant.

There is some information at the end of the chapter that can help people get set up if they are using a database other than InterBase, MySQL, or Access. In particular, you will find SQL statements defining the metadata for the tables, as well as pointers to text files that contain very generic SQL statements for loading the data into a database.

Working with Different Databases

The CD that accompanies this book contains a database called jbbook. There are a number of tables in that database, most of which are referenced by one or more of the sample programs on the CD.

I have provided a copy of the jbbook database for Access, MySQL, and InterBase users. However, I will pick MySQL as the primary database I use in the examples I discuss. Please read this chapter and the index.html file on the CD to find out how to set up these databases.

As a rule, it should be very simple to switch back and forth between these different versions of the database. Many of the programs I provide will let you make the switch by changing a single variable in your program.

If you don't have much understanding of databases and SQL, I would suggest installing MySQL and stepping through the tutorials outlined over the next few pages. In this chapter I spend quite a bit of time reviewing the basic commands you can give to an SQL database and provide an overview of how to access basic features of these powerful tools.

MySQL is one of the most powerful databases available. Having an understanding of how to use this extraordinary program is an extremely useful skill.

The first pages of this chapter are about doing things from the command line. Once you have the database installed properly and understand how to access jbbook data, you can move on to the next chapter. There you will see how JBuilder fits into the picture.

NOTE: There are some GUI front ends for use with MySQL. However, the ones I have seen are not particularly appealing to me. Furthermore, the command prompt is the only real OS-neutral way of accessing MySQL.

Setting up MySQL on Windows

MySQL is a very fast, full-featured, open source database. It amazes me that a database this powerful and this reliable is available for free. Popular web sites run this server. Mainstream companies such as Yahoo, MP3.com, Motorola, NASA, Silicon Graphics, and Texas Instruments use it to handle huge databases in mission-critical situations. There are over 2 million installations of MySQL worldwide.

You can download MySQL from http://www.mysql.org or http://www.mysql.com. Make sure you get the MySQL Max version of the program, as it provides support for InnoDB. MySQL is free for personal and non-commercial development under the GNU public license. If you want to use it in a commercial setting, you should pay a fee, which is low compared to the price of other databases.

The download from mysql.org includes a standard Windows setup program. Go ahead and run the install as you would for any other Windows program. (In short, this is a forehead install and therefore needs no commentary.)

In the root mysql directory that the install created, there are some files called my_small.cnf, my-medium.cnf, my-large.cnf, and so on. Move and rename the first of these files so that it ends up being called **c:\my.cnf**. Please take this quite literally. Even if you boot Windows from some other drive, still place the file in the root of the C drive.

You should place a second, identical copy of this file in your Windows directory. Give it a slightly different name: **c:\windows\my.ini**. Probably only one of these two files will be used by MySQL, but it is best to include them both unless you are absolutely sure that only one is being accessed. (If you are on Windows 2000 or an old NT box, the second file would be called in c:\winnt\my.ini.)

NOTE: I'm going to ask you to make more changes to both of these files. As a result, you might want to keep them both open in a text editor, such as JBuilder's, that handles multiple files.

The question of which file MySQL uses can ultimately be answered once you have the system up and running. At that time, you can give the **show variables** command at the mysql monitor prompt, as explained later in this chapter. You will then be able to see what values are set for basedir, key_buffer_size, etc. By changing these values in one file but not the other, you can ultimately detect which file MySQL is actually using.

Also, be careful to get the extensions for these files set up correctly. In Windows, particularly when using NotePad, it is easy to end up with files that have odd names, such as my.ini.ini or my.sql.ini. The best way to check this is to go to the command line and use the dir command to view the files. Don't trust the Windows Explorer to report the extension of a file correctly.

Under the mysqld section of my.cnf and my.ini, you should add text to point to the directory where you installed MySQL. This involves adding three nodes called basedir, datadir, and language:

```
port          = 3306
socket        = c:/temp/mysql.sock

[mysqld]
basedir=f:/mysql
datadir=f:/mysql/data
language=f:/mysql/share/english
port          = 3306
socket        = c:/temp/mysql.sock
skip-locking
set-variable= key_buffer=16K
set-variable= max_allowed_packet=1M
set-variable= thread_stack=64K
set-variable= table_cache=4
set-variable= sort_buffer=64K
set-variable= net_buffer_length=2K
server-id     = 1
```

Notice also that I have twice set the socket directory to a place on my system that is convenient for me. The port can usually stay with the default value of 3306.

The important part of this code excerpt is the first three lines after [mysqld] and the bit about c:/temp/mysql.sock. The rest I am including for context. You should, however, scan through the file and make sure that all the path entries make sense. In particular, they may be set up by default with Linux paths. Change any Linux paths that you see to Windows paths.

NOTE: I have included my my.cnf file in the Database directory on the CD. You can compare your work to mine by examining that file and by checking the www.elvenware.com site for updates.

As far as I can see, it does not matter where on your hard drive you install the MySQL database, as long as you create the configuration file and put a copy of it in your C drive and in your Windows directory. For instance, on my system, I am currently using this setup:

```
basedir=g:/Utilities/mysql
datadir=g:/Utilities/mysql/data
language=g:/Utilities/mysql/share/English
```

NOTE: On my XP system, I had trouble including comments on the line that is being parsed from the configuration file. It is easy to include these comments, as they are part of the suggested setup in at least some of the older versions of the product documentation. For instance, this line is included in some versions of the help system:

```
datadir=f:/mysql/data     # don't include comments here.
```

You should delete the comment or move it onto its own line:

```
# Place comments on their own line
datadir=f:/mysql/data
```

On Windows, the actual program you execute to start MySQL is called mysqld.exe, msqld-max.exe, msqld-max-nt.exe, or some variation thereof. These files come with the standard installation and are stored in the /mysql/bin directory. In the next few paragraphs I will explain why these different versions of the executable exist.

MySQL supports a powerful database standard called InnoDB. Without this addition to MySQL, I was not able to properly set up foreign keys. MySQL works perfectly well without InnoDB, but if you want the full benefits of MySQL, you should enable InnoDB. You can read about this technology at www.innodb.com.

The InnoDB support comes in the versions of MySQL that contain the word "max." For instance, mysqld-max-nt.exe is one such program. InnoDB is not included in mysqld.exe.

Just running mysqld-max-nt.exe is not enough to turn on the InnoDB feature. You also need to uncomment these lines in your my.cnf or my.ini file and point some of the variables at your install image:

```
innodb_data_file_path = ibdata1:100M
innodb_data_home_dir = g:/Utilities/mysql/data
innodb_log_group_home_dir = g:/Utilities/mysql/data
innodb_log_arch_dir = g:/Utilities/mysql/data
set-variable = innodb_mirrored_log_groups=1
set-variable = innodb_log_files_in_group=3
set-variable = innodb_log_file_size=5M
set-variable = innodb_log_buffer_size=8M
innodb_flush_log_at_trx_commit=1
innodb_log_archive=0
set-variable = innodb_buffer_pool_size=16M
set-variable = innodb_additional_mem_pool_size=2M
set-variable = innodb_file_io_threads=4
set-variable = innodb_lock_wait_timeout=50
```

Notice in particular that innodb_data_home_dir, innodb_log_group_home_dir, and innodb_log_arch_dir have been edited to point at directories on my system.

NOTE: On some systems, you may need to specify the path to the ibdata1:100M file: g:/Utilities/mysql/data/ibdata1:100M. This seemed to help in one case, but usually I believe it is better to omit the path.

If you have set up your configuration files properly, starting MySQL will create a 100 MB file called ibdata1. This file will hold your InnoDB tables. It will appear in your innodb_data_home_dir specified in the my.cnf script. In other words, you can check for the presence of this file as one way of confirming that you have turned on InnoDB support.

If 100 MB is too big for you, you can make ibdata1 smaller and still work with the databases included in this book. For instance, you can change the data file path line like this:

```
innodb_data_file_path = ibdata1:25M
```

If you want to make the file larger later, you should append a second filename to this first name:

```
innodb_data_file_path = ibdata1:25M;ibdata2:2000M
```

The command above should appear all on one line.

Starting MySQL as a Stand-alone Application on Windows

The first time you start the server, you should run it as a stand-alone application, which takes up its own space in a command window. In the next section, I will explain how to start MySQL as a service. Running as a service is probably the preferred method in most cases, but you should run as a stand-alone app when you are getting your system set up.

From the mysql\bin directory, start the server as follows from the command line on a 2000 or XP box:

```
mysqld-max-nt.exe --standalone
```

By default, the server does not give you any information at all but simply goes to the next line in your command window and sits there. If you see output from the server, something is wrong. If you have errors, it is probably a problem in the paths you declared in your my.ini or my.cnf file. Also, check the mysql/data directory for a file called mysql.err or other recently created text files.

Go to a second command window, enter the mysql\bin directory, and type **mysql** to launch the mysql monitor. If all is well, you will be taken to a simple command prompt that looks something like this:

```
[f:\mysql\bin]mysql.exe
Welcome to the MySQL monitor. Commands end with ; or \g.
Your MySQL connection id is 4 to server version: 3.23.49-max-nt

Type 'help;' or '\h' for help. Type '\c' to clear the buffer.

mysql>
```

The mere fact that you are in mysql is confirmation that things are going well. Congratulations, you are now at the helm of one humongously powerful database!

However, just to be sure, type **status** at the mysql prompt:

```
mysql> status
--------------
mysql.exe  Ver 11.16 Distrib 3.23.49, for Win95/Win98 (i32)

Connection id:          4
Current database:
Current user:           ODBC@localhost
Server version:         3.23.49-max-nt
Protocol version:       10
Connection:             . via named pipe
Client characterset:    latin1
Server characterset:    latin1
UNIX socket:            c:/temp/mysql.sock
Uptime:                 16 min 17 sec
```

```
Threads: 2  Questions: 20  Slow queries: 0  Opens: 7  Flush tables: 1  Open tables:
1 Queries per second avg: 0.020
--------------
```

If you get output similar to this, you can be fairly sure that MySQL is working.

Shutting Down the MySQL Stand-alone Server on Windows

If you want to shut down the server, first exit the mysql monitor by issuing the exit command:

```
mysql> exit;
Bye

[g:\utilities\mysql\bin]
```

In general, all the commands you give in the mysql monitor should end with a semicolon.

The command to shut down mysql when it is running as an application looks like this:

```
g:\Utilities\mysql\mysqladmin.exe shutdown
```

The next section explains how to start and stop the server when you run it as a service. Running as a service is definitely the simplest way to run the server.

Starting and Stopping MySQL as a Windows Service

Programs that run as a service will be started automatically when your computer starts. When you shut down your computer, they will be stopped automatically. If this is the behavior you want, you should run MySQL as a service.

If you have everything running correctly from the command prompt, you should now stop the stand-alone server, as shown in the previous section. Then install MySQL as a service:

```
[g:\utilities\mysql\bin]mysqld-max-nt.exe -install
Service successfully installed.

[g:\utilities\mysql\bin]net start mysql
The MySql service is starting.
The MySql service was started successfully.
```

You can always find out what services you are running by typing net start at the command prompt. If you prefer to use the GUI tools, go to the **Control Panel**, choose **Administrative Tools**, and look in the list of Services.

If you want to remove the service, first stop it, and then use the mysql tools to remove it:

```
[g:\utilities\mysql\bin]net stop mysql
The MySql service is stopping.
The MySql service was stopped successfully.

[g:\utilities\mysql\bin]mysqld-max-nt.exe -remove
Service successfully removed.
```

If you run MySQL as a service, you don't need to worry about shutting it down if you turn off your system at the end of the day. Just do a normal Windows shutdown, and your database should be stopped automatically.

Setting up MySQL on Linux

As is the case with many open source tools, you will find that it is much easier to set up MySQL on Linux than it is on Windows. In fact, MySQL may already be installed for you on Linux.

If it is not installed, download the appropriate rpms from www.mysql.org and install them.

NOTE: RPM stands for the Redhat Package Manager. It is a tool for automatically installing or uninstalling programs on Linux. It is a command line program designed to do all the things an InstallShield program would on Windows.

After downloading the files, you install them like this:

```
rpm -Uhv MySQL-3.23.49a-1.i386.rpm
rpm -Uhv MySQL-Max-3.23.49a-1.i386.rpm
rpm -Uhv MySQL-client-3.23.49a-1.i386.rpm
rpm -Uhv MySQL-shared-3.23.49a-1.i386.rpm
rpm -Uhv MyODBC-3.51.02-1.i386.rpm
```

The actual versions of the files you get should not matter, as long as you get a version at least as recent as the ones I show here. Note that the MySQL-Max file is the one that gives you support for InnoDB. To use InnoDB, you will have to copy my-small.cnf to /etc/my.cnf and uncomment the options that give you InnoDB support. All the rest of the paths in the file will probably be correct, but you will have to add the basedir and datadir entries:

```
[mysqld]
basedir = /var/lib/mysql/
datadir = /var/lib/mysql/
language = /usr/share/mysql/english
```

Be sure that there is enough room in your var partition to have a database there. For instance, on one of my systems, I keep the actual size of the InnoDB file to 25 MB, as specified in /etc/my.cnf:

```
# Uncomment the following if you are using Innobase tables
innodb_data_file_path = ibdata1:25M
innodb_data_home_dir = /var/lib/mysql/
innodb_log_group_home_dir = /var/lib/mysql/
innodb_log_arch_dir = /var/lib/mysql/
set-variable = innodb_mirrored_log_groups=1
set-variable = innodb_log_files_in_group=3
set-variable = innodb_log_file_size=5M
set-variable = innodb_log_buffer_size=8M
innodb_flush_log_at_trx_commit=1
innodb_log_archive=0
set-variable = innodb_buffer_pool_size=16M
set-variable = innodb_additional_mem_pool_size=2M
set-variable = innodb_file_io_threads=4
set-variable = innodb_lock_wait_timeout=50
```

Make sure that a file called ibdata1 exists in your /var/lib/mysql directory. The existence of this file is one clue that InnoDB is set up correctly. Also check the .err files in your /var/lib/mysql directory.

The last rpm command installs the ODBC drivers. That may not be necessary on your system, as you will probably end up using the JDBC driver instead. But I'm getting ahead of myself. I will talk about the drivers in the next chapter.

The steps you have taken so far should set things up so that MySQL will automatically start and stop when you boot and shut down your machine. Here is how to explicitly stop and start MySQL on Linux:

```
mysqladmin shutdown
/usr/bin/safe_mysqld
```

If you need to supply a password, submit it as in either of these examples:

```
mysqladmin -p shutdown
mysqladmin --password=foo shutdown
```

The first example will prompt you for a password, while the second allows you to enter it on the command line.

To specify a user and a password, use this syntax:

```
mysqladmin --user=root --password=foo
```

By default, on a new install, there will be only two users: root and the blank user. Neither of these users will have a password assigned. Under these circumstances, you should be able to issue commands without specifying the user or a password. After you assign a password to root and delete the blank user, you will have to give a password each time you use the MySQL tools. If you are signed on to Linux as root, you can use MySQL without specifying a user name. If you are signed on as a user and you have created an account for that user on MySQL, you do not need to specify a user name when using the MySQL tools. I will talk more about users and passwords in the next few sections of the text.

Before trying to start the server, be sure to run the mysql_install_db script usually found in the /usr/bin directory. This creates the tables that are needed for mysql to run correctly.

To restart the server manually, do this:

```
[root@bree root]# /usr/bin/safe_mysqld
Starting mysqld-max daemon with databases from /var/lib/mysql/
```

NOTE: If you have trouble starting the server, one possible cause is that you do not have the correct privileges in the directory that holds the MySQL databases. In particular, this can be the cause of the host.frm error. To fix the problem, you could try changing the privileges with chown to mysql.root:

```
chown -R mysql.root var/lib/mysql;
```

When this or other troubles occur, be sure to read the automatically generated error file called X.err file, located in the /var/lib/mysql directory.

If you have InnoDB installed and set up properly, safe_mysqld will start mysqld-max rather than mysqld. If you want to start the server and get back to the command prompt, use the classic ampersand trick:

```
[root@bree root]# /usr/bin/safe_mysqld &
[1] 2194
[root@bree root]# Starting mysqld-max daemon with databases from /var/lib/mysql/

[root@bree root]# jobs
[1]+  Running                 /usr/bin/safe_mysqld &
```

Notice that after starting the server in the background, I was able to type **jobs** at the shell prompt to see that it was running.

Now start the mysql monitor and type **status** to confirm that things are working:

```
[ccalvert@bree ccalvert]$ mysql --user=root --password=foo
Welcome to the MySQL monitor.  Commands end with ; or \g.
Your MySQL connection id is 54 to server version: 3.23.49a-Max

Type 'help;' or '\h' for help. Type '\c' to clear the buffer.

mysql> status
--------------
mysql  Ver 11.17 Distrib 3.23.49a, for pc-linux-gnu (i686)

Connection id:          54
Current database:
Current user:           root@localhost
Current pager:          stdout
Using outfile:          ''
Server version:         3.23.49a-Max
Protocol version:       10
Connection:             Localhost via UNIX socket
Client characterset:    latin1
Server characterset:    latin1
UNIX socket:            /var/lib/mysql/mysql.sock
Uptime:                 15 hours 53 min 48 sec

Threads: 1  Questions: 1172  Slow queries: 0  Opens: 84  Flush tables: 1  Open tables:
4 Queries per second avg: 0.020
--------------

mysql>
```

If you try to use the mysql monitor and you get a message back about not being able to connect through a socket, the server is probably not running.

Here is how to start the msyql database as a Linux service that runs automatically at startup:

```
[root@bree mysql]# /usr/share/mysql/mysql.server start &
[1] 2664
[root@bree mysql]# Starting mysqld-max daemon with databases from /var/lib/mysql/

[1]+  Done                    /usr/share/mysql/mysql.server start
[root@bree mysql]#
```

Here is how to stop the service:

```
[root@bree mysql]# ./mysql.server stop
Killing mysqld with pid 2714
Wait for mysqld to exit\c
.\c
.\c
.\c
.\c
```

```
 .\c
 .\c
 .\c
  done
 [root@bree mysql]#
```

Once you have the server up and running, don't forget to run /usr/bin/mysql_install_db. This will create the default tables in /var/lib/mysql.

A GUI Front End for MySQL

Once you have MySQL set up, you can begin to use a front end to manage it. There are two GUI front ends available for download on the www.mysql.org site — MySQLGUI and MyCC. Both front ends are free, and both work on Linux and Windows.

My experience, on both Linux and Windows, was that MySQLGUI was not particularly stable. It was better on Linux but still crashed fairly frequently. It was easy to use and well laid out in a blessedly quirky fashion, but it just wasn't very stable. Still, it was so easy to use that you might want to install it. If the parts of the program you want to use are working, you can get a job done very quickly. You can see the MySQLGUI front end in Figure 39-1.

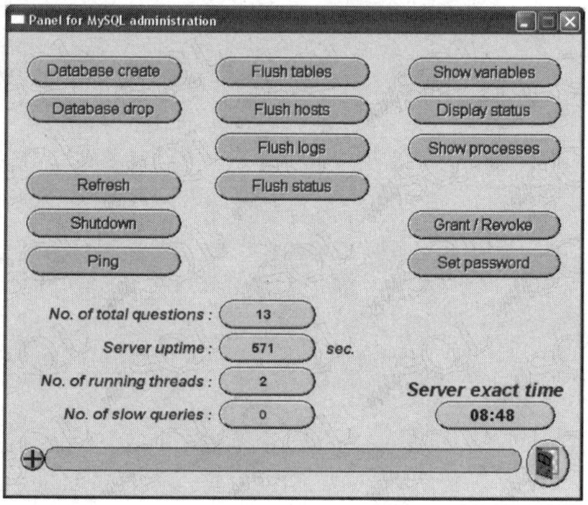

Figure 39-1: The Administrator panel from MySQLGUI

MyCC was still in alpha at the time of publication. However, it looks to be quite a promising tool. It still has many rough edges and much missing functionality, but it is quite stable. You can see one of the many views available in MyCC in Figure 39-2.

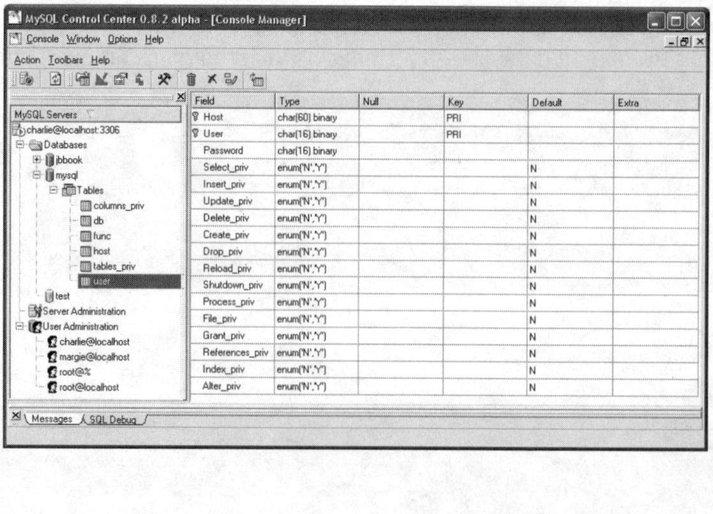

Figure 39-2: Browsing the metadata for the USER table in MyCC

I'm going to use MyCC in the examples in this text. However, you must remember that I am working with an alpha version of the product, and there is no guarantee that everything will be quite the same by the time you download a new version and try it out.

NOTE: In this chapter, I will show you how to perform most actions both at the command prompt and using a GUI. The command line tools are very stable and are unlikely to change. As a result, all the information you need is certain to be in the text of this chapter in the form of comments on how to use the command line tools. Having a GUI front end makes life much easier, so I would use one when possible. However, you can be sure that the command line tools won't fail you; they are rock solid.

When you first start MyCC, you will want to add a connection to a server, as shown in Figure 39-3. To reach this dialog, select **Action | Register Server** from the MyCC menu. The host name will probably be localhost for your first connection. Add a user name and password. If you are working with a brand new install of MySQL, there should be an account for user root, who will have no password. So put **root** in the user field and leave the password field blank. In the next section you will learn how to add a password. If you have a password, there is an option to prompt for it on startup. MyCC can also remember your password for you so that you will never be prompted for it.

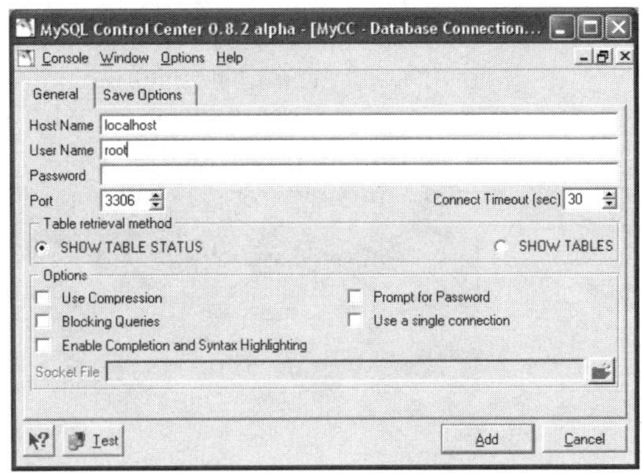

Figure 39-3: Adding a connection to a server

You may or may not need to point to the socket file. On Linux, that would normally be /var/lib/mysql/mysql.sock. On Windows, it would normally be c:\temp\mysql.sock. On Windows, I never had to fill this value in. On Linux, I type it in directly.

If all is working properly for you, you should be able to press the **Add** button, cancel out of the dialog, and return to the main screen of MyCC. Right-click on the node you have created, and choose **Connect**. The node should open up, as shown in Figure 39-4.

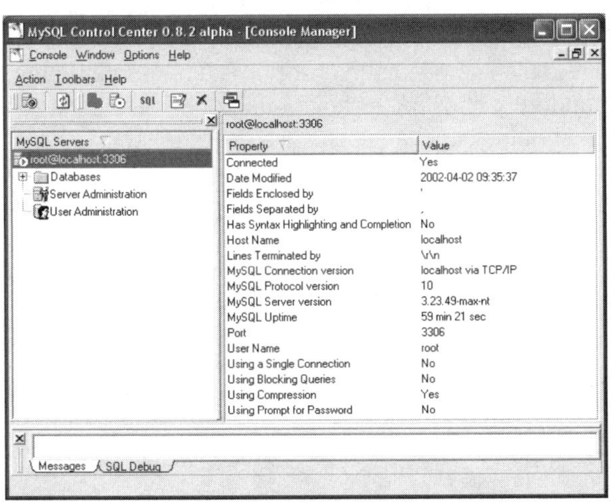

Figure 39-4: A successful connection to a MySQL database from MyCC

At this stage you have a GUI front end that you can use with MySQL. If you want, you can connect to servers on remote machines, filling out the dialog shown in Figure 39-3 but putting in the name of a server rather than localhost.

Creating Users and Passwords in MySQL

Once you have MySQL up and running on either Linux or Windows, you should set up users and passwords. I will first show you how to do it with the GUI and then walk you through the process at the command line.

Right-click on the **User Administration** node in MySQL, as shown in Figure 39-4. Choose **Add User** from the menu. The dialog shown in Figure 39-5 appears. Type in your user name, the host machine, and a password. Your first user is probably one who you want to make all-powerful, so select **All Privileges**, **With GRANT option**, and **Global Privileges** from the options available. Click the **Add** button and then **Cancel** to finish up. When you are done, the new user should appear in the list of users beneath the User Administration node.

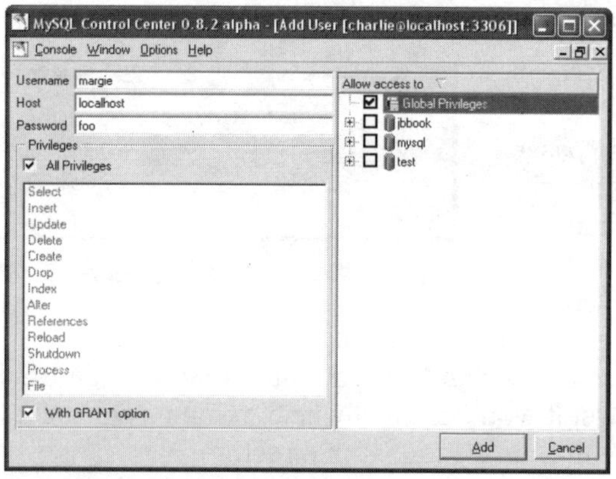

Figure 39-5: Setting up a user in MyCC

By default, in a new setup, there will also be "a node with no name." If you care about security, you should delete that node.

You will also want to change the password of the default root user. Right-click on **root@localhost**, and choose **Edit** from the menu. Use the dialog to change the password for the user. You will notice that there is also a node called root@%. The percent sign (%) is a wild card that can stand for any randomly chosen server. Thus, root@% means root signing on from some other machine. You should also change the password for this user.

I will now show you how to do the same thing from the command line. This information is useful since the MySQL GUIs are not totally stable and because command line routines like this can be scripted, and hence automated.

Here is a complete session to set up a user and password at the command line:

```
[f:\mysql\bin]mysql mysql
Welcome to the MySQL monitor.  Commands end with ; or \g.
Your MySQL connection id is 10 to server version: 3.23.49-max-nt

Type 'help;' or '\h' for help. Type '\c' to clear the buffer.

mysql> DELETE FROM user WHERE Host='localhost' AND User='';
```

```
Query OK, 1 row affected (0.05 sec)

mysql> GRANT ALL PRIVILEGES ON *.* TO charlie@localhost
         IDENTIFIED BY 'foo' WITH GRANT OPTION;

mysql> GRANT ALL PRIVILEGES ON *.* TO charlie@"%"
         IDENTIFIED BY 'foo' WITH GRANT OPTION;

mysql> update user set password=PASSWORD("foo") where user="charlie";

mysql> QUIT
Bye

[f:\mysql\bin]mysqladmin --user=charlie --password=foo reload

[f:\mysql\bin]mysqladmin -u root password mypassword
```

The first command in this series enters the mysql monitor utility using the mysql database. The mysql database comes with the product. It is where you define users and their privileges. If you did not specify a database when starting the mysql monitor, type **use mysql** at the mysql prompt to begin using the system database:

```
mysql> use mysql;
Database changed
```

The system database, called mysql, is where the list of users, their passwords, and their privileges is stored.

Once inside the MySQL monitor, you should delete the blank or empty user:

```
mysql> DELETE FROM user WHERE Host='localhost' AND User='';
```

After doing this, you will no longer be able to enter mysql by simply typing mysql at the command prompt. Instead, you will have to supply a user name, as explained below.

After deleting the blank user, the next step is to add a new user, granting him what amounts to super user privileges. Notice that you grant the user privileges twice, once as a local user and once with the % symbol to allow him or her to sign on from a remote machine:

```
mysql> GRANT ALL PRIVILEGES ON *.* TO charlie@localhost
         IDENTIFIED BY 'foo' WITH GRANT OPTION;

mysql> GRANT ALL PRIVILEGES ON *.* TO charlie@"%"
         IDENTIFIED BY 'foo' WITH GRANT OPTION;
```

NOTE: Adding these kinds of grant options are the key to solving the "host 'x' is not allowed to connect to this SQL server" problem.

Change the new user's password to "foo" or some more robust password of your own choice:

```
mysql> update user set password=PASSWORD("foo") where user="charlie";
```

Exit the mysql monitor, and then reload the database:

```
[f:\mysql\bin]mysqladmin --user=charlie --password=foo reload
```

Reloading is necessary after you change the system tables in the mysql database. It is not necessary when changing ordinary tables.

The next to last line shows a second way to set the password for a user. If you had already set the password once for the user, the line to set a new password would look like this:

```
[/usr/bin/]mysqladmin --user=root --password password 'foo'
[f:\mysql\bin]mysqladmin --user=root --password=foo password newpw
```

The first example shows what to do if there is no password on the server when you begin, and the second example shows what to do if there is a password.

If you assign the user a password, you will also have to specify the password when starting the mysql monitor:

```
[g:\utilities\mysql\bin]mysql --user=charlie --password=foo
```

More on Working with User Accounts

You already know how to get a list of users on the system when inside of MyCC. As you know, the list of users is stored in a table. Go to the **Databases** node in MyCC and open it. Select the **mysql** database, and find the USER table, as shown near the beginning of this chapter in Figure 39-2. Double-click on the **user** node to bring up a view of that table, as shown in Figure 39-6.

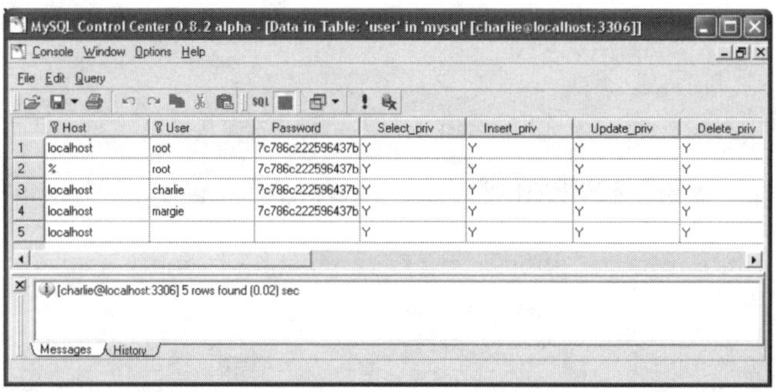

Figure 39-6: Viewing the list of users stored in the mysql database in the USER table

In this view you can see that Host and User are primary key fields. The various privileges assigned to each user are also visible. A Y for "yes" means the user has a privilege, and an N for "no" means the user is denied that privilege.

At the top of the view shown in Figure 39-6 is an SQL button. If you press that button, you can enter SQL statements to run against the currently selected node. For instance, in Figure 39-7, you can see a query run against the user table to select on the records of the root user. Notice that there is a history window for keeping track of the commands you have issued.

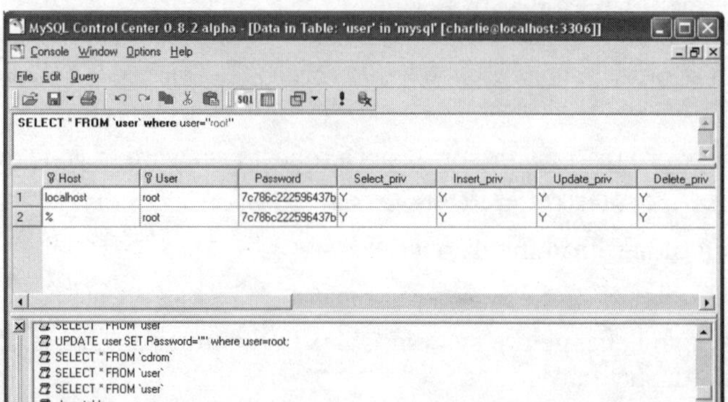

Figure 39-7: Issuing queries in MyCC

Here is how to get the list of users from the USER table when working at the command prompt:

```
[g:\utilities\mysql\bin]mysql --user=root --password=foo mysql
Welcome to the MySQL monitor.  Commands end with ; or \g.
Your MySQL connection id is 5 to server version: 3.23.49-max-nt

Type 'help;' or '\h' for help. Type '\c' to clear the buffer.

mysql> select host, user from user;
+-----------+------+
| host      | user |
+-----------+------+
| %         |      |
| %         | root |
| localhost |      |
| localhost | root |
+-----------+------+
4 rows in set (0.00 sec)

mysql>
```

Notice that when I signed on, I specified not only my user name and password but also the database I wanted to use. The mysql database is where all the key metadata, such as user information, is stored.

Here is what happens if you delete a user:

```
mysql> delete from user where host='localhost' and user='';
Query OK, 1 row affected (0.01 sec)

mysql> select host, user from user;
+-----------+------+
| host      | user |
+-----------+------+
| %         |      |
| %         | root |
| localhost | root |
+-----------+------+
3 rows in set (0.00 sec)
```

As you can see, the user with no name on the localhost has been deleted, but the one from any machine (%) is still there. The empty user from any machine (%) has no privileges by default. (You can issue this same kind of command in MyCC, using the view shown in Figure 39-7.)

Here is how to add a single user using SQL and the way the database looks after you do it:

```
mysql> grant all privileges on *.* to charlie@localhost
    -> identified by 'foo' with grant option;
Query OK, 0 rows affected (0.00 sec)

mysql> select host, user from user;
+-----------+---------+
| host      | user    |
+-----------+---------+
```

```
| %         |         |
| %         | root    |
| localhost | charlie |
| localhost | root    |
+-----------+---------+
4 rows in set (0.00 sec)
```

Here are the fields of the USER table:

```
Host
User
Password
Select_priv
Insert_priv
Update_priv
Delete
_priv
Create_priv
Drop_priv
Reload_priv
Shutdown_priv
Process_priv
File_priv
Grant_priv
References_priv
Index_priv
Alter_priv
```

Given this information, it is easy to determine what a particular user can do:

```
mysql> select host, user, insert_priv, shutdown_priv, update_priv from user;
+-----------+---------+-------------+---------------+-------------+
| host      | user    | insert_priv | shutdown_priv | update_priv |
+-----------+---------+-------------+---------------+-------------+
| localhost | root    | Y           | Y             | Y           |
| %         | root    | Y           | Y             | Y           |
| localhost | charlie | Y           | Y             | Y           |
| %         |         | N           | N             | N           |
+-----------+---------+-------------+---------------+-------------+
4 rows in set (0.00 sec)
```

Note that the blank user from any machine has no privileges. Selecting data from the USER table can also be a quick way to find out who has a password and who doesn't:

```
mysql> select host, user, password from user;
+-----------+---------+------------------+
| host      | user    | password         |
+-----------+---------+------------------+
| localhost | root    |                  |
| %         | root    |                  |
| localhost | charlie | 34bd5ce05ed376e6 |
| %         |         |                  |
+-----------+---------+------------------+
4 rows in set (0.00 sec)
```

NOTE: All this changing of passwords can get you in a weird state if you are not careful. If you are in MyCC and suddenly nodes won't open or respond correctly, the problem can be that you changed the password at the command prompt, thereby invalidating your current MyCC session. To fix the situation, just sync up the passwords in MyCC and mysql monitor.

Just for the sake of clarity, let's review giving the user a password and then see what the database looks like when all but the powerless anonymous remote user has a password:

```
mysql> update user set password=password('mypassword')
    -> where user='root';
Query OK, 2 rows affected (0.00 sec)
Rows matched: 2  Changed: 2  Warnings: 0

mysql> select host, user, password from user;
+-----------+---------+------------------+
| host      | user    | password         |
+-----------+---------+------------------+
| localhost | root    | 34bd5ce05ed376e6 |
| %         | root    | 34bd5ce05ed376e6 |
| localhost | charlie | 34bd5ce05ed376e6 |
| %         |         |                  |
+-----------+---------+------------------+
4 rows in set (0.00 sec)
```

At this stage, you know the minimal number of things that you absolutely have to be cognizant of to get MySQL up and running on Windows or Linux.

Creating Simple Databases and Tables

Once you have the system up and running on either Linux or Windows, you will want to create a database and a simple table. The following is shown on Windows, but more or less the same thing happens on Linux. For instance, instead of typing mysql.exe, type mysql. Or, if you are using the GUI, start up mycc rather than MyCC.exe. Once you are inside mysql or MyCC, everything else is exactly the same.

NOTE: This is not the section of this chapter where I show how to load the jbbook database that contains the data used in the sample programs. That section appears near the end of the chapter.

At the time of publication, neither MyCC nor MySQLGUI could give you much help creating tables. The best that either tool appears to offer is a chance to enter SQL statements. This is in fact my primary and preferred means for creating a table. But given the current lack of good GUI tools, I am going to simply explain how to do things from the command line.

There is a default MySQL database called test that you can use for experiments:

```
[g:\utilities\mysql\bin]mysql.exe --user=charlie --password=foo test
Welcome to the MySQL monitor.  Commands end with ; or \g.
Your MySQL connection id is 25 to server version: 3.23.49-max-nt

Type 'help;' or '\h' for help. Type '\c' to clear the buffer.

mysql> create table test_table (test_field int);
Query OK, 0 rows affected (0.02 sec)
```

Note that on the initial command line I specified a desire to work with the test database. If I did not, my first command inside mysql monitor would be use test.

In the session shown here, a CREATE TABLE command is used to create a simple table with one field in the test database. The table name is TEST_TABLE, and the sole field created is of type int and is called test_field:

```
mysql> create table test_table (test_field int);
```

To enter data into your table and then view the data, type the following:

```
mysql> insert into test_table values(1);
Query OK, 1 row affected (0.00 sec)

mysql> select * from test_table;
+------------+
| test_field |
+------------+
|          1 |
+------------+
1 row in set (0.00 sec)
```

The first command entered the data, and the second gave you a chance to view it.

NOTE: In case you are worried, let me assure you that I will, over time, show you how to do all these things inside of JBuilder. However, it is best to lay the foundation for your work inside of JBuilder by first learning how the database you use operates on its own.

Figure 39-2 showed you how to view the metadata from a table. Here is how to see the columns in your table if you are working in the mysql monitor:

```
mysql> show columns from test_table;
+--------------+---------+------+-----+---------+-------+
| Field        | Type    | Null | Key | Default | Extra |
+--------------+---------+------+-----+---------+-------+
| test_field   | int(11) | YES  |     | NULL    |       |
+--------------+---------+------+-----+---------+-------+
1 row in set (0.03 sec)
```

Once you have created a table or two, you will be ready to create your own database. To create the database, enter the following command:

```
mysql> create database mydatabase;
Query OK, 1 row affected (0.00 sec)
```

Now type **use mydatabase**, and you can begin creating the tables you want to use in your programs.

To create a database in MyCC, right-click on the **Databases** node and select **Create new database**. A dialog will pop up, allowing you to fill in the name of the database.

To see the variables you set in your my.cnf and my.ini files, you can type **Show variables** at the mysql monitor prompt. In MyCC, you can see the same information by right-clicking on the **Server Administration** node and choosing **Show Variables** from the pop-up menu. As explained earlier in the chapter, you can use the values of these variables to determine which configuration file your system is using.

Introduction to InterBase

The goal of this section is to get InterBase installed on your system. InterBase is a powerful relational database. As you will learn in the next chapter, you can use a tool called InterClient to achieve a JDBC connection between your InterBase database and the worlds of Java and JBuilder.

InterBase had its roots at various companies, including DEC and Ashton-Tate. It became part of the Borland product line after Borland bought Ashton-Tate. Though it never was a big product for Borland, it remained a steady source of income into 2000, when it suffered from political battles between the developers and Borland's administration.

As a happy result of these battles, Borland released InterBase as an open source tool. The actual launch of the open source product, however, once again proved fractious. There are now at least two versions of InterBase, one of them a commercial product released by Borland and the other an open source product released under the name Firebird. (Borland has also released an open source version of the product, but most of their effort is aimed at the commercial version.)

Despite all these problems, I have always had, and will always have, a strong admiration for InterBase. The technology industry has many tales to tell about good technologies being left behind while inferior technologies gain wide acceptance. In my opinion, the history of InterBase is one of those tales of shame, in which we are all to blame for allowing this astounding database to be passed over in favor of inferior products. In part, the angry episodes in the last few years of InterBase's history are a result of the frustration felt by managers and developers who spent years developing and promoting a superior product, sold at a shamefully low price, that often lost out to competitors for no good reason. This is not to say that InterBase is not being used at major, mission-critical sites throughout the world. InterBase has been around for a long time, and it has a long list of supporters from companies such as the U.S. Department of Labor, Hewlett-Packard, SAP, NEC Electronics, and many, many others.

Downloading InterBase

The Firebird open source version of InterBase is available at http://firebird.sourceforge.net/.

You can download both InterBase and InterClient from this site. I use the super-server version of the database.

Some links to Borland's open source version of InterBase are http://sourceforge.net/projects/interbase and http://www.borland.com/devsupport/interbase/opensource/.

The home page for Borland's commercial version of the product is http://www.borland.com/interbase/.

If you've been using Borland products, there is a chance that InterBase is already installed on your system. There are several different ways to find out if this is the case. On Windows, you can type **net start** at the command prompt and look for the InterBase service. It should be listed under both the InterBase Guardian and InterBase Server. Another approach is to look in the Services page found through Control Panel\Administrative Tools; there should be an applet called the InterBase manager added to the main page of the Control Panel. Figure 39-8 shows what it looks like if both InterBase and InterClient are installed as services.

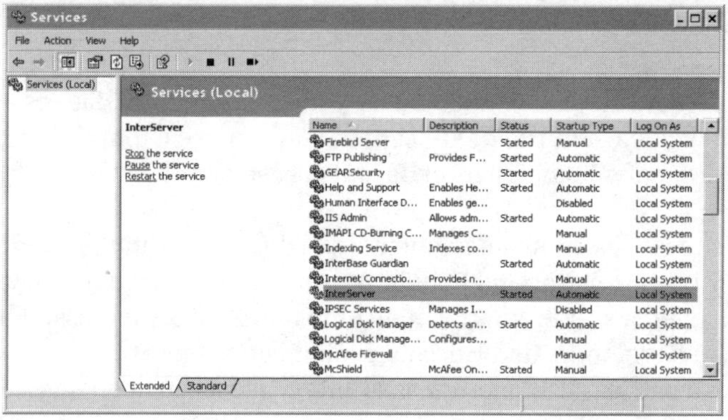

Figure 39-8: InterBase (Firebird), InterBase Guardian, and InterClient (InterServer) all installed as services in the Windows Control Panel

NOTE: The InterBase Guardian is a tool used to ensure that the InterBase server stays loaded and will automatically reload if there is a crash.

On Linux, InterBase is usually installed by default in the /opt/interbase directory. The main program, stored in the bin directory, is called ibserver. A file called libgds.so should be found in your /usr/lib directory.

An entry for InterClient should be made in your services file. This file is found in the etc directory on Linux. On Windows, it should appear in the /windows/system32/drivers/etc directory. (Windows 2000 and older NT products use the /winnt/system32/drivers/etc directory.)

```
gds_db          3050/tcp                # InterBase InterServer
interserver     3060/tcp                # interclient
```

Installing InterBase on Windows and Linux

If you have downloaded Firebird or have a copy of Borland's version of InterBase, the install is very straightforward. For instance, you would type this to install Firebird on Windows:

```
[g:\downloads\partsi-s\interbase]Firebird-1.0.0.796-Win32.exe
```

You will then be stepped through a simple set of standard install dialogs.

On Linux, you would type this to install Firebird InterBase:

```
rpm -Uhv FirebirdSS-1.0.0.796-0.i386.rpm
```

Here is the command for starting one of the versions of InterBase from Borland on Linux:

```
rpm -Uhv InterBaseSS_LI_kylix2-V6.0.1-1.i386.rpm
```

To stop and start InterBase as a service on Windows, you would either select **Control Panel | Administrative Tools | Services** or type the following at the command prompt:

```
[g:\downloads\partsi-s\interbase]net start "InterBase Guardian"
The InterBase Guardian service is starting.
The InterBase Guardian service was started successfully.

[g:\downloads\partsi-s\interbase]net stop "InterBase Guardian"
The InterBase Guardian service is stopping.
The InterBase Guardian service was stopped successfully.
```

You only need to stop and start the InterBase Guardian. The InterBase server itself will follow the Guardian's lead.

On Linux, you can change to /opt/interbase/bin directory and start the server like this:

```
./ibmgr -start -forever -user sysdba -password masterkey
```

To stop the server, type:

```
./ibmgr -shut -user sysdba -password masterkey
```

Note that InterBase runs as a xinetd service. To make that work, the following text file, called firebird, is placed in /etc/xinetd at install time:

```
service gds_db
{
        flags                   = REUSE
        socket_type             = stream
        wait                    = no
        user                    = root
        log_on_success          += USERID
        log_on_failure          += USERID
        server                  = /opt/interbase/bin/gds_inet_server
        disable                 = no
}
```

The presence of this file is enough to ensure that InterBase will be started at install time. xinetd gives you the following options:

```
[root@bree bin]# /etc/init.d/xinetd --help
Usage: /etc/init.d/xinetd {start|stop|status|restart|condrestart|reload}
```

So one rather brute force way to start the service is to type:

```
[root@bree bin]# /etc/init.d/xinetd restart
Stopping xinetd:                                          [  OK  ]
Starting xinetd:                                          [  OK  ]
```

At the command prompt, you should type **cat /var/log/messages** to make sure no errors occurred during the restart operation. This command will print the messages file to the screen. At the end of this usually very long file, you should see a report on your latest operation. If any errors occurred while restarting xinitd, they should be appended to the end of the messages file.

Testing InterBase on Windows and Linux

The Windows release of Borland's version of InterBase comes with an excellent front end called IBConsole. You can download the indefatigable Jeff Overcash's free version of IBConsole for use with Firebird from the CodeCentral site found on http://community.borland.com. More particularly, try this link: http://codecentral.borland.com/codecentral/ccweb.exe/listing?id=17154. A replacement for IBConsole called IBExpert Personal Edition is available from the IBPhoenix site at http://www.ibphoenix.com/. Source (which may be a bit out of date) for IBConsole is also available from the IBPhoenix site. All these programs are similar to the MyCC program examined earlier in this chapter. Because of space considerations and the intuitive nature of the product, I won't bother discussing it here at this time. I do, however, highly recommend it.

You can run an InterBase command line tool called isql to see if Linux is working properly. This tool is roughly equivalent to the mysql monitor that we looked at earlier in this chapter.

With InterBase, you don't need to set up your password ahead of time. You can assume that there is a super user named sysdba that has a password of masterkey.

Here is a simple isql session that you can use to test whether or not InterBase is installed:

```
[g:\compilers\interbase\bin]isql g:\data\employee.gdb -u sysdba -p masterkey
Database:  g:\data\employee.gdb, User: sysdba
SQL>
SQL> select first_name, last_name from employee where last_name = "Nelson";

FIRST_NAME      LAST_NAME
=============== ====================


Robert          Nelson

SQL>
```

You will have to edit the line to point to your copy of the employee.gdb database that ships with InterBase. The command looks exactly the same on Linux, other than the direction of your slashes and the location of employee.gdb.

Here is how to check which tables are installed in your database:

```
SQL> show tables;
       COUNTRY                                CUSTOMER
       DEPARTMENT                             EMPLOYEE
       EMPLOYEE_PROJECT                       JOB
       PHONE_LIST                             PROJECT
       PROJ_DEPT_BUDGET                       SALARY_HISTORY
       SALES
SQL>
```

Rather than going into more depth, I'm going to stop here and not explain any more about InterBase. However, there is an active InterBase community both on the Borland newsgroups at forums.borland.com and on the firebird.sourceforge.net web sites. There are numerous articles available on the subject, including those found at www.interbase.com and www.ibphoenix.com.

Creating Data for Use with this Book

The tables that you will use in this book are available both on the CD and at http://www.elvenware.com. It is easy to give you the databases for InterBase and Access since they come as discrete files:

- For Access, locate jbbook.mdb and jbbook.ldb on this book's CD.
- For InterBase, locate jbbook.gdb on this book's CD.

Also, read the index.html file on the root of the CD for any last-minute updates. For further questions about or updates to the Access and InterBase data, check www.elvenware.com.

The InnoDB files for MySQL, on the other hand, are a bit harder to share. As a result, I will provide that data in script form and then give you scripts that will run on either Windows or Linux for automatically importing the data into MySQL. Having the data in text form allows you to recreate the tables if they get corrupted while you are experimenting with them. The command for creating the tables is very, very simple to execute. You can read about it in the following section.

In the next few sections of this book I include the SQL commands you can give to MySQL, InterBase, and Access in order to create the tables used in this text. These commands don't insert data into the tables; they only create the metadata for the tables. I do, however, provide means to repopulate the databases with data.

It is interesting to see that there are slight differences in the commands you give to load a database on the various different platforms. After this paragraph is the command for creating a table called BOOK when using MySQL. Don't try to type this in, as it won't work unless you have already defined the TYPES, MEDIUM, and ARTIST tables referenced in the foreign keys. I show how to create those tables later. For now, look at this SQL syntax so that we can discuss it:

```
CREATE TABLE BOOK
(
  CODE      INT NOT NULL,
  TYPES     INT NOT NULL,
  MEDIUM    INT NOT NULL,
  RATING    INT NOT NULL,
  COMMENT   TEXT,
  GROUPCODE INT NOT NULL,
  BOOK      VARCHAR(50),
  INDEX INDEX_TYPES (TYPES),
  FOREIGN KEY(TYPES) REFERENCES TYPES(CODE),
  INDEX INDEX_MEDIM (MEDIUM),
  FOREIGN KEY(MEDIUM) REFERENCES MEDIUM(CODE),
  INDEX INDEX_GROUPCODE (GROUPCODE),
  FOREIGN KEY(GROUPCODE) REFERENCES ARTIST(CODE),
  PRIMARY KEY (CODE)
) TYPE=INNODB;
```

This syntax provides very clear statements for creating a foreign key and adding an index.

MySQL requires that you place an index on foreign keys that reference the primary key of another table. Notice the specification of the InnoDB table type. Finally, notice the simple command for creating a text field, which is a kind of BLOB.

NOTE: A BLOB is a Binary Large Object. BLOB fields are designed to hold any kind of undefined data, such as an image or large text field. In MySQL you can use either the Text or the BLOB type, depending on your needs. The subtypes include TINYBLOB, BLOB, MEDIUMBLOB, LONGBLOB, TINYTEXT, TEXT, MEDIUMTEXT, and LONGTEXT. If you want the text to show up in Java text fields, it is best to use the TEXT types.

Here is the same table defined for InterBase. Again, I ask that you don't try to type this in, but only study it:

```
CREATE TABLE BOOK
(
  CODE      INT NOT NULL,
  TYPES     INT NOT NULL,
  MEDIUM    INT NOT NULL,
  RATING    INT NOT NULL,
  COMMENT   BLOB SUB_TYPE TEXT SEGMENT SIZE 80,
```

```
  GROUPCODE INT NOT NULL,
  BOOK      VARCHAR(50),
  FOREIGN KEY(TYPES) REFERENCES TYPES(CODE),
  FOREIGN KEY(MEDIUM) REFERENCES MEDIUM(CODE),
  FOREIGN KEY(GROUPCODE) REFERENCES ARTIST(CODE),
  PRIMARY KEY (CODE)
);
```

The BLOB is a bit more complex to declare, but it allows us to specify its subtype. In InterBase, you do not need to create an index on the foreign keys, and there is no way to do that chore inside of the create table statement itself.

Finally, here is the code for creating the table in Access:

```
CREATE TABLE BOOK
(
  CODE      INT NOT NULL,
  TYPES     INT NOT NULL,
  MEDIUM    INT NOT NULL,
  RATING    INT NOT NULL,
  COMMENT   MEMO,
  GROUPCODE INT NOT NULL,
  BOOK      VARCHAR(50),
  FOREIGN KEY(TYPES) REFERENCES TYPES(CODE),
  FOREIGN KEY(MEDIUM) REFERENCES MEDIUM(CODE),
  FOREIGN KEY(GROUPCODE) REFERENCES ARTIST(CODE),
  PRIMARY KEY (CODE)
);
```

In this case everything is the same as in InterBase, except for the BLOB field, which is now called a Memo.

I also found some small differences between the databases. For instance, if I used a SMALLINT field in one table and an INT field in a second table and then linked the tables with a foreign key on the field in question, everything would work in InterBase but fail when I tried to insert a record in MySQL. The Access table did not support the SMALLINT type. The end result is that I have used INT everywhere.

But most of these differences are fairly minor. Overall, these three types of databases were fairly interchangeable.

Creating Tables for MySQL

Because of the way the InnoDB database files work, I do not ship the jbbook database for MySQL in binary format. Instead, I ask that you create the binary file yourself from a script that I provide. The script is stored in a 200 KB text file called jbbook-backup.sql, which is found in the Database directory on the CD.

If you are creating the database from scratch, issue these commands:

```
[g:\srcjava\jbbook\database]mysql --user=charlie --password=foo
Welcome to the MySQL monitor.  Commands end with ; or \g.
Your MySQL connection id is 124 to server version: 3.23.49-max-nt

Type 'help;' or '\h' for help. Type '\c' to clear the buffer.

mysql> create database jbbook;
```

```
Query OK, 1 row affected (0.00 sec)

mysql> use jbbook;
Database changed
mysql> source jbbook-backup.sql;
```

Here is the command to create, recreate, or restore the database from a text file if the database already exists:

```
mysql --user=charlie --password=foo jbbook < jbbook-backup.sql
```

Here is the command I used to create the backup file:

```
mysqldump --user=charlie --password=foo --opt jbbook > jbbook-backup.sql
```

NOTE: Tiny batch files and shell scripts on the CD contain these commands. For instance, the latter command is stored in mysql-backup-jbbook.bat and the former in restore-mysql-jbbook.bat.

In Listing 39-1 you will find the data definition for the MySQL database. Please check the index.html on the root of the CD and the file called create-music-mysql.sql in the Database/scripts directory on the CD for any last-minute updates.

Listing 39-1: Creating the Music database for MySQL

```
CREATE TABLE TYPES
(
  TYPES     VARCHAR(15) NOT NULL,
  CODE      INTEGER NOT NULL,
  PRIMARY KEY (CODE)
) TYPE=INNODB;

CREATE TABLE ARTIST
(
  CODE      INT NOT NULL,
  LAST      VARCHAR(30),
  FIRST     VARCHAR(30),
  BORN      TIMESTAMP,
  DIED      TIMESTAMP,
  BIRTHPLACE VARCHAR(35),
  COMMENT   BLOB,
  ARTISTTYPE INTEGER NOT NULL,
  PRIMARY KEY (CODE)
) TYPE=INNODB;

CREATE TABLE LOUDNESS
(
  LOUDNESS  VARCHAR(15) NOT NULL,
  CODE      INTEGER NOT NULL,
 PRIMARY KEY (CODE)
) TYPE=INNODB;

CREATE TABLE MEDIUM
(
  MEDIUM    VARCHAR(15) NOT NULL,
  CODE      INTEGER NOT NULL,
```

```
 PRIMARY KEY (CODE)
) TYPE=INNODB;

CREATE TABLE ALBUM
(
  CODE       INT NOT NULL,
  ALBUM      VARCHAR(45) NOT NULL,
  TYPES      SMALLINT,
  LOUDNESS   INT,
  MEDIUM     INT,
  RATING     INT,
  GROUPCODE  INT NOT NULL,
  CDDBID     VARCHAR(20),
  CDDBNAME   VARCHAR(40),
  INDEX INDEX_TYPES (TYPES),
  FOREIGN KEY(TYPES) REFERENCES TYPES(CODE),
  INDEX INDEX_LOUDNESS (LOUDNESS),
  FOREIGN KEY(LOUDNESS) REFERENCES LOUDNESS(CODE),
  INDEX INDEX_MEDIM (MEDIUM),
  FOREIGN KEY(MEDIUM) REFERENCES MEDIUM(CODE),
  INDEX INDEX_GROUPCODE (GROUPCODE),
  FOREIGN KEY(GROUPCODE) REFERENCES ARTIST(CODE),
  PRIMARY KEY (CODE)
) TYPE=INNODB;

CREATE TABLE ALBUMINFO
(
  CODE       INT NOT NULL,
  COMMENT    TEXT,
  CDDBDATA   TEXT,
  ALBUMCODE  INT NOT NULL,
  INDEX INDEX_ALBUMCODE (ALBUMCODE),
  FOREIGN KEY(ALBUMCODE) REFERENCES ALBUM(CODE),
  PRIMARY KEY (CODE)
) TYPE=INNODB;

CREATE TABLE ARTISTTYPE
(
  ARTISTTYPEVARCHAR(15) NOT NULL,
  CODE       INTEGER NOT NULL,
  PRIMARY KEY (CODE)
) TYPE=INNODB;

CREATE TABLE BOOK
(
  CODE       INT NOT NULL,
  TYPES      INT NOT NULL,
  MEDIUM     INT NOT NULL,
  RATING     INT NOT NULL,
  COMMENT    TEXT,
  GROUPCODE  INT NOT NULL,
```

```
  BOOK      VARCHAR(50),
  INDEX INDEX_TYPES (TYPES),
  FOREIGN KEY(TYPES) REFERENCES TYPES(CODE),
  INDEX INDEX_MEDIM (MEDIUM),
  FOREIGN KEY(MEDIUM) REFERENCES MEDIUM(CODE),
  INDEX INDEX_GROUPCODE (GROUPCODE),
  FOREIGN KEY(GROUPCODE) REFERENCES ARTIST(CODE),
  PRIMARY KEY (CODE)
) TYPE=INNODB;

CREATE TABLE CDROM
(
  CODE              INT NOT NULL,
  LOCATIONCODE      INTEGER,
  NAME              VARCHAR(50),
  IDVALUE           VARCHAR(50),
  KEYVALUE          VARCHAR(50),
  COMMENT           TEXT,
  TYPES             INTEGER,
 PRIMARY KEY (CODE)
) TYPE=INNODB;

CREATE TABLE LOCATION
(
  CODE              INTEGER,
  LOCATION          VARCHAR(25)
) TYPE=INNODB;

CREATE TABLE SONGS
(
  CODE              INT NOT NULL,
  SONG              VARCHAR(65) NOT NULL,
  WRITER            VARCHAR(45),
  RATING            SMALLINT,
  ALBUMCODE         INT NOT NULL,
  SONGNUMBER        SMALLINT,
  INDEX INDEX_ALBUMCODE (ALBUMCODE),
  FOREIGN KEY(ALBUMCODE) REFERENCES ALBUM(CODE),
  PRIMARY KEY (CODE)
) TYPE=INNODB;
```

The text shown here will run as a script inside of MySQL. To have the database read it in, enter this command, changing the user and password to suit your system:

```
mysql --password="foo" --user="charlie" jbbook < create-music-mysql.sql
```

You will find other scripts available, such as ones for deleting all the tables and entering the data into empty tables.

Creating Tables for InterBase

There is no need to create the tables for InterBase. Instead, you can just use the jbbook.gbd database that you will find on the CD. The final metadata for the database is stored in

InterBase-jbbook-metadata.txt, found in the Database directory on the CD. In the next chapter I will explain how to connect to that database from JBuilder.

Listing 39-2: Creating the Music database for InterBase

```
CREATE TABLE LOUDNESS
(
  LOUDNESS  VARCHAR(15) NOT NULL,
  CODE      INTEGER NOT NULL,
  PRIMARY KEY (CODE)
);

CREATE TABLE MEDIUM
(
  MEDIUM    VARCHAR(15) NOT NULL,
  CODE      INTEGER NOT NULL,
  PRIMARY KEY (CODE)
);

CREATE TABLE TYPES
(
  TYPES     VARCHAR(15) NOT NULL,
  CODE      INTEGER NOT NULL,
 PRIMARY KEY (CODE)
);

CREATE TABLE ARTIST
(
  CODE      INT NOT NULL,
  LAST      VARCHAR(30),
  FIRST     VARCHAR(30),
  BORN      TIMESTAMP,
  DIED      TIMESTAMP,
  BIRTHPLACE VARCHAR(35),
  COMMENT   BLOB SUB_TYPE TEXT SEGMENT SIZE 80,
  ARTISTTYPE INTEGER NOT NULL,
 PRIMARY KEY (CODE)
);

CREATE TABLE ALBUM
(
  CODE      INT NOT NULL,
  ALBUM     VARCHAR(45) NOT NULL,
  TYPES     SMALLINT,
  LOUDNESS  SMALLINT,
  MEDIUM    SMALLINT,
  RATING    SMALLINT,
  GROUPCODE INT NOT NULL,
  CDDBID    VARCHAR(20),
  CDDBNAME  VARCHAR(40),
  FOREIGN KEY(TYPES) REFERENCES TYPES(CODE),
  FOREIGN KEY(LOUDNESS) REFERENCES LOUDNESS(CODE),
```

```
  FOREIGN KEY(MEDIUM) REFERENCES MEDIUM(CODE),
  FOREIGN KEY(GROUPCODE) REFERENCES ARTIST(CODE),
  PRIMARY KEY (CODE)
);

CREATE TABLE ALBUMINFO
(
  CODE      INT NOT NULL,
  COMMENT   BLOB SUB_TYPE TEXT SEGMENT SIZE 80,
  CDDBDATA  BLOB SUB_TYPE TEXT SEGMENT SIZE 80,
  ALBUMCODE INT NOT NULL,
  FOREIGN KEY (ALBUMCODE) REFERENCES ALBUM,
  PRIMARY KEY (CODE)
);

CREATE TABLE ARTISTTYPE
(
  ARTISTTYPE VARCHAR(15) NOT NULL,
  CODE       INTEGER NOT NULL,
 PRIMARY KEY (CODE)
);

CREATE TABLE BOOK
(
  CODE      INT NOT NULL,
  TYPES     INT NOT NULL,
  MEDIUM    INT NOT NULL,
  RATING    INT NOT NULL,
  COMMENT   BLOB SUB_TYPE TEXT SEGMENT SIZE 80,
  GROUPCODE INT NOT NULL,
  BOOK      VARCHAR(50),
  FOREIGN KEY(TYPES) REFERENCES TYPES(CODE),
  FOREIGN KEY(MEDIUM) REFERENCES MEDIUM(CODE),
  FOREIGN KEY(GROUPCODE) REFERENCES ARTIST(CODE),
  PRIMARY KEY (CODE)
);

CREATE TABLE CDROM
(
  CODE            INT NOT NULL,
  LOCATIONCODE    INTEGER,
  NAME            VARCHAR(50),
  IDVALUE         VARCHAR(50),
  KEYVALUE        VARCHAR(50),
  COMMENT         BLOB SUB_TYPE TEXT SEGMENT SIZE 80,
  TYPES           INTEGER,
 PRIMARY KEY (CODE)
);

CREATE TABLE LOCATION
(
```

```
  CODE            INTEGER,
  LOCATION        VARCHAR(25)
);

CREATE TABLE SONGS
(
  CODE            INT NOT NULL,
  SONG            VARCHAR(65) NOT NULL,
  WRITER          VARCHAR(45),
  RATING          SMALLINT,
  ALBUMCODE       INT NOT NULL,
  SONGNUMBER      SMALLINT,
  FOREIGN KEY (ALBUMCODE) REFERENCES ALBUM (CODE),
  PRIMARY KEY (CODE)
);
```

Creating Tables for Access

The Access database for this book is stored in a file called jbbook.mdb on the CD. Listing 39-3 shows the metadata for that database.

Listing 39-3: The metadata for the data stored in the jbbook Access database

```
CREATE TABLE LOUDNESS
(
  LOUDNESS  VARCHAR(15) NOT NULL,
  CODE      INTEGER NOT NULL,
  PRIMARY KEY (CODE)
);

CREATE TABLE MEDIUM
(
  MEDIUM    VARCHAR(15) NOT NULL,
  CODE      INTEGER NOT NULL,
  PRIMARY KEY (CODE)
);

CREATE TABLE TYPES
(
  TYPES     VARCHAR(15) NOT NULL,
  CODE      INTEGER NOT NULL,
 PRIMARY KEY (CODE)
);

CREATE TABLE ARTIST
(
  CODE      INT NOT NULL,
  LAST      VARCHAR(30),
  FIRST     VARCHAR(30),
  BORN      TIMESTAMP,
  DIED      TIMESTAMP,
  BIRTHPLACE VARCHAR(35),
  COMMENT   MEMO,
```

```
  ARTISTTYPE INTEGER NOT NULL,
 PRIMARY KEY (CODE)
);

CREATE TABLE ALBUM
(
  CODE       INT NOT NULL,
  ALBUM      VARCHAR(45) NOT NULL,
  TYPES      INT,
  LOUDNESS   INT,
  MEDIUM     INT,
  RATING     INT,
  GROUPCODE  INT NOT NULL,
  CDDBID     VARCHAR(20),
  CDDBNAME   VARCHAR(40),
  FOREIGN KEY(TYPES) REFERENCES TYPES(CODE),
  FOREIGN KEY(LOUDNESS) REFERENCES LOUDNESS(CODE),
  FOREIGN KEY(MEDIUM) REFERENCES MEDIUM(CODE),
  FOREIGN KEY(GROUPCODE) REFERENCES ARTIST(CODE),
  PRIMARY KEY (CODE)
);

CREATE TABLE ALBUMINFO
(
  CODE       INT NOT NULL,
  COMMENT    MEMO,
  CDDBDATA   MEMO,
  ALBUMCODE  INT NOT NULL,
  FOREIGN KEY (ALBUMCODE) REFERENCES ALBUM,
 PRIMARY KEY (CODE)
);

CREATE TABLE ARTISTTYPE
(
  ARTISTTYPE VARCHAR(15) NOT NULL,
  CODE       INTEGER NOT NULL,
 PRIMARY KEY (CODE)
);

CREATE TABLE BOOK
(
  CODE       INT NOT NULL,
  TYPES      INT,
  MEDIUM     INT,
  RATING     INT,
  COMMENT    MEMO,
  GROUPCODE  INT NOT NULL,
  BOOK       VARCHAR(50),
  FOREIGN KEY(TYPES) REFERENCES TYPES(CODE),
  FOREIGN KEY(MEDIUM) REFERENCES MEDIUM(CODE),
  FOREIGN KEY(GROUPCODE) REFERENCES ARTIST(CODE),
```

```
  PRIMARY KEY (CODE)
);

CREATE TABLE CDROM
(
  CODE              INT NOT NULL,
  LOCATIONCODE      INTEGER,
  NAME              VARCHAR(50),
  IDVALUE           VARCHAR(50),
  KEYVALUE          VARCHAR(50),
  COMMENT           MEMO,
  TYPES             INTEGER,
 PRIMARY KEY (CODE)
);

CREATE TABLE LOCATION
(
  CODE              INTEGER,
  LOCATION          VARCHAR(25)
);

CREATE TABLE SONGS
(
  CODE              INT NOT NULL,
  SONG              VARCHAR(65) NOT NULL,
  WRITER VARCHAR(45),
  RATING SMALLINT,
  ALBUMCODE INT NOT NULL,
  SONGNUMBER SMALLINT,
  FOREIGN KEY (ALBUMCODE) REFERENCES ALBUM (CODE),
  PRIMARY KEY (CODE)
);
```

Loading the Raw Data

In the Database/data directory on the CD, you will find a number of files with names like album.sql and artist.sql. These files contain the raw data used in the jbbook database. There are scripts available for loading this data into MySQL, but these scripts are primarily meant to serve as examples to users of other databases who want to load this data.

For instance, here is one of the simplest files in the data directory:

```
insert into LOUDNESS (LOUDNESS, CODE) values("UNKNOWN", 0);
insert into LOUDNESS (LOUDNESS, CODE) values("PEACEFUL", 1);
insert into LOUDNESS (LOUDNESS, CODE) values("MODERATE", 2);
insert into LOUDNESS (LOUDNESS, CODE) values("LOUD", 3);
```

If the LOUDNESS table already exists, this simple script will load data into it. Not all the sql files found in that directory are this simple. Some contain hundreds of records stored in many fields, some of which are BLOBs. Those files are more intimidating than this one.

I used these files to port my data from InterBase to MySQL and Access. You can use them to port the data to other databases. Simple scripts like these can grant a significant degree of power in the database world. If you are interested, you can view the JBuilder programs on the CD called AccessSetup, ConvertAddress, CountryData, and MusicConvert. These Java projects work with simple scripts like the ones shown here. The HTML files found in the root directory of these programs explain their purpose.

Setting Up Your Windows Environment

The JBuilder database code relies on a number of JAR files that ship with JBuilder. In particular, you will need to place dx.jar, dbswing.jar, and interclient.jar on your classpath. This won't matter when you are inside of JBuilder, but it will matter if you want to compile from the command prompt. In particular, if you are using Ant, you will want to include these files in your classpath.

To set up your command line environment correctly on Windows, run the batch file shown in Listing 39-4. On Linux, run the script shown in Listing 39-5.

The paths in these files will need to be changed to reflect the location of specific files on your system. These scripts are written so that you only need to edit a few variables at the top of each file. After you do that, the rest of the file should fall into place without much trouble.

On some occasions, particularly if you are using a version control system, you might want to share scripts like these between multiple developers. In the Windows batch file, I show you how to have two different users.

Listing 39-4: A simple batch file for setting up the environment for a Windows machine

```
@echo off

rem -----------------------------------------------------------------------
rem Set up the environment for your machine.
rem You will need to tweak the first four items in each users section
rem The CLASSESDIR is a place for storing some globally needed jar files
rem -----------------------------------------------------------------------

if %1==1 goto charlie
if %1==2 goto margie

echo Set up the environment for your machine.
echo You can define more than one user
echo You will probably need to edit this for your personal system

echo 1: Charlie
echo 2: Margie

goto end

rem - Margie --------------------------------
:charlie
set ANT_HOME=g:/SrcJava/ant
set JAVA_HOME=g:/Compilers/j2sdk1.4.0
set JBUILDER_HOME=g:/jb7
set CLASSESDIR=g:/utils/classes
set INTERCLIENT_JAR=g:/Compilers/interbase/InterClient/interclient.jar

rem some miscelaneous jar files
set CLASSPATH=%CLASSESDIR%/jaxp.jar;%CLASSESDIR%/codebox.jar
rem setup Borland data express stuff
```

```
set CLASSPATH=%CLASSPATH;%JBUILDER_HOME/lib/dx.jar; \
      %JBUILDER_HOME/lib/dbswing.jar;%JBUILDER_HOME/lib/jbcl.jar; \
      %JBUILDER_HOME%/lib/junit.jar;

rem set up mm.mysql
set CLASSPATH=%CLASSPATH;%CLASSESDIR/mm.mysql-2.0.11-bin.jar
rem set up interbase
set CLASSPATH=%CLASSPATH:%INTERCLIENT_JAR

set PATH=%PATH%;%ANT_HOME/bin

rem - Margie --------------------------------
:margie
set ANT_HOME=g:/src/srcjava/jakarta-ant-1.4.1
set JAVA_HOME=E:/Compilers/j2sdk1.4.0
set JBUILDER_HOME=E:/Utilities/JBuilder
set CLASSESDIR=g:/utils/classes

rem some miscelaneous jar files
set CLASSPATH=%CLASSESDIR%/jaxp.jar;%CLASSESDIR%/codebox.jar
rem setup Borland data express stuff
set CLASSPATH=%CLASSPATH;%JBUILDER_HOME/lib/dx.jar; \
      %JBUILDER_HOME/lib/dbswing.jar;%JBUILDER_HOME \
      %/lib/junit.jar;%JBUILDER_HOME%/lib/jbcl.jar

rem set up mm.mysql
set CLASSPATH=%CLASSPATH;%CLASSESDIR/mm.mysql-2.0.11-bin.jar

set PATH=%PATH%;%ANT_HOME/bin

:end
```

Setting Up Your Linux Environment

Listing 39-5 shows the script for use in Linux.

Listing 39-5: A simple script for setting up your environment on a Linux machine

```
#! /bin/bash

# You will need to tweak the first four items in the code for this file
# The CLASSESDIR is a place for storing some globally needed jar files
# The most important file in the CLASSESDIR is codebox, which you can
# build by running ant in the src directory for the files that come
# with this book.
# You will also need to get mm.mysql-2.0.11-bin.jar file from the
# internet or from this cd.
export ANT_HOME=/home/ccalvert/src/srcjava/jakarta-ant-1.4.1
export JAVA_HOME=/usr/java/j2sdk1.4.0
export JBUILDER_HOME=/home/ccalvert/jb7
export CLASSESDIR=/home/ccalvert/classes
export INTERCLIENT_JAR=/usr/interclient/interclient.jar
```

```
export CLASSPATH=$CLASSESDIR/jaxp.jar:$CLASSESDIR/codebox.jar
export CLASSPATH=$CLASSPATH:$JBUILDER_HOME/lib/dx.jar:$JBUILDER_HOME/lib/
        dbswing.jar:$JBUILDER_HOME/lib/jbcl.jar:$JBUILDER_HOME/junit.jar

# ------------------------------------
# Database section
# ------------------------------------
# mm.mysql.jar is a symbolix link to the current mm.mysql-2.0.11-bin.jar
export CLASSPATH=$CLASSPATH:$CLASSESDIR/mm.mysql.jar
export CLASSPATH=$CLASSPATH:$INTERCLIENT_JAR

# ------------------------------------
# Paths
# ------------------------------------
PATH=$PATH:/home/ccalvert/src/srcjava/jakarta-ant-1.4.1/bin
```

Setting Up Ant

Listing 39-6 shows a typical Ant file that I use in this part of the book. To adapt it for another project, simply change the properties at the top called small-name, caps-name, and camel-name.

If you have Ant set up properly on your system, you can enter the following commands:

Command	Purpose
ant	Build the project and place it in a JAR file.
ant run	Compile the project, put it in a JAR file, and run it.
ant clean	Delete the classes directory, the JAR file, and other extraneous files.

Listing 39-6: Use this Ant file by typing ant, ant clean, or ant run at the command prompt.

```
<project name="MasterDetail" default="dist" basedir=".">

      <target name="init">
            <!-- set global properties for this build -->
            <property name="src" value="src"/>
            <property name="build" value="classes"/>
            <property name="dist"  value="lib"/>
            <property name="doc" value="doc"/>
            <!-- You should only have to edit these -->
            <property name="small-name" value="masterdetail"/>
            <property name="camel-name" value="masterDetail"/>
            <property name="caps-name" value="MasterDetail"/>
            <!-- End edit section -->
            <property name="project-jar" value="${dist}\${small-name}.jar"/>
            <echo message="project jar = ${project-jar}"/>
            <!-- Create the time stamp -->
            <tstamp/>
      </target>

      <target name="compile" depends="init">
```

```
            <!-- Create the build directory structure used by compile -->
            <mkdir dir="${build}"/>
            <!-- Compile the java code from ${src} into ${build} -->
            <javac srcdir="${src}" destdir="${build}"/>
            <copy todir="${build}/${small-name}">
                  <fileset dir="${src}/${small-name}/">
                  <exclude name="**/*.java"/>
                  </fileset>
            </copy>
      </target>

      <target name="dist" depends="compile">
            <!-- Create the distribution directory -->
            <mkdir dir="${dist}"/>
        <jar jarfile="${project-jar}" basedir="${build}"/>
      </target>

      <target name="run" depends="dist">
            <java classname="${small-name}.${caps-name}" fork="yes">
                  <classpath>
                        <pathelement location="${project-jar}"/>
                        <pathelement path="${java.class.path}"/>
                  </classpath>
            </java>
      </target>

      <target name="clean" depends="init">
            <!-- Delete the ${build} and ${dist} directory trees -->
            <delete dir="${build}"/>
            <delete dir="${dist}"/>
            <delete dir="${doc}"/>
            <delete file="${caps-name}.jpx.local"/>
            <delete file="${caps-name}.jpx.local~"/>
            <delete file="${caps-name}.jpx~"/>
            <delete file="${caps-name}.html~"/>
      </target>
</project>
```

Listing 39-6 will only work if you have first set up your classpath, as shown in Listings 39-4 and 39-5. An alternative would be to do something like this, where certain values are drawn from the system environment but the paths to JAR files are explicitly declared in the Ant build file:

```
<target name="set-name">
        <property environment="env"/>
      <!-- Set up class path. See index.html in root dir. -->
        <property name="classes-dir" value="${env.CLASSESDIR}"/>
      <property name="jbuilder-home" value="${env.JBUILDER_HOME}"/>
      <property name="dx-jar" value="${jbuilder-home}/lib/dx.jar"/>
      <property name="dbswing" value="${jbuilder-home}/lib/dbswing.jar"/>
```

```
        <property name="junit-jar" value="${classes-dir}/junit.jar"/>
          <echo message="dx-jar=${dx-jar}"/>
        <echo message="junit-jar=${junit-jar}"/>
        <echo message="junit-jar=${dbswing}"/>
    </target>
```

Too Many Options?

In this chapter I have presented a lot of options. If you are feeling overwhelmed or confused by all these choices, I would suggest you do the following, if possible:

- Install MySQL on a Linux machine.
- Put all your data in your Linux-based MySQL database.
- Use pure JDBC drivers to connect to the data, as explained in the next chapter.

If you follow these recommendations, you will be prepared to do some very serious database programming. Big companies with very serious database loads have found that a solution like this meets their needs. Best of all, it's all free software!

If you are locked into some other database or you don't have a Linux box you can use for this kind of chore, you can't do this. But if you can set things up this way, my advice is to do it.

Summary

In this chapter you have been introduced in some depth to both MySQL and InterBase. For those who are new to SQL, I have given some hints as to what you can do with the language. I have also provided a solution for people who would prefer to use Access.

Toward the end of the chapter I explained how to access the data for the example programs used in this book. I also showed how to set up your environment so that you can run JBuilder database programs from the command line. A short section at the very end of the chapter gave Ant users all the information they need to get up and running.

In the next chapter, you will finally learn how to access these databases from JBuilder. The main purpose of the chapter is to introduce you to ODBC and JDBC drivers that form the link between Java and all the databases discussed in this chapter.

Chapter 40

Connecting to Databases from JBuilder

Charlie Calvert

In this chapter you will learn how to connect JBuilder to the databases you have set up. This is done by means of database drivers.

There are two primary kinds of drivers discussed in this chapter. One is a JDBC driver. JDBC drivers are written entirely in Java. They should run on any platform, as long as the right JVM is installed.

The other kind of connectivity tool is an ODBC driver. ODBC is also a cross-platform standard, but it is most commonly used on Windows. The same JDBC driver will work on Windows, Linux, and other platforms. You will need to get multiple ODBC drivers to perform the same chore, one written for Windows, one for Linux, etc.

One of the great advantages of an ODBC driver is its virtual ubiquity. There are free ODBC drivers for many of the most popular databases, including Access, Paradox, dBASE, FoxPro, MSSQL, InterBase, and MySQL. The great advantage of JDBC is that usually one driver, written entirely in Java, will work on multiple platforms.

Connecting to ODBC drivers from Java is easy because your JVM ships with a JDBC-ODBC Bridge created by Sun. This bridge was designed to help jump-start Java database development. Its presence means that you can always connect from Java and JBuilder to virtually any database that has a valid ODBC driver for your platform. The bridge is present on both Linux and Windows.

In this chapter I will cover the following JDBC drivers:

- mm.mysql for connectivity between JBuilder and MySQL
- InterClient for connectivity between JBuilder and InterBase (At the time of publication, the Firebird project was in the process of creating a newer, more powerful JDBC driver for InterBase.)

I will also cover the following ODBC drivers, which I recommend if you can't use the JDBC drivers:

- myodbc for connectivity between JBuilder and MySQL
- MSAccess, the Microsoft ODBC driver for Access

I am going to show you the drivers in the following order: first both MySQL drivers, then the InterBase InterClient driver, and then the Access driver.

I want to stress that I am covering ODBC for two reasons:

- It is the only way I know to connect to Access from JBuilder.
- The ODBC drivers seem to provide better support when you are debugging. You therefore might want to use ODBC during development and then switch to JDBC when you ship. However, not all drivers act the same, so you should check your code

regularly under JDBC if you plan to ship with it. Because it is a small, fast, cross-platform solution, I definitely recommend that you use JDBC with your shipping code whenever possible.

In this chapter and throughout the rest of the book, I'm going to default to using the MySQL JDBC driver. As a result, everyone ought to read that section of this chapter in full. I will then go over as quickly as possible connecting with the other types of drivers. If you are having trouble setting up a connection to InterBase or Access, read over the mm.mysql section in detail, as you might find tips there. The end of the chapter contains a section of general interest called "Testing Your Work."

Installing MySQL Drivers

The next few sections cover installing drivers for connecting to MySQL from JBuilder. The first two sections cover JDBC connectivity, and the third covers ODBC connectivity.

Installing mm.mysql

Now that you have MySQL installed and working correctly, the next step is to access it from JBuilder. To do this, you need to install a database driver.

mm.mysql is an open source, all-Java driver that allows you to connect to MySQL from JBuilder. My experience with this driver has been excellent. It is easy to install and works beautifully on both Linux and Windows.

You can download mm.mysql from this web address: http://mmmysql.sourceforge.net/. You should get the latest version, not the version that I happen to be using here.

Download the files and unjar the package it comes in using the following command:

```
jar xvf mm.mysql-2.0.11-you-must-unjar-me.jar
```

All readers of this book have the jar utility on their system, since it ships with the JDK. Just make sure the jdk or jre bin directory is on your path. You can also decompress this file using WinZip or any other zip file utility. You can download WinZip from www.winzip.com.

NOTE: In this case, the version of the mm.mysql is 2.0.11. This is the part of the filename that will change if you pull down an updated version of the driver.

Locate the file with a name similar to mm.mysql-2.0.11-bin.jar. This is the JDBC driver. Place it in a directory of your choosing. Close JBuilder and add the directory where you stored the file to your JBuilder.config file:

```
addjars g:/utils/classes
```

The JBuilder.config file is located in your JBuilder7/bin directory.

If you want to run your programs from the command line, I would also recommend putting this JAR file on your classpath via the script files shown at the end of the previous chapter. Here is an excerpt from those files:

```
set JBUILDER_HOME=g:/jb7
set CLASSESDIR=g:/utils/classes
set INTERCLIENT_JAR=g:/Compilers/interbase/InterClient/interclient.jar

rem some miscellaneous jar files
set CLASSPATH=%CLASSESDIR%/jaxp.jar;%CLASSESDIR%/codebox.jar
rem setup Borland data express stuff
```

```
set CLASSPATH=%CLASSPATH;%JBUILDER_HOME/lib/dx.jar; \
      %JBUILDER_HOME/lib/dbswing.jar;%JBUILDER_HOME/lib/jbcl.jar; \
      %JBUILDER_HOME%/lib/junit.jar;

rem set up mm.mysql
set CLASSPATH=%CLASSPATH;%CLASSESDIR/mm.mysql-2.0.11-bin.jar
```

When looking at this file, notice that the variable CLASSESDIR is set to the same directory where you put the driver. Look further at the last line in this code excerpt from the previous chapter. There you will see a specific reference to this driver. Alternatively, you can add items to your classpath by opening the Windows Control Panel, selecting the System applet, turning to the Advanced page, and selecting the Environment Variables button.

Now restart JBuilder. Choose **Tools | Database Pilot** to bring up the Database Pilot, a feature of JBuilder Enterprise. Choose **View | Options** from the Pilot menu and turn to the **Drivers** page. Choose the **Add** button and paste in the following string:

```
org.gjt.mm.mysql.Driver
```

NOTE: Alternatively, you can start JBuilder and create a new library that points at the mm.mysql-2.0.11-bin.JAR file. Then choose Tools | Enterprise setup, and turn to the Database Drivers page. Choose the Add button and select your library. Now choose View | Options from the Pilot menu and enter the driver string, as explained in the previous paragraph.

Close and restart JBuilder. At this stage you should have successfully completed the installation of the driver. To test this, go to the **Database Pilot**, close any open databases, and select **File | New**. Open the **Driver** field and browse down the list looking for the string "org.gjt.mm.mysql.Driver." If you see it, and if its color is black, you are on track. If it is in red, something is wrong and you should review the steps outlined in the last few pages.

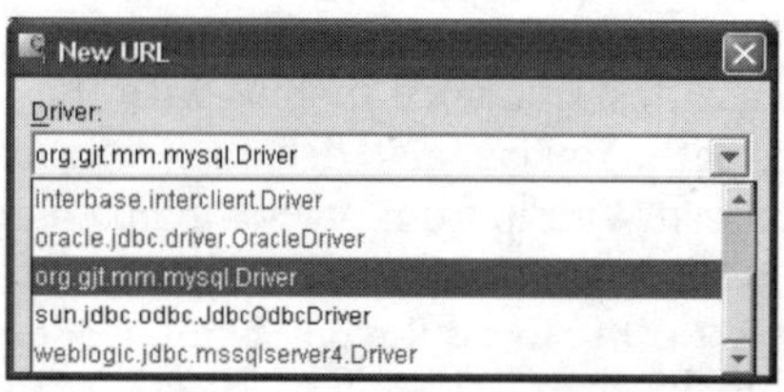

Figure 40-1: Viewing the listing for the MySQL driver in the Database Pilot

Working with the Installed mm.mysql Driver

Now that the driver is installed, you want to again bring up the Database Pilot. Choose **File | New** from its menu. Select **org.gjt.mm.mysql.Driver** from the list of available drivers, as shown in Figure 40-1. For the URL, enter **jdbc:mysql://localhost/jbbook**, as shown in Figure 40-2. As you recall, jbbook is the database that you created at the end of the last chapter. If you want to connect to a database on a remote server, type in the name of the remote server instead of the name of the local machine. If your server was named bree, you might type the following string: jdbc:mysql://bree/jbbook.

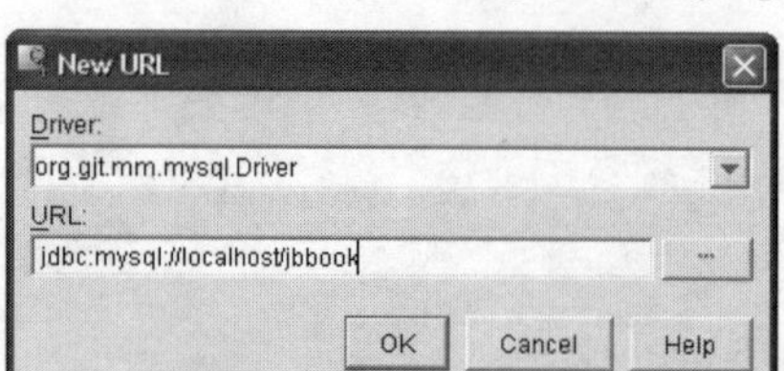

Figure 40-2: Setting up the connection to a MySQL database

NOTE: There is an ellipsis button to the right of the URL field in the New URL dialog. You can always use this button when setting up ODBC databases, but you may or may not be able to use it when looking for JDBC databases. If it is not enabled, don't worry; just type in the string. Click the plus sign in front of the new URL you have created. You will be prompted for a user name and password. Enter the values you used when you created a MySQL user. If you entered the values correctly, you can now open up the node and view the tables and procedures in the database, as shown in Figure 40-2.

Java is going to parse the information you just entered and use it to connect you to your database. You are supplying the JVM with the information it needs to make the connection. The first string you entered tells JBuilder the driver to use. It cannot use the driver unless it is on your classpath, in a library, or in your JBuilder config file, as explained in the previous section of this chapter.

NOTE: The previous paragraph may cause you to think about deploying database applications. A discussion of that topic is included near the end of Chapter 43 in the section called "Wrapping Up Your Application in a JAR File or Executable."

Once the JVM has found the driver, the next step is to tell it which database to use. The second string you entered communicates this information. You perhaps recall that the string looked like this: jdbc:mysql://localhost/jbbook. As I have explained previously, the first part of this string tells the protocol to use jdbc. The second part tells the database to use mysql. The third part specifies the server to use //localhost. The fourth part tells the database to use on that server /jbbook.

In Figure 40-3 you can see the way your new connection looks in the Database Pilot. On the right you can see the URL and Driver strings that you entered. Below these is a field called UserName. Here you can optionally enter the name of a user on your database server. An extensive discussion of setting up users appears in the previous chapter. In this field you will probably want to enter either root or your user name on the database — not your user name on Windows or Linux, but your user name on the database server.

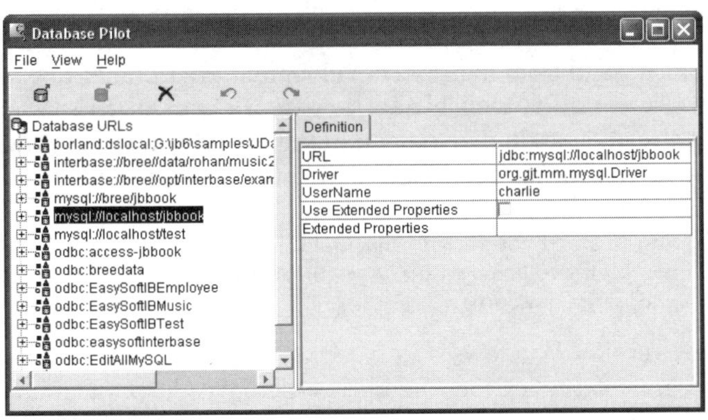

Figure 40-3: Viewing a connection, complete with user name, to the jbbook database

When you ship, you will probably want to leave the UserName field in the data module for your application blank so that the user can enter it at that time. But during development, it saves you the trouble of typing it in if you hard-code the string into your application. There will be another place where you can decide whether or not to include this name in your finished program, so here you might as well enter it.

NOTE: I will cover this subject in more depth in the next chapter, but I should perhaps mention that JBuilder allows you to decide whether or not to automatically prompt the user for a user name and password at run time. If you have a completed data module that includes a database, select the connection property for the database and check or uncheck the option labeled Prompt user password. Don't worry if this does not quite make sense to you yet, as data modules and database classes will be covered in more depth in the next chapter.

You should now right-click on the plus to the left of the new connection you made. Enter your password. When you are done, you should be able to see the tables in your database, as shown in Figure 40-4.

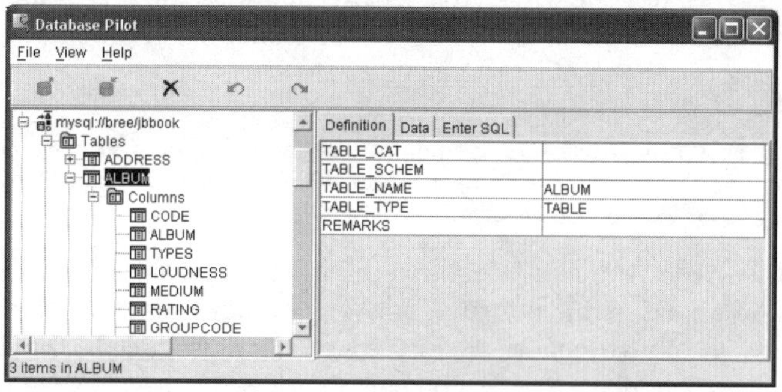

Figure 40-4: Viewing the tables for a database in the Database Pilot

If you plan to use MySQL and JDBC connectivity, which is the recommended course of action in this book, you are now all set to begin building database applications in JBuilder. Before you begin, however, I would recommend reading the section at the end of this chapter called "Testing Your Work." If you want to connect to some other database, I think the experience you will get by working through the rest of this chapter will be quite valuable.

Installing MyODBC on Windows or Linux

If you are working with JBuilder and Java, there is little doubt that pure JDBC drivers like mm.mysql have a great deal of appeal. However, ODBC drivers can sometimes help you when debugging, and they can be accessed from multiple development environments, such as Delphi, Perl, PHP, Python, or C++. It is arguably easier to work with ODBC drivers, since the JDBC-ODBC Bridge is already installed by default in the JBuilder Database Pilot and does not require the driver installation process described in the previous section.

NOTE: In this book, I am going to show you how to use ODBC drivers on Windows. If you want to connect using ODBC on Linux, try these links: http://www.unixodbc.org/, http://www.jepstone.net/FreeODBC/, and http://www.openlinksw.com/.

There are MySQL ODBC drivers for Windows, Linux, Solaris, and MacOS available from the www.mysql.org site. At the time of publication, the link to them was http://www.mysql.org/products/myodbc/index.html. Download the Windows driver.

The install program comes as a zip file. Unzip the contents of the file to a temp directory, and then run Setup.exe from that directory. This is a simple forehead install program, but I want you to cancel out of the last dialog it gives you. When you get to the end of the install, a Data Sources dialog will pop up, as shown in Figure 40-5. This will allow you to configure the driver. For now, I would suggest choosing **Close**. This dialog can only be reached by the install program, and it is better to learn how to access ODBC configuration through the technique laid out in the next paragraphs.

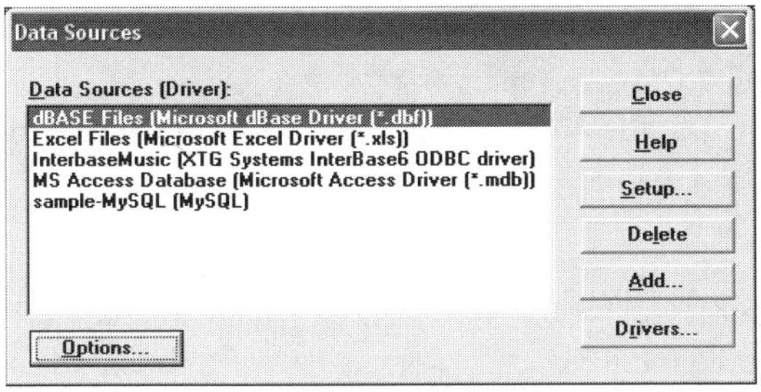

Figure 40-5: Choose Close from the last dialog in the install program for MyODBC.

After you have installed the drivers, open the Windows Control Panel, and choose **Administrative Tools | Data Source (ODBC)**. Turn to the **System DSN** page and choose the **Add** button. You will be asked to select the driver you want to use, as shown in Figure 40-6.

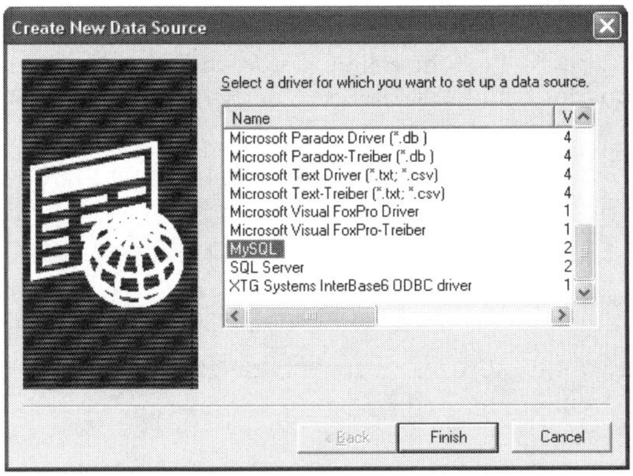

Figure 40-6: Electing to use the MySQL ODBC driver in the Windows XP ODBC configuration tool found in the Control Panel

The next step is to fill in the fields of the dialog, as shown in Figure 40-7. The key field is the name, which should be as descriptive as possible: **ODBC-MySQL-JBBook-2**. Then add the host name, which can be **localhost** or the name of your database server machine. The name of the database is next: **jbbook**. Finally, add your user name and password. Again, these last two are optional, but I would fill them in for now.

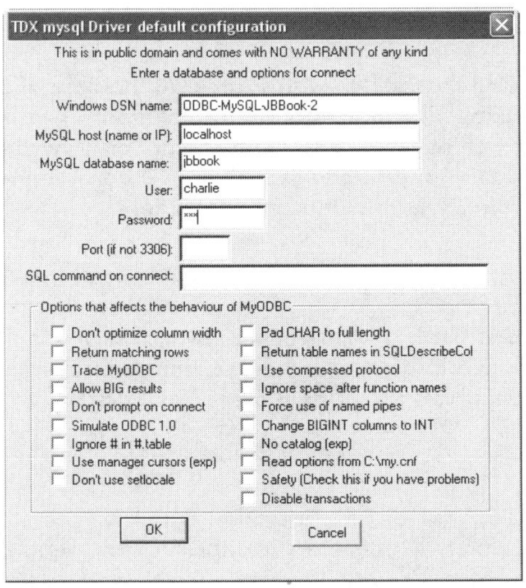

Figure 40-7: Describing the connection to your database in the Windows XP ODBC configuration tool

If you were connecting to a remote MySQL database server, you would put in the IP address or name of that server rather than your local server.

Now go to JBuilder and bring up the Database Pilot. Choose **New** from the menu and fill in the dialog as shown in Figure 40-8. The URL field should contain something like this: **jdbc:odbc:ODBC-MySQL-JBBook-2**. The Driver field should look like this: **sun.jdbc.odbc.JdbcOdbcDriver**. You should be able to pick both items from the drop-down lists. If you have to type things in, something is probably wrong. (Sadly, I have no idea what might have gone wrong, but this could be a clue that <u>something</u> is amiss!) Close the dialog when you are done.

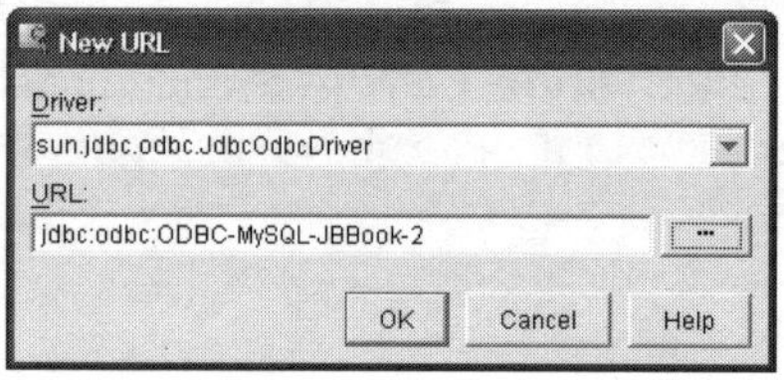

Figure 40-8: Connecting to a MySQL database from the JBuilder Database Pilot

Right-click on your alias in the Database Pilot and choose **Open**. A dialog will pop up prompting you for your user name and password. Enter them. If all is working correctly, you should be able to see some new nodes in the Database Pilot. Select the one that says **Tables** and expand it. If you choose the **Data** tab, you should be able to see the data from your database, much as you could in Figure 40-4.

At this stage you can optionally read about setting up InterBase and Access, or else skip to the end of the chapter and read the last section called "Testing Your Work."

Setting up InterBase

The next sections describe connecting to InterBase via JDBC with InterClient and via ODBC.

During this discussion remember that Firebird is the name of the open source InterBase project. This project is also frequently referred to as IBPhoenix. The Firebird project has an active community, as does the Borland commercial version of the product. The Borland open source version is not used very heavily.

NOTE: There is a free ODBC driver for Firebird that comes with source. At the time of publication, the link to it was http://www.ibphoenix.com/ibp_60_odbc.html. If this link doesn't work for you, or if you are looking for updates, start your search at Firebird.sourceforge.net or www.ibphoenix.com. I had a little struggle getting it running, so I am not going to recommend it here. Anyway, right now the best way to connect to InterBase from JBuilder is through InterClient.

NOTE: The upcoming Firebird pure JDBC driver looks very promising, but it was in the early stages of beta development at the time of publication.

At the time of publication, the new Firebird JDBC-JCA driver was available at this address: http://prdownloads.sourceforge.net/firebird/FirebirdSQL-1.0_beta_1.zip. Hopefully they will be well beyond beta 1 by the time you read this. If you can't find it there, fall back on http://firebird.sourceforge.net/.

Setting up InterClient on Windows

Unlike mm.mysql, InterClient consists of two portions, a server and a client. The server, called InterServer, needs to be installed on the same machine as your InterBase server and requires at least a minimal amount of setup. The client is a single file, interclient.jar. When you are on a client machine, this one JAR file is the only file you need, other than your program, when you want to talk to the InterBase server.

The only requirement to use the interclient.JAR file is that it be on the classpath. There are some complications, however. There can be an impedance mismatch between a particular version of interclient.jar and a particular InterServer installation. In particular, the versions of Firebird InterClient don't get along with Borland's version of InterServer. Furthermore, some versions of interclient.jar need to run on a particular JVM. I find that if I get the one intended for use on 1.3, it will also work on 1.4. However, a problem arises if you get the one intended for use on 1.2 and try to use it with 1.3 or 1.4.

There are many different ways to install InterClient. Firebird has one version, while Borland has different install programs for different platforms and versions of the product. As a rule, all of these installs are forehead installs.

InterServer can be run as either a service or a stand-alone application. The iscclient.exe program that comes with InterClient will be run automatically near the end of the install. Use this client to help you configure InterClient, as shown in Figure 40-9. This program is stored in the InterClient\Bin directory. I recommend running InterServer as a service. The second page of the application will allow you to stop and start the service.

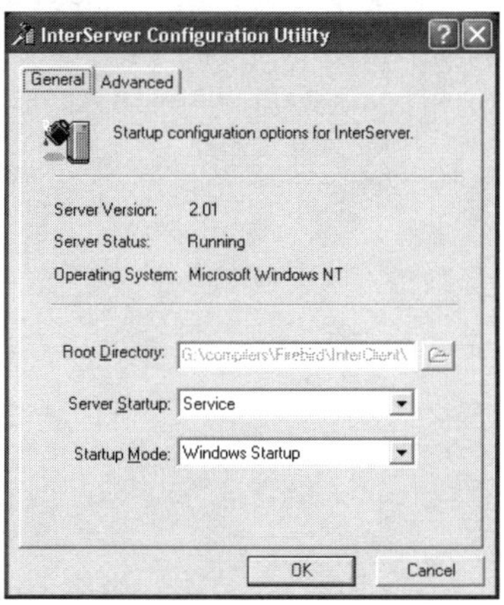

Figure 40-9: Run the isconfig program to configure the InterServer on Windows.

Setting up InterClient on Linux

On Linux, InterClient sometimes appears as a tar file. Un-tar it, and three files will be created. Run the install script:

```
sh install.sh
```

By default, InterClient will be installed into /usr/interclient.

Make sure that interclient.jar is on your classpath:

```
export CLASSPATH=/usr/interclient/interclient.jar:$CLASSPATH
```

NOTE: If you have InterServer running on a particular box, stick with the version of interclient.jar that you have on that machine. There is no real need to get the Windows version of InterClient to connect to an InterServer that is running on Linux. Just use the same interclient.jar file on both machines. That way, it will be unlikely that you will have a mismatch between versions of InterClient.

When using FireBird, the interserver itself should be placed in the /opt/interbase/interclient/ directory as part of the install process. It will be started by a file called interserver that is placed in the /etc/xinit.d directory. To start interserver, enter the following command:

```
/etc/init.d/xinitd restart
```

You should check /var/log/messages after giving the command to make sure there are no errors. A common error is to forget to set the execute permissions for interserver:

```
chmod x+ug /opt/interbase/interclient/interserver
```

Don't forget to check /etc/services and see that the interserver (3060) entry has been added, as explained in the last chapter.

Testing InterClient

Once you have InterClient installed on either Windows or Linux, you should run the test program. Make sure InterClient is on your classpath, Java is on your path, and InterServer is running. Then type this command:

```
java interbase.interclient.utils.CommDiag
```

A dialog like the one shown in Figure 40-10 will appear. Enter the name of the server that is running InterServer. Then type in the name of the database to which you want to connect. InterBase comes with a sample database called employee.gdb. Type in a valid user name and password. By default, InterBase comes with a super user called sysdba with a password of masterkey.

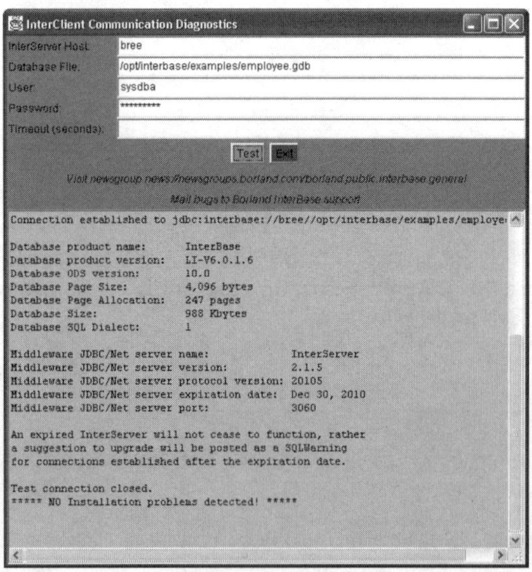

Figure 40-10: Running the CommDiag test to make sure that InterClient is working correctly

If you have trouble running the test, the most likely problem is that you forgot to start InterServer or InterBase as services, or you did not start ibmgr on Linux. Another likely problem is a mismatch between versions of InterClient or between InterClient and your current SDK.

InterBase and JBuilder on Windows

Once you have installed InterClient, you need to get JBuilder set up to use it. Go to the JBuilder bin directory and open up JBuilder.config in a text editor. Add a section to this file that looks something like this, with the path conforming to the setup on your system:

```
#Interclient section added by csc
addjars G:/Utilities/InterClient
```

Now restart JBuilder. Select **Tools | Database Pilot**, and then select **File | New**. Drop down the driver list; you should see interbase.interclient.Driver listed in black, as shown in Figure 40-11. The items listed in red are not ready to use, while those listed in black are all set to go.

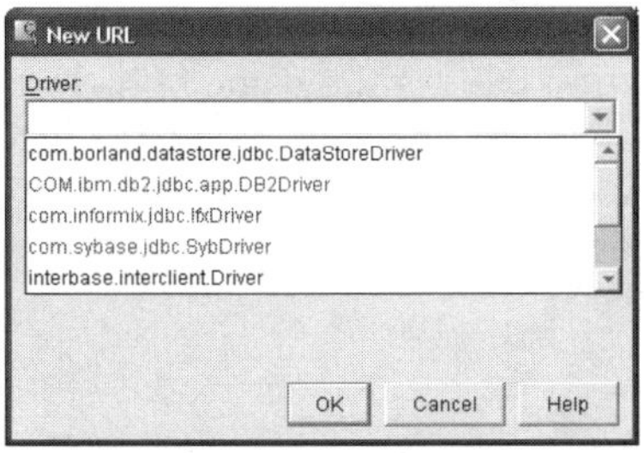

Figure 40-11: The listing for interbase.interclient.Driver should show up in black.

In the URL section, click the ellipsis button and browse for an InterBase database. InterBase files end, by default, with a .gdb extension. One called employee.gdb ships in the examples directory of most InterBase distributions. The jbbook.gdb file from this book's CD also works. The correctly filled out dialog looks like the image shown in Figure 40-12.

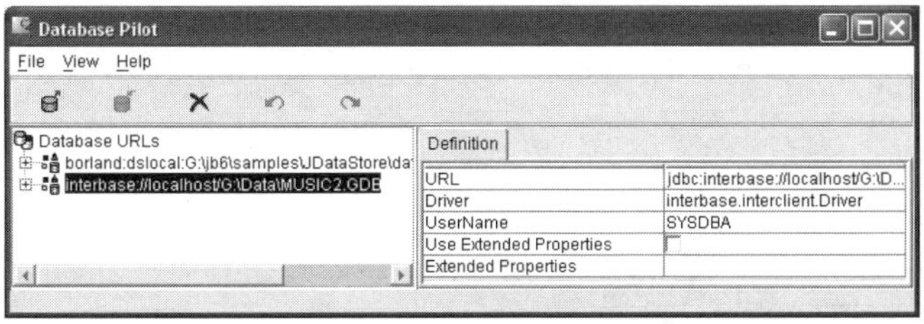

Figure 40-12: Connecting to a database using the InterBase InterClient driver

Let's take a quick look at that connection string:

```
jdbc:interbase://localhost/G:\Data\jbbook.gdb
```

The jdbc:interbase part points at the driver, which in this case in InterClient. Then the //localhost/ part points at the host of the server, which in this case is my local machine. Finally, the G:\Data\jbook.gdb part points at the particular InterBase database in use.

NOTE: Each InterBase database can contain one or more files. It is the norm for an entire database, consisting of hundreds of files and gigabytes of data, to be stored in a single GDB file. You can have up to 64,000 tables in one database, and each table can be up to 32 terabytes in size. Note, however, that Borland says that the largest known InterBase database in production use is 200 GB in size.

You will then be taken to a dialog like the one shown in Figure 40-12. Set the UserName field to **SYSDBA**. By default, the password is masterkey.

InterBase and JBuilder on Linux

By this time, you have everything set up, and all you need to do is get JBuilder talking to the system. The process here is more or less identical to what you did for Windows. Close JBuilder and edit JBuilder.config, adding this statement:

```
addjars /usr/interclient
```

NOTE: There are multiple JAR files in the /usr/interclient directory. However, the file called interclient.jar contains the code included in the other JAR files.

Now bring up the Database Pilot and define a new connection string:

```
jdbc:interbase://localhost//opt/interbase/examples/employee.gdb
```

The pattern here should be very familiar to you by now. jdbc is the name of the protocol, interbase is the name of the driver, localhost is the name of the server, and the last bit is the name of the database you want to access. The same syntax is used to access a MySQL database, except that you substitute "mysql" for the word "interbase."

Installing ODBC for Access

If you have Access installed on your system, it should be quite easy to use it from JBuilder. The standard installs for Access include a complete installation of their ODBC driver. This means that you only need to set up an ODBC System DSN and then connect to it from the Database Pilot.

Use the Windows Start menu to bring up the Control Panel. Go to the **Administrative Tools**, and bring up the **ODBC Data Sources** applet. Turn to the **System DSN** page. Click the **Add** button, and choose the **Microsoft Access Driver**, as shown in Figure 40-13. Click the **Finish** button.

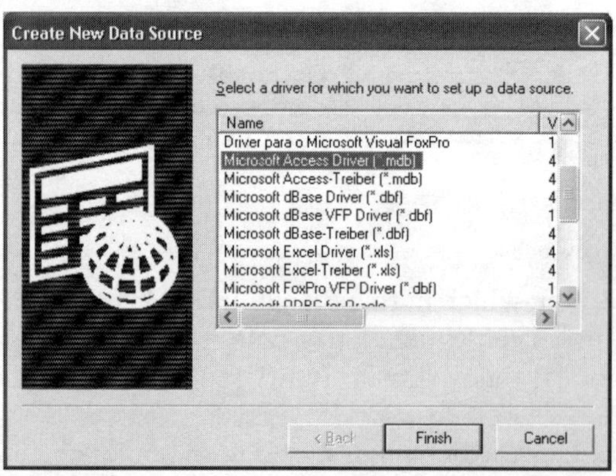

Figure 40-13: Choosing the Microsoft Access Driver in the ODBC Data Sources applet

You should now be in the ODBC Microsoft Access Setup dialog, as shown in Figure 40-14. At the top of the dialog, give your new DSN a descriptive name, such as ODBC-Access-jbbook. Click the **Select** button and then browse for the name of the Access database that you want to use. In this case, it will be the jbbook.mdb file from this book's CD. You can also download this file from my web site at www.elvenware.com. (If you have trouble getting the file, write me at charlie@elvenware.com.) Make sure the database has been copied onto your hard drive and that it is not read-only. Click the **OK** button to complete the process.

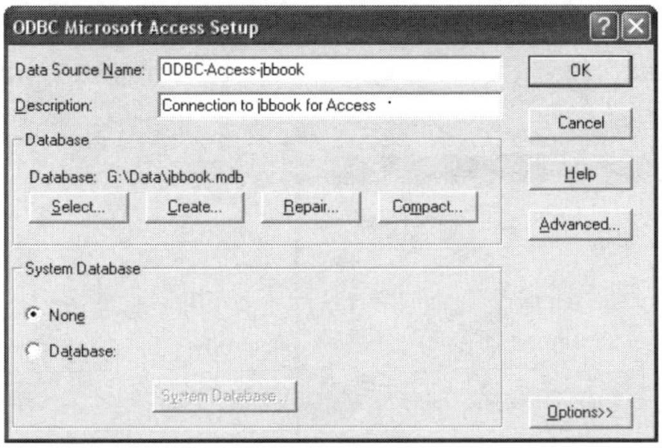

Figure 40-14: Filling in the configuration dialog for an Access ODBC DSN

Now open up JBuilder and choose **Tools | Database Pilot**. In the Database Pilot choose **File | New**. Select the **sun.jdbc.odbc.Jdbc-OdbcDriver** driver in the Driver field. Click the ellipsis button to browse for the name of the connection, as shown in Figure 40-15. When you are done, click the **OK** button.

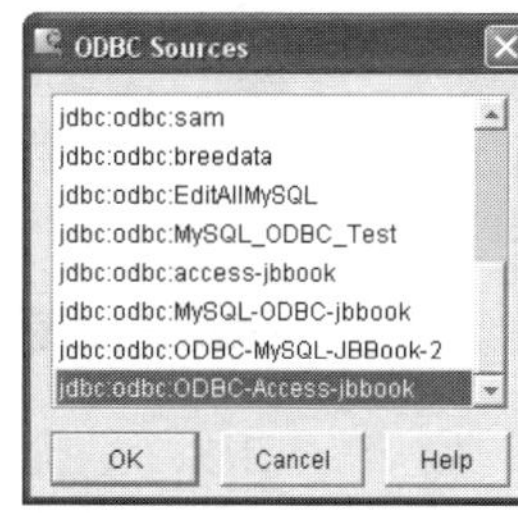

Figure 40-15: Using the Database Pilot to select the DSN you created to connect to an Access database

At this stage, all you need to do is right-click on the new connection you have created. Choose **Open**, and press the **OK** button. By default, there should be no user name and password for an Access database.

Testing Your Work

It is now time to connect to your database from a JBuilder application. I will explain this process in depth in the next several chapters. For now, let's just get an application up and running as quickly as possible.

Start JBuilder and begin a new project. Do not create an application in the usual way, as there is a special technique for developing database applications. All we need for now is a project.

Select **File | New** and create a new data module from the General Page. Make sure that **Invoke Data Modeler** is checked, as shown in Figure 40-16.

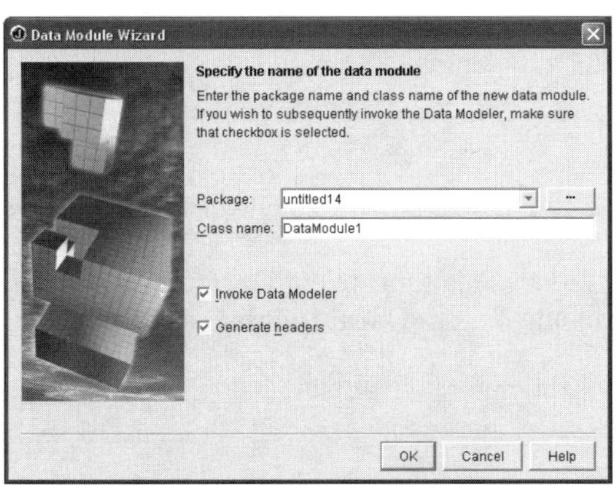

Figure 40-16: Creating a data module in JBuilder

In the Data Modeler you will see a list of connections that you created in the Database Pilot. Scroll down and choose the one you want. In my case, I chose the JDBC mysql connection to jbbook, as shown in Figure 40-17.

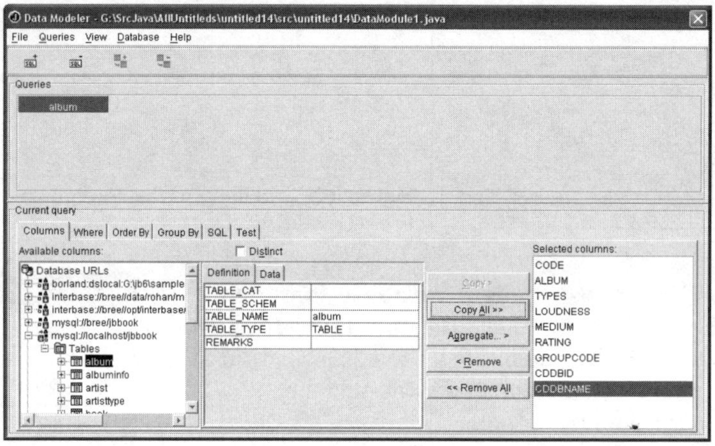

Figure 40-17: Selecting the connection you want to use in your JBuilder application

Click on the plus sign in front of the connection to open it. You will be prompted for your user name and password. Select the table you want to use from the database, as shown in Figure 40-17. Choose the **Copy All** button to copy all the fields into the Selected Columns list. Choose **File | Save** and then **File | Exit** from the Data Modeler menu.

There should now be a new node called DataModule1.java in the project pane and source in the content pane, as shown in Figure 40-18. This file contains the code for connecting and querying your data source. It will be explained in considerable depth in the following chapters. For now, just pretend that it is a black box.

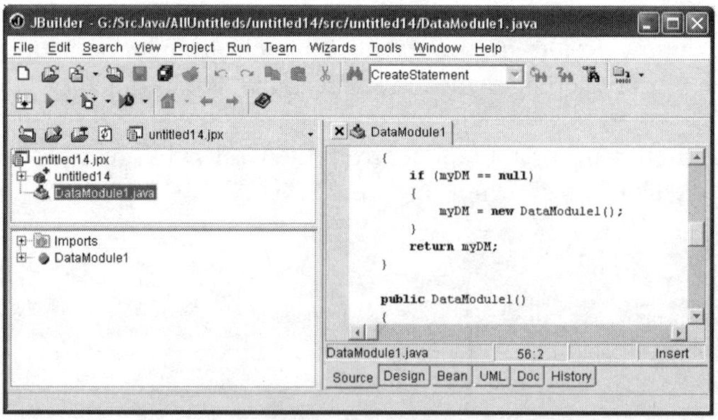

Figure 40-18: The newly created data module in the JBuilder project pane

Choose **File | New** from the JBuilder menu. This time select **Data Module Application** from the General page. Set the Data Module field to **DataModule1**, as shown in Figure 40-19. Click the **OK** button.

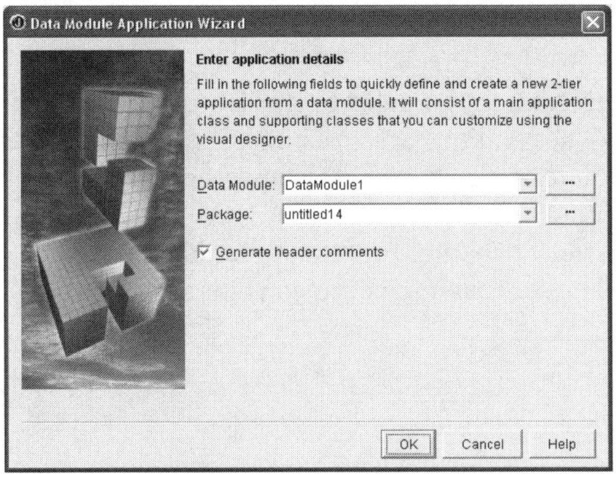

Figure 40-19: Selecting the data module on which you wish to base your application

To see your app in action, right-click on **DataModule1TwoTierApp.java** in the project pane, and choose **Run** from the menu. The application should appear as it does in Figure 40-20.

NOTE: If you want to start the application using the green run button, you may have to set up the run-time configuration in the Project | Project Properties dialog available from the JBuilder menu. Turn to the Run page, choose New, and use the ellipsis button to set DataModule1TwoTierApp as the main class.

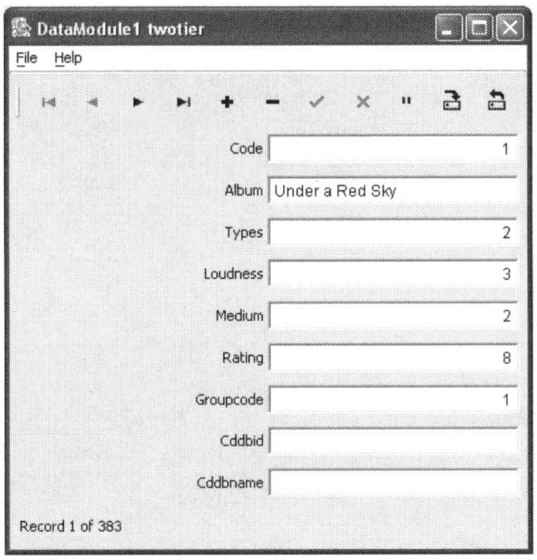

Figure 40-20: A completed JBuilder database application

If all has gone well, congratulations! You have created a fully functional JBuilder database application.

NOTE: One rather confusing error may occur when you try to run your application. In particular, you may have a firewall problem if all the other steps in this chapter work properly, but you get an error at run time that looks something like this: "Cannot connect to MySQL server on localhost:3306." For instance, if you can connect to the database from the Database Pilot and the Data Modeler Wizard but cannot run your application, it may be your firewall that is causing trouble. You should either take your firewall down or make sure it is not blocking either your database or Java.

Summary

In this chapter you have learned how to connect JBuilder to a JDBC or ODBC data source. You had a chance to learn how to install several drivers and how to use these drivers inside of JBuilder. Two of the important tools you learned about in this chapter were the Database Pilot and the Microsoft ODBC Data Source tool.

At the end of the chapter, you had a very brief introduction to building database applications in JBuilder. The next few chapters will cover that subject in considerable depth.

Chapter 41

Database Basics

Charlie Calvert

It is now time to learn a few things you need to know to begin building simple databases in JBuilder. The text explains how to automatically build an application that opens a database, selects a table, and allows the user to browse and edit the data found in the table.

More complex subjects, such as master-detail relationships, lookups, and calculated fields, will be discussed in the next two chapters. Here the emphasis is on the most basic database tools JBuilder has in its repertoire.

It would be a mistake, however, to assume that this chapter is just for beginners. Parts of the discussion, such as the coverage of how JBuilder retrieves data from the database, become quite complex.

The code shown in this chapter will all be generated automatically by JBuilder. I will, however, show how to tweak the templates from which the code is generated. By changing these templates, you can — at least in theory — change the look and feel of the applications that JBuilder generates.

Some of the material in this chapter was touched on in the last paragraphs of the previous chapter. However, we are now going to go over that material in more depth. The goal is to not just see what JBuilder does but understand why it does it. The main program discussed in this chapter can be found on the accompanying CD in the directory called SimpleAuto.

Data Modules

I'm going to begin by talking about a means for separating your database code from your UI objects. In JBuilder, this useful task is performed by a tool called a data module.

Data modules are not strictly necessary. You can, if you are so inclined, place your database connection objects, such as QueryDataSet or Database, directly inside a JFrame, JPanel, or JDialog. I will, however, encourage you not to adopt that practice since it mixes up your UI code and your back-end code. Rather than make such a hash of your work, I recommend placing your database code in a separate class called a data module. You will, of course, often place data-aware components, such as a JdbTextField, inside a JFrame or JPanel.

Creating a Data Module

Let's go through the steps necessary to create a data module. To begin, create a new project, but this time I'll ask you not to begin by putting an application in it. Instead, we are going to first create a data module and then have JBuilder automatically generate our application based on this data module.

NOTE: Most of the work I'm going to show you in the next few chapters will not be based on these automatically generated applications. But even if you do use them as the start for your project, you will find that the generated code is well written and easy to extend. As I have said before, JBuilder has no black boxes, and the code that it generates is designed to be easy to edit. In fact, we are going to look at it quite closely to see what we can learn from the experts who put this code together.

Choose **File | New**, turn to the **General** page, and select the **Data Module Wizard.** This is a very simple, one-step dialog. Fill it out as shown in Figure 41-1, changing the name of the class to **AlbumDataModule** and selecting **Invoke Data Modeler** and **Generate headers.**

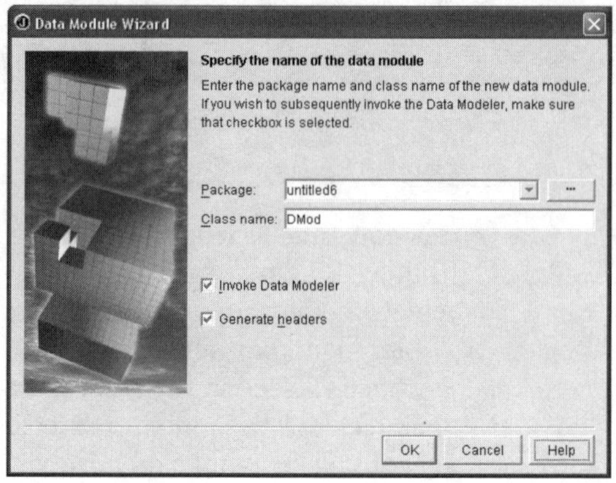

Figure 41-1: The simple one-step process for creating a data module is accomplished by clicking OK in the Data Module dialog.

In Figure 41-1 you can see that I have checked the option for invoking the Data Modeler. The Data Modeler will help you automatically create the queries for selecting the data exposed in your application.

Invoking the Data Modeler is an optional step. However, in many cases it is probably simplest to use this powerful tool. In later chapters I will explain what to do if you don't want to begin by invoking the Data Modeler. In some instances, the Data Modeler is absolutely the wrong tool to use. But if you can use it, then use it.

NOTE: The JBuilder Data Modeler is by no means the most powerful tool of its kind in existence. Some third-party data modelers are major applications in their own right, comparable in scope and complexity to JBuilder itself. This data modeler is not built on that kind of scale, but it gets the job done. You should have no trouble integrating third-party data modelers with the tools discussed in this chapter and in the next few chapters.

After clicking **OK** in the Data Module Wizard, you will see the Data Modeler, as shown in Figure 41-2. (Don't mix up your data modules and data modelers!)

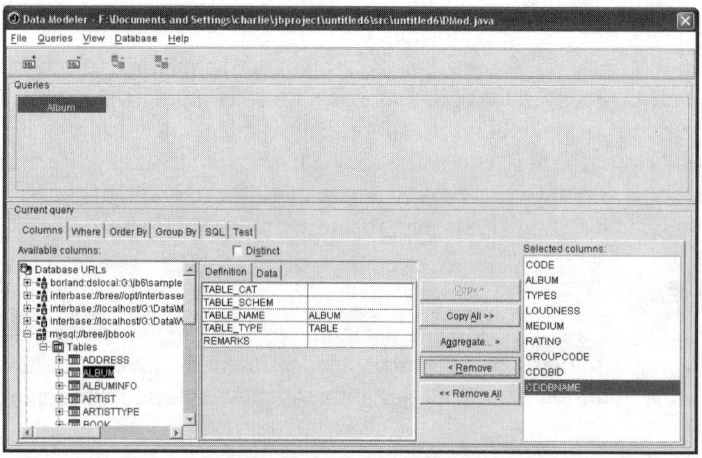

Figure 41-2: The Data Modeler with a database open, a table selected, and all the columns in the table selected to use in a query

You will recognize the Available Columns portion of the Data Modeler dialog from the Database Pilot discussed in the previous chapter. You can use the available columns to select and open the database that you want to use. In this case, I am working with the jbbook database that is on the CD that accompanies this book. It was explained in the previous chapter.

NOTE: As explained in the previous chapter, I have created Access, InterBase, and MySQL versions of the jbbook database. As a result, it is up to you to choose the type of connection you want to use. In most of the examples I discuss in this book, I use MySQL. To switch to another database, just specify the type of driver you want to use, as described in the previous chapter.

In Figure 41-2 you can see that I have opened the jbbook database. This involved typing in a user name and password, as described in the previous chapter. I then selected the ALBUM table and picked the Copy All button. In this way I ensure that the user will have access to all the fields in this table. More particularly, what I have done is create a simple SQL statement that will select all the data from the ALBUM table. You can view and edit the SQL statement in the SQL tab of the Data Modeler, as shown in Figure 41-3.

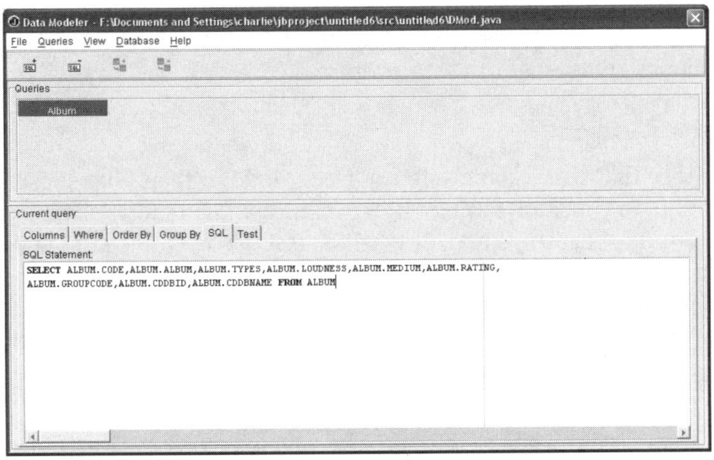

Figure 41-3: Viewing the SQL statement generated by the Data Modeler

If you are satisfied with the appearance of your SQL statement, you can test it in the Test pane of the Data Modeler, as shown in Figure 41-4. You can resize the columns, and the entire dialog if you want, to get a better view of the data.

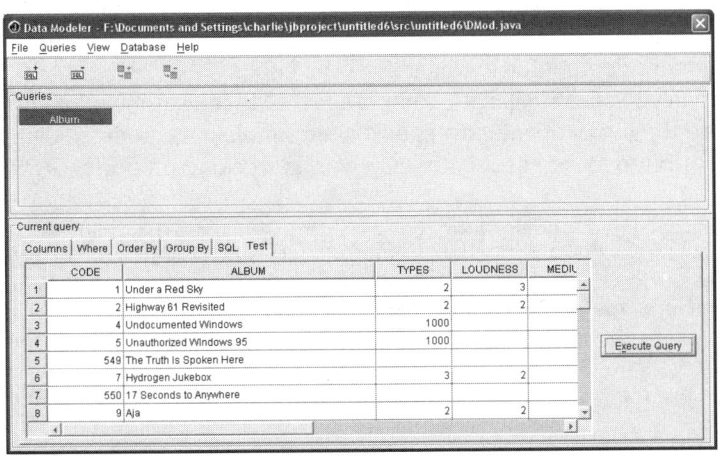

Figure 41-4: Viewing the results of the query you created in the Data Modeler

At this stage, you should save your work. Before doing so, make sure that the View | Options | Generate Entities menu item is not checked. Now choose **File | Save** from the Data Modeler menu. This will save your work to the data module that you are creating. The only storage for your work in the Data Modeler is the java file (data module) that you are in the process of creating. You can think of "saving" the data module as the step that actually generates your data module. You can generate the data module over and over again up until the time you leave the Data Modeler. After you leave the Data Modeler, you cannot invoke the Data Modeler again, unless you create a new data module. In other words, you can't reload a data module into the Data Modeler.

Not being able to invoke the Data Modeler again without stating a new data module is not quite as serious a problem as it might at first seem. At any point in your development, you will be able to access most of the Data Modeler's functionality through utilities built into JBuilder. For instance, you can access all the parts of the Data Modeler that allow you to create queries. Other automated visual tools allow you to create master-detail relationships, lookups, etc., at any time from inside the JBuilder editor. I will explain those tools later in this chapter and over the course of the next two chapters.

Before Leaving the Data Modeler

I'm sure you have noticed that there is more to the Data Modeler than I have discussed so far. Let's take a few moments to consider some of these features. I do not, however, want to explore them in depth in this chapter, since they will distract us from the simple foundation in JBuilder's database tools that we are currently building.

If you look in the Queries section, seen in Figure 41-4, you can see a node called Album. This represents the work you have done so far with the ALBUM table. You can add additional nodes here, one for each query you create. You can create multiple queries on one or more tables. When you are done, you will have a series of nodes, rather than one node called Album.

You can establish relationships between the queries you create. For instance, you can create master-detail relationships that will be graphically depicted, in a simplistic fashion, in the Queries section of the Data Modeler.

Looking at the tabs in the bottom half of the Data Modeler, you can see that it is possible to create WHERE clauses, ORDER BY clauses, and GROUP BY clauses. These words designate the various kinds of queries that you can create when you want to select data from a database. I will discuss them in more depth later in this part of the book.

At this stage, you can choose **File | Exit** from the Data Modeler. You will be taken back to JBuilder proper, where the project pane now shows your simple data module. Compile, but don't run, your application to make sure that everything is working properly.

NOTE: One feature of the Data Modeler that I have only touched on is the ability to create entities. Choose View | Options from the Data Modeler menu. Check the Generate Entities box. This approach will divide your code into several more classes and an interface, all based on the EntityDataSet architecture. You should, however, make sure that this option is not selected during this exercise.

Letting JBuilder Construct Your Application

We now want to generate an application based on the data module we created. As you saw in the last chapter, this is an extremely simple step.

To have JBuilder automatically generate the code for your application, choose **File | New** from the menu and then select **Data Module Application** from the General page. There is no need to make any changes; simply click the **OK** button. A fully functional database application will be generated. When you run the program, it appears as shown in Figure 41-5.

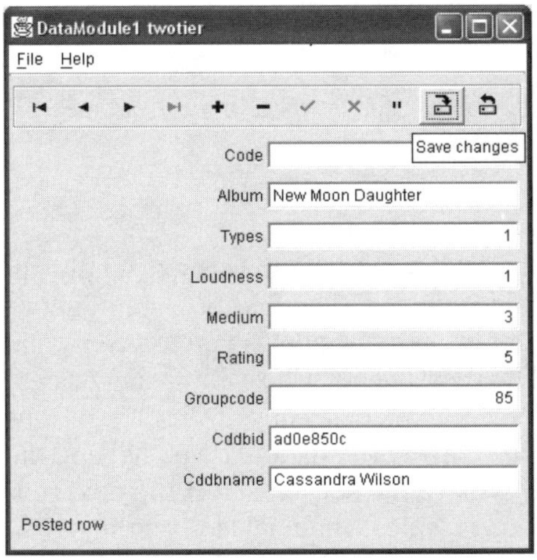

Figure 41-5: A simple database application automatically generated by JBuilder

To run the program, simply right-click on **AlbumDataModuleTwoTierApp** in the project pane. Choose **Run using defaults** from the menu. There are, however, three things that can go wrong at this stage:

- If you press the green run button, the program will not launch automatically. Instead, the Project Properties dialog will appear, open to the Run page. To set things up properly, choose the **New** button from the Project Properties dialog, and browse for the main file in your project. In this case, that will be the source file called AlbumDataModuleTwoTierApp.java. Configuring the main application for your project is covered in more depth in Chapter 31 and in Part V: Project Management.
- The second problem can be a classpath issue involving the driver for your database. In particular, you might get an error similar to "The driver: org.gjt.mm.mysql could not be loaded." You may or may not have this problem, depending on the driver you are using and the libraries you have set up. For instance, if the mm-mysql-version.jar file is not in a library, and therefore not on JBuilder's view of your classpath, your program probably won't be able to run correctly. First try to run the program, and then if you have the problem, try the fix shown here. To solve the problem, create a new library in your User Home directory that points at the JAR file for your driver. Choose **Project | Project Properties | Required Libraries** from the JBuilder menu. Select the **Add** button and choose **New** from the bottom of the Select One or More Libraries dialog. Call the new library **mm-mysql** or some name appropriate to the driver you are using. If you have the option, make sure the Location field is set to **User Home** and not to Project Home. Press the **Add** button and browse for the JAR file for your driver. Click **OK** four times to close all the dialogs you have opened. Now try running your application and see if the error has gone away. The simple creation of this library in your User

Home area should ensure that in future database projects this library will be automatically added to the Required Libraries section of your Project Properties. If you need more help on working with libraries, see the appropriate chapters in Part V: Project Management.

- A third thing that can go wrong at this stage is that you accidentally selected the Generate Entities button in the View | Options menu of the Data Modeler. If so, you will have generated the wrong kind of application. Unless you want to work with entities, you will find it simplest to fix the problem by starting a new project from the beginning. Once you get the hang of it, you can run through all the steps outlined so far in just a few seconds.

The program you created allows you to iterate through the data in your dataset. You can edit the rows and post the data to the dataset.

Saving Data: The Nav Bar

Across the top of the application, you can see a JdbNavToolBar. This extremely important and very commonly used component has several icons on it. The four on the left allow you to move through your dataset. The next icon, a plus symbol, allows you to insert a new row. The minus symbol allows you to delete a row. The next two icons are for saving or canceling your edits on a row. The double quote icon allows you to make a copy of the current row.

All of these changes are applied only to the copy of the data that you have in the dataset on your local machine. To actually commit the work to the server, select the next to last icon on the nav bar. To refresh your data from the server, select the final icon on the nav bar. This will overwrite any data you haven't saved. If you don't use the next to last icon ("save changes"), you are only working with a local copy of the data and not saving your work to the server.

In this example, I have tried to show you the simplest possible automatically generated database program. You can, however, have JBuilder create more complex examples, as shown in the next chapter.

A Singular Manner for Constructing the Data Module

It is now time to take a moment to examine the code we have created. You can view the complete source for the data module in Listing 41-1. On this book's CD, the program is called SimpleAuto.

Listing 41-1: The source for a simple DataModule descendant created by the Data Modeler

```
package untitled6;

import java.awt.*;
import java.awt.event.*;
import com.borland.dx.dataset.*;
import com.borland.dx.sql.dataset.*;

public class DataModule1 implements DataModule
{
      private static DataModule1 myDM;
      Database database1 = new Database();
      QueryDataSet album = new QueryDataSet();
```

```
    public static DataModule1 getDataModule()
    {
        if(myDM == null)
        {
            myDM = new DataModule1();
        }
        return myDM;
    }

    public DataModule1()
    {
        try
        {
            jbInit();
        }
        catch(Exception e)
        {
            e.printStackTrace();
        }
    }

    private void jbInit() throws Exception
    {
        album.setQuery(
            new QueryDescriptor(database1,
            "SELECT ALBUM.CODE,ALBUM.ALBUM,ALBUM.TYPES,"+
            "ALBUM.LOUDNESS,ALBUM.MEDIUM,ALBUM.RATING,"+
            "ALBUM.GROUPCODE,ALBUM.CDDBID," +
            "ALBUM.CDDBNAME FROM ALBUM",
            null, true, Load.ALL));

        database1.setConnection(
            new ConnectionDescriptor(
            "jdbc:mysql://bree/jbbook",
            "root",
            "foo",
            false,
            "org.gjt.mm.mysql.Driver"));
    }

    public Database getDatabase1()
    {
        return database1;
    }

    public QueryDataSet getAlbum()
    {
        return album;
    }
}
```

The first thing you might notice about this code is that it implements a modified version of the singleton pattern:

```
        private static DataModule1 myDM;

        // Singleton pattern
        public static DataModule1 getDataModule()
        {
                if(myDM == null)
                {
                        myDM = new DataModule1();
                }
                return myDM;
        }

        // Constructor
        public DataModule1()
        {
                try
                {
                        jbInit();
                }
                catch(Exception e)
                {
                        e.printStackTrace();
                }
        }
```

The singleton pattern is designed to ensure that one, and only one, instance of an object is ever created. Opening up a database is expensive in terms of both time and memory. As a result, you don't want to have multiple copies of this item in memory. To enforce this rule, it is suggested that you call getDataModule rather than accessing the constructor directly:

```
AlbumDataModule AlbumDataModule =
  untitled6.AlbumDataModule.getDataModule();
```

NOTE: As you will see later in the book, there is a JBuilder wizard called the Use DataModule Wizard. It will automatically call this method or the constructor, depending on your whims. If in doubt, I suggest calling the getDataModule method. In the wizard, this is known as "sharing the static instance of the data module."

To really make the singleton pattern stick, the constructor should be declared private:

```
private DataModule1()
{
        try
        {
                jbInit();
        }
        catch(Exception e)
        {
                e.printStackTrace();
        }
}
```

If the constructor is private, there is no way to create this object other than to call getDataModule. This ensures that there is only one copy of the data module. As a result, I suggest that you take this step in your applications and change the signature for the constructor in data modules to private. If you want to access the object, call getDataModule.

NOTE: There are, in fact, legitimate reasons why you might want two copies of a data module in memory. If you know what you are doing, by all means proceed apace. But by default, I would suggest sharing a single instance of the data module.

Opening a Database

Of course, the construction of the data module is merely an implementation detail. What matters to us is the data itself.

JBuilder puts the code for opening a table in jbInit:

```
Database database1 = new Database();
QueryDataSet album = new QueryDataSet();

private void jbInit() throws Exception
{
    database1.setConnection(new ConnectionDescriptor(
                "jdbc:mysql://bree/jbbook",
                "root",
                "foo",
                false,
                "org.gjt.mm.mysql.Driver"));

    album.setQuery(new QueryDescriptor(database1,
            "SELECT ALBUM.CODE,ALBUM.ALBUM,ALBUM.TYPES,"+
            "ALBUM.LOUDNESS,ALBUM.MEDIUM,ALBUM.RATING,"+
            "ALBUM.GROUPCODE,ALBUM.CDDBID," +
            "ALBUM.CDDBNAME FROM ALBUM",
            null, true, Load.ALL));
}
```

To connect to your database, call database1.setConnection. To complete the call, you must first create a ConnectionDescriptor object. This object seems complicated because it has a long name and the generated code specifies the full path to its package:

```
com.borland.dx.sql.dataset.ConnectionDescriptor
```

However, ConnectionDescriptor is at heart a very simple class. It does little more than provide a wrapper for the data you need in order to create a connection to a JDBC database. Here, for instance, is one of the object's most commonly used constructors:

```
public ConnectionDescriptor(String connectionURL,
      String userName,
      String password,
      boolean promptPassword,
      String driver)
{
    this.connectionURL = connectionURL;
    this.userName      = userName;
```

```
        this.password       = password;
        this.promptPassword= promptPassword;
        this.driver         = driver;
    }
```

This is also one of the more complex methods in the ConnectionDescriptor object! To create a connection, JDBC needs to know your preferred connectionURL, user name, password, and driver. The ConnectionDescriptor is a simple object designed to allow JBuilder to keep track of that information.

NOTE: The code in DataExpress is built on top of JDBC. The data in ConnectionDescriptor is really just passed on to the standard JDBC commands that do the actual work of connecting to the database. I will talk a little about using JDBC at various points over the next few chapters. In the JdbcTests directory on the book's CD, you will find example programs that use JDBC exclusively. You will need to edit these simple programs to point at databases and drivers loaded on your system or network.

The most important piece of information you are passing in is the connectionURL:

```
    "jdbc:mysql://bree/jbbook"
```

The jdbc part of this string says that we want to use the Java Database Connectivity tools built into the Java Virtual Machine. The mysql part of the statement says that we want to use a mysql driver to connect to the database. JDBC uses this string to look up the class name of the driver that you want to use. In this case, it is org.gjt.mm.mysql.Driver.

Bree is the name of the machine where the database is stored. In many cases, you might want to change that name to LocalHost or to the name of another server on your system. jbbook is the name of the MySQL database that this program will access.

NOTE: In the code found on the CD for this book, I made every effort to change all references to Bree or other servers on my system to LocalHost. However, it is possible that I forgot to do this in some cases. If you have trouble using the programs, check this part of the code to make sure it is not causing problems. Check also the user name and password.

The portable nature of JDBC is such that, in theory, you can change the database that you want to access by simply changing one word of this string:

```
    "jdbc:interbase://bree/jbbook"
```

Here I have changed "mysql" to "interbase." Assuming you have also changed the driver string in the last parameter, this connection URL will access InterBase rather than MySQL. If you have the same data stored on both servers, the rest of your application can, at least in theory, remain the same. In tests that I have run, I have been able to successfully make switches of this kind. In some cases, however, you might embed SQL statements in your program that work on one type of database server and not on another.

NOTE: It is, of course, unlikely that you have the same set of tables with the same metadata on two different types of database servers. But if you do want to do such a thing, it is at least theoretically possible. My case is unique, since the CD with this book includes databases for MySQL, Access, and InterBase. I went out of my way to create the same database on multiple servers. Programs found on the CD such as MusicConvert and ConvertAddress helped me in this endeavor.

The next few fields of the connection string are easier to understand:

```
                        "root",
                        "foo",
```

```
                    false,
                    "org.gjt.mm.mysql.Driver"));
```

root is the user name of the person who will connect to the database. “foo” is that user’s impregnable password.

The Boolean value false says that I don’t want to be prompted for a password. If you set this value to true, you will be prompted for a user name and password when the application is first launched. Please remember this fact. There is no need for you to write code that prompts the user for a user name and password. It is built into the Borland database tools.

NOTE: I should perhaps qualify what I said in the last paragraph by pointing out that some users may find the Borland dialog less than completely user friendly. If it does not meet your needs, you might need to write code of your own.

The final string is the name of the driver that JDBC can use to talk to the database. We talked about drivers in some depth in the previous chapter.

Once you are done with this step, the Database object you are using is fully initialized. You will use this object to access the tables in your database. The Database object represents your connection to the actual data in your MySQL, InterBase, Oracle, MSSQL, JDataStore, or Access database.

QueryDataSet and Querying a Database

The jbInit method we are studying also has a call to specify the SQL query itself:

```
album.setQuery(
      new com.borland.dx.sql.dataset.QueryDescriptor(database1,
      "SELECT ALBUM.CODE,ALBUM.ALBUM,ALBUM.TYPES,ALBUM.LOUDNESS," +
      "ALBUM.MEDIUM,ALBUM.RATING,ALBUM.GROUPCODE,ALBUM.CDDBID," +
      "ALBUM.CDDBNAME FROM ALBUM", null, true, Load.ALL));
```

The variable album is of type QueryDataSet. A QueryDataSet is the workhorse component of the JBuilder database world. You will use this component over and over again.

Conceptually, QueryDataSet is very easy to understand. It is the tool you use to retrieve data from the database. You can also use it to access the tools that save and update data.

You don’t need QueryDataSet SQL statements for doing anything other than retrieving data. Instead, use methods of QueryDataSet when you want to update, delete, or insert rows into a table. I ask that you focus on this point for just one moment, as it is very important: Use SQL to retrieve data from the dataset, but use methods to update, delete, or insert rows of data. Make sure you understand the idea I’m describing here before you move on. I will, of course, explain how to delete and update data later in this chapter and the next.

NOTE: In many other database environments, you would use SQL to query, insert, delete, and update data. In fact, behind the scenes, JBuilder is using SQL for all these tasks. But part of the job of QueryDataSet and a related class called a resolver is to hide the complexity of updating the dataset. Instead of composing SQL statements, you give simple commands such as album.setString or album.saveChanges. All of this will be discussed in more depth in its proper place. In particular, see the section near the end of this chapter called “Monitoring SQL Activity.” That section describes how you can view the SQL that JBuilder is creating for you.

In most cases, a QueryDataSet is created by dropping the component on your data module. You can, of course, create such an object in code if you want. The call to create a QueryDataSet is very simple:

```
QueryDataSet album = new QueryDataSet();
```

As you will learn later on, you can open a QueryDataSet and display its contents in a grid with these two calls:

```
JdbTable JdbTable1 = new JdbTable();
JdbTable1.setDataSet(AlbumDataModule1.getAlbum());
```

In short, JBuilder makes it very simple for you to display live, editable data to a user. You can then use the JdbNavToolBar to give commands such as refresh, post, or save. These kinds of tools are part of the reason why you might want to use JBuilder's database tools rather than raw JDBC code. The JDBC is very elegant, but it is not as powerful as the tools shown here.

The only really tricky part of the process is requesting the data. As you have seen, the Data Modeler automatically generates that request for you. However, we need to examine the request in some detail in order to understand it.

As you recall, our QueryDataSet, called album, is assigned a QueryDescriptor. The QueryDescriptor constructor looks like this:

```
public QueryDescriptor(Database database,
                       String query,
                       ReadWriteRow parameters,
                       boolean executeOnOpen,
                       int loadOption)
```

The first two parameters are quite straightforward. The first is the Database object that you are using, and the second is the query you have created. A ReadWriteRow will come into use in Chapter 43 when we start talking about parameterized queries. Use parameterized queries to easily modify a query just before you submit it. For instance, it will allow you to specify at run time that you want to select all the rows from a database where a field called Artist has a particular value, such as "Vivaldi" or "Bartok."

The executeOnOpen parameter is perhaps most useful if you don't want to retrieve the dataset automatically at design time because it is too large or the connection is slow. Set this value to false, and you will be able to edit your visual components inside of JBuilder without having to retrieve a dataset from your server. Most of the time this is not necessary, but the option is available to you if you need it. There are, of course, other reasons why you might want to set this parameter to false. In general, its presence gives you a degree of flexibility.

So far, all has been pretty straightforward. The last field, called loadOption, is a bit trickier to understand. Its general purpose is to determine the way the data you requested is retrieved from the dataset. This can be a complex subject. As a result, I will treat it in its own section.

How JBuilder Retrieves Data

The loadOption parameter of the QueryDescriptor has the following possible values:

```
public interface Load
{
  public static final int ALL          = 0;
  public static final int ASYNCHRONOUS = 1;
  public static final int AS_NEEDED    = 2;
  public static final int UNCACHED     = 4;
}
```

I suggest that you always set this value to Load.ALL, until you become intimately familiar with DataExpress. The other options, while very useful, can, on rare occasions, lead to trouble if you are not careful.

Here is a quick overview of the options available to you:

- ALL: Use this option to retrieve all the rows from a dataset. As discussed in the previous chapter, a command like this can bring back megabytes of data. As a result, you can set the QueryDataSet's maxRows property to some useful number, such as 500, in order to limit the number of records you see. Even better, modify your query to bring back a smaller dataset. After all, what exactly is the user going to do with 10,000 records? By default, maxRows is set to –1, which means that DataExpress will attempt to retrieve all the available rows.
- ASYNCHRONOUS: Use this option to run the query on a separate thread. You would want to do this if a long query is causing your application to appear to lock up. If your application is really locking up, this won't fix it. The point is that if getting the dataset takes a long time, this will allow users to access the menus of your application even while it is retrieving a dataset. The JBuilder docs state that this option could result in a thread deadlock under some circumstances. You can call QueryDataSet.closeProvider to force the operation to finish before anything else happens. Choosing this option would, in effect, change the ASYNCHRONOUS option back into the ALL option. You might want to force a completion if you want to perform an operation on all the rows you requested.
- AS_NEEDED: This option can also radically improve the perceived performance of your application. The idea here is that you will see only one screen full of data at a time in a grid. If you move down below the bottom of the grid, new data will be retrieved from the server. You can use maxRows and maxDesignRows to tweak the number of rows you display. If you select AS_NEEDED, maxRows defaults to 25 rather than the unlimited number it normally defaults to.
- UNCACHED: This is similar to AS_NEEDED, but instead of retrieving a screenful (25 rows) at a time, it retrieves only one record at a time. In many cases, retrieving a single record from a server can be almost instantaneous. As a result, this can be a good option for you if you do not have a good connection to your server. Needless to say, it works best when you are not using a grid to display data.

There are several different ways to learn about the loadOption field, which I will discuss in the next section.

Monitoring SQL Activity

One way to start learning about the loadOption technology is to place a JdbStatusLabel at the bottom of your form and point it at your dataset:

```
jdbStatusLabel1.setDataSet(myDataSet).
```

This was done for you automatically in the default application we just finished creating. This label can help you track exactly how many rows of your query have been returned from the server.

To learn more about the loadOption, set it to **Load.AS_NEEDED**:

```
album.setQuery(
      new com.borland.dx.sql.dataset.QueryDescriptor(database1,
      "SELECT ALBUM.CODE,ALBUM.ALBUM,ALBUM.TYPES,ALBUM.LOUDNESS," +
```

```
        "ALBUM.MEDIUM,ALBUM.RATING,ALBUM.GROUPCODE,ALBUM.CDDBID," +
        "ALBUM.CDDBNAME FROM ALBUM", null, true, Load.AS_NEEDED));
```

When you first launch your program, you will see by looking at your jdStatusLabel that rather than loading several hundred rows of data, only 25 rows from the dataset are loaded. Then, as you scroll down the grid, you can watch the status label to see when additional rows are loaded.

There are, however, better ways to learn even more about what is going on. One is to use the JDBC Monitor button in your application. To use this button, first choose **Project | Project Properties**, turn to the **Required Libraries** page, and add **JBCL** to your list of libraries. Close the dialog, select the **Bean Chooser**, and browse for the following class: com.borland.jbcl.sql.monitor.MonitorButton. Drop the button on a visual form of your choice, such as the bottom of the AlbumUIBean. Run your program, and press the button to view the output.

NOTE: My experience is that not all drivers will readily print data to the JDBC Monitor or the DriveManager file streams mentioned below. For instance, I tend to have trouble with JDBC drivers, while ODBC drivers for Access or InterBase seem to work just fine. Even if you want to ship using the JDBC driver for InterBase or MySQL, you might try debugging using the ODBC drivers. Fortunately, it is easy to switch back and forth between these drivers, as described in the section of this chapter called "Opening a Database."

If you don't want to use the MonitorButton, you can insert either of these statements before you do anything else in your data module:

```
java.sql.DriverManager.setLogStream(System.out);
java.sql.DriverManager.setLogWriter(new java.io.PrintWriter(System.out));
```

The first statement is for use with JDBC 1.0, and the second is for JDBC 2.0. The first statement should work in either case. A good place to put them is in the constructor for your data module before you call jbInit.

If all is working well, calling setLogStream and setting loadOptions to **ALL** should cause a huge amount of data to be dumped to your JBuilder message window. Choosing AS_NEEDED should generate a small amount of data. As you scroll through the dataset, each time a new set of 25 rows is pulled down, you will see another chunk of data in your message window. If you choose UNCACHED, you will see one record come down at a time whenever you click the Next button in the nav bar.

For the UNCACHED option, the act of pulling down one row of data while using setLogStream might look like this:

```
Get integer data (SQLGetData), hStmt=189276352, column=1
value=4
Get string data (SQLGetData), hStmt=189276352, column=2, maxLen=46
Undocumented Windows
Get integer data (SQLGetData), hStmt=189276352, column=3
value=1000
Get integer data (SQLGetData), hStmt=189276352, column=4
NULL
Get integer data (SQLGetData), hStmt=189276352, column=5
value=1000
Get integer data (SQLGetData), hStmt=189276352, column=6
value=7
Get integer data (SQLGetData), hStmt=189276352, column=7
```

```
value=3
Get string data (SQLGetData), hStmt=189276352, column=8, maxLen=21
Get string data (SQLGetData), hStmt=189276352, column=9, maxLen=41
```

The key thing to look for here is the column field, followed by the value stored in the column. For instance, Column 2, which has a max length of 46, is set to the value "Undocumented Windows."

If you press the Next button in the nav bar, you will see one more record this size get pulled down. It is this incremental transaction rate that makes the program so responsive.

Another alternative is to set loadOption to **ASYNCHRONOUS**. If you are monitoring the SQL action with setLogStream, you will probably see your UI appear while data is still scrolling in the message pane. The delay caused by setLogStream is in fact enough to make the ASYNCHRONOUS option genuinely useful in this application.

You can see that two threads are at work; one is busy loading the data and reporting the progress in your message window. The other thread shows you the first parts of the data as soon as it is available. The UI is active, and the user can scan through the available data even while it is still being pulled down from the server.

NOTE: In Chapter 42, you will learn about the DBEventMonitor component. This component can help you explore events in JBuilder DataExpress code. Its functionality is different from the monitoring techniques shown in this chapter, since it is focused on the Borland tools and not the underlying JDBC code. Nevertheless, it is still another tool used to look inside your database code and get reports on exactly what is going on behind the scenes.

If you find all this a bit confusing, it probably is not important that you fully understand it as a newcomer. In most cases, your databases will be small enough to allow you to work with the default loadOptions.ALL value. However, if you begin working with larger datasets, or if your connection to your database is slow, then it will be nice to know about these alternative values.

Data Module Access Methods

As you recall, we are still in the process of making our way through the automatically generated code for your data module. We are proceeding pretty much line by line, as this code is very important.

The final lines of code in the data module look like this:

```
    public Database getDatabase1()
    {
        return database1;
    }

    public QueryDataSet getAlbum()
    {
        return album;
    }
```

The purpose of this code is clear: It gives you access to the two main objects in the class. It probably won't surprise you to hear that I believe it might be a good idea to delete this code. A data module should stand on its own. These methods export the guts of the data module and let other classes play with them. In most cases, this is simply not good for the health of your project.

Examining the Generated Application

We took an in-depth look at the data module. There is no need to go into such depth with the application that JBuilder generates. However, a few things should be said about this code.

Let's look at the files that JBuilder generated:

```
Main Package:
AlbumDataModuleTwoTierApp.java
AlbumDataModule.java

UI Package
AlbumUIBean.java
ClientAboutBoxDialog.java
ClientFrame.java
ClientResources.java
```

The layout of this application makes good sense to me. One set of files, both non-visual, are kept in the main package. All of the code having to do with the interface is kept in a separate package. Again, this is the proper way to partition an application. Let those who have eyes see and those who have ears hear!

AlbumDataModuleTwoTierApp.java and ClientFrame.java are more or less identical to the first two files generated when you create any other JBuilder application. In other words, they are just slight variations on the standard Application1.java and Frame1.java that the JBuilder Application Wizard generates. The ClientAboutBoxDialog.java is also similar to what the JBuilder Application Wizard can produce. Certainly there is not much of interest to say about it in this context.

That really leaves us with only two files: ClientResources and AlbumUIBean. The client resource isn't really germane to our current conversation, but I find it interesting in its own right. As a result, I will discuss it later in this chapter. The main focus here will be on the AlbumUIBean.java, which is not a particularly difficult or startling piece of code.

I will not reproduce the AlbumUIBean in full. It is mostly just a series of JLabel and JdbTextFields on a small JPanel that uses a GridLayout and then is inserted into a larger JPanel using GridBagLayOut:

```
    JdbTextField fieldCODE;

    labelCODE.setText("Code");
    fieldCODE.setColumnName("CODE");
    fieldCODE.setDataSet(dataSet);

    panelCODE.setLayout(gridLayout1);
    labelCODE.setHorizontalAlignment(SwingConstants.RIGHT);
    panelCODE.add(labelCODE);
    panelCODE.add(fieldCODE);
    this.add(panelCODE,
      new GridBagConstraints(1, 2, 2, 1, 1.0, 1.0,
          GridBagConstraints.NORTH, GridBagConstraints.HORIZONTAL,
          new Insets(3, 0, 3, 3), 0, 0));
```

fieldCODE is the JdbTextField component. This is a visual component created by Borland for the purpose of showing a single field from a table. You need to simply tell a JdbTextField which dataset you want to associate it with and which field from the dataset you want it to display:

```
fieldCODE.setColumnName("CODE");
fieldCODE.setDataSet(dataSet);
```

After you do this, fieldCODE will act like a normal JTextField, only it will contain a field from your dataset. If you press the Save icon in the nav tool bar, the edits you make to this field will be saved back to the dataset as long as they don't break any integrity rules of the database.

The rest of the code from this class simply arranges the panel and text field components next to each other on a panel and then inserts the panel into the larger view that contains the controls for displaying the whole set of database fields.

Code Generation and Templates

The code that JBuilder generates is not hard-coded into JBuilder itself. Instead, a system exists that allows you to change the code that JBuilder generates.

The code that was generated in the AlbumUIBean is drawn from resources kept in the templates directory found off the root JBuilder install directory. For instance, you might find these files in C:\JBuilder7\templates or in /home/user-name/jbuilder7/templates.

The templates are not pretty to look at. They do, however, contain the code fragments from which these applications are drawn.

In this particular case, you want to look at the ColumnarUIBean.java.template text file from the JBuilder7/templates directory. Look for a line of code that resembles this one:

```
this.add(panel[MakeProperCase(this)],
      new java.awt.GridBagConstraints(1,
      [IncrementNumericHint("NumericHint")], 2, 1, 1.0, 1.0,
      java.awt.GridBagConstraints.NORTH,
      java.awt.GridBagConstraints.HORIZONTAL,
      new Insets(3, 0, 3, 3), 0, 0));
```

Most of the code here makes it intact into the final AlbumUIBean. The parts that look funny, such as IncrementNumericHint, are macros in the JBuilder template language. You can find some of these macros in Macros.template from the templates directory:

```
[MACRO IncrementNumericHint]
  [IF TYPE == "stringObject"]
    [FOR get(VALUE)]
      [put(stringObject.VALUE, 1 + VALUE)]
      [RETURN 1 + VALUE]
    [END]
  [ENDIF]

  [RETURN 0]
[END]
```

If you want to change the code that JBuilder produces, you can just start editing the code in these templates. For instance, if you change the code fragment new Insets(3, 0, 3, 3) to new Insets(5, 0, 5, 5), the GridBag code JBuilder produces will include fives instead of threes.

Whether you really want to get involved in editing these templates is up to you. Frankly, I don't find the code inside them very inspiring. However, if you do want to start making some changes — well, here are the files, and you are free to go at it.

The ClientResource

There is one last file that you should at least glance at when you are exploring the code that JBuilder produced for your project. ClientResources.java encapsulates a ClientResource-Bundle that contains all the strings that are used in the application. The source for it can be seen in Listing 41-3.

Listing 41-3: The ClientResources.java file contains the strings used in the application.

```
package untitled8._AlbumDataModule.twotier;

import java.text.MessageFormat;

public class ClientResources extends java.util.ListResourceBundle
{
  static final Object[][] contents =
  {
    { "File",              "File" },
    { "FileShortcut",      "F" },
    { "Exit",              "Exit" },
    { "ExitShortcut",      "x" },
    { "Actions",           "Actions" },
    { "ActionsShortcut",   "A" },
    { "RemoveTab",         "Remove Tab" },
    { "RemoveTabShortcut", "R" },
    { "Help",              "Help" },
    { "HelpShortcut",      "H" },
    { "About",             "About" },
    { "AboutShortcut",     "A" },
    { "Version",           "Version 1.0" },
    { "Copyright",         "Copyright (c)" },
    { "Comments",          "JBuilder Generated Application" },
    { "OK",                "OK" },
    { "Refresh",           "Refresh" },
    { "Save",              "Save" },
    { "SaveAll",           "Save All" },
    { "result",            "result" },
  };

  public Object[][] getContents()
  {
    return contents;
  }

  public static String format(String pattern, Object p1)
  {
    return MessageFormat.format(pattern, new Object[] {p1});
  }

  public static String format(String pattern, Object p1, Object p2)
  {
    return MessageFormat.format(pattern, new Object[] {p1, p2});
```

```
    }

    public static String format(String pattern, Object p1, Object p2, Object p3)
    {
      return MessageFormat.format(pattern, new Object[] {p1, p2, p3});
    }

    public static String format(String pattern, Object[] objects)
    {
      return MessageFormat.format(pattern, objects);
    }
  }
```

There are pairs of strings in this file. The first item in the pair is the name of a string resource and the second item is the resource itself. You would use the file like this:

```
java.util.ResourceBundle res =
      getBundle("untitled8._AlbumDataModule.twotier.ClientResources");

menuHelp.setText(res.getString("Help"));
menuHelp.setMnemonic(res.getString("HelpShortcut").charAt(0));
menuHelpAbout.setText(res.getString("About"));
menuHelpAbout.setMnemonic(res.getString("AboutShortcut").charAt(0));
```

Here you can see that the strings in the menu for the application are pulled from this resource.

The beauty of this system is twofold:

- You can store and easily access your strings in one place.
- You can easily swap in another set of strings if you want to work with a different language, create a different mood, or target a different audience.

NOTE: In some of the example programs found in this book, you will see that I use resource bundles for storing the queries I pass to a QueryDataSet.

I've taken the time to show you the ResourceBundle object simply because it represents good programming practice. In fact, all the code generated in this example is relatively well written, especially the nice separation between the UI code in one package and the non-visual code in a separate package. This is an example of exactly the right technique to use when creating a Java application.

NOTE: Some editions of JBuilder include a Resource Strings Wizard. You can reach it by choosing Wizards | Resource Strings from the JBuilder menu.

Summary

In this chapter you have been introduced to the JBuilder tools for automatically generating an application. I have tried to do more than simply step you through the act of creating the code. There has been a certain amount of code analysis and an attempt to explain what JBuilder is doing and why.

Later chapters will show you how to go under the hood and create database applications by hand. The next chapter, however, will simply show a few of the more advanced things you can do when using the JBuilder database application generator.

Chapter 42

Database Techniques

Charlie Calvert

This chapter covers some basic techniques you need to know to create useful database applications. Included is coverage of one-to-many applications and calculated fields.

This chapter contains a mixture of application generation tools and more hard-core tools for tweaking the settings of your data modules.

All of these tools are very simple to use, so there is really nothing advanced about the material in this chapter. However, the applications that we will be building have some fairly powerful database features in them, so there is much important ground covered in this chapter.

Two applications will be developed in this chapter. The first one is quite simple. You will find it on the CD under the name InsertDelete. The second is a bit more complex, but also a bit more interesting. It is found on the CD as OneToManyCalc. You can also download code for this book from the www.elvenware.com web site.

One-to-Many Relationships

In this part of the text you will learn about creating one-to-many relationships between two tables. A one-to-many relationship is sometimes called a master-detail relationship.

In these examples we will link the ALBUM table to the ARTIST table. When we are done, viewing one record in the ARTIST table will allow us to see all the associated records in the ALBUM table. For instance, when looking at the artist Pat Metheny, we will be able to see all the albums that he made in our database.

You will see two different ways to establish the relationship between two tables. In the first example, you will use the Data Modeler to create the one-to-many relationship. In the second example, you will use tools built into the JBuilder IDE itself. Use the first technique to create a data module from scratch and the second technique to edit an existing data module.

Creating a One-to-Many Relationship with the Data Modeler

It is time to walk through the steps necessary to create a one to-many relationship between two tables.

Here are the opening steps:

- Select **File | New Project** from the JBuilder menu.
- Select **File | New DataModule** from the JBuilder menu.
- Make sure **Invoke Data Modeler** is checked, and then press the **OK** button.
- Open up the jbbook database. (See Chapter 39 for information on the jbbook database.)
- Select the **ARTIST** table and choose the **Copy All** button.
- Choose **Queries | Add** from the Data Modeler menu.
- Select the **ALBUM** table and choose the **Copy All** button.

- Choose **Queries | Link** from the menu.
- From the ARTIST table, choose **Code**. From the ALBUM table, choose **GroupCode**. Check the **Allow cascading deletes** and **Allow cascading updates** options. See Figure 42-1 for help on this step.
- Click the **OK** button in the Link Queries dialog. You should now be able to see a visual representation of the relationship between the two tables, as shown in Figure 42-2.

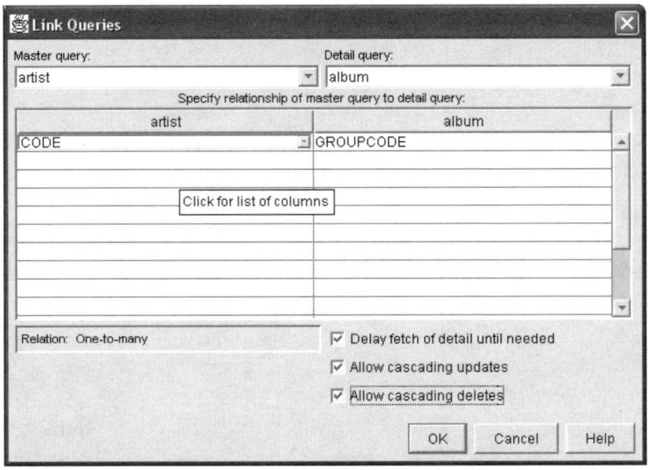

Figure 42-1: Creating a one-to-many relationship with cascading deletes and updates between the ARTIST and ALBUM tables

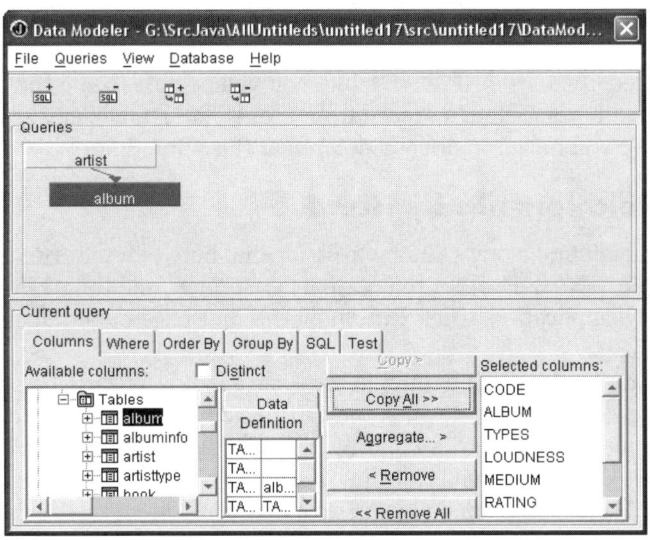

Figure 42-2: Using the Data Modeler to view a visual representation of the relationship between two tables

Choose **File | Save** and **File | Exit** from the Data Modeler menu. These actions will generate the code for your data module.

Choose **File | New | Data Module Application** from the JBuilder menu. Click the **OK** button in the Application Wizard.

At this stage you have completed generating your application. Select **Project | Project Properties**, turn to the **Run** page, and select the **New** button. Browse for the main file in your application, which will have a name somewhat like DataModule1TwoTierApp.

Click the **OK** button in two dialogs to get back to the main window of the JBuilder IDE. Press the green run button. You should now be able to see your running application, as shown in Figure 42-3.

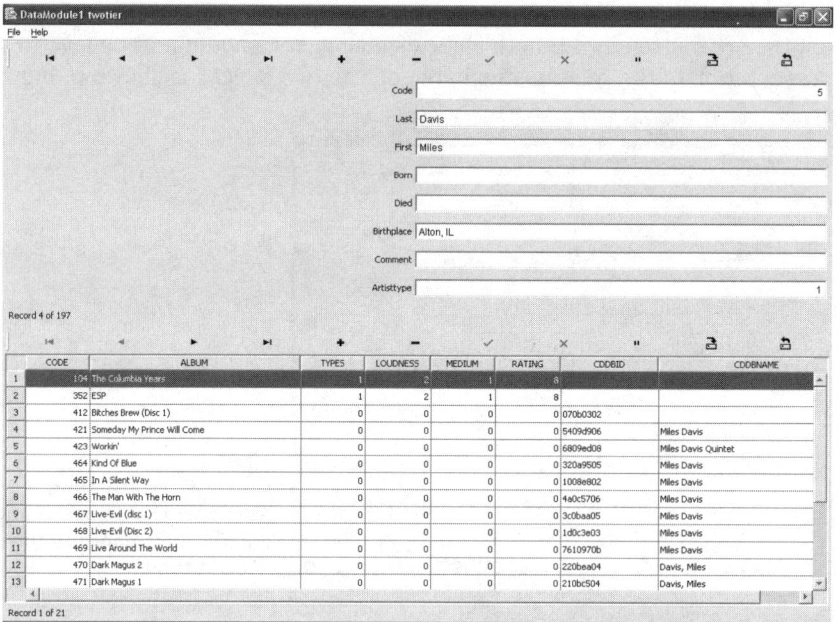

Figure 42-3: An automatically generated one-to-many application created by JBuilder 7

As you move through the records in the ARTIST table, you will be able to see the associated records in the ALBUM table. If you delete a record from the ARTIST table, any associated records in the ALBUM table will be automatically deleted at the same time.

Creating a One-to-Many Relationship by Hand

In this example we will again define a one-to-many relationship between the ARTIST and ALBUM tables. Choose **File | New Project** to create a new project and then **File | New | Application** to create a new application. Click **Finish** on the first page of both dialogs, accepting all the default values.

Choose **File | New Data Module.** This time, in the Data Module Wizard, be sure that the Invoke Data Modeler option is not selected. Click the **OK** button to close the dialog.

Focus the new data module in the JBuilder content pane and switch to design view. Turn to the DataExpress page in the component palette. Choose the first icon on the far left, labeled com.borland.dx.sql.dataset.Database. Drop an instance of this component on the data access node in the structure pane, as shown in Figure 42-4.

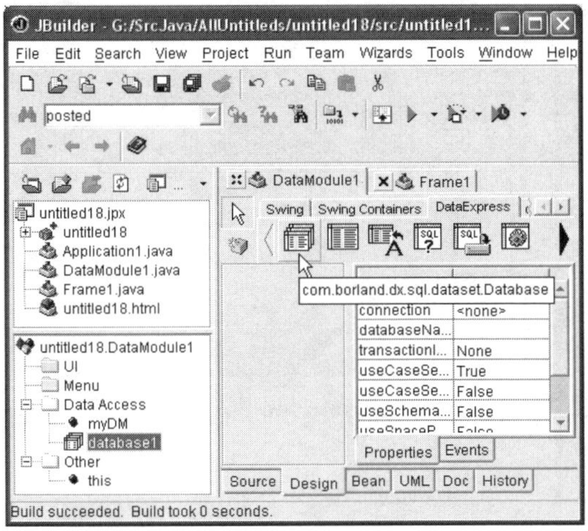

Figure 42-4: Picking the Database object from the far left of the DataExpress page of the component palette and dropping it on the Data Access node of the structure pane

In the Inspector, choose the ellipsis button of the connection property to bring up the Connection dialog, as shown in Figure 42-5. Select the **Choose Existing Connection** button and browse for the jbbook database. Type in your user name and password and select the **Test Connection** button.

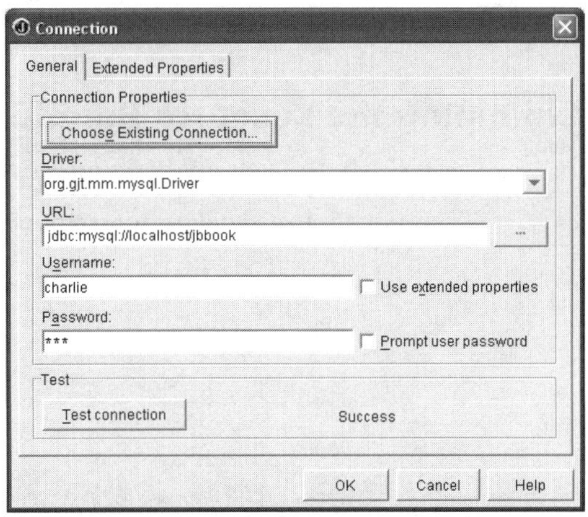

Figure 42-5: Selecting and testing a connection to a database

If you want to have the user be prompted for the password, select the **Prompt user password** option. Otherwise, the password will be hard-coded into your application. This latter option is actually the preferred choice during application development, as you don't want to waste time typing in the password. Click **OK** to close the dialog.

You now want to query the database for both the ARTIST and ALBUM tables. Select the fourth component in on the DataExpress page of the component palette. This component is called com.borland.dx.sql.dataset.QueryDataSet. Drop two instances of this component onto the Data Access node of the structure pane. Use the Inspector to name the first one **queryDataSetArtist** and the second one **queryDataSetAlbum**. At the same time, you might rename database1 to **database**.

Select **queryDataSetArtist** and click the ellipsis button in the query property found in the Inspector. The Query dialog should appear, as shown in Figure 42-6. Set the Database field to the database you created. Select the **SQL Builder** button and open up the database node to reveal the tables. Select the **ARTIST** table and choose the **Copy All** button, as shown in Figure 42-7. Click the **OK** button. The Query dialog should now look as it does in Figure 42-6. Choose the **Test Query** button to confirm that you have entered a valid query. This last step is optional, but I prefer to choose the **Place SQL text in resource bundle** option. If you select this item, you will be prompted to confirm the name of the resource bundle after choosing the OK button at the bottom of the Query dialog. Confirm, but do not change, the name of the resource bundle.

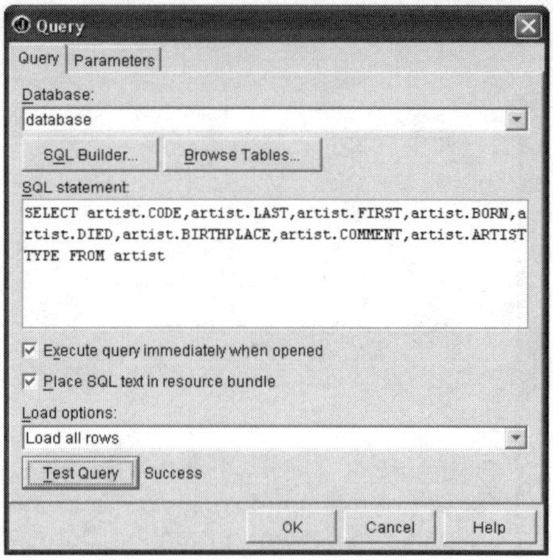

Figure 42-6: Setting up and testing a query in the Query dialog

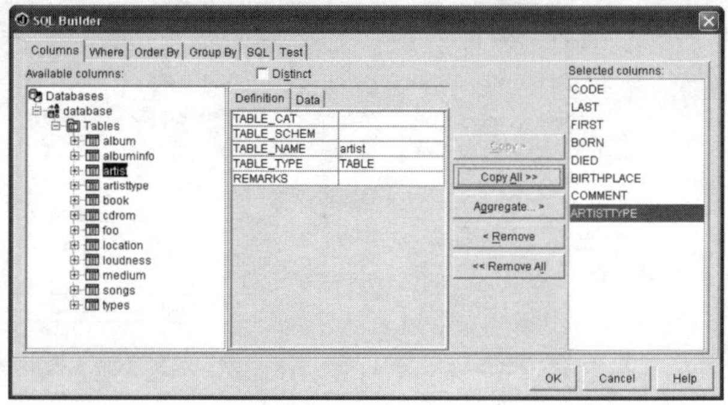

Figure 42-7: Using the SQL Builder to create a query

Examining the Resource Bundle

At this stage you might be interested in viewing the resource bundle, shown in Listing 42-1.

Listing 42-1: A simple resource bundle containing a query on the ARTIST table

```
package untitled18;

import java.util.*;

public class SqlRes extends java.util.ListResourceBundle
{

    static final Object[][] contents = new String[][]{
      { "artist", "SELECT artist.CODE,artist.LAST,artist.FIRST," +
      "artist.BORN,artist.DIED,artist.BIRTHPLACE,artist.COMMENT," +
      "artist.ARTISTTYPE FROM artist" }};

    public Object[][] getContents()
    {
        return contents;
    }
}
```

The contents array in the resource bundle contains a string pair. The first item in the pair is called artist. Use this string to retrieve the actual query:

```
ResourceBundle sqlRes = ResourceBundle.getBundle("untitled18.SqlRes");
String myquery = sqlRes.getString("artist")
```

But let's not linger too long over the resource bundle. There is still more work to do.

Select the **queryDataSetAlbum** component. Turn to the query property in the Inspector and repeat all the steps for the queryDataSetArtist component. The only difference is that this time you will select all the fields from the ALBUM table rather than the ARTIST table. If you choose to use the resource bundle, new code will be added to the resource bundle to record your new query:

```
static final Object[][] contents = new String[][]{
  { "artist", "SELECT artist.CODE,artist.LAST,artist.FIRST," +
  artist.BORN,artist.DIED,artist.BIRTHPLACE,artist.COMMENT," +
  "artist.ARTISTTYPE FROM artist" },

  { "album", "SELECT album.CODE,album.ALBUM,album.TYPES,album.LOUDNESS," +
  "album.MEDIUM,album.RATING,album.GROUPCODE,album.CDDBID, " +
  "album.CDDBNAME FROM album" }};
```

Now you can call SqlRes.getString("album") to retrieve the album query.

So far, everything has been quite straightforward. The next step is a bit trickier but still relatively easy.

To create the actual one-to-many relationship between the two tables, choose the **masterLink** property in the Inspector for the queryDataSetAlbum component. Select the **queryDataSetArtist** component in the Master dataset field. Select the **Code** field for the Master link columns. Select the **GroupCode** field for the Detail link columns field. Select all the options at the bottom of the dialog, as shown in Figure 42-8. These options allow you to delay the fetch of the detail rows until they are needed and use cascading updates and deletes. If you choose to delay the fetch, the test button will probably fail. You should probably uncheck that button long enough to run the test and confirm that your query works. If everything looks okay, select the option again, as it will often improve the performance of your application and cut down on network traffic.

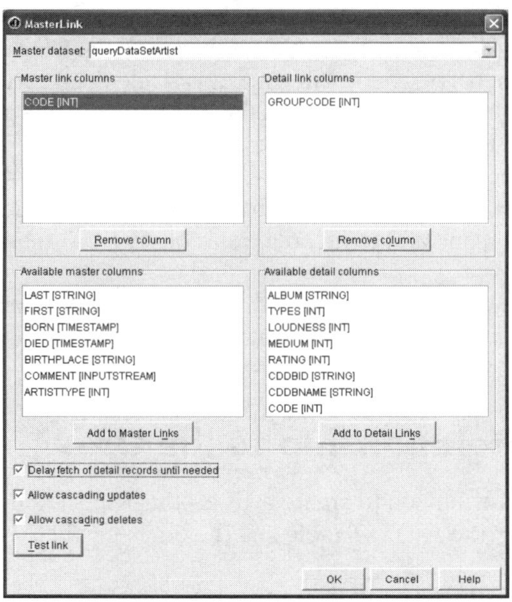

Figure 42-8: Creating a master-detail relationship in the MasterLink dialog

In the previous chapter, I explained the code that was generated for creating a database connection and querying a dataset. You still need, however, to see the code that creates a master-detail link between two tables:

```
queryDataSetAlbum.setMasterLink(new MasterLinkDescriptor(queryDataSetArtist,
      new String[] {"CODE"},
      new String[] {"GROUPCODE"},
      true, true, true));
```

NOTE: In the code produced by JBuilder, you will see the following syntax: com.borland.dx.dataset.MasterLinkDescriptor. In this case, as in many other places throughout this section of the text, I have removed the com.Borland.dx.dataset part of the code. In my mind, it is redundant, since we have already included an import statement that references this package at the top of the source file: import com.borland.dx.sql.dataset.*. My feeling is that all this additional syntax just obscures the intention of the code. As a result, I often remove it, hoping to produce code that is easier to read.

The first three parameters passed to the setMasterLink method of a QueryDataSet component are all but self-explanatory. The first field is the dataset to which you want to link the ALBUM table. The second field is the field or fields from the master table that help establish the link. The third field is the field from the detail table that is used in the link.

NOTE: I talked earlier about the nature of the link between two tables. In this case, Code is the primary key of the ARTIST table and GroupCode is a foreign key in the ALBUM table. If the Code field for the Pat Metheny record in the ARTIST table is 11, placing 11 in the GroupCode field of the ALBUM table indicates that the selected album was created by Pat Metheny.

At the same time that these changes were made, a parameterized query should have been created in your resource bundle:

```
{ "album", "SELECT album.CODE,album.ALBUM,album.TYPES,album.LOUDNESS, " +
      "album.MEDIUM,album.RATING,album.GROUPCODE," +
      "album.CDDBID,album.CDDBNAME FROM album where GROUPCODE=:CODE" }};
```

Notice that this code has been modified to include a WHERE clause. In particular, we are going to select from the ALBUM table all those records where the GROUPCODE equals some as-yet-to-be-determined value. In particular, it will equal a variable designated by the :CODE syntax. The presence of the colon before the word CODE designates this as a parameter or run-time variable. The value of the CODE will be assigned at run time by the JBuilder DataExpress code. When the user selects an artist, the value of the CODE field for that artist will be plugged into our SQL statement in place of the variable :CODE. For instance, if Pat Metheny is selected, Code will equal 11, and all the records from the ALBUM table that have a GroupCode of 11 will be selected.

That is all that you need to do to make sure the query is properly selected. Check all the elements in your code to be sure they are valid. In particular, make certain that the WHERE clause is set up properly. If it is not, insert that code manually.

Displaying the One-to-Many Relationship to the User

To show this relationship to a user, you will need to create a UI for this application. Begin by creating two panel components, one for the ARTIST table and the other for the ALBUM table.

Choose **File | New Class** from the JBuilder menu. Set the base class of the new component to **javax.swing.JPanel**. Set the package name to the name of your main package plus a subpackage called ui: untitled18.ui. Name your new component **ArtistView**, as shown in Figure 42-9.

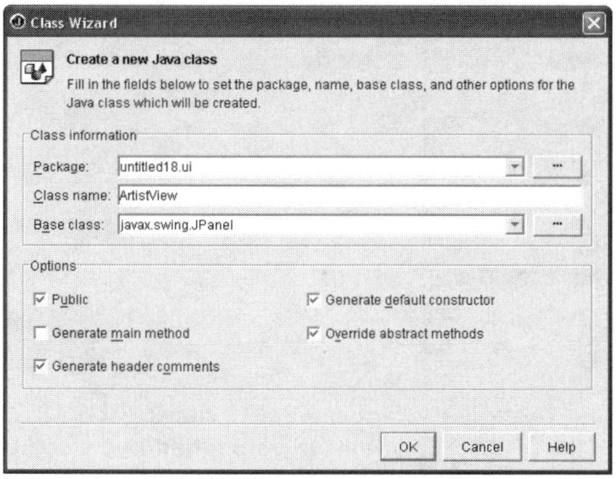

Figure 42-9: Creating a home for the visual view of the ARTIST table

Place your new component in design mode. Set the layout for your component to **BorderLayout**. Turn to the dbSwing page of the component palette and drop down a TableScrollPane, setting its constraints property to **Center**. Drop down a JdbTable component on top of the TableScrollPane and call it **tableArtist**.

Compile your code to make sure that everything is working correctly at this stage. You need to do this before taking the next step. The Data Module Wizard will only work correctly with compiled code.

While still in design view on the ArtistView dialog, choose **Wizards | Use DataModule** from the JBuilder menu. In the Use DataModule Wizard, set the field name to **dMod** and the DataModule class to the name of your data module. Elect to share a static instance of the data module, as shown in Figure 42-10. As explained in the previous chapter, this wizard will enable you to use the singleton pattern to ensure that only one instance of your data module is created.

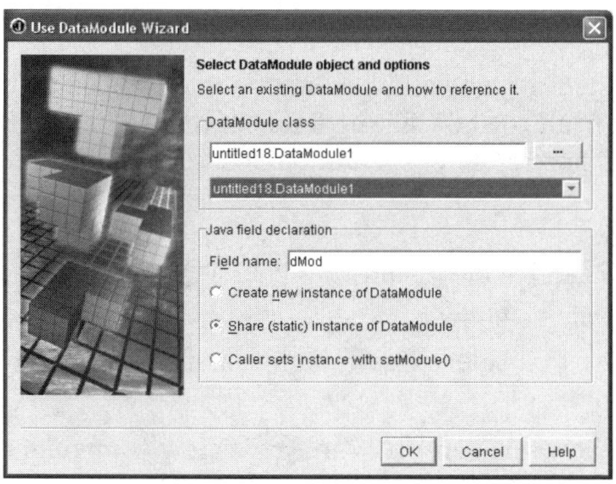

Figure 42-10: Using the Use DataModule Wizard to get access to the data module that you created

The code generated by the Data Module Wizard looks like this:

```
DataModule1 dMod;
dMod = untitled18.DataModule1.getDataModule();
```

Select the **tableArtist** component and use its dataSet property to select the queryDataSetARTIST table from the data module. When you are done, you should see the table in your panel component, as shown in Figure 42-11.

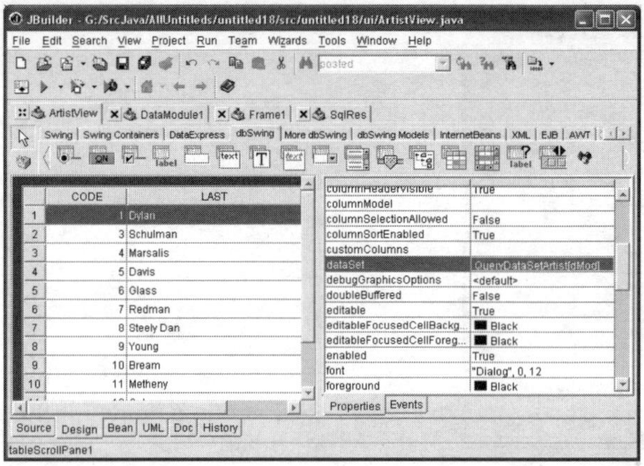

Figure 42-11: Viewing the ARTIST table in a JdbTable embedded in a scroll pane on your panel component

You now want to repeat this entire process with the ALBUM table. Create a new JPanel descendant with BorderLayout called **AlbumView** and place it in the ui package. Drop down a TableScrollPane and JdbTable component from the dbSwing page. First compile your program, and then use the Use DataModule Wizard to connect the new visual component to your data module. Set the dataSet property of the JdbTable property to **queryDataSetAlbum.** When you complete this last step, you probably won't get any visual confirmation that it worked. In fact, it may appear that the JdbTable component completely disappeared. Don't let this trouble you; it is entirely normal.

Turn back to Frame1 and go into design mode. Use the Bean Chooser, located way on the left of the component palette, to select the two new components that you created. A detailed explanation of this process is presented in Part VII: JavaBeans.

Drop down the ArtistView component on Frame1, and set its constraints property to **WEST**. Drop down the AlbumView component on Frame1 and set its constraints property to **CENTER**.

After placing the components on Frame1, you will likely notice that things don't look quite right. In particular, it is going to be difficult to show all the fields of the ARTIST table and still get a good look at the ALBUM table. There simply is not enough screen real estate to pull this off with any grace.

At this stage, you have three choices:

- Select fewer fields from the ARTIST table by altering your SQL statement.
- Hide the fields that you don't want to show.
- Find some middle ground, where you select viewer fields, and then hide any additional ones that you don't want to show.

I will elect the second option. Here is how you can alter the ArtistView component so that only the FIRST and LAST fields are visible. Doing this leaves the CODE field intact, which is important, since it is used in the one-to-many relationship with the ALBUM table:

```
private void jbInit() throws Exception
{
      // Code omitted here…
      tableArtist.setHiddenColumns(new int[]{0,3,4,5,6,7});
}
```

As you can see, the setHiddenColumns method of the JdbTable component allows you to designate any fields that you want to hide.

At this stage, when you run your application, you can see two fields from the ARTIST table and all the fields from the designated row of the ALBUM table, as shown in Figure 42-12.

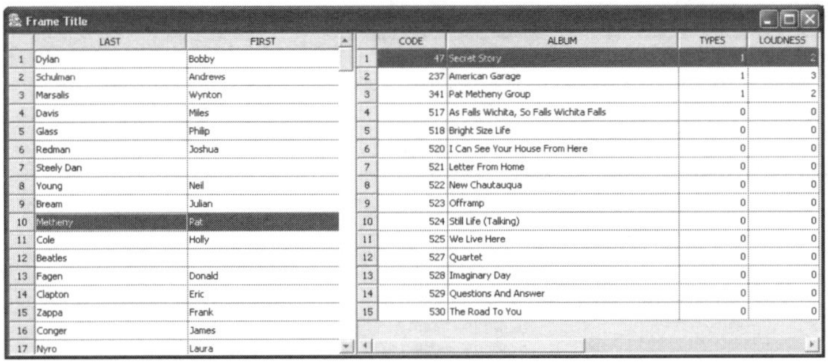

Figure 42-12: The handmade one-to-many relationship, version 0.5

As you can tell, things still don't look quite right. To fix things further, however, we will need to learn about a new technique called a calculated field.

At this stage you know the basic facts needed to create one-to-many relationships between two tables. On this book's CD, you will find a program called MasterDetail, which illustrates exactly how this process works in practice.

Calculated Fields

A *calculated field* is a new column added to your table with a value calculated at run time. In our case, we are showing the user the first and last names from the ALBUM table. The user doesn't really need, or even want, to see these fields as two separate columns. Instead, the user would probably rather see them both as a single field with the two names combined: Pat Metheny, Andres Segovia, Steve Gordon, Leona Boyd, Joe Sample, etc.

Open up queryDataSetArtist in the structure pane and choose the field labeled **<new column>**, as shown in Figure 42-13.

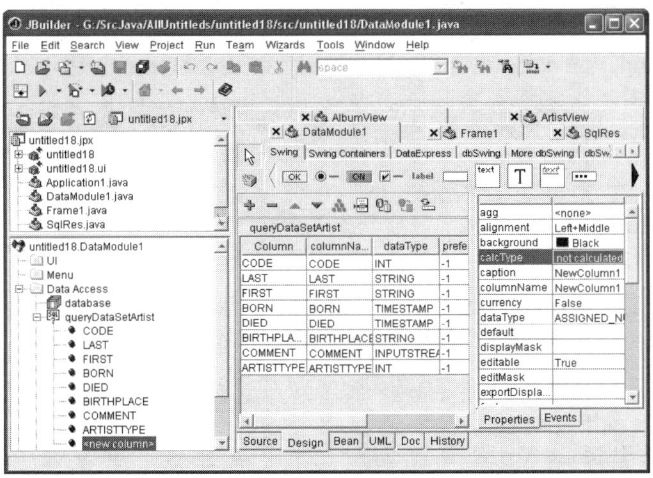

Figure 42-13: Viewing the columns in the queryDataSetArtist component and selecting the new column

Change the columnName property to **firstLastCalc** and set the caption property to **Name**. Set the calcType property to **Calculated**. At this stage, you will be able to scroll up to the top of the Inspector and fill in the name property, which should read firstLastCalc. When you are done, things should look much as they do in Figure 42-14.

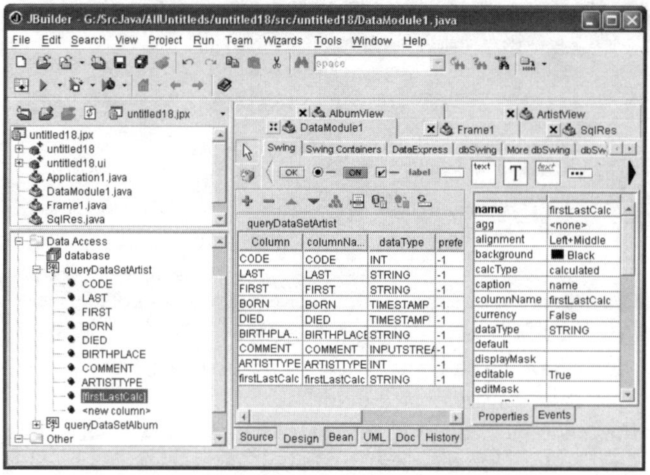

Figure 42-14: Filling in the fields for a calculated column

Select **queryDataSetArtist** in the structure pane. In the Inspector, turn to the Events page. Create an entry for the calcFields event that looks like this:

```
void queryDataSetArtist_calcFields(ReadRow changedRow,
      DataRow calcRow, boolean isPosted)
{
      if (isPosted)
      {
            String calculatedValue = changedRow.getString("FIRST");
            calculatedValue += " " + changedRow.getString("LAST");
            calcRow.setString("firstLastCalc", calculatedValue);
      }
}
```

After you insert this method, you can run the application. It will look much as it did before, but there will now be a third field in the ARTIST table. Besides the first name and last name fields, there will also be a new field containing both the first and last names. You may have to use the scroll bar at the bottom of the application to see this field, as shown in Figure 42-15. Later in the text, we will further modify this setup to give an appearance more in line with the user's expectations.

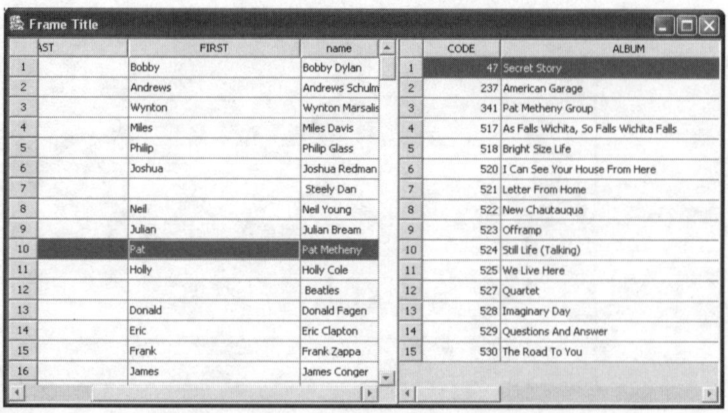

Figure 42-15: Viewing the new calculated field added to our simple database application

The calcFields method is called once for each row in your dataset. You are passed a copy of the current state of each row and a place to enter your changes to the row. Finally, you are passed a Boolean value referencing the current state of the row. Here are the three parameters passed to the handler for the calcFields event:

- changedRow: Here you will find the values of the fields in the current row.
- calcRow: Use this variable to return to DataExpress the new values that you want to insert. You can change any of the fields in the row, but usually you will want to change only the calculated row.
- isPosted: This value will be true if the fields are about to be posted. In my experience, this value is almost always true, unless the user is actually in the process of editing a row. At such times, you probably don't want to bother trying to make the calculation on the row. So you should wait until isPosted is set to true, and then calculate the value. A row will be posted whenever the user chooses a menu item or button to post it or moves the focus off the row to any other row.

It is helpful to understand when the calcFields method is called. The best way to do this is to actually insert some code into the method that will give you explicit feedback about its state:

```
int value = 0;

void queryDataSetArtist_calcFields(ReadRow changedRow,
      DataRow calcRow, boolean isPosted)
{
      value++;
      System.out.println("Value: " + value + " " + isPosted);

      if (isPosted)
      {
            String calculatedValue = changedRow.getString("FIRST");
            calculatedValue += " " + changedRow.getString("LAST");
            calcRow.setString("firstLastCalc", calculatedValue);
      }
}
```

The println statement shown here will be very busy when the application first starts. It will be called once for each row in the dataset, which in this case should be approximately 200 times. The method will then be silent until you begin editing one of the rows. While you are editing the row, isPosted will be false. When you post the row, by using a button or menu option or moving to the next row, isPosted will be set to true.

At this stage, you probably want to make the FIRST and LAST columns invisible so that the user sees only your new calculated field, as shown in Figure 42-16. To do this, simply modify your setHiddenColumns statement in the ArtistView class:

```
tableArtist.setHiddenColumns(new int[]{0,1,2,3,4,5,6,7});
tableArtist.setRowHeaderVisible(false);
```

The addition of fields 1 and 2 in the setHiddenColumns method hides the FIRST and LAST fields. The new field, the firstLastCalc column, is column 8, so it remains visible. I have also added code that makes the row number fields on the far left of each row invisible. These fields are called row headers. Finally, I selected the data module, went into design mode, selected the firstLastCalc row, and set its width property to 25. In code view, the result looked like this:

```
firstLastCalc.setWidth(25);
```

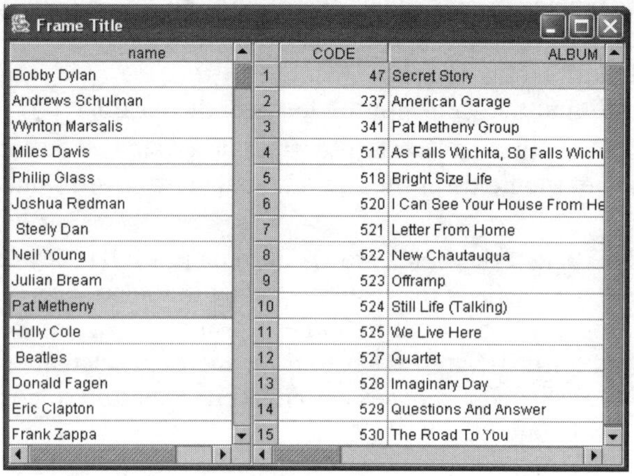

Figure 42-16: Changing the view so that the FIRST and LAST columns are hidden. All you see is the new calculated column without a row header.

When you look at Figure 42-16, you can see that the arrangement of the components on Frame1 has changed. In particular, the new column now takes up only a small amount of room, and there is more room for the ALBUM table. To make this change, open up Frame1, select the artistView1 component in the structure pane, and set its preferred size to 200, 425, and make sure its minimum size is a smaller value, such as 28, 28.

The last change to the appearance of the application is entirely aesthetic. The default Windows look and feel doesn't suit this kind of application. As a result, I would open up Application1.java and edit the look and feel line so that it has this appearance:

```
UIManager.setLookAndFeel("javax.swing.plaf.metal.MetalLookAndFeel");
```

The metal look and feel makes the divisions between the components of your application more pronounced.

NOTE: The main purpose of this chapter is to show how the basic JBuilder database features work. I've tried to create a simple and easy-to-build interface to accompany this lesson. In your programs, you will probably want to spend more time building a fancy interface. However, even the simple interface we have constructed here has given you a chance to learn about a few of the features available for changing the appearance of your application. As you begin to examine these features, you will find that they are quite varied and complex.

Editing Your Data

In the application we have created, the ARTIST table is entirely read-only. The ALBUM table can be edited, but we have not given the user a means of saving changes to the database. In particular:

- The calculated fields we have created are entirely read-only. There is no way for the user to edit this data.
- The ALBUM table can be edited. When you make changes to the data in a row and then move off the row, your changes will be posted back to the local dataset. However, there is no means in the application for saving the changes to the local dataset back to the database server.

We will fix the second problem first, since it is the easiest to remedy. One solution is simply to paste a nav bar into the top of Frame1, as shown in Figure 42-17.

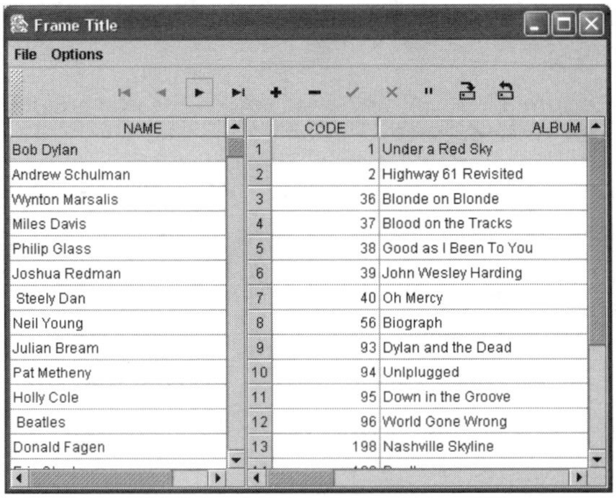

Figure 42-17: An updated version of the application with a navigation bar along the top and a menu

The navigation bar is found on the dbSwing page of the component palette. It is the last item on the right, a JdbNavToolBar. After dropping the component onto the contentPane in the structure pane, you should set its constraints to **North**.

Now you need to attach the nav bar to queryDataSetAlbum. To do this, first use the Data Module Wizard to share a static instance of the data module, as described earlier in this chapter and in the previous chapter. Compile the code once to be sure JBuilder is aware of the current state of your application. Now click on the nav bar to focus it, go to the Inspector, and set the dataSet field to **dMod.queryDataSetAlbum**.

If you now run the application, you will be able to use the buttons on the far right of the nav bar to commit your work to the database or retrieve the current state of the dataset. Remember that posting data by just moving off a row or pressing the check button on the nav bar only changes the local copy of your dataset. You need to use the buttons on the far right to commit the data back to the server.

Editing the Calculated Field

In many cases, a calculated field contains a numeric calculation that you do not want the user to edit. However, in this case, the user might want to edit the contents of this field. To do that, we need to take some special steps.

You will need to add a menu to the application. Go to the Swing Containers page and drop down a JMenuBar onto the Menu node in the structure pane. Right-click on the JMenuBar in the structure pane and choose **Activate Designer**. Create a File | Exit menu and an Options | Edit Artist menu. In the handlers for File | Exit, enter **System.exit(0)**. I will explain the code for handling the Edit Artist menu item in the next few paragraphs. If you need help creating a menu, see Chapter 13. Be sure to add the following line to the end of your jbInit():

```
this.setJMenuBar(jMenuBar1);
```

I have added a menu to the application. If you select Options | Edit Artist from the menu, the dialog shown in Figure 42-18 will appear. The source is shown in Listing 42-2. This dialog will allow the user to edit the contents of the first and last names from the current row.

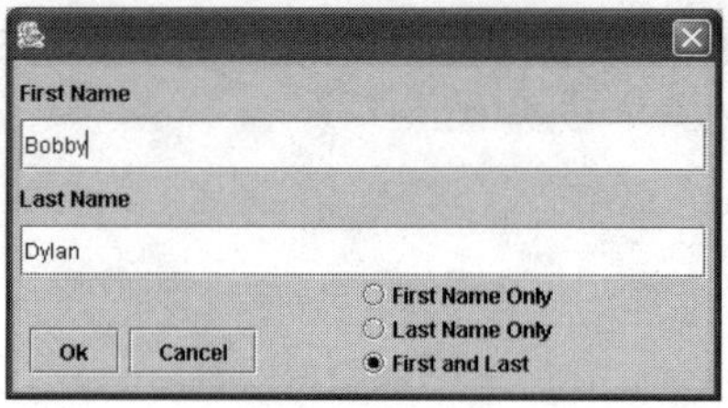

Figure 42-18: A dialog for editing the first and last name of the Artist dataset

Listing 42-2: The FirstLastInput dialog

```
package onetomanycalc.ui;

import javax.swing.*;
import java.awt.*;
import javax.swing.border.*;
import java.awt.event.*;
import onetomanycalc.*;

/**
 * <p>Title: </p>
 * <p>Description: </p>
 * <p>Copyright: Copyright (c) 2002</p>
 * <p>Company: </p>
 * @author unascribed
 * @version 1.0
 */

public class FirstLastInput extends JDialog implements ActionListener
{
      // Enumerate type, see the DialogState member class
      String fName;
      String lName;
      private DialogState dlgState = DialogState.FIRST_LAST;
      private DataModule1 dMod = null;
      Border border1;
      BorderLayout borderLayout1 = new BorderLayout();
      BorderLayout borderLayout2 = new BorderLayout();
      ButtonGroup buttonGroup1 = new ButtonGroup();
      FlowLayout flowLayout1 = new FlowLayout();
      FlowLayout flowLayout2 = new FlowLayout();
      GridLayout gridLayout1 = new GridLayout();
      GridLayout gridLayout2 = new GridLayout();
      GridLayout gridLayout3 = new GridLayout();
      GridLayout gridLayout4 = new GridLayout();
      GridLayout gridLayout5 = new GridLayout();
      JButton jButtonCancel = new JButton();
      JButton jButtonOk = new JButton();
      JLabel jLabelFirstName = new JLabel();
      JLabel jLabelLastName = new JLabel();
      JPanel jPanel1 = new JPanel();
      JPanel jPanel2 = new JPanel();
      JPanel jPanel3 = new JPanel();
```

```
JPanel jPanel4 = new JPanel();
JPanel jPanel5 = new JPanel();
JPanel jPanel6 = new JPanel();
JPanel jPanel7 = new JPanel();
JPanel jPanel8 = new JPanel();
JPanel jPanel9 = new JPanel();
JRadioButton jRadioButton4 = new JRadioButton();
JRadioButton jRadioButton5 = new JRadioButton();
JRadioButton jRadioButton6 = new JRadioButton();
JRadioButton jRadioButtonBoth = new JRadioButton();
JRadioButton jRadioButtonFirst = new JRadioButton();
JRadioButton jRadioButtonLast = new JRadioButton();
JTextField jTextFieldFirstName = new JTextField();
JTextField jTextFieldLastName = new JTextField();

public FirstLastInput(JFrame parent, DataModule1 dMod)
{
      super(parent);
      this.fName = dMod.getFirstName();
      this.lName = dMod.getLastName();
      this.dMod = dMod;
      enableEvents(AWTEvent.WINDOW_EVENT_MASK);
      try
      {
            jbInit();
      }
      catch(Exception e)
      {
            e.printStackTrace();
      }
      setSize(400, 220);
      jTextFieldFirstName.setText(this.fName);
      jTextFieldLastName.setText(this.lName);
}

private void jbInit() throws Exception
{
      border1 = BorderFactory.createMatteBorder(4,4,4,4,Color.pink);
      this.getContentPane().setLayout(borderLayout2);
      //setResizable(false);
      jLabelFirstName.setText("First Name");
      jPanel1.setLayout(gridLayout2);
      gridLayout2.setColumns(1);
      gridLayout2.setRows(2);
      jPanel3.setLayout(gridLayout3);
      gridLayout3.setColumns(1);
      gridLayout3.setRows(2);
      jLabelLastName.setText("Last Name");
      jPanel2.setLayout(gridLayout4);
      jPanel4.setLayout(gridLayout1);
```

```
gridLayout1.setColumns(1);
gridLayout1.setRows(3);
jPanel4.setBorder(border1);
gridLayout4.setColumns(2);
jRadioButton4.setText("jRadioButton3");
jRadioButton6.setText("jRadioButton1");
jPanel5.setLayout(borderLayout1);
jPanel8.setLayout(flowLayout2);
flowLayout2.setAlignment(FlowLayout.LEFT);
jRadioButtonFirst.setText("First Name Only");
jRadioButtonFirst.addItemListener(new
      FirstLastInput_jRadioButtonFirst_itemAdapter(this));
jRadioButtonLast.setText("Last Name Only");
jRadioButtonLast.addItemListener(new
      FirstLastInput_jRadioButtonLast_itemAdapter(this));
jRadioButtonBoth.setSelected(true);
jRadioButtonBoth.setText("First and Last");
jRadioButtonBoth.addItemListener(new
      FirstLastInput_jRadioButtonBoth_itemAdapter(this));
jPanel6.setLayout(gridLayout5);
gridLayout5.setColumns(1);
gridLayout5.setRows(3);
jButtonCancel.setText("Cancel");
jButtonCancel.addActionListener(this);
jButtonOk.setActionCommand("Ok");
jButtonOk.setText("Ok");
jButtonOk.addActionListener(this);
jPanel7.setLayout(flowLayout1);
flowLayout1.setAlignment(FlowLayout.LEFT);
jPanel1.add(jLabelFirstName, null);
jPanel1.add(jTextFieldFirstName, null);
this.getContentPane().add(jPanel4,  BorderLayout.CENTER);
jPanel4.add(jPanel1, null);
jPanel4.add(jPanel3, null);
jPanel4.add(jPanel2, null);
jPanel3.add(jLabelLastName, null);
jPanel3.add(jTextFieldLastName, null);

jPanel2.add(jPanel5, null);
jPanel2.add(jPanel6, null);
jPanel6.add(jRadioButtonFirst, null);
jPanel6.add(jRadioButtonLast, null);
jPanel6.add(jRadioButtonBoth, null);

jPanel5.add(jPanel7,  BorderLayout.SOUTH);
jPanel7.add(jButtonOk, null);
jPanel7.add(jButtonCancel, null);
jPanel5.add(jPanel9,  BorderLayout.CENTER);
buttonGroup1.add(jRadioButtonBoth);
buttonGroup1.add(jRadioButtonLast);
```

```
        buttonGroup1.add(jRadioButtonFirst);

    }

//Overridden so we can exit when window is closed
    protected void processWindowEvent(WindowEvent e)
    {
        if (e.getID() == WindowEvent.WINDOW_CLOSING)
        {
            cancel();
        }
        super.processWindowEvent(e);
    }

    void cancel()
    {
        this.dispose();
    }

    public String getFirst()
    {
        return jTextFieldFirstName.getText();
    }

    public String getLast()
    {
        return jTextFieldLastName.getText();
    }

    public void actionPerformed(ActionEvent e)
    {
        if (e.getSource() == jButtonCancel)
        {
            cancel();
        }
        else
        {
            if (dlgState == DialogState.FIRST_ONLY)
            {
                dMod.setFirstName(jTextFieldFirstName.getText());
            }
            else if (dlgState == DialogState.LAST_ONLY)
            {
                dMod.setLastName(jTextFieldLastName.getText());
            }
            else
            {
                dMod.setFirstLastName(jTextFieldFirstName.getText(),
                    jTextFieldLastName.getText());
            }
            cancel();
```

```
            }
        }

        private void configureState()
        {
            if (dlgState == DialogState.FIRST_ONLY)
            {
                jTextFieldLastName.setEnabled(false);
                jTextFieldFirstName.setEnabled(true);
                jLabelLastName.setEnabled(false);
                jLabelFirstName.setEnabled(true);
            }
            else if (dlgState == DialogState.LAST_ONLY)
            {
                jTextFieldLastName.setEnabled(true);
                jTextFieldFirstName.setEnabled(false);
                jLabelLastName.setEnabled(true);
                jLabelFirstName.setEnabled(false);
            }
            else
            {
                jTextFieldLastName.setEnabled(true);
                jTextFieldFirstName.setEnabled(true);
                jLabelLastName.setEnabled(true);
                jLabelFirstName.setEnabled(true);
            }

        }

        void jRadioButtonFirst_itemStateChanged(ItemEvent e)
        {
            if (e.getStateChange() == ItemEvent.SELECTED)
            {
                dlgState = DialogState.FIRST_ONLY;
                configureState();
            }

        }

        void jRadioButtonLast_itemStateChanged(ItemEvent e)
        {
            if (e.getStateChange() == ItemEvent.SELECTED)
            {
                dlgState = DialogState.LAST_ONLY;
                configureState();
            }
        }

        void jRadioButtonBoth_itemStateChanged(ItemEvent e)
        {
            if (e.getStateChange() == ItemEvent.SELECTED)
```

```
            {
                dlgState = DialogState.FIRST_LAST;
                configureState();
            }
        }

        /**
         * An enumeration class. Creates an enumerated type for use in Java.
         */
        private final static class DialogState
        {
            private final String name;

            private DialogState(String name)
            {
                this.name = name;
            }

            public String toString()
            {
                return name;
            }

            static final DialogState FIRST_ONLY = new DialogState("FIRST_ONLY");
            static final DialogState LAST_ONLY = new DialogState("LAST_ONLY");
            static final DialogState FIRST_LAST = new DialogState("FIRST_ONLY");
        }

    }

    class FirstLastInput_jRadioButtonFirst_itemAdapter implements java.awt.event.ItemListener
    {
        FirstLastInput adaptee;

        FirstLastInput_jRadioButtonFirst_itemAdapter(FirstLastInput adaptee)
        {
            this.adaptee = adaptee;
        }
        public void itemStateChanged(ItemEvent e)
        {
            adaptee.jRadioButtonFirst_itemStateChanged(e);
        }
    }

    class FirstLastInput_jRadioButtonLast_itemAdapter implements java.awt.event.ItemListener
    {
        FirstLastInput adaptee;

        FirstLastInput_jRadioButtonLast_itemAdapter(FirstLastInput adaptee)
        {
            this.adaptee = adaptee;
```

```
        }
        public void itemStateChanged(ItemEvent e)
        {
              adaptee.jRadioButtonLast_itemStateChanged(e);
        }
  }

  class FirstLastInput_jRadioButtonBoth_itemAdapter implements java.awt.event.ItemListener
  {
        FirstLastInput adaptee;

        FirstLastInput_jRadioButtonBoth_itemAdapter(FirstLastInput adaptee)
        {
              this.adaptee = adaptee;
        }
        public void itemStateChanged(ItemEvent e)
        {
              adaptee.jRadioButtonBoth_itemStateChanged(e);
        }
  }
  The code for launching the dialog looks like this:
  FirstLastInput firstLastDlg = new FirstLastInput(this, dMod);
  firstLastDlg.show();
```

The most important feature of this code is that it never touches the innards of either the program's data module or the FirstLastInput dialog. This is essentially important if you want to create reusable code that is easy to maintain.

Inside the FirstLast Input dialog, the interactions with the data module are kept to a minimum:

```
  public FirstLastInput(JFrame parent, DataModule1 dMod)
  {
        super(parent);
        this.fName = dMod.getFirstName();
        this.lName = dMod.getLastName();
        this.dMod = dMod;
        enableEvents(AWTEvent.WINDOW_EVENT_MASK);
        try
        {
              jbInit();
        }
        catch(Exception e)
        {
              e.printStackTrace();
        }
        setSize(400, 220);
        jTextFieldFirstName.setText(this.fName);
        jTextFieldLastName.setText(this.lName);
  }
```

The constructor of the FirstLastInput dialog uses methods of the data module called getFirstName and getLastName to retrieve the data from the current row. Notice that it is up to the data module to actually retrieve the data from the Artist dataset. To have the FirstLastInput dialog perform that task would be indiscreet.

Here is the relevant code from the data module:

```
private final static String firstNameField = "FIRST";
private final static String lastNameField= "LAST";

public String getFirstName()
{
      return queryDataSetArtist.getString(firstNameField);
}

public String getLastName()
{
      return queryDataSetArtist.getString(lastNameField);
}
```

These methods could not be more straightforward.

The following method of the FirstLastInput dialog sets the new data after the user has edited it:

```
public void actionPerformed(ActionEvent e)
{
      if (e.getSource() == jButtonCancel)
      {
            cancel();
      }
      else
      {
            if (dlgState == DialogState.FIRST_ONLY)
            {
                  dMod.setFirstName(jTextFieldFirstName.getText());
            }
            else if (dlgState == DialogState.LAST_ONLY)
            {
                  dMod.setLastName(jTextFieldLastName.getText());
            }
            else
            {
                  dMod.setFirstLastName(jTextFieldFirstName.getText(),
                        jTextFieldLastName.getText());
            }
            cancel();
      }
}
```

If the user presses the Cancel button, the whole operation is canceled, as if nothing had occurred. If the user wants to change the data, one of several methods is called, depending on whether the data to be changed is the first name, last name, or both names. The choice made by the user is determined by a small Java class designed to have the same functionality as an enumerated type would in Pascal or C++:

```
      private final static class DialogState
      {
```

```
        private final String name;

        private DialogState(String name)
        {
            this.name = name;
        }

        public String toString()
        {
            return name;
        }

        static final DialogState FIRST_ONLY = new DialogState("FIRST_ONLY");
        static final DialogState LAST_ONLY = new DialogState("LAST_ONLY");
        static final DialogState FIRST_LAST = new DialogState("FIRST_ONLY");
    }
```

These kinds of classes are discussed in Chapter 16.

Here is the code from the data module that is used to actually post the data to the dataset:

```
public void setFirstName(String firstName)
{
    queryDataSetArtist.setString(firstNameField, firstName);
    queryDataSetArtist.post();
}

public void setLastName(String lastName)
{
    queryDataSetArtist.setString(lastNameField, lastName);
    queryDataSetArtist.post();
}

public void setFirstLastName(String firstName, String lastName)
{
    queryDataSetArtist.setString(firstNameField, firstName);
    queryDataSetArtist.setString(lastNameField, lastName);
    queryDataSetArtist.post();
}
```

The first two methods set the values for the local copy of the dataset.

The key function is our calculated fields method from DataModule1.java, which has been rewritten to call queryDataSetArtist.saveChanges():

```
void queryDataSetArtist_calcFields(ReadRow changedRow, DataRow calcRow, boolean isPosted)
{
   String calculatedValue = changedRow.getString(firstNameField);
   calculatedValue += " " + changedRow.getString(lastNameField);
   calcRow.setString("firstLastCalc", calculatedValue);
   if (!isPosted)
   {
       queryDataSetArtist.saveChanges();
   }
}
```

This method was discussed in some depth earlier in the chapter. It is still the same method, except it has been modified to call saveChanges. It is this saveChanges method, and not the queryDataSetArtist.post() method, that will actually post the data back to the database server.

The calcFields method will be called automatically after either of the first two methods is called. Any changes to the current row will cause our calcFields method to be called. As suggested earlier in the chapter, you might want to add a System.out.println method (or a breakpoint) to this routine so that you can see when it is called:

```
if (!isPosted)
{
    System.out.println("queryDataSetArtist_calcFields Posted");
    queryDataSetArtist.saveChanges();
}
```

Notice that the code reverses the order of operations from our previous examples of this method. In this case, we really only care if the data is not posted. If that is the case, then we call saveChanges. If the data has not been posted, you can assume that new changes have occurred to the dataset.

NOTE: There are other logical ways to solve the problem described here. I am choosing this one simply because it illustrates the nature of the event handler for a calculated field.

Using the dbDisposeMonitor and Other Utilities

When you are creating a form that hosts data-aware controls, you will often want to add a dbDisposeMonitor from the More dbSwing page. This component will ensure that all the data-aware components on your JFrame or JPanel have their dataSet properties set to null when you close the window that owns them. Doing so will allow Java to more effectively clean up memory for your applications that use data-aware controls. In particular, it will allow the garbage collector to do its work.

As a general rule, I would suggest placing a dbDisposeMonitor on all your frames or panels that use data-aware controls. Simply use the Inspector to set the dataAwareComponentContainer property of the dbDisposeMonitor to **this**, and you should be fine.

It is possible to do a little more fine tuning of a dbDisposeMonitor. For instance, there are Boolean properties specifying whether or not you want to close database connections on your component. There is also a non-visual property called dataSetAwareComponents that takes an array of data-aware components. To use the property, type in syntax that looks like this:

```
dBDisposeMonitor1.setDataSetAwareComponents( new DataSetAware[] {albumView1.jdbTable1});
```

You would use this property in lieu of the dataAwareComponentContainer property. If you set the dataAwareComponentContainer, the dataSetAwareComponents property is ignored. The executeOnWindowClosing property designates whether the control frees up resources when a window simply closes, rather than when it is disposed.

Other utilities that you might want to use include the DBExceptionHandler for displaying an error when DataSetException occurs.

The DBEventMonitor helps you debug your component by reporting the events fired by your datasets. The dBEventMonitor1.setPrintStream() method can be used to set the print stream to a text file. Or you can simply have the output sent to standard out, which is where it goes by default.

Simply drop the DBEventMonitor from the More dbSwing page of the component palette onto a JFrame or JPanel where you have data-aware controls. Set the dataAwareComponent-Container property to bold or to a control that you want to monitor. Now run your application. As you work with your dataset, data about events occurring to it will be sent to standard out. Here are a few lines of output from the monitor. Please note that I have used the \ character to wrap long bits of text to the next line:

```
DBEventMonitor[Sun Apr 14 17:28:02 PDT 2002] source: \
  HOUSEADDRESS, NavigateListener.navigated()
DBEventMonitor[Sun Apr 14 17:28:06 PDT 2002] \
  EditListener.modifying(dataSet: HOUSEADDRESS)
DBEventMonitor[Sun Apr 14 17:28:06 PDT 2002] source: \
  HOUSEADDRESS StatusListener.statusMessage:
StatusEvent.EDIT_STARTED or StatusEvent.SORTING
DBEventMonitor[Sun Apr 14 17:28:09 PDT 2002]source: \
  HOUSEADDRESS DataChangeListener.dataChanged: \
  DataChangeEvent.ROW_CHANGED, rowAffected: 2
DBEventMonitor[Sun Apr 14 17:28:09 PDT 2002] source: \
  HOUSEADDRESS DataChangeListener.postRow(): \
  DataChangeEvent.POST_ROW, rowAffected: -1
```

In Listing 42-3 you will find methods that can be used to open and close a stream that can be written to by a DBEventMonitor. Notice that I call closeStream from inside the default processWindowEvent method, which JBuilder creates for all standard JFrame objects.

Listing 42-3: The getStream and closeStreams methods can be used to create a file stream that can be passed to the dbEventMonitor.

```
FileOutputStream fw;
PrintStream ps;

private PrintStream getStream(String fileName)
{
      fw = null;
      ps = null;
      try
      {
            fw = new FileOutputStream(fileName);
            ps = new PrintStream(fw);
      }
      catch(IOException e)
      {
            System.out.println(e);
      }
      return ps;
}

private void closeStream()
{
      try
      {
            ps.close();
            fw.close();
```

```
        }
        catch(IOException e)
        {
            System.out.println(e);
        }
    }

    // Standard constructor with code to initialize the dbEventMonitor
    public Frame1()
    {
        enableEvents(AWTEvent.WINDOW_EVENT_MASK);
        try
        {
            jbInit();
        } catch(Exception e)
        {
            e.printStackTrace();
        }
        String fileName = FileBox.makeHomeDirectory("elvenware") + "one2mn.txt";
        PrintStream stream = getStream(fileName);
        dBEventMonitor1.setPrintStream(stream);
    }

    protected void processWindowEvent(WindowEvent e)
    {
        super.processWindowEvent(e);
        if (e.getID() == WindowEvent.WINDOW_CLOSING)
        {
            closeStream();
            System.exit(0);
        }
    }
```

An example of using the DBEventMonitor is included in the OneToManyCalc program found on the CD that accompanies this book. Remember, however, that to get the monitor to write to standard out, all you have to do is set the DBEventMonitor dataAwareComponent-Container property to a JFrame, JPanel, or some other appropriate control. The code shown here is only necessary if you want to write to a text file rather than to standard out.

I should add that there is a bit more flexibility in the DBEventMonitor component than I have shown here. For instance, you can associate it with a specific dataset via the DBEvent-Monitor setDataSets property. This is useful if you want to use the component in a non-visual component. You can also monitor particular components if you choose. Here is how to proceed:

```
dBEventMonitor1.setDataSetAwareComponents(new DataSetAware[] {artistView1.dbTable1});
```

In this code, I am accessing the table that we dropped onto the ArtistView panel. By default, that table will have protected access. You should explicitly set it to have public access, since it does not reside in the same package as Frame1. You will probably also have to add an import com.Borland.dx.dataset.* statement to the top of Frame1. When you are done, however, you can see an output of only the events that occur to the JdbTable object in the ArtistView component. The following shows some of the code that is generated when you open the table and edit the first record:

```
DBEventMonitor[Mon Apr 15 12:57:38 PDT 2002] source: artist LoadListener.dataLoaded()
DBEventMonitor[Mon Apr 15 12:57:38 PDT 2002] source: artist AccessListener.accessChange()
AccessEvent.OPEN, reason: , AccessEvent.UNSPECIFIED
DBEventMonitor[Mon Apr 15 12:58:57 PDT 2002] EditListener.modifying(dataSet: artist)
DBEventMonitor[Mon Apr 15 12:58:57 PDT 2002] source: artist StatusListener.statusMessage:
StatusEvent.EDIT_STARTED or StatusEvent.SORTING
Value: 198 false
DBEventMonitor[Mon Apr 15 12:58:57 PDT 2002]source: artist DataChangeListener.dataChanged:
DataChangeEvent.ROW_CHANGED, rowAffected: 0
DBEventMonitor[Mon Apr 15 12:58:57 PDT 2002] EditListener.updating(dataSet: artist, newRow:
com.borland.dx.sql.dataset.QueryDataSet@6bade9:CODE=1:LAST=Dylan:FIRST=Bobby:BORN=2001-07-15
00:00:00.0:DIED=2-11-30 00:00:00.0:BIRTHPLACE=Hibbing
MN:COMMENT=com.borland.jb.io.InputStreamToByteArray@59a68:ARTISTTYPE=1:firstLastCalc=, oldRow:
com.borland.dx.dataset.InternalRow@5c62bc:CODE=1:LAST=Dylan:FIRST=Bob:BORN=2001-07-15
00:00:00.0:DIED=2-11-30 00:00:00.0:BIRTHPLACE=Hibbing
MN:COMMENT=com.borland.jb.io.InputStreamToByteArray@59a68:ARTISTTYPE=1:firstLastCalc=Bob Dylan)
```

If you wanted to work with the ALBUM table rather than the ARTIST table, you would add code that works with the albumView1 variable rather than the artistView1 variable:

```
dBEventMonitor1.setDataSetAwareComponents(new DataSetAware[] {albumView1.dbTable1});
```

DBPassword promptor will pop up a password dialog to the user at the appropriate time. The easiest way to use this latter control is to check the password option on the Connection dialog you access when selecting the Database component in your data module and click on the ellipsis in the connection property. This changes the way your call to setConnection looks. In this example, you are not prompted for a password:

```
database.setConnection(
      new ConnectionDescriptor(
      "jdbc:mysql://localhost/jbbook",
      "charlie",
      "foo",                        // This is the password itself
      false,                        // Don't prompt for password
      "org.gjt.mm.mysql.Driver"));
```

In this example, you are prompted for a password:

```
database.setConnection(
      new ConnectionDescriptor(
      "jdbc:mysql://localhost/jbbook",
      "charlie",
      null,                         // Password set to null
      true,                         // Prompt the user for a password
      "org.gjt.mm.mysql.Driver"));
```

Summary

In this chapter you have learned about one-to-many relationships and calculated fields. The material presented here should also give you a good sense of how to go about developing database applications in JBuilder. In particular, there was less reliance on application generators in this chapter. Instead, you had to get your hands dirty manipulating the database-aware controls themselves via the properties exposed in the Inspector.

The very end of the chapter mentioned the DBDisposeMonitor, which can be used to help you clean up database resources.

Chapter 43

Database Strategies

Charlie Calvert

In this chapter you will learn about various strategies for creating powerful database applications. Subjects covered include searching, lookups, and wrapping up your application in a JAR file.

This chapter is a continuation of the same type of material covered in the previous chapter. The goal is simply to round out the basic information you need to create powerful database applications.

Searching

There are two different techniques you can use in JBuilder to search through the records in a dataset. One involves using a component called the JdbNavField, which is found on the More dbSwing page of the component palette. The second technique involves methods of QueryDataSet called locate and lookup. I will handle each technique in turn, beginning with the JdbNavField.

NOTE: Do not confuse the JdbNavField with the JdbNavToolBar.

Using JdbNavField

The JdbNavField is an easy-to-use Borland component that helps you search through the rows in your dataset. On string fields, it will perform an incremental search, moving to the next closest match in the dataset as the user types in values. For instance, if the user types in "J," he or she will be moved to the first record that has an entry in a particular field beginning with a "J." If the user types in "Ja," he or she will be moved to the first record with a field containing data that begins with a "Ja," and so on.

I'll begin with a quick summary of how to use a JdbNavField. After you get a feeling for how easy it is to use the component, I will explain in more detail how to build an application that uses it:

- Create a sample database application using the JBuilder wizards or tools.
- Display a dataset in a JdbTable.
- Drop down a JdbNavField and hook its dataset property to your QueryDataSet.
- Run your application.

At run time, you can select the field you want to search on by clicking on the JdbTable grid itself. At first, click on any string field in your JdbTable. Type something in the JdbNavField; you should be able to do an incremental search on the values in that field. For numerical fields, enter the value you want to search for and press Enter to perform the search. You can perform a case-insensitive search by typing only lowercase letters. Uppercase or mixed case letters initialize a case-sensitive search. By default, the control will use your status bar to display information.

The JdbNavField has a columnName property that can be used to focus the control on a particular field, regardless of which column the user clicks on. To put the matter somewhat differently, if you use the columnName field, the user loses the ability to dynamically change the field on which he or she is searching. Instead, the control is hard-coded to use the field you selected.

Here is a more detailed tutorial for creating a test program that uses a JdbNavField:

- Create a new project.
- Select **File | New | Data Module** from the menu. Make sure the **Invoke Data Modeler** option is selected.
- In the Data Modeler, choose the **jbbook** database. (This database was explained in Chapter 39.)
- Select the **HOUSEADDRESS** table and choose the **Copy All** button.
- Select **File | Save** and then **File | Exit** from the Data Modeler menu.
- Choose **File | New | Data Module Application** from the menu. Click **OK** in the first screen of the wizard to create the application.
- Perform a build in your application and then use the project pane to select the automatically generated HouseAddressUIBean from the DataModule1.twotier package.
- Go into design mode on HouseAddressUIBean and delete the navigator control from the top of the application.
- Turn to the **More dbSwing** page in the component palette and select the **JdbNavField**. Drop it down into the structure pane on the node labeled "this." The nav field should now occupy the place previously held by the navigation control.
- Click on the ellipsis in the constraints property for the JdbNavField to pop up a GridBagLayout dialog. Set the fill property at the bottom of the dialog to **Both**. Close the GridBagLayout dialog. Select the dataset property and set it to **dataset**. Select the columnName property and use the drop-down list to set it to the **NAME** field.
- We now need to configure JBuilder so that a click on the green run button will launch your newly created application. Choose **Project | Project Properties** and turn to the **Run** page. Press the **New** button and set up DataModule1TwoTierApp as the main class for your program.
- Run the application and type words into the JdbNavField. For instance, try typing in **Sam**, as shown in Figure 43-1.

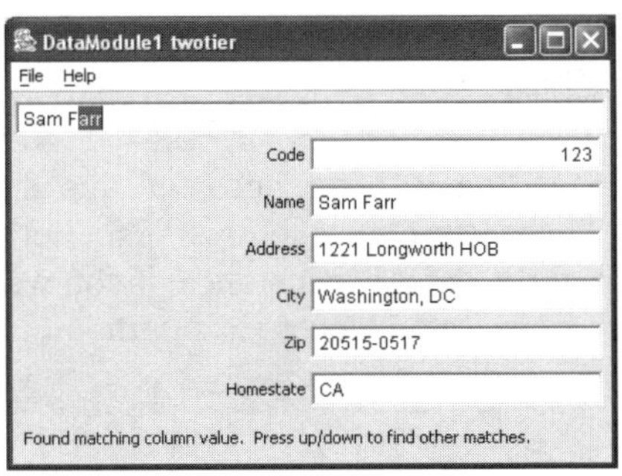

Figure 43-1: Using the JdbNavTool to search on the NAME field in the HouseAddress table

A somewhat more complex example program called NavTool is available on the CD that accompanies this book. In that example program, there are two pages, one similar to Figure 43-1. The second page will allow you to experiment with the ability to click on the JdbTable in order to select a new field on which to search. Remember that when searching on numeric fields, you need to enter the number, and then press Enter to complete the search. The NavTool program is shown in Figure 43-2.

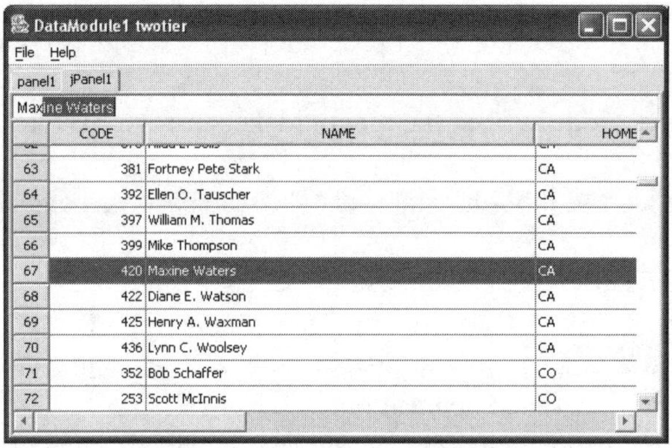

Figure 43-2: The JdbNavTool can be set up so that the user can click on a field in the JdbTable grid in order to select the column they wish to search on.

The NavTool example program is one in which the ability to drag a column into a new position can be useful. For instance, in Figure 43-2, the HomeState column, by default, appears in the last column of the dataset. I used the mouse to enlarge it and then drag it next to the Name field. This is a built-in feature of JdbTable.

Searching with Locate and Lookup

The second way to search through a dataset is to use the locate method. Here is the declaration for the method as it is appears in com.borland.dx.dataset.DataSet:

```
public final boolean locate(ReadRow rowLocate, int locateOptions)
```

We have encountered the ReadRow object before, but it is time now to take a closer look at it. ReadRow is a class designed to give you read-only access to one row of data from a dataset. Its companion object is ReadWriteRow, which gives you read and write access to a row.

The majority of methods in ReadRow are getters custom made for each of the possible types supported by a column in a dataset:

```
public final byte          getByte(int ordinal)
public final boolean       getBoolean(int ordinal)
public final java.sql.Date getDate(int ordinal)
public final int           getInt(int ordinal)
public final String        getString(int ordinal)
```

There are many more of these methods than I have shown here, but this should be enough to give you an idea of what they are about. The parameter taken by these methods is the number of the column from which you want to draw the data. For instance, if you want to retrieve data from the fifth column in the currently active row, you would pass in the number 4:

```
getString(4); // Zero based, so 4 is the fifth column.
```

You can also access the methods by column name rather than by the column offset. For instance, if you had a database with the fields Code, FirstName, LastName, Address, and Zip, you could access the FirstName field as follows:

```
String firstName = getString("FirstName");
```

A ReadWriteRow will, of course, have a corresponding set of setters to go with each of these get methods. The ReadRow and ReadWriteRow objects also have the ability to copy themselves to another row. This results in duplicating the row.

By now it should be fairly easy to guess how the locate method works. You create and fill in the values of a ReadRow object, and DataExpress attempts to locate the object for you.

```
public void locateField(String colName, String searchStr)
{
      // Create a DataRow object to define the row we want to find.
      DataRow datarow = new DataRow(address, colName);

      // Insert our search string into the DataRow
      datarow.setString(colName, searchStr);

      // Locate the new row
      address.locate(datarow, options);
}
```

In this example, address is a standard QueryDataSet of the kind we have been looking at over and over again in the last few chapters. In an example like this, the locate method would, by default, find the first instance of a row that contained the string on which we were searching. This is defined by the options parameter to the locate method. The contents of the options variable will be discussed later in this chapter.

You may have noticed that this code works with a DataRow, rather than a ReadRow or ReadWriteRow. A DataRow is a descendant of ReadWriteRow custom made for performing searches, inserts, and updates.

Notice also that the code uses the address QueryDataSet when creating the DataRow:

```
DataRow datarow = new DataRow(address, colName);
```

This is necessary in order to ensure that the row will work correctly with this particular dataset. If the dataset were restructured at run time, you would need to create a new instance of DataRow.

It should not come as a surprise to hear that you can search on multiple fields:

```
public void locateFirstLast(String firstName, String lastName)
{
      // The name of the column to search on
      String firstColName = "FNAME";
      String lastColName = "LNAME";

      // Create a DataRow object to define the row we want to find.
      DataRow datarow = new DataRow(address, new String[] {firstColName, lastColName});

      // Insert our search string into the DataRow
      datarow.setString(firstColName, firstName);
      datarow.setString(lastColName, lastName);
```

```
        // Locate the new row
        address.locate(datarow, options);
    }
```

In this code the DataRow object has two columns defined, one for searching on the first name field and one for searching on the last name field. This will allow you to make a much more specific search.

The locate method, besides taking a DataRow, also takes an option parameter of type Locate:

```
interface Locate
{
        public static final int PARTIAL          = 0x1;
        public static final int NEXT             = 0x2;
        public static final int PRIOR            = 0x4;
        public static final int CASE_INSENSITIVE = 0x8;
        public static final int FIRST            = 0x20;
        public static final int LAST             = 0x40;
        public static final int FAST             = 0x80;
        static final int DETAIL                  = 0x100;
        public static final int NEXT_FAST        = NEXT|FAST;
        public static final int PRIOR_FAST       = PRIOR|FAST;
        static final       int START_MASK       = (FIRST|LAST|NEXT|PRIOR);
}
```

This interface is fairly intuitive. For instance, the first member, PARTIAL, allows you to perform searches on partial matches on string columns. For instance, "Ja" would match the word "Java." You can also search for the next or previous instance of a match. The FAST option allows you to use values from the previous search, which cuts down a bit on the search time. The START_MASK and DETAIL options are for internal use of the DataExpress engine.

You can, and often will, combine more than one of these fields from the Locate interface using the pipe symbol:

```
private final static int options = Locate.CASE_INSENSITIVE | Locate.FIRST | Locate.PARTIAL;
```

NOTE: The Locate interface can be a bit troublesome at times. In particular, it is not included in the compiled version of dx.jar included in either JBuilder 6 or 7. As a result, it can be difficult to run a version of a program that uses it from the command line. One solution is to use the Archive Builder to create a JAR file that includes the appropriate source. Another solution is to take the code from the src directory and create your own version of the Locate.class file. All of these options will be discussed in the section of this chapter on creating database JAR files.

On the CD you will find an example program called ElfAddress. The example code you have been looking at is drawn from that program.

The search dialog from ElfAddress is shown in Figure 43-3. A dialog very similar to this made an appearance in a program from the previous chapter. This time, the main purpose of the dialog is to allow the user to search on the first name field, last name field, or both.

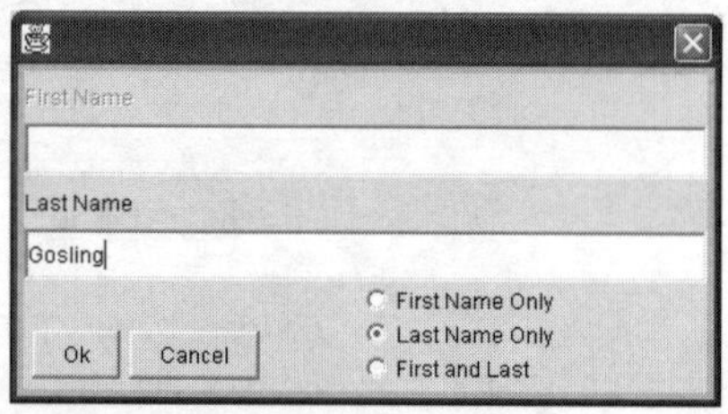

Figure 43-3: Searching for data in the ADDRESS table

Here is the code from the LookupDialog that calls the methods that do the searching:

```
// dMod is an instance of the data module
DMod dMod;

if (dlgState == DialogState.FIRST_ONLY)
{
      dMod.locateFirst(jTextFieldFirstName.getText());
}
else if (dlgState == DialogState.LAST_ONLY)
{
      dMod.locateLast(jTextFieldLastName.getText());
}
else
{
      dMod.locateFirstLast(jTextFieldFirstName.getText(),
            jTextFieldLastName.getText());
}
```

As you perhaps recall from an earlier chapter, the DialogState type is an "enumerated class," designed to emulate enumerated types in a Java program.

Listing 43-1 shows several methods from the data module that perform different types of searches.

Listing 43-1: Here is a series of methods for locating data in a dataset. The first three methods use locate, while the fourth method is a call to the lookup method.

```
private final static int options =
            Locate.CASE_INSENSITIVE | Locate.FIRST | Locate.PARTIAL;

public void locateField(String colName, String searchStr)
{

      // Create a DataRow object to define the row we want to find.
      DataRow datarow = new DataRow(address, colName);

      // Insert our search string into the DataRow
      datarow.setString(colName, searchStr);

      // Locate the new row
      address.locate(datarow, options);
}

public void locateFirst(String searchStr)
{
      locateField("FNAME", searchStr);
}

/**
 * Locate a row in the data set
 *
 * @param searchStr The string to search for
 */
```

```
public void locateLast(String searchStr)
{
      locateField("LNAME", searchStr);
}

/**
 * Locate a row in a dataset and move the users view to that position.
 *
 * @param firstName The first name of the row you want to find
 * @param lastName The last name of the row you want to find.
 */
public void locateFirstLast(String firstName, String lastName)
{
      // The name of the column to search on
      String firstColName = "FNAME";
      String lastColName = "LNAME";

      // Create a DataRow object to define the row we want to find.
      DataRow datarow = new DataRow(address, new String[] {firstColName, lastColName});

      // Insert our search string into the DataRow
      datarow.setString(firstColName, firstName);
      datarow.setString(lastColName, lastName);

      // Locate the new row
      address.locate(datarow, options);
}

/**
 * Lookup a row in the data set. This option finds the row, but does
 * not move you to it.
 *
 *
 * @param searchStr The string to search for
 */
public void lookupFirstLast(String firstName, String lastName)
{
      // The name of the columns to search on
      String lastColName = "LNAME";
      String firstColName = "FNAME";

      // Create a row to search for
      DataRow rowToFind = new DataRow(address, new String[] {firstColName, lastColName});

      // Insert our search strings into the DataRow
      rowToFind.setString(firstColName, firstName);
      rowToFind.setString(lastColName, lastName);

      // Create a DataRow object to define the returned row.
      DataRow returnRow = new DataRow(address);
```

```
        // Locate the new row with specific options
        address.lookup(rowToFind, returnRow, options);

        // Report the results
        System.out.println("row: " + returnRow.getString(lastColName) +
             ", " +   returnRow.getString(firstColName));
    }
```

You may have noticed that I have thrown you a wild card here in the very last method. At first glance, it might look very much like the previous method, locateFirstLast. The last method, however, calls lookup instead of locate. The difference is that lookup returns a copy of the row it found but does not navigate to that row. locate, on the other hand, does not return a copy of the row, but rather moves the cursor on the dataset to the row that it found. You would use locate if the user wanted to view a particular row and lookup when you wanted to write background code that needed to search a particular location.

NOTE: A database cursor points at the currently selected row in a dataset. One of the features of a JBuilder dataset is that it supports the concept of a cursor. You can move the cursor using methods such as first(), last(), next(), and prior().

Lookups and Picklists

I am now going to discuss a tool called a lookup, or picklist. In this context, the word "lookup" is completely distinct from the lookup method discussed in the previous section.

A lookup is a bit like a one-to-many relationship in that it defines a connection between two tables based on certain fields. It also is a little bit like a database equivalent of an enumerated type. In JBuilder, a lookup is often referred to as a picklist.

NOTE: As you will see, lookups are — at least conceptually — quite simple. The basic task you want to perform is not difficult. For reasons that are not entirely clear to me, JBuilder can make it quite trying for you to actually use a lookup in your program. In my opinion, this is just one of the areas where JBuilder didn't get it quite right. Nevertheless, this is a subject that you can master if you just take a little time with it.

Before showing you how to build a lookup, let's spend a second understanding how one is put together. This part of the process should be quite straightforward and easy to understand.

Suppose you have a set of categories, such as Good, Bad, and Ugly. You could encapsulate these values inside a simple table called RATING that looks like this:

1	Good
2	Bad
3	Ugly

You should make the first field of the RATING table a primary key.

In your main table, you might want to rate certain entries via a numeric lookup into the RATING table:

1	Clint Eastwood	Blondie	1
2	Lee Van Cleef	Sentenza	2
3	Eli Wallach	Tuco	3
4	Sergio Leone	Director	1

In this table, the fourth column is a lookup column into the RATING table. The numbers in the fourth column refer to rows in the RATING table. The number 1 references the row with the word Good in it, and so on.

NOTE: Though it may not be strictly necessary in all databases, I think it is best to set a column like the fourth one shown here as a foreign key that references the RATING table. That way you can ensure that the values entered into the main table refer to real values in the lookup table.

In a parallel universe, the second table could have looked like this:

1	Clint Eastwood	Blondie	Good
2	Lee Van Cleef	Sentenza	Bad
3	Eli Wallach	Tuco	Ugly
4	Sergio Leone	Director	Good

There are three reasons that this second version is inferior to the first:

- The words Good, Bad, and Ugly take up more room than the numbers 1, 2, and 3.
- If the users have to type in the values Good, Bad, and Ugly, they might make spelling errors.
- Finally, users might start making up their own inappropriate categories, such as Pretty or Dainty. (If you've seen the movie, you would understand that categories such as Dainty simply don't apply in this case!)

So now you know why a string field is not a good option for the fourth column in the previous table. There are, however, also problems with the idea of using numbers that represent words.

The problem with inserting numbers such as 1, 2, and 3 into the table is that they are, in and of themselves, meaningless. This is the same problem that enumerated types are designed to solve. If you associate the number 1 with the word Good, you can simply use the word Good whenever you want to refer to the number 1. In many cases, a mnemonic of that sort can help stave off confusion. However, you have to provide some means of connecting the number 1 with the word Good, or users will get confused.

Lookup fields are designed to solve this problem. They perform a small miracle, or rather a sleight of hand, that allows you to simultaneously use the number 1 for the fourth column in this table and the word Good. Let me explain.

A lookup field inserts a drop-down list of values directly into a JdbTable object. In this case, it will put the drop-down list in the fourth field of the table.

When the user wants to make a change to the fourth field of this table, he can simply pick the appropriate value from a drop-down list that appears automatically in the JdbTable itself. You can see an example of this in Figure 43-4. Here the lookup table contains the words Unknown, Compact Disk, Tape, etc., rather than the words Good, Bad, and Ugly. The theory behind the technology, however, is unchanged. Instead of seeing numbers, the user is given a list of strings from which to choose.

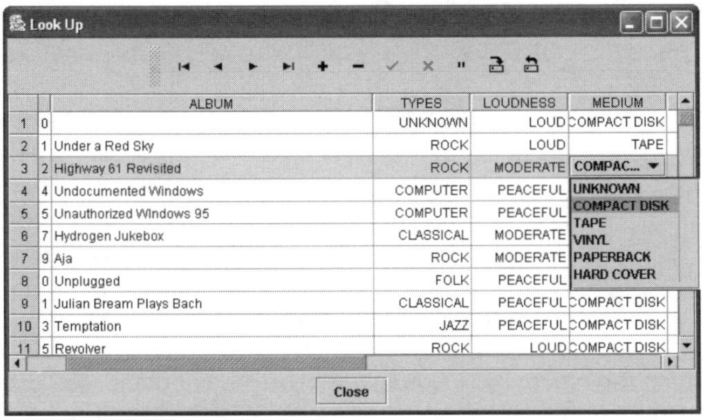

Figure 43-4: The Lookup project on the CD shows how to build a lookup.

Creating a Program that Contains Lookups

NOTE: In this section you will find that there are both tables and fields with the names LOUDNESS, MEDIUM, and TYPES. When you are writing code, this ends up being a simple and clean way to proceed. However, it can be confusing to read about at times. I will try to state specifically whether I am talking about a field or a table, and I will present some special examples that will help to make the distinction completely clear.

To create your own lookup program like the one shown in Figure 43-4, you can use the ALBUM, LOUDNESS, MEDIUM, and TYPES tables from the jbbook database. See Chapter 39 for details on creating the jbbook database.

The ALBUM table contains a list of albums. There are three lookup fields in the table called LOUDNESS, MEDIUM, and TYPES. They are all of type integer. The LOUDNESS table contains lookup values such as Peaceful, Moderate, and Loud. The MEDIUM table is shown in Figure 43-4. The TYPES table contains values such as Classical, Jazz, Folk, New Age, etc.

To begin, create a new default JBuilder project and add a default application. Choose **File | New DataModule** and deselect the **Invoke Data Modeler** option. Click **OK** to create a default data module.

Focus the data module in the content pane and switch to design mode. Turn to the DataExpress page on the component palette and drop down a Database and QueryDataSet object onto the Data Access node in the structure pane. Call the Database **jbbook** and the QueryDataSet **queryDataSetAlbum**, as shown in Figure 43-5.

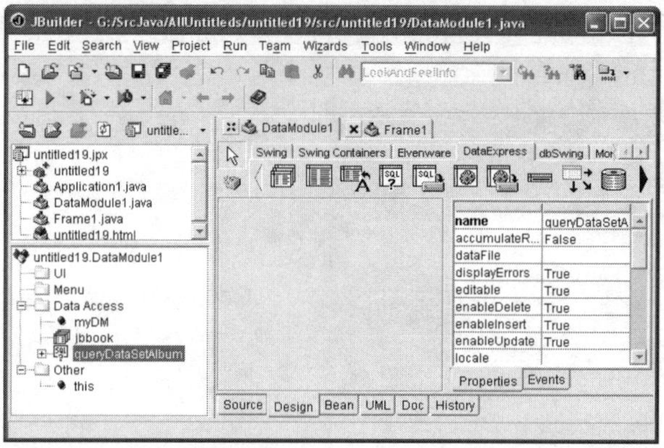

Figure 43-5: Setting up the Database and QueryDataSet objects in a simple data module

Click on the ellipsis button for the connection property of the jbbook database object. Click **Choose Existing Connection** and pick a connection to your jbbook database, as described in Chapters 39 and 42. Type in a password and test the connection, as shown in Figure 43-6.

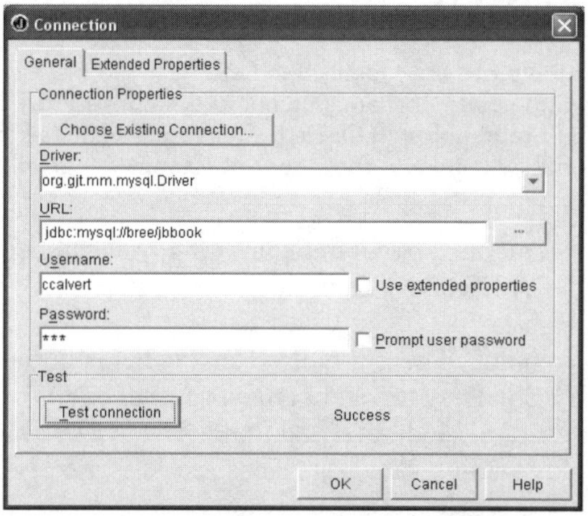

Figure 43-6: Creating a connection to a database. You should have set up existing connections in Chapter 39.

Click on the **queryDataSetAlbum** component and select the query property in the Inspector. Use the tools to create a SELECT statement for all the fields in the ALBUM table, as shown in Figure 43-7. This operation has been described numerous times so far in the book, so I'll let you carry it out without further description.

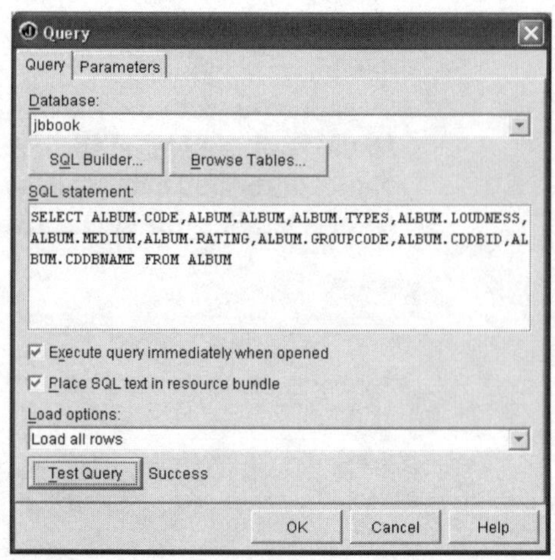

Figure 43-7: Using the JBuilder tools to create a simple query on the ALBUM table

You should now repeat this same process for the LOUDNESS, TYPES, and MEDIUM tables. Drop down a QueryDataSet for each table, name it appropriately, and select all the fields from each table. Put all your queries into a resource bundle. If you forget to use the resource bundle the first time, simply open the query again, check the appropriate option, and click the **OK** button. When you are done, your data module should look as it does in Figure 43-8.

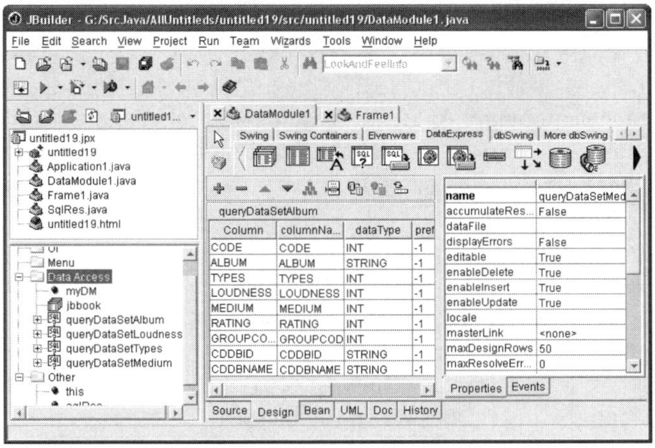

Figure 43-8: Setting up the data module to support the LOUDNESS, TYPES, and MEDIUM tables. Notice the structure pane in particular.

At last all the setup work is done, and it is time to begin defining the lookups themselves. In JBuilder a lookup is sometimes referred to as a picklist. Picklists are defined not on QueryDataSets but on columns. You access the columns for a table by clicking the plus sign to the left of a QueryDataSet component in the structure pane, as shown in Figure 43-9.

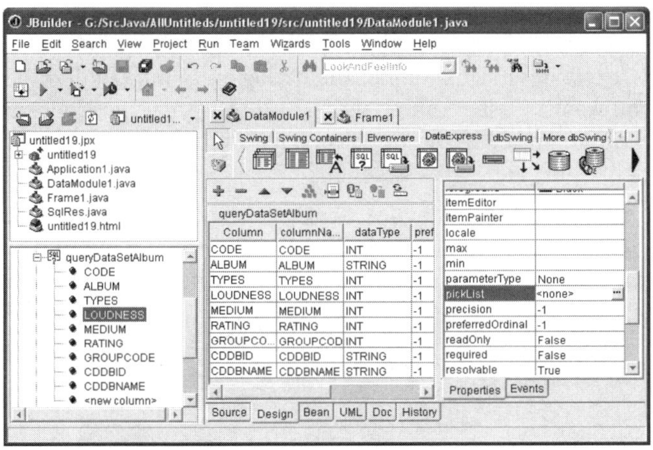

Figure 43-9: Selecting the pickList property for the LOUDNESS column in the ALBUM table

Select the pickList property to pop up the PickList dialog, as shown in Figure 43-10. This dialog is not easy to use.

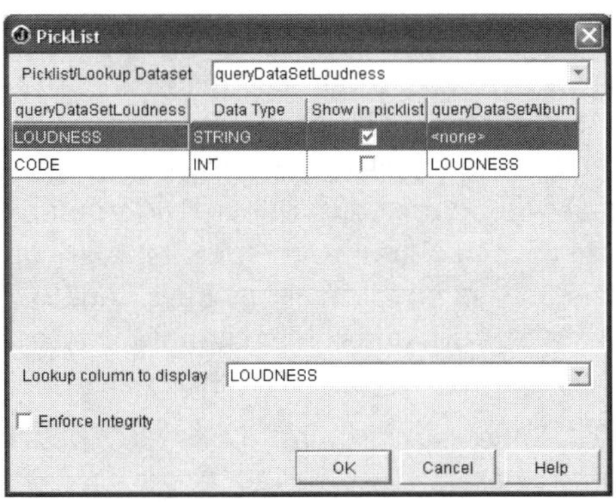

Figure 43-10: Filling in the PickList dialog to establish a relationship between the ALBUM and LOUDNESS table such that that the user can pick values from the LOUDNESS table

When thinking about the PickList dialog, consider the following facts:

- The main table and column that you are using are already selected because you are working with the Loudness field of the ALBUM table. If you think of a lookup operation as a master-detail relationship, ALBUM is the master table and LOUDNESS is the detail table. You don't need to specify the ALBUM table in this dialog because you used the ALBUM table to reach the dialog. In particular, you used the LOUDNESS column of the ALBUM table.
- The Picklist/Lookup Dataset at the top, called queryDataSetLoudness, is the dataset on which you want to perform the lookup. It is the detail half of this relationship.
- After selecting the LOUDNESS dataset, you can see its fields, called LOUDNESS and CODE, in the table that takes up the approximate center of the dialog. The first line in this table states that you want to display the values from the Loudness field of the LOUDNESS table when the user drops down the picklist. Therefore, check the **Show in picklist** box for this line of the table. You also want to associate the CODE field of the LOUDNESS table with the Loudness field of the ALBUM table. Therefore, use the second line of the table to specify that the integer Code field of the LOUDNESS table is linked to the integer Loudness field of the ALBUM table.
- At the bottom of the dialog, choose the column of the ALBUM table where you want to display the default value from the LOUDNESS table. If the Loudness field of the ALBUM table is set to the value 2, you don't want to show that integer value; instead, you want to show a String value from the LOUDNESS table that is associated with the number 2. What you are doing in this field of the dialog is telling JBuilder which field of the ALBUM table you want to use to show the String. And yes, the Loudness field of the ALBUM table is of type integer, but the "miracle" of the picklist technology is that it replaces these abstract integers with strings.

If you give up on using the dialog (and I usually do), or if you give up on trying to parse my explanation of the dialog (for which I can't blame you), you will find that typing in the code is not too difficult. Go to the jbInit of your data module and type in the following code:

```
column1.setPickList(
      new PickListDescriptor(
            QueryDataSetLoudness,
            new String[] {"CODE"},
            new String[] {"LOUDNESS"},
            new String[] {"LOUDNESS"},
            "LOUDNESS",
            false));
```

The parameters here are tricky. The first is the dataset containing the lookup values. The second parameter is the column in the lookup (pick) list that the link is made on. For instance, in the LOUDNESS table, that would be the CODE column. The third parameter is the column from the picklist that contains the values you want to display in the drop-down list. The fourth parameter is the field from the master list that will be linked to the CODE column in the picklist table. The fifth parameter is the name of the column in the picklist that contains the value you want to display in the grid when the user is not actively picking items. The final parameter, which you can ignore for now, has to do with enforcing data integrity constraints on the data added to the columns.

```
new PickListDescriptor(
  QueryDataSetTypes,        // Dataset containing the lookup values.
```

```
    new String[] {"CODE"},    // The link column in the pick list.
    new String[] {"LOUDNESS"},// The column from pick to display in drop down.
    new String[] {"LOUDNESS"},// The column to show values in.
    "LOUDNESS",               // Column from the pick list to display in grid
    true));
```

It is, I believe, appropriate to name the fields of the two tables as I have here. However, in this case, there may be some confusion because the tables use the same names for associated fields. For the sake of clarity, let me show you what things would look like were we linking in the GOOD_BAD_AND_UGLY table rather than the LOUDNESS table:

```
create table GOOD_BAD_AND_UGLY
(
      GBUCode int NOT NULL,
      Description VARCHAR(10),
      PRIMARY KEY (GBUCode)
) TYPE=INNODB;
insert into GOOD_BAD_AND_UGLY values (1, "GOOD");
insert into GOOD_BAD_AND_UGLY values (2, "BAD");
insert into GOOD_BAD_AND_UGLY values (3, "UGLY");
```

NOTE: This table should be in the jbbook database. If it is not, and you want to follow along, you can simply open the jbbook database in the Database Pilot. Turn to the Enter SQL page and type in the lines shown here. Press the Execute button. In this example, I have included the TYPE=INNODB clause, which should only be used if you are using MySQL.

Add a new QueryDataSet to your example. Use its query property to select all the fields of the GOOD_BAD_AND_UGLY table, just as you did for the other QueryDataSets. Select the Medium field of the QUERYDATASETALBUM table. Pop up the PickList dialog and fill in the values, as shown in Figure 43-11.

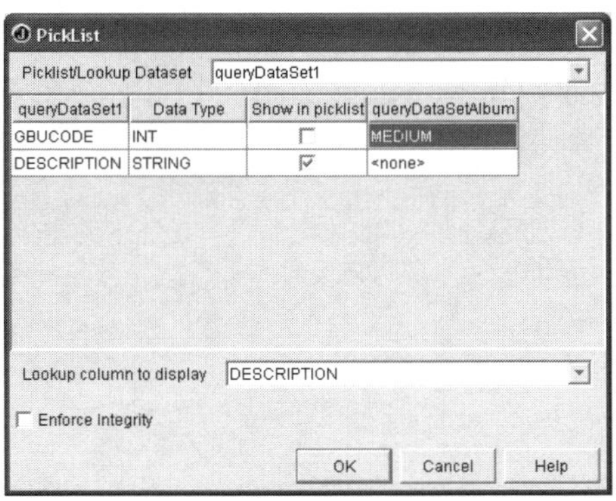

Figure 43-11: Linking in the Good, the Bad, and the Ugly

Here is the code produced by the dialog shown in Figure 43-11:

```
column2.setPickList(new PickListDescriptor(
      QueryDataSetGBU,               // Query data set containinglookup
      new String[] {"GBUCODE"},      // Field(s) in lookup table to link on
      new String[] {"DESCRIPTION"},  // Row containing values for dropdown
      new String[] {"MEDIUM"},       // Column in main table to display in
      "DESCRIPTION",                 // Field from lookup to display in grid
      false));                       // Whether or not to enforce integrity
```

It should now be easier to see which fields come from the lookup table and which from the main table.

NOTE: The most confusing items in the PickListDescripter are the third and fifth. The point here is that you might not use the same field of the lookup table to display in the grid and in the drop down. I am not sure why that is considered useful, but the option is available to you.

Because this is a difficult subject, let me try to hammer the point home by showing you the actual declaration of the PickListDescriptor in the JBuilder source code:

```
public PickListDescriptor
(
  DataSet   pickListDataSet,       // Dataset containing the lookup fields
  String[]  pickListColumns,       // Column or columns in lookup to link on
  String[]  pickListDisplayColumns,// Column(s) to show in the drop-down list
  String[]  destinationColumns,    // Column(s) in main table to display in
  String    lookupDisplayColumn,   // Column from lookup to display in grid
  boolean   enforceIntegrity       // Use data integrity?
)
```

When looking at these columns, remember that you knew from the beginning which column was the main table and which field in the main table you would link to the pickListColumns in the lookup table. Other matters, such as why some fields are called pickListXXX and others are called lookupXXX, I will leave for the reader to contemplate.

An Introduction to the JBuilder Column Object

In the next few paragraphs I am going to introduce you to one of the key concepts in DataExpress: the Column class. Columns play a key role in JDBC programming, and since DataExpress is based on the JDBC, columns have also come to play an important role in DataExpress.

By studying columns, you will be able to complete your understanding of what is happening when you create a lookup. So far, I have only shown you a portion of the code generated when you work in the PickListDialog. Here is the complete code:

```
columnMedium.setColumnName("MEDIUM");
columnMedium.setDataType(com.borland.dx.dataset.Variant.INT);
columnMedium.setPickList(new PickListDescriptor(QueryDataSetGBU,
      new String[] {"GBUCODE"},
      new String[] {"DESCRIPTION"},
      new String[] {"MEDIUM"},
      "DESCRIPTION",
      false));
columnMedium.setTableName("ALBUM");
columnMedium.setServerColumnName("MEDIUM");
columnMedium.setSqlType(4);
```

When you start working with a particular column for a QueryDataSet, JBuilder will often create an instance of the column for you, as shown in Figure 43-12. You can tell that JBuilder has created a Column object for you by noting that the word MEDIUM in the structure pane has brackets around it.

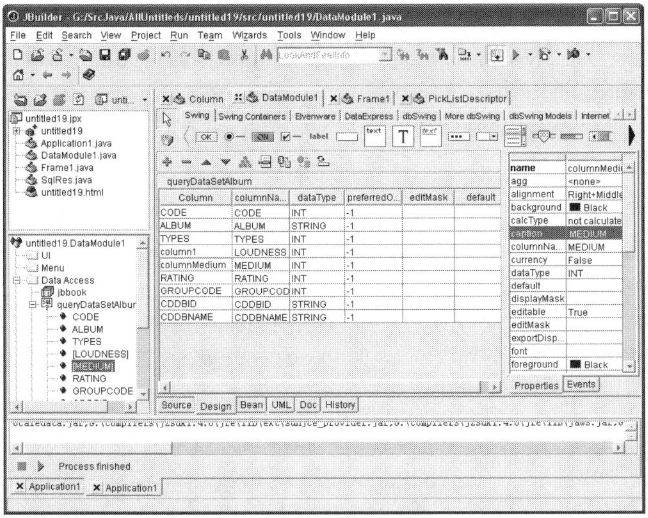

Figure 43-12: In the structure pane, notice that MEDIUM is set off with brackets and the new column is shown in the content pane and the Inspector. This means an explicit instance of a Column object has been created for you in your source code.

In Figure 43-12, I have renamed the column from its default name of column2 to columnMedium. I have also set the caption property for the component to Medium. By default, it contained the name of the display field from the lookup table. In this case, that name was Description.

Looking at the code that was generated, you can see that setTableName was called to link the column to a particular table. The setColumnName method was used to choose the column from the table used by this Column object. setServerColumnName is the column in the main table on the database server that will be used to resolve updates to this column. If this field is not set, the columnName property is used instead.

NOTE: The data type of the column is also defined. Note that MySQL databases will rightfully complain if you try to link an INT field with SMALLINT field in a lookup.

I will talk more about Column objects later in this section of the text. For now, you need only know that JBuilder always creates a Column object for each field in your tables. However, if you need to perform certain discrete operations on a field or table, JBuilder will help you create an explicit Column object of the type shown in this section. It does not take extra memory or resources for you to create an explicit instance of a Column object. JBuilder already created Column objects for all the fields of your table. The point is that an explicit instance of a Column object gives you a chance to customize how the column will behave. You can always tell that a Column object has been created by looking at the source code in your jbInit method. However, a second clue is provided by the brackets you see around a column name in the content pane. The brackets designate that an explicit instance of the Column object has been created.

Restoring Your Program

To finish the program, delete the lookup on the GOOD_BAD_AND_UGLY table. Create new lookups on the MEDIUM and TYPES tables. When you are done, your application should look like the program shown earlier in the chapter in Figure 43-4.

There is nothing new to be learned by setting up these additional fields. However, I find that practicing setting up a lookup a few times can be helpful. Despite all the time and explanation I have put into this subject, the actual act of setting up the lookup is not so terribly difficult if you know what you are doing. Even if the dialog does not quite work for you, it will at least set up the Column object for you properly. With it set up, it is easy to fill in the values for the PickListDescriptor. If you need additional help, view the Lookup example on the CD.

Wrapping Up Your Application in a JAR File or Executable

The final subject I want to cover in this chapter has to do with wrapping up your database project in a JAR file so that it can be easily distributed. This general subject is covered in some detail in Chapter 28. Here I will simply step you through the process quickly, since this is a subject that many people will need to understand.

The reason this subject is important is that your JBuilder database code relies on the dx.jar file and dbSwing.jar files that are not standard parts of the JDK. In particular, these two JAR files are created by Borland. What we want to do is link the necessary code from these JAR files directly into a single JAR file with the main code from your program.

To get started, choose **Wizards | Archive** from the JBuilder menu. Set the Archive Type to **Application**, as shown in Figure 43-13.

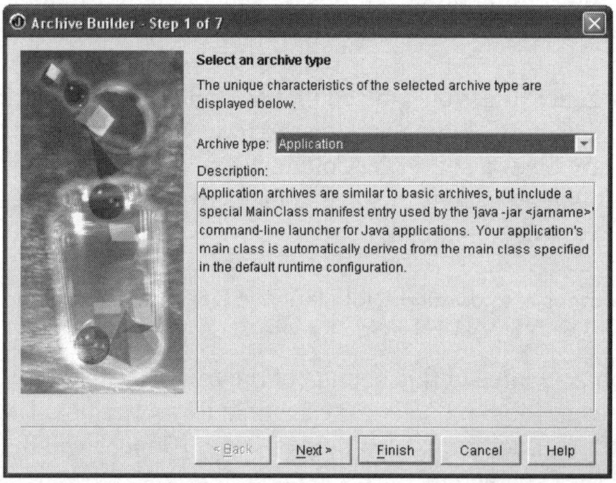

Figure 43-13: Preparing to create a JAR file that contains your newly built application

Click the **Next** button and fill in the second page of the wizard, as shown in Figure 43-14. Give your new archive node an appropriate name to display in the project pane. For instance, **Create Lookup Jar File** would do nicely in this case. Choose the name of the JAR file that you want to create. You will probably want to compress the contents of the JAR file, and you probably don't want to go through the lengthy step of creating the JAR file each time you compile.

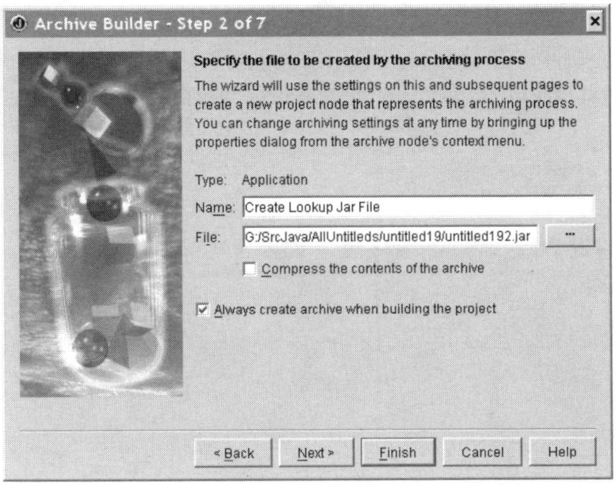

Figure 43-14: Specifying the name for your JAR file, the name for its node in the project pane, whether you want to create it each time you compile, and whether or not to compress it

Select the **Next** button and choose **Always include all classes and resources.** Sometimes you can save some space by specifying the individual packages you want to include. In our case, however, it will be simplest just to wrap up the whole ball of wax.

Select the **Next** button and choose **Always include all classes and resources** from DataExpress, dbSwing, and your database driver, as shown in Figure 43-15. You need to perform the operation three times, once for each JAR file. The database driver may not be necessary in some cases, such as if you are using ODBC to link to Access. You can usually save space by choosing to include only the required classes and all known resources, but I recommend at least starting out by choosing everything and narrowing your focus later.

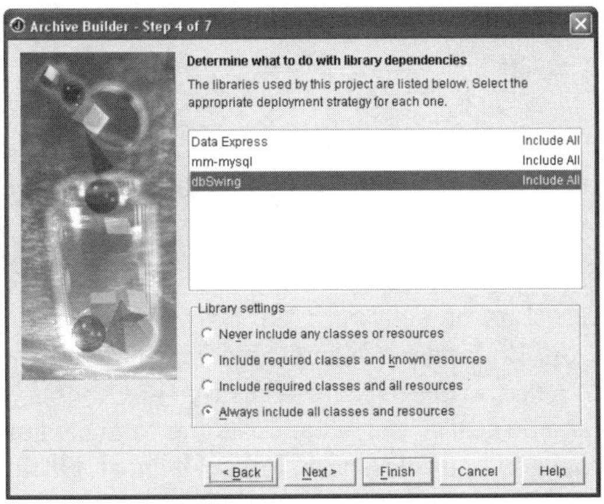

Figure 43-15: Choosing to link in the Borland database code and the code for your driver

NOTE: If you are planning on running your program only on your development machine, you do not need to include the dx.jar, dbSwing.jar, or your SQL driver in the JAR file that you are creating. Furthermore, if you are distributing a suite of applications, it may be simpler to distribute the dx.jar, dbSwing, and SQL driver as separate files rather than linking them into multiple JAR files.

In Step 5 of the wizard, accept the default values to include a manifest and create a manifest. In Step 6, select **Use the main class specified in the default run time.** This refers to the class you selected when you chose Project | Project Properties and then turned to the Run page.

Starting with JBuilder 7, Step 7 of the wizard allows you to wrap your project in an executable custom made for various platforms. In Figure 43-16, you can see that I have wrapped this project up in a Windows GUI application. This step can be helpful to users who are not used to working with JAR files.

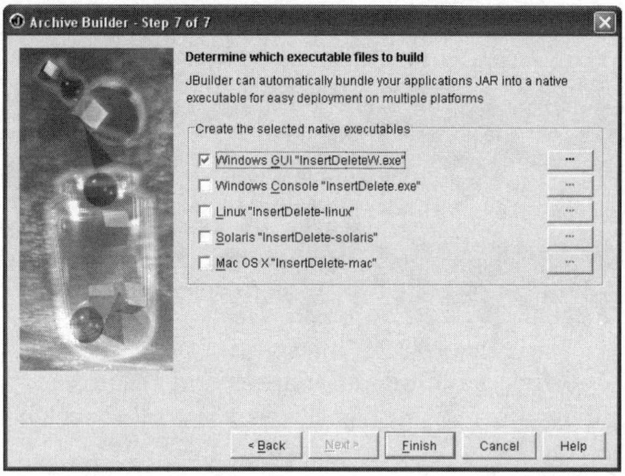

Figure 43-16: A new feature in JBuilder 7 allows you to wrap your project in an executable.

Click the **Finish** button. A new node should now appear in your project pane right next to Application1.java, Frame1.java, etc. Right-click on this node and choose either **Make** or **Rebuild**.

To run your program, go to the command prompt and type **dir** or **ls** in the main root directory for your project:

```
4/14/02   9:38          887  untitled19.html
4/14/02  12:04    1,053,047  untitled19.jar
4/14/02  10:08        2,898  untitled19.jpx
4/14/02  12:04    1,132,919  untitled19W.exe
```

You can run untitled19W.exe directly as a standard Windows executable. To run the JAR file, type the following at the command prompt:

```
java -jar untitled19.jar
```

Assuming that you have the JDK bin directory on your path, either of these commands should launch your application. In the exe option, Borland performs some very useful hand-waving that can sometimes result in your code discovering JDKs or JREs that are not on your path.

Before distributing your code, you should test it on a clean machine to make sure it does not rely on any files that just happen to be on your classpath. (You can cheat a little by setting your classpath to an empty string, but I still recommend trying a clean machine before distributing your code.) By a clean machine, I mean one that does not contain JBuilder or any other files used during development. You can also try tweaking the settings in your archive project to see if you can create JAR or executable files that are a bit smaller.

Just so you can understand some of what is happening here, I will show you how big the JAR and exe files are if you elect to use dx.jar, dbSwing.jar, and your SQL driver in their stand-alone JAR files:

```
4/14/02  12:15        5,112  untitled19.jar
4/14/02  12:15        4,039  untitled19.jpx
4/14/02  12:15       84,984  untitled19W.exe
```

Whoa! The JAR file went from 1,000 KB in size to 5 KB. Clearly, you pay a heavy price for linking the database tools directly into your project. However, in some cases, this is going to be by far the simplest way to distribute your database project. Remember what I said earlier: If you are distributing a suite of applications, you can save a lot of disk space by distributing dx.jar, dbSwing.jar, your SQL driver, and your application in separate JAR files. However, if you just want to distribute one file to a target machine, then use the techniques shown here.

Summary

In this chapter you have learned about searching for data in a dataset and performing lookups. At the end of the chapter, you also got a look at how to wrap your database application up in a single JAR file. A small section in the text introduced you to the Column object, which will be discussed in more depth in Chapters 44 and 45.

Chapter 44

Data Control

Charlie Calvert

This chapter focuses on advanced techniques for updating, inserting, and deleting data. Coverage of parameterized queries is included in the next chapter. Several sections in the middle of this chapter focus on using SQL statements. Additional material on using SQL in JBuilder will be covered in the next chapter.

This chapter has several important passages that are MySQL specific. The current state of databases is such that there are times when one really needs to do things the "MySQL way" or the "InterBase way" or the "Access way." When I can't find a standard way to do things, the focus in this book is on MySQL.

NOTE: In this chapter I present a number of SQL statements. I have found that when using MySQL on Windows, case sensitivity for table names and fields is not important. On Linux, however, getting the case right can be important. In particular, table names used in the programs for this book should usually be uppercase. I sometimes cut and paste into this document from Windows tools, and once or twice the case got mangled. I have tried to correct the errors, typing "select * from MY_TABLE," not "select * from my_table." If you have questions about this subject, refer to the code on the CD. It should serve as a reliable reference, since it was tested on both platforms.

Updating, Inserting, and Deleting

A fundamental feature of database applications is the ability to insert, delete, and update data. You have already learned something about these features by using the Save and Update buttons on the JdbNavToolBar from the SimpleAuto application in Chapter 41.

The JdbNavToolBar is very powerful. You will probably want to use it in many, probably even most, of your database applications. However, you may need more direct control over inserting and deleting records from a database. In this section you will see how to perform these operations manually. The goal is to give a more in-depth explanation of the underlying structure of DataExpress and how to get tight control over your data.

Let's begin our examination by talking in very general terms about the StorageDataSet class. This is the class from which QueryDataSet descends:

```
java.lang.Object
   +----com.borland.dx.dataset.ReadRow
         +----com.borland.dx.dataset.ReadWriteRow
               +----com.borland.dx.dataset.DataSet
                     +----com.borland.dx.dataset.StorageDataSet
                           +----com.borland.dx.sql.dataset.QueryDataSet
```

JBuilder uses it to help you save your data. In particular, StorageDataSet has properties called resolver and provider. In a QueryDataSet component, the provider property fetches data from a dataset. The resolver saves the data. Logically enough, the resolver property is of type Resolver. If you want to change the default behavior DataExpress uses when resolving data, you can set the resolver property to a custom class that you create. Often this involves working with a descendant of Resolver called a QueryResolver.

If you want to dig more into the behavior of the QueryDataSet, you can explore the classes mentioned in the previous paragraph. In this chapter, however, we will explore the default behavior of the built-in QueryResolver object.

NOTE: JBuilder uses transactions by default. The best way to handle transactions in JBuilder is to let the database tools work as they would normally. A brief discussion of how to change transaction isolation levels is included at the end of the next chapter.

Insertions and Auto-Increment Fields

There is frequently a serious problem that must be overcome when inserting a new row into a dataset. Consider the ALBUM or ARTIST tables used in the jbbook database. Each of these tables starts with a primary key called CODE that is of type int and declared to be not null. This means that each row added to the database must have a unique integer value in this field. For instance, the first row might have CODE set to 1, the next might set CODE to 2, the third to 3, etc. It would be an error if you inserted two rows that had the same CODE value or if you tried to leave this field blank. The question, then, is how can you ensure that you are inserting a unique value into each row?

Foreseeing this problem, some databases provide a very simple solution called an auto-increment field. Here, for instance, is the declaration for a very simple MySQL table that uses the auto-increment field:

```
CREATE TABLE AUTOINC_TEST
(
      CODE INT NOT NULL AUTO_INCREMENT,
      NAME VARCHAR(25),
      PRIMARY KEY(CODE)
);
```

Notice the declaration for the CODE field; it is declared to be an AUTO_INCREMENT field. Including that simple declaration is all you need to do to get MySQL to generate unique values for the CODE field. The database will automatically insert these values into the table whenever you add a new row.

The example program we are about to create will only work if you are using MySQL or Access. InterBase does not support auto-increment fields. Instead, it uses a system called a generator. You might want to use a combination of a generator and a stored procedure to solve the auto-increment problem in InterBase, as shown in the ElfAddress program found on the CD.

NOTE: In Access, you would create the same table with this code:

```
CREATE TABLE AUTOINC_TEST
(
  CODE COUNTER  NOT NULL,
  NAME VARCHAR(25),
  PRIMARY KEY(CODE)
)
```

The following syntax is a bit more terse, but it will also work:

```
CREATE TABLE AUTOINC_TEST
(
  CODE COUNTER  NOT NULL PRIMARY KEY,
  NAME VARCHAR(25)
)
```

The COUNTER type creates an AutoNumber field, which is the Microsoft equivalent of an auto-increment field.

To create a table in Access using SQL, first open your database. Turn to the Objects page, choose Queries, and double-click on Create Query in Design View. Close the Show Table dialog. Choose Query | SQL Specific | Data Definition from the Access menu. In the Data Definition Query dialog, type in one of the CREATE TABLE statements shown in this note.

Choose Query | Run from the Access menu. Close your dialog, saving your work if you wish.

Go back to Tables mode. Right-click on your new table, AUTOINC_TEST, and choose Design View. You should see that the first field, called CODE, has a data type of AutoNumber. You have now created a table that will automatically insert values into the Code field each time you insert a new record.

You can also change an existing Access Number field to AutoNumber. I have found that if I open Access, go into design mode on a table, and set the first field in a table to AutoNumber, I can achieve the same effect as using the AUTO_INCREMENT syntax in a MySQL table.

Creating an Auto-Increment Program

Let's create a simple database program that uses the AUTO_INCREMENT table. You can find a finished version of this project on the CD under the title AutoIncInsert.

NOTE: When describing this program, I will, in some places, first show you a wrong or incomplete way to do things and then provide a more thorough explanation of how to proceed. This can be frustrating for the reader. The problem is that I will show you a technique and then "take it away from you" by explaining what is wrong with it. Nevertheless, if you have the patience to bear with me, I believe that you will ultimately end up learning more than if I simply showed you the answer without explaining how I arrived at that particular solution.

To create the program, begin a new project in JBuilder and insert a new application into it. Choose **File | New | Data Module** and build a new data module called **DMod.** Do not use the Data Modeler.

NOTE: It would not be wrong to use the Data Modeler at this point. I just think it might be a useful exercise to build this part of the program by hand.

Take the data module into design mode. Drop down a Database and a QueryDataSet onto the Data Access node in the structure pane. Name the database **jbbook** and the QueryDataSet **queryDataSetAutoInc**, as shown in Figure 44-1.

Connect the jbbook database component to the MySQL jbbook database, as shown in Figure 44-2. This should simply be a matter of choosing one of the connections you defined in Chapter 39.

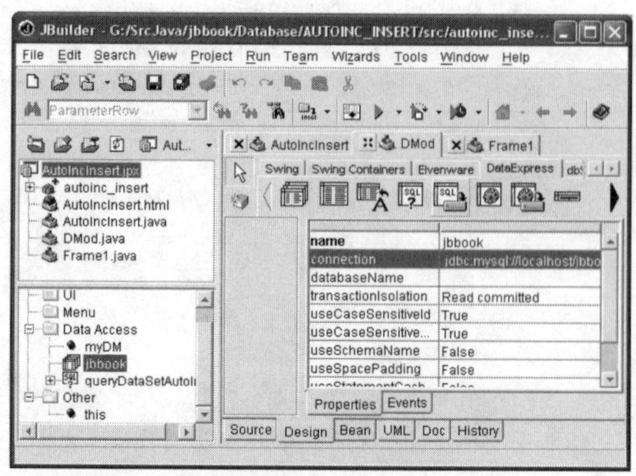

Figure 44-1: Preparing to build a simple database application in JBuilder. In the structure pane you can see a database called jbbook.

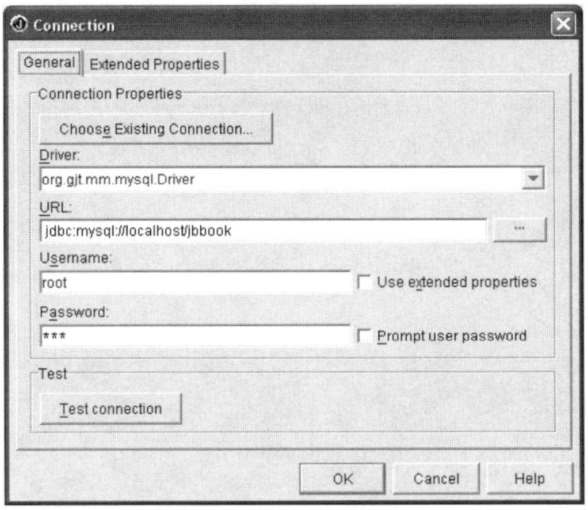

Figure 44-2: Connecting to the jbbook database using the built-in JBuilder tools

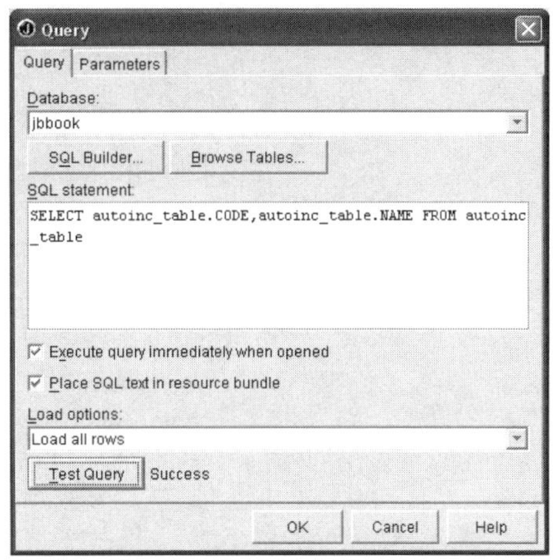

Figure 44-3: Creating a simple query to select all the rows from the AUTOINC_ TEST table

Create a query on the QueryDataSetAutoInc component to select all the data from the AUTOINC_ TABLE table, as shown in Figure 44-3. You might prefer to store the data in an SQL bundle. Test your query before closing the dialog.

Focus **Frame1** in the content pane and move into design mode. Turn to the dbSwing page in the component palette and drop down a TableScrollPane. Place a JdbTable on top of the scroll pane. Build your project, and then select **Wizards | Use Data Module** from the JBuilder menu. From the options available, choose **Share (static) instance of data module**. Once again, compile or build your project. Select the **jdbTable1** component in the structure pane and set its dataSet property to **QueryDataSetAutoInc**. You should be able to pick the dataset directly in a drop-down list from the dataset property editor.

You now need to add some kind of interface that will allow you to add and delete items from your dataset. In this case, adding a menu is probably most appropriate. Turn to the Swing Containers page of the component palette and drop down a JMenuBar onto the Menu node in the structure pane. Right-click on the menu bar and choose **Activate designer**. Add a File menu with an Exit menu item. Add an Options menu with Insert, Insert and Save, Add, Save, Empty Dataset, and Delete Record menu items. At the end of the jbInit method, add a call to **this.setJMenuBar(jMenuBar1)**. If you need help working with the menu designer, see Chapter 13.

Add event handlers for the Exit, Add, Insert, Insert and Save, Save, Empty Dataset, and Delete Record menu items:

```
Random random = new java.util.Random();

private String getDurrell()
{
      String books[] = new String[] {"Bitter Lemons", "Justine", "Clea",
      "Balthazar", "Mountolive", "Tunc", "Nunquam", "Livia", "Constance"};
```

```
        int num = random.nextInt(books.length);
        return books[num];
    }

    void jMenuItemInsert_actionPerformed(ActionEvent e)
    {
        dMod1.insertRow(getDurrell(), false);
    }

    void jMenuItemInsertAndSave_actionPerformed(ActionEvent e)
    {
        dMod1.insertRow(getDurrell(), true);
    }

    void jMenuItemDelete_actionPerformed(ActionEvent e)
    {
        dMod1.deleteCurrentRow(this);
    }

    void jMenuItemAddRow_actionPerformed(ActionEvent e)
    {
        String prompt = "Number of rows to add to the database";
        String numRowsStr = (String)JOptionPane.showInputDialog(this, prompt,
            "Add rows", JOptionPane.QUESTION_MESSAGE,
            null , null, "1000");
        int numRows = Integer.parseInt(numRowsStr);
        for (int i = 0; i < numRows; i++)
        {
            dMod1.addRow(getDurrell());
        }
        dMod1.save();
        dMod1.last();
    }

    void jMenuItemEmpty_actionPerformed(ActionEvent e)
    {
        dMod1.clear(this);
    }

    void jMenuItemSave_actionPerformed(ActionEvent e)
    {
        dMod1.save();
    }

    void jMenuItemExit_actionPerformed(ActionEvent e)
    {
        System.exit(0);
    }
```

Most of these methods are one-liners that call routines in the data module. Some of the routines in the data module are very simple. For instance, the last method is really just a wrapper:

```
public void last()
{
      queryDataSetAutoInc.last();
}
```

I'm including this routine just to make sure the interface for the program doesn't need to know any details about how the data module does its job. The last routine in the series is the simple handler for the Exit menu item. That routine is so simple that it need not be commented on.

Some of the other routines are more complex. I will cover all of them in later sections of this chapter.

Before moving on, you should note the getDurrell method. This routine will generate strings that can be inserted into the dataset. The point of this program is to let you study how to go about inserting and deleting rows of data. I don't want to bother you with having to actually type something into the rows; this method relieves you of that responsibility. You still can type something in if you want, but you don't have to.

The getDurrell method declares an array of String. The strings in the array are book titles written by the English author Lawrence Durrell. The Java Random class is used to produce indices into the array.

Deleting a Row

I am now going to begin examining the code in the data module. Here is the method to delete a single row of data:

```
private static final String nameCol = "NAME";

/**
 * Delete one row from the dataset.
 * @param frame The frame of the window making the request.
 */
public void deleteCurrentRow(JFrame frame)
{
      // Set up the prompt string
      String data = "Are you sure you want to delete: ";

      // Find the data from the row that will be deleted
      data += QueryDataSetAutoInc.getString(nameCol);

      // Prompt the user to see if he wants to delete
      if (JOptionPane.showConfirmDialog(frame, data) == JOptionPane.OK_OPTION)
      {
            // Delete the currently selected row
            QueryDataSetAutoInc.deleteRow();

            // Save the changes
            QueryDataSetAutoInc.saveChanges();
      }
}
```

The actual command to delete the row is simply **QueryDataSetAutoInc.deleteRow()**. When using this method, the row that will be deleted is the currently selected row. Nothing could be much simpler.

Notice the code that is used to retrieve the current value in the NAME column:

```
String data = "Are you sure you want to delete: ";
data += QueryDataSetAutoInc.getString(nameCol);
```

You can get and set values in the currently selected row by calling methods of this type. For instance, there is a setString method, a getInt method, a getBoolean method, a setBoolean method, etc. Simply pass in the name or number of the column you want to get or set.

When you are done with the operation, you could post the data to the local dataset. But the code shown here does more than that; it makes the deletion permanent by calling saveChanges:

```
QueryDataSetAutoInc.saveChanges();
```

Calling saveChanges has the same result as pressing the next to last icon on the right-hand side of the JdbNavToolBar: It sends the data back to the database server for storage.

By default, the saveChanges method starts a transaction, deletes the row from the database, and then commits the transaction. I will discuss more about transactions at the end of the next chapter.

Inserting a Row

There are two different ways to add a new row to the current dataset. A call to insertRow adds an empty row to the dataset. A call to addRow adds a complete DataRow object to the dataset. The JBuilder documentation says that you should use addRow if you want to perform many insertions in a rapid-fire manner. Indeed, the AutoIncInsert program on the CD for this book allows you to do just that.

Listing 44-1 includes fairly complex code for inserting a row into a dataset. Inserting a row in JBuilder is actually a very simple operation. But a lot of things can happen when you insert a row. As a result, I've taken this simple operation and expanded on it by showing you how to cope with a range of related issues.

Listing 44-1: Code from AutoIncInsert for inserting a row. These methods cope with more problems than you will likely face in a standard database program.

```
private static boolean isMySQL = true;
private static final boolean debug = true;

/**
 * Given an autoIncrement value inserted into a MySQL table, retrieve
 * the most recently generated auto_increment value
 *
 * The LAST_INSERT_ID macro is specific to MySQL. MAX ought to work on
 * most databases.
 */
private long getNewAutoIncValue()
{
      String sqlStatement;
      if (isMySQL)
      {
```

```
            sqlStatement = "select LAST_INSERT_ID();";
        }
        else
        {
            sqlStatement = "select MAX(CODE) from AUTOINC_TEST;";
        }
        QueryDataSet dataSet = new QueryDataSet();
        dataSet.setQuery(new com.borland.dx.sql.dataset.QueryDescriptor(
                jbbook, sqlStatement, null, true, Load.ALL));
        dataSet.open();
        if (isMySQL)
        {
            return dataSet.getLong(0);
        }
        else
        {
            return dataSet.getInt(0);
        }
    }

    public void locate(DataSet dataset, long code)
    {
        // Create a DataRow object to define the row we want to find.
        DataRow datarow = new DataRow(dataset, new String[] {codeName});

        // Insert our search string into the DataRow
        datarow.setInt(codeName, (int)code);

        // Locate the new row
        dataset.locate(datarow, Locate.CASE_INSENSITIVE | Locate.FIRST);
    }

    /**
     * Insert a row into the data set.
     *
     * Compare this method with the addRow method, shown below. This method
     * inserts a row, and then allows you to start editing it. The other method
     * creates the whole row first, and then inserts it.
     *
     * @param insertStr
     */
    public void insertRow(String insertStr, boolean saveToServer)
    {
        // Declare the column to save the new string into.
        String colName = nameCol;

        // Print debug info if requested
        if (this.debug) System.out.println("Inserting string: " + insertStr);

        // Insert a new row in the database and set the the album field
        QueryDataSetAutoInc.insertRow(false);
```

```
        QueryDataSetAutoInc.setString(colName, insertStr);

        if (!saveToServer)
        {
            // Save our work to the local data set
            QueryDataSetAutoInc.post();
        }
        else
        {
            QueryDataSetAutoInc.saveChanges();

            // Pull our work back from the server so we can view it.
            QueryDataSetAutoInc.refresh();

            // Discover the autoincrement value we created
            long newAutoIncValue = getNewAutoIncValue();
            if (this.debug) System.out.println("Inserting code: " +
                newAutoIncValue);

            // Move the user to the new row that we have inserted
            locate(QueryDataSetAutoInc, newAutoIncValue);
        }
    }
```

As I said before, the basic work of inserting the row is very simple. All you need to do is call QueryDataSetAutoInc.insertRow(false), and the new empty row will be added to the dataset. You will be automatically taken to the newly inserted row. It's that simple. In many programs, you won't have to do anything more than call that one function. But sometimes you want to do a little more than that, and so I'm giving you code that surfaces some of the complexities inherent in this situation.

I said earlier that insertRow creates an empty row. That is true, but it is not a simple truth. As you know, the auto_increment feature will fill in the value of the CODE field. You will not, however, see this value right away. Indeed, it will not even be generated right away. The CODE field was, or will be, generated on the server, but you are way back on the client. A call to insertRow affects only your local copy of the data. It does not affect the server and thus does not cause an Auto_Increment number to be generated. And even if it did affect the server, you would not automatically be informed of what is happening on the server unless you refreshed the data.

insertRow takes a single Boolean parameter. If set to true, the row will be added before the currently selected row. If set to false, it will be added after the currently selected row. In either case, JBuilder will take you to the newly inserted row. If the grid is sorted, the record may appear in sorted order rather than in the order in which it was inserted into the table. But if you do nothing more than call insert, you do not need to worry, as JBuilder will take the user to the newly inserted row.

Once you have inserted the row, the next step is to fill in the data. In some cases, the user might do this for you. However, you can make the additions by using code, as I do in this program. Here you can see a call to QueryDataSetAutoInc.setString(), passing in the name of the column to be changed and the value to be inserted:

```
private static final String colName = "NAME";

QueryDataSetAutoInc.insertRow(false);
QueryDataSetAutoInc.setString(colName, insertStr);
```

Instead of the name of the column, you can pass in the number of the column. In general, I believe it is best to refer to a column by name. The order or number of columns in a dataset can change for a number of reasons, but the name of a column is much less likely to change. In particular, a simple change to an SQL SELECT statement can change both the order and number of columns in a dataset. Hence, the preferred way to call setString is by column name.

In this program, the table we are working with is very simple, so I only need to insert a single string. A more complex dataset would require repeated calls to fill in all the values for the columns. As I mentioned earlier, DataExpress provides a range of functions for inserting data, such as setBoolean, setString, setInt, etc. You can also use a method called updateRow, which will be discussed later in a section titled "Updating a Row."

So far, everything is very straightforward. JBuilder is allowing you to insert data into your dataset with a few lines of code. That is all you will need to do in most cases.

But inserting a new row and adding some data to it is not always the whole story. A few things still need to be done to complete the operation. In particular, you now have two choices. The first is almost always quite simple, and the other is often complex:

- You can call QueryDataSet.post() and save your changes to the local copy of the dataset.
- You can call QueryDataSet.saveChanges and save your changes back to the server.

In most normal database programs, the first option will go off without a hitch. Furthermore, it will be by far the simplest to implement. In particular, the whole problem of keeping track of the row you are editing will be a moot issue. JBuilder will handle that for you. After the post, the cursor will be on the newly added row.

NOTE: Calling post() is roughly equivalent to selecting the check icon from the navigation toolbar.

Notice, however, that your newly posted row will not have a new CODE field value after you call post(), as shown in Figure 44-4. Calling post() only affects the local copy of the dataset, and as you know, the new CODE value will be generated on the server. The server doesn't know that you have called post; it only knows that something has happened after you call saveChanges.

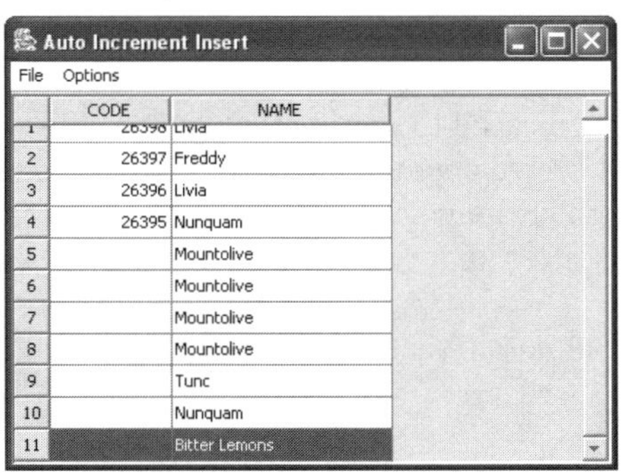

Figure 44-4: After calling insertRow and post, there is no sign of a value in the CODE field.

NOTE: The problem I am showing you here is not likely to be a problem in a real-world program. In those programs, you would want to hide the CODE field from the user. It is never the user's responsibility to edit this field. Indeed, any attempts to edit it will often cause a primary key violation either immediately or at some later date. So, from the end user's perspective, this is a moot issue. But as developers, we do care about the values that are placed in the CODE field. The end user might not need them, but we do.

In order to have auto-increment values generated on the server, you need to call saveChanges. To see these values back on the client, you need to call both saveChanges and refresh:

```
public void save()
{
      QueryDataSetAutoInc.saveChanges();
      QueryDataSetAutoInc.refresh();
      long lastCode = getNewAutoIncValue();
      locate(QueryDataSetAutoInc, lastCode);
      if (this.debug) System.out.println("Save and refresh called");
}
```

The first two lines of this method post the data to the server and then pull back the newly generated CODE values so you can view them, as shown in Figure 44-5. When you call saveChanges, the server will automatically generate the CODE values for you. In order to see them, you need to call refresh. This is roughly the same thing as pressing the two broken arrow icons way over on the far right of the navigation toolbar.

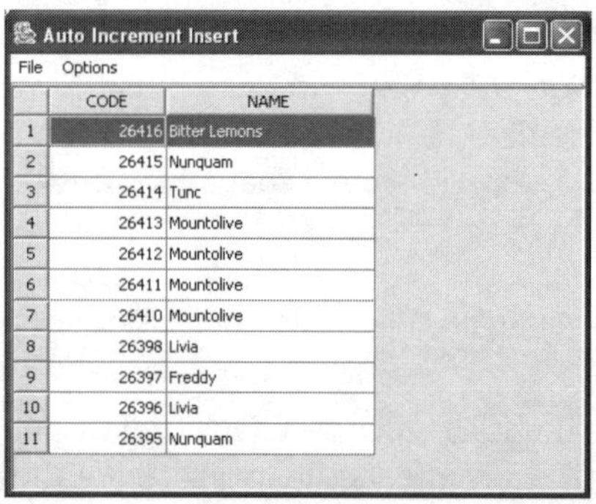

Figure 44-5: After you call saveChanges and refresh the data from the server, you can see the newly generated autoInc values.

There is, however, a problem that arises when you perform these kinds of operations. After you call refresh, you will have lost your place in the dataset. You have completely refreshed the dataset, which means that DataExpress has lost track of your location. Or rather, your location has been reset back to record one.

The last few lines of the save method are dedicated to getting you back to the record you were on when you called refresh. I know that I have spent some time building up to this moment, but I'm going to ask you to wait just a bit longer before you learn about these last three lines. I will, however, cover this subject after showing you a few additional simple lines of code.

Take a look back at Listing 44-1 and you will notice that the insertRow method takes a Boolean saveToServer parameter:

```
      if (!saveToServer)
      {
```

```
            // Save our work to the local data set
            QueryDataSetAutoInc.post();
        }
        else
        {
            QueryDataSetAutoInc.saveChanges();

            // Pull our work back from the server so we can view it.
            QueryDataSetAutoInc.refresh();


            // Discover the autoincrement value we created
            long newAutoIncValue = getNewAutoIncValue();
            if (this.debug) System.out.println("Inserting code: " +
                 newAutoIncValue);

            // Move the user to the new row that we have inserted
            locate(QueryDataSetAutoInc, newAutoIncValue);
        }
```

If saveToServer is false, the first of our two options was taken. As predicted, the code to handle that situation is simple. But the other branch has code that is considerably more complex.

Refinding Your Place in a Dataset with Simple Searches

This second option in the insertRow method starts out with code just like the code in the save method. In particular, there are calls to saveChanges and refresh. After the call to refresh, however, a funny thing has happened. The whole dataset has been refreshed, and the cursor is on the top row. The top row, of course, is not likely to be the row that the user was editing.

NOTE: In some cases, it doesn't matter that you are not on the row the user was editing. For instance, the user might have queried a dataset for a particular name. You showed them that record, and no others, and then posted the record when they were through editing it. In that situation, which is not at all uncommon, you don't need to get back to the row that the user was editing. So you would be through, regardless of whether you called post or saveChanges. I have employed a technique of this type in many programs, as it avoids all the problems currently under discussion.

In this chapter I'm trying to show you not the simplest cases, but the trickier ones. In this case, let's assume you do have to get back to the record that the user inserted. Or, in the case of batch posts, let's say you want to get back to the last record the user posted.

If we were appending data onto the end of the dataset, we could simply call QueryDataSet.last(), and we would be taken to the new row appended to the end of the dataset. But again, that is too simple. We are not doing an append, but an insert.

In many cases, there will be a fairly simple solution to this problem. Let's suppose that the CODE field is not the only unique value in the dataset. For instance, let's assume that you also have First and Last name fields that you know, when taken together, to be unique. Or, if they are not unique, you know they are listed in your dataset in the order in which they were inserted. In either of those cases, it generally works to search for the last instance in the dataset of the newly added First and Last name values.

To search on the first and last names, you can call the QueryDataSetAutoInc.locate function. The technology for this kind of call was discussed in depth in the previous chapter. Here I show the code for locating the record, but I'll ask that you look at Chapter 43 for an explanation of how it works:

```
private final static String firstNameCol = "FIRST_NAME";
private final static String lastNameCol = "LAST_NAME";

/**
 * Locate a row in the data set
 *
 * @param colName The name of the column to search on
 * @param searchStr The string to search for
 */
public void locate(DataSet dataset, String firstName, String lastName)
{
      // Create a DataRow object to define the row we want to find.
      DataRow datarow = new DataRow(dataset, new String[] {firstNameCol,
            lastNameCol});

      // Insert our search string into the DataRow
      datarow.setString(firstNameCol, firstName);
      datarow.setString(lastNameCol, lastName);

      // Locate the new row
      dataset.locate(datarow, Locate.CASE_INSENSITIVE | Locate.LAST);
}
```

Notice that the options in the last parameter to dataset.locate include the Locate.LAST option. This will find the last instances of the string in the dataset.

But once again, this solution is too easy. Yes, there are cases when it will work, but what do you do if there are no unique strings in the dataset for you to use when locating the record?

NOTE: If we did an edit rather than an insert, the issue under discussion is moot. In an edit, the CODE field has already been generated, and you can search on it. No one but you will ever edit the CODE field, and it should only be edited once: during the original insertion of the row.

Here is code for finding a record based on its ID:

```
      private static final String codeName = "CODE";

      public void locate(DataSet dataset, long code)
      {
            // Create a DataRow object to define the row we want to find.
            DataRow datarow = new DataRow(dataset, new String[] {codeName});

            // Insert our search string into the DataRow
            datarow.setInt(codeName, (int)code);

            // Locate the new row
            dataset.locate(datarow, Locate.CASE_INSENSITIVE | Locate.FIRST);
      }
```

This code is simple enough. It performs a simple search based on the locate method discussed in the previous chapter. The only problem is that this method won't work unless you know the proper code generated by the auto-increment technology on the server. An explanation of how to get that value is discussed in the next sections of this chapter.

A First Try at Getting the Auto-Increment Value from a Server

It appears that we are finally down to the nub of the matter, which is: How do I get the value set by the auto-increment routine back on the server? That's the $64,000 question. Let's see if we can come up with a $64,000 answer (or at least one that's worth a crisp new C note).

Some databases are very busy. I will show you how to handle them later in the chapter. On the other hand, many databases have very little activity. In those databases, inserts are done once an hour on a busy day, and on most days there are no new inserts at all. In such cases, you can use this simple and quite standard SQL query to retrieve the value of the new CODE field:

```
select MAX(CODE) from AUTOINC_TEST
```

This statement asks for the max value in the CODE field of the AUTOINC_TEST table. Here is code that you can use to get this value from the server:

```
private long getNewAutoIncValue()
{
      String sqlStatement;
      sqlStatement = "select MAX(CODE) from AUTOINC_TEST;";

      QueryDataSet dataSet = new QueryDataSet();
      dataSet.setQuery(new com.borland.dx.sql.dataset.QueryDescriptor(
            jbbook, sqlStatement, null, true, Load.ALL));
      dataSet.open();
      return dataSet.getInt(0);
}
```

This is quite standard code that should work when run against most database servers. It was created without the use of any visual tools. Nevertheless, the code parallels that found in the initialization section of the data module and in jbInit.

The getNewAutoIncValue method creates a new QueryDataSet for you and then initializes it with a query that you create:

```
QueryDataSet dataSet = new QueryDataSet();
dataSet.setQuery(new com.borland.dx.sql.dataset.QueryDescriptor(
      jbbook, sqlStatement, null, true, Load.ALL));
```

Once you have the QueryDataSet, you can use a get method to retrieve values from it:

```
int newCodeValue = codeData.getInt("artistcode");
```

Or you can do as we do here and just pass in an integer value to indicate the column:

```
return dataSet.getInt(0);
```

NOTE: In real database programs, you will often need to query a dataset without having any interaction from the user. Furthermore, you might need to query dozens of tables. In situations like these, the JBuilder visual database tools really don't do you much good, and they can be a waste of resources. You should therefore use non-visual code like that shown in getNewAutoIncValue.

There is a second way to think about this same issue. The QueryDataSet works well in a visual programming environment. However, it works equally well if you want to query a database behind

the scenes without input from the user. Lots of good database programs make heavy use of QueryDataSets behind the scenes, without any help from the JBuilder visual tools.

The solution shown in getNewAutoIncValue is a nice solution, since it will work on MySQL, Access, and many other databases.

There is, however, a potential problem. Some other user may have inserted a row into the dataset between the time that you inserted your row and the time that you requested a value back from the server.

This is not likely to happen, but it is possible. And so, once again, we reject this solution as too simple.

An Improved Way to Get the Auto-Increment Value from the Server

In this case, a proprietary solution specific to a particular database is required. For instance, if we were using InterBase, a solution could be found using a generator and a stored procedure. With MySQL, you use the following syntax in an SQL statement:

```
"select LAST_INSERT_ID();";
```

This SQL statement will retrieve the last auto-increment value generated for your connection. If another user generates a new number at the same time, you will not see it. It is only numbers generated for your connection that will be reported to you.

Here is a rewritten version of the getNewAutoIncValue function that includes code specific to MySQL:

```
private long getNewAutoIncValue()
{
    String sqlStatement;
    if (isMySQL)
    {
        sqlStatement = "select LAST_INSERT_ID();";
    }
    else
    {
        sqlStatement = "select MAX(CODE) from AUTOINC_TEST;";
    }
    QueryDataSet dataSet = new QueryDataSet();
    dataSet.setQuery(new com.borland.dx.sql.dataset.QueryDescriptor(
            jbbook, sqlStatement, null, true, Load.ALL));
    dataSet.open();
    if (isMySQL)
    {
        return dataSet.getLong(0);
    }
    else
    {
        return dataSet.getInt(0);
    }
}
```

If a Boolean value called isMySQL is set to true, the query we post involves the LAST_INSERT_ID() method that MySQL supports. Also examine the code near the end of the method. getLong is called if LAST_INSERT_ID was used, and getInt is called if

MAX(CODE) was used. MySQL returns a long, not an int, when you make a request for the last auto_increment value that was generated for your connection to the database.

At long last, we have reached the end of our search for a way to handle even the worst-case insert methods that involve an auto-increment value. If you call LAST_INSERT_ID, you have a solution that is robust and trustworthy even under difficult circumstances. Most databases do provide you with some kind of solution to this problem, but in this book, I'm only going to focus in this kind of detail on MySQL.

Adding or Appending a Row to a Dataset

The act of adding or appending a row to a dataset is quite different from inserting a row. When you add a row, you first create the new row as a stand-alone entity and then add the new row to the data set itself.

The code in the AutoIncInsert program allows you to insert from 1 to x number of rows. Inserting large numbers of rows, say 5,000 or more, can be problematic. When I tried it on my home system, I thought a request to insert that many rows had locked up my program. But the method did eventually return and the data was inserted correctly. On my 1700 MHZ AMD machine with a reported 480 MB of RAM, I found DataExpress did a good job of handling a thousand or so rows of data at once.

NOTE: The above paragraph is a statement about how well the Borland database tools and Java SQL tools work, and not a statement about the performance of MySQL. You would want to write a different kind of program if you wanted to benchmark MySQL. As I said earlier, MySQL is one of the fastest databases around. In tests that I have seen, only Oracle could compete with it in terms of raw performance, and there the results were pretty much a draw.

Listing 44-2 shows code for adding a new row. Again, the code I've written is more complex than you will find necessary in most programs.

Listing 44-2: The three methods shown here provide flexibility when you want to add rows to a dataset.

```
/**
 * Append a new row onto the end of the dataset. Create the row first,
 * then insert it. The insertRow method shown above will first insert the
 * row, then allow you to fill it in.
 *
 * The JBuilder documentation states that this method is better to
 * use if you want to perform a batch insert of many rows.
 *
 * @param insertStr The string to insert.
 */
public void addRow(String insertStr)
{
    // Set up a local copy of the new row
    DataRow newRow = new DataRow(QueryDataSetAutoInc, nameCol);
    newRow.setString(nameCol, insertStr);

    // Append the new row
    QueryDataSetAutoInc.addRow(newRow);

    // Post your changes
```

```
        QueryDataSetAutoInc.post();
    }

    /**
     * Add a row and save the information associated with it.
     *
     * @param insertStr
     */
    public void addRowSave(String insertStr)
    {
        // Call local function to perform insert
        addRow(insertStr);

        // Save our work to the server
        QueryDataSetAutoInc.saveChanges();

        // Pull our work back from the server so we can view it.
        QueryDataSetAutoInc.refresh();

        long newCode = getNewAutoIncValue();
        // Move the user to the new row that we have inserted
        locate(QueryDataSetAutoInc, newCode);
    }

    public void save()
    {
        QueryDataSetAutoInc.saveChanges();
        QueryDataSetAutoInc.refresh();
        long lastCode = getNewAutoIncValue();
        locate(QueryDataSetAutoInc, lastCode);
        if (this.debug) System.out.println("Save and refresh called");
    }
```

The addRow method performs the actual adding of a row. The addRowSave method adds a row and then saves it. The third method is the save routine, discussed earlier. (If you are typing in the code as you read through the chapter, note that you have probably already typed in the save method.) If you used the addRow method to insert multiple rows, you would want to call save after the insertions.

To create the new row that you want to add onto the dataset, create a new instance of a DataRow and use a set method to insert the data into the row:

```
DataRow newRow = new DataRow(QueryDataSetAutoInc, nameCol);
newRow.setString(nameCol, insertStr);

// Append the new row
QueryDataSetAutoInc.addRow(newRow);
```

As you recall, the DataRow object represents one or more fields from a single row of data.

NOTE: There are actually several different constructors for the DataRow class. One of them does not require that you specify the columns you want to include in the new row. Instead, it includes initialized space for all the fields in the row.

If you are done adding a group of rows, simply repeat the operations you performed when inserting a row. In particular, the code shown here saves the changes to the server, then retrieves the new CODE field from the server, and finally locates the cursor on the newly inserted row. In most cases, you can locate the row by simply moving to the end of the dataset. If that does not work, try using the "select LAST_INSERT_ID();" technique and then calling the locate function.

Updating a Row

There is no explicit method in the AutoIncInsert program for updating a record. However, there are several "stealth" examples of updating a dataset in the program. In particular, if you first insert the row and then add data to it, you are really involved in a two-step process — the first an insert and the second an update.

When updating, you will often move to the row you want to edit and then use setString, setInt, setBoolean, etc., to edit the data in the dataset. Then call either post to save the data to the local copy of the dataset or saveChanges if you want to post the data to the server.

If you are letting the user edit the data, the process is even simpler. The user moves to a particular row. By starting to type in a data-aware control, the user puts the dataset into edit mode. When he or she moves off the row, it will automatically be posted to the local copy of the dataset. To save the data to the server, you must explicitly call saveChanges or the user must press the rightmost button in the JdbNavToolBar.

An alternative to calling setString, setInt, setBoolean, etc., is to call the method QueryDataSet.updateRow. In the following example, entryList is a QueryDataSet:

```
entryList.insertRow(false);
DataRow dataRow = new DataRow(entryList);
dataRow.setString(1, dir);
dataRow.setInt(2, id);
entryList.updateRow(dataRow);
database1.saveChanges(entryList);
```

As you recall, the alternative looks like this:

```
entryList.insertRow(false);
entryList.setString(1, dir);
entryList.setInt(2, id);
database1.saveChanges(entryList);
```

The second method takes fewer lines of code. However, each call to a set method in the second example involves using a QueryDataSet. I have not benchmarked these two routines, but it may be faster to first update a DataRow and then post the whole DataRow to the QueryDataSet.

The ElfTracker program on the CD has an example of using the updateRow method. In fact, the code shown in this section is taken from that program.

Emptying a Dataset

The code for emptying a dataset is very straightforward. It consists of nothing more than a call to QueryDataSetAutoInc.deleteAllRows() followed by a call to save your changes:

```
public void clear(JFrame frame)
{
     // Set up the prompt string
```

```
        String data = "Are you sure you want to permanently delete all " +
              "the data in the table?";

        // Prompt the user to see if he wants to delete
        if (JOptionPane.showConfirmDialog(frame, data) == JOptionPane.OK_OPTION)
        {
              QueryDataSetAutoInc.deleteAllRows();
              QueryDataSetAutoInc.saveChanges();
        }
    }
```

The QueryDataSet.empty() method will empty the local copy of your dataset, but it will not affect the data back on the server. Calling empty and then saveChanges() does not work either. Call deleteAllRows if you want to empty the table in your database.

The effect of calling deleteAllRows will differ depending on whether you brought down all or part of a dataset in your query. If you brought down only a portion of the dataset, you will delete only the portion you retrieved. The following SQL statement will delete all the rows in a table:

```
delete from AUTOINC_TEST
```

In earlier sections of this chapter I showed how to create a QueryDataSet in code rather than using the visual tools. The text then went on to explain how to execute a query using that QueryDataSet. You might use a similar technology to execute the delete query shown here.

Summary

In this chapter the text covered inserting and adding rows of data, as well as deleting data. You had a chance to study the differences between posting data to your local dataset and saving the changes back to the server.

You learned about working with auto-increment fields. You saw that they are declared one way in Access and a second way in MySQL, and they are dealt with via the generator mechanism in InterBase.

You also learned some strategies for retrieving newly inserted auto-increment fields and ways to locate records that seemed to disappear after the user saved them. In the process, you were introduced to some advanced techniques for working with SQL queries.

The subject of working with queries will be picked up again in the next chapter. There you will learn how to use parameterized queries. A discussion of transactions will also be included in that chapter, along with several other important topics.

Chapter 45

SQL Queries, Parameterized Queries, Columns, and Transactions

Charlie Calvert

This chapter will give you a look at some new ways to handle queries. In particular, you will learn about parameterized queries and writing queries using raw JDBC code.

Parameterized queries help you customize an SQL statement at run time. For instance, you might compose an SQL statement to retrieve all the records from a particular state. In an ideal world, you would want to decide which state to query on at run time, rather than having to hard-code the value at design time. A parameterized query will help you treat part of the query as a variable that can be filled in at run time.

When working with parameterized queries, you will also get a chance to explore the Column object in more depth. The Column object plays a major role in JBuilder database programming, and you will be well served if you understand how it works.

A section in the middle of the chapter explores techniques for slipping past the DataExpress wrappers, so you can get down with the raw JDBC code. This can be helpful when you want to optimize your code or access infrequently used features that might not be included in DataExpress.

The chapter also includes a brief overview of how transactions are built into standard DataExpress routines. This is not a subject that you need to understand in order to use the JBuilder database tools, but it is valuable information that can help you understand the limits and strengths of your program.

The chapter will end with a very brief overview of a few more complex example programs that are included on the CD. These example programs allow you to see the techniques discussed in the last few chapters in a more real-world setting.

Getting More Control of SQL Queries

In this first section of the chapter we will look at a program called InsertDelete. You can find the source on the CD that accompanies this book and at www.elvenware.com. This program will give you a look at some new ways that you can use SQL. The InsertDelete program is shown in Figure 45-1.

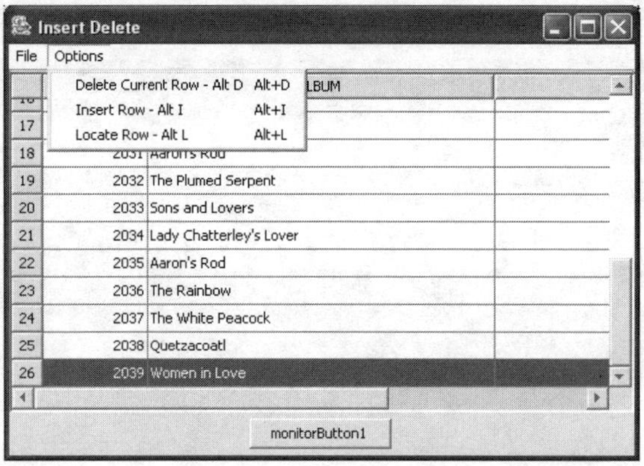

Figure 45-1: The simple interface to the InsertDelete program

If it is at all possible, you should use auto-increment fields, as described in the previous chapter. They are designed to ensure that your insert goes smoothly. If that fails, try using stored procedures, which are not covered in this book due to time and space constraints. Also, stored procedures won't be available in MySQL for a few more months, and this book is focused on MySQL.

There are occasions, however, when an auto-increment field or a stored procedure won't work for you for one reason or another. The best reason, of course, would be that your current database doesn't support them. Fortunately, there is a time-honored method of dealing with this problem.

The solution I'm going to show you is not a perfect solution, but it will work in most programs. More importantly, it will give us a very good excuse to start examining exactly how to start using SQL queries in a much more flexible and advanced manner than we have so far.

Consider the following very simple table, designed to hold a single row of data:

```
CREATE TABLE CODE_VALUES
(
   ARTISTCODE int,
   ALBUMCODE int
) TYPE=INNODB;
INSERT INTO CODE_VALUES VALUES(2000, 2000);
```

This table is designed to hold two integers. One integer will be the current value for the CODE field of the ARTIST table and the other the current value of the CODE field for the ALBUM table. When you do an insert into the ALBUM table, you can retrieve the current value of ALBUMCODE from the CODE_VALUES table and use it as the next value for the ALBUM table. You then increment the ALBUMCODE value and put it back into the CODE_VALUES table. For instance, if CODE_VALUES currently has the ALBUMCODE value of 1000, you would want to increment it to 1001 and then insert the new value back in the table. In this way you have a single value, kept in a single field, of a single row, of a single table that will always be used as the next value for the CODE field of the ALBUM table. Large, untold numbers of database programs have been written over the years using this algorithm.

There is, needless to say, one serious problem with this scenario. It is similar to the problem we had when working with inserts for auto-increment fields. There is a window of opportunity for disaster to strike between the time you do a read on the ARTISTCODE field and the time you reinsert the incremented value in the CODE_VALUES table.

It is very unlikely that this tiny window of opportunity will ever be big enough for anyone to fall through. And yet, it is not impossible. So a solution needs to be found. The following section discusses one such solution.

Locking Tables

The solution to the window of opportunity problem that I will implement here involves locking the CODE_VALUES table, reading from it, incrementing and inserting the new number, and then unlocking the table. While the table is locked, no one else can access it. They can't even do a read on it.

The best way to understand locking tables is to see it in action. Perhaps the simplest way to view this interesting technology is to open two command line windows with MySQL monitor running in each of them. You could also use MyCC. MySQL monitor and MyCC were discussed in Chapter 39.

Create the CODE_VALUES table using the SQL code from the previous section. After you create it, use the show tables status command in the MySQL monitor to ensure that you have indeed created an InnoDB table.

In the first of your two command windows that are running the MySQL monitor, enter the following two lines of code:

```
LOCK TABLES CODE_VALUES WRITE;
select * from CODE_VALUES;
```

Now open a second window MySQL monitor window, and enter this code:

```
select * from CODE_VALUES;
```

This simple SQL statement will hang, as shown in Figure 45-2. It will just sit there, unable to move, because it cannot access CODE_VALUES until the first session enters the following text:

```
UNLOCK TABLES;
```

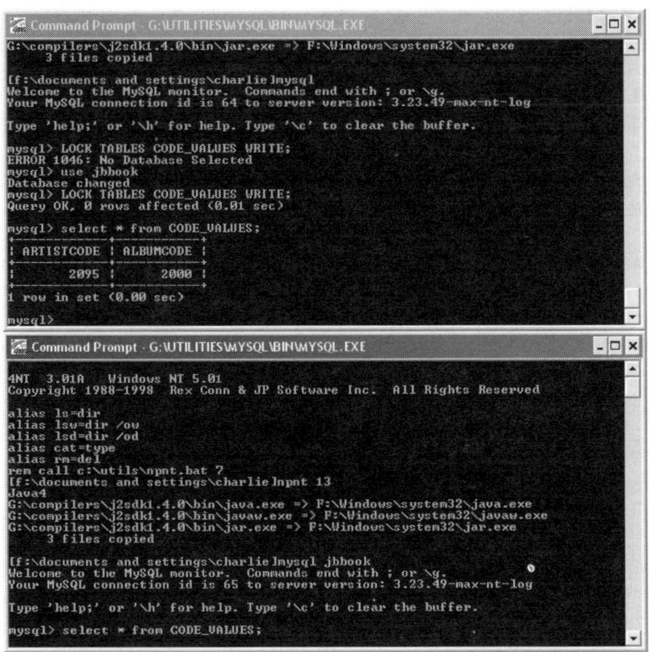

Figure 45-2: The MySQL session in the lower command window is hung, waiting for the first session to release its lock.

The moment the UNLOCK TABLES command is given, the second command session will be allowed to finish its request:

```
mysql> select * from CODE_VALUES;
+------------+-----------+
| ARTISTCODE | ALBUMCODE |
+------------+-----------+
|       2095 |      2000 |
+------------+-----------+
1 row in set (6 min 49.23 sec)
```

You can see here that it took 6 minutes 49.23 seconds to complete the request. That gives you some idea of how long it takes me to take a screen shot, edit it, and type in a few words of explanation.

Here is how long the original select request took in the upper command window:

```
mysql> select * from CODE_VALUES;
+------------+-----------+
| ARTISTCODE | ALBUMCODE |
+------------+-----------+
|       2095 |      2000 |
+------------+-----------+
1 row in set (0.00 sec)
```

The point here is that nothing could happen in the second command window until the first command window unlocked the table.

If you are unfamiliar with locking tables, I would recommend actually performing this little experiment. There is nothing like getting your hands dirty to help you get a feeling for how a technology like this actually works.

NOTE: This example program illustrates one of the dangers of locking tables. If you are not careful, you can end up in a deadlocked situation where two or more instances of your program are hung. The danger inherent in locking a table is why I prefer to use auto-increment values. If you are using auto-increment values correctly, there is little risk that anything will go wrong. InterBase programs using generators and stored procedures are also safe from the danger of locking.

Having said all this, I should add that locking tables in the manner shown here is extremely unlikely to cause trouble. Locking usually becomes dangerous when code more complex than that shown here is executed.

This discussion of the dangers inherent in locking tables will be continued at the end of the chapter, when transactions are discussed. A kind of locking can take place during a transaction, but it is usually less severe than the locking we are currently discussing. In particular, some types of transactions lock write procedures, but not read procedures. Other types of transactions don't lock tables at all. Finally, there are some types of transactions that can lead to problems similar to those discussed here. The default transaction mode used by the QueryDataSet will not lead to lockups. But I am getting ahead of myself. Transactions will be discussed near the end of this chapter.

The InsertDelete program works with the CODE_VALUES table and a small scratch table I created called TINYALBUM. I created this second table so that we could experiment all we wanted with this technology without actually messing up the real ALBUM table. Here is the definition for the TINYALBUM table:

```
CREATE TABLE TINYALBUM
(
  CODE   INT NOT NULL,
```

```
  ALBUM        VARCHAR(45) NOT NULL,
  COMMENT   VARCHAR(75),
  PRIMARY KEY(CODE)
) TYPE = INNODB;
```

The only important field in this table is the CODE field. That's the one we are focusing on. The rest of the fields are just there to give us some context and verisimilitude.

As you recall, we want to get the value of the ALBUMCODE, increment it by one, and then put it back in the CODE_VALUES table. We can then use the value we retrieved from the ALBUMCODE field as a unique value for the CODE field, which is the primary key in the TINYALBUM table.

When using this technology, an insert method looks almost exactly as it did in the previous example using the auto-increment field. The only difference is that you need to have a way to retrieve the new value for the code field via a custom method called getNextCodeValue. In the example shown here, tinyAlbum is the name of the QueryDataSet used in this data module:

```
/**
 * Insert a new row into the database
 */
public void insertRow(String insertStr)
{
      // Declare the column to save the new string into.
      String colName = "ALBUM";

      // Print debug info if requested
      if (this.debug)System.out.println("Inserting string: " + insertStr);

      // Insert a new row in the database and set the album field
      tinyAlbum.insertRow(false);
      int codeValue = getNextCodeValue();
      tinyAlbum.setInt(codeField, codeValue);
      tinyAlbum.setString(colName, insertStr);

      // Save our work to the server
      save();

      // Pull our work back from the server so we can view it.
      tinyAlbum.refresh();

      // Move the user to the new row that we have inserted
      locate(colName, insertStr, codeValue);
}
```

Right after the call to insertRow, you will see the call to getNextCodeValue. Once the value is retrieved, you can use setInt to insert it into the dataset's CODE field.

Here is the call to getNextCodeValue and interesting related methods called doSQL and doQuery:

```
private int doQuery(String sql)
{
      Statement statement = database1.createStatement();
      int codeValue = 0;
```

```
        try
        {
            ResultSet set = statement.executeQuery(sql);
            set.first();
            codeValue = set.getInt(albumCodeField);
            System.out.println("jdbc value: " + codeValue);
        }
        catch (SQLException e)
        {
            System.out.println(e);
        }
        return codeValue;
    }

    private void doSQL(Statement updateStatement, String sql)
    {
        try
        {
            updateStatement.executeUpdate(sql);
        }
        catch (java.sql.SQLException e)
        {
            System.err.println(e);
        }
    }

    /**
     * This is the old fashioned way to get a new unique value for the primary
     * key of artist data set. The goal is to keep the current value of CODE in
     * a very small, one row table. Then retrieve and increment that number
     * each time you want to add a row to the artist data set.
     *
     * @return The new unique value.
     */
    private int getNextCodeValue()
    {
        // Create a statement and Lock the table so no one can talk to it.
        Statement updateStatement = database1.createStatement();
        String sql = "LOCK TABLES CODE_VALUES WRITE;";
        doSQL(updateStatement, sql);

        // get the current value of the AlbumCode, this is what we are after
        sql = "select * from CODE_VALUES";
        int newCodeValue = doQuery(sql);

        // Compose update so code_values has a unique number next time
        sql = "update CODE_VALUES set ALBUMCODE = " + (newCodeValue + 1);
        sql += " where ALBUMCODE = " + newCodeValue; // codeData.getInt("ALBUMCODE");

        // Use the JDBC statement and run the update
        doSQL(updateStatement, sql);
```

```
        sql = "UNLOCK TABLES";
        doSQL(updateStatement, sql);

        return newCodeValue;
    }
```

The interesting thing about this code is that it relies almost entirely upon JDBC code, rather than DataExpress code. It lets the Database object manage the connection, but all the retrieving and inserting data into tables is done through raw JDBC functions from the JDK.

NOTE: I am relying on the JDK SQL code heavily here, in part just to show you how to write this kind of code if you want to write it. Furthermore, I want to show that DataExpress is just a wrapper around JDBC. Borland code is usually flexible, and true to form it lets you get down to the underlying layer if that is what you want to do. There is, however, another reason why I chose to use JDK SQL code in this case. You can't use the QueryDataSet to update this field without customizing it for the current dataset. In particular, you need to start working with Column objects, which seems like overkill in a situation like this. To avoid all that work, you can create your own query for updating a value.

The createStatement or createPreparedStatement methods of the Database object give you the key to getting at the lower-level JDK code. These are simple, very short wrappers around JDBC code. Here you are really asking for access to JDBC itself so that you can perform some queries for updating a dataset.

Experienced database programmers know that significant work can be done by simply issuing SQL statements. The technology I am showing you here gives you the ability to start issuing these statements at will. The Borland visual tools are very useful for creating the interface of your program. But when it comes time to start manipulating data behind the scenes, all you really need is the ability to create a simple SQL statement and execute it.

Here is the code for creating an SQL statement that can be used for an update:

```
// Create a JDBC update statement and run the update
java.sql.Statement updateStatement = database1.createStatement();
try
{
    updateStatement.executeUpdate(sql);
}
catch (java.sql.SQLException e)
{
    System.err.println(e);
}
```

Call DataBase.createStatement to create an instance of the java.sql.Statement type. As mentioned earlier, this is simply a wrapper around the JDBC call to Connection.CreateStatement. The Statement class was not created at Borland. If it were, it would be named something like com.borland.dx.dataset.Statement. Instead, it is part of the built-in JDBC code that is part of Java itself. You are using Borland's tools to access this class, but the class itself is part of the built-in substructure that underlies DataExpress.

NOTE: One reason that I am stressing this so much is that it illustrates the flexibility of DataExpress. As you have seen, the DataExpress tools are very helpful when you want to create the visual interface for your program. But if all you want to do is issue SQL statements, DataExpress seems like overkill. In such cases, DataExpress wrapper code would just cause performance problems without really aiding you in writing these kinds of statements. My point here is that you can use DataExpress when you need it and then switch to raw SQL when you want to

hone a bit closer to the metal (if one can talk about being close to the metal when using a VM!). I should add, however, that well-written wrapper code is often much more efficient than the quickly hacked together solutions that developers, including myself, paste together under the pressure of a deadline.

Once you have an instance of the Statement class, you can simply pass it a String containing an SQL statement. For instance, you might pass it a string such as:

```
update MYTABLE set LAST_NAME = "Tagore" where FIRST_NAME="Rabindranath".
```

Now call Statement.executeUpdate, and you are done:

```
updateStatement.executeUpdate(sql);
```

The whole process takes three or four lines of code. It is a simple, flexible, and very powerful technique.

The process is a little more complicated if you want to send a query that returns a dataset:

```
private static final String albumCodeField = "ALBUMCODE";

private int doQuery(String sql)
{
      Statement statement = database1.createStatement();
      int codeValue = 0;
      try
      {
            ResultSet set = statement.executeQuery(sql);
            set.first();
            codeValue = set.getInt(albumCodeField);
            System.out.println("jdbc value: " + codeValue);
      }
      catch (SQLException e)
      {
            System.out.println(e);
      }
      return codeValue;
}
```

The opening lines are similar to the code in the executeUpdate method, as you first create a Statement. But instead of calling executeUpdate, this time you call executeQuery. In return you get a ResultSet. ResultSet is — in a very loose sense — the class that QueryDataSet is built around. It wraps the data retrieved from the database. Like QueryDataSet, it is a series of getter and setter methods, one for each of the major Java types. In our case, we are only interested in calling getInt. Pass in the name of the field that you want to access as the sole parameter to the method. Once we have the return value, the method exits. The next step is to increment that value and update the dataset, as explained earlier in this section.

NOTE: **The com.elvenware.database.BasicQuery object has a few more methods of this type in it. The methods are quite simple, but they are designed to generalize this kind of access to databases. The TestBasicQuery JUnit test in the src/test directory from the CD shows how to use those routines. In particular, note this method for wrapping a row of data in an ArrayList:**

```
public static ArrayList rowToArrayList(ResultSet resultSet, int row)
{
      ArrayList list = new ArrayList();
      try
```

```
    {
          // Move to the row the user wants to see
          resultSet.first();
          resultSet.relative(row);

          // Find out the number of columns
          int colCount = resultSet.getMetaData().getColumnCount();

          // Add the row to the array
          for (int i = 1; i <= colCount; i++)
          {
                list.add(resultSet.getObject(i));
          }
    }
    catch (SQLException e)
    {
          System.out.println(e);
    }

    // Return an array containing one row of data
    return list;
}
```

Note the call to resultSet.first(). When you first get it, a ResultSet is not pointing at any data. You need to move to the first record or you end up accessing null values. The ResultSet.relative() method moves to a row number calculated from a particular point in a dataset. Note also the call to getMetaData(), which can return an object that describes the dataset you are using. Look at the for statement, and you will see that the first field of a row is at offset 1, not at offset 0. Borland, and most C programmers, always (almost always?) use 0 as the first element of an array, so this one can catch you off guard.

This is the end of any serious discussion of JDBC-specific code. However, the topic of working with SQL will be continued in the next section. There you will learn more about the SQL queries and explore something called parameterized queries.

Parameterized Queries and Column Objects

Parameterized queries are a powerful technique that can help you create flexible SQL statements. You have actually used parameterized queries in the one-to-many relationships established in Chapter 42. However, there are many occasions when you will want to use this technique in code explicitly written by hand, rather than in code auto-generated by the IDE. This section of the chapter will explain how to achieve that goal. Two sample programs called EasySQL and Params are available on the CD. We will look at the Params example first and then take a quick look at EasySQL.

NOTE: In this section you are again going to spend a considerable amount of time working with the DataExpress Column object. Column objects play an important role in parameterized queries and are also helpful when you customize the appearance of JdbTable objects. Column objects are an important part of DataExpress, and you should pay close attention to the discussion of them in this section of the text.

I should perhaps add that Column objects play such a big role in DataExpress because they play a big role in JDBC programming. The Java JDK classes on which DataExpress is built certainly have a major impact on the structure of DataExpress. If you are a Delphi programmer, and some-

times wish that DataExpress were more like Delphi, issues like this can help you understand why DataExpress took a form somewhat different than the award-winning database tools found in Delphi.

The goal of a parameterized query is to give you more flexibility at run time as to exactly what values will be used in an SQL statement. For instance, you might want to select a limited range of data, such as all the people from a database that live in a particular state or have a particular zip code. At design time, you won't know which zip code or state to use in SQL statements. Parameterized queries allow you to fill in that value at run time.

The basic syntax for selecting a range of people looks like this:

```
select * from MY_TABLE where STATE="AZ";
```

The problem with this statement is that the state you want to reference, Arizona, is hard-coded into the statement. To make this into a parameterized query, you should come up with syntax that looks like this:

```
select * from MY_TABLE where STATE=:STATE;
```

By adding a colon, followed by the word STATE, you are turning the last part of the statement into a variable that can be changed at run time. For instance, you could set STATE to "CA," "MD," "MA," or some other value. After making the change, you would refresh the query, thereby gaining access to a new result set with information about a particular state.

To use parameterized queries, you should first create an application with a data module in it that gives you access to the fields of the ALBUM table from the jbbook database. We have done this kind of thing so many times that I won't take you through all the details of this operation. The key steps are to create a new application and add a data module to it. Either use the Data Modeler or drop down Database and QueryDataset objects. Make sure Database is hooked up to the jbbook database and QueryDataSet to the ALBUM table. If you are having trouble, take a look at the Params example on the CD or reread some of the earlier chapters in this part of the book.

Now that you have the basic app set up, it is time to add the parameterized query. In this case, what we want to do is select all the records from the ALBUM table that have a particular rating. For instance, we want to find all the albums with a rating of 8 or higher. But the key is that we want to supply the actual rating value at run time. The parameter in our parameterized query will be the RATING field of the ALBUM table. (If you are having trouble setting up the ALBUM table and jbbook database, see Chapter 39.)

To get started adding the parameterized query, first add a third component to the Data Access node of the structure pane. The new component is from the DataExpress tab and is called a ParameterRow. You can see it in Figure 45-3.

In the content pane shown in Figure 45-3, you can see that a new column called rating has been added to the component. To add a column, press the plus button

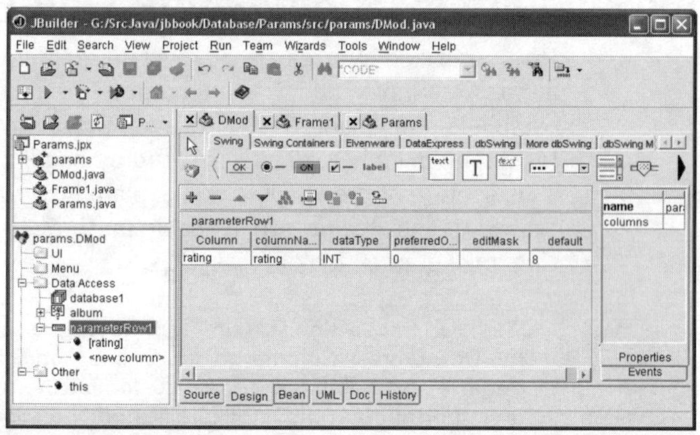

Figure 45-3: A ParameterRow component in a data module being edited in the content pane. The tool you use in the content pane is called a Column editor.

directly beneath the Bean Chooser and to the right of the word Params.java in the project pane.

NOTE: After you drop a ParameterRow on the structure pane, you may have to double-click on it before the Column editor will appear in the content pane.

In Figure 45-3, the content pane presents a custom-made view of the properties of the new Column component. In particular, you can see the Column, columnName, dataType, preferredOrdinal, editMask, and default properties. You could, if you wanted, use the Inspector to change all of these properties. The content pane is simply giving you a filtered view of these properties. You can add or delete any of these properties from the content pane by choosing the fifth icon over from the plus symbol you pressed to create the column.

NOTE: The columnName and dataType properties are self-explanatory. The preferredOrdinal property designates the position of the column in the dataset. By default, the CODE field is in position 0, the first position, since it is the first field of the dataset. If you wanted to move a column to a different position, you could use this field. The editMask property can help you define what values a user can enter into a field. For instance, you can limit users to typing in only integers or help guide them when typing in a date field. Unfortunately, I do not have room to discuss this important property in this book. The default value defines the default setting you want to give a field. For instance, you might want to set the default value of the RATING column to 8 or the default value of a STATE column to MA.

Set the column and columnName properties to **RATING**. Set the dataType to **INT** and the default value to **8**. This default value will be the default value assigned to the rating field. In other words, by default, we are asking for a view of all albums that have a rating of 8 or higher.

Click on the QueryDataSet that points at the ALBUM table. Choose the ellipsis icon in the query property to pop up the Query dialog shown in Figure 45-4.

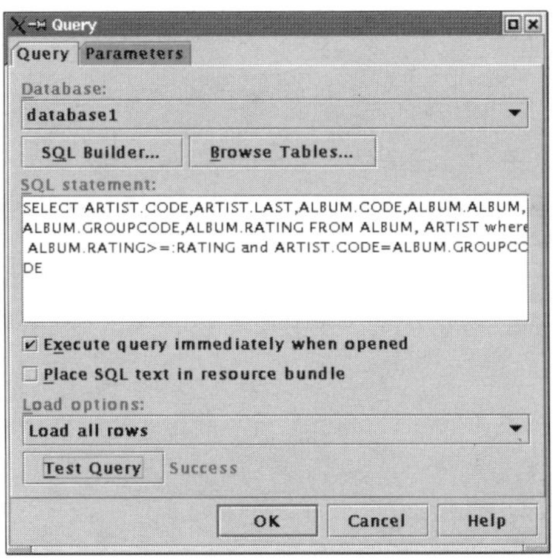

Figure 45-4: The Query dialog, set up to handle a parameterized query

Modify the query in the dialog so that it reads as follows:

```
SELECT ALBUM.CODE,ALBUM.ALBUM,ALBUM.RATING
      FROM ALBUM where ALBUM.RATING>=:RATING;
```

Here you can see that the variable in your parameterized query is the word :RATING. The colon before the word marks it as a variable that will be filled in at run time.

Turn to the Parameters page of the Query dialog and use the drop-down list to select the value parameterRow1, as shown in Figure 45-5. This will associate the ParameterRow component you created with the query.

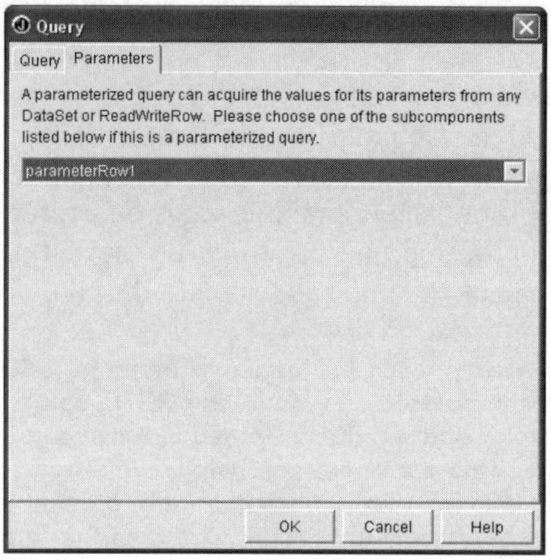

Figure 45-5: Associating a ParameterRow object with your query

You can test the work you have done by pressing the Test Query button at the bottom of the first page of the Query dialog. The word "Success" should appear next to the button, as shown in Figure 45-4. If something goes wrong, the most likely problem is that the ParameterRow component is not associated with the query, as shown in Figure 45-5.

Click the **OK** button in the Query dialog, and switch to source mode. You should now see the following code in your jbInit for the data module:

```
album.setQuery(new QueryDescriptor(
      database1,
      "SELECT album.CODE,album.ALBUM,album.RATING " +
      "FROM album where album.RATING>=:rating",
      parameterRow1, true, Load.ALL));
```

Notice the presence of your database, the SQL statement you composed, the ParameterRow component, a Boolean request to automatically execute the query, and a constant designating your desire to pull down all the rows.

Other code in the jbInit section and class initialization section is equally important. Notice in particular this code for setting up the rating column of the parameterRow1 variable:

```
Column rating = new Column();

rating.setColumnName("rating");
rating.setDataType(com.borland.dx.dataset.Variant.INT);
rating.setDefault("8");
rating.setPreferredOrdinal(0);
rating.setServerColumnName("NewColumn1");
rating.setSqlType(0);
parameterRow1.setColumns(new Column[] {rating});
```

The code shown here is the result of the work you did with the ParameterRow component. In particular, it shows what happened when you pressed the green plus button to add a new column to the component. Rather than use the default name of column1, I have renamed the Column instance to rating.

The code to actually complete this request is now extremely simple. Add a method to your data module that looks like this:

```
public void doQuery(int rangeNumber)
{
      parameterRow1.setInt("RATING", rangeNumber);
      album.refresh();
}
```

This code sets the value of the rating column that you added to the ParameterRow component. You might, for instance, set this value to 9, or 5, or 3, or any ordinal value from 1 and 10. The call to QueryDataSet.refresh() actually executes your query and pulls down the new values to show in the main form of the component. After you have completed the rest of the program, the call to refresh produces the results shown in Figure 45-6.

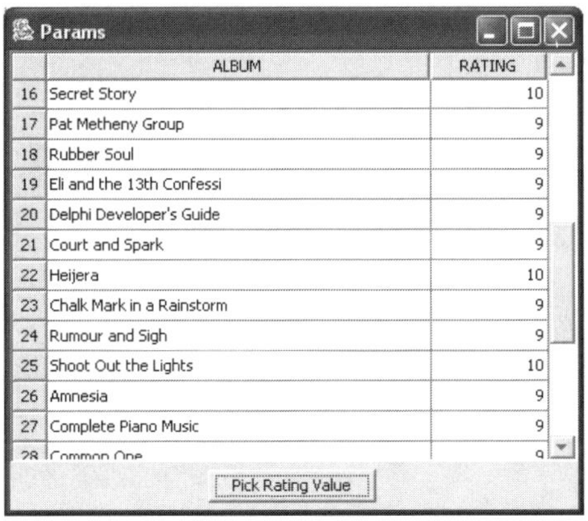

Figure 45-6: The simple interface for the Params program

To make the interface shown in Figure 45-6, add two JPanels to Frame1. Set the top panel's constraints property to **CENTER** and the bottom one to **SOUTH**.

It's now time to write the interface-related code that will call the doQuery method you inserted into the data module. To ensure that Frame1 can call the data module, focus **Frame1** in the content pane, select the **Use Data Module wizard**, and choose **Share static instance of data module** from the options it presents.

Drop a button in the bottom panel and set its text field to **Pick Rating Value**, as shown in Figure 45-6. I associated the following method with the button's actionPerformed event:

```
void jButton1_actionPerformed(ActionEvent e)
{
      String input = JOptionPane.showInputDialog(this,
            "Enter a number between 1 and 10");
      if (input != null)
      {
            int rangeNumber = Integer.parseInt(input);
            if ((rangeNumber > 0) && (rangeNumber < 11))
            {
                  dMod.doQuery(rangeNumber);
            }
      }
}
```

This code retrieves a value from the user, translates the value into a number, ensures that the number is between 1 and 10, and passes the number to the data module for processing by the doQuery method.

NOTE: Additional error checking would be needed to make this method withstand the onslaught of invalid input that a careless user would be likely to generate.

The center panel in Frame1 has a TableScrollPanel with a JdbTable placed on top of it. The dataSet property of the JdbTable component is set to the Album QueryDataSet component found on the data module:

```
jdbTable1.setDataSet(dMod.getAlbum());
```

If you have any questions about how to lay out the Params program, you can find the program on the CD. Any possible updates to the program can be found on www.elvenware.com.

Adding a Join to the Params Program

The Params program could be improved if you could easily see the artist who is associated with a particular album, as shown in Figure 45-7.

Figure 45-7: A join between the ARTIST and ALBUM tables allows us to see which artist is associated with which album.

A standard bit of SQL syntax allows you to link fields from one table with fields from a second table to create a dataset that combines values from both tables. In a sense, a join accomplishes something very much like what is achieved by a one-to-many relationship. The difference is that a one-to-many relationship is displayed in two datasets, while a join is displayed in a single dataset.

NOTE: Your ability to automatically edit and save the values in a join can be somewhat problematic. To find out exactly what capabilities you have, you should experiment. For instance, you might not be able to edit the fields at all or you might be able to edit only the fields from one table. A common solution to this problem is to pop up a dialog with the values from the dataset shown in ordinary JTextFields. After the user presses the OK button in the dialog, extract the values from the text fields, compose an SQL update statement, and insert the new values into the database. The version of the Params program included on the disk has a Save button on it so that you can experiment with your ability to save fields of the dataset.

Here is how to edit the SQL in the Params program so that you can have a join between the ARTIST and ALBUM table:

```
album.setQuery(new dataset.QueryDescriptor(
      database1,
      "SELECT ARTIST.CODE,ARTIST.LAST,ALBUM.CODE,ALBUM.ALBUM,"+
      "ALBUM.GROUPCODE,ALBUM.RATING FROM ALBUM, ARTIST " +
      "where ALBUM.RATING>=:RATING and ARTIST.CODE=ALBUM.GROUPCODE",
      parameterRow1,
      true,
      Load.ALL));
```

There is a degree of complexity in this new SQL statement. Notice first that there are selections from both the ARTIST and ALBUM tables: artist.CODE, album.CODE. You can still see our initial where clause, which specified the rating variable: where album.RATING>= :RATING. Now, however, a second WHERE clause has been added:

```
and ARTIST.CODE=ALBUM.GROUPCODE"
```

This second WHERE clause requests the records from the ARTIST table where ARTIST.CODE equals album.GROUPCODE. As you perhaps recall, GROUPCODE is the foreign key in the ALBUM table that links to the CODE field in the ARTIST table. In other words, if an artist has a CODE of 1 and an album has a GROUPCODE of 1, that means the artist was the creator of that particular album. This WHERE clause thereby matches artists with albums. For instance, if you are looking at the album *Secret Story*, you will see that it has a GROUPCODE of 11. This WHERE clause instructs the database to look in the ARTIST table for the artist with a CODE of 11. It finds Pat Metheny, and then extracts a value in the LAST field from the ARTIST table and inserts it into the LAST field of the joined table.

This SQL statement selects some fields that we do not really want to show in the grid. As a result, the following statement is added to the jbInit method of Frame1:

```
jdbTable1.setHiddenColumns(new int[] {0,2,4});
```

This code ensures that the artist.CODE, album.CODE, and album.GROUPCODE fields are not displayed in jdbTable1.

More on the Column Class

The new join that we have created results in a JdbTable instance with an awkward size. It is just wide enough to be wider than a standard Java form. If only we could make it just a bit narrower, it would fit easily into a window. One way to accomplish this goal is to make the widths of some of the fields just a bit narrower than the size assigned to them by default. If we do this, perhaps one or two LAST or ALBUM fields won't quite fit in the displayed area, but most of them will fit handily.

At first, you might want to make a change like this by editing the JdbTable class. You can sometimes get work done that way, but often it is simplest to use the Column object. In particular, you can do this by changing the width property of the Column component in the Inspector.

Editing the width property of a column is simple, but it has wide-ranging effects. Let's take a moment to consider those effects.

Every QueryDataSet creates a default Column object for each field in your dataset. In many cases, you will want to override those default columns by creating custom Column objects of your own. We have done that already several times in our code. In particular, you created custom Column objects in the ParameterRow object we have just been looking at.

In Figure 45-8, you can see the ALBUM table from the Params program. Notice that the LAST and ALBUM fields have their names surrounded by brackets when they are displayed in the structure pane. These brackets signify that you have created a custom instance of the Column object rather than using the default one created by DataExpress.

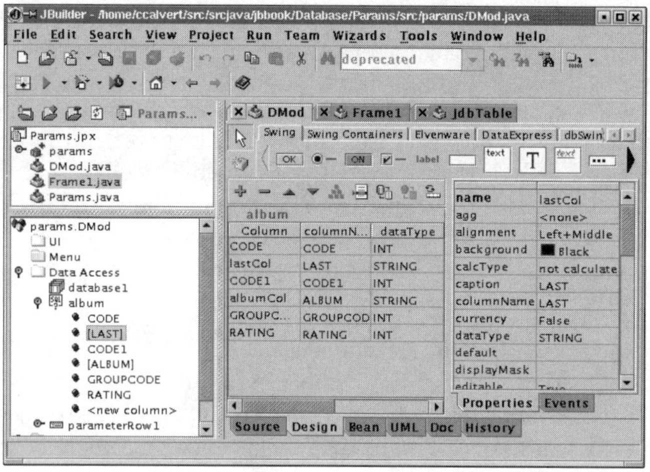

Figure 45-8: If you create a custom column, JBuilder will display it set off by brackets in the structure pane.

To create the custom component, all I needed to do was start editing the properties of the field in the Inspector. The moment you start to change these properties, a custom instance of the Column component is created, and its name in the structure pane is surrounded by brackets.

Since DataExpress has already created a Column object for you, there is no additional overhead in supplying a custom one of your own. However, the addition of these objects does add to the already heavily cluttered scene in your jbInit:

```
lastCol.setColumnName("LAST");
lastCol.setDataType(com.borland.dx.dataset.Variant.STRING);
lastCol.setPrecision(30);
lastCol.setTableName("ARTIST");
lastCol.setWidth(15);
lastCol.setServerColumnName("LAST");
lastCol.setSqlType(12);
albumCol.setColumnName("ALBUM");
albumCol.setDataType(com.borland.dx.dataset.Variant.STRING);
albumCol.setPrecision(45);
albumCol.setTableName("ALBUM");
albumCol.setWidth(25);
albumCol.setServerColumnName("ALBUM");
albumCol.setSqlType(12);
```

All of this code was generated automatically by JBuilder the moment I started editing the width property of the lastCol and albumCol objects. Notice that I also changed the default names of these columns from something like column1 or column2 to lastCol and albumCol. Giving your column a reasonable name can help you have some chance of making sense of what is taking place in your jbInit method.

Here you can see that I have set the width of these two columns to 15 characters in one case and 25 in the other. Changes to the width property can also affect the precision property and vice versa.

A Quick Glance at the EasySQL Program

The EasySQL program, shown in Figure 45-9, offers some glimpses at technology that extends our use of parameterized queries. The program is found on the CD. It is similar in structure to the Params program you have just seen. As a result, I will not explore it in much depth. To create the program, simply go through all the steps discussed in the Params program, but customize your query as described below and insert a slightly different interface.

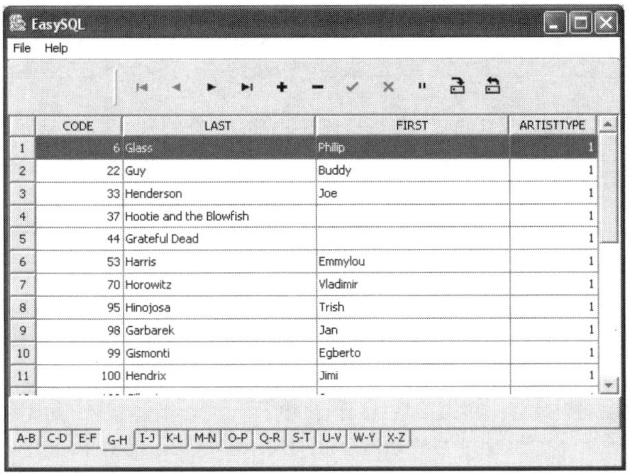

Figure 45-9: The EasySQL program allows the user to use tabs to select a range of data from the dataset.

The program selects data from the ARTIST table using the following setQuery statement:

```
country_name.setQuery(new
        QueryDescriptor(database1,
        "SELECT ARTIST.CODE,ARTIST.LAST,ARTIST.FIRST," +
        "ARTIST.ARTISTTYPE FROM ARTIST "+
        "where LAST like :StartCode or LAST like :EndCode",
        parameterRow1, true, Load.ALL));
```

Here you can see that a few choice fields from the ARTIST table are selected. The SQL statement ends with some rather peculiar-looking syntax:

```
"where LAST like :StartCode or LAST like :EndCode",
```

When the parameters use this syntax, the run-time code after substitutions might look like this:

```
"where LAST like "A%" or LAST like "B%",
```

This translates into a request to retrieve all the records from the ARTIST table where the last field begins with the letter A or the letter B. The percent sign after the letters A and B is a SQL wild card, meaning that it can be matched by any values. Most, but perhaps not all, SQL databases support syntax of this kind. In effect you are saying, "Just give me all the artists whose last names begin with an A or a B."

The ParameterRow component used in the program is set up as shown in Figure 45-10. Notice that the data type for the two new columns is of type String, and default values of A and B are included in the rows.

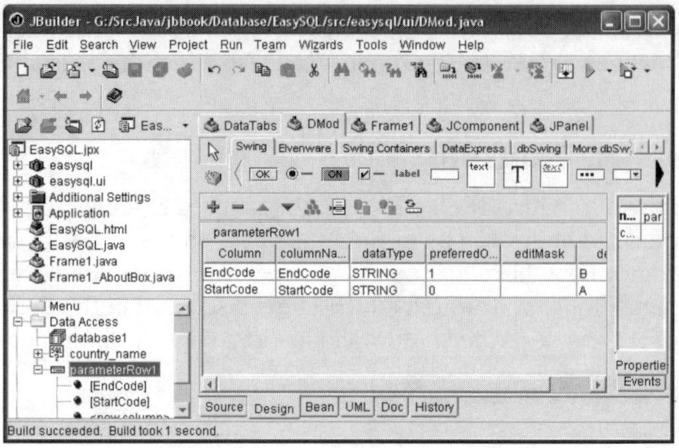

Figure 45-10: Setting up the ParameterRow component to handle the StartCode and EndCode fields used in the SQL transaction

The code for actually running the query is very straightforward:

```
public void runParameterizedQuery(String startCode, String endCode)
{
      parameterRow1.setString("STARTCODE", startCode);
      parameterRow1.setString("ENDCODE", endCode);
      country_name.refresh();
}
```

You can see that the parameterRow component has its two custom column fields set to explicit values at run time. As you may recall, the parameterRow component was associated with the country_name QueryDataSet during the call to setQuery. Therefore, DataExpress finds it possible to register your changes to the ParameterRow object in response to a call to country_name.refresh. In other words, when you call refresh, DataExpress extracts the values you inserted into the ParameterRow object and conspires with the JDBC to compose a new SQL statement that will pull down the values you requested.

The code to create the tabbed panes at the bottom of the EasySQL interface was actually quite simple to compose — once I got the hang of how to do it! I used the visual tools to put the control together, but the generated Swing code looks like this:

```
          this.add(jTabbedPanel,  BorderLayout.CENTER);

          jTabbedPanel.add(jPanel1,  "A-B");
          jTabbedPanel.add(jPanel2,  "C-D");
          jTabbedPanel.add(jPanel3,  "E-F");
          jTabbedPanel.add(jPanel4,  "G-H");
          jTabbedPanel.add(jPanel5,  "I-J");
          jTabbedPanel.add(jPanel6,  "K-L");
          jTabbedPanel.add(jPanel7,  "M-N");
          jTabbedPanel.add(jPanel8,  "O-P");
          jTabbedPanel.add(jPanel9,  "Q-R");
          jTabbedPanel.add(jPanel10,  "S-T");
          jTabbedPanel.add(jPanel11,  "U-V");
          jTabbedPanel.add(jPanel12,  "W-Y");
          jTabbedPanel.add(jPanel13,  "X-Z");
```

I have saved this component in a separate bean file called DataTabs.java. As a result, it is a reusable component that could be easily inserted into your programs. You will find a generalized version of this component in the com.elvenware.comp package.

I'm not going to go into any more detail on the EasySQL component, as it is merely adding incrementally to your knowledge about parameterized queries. Take a look at the program on the CD and see how you can flip through all the letters of the alphabet by choosing the tabs at the bottom of the dialog.

Transactions

Transactions are going on by default in your DataExpress code almost every time your program interacts with the database server. Because the code is built into DataExpress, you usually don't have to think about it. However, there are occasions when you are going to care about the transaction mode of your program, and so a few words of explanation are in order.

NOTE: Transactions are really a huge subject, and if this were a book solely about databases, I would go on about it at some length. But this book is about JBuilder in general, and there has to be some point at which I call cease and desist on all this talk about databases and, indeed, on many of the other topics discussed in this book. Otherwise, there would be no end to the text.

When you are working in the data module in design view, you can select your Database object to see its transaction status. In particular, you want to look at the Boolean useTransactions property and the more complex transactionIsolation property, shown in Figure 45-11.

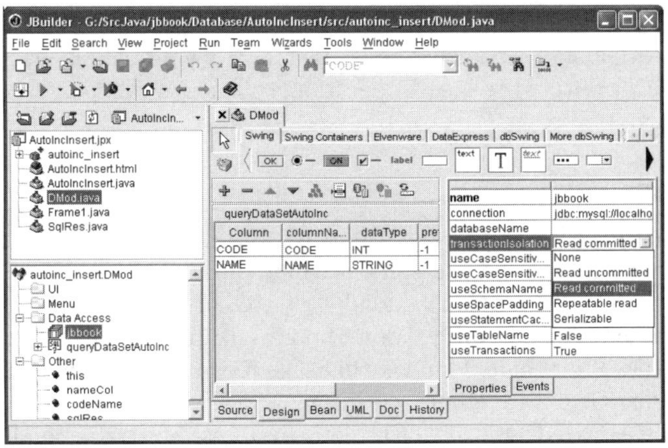

Figure 45-11: The Inspector shows the transactionIsolation levels you can set when viewing a Database object from a data module.

If you want more specific control over transactions, you could, at least in theory, use the database methods start, commit, and rollback:

```
database1.commit();
database1.rollback();
database1.start();
```

It is not recommended that you use these methods. They are really only for internal use by DataExpress. But there are ways to get control over this process, as you will learn if you read on.

The saveChanges method of the Database object can take a Boolean parameter called doTransactions. By default, this value is set to true. If you pass in the parameter and set it to false, a transaction will not be used when committing the data. The useTransactions property of the Database object is what usually determines if saveChanges will use transactions or not.

NOTE: Ironically, one way for you to get control over transactions in a DataExpress program is to turn the useTransactions property off. Then you can start and stop the transactions when you want, and DataExpress will simply be used to post the data to the server.

Most calls to SaveChanges end up calling code in the DataExpress class called Resolution-Manager, which looks something like this:

```
transactionSupport.start();

transactionStarted  = true;

processDataSetDeletes(resOrder);

if (insertsFirst) {
  processDataSetInserts(resOrder);
  processDataSetUpdates(resOrder);
}
else {
  processDataSetUpdates(resOrder);
  processDataSetInserts(resOrder);
}

transactionSupport.commit();
```

In short, when you call saveChanges, a transaction is started, and your data is inserted and committed. If any errors occur during the insert operation, rollback is called:

```
transactionSupport.rollback();
```

Transaction Isolation Levels

Not all transactions behave the same way. In fact, there are four distinct types of transactions. A couple of them are fairly closely related, but some are quite unique.

The following descriptions of the four transaction levels are combinations of my own words and text taken from the JBuilder docs. Frankly, I don't find the JBuilder information particularly helpful in this regard, but I'll include it anyway because it can provide some interesting hints as to how this technology is put together:

- TRANSACTION_READ_UNCOMMITTED: This first type of transaction has a very low level of intrusion on the default behavior of a table. Here is how it works: If you update a table, the other users can see the changes the moment a table is changed, even if a commit has not yet been called. In short, this is what would happen if you weren't using transactions at all, only you have the ability to roll back, or undo, your update. In short, you can perform any number of updates to the database, and they will appear to other users the moment you make them. They will not be permanent, however, until you call commit. At any time you can call rollback and the database will be put back in the order it was in before you began making commits. The problem with this is that I might roll back my transaction, thereby invalidating your view of the data. In other words, you could be looking at the result of an update that I later decided to undo, or roll back. From the JBuilder docs: "*Suitable for single user applications for reports that do not mind transactionally inconsistent views of the data. Especially useful when browsing JDataStore tables with dbswing and DataExpress DataSet components. This isolation level incurs minimal locking overhead."* My understanding of this is simply that you should not try to use this kind of transaction if you expect multiple users to be trying to update the database at the same time.

- TRANSACTION_READ_COMMITTED: This is the default technology used by JBuilder. When you use this transaction level while updating the dataset, no one else will see the changes you make to a dataset until you commit the transaction. Therefore, other users could do a read and get what will eventually prove to be an outdated view of the data. If you then commit your data, you might invalidate some action they want to take. For instance, you might delete the row they are editing or delete a master row on which the detail set they are editing depends. In such cases, JBuilder will surface the error to the second user, informing him or her about what has gone wrong. As a rule, the second person is out of luck, but no serious damage is done to the database. From the JBuilder docs: *"Commonly used for high performance applications. Ideal for data access models that use Optimistic concurrency control. DataExpress QueryDataSet and Borland Application Server use Optimistic concurrency control approaches to data access. In these data access models, read operations are largely performed first. In some cases, read operations are actually performed in a separate transaction from the write operations."*
- TRANSACTION_REPEATABLE_READ: From the moment you start this kind of transaction you will see a static view of the dataset, even if other users change it. This is sometimes called a "snapshot" view of the dataset, since it freezes your view of the data in time until you reach the end of your transaction. If you want to perform calculations on a set of data, this is the ideal mode to use. For instance, if you are calculating who won the most games in a season, you want to ensure that all teams have played the same number of games. Pick such a moment, and begin the transaction. Even if another user attempts to insert a row into the database while you are performing your calculations, your data will still be valid for the point of time at which you began the transaction. From the JBuilder docs: *Provides more protection for transactionally consistent data access without the reduced concurrency of TRANSACTION_SERIALIZABLE. This isolation level, however, results in increased locking overhead because row locks must be acquired and held for the duration of the transaction.*
- TRANSACTION_SERIALIZABLE: This option specifies that all interactions with the dataset must occur serially. In effect, nobody can read the data while I'm working with it. From the JBuilder docs: *"Provides complete serializability of transactions at the risk of reduced concurrency and increased potential for deadlocks. Although row locks can still be used for common operations with this isolation level, some operations cause the JDataStore lock manager to escalate to using table locks."*

Additional Sample Programs

I have run out of both the time and room needed to discuss databases at any greater length. Hopefully I have laid the groundwork on which you can begin building your own database applications. If you are hoping to get information on multi-tier databases, see *JBuilder 7.0 EJB Programming* from Wordware Publishing.

On the CD that accompanies this book, you will find several example programs that expand and illustrate the topics we have been discussing. These example programs attempt to fulfill certain real-world requirements and explore interesting aspects of database development. Note in particular the ElfAddress, ElfMusic, and ElfTracker database programs.

ElfAddress, shown in Figure 45-12, demonstrates how to create a simple real-world database program for maintaining a list of addresses. It uses a single table and has a very simple structure.

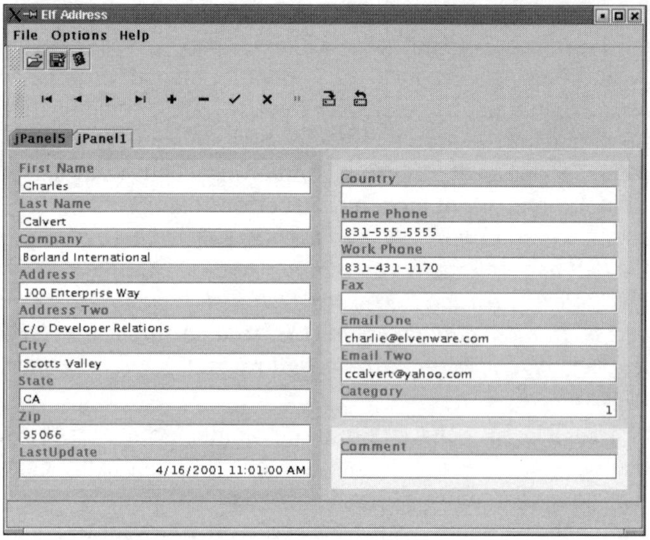

Figure 45-12: The ElfAddress program gives you two views of your data, in table form and in card form. It allows you to search for records, as well as insert and delete them.

The ElfMusic program pulls together all the pieces that we have spread out over several example programs to show how to present a single view of a fairly complex set of interrelated tables. The master-detail view is shown in Figure 45-13, and the lookup view is shown in Figure 45-14.

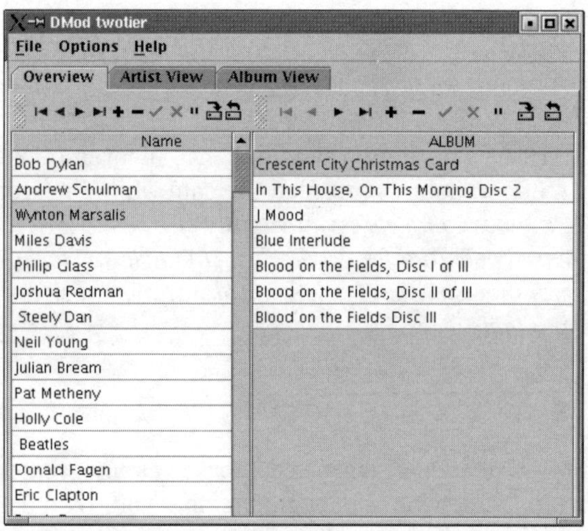

Figure 45-13: Using a one-to-many relationship between the ARTIST and ALBUM tables to allow people to browse all the music associated with a set of artists

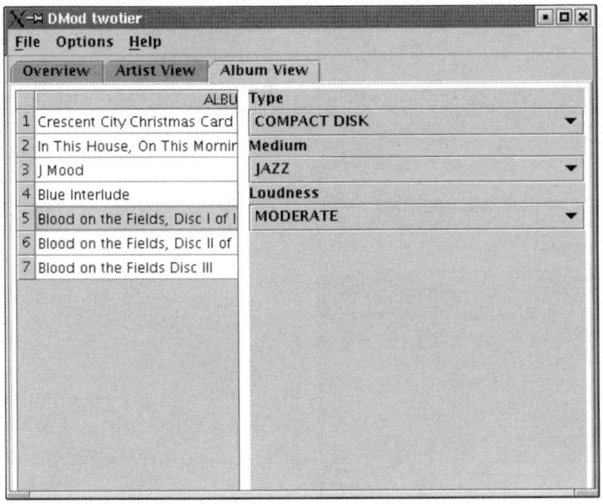

Figure 45-14: This custom view of the ALBUM table uses lookups to make it easy for users to drop down combo boxes and choose the properties for an album.

Of course, the ElfMusic program is based around things like albums and tapes and some really old technology called vinyl records. Many younger readers probably don't even know what these things are.

To come up to date with the modern music world, I have provided the ElfTracker program, which scans CD-ROMs filled with MP3 files and allows you to store the information in a database. In Figure 45-15, you can see the main interface for the program, showing the results of a scan across a drive on my system that holds some MP3 files. Figure 45-16 shows what the entries look like once they are stored in a searchable MySQL database.

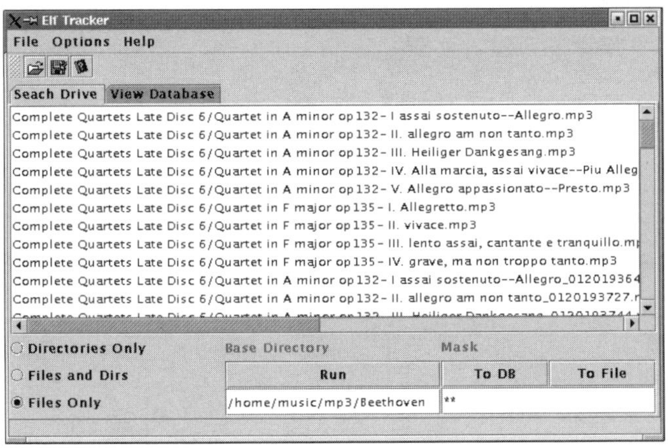

Figure 45-15: Select a drive on your system, and this program will recursively scan through the subdirectories of the drive, looking for files of any type that you specify.

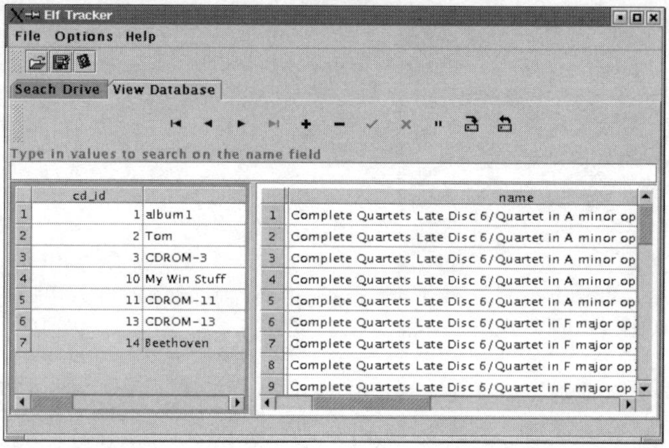

Figure 45-16: If you like the results of your scan, store them to a text file or into the database tables shown here.

The Elf Tracker program takes advantage of some routines built into the Apache Jakarta Ant tool. One of the interesting things about Java is that you can use any classes that happen to be sitting around on your system, whether you wrote them or not. Of course, there is nothing wrong with using open source code like that provided with Ant. However, I will need to come up with another solution if I want to distribute this app to people who do not have Ant installed. Needless to say, the program won't run unless Ant.jar is on your class path. To run it from the JBuilder IDE, you need to set up a library.

The ListTables program, shown in Figure 45-17, is interesting in that it includes no DataExpress code. Instead, it uses JDBC code to get the metadata information about all the tables from a particular database.

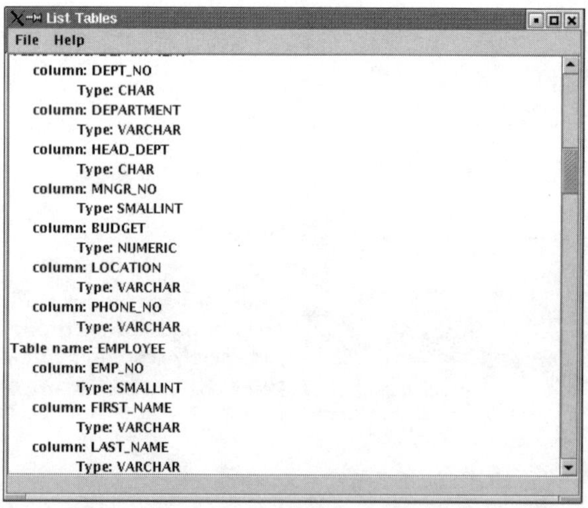

Figure 45-17: Using JDBC to query an InterBase database, discover all the tables in the database, and then find the fields and their types

Because it uses JDBC, the ListTables program is quite flexible and should work with pretty much any database to which you connect. At the time of publication, however, this program was set up to connect to the EMPLOYEE table that comes with InterBase. This information is hard-coded into the program, and you will probably need to change it to query a database on your system.

Details about the programs discussed here can be found on the CD. Each program comes with an HTML file and additional Javadoc files describing how it works. You might check the Elvenware site to see if I have updated any of these programs.

Summary

This chapter showed some of the fancier things you can do with SQL queries, including using JDBC statements to create SQL for updating or deleting values. This book is not intended to explore low-level APIs like java.sql.Statement in any depth, regardless of how useful they might be. You might, however, want to take some time to explore this area on your own. Take a look at the Java documentation for statements and prepared statements. These are available at the following fairly stable URLs: http://java.sun.com/j2se/1.4/docs/api/java/sql/Statement.html and http://java.sun.com/j2se/1.4/docs/api/java/sql/class-use/Statement.html.

Both statements and prepared statements are fully supported by the DataExpress Database component. You should also look at the InsertDelete program on the CD.

The middle of the chapter covered parameterized queries. Besides showing you the ParameterRow component, that discussion also focused on the use of powerful SQL syntax, such as joins and LIKE clauses.

You also had a chance to learn about the Column component and some of the useful things it can do for you. The DataExpress components use Column objects quite heavily, and getting at least a basic understanding of how they work can be very helpful.

The last sections of the chapter briefly explored transactions and then mentioned a few sample programs that can be found on the CD and on www.elvenware.com. Exploring these programs can help you see how to use database code in real-world situations.

This is the end of Part VIII, which focused on database code. We have been able to cover most of the major topics needed by database programmers. If you want to extend your knowledge, you might begin by looking at the DataExpress support for stored procedures and working with text files.

Another major subject not explored in this book is JDataStore. JDataStore is a database built by Borland entirely in Java. Needless to say, the great advantage of JDataStore is that you can deploy it on virtually any platform that supports Java. There is a fee associated with deploying JDataStore applications.

Appendix A

Additional Technical Resources

This appendix lists various sites on the web where you can get information about JBuilder or Java. It is kept in three places:

- This appendix.
- The CD that comes with this JBuilder book. The CD version can be viewed on a computer so that you can take advantage of the hyperlinks.
- The version on Charlie and Margie's web site at http://www.elvenware.com/charlie/java/links.html can be viewed on a computer and updated.

These items are listed in the reverse order of usefulness. Articles of this type are best viewed online so you can take advantage of hyperlinked text. Furthermore, the version on our web site can be updated as links change and new sites are discovered. Therefore, the version in the book itself is least useful, while the one on our web site is most useful.

You will notice that in many cases I do not list the actual URLs. Admittedly, that makes the text-based version less than entirely useful. However, many of the URLs shown here are long, ungainly, and likely to change. As a result, the printed version is really meant to point you to the online version and give you some sense of what you can expect when you reach it. Needless to say, the online version uses hyperlinks to take you to the actual web pages associated with the subjects listed here.

The problem with the web is that it is so huge that it is hard to focus on useful and valuable material. Instead, one can wander for hours in byways that serve to obscure the core functionality one wants to access. This short article is designed to help you focus on truly valuable web resources. If you feel that I am missing something important, write me at mailto: charlie@elvenware and put "JBuilder Companion" in the Subject line.

JDK Information

- The Java Standard edition site: http://java.sun.com/j2se/
- JDK 1.4 overview: http://java.sun.com/j2se/1.4/docs/relnotes/features.html
- JDK 1.4 API Docs: http://java.sun.com/j2se/1.4/docs/api/index.html
- Java Enterprise edition site: http://java.sun.com/j2ee/

JavaBeans Specification

- JavaBeans home page: http://java.sun.com/products/javabeans/
- The Sun Java and XML web site

- The Sun Java tutorials site
- The Sun Java code samples site

Basic Java Newsgroups and Community

If you have questions about how to program, post them in the Borland/Inprise newsgroups.

- The Borland newsgroups at: http://www.borland.com/newsgroups
- The Borland community site: http://community.borland.com
- The all-important comp.lang.java newsgroups on Google
- The useful elists site for mailing lists has a JBuilder node: http://www.elists.org/mailman/listinfo/

Newsgroups are a great free way to get information and share your knowledge with the programming community. Given the nature of our computer-based electronic forums, it simply does not make sense for anyone to ask questions in a one-to-one exchange of messages when more knowledge can be disseminated in a broader forum, such as a newsgroup.

OpenTools and Code Downloads

If you want to find code samples, utilities, or components, here are some good places to look:

- The JBuilder OpenTools Repository: http://jbopentools.sourceforge.net/
- JBuilder submissions on CodeCentral
- The impressive and extensive list of OpenTools on John Kaster's CodeCentral
- Java Builders lists a small number of fairly high-quality OpenTools
- JBuilder OpenTools links on the Borland site

Here are some specific OpenTool sites:

- http://antrunner.sourceforge.net/
- http://jrefactory.sourceforge.net/
- http://www.javabuilders.com/opentools/codetemplates.html

General-purpose Java Sites

Other important sites include:

- JBuilder FAQs on http://www.jguru.com
- JBuilders Journal
- Java Developers Journal
- Dr. Bob's JBuilder site
- The SlashDot Java Articles (a great way spend some time thinking about Java from the meta level)
- The JavaRanch (a wide range of Java resources presented in a friendly and humorous manner)

Complete Books from Sun Available Online

Sun makes most of the books in their press available online at http://java.sun.com/docs/books/. In most cases you can view the books online, and in some cases you can download the HTML for use on your home machine. The HTML versions usually contain hyperlinked text, which can be very helpful. Here is a selected view of key books:

- The Java Language Specification: The blow-by-blow description of the language by its creators makes an excellent resource for masochists.
- The Java Tutorial: A more humane approach to learning the language than you get in the more rigorous language specification.
- Java Platform Performance: Described thusly on Sun's site: "Platform Performance is a comprehensive field manual full of battle-tested strategies and tactics for developing high-performance applications and applets with Java technology."
- *Effective Java*: This excellent book, which is not available online, describes techniques for writing robust, elegant Java code. It is one of the most valuable resources available on the Java language.

Borland TechPubs Web Site

The complete documentation for the JBuilder product, plus updates, is available on the Borland web site at: http://www.borland.com/techpubs/jbuilder/.

For instance, here is a link to the JBuilder 6 docs: http://www.borland.com/techpubs/jbuilder/jbuilder6/index1024x768-ent.html.

Here is a link to the section of the docs on refactoring: http://www.borland.com/techpubs/jbuilder/jbuilder6/pg/whatsnew.html#refactoring.

Appendix B

CD Overview

Charlie Calvert

Introduction

This appendix describes how to compile and run the code found on the CD for this book. It is maintained in three places:

- A shortened version is printed here.
- A second longer and more complete version is stored as index.html on the CD that comes with this book. This version allows you to view descriptions of the programs by clicking on a hyperlink list.
- Finally, I have linked to a third version from http://www.elvenware.com/charlie/java/index.html. This third version may contain updates or late-breaking news regarding the code found on the CD. The online versions are superior to the printed text in that they are longer and make heavy use of hyperlinks — a mechanism that is particularly useful in an article of this type.

There are two key steps you must take before trying to use the code that comes with this book:

- First, and most importantly, you must set up codebox.jar. This involves setting up a JBuilder library called codebox that points at codebox.jar.
- And if you want to compile from the command line, set up and run **set-classpath.bat**. The key is to edit the variables in that program so that they point to the right directories on your system.

Let me add that you can download updates to this code from http://sourceforge.net/projects/elvenware. The code is available there as an open source project. You can download updates as a zip file, or you can get the most recent version by using CVS. Hopefully the SourceForge project will be very long running. If by some chance you can't reach it, try http://www.elvenware.com, an address which I intend to keep available for the foreseeable future.

Late-Breaking News

The mm.mysql driver by Mark Matthews that is used extensively in Part VIII: Databases has been folded into the official MYSQL family. You can still download the old drivers at the SourceForge site mentioned in the book, but you can also get them at the official MySQL site. The code and functionality of the library is still more or less identical to what is described in this book. The only real difference is that the project is now an official part of MySQL, rather than a third-party add-on.

The name of the mm.mysql project has changed to MySQL Connector/J, and the name of the JAR file that contains the drivers has changed to mysql-connector-java-version-bin.jar. There are very few changes you need to make to adapt to this new situation. My tests show that the new JAR file should now be referenced from your JBuilder mm.mysql library and placed on your path when working from the command line. I do not believe any changes need be made to your source code. Just change the library itself.

Overview of the CD

On the CD, the programs are stored not by chapter but by the name of the section of the book in which they were discussed. Some exceptions include the layout programs from the Fundamentals section, which are mostly stored in a directory called Layout. The OpenTools examples are in a directory called OpenTools. The project management chapters are mostly in a directory called ComplexProjects. The rest are where you would expect to find them. For instance, the database examples are in the Database directory, the Getting Started examples are in the GettingStarted directory, and the Fundamental examples (except for the layouts) are in the Fundamentals directory.

If you have the Enterprise version of JBuilder, the simplest way to get started is to first install the Apache project called Jakarta Ant. If you have Ant installed, you can just type **Ant** in the root directory of the code for this book to compile all the included projects. If you have the SE version of JBuilder, everything should compile when you type **Ant** if you remove the references to the database section in the file called build.xml. If you have the Personal edition, all but the database projects and maybe three or four other projects, most of which are in the layouts section, will compile. In other words, if you leave the database examples out of the picture, 98 percent of the projects on the CD will compile in the Personal edition.

Each subdirectory will also have its own Ant project. If you are in a project directory, just type **ant run** to run the project. This will work for all but the OpenTools projects, which can't be run. For instance, if you are in the /Database/EasySQL directory, type **ant run** to run the project. You can clean up the project by typing **ant clean**. This will remove the .class files and other extraneous files created during compilation of the projects.

The database projects require considerable setup before the drivers will be in place. As a result, they probably will not compile until you have set up your system properly for handling databases. A discussion of how to set up databases is covered in depth in the text of this book. (This book was originally not targeted for users of the Enterprise version of the product. It came as a total and completely unexpected surprise to me when Borland decided to move the database tools into the Enterprise edition.)

Many, if not most, of the programs require JDK 1.3.1 to be installed. This is the default JDK that comes with JBuilder 7. I believe that all of the programs have also been tested and found to run correctly under JDK 1.4.0. I have tried to remove the dependencies to JDK 1.4 from all the projects except one or two. For instance, in the Utilities directory there is a project that uses the JDK 1.4 logging facilities, and I believe that another project uses assertions. The assertion project will work with JDK 1.3.1 from inside the JBuilder IDE, but you will have trouble compiling and running the assertion example from the command line unless you are using JDK 1.4.0 or higher. If you can easily download JDK 1.4, life will be simpler for you if you just download it and use it as your default JDK. This is described in more depth in the version of this appendix on the CD.

Project Layout

Almost all the projects have a main class named after the project. For instance, a project called MyProject will be stored in a package called myproject and the main class for the project will be called MyProject. Thus you would launch the project from the command line by typing something like:

```
java -cp .;classes myproject.MyProject
```

There are some projects that do not work that way. For instance, the projects in the OpenTools directory and some of the projects in the ComplexProjects directory follow a different pattern. Typing **ant run** should work for those projects and for almost all the other projects on the CD.

In the root directory for the CD, where this file is stored, you will find two scripts called set-classpath.sh (Linux) and setclasspath-bat (Windows). For many projects, you will need to run the appropriate version of these scripts before trying to compile or launch from the command line many of the projects included on the CD. You will need to edit these scripts to set up the path appropriately for your system. See the version of this appendix on the CD for more information on this subject.

Using the Personal Edition

Leaving the database programs aside, you will find that most of the programs that come with this book will run in the Personal edition. This was a conscious decision. The code for this book is designed to be as useful as possible to people who have the Personal edition.

When getting the programs ready to run in the Personal edition, I discovered that it is essential to explicitly include all the files in the program as part of the project. In the higher end editions, it is not necessary to explicitly include a graphic or Java file in the project in order to compile that file and copy it to the classes directory. Simply having the file in the right package is enough. In the Personal edition, however, you must explicitly include files you want to use in your project. I tried to go through all the programs and make sure I have explicitly included all the necessary files, but I cannot be positive that I have done that. If you run a program and receive a null exception when you try to launch its About box, there is a high likelihood that the problem is that a PNG or GIF file is not being copied to the classes directory. To correct the problem, simply add the file to the project.

As mentioned in the book, there are a number of powerful OpenTools add-ins that can be used with the Personal edition. For instance, there is support for adding Ant files to your project, as well as support for adding in refactoring tools. The OpenTools site on SourceForge can be a good place to get started looking for add-ins. You might also take a look at Code Central. There you will find pointers to both JRefactory and AntRunner. If you don't know about OpenTools, please read the relevant chapter in the book.

Extra Programs: Games and Internet

There are a number of programs on the CD that never made it into the book. In particular, see the Games directory and the Internet directory. At least one of the games, called Breakout, has the option to run full screen on Windows. This is a JDK 1.4 feature, so you will need to install JDK 1.4 to run that program.

Summary

Each of the projects on the CD is accompanied by a file called index.html, which provides at least a brief description of the program. A file called DocLinks.html in the root directory of the CD provides links to most of these files.

Hopefully you now have enough information to run most of the programs on the CD with little or no trouble. If you are absolutely stuck and can't get some of the code to run, first look at http://www.elvenware.com and see if there is a solution to your problem. If that fails, write to me at mailto:charlie@elvenware.com. I can provide help on getting the programs on the CD to run, but I cannot provide general programming support or do your homework for you.

I hope you enjoy the code presented here and can find a way to make use of it in your own programs. You are free to do pretty much whatever you want with it as long as you don't try to claim it as your own or use it as material for your own books.

Index

About the CD

The CD that accompanies this book contains example code and programs organized by the part of the book in which they are discussed. Each of the projects is accompanied by a file called index.html, which provides a brief description of the program.

Please see Appendix B for more information about the CD contents and how to get started using the CD. A more complete version of Appendix B with hyperlinks that allow you to view descriptions of the programs is in the index.html file on the root.

NOTE: Borland has a short release cycle for the JBuilder product. This title is current through version 7. Information about subsequent JBuilder releases and updates to the text of this book or the included code examples are available at www.wordware.com/calvert.

CAUTION: By opening the CD package, you accept the terms and conditions of the CD/Source Code Usage License Agreement.

Additionally, opening the CD package makes this book non-returnable.

CD/Source Code Usage License Agreement

Please read the following CD/Source Code usage license agreement before opening the CD and using the contents therein:

1. By opening the accompanying software package, you are indicating that you have read and agree to be bound by all terms and conditions of this CD/Source Code usage license agreement.
2. The compilation of code and utilities contained on the CD and in the book are copyrighted and protected by both U.S. copyright law and international copyright treaties, and is owned by Wordware Publishing, Inc. Individual source code, example programs, help files, freeware, shareware, utilities, and evaluation packages, including their copyrights, are owned by the respective authors.
3. No part of the enclosed CD or this book, including all source code, help files, shareware, freeware, utilities, example programs, or evaluation programs, may be made available on a public forum (such as a World Wide Web page, FTP site, bulletin board, or Internet news group) without the express written permission of Wordware Publishing, Inc. or the author of the respective source code, help files, shareware, freeware, utilities, example programs, or evaluation programs.
4. You may not decompile, reverse engineer, disassemble, create a derivative work, or otherwise use the enclosed programs, help files, freeware, shareware, utilities, or evaluation programs except as stated in this agreement.
5. The software, contained on the CD and/or as source code in this book, is sold without warranty of any kind. Wordware Publishing, Inc. and the authors specifically disclaim all other warranties, express or implied, including but not limited to implied warranties of merchantability and fitness for a particular purpose with respect to defects in the disk, the program, source code, sample files, help files, freeware, shareware, utilities, and evaluation programs contained therein, and/or the techniques described in the book and implemented in the example programs. In no event shall Wordware Publishing, Inc., its dealers, its distributors, or the authors be liable or held responsible for any loss of profit or any other alleged or actual private or commercial damage, including but not limited to special, incidental, consequential, or other damages.
6. One (1) copy of the CD or any source code therein may be created for backup purposes. The CD and all accompanying source code, sample files, help files, freeware, shareware, utilities, and evaluation programs may be copied to your hard drive. With the exception of freeware and shareware programs, at no time can any part of the contents of this CD reside on more than one computer at one time. The contents of the CD can be copied to another computer, as long as the contents of the CD contained on the original computer are deleted.
7. You may not include any part of the CD contents, including all source code, example programs, shareware, freeware, help files, utilities, or evaluation programs in any compilation of source code, utilities, help files, example programs, freeware, shareware, or evaluation programs on any media, including but not limited to CD, disk, or Internet distribution, without the express written permission of Wordware Publishing, Inc. or the owner of the individual source code, utilities, help files, example programs, freeware, shareware, or evaluation programs.
8. You may use the source code, techniques, and example programs in your own commercial or private applications unless otherwise noted by additional usage agreements as found on the CD.

CAUTION: By opening the CD package, you accept the terms and conditions of the CD/Source Code Usage License Agreement.

Additionally, opening the CD package makes this book non-returnable.